LAW I - Business Law 201

Selected Chapters and New York Cases
Monroe Community College

Fifth Edition

Gaylord A. Jentz | Roger LeRoy Miller | Frank B. Cross |
Karen Morris | Jim Petrosino

CENGAGE
Learning™

Australia • Brazil • Japan • Korea • Mexico • Singapore • Spain • United Kingdom • United States

CENGAGE
Learning™

LAW I - Business Law 201
Selected Chapters and New York Cases
MCC 5th Edition

Executive Editors:
 Maureen Staudt
 Michael Stranz

Senior Project Development Manager:
 Linda deStefano

Marketing Specialist:
 Courtney Sheldon

Senior Production/Manufacturing Manager:
 Donna M. Brown

PreMedia Manager:
 Joel Brennecke

Sr. Rights Acquisition Account Manager:
 Todd Osborne

Cover Image:
 Getty Images*

*Unless otherwise noted, all cover images used by Custom Solutions, a part of Cengage Learning, have been supplied courtesy of Getty Images with the exception of the Earthview cover image, which has been supplied by the National Aeronautics and Space Administration (NASA).

For product information and technology assistance, contact us at
Cengage Learning Customer & Sales Support, 1-800-354-9706

For permission to use material from this text or product,
submit all requests online at **cengage.com/permissions**
Further permissions questions can be emailed to
permissionrequest@cengage.com

This book contains select works from existing Cengage Learning resources and was produced by Cengage Learning Custom Solutions for collegiate use. As such, those adopting and/or contributing to this work are responsible for editorial content accuracy, continuity and completeness.

Cengage Learning
5191 Natorp Boulevard
Mason, Ohio 45040
USA
Cengage Learning is a leading provider of customized learning solutions with office locations around the globe, including Singapore, the United Kingdom, Australia, Mexico, Brazil, and Japan. Locate your local office at:
international.cengage.com/region.

Cengage Learning products are represented in Canada by Nelson Education, Ltd.
For your lifelong learning solutions, visit **www.cengage.com/custom.**
Visit our corporate website at **www.cengage.com.**

Printed in the United States of America

Table of Contents

CHAPTER 1

Introduction to Law and Legal Reasoning

One of the important functions of law in any society is to provide stability, predictability, and continuity so that people can be sure of how to order their affairs. If any society is to survive, its citizens must be able to determine what is legally right and legally wrong. They must know what sanctions will be imposed on them if they commit wrongful acts. If they suffer harm as a result of others' wrongful acts, they must know how they can seek redress. By setting forth the rights, obligations, and privileges of citizens, the law enables individuals to go about their business with confidence and a certain degree of predictability. The stability and predictability created by the law provide an essential framework for all civilized activities, including business activities.

What do we mean when we speak of "the law"? Although this term has had, and will continue to have, different definitions, they are all based on a general observation: at a minimum, **law** consists of *enforceable rules governing relationships among individuals and between individuals and their society.* These "enforceable rules" may consist of unwritten principles of behavior established by a nomadic tribe. They may be set forth in a law code, such as the Code of Hammurabi in ancient Babylon (c. 1780 B.C.E.) or the law code of one of today's European nations. They may consist of written laws and court decisions created by modern legislative and judicial bodies, as in the United States. Regardless of how such rules are created, they all have one thing in common: they establish rights, duties, and privileges that are consistent with the values and beliefs of their society or its ruling group.

Those who embark on a study of law will find that these broad statements leave unanswered some important questions concerning the nature of law. Part of the study of law, often referred to as **jurisprudence,** involves learning about different schools of jurisprudential thought and discovering how the approaches to law characteristic of each school can affect judicial decision making.

We open this introductory chapter with an examination of that topic. We then look at an important question for any student reading this text: How does the legal environment affect business decision making? We next describe the basic sources of American law, the common law tradition, and some general classifications of law. We conclude the chapter with sections offering practical guidance on several topics, including how to find the sources of law discussed in this chapter (and referred to throughout the text) and how to read and understand court opinions.

Schools of Jurisprudential Thought

You may think that legal philosophy is far removed from the practical study of business law and the legal environment. In fact, it is not. As you will learn in the chapters of this text, how judges apply the law to specific disputes, including disputes relating to the business world, depends in part on their philosophical approaches to law.

Clearly, judges are not free to decide cases solely on the basis of their personal philosophical views or on their opinions about the issues before the court. A judge's function is not to *make* the laws—that is the function of the legislative branch of government—but to interpret and apply them. From a practical point of view, however, the courts play a significant role in defining what the law is. This is because laws enacted by legislative bodies tend to be expressed in general terms. Judges thus have some flexibility in interpreting and applying the law. It is because of this flexibility that different courts can, and often do, arrive at different conclusions in cases that involve nearly identical issues, facts, and applicable laws. This flexibility also means that each judge's unique personality, legal philosophy, set of values, and intellectual attributes necessarily frame the judicial decision-making process to some extent.

Over time several significant schools of legal, or jurisprudential, thought have evolved. We now look at some of them.

The Natural Law School

An age-old question about the nature of law has to do with the finality of a nation's laws, such as the laws of the United States at the present time. For example, what if a particular law is deemed to be a "bad" law by a substantial number of that nation's citizens? Must a citizen obey the law if it goes against his or her conscience to do so? Is there a higher or universal law to which individuals can appeal? One who adheres to the natural law tradition would answer these questions in the affirmative. **Natural law** denotes a system of moral and ethical principles that are inherent in human nature and that people can discover through the use of their natural intelligence, or reason.

The natural law tradition is one of the oldest and most significant schools of jurisprudence. It dates back to the days of the Greek philosopher Aristotle (384–322 B.C.E.), who distinguished between natural law and the laws governing a particular nation. According to Aristotle, natural law applies universally to all humankind.

The notion that people have "natural rights" stems from the natural law tradition. Those who claim that a specific foreign government is depriving certain citizens of their human rights implicitly are appealing to a higher law that has universal applicability. The question of the universality of basic human rights also comes into play in the context of international business operations. Should rights extended to workers in the United States, such as the right to be free of discrimination in the workplace, be extended to workers employed by a U.S. firm doing business in another country that does not provide for such rights? This

question is rooted implicitly in a concept of universal rights that has its origins in the natural law tradition.

The Positivist School

In contrast, **positive law,** or national law (the written law of a given society at a particular point in time), applies only to the citizens of that nation or society. Those who adhere to the **positivist school** believe that there can be no higher law than a nation's positive law. According to the positivist school, there is no such thing as "natural rights." Rather, human rights exist solely because of laws. If the laws are not enforced, anarchy will result. Thus, whether a law is "bad" or "good" is irrelevant. The law is the law and must be obeyed until it is changed—in an orderly manner through a legitimate lawmaking process. A judge with positivist leanings probably would be more inclined to defer to an existing law than would a judge who adheres to the natural law tradition.

The Historical School

The **historical school** of legal thought emphasizes the evolutionary process of law by concentrating on the origin and history of the legal system. Thus, this school looks to the past to discover what the principles of contemporary law should be. The legal doctrines that have withstood the passage of time—those that have worked in the past—are deemed best suited for shaping present laws. Hence, law derives its legitimacy and authority from adhering to the standards that historical development has shown to be workable. Adherents of the historical school are more likely than those of other schools to strictly follow decisions made in past cases.

Legal Realism

In the 1920s and 1930s, a number of jurists and scholars, known as legal realists, rebelled against the historical approach to law. **Legal realism** is based on the idea that law is just one of many institutions in society and that it is shaped by social forces and needs. The law is a human enterprise, and judges should take social and economic realities into account when deciding cases. Legal realists also believe that the law can never be applied with total uniformity. Given that judges are human beings with unique personalities, value systems, and intellects, different judges will obviously bring different reasoning processes to the same case.

Legal realism strongly influenced the growth of what is sometimes called the **sociological school** of jurisprudence. This school views law as a tool for promoting justice in society. In the 1960s, for example, the justices of the United States Supreme Court played a leading role in the civil rights movement by upholding long-neglected laws calling for equal treatment for all Americans, including African Americans and other minorities. Generally, jurists who adhere to this philosophy of law are more likely to depart from past decisions than are those jurists who adhere to the other schools of legal thought. *Concept Summary 1.1* reviews the schools of jurisprudential thought.

Business Activities and the Legal Environment

As those entering the world of business will learn, laws and government regulations affect virtually all business activities—from hiring and firing decisions to workplace safety, the manufacturing and marketing of products, business financing, and more. To make good business decisions, a basic knowledge of the laws and regulations governing these activities is beneficial—if not essential. Realize also that in today's world a knowledge of "black-letter" law is not enough. Businesspersons are also pressured to make ethical decisions. Thus, the study of business law necessarily involves an ethical dimension.

Many Different Laws May Affect a Single Business Transaction

As you will note, each chapter in this text covers a specific area of the law and shows how the legal rules in that area affect business activities. Though compartmentalizing the law in this fashion promotes conceptual clarity, it does not indicate the extent to which a number of different laws may apply to just one transaction.

Consider an example. Suppose that you are the president of NetSys, Inc., a company that creates and maintains computer network systems for its clients, including business firms. NetSys also markets software for customers who require an internal computer network. One day, Hernandez, an operations officer for Southwest Distribution Corporation (SDC), contacts you by e-mail about a possible contract concerning SDC's computer network. In deciding whether to enter

---

CONCEPT SUMMARY 1.1
Schools of Jurisprudential Thought

School of Thought	Description
THE NATURAL LAW SCHOOL	One of the oldest and most significant schools of legal thought. Those who believe in natural law hold that there is a universal law applicable to all human beings. This law is discoverable through reason and is of a higher order than positive (national) law.
THE POSITIVIST SCHOOL	A school of legal thought centered on the assumption that there is no law higher than the laws created by the government. Laws must be obeyed, even if they are unjust, to prevent anarchy.
THE HISTORICAL SCHOOL	A school of legal thought that stresses the evolutionary nature of law and that looks to doctrines that have withstood the passage of time for guidance in shaping present laws.
LEGAL REALISM	A school of legal thought, popular during the 1920s and 1930s, that left a lasting imprint on American jurisprudence. Legal realists generally advocated a less abstract and more realistic and pragmatic approach to the law, an approach that would take into account customary practices and the circumstances in which transactions take place. Legal realism strongly influenced the growth of the *sociological school* of jurisprudence, which views law as a tool for promoting social justice.

into a contract with SDC, you should consider, among other things, the legal requirements for an enforceable contract. Are there different requirements for a contract for services and a contract for products? What are your options if SDC **breaches** (breaks, or fails to perform) the contract? The answers to these questions are part of contract law and sales law.

Other questions might concern payment under the contract. How can you guarantee that NetSys will be paid? For example, if payment is made with a check that is returned for insufficient funds, what are your options? Answers to these questions can be found in the laws that relate to negotiable instruments (such as checks) and creditors' rights. Also, a dispute may occur over the rights to NetSys's software, or there may be a question of liability if the software is defective. Questions may even be raised as to whether you and Hernandez had the authority to make the deal in the first place. A disagreement may arise from other circumstances, such as an accountant's evaluation of the contract. Resolutions of these questions may be found in areas of the law that relate to intellectual property, e-commerce, torts, product liability, agency, business organizations, or professional liability.

Finally, if any dispute cannot be resolved amicably, then the laws and the rules concerning courts and court procedures spell out the steps of a lawsuit. Exhibit 1–1 illustrates the various areas of law that may influence business decision making.

PREVENTING LEGAL DISPUTES

To prevent potential legal disputes, businesspersons need to be aware of the many different laws that may apply to a single business transaction. It is equally important for businesspersons to understand enough about the law to know when to turn to an attorney for advice.

Ethics and Business Decision Making

Merely knowing the areas of law that may affect a business decision is not sufficient in today's business world. Businesspersons must also take ethics into account. As you will learn in Chapter 5, *ethics* is generally defined as the study of what constitutes right or wrong behavior. Today, business decision makers

EXHIBIT 1–1 • **Areas of the Law That May Affect Business Decision Making**

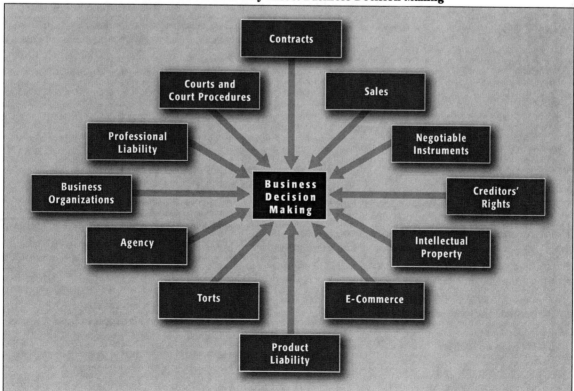

need to consider not just whether a decision is legal, but also whether it is ethical.

Throughout this text, you will learn about the relationship between the law and ethics, as well as about some of the types of ethical questions that often arise in the business context. For example, the unit-ending *Focus on Ethics* features in this text are devoted solely to the exploration of ethical questions pertaining to selected topics treated within the unit. We have also added several new features for this edition that stress the importance of ethical considerations in today's business climate. These include the new *Ethical Dimension* questions that conclude many of the cases presented in this text and the *Insight into Ethics* features that appear in selected chapters. We have also included *A Question of Ethics* case problems at the ends of the chapters to introduce you to the ethical aspects of specific cases involving real-life situations. Additionally, Chapter 5 offers a detailed look at the importance of ethical considerations in business decision making.

Sources of American Law

There are numerous sources of American law. *Primary sources of law*, or sources that establish the law, include the following:

1. The U.S. Constitution and the constitutions of the various states.
2. Statutory law—including laws passed by Congress, state legislatures, or local governing bodies.
3. Regulations created by administrative agencies, such as the Food and Drug Administration.
4. Case law and common law doctrines.

We describe each of these important sources of law in the following pages.

Secondary sources of law are books and articles that summarize and clarify the primary sources of law. Examples include legal encyclopedias, treatises, articles in law reviews, and compilations of law, such as the *Restatements of the Law* (which will be discussed shortly). Courts often refer to secondary sources of law for guidance in interpreting and applying the primary sources of law discussed here.

Constitutional Law

The federal government and the states have separate written constitutions that set forth the general organi-

zation, powers, and limits of their respective governments. **Constitutional law** is the law as expressed in these constitutions.

According to Article VI of the U.S. Constitution, the Constitution is the supreme law of the land. As such, it is the basis of all law in the United States. A law in violation of the Constitution, if challenged, will be declared unconstitutional and will not be enforced, no matter what its source. Because of its importance in the American legal system, we present the complete text of the U.S. Constitution in Appendix B.

The Tenth Amendment to the U.S. Constitution reserves to the states all powers not granted to the federal government. Each state in the union has its own constitution. Unless it conflicts with the U.S. Constitution or a federal law, a state constitution is supreme within the state's borders.

Statutory Law

Laws enacted by legislative bodies at any level of government, such as the statutes passed by Congress or by state legislatures, make up the body of law generally referred to as **statutory law.** When a legislature passes a statute, that statute ultimately is included in the federal code of laws or the relevant state code of laws (these codes are discussed later in this chapter).

Statutory law also includes local **ordinances**— statutes (laws, rules, or orders) passed by municipal or county governing units to govern matters not covered by federal or state law. Ordinances commonly have to do with city or county land use (zoning ordinances), building and safety codes, and other matters affecting the local community.

A federal statute, of course, applies to all states. A state statute, in contrast, applies only within the state's borders. State laws thus may vary from state to state. No federal statute may violate the U.S. Constitution, and no state statute or local ordinance may violate the U.S. Constitution or the relevant state constitution.

Uniform Laws The differences among state laws were particularly notable in the 1800s, when conflicting state statutes frequently made trade and commerce among the states difficult. To counter these problems, in 1892 a group of legal scholars and lawyers formed the National Conference of Commissioners on Uniform State Laws (NCCUSL) to draft **uniform laws,** or model laws, for the states to consider adopting. The NCCUSL still exists today and continues to issue uniform laws.

Each state has the option of adopting or rejecting a uniform law. *Only if a state legislature adopts a uniform law does that law become part of the statutory law of that state.* Note that a state legislature may adopt all or part of a uniform law as it is written, or the legislature may rewrite the law however the legislature wishes. Hence, even though many states may have adopted a uniform law, those states' laws may not be entirely "uniform."

The earliest uniform law, the Uniform Negotiable Instruments Law, was completed by 1896 and adopted in every state by the early 1920s (although not all states used exactly the same wording). Over the following decades, other acts were drawn up in a similar manner. In all, more than two hundred uniform acts have been issued by the NCCUSL since its inception. The most ambitious uniform act of all, however, was the Uniform Commercial Code.

The Uniform Commercial Code The Uniform Commercial Code (UCC), which was created through the joint efforts of the NCCUSL and the American Law Institute,[1] was first issued in 1952. All fifty states,[2] the District of Columbia, and the Virgin Islands have adopted the UCC. It facilitates commerce among the states by providing a uniform, yet flexible, set of rules governing commercial transactions. The UCC assures businesspersons that their contracts, if validly entered into, normally will be enforced. Because of its importance in the area of commercial law, we cite the UCC frequently in this text. We also present the full text of the UCC in Appendix C.

Administrative Law

Another important source of American law is **administrative law,** which consists of the rules, orders, and decisions of administrative agencies. An **administrative agency** is a federal, state, or local government agency established to perform a specific function. Administrative law and procedures, which will be examined in detail in Chapter 43, constitute a dominant element in the regulatory environment of business. Rules issued by various administrative agencies now affect virtually every aspect of a business's operations, including its capital structure and financing, its hiring and firing procedures, its relations with employees and unions, and the way it manufactures and markets its products.

Federal Agencies At the national level, numerous **executive agencies** exist within the cabinet departments of the executive branch. The U.S. Food and Drug Administration, for example, is an agency within the U.S. Department of Health and Human Services. Executive agencies are subject to the authority of the president, who has the power to appoint and remove officers of federal agencies. There are also major **independent regulatory agencies** at the federal level, such as the Federal Trade Commission, the Securities and Exchange Commission, and the Federal Communications Commission. The president's power is less pronounced in regard to independent agencies, whose officers serve for fixed terms and cannot be removed without just cause.

State and Local Agencies There are administrative agencies at the state and local levels as well. Commonly, a state agency (such as a state pollution-control agency) is created as a parallel to a federal agency (such as the U.S. Environmental Protection Agency). Just as federal statutes take precedence over conflicting state statutes, so federal agency regulations take precedence over conflicting state regulations.

Case Law and Common Law Doctrines

The rules of law announced in court decisions constitute another basic source of American law. These rules of law include interpretations of constitutional provisions, of statutes enacted by legislatures, and of regulations created by administrative agencies. Today, this body of judge-made law is referred to as **case law.** Case law—the doctrines and principles announced in cases—governs all areas not covered by statutory law or administrative law and is part of our common law tradition. We look at the origins and characteristics of the common law tradition in some detail in the pages that follow. See *Concept Summary 1.2* on the next page for a review of the sources of American law.

The Common Law Tradition

Because of our colonial heritage, much of American law is based on the English legal system, which originated in medieval England and continued to evolve in the following centuries. Knowledge of this system is necessary to understanding the American legal system today.

---

1. This institute was formed in the 1920s and consists of practicing attorneys, legal scholars, and judges.

2. Louisiana has not adopted Articles 2 and 2A (covering contracts for the sale and lease of goods), however.

CONCEPT SUMMARY 1.2
Sources of American Law

Source	Description
CONSTITUTIONAL LAW	The law as expressed in the U.S. Constitution and the state constitutions. The U.S. Constitution is the supreme law of the land. State constitutions are supreme within state borders to the extent that they do not violate a clause of the U.S. Constitution or a federal law.
STATUTORY LAW	Laws (statutes and ordinances) created by federal, state, and local legislatures and governing bodies. None of these laws may violate the U.S. Constitution or the relevant state constitution. Uniform statutes, when adopted by a state, become statutory law in that state.
ADMINISTRATIVE LAW	The rules, orders, and decisions of federal, state, or local government administrative agencies.
CASE LAW AND COMMON LAW DOCTRINES	Judge-made law, including interpretations of constitutional provisions, of statutes enacted by legislatures, and of regulations created by administrative agencies.

Early English Courts

The origins of the English legal system—and thus the U.S. legal system as well—date back to 1066, when the Normans conquered England. William the Conqueror and his successors began the process of unifying the country under their rule. One of the means they used to do this was the establishment of the king's courts, or *curiae regis*. Before the Norman Conquest, disputes had been settled according to the local legal customs and traditions in various regions of the country. The king's courts sought to establish a uniform set of customs for the country as a whole. What evolved in these courts was the beginning of the **common law**—a body of general rules that applied throughout the entire English realm. Eventually, the common law tradition became part of the heritage of all nations that were once British colonies, including the United States.

Courts of Law and Remedies at Law The early English king's courts could grant only very limited kinds of **remedies** (the legal means to enforce a right or redress a wrong). If one person wronged another in some way, the king's courts could award as compensation one or more of the following: (1) land, (2) items of value, or (3) money. The courts that awarded this compensation became known as **courts of law,** and the three remedies were called **remedies at law.** (Today, the remedy at law normally takes the form of monetary **damages**—an amount given to a party whose legal interests have been injured.) Even though the system introduced uniformity in the settling of disputes, when a complaining party wanted a remedy other than economic compensation, the courts of law could do nothing, so "no remedy, no right."

Courts of Equity and Remedies in Equity Equity is a branch of law, founded on what might be described as notions of justice and fair dealing, that seeks to supply a remedy when no adequate remedy at law is available. When individuals could not obtain an adequate remedy in a court of law, they petitioned the king for relief. Most of these petitions were decided by an adviser to the king, called a **chancellor,** who had the power to grant new and unique remedies. Eventually, formal chancery courts, or **courts of equity,** were established.

The remedies granted by the equity courts became known as **remedies in equity,** or equitable remedies. These remedies include *specific performance* (ordering a party to perform an agreement as promised), an *injunction* (ordering a party to cease engaging in a specific activity or to undo some wrong or injury), and *rescission* (the cancellation of a contractual obligation). We discuss these and other equitable remedies in more detail at appropriate points in the chapters that follow, particularly in Chapter 18.

As a general rule, today's courts, like the early English courts, will not grant equitable remedies unless the remedy at law—monetary damages—is inadequate. For example, suppose that you form a contract (a legally binding agreement—see Chapter 10) to purchase a parcel of land that you think will be just perfect for your future home. Further suppose that the seller breaches this agreement. You could sue the seller for the return of any deposits or down payment you might have made on the land, but this is not the remedy you really seek. What you want is to have the court order the seller to go through with the contract. In other words, you want the court to grant the equitable remedy of specific performance because monetary damages are inadequate in this situation.

Equitable Maxims In fashioning appropriate remedies, judges often were (and continue to be) guided by so-called **equitable maxims**—propositions or general statements of equitable rules. Exhibit 1–2 lists some important equitable maxims. The last maxim listed in that exhibit—"Equity aids the vigilant, not those who rest on their rights"—merits special attention. It has become known as the equitable doctrine of **laches** (a term derived from the Latin *laxus*, meaning "lax" or "negligent"), and it can be used as a defense. A **defense** is an argument raised by the **defendant** (the party being sued) indicating why the **plaintiff** (the suing party) should not obtain the remedy sought. (Note that in equity proceedings, the party bringing a lawsuit is called the **petitioner**, and the party being sued is referred to as the **respondent**.)

The doctrine of laches arose to encourage people to bring lawsuits while the evidence was fresh. What constitutes a reasonable time, of course, varies according to the circumstances of the case. Time periods for different types of cases are now usually fixed by

statutes of limitations. After the time allowed under a statute of limitations has expired, no action (lawsuit) can be brought, no matter how strong the case was originally.

Legal and Equitable Remedies Today

The establishment of courts of equity in medieval England resulted in two distinct court systems: courts of law and courts of equity. The systems had different sets of judges and granted different types of remedies. During the nineteenth century, however, most states in the United States adopted rules of procedure that resulted in the combining of courts of law and equity. A party now may request both legal and equitable remedies in the same action, and the trial court judge may grant either or both forms of relief.

The distinction between legal and equitable remedies remains relevant to students of business law, however, because these remedies differ. To seek the proper remedy for a wrong, one must know what remedies are available. Additionally, certain vestiges of the procedures used when there were separate courts of law and equity still exist. For example, a party has the right to demand a jury trial in an action at law, but not in an action in equity. Exhibit 1–3 on page 10 summarizes the procedural differences (applicable in most states) between an action at law and an action in equity.

The Doctrine of *Stare Decisis*

One of the unique features of the common law is that it is *judge-made* law. The body of principles and doctrines that form the common law emerged over time as judges decided legal controversies.

EXHIBIT 1–2 • Equitable Maxims

1. *Whoever seeks equity must do equity.* (Anyone who wishes to be treated fairly must treat others fairly.)

2. *Where there is equal equity, the law must prevail.* (The law will determine the outcome of a controversy in which the merits of both sides are equal.)

3. *One seeking the aid of an equity court must come to the court with clean hands.* (Plaintiffs must have acted fairly and honestly.)

4. *Equity will not suffer a wrong to be without a remedy.* (Equitable relief will be awarded when there is a right to relief and there is no adequate remedy at law.)

5. *Equity regards substance rather than form.* (Equity is more concerned with fairness and justice than with legal technicalities.)

6. *Equity aids the vigilant, not those who rest on their rights.* (Equity will not help those who neglect their rights for an unreasonable period of time.)

EXHIBIT 1-3 • Procedural Differences between an Action at Law and an Action in Equity

Procedure	Action at Law	Action in Equity
Initiation of lawsuit	By filing a complaint	By filing a petition
Parties	Plaintiff and defendant	Petitioner and respondent
Decision	By jury or judge	By judge (no jury)
Result	Judgment	Decree
Remedy	Monetary damages	Injunction, specific performance, or rescission

Case Precedents and Case Reporters
When possible, judges attempted to be consistent and to base their decisions on the principles suggested by earlier cases. They sought to decide similar cases in a similar way and considered new cases with care because they knew that their decisions would make new law. Each interpretation became part of the law on the subject and served as a legal **precedent**—that is, a decision that furnished an example or authority for deciding subsequent cases involving similar legal principles or facts.

In the early years of the common law, there was no single place or publication where court opinions, or written decisions, could be found. By the early fourteenth century, portions of the most important decisions of each year were being gathered together and recorded in *Year Books*, which became useful references for lawyers and judges. In the sixteenth century, the *Year Books* were discontinued, and other forms of case publication became available. Today, cases are published, or "reported," in volumes called **reporters,** or *reports*. We describe today's case reporting system in detail later in this chapter.

***Stare Decisis* and the Common Law Tradition** The practice of deciding new cases with reference to former decisions, or precedents, became a cornerstone of the English and American judicial systems. The practice formed a doctrine known as **stare decisis**[3] (a Latin phrase meaning "to stand on decided cases").

Under this doctrine, judges are obligated to follow the precedents established within their jurisdictions. The term *jurisdiction* refers to an area in which a court or courts have the power to apply the law—see

Chapter 2. Once a court has set forth a principle of law as being applicable to a certain set of facts, that court and courts of lower rank (within the same jurisdiction) must adhere to that principle and apply it in future cases involving similar fact patterns. Thus, *stare decisis* has two aspects: first, that decisions made by a higher court are binding on lower courts; and second, that a court should not overturn its own precedents unless there is a compelling reason to do so.

The doctrine of *stare decisis* helps the courts to be more efficient because if other courts have carefully analyzed a similar case, their legal reasoning and opinions can serve as guides. *Stare decisis* also makes the law more stable and predictable. If the law on a given subject is well settled, someone bringing a case to court can usually rely on the court to make a decision based on what the law has been in the past.

A Typical Scenario To illustrate how the doctrine of *stare decisis* works, consider an example. Suppose that the lower state courts in Georgia have reached conflicting conclusions on whether drivers are liable for accidents they cause while merging into freeway traffic. Some courts have held drivers liable even though the drivers looked and did not see any oncoming traffic and even though witnesses (passengers in their cars) testified to that effect. To settle the law on this issue, the Georgia Supreme Court decides to review a case involving this fact pattern. The court rules that, in such a situation, the driver who is merging into traffic is liable for any accidents caused by that driver's failure to yield to freeway traffic—even if that driver looked carefully and did not see an approaching vehicle.

The Georgia Supreme Court's decision on this matter is a **binding authority**—a case precedent, statute, or other source of law that a court must follow when

---

3. Pronounced *ster*-ay dih-*si*-ses.

deciding a case. In other words, the Georgia Supreme Court's decision will influence the outcome of all future cases on this issue brought before the Georgia state courts. Similarly, a decision on a given question by the United States Supreme Court (the nation's highest court), no matter how old, is binding on all courts.

Departures from Precedent Although courts are obligated to follow precedents, sometimes a court will depart from the rule of precedent if it decides that the precedent should no longer be followed. If a court decides that a ruling precedent is simply incorrect or that technological or social changes have rendered the precedent inapplicable, the court might rule contrary to the precedent. Cases that overturn precedent often receive a great deal of publicity.

Note that judges do have some flexibility in applying precedents. For example, a lower court may avoid applying a precedent set by a higher court in its jurisdiction by distinguishing the two cases based on their facts. When this happens, the lower court's ruling stands unless it is appealed to a higher court and that court overturns the decision.

When There Is No Precedent Occasionally, the courts must decide cases for which no precedents exist, called *cases of first impression.* For example, as you will read throughout this text, the extensive use of the Internet has presented many new and challenging issues for the courts to decide. In deciding cases of first impression, courts often look at *persuasive authorities* (precedents from other jurisdictions) for guidance. A court may also consider a number of factors, including legal principles and policies underlying previous court decisions or existing statutes, fairness, social values and customs, **public policy** (governmental policy based on widely held societal values), and data and concepts drawn from the social sciences. Which of these sources is chosen or receives the greatest emphasis depends on the nature of the case being considered and the particular judge or judges hearing the case.

Stare Decisis and Legal Reasoning

Legal reasoning is the reasoning process used by judges in deciding what law applies to a given dispute and then applying that law to the specific facts or circumstances of the case. Through the use of legal reasoning, judges harmonize their decisions with those that have been made before, as the doctrine of *stare decisis* requires.

Students of business law and the legal environment also engage in legal reasoning. For example, you may be asked to provide answers for some of the case problems that appear at the end of every chapter in this text. Each problem describes the facts of a particular dispute and the legal question at issue. If you are assigned a case problem, you will be asked to determine how a court would answer that question, and why. In other words, you will need to give legal reasons for whatever conclusion you reach.[4] We look here at the basic steps involved in legal reasoning and then describe some forms of reasoning commonly used by the courts in making their decisions.

Basic Steps in Legal Reasoning At times, the legal arguments set forth in court opinions are relatively simple and brief. At other times, the arguments are complex and lengthy. Regardless of the length of a legal argument, however, the basic steps of the legal reasoning process remain the same. These steps, which you also can follow when analyzing cases and case problems, form what is commonly referred to as the *IRAC method* of legal reasoning. IRAC is an acronym formed from the first letters of the following words: Issue, Rule, Application, and Conclusion. To apply the IRAC method, you would ask the following questions:

1. *What are the key facts and issues?* For example, a plaintiff comes before the court claiming *assault* (a wrongful and intentional action in which one person makes another fearful of immediate physical harm—part of a class of actions called *torts*). The plaintiff claims that the defendant threatened her while she was sleeping. Although the plaintiff was unaware that she was being threatened, her roommate heard the defendant make the threat. The legal issue, or question, raised by these facts is whether the defendant's actions constitute the tort of assault, given that the plaintiff was not aware of those actions at the time they occurred.

2. *What rules of law apply to the case?* A rule of law may be a rule stated by the courts in previous decisions, a state or federal statute, or a state or federal administrative agency regulation. In our hypothetical case, the plaintiff **alleges** (claims) that the defendant committed a tort. Therefore, the applicable law is the common law of torts—specifically, tort law governing assault (see Chapter 6 for more

---

4. See Appendix A for further instructions on how to analyze case problems.

detail on intentional torts). Case precedents involving similar facts and issues thus would be relevant. Often, more than one rule of law will be applicable to a case.

3. *How do the rules of law apply to the particular facts and circumstances of this case?* This step is often the most difficult because each case presents a unique set of facts, circumstances, and parties. Although cases may be similar, no two cases are ever identical in all respects. Normally, judges (and lawyers and law students) try to find **cases on point**—previously decided cases that are as similar as possible to the one under consideration. (Because of the difficulty—and importance—of this step in the legal reasoning process, we discuss it in more detail in the next subsection.)

4. *What conclusion should be drawn?* This step normally presents few problems. Usually, the conclusion is evident if the previous three steps have been followed carefully.

Forms of Legal Reasoning Judges use many types of reasoning when following the third step of the legal reasoning process—applying the law to the facts of a particular case. Three common forms of reasoning are deductive reasoning, linear reasoning, and reasoning by analogy.

Deductive Reasoning. Deductive reasoning is sometimes called *syllogistic reasoning* because it employs a **syllogism**—a logical relationship involving a major premise, a minor premise, and a conclusion. Consider the hypothetical case presented earlier, in which the plaintiff alleged that the defendant committed assault by threatening her while she was sleeping. The judge might point out that "under the common law of torts, an individual must be *aware* of a threat of danger for the threat to constitute assault" (major premise); "the plaintiff in this case was unaware of the threat at the time it occurred" (minor premise); and "therefore, the circumstances do not amount to an assault" (conclusion).

Linear Reasoning. A second important form of legal reasoning that is commonly employed might be thought of as "linear" reasoning because it proceeds from one point to another, with the final point being the conclusion. A comparison will help make this form of reasoning clear. Imagine a knotted rope, with each knot tying together separate pieces of rope to form a tightly knotted length. As a whole, the rope represents a linear progression of thought logically connecting various points, with the last point, or knot, representing the conclusion. Suppose that a tenant in an apartment building sues the landlord for damages for an injury resulting from an allegedly inadequately lit stairway. The court may engage in a reasoning process involving the following "pieces of rope":

1. The landlord, who was on the premises the evening the injury occurred, testifies that none of the other nine tenants who used the stairway that night complained about the lights.

2. The fact that none of the tenants complained is the same as if they had said the lighting was sufficient.

3. That there were no complaints does not prove that the lighting was sufficient but does prove that the landlord had no reason to believe that it was not.

4. The landlord's belief was reasonable because no one complained.

5. Therefore, the landlord acted reasonably and was not negligent with respect to the lighting in the stairway.

From this reasoning, the court concludes that the tenant is not entitled to compensation on the basis of the stairway's allegedly insufficient lighting.

Reasoning by Analogy. Another important type of reasoning that judges use in deciding cases is reasoning by *analogy*. To reason by **analogy** is to compare the facts in the case at hand to the facts in other cases and, to the extent that the patterns are similar, to apply the same rule of law to the present case. To the extent that the facts are unique, or "distinguishable," different rules may apply. For example, in case A, the court held that a driver who crossed a highway's center line was negligent. Case B involves a driver who crosses the line to avoid hitting a child. In determining whether case A's rule applies in case B, a judge would consider what the reasons were for the decision in A and whether B is sufficiently similar for those reasons to apply. If the judge holds that B's driver is not liable, that judge must indicate why case A's rule is not relevant to the facts presented in case B.

There Is No One "Right" Answer

Many persons believe that there is one "right" answer to every legal question. In most situations involving a legal controversy, however, there is no single correct result. Good arguments can often be made to support either side of a legal controversy. Quite often, a case does not involve a "good" person suing a "bad" person. In many cases, both parties have acted in good faith in some measure or in bad faith to some degree.

Additionally, each judge has her or his own personal beliefs and philosophy, which shape, at least to some extent, the process of legal reasoning. This means that the outcome of a particular lawsuit before a court cannot be predicted with absolute certainty. In fact, in some cases, even though the weight of the law would seem to favor one party's position, judges, through creative legal reasoning, have found ways to rule in favor of the other party in the interests of preventing injustice. Legal reasoning and other aspects of the common law tradition are reviewed in *Concept Summary 1.3*.

The Common Law Today

Today, the common law derived from judicial decisions continues to be applied throughout the United States. Common law doctrines and principles govern all areas *not* covered by statutory or administrative law. In a dispute concerning a particular employment practice, for example, if a statute regulates that practice, the statute will apply rather than the common law doctrine that applied prior to the enactment of the statute.

The Continuing Importance of the Common Law

Because the body of statutory law has expanded greatly since the beginning of this nation, thus narrowing the applicability of common law doctrines, it might seem that the common law has dwindled in importance. This is not true, however. Even in areas governed by statutory law, there is a significant interplay between statutory law and the common law. For example, many statutes essentially codify existing common law rules, and regulations issued by various administrative agencies usually are based, at least in part, on common law principles. Additionally, the courts, in interpreting statutory law, often rely on the

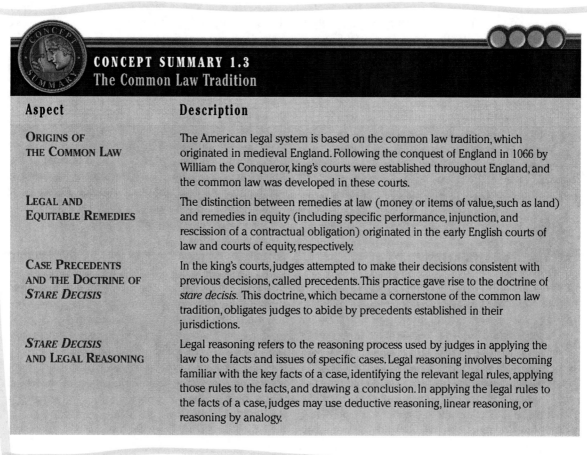

CONCEPT SUMMARY 1.3
The Common Law Tradition

Aspect	Description
ORIGINS OF THE COMMON LAW	The American legal system is based on the common law tradition, which originated in medieval England. Following the conquest of England in 1066 by William the Conqueror, king's courts were established throughout England, and the common law was developed in these courts.
LEGAL AND EQUITABLE REMEDIES	The distinction between remedies at law (money or items of value, such as land) and remedies in equity (including specific performance, injunction, and rescission of a contractual obligation) originated in the early English courts of law and courts of equity, respectively.
CASE PRECEDENTS AND THE DOCTRINE OF *STARE DECISIS*	In the king's courts, judges attempted to make their decisions consistent with previous decisions, called precedents. This practice gave rise to the doctrine of *stare decisis*. This doctrine, which became a cornerstone of the common law tradition, obligates judges to abide by precedents established in their jurisdictions.
STARE DECISIS AND LEGAL REASONING	Legal reasoning refers to the reasoning process used by judges in applying the law to the facts and issues of specific cases. Legal reasoning involves becoming familiar with the key facts of a case, identifying the relevant legal rules, applying those rules to the facts, and drawing a conclusion. In applying the legal rules to the facts of a case, judges may use deductive reasoning, linear reasoning, or reasoning by analogy.

common law as a guide to what the legislators intended.

Furthermore, how the courts interpret a particular statute determines how that statute will be applied. If you wanted to learn about the coverage and applicability of a particular statute, for example, you would necessarily have to locate the statute and study it. You would also need to see how the courts in your jurisdiction have interpreted and applied the statute. In other words, you would have to learn what precedents have been established in your jurisdiction with respect to that statute. Often, the applicability of a newly enacted statute does not become clear until a body of case law develops to clarify how, when, and to whom the statute applies.

Restatements of the Law

The American Law Institute (ALI) has drafted and published compilations of the common law called *Restatements of the Law*, which generally summarize the common law rules followed by most states. There are *Restatements of the Law* in the areas of contracts, torts, agency, trusts, property, restitution, security, judgments, and conflict of laws. The *Restatements*, like other secondary sources of law, do not in themselves have the force of law, but they are an important source of legal analysis and opinion on which judges often rely in making their decisions.

Many of the *Restatements* are now in their second, third, or fourth editions. We refer to the *Restatements* frequently in subsequent chapters of this text, indicating in parentheses the edition to which we are referring. For example, we refer to the second edition of the *Restatement of the Law of Contracts* as simply the *Restatement (Second) of Contracts*.

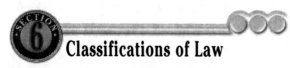

Classifications of Law

The substantial body of the law may be broken down according to several classification systems. For example, one classification system divides law into substantive law and procedural law. **Substantive law** consists of all laws that define, describe, regulate, and create legal rights and obligations. **Procedural law** consists of all laws that delineate the methods of enforcing the rights established by substantive law. Other classification systems divide law into federal law and state law, private law (dealing with relationships between pri-

vate entities) and public law (addressing the relationship between persons and their governments), and national law and international law. Here we look at still another classification system, which divides law into civil law and criminal law, as well as at what is meant by the term *cyberlaw*.

Civil Law and Criminal Law

Civil law spells out the rights and duties that exist between persons and between persons and their governments, as well as the relief available when a person's rights are violated. Typically, in a civil case, a private party sues another private party (although the government can also sue a party for a civil law violation) to make that other party comply with a duty or pay for the damage caused by failure to comply with a duty. Much of the law that we discuss in this text is civil law. Contract law, for example, covered in Chapters 10 through 19, is civil law. The whole body of tort law (see Chapters 6 and 7) is also civil law.

Criminal law, in contrast, is concerned with wrongs committed *against the public as a whole.* Criminal acts are defined and prohibited by local, state, or federal government statutes. Criminal defendants are thus prosecuted by public officials, such as a district attorney (D.A.), on behalf of the state, not by their victims or other private parties. (See Chapter 9 for a further discussion of the distinction between civil law and criminal law.)

Cyberlaw

As mentioned, the use of the Internet to conduct business transactions has led to new types of legal issues. In response, courts have had to adapt traditional laws to situations that are unique to our age. Additionally, legislatures have created laws to deal specifically with such issues. Frequently, people use the term **cyberlaw** to refer to the emerging body of law that governs transactions conducted via the Internet. Cyberlaw is not really a classification of law, nor is it a new *type* of law. Rather, it is an informal term used to describe traditional legal principles that have been modified and adapted to fit situations that are unique to the online world. Of course, in some areas new statutes have been enacted, at both the federal and the state levels, to cover specific types of problems stemming from online communications. Throughout this book, you will read how the law in a given area is evolving to govern specific legal issues that arise in the online context.

How to Find Primary Sources of Law

This text includes numerous citations to primary sources of law—federal and state statutes, the U.S. Constitution and state constitutions, regulations issued by administrative agencies, and court cases. (A **citation** is a reference to a publication in which a legal authority—such as a statute or a court decision or other source—can be found.) In this section, we explain how you can use citations to find primary sources of law. Note that in addition to the primary sources being published in sets of books as described next, most federal and state laws and case decisions are also available online.

Finding Statutory and Administrative Law

When Congress passes laws, they are collected in a publication titled *United States Statutes at Large.* When state legislatures pass laws, they are collected in similar state publications. Most frequently, however, laws are referred to in their codified form—that is, the form in which they appear in the federal and state codes. In these codes, laws are compiled by subject.

United States Code The *United States Code* (U.S.C.) arranges all existing federal laws by broad subject. Each of the fifty subjects is given a title and a title number. For example, laws relating to commerce and trade are collected in Title 15, "Commerce and Trade." Titles are subdivided by sections. A citation to the U.S.C. includes both title and section numbers. Thus, a reference to "15 U.S.C. Section 1" means that the statute can be found in Section 1 of Title 15. ("Section" may also be designated by the symbol §, and "Sections," by §§.) In addition to the print publication of the U.S.C., the federal government also provides a searchable online database of the *United States Code* at **www.gpoaccess.gov/uscode/index.html**.

Commercial publications of federal laws and regulations are also available. For example, West Group publishes the *United States Code Annotated* (U.S.C.A.). The U.S.C.A. contains the official text of the U.S.C., plus notes (annotations) on court decisions that interpret and apply specific sections of the statutes. The U.S.C.A. also includes additional research aids, such as cross-references to related statutes, historical notes, and library references. A citation to the U.S.C.A. is similar to a citation to the U.S.C.: "15 U.S.C.A. Section 1."

State Codes State codes follow the U.S.C. pattern of arranging law by subject. They may be called codes, revisions, compilations, consolidations, general statutes, or statutes, depending on the preferences of the states. In some codes, subjects are designated by number. In others, they are designated by name. For example, "13 Pennsylvania Consolidated Statutes Section 1101" means that the statute can be found in Title 13, Section 1101, of the Pennsylvania code. "California Commercial Code Section 1101" means that the statute can be found under the subject heading "Commercial Code" of the California code in Section 1101. Abbreviations are often used. For example, "13 Pennsylvania Consolidated Statutes Section 1101" is abbreviated "13 Pa. C.S. § 1101," and "California Commercial Code Section 1101" is abbreviated "Cal. Com. Code § 1101."

Administrative Rules Rules and regulations adopted by federal administrative agencies are initially published in the *Federal Register,* a daily publication of the U.S. government. Later, they are incorporated into the *Code of Federal Regulations* (C.F.R.). Like the U.S.C., the C.F.R. is divided into fifty titles. Rules within each title are assigned section numbers. A full citation to the C.F.R. includes title and section numbers. For example, a reference to "17 C.F.R. Section 230.504" means that the rule can be found in Section 230.504 of Title 17.

Finding Case Law

Before discussing the case reporting system, we need to look briefly at the court system (which will be discussed in detail in Chapter 2). There are two types of courts in the United States, federal courts and state courts. Both the federal and the state court systems consist of several levels, or tiers, of courts. *Trial courts,* in which evidence is presented and testimony given, are on the bottom tier (which also includes lower courts that handle specialized issues). Decisions from a trial court can be appealed to a higher court, which commonly is an intermediate *court of appeals,* or an *appellate court.* Decisions from these intermediate courts of appeals may be appealed to an even higher court, such as a state supreme court or the United States Supreme Court.

State Court Decisions Most state trial court decisions are not published in books (except in New

York and a few other states, which publish selected trial court opinions). Decisions from state trial courts are typically filed in the office of the clerk of the court, where the decisions are available for public inspection. Written decisions of the appellate, or reviewing, courts, however, are published and distributed (both in print and via the Internet). As you will note, most of the state court cases presented in this book are from state appellate courts. The reported appellate decisions are published in volumes called *reports* or *reporters*, which are numbered consecutively. State appellate court decisions are found in the state reporters of that particular state. Official reports are volumes that are published by the state, whereas unofficial reports are privately published.

Regional Reporters. State court opinions appear in regional units of the National Reporter System, published by West Group. Most lawyers and libraries have the West reporters because they report cases more quickly, and are distributed more widely, than the state-published reporters. In fact, many states have eliminated their own reporters in favor of West's National Reporter System. The National Reporter System divides the states into the following geographic areas: *Atlantic* (A. or A.2d), *North Eastern* (N.E. or N.E.2d), *North Western* (N.W. or N.W.2d), *Pacific* (P., P.2d, or P.3d), *South Eastern* (S.E. or S.E.2d), *South Western* (S.W., S.W.2d, or S.W.3d), and *Southern* (So. or So.2d). (The *2d* and *3d* in the preceding abbreviations refer to *Second Series* and *Third Series,* respectively.) The states included in each of these regional divisions are indicated in Exhibit 1–4, which illustrates West's National Reporter System.

Case Citations. After appellate decisions have been published, they are normally referred to (cited) by the name of the case; the volume, name, and page number of the state's official reporter (if different from West's National Reporter System); the volume, name, and page number of the National Reporter; and the volume, name, and page number of any other selected reporter. (Citing a reporter by volume number, name, and page number, in that order, is common to all citations; often, as in this book, the year the decision was issued will be included in parentheses, just after the citations to reporters.) When more than one reporter is cited for the same case, each reference is called a *parallel citation.*

Note that some states have adopted a "public domain citation system" that uses a somewhat different format for the citation. For example, in Wisconsin, a Wisconsin Supreme Court decision might be designated "2008 WI 40," meaning that the case was decided in the year 2008 by the Wisconsin Supreme Court and was the fortieth decision issued by that court during that year. Parallel citations to the *Wisconsin Reports* and West's *North Western Reporter* are still included after the public domain citation.

Consider the following case citation: *Ramirez v. Health Net of Northeast, Inc.,* 285 Conn. 1, 938 A.2d 576 (2008). We see that the opinion in this case can be found in Volume 285 of the official *Connecticut Reports,* which reports only the decisions of the Supreme Court of Connecticut, on page 1. The parallel citation is to Volume 938 of the *Atlantic Reporter, Second Series,* page 576. In presenting opinions in this text, in addition to the reporter, we give the name of the court hearing the case and the year of the court's decision. Sample citations to state court decisions are explained in Exhibit 1–5 on pages 18–20.

Federal Court Decisions Federal district (trial) court decisions are published unofficially in West's *Federal Supplement* (F.Supp. or F.Supp.2d), and opinions from the circuit courts of appeals (reviewing courts) are reported unofficially in West's *Federal Reporter* (F., F.2d, or F.3d). Cases concerning federal bankruptcy law are published unofficially in West's *Bankruptcy Reporter* (Bankr. or B.R.).

The official edition of the United States Supreme Court decisions is the *United States Reports* (U.S.), which is published by the federal government. Unofficial editions of Supreme Court cases include West's *Supreme Court Reporter* (S.Ct.) and the *Lawyers' Edition of the Supreme Court Reports* (L.Ed. or L.Ed.2d). Sample citations for federal court decisions are also listed and explained in Exhibit 1–5.

Unpublished Opinions Many court opinions that are not yet published or that are not intended for publication can be accessed through Westlaw® (abbreviated in citations as "WL"), an online legal database maintained by West Group. When no citation to a published reporter is available for cases cited in this text, we give the WL citation (see Exhibit 1–5 for an example). Can a court consider unpublished decisions as persuasive precedent? See this chapter's *Insight into E-Commerce* feature on pages 22 and 23 for a discussion of this issue.

EXHIBIT 1–4 • **West's National Reporter System—Regional/Federal**

Regional Reporters	Coverage Beginning	Coverage
Atlantic Reporter (A. or A.2d)	1885	Connecticut, Delaware, District of Columbia, Maine, Maryland, New Hampshire, New Jersey, Pennsylvania, Rhode Island, and Vermont.
North Eastern Reporter (N.E. or N.E.2d)	1885	Illinois, Indiana, Massachusetts, New York, and Ohio.
North Western Reporter (N.W. or N.W.2d)	1879	Iowa, Michigan, Minnesota, Nebraska, North Dakota, South Dakota, and Wisconsin.
Pacific Reporter (P., P.2d, or P.3d)	1883	Alaska, Arizona, California, Colorado, Hawaii, Idaho, Kansas, Montana, Nevada, New Mexico, Oklahoma, Oregon, Utah, Washington, and Wyoming.
South Eastern Reporter (S.E. or S.E.2d)	1887	Georgia, North Carolina, South Carolina, Virginia, and West Virginia.
South Western Reporter (S.W., S.W.2d, or S.W.3d)	1886	Arkansas, Kentucky, Missouri, Tennessee, and Texas.
Southern Reporter (So. or So.2d)	1887	Alabama, Florida, Louisiana, and Mississippi.
Federal Reporters		
Federal Reporter (F., F.2d, or F.3d)	1880	U.S. Circuit Courts from 1880 to 1912; U.S. Commerce Court from 1911 to 1913; U.S. District Courts from 1880 to 1932; U.S. Court of Claims (now called U.S. Court of Federal Claims) from 1929 to 1932 and since 1960; U.S. Courts of Appeals since 1891; U.S. Court of Customs and Patent Appeals since 1929; U.S. Emergency Court of Appeals since 1943.
Federal Supplement (F.Supp. or F.Supp.2d)	1932	U.S. Court of Claims from 1932 to 1960; U.S. District Courts since 1932; U.S. Customs Court since 1956.
Federal Rules Decisions (F.R.D.)	1939	U.S. District Courts involving the Federal Rules of Civil Procedure since 1939 and Federal Rules of Criminal Procedure since 1946.
Supreme Court Reporter (S.Ct.)	1882	United States Supreme Court since the October term of 1882.
Bankruptcy Reporter (Bankr.)	1980	Bankruptcy decisions of U.S. Bankruptcy Courts, U.S. District Courts, U.S. Courts of Appeals, and the United States Supreme Court.
Military Justice Reporter (M.J.)	1978	U.S. Court of Military Appeals and Courts of Military Review for the Army, Navy, Air Force, and Coast Guard.

NATIONAL REPORTER SYSTEM MAP

■ Pacific
□ North Western
□ South Western
■ North Eastern
■ Atlantic
■ South Eastern
■ Southern

EXHIBIT 1–5 • **How to Read Citations**

STATE COURTS

274 Neb. 796, 743 N.W.2d 632 (2008)[a]

> *N.W.* is the abbreviation for West's publication of state court decisions rendered in the *North Western Reporter* of the National Reporter System. *2d* indicates that this case was included in the *Second Series* of that reporter. The number 743 refers to the volume number of the reporter; the number 632 refers to the page in that volume on which this case begins.

> *Neb.* is an abbreviation for *Nebraska Reports*, Nebraska's official reports of the decisions of its highest court, the Nebraska Supreme Court.

159 Cal.App.4th 1114, 72 Cal.Rptr.3d 81 (2008)

> *Cal.Rptr.* is the abbreviation for West's unofficial reports—titled *California Reporter*—of the decisions of California courts.

8 N.Y.3d 422, 867 N.E.2d 381, 835 N.Y.S.2d 530 (2007)

> *N.Y.S.* is the abbreviation for West's unofficial reports—titled *New York Supplement*—of the decisions of New York courts.

> *N.Y.* is the abbreviation for *New York Reports*, New York's official reports of the decisions of its court of appeals. The New York Court of Appeals is the state's highest court, analogous to other states' supreme courts. In New York, a supreme court is a trial court.

289 Ga.App. 85, 656 S.E.2d 222 (2008)

> *Ga.App.* is the abbreviation for *Georgia Appeals Reports*, Georgia's official reports of the decisions of its court of appeals.

FEDERAL COURTS

____ U.S. ___, 128 S.Ct. 1184, 170 L.Ed.2d 151 (2008)

> *L.Ed.* is an abbreviation for *Lawyers' Edition of the Supreme Court Reports*, an unofficial edition of decisions of the United States Supreme Court.

> *S.Ct.* is the abbreviation for West's unofficial reports—titled *Supreme Court Reporter*—of decisions of the United States Supreme Court.

> *U.S.* is the abbreviation for *United States Reports*, the official edition of the decisions of the United States Supreme Court. The blank lines in this citation (or any other citation) indicate that the appropriate volume of the case reporter has not yet been published and no page number is available.

a. The case names have been deleted from these citations to emphasize the publications. It should be kept in mind, however, that the name of a case is as important as the specific page numbers in the volumes in which it is found. If a citation is incorrect, the correct citation may be found in a publication's index of case names. In addition to providing a check on errors in citations, the date of a case is important because the value of a recent case as an authority is likely to be greater than that of older cases from the same court.

EXHIBIT 1–5 • **How to Read Citations—Continued**

FEDERAL COURTS (Continued)

512 F.3d 582 (9th Cir. 2008)

9th Cir. is an abbreviation denoting that this case was decided in the U.S. Court of Appeals for the Ninth Circuit.

533 F.Supp.2d 740 (W.D.Mich. 2008)

W.D.Mich. is an abbreviation indicating that the U.S. District Court for the Western District of Michigan decided this case.

ENGLISH COURTS

9 Exch. 341, 156 Eng.Rep. 145 (1854)

Eng.Rep. is an abbreviation for *English Reports, Full Reprint,* a series of reports containing selected decisions made in English courts between 1378 and 1865.

Exch. is an abbreviation for *English Exchequer Reports,* which includes the original reports of cases decided in England's Court of Exchequer.

STATUTORY AND OTHER CITATIONS

18 U.S.C. Section 1961(1)(A)

U.S.C. denotes *United States Code,* the codification of *United States Statutes at Large.* The number 18 refers to the statute's U.S.C. title number and 1961 to its section number within that title. The number 1 in parentheses refers to a subsection within the section, and the letter A in parentheses to a subdivision within the subsection.

UCC 2–206(1)(b)

UCC is an abbreviation for *Uniform Commercial Code.* The first number 2 is a reference to an article of the UCC, and 206 to a section within that article. The number 1 in parentheses refers to a subsection within the section, and the letter b in parentheses to a subdivision within the subsection.

Restatement (Second) of Torts, Section 568

Restatement (Second) of Torts refers to the second edition of the American Law Institute's *Restatement of the Law of Torts.* The number 568 refers to a specific section.

17 C.F.R. Section 230.505

C.F.R. is an abbreviation for *Code of Federal Regulations,* a compilation of federal administrative regulations. The number 17 designates the regulation's title number, and 230.505 designates a specific section within that title.

EXHIBIT CONTINUES

EXHIBIT 1–5 • How to Read Citations—Continued

WESTLAW® CITATIONS[b]

2008 WL 427478

WL is an abbreviation for Westlaw. The number 2008 is the year of the document that can be found with this citation in the Westlaw database. The number 427478 is a number assigned to a specific document. A higher number indicates that a document was added to the Westlaw database later in the year.

UNIFORM RESOURCE LOCATORS (URLs)

http://www.westlaw.com[c]

The suffix *com* is the top level domain (TLD) for this Web site. The TLD *com* is an abbreviation for "commercial," which usually means that a for-profit entity hosts (maintains or supports) this Web site.

westlaw is the host name—the part of the domain name selected by the organization that registered the name. In this case, West Group registered the name. This Internet site is the Westlaw database on the Web.

www is an abbreviation for "World Wide Web." The Web is a system of Internet servers that support documents formatted in *HTML* (hypertext markup language). HTML supports links to text, graphics, and audio and video files.

http://www.uscourts.gov

This is "The Federal Judiciary Home Page." The host is the Administrative Office of the U.S. Courts. The TLD *gov* is an abbreviation for "government." This Web site includes information and links from, and about, the federal courts.

http://www.law.cornell.edu/index.html

This part of a URL points to a Web page or file at a specific location within the host's domain. This page is a menu with links to documents within the domain and to other Internet resources.

This is the host name for a Web site that contains the Internet publications of the Legal Information Institute (LII), which is a part of Cornell Law School. The LII site includes a variety of legal materials and links to other legal resources on the Internet. The TLD *edu* is an abbreviation for "educational institution" (a school or a university).

http://www.ipl.org/div/news

This part of the Web site points to a static *news* page at this Web site, which provides links to online newspapers from around the world.

div is an abbreviation for "division," which is the way that the Internet Public Library tags the content on its Web site as relating to a specific topic.

ipl is an abbreviation for "Internet Public Library," which is an online service that provides reference resources and links to other information services on the Web. The IPL is supported chiefly by the School of Information at the University of Michigan. The TLD *org* is an abbreviation for "organization" (normally nonprofit).

b. Many court decisions that are not yet published or that are not intended for publication can be accessed through Westlaw, an online legal database.
c. The basic form for a URL is "service://hostname/path." The Internet service for all of the URLs in this text is *http* (hypertext transfer protocol). Because most Web browsers add this prefix automatically when a user enters a host name or a hostname/path, we have omitted the http:// from the URLs listed in this text.

Old Case Law On a few occasions, this text cites opinions from old, classic cases dating to the nineteenth century or earlier; some of these are from the English courts. The citations to these cases may not conform to the descriptions given above because the reporters in which they were published were often known by the names of the persons who compiled the reporters and have since been replaced.

How to Read and Understand Case Law

The decisions made by the courts establish the boundaries of the law as it applies to virtually all business relationships. It thus is essential that businesspersons know how to read and understand case law. The cases that we present in this text have been condensed from the full text of the courts' opinions and are presented in a special format. In each case, we have summarized the background and facts, as well as the court's decision and rationale, in our own words and have included only selected portions of the court's opinion. For those who wish to review court cases as part of research projects or to gain additional legal information, the following sections will provide useful insights into how to read and understand case law.

Case Titles

The title of a case, such as *Adams v. Jones,* indicates the names of the parties to the lawsuit. The *v.* in the case title stands for *versus,* which means "against." In the trial court, Adams was the plaintiff—the person who filed the suit. Jones was the defendant. If the case is appealed, however, the appellate court will sometimes place the name of the party appealing the decision first, so the case may be called *Jones v. Adams* if Jones is appealing. Because some appellate courts retain the trial court order of names, it is often impossible to distinguish the plaintiff from the defendant in the title of a reported appellate court decision. You must carefully read the facts of each case to identify the parties. Otherwise, the discussion by the appellate court may be difficult to understand.

Terminology

The following terms, phrases, and abbreviations are frequently encountered in court opinions and legal publications. Because it is important to understand what is meant by these terms, phrases, and abbreviations, we define and discuss them here.

Parties to Lawsuits As mentioned previously, the party initiating a lawsuit is referred to as the *plaintiff* or *petitioner,* depending on the nature of the action, and the party against whom a lawsuit is brought is the *defendant* or *respondent.* Lawsuits frequently involve more than one plaintiff and/or defendant. When a case is appealed from the original court or jurisdiction to another court or jurisdiction, the party appealing the case is called the **appellant.** The **appellee** is the party against whom the appeal is taken. (In some appellate courts, the party appealing a case is referred to as the *petitioner,* and the party against whom the suit is brought or appealed is called the *respondent.*)

Judges and Justices The terms *judge* and *justice* are usually synonymous and represent two designations given to judges in various courts. All members of the United States Supreme Court, for example, are referred to as justices, and justice is the formal title often given to judges of appellate courts, although this is not always the case. In New York, a *justice* is a judge of the trial court (which is called the Supreme Court), and a member of the Court of Appeals (the state's highest court) is called a *judge.* The term *justice* is commonly abbreviated to J., and *justices,* to JJ. A Supreme Court case might refer to Justice Alito as Alito, J., or to Chief Justice Roberts as Roberts, C.J.

Decisions and Opinions Most decisions reached by reviewing, or appellate, courts are explained in written **opinions.** The opinion contains the court's reasons for its decision, the rules of law that apply, and the judgment.

Unanimous, Concurring, and Dissenting Opinions. When all judges or justices unanimously agree on an opinion, the opinion is written for the entire court and can be deemed a *unanimous opinion.* When there is not a unanimous opinion, a *majority opinion* is written; the majority opinion outlines the view supported by the majority of the judges or justices deciding the case. If a judge agrees, or concurs, with the majority's decision, but for different reasons, that judge may write a *concurring opinion.* A *dissenting opinion* presents the views of one or more judges who disagree with the majority's decision. The dissenting opinion is important because it may form the basis of the arguments used years later in overruling the precedential majority opinion.

Other Types of Opinions. Occasionally, a court issues a *per curiam* opinion. *Per curiam* is a Latin phrase meaning "of the court." In *per curiam* opinions, there is no indication as to which judge or justice authored the opinion. This term may also be used for an announcement of a court's disposition of a case that is not accompanied by a written opinion. Some of the cases presented in this text are *en banc* decisions.

When an appellate court reviews a case *en banc,* which is a French term (derived from a Latin term) for "in the bench," generally all of the judges "sitting on the bench" of that court review the case.

A Sample Court Case

Knowing how to read and understand court opinions and the legal reasoning used by the courts is an essential step in undertaking accurate legal research. A further step is "briefing," or summarizing, the case. Legal researchers routinely brief cases by reducing the texts of the opinions to their essential elements. Instructions on how to brief a case are given in Appendix A.

The cases within the chapters in this text have already been analyzed and briefed by the authors, and the essential aspects of each case are presented precedent to some extent because they are so publicly accessible.

Another argument against allowing unpublished decisions to be precedent concerns the quality of the legal reasoning set forth in these decisions. Staff attorneys and law clerks frequently write unpublished opinions so that judges can spend more time on the opinions intended for publication. Consequently, some claim that allowing unpublished decisions to establish precedent could result in bad precedents because the reasoning may not be up to par. If the decision is regarded merely as persuasive precedent, however, then judges who disagree with the reasoning are free to reject the conclusion.

The United States Supreme Court Changes Federal Rules on Unpublished Opinions after 2007

In spite of objections from several hundred judges and lawyers, the United States Supreme Court made history in 2006 when it announced that it would allow lawyers to refer to (cite) unpublished decisions in all federal courts. The new rule, Rule 32.1 of the Federal Rules of Appellate Procedure, states that federal courts may not prohibit or restrict the citation of federal judicial opinions that have been designated as "not for publication," "non-precedential," or "not precedent." The rule applies only to federal courts and only to unpublished opinions issued after January 1, 2007. It does not specify the effect that a court must give to one of its unpublished opinions or to an unpublished opinion from another court. Basically, the rule simply makes all the federal courts follow a uniform rule that allows attorneys to cite—and judges to consider as persuasive precedent—unpublished decisions beginning in 2007.

The impact of this new rule remains to be seen. At present, the majority of states do not allow their state courts to consider the rulings in unpublished cases as persuasive precedent, and this rule does not affect the states. The Supreme Court's decision, however, provides an example of how technology—the availability of unpublished opinions over the Internet—has affected the law.

CRITICAL THINKING

INSIGHT INTO THE SOCIAL ENVIRONMENT

Now that the Supreme Court is allowing unpublished decisions to form persuasive precedent in federal courts, should state courts follow? Why or why not?

in a convenient format consisting of two sections: *Background and Facts* and *Decision and Rationale*. This format is illustrated in the sample court case in Exhibit 1–6 on pages 24 and 25, which has been annotated to explain the kind of information that is contained in each section. In the remaining chapters of this book, the basic format is often expanded to include special introductory sections, or special comments or considerations following the cases.

The case we present and annotate in Exhibit 1–6 is an actual case that the U.S. Court of Appeals for the Ninth Circuit decided in 2008. The Seattle Center is an entertainment "zone" near downtown Seattle, Washington, that attracts almost ten million tourists every year. The center encompasses theaters, arenas, museums, exhibition halls, conference rooms, outdoor stadiums, and restaurants. Street performers add to the festive atmosphere. Under the authority of the city, the center's director issued rules to address safety concerns and other matters. Staff at the Seattle Center cited one of the street performers, a balloon artist, for several rule violations. The artist filed a suit in a federal district court against the city and others, alleging that the rules violated his rights under the U.S. Constitution. The court issued a judgment in the plaintiff's favor. The city appealed to the U.S. Court of Appeals for the Ninth Circuit.

EXHIBIT 1–6 ● **A Sample Court Case**

> This section contains the citation—the name of the case, the name of the court that heard the case, the year of the decision, and the reporter in which the court's opinion can be found.

> This section identifies the parties and describes the events leading up to the trial and its appeal. The decision of the lower court is included, as well as the issue to be decided by the U.S. Court of Appeals for the Ninth Circuit.

> A document that, when filed with a court, initiates a lawsuit.

> A court decree ordering a person to do or refrain from doing a certain act.

> The First Amendment to the Constitution guarantees, among other freedoms, the right of free speech—to express one's views without governmental restrictions.

> A judgment that a court enters without beginning or continuing a trial. It can be entered only if no facts are in dispute and the only question is how the law applies.

> This section contains the court's decision and reasoning on the issue before it. An appellate court's decision is often phrased with reference to the decision of the lower court from which the case was appealed. For example, an appellate court may "affirm" or "reverse" a lower court's ruling. A court's rationale indicates the relevant laws and legal principles, and the court's reasoning that led to its conclusion.

> Sent back.

> A federal court that hears appeals from the federal district courts located within its geographical boundaries.

BERGER v. CITY OF SEATTLE

U.S. Court of Appeals,

Ninth Circuit, 2008.

512 F.3d 582.

Background and Facts In the heart of the city of Seattle, Washington, is the Seattle Center, an entertainment zone covering eighty acres of land. Within this area, the city requires that all street performers follow the so-called Campus Rules. One such rule, Rule F.1, requires a permit for street performers and requires badges to be worn during street performances. Michael Berger, a street performer, has been performing there since the 1980s. After the Campus Rules were enacted in 2002, Berger obtained a permit. Thereafter, Seattle Center authorities received numerous publicly filed complaints alleging that Berger had exhibited threatening behavior. Also, the Seattle Center staff reported several rule violations. In 2003, Berger filed a **complaint** seeking damages and an **injunctive relief**, alleging that the Campus Rules violated the **First Amendment** to the U.S. Constitution. In 2005, a federal district court granted **summary judgment** to Berger. The city appealed the district court's order of summary judgment to the U.S. Court of Appeals for the Ninth Circuit and sought to reverse with instructions to enter summary judgment in its favor.

Decision and Rationale The U.S. Court of Appeals for the Ninth Circuit reversed the summary judgment to Berger and **remanded** the case to the district court for further proceedings consistent with the appellate court's opinion. The **appellate court** stated that restrictions on oral or written speech "must be justified without reference to the content of the regulated speech, [and] they must be narrowly tailored to serve a significant government interest. * * * " If a licensing statute affects only certain messages, it would lack neutrality. Seattle's licensing requirement for the Seattle Center did not, according to the court, discriminate based on content. Further, the court stated

EXHIBIT 1–6 • **A Sample Court Case—Continued**

that "The Seattle Center authorities enacted the permit requirement after encountering 'chronic' territorial disputes between
performers and threats to public citizens by street performers."
The court was convinced that street performers did pose a threat
to the city's interest in maintaining order in the Seattle Center. It
stated that the Seattle Center rules satisfied "requirements for
valid restrictions on expression under the First Amendment."

REVIEWING Introduction to Law and Legal Reasoning

Suppose that the California legislature passes a law that severely restricts carbon dioxide
emissions from automobiles in that state. A group of automobile manufacturers files a suit
against the state of California to prevent the enforcement of the law. The automakers claim that a federal
law already sets fuel economy standards nationwide and that fuel economy standards are essentially the
same as carbon dioxide emission standards. According to the automobile manufacturers, it is unfair to
allow California to impose more stringent regulations than those set by the federal law. Using the
information presented in the chapter, answer the following questions.

1. Who are the parties (the plaintiffs and the defendant) in this lawsuit?
2. Are the plaintiffs seeking a legal remedy or an equitable remedy? Why?
3. What is the primary source of the law that is at issue here?
4. Where would you look to find the relevant California and federal laws?

TERMS AND CONCEPTS

administrative agency
administrative law
allege
analogy
appellant
appellee
binding authority

breach
case law
case on point
chancellor
citation
civil law
common law
constitutional law
court of equity
court of law

criminal law
cyberlaw
damages
defendant
defense
equitable maxims
executive agency
historical school
independent regulatory
  agency

jurisprudence 2

laches 9

law 2

legal realism 3

legal reasoning 11

natural law 3

opinion 21

ordinance 6

petitioner 9

plaintiff 9

positive law 3

positivist school 3

precedent 10

procedural law 14

public policy 11

remedy 8

remedy at law 8

remedy in equity 8

reporter 10

respondent 9

sociological school 4

stare decisis 10

statute of limitations 9

statutory law 6

substantive law 14

syllogism 12

uniform law 6

QUESTIONS AND CASE PROBLEMS

1-1. How does statutory law come into existence? How does it differ from the common law? If statutory law conflicts with the common law, which law will govern?

1-2. QUESTION WITH SAMPLE ANSWER

After World War II, which ended in 1945, an international tribunal of judges convened at Nuremberg, Germany. The judges convicted several Nazis of "crimes against humanity." Assuming that the Nazi war criminals who were convicted had not disobeyed any law of their country and had merely been following their government's (Hitler's) orders, what law had they violated? Explain.

- **For a sample answer to Question 1-2, go to Appendix C at the end of this text.**

1-3. Assume that you want to read the entire court opinion in the case of *Menashe v. V Secret Catalogue, Inc.,* 409 F.Supp.2d 412 (S.D.N.Y. 2006). The case focuses on whether "SEXY LITTLE THINGS" is a suggestive or descriptive trademark and on which of the parties to the suit used the mark first in commerce. (Note that this case is presented in Chapter 8 of this text as Case 8.2.) Refer to the subsection entitled "Finding Case Law" in this chapter, and then explain specifically where you would find the court's opinion.

1-4. This chapter discussed a number of sources of American law. Which source of law takes priority in the following situations, and why?

(a) A federal statute conflicts with the U.S. Constitution.
(b) A federal statute conflicts with a state constitutional provision.
(c) A state statute conflicts with the common law of that state.
(d) A state constitutional amendment conflicts with the U.S. Constitution.

1-5. In the text of this chapter, we stated that the doctrine of *stare decisis* "became a cornerstone of the English and American judicial systems." What does *stare decisis* mean, and why has this doctrine been so fundamental to the development of our legal tradition?

1-6. What is the difference between a concurring opinion and a majority opinion? Between a concurring opinion and a dissenting opinion? Why do judges and justices write concurring and dissenting opinions, given that these opinions will not affect the outcome of the case at hand, which has already been decided by majority vote?

1-7. Courts can overturn precedents and thus change the common law. Should judges have the same authority to overrule statutory law? Explain.

1-8. "The judge's role is not to make the law but to uphold and apply the law." Do you agree or disagree with this statement? Discuss fully the reasons for your answer.

1-9. Assume that Arthur Rabe is suing Xavier Sanchez for breaching a contract in which Sanchez promised to sell Rabe a Van Gogh painting for $3 million.

(a) In this lawsuit, who is the plaintiff and who is the defendant?
(b) Suppose that Rabe wants Sanchez to perform the contract as promised. What remedy would Rabe seek from the court?
(c) Now suppose that Rabe wants to cancel the contract because Sanchez fraudulently misrepresented the painting as an original Van Gogh when in fact it is a copy. What remedy would Rabe seek?
(d) Will the remedy Rabe seeks in either situation be a remedy at law or a remedy in equity? What is the difference between legal and equitable remedies?
(e) Suppose that the trial court finds in Rabe's favor and grants one of these remedies. Sanchez then appeals the decision to a higher court. On appeal, which party will be the appellant (or petitioner), and which party will be the appellee (or respondent)?

1–10. A QUESTION OF ETHICS

On July 5, 1884, Dudley, Stephens, and Brooks— "all able-bodied English seamen"—and a teenage English boy were cast adrift in a lifeboat following a storm at sea. They had no water with them in the boat, and all they had for sustenance were two one-pound tins of turnips. On July 24, Dudley proposed that one of the four in the lifeboat be sacrificed to save the others. Stephens agreed with Dudley, but Brooks refused to consent—and the boy was never asked for his opinion. On July 25, Dudley killed the boy, and the three men then fed on the boy's body and blood. Four days later, a passing vessel rescued the men. They were taken to England and tried for the murder of the boy. If the men had not fed on the boy's body, they would probably have died of starvation within the four-day period. The boy, who was in a much weaker condition, would likely have died before the rest. [Regina v. Dudley and Stephens, 14 Q.B.D. (Queen's Bench Division, England) 273 (1884)]

(a) The basic question in this case is whether the survivors should be subject to penalties under English criminal law, given the men's unusual circumstances. Were the defendants' actions necessary but unethical? Explain your reasoning. What ethical issues might be involved here?

(b) Should judges ever have the power to look beyond the written "letter of the law" in making their decisions? Why or why not?

LAW ON THE WEB

Today, business law and legal environment professors and students can go online to access information on almost every topic covered in this text. A good point of departure for online legal research is the Web site for *Business Law: Alternate Edition,* Eleventh Edition, which can be found at **www.cengage.com/blaw/jentz**. There you will find numerous materials relevant to this text and to business law generally, including links to various legal resources on the Web. Additionally, every chapter in this text ends with a *Law on the Web* feature that contains selected Web addresses.

You can access many of the sources of law discussed in Chapter 1 at the FindLaw Web site, which is probably the most comprehensive source of free legal information on the Internet. Go to

www.findlaw.com

The Legal Information Institute (LII) at Cornell Law School, which offers extensive information about U.S. law, is also a good starting point for legal research. The URL for this site is

www.law.cornell.edu

The Library of Congress offers extensive links to state and federal government resources at

www.loc.gov

Legal Research Exercises on the Web

Go to **www.cengage.com/blaw/jentz**, the Web site that accompanies this text. Select "Chapter 1" and click on "Internet Exercises." There you will find the following Internet research exercises that you can perform to learn more about some of the important sources of law discussed in Chapter 1 and other useful legal sites on the Web.

Internet Exercise 1–1: Legal Perspective
                Internet Sources of Law

Internet Exercise 1–2: Management Perspective
                Online Assistance from Government Agencies

Internet Exercise 1–3: Social Perspective
                The Case of the Speluncean Explorers

CHAPTER 2

Courts and Alternative Dispute Resolution

Today in the United States there are fifty-two court systems—one for each of the fifty states, one for the District of Columbia, and a federal system. Keep in mind that the federal courts are not superior to the state courts; they are simply an independent system of courts, which derives its authority from Article III, Section 2, of the U.S. Constitution. By the power given to it under Article I of the U.S. Constitution, Congress has extended the federal court system beyond the boundaries of the United States to U.S. territories such as Guam, Puerto Rico, and the Virgin Islands.[1] As we shall see, the United States Supreme Court is the final controlling voice over all of these fifty-two systems, at least when questions of federal law are involved.

Every businessperson will likely face a lawsuit at some time in his or her career. Thus, anyone involved in business needs to have an understanding of the American court systems, as well as the various methods of dispute resolution that can be pursued outside the courts. In this chapter, after examining the judiciary's role in the American governmental system, we discuss some basic requirements that must be met before a party may bring a lawsuit in front of a particular court. We then look at the court systems of the United States in some detail. We conclude the chapter with an overview of some alternative methods of settling disputes, including online dispute resolution.

---

1. In Guam and the Virgin Islands, territorial courts serve as both federal courts and state courts; in Puerto Rico, they serve only as federal courts.

The Judiciary's Role in American Government

As you learned in Chapter 1, the body of American law includes the federal and state constitutions, statutes passed by legislative bodies, administrative law, and the case decisions and legal principles that form the common law. These laws would be meaningless, however, without the courts to interpret and apply them. This is the essential role of the judiciary—the courts—in the American governmental system: to interpret the laws and apply them to specific situations.

As the branch of government entrusted with interpreting the laws, the judiciary can decide, among other things, whether the laws or actions of the other two branches are constitutional. The process for making such a determination is known as **judicial review.** The power of judicial review enables the judicial branch to act as a check on the other two branches of government, in line with the system of checks and balances established by the U.S. Constitution.[2]

The power of judicial review is not mentioned in the Constitution (although many constitutional scholars conclude that the founders intended the judiciary to have this power). Rather, this power was explicitly established by the United States Supreme Court in 1803 by its decision in *Marbury v. Madison*,[3] in which the Supreme Court stated, "It is emphatically the province and duty of the Judicial Department to say

---

2. In a broad sense, judicial review occurs whenever a court "reviews" a case or legal proceeding—as when an appellate court reviews a lower court's decision. When referring to the judiciary's role in American government, however, the term *judicial review* is used to indicate the power of the judiciary to decide whether the actions of the other two branches of government do or do not violate the U.S. Constitution.

3. 5 U.S. (1 Cranch) 137, 2 L.Ed. 60 (1803).

what the law is. . . . If two laws conflict with each other, the courts must decide on the operation of each. . . . So if the law be in opposition to the Constitution . . . [t]he Court must determine which of these conflicting rules governs the case. This is the very essence of judicial duty." Since the *Marbury v. Madison* decision, the power of judicial review has remained unchallenged. Today, this power is exercised by both federal and state courts.

Basic Judicial Requirements

Before a lawsuit can be brought before a court, certain requirements must be met. These requirements relate to jurisdiction, venue, and standing to sue. We examine each of these important concepts here.

Jurisdiction

In Latin, *juris* means "law," and *diction* means "to speak." Thus, "the power to speak the law" is the literal meaning of the term **jurisdiction.** Before any court can hear a case, it must have jurisdiction over the person (or company) against whom the suit is brought (the defendant) or over the property involved in the suit. The court must also have jurisdiction over the subject matter of the dispute.

Jurisdiction over Persons or Property

Generally, a particular court can exercise *in personam* **jurisdiction** (personal jurisdiction) over any person or business that resides in a certain geographic area. A state trial court, for example, normally has jurisdictional authority over residents (including businesses) of a particular area of the state, such as a county or district. A state's highest court (often called the state supreme court)[4] has jurisdictional authority over all residents within the state.

A court can also exercise jurisdiction over property that is located within its boundaries. This kind of jurisdiction is known as *in rem* **jurisdiction,** or "jurisdiction over the thing." Suppose that a dispute arises over the ownership of a boat in dry dock in Fort Lauderdale, Florida. The boat is owned by an Ohio resident, over whom a Florida court normally cannot exercise per-

sonal jurisdiction. The other party to the dispute is a resident of Nebraska. In this situation, a lawsuit concerning the boat could be brought in a Florida state court on the basis of the court's *in rem* jurisdiction.

Long Arm Statutes. Under the authority of a state **long arm statute,** a court can exercise personal jurisdiction over certain out-of-state defendants based on activities that took place within the state. Before a court can exercise jurisdiction over an out-of-state defendant under a long arm statute, though, it must be demonstrated that the defendant had sufficient contacts, or *minimum contacts,* with the state to justify the jurisdiction.[5] Generally, this means that the defendant must have enough of a connection to the state for the judge to conclude that it is fair for the state to exercise power over the defendant. For example, if an out-of-state defendant caused an automobile accident or sold defective goods within the state, a court will usually find that minimum contacts exist to exercise jurisdiction over that defendant. Similarly, a state may exercise personal jurisdiction over a nonresident defendant who is sued for breaching a contract that was formed within the state.

Corporate Contacts. Because corporations are considered legal persons, courts use the same principles to determine whether it is fair to exercise jurisdiction over a corporation.[6] A corporation normally is subject to personal jurisdiction in the state in which it is incorporated, has its principal office, and is doing business. Courts apply the minimum-contacts test to determine if they can exercise jurisdiction over out-of-state corporations.

The minimum-contacts requirement is usually met if the corporation advertises or sells its products within the state, or places its goods into the "stream of commerce" with the intent that the goods be sold in the state. Suppose that a business is incorporated under the laws of Maine but has a branch office and manufacturing plant in Georgia. The corporation also advertises and sells its products in Georgia. These activities would likely constitute sufficient contacts with the state of Georgia to allow a Georgia court to exercise jurisdiction over the corporation.

---

4. As will be discussed shortly, a state's highest court is often referred to as the state supreme court, but there are exceptions. For example, the court that is labeled the Supreme Court in New York is actually a trial court.

5. The minimum-contacts standard was first established in *International Shoe Co. v. State of Washington,* 326 U.S. 310, 66 S.Ct. 154, 90 L.Ed. 95 (1945).

6. In the eyes of the law, corporations are "legal persons"—entities that can sue and be sued. See Chapter 38.

Some corporations, however, do not sell or advertise products or place any goods in the stream of commerce. Determining what constitutes minimum contacts in these situations can be more difficult, as the following case—involving a resort hotel in Mexico and a hotel guest from New Jersey—illustrates.

C A S E   2.1   Mastondrea v. Occidental Hotels Management S.A.
Superior Court of New Jersey, Appellate Division, 2007. 391 N.J.Super. 261, 918 A.2d 27.
lawlibrary.rutgers.edu/search.shtml[a]

● **Background and Facts** Libgo Travel, Inc., in Ramsey, New Jersey, with Allegro Resorts Management Corporation (ARMC), a marketing agency in Miami, Florida, placed an ad in the *Newark Star Ledger,* a newspaper in Newark, New Jersey, to tout vacation packages for accommodations at the Royal Hideaway Playacar, an all-inclusive resort hotel in Quintana Roo, Mexico. ARMC is part of Occidental Hotels Management, B.V., a Netherlands corporation that owns the hotel with Occidental Hoteles Management S.A., a Spanish company. In response to the ad, Amanda Mastondrea, a New Jersey resident, bought one of the packages through Liberty Travel, a chain of travel agencies in the eastern United States that Libgo owns and operates. On June 16, 2003, at the resort, Mastondrea slipped and fell on a wet staircase, breaking her ankle. She filed a suit in a New Jersey state court against the hotel, its owners, and others, alleging negligence. The defendants asked the court to dismiss the suit on the ground that it did not have personal jurisdiction over them. The court ruled in part that it had jurisdiction over the hotel. The hotel appealed this ruling to a state intermediate appellate court.

● **Decision and Rationale** The state intermediate appellate court affirmed the lower court's ruling. "This evidence was sufficient to support the assertion of * * * personal jurisdiction over the Hotel in this State." The appellate court noted that the hotel's operations were located entirely in Mexico and that the hotel was not registered, licensed, or otherwise authorized to do business in New Jersey. In spite of this lack of business presence in that state, the reviewing court looked at the "Tour Operators Agreements" in effect between the hotel and Libgo Travel. A specific number of rooms were allotted to clients of Libgo at agreed-upon rates. Libgo was required to provide the hotel with weekly sales reports. Libgo had to confirm all reservations in writing. Moreover, the hotel "purposely and successfully" sought vacationers from New Jersey, and it derived a profit from them. Finally, the owners of the hotel entered into cooperative marketing agreements with Libgo Travel.

● **What If the Facts Were Different?** *If Mastondrea had not seen Libgo and Allegro's ad, but had bought a Royal Hideaway vacation package on the recommendation of a Liberty Travel agent, is it likely that the result in this case would have been different? Why or why not?*

● **The Global Dimension** *What do the circumstances and the holding in this case suggest to a business firm that actively attempts to attract customers in a variety of jurisdictions?*

a. In the "SEARCH THE N.J. COURTS DECISIONS" section, type "Mastondrea" in the box, and click on "Search!" In the result, click on the case name to access the opinion. Rutgers University Law School in Camden, New Jersey, maintains this Web site.

Jurisdiction over Subject Matter Subject-matter jurisdiction refers to the limitations on the types of cases a court can hear. Certain courts are empowered to hear certain kinds of disputes.

General and Limited Jurisdiction. In both the federal and the state court systems, there are courts of *general* (unlimited) *jurisdiction* and courts of *limited jurisdiction.* A court of general jurisdiction can decide cases involving a broad array of issues. An example of a court of general jurisdiction is a state trial court or a federal district court. An example of a state court of limited jurisdiction is a probate court. **Probate courts** are state courts that handle only matters relating to the transfer of a person's assets and obligations after that person's death, including issues relating to the custody and guardianship of children. An example of a federal court of limited subject-matter jurisdiction is a bankruptcy court. **Bankruptcy courts** handle only bankruptcy proceedings, which are governed by federal bankruptcy law (discussed in Chapter 30).

A court's jurisdiction over subject matter is usually defined in the statute or constitution creating the court. In both the federal and the state court systems, a court's subject-matter jurisdiction can be limited not only by the subject of the lawsuit but also by the sum in controversy, whether the case is a felony (a more serious type of crime) or a misdemeanor (a less serious type of crime), or whether the proceeding is a trial or an appeal.

Original and Appellate Jurisdiction. A court's subject-matter jurisdiction is also frequently limited to hearing cases at a particular stage of the dispute. Courts in which lawsuits begin, trials take place, and evidence is presented are referred to as *courts of original jurisdiction*. Courts having original jurisdiction are courts of the first instance, or trial courts. In the federal court system, the *district courts* are trial courts. In the various state court systems, the trial courts are known by different names, as will be discussed shortly.

Courts having appellate jurisdiction act as reviewing courts, or appellate courts. In general, cases can be brought before appellate courts only on appeal from an order or a judgment of a trial court or other lower court. In other words, the distinction between courts of original jurisdiction and courts of appellate jurisdiction normally lies in whether the case is being heard for the first time.

Jurisdiction of the Federal Courts

Because the federal government is a government of limited powers, the jurisdiction of the federal courts is limited. Federal courts have subject-matter jurisdiction in two situations.

Federal Questions. Article III of the U.S. Constitution establishes the boundaries of federal judicial power. Section 2 of Article III states that "[t]he judicial Power shall extend to all Cases, in Law and Equity, arising under this Constitution, the Laws of the United States, and Treaties made, or which shall be made, under their Authority." In effect, this clause means that whenever a plaintiff's cause of action is based, at least in part, on the U.S. Constitution, a treaty, or a federal law, a **federal question** arises. Any lawsuit involving a federal question comes under the judicial authority of the federal courts and can originate in a federal court. People who claim that their constitutional rights have been violated, for example, can begin their suits in a federal court. Note that in a case based on a federal question, a federal court will apply federal law.

Diversity of Citizenship. Federal district courts can also exercise original jurisdiction over cases involving **diversity of citizenship.** This term applies whenever a federal court has jurisdiction over a case that does not involve a question of federal law. The most common type of diversity jurisdiction has two requirements:[7] (1) the plaintiff and defendant must be residents of different states, and (2) the dollar amount in controversy must exceed $75,000. For purposes of diversity jurisdiction, a corporation is a citizen of both the state in which it is incorporated and the state in which its principal place of business is located. A case involving diversity of citizenship can be filed in the appropriate federal district court. If the case starts in a state court, it can sometimes be transferred, or "removed," to a federal court. A large percentage of the cases filed in federal courts each year are based on diversity of citizenship.

As noted, a federal court will apply federal law in cases involving federal questions. In a case based on diversity of citizenship, in contrast, a federal court will apply the relevant state law (which is often the law of the state in which the court sits).

Exclusive versus Concurrent Jurisdiction

When both federal and state courts have the power to hear a case, as is true in suits involving diversity of citizenship, **concurrent jurisdiction** exists. When cases can be tried only in federal courts or only in state courts, **exclusive jurisdiction** exists. Federal courts have exclusive jurisdiction in cases involving federal crimes, bankruptcy, and most patent and copyright claims; in suits against the United States; and in some areas of admiralty law (law governing transportation on ocean waters). State courts also have exclusive jurisdiction over certain subjects—for example, divorce and adoption. When concurrent jurisdiction exists, a party may choose to bring a suit in either a federal court or a state court.

---

7. Diversity jurisdiction also exists in cases between (1) a foreign country and citizens of a state or of different states and (2) citizens of a state and citizens or subjects of a foreign country. These bases for diversity jurisdiction are less commonly used.

Jurisdiction in Cyberspace

The Internet's capacity to bypass political and geographic boundaries undercuts the traditional basis on which courts assert personal jurisdiction. This basis includes a party's contacts with a court's geographic jurisdiction. As already discussed, for a court to compel a defendant to come before it, there must be at least minimum contacts—the presence of a salesperson within the state, for example. Are there sufficient minimum contacts if the only connection to a jurisdiction is an ad on a Web site originating from a remote location?

The "Sliding-Scale" Standard Gradually, the courts are developing a standard—called a "sliding-scale" standard—for determining when the exercise of personal jurisdiction over an out-of-state Internet-based defendant is proper. In developing this standard, the courts have identified three types of Internet business contacts: (1) substantial business conducted over the Internet (with contracts and sales, for example); (2) some interactivity through a Web site; and (3) passive advertising. Jurisdiction is proper for the first category, is improper for the third, and may or may not be appropriate for the second.[8] An Internet communication is typically considered passive if people have to voluntarily access it to read the message and active if it is sent to specific individuals.

In certain situations, even a single contact can satisfy the minimum-contacts requirement. A Louisiana man, Daniel Crummey, purchased a used recreational vehicle (RV) from sellers in Texas after viewing numerous photos of the RV on eBay. The sellers' statements on eBay stated that "everything works great on this RV and will provide comfort and dependability for years to come. This RV will go to Alaska and back without problems!" Crummey picked up the RV in Texas but on the drive back to Louisiana, the RV quit working. He filed a lawsuit in Louisiana against the sellers alleging that the vehicle was defective. The sellers claimed that the Louisiana court lacked jurisdiction, but the court held that because the sellers had used eBay to market and sell the RV to a Louisiana buyer, jurisdiction was proper.[9]

PREVENTING LEGAL DISPUTES

Today's entrepreneurs are often eager to establish Web sites to promote their products and solicit orders. Many of these individuals may not be aware that defendants can be sued in states in which they have never been physically present, provided they have had sufficient contacts with that state's residents over the Internet. Businesspersons who contemplate making their Web sites the least bit interactive should consult an attorney to find out whether by doing so they will be subjecting themselves to jurisdiction in every state. Becoming informed about the extent of potential exposure to lawsuits in various locations is an important part of preventing litigation.

International Jurisdictional Issues

Because the Internet is international in scope, international jurisdictional issues have understandingly come to the fore. The world's courts seem to be developing a standard that echoes the requirement of "minimum contacts" applied by the U.S. courts. Most courts are indicating that minimum contacts—doing business within the jurisdiction, for example—are enough to exercise jurisdiction over a defendant. The effect of this standard is that a business firm may have to comply with the laws in any jurisdiction in which it actively targets customers for its products.

To understand some of the problems created by Internet commerce, consider a French court's judgment against the U.S.-based Internet company Yahoo!, Inc. Yahoo operates an online auction site on which Nazi memorabilia have been offered for sale. In France, the display of any objects depicting symbols of Nazi ideology is illegal and leads to both criminal and civil liability. The International League against Racism and Anti-Semitism filed a suit in Paris against Yahoo for displaying Nazi memorabilia and offering them for sale via its Web site.

The French court asserted jurisdiction over Yahoo on the ground that the materials on the company's U.S.-based servers could be viewed on a Web site accessible in France. The French court ordered Yahoo to eliminate all Internet access in France to the Nazi memorabilia offered for sale through its online auctions. Yahoo then took the case to a federal district court in the United States, claiming that the French court's order violated the First Amendment to the U.S. Constitution. Although the federal district court ruled in favor of Yahoo, the U.S. Court of Appeals for the

---

8. For a leading case on this issue, see *Zippo Manufacturing Co. v. Zippo Dot Com, Inc.*, 952 F.Supp. 1119 (W.D.Pa. 1997).

9. *Crummey v. Morgan*, 965 So.2d 497 (La.App. 1st Cir. 2007).

CONCEPT SUMMARY 2.1
Jurisdiction

Type of Jurisdiction	Description
PERSONAL	Exists when a defendant is located within the territorial boundaries within which a court has the right and power to decide cases. Jurisdiction may be exercised over out-of-state defendants under state long arm statutes. Courts have jurisdiction over corporate defendants that do business within the state, as well as corporations that advertise, sell, or place goods into the stream of commerce in the state.
PROPERTY	Exists when the property that is subject to a lawsuit is located within the territorial boundaries within which a court has the right and power to decide cases.
SUBJECT MATTER	Limits the court's jurisdictional authority to particular types of cases. 1. *Limited jurisdiction*—Exists when a court is limited to a specific subject matter, such as probate or divorce. 2. *General jurisdiction*—Exists when a court can hear cases involving a broad array of issues.
ORIGINAL	Exists with courts that have the authority to hear a case for the first time (trial courts).
APPELLATE	Exists with courts of appeal and review. Generally, appellate courts do not have original jurisdiction.
FEDERAL	1. *Federal questions*—When the plaintiff's cause of action is based at least in part on the U.S. Constitution, a treaty, or a federal law, a federal court can exercise jurisdiction. 2. *Diversity of citizenship*—In cases between citizens of different states when the amount in controversy exceeds $75,000 (or in cases between a foreign country and citizens of a state or of different states and in cases between citizens of a state and citizens or subjects of a foreign country), a federal court can exercise jurisdiction.
CONCURRENT	Exists when both federal and state courts have authority to hear the same case.
EXCLUSIVE	Exists when only state courts or only federal courts have authority to hear a case.
JURISDICTION IN CYBERSPACE	Because the Internet does not have physical boundaries, traditional jurisdictional concepts have been difficult to apply in cases involving activities conducted via the Web. Gradually, the courts are developing standards to use in determining when jurisdiction over a Web site owner or operator in another state is proper. A significant legal challenge with respect to cyberspace transactions has to do with resolving jurisdictional disputes in the international context.

Ninth Circuit reversed. According to the appellate court, U.S. courts lacked personal jurisdiction over the French groups involved.[10] The *Yahoo* case represents the first time a U.S. court was asked to decide whether to honor a foreign judgment involving business conducted over the Internet. The federal appeals court's ruling leaves open the possibility that Yahoo, and anyone else who posts anything on the Internet, could be held answerable to the laws of any country in which the message might be received. *Concept Summary 2.1* reviews the various types of jurisdiction, including jurisdiction in cyberspace.

---

10. *Yahoo! Inc. v. La Ligue Contre le Racisme et l'Antisemitisme,* 379 F.3d 1120 (9th Cir. 2004), *cert.* denied, __ U.S. __, 126 S.Ct. 2332, 164 L.Ed.2d 841 (2006).

Venue

Jurisdiction has to do with whether a court has authority to hear a case involving specific persons, property, or subject matter. **Venue**[11] is concerned with the most appropriate location for a trial. For example, two state courts (or two federal courts) may have the authority to exercise jurisdiction over a case, but it may be more appropriate or convenient to hear the case in one court than in the other.

Basically, the concept of venue reflects the policy that a court trying a suit should be in the geographic neighborhood (usually the county) where the incident leading to the lawsuit occurred or where the parties involved in the lawsuit reside. Venue in a civil case typically is where the defendant resides, whereas venue in a criminal case is normally where the crime occurred. Pretrial publicity or other factors, though, may require a change of venue to another community, especially in criminal cases in which the defendant's right to a fair and impartial jury has been impaired.

Standing to Sue

In order to bring a lawsuit before a court, a party must have **standing to sue,** or a sufficient "stake" in a matter to justify seeking relief through the court system. In other words, to have standing, a party must have a legally protected and tangible interest at stake in the litigation. The party bringing the lawsuit must have suffered a harm or been threatened with a harm by the action about which she or he has complained. At times, a person can have standing to sue on behalf of another person. For example, suppose that a child suffers serious injuries as a result of a defectively manufactured toy. Because the child is a minor, another person, such as a parent or a legal guardian, can bring a lawsuit on the child's behalf.

Standing to sue also requires that the controversy at issue be a **justiciable**[12] **controversy**—a controversy that is real and substantial, as opposed to hypothetical or academic. For example, to entice DaimlerChrysler Corporation to build a $1.2 billion Jeep assembly plant in the area, the city of Toledo, Ohio, gave the company a ten-year local property tax exemption as well as a state franchise tax credit. Toledo taxpayers filed a lawsuit in state court, claiming that the tax breaks violated the commerce clause

in the U.S. Constitution. The taxpayers alleged that the tax exemption and credit injured them because they would have to pay higher taxes to cover the shortfall in tax revenues. In 2006, the United States Supreme Court ruled that the taxpayers lacked standing to sue over the incentive program because their alleged injury was "conjectural or hypothetical"—that is, there was no justiciable controversy.[13]

The State and Federal Court Systems

As mentioned earlier in this chapter, each state has its own court system. Additionally, there is a system of federal courts. Although no two state court systems are exactly the same, the right-hand side of Exhibit 2–1 illustrates the basic organizational framework characteristic of the court systems in many states. The exhibit also shows how the federal court system is structured. We turn now to an examination of these court systems, beginning with the state courts. (See this chapter's *Insight into Ethics* feature on pages 36–37 for a discussion of the impact that the use of private judges and out-of-court settlements is having on the nation's court systems and our notions of justice.)

State Court Systems

Typically, a state court system includes several levels, or tiers, of courts. As indicated in Exhibit 2–1, state courts may include (1) local trial courts of limited jurisdiction, (2) state trial courts of general jurisdiction, (3) state courts of appeals (intermediate appellate courts), and (4) the state's highest court (often called the state supreme court). Generally, any person who is a party to a lawsuit has the opportunity to plead the case before a trial court and then, if he or she loses, before at least one level of appellate court. Finally, if the case involves a federal statute or federal constitutional issue, the decision of a state supreme court on that issue may be further appealed to the United States Supreme Court.

The states use various methods to select judges for their courts. Usually, voters elect judges, but in some states judges are appointed. For example, in Iowa, the

---

11. Pronounced *ven*-yoo.
12. Pronounced jus-*tish*-a-bul.

13. *DaimlerChrysler v. Cuno,* 547 U.S. 332, 126 S.Ct.1854, 164 L.Ed.2d 589 (2006).

EXHIBIT 2–1 • **The State and Federal Court Systems**

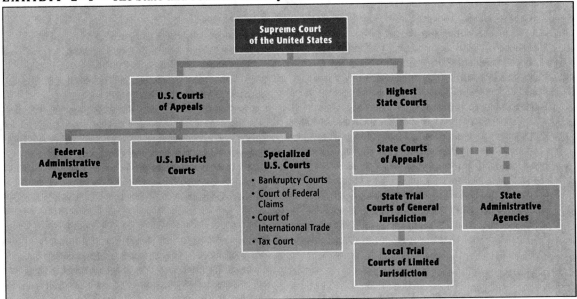

governor appoints judges, and then the general population decides whether to confirm their appointment in the next general election. The states usually specify the number of years that judges will serve. In contrast, as you will read shortly, judges in the federal court system are appointed by the president of the United States and, if they are confirmed by the Senate, hold office for life—unless they engage in blatantly illegal conduct.

Trial Courts Trial courts are exactly what their name implies—courts in which trials are held and testimony is taken. State trial courts have either general or limited jurisdiction. Trial courts that have general jurisdiction as to subject matter may be called county, district, superior, or circuit courts.[14] State trial courts of general jurisdiction have jurisdiction over a wide variety of subjects, including both civil disputes and criminal prosecutions. In some states, trial courts of general jurisdiction may hear appeals from courts of limited jurisdiction.

Courts of limited jurisdiction as to subject matter are often called special inferior trial courts or minor judiciary courts. **Small claims courts** are inferior trial courts that hear only civil cases involving claims of less

than a certain amount, such as $5,000 (the amount varies from state to state). Suits brought in small claims courts are generally conducted informally, and lawyers are not required (in a few states, lawyers are not even allowed). Decisions of small claims courts and municipal courts may sometimes be appealed to a state trial court of general jurisdiction.

Other courts of limited jurisdiction include domestic relations courts, which handle primarily divorce actions and child-custody disputes; local municipal courts, which mainly deal with traffic cases; and probate courts, as mentioned earlier.

Appellate, or Reviewing, Courts Every state has at least one court of appeals (appellate court, or reviewing court), which may be an intermediate appellate court or the state's highest court. About three-fourths of the states have intermediate appellate courts. Generally, courts of appeals do not conduct new trials, in which evidence is submitted to the court and witnesses are examined. Rather, an appellate court panel of three or more judges reviews the record of the case on appeal, which includes a transcript of the trial proceedings, and then determines whether the trial court committed an error.

Usually, appellate courts focus on questions of law, not questions of fact. A **question of fact** deals with what really happened in regard to the dispute being tried—

---

14. The name in Ohio and Pennsylvania is Court of Common Pleas; the name in New York is Supreme Court, Trial Division.

such as whether a party actually burned a flag. A **question of law** concerns the application or interpretation of the law—such as whether flag-burning is a form of speech protected by the First Amendment to the Constitution. Only a judge, not a jury, can rule on questions of law. Appellate courts normally defer to the trial court's findings on questions of fact because the trial court judge and jury were in a better position to evaluate testimony—by directly observing witnesses' gestures, demeanor, and other nonverbal behavior during the trial. At the appellate level, the judges review the written transcript of the trial, which does not include these nonverbal elements. Thus, an appellate court will not tamper with a trial court's finding of fact unless it is clearly erroneous (contrary to the evidence presented at trial) or when there is no evidence to support the finding.

Highest State Courts The highest appellate court in a state is usually called the supreme court but may be designated by some other name. For example, in both New York and Maryland, the highest state court is called the Court of Appeals. In Maine and Massachusetts, the highest court is labeled the Supreme Judicial Court. In West Virginia, the highest state court is the Supreme Court of Appeals.

The decisions of each state's highest court on all questions of state law are final. Only when issues of federal law are involved can the United States Supreme Court overrule a decision made by a state's highest court. Suppose that a city ordinance prohibits citizens from engaging in door-to-door advocacy without first registering with the mayor's office and receiving a permit. Further suppose that a religious group sues the city, arguing that the law violates the freedoms of speech and religion guaranteed by the First Amendment. If the state supreme court upholds the law, the group could appeal the decision to the United States Supreme Court—because a constitutional (federal) issue is involved.

The Federal Court System

The federal court system is basically a three-tiered model consisting of (1) U.S. district courts (trial courts of

In Ohio, for example, a state statute allows the parties to any civil action to have their dispute tried by a retired judge of their choosing who will make a decision in the matter.[a] Recently, though, private judging came under criticism in that state because private judges were conducting jury trials in county courtrooms at taxpayers' expense. A public judge, Nancy Margaret Russo, refused to give up jurisdiction over one case on the ground that private judges are not authorized to conduct jury trials. The Ohio Supreme Court agreed. As the state's highest court noted, private judging raises significant public-policy issues that the legislature needs to consider.[b]

One issue is that private judges charge relatively large fees. This means that litigants who are willing and able to pay the extra cost can have their case heard by a private judge long before they would be able to set a trial date in a regular court. Is it fair that those who cannot afford private judges should have to wait longer for justice? Similarly, is it ethical to allow parties to pay extra for secret proceedings before a private judge and thereby avoid the public scrutiny of a regular trial? Some even suggest that the use of private judges is leading to two different systems of justice.

a. See Ohio Revised Code Section 2701.10.
b. *State ex rel. Russo v. McDonnell,* 110 Ohio St.3d 144, 852 N.E.2d 145 (2006). (The term *ex rel.* is Latin for *ex relatione.* This phrase refers to an action brought on behalf of the state, by the attorney general, at the instigation of an individual who has a private interest in the matter.)

A Threat to the Common Law System?

The decline in the number of civil trials may also be leading to the erosion of this country's common law system. As discussed in Chapter 1, courts are obligated to consider precedents—the decisions rendered in previous cases with similar facts and issues—when deciding the outcome of a dispute. If fewer disputes go to trial because they are arbitrated or heard by a private judge, then they will never become part of the body of cases and appeals that form the case law on that subject. With fewer precedents on which to draw, individuals and businesses will have less information about what constitutes appropriate business behavior in today's world. Furthermore, private dispute resolution does not allow our case law to keep up with new issues related to areas such as biotechnology and the online world. Thus, the long-term effects of the decline of public justice could be a weakening of the common law itself.

CRITICAL THINKING
INSIGHT INTO THE SOCIAL ENVIRONMENT
If wealthier individuals increasingly use private judges, how will our justice system be affected in the long run?

---

general jurisdiction) and various courts of limited jurisdiction, (2) U.S. courts of appeals (intermediate courts of appeals), and (3) the United States Supreme Court.

Unlike state court judges, who are usually elected, federal court judges—including the justices of the Supreme Court—are appointed by the president of the United States, subject to confirmation by the U.S. Senate. Article III of the Constitution states that federal judges "hold their offices during good Behaviour." In effect, this means that federal judges have lifetime appointments. Although they can be impeached (removed from office) for misconduct, this is rarely done. In the entire history of the United States, only seven federal judges have been removed from office through impeachment proceedings.

U.S. District Courts At the federal level, the equivalent of a state trial court of general jurisdiction is the district court. U.S. district courts have original jurisdiction in federal matters, and federal cases typically originate in district courts. There are other federal courts with original, but special (or limited), jurisdic-

tion, such as the federal bankruptcy courts and others shown earlier in Exhibit 2–1 on page 35.

There is at least one federal district court in every state. The number of judicial districts can vary over time, primarily owing to population changes and corresponding changes in caseloads. Currently, there are ninety-four federal judicial districts. Exhibit 2–2 on the next page shows the boundaries of the U.S. district courts, as well as the U.S. courts of appeals.

U.S. Courts of Appeals In the federal court system, there are thirteen U.S. courts of appeals—referred to as U.S. circuit courts of appeals. Twelve of the federal courts of appeals (including the Court of Appeals for the D.C. Circuit) hear appeals from the federal district courts located within their respective judicial circuits, or geographic boundaries (shown in Exhibit 2–2).[15] The Court of Appeals for the Thirteenth Circuit, called

---

15. Historically, judges were required to "ride the circuit" and hear appeals in different courts around the country, which is at the origin of the name "circuit court."

EXHIBIT 2–2 • Geographic Boundaries of the U.S. Courts of Appeals and U.S. District Courts

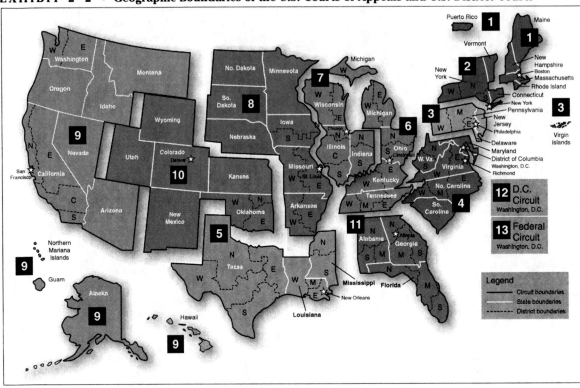

Source: Administrative Office of the United States Courts.

the Federal Circuit, has national appellate jurisdiction over certain types of cases, such as those involving patent law and those in which the U.S. government is a defendant. The decisions of a circuit court of appeals are binding on all courts within the circuit court's jurisdiction and are final in most cases, but appeal to the United States Supreme Court is possible.

United States Supreme Court At the highest level in the three-tiered federal court system is the United States Supreme Court. According to the language of Article III of the U.S. Constitution, there is only one national Supreme Court. All other courts in the federal system are considered "inferior." Congress is empowered to create other inferior courts as it deems necessary. The inferior courts that Congress has created include the second tier in our model—the U.S. circuit courts of appeals—as well as the district courts and the various federal courts of limited, or specialized, jurisdiction.

The United States Supreme Court consists of nine justices. Although the Supreme Court has original, or trial, jurisdiction in rare instances (set forth in Article III, Sections 1 and 2), most of its work is as an appeals court. The Supreme Court can review any case decided by any of the federal courts of appeals, and it

also has appellate authority over cases involving federal questions that have been decided in the state courts. The Supreme Court is the final arbiter of the Constitution and federal law.

Appeals to the Supreme Court. To bring a case before the Supreme Court, a party requests the Court to issue a writ of *certiorari*.[16] A **writ of *certiorari*** is an order issued by the Supreme Court to a lower court requiring the latter to send it the record of the case for review. The Court will not issue a writ unless at least four of the nine justices approve of it. This is called the **rule of four.** Whether the Court will issue a writ of *certiorari* is entirely within its discretion, and most petitions for writs are denied. (Thousands of cases are filed with the Supreme Court each year, yet it hears, on average, fewer than one hundred of these cases.[17]) A denial is not a decision on the merits of a case, nor does it indicate agreement with the lower court's opin-

---

16. Pronounced sur-shee-uh-*rah*-ree.

17. From the mid-1950s through the early 1990s, the Supreme Court reviewed more cases per year than it has since then. In the Court's 1982–1983 term, for example, the Court issued written opinions in 151 cases. In contrast, during the Court's 2007–2008 term, the Court issued written opinions in only 72 cases.

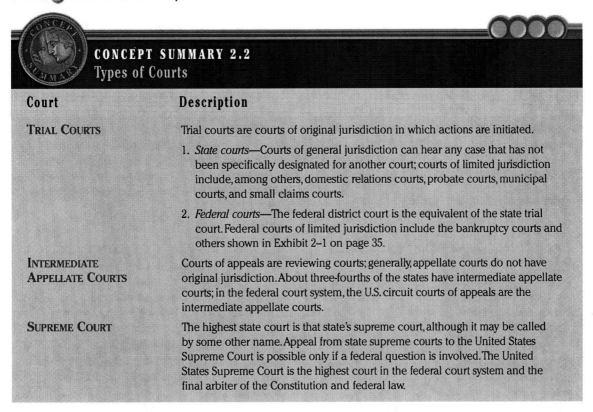

CONCEPT SUMMARY 2.2
Types of Courts

Court	Description
TRIAL COURTS	Trial courts are courts of original jurisdiction in which actions are initiated.
	1. *State courts*—Courts of general jurisdiction can hear any case that has not been specifically designated for another court; courts of limited jurisdiction include, among others, domestic relations courts, probate courts, municipal courts, and small claims courts.
	2. *Federal courts*—The federal district court is the equivalent of the state trial court. Federal courts of limited jurisdiction include the bankruptcy courts and others shown in Exhibit 2–1 on page 35.
INTERMEDIATE APPELLATE COURTS	Courts of appeals are reviewing courts; generally, appellate courts do not have original jurisdiction. About three-fourths of the states have intermediate appellate courts; in the federal court system, the U.S. circuit courts of appeals are the intermediate appellate courts.
SUPREME COURT	The highest state court is that state's supreme court, although it may be called by some other name. Appeal from state supreme courts to the United States Supreme Court is possible only if a federal question is involved. The United States Supreme Court is the highest court in the federal court system and the final arbiter of the Constitution and federal law.

ion. Also, denial of the writ has no value as a precedent. Denial simply means that the lower court's decision remains the law in that jurisdiction.

Petitions Granted by the Court. Typically, the Court grants petitions in cases that raise important constitutional questions or when the lower courts have issued conflicting decisions on a significant issue. The justices, however, never explain their reasons for hearing certain cases and not others, so it is difficult to predict which type of case the Court might select. (See *Concept Summary 2.2* to review the various types of courts in the federal and state court systems.)

Alternative Dispute Resolution

Litigation—the process of resolving a dispute through the court system—is expensive and time consuming. Litigating even the simplest complaint is costly, and because of the backlog of cases pending in many courts, several years may pass before a case is actually tried. For these and other reasons, more and more

businesspersons are turning to **alternative dispute resolution (ADR)** as a means of settling their disputes.

The great advantage of ADR is its flexibility. Methods of ADR range from the parties sitting down together and attempting to work out their differences to multinational corporations agreeing to resolve a dispute through a formal hearing before a panel of experts. Normally, the parties themselves can control how the dispute will be settled, what procedures will be used, whether a neutral third party will be present or make a decision, and whether that decision will be legally binding or nonbinding. ADR also offers more privacy than court proceedings and allows disputes to be resolved relatively quickly.

Today, more than 90 percent of civil lawsuits are settled before trial using some form of ADR. Indeed, most states either require or encourage parties to undertake ADR prior to trial. Many federal courts have instituted ADR programs as well. In the following pages, we examine the basic forms of ADR.

Negotiation

The simplest form of ADR is **negotiation,** a process in which the parties attempt to settle their dispute informally, with or without attorneys to represent them. Attorneys frequently advise their clients to negotiate a settlement voluntarily before they proceed to trial. In some courts, pretrial negotiation is mandatory before parties can proceed to trial. Parties may even try to negotiate a settlement during a trial or after the trial but before an appeal. Negotiation traditionally involves just the parties themselves and (typically) their attorneys. The attorneys, though, are advocates—they are obligated to put their clients' interests first.

Mediation

In **mediation,** a neutral third party acts as a mediator and works with both sides in the dispute to facilitate a resolution. The mediator normally talks with the parties separately as well as jointly, emphasizes points of agreement, and helps the parties to evaluate their options. Although the mediator may propose a solution (called a mediator's proposal), he or she does not make a decision resolving the matter. The mediator, who need not be a lawyer, usually charges a fee for his or her services (which can be split between the parties). States that require parties to undergo ADR before trial often offer mediation as one of the ADR options or (as in Florida) the only option.

One of the biggest advantages of mediation is that it is not as adversarial in nature as litigation. In mediation, the mediator takes an active role and attempts to bring the parties together so that they can come to a mutually satisfactory resolution. The mediation process tends to reduce the antagonism between the disputants, allowing them to resume their former relationship while minimizing hostility. For this reason, mediation is often the preferred form of ADR for disputes involving business partners, employers and employees, or other parties involved in long-term relationships.

Today, characteristics of mediation are being combined with those of arbitration (to be discussed next). In *binding mediation,* for example, the parties agree that if they cannot resolve the dispute, the mediator can make a legally binding decision on the issue. In *mediation-arbitration,* or "med-arb," the parties first attempt to settle their dispute through mediation. If no settlement is reached, the dispute will be arbitrated.

Arbitration

A more formal method of ADR is **arbitration,** in which an arbitrator (a neutral third party or a panel of experts) hears a dispute and imposes a resolution on the parties. Arbitration differs from other forms of ADR in that the third party hearing the dispute makes a decision for the parties. Exhibit 2–3 outlines the basic differences among the three traditional forms of ADR. Usually, the parties in arbitration agree that the third party's decision will be *legally binding,* although the parties can also agree to *nonbinding* arbitration. (Additionally, arbitration that is mandated by the courts often is not binding on the parties.) In nonbinding arbitration, the parties can go forward with a lawsuit if they do not agree with the arbitrator's decision.

The Arbitration Process In some respects, formal arbitration resembles a trial, although usually the procedural rules are much less restrictive than those governing litigation. In a typical arbitration, the par-

EXHIBIT 2–3 ● **Basic Differences in the Traditional Forms of ADR**

Type of ADR	Description	Neutral Third Party Present	Who Decides the Resolution
Negotiation	Parties meet informally with or without their attorneys and attempt to agree on a resolution.	No.	The parties themselves reach a resolution.
Mediation	A neutral third party meets with the parties and emphasizes points of agreement to bring them toward resolution of their dispute.	Yes.	The parties, but the mediator may suggest or propose a resolution.
Arbitration	The parties present their arguments and evidence before an arbitrator at a hearing, and the arbitrator renders a decision resolving the parties' dispute.	Yes.	The arbitrator imposes a resolution on the parties that may be either binding or nonbinding.

ties present opening arguments and ask for specific remedies. Evidence is then presented, and witnesses may be called and examined by both sides. The arbitrator then renders a decision, called an **award.**

An arbitrator's award is usually the final word on the matter. Although the parties may appeal an arbitrator's decision, a court's review of the decision will be much more restricted in scope than an appellate court's review of a trial court's decision. The general view is that because the parties were free to frame the issues and set the powers of the arbitrator at the outset, they cannot complain about the results. The award will be set aside only if the arbitrator's conduct or "bad faith" substantially prejudiced the rights of one of the parties, if the award violates an established public policy, or if the arbitrator exceeded her or his powers (by arbitrating issues that the parties did not agree to submit to arbitration).

Arbitration Clauses and Statutes Virtually any commercial matter can be submitted to arbitration. Frequently, parties include an **arbitration clause** in a contract (a written agreement—see Chapter 10) specifying that any dispute arising under the contract will be resolved through arbitration rather than through the court system. Parties can also agree to arbitrate a dispute after it arises.

Most states have statutes (often based in part on the Uniform Arbitration Act of 1955) under which arbitration clauses will be enforced, and some state statutes compel arbitration of certain types of disputes, such as those involving public employees. At the federal level, the Federal Arbitration Act (FAA), enacted in 1925, enforces arbitration clauses in contracts involving maritime activity and interstate commerce. Because of the breadth of the commerce clause (see Chapter 4), arbitration agreements involving transactions only slightly connected to the flow of interstate commerce may fall under the FAA.

The question in the following case was whether a court or an arbitrator should consider a claim that an entire contract, including its arbitration clause, is rendered void by the alleged illegality of a separate provision in the contract.

C A S E   **2.2   Buckeye Check Cashing, Inc. v. Cardegna**
Supreme Court of the United States, 2006. 546 U.S. 440, 126 S.Ct. 1204, 163 L.Ed.2d 1038.
www.law.cornell.edu/supct/index.html[a]

● **Background and Facts** Buckeye Check Cashing, Inc., cashes personal checks for consumers in Florida. Buckeye agrees to delay submitting a check for payment in exchange for a consumer's payment of a "finance charge." For each transaction, the consumer signs a "Deferred Deposit and Disclosure Agreement," which states, "By signing this Agreement, you agree that i[f] a dispute of any kind arises out of this Agreement * * * th[e]n either you or we or third-parties involved can choose to have that dispute resolved by binding arbitration." John Cardegna and others filed a suit in a Florida state court against Buckeye, alleging that the "finance charge" represented an illegally high interest rate in violation of Florida state laws, rendering the agreement "criminal on its face." Buckeye filed a motion to compel arbitration. The court denied the motion. On Buckeye's appeal, a state intermediate appellate court reversed this denial, but on the plaintiffs' appeal, the Florida Supreme Court reversed the lower appellate court's decision. Buckeye appealed to the United States Supreme Court.

● **Decision and Rationale** The United States Supreme Court reversed the judgment of the Florida Supreme Court and remanded the case for further proceedings. The Court ruled that a challenge to the validity of a contract as a whole, and not specifically to an arbitration clause contained in the contract, must be resolved by an arbitrator. The Court set out three propositions. "First, as a matter of substantive federal arbitration law, an arbitration provision is severable [capable of being legally separated] from the remainder of the contract. Second, unless the challenge is to the arbitration clause itself, the issue of the contract's validity is considered by the arbitrator in the first instance. Third, this arbitration law applies in state as well as federal courts." The Court concluded that here, because the plaintiffs challenged the contract's "finance charge," but not its arbitration provisions, those provisions were enforceable apart from the remainder of the contract. "The

---

a. In the "Supreme Court Collection" menu at the top of the page, click on "Search." When that page opens, in the "Search for:" box, type "Buckeye Check," choose "All decisions" in the accompanying list, and click on "Search." In the result, scroll to the name of the case and click on the appropriate link to access the opinion.

CASE CONTINUES

CASE 2.2 CONTINUED challenge should therefore be considered by an arbitrator, not a court." The plaintiffs also argued that the only arbitration agreements to which the Federal Arbitration Act (FAA) applies are those involving contracts and that the Buckeye agreement was not a contract because it was "void *ab initio*" (from the beginning). The FAA allows a challenge to an arbitration provision "upon such grounds as exist at law or in equity for the revocation [cancellation] of any contract." The Court reasoned that this includes contracts that later prove to be void. "Otherwise, the grounds for revocation would be limited to those that rendered a contract voidable—which would mean (implausibly) that an arbitration agreement could be challenged as voidable but not as void."

● **The Ethical Dimension** *Does the holding in this case permit a court to enforce an arbitration agreement in a contract that the arbitrator later finds to be void? Is this fair? Why or why not?*

● **The Legal Environment Dimension** *As indicated in the parties' arguments and the Court's reasoning in this case, into what categories can contracts be classified with respect to their enforceability?*

Arbitrability When a dispute arises as to whether the parties to a contract with an arbitration clause have agreed to submit a particular matter to arbitration, one party may file suit to compel arbitration. The court before which the suit is brought will not decide the basic controversy but must decide the issue of *arbitrability*—that is, whether the matter is one that must be resolved through arbitration. If the court finds that the subject matter in controversy is covered by the agreement to arbitrate, then a party may be compelled to arbitrate the dispute. Even when a claim involves a violation of a statute passed to protect a certain class of people, a court may determine that the parties must nonetheless abide by their agreement to arbitrate the dispute. Usually, a court will allow the claim to be arbitrated if the court, in interpreting the statute, can find no legislative intent to the contrary.

No party, however, will be ordered to submit a particular dispute to arbitration unless the court is con-

vinced that the party has consented to do so.[18] Additionally, the courts will not compel arbitration if it is clear that the prescribed arbitration rules and procedures are inherently unfair to one of the parties.[19]

The terms of an arbitration agreement can limit the types of disputes that the parties agree to arbitrate. When the parties do not specify limits, however, disputes can arise as to whether the particular matter is covered by the arbitration agreement, and it is up to the court to resolve the issue of arbitrability. In the following case, the parties had previously agreed to arbitrate disputes involving their contract to develop software, but the dispute involved claims of copyright infringement (see Chapter 8). The question was whether the copyright infringement claims were beyond the scope of the arbitration clause.

---

18. See, for example, *Wright v. Universal Maritime Service Corp.*, 525 U.S. 70, 119 S.Ct. 391, 142 L.Ed.2d 361 (1998).

19. *Hooters of America, Inc. v. Phillips*, 173 F.3d 933 (4th Cir. 1999).

C A S E **2.3 NCR Corp. v. Korala Associates, Ltd.**
United States Court of Appeals, Sixth Circuit, 2008. 512 F.3d 807.
www.ca6.uscourts.gov[a]

● **Background and Facts** In response to a need to upgrade the security of its automated teller machines (ATMs), NCR Corporation developed a software solution to install in all of its machines. At the same time, Korala Associates, Ltd. (KAL), claimed to have developed a similar security upgrade for NCR's ATMs. Indeed, KAL had entered into a contract with NCR in 1998 (the "1998 Agreement") to develop such software. To enable KAL to do so, NCR loaned to KAL a proprietary ATM that contained copyrighted software called APTRA XFS. NCR alleged that KAL "obtained access to, made unauthorized use of, and engaged in unauthorized copying of the APTRA XFS software." By so doing, KAL

---

a. Click on "Opinions Search" and then on "Short Title;" and type "NCR." Click on "Submit Query." Next, click on the opinion link in the first column of the row corresponding to the name of this case.

CASE 2.3 CONTINUED developed its own version of a security upgrade for NCR's ATMs. When NCR brought a suit against KAL, the latter moved to compel arbitration under the terms of the 1998 Agreement between the two companies. At trial, KAL prevailed. NCR appealed the order compelling arbitration to the U.S. Court of Appeals for the Sixth Circuit.

● **Decision and Rationale** The U.S. Court of Appeals for the Sixth Circuit affirmed the judgment compelling arbitration as to NCR's claims relating to direct copyright infringement of certain software. The court pointed out that the 1998 Agreement clearly provided for arbitration. The court still faced the issue of determining whether NCR's claims fell within the substantive scope of the Agreement. "As a matter of Federal law, any doubts concerning the scope of arbitrable issues should be resolved in favor of arbitration." Because the arbitration clause in the 1998 Agreement was so broad, the appellate court reasoned that a trial court should follow the "presumption of arbitration and resolve doubts in favor of arbitration." Consequently, the court found that the copyright infringement claim that NCR alleged fell within the scope of the arbitration agreement.

● **The Ethical Dimension** *Could NCR have a claim that KAL had engaged in unfair competition because KAL had engaged in unethical business practices? (Hint: Unfair competition may occur when one party deceives the public into believing that his or her goods are the goods of another.) Why or why not?*

● **The Legal Environment Dimension** *Why do you think that NCR did not want its alleged claims decided by arbitration?*

Mandatory Arbitration in the Employment Context

A significant question in the last several years has concerned mandatory arbitration clauses in employment contracts. Many claim that employees' rights are not sufficiently protected when they are forced, as a condition of being hired, to agree to arbitrate all disputes and thus waive their rights under statutes specifically designed to protect employees. The United States Supreme Court, however, has held that mandatory arbitration clauses in employment contracts are generally enforceable.[20] (Recently, however, some courts have been striking arbitration clauses because they shocked the conscience of the courts. See the *Business Application* feature on the following page.)

PREVENTING LEGAL DISPUTES

The United States Supreme Court has made it clear that arbitration clauses in employment contracts are enforceable under the FAA. Nevertheless, to prevent future disputes, business owners and managers would be wise to exercise caution when drafting such clauses and requiring employees to sign them. It is especially important to make certain that the terms of the agreement (including how the parties will split the costs of the arbitration procedure, for example) are not so one sided and unfair that a court could declare the entire agreement unenforceable.

Other Types of ADR

The three forms of ADR just discussed are the oldest and traditionally the most commonly used forms. As mentioned earlier, a variety of new types of ADR have emerged in recent years, including those described here.

1. In **early neutral case evaluation,** the parties select a neutral third party (generally an expert in the subject matter of the dispute) to evaluate their respective positions. The parties explain their positions to the case evaluator, and the case evaluator assesses the strengths and weaknesses of each party's claims.

2. In a **mini-trial,** each party's attorney briefly argues the party's case before the other and a panel of representatives from each side who have the authority to settle the dispute. Typically, a neutral third party (usually an expert in the area being disputed) acts as an adviser. If the parties fail to reach an agreement, the adviser renders an opinion as to how a court would likely decide the issue.

3. Numerous federal courts now hold **summary jury trials (SJTs),** in which the parties present their arguments and evidence and the jury renders a verdict.

20. For a landmark decision on this issue, see *Gilmer v. Interstate/Johnson Lane Corp.*, 500 U.S. 20, 111 S.Ct. 1647, 114 L.Ed.2d 26 (1991).

MANAGEMENT FACES A LEGAL ISSUE

Arbitration is normally simpler, speedier, and less costly than litigation. For that reason, business owners and managers today often include arbitration clauses in their contracts, including employment contracts. What happens, though, if a job candidate whom you wish to hire (or an existing employee whose contract is being renewed) objects to one or more of the provisions in an arbitration clause? If you insist that signing the agreement to arbitrate future disputes is a mandatory condition of employment, will such a clause be enforceable? Put another way, in which situations might a court invalidate an arbitration agreement because it is considered *unconscionable* (morally unacceptable—shocks the conscience)?

WHAT THE COURTS SAY

The United States Supreme Court has consistently taken the position that because the Federal Arbitration Act (FAA) favors the arbitration of disputes, arbitration clauses in employment contracts should generally be enforced. Nonetheless, some courts have held that arbitration clauses in employment contracts should not be enforced if they are too one sided and unfair to the employee. In one case, for example, the U.S. Court of Appeals for the Ninth Circuit refused to enforce an arbitration clause on the ground that the agreement was unconscionable—so one sided and unfair as to be unenforceable under "ordinary principles of state contract law." The agreement was a standard-form contract drafted by the employer (the party with superior bargaining power), and the employee had to sign it without any modification as a prerequisite to employment. Moreover, only the employees were required to arbitrate their disputes, while the employer remained free to litigate any claims it had against its employees in court. Among other things, the contract also severely limited the relief that was available to employees. For these reasons, the court held the entire arbitration agreement unenforceable.[a] Other courts have cited

similar reasons for deciding not to enforce one-sided arbitration clauses.[b]

In a more recent case, employees of a large California law firm were given copies of that firm's new dispute-resolution program. The program culminated in final binding arbitration for most employment-related claims by and against the firm's employees. The new program became effective three months after it was distributed. After leaving employment at the law firm, an employee filed a lawsuit alleging failure to pay overtime wages. She also claimed that her former employer's dispute-resolution program was unconscionable. The reviewing court found that the dispute-resolution program was presented to the employees on a take-it-or-leave-it basis and was therefore procedurally unconscionable. The court also found that the program was substantively unconscionable because it required employees to waive claims if those employees failed to give the firm notice and demand for mediation within one year from the time when the claim was known.[c]

IMPLICATIONS FOR MANAGERS

Although the United States Supreme Court has made it clear that arbitration clauses in employment contracts are enforceable under the FAA, managers should be careful when drafting such clauses. It is especially important to make sure that the terms of the agreement are not so one sided that a court could declare the entire agreement unconscionable.

Managers should also be aware that the proposed Arbitration Fairness Act might eventually become law. This planned "consumer protection" bill would render unenforceable all predispute mandatory arbitration provisions in consumer, employment, and franchise contracts. It would amend the FAA and seriously restrict the ability of firms to require arbitration.

a. *Circuit City Stores, Inc. v. Adams,* 279 F.3d 889 (9th Cir. 2002). (This was the Ninth Circuit's decision, on remand, after the United States Supreme Court reviewed the case.)

b. See, for example, *Hooters of America, Inc. v. Phillips,* 173 F.3d 933 (4th Cir. 1999); and *Hardwick v. Sherwin Williams Co.,* 2002 WL 31992364 (Ohio App. 8 Dist. 2003).
c. *Davis v. O'Melveny & Myers, LLC,* 485 F.3d 1066 (9th Cir. 2007).

The jury's verdict is not binding, but it does act as a guide to both sides in reaching an agreement during the mandatory negotiations that immediately follow the trial.

4. Other alternatives being employed by the courts include summary procedures for commercial litigation and the appointment of special masters to assist judges in deciding complex issues.

Providers of ADR Services

Both government agencies and private organizations provide ADR services. A major provider of ADR services is the **American Arbitration Association (AAA),** which was founded in 1926 and now handles more than two hundred thousand claims each year in its numerous offices around the country. Cases brought before the AAA are heard by an expert or a panel of experts in the area relating to the dispute and are usually settled quickly. Generally, about half of the panel members are lawyers. To cover its costs, the AAA charges a fee, paid by the party filing the claim. In addition, each party to the dispute pays a specified amount for each hearing day, as well as a special additional fee in cases involving personal injuries or property loss.

Hundreds of for-profit firms around the country also provide dispute-resolution services. Typically, these firms hire retired judges to conduct arbitration hearings or otherwise assist parties in settling their disputes. The judges follow procedures similar to those of the federal courts and use similar rules. Usually, each party to the dispute pays a filing fee and a designated fee for a hearing session or conference.

Online Dispute Resolution

An increasing number of companies and organizations are offering dispute-resolution services using the Internet. The settlement of disputes in these online forums is known as **online dispute resolution (ODR).** The disputes resolved in these forums have most commonly involved disagreements over the rights to domain names (Web site addresses—see Chapter 8) or the quality of goods sold via the Internet, including goods sold through Internet auction sites.

At this time, ODR may be best for resolving small- to medium-sized business liability claims, which may not be worth the expense of litigation or traditional ADR methods. Rules being developed in online forums, however, may ultimately become a code of conduct for everyone who does business in cyberspace. Most online forums do not automatically apply the law of

any specific jurisdiction. Instead, results are often based on general, more universal legal principles. As with offline methods of dispute resolution, any party may appeal to a court at any time.

International Dispute Resolution

Businesspersons who engage in international business transactions normally take special precautions to protect themselves in the event that a party with whom they are dealing in another country breaches an agreement. Often, parties to international contracts include special clauses in their contracts providing for how disputes arising under the contracts will be resolved.

Forum-Selection and Choice-of-Law Clauses

As you will read in Chapter 20, parties to international transactions often include forum-selection and choice-of-law clauses in their contracts. These clauses designate the jurisdiction (court or country) where any dispute arising under the contract will be litigated and the nation's law that will be applied. When an international contract does not include such clauses, any legal proceedings arising under the contract will be more complex and attended by much more uncertainty. For example, litigation may take place in two or more countries, with each country applying its own national law to the particular transactions.

Furthermore, even if a plaintiff wins a favorable judgment in a lawsuit litigated in the plaintiff's country, the defendant's country could refuse to enforce the court's judgment. As will be discussed in Chapter 52, for reasons of courtesy, the judgment may be enforced in the defendant's country, particularly if the defendant's country is the United States and the foreign court's decision is consistent with U.S. national law and policy. Other nations, however, may not be as accommodating as the United States, and the plaintiff may be left empty-handed.

Arbitration Clauses

Parties to international contracts also often include arbitration clauses in their contracts that require a neutral third party to decide any contract disputes. In international arbitration proceedings, the third party may be a neutral entity (such as the International Chamber of Commerce), a panel of individuals representing both parties' interests, or some other group or organization. The United Nations Convention on the Recognition and Enforcement of Foreign Arbitral Awards[21]—which has been implemented in more than fifty countries, including the United States—assists in the enforcement of arbitration clauses, as do provisions in specific treaties among nations. The American Arbitration Association provides arbitration services for international as well as domestic disputes.

21. June 10, 1958, 21 U.S.T. 2517, T.I.A.S. No. 6997 (the "New York Convention").

REVIEWING Courts and Alternative Dispute Resolution

Stan Garner resides in Illinois and promotes boxing matches for SuperSports, Inc., an Illinois corporation. Garner created the concept of "Ages" promotion—a three-fight series of boxing matches pitting an older fighter (George Foreman) against a younger fighter, such as John Ruiz or Riddick Bowe. The concept included titles for each of the three fights ("Challenge of the Ages," "Battle of the Ages," and "Fight of the Ages"), as well as promotional epithets to characterize the two fighters ("the Foreman Factor"). Garner contacted George Foreman and his manager, who both reside in Texas, to sell the idea, and they arranged a meeting at Caesar's Palace in Las Vegas, Nevada. At some point in the negotiations, Foreman's manager signed a nondisclosure agreement prohibiting him from disclosing Garner's promotional concepts unless the parties signed a contract. Nevertheless, after negotiations between Garner and Foreman fell through, Foreman used Garner's "Battle of the Ages" concept to promote a subsequent fight. Garner filed a suit against Foreman and his manager in a federal district court located in Illinois, alleging breach of contract. Using the information presented in the chapter, answer the following questions.

1. On what basis might the federal district court in Illinois exercise jurisdiction in this case?
2. Does the federal district court have original or appellate jurisdiction?
3. Suppose that Garner had filed his action in an Illinois state court. Could an Illinois state court exercise personal jurisdiction over Foreman or his manager? Why or why not?
4. Assume that Garner had filed his action in a Nevada state court. Would that court have personal jurisdiction over Foreman or his manager? Explain.

TERMS AND CONCEPTS

alternative dispute
 resolution (ADR)
American Arbitration
 Association (AAA)
arbitration
arbitration clause
award
bankruptcy court
concurrent jurisdiction
diversity of citizenship

early neutral case evaluation
exclusive jurisdiction
federal question
in personam jurisdiction
in rem jurisdiction
judicial review
jurisdiction
justiciable controversy
litigation
long arm statute
mediation
mini-trial

negotiation
online dispute
 resolution (ODR)
probate court
question of fact
question of law
rule of four
small claims court
standing to sue
summary jury trial (SJT)
venue
writ of *certiorari*

QUESTIONS AND CASE PROBLEMS

2–1. In an arbitration proceeding, the arbitrator need not be a judge or even a lawyer. How, then, can the arbitrator's decision have the force of law and be binding on the parties involved?

2–2. QUESTION WITH SAMPLE ANSWER

The defendant in a lawsuit is appealing the trial court's decision in favor of the plaintiff. On appeal, the defendant claims that the evidence presented at trial to support the plaintiff's claim was so scanty that no reasonable jury could have found for the plaintiff. Therefore, argues the defendant, the appellate court should reverse the trial court's decision. Will an appellate court ever reverse a trial court's findings with respect to questions of fact? Discuss fully.

- **For a sample answer to Question 2–2, go to Appendix C at the end of this text.**

2–3. Appellate courts normally see only written transcripts of trial proceedings when they are reviewing cases. Today, in some states, videotapes are being used as the official trial reports. If the use of videotapes as official reports continues, will this alter the appellate process? Should it? Discuss fully.

2–4. Marya Callais, a citizen of Florida, was walking along a busy street in Tallahassee, Florida, when a large crate flew off a passing truck and hit her, causing numerous injuries. She experienced a great deal of pain and suffering, incurred significant medical expenses, and could not work for six months. She wants to sue the trucking firm for $300,000 in damages. The firm's headquarters are in Georgia, although the company does business in Florida. In what court might Callais bring suit—a Florida state court, a Georgia state court, or a federal court? What factors might influence her decision?

2–5. E-Jurisdiction. American Business Financial Services, Inc. (ABFI), a Pennsylvania firm, sells and services loans to businesses and consumers. First Union National Bank, with its principal place of business in North Carolina, provides banking services. Alan Boyer, an employee of First Union, lives in North Carolina and has never been to Pennsylvania. In the course of his employment, Boyer learned that the bank was going to extend a $150 million line of credit to ABFI. Boyer then attempted to manipulate the price of ABFI's stock for personal gain by sending disparaging e-mails to ABFI's independent auditors in Pennsylvania. Boyer also posted negative statements about ABFI and its management on a Yahoo bulletin board. ABFI filed a suit in a Pennsylvania state court against Boyer, First Union, and others, alleging wrongful interference with a contractual relationship, among other things. Boyer filed a motion to dismiss the complaint for lack of personal jurisdiction. Could the court exercise jurisdiction over Boyer? Explain. [*American Business Financial Services, Inc. v. First Union National Bank,* __ A.2d __ (Pa.Comm.Pl. 2002)]

2–6. Arbitration. Alexander Little worked for Auto Stiegler, Inc., an automobile dealership in Los Angeles County, California, eventually becoming the service manager. While employed, Little signed an arbitration agreement that required the submission of all employment-related disputes to arbitration. The agreement also provided that any award over $50,000 could be appealed to a second arbitrator. Little was later demoted and terminated. Alleging that these actions were in retaliation for investigating and reporting warranty fraud and thus were in violation of public policy, Little filed a suit in a California state court against Auto Stiegler. The defendant filed a motion with the court to compel arbitration. Little responded that the arbitration agreement should not be enforced because, among other things, the appeal provision was unfairly one sided. Is this provision enforceable? Should the court grant Auto Stiegler's motion? Why or why not? [*Little v. Auto Stiegler, Inc.,* 29 Cal.4th 1064, 63 P.3d 979, 130 Cal.Rptr.2d 892 (2003)]

2–7. Jurisdiction. KaZaA BV was a company formed under the laws of the Netherlands. KaZaA distributed KaZaA Media Desktop (KMD) software, which enabled users to exchange digital media, including movies and music, via a peer-to-peer transfer network. KaZaA also operated the KaZaA.com Web site, through which it distributed the KMD software to millions of California residents and other users. Metro-Goldwyn-Mayer Studios, Inc., and other parties in the entertainment industries based in California filed a suit in a federal district court against KaZaA and others, alleging copyright infringement. KaZaA filed a counterclaim, but while legal action was pending, the firm passed its assets and its Web site to Sharman Networks, Ltd., a company organized under the laws of Vanuatu (an island republic east of Australia) and doing business principally in Australia. Sharman explicitly disclaimed the assumption of any of KaZaA's liabilities. When the plaintiffs added Sharman as a defendant, Sharman filed a motion to dismiss on the ground that the court did not have jurisdiction. Would it be fair to subject Sharman to suit in this case? Explain. [*Metro-Goldwyn-Mayer Studios, Inc. v. Grokster, Ltd.,* 243 F.Supp.2d 1073 (C.D.Cal. 2003)]

2–8. CASE PROBLEM WITH SAMPLE ANSWER

Michael and Karla Covington live in Jefferson County, Idaho. When they bought their home, a gravel pit was across the street. In 1995, the county converted the pit to a landfill. Under the county's operation, the landfill accepted major appliances, household garbage, spilled grain, grass clippings, straw, manure, animal carcasses, containers with hazardous content warnings, leaking car batteries, and waste oil, among other things. The deposits were often left uncovered, attracting insects and other scavengers and contaminating the groundwater. Fires broke out, including at least one started by an intruder who entered the property through an unlocked gate. The Covingtons complained to the state, which inspected the landfill, but no changes were made to address their concerns. Finally, the Covingtons filed a suit in a federal district court against the county and the state, charging violations of federal environmental laws. Those laws were designed to minimize the risks of injuries from fires, scavengers, groundwater contamination, and other pollution dangers. Did the Covingtons have standing to sue? What principles apply? Explain. [*Covington v. Jefferson County*, 358 F.3d 626 (9th Cir. 2004)]

- **To view a sample answer for Problem 2–8, go to this book's Web site at www.cengage. com/blaw/jentz, select "Chapter 2," and click on "Case Problem with Sample Answer."**

2–9. E-Jurisdiction. Xcentric Ventures, LLC, is an Arizona firm that operates the Web sites RipOffReport.com and BadBusinessBureau.com. Visitors to the sites can buy a copy of a book titled *Do-It-Yourself Guide: How to Get Rip-Off Revenge*. The price ($21.95) includes shipping to anywhere in the United States, including Illinois, to which thirteen copies have been shipped. The sites accept donations and feature postings by individuals who claim to have been "ripped off." Some visitors posted comments about George S. May International Co., a management consulting firm. The postings alleged fraud, larceny, possession of child pornography, and possession of controlled substances (illegal drugs). May filed a suit in a federal district court in Illinois against Xcentric and others, charging, among other things, "false descriptions and representations." The defendants filed a motion to dismiss for lack of jurisdiction. What is the standard for exercising jurisdiction over a party whose only connection to a jurisdiction is over the Web? How would that standard apply in this case? Explain. [*George S. May International Co. v. Xcentric Ventures, LLC*, 409 F.Supp.2d 1052 (N.D.Ill. 2006)]

2–10. Jurisdiction. In 2001, Raul Leal, the owner and operator of Texas Labor Contractors in East Texas, contacted Poverty Point Produce, Inc., which operates a sweet potato farm in West Carroll Parish, Louisiana, and offered to provide field workers. Poverty Point accepted the offer. Jeffrey Brown, an owner of, and field manager for, the farm, told Leal the number of workers needed and gave him forms for them to fill out and sign. Leal placed an ad in a newspaper in Brownsville, Texas. Job applicants were directed to Leal's car dealership in Weslaco, Texas, where they were told the details of the work. Leal recruited, among others, Elias Moreno, who lives in the Rio Grande Valley in Texas, and transported Moreno and the others to Poverty Point's farm. At the farm, Leal's brother Jesse oversaw the work with instructions from Brown, lived with the workers in the on-site housing, and gave them their paychecks. When the job was done, the workers were returned to Texas. Moreno

and others filed a suit in a federal district court against Poverty Point and others, alleging, in part, violations of Texas state law related to the work. Poverty Point filed a motion to dismiss the suit on the ground that the court did not have personal jurisdiction. All of the meetings between Poverty Point and the Leals occurred in Louisiana. All of the farmwork was done in Louisiana. Poverty Point has no offices, bank accounts, or phone listings in Texas. It does not advertise or solicit business in Texas. Despite these facts, can the court exercise personal jurisdiction? Explain. [*Moreno v. Poverty Point Produce, Inc.*, 243 F.R.D. 275 (S.D.Tex. 2007)]

2–11. A QUESTION OF ETHICS

Linden Research, Inc., operates a multiplayer role-playing game in the virtual world known as "Second Life" at secondlife.com. Participants create avatars to represent themselves on the site. In 2003, Second Life became the only virtual world to recognize participants' rights to buy, own, and sell digital content— virtual property, including "land." Linden's chief executive officer, Philip Rosedale, joined efforts to publicize this recognition and these rights in the real-world media. Rosedale also created an avatar to tout the rights in Second Life town meetings. March Bragg, an experienced Pennsylvania attorney, was a Second Life participant whose avatar attended the meetings, after which Bragg began to invest in Second Life's virtual property. In April 2006, Bragg bought "Taessot," a parcel of virtual land. Linden decided that the purchase was improper, however, and took Taessot from Bragg. Linden also froze Bragg's account, effectively confiscating all of his virtual property and currency. Bragg filed a suit against Linden and Rosedale, claiming that the defendants acted unlawfully. [Bragg v. Linden Research, Inc., 487 F.Supp.2d 593 (E.D.Pa. 2007)]

(a) In the federal district court in Pennsylvania that was hearing the suit, Rosedale, who lives in California, filed a motion to dismiss the claim against him for lack of personal jurisdiction. On what basis could the court deny this motion and assert jurisdiction? Is it fair to require Rosedale to appear in a court in a distant location? Explain.

(b) To access Second Life, a participant must accept its "Terms of Service" (TOS) by clicking an "accept" button. Under the TOS, Linden has the right "at any time for any reason or no reason to suspend or terminate your Account," to refuse to return a participant's money, and to amend the terms at its discretion. The terms also stipulate that any dispute be resolved by binding arbitration in California. Is there anything unfair about the TOS? Should the court compel Bragg to arbitrate this dispute? Discuss.

2-12. VIDEO QUESTION

Go to this text's Web site at **www.cengage.com/blaw/jentz** and select "Chapter 2." Click on "Video Questions" and view the video titled *Jurisdiction in Cyberspace*. Then answer the following questions.

(a) What standard would a court apply to determine whether it has jurisdiction over the out-of-state computer firm in the video?

(b) What factors is a court likely to consider in assessing whether sufficient contacts existed when the only connection to the jurisdiction is through a Web site?

(c) How do you think the court would resolve the issue in this case?

LAW ON THE WEB

For updated links to resources available on the Web, as well as a variety of other materials, visit this text's Web site at

www.cengage.com/blaw/jentz

For the decisions of the United States Supreme Court, as well as information about the Supreme Court and its justices, go to either

www.supremecourtus.gov

or

www.oyez.org

The Web site for the federal courts offers information on the federal court system and links to all federal courts at

www.uscourts.gov

The National Center for State Courts (NCSC) offers links to the Web pages of all state courts. Go to

www.ncsconline.org

For information on alternative dispute resolution, go to the American Arbitration Association's Web site at

www.adr.org

Legal Research Exercises on the Web

Go to **www.cengage.com/blaw/jentz**, the Web site that accompanies this text. Select "Chapter 2" and click on "Internet Exercises." There you will find the following Internet research exercises that you can perform to learn more about the topics covered in this chapter.

Internet Exercise 2–1: Legal Perspective
                       Alternative Dispute Resolution

Internet Exercise 2–2: Management Perspective
                       Resolve a Dispute Online

Internet Exercise 2–3: Historical Perspective
                       The Judiciary's Role in American Government

COURT INFORMATION

I. TOWN COURT

- Every town has a Town Court.

- Jurisdiction includes: traffic matters; misdemeanors; felonies-arraignments and preliminary hearing only; town ordinance violations; eviction proceedings; civil suits seeking up to $3,000. Small Claims Court is a division of Town Court in which procedural rules are relaxed. An objective of Small Claims Court is to enable persons with relatively small claims to bring their cases to court without the necessity of incurring lawyer's fees.

- Judges of Town Court are elected for a four-year term.

II. CITY COURT

- Every city but New York City has a City Court.

- Criminal jurisdiction is the same as Town Courts; civil jurisdiction cases in which plaintiff is seeking up to $15,000.00, and eviction proceedings. Also City Court includes a Commercial Claims Part in which claims made by corporations, partnerships and business associations up to $3,000.00 are heard and court procedural rules are relaxed. Like Small Claims Court, an objective of Commercial Claims Part is to enable businesses with relatively small claims to bring their case to court without the necessity of incurring lawyer's fees.

- Judges of City Court are elected for a ten-year term.

III. NEW YORK CITY CIVIL COURT

- This court is found in New York City only.

- Jurisdiction includes civil suits seeking up to $25,000.00 and eviction proceedings.

- Judges are appointed by the Mayor of New York City for a ten-year term.

IV. NEW YORK CITY CRIMINAL COURT

- This court is found in New York City only.

- Jurisdiction includes: misdemeanors; felonies-arraignments and preliminary hearings only.

- Judges are appointed by the Mayor of New York City for a ten-year term.

V. DISTRICT COURT

- This court is found in Nassau and Suffolk Counties only.

- Jurisdiction includes: all civil suits seeking up to $15,000.00; eviction proceedings; misdemeanors; felonies-arraignments and preliminary hearings only; and Commercial Claims, as in City Court. (see II)

- Judges are elected for a ten-year term.

VI. FAMILY COURT

- Every county has a Family Court.

- Jurisdiction includes: juvenile delinquency proceedings, adoptions, child neglect and abuse matters; spousal abuse cases; support proceedings; custody disputes; paternity cases, and appointments of guardians for minors.

- Judges are elected for a ten-year term except in New York City where the judges are appointed by the mayor for a ten-year term.

VII. COURT OF CLAIMS

- Jurisdiction includes lawsuits in which New York State or certain of its subdivisions is the defendant.

- Judges are appointed by the governor and must be approved by the senate. Their term is nine years.

- All cases are tried by a judge without a jury.

VIII. SURROGATE COURT

- Every county has a Surrogate Court.

- Jurisdiction includes probate of wills, administration of estates, and adoptions.

- Judges are elected for a ten-year term except in the City of New York where they are elected to 14 year terms.

IX. COUNTY COURT

- Every county has a County Court except the counties comprising New York City (Bronx, Kings, New York, Queens, Richmond).

- Jurisdiction includes: civil suits seeking up to $25,000.00; felonies and indicted misdemeanors; appeals from City and Town Courts except in counties having an Appellate Term. In those counties appeals from City and Town Courts are heard by the Appellate Term rather than County Court.

- Judges are elected for a ten-year term.

X. SUPREME COURT

- The state is divided into twelve judicial districts, each of which has a Supreme Court.

- Jurisdiction includes unlimited original jurisdiction. This court can hear any type of case the first time it is heard by a court. However, cased falling within the jurisdiction of other courts are normally referred to those other courts.

- Judges are elected for a fourteen year term.

XI. APPELLATE TERM

- The state is divided into four geographic divisions, each of which is referred to as a department. The First and Second Departments each have an Appellate Term. Those Departments include the following counties: Bronx, Dutchess, Kings, Nassau, New York, Orange, Queens, Putnam, Richmond, Rockland, Suffolk and Westchester. The Appellate Term does not exist in other counties in New York State.

- Jurisdiction includes appeals from District Courts, Town Courts, City Courts, New York City Civil Court and New York City Criminal Court.

- Judges are appointed by the presiding judge of the Appellate Division within which the Appellate Term is located, but must be Supreme Court Judges at the time of appointment.

XII. APPELLATE DIVISION

- This court is an intermediate appellate court.

- The state is divided into four geographic divisions, each of which is referred to as a department. Each of the four departments has an Appellate Division.

- Jurisdiction is primarily appellate. This court hears appeals from Family Court, County Court, Supreme Court, Surrogate Court, and civil cases from Appellate Term. It has original jurisdiction to hear special proceedings involving lawyers and certain judges.

- Judges are appointed by the governor but must be Supreme Court Judges at the time of appointments. The appointment is for five years but not longer than the remaining period of a judge's fourteen-year term.

- Each case is heard by a panel of five judges.

XIII. COURT OF APPEALS

- The state has only one Court of Appeals which is located in Albany.

- Jursidiction is primarily appellate. The court hears appeals from the Appellate Division, and from other courts sitting as intermediate appellate courts.

- Judges are appointed by the governor for a fourteen-year term. The court consists of seven judges.

COURT CHART I
UPSTATE COUNTIES OF NEW YORK STATE[1]

(Arrow indicate the court to which cases are appealed)

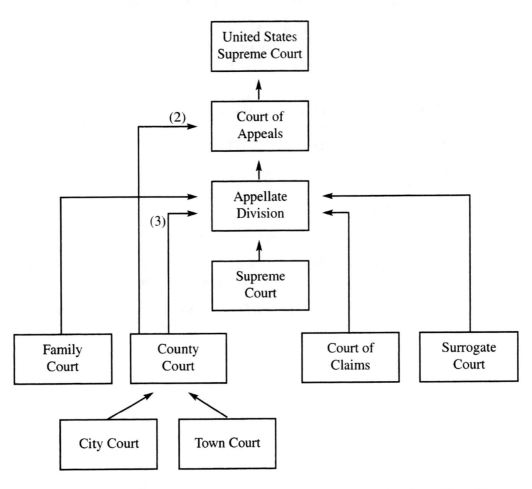

1) This chart does not apply to the following downstate counties: Bronx, Dutchess, Kings, Nassau, New York, Orange, Putnam, Queens, Richmond, Rockland, Suffolk and Westchester. See Court Chart II for those counties.

2) Criminal cases but not civil cases appealed to County Court from a Town or City Court, and thereafter appealed from County Court, are heard by the Court of Appeals.

3) All cases appealed from County Court, except those identified in footnote 2, are heard by the Appellate Division.

COURT CHART II
DOWNSTATE COUNTIES OF NEW YORK STATE[1]
(Arrow indicate the court to which cases are appealed)

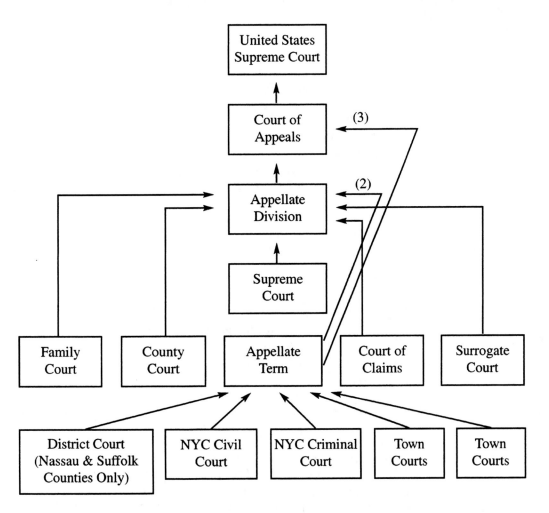

1) This chart applies to the following counties: Bronx, Dutchess, Kings, Nassau, New York, Orange, Putnam, Queens, Richmond, Rockland, Suffolk and Westchester. See Court Chart I for the other counties in New York State.

2) Civil cases but not criminal cases appealed from Appellate Term are heard by the Appellate Division.

3) Criminal cases but not civil cases appealed from Appellate Term are heard by the Court of Appeals.

CHAPTER 3

Court Procedures

American and English courts follow the *adversarial system of justice*. Although clients are allowed to represent themselves in court (called *pro se* representation),[1] most parties to lawsuits hire attorneys to represent them. Each lawyer acts as his or her client's advocate, presenting the client's version of the facts in such a way as to convince the judge (or the judge and jury, in a jury trial) that this version is correct.

Most of the judicial procedures that you will read about in the following pages are rooted in the adversarial framework of the American legal system. In this chapter, after a brief overview of judicial procedures, we illustrate the steps involved in a lawsuit with a hypothetical civil case (criminal procedures will be discussed in Chapter 9).

---

1. This right was definitively established in *Faretta v. California,* 422 U.S. 806, 95 S.Ct. 2525, 45 L.Ed.2d 562 (1975).

Procedural Rules

The parties to a lawsuit must comply with the procedural rules of the court in which the lawsuit is filed. Although most people, when considering the outcome of a case, think of matters of substantive law, procedural law can have a significant impact on one's ability to assert a legal claim. Procedural rules provide a framework for every dispute and specify what must be done at each stage of the litigation process. All civil trials held in federal district courts are governed by the **Federal Rules of Civil Procedure (FRCP).**[2] Each state also has rules of civil procedure that apply to all courts within that state. In addition, each court has its own local rules of procedure that supplement the federal or state rules.

Stages of Litigation

Broadly speaking, the litigation process has three phases: pretrial, trial, and posttrial. Each phase involves specific procedures, as discussed throughout this chapter. Although civil lawsuits may vary greatly in terms of complexity, cost, and detail, they typically progress through the specific stages charted in Exhibit 3–1.

To illustrate the procedures involved in a civil lawsuit, we will use a simple hypothetical case. The case arose from an automobile accident, which occurred when a car driven by Antonio Carvello, a resident of New Jersey, collided with a car driven by Jill Kirby, a resident of New York. The accident took place at an intersection in New York City. Kirby suffered personal injuries, which caused her to incur medical and hospital expenses as well as lost wages for four months. In all, she calculated that the cost to her of the accident was $100,000.[3] Carvello and Kirby have been unable to agree on a settlement, and Kirby now must decide whether to sue Carvello for the $100,000 compensation she feels she deserves.

---

2. The United States Supreme Court has authority to set forth these rules, as spelled out in 28 U.S.C. Sections 2071–2077. Generally, though, the federal judiciary appoints committees that make recommendations to the Supreme Court. The Court then publishes any proposed changes in the rules and allows for public comment before finalizing the rules.

---

3. In this example, we are ignoring damages for pain and suffering or for permanent disabilities. Often, plaintiffs in personal-injury cases seek such damages.

EXHIBIT 3–1 • Stages in a Typical Lawsuit

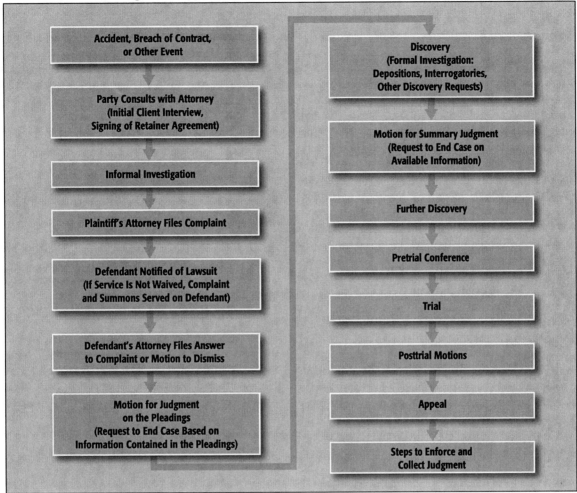

The First Step: Consulting with an Attorney

As mentioned, rules of procedure often affect the outcome of a dispute—a fact that highlights the importance of obtaining the advice of counsel. The first step taken by virtually anyone contemplating a lawsuit is to seek the guidance of a qualified attorney.[4] In the hypothetical Kirby-Carvello case, assume that Kirby consults with a lawyer. The attorney will advise her regarding what she can expect in a lawsuit, her probability of success at trial, and the procedures that will be involved. If more than one court would have jurisdic-

tion over the matter, the attorney will also discuss the advantages and disadvantages of filing in a particular court. Depending on the court hearing the case, the attorney will give Kirby an idea of how much time it will take to resolve the dispute through litigation and provide an estimate of the costs involved.

The attorney will also inform Kirby of the legal fees that she will have to pay in an attempt to collect damages from the defendant, Carvello. Attorneys base their fees on such factors as the difficulty of a matter, the amount of time involved, the experience and skill of the attorney in the particular area of the law, and the cost of doing business. In the United States, legal fees range from $125 to $600 per hour or even higher (the average fee per hour is between $175 and $300). In addition, the client is also responsible for paying

---

4. See Chapter 42 for a discussion of the importance of obtaining legal counsel and for guidelines on how to locate attorneys and retain their services.

various expenses related to the case (called "out-of-pocket" costs), including court filing fees, travel expenses, and the cost of expert witnesses and investigators, for example.

Types of Attorneys' Fees For a particular legal matter, an attorney may charge one type of fee or a combination of several types. *Fixed fees* may be charged for the performance of such services as drafting a simple will. *Hourly fees* may be computed for matters that will involve an indeterminate period of time. Any case brought to trial, for example, may involve an expenditure of time that cannot be precisely estimated in advance. *Contingency fees* are fixed as a percentage (usually between 25 and 40 percent) of a client's recovery in certain types of lawsuits, such as a personal-injury lawsuit.[5] If the lawsuit is unsuccessful, the attorney receives no fee, but the client will have to reimburse the attorney for any out-of-pocket costs incurred. Because Kirby's claim involves a personal injury, her lawyer will likely take the case on a contingency-fee basis, but she may have to pay an amount up front to cover the court costs.

In some cases, the winning party may be able to recover at least some portion of her or his attorneys' fees from the losing party. Many state and federal statutes provide for an award of attorneys' fees in certain legal actions, such as probate matters (settling a person's estate after death). In these situations, the judge sets the amount of the fee, which may be specified by statute or based on other factors, such as the fee customarily charged for similar services in the area. An attorney will advise the client as to whether she or he would be entitled to recover some or all of the attorneys' fees in a case.

Settlement Considerations Once an attorney has been retained, the attorney is required to pursue a resolution of the matter on the client's behalf. Nevertheless, the amount of energy an attorney will spend on a given case is also determined by how much time and funds the client wishes to devote to the process. If the client is willing to pay for a lengthy trial and one or more appeals, the attorney may pursue those actions. Often, however, once a client learns the substantial costs involved in litigation, he or she may

decide to pursue a settlement of the claim. Attempts to settle the case may be ongoing throughout the litigation process.

Another important factor in deciding whether to pursue litigation is the defendant's ability to pay the damages sought. Even if Kirby is awarded damages, it may be difficult to enforce the court's judgment if, for example, the amount exceeds the limits of Carvello's automobile insurance policy. (We will discuss the problems involved in enforcing a judgment later in this chapter.)

Pretrial Procedures

The pretrial litigation process involves the filing of the *pleadings*, the gathering of evidence (called *discovery*), and possibly other procedures, such as a pretrial conference and jury selection.

The Pleadings

The *complaint* and *answer* (and other legal documents discussed below), taken together, are known as the **pleadings.** The pleadings inform each party of the other's claims and specify the issues (disputed questions) involved in the case. Because the rules of procedure vary depending on the jurisdiction of the court, the style and form of the pleadings may be different from those shown in this chapter.

The Plaintiff's Complaint Kirby's action against Carvello commences when her lawyer files a **complaint**[6] with the clerk of the appropriate court. The complaint contains a statement alleging (1) the facts showing that the court has jurisdiction, (2) the facts establishing the plaintiff's basis for relief, and (3) the remedy the plaintiff is seeking. Complaints can be lengthy or brief, depending on the complexity of the case and the rules of the jurisdiction.

Exhibit 3–2 illustrates how a complaint in the Kirby-Carvello case might appear. The complaint asserts facts indicating that the federal district court has jurisdiction because of diversity of citizenship. It then gives a brief statement of the facts of the accident and alleges that Carvello negligently drove his vehicle through a red light, striking Kirby's car and causing

---

5. Note that attorneys may charge a contingency fee in only certain types of cases and are typically prohibited from entering into this type of fee arrangement in criminal cases, divorce cases, and cases involving the distribution of assets after death.

6. Sometimes, the document filed with the court is called a *petition* or a *declaration* instead of a complaint.

EXHIBIT 3-2 • A Typical Complaint

IN THE UNITED STATES DISTRICT COURT
FOR THE SOUTHERN DISTRICT OF NEW YORK

JILL KIRBY

                    Plaintiff,

v.

ANTONIO CARVELLO

                    Defendant.

CIVIL NO. 09-1047

COMPLAINT

The plaintiff brings this cause of action against the defendant, alleging as follows:

1. This action is between the plaintiff, who is a resident of the State of New York, and the defendant, who is a resident of the State of New Jersey. There is diversity of citizenship between the parties.
2. The amount in controversy, exclusive of interest and costs, exceeds the sum of $75,000.
3. On September 10th, 2008, the plaintiff, Jill Kirby, was exercising good driving habits and reasonable care in driving her car through the intersection of Boardwalk and Pennsylvania Avenue, New York City, New York, when the defendant, Antonio Carvello, negligently drove his vehicle through a red light at the intersection and collided with the plaintiff's vehicle.
4. As a result of the collision, the plaintiff suffered severe physical injury, which prevented her from working, and property damage to her car.

WHEREFORE, the plaintiff demands judgment against the defendant for the sum of $100,000 plus interest at the maximum legal rate and the costs of this action.

By _*Joseph Roe*_____

Joseph Roe
Attorney for Plaintiff
100 Main Street
New York, New York

1/2/09

---

serious personal injury and property damage. The complaint goes on to state that Kirby is seeking $100,000 in damages, although in some state civil actions the plaintiff need not specify the amount of damages sought.

Service of Process. Before the court can exercise jurisdiction over the defendant (Carvello)—in effect, before the lawsuit can begin—the court must have proof that the defendant was notified of the lawsuit.

Formally notifying the defendant of a lawsuit is called **service of process.** The plaintiff must deliver, or serve, a copy of the complaint and a **summons** (a notice requiring the defendant to appear in court and answer the complaint) to the defendant. The summons notifies Carvello that he must file an answer to the complaint within a specified time period (twenty days in the federal courts) or suffer a default judgment against him. A **default judgment** in Kirby's favor would mean that she would be awarded the damages alleged in her

EXHIBIT 3-3 • **A Typical Summons**

UNITED STATES DISTRICT COURT
FOR THE SOUTHERN DISTRICT OF NEW YORK

CIVIL ACTION, FILE NO. 09-1047

JILL KIRBY

Plaintiff,

v.

SUMMONS

ANTONIO CARVELLO

Defendant.

To the above-named Defendant:

You are hereby summoned and required to serve upon Joseph Roe, plaintiff's attorney, whose address is 100 Main Street, New York, NY, an answer to the complaint which is herewith served upon you, within 20 days after service of this summons upon you, exclusive of the day of service. If you fail to do so, judgment by default will be taken against you for the relief demanded in the complaint.

C. H. Hynek
_____
CLERK

January 2, 2009
_____
DATE

John Dolan
_____
BY DEPUTY CLERK

complaint because Carvello failed to respond to the allegations. A typical summons is shown in Exhibit 3–3.

Method of Service. How service of process occurs depends on the rules of the court or jurisdiction in which the lawsuit is brought. Under the Federal Rules of Civil Procedure, anyone who is at least eighteen years of age and is not a party to the lawsuit can serve process in federal court cases. In state courts, the process server is often a county sheriff or an employee of an independent company that provides process service in the local area. Usually, the server hands the summons and complaint to the defendant personally or leaves it at the defendant's residence or place of business. In some states, process can be served by mail if the defendant consents (accepts service). When the defendant cannot be reached, special rules provide for alternative means of service, such as publishing a notice in the local newspaper. In some situations, such

as when the parties are in other countries or no other alternative is available, courts have even allowed service of process via e-mail, provided that it is reasonably calculated to provide notice and an opportunity to respond.[7]

In cases involving corporate defendants, the summons and complaint may be served on an officer or on a *registered agent* (representative) of the corporation. The name of a corporation's registered agent can usually be obtained from the secretary of state's office in the state where the company incorporated its business (and, frequently, from the secretary of state's office in any state where the corporation does business).

Did the plaintiff in the following case effect proper service of the summons and the complaint on an out-of-state corporation?

---

7. See, for example, *Rio Properties, Inc. v. Rio International Interlink,* 284 F.3d 1007 (9th Cir. 2002).

C A S E **3.1**   **Cruz v. Fagor America, Inc.**
California Court of Appeal, Fourth District, Division 1, 2007.
52 Cal.Rptr.3d 862, 146 Cal.App.4th 488.

● **Background and Facts** At the San Diego County Fair in California in the summer of 2001, Alan Cruz's parents bought a pressure cooker distributed by Fagor America, Inc. On September 10, sixteen-year-old Cruz tried to take the lid off of the pressure cooker and was burned on the left side of his torso and thigh. Cruz's parents e-mailed Fagor to alert the company to what had happened. Fagor denied liability. Cruz filed a suit in a California state court against Fagor, alleging negligence and product liability (see Chapters 7 and 23). Cruz mailed a summons and a copy of the complaint to Fagor by certified mail, return receipt requested. The envelope was addressed to "Patricio Barriga, Chairman of the Board, FAGOR AMERICA, INC., A Delaware Corporation, 1099 Wall Street, Lyndhurst, NJ 07071-3678." The receipt was returned with the signature of "Tina Hayes." When Fagor did not file an answer to Cruz's complaint, Cruz obtained a default judgment and was awarded damages of $259,114.50. More than nine months later, Barriga claimed that he had not been notified of the suit, and Fagor filed a motion to set aside the judgment. The court granted the motion, in part, on the ground that Cruz's service of process had not been effective. Cruz appealed to a state intermediate appellate court.

● **Decision and Rationale** The state intermediate appellate court reversed the decision of the lower court, ruling that it erred in concluding that the judgment against Fagor was void for the lack of a valid service of process. The appellate court concluded that Cruz met all of the requirements for serving an out-of-state corporation. In compliance with a California state statute, Cruz sent the summons and a copy of the complaint via first-class mail, return receipt requested. Significantly, Cruz addressed the service to Barriga, Fagor's president, not to the corporation itself. Barriga did not sign the receipt, but Hayes did. Under a state statute, service is proper when the summons and a copy of the complaint are delivered to "a person authorized by the corporation to receive service." According to a representative of the U.S. Postal Service, Hayes was a Fagor employee who regularly received mail on her employer's behalf. "The only reasonable inference from the evidence in the record is that Hayes was authorized to accept mail on behalf of Fagor's president at the time she signed the return receipt for the summons and complaint." Furthermore, reasoned the court, "By virtue of her authority to accept mail on Fagor's behalf, Hayes's notice of the action is imputed to Fagor and its officers. *   *   * To hold otherwise would be to ignore the realities of corporate life, in which the duty to sign for mail received often resides with a designated mailroom employee, a receptionist, a secretary, or an assistant."

● **What If the Facts Were Different?** *Suppose that Cruz had misaddressed the envelope but the summons had still reached Hayes, and Cruz could prove it. Would this have been sufficient to establish valid service? Explain.*

● **The Ethical Dimension** *Should a plaintiff be required to serve a defendant with a summons and a copy of a complaint more than once? Why or why not?*

Waiver of Formal Service of Process. In many instances, the defendant is already aware that a lawsuit is being filed and is willing to waive (give up) her or his right to be served personally. The Federal Rules of Civil Procedure (FRCP) and many states' rules allow defendants to waive formal service of process, provided that certain procedures are followed. Kirby's attorney, for example, could mail to defendant Carvello a copy of the complaint, along with "Waiver of Service of Summons" forms for Carvello to sign. If Carvello signs and returns the forms within thirty days, formal service of process is waived. Moreover, under the FRCP, defendants who agree to waive formal service of process receive additional time to respond to the complaint (sixty days, instead of twenty days). Some states provide similar incentives to encourage defendants to waive formal service of process and thereby reduce associated costs and foster cooperation between the parties.

The Defendant's Response Typically, the defendant's response to the complaint takes the form of an **answer.** In an answer, the defendant either admits or denies each of the allegations in the plaintiff's complaint and may also set forth defenses to those allegations. Under the federal rules, any allegations that are not denied by the defendant will be deemed by the court to have been admitted. If Carvello admits to all of Kirby's allegations in his answer, a judgment will be entered for Kirby. If Carvello denies Kirby's allegations, the matter will proceed further.

Affirmative Defenses. Carvello can also admit the truth of Kirby's complaint but raise new facts to show that he should not be held liable for Kirby's damages. This is called raising an **affirmative defense.** As will be discussed in subsequent chapters, defendants in both civil and criminal cases can raise affirmative defenses. For example, Carvello could assert Kirby's own negligence as a defense by alleging that Kirby was driving negligently at the time of the accident. In some states, a plaintiff's contributory negligence operates as a complete defense. In most states, however, the plaintiff's own negligence constitutes only a partial defense (see Chapter 7).

Counterclaims. Carvello could also deny Kirby's allegations and set forth his own claim that the accident occurred as a result of Kirby's negligence and that therefore she owes Carvello for damage to his car. This is appropriately called a **counterclaim.** If Carvello files a counterclaim, Kirby will have to submit an answer to the counterclaim.

Dismissals and Judgments before Trial

Many actions for which pleadings have been filed never come to trial. The parties may, for example, negotiate a settlement of the dispute at any stage of the litigation process. There are also numerous procedural avenues for disposing of a case without a trial. Many of them involve one or the other party's attempts to get the case dismissed through the use of various motions.

A **motion** is a procedural request submitted to the court by an attorney on behalf of her or his client. When one party files a motion with the court, that party must also send to, or serve on, the opposing party a *notice of motion.* The notice of motion informs the opposing party that the motion has been filed. **Pretrial motions** include the motion to dismiss, the motion for judgment on the pleadings, and the motion for summary judgment, as well as the other motions listed in Exhibit 3–4.

Motion to Dismiss Either party can file a **motion to dismiss** requesting the court to dismiss the case for the reasons stated in the motion, although normally it is the defendant who requests dismissal. A defendant could file a motion to dismiss if the plaintiff's complaint fails to state a claim for which relief (a remedy) can be granted. Such a motion asserts that even if the facts alleged in the complaint are true, they do not give rise to any legal claim against the defendant. For example, if the allegations in Kirby's complaint do not constitute negligence on Carvello's part, Carvello could move to dismiss the case for failure to state a claim. Defendant Carvello could also file a motion to dismiss on the grounds that he was not properly served, that the court lacked jurisdiction, or that the venue was improper.

If the judge grants the motion to dismiss, the plaintiff generally is given time to file an amended complaint. If the judge denies the motion, the suit will go forward, and the defendant must then file an answer. Note that if Carvello wishes to discontinue the suit because, for example, an out-of-court settlement has been reached, he can likewise move for dismissal. The court can also dismiss a case on its own motion.

Motion for Judgment on the Pleadings At the close of the pleadings, either party may make a **motion for judgment on the pleadings,** which asks the court to decide the issue solely on the pleadings without proceeding to trial. The judge will grant the motion only when there is no dispute over the facts of the case and the sole issue to be resolved is a question of law. For example, in the Kirby-Carvello case, if Carvello had admitted to all of Kirby's allegations in his answer and had raised no affirmative defenses, Kirby could file a motion for judgment on the pleadings.

In deciding a motion for judgment on the pleadings, the judge may consider only the evidence contained in the pleadings. In contrast, in a motion for summary judgment, discussed next, the court may consider evidence outside the pleadings, such as sworn statements and other materials that would be admissible as evidence at trial.

Motion for Summary Judgment Either party can file a **motion for summary judgment,** which asks the court to grant a judgment in that party's favor without a trial. As with a motion for judgment on the pleadings, a court will grant a motion for summary judgment only if it determines that no facts are in dis-

EXHIBIT 3-4 • Pretrial Motions

MOTION TO DISMISS

A motion normally filed by the defendant in which the defendant asks the court to dismiss the case for a specified reason, such as improper service, lack of personal jurisdiction, or the plaintiff's failure to state a claim for which relief can be granted.

MOTION TO STRIKE

A motion filed by the defendant in which the defendant asks the court to strike (delete) from the complaint certain paragraphs contained in the complaint. Motions to strike help to clarify the underlying issues that form the basis for the complaint by removing paragraphs that are redundant or irrelevant to the action.

MOTION TO MAKE MORE DEFINITE AND CERTAIN

A motion filed by the defendant to compel the plaintiff to clarify the basis of the plaintiff's cause of action. The motion is filed when the defendant believes that the complaint is too vague or ambiguous for the defendant to respond to it in a meaningful way.

MOTION FOR JUDGMENT ON THE PLEADINGS

A motion that may be filed by either party in which the party asks the court to enter a judgment in his or her favor based on information contained in the pleadings. A judgment on the pleadings will be made only if there are no facts in dispute and the only question is how the law applies to a set of undisputed facts.

MOTION TO COMPEL DISCOVERY

A motion that may be filed by either party in which the party asks the court to compel the other party to comply with a discovery request. If a party refuses to allow the opponent to inspect and copy certain documents, for example, the party requesting the documents may make a motion to compel production of those documents.

MOTION FOR SUMMARY JUDGMENT

A motion that may be filed by either party in which the party asks the court to enter judgment in his or her favor without a trial. Unlike a motion for judgment on the pleadings, a motion for summary judgment can be supported by evidence outside the pleadings, such as witnesses' affidavits, answers to interrogatories, and other evidence obtained prior to or during discovery.

pute and the only question is how the law applies to the facts. A motion for summary judgment can be made before or during a trial, but it will be granted only if, when the evidence is viewed in the light most favorable to the other party, there clearly are no factual disputes in contention.

To support a motion for summary judgment, one party can submit evidence obtained at any point prior to trial that refutes the other party's factual claim. The evidence may consist of **affidavits** (sworn statements by parties or witnesses) or documents, such as a contract. Of course, the evidence must be *admissible* evidence—that is, evidence that the court would allow to be presented during the trial. As mentioned, the use of additional evidence is one feature that distinguishes the motion for summary judgment from the motion to dismiss and the motion for judgment on the pleadings.

Discovery

Before a trial begins, the parties can use a number of procedural devices to obtain information and gather evidence about the case. Kirby, for example, will want to know how fast Carvello was driving, whether he had been drinking or was under the influence of any medication, and whether he was wearing corrective lenses if he was required by law to do so while driving. The process of obtaining information from the opposing party or from witnesses prior to trial is known as **discovery.** Discovery includes gaining access to witnesses, documents, records, and other types of evidence. In federal courts, the parties are required to make initial disclosures of relevant evidence to the opposing party.

The Federal Rules of Civil Procedures and similar state rules set forth the guidelines for discovery activity. Generally, discovery is allowed regarding any matter that is relevant to the claim or defense of any party. Discovery rules also attempt to protect witnesses and parties from undue harassment, and to safeguard privileged or confidential material from being disclosed. Only information that is relevant to the case at hand—or likely to lead to the discovery of relevant information—is discoverable. If a discovery request involves privileged or confidential business information, a court can deny the request and can limit the scope of discovery in a number of ways. For example, a court can require the party to submit the materials to the judge in a sealed envelope so that the judge can decide if they should be disclosed to the opposing party.

Discovery prevents surprises at trial by giving both parties access to evidence that might otherwise be hidden. This allows the litigants to learn as much as they can about what to expect at a trial before they reach the courtroom. Discovery also serves to narrow the issues so that trial time is spent on the main questions in the case.

Depositions and Interrogatories Discovery can involve the use of depositions or interrogatories, or both. A **deposition** is sworn testimony by a party to the lawsuit or by any witness, recorded by an authorized court official. The person deposed gives testimony and answers questions asked by the attorneys from both sides. The questions and answers are recorded, sworn to, and signed. These answers, of course, will help the attorneys prepare their cases. Depositions also give attorneys the opportunity to evaluate how their witnesses will conduct themselves at trial. In addition, depositions can be employed in court to *impeach* (challenge the credibility of) a party or a witness who changes testimony at the trial. A deposition can also be used as testimony if the witness is not available at trial.

Interrogatories are written questions for which written answers are prepared and then signed under oath. The main difference between interrogatories and written depositions is that interrogatories are directed to a party to the lawsuit (the plaintiff or the defendant), not to a witness, and the party can prepare answers with the aid of an attorney. Whereas depositions are useful for eliciting candid responses from a party and answers not prepared in advance, interrogatories are designed to obtain accurate information about specific topics, such as, for example, how many contracts were signed and when. The scope of interrogatories is also broader because parties are obligated to answer questions, even if that means disclosing information from their records and files.

Requests for Admissions One party can serve the other party with a written request for an admission of the truth of matters relating to the trial. Any fact admitted under such a request is conclusively established as true for the trial. For example, Kirby can ask Carvello to admit that his driver's license was suspended at the time of the accident. A request for admission shortens the trial because the parties will not have to spend time proving facts on which they already agree.

Requests for Documents, Objects, and Entry upon Land A party can gain access to documents and other items not in her or his possession in order to inspect and examine them. Carvello, for example, can gain permission to inspect and copy Kirby's car repair bills. Likewise, a party can gain "entry upon land" to inspect the premises.

Request for Examinations When the physical or mental condition of one party is in question, the opposing party can ask the court to order a physical or mental examination by an independent examiner. If the court agrees to make the order, the opposing party can obtain the results of the examination. Note that the court will make such an order only when the need for the information outweighs the right to privacy of the person to be examined.

Electronic Discovery Any relevant material, including information stored electronically, can be the object of a discovery request. The federal rules and most state rules (as well as court decisions) now specifically allow individuals to obtain discovery of electronic "data compilations." Electronic evidence, or **e-evidence,** consists of all computer-generated or electronically recorded information, such as e-mail, voice mail, spreadsheets, word-processing documents, and other data. E-evidence can reveal significant facts that are not discoverable by other means. For example, computers automatically record certain information about files—such as who created the file and when, and who accessed, modified, or transmitted it—on their hard drives. This information can only be obtained from the file in its electronic format—not from printed-out versions.

Amendments to the Federal Rules of Civil Procedure that took effect in December 2006 deal specifically with the preservation, retrieval, and production of electronic data. Although traditional means, such as interrogatories and depositions, are still used to find out whether e-evidence exists, a party must usually hire an expert to retrieve the evidence in its electronic format. The expert uses software to reconstruct e-mail exchanges to establish who knew what and when they knew it. The expert can even recover files from a computer that the user thought had been deleted. Reviewing back-up copies of documents and e-mail can provide useful—and often quite damaging—information about how a particular matter progressed over several weeks or months.

Electronic discovery has significant advantages over paper discovery, but it is also time consuming and expensive. These costs are amplified when the parties involved in the lawsuit are large corporations with many offices and employees. Who should pay the costs associated with electronic discovery? For a discussion of how the courts are handling this issue, see this chapter's *Emerging Trends* feature on pages 62 and 63.

Pretrial Conference

After discovery has taken place and before the trial begins, the attorneys may meet with the trial judge in a **pretrial conference,** or hearing. Usually, the hearing consists of an informal discussion between the judge and the opposing attorneys after discovery has taken place. The purpose of the hearing is to explore the possibility of a settlement without trial and, if this is not possible, to identify the matters that are in dispute and to plan the course of the trial. In particular, the parties may attempt to establish ground rules to restrict the number of expert witnesses or discuss the admissibility or costs of certain types of evidence.

The Right to a Jury Trial

The Seventh Amendment to the U.S. Constitution guarantees the right to a jury trial for cases at law in *federal* courts when the amount in controversy exceeds $20. Most states have similar guarantees in their own constitutions (although the threshold dollar amount is higher than $20). The right to a trial by jury need not be exercised, and many cases are tried without a jury. In most states and in federal courts, one of the parties must request a jury, or the judge presumes the parties waive this right. If there is no jury, the judge determines the truth of the facts alleged in the case.

Jury Selection

Before a jury trial commences, a panel of jurors must be selected. Although some types of trials require twelve-person juries, most civil matters can be heard by six-person juries. The jury selection process is known as **voir dire.**[8] During *voir dire* in most jurisdictions, attorneys for the plaintiff and the defendant ask prospective jurors oral questions to determine whether a potential jury member is biased or has any connection with a party to the action or with a prospective witness. In some jurisdictions, the judge may do all or part of the questioning based on written questions submitted by counsel for the parties.

During *voir dire,* a party may challenge a certain number of prospective jurors *peremptorily*—that is, ask that an individual not be sworn in as a juror without providing any reason. Alternatively, a party may challenge a prospective juror *for cause*—that is, provide a reason why an individual should not be sworn in as a juror. If the judge grants the challenge, the individual is asked to step down. A prospective juror, however, may not be excluded by the use of discriminatory challenges, such as those based on racial criteria or gender. (See *Concept Summary 3.1* on the following page for a review of pretrial procedures.)

The Trial

Various rules and procedures govern the trial phase of the litigation process. There are rules governing what kind of evidence will or will not be admitted during the trial, as well as specific procedures that the participants in the lawsuit must follow.

Opening Statements

At the beginning of the trial, both attorneys are allowed to make **opening statements** setting forth the facts that they expect to prove during the trial. The opening statement provides an opportunity for each lawyer to give a brief version of the facts and the supporting evidence that will be used during the trial. Then the plaintiff's case is presented. In our hypothetical case, Kirby's lawyer would introduce evidence (relevant documents, exhibits, and the testimony of witnesses) to support Kirby's position.

---

8. Pronounced *vwahr deehr.* These old French verbs mean "to speak the truth." In legal language, the phrase refers to the process of questioning jurors to learn about their backgrounds, attitudes, and similar attributes.

Rules of Evidence

Whether evidence will be admitted in court is determined by the **rules of evidence**—a series of rules that have been created by the courts to ensure that any evidence presented during a trial is fair and reliable. The Federal Rules of Evidence govern the admissibility of evidence in federal courts.

Evidence Must Be Relevant to the Issues

Evidence will not be admitted in court unless it is relevant to the matter in question. **Relevant evidence** is evidence that tends to prove or disprove a fact in question or to establish the degree of probability of a fact or action. For example, evidence that a suspect's gun was in the home of another person when a victim was shot would be relevant—because it would tend to prove that the suspect did not shoot the victim.

Even relevant evidence may not be admitted in court if its reliability is questionable or if its probative (proving) value is substantially outweighed by other important considerations of the court. For example, a

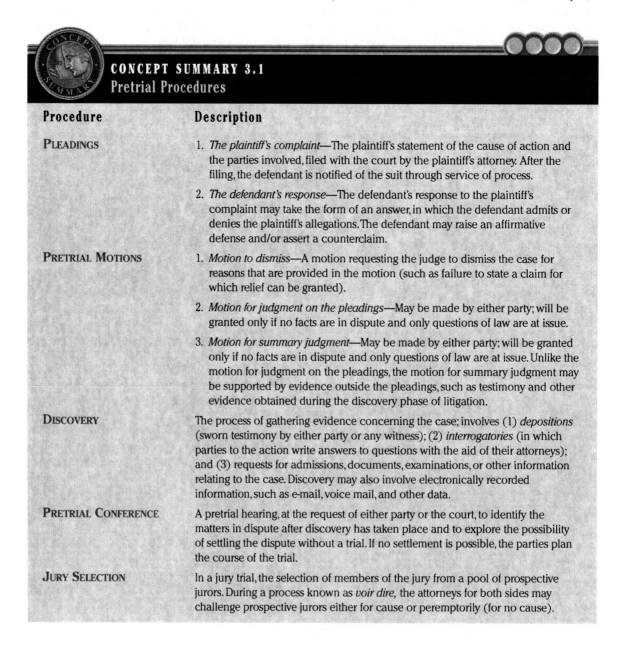

CONCEPT SUMMARY 3.1
Pretrial Procedures

Procedure	Description
PLEADINGS	1. *The plaintiff's complaint*—The plaintiff's statement of the cause of action and the parties involved, filed with the court by the plaintiff's attorney. After the filing, the defendant is notified of the suit through service of process.
	2. *The defendant's response*—The defendant's response to the plaintiff's complaint may take the form of an answer, in which the defendant admits or denies the plaintiff's allegations. The defendant may raise an affirmative defense and/or assert a counterclaim.
PRETRIAL MOTIONS	1. *Motion to dismiss*—A motion requesting the judge to dismiss the case for reasons that are provided in the motion (such as failure to state a claim for which relief can be granted).
	2. *Motion for judgment on the pleadings*—May be made by either party; will be granted only if no facts are in dispute and only questions of law are at issue.
	3. *Motion for summary judgment*—May be made by either party; will be granted only if no facts are in dispute and only questions of law are at issue. Unlike the motion for judgment on the pleadings, the motion for summary judgment may be supported by evidence outside the pleadings, such as testimony and other evidence obtained during the discovery phase of litigation.
DISCOVERY	The process of gathering evidence concerning the case; involves (1) *depositions* (sworn testimony by either party or any witness); (2) *interrogatories* (in which parties to the action write answers to questions with the aid of their attorneys); and (3) requests for admissions, documents, examinations, or other information relating to the case. Discovery may also involve electronically recorded information, such as e-mail, voice mail, and other data.
PRETRIAL CONFERENCE	A pretrial hearing, at the request of either party or the court, to identify the matters in dispute after discovery has taken place and to explore the possibility of settling the dispute without a trial. If no settlement is possible, the parties plan the course of the trial.
JURY SELECTION	In a jury trial, the selection of members of the jury from a pool of prospective jurors. During a process known as *voir dire*, the attorneys for both sides may challenge prospective jurors either for cause or peremptorily (for no cause).

video or a photograph that shows in detail the severity of a victim's injuries would be relevant evidence, but the court might exclude this evidence on the ground that it would emotionally inflame the jurors.

Hearsay Evidence Not Admissible Generally, hearsay is not admissible as evidence. **Hearsay** is defined as any testimony given in court about a statement made by someone else who was not under oath at the time of the statement. Literally, it is what someone heard someone else say. For example, if a witness in the Kirby-Carvello case testified in court concerning what he or she heard another observer say about the accident, that testimony would be hearsay, or second-hand knowledge. Admitting hearsay into evidence carries many risks because, even though it may be relevant, there is no way to test its reliability.

In the following case, the plaintiff's evidence consisted in part of printouts of Web pages purporting to indicate how the pages appeared at a prior point in time. The defendant challenged this evidence as hearsay.

C A S E 3.2   Novak v. Tucows, Inc.
United States District Court, Eastern District of New York, 2007. __ F.Supp.2d __.

● **Background and Facts** In 1997, Robert Novak registered the domain name **petswarehouse.com** and began selling pet supplies and livestock online. Within two years, the site had become one of the most popular sites for pet supplies in the United States. Novak obtained a trademark for the **petswarehouse.com** name and transferred its registration to Nitin Networks, Inc., which was owned by Tucows, Inc., a Canadian firm. In an unrelated matter, John Benn obtained a judgment against Novak in an Alabama state court. Tucows transferred the name to the court on its order on May 1, 2003. After a state intermediate appellate court reversed the judgment, the name was returned to Novak on October 1, 2004. Novak filed a suit in a federal district court against Tucows and Nitin, arguing that the transfer of the name out of his control for seventeen months destroyed his pet-supply business. Novak alleged several violations of federal and state law, including trademark infringement and conversion. Tucows responded with, among other things, a motion to strike some of Novak's exhibits.

● **Decision and Rationale** The court granted Tucows's motion to strike Novak's exhibits. The defendants had contended that Novak's exhibits were printouts of Internet pages and that as such they constituted inadmissible hearsay. Further, one of the exhibits was a printout from **RegisterSite.com** as it purportedly appeared in 2003. Novak had obtained this printout through a Web site called Internet Archive, which provides access to a digital library of Internet sites. The court concluded that "where postings from Internet Web sites are not statements made by declarants testifying at trial and are offered to prove the truth of the matter asserted, such postings generally constitute hearsay under [the Federal Rules of Evidence]. Furthermore, such documents have not been properly authenticated pursuant to [the Federal Rules of Evidence]. Therefore, in the absence of any authentication of plaintiff's Internet printouts, combined with lack of any assertion that such printouts fall under a viable exception to the hearsay rule, defendant's motion to strike [certain exhibits] is granted."

● **The Ethical Dimension** *Hearsay is literally what a witness says he or she heard another person say. What makes the admissibility of such evidence potentially unethical?*

● **The E-Commerce Dimension** *In this case, the plaintiff offered as evidence the printouts of Web pages that he claimed once appeared on others' Web sites. What makes such evidence questionable until proved accurate?*

EMERGING TRENDS IN BUSINESS LAW
E-Discovery and Cost-Shifting

Before the computer age, discovery involved searching through paper records—physical evidence. Today, less than 0.5 percent of new information is created on paper. Instead of sending letters and memos, for example, people send e-mails—almost 600 billion of them annually in the United States. The all-inclusive nature of electronic information means that electronic discovery (e-discovery) now plays an important role in almost every business lawsuit.

Changes in the Federal Rules of Civil Procedure

As e-discovery has become ubiquitous, the Federal Rules of Civil Procedure (FRCP) have changed to encompass it. Amended Section 26(f) of the FRCP, for example, requires that the parties confer about "preserving discoverable information" and discuss "any issues relating to . . . discovery of electronically stored information, including the electronic forms in which it should be produced."

The most recent amendment to Section 34(a) of the FRCP expressly permits one party to a lawsuit to request that the other produce "electronically stored information— including . . . data compilation stored in any medium from which information can be obtained." The new rule has put in place a two-tiered process for discovery of electronically stored information. Relevant and nonprivileged information that is reasonably accessible is discoverable as a matter of right. Discovery of less accessible— and therefore more costly to obtain— electronic data may or may not be allowed by the court. The problem of the costs of e-discovery is discussed further below.

The *Ameriwood* Three-Step Process

The new federal rules were applied in *Ameriwood Industries, Inc. v. Liberman,* a major case involving e-discovery in which the court developed a three-step procedure for obtaining electronic data.[a] In the first step, *imaging,* mirror images of a

a. 2007 WL 685623 (E.D.Mo. 2007).

party's hard drives can be required. The second step involves *recovering* available word-processing documents, e-mails, PowerPoint presentations, spreadsheets, and other files. The final step is *full disclosure* in which a party sends the other party all responsive and nonprivileged documents and information obtained in the previous two steps.

Limitations on E-Discovery and Cost-Shifting

Complying with requests for electronically discoverable information can cost hundreds of thousands, if not millions, of dollars, especially if a party is a large corporation with thousands of employees creating millions of electronic documents. Consequently, there is a trend toward limiting e-discovery. Under the FRCP, a court can limit electronic discovery (1) when it would be unreasonably cumulative or duplicative, (2) when the requesting party has already had ample opportunity during discovery to obtain the information, or (3) when the burden or expense outweighs the likely benefit.

Examination of Witnesses

Because Kirby is the plaintiff, she has the burden of proving that her allegations are true. Her attorney begins the presentation of Kirby's case by calling the first witness for the plaintiff and examining, or questioning, the witness. (For both attorneys, the types of questions and the manner of asking them are governed by the rules of evidence.) This questioning is called **direct examination.** After Kirby's attorney is finished, the witness is subject to **cross-examination** by Carvello's attorney. Then Kirby's attorney has another opportunity to question the witness in *redirect examination,* and Carvello's attorney may follow the redirect examination with a *recross-examination.* When both attorneys have finished with the first wit-

ness, Kirby's attorney calls the succeeding witnesses in the plaintiff's case, each of whom is subject to examination by the attorneys in the manner just described.

Potential Motion and Judgment At the conclusion of the plaintiff's case, the defendant's attorney has the opportunity to ask the judge to direct a verdict for the defendant on the ground that the plaintiff has presented no evidence to support her or his claim. This is called a **motion for a judgment as a matter of law** (or a **motion for a directed verdict** in state courts). In considering the motion, the judge looks at the evidence in the light most favorable to the plaintiff and grants the motion only if there is insufficient

Many courts are allowing responding parties to object to e-discovery requests on the ground that complying with the request would cause an undue financial burden. In a suit between E*Trade and Deutsche Bank, for example, the court denied E*Trade's request that the defendant produce its hard drives because doing so would create an undue burden.[b]

In addition, sometimes when a court finds that producing the requested information would create an undue financial burden, the court orders the party to comply but shifts the cost to the requesting party (usually the plaintiff). A major case in this area involved Rowe Entertainment and the William Morris Agency. When the e-discovery costs were estimated to be as high as

$9 million, the court determined that cost-shifting was warranted.[c] In deciding whether to order cost-shifting, courts increasingly take into account the amount in controversy and each party's ability to pay. Sometimes, a court may require the responding party to restore and produce representative documents from a small sample of the requested medium to verify the relevance of the data before the party incurs significant expenses.[d]

IMPLICATIONS FOR THE BUSINESSPERSON

1. Whenever there is a "reasonable anticipation of litigation," all the relevant documents must be preserved. Preserving data can be a challenge, particularly for large corporations that have electronic data scattered across multiple networks, servers, desktops, laptops, handheld devices, and even home computers.

2. Even though an e-mail is deleted, it is not necessarily eliminated from one's hard drive, unless it is completely overwritten by new data. Thus, businesspersons should be aware that their hard drives can contain information they presumed no longer existed.

FOR CRITICAL ANALYSIS

1. How might a large corporation protect itself from allegations that it intentionally failed to preserve electronic data?

2. Given the significant and often burdensome costs associated with electronic discovery, should courts consider cost-shifting in every case involving electronic discovery? Why or why not?

RELEVANT WEB SITES

To locate information on the Web concerning the issues discussed in this feature, go to this text's Web site at **www.cengage.com/blaw/jentz**, select "Chapter 3," and click on "Emerging Trends."

b. *E*Trade Securities, LLC v. Deutsche Bank A.G.,* 230 F.R.D. 582 (D.Minn. 2005). This is a *Federal Rules Decision* not designated for publication in the *Federal Supplement,* citing *Zubulake v. UBS Warburg, LLC,* 2003 WL 21087884 (S.D.N.Y. 2003).

c. *Rowe Entertainment, Inc., v. William Morris Agency, Inc.,* 2002 WL 975713 (S.D.N.Y. 2002).
d. See, for example, *Quinby v. WestLB AG,* 2006 WL 2597900 (S.D.N.Y. 2006).

evidence to raise an issue of fact. (Motions for directed verdicts at this stage of a trial are seldom granted.)

Defendant's Evidence The defendant's attorney then presents the evidence and witnesses for the defendant's case. Witnesses are called and examined by the defendant's attorney. The plaintiff's attorney has the right to cross-examine them, and there may be a redirect examination and possibly a recross-examination. At the end of the defendant's case, either attorney can move for a directed verdict, and the test again is whether the jury can, through any reasonable interpretation of the evidence, find for the party against whom the motion has been made. After

the defendant's attorney has finished introducing evidence, the plaintiff's attorney can present a **rebuttal,** which includes additional evidence to refute the defendant's case. The defendant's attorney can, in turn, refute that evidence in a **rejoinder.**

Closing Arguments, Jury Instructions, and Verdict

After both sides have rested their cases, each attorney presents a closing argument. In the **closing argument,** each attorney summarizes the facts and evidence presented during the trial and indicates why the facts and evidence support his or her client's claim. In addition to generally urging a verdict in favor of the client, the closing arguments typically reveal the shortcomings of the points made by the opposing party during the trial.

Attorneys generally present closing arguments whether or not the trial was heard by a jury. If it was a jury trial, the judge then instructs the jury in the law that applies to the case (these instructions are often called *charges*), and the jury retires to the jury room to deliberate a verdict. In most civil cases, the standard of proof is a *preponderance of the evidence.*[9] In other words, the plaintiff (Kirby in our hypothetical case) need only show that her factual claim is more likely to be true than the defendant's. (As you will read in Chapter 9, in a criminal trial the prosecution has a higher standard of proof to meet—it must prove its case *beyond a reasonable doubt.*)

Once the jury has reached a decision, it issues a **verdict** in favor of one party; the verdict specifies the jury's factual findings. In some cases, the jury also

---

9. Note that some civil claims must be proved by "clear and convincing evidence," meaning that the evidence must show that the truth of the party's claim is highly probable. This standard is often applied in situations that present a particular danger of deception, such as allegations of fraud.

decides on the amount of the *award* (the compensation to be paid to the prevailing party). After the announcement of the verdict, which marks the end of the trial itself, the jurors are dismissed. (See *Concept Summary 3.2* for a review of trial procedures.)

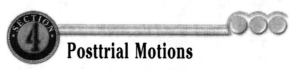

Posttrial Motions

After the jury has rendered its verdict, either party may make a posttrial motion. The prevailing party usually requests that the court enter a judgment in accordance with the verdict. The nonprevailing party frequently files one of the motions discussed next.

Motion for a New Trial

At the end of the trial, a motion can be made to set aside an adverse verdict and any judgment and to hold a new trial. The **motion for a new trial** will be granted only if the judge is convinced, after looking at all the evidence, that the jury was in error, but does not feel it

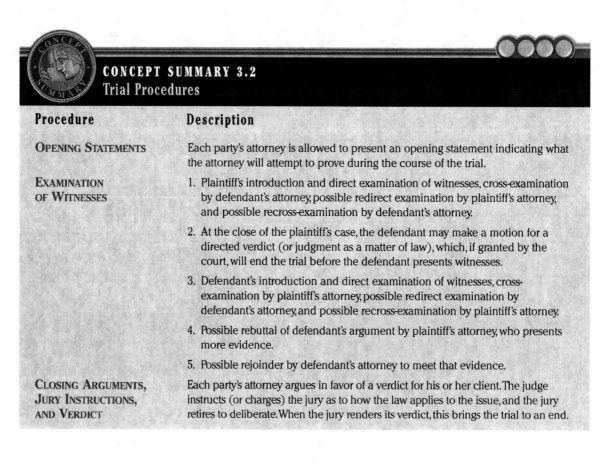

CONCEPT SUMMARY 3.2
Trial Procedures

Procedure	Description
OPENING STATEMENTS	Each party's attorney is allowed to present an opening statement indicating what the attorney will attempt to prove during the course of the trial.
EXAMINATION OF WITNESSES	1. Plaintiff's introduction and direct examination of witnesses, cross-examination by defendant's attorney, possible redirect examination by plaintiff's attorney, and possible recross-examination by defendant's attorney.
	2. At the close of the plaintiff's case, the defendant may make a motion for a directed verdict (or judgment as a matter of law), which, if granted by the court, will end the trial before the defendant presents witnesses.
	3. Defendant's introduction and direct examination of witnesses, cross-examination by plaintiff's attorney, possible redirect examination by defendant's attorney, and possible recross-examination by plaintiff's attorney.
	4. Possible rebuttal of defendant's argument by plaintiff's attorney, who presents more evidence.
	5. Possible rejoinder by defendant's attorney to meet that evidence.
CLOSING ARGUMENTS, JURY INSTRUCTIONS, AND VERDICT	Each party's attorney argues in favor of a verdict for his or her client. The judge instructs (or charges) the jury as to how the law applies to the issue, and the jury retires to deliberate. When the jury renders its verdict, this brings the trial to an end.

is appropriate to grant judgment for the other side. This will usually occur when the jury verdict is obviously the result of a misapplication of the law or a misunderstanding of the evidence presented at trial. A new trial can also be granted on the grounds of newly discovered evidence, misconduct by the participants during the trial (such as when an attorney has made prejudicial and inflammatory remarks), or error by the judge.

Motion for Judgment *N.O.V.*

If Kirby wins, and if Carvello's attorney has previously moved for a directed verdict, then Carvello's attorney can now make a **motion for judgment *n.o.v.***—from the Latin *non obstante veredicto,* meaning "notwithstanding the verdict." (Federal courts use the term *judgment as a matter of law* instead of *judgment n.o.v.*) Such a motion will be granted only if the jury's verdict was unreasonable and erroneous. If the judge grants the motion, then the jury's verdict will be set aside, and a judgment will be entered in favor of the opposing party (Carvello). If the motion is denied, Carvello may then appeal the case. (Kirby may also appeal the case, even though she won at trial. She might appeal, for example, if she received a smaller monetary award than she had sought.)

The Appeal

Either party may appeal not only the jury's verdict but also the judge's ruling on any pretrial or posttrial motion. Many of the appellate court cases that appear in this text involve appeals of motions for summary judgment or other motions that were denied by trial court judges. Note that a party must have legitimate grounds to file an appeal (some legal error) and that few trial court decisions are reversed on appeal. Moreover, the expenses associated with an appeal can be considerable.[10]

Filing the Appeal

If Carvello decides to appeal the verdict in Kirby's favor, then his attorney must file a *notice of appeal* with the clerk of the trial court within a prescribed period of time. Carvello then becomes the *appellant* or *petitioner.* The clerk of the trial court sends to the reviewing court (usually an intermediate court of appeals) the *record on appeal.* The record contains all the pleadings, motions, and other documents filed with the court and a complete written transcript of the proceedings, including testimony, arguments, jury instructions, and judicial rulings.

Carvello's attorney will file an appellate *brief* with the reviewing court. The **brief** is a formal legal document outlining the facts and issues of the case, the judge's rulings or jury's findings that should be reversed or modified, the applicable law, and arguments on Carvello's behalf (citing applicable statutes and relevant cases as precedents). The attorney for the *appellee* (Kirby, in our hypothetical case) usually files an answering brief. Carvello's attorney can file a reply, although it is not required. The reviewing court then considers the case.

Appellate Review

As mentioned in Chapter 2, a court of appeals does not hear any evidence. Rather, it reviews the record for errors of law. Its decision concerning a case is based on the record on appeal and the briefs and arguments. The attorneys present oral arguments, after which the case is taken under advisement. The court then issues a written opinion. In general, appellate courts do not reverse findings of fact unless the findings are unsupported or contradicted by the evidence.

An appellate court has the following options after reviewing a case:

1. The court can *affirm* the trial court's decision.
2. The court can *reverse* the trial court's judgment if it concludes that the trial court erred or that the jury did not receive proper instructions.
3. The appellate court can *remand* (send back) the case to the trial court for further proceedings consistent with its opinion on the matter.
4. The court might also affirm or reverse a decision *in part.* For example, the court might affirm the jury's finding that Carvello was negligent but remand the case for further proceedings on another issue (such as the extent of Kirby's damages).
5. An appellate court can also *modify* a lower court's decision. If the appellate court decides that the jury awarded an excessive amount in damages, for example, the court might reduce the award to a more appropriate, or fairer, amount.

---

10. See, for example, *Phansalkar v. Andersen Weinroth & Co.*, 356 F.3d 188 (2d Cir. 2004).

Appellate courts apply different standards of review depending on the type of issue involved and the lower courts' rulings. Generally, these standards require the reviewing court to give a certain amount of deference, or weight, to the findings of lower courts on specific issues. The following case illustrates the importance of standards of review as a means of exercising judicial restraint.

CASE 3.3 Evans v. Eaton Corp. Long Term Disability Plan
United States Court of Appeals, Fourth Circuit, 2008. 514 F.3d 315.

● **Background and Facts** Eaton Corporation is a multinational manufacturing company that funds and administers a long-term disability benefits plan for its employees. Brenda Evans was an employee at Eaton. In 1998, due to severe rheumatoid arthritis, Evans quit her job at Eaton and filed for disability benefits. Eaton paid disability benefits to Evans without controversy prior to 2003, but that year, Evans's disability status became questionable. Her physician had prescribed a new medication that had dramatically improved Evans's arthritis. In addition, Evans had injured her spine in a car accident in 2002 and was claiming to be disabled by continuing back problems as well as arthritis. But diagnostic exams during that period indicated that the injuries to Evans's back were not severe, and she could cook, shop, do laundry, wash dishes, and drive about seven miles a day. By 2004, several physicians who reviewed Evans's file had determined that she could work and was no longer totally disabled, and Eaton terminated Evans's disability benefits. Evans filed a complaint in the U.S. District Court for South Carolina alleging violations of the Employee Retirement Income Security Act of 1974 (ERISA, which is a federal law regulating pension plans, will be discussed in Chapter 33). The district court examined the evidence in great detail and concluded that Eaton's termination of Evans's benefits was an abuse of discretion because the physicians who testified in Evans's favor were more believable than the reviewing physicians. Eaton appealed to the U.S. Court of Appeals for the Fourth Circuit.

● **Decision and Rationale** The U.S. Court of Appeals for the Fourth Circuit reversed the district court's award of benefits to Evans and remanded the case with instructions that the district court enter a judgment in favor of Eaton. The appellate court pointed out that Eaton had numerous years of experience in administering its long-term disability benefits plan. The plan clearly gave the company discretionary authority to determine eligibility for benefits in addition to the power and discretion to determine all questions of fact arising with the plan's administration, interpretation, and application. Courts "when faced with discretionary language like that in the planned instrument in this case" can never forget their duty of deference and their secondary "rather than primary role in determining a claimant's right to benefits." Eaton's discretionary standards protect important values such as the enhanced prospects of achieving consistent application of the plan's provisions. Had the appellate court allowed the trial court's decision to stand, it would not have preserved the "plan's decision makers' functions against judicial intrusion."

● **What If the Facts Were Different?** *Suppose that the district court had concluded that Eaton Corporation's termination of Evans's benefits was not an abuse of discretion, and Evans had appealed. In that situation, would Evans have had any grounds for appealing the district court's decision? Explain.*

● **The Ethical Dimension** *The appellate court noted in this case that the district court's decision—which granted benefits to Evans—may arguably have been a better decision under these facts. If the appellate court believed that the district court's conclusion was right, then why did it reverse the decision? What does this tell you about the standards for review that judges use?*

Higher Appellate Courts

If the reviewing court is an intermediate appellate court, the losing party may decide to appeal the decision to the state's highest court, usually called its supreme court. Although the losing party has a right to ask (petition) a higher court to review the case, the party does not have a right to have the case heard by the higher appellate court. Appellate courts normally have discretionary power and can accept or reject an appeal. As with the United States Supreme Court, getting a case heard in most state supreme courts is unlikely. If the petition is granted, new briefs must be filed before the state supreme court, and the attorneys may be allowed or requested to present oral arguments. Like the intermediate appellate courts, the supreme court can reverse or affirm the lower appellate court's decision or remand the case. At this point, the case typically has reached its end (unless a federal question is at issue and one of the parties has legiti-

mate grounds to seek review by a federal appellate court). *Concept Summary 3.3* reviews the options that the parties may pursue after the trial.

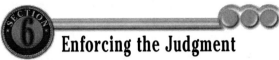

Enforcing the Judgment

The uncertainties of the litigation process are compounded by the lack of guarantees that any judgment will be enforceable. Even if the jury awards Kirby the full amount of damages requested ($100,000), for example, Carvello's auto insurance coverage might have lapsed, in which event the company would not pay any of the damages. Alternatively, Carvello's insurance policy might be limited to $50,000, meaning that Carvello personally would have to pay the remaining $50,000.

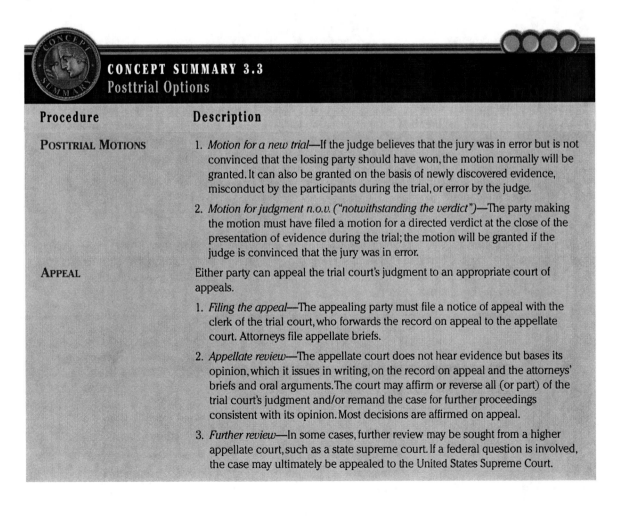

CONCEPT SUMMARY 3.3
Posttrial Options

Procedure	Description
POSTTRIAL MOTIONS	1. *Motion for a new trial*—If the judge believes that the jury was in error but is not convinced that the losing party should have won, the motion normally will be granted. It can also be granted on the basis of newly discovered evidence, misconduct by the participants during the trial, or error by the judge.
	2. *Motion for judgment n.o.v. ("notwithstanding the verdict")*—The party making the motion must have filed a motion for a directed verdict at the close of the presentation of evidence during the trial; the motion will be granted if the judge is convinced that the jury was in error.
APPEAL	Either party can appeal the trial court's judgment to an appropriate court of appeals.
	1. *Filing the appeal*—The appealing party must file a notice of appeal with the clerk of the trial court, who forwards the record on appeal to the appellate court. Attorneys file appellate briefs.
	2. *Appellate review*—The appellate court does not hear evidence but bases its opinion, which it issues in writing, on the record on appeal and the attorneys' briefs and oral arguments. The court may affirm or reverse all (or part) of the trial court's judgment and/or remand the case for further proceedings consistent with its opinion. Most decisions are affirmed on appeal.
	3. *Further review*—In some cases, further review may be sought from a higher appellate court, such as a state supreme court. If a federal question is involved, the case may ultimately be appealed to the United States Supreme Court.

Requesting Court Assistance in Collecting the Judgment

If the defendant does not have the funds available to pay the judgment, the plaintiff can go back to the court and request that the court issue a *writ of execution*. A **writ of execution** is an order directing the sheriff to seize and sell the defendant's nonexempt assets, or property (certain assets are exempted by law from creditors' actions). The proceeds of the sale would then be used to pay the damages owed, and any excess proceeds would be returned to the defendant. Alternatively, the nonexempt property itself could be transferred to the plaintiff in lieu of an outright payment. (Creditors' remedies, including those of judgment creditors, as well as exempt and nonex-

empt property, will be discussed in more detail in Chapter 28.)

Availability of Assets

The problem of collecting a judgment is less pronounced, of course, when a party is seeking to satisfy a judgment against a defendant with substantial assets that can be easily located, such as a major corporation. Usually, one of the factors considered by the plaintiff and his or her attorney before a lawsuit is initiated is whether the defendant has sufficient assets to cover the amount of damages sought. In addition, during the discovery process, attorneys routinely seek information about the location of the defendant's assets that might potentially be used to satisfy a judgment.

REVIEWING Court Procedures

Ronald Metzgar placed his fifteen-month-old son, Matthew, awake and healthy, in his playpen. Ronald left the room for five minutes and on his return found Matthew lifeless. A toy block had lodged in the boy's throat, causing him to choke to death. Ronald called 911, but efforts to revive Matthew were to no avail. There was no warning of a choking hazard on the box containing the block. Matthew's parents hired an attorney and sued Playskool, Inc., the manufacturer of the block, alleging that the manufacturer had been negligent in failing to warn of the block's hazard. Playskool filed a motion for summary judgment, arguing that the danger of a young child choking on a small block was obvious. Using the information presented in the chapter, answer the following questions.

1. Suppose that the attorney the Metzgars hired agreed to represent them on a contingency-fee basis. What does that mean?
2. How would the Metzgars' attorney likely have served process (the summons and complaint) on Playskool, Inc.?
3. Should Playskool's request for summary judgment be granted? Why or why not?
4. Suppose that the judge denied Playskool's motion and the case proceeded to trial. After hearing all the evidence, the jury found in favor of the defendant. What options do the plaintiffs have at this point if they are not satisfied with the verdict?

TERMS AND CONCEPTS

	answer	cross-examination
	brief	default judgment
	closing argument	deposition
affidavit	complaint	direct examination
affirmative defense	counterclaim	discovery

e-evidence

Federal Rules of Civil
Procedure (FRCP)

hearsay

interrogatories

motion

motion for a directed verdict

motion for a judgment as a
matter of law

motion for a new trial

motion for judgment *n.o.v.*

motion for judgment on the
pleadings

motion for summary
judgment

motion to dismiss

opening statement

pleadings

pretrial conference

pretrial motion

rebuttal

rejoinder

relevant evidence

rules of evidence

service of process

summons

verdict

voir dire

writ of execution

QUESTIONS AND CASE PROBLEMS

3–1. Attorneys in personal-injury and other tort lawsuits (see Chapters 6 and 7) frequently charge clients on a contingency-fee basis; that is, a lawyer will agree to take on a client's case in return for, say, 30 percent of whatever damages are recovered. What are some of the social benefits and costs of the contingency-fee system? In your opinion, do the benefits of this system outweigh the costs?

3–2. QUESTION WITH SAMPLE ANSWER

When and for what purpose is each of the following motions made? Which of them would be appropriate if a defendant claimed that the only issue between the parties was a question of law and that the law was favorable to the defendant's position?

(a) A motion for judgment on the pleadings.
(b) A motion for a directed verdict.
(c) A motion for summary judgment.
(d) A motion for judgment *n.o.v.*

• For a sample answer to Question 3–2, go to Appendix C at the end of this text.

3–3. In the past, the rules of discovery were very restrictive, and trials often turned on elements of surprise. For example, a plaintiff would not necessarily know until the trial what the defendant's defense was going to be. In the last several decades, however, new rules of discovery have substantially changed this situation. Now each attorney can access practically all of the evidence that the other side intends to present at trial, with the exception of certain information—namely, the opposing attorney's work product. Work product is not a clear concept. Basically, it includes all of the attorney's thoughts on the case. Can you see any reason why such information should not be made available to the opposing attorney? Discuss fully.

3–4. Washoe Medical Center, Inc., admitted Shirley Swisher for the treatment of a fractured pelvis. During her

stay, Swisher suffered a fatal fall from her hospital bed. Gerald Parodi, the administrator of her estate, and others filed an action against Washoe seeking damages for the alleged lack of care in treating Swisher. During *voir dire,* when the plaintiffs' attorney returned a few minutes late from a break, the trial judge led the prospective jurors in a standing ovation. The judge joked with one of the prospective jurors, whom he had known in college, about his fitness to serve as a judge and personally endorsed another prospective juror's business. After the trial, the jury returned a verdict in favor of Washoe. The plaintiffs moved for a new trial, but the judge denied the motion. The plaintiffs then appealed, arguing that the tone set by the judge during *voir dire* prejudiced their right to a fair trial. Should the appellate court agree? Why or why not?

3–5. Advance Technology Consultants, Inc. (ATC), contracted with RoadTrac, L.L.C., to provide software and client software systems for the products of global positioning satellite (GPS) technology being developed by RoadTrac. RoadTrac agreed to provide ATC with hardware with which ATC's software would interface. Problems soon arose, however. ATC claimed that RoadTrac's hardware was defective, making it difficult to develop the software. RoadTrac contended that its hardware was fully functional and that ATC had simply failed to provide supporting software. ATC told RoadTrac that it considered their contract terminated. RoadTrac filed a suit in a Georgia state court against ATC alleging breach of contract. During discovery, RoadTrac requested ATC's customer lists and marketing procedures. ATC objected to providing this information because RoadTrac and ATC had become competitors in the GPS industry. Should a party to a lawsuit have to hand over its confidential business secrets as part of a discovery request? Why or why not? What limitations might a court consider imposing before requiring ATC to produce this material?

3–6. Jury Selection. Ms. Thompson filed a suit in a federal district court against her employer, Altheimer & Gray, seeking damages for alleged racial discrimination in violation of federal law. During *voir dire*, the judge asked the prospective jurors whether "there is something about this kind of lawsuit for money damages that would start any of you leaning for or against a particular party?" Ms. Leiter, one of the prospective jurors, raised her hand and explained that she had "been an owner of a couple of businesses and am currently an owner of a business, and I feel that as an employer and owner of a business that will definitely sway my judgment in this case." She explained, "I am constantly faced with people that want various benefits or different positions in the company or better contacts or, you know, a myriad of issues that employers face on a regular basis, and I have to decide whether or not that person should get them." Asked by Thompson's lawyer whether "you believe that people file lawsuits just because they don't get something they want," Leiter answered, "I believe there are some people that do." In answer to another question, she said, "I think I bring a lot of background to this case, and I can't say that it's not going to cloud my judgment. I can try to be as fair as I can, as I do every day." Explain the purpose of *voir dire* and how Leiter's response should be treated in light of that purpose. [*Thompson v. Altheimer & Gray,* 248 F.3d 621 (7th Cir. 2001)]

3–7. CASE PROBLEM WITH SAMPLE ANSWER

To establish a Web site, a person must have an Internet service provider or hosting company, register a domain name, and acquire domain name servicing. Pfizer, Inc., Pfizer Ireland Pharmaceuticals, and Warner-Lambert Co. (collectively, Pfizer) filed a suit in a federal district court against Domains By Proxy, Inc., and other persons alleged to be behind two Web sites—genericlipitors.com and econopetcare.com. Among the defendants were an individual and a company that, according to Pfizer, were located in a foreign country. Without investigating other means of serving these two defendants, Pfizer asked the court for permission to accomplish service of process via e-mail. Under what circumstances is service via e-mail proper? Would it be appropriate in this case? Explain. [*Pfizer, Inc. v. Domains By Proxy,* ___ F.Supp.2d ___ (D.Conn. 2004)]

- **To view a sample answer for Problem 3–7, go to this book's Web site at www.cengage.com/blaw/jentz, select "Chapter 3," and click on "Case Problem with Sample Answer."**

3–8. Motion for Judgment *n.o.v.* Gerald Adams worked as a cook for Uno Restaurants, Inc., at Warwick Pizzeria Uno Restaurant & Bar in Warwick, Rhode Island. One night, shortly after Adams's shift began, he noticed that the kitchen floor was saturated with a foul-smelling liquid coming from the drains and backing up water onto the

floor. He complained of illness and went home, where he contacted the state health department. A department representative visited the restaurant and closed it for the night, leaving instructions to sanitize the kitchen and clear the drains. Two days later, in the restaurant, David Badot, the manager, shouted at Adams in the presence of other employees. When Adams shouted back, Badot fired Adams and had him arrested. Adams filed a suit in a Rhode Island state court against Uno, alleging that he had been unlawfully terminated for contacting the health department. A jury found in favor of Adams. Arguing that Adams had been fired for threatening Badot, Uno filed a motion for judgment *n.o.v.* (also known as a motion for judgment as a matter of law). What does a court weigh in considering whether to grant such a motion? Should the court grant the motion in this case? Why or why not? [*Adams v. Uno Restaurants, Inc.,* 794 A.2d 489 (R.I. 2002)]

3–9. A QUESTION OF ETHICS

Narnia Investments, Ltd., filed a suit in a Texas state court against several defendants, including *Harvestons Securities, Inc.,* a securities dealer. (Securities are documents evidencing the ownership of a corporation, in the form of stock, or debts owed by it, in the form of bonds.) Harvestons is registered with the state of Texas and thus may be served with a summons and a copy of a complaint by serving the Texas Securities Commissioner. In this case, the return of service indicated that process was served on the commissioner "by delivering to JoAnn Kocerek defendant, in person, a true copy of this [summons] together with the accompanying copy(ies) of the [complaint]." Harvestons did not file an answer, and Narnia obtained a default judgment against the defendant for $365,000, plus attorneys' fees and interest. Five months after this judgment, Harvestons filed a motion for a new trial, which the court denied. Harvestons appealed to a state intermediate appellate court, claiming that it had not been served in strict compliance with the rules governing service of process. [Harvestons Securities, Inc. v. Narnia Investments, Ltd., *218 S.W.3d 126 (Tex.App.—Houston [14 Dist.] 2007)]*

(a) Harvestons asserted that Narnia's service was invalid in part because "the return of service states that process was delivered to 'JoAnn Kocerek'" and did not show that she "had the authority to accept process on behalf of Harvestons or the Texas Securities Commissioner." Should such a detail, if it is required, be strictly construed and applied? Should it apply in this case? Explain.

(b) Whose responsibility is it to see that service of process is accomplished properly? Was it accomplished properly in this case? Why or why not?

For updated links to resources available on the Web, as well as a variety of other materials, visit this text's Web site at

www.cengage.com/blaw/jentz

If you are interested in learning more about the Federal Rules of Civil Procedure (FRCP) and the Federal Rules of Evidence (FRE), you can access them via the Internet at the following Web site:

www.law.cornell.edu

Procedural rules for several of the state courts are also online and can be accessed via the courts' Web pages. You can find links to the Web pages for state courts at the Web site of the National Center for State Courts. Go to

www.ncsconline.org

The American Bar Association maintains a gateway to information on legal topics, including the court systems and court procedures, at

www.abalawinfo.org

Legal Research Exercises on the Web

Go to **www.cengage/com/blaw/jentz**, the Web site that accompanies this text. Select "Chapter 3" and click on "Internet Exercises." There you will find the following Internet research exercises that you can perform to learn more about the topics covered in this chapter.

Internet Exercise 3–1:   Legal Perspective
                        Civil Procedure

Internet Exercise 3–2:   Management Perspective
                        Small Claims Courts

Internet Exercise 3–3:   Technological Perspective
                        Virtual Courtrooms

CHAPTER 4

Intentional Torts

Part of doing business today—and, indeed, part of everyday life—is the risk of being involved in a lawsuit. The list of circumstances in which businesspersons can be sued is long and varied. A customer who is injured by a security guard at a business establishment, for example, may attempt to sue the business owner, claiming that the security guard's conduct was wrongful. Any time that one party's allegedly wrongful conduct causes injury to another, an action may arise under the law of **torts** (the word *tort* is French for "wrong"). Through tort law, society compensates those who have suffered injuries as a result of the wrongful conduct of others.

Many of the lawsuits brought by or against business firms are based on the tort theories discussed in this chapter, which covers intentional torts, and the next chapter, which discusses unintentional torts. *Intentional torts* arise from intentional acts, whereas *unintentional torts* often result from carelessness (as when an employee at a store knocks over a display case, injuring a customer). In addition, this chapter discusses how tort law applies to wrongful actions in the online environment. Tort theories also come into play in the context of product liability (liability for defective products), which will be discussed in detail in Chapter 23.

The Basis of Tort Law

Two notions serve as the basis of all torts: wrongs and compensation. Tort law is designed to compensate those who have suffered a loss or injury due to another person's wrongful act. In a tort action, one person or group brings a lawsuit against another person or group to obtain compensation (monetary damages) or other relief for the harm suffered.

The Purpose of Tort Law

The basic purpose of tort law is to provide remedies for the invasion of various *protected interests*. Society recognizes an interest in personal physical safety, and tort law provides remedies for acts that cause physical injury or that interfere with physical security and freedom of movement. Society recognizes an interest in protecting property, and tort law provides remedies for acts that cause destruction or damage to property. Society also recognizes an interest in protecting cer-

tain intangible interests, such as personal privacy, family relations, reputation, and dignity, and tort law provides remedies for violation of these interests.

Damages Available in Tort Actions

Because the purpose of tort law is to compensate the injured party for the damage suffered, you need to have an understanding of the types of damages that plaintiffs seek in tort actions. The high cost to society of sizable damages awards in tort cases has fueled the tort reform movement, which is discussed in this chapter's *Contemporary Legal Debates* feature on pages 118 and 119.

Compensatory Damages Compensatory **damages** are intended to compensate or reimburse a plaintiff for actual losses—to make the plaintiff whole and put her or him in the same position that she or he would have been had the tort not occurred. Compensatory damages awards are often broken down into special damages and general damages. *Special damages* compensate the plaintiff for quantifiable monetary losses, such as medical expenses, lost wages and benefits (now and in the future), extra costs, the loss of irreplaceable items, and the costs of repairing or replacing damaged property. *General damages* compensate individuals (not companies) for the nonmonetary aspects of the harm suffered, such as pain and suffering. A court might award general damages for physical or emotional pain and suffering, loss of companionship, loss of consortium (losing the emotional and physical benefits of a spousal relationship), disfigurement, loss of reputation, or loss or impairment of mental or physical capacity.

Punitive Damages Occasionally, the courts may also award **punitive damages** in tort cases to punish the wrongdoer and deter others from similar wrongdoing. Punitive damages are appropriate only when the defendant's conduct was particularly egregious or reprehensible. Usually, this means that punitive damages are available mainly in intentional tort actions and only rarely in negligence lawsuits (*negligence* actions will be discussed in Chapter 7). They may be awarded, however, in suits involving *gross negligence*, which can be defined

as an intentional failure to perform a manifest duty in reckless disregard of the consequences of such a failure for the life or property of another.

Courts exercise great restraint in granting punitive damages to plaintiffs in tort actions because punitive damages are subject to the limitations imposed by the due process clause of the U.S. Constitution (discussed in Chapter 2). In *State Farm Mutual Automobile Insurance Co. v. Campbell,*[1] the United States Supreme Court held that to the extent an award of punitive damages is grossly excessive, it furthers no legitimate purpose and violates due process requirements. Although this case dealt with intentional torts (fraud and intentional infliction of emotional distress), the Court's holding applies equally to punitive damages awards in gross negligence cases (as well as to product liability cases).

Although the following case involved a product liability claim (which will be discussed in Chapter 23), the decision illustrates how courts analyze whether punitive damages awards are excessive.

---

1. 538 U.S. 408, 123 S.Ct. 1513, 155 L.Ed.2d 585 (2003).

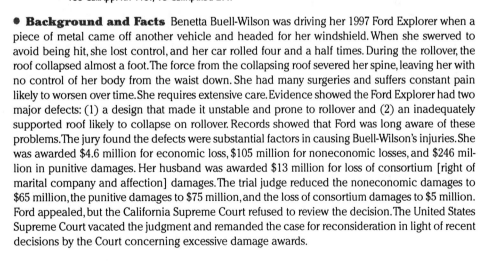

C A S E **4.1** **Buell-Wilson v. Ford Motor Co.**
Court of Appeal, Fourth District, Division 1, California, 2008.
160 Cal.App.4th 1107, 73 Cal.Rptr.3d 277.

● **Background and Facts** Benetta Buell-Wilson was driving her 1997 Ford Explorer when a piece of metal came off another vehicle and headed for her windshield. When she swerved to avoid being hit, she lost control, and her car rolled four and a half times. During the rollover, the roof collapsed almost a foot. The force from the collapsing roof severed her spine, leaving her with no control of her body from the waist down. She had many surgeries and suffers constant pain likely to worsen over time. She requires extensive care. Evidence showed the Ford Explorer had two major defects: (1) a design that made it unstable and prone to rollover and (2) an inadequately supported roof likely to collapse on rollover. Records showed that Ford was long aware of these problems. The jury found the defects were substantial factors in causing Buell-Wilson's injuries. She was awarded $4.6 million for economic loss, $105 million for noneconomic losses, and $246 million in punitive damages. Her husband was awarded $13 million for loss of consortium [right of marital company and affection] damages. The trial judge reduced the noneconomic damages to $65 million, the punitive damages to $75 million, and the loss of consortium damages to $5 million. Ford appealed, but the California Supreme Court refused to review the decision. The United States Supreme Court vacated the judgment and remanded the case for reconsideration in light of recent decisions by the Court concerning excessive damage awards.

● **Decision and Rationale** The California Court of Appeal considered the amount of damages on remand. The court held that the $65 million in noneconomic damages awarded to a forty-six-year-old plaintiff who had been healthy prior to the accident was excessive and would be reduced to $18 million. That amount is one that "a reasonable person would estimate as fair compensation" in this case. The large award was granted by a jury that acted out of "passion and prejudice." Ford also contended that the punitive damages award "is excessive under the federal due

CASE CONTINUES

CASE 4.1 CONTINUED process clause of the 14th Amendment to the United States Constitution." The court concluded that "after reducing the noneconomic damage award to Mrs. Wilson to $18 million, the award of punitive damages is excessive and is, therefore, reduced to $55 million, an approximate two-to-one ratio of the total compensatory damage award ($4.6 million in economic damages + $18 million in noneconomic damages + $5 million in loss of consortium damages = $27.6 million × 2 = $55.2 million)." This is more in line with the guidelines set by the United States Supreme Court regarding punitive damages.[a]

● **The Ethical Dimension** *The court stated that punitive damages are designed to punish the defendant for reprehensible behavior. If so, should the punitive damages go to one plaintiff or be shared by all buyers of Ford products or by the general public? Why or why not?*

● **The Legal Environment Dimension** *Why did the appellate court indicate that the plaintiff had been "healthy prior to the accident"?*

---

a. The Supreme Court of California granted review of this case and had not yet issued a decision at the time this book went to press [187 P.3d 887, 80 Cal.Rptr.3d 27 (2008)].

Intentional Torts against Persons

An **intentional tort,** as the term implies, requires intent. The **tortfeasor** (the one committing the tort) must intend to commit an act, the consequences of which interfere with the personal or business interests of another in a way not permitted by law. An evil or harmful motive is not required—in fact, the actor may even have a beneficial motive for committing what turns out to be a tortious act. In tort law, *intent* means only that the actor intended the consequences of his or her act or knew with substantial certainty that specific consequences would result from the act. The law generally assumes that individuals intend the *normal* consequences of their actions. Thus, forcefully pushing another—even if done in jest and without any evil motive—is an intentional tort (if injury results), because the object of a strong push can ordinarily be expected to be abruptly displaced.

Intentional torts against persons include assault and battery, false imprisonment, infliction of emotional distress, defamation, invasion of privacy, appropriation, fraudulent misrepresentation, and torts related to misuse of litigation. We discuss these torts in the following subsections.

Assault and Battery

Any intentional, unexcused act that creates in another person a reasonable apprehension of immediate harmful or offensive contact is an **assault.** Note that apprehension is not the same as fear. If a contact is such that a reasonable person would want to avoid it, and if there is a reasonable basis for believing that the contact will occur, then the plaintiff suffers apprehension whether or not she or he is afraid. The interest protected by tort law concerning assault is the freedom from having to expect harmful or offensive contact. The arousal of apprehension is enough to justify compensation.

The *completion* of the act that caused the apprehension, if it results in harm to the plaintiff, is a **battery,** which is defined as an unexcused and harmful or offensive physical contact *intentionally* performed. For example, Ivan threatens Jean with a gun, then shoots her. The pointing of the gun at Jean is an assault; the firing of the gun (if the bullet hits Jean) is a battery. The interest protected by tort law concerning battery is the right to personal security and safety. The contact can be harmful, or it can be merely offensive (such as an unwelcome kiss). Physical injury need not occur. The contact can involve any part of the body or anything attached to it—for example, a hat or other item of clothing, a purse, or a chair or an automobile in which one is sitting. Whether the contact is offensive is determined by the *reasonable person standard.*[2] The contact can be made by the defendant or by some force the defendant sets in motion—for example, a rock thrown, food poisoned, or a stick swung.

Compensation If the plaintiff shows that there was contact, and the jury (or judge, if there is no jury) agrees that the contact was offensive, then the plaintiff

---

2. The *reasonable person standard* is an "objective" test of how a reasonable person would have acted under the same circumstances. See the subsection entitled "The Duty of Care and Its Breach" in Chapter 7.

has a right to compensation. There is no need to establish that the defendant acted out of malice. The underlying motive does not matter, only the intent to bring about the harmful or offensive contact to the plaintiff. In fact, proving a motive is never necessary. A plaintiff may be compensated for the emotional harm or loss of reputation resulting from a battery, as well as for physical harm.

Defenses to Assault and Battery A defendant who is sued for assault, battery, or both can raise any of the following legally recognized defenses:

1. *Consent.* When a person consents to the act that is allegedly tortious, there may be a complete or partial defense to liability.
2. *Self-defense.* An individual who is defending her or his life or physical well-being can claim self-defense. In a situation of either *real* or *apparent* danger, a person may normally use whatever force is *reasonably* necessary to prevent harmful contact (see Chapter 9 for a more detailed discussion of self-defense).
3. *Defense of others.* An individual can act in a reasonable manner to protect others who are in real or apparent danger.
4. *Defense of property.* Reasonable force may be used in attempting to remove intruders from one's home, although force that is likely to cause death or great bodily injury normally cannot be used just to protect property.

False Imprisonment

False imprisonment is defined as the intentional confinement or restraint of another person's activities without justification. It involves interference with the freedom to move without restriction. The confinement can be accomplished through the use of physical barriers, physical restraint, or threats of physical force. Moral pressure does not constitute false imprisonment. Furthermore, it is essential that the person being restrained not agree to the restraint.

Businesspersons often face suits for false imprisonment after they have attempted to confine a suspected shoplifter for questioning. Under the laws of most states, merchants may detain persons suspected of shoplifting and hold them for the police. Although laws vary from state to state, normally only a merchant's security personnel—not salesclerks or other employees—have the right to detain suspects. Reasonable or probable cause must exist to believe that the person being detained has committed a theft.

Additionally, most states require that any detention be conducted in a *reasonable* manner and for only a *reasonable* length of time. Tackling a customer suspected of theft in the parking lot would be considered unreasonable in many jurisdictions.

PREVENTING LEGAL DISPUTES

Businesspersons who operate retail establishments need to make sure that their employees are aware of the limitations on the privilege to detain. Even if someone is suspected of shoplifting, businesspersons (and employees) must have probable cause to stop and question the person and must behave reasonably and detain the person for only a sensible amount of time. Undue force or unreasonable detention can lead to liability for the business.

Intentional Infliction of Emotional Distress

The tort of *intentional infliction of emotional distress* can be defined as an intentional act that amounts to extreme and outrageous conduct resulting in severe emotional distress to another. To be **actionable** (capable of serving as the ground for a lawsuit), the act must be extreme and outrageous to the point that it exceeds the bounds of decency accepted by society. For example, a prankster telephones a pregnant woman and says that her husband and two sons have just been killed in a horrible accident (although they have not). As a result, the woman suffers intense mental pain and has a miscarriage. In that situation, the woman would be able to sue for intentional infliction of emotional distress.

Courts in most jurisdictions are wary of emotional distress claims and confine them to situations involving truly outrageous behavior. Acts that cause indignity or annoyance alone usually are not sufficient. Many times, however, repeated annoyances (such as those experienced by a person who is being stalked), coupled with threats, are enough.

Note that when the outrageous conduct consists of speech about a public figure, the First Amendment's guarantee of freedom of speech also limits emotional distress claims. For example, *Hustler* magazine once printed a fake advertisement that showed a picture of Reverend Jerry Falwell and described him as having lost his virginity to his mother in an outhouse while he was drunk. Falwell sued the magazine for intentional

CONTEMPORARY LEGAL DEBATES
Tort Reform

The question of whether our tort law system is in need of reform has aroused heated debate. While some argue that the current system imposes excessive costs on society, others contend that the system protects consumers from unsafe products and practices.

"End the Tort Tax and Frivolous Lawsuits," Say the Critics

Critics of the current tort law system contend that it encourages too many frivolous lawsuits, which clog the courts, and is unnecessarily costly. In particular, they say, damages awards are often excessive and bear little relationship to the actual damage suffered. Such large awards encourage plaintiffs to bring frivolous suits, hoping that they will "hit the jackpot." Trial lawyers, in turn, are eager to bring the suits because they are paid on a contingency-fee basis, meaning that they receive a percentage of the damages awarded.

The result, in the critics' view, is a system that disproportionately rewards a few lucky plaintiffs while imposing enormous costs on business and society as a whole. They refer to the economic burden that the tort system imposes on society as the "tort tax." According to one recent study, more than $300 billion per year is expended on tort litigation, including plaintiffs' and defendants' attorneys' fees, damages awards, and other costs. Most of the costs are from class-action lawsuits involving product liability or medical malpractice.[a] (A *class action* is a

a. Lawrence J. McQuillan, Hovannes Abramyan, and Anthony P. Archie, *Jackpot Justice: The True Cost of America's Tort System* (San Francisco: Pacific Research Institute, 2007).

lawsuit in which a single person or a small group of people represents the interests of a larger group.) Although even the critics would not contend that the tort tax encompasses the entire $300 billion, they believe that it includes a sizable portion of that amount. Furthermore, they say, the tax appears in other ways. Because physicians, hospitals, and pharmaceutical companies are worried about medical malpractice suits, they have changed their behavior. Physicians, for example, engage in defensive medicine by ordering more tests than necessary. PricewaterhouseCoopers has calculated that the practice of defensive medicine increases health-care costs by more than $100 billion per year.

To solve the problems they perceive, critics want to reduce both the number of tort cases brought each year and the amount of damages awards. They advocate the following tort reform measures: (1) limit the amount of punitive damages that can be awarded; (2) limit the amount of general noneconomic damages that can be awarded (for example, for pain and suffering); (3) limit the amount that attorneys can collect in contingency fees; and (4) to discourage the filing of meritless suits, require the losing party to pay both the plaintiff's and the defendant's expenses.

"The Current System Promotes Fairness and Safety," Say Their Opponents

Others are not so sure that the current system needs such drastic reform. They say that the prospect of tort lawsuits encourages companies to produce safer products and deters them from putting dangerous products on the market. In the health-care industry,

---

infliction of emotional distress and won, but the United States Supreme Court overturned the decision. The Court held that creators of parodies of public figures are protected under the First Amendment from intentional infliction of emotional distress claims. (The Court used the same standards that apply to public figures in defamation lawsuits, discussed next.)[3]

3. *Hustler Magazine, Inc. v. Falwell*, 485 U.S. 46, 108 S.Ct. 876, 99 L.Ed.2d 41 (1988). For another example of how the courts protect parody, see *Busch v. Viacom International, Inc.*, 477 F.Supp.2d 764 (N.D.Tex. 2007), involving a fake endorsement of televangelist Pat Robertson's diet shake.

Defamation

As discussed in Chapter 4, the freedom of speech guaranteed by the First Amendment is not absolute. In interpreting the First Amendment, the courts must balance the vital guarantee of free speech against other pervasive and strong social interests, including society's interest in preventing and redressing attacks on reputation.

Defamation of character involves wrongfully hurting a person's good reputation. The law imposes a general duty on all persons to refrain from making false, defamatory *statements of fact* about others. Breaching

the potential for medical malpractice suits has led to safer and more effective medical practices.

Imposing limits on the amount of punitive and general noneconomic damages would be unfair, say the system's defenders, and would reduce efficiency in our legal and economic system. After all, corporations conduct cost-benefit analyses when they decide how much safety to build into their products. Any limitation on potential damages would mean that corporations would have less incentive to build safer products. Indeed, Professor Stephen Teret of the Johns Hopkins University School of Public Health says that tort litigation is an important tool for preventing injuries because it forces manufacturers to opt for more safety in their products rather than less.[b] Limiting contingency fees would also be unfair, say those in favor of the current system, because low-income consumers who have been injured could not afford to pay an attorney to take a case on an hourly fee basis—and an attorney would not expend the time needed to pursue a case without the prospect of a large reward in the form of a contingency fee.

Tort Reform in Reality

While the debate continues, the federal government and a number of states have begun to take some steps toward tort reform. At the federal level, the Class Action Fairness Act (CAFA) of 2005[c] shifted jurisdiction over large interstate tort and product liability class-action lawsuits from the state courts to the federal courts. The intent was to prevent plaintiffs' attorneys from shopping around for a state court that might be predisposed to be sympathetic to their clients' cause and to award large damages in class-action suits.

At the state level, more than twenty states have placed caps ranging from $250,000 to $750,000 on noneconomic damages, especially in medical malpractice suits. More than thirty states have limited punitive damages, with some imposing outright bans.

WHERE DO YOU STAND?

Large damages awards in tort litigation have to be paid by someone. If the defendant is insured, then insurance companies foot the bill. Ultimately, though, high insurance rates are passed on to consumers of goods and services in the United States. Consequently, tort reform that reduces the size and number of damages awards ultimately will mean lower costs of goods and services to consumers. The downside of these lower costs, though, might be higher risks of medical malpractice and dangerous products. Do you believe that this trade-off is real? Why or why not?

---

b. "Litigation Is an Important Tool for Injury and Gun Violence Prevention," Johns Hopkins University Center for Gun Policy and Research, July 15, 2006.
c. 28 U.S.C.A. Sections 1711–1715, 1453.

---

this duty in writing or other permanent form (such as an electronic recording) involves the tort of **libel.** Breaching this duty orally involves the tort of **slander.** The tort of defamation also arises when a false statement of fact is made about a person's product, business, or legal ownership rights.

Note that generally only false statements that represent something as a fact (such as "Vladik cheats on his taxes") constitute defamation. Expressions of personal opinion (such as "Vladik is a jerk") are protected by the First Amendment and normally cannot lead to tort liability.

The Publication Requirement The basis of the tort of defamation is the publication of a statement or statements that hold an individual up to contempt, ridicule, or hatred. *Publication* here means that the defamatory statements are communicated (either intentionally or accidentally) to persons other than the defamed party. If Thompson writes Andrews a private letter falsely accusing him of embezzling funds, the action does not constitute libel. If Peters falsely states that Gordon is dishonest and incompetent when no one else is around, the action does not constitute slander. In neither case was the message communicated to a third party.

The courts have generally held that even dictating a letter to a secretary constitutes publication, although the publication may be privileged (a concept that will be explained shortly). Moreover, if a third party merely overhears defamatory statements by chance, the courts usually hold that this also constitutes publication. Defamatory statements made via the Internet are actionable as well. Note also that any individual who repeats or republishes defamatory statements normally is liable even if that person reveals the source of the statements.

Damages for Libel Once a defendant's liability for libel is established, *general damages* are presumed as a matter of law. General damages are designed to compensate the plaintiff for nonspecific harms such as disgrace or dishonor in the eyes of the community, humiliation, injured reputation, and emotional distress—harms that are difficult to measure. In other words, to recover damages in a libel case, the plaintiff need not prove that he or she was actually injured in any way as a result of the libelous statement.

Damages for Slander In contrast to cases alleging libel, in a case alleging slander, the plaintiff must prove *special damages* to establish the defendant's liability. The plaintiff must show that the slanderous statement caused her or him to suffer actual economic or monetary losses. Unless this initial hurdle of proving special damages is overcome, a plaintiff alleging slander normally cannot go forward with the suit and recover any damages. This requirement is imposed in slander cases because oral statements have a temporary quality. In contrast, a libelous (written) statement has the quality of permanence, can be circulated widely, and usually results from some degree of deliberation on the part of the author.

Exceptions to the burden of proving special damages in cases alleging slander are made for certain types of slanderous statements. If a false statement constitutes "slander *per se*," no proof of special damages is required for it to be actionable. In most states, the following four types of utterances are considered to be slander *per se:*

1. A statement that another has a loathsome disease (historically, leprosy and sexually transmitted diseases, but now also including allegations of mental illness).
2. A statement that another has committed improprieties while engaging in a profession or trade.
3. A statement that another has committed or has been imprisoned for a serious crime.

4. A statement that a person (usually only an unmarried person and sometimes only a woman) is unchaste or has engaged in serious sexual misconduct.

Defenses to Defamation Truth is normally an absolute defense against a defamation charge. In other words, if a defendant in a defamation case can prove that the allegedly defamatory statements of fact were true, normally no tort has been committed. Other defenses to defamation may exist if the speech is *privileged* or concerns a public figure. Note that the majority of defamation actions are filed in state courts, and state laws differ somewhat in the defenses they allow, such as privilege (discussed next).

Privileged Speech. In some circumstances, a person will not be liable for defamatory statements because she or he enjoys a **privilege**, or immunity. With respect to defamation, privileged communications are of two types: absolute and qualified.[4] Only in judicial proceedings and certain government proceedings is an *absolute privilege* granted. For example, statements made by attorneys and judges in the courtroom during a trial are absolutely privileged. So are statements made by government officials during legislative debate, even if the legislators make such statements maliciously—that is, knowing them to be untrue. An absolute privilege is granted in these situations because judicial and government personnel deal with matters that are so much in the public interest that the parties involved should be able to speak out fully and freely and without restriction.

In other situations, a person will not be liable for defamatory statements because he or she has a *qualified*, or *conditional, privilege.* An employer's statements in written evaluations of employees are an example of a qualified privilege. Generally, if the statements are made in good faith and the publication is limited to those who have a legitimate interest in the communication, the statements fall within the area of qualified privilege. The concept of conditional privilege rests on the common law assumption that in some situations, the right to know or speak is equal in importance to the right not to be defamed. If a communication is conditionally privileged, to recover damages, the plaintiff must show that the privilege was abused.

---

4. Note that the term *privileged communication* in this context is not the same as privileged communication between a professional, such as an attorney, and his or her client. The latter type of privilege will be discussed in Chapter 51, in the context of the liability of professionals.

Public Figures. Public officials who exercise substantial governmental power and any persons in the public limelight are considered *public figures.* In general, public figures are considered "fair game," and false and defamatory statements about them that are published in the press will not constitute defamation unless the statements are made with **actual malice.** To be made with actual malice, a statement must be made *with either knowledge of its falsity or a reckless disregard of the truth.*[5]

Statements made about public figures, especially when they are communicated via a public medium, are usually related to matters of general public interest; they refer to people who substantially affect all of us. Furthermore, public figures generally have some access to a public medium for answering disparaging falsehoods about themselves; private individuals do not. For these reasons, public figures have a greater burden of proof in defamation cases (they must prove actual malice) than do private individuals.

Invasion of Privacy

A person has a right to solitude and freedom from prying public eyes—in other words, to privacy. As mentioned in Chapter 4, the courts have held that certain amendments to the U.S. Constitution imply a right to privacy. Some state constitutions explicitly provide for privacy rights, as do a number of federal and state

---

5. *New York Times Co. v. Sullivan,* 376 U.S. 254, 84 S.Ct. 710, 11 L.Ed.2d 686 (1964). As mentioned earlier, the First Amendment protects the creator of a parody from liability for defamation of a public figure.

statutes. Tort law also safeguards these rights through the tort of *invasion of privacy.* Four acts qualify as invasions of privacy:

1. *Appropriation of identity.* Under the common law, using a person's name, picture, or other likeness for commercial purposes without permission is a tortious invasion of privacy. Most states today have also enacted statutes prohibiting *appropriation* (discussed further in the next subsection).

2. *Intrusion into an individual's affairs or seclusion.* For example, invading someone's home or searching someone's personal computer without authorization is an invasion of privacy. This tort has been held to extend to eavesdropping by wiretap, unauthorized scanning of a bank account, compulsory blood testing, and window peeping.

3. *False light.* The publication of information that places a person in a false light is another category of invasion of privacy. This could be a story attributing to someone ideas not held or actions not taken by that person. (The publication of such a story could involve the tort of defamation as well.)

4. *Public disclosure of private facts.* This type of invasion of privacy occurs when a person publicly discloses private facts about an individual that an ordinary person would find objectionable or embarrassing. A newspaper account of a private citizen's sex life or financial affairs could be an actionable invasion of privacy, even if the information revealed is true, because it is not of public concern.

The following case included an allegation of an intrusion into an individual's affairs or seclusion.

C A S E **4.2 Anderson v. Mergenhagen**
Court of Appeals of Georgia, 2007. 283 Ga.App. 546, 642 S.E.2d 105.

● **Background and Facts** After Dick and Karyn Anderson's marriage collapsed and they divorced, Karyn harassed Dick's new wife, Maureen, until Maureen obtained a warrant for Karyn's arrest. According to Maureen, Karyn's new boyfriend, Paul Mergenhagen, then began following Maureen. On more than a dozen occasions between mid-2003 and mid-2005, Paul took photos of, and made obscene gestures to, Maureen as she was driving in her car or walking with her children. Frightened and upset, Maureen called the police several times. Paul admitted that he had followed Maureen at least four times and had taken at least forty photos of her car. The security guard at the entrance to the Andersons' subdivision corroborated Maureen's account that Paul often lay in wait for her and that she was "visibly shaken and upset, almost to the point of tears," at least once. Maureen filed a suit in a Georgia state court against Paul, alleging, among other things, invasion of privacy. The court issued a summary judgment in Paul's favor on this charge. Maureen appealed to a state intermediate appellate court.

CASE CONTINUES

CASE 4.2 CONTINUED • **Decision and Rationale** The state intermediate appellate court reversed the grant of summary judgment to Paul on Maureen's invasion of privacy claim. The court remanded the case for trial on the issue of whether Maureen was followed and photographed so frequently as to amount to an intrusion into her privacy. As the appellate court stated, "The right of privacy is embraced within the absolute rights of personal security and personal liberty * * * ." The court stated that this was indeed a situation of intrusion upon seclusion or solitude. Unreasonable intrusion involves a prying or intrusion that would be offensive or objectionable to a reasonable person. Having one's photograph taken changes from a relatively harmless activity to a tortious one when there is repetition. Repeatedly following a pregnant woman and photographing her at least forty times "creates a jury question as to whether the defendant's actions amounted to a course of hounding the plaintiff that intruded upon her privacy."

• **What If the Facts Were Different?** *Suppose that Dick and Karyn had two children and Dick had been awarded custody of them. If Paul had been watching Maureen to determine her fitness to care for the children, would the result in this case have been different? Explain.*

• **The Legal Environment Dimension** *To succeed on a claim of intrusion into an individual's affairs or seclusion, should a plaintiff have to prove a physical intrusion? Why or why not?*

Appropriation

The use of another person's name, likeness, or other identifying characteristic, without permission and for the benefit of the user, constitutes the tort of **appropriation** (sometimes referred to as the *right of publicity*). Under the law, normally an individual's right to privacy includes the right to the exclusive use of his or her identity. For example, in one early case, Vanna White, the hostess of the popular *Wheel of Fortune* game show, brought a case against Samsung Electronics America, Inc. Without permission, Samsung had included in an advertisement a robotic image dressed in a wig, gown, and jewelry, in a setting that resembled the *Wheel of Fortune* set, in a stance for which White is famous. The court ruled in White's favor, holding that the tort of appropriation does not require the use of a celebrity's name or actual likeness. The court stated that Samsung's robot ad left "little doubt" as to the identity of the celebrity that the ad was meant to depict.[6]

Degree of Likeness In recent cases, courts have reached different conclusions as to the degree of likeness that is required to impose liability for the tort of appropriation. In one case, a former professional hockey player, Anthony "Tony" Twist, who had a reputation for fighting, sued the publishers of the comic book *Spawn*, which included an evil character named Anthony Tony Twist Twistelli. The Missouri Supreme

Court held that the use of Tony Twist's name alone was sufficient proof of likeness to support a misappropriation claim.[7] Ultimately, the hockey player was awarded $15 million in damages.[8]

In California, in contrast, Keirin Kirby, the lead singer in a 1990s funk band called Deee-Lite, lost her appropriation claim against the makers of the video game *Space Channel 5*. Although the video game's character "Ulala" had some of Kirby's distinctive traits—hot pink hair, short skirt, platform shoes, and dance moves—there were not enough similarities, according to the state appellate court, to constitute misappropriation.[9]

Right of Publicity as a Property Right As mentioned, the common law tort of appropriation in many states has become known as the right of publicity.[10] Rather than being aimed at protecting a person's right to be left alone (privacy), this right aims to protect an individual's pecuniary (financial) interest in the commercial exploitation of his or her identity. In other words, it gives public figures, celebrities, and entertainers a right to sue anyone who uses their images for commercial benefit without their permission. Cases involving the right of publicity generally turn on whether the use was commercial. For instance, if a tel-

---

6. *White v. Samsung Electronics America, Inc.*, 971 F.2d 1395 (9th Cir. 1992).

7. *Doe v. TCI Cablevision*, 110 S.W.3d 363 (Mo. 2003).

8. The amount of damages was appealed and subsequently affirmed. See *Doe v. McFarlane*, 207 S.W.3d 52 (Mo.App. 2006).

9. *Kirby v. Sega of America, Inc.*, 144 Cal.App.4th 47, 50 Cal.Rptr.3d 607 (2006).

10. See, for example, California Civil Code Sections 3344 and 3344.1.

evision news program reports on a celebrity and shows an image of the person, the use likely would not be classified as commercial; in contrast, including the celebrity's image on a poster without his or her permission would be a commercial use.

Because the right of publicity is similar to a property right, most states have concluded that the right is inheritable and survives the death of the person who held the right. Normally, though, the person must provide for the passage of the right to another in her or his will. In 2007, for example, a court held that because Marilyn Monroe's will did not specifically state a desire to pass the right to publicity to her heirs, the beneficiaries under her will did not have a right to prevent a company from marketing T-shirts and other merchandise using Monroe's name, picture, and likeness.[11]

Fraudulent Misrepresentation

A misrepresentation leads another to believe in a condition that is different from the condition that actually exists. This is often accomplished through a false or an incorrect statement. Although persons sometimes make misrepresentations accidentally because they are unaware of the existing facts, the tort of **fraudulent misrepresentation,** or *fraud,* involves *intentional* deceit for personal gain. The tort includes several elements:

1. A misrepresentation of material facts or conditions with knowledge that they are false or with reckless disregard for the truth.
2. An intent to induce another party to rely on the misrepresentation.
3. A justifiable reliance on the misrepresentation by the deceived party.
4. Damages suffered as a result of that reliance.
5. A causal connection between the misrepresentation and the injury suffered.

For fraud to occur, more than mere **puffery,** or *seller's talk,* must be involved. Fraud exists only when a person represents as a fact something he or she knows is untrue. For example, it is fraud to claim that the roof of a building does not leak when one knows that it does. Facts are objectively ascertainable, whereas seller's talk—such as "I am the best accountant in town"—is not, because the speaker is representing a subjective view.

Normally, the tort of fraudulent misrepresentation occurs only when there is reliance on a *statement of fact.* Sometimes, however, reliance on a *statement of opinion* may involve the tort of fraudulent misrepresentation if the individual making the statement of opinion has superior knowledge of the subject matter. For example, when a lawyer makes a statement of opinion about the law in a state in which the lawyer is licensed to practice, a court would construe reliance on such a statement to be equivalent to reliance on a statement of fact.

Abusive or Frivolous Litigation

Persons or businesses generally have a right to sue when they have been injured. In recent years, however, an increasing number of meritless lawsuits have been filed—sometimes simply to harass the defendant. Defending oneself in any legal proceeding can be costly, time consuming, and emotionally draining. Tort law recognizes that people have a right not to be sued without a legally just and proper reason. It therefore protects individuals from the misuse of litigation. Torts related to abusive litigation include malicious prosecution and abuse of process.

If the party that initiated a lawsuit did so out of malice and without probable cause (a legitimate legal reason), and ended up losing that suit, the party can be sued for *malicious prosecution.* In some states, the plaintiff (who was the defendant in the first proceeding) must also prove injury other than the normal costs of litigation, such as lost profits. *Abuse of process* can apply to any person using a legal process against another in an improper manner or to accomplish a purpose for which the process was not designed. The key difference between the torts of abuse of process and malicious prosecution is the level of proof. Abuse of process does not require the plaintiff to prove malice or show that the defendant (who was previously the plaintiff) lost in a prior legal proceeding.[12] Abuse of process is also not limited to prior litigation. It can be based on the wrongful use of subpoenas, court orders to attach or seize real property, or other types of formal legal process. *Concept Summary 4.1* on the following page reviews intentional torts against persons.

---

11. *Shaw Family Archives, Ltd. v. CMG Worldwide, Inc.,* 486 F. Supp. 2d 309 (S.D.N.Y. 2007), presented as Case 50.1.

12. *Bernhard-Thomas Building Systems, LLC v. Duncan,* 918 A.2d 889 (Conn. App. 2007); and *Hewitt v. Rice,* 154 P.3d 408 (Colo. 2007).

CONCEPT SUMMARY 4.1
Intentional Torts against Persons

Name of Tort	Description
ASSAULT AND BATTERY	Any unexcused and intentional act that causes another person to be apprehensive of immediate harm is an assault. An assault resulting in physical contact is battery.
FALSE IMPRISONMENT	An intentional confinement or restraint of another person's movement without justification.
INTENTIONAL INFLICTION OF EMOTIONAL DISTRESS	An intentional act that amounts to extreme and outrageous conduct resulting in severe emotional distress to another.
DEFAMATION (LIBEL OR SLANDER)	A false statement of fact, not made under privilege, that is communicated to a third person and that causes damage to a person's reputation. For public figures, the plaintiff must also prove that the statement was made with actual malice.
INVASION OF PRIVACY	Publishing or otherwise making known or using information relating to a person's private life and affairs, with which the public has no legitimate concern, without that person's permission or approval.
APPROPRIATION	The use of another person's name, likeness, or other identifying characteristic without permission and for the benefit of the user.
FRAUDULENT MISREPRESENTATION (FRAUD)	A false representation made by one party, through misstatement of facts or through conduct, with the intention of deceiving another and on which the other reasonably relies to his or her detriment.
ABUSIVE LITIGATION	The filing of a lawsuit without legitimate grounds and with malice or the use of a legal process in an improper manner.

Business Torts

Most torts can occur in any context, but a few torts, referred to as **business torts,** apply only to wrongful interferences with the business rights of others. Business torts generally fall into two categories—interference with a contractual relationship and interference with a business relationship.

Wrongful Interference with a Contractual Relationship

The body of tort law relating to *wrongful interference with a contractual relationship* has increased greatly in recent years. A landmark case in this area involved an opera singer, Joanna Wagner, who was under contract to sing for a man named Lumley for a specified period of years. A man named Gye, who knew of this contract, nonetheless "enticed" Wagner to refuse to carry out the agreement, and Wagner began to sing for Gye. Gye's action constituted a tort because it inter-fered with the contractual relationship between Wagner and Lumley. (Of course, Wagner's refusal to carry out the agreement also entitled Lumley to sue Wagner for breach of contract.)[13]

Three elements are necessary for wrongful interference with a contractual relationship to occur:

1. A valid, enforceable contract must exist between two parties.
2. A third party must know that this contract exists.
3. This third party must *intentionally induce* a party to the contract to breach the contract.

In principle, any lawful contract can be the basis for an action of this type. The contract could be between a firm and its employees or a firm and its customers. Sometimes, a competitor of a firm draws away one of the firm's key employees. Only if the original employer can show that the competitor knew of the contract's existence, and intentionally induced the breach, can damages be recovered from the competitor.

---

13. *Lumley v. Gye,* 118 Eng.Rep. 749 (1853).

Wrongful Interference with a Business Relationship

Businesspersons devise countless schemes to attract customers, but they are prohibited from unreasonably interfering with another's business in their attempts to gain a greater share of the market. There is a difference between *competitive practices* and *predatory behavior*—actions undertaken with the intention of unlawfully driving competitors completely out of the market.

Attempting to attract customers in general is a legitimate business practice, whereas specifically targeting the customers of a competitor is more likely to be predatory. For example, the mall contains two athletic shoe stores: Joe's and Sprint. Joe's cannot station an employee at the entrance of Sprint to divert customers to Joe's and tell them that Joe's will beat Sprint's prices. Doing this would constitute the tort of wrongful interference with a business relationship because it would interfere with a prospective (economic) advantage; such behavior is commonly considered to be an unfair trade practice. If this type of activity were permitted, Joe's would reap the benefits of Sprint's advertising.

Although state laws vary on wrongful interference with a business relationship, generally a plaintiff must prove that the defendant used predatory methods to intentionally harm an established business relationship or prospective economic advantage. The plaintiff must also prove that the defendant's interference caused the plaintiff to suffer economic harm.

Defenses to Wrongful Interference

A person will not be liable for the tort of wrongful interference with a contractual or business relationship if it can be shown that the interference was justified, or permissible. Bona fide competitive behavior is a permissible interference even if it results in the breaking of a contract.

For example, if Jerrod's Meats advertises so effectively that it induces Sam's Restaurant to break its contract with Burke's Meat Company, Burke's Meat Company will be unable to recover against Jerrod's Meats on a wrongful interference theory. After all, the public policy that favors free competition through advertising outweighs any possible instability that such competitive activity might cause in contractual relations. Although luring customers away from a competitor through aggressive marketing and advertising strategies obviously interferes with the competitor's

relationship with its customers, courts typically allow such activities in the spirit of competition.

Intentional Torts against Property

Intentional torts against property include trespass to land, trespass to personal property, conversion, and disparagement of property. These torts are wrongful actions that interfere with individuals' legally recognized rights with regard to their land or personal property. The law distinguishes real property from personal property (see Chapter 47). *Real property* is land and things permanently attached to the land. *Personal property* consists of all other items, which are basically movable. Thus, a house and lot are real property, whereas the furniture inside a house is personal property. Cash and securities are also personal property.

Trespass to Land

The tort of **trespass to land** occurs any time a person, without permission, enters onto, above, or below the surface of land that is owned by another; causes anything to enter onto the land; or remains on the land or permits anything to remain on it. Actual harm to the land is not an essential element of this tort because the tort is designed to protect the right of an owner to exclusive possession. Common types of trespass to land include walking or driving on another's land; shooting a gun over another's land; throwing rocks at or spraying water on a building that belongs to someone else; building a dam across a river, thereby causing water to back up on someone else's land; and constructing one's building so that it extends onto an adjoining landowner's property.

Trespass Criteria, Rights, and Duties
Before a person can be a trespasser, the real property owner (or other person in actual and exclusive possession of the property, such as a person who is leasing the property) must establish that person as a trespasser. For example, "posted" trespass signs expressly establish as a trespasser a person who ignores these signs and enters onto the property. Any person who enters onto another's property to commit an illegal act (such as a thief entering a lumberyard at night to steal lumber) is established impliedly as a trespasser, without posted signs.

At common law, a trespasser is liable for damages caused to the property and generally cannot hold the owner liable for injuries that the trespasser sustains on the premises. This common law rule is being abandoned in many jurisdictions, however, in favor of a "reasonable duty" rule that varies depending on the status of the parties. For example, a landowner may have a duty to post a notice that the property is patrolled by guard dogs. Also, under the "attractive nuisance" doctrine, a landowner may be held liable for injuries sustained by young children on the landowner's property if the children were attracted to the premises by some object, such as a swimming pool or an abandoned building. Finally, an owner can remove a trespasser from the premises—or detain a trespasser on the premises for a reasonable time—through the use of reasonable force without being liable for assault, battery, or false imprisonment.

Defenses against Trespass to Land

Trespass to land involves wrongful interference with another person's real property rights. If it can be shown that the trespass was warranted, however, as when a trespasser enters to assist someone in danger, a defense exists. Another defense exists when the trespasser can show that he or she had a license to come onto the land. A *licensee* is one who is invited (or allowed to enter) onto the property of another for the licensee's benefit. A person who enters another's property to read an electric meter, for example, is a licensee. When you purchase a ticket to attend a movie or sporting event, you are licensed to go onto the property of another to view that movie or event. Note that licenses to enter onto another's property are *revocable* by the property owner. If a property owner asks a meter reader to leave and the meter reader refuses to do so, the meter reader at that point becomes a trespasser.

Trespass to Personal Property

Whenever any individual, without consent, takes or harms the personal property of another or otherwise interferes with the lawful owner's possession and enjoyment of personal property, **trespass to personal property** occurs. This tort may also be called *trespass to chattels* or *trespass to personalty.* In this context, harm means not only destruction of the property, but also anything that diminishes its value, condition, or quality. Trespass to personal property involves intentional meddling with a possessory interest (an interest arising from possession), including barring an owner's access to personal property. If Kelly takes Ryan's business law book as a practical joke and hides it so that Ryan is unable to find it for several days prior to the final examination, Kelly has engaged in a trespass to personal property.

If it can be shown that trespass to personal property was warranted, then a complete defense exists. Most states, for example, allow automobile repair shops to hold a customer's car (under what is called an *artisan's lien,* discussed in Chapter 28) when the customer refuses to pay for repairs already completed.

Conversion

Whenever a person wrongfully possesses or uses the personal property of another as if the property belonged to her or him, the tort of **conversion** occurs. Any act that deprives an owner of personal property or of the use of that property without that owner's permission and without just cause can be conversion. Often, when conversion occurs, a trespass to personal property also occurs because the original taking of the personal property from the owner was a trespass, and wrongfully retaining it is conversion. Conversion requires a more serious interference with the personal property than trespass, in terms of the duration and extensiveness of use.

Conversion is the civil side of crimes related to theft, but it is not limited to theft. Even when the rightful owner consented to the initial taking of the property so there was no theft or trespass, a failure to return the personal property may still be conversion. For example, Chen borrows Marik's iPod to use while traveling home from school for the holidays. When Chen returns to school, Marik asks for his iPod back, but Chen says that he gave it to his little brother for Christmas. In this situation, Marik can sue Chen for conversion, and Chen will have to either return the iPod or pay damages equal to its value.

Similarly, even if a person mistakenly believed that she or he was entitled to the goods, a tort of conversion may still have occurred. In other words, good intentions are not a defense against conversion; in fact, conversion can be an entirely innocent act. Someone who buys stolen goods, for example, has committed the tort of conversion even if he or she did not know the goods were stolen. Note that even the taking of electronic records and data may form the basis of a common law conversion claim.[14] So can the wrongful taking of a

---

14. See *Thyroff v. Nationwide Mutual Insurance Co.,* 8 N.Y.3d 283, 864 N.E.2d 1272 (2007).

domain name.[15] Thus, the personal property need not be tangible (physical) property.

Disparagement of Property

Disparagement of property occurs when economically injurious falsehoods are made about another's product or property rather than about another's reputation (as in the tort of defamation). *Disparagement of property* is a general term for torts that can be more specifically referred to as *slander of quality* or *slander of title*.

Slander of Quality Publishing false information about another's product, alleging it is not what its seller claims, constitutes the tort of **slander of quality,** or **trade libel.** The plaintiff must prove that actual damages proximately resulted from the slander of quality. In other words, the plaintiff must show not only that a third person refrained from dealing with the plaintiff because of the improper publication but also that the plaintiff suffered damages because the third person refrained from dealing with him or her. The economic calculation of such damages—they are, after all, conjectural—is often extremely difficult.

An improper publication may be both a slander of quality and a defamation of character. For example, a statement that disparages the quality of a product may also, by implication, disparage the character of a person who would sell such a product.

---

15. See *Kremen v. Cohen,* 325 F. 3d 1035 (9th Cir. 2003).

Slander of Title When a publication falsely denies or casts doubt on another's legal ownership of property, resulting in financial loss to the property's owner, the tort of **slander of title** occurs. Usually, this is an intentional tort in which someone knowingly publishes an untrue statement about another's ownership of certain property with the intent of discouraging a third person from dealing with the person slandered. For example, it would be difficult for a car dealer to attract customers after competitors published a notice that the dealer's stock consisted of stolen autos. See *Concept Summary 4.2* for a review of intentional torts against property.

Cyber Torts

Torts can also be committed in the online environment. Torts committed via the Internet are often called **cyber torts.** Over the years, the courts have had to decide how to apply traditional tort law to torts committed in cyberspace. Consider, for example, issues of proof. How can it be proved that an online defamatory remark was "published" (which requires that a third party see or hear it)? How can the identity of the person who made the remark be discovered? Can an Internet service provider (ISP), such as America Online, Inc. (AOL), be forced to reveal the source of an anonymous comment? We explore some of these questions in this section, as well as some legal issues that have arisen with respect to bulk e-mail advertising.

CONCEPT SUMMARY 4.2
Intentional Torts against Property

Name of Tort	Description
TRESPASS TO LAND	The invasion of another's real property without consent or privilege. Once a person is expressly or impliedly established as a trespasser, the property owner has specific rights, which may include the right to detain or remove the trespasser.
TRESPASS TO PERSONAL PROPERTY	The intentional interference with an owner's right to use, possess, or enjoy his or her personal property without the owner's consent.
CONVERSION	The wrongful possession or use of another person's personal property without just cause.
DISPARAGEMENT OF PROPERTY	Any economically injurious falsehood that is made about another's product or property; an inclusive term for the torts of *slander of quality* and *slander of title.*

Defamation Online

Recall from the discussion of defamation earlier in this chapter that one who repeats or otherwise republishes a defamatory statement is subject to liability as if he or she had originally published it. Thus, publishers generally can be held liable for defamatory contents in the books and periodicals that they publish. Now consider online message forums. These forums allow anyone—customers, employees, or crackpots—to complain about a business firm's personnel, policies, practices, or products. Regardless of whether the complaint is justified and whether it is true, it might have an impact on the firm's business. One of the early questions in the online legal arena was whether the providers of such forums could be held liable, as publishers, for defamatory statements made in those forums.

Immunity of Internet Service Providers

Newspapers, magazines, and television and radio stations may be held liable for defamatory remarks that they disseminate, even if those remarks are prepared or created by others. Prior to the passage of the Communications Decency Act (CDA) of 1996, the courts grappled on several occasions with the question of whether ISPs should be regarded as publishers and thus be held liable for defamatory messages made by users of their services. The CDA resolved the issue by stating that "[n]o provider or user of an interactive computer service shall be treated as the publisher or speaker of any information provided by another information content provider."[16] In other words, Internet publishers are treated differently from publishers in print, television, and radio, and are not liable for publishing defamatory statements, provided that the material came from a third party.

In a leading case on this issue, decided the year after the CDA was enacted, America Online, Inc. (AOL, now part of Time Warner, Inc.), was not held liable even though it failed to promptly remove defamatory messages of which it had been made aware. In upholding a district court's ruling in AOL's favor, a federal appellate court stated that the CDA "plainly immunizes computer service providers like AOL from liability for information that originates with third parties." The court explained that the purpose of the statute is "to maintain the robust nature of Internet communication and, accordingly, to keep government interference in the medium to a minimum."[17] The courts have reached similar conclusions in subsequent cases, extending the CDA's immunity to Web message boards, online auction houses, Internet dating services, and any business that provides e-mail and Web browsing services.[18]

In the following case, the court considered the scope of immunity that could be accorded to an online roommate-matching service under the CDA.

---

16. 47 U.S.C. Section 230.

17. *Zeran v. America Online, Inc.,* 129 F.3d 327 (4th Cir. 1997); *cert.* denied, 524 U.S. 937, 118 S.Ct. 2341, 141 L.Ed.2d 712 (1998).

18. See *Universal Communications Systems, Inc. v. Lycos, Inc.,* 478 F.3d 413 (1st Cir. 2007); *Barrett v. Rosenthal,* 40 Cal.4th 33, 51 Cal.Rptr.3d 55 (2006); *Delfino v. Agilent Technologies, Inc.,* 145 Cal.App. 4th 790, 52 Cal.Rptr.3d 376 (2006); *Noah v. AOL Time Warner, Inc.,* 261 F.Supp.2d 532 (E.D.Va. 2003); and *Carafano v. Metrosplash.com, Inc.,* 339 F.3d 1119 (9th Cir. 2003).

C A S E **4.3** **Fair Housing Council of San Fernando Valley v. Roommate.com, LLC**

United States Court of Appeals, Ninth Circuit, 2008. 521 F.3d 1157.

● **Background and Facts** Roommate.com, LLC (Roommate), operates an online roommate-matching Web site at **www.roommates.com**. The site helps individuals find roommates based on their descriptions of themselves and their roommate preferences. Roommate has approximately 150,000 active listings and receives about a million user views per day. To become members of Roommate, users respond to a series of online questions, choosing from answers in drop-down and select-a-box menus. Users disclose information about themselves and their roommate preferences based on age, gender, and other characteristics, as well as on whether children will live in the household. Members can create personal profiles, search lists of compatible roommates, and send "roommail" messages to other members. Roommate also e-mails newsletters to members seeking housing, listing compatible members who have places to rent. The Fair Housing Councils of San Fernando Valley and San Diego, California, filed a suit in a federal district court against Roommate, claiming that the defendant violated the Fair Housing Act (FHA) by asking for and distributing the information in its member profiles. The court held that the Communications Decency Act (CDA) barred this claim and dismissed it. The councils appealed to the U.S. Court of Appeals for the Ninth Circuit.

CASE 4.3 CONTINUED ● **Decision and Rationale** The U.S. Court of Appeals for the Ninth Circuit concluded that the CDA does not provide immunity to Roommate for all of the content of its Web site and e-mail newsletters. "Roommate[s] created the questions and choice of answers, and designed its Web site registration process around them." Therefore, Roommate is "the 'information content provider' as to the questions and can claim no immunity for posting them on its Web site, or for forcing subscribers to answer them as a condition of using its services." Because Roommate forced subscribers to answer questions in which they divulged protected characteristics, it was responsible, at least in part, for the development of the content and could be held liable for any unlawful content. The court noted that asking questions "certainly can violate the Fair Housing Act and analogous laws in the physical world" and reasoned that illegal questions "don't magically become lawful when asked electronically online." The appellate court reversed the lower court's dismissal and remanded the case to the lower court to determine "whether the alleged actions for which Roommate is not immune violated the Fair Housing Act."

● **The Ethical Dimension** *Do Internet service providers have an ethical duty to advise their users if the information that the users provide for distribution through the Internet service providers might violate the law? Explain.*

● **The E-Commerce Dimension** *Should the courts continue to regard the CDA's grant of immunity to Internet service providers as vigorously as in the past? Why or why not?*

Piercing the Veil of Anonymity A threshold barrier to anyone who seeks to bring an action for online defamation is discovering the identity of the person who posted the defamatory message online. ISPs can disclose personal information about their customers only when ordered to do so by a court. Consequently, businesses and individuals often resort to filing lawsuits against "John Does" (John Doe is a fictitious name that is used when the name of the particular person is not known). Then, using the authority of the courts, they attempt to obtain from the ISPs the identities of the persons responsible for the messages. This strategy has worked in some cases,[19] but not in others.[20] Courts typically are reluctant to deter those who would potentially post messages on the Internet from exercising their First Amendment right to speak anonymously. After all, speaking anonymously is part of the nature of the Internet and helps to make it a useful forum for public discussion.

Spam

Bulk, unsolicited e-mail ("junk" e-mail) sent to all of the users on a particular e-mailing list or all of the members of a newsgroup is often called **spam**.[21]

Typically, spam consists of product ads. Spam can waste user time and network bandwidth (the amount of data that can be transmitted within a certain time). It also imposes a burden on an ISP's equipment as well as on an e-mail recipient's computer system.[22] Because of the problems associated with spam, the majority of states now have laws regulating its transmission. In 2003, the U.S. Congress also enacted a law to regulate the use of spam, although the volume of spam has actually increased since the law was enacted.

Statutory Regulation of Spam In an attempt to combat spam, thirty-six states have enacted laws that prohibit or regulate its use. Many state laws regulating spam require the senders of e-mail ads to instruct the recipients on how they can "opt out" of further e-mail ads from the same sources. For instance, in some states an unsolicited e-mail ad must include a toll-free phone number or return e-mail address through which the recipient can contact the sender to request that no more ads be e-mailed. The most stringent state law is California's antispam law, which went into effect on January 1, 2004. That law follows the "opt-in" model favored by consumer groups and antispam advocates. In other words, the law prohibits any person or business from sending e-mail ads to or from any e-mail address in California unless the recipient has

---

19. *Does v. Hvide,* 770 So.2d 1237 (Fla.App.3d 2000).

20. See, for example, *Doe v. Cahill,* 884 A.2d 451 (Del.Supr. 2005); and *Dendrite International, Inc. v. Doe No. 3,* 342 N.J.Super. 134, 775 A.2d 756 (2001).

21. The term *spam* is said to come from a Monty Python song with the lyrics, "Spam spam spam spam, spam spam spam spam, lovely spam, wonderful spam." Like these lyrics, spam online is often considered to be a repetition of worthless text.

22. For an early case in which a court found that spam constituted a trespass to personal property because of the burden on the ISP's equipment, see *CompuServe, Inc. v. Cyber Promotions, Inc.,* 962 F.Supp. 1015 (S.D. Ohio 1997).

expressly agreed to receive e-mails from the sender. An exemption is made for e-mail sent to consumers with whom the advertiser has a "preexisting or current business relationship."

The Federal CAN-SPAM Act In 2003, Congress enacted the Controlling the Assault of Non-Solicited Pornography and Marketing (CAN-SPAM) Act, which took effect on January 1, 2004. The legislation applies to any "commercial electronic mail messages" that are sent to promote a commercial product or service. Significantly, the statute preempts state antispam laws except for those provisions in state laws that prohibit false and deceptive e-mailing practices.

Generally, the act permits the use of unsolicited commercial e-mail but prohibits certain types of spamming activities, including the use of a false return address and the use of false, misleading, or deceptive information when sending e-mail. The statute also prohibits the use of "dictionary attacks"—sending messages to randomly generated e-mail addresses—and the "harvesting" of e-mail addresses from Web sites through the use of specialized software. Notwithstanding the requirements of the federal act, the reality is that the problem of spam is difficult to address because much of it is funneled through foreign servers.

REVIEWING Intentional Torts

Two sisters, Darla and Irene, are partners in an import business located in a small town in Rhode Island. Irene is married to a well-known real estate developer and is campaigning to be the mayor of their town. Darla is in her mid-thirties and has never been married. Both sisters travel to other countries to purchase the goods they sell at their retail store. Irene buys Indonesian goods, and Darla buys goods from Africa. After a tsunami (tidal wave) destroys many of the cities in Indonesia to which Irene usually travels, she phones one of her contacts there and asks him to procure some items and ship them to her. He informs her that it will be impossible to buy these items now because the townspeople are being evacuated due to a water shortage. Irene is angry and tells the man that if he cannot purchase the goods, he should just take them without paying for them after the town has been evacuated. Darla overhears her sister's instructions and is outraged. They have a falling-out, and Darla decides that she no longer wishes to be in business with her sister. Using the information presented in the chapter, answer the following questions.

1. Suppose that Darla tells several of her friends about Irene's instructing the man to take goods without paying for them after the tsunami disaster. Under which intentional tort theory discussed in this chapter might Irene attempt to sue Darla? Would Irene's suit be successful? Why or why not?
2. Now suppose that Irene wins the election and becomes the city's mayor. Darla then writes a letter to the editor of the local newspaper disclosing Irene's misconduct. What intentional tort might Irene accuse Darla of committing? What defenses could Darla assert?
3. If Irene accepts goods shipped from Indonesia that were wrongfully obtained, has she committed an intentional tort against property? Explain.
4. Suppose now that Irene, who is angry with her sister for disclosing her business improprieties, writes a letter to the editor falsely accusing Darla of having sexual relations with her neighbor's thirteen-year-old son. For what intentional tort or torts could Darla sue Irene in this situation?

TERMS AND CONCEPTS

actionable

actual malice

appropriation

assault

battery

business tort

compensatory damages

conversion

cyber tort

defamation

disparagement of property

fraudulent misrepresentation

intentional tort

libel

privilege

puffery

punitive damages

slander

slander of quality

slander of title

spam

tort

tortfeasor

trade libel

trespass to land

trespass to personal property

QUESTIONS AND CASE PROBLEMS

6-1. Richard is an employee of the Dun Construction Corp. While delivering materials to a construction site, he carelessly backs Dun's truck into a passenger vehicle driven by Green. This is Richard's second accident in six months. When the company owner, Dun, learns of this latest accident, a heated discussion ensues, and Dun fires Richard. Dun is so angry that he immediately writes a letter to the union of which Richard is a member and to all other construction companies in the community, stating that Richard is the "worst driver in the city" and that "anyone who hires him is asking for legal liability." Richard files a suit against Dun, alleging libel on the basis of the statements made in the letters. Discuss the results.

6-2. QUESTION WITH SAMPLE ANSWER

Lothar owns a bakery. He has been trying to obtain a long-term contract with the owner of Martha's Tea Salons for some time. Lothar starts a local advertising campaign on radio and television and in the newspaper. This advertising campaign is so persuasive that Martha decides to break the contract she has had with Harley's Bakery so that she can patronize Lothar's bakery. Is Lothar liable to Harley's Bakery for the tort of wrongful interference with a contractual relationship? Is Martha liable for this tort?

- **For a sample answer to Question 6–2, go to Appendix C at the end of this text.**

6-3. Gerrit is a former employee of ABC Auto Repair Co. He enters ABC's repair shop, claiming that the company owes him $800 in back wages. Gerrit argues with ABC's general manager, Steward, and Steward orders him off the property. Gerrit refuses to leave, and Steward tells two mechanics to throw him off the property. Gerrit runs to his truck, but on the way, he grabs some tools valued at $800; then he drives away. Gerrit refuses to return the tools.

(a) Discuss whether Gerrit has committed any torts.

(b) If the mechanics had thrown Gerrit off the property, would ABC be guilty of assault and battery? Explain.

6-4. Bombardier Capital, Inc., provides financing to boat and recreational vehicle dealers. Bombardier's credit policy requires dealers to forward immediately to Bombardier the proceeds of boat sales. When Howard Mulcahey, Bombardier's vice president of sales and marketing, learned that dealers were not complying with this policy, he told Frank Chandler, Bombardier's credit director, of his concern. Before Chandler could obtain the proceeds, Mulcahey falsely told Jacques Gingras, Bombardier's president, that Chandler was, among other things, trying to hide the problem. On the basis of Mulcahey's statements, Gingras fired Chandler and put Mulcahey in charge of the credit department. Under what business tort theory discussed in this chapter might Chandler recover damages from Mulcahey? Explain.

6-5. Trespass to Property. America Online, Inc. (AOL), provides services to its customers or members, including the transmission of e-mail to and from other members and across the Internet. To become a member, a person must agree not to use AOL's computers to send bulk, unsolicited, commercial e-mail (spam). AOL uses filters to block spam, but bulk e-mailers sometimes use other software to thwart the filters. National Health Care Discount, Inc. (NHCD), sells discount optical and dental service plans. To generate leads for NHCD's products, sales representatives, who included AOL members, sent more than 300 million pieces of spam through AOL's computer system. Each item cost AOL an estimated $0.00078 in equipment expenses. Some of the spam used false headers and other methods to hide the source. After receiving more than 150,000 complaints from its members, AOL asked NHCD to stop. When the spam continued, AOL filed a suit in a federal district court against NHCD, alleging, in part, trespass to chattels—an unlawful interference with another's rights to possess personal property. AOL asked the court for a summary judgment on this claim. Did the spamming constitute trespass to chattels? Explain. [*America Online, Inc. v. National Health Care Discount, Inc.,* 121 F.Supp.2d 1255 (N.D. Iowa 2000)]

6–6. Intentional Torts against Property. In 1994, Gary Kremen registered the domain name "sex.com" with Network Solutions, Inc., to the name of Kremen's business, Online Classifieds. Later, Stephen Cohen sent Network Solutions a letter that he claimed to have received from Online Classifieds. It stated that "we have no objections to your use of the domain name sex.com and this letter shall serve as our authorization to the Internet registrar to transfer sex.com to your corporation." Without contacting Kremen, Network Solutions transferred the name to Cohen, who subsequently turned sex.com into a lucrative business. Kremen filed a suit in a federal district court against Cohen and others, seeking the name and Cohen's profits. The court ordered Cohen to return the name to Kremen and pay $65 million in damages. Cohen ignored the order and disappeared. Against what other parties might Kremen attempt to obtain relief? Under which theory of intentional torts against property might Kremen be able to file an action? What is the likely result, and why? [*Kremen v. Cohen,* 337 F.3d 1024 (9th Cir. 2003)]

6–7. Invasion of Privacy. During the spring and summer of 1999, Edward and Geneva Irvine received numerous "hang-up" phone calls, including three calls in the middle of the night. With the help of their local phone company, the Irvines learned that many of the calls were from the telemarketing department of the *Akron Beacon Journal* in Akron, Ohio. The *Beacon's* sales force was equipped with an automatic dialing machine. During business hours, the dialer was used to maximize productivity by calling multiple phone numbers at once and connecting a call to a sales representative only after it was answered. After business hours, the *Beacon* programmed its dialer to dial a list of disconnected numbers to determine whether they had been reconnected. If the dialer detected a ring, it recorded the information and dropped the call. If the automated dialing system crashed, which it did frequently, it redialed the entire list. The Irvines filed a suit in an Ohio state court against the *Beacon* and others, alleging, among other things, an invasion of privacy. In whose favor should the court rule, and why? [*Irvine v.*

Akron Beacon Journal, 147 Ohio App.3d 428, 770 N.E.2d 1105 (9 Dist. 2002)]

6–8. Defamation. Lydia Hagberg went to her bank, California Federal Bank, FSB, to cash a check made out to her by Smith Barney (SB), an investment services firm. Nolene Showalter, a bank employee, suspected that the check was counterfeit. Showalter called SB and was told that the check was not valid. As she phoned the police, Gary Wood, a bank security officer, contacted SB again and was informed that its earlier statement was "erroneous" and that the check was valid. Meanwhile, a police officer arrived, drew Hagberg away from the teller's window, spread her legs, patted her down, and handcuffed her. The officer searched her purse, asked her whether she had any weapons or stolen property and whether she was driving a stolen vehicle, and arrested her. Hagberg filed a suit in a California state court against the bank and others, alleging, among other things, slander. Should the absolute privilege for communications made in judicial or other official proceedings apply to statements made when a citizen contacts the police to report suspected criminal activity? Why or why not? [*Hagberg v. California Federal Bank*, FSB, 32 Cal.4th 350, 81 P.3d 244, 7 Cal.Rptr.3d 803 (2004)]

6–9. CASE PROBLEM WITH SAMPLE ANSWER

Between 1996 and 1998, Donna Swanson received several anonymous, handwritten letters that, among other things, accused her husband, Alan, of infidelity. In 1998, John Grisham, Jr., the author of *The Firm* and many other best-selling novels, received an anonymous letter that appeared to have been written by the same person. Grisham and the Swansons suspected Katherine Almy, who soon filed a suit in a Virginia state court against them, alleging, among other things, intentional infliction of emotional distress. According to Almy, Grisham intended to have her "really, really, suffer" for writing the letters, and the three devised a scheme to falsely accuse her. They gave David Liebman, a handwriting analyst, samples of Almy's handwriting. These included copies of confidential documents from her children's files at St. Anne's–Belfield School in Charlottesville, Virginia, where Alan taught and Grisham served on the board of directors. In Almy's view, Grisham influenced Liebman to report that Almy might have written the letters and misrepresented this report as conclusive, which led the police to confront Almy. She claimed that she then suffered severe emotional distress and depression, causing "a complete disintegration of virtually every aspect of her life" and requiring her "to undergo extensive therapy." In response, the defendants asked the court to dismiss the complaint for failure to state a claim. Should the court grant this request? Explain. [*Almy v. Grisham,* 273 Va. 68, 639 S.E.2d 182 (2007)]

• **To view a sample answer for Problem 6–9,**

go to this book's Web site at www.cengage.com/blaw/jentz, select "Chapter 6," and click on "Case Problem with Sample Answer."

6-10. A QUESTION OF ETHICS

White Plains Coat & Apron Co. is a New York–based linen rental business. Cintas Corp. is a nationwide business that rents similar products. White Plains had five-year exclusive contracts with some of its customers. As a result of Cintas's soliciting of business, dozens of White Plains' customers breached their contracts and entered into rental agreements with Cintas. White Plains demanded that Cintas stop its solicitation of White Plains' customers. Cintas refused. White Plains filed a suit in a federal district court against Cintas, alleging wrongful interference with existing contracts. Cintas argued that it had no knowledge of any contracts with White Plains and had not induced any breach. The court dismissed the suit, ruling that Cintas had a legitimate interest as a competitor to solicit business and make a profit. White Plains appealed to the U.S. Court of Appeals for the Second Circuit. *[White Plains Coat & Apron Co. v. Cintas Corp., 8 N.Y.3d 422, 867 N.E.2d 381 (2007)]*

(a) What are the two important policy interests at odds in wrongful interference cases? When there is an existing contract, which of these interests should be accorded priority?

(b) The U.S. Court of Appeals for the Second Circuit asked the New York Court of Appeals to answer a question: Is a general interest in soliciting business for profit a sufficient defense to a claim of wrongful interference with a contractual relationship? What do you think? Why?

LAW ON THE WEB

For updated links to resources available on the Web, as well as a variety of other materials, visit this text's Web site at

www.cengage.com/blaw/jentz

You can find cases and articles on torts, including business torts, in the tort law library at the Internet Law Library's Web site. Go to

www.lawguru.com/ilawlib

Legal Research Exercises on the Web

Go to **www.cengage.com/blaw/jentz**, the Web site that accompanies this text. Select "Chapter 6" and click on "Internet Exercises." There you will find the following Internet research exercises that you can perform to learn more about the topics covered in this chapter.

Internet Exercise 6–1:   Legal Perspective
Online Defamation

Internet Exercise 6–2:   Management Perspective
Legal and Illegal Uses of Spam

Torts

Case No. 1

ASSAULT AND BATTERY

Pastre v. Weber, et al.

Federal District Court, Southern District of New York

717 F.Supp 992 (1989)

FACTS: Plaintiff Scott Pastre (Pastre) was driving a car while intoxicated and ran a red light. With him were several friends who were also intoxicated. Defendant New York State Troopers Thomas L. Weber (Weber) and Robert Pineau witnessed the traffic violation, turned on their flashing lights, and gave chase. The 70 mph chase took place over winding country roads and ended when one of Pastre's tires blew out. Pastre and his friends then remained in the car and locked the doors.

Officer Weber, angry from the risky chase, smashed the driver's side window, unlocked the door and opened it. Pastre kicked Weber several times. Weber removed Pastre from the car, addressed him using profanity, and kicked him in the head, arms, ribs, stomach, and groin.

Pastre sued Weber for assault and battery, seeking compensatory and punitive damages.

FIRST ISSUE: When a police officer loses his temper after a life-threatening situation, and roughs up an arrestee by striking and kicking him, is the officer guilty of the tort of assault and battery?

DECISION: Yes, judgment for Pastre.

REASONING: Even though the court acknowledged that Weber was "extremely provoked" by the chase and locked car doors, Weber used force that was neither reasonable nor necessary. The court stated that Weber had no basis to address a citizen using an obscenity or to "clobber him".

SECOND ISSUE: Is Pastre entitled to punitive damages? (Punitive damages is an award of money in excess of actual damages, to punish the wrongdoer.)

DECISION: No.

REASONING: Punitive damages are generally awarded only where willful and malicious conduct is involved. In this case, Weber was provoked by Pastre's actions; therefore, the facts did not support the conclusion that Weber's behavior was a "callous disregard of, or indifference to, the rights or safety of others".

* * * QUESTION * * *
(See back of text for answer)

1)   Do you agree with the court's ruling on the punitive damages issue? Why or why not?

Case No. 2

ASSAULT

Holtz v. Widenstein & Co., Inc.

Appellate Division, First Department

261 AD2d 336, 693 NYS2d 516 (1999)

FACTS: In this civil assault action, an employee is suing her employer based on conduct of her supervisor. Plaintiff alleged that she was in her supervisor's office and the latter made "an impulsive reaching motion in plaintiff's direction". Plaintiff avoided contact by "briskly" leaving the supervisor's office.

ISSUE: Do the facts alleged constitute the tort of assault?

DECISION: No.

REASONING: To sustain a claim for assault there must be proof that defendant engaged in conduct that placed plaintiff in imminent fear of harmful contact. The conduct attributed to plaintiff's supervisor, coupled with plaintiff's prompt departure from the supervisor's office, could not have generated in plaintiff the requisite imminent apprehension of harmful contact.

Judgment for the employer.

Case No. 3

DEFAMATION

<u>Cardiff v. Brooklyn Eagle, Inc.</u>

Supreme Court, Kings County

75 N.Y.S.2d 222 (1947)

FACTS: Defendant Brooklyn Eagle, Inc. (Brooklyn Eagle) published a newspaper which contained an obituary notice stating that plaintiff John Cardiff (Cardiff) had died and his body was lying in state at a specified address. The notice was incorrect; Cardiff was "very much alive" at the time of the publication. Further, the address identified in the notice as the place where Cardiff was lying in state was his own place of business, a bar and grill.

Cardiff sued Brooklyn Eagle for libel.

ISSUE: Does the publication in a newspaper of an announcement Of a person's death constitute libel where the person has not died?

DECISION: No, judgment for Brooklyn Eagle.

REASONING: To constitute libel a false statement must be published in writing and expose the subject to hatred, contempt, ridicule or disgrace. The false publication of a person's death does not have that effect.

Death is an event beyond a person's control. While the false obituary notice may have annoyed Cardiff and caused him to become the butt of jokes among his friends and acquaintances, it did not reach the level of libel.

* * * QUESTIONS * * *
(See back of text for answers)

1) What effect does the fact that death is an event beyond a person's control have on the decision?

2) Assume the newspaper falsely reported that Cardiff had been arrested for selling illegal drugs. Could Cardiff successfully sue the newspaper for libel?

3) Assume the following additional facts: Cardiff was a well-known rock singer; the newspaper falsely reported he was arrested for purchasing illegal drugs; the newspaper's story was based on statements made by an unidentified caller. Would Cardiff be able to sue successfully the newspaper for libel?

Case No. 4

DEFAMATION, LIBEL

Mahoney v. Adirondack Publishing Company

Court of Appeals

71 N.Y.2d 31, 523 N.Y.S.2d 480 (1987)

FACTS: Defendant Adirondack Publishing Co. (Adirondack) published a newspaper article which described a football game between St. Lawrence Central High School and Tupper Lake High School. The article reported extensively on the behavior of the plaintiff— St. Lawrence coach Jerry Mahoney (Mahoney)—on the sidelines during the game and in the locker room afterwards.

Reporter Thomas Bengston wrote that Mahoney "cursed and belittled his players from the sidelines...", "screamed at his players so loudly in the locker room after the game that he easily could be heard by embarrassed fans...", and his verbal abuse of the players was mixed with profanities. The story reported that St. Lawrence "...quarterback Kevin Hartson completed 14 passes and was intercepted six times. Each time Hartson came off the field after throwing an interception, he was greeted with ...'Come on, get your head out of your &(!! (&. Play the game.'"

Mahoney sued Adirondack for libel, claiming that portions of the article were false and harmed his reputation as a coach and educator. During the trial, Mahoney admitted that he had used the words "hell", "damn", and "goddamn" when dealing with his team during and after the game, and he conceded that he was a "public figure". Many people at the game, including game officials, quarterback Hartson's father, Mahoney's wife, and the St. Lawrence cheerleading coach, all testified that they did not hear or observe any offensive or profane language from Mahoney. Several people also testified that Mahoney had encouraged quarterback Hartson by saying "Get your head up" rather than "get your head out of your &!(!!(&", as reported in the article.

FIRST ISSUE: Did the article contain defamatory statements?

DECISION: Yes.

REASONING: To constitute defamation, a false statement must be made that exposes the subject to hatred, contempt, ridicule or disgrace, thereby wrongfully harming the person's good reputation.

The evidence presented at trial convinced the trier of fact that portions of the article were false. Mahoney's admission to using profanity negated his claim of falsity concerning the article's statement that he used profanity. However, the evidence established that Mahoney did not say "get your head out of your &!(!!(&", as reported. Further, the general thrust of the article condemned Mahoney's behavior and, taken as a whole, cast doubt on his fitness as a coach and educator.

SECOND ISSUE: Is Adirondack liable for defamation?

DECISION: No, judgment for Adirondack.

REASONING: Although the article was defamatory, more is needed for a public figure to successfully pursue a defamation action. Actual malice must be proven. The plaintiff must show that the defendant acted with knowledge of the falsity or with a reckless disregard for the truth. The court determined that the reporter's account of the statement about Hartson's head was more the result of misperception than fabrication. Thus, Mahoney failed to establish that the statement was published with actual malice, thereby defeating his action for libel.

* * * QUESTION * * *
(See back of text for answer)

1) In this case the reporter observed the reported events from approximately 30 feet away and during a part of the football game when the crowd was cheering loudly. How do these facts affect Mahoney's contention that the falsity was published with actual malice?

Case No. 5

DEFAMATION

Costanza v. Seinfeld

Supreme Court, New York County

181 M2d 562, 693 NYS2d897 (1999)

FACTS: Plaintiff Michael Costanza is suing Jerry Seinfeld the actor, the television show "Seinfeld", the production companies, and NBC for $100 million for defamation. Plaintiff claims that defendants used his name and likeness without his permission. Specifically, he claims that the show's fictional character of George Costanza is based on him.

In the show George Costanza was a long-time friend of the lead character, Jerry Seinfeld. George Costanza constantly had employment problems, disastrous romantic relationships, conflicts with his parents and general self-absorption. These traits were part of the comedic interplay with Jerry Seinfeld and the other actors that led to the great success of the Seinfeld television show. At the time of the final episode of Seinfeld, plaintiff published a book entitled, "The Real Seinfeld". The show's spokesperson described plaintiff to the media as a "flagrant opportunist" seeking to cash in on the show's publicity and appeal. Plaintiff's lawsuit includes a claim for defamation based on these statements.

To bolster plaintiff's claim that his name and likeness are being appropriated, plaintiff points to various similarities between himself and the character George Costanza. He claims that, like him, George Costanza is short, fat, and bald. Plaintiff claims the self-centered nature and unreliability of the character George Costanza are attributed to him by others and this humiliates him.

FIRST ISSUE: Does the cause of action for invasion of privacy cover the use of a person's name on a fictional television show?

DECISION: No, the cause of action for invasion of privacy is dismissed.

REASONING: Invasion of privacy is based on a statutory provision, Civil Rights Law §§ 50 and 51. The relief provided by the statute is limited to use of someone's name or likeness without permission for trade or advertising purposes. The type of commercial exploitation prohibited by the statute is use by a defendant of plaintiff's name or picture to solicit customers. Works of fiction and satire do not fall within the scope of the statutory phrase "advertising" and "trade". The Seinfeld television program was a fictional comedic presentation and thus does not fall within the scope of trade or advertising.

SECOND ISSUE: Did the statement made by Seinfeld's spokesperson describing plaintiff as a flagrant opportunist constitute defamation?

DECISION: No, the cause of action for defamation is dismissed.

REASONING: The use of the phrase "flagrant opportunist" was, under the particular circumstances of its utterance, an expression of opinion and not of fact. Those circumstances include the close proximity to publication of plaintiff's book and the heightened publicity surrounding the show's final episode. Statements of opinion do not support a defamation action.

* * * QUESTION* * *
(See back of text for answers)

1) Why do statements of opinion not form the basis of a defamation action?

Case No. 6

DEFAMATION

DRT Construction Company, Inc. v.
Andrew Lenkel and Mapleleaf Homeowners Association

Appellate Division, Fourth Department

—App. Div.2d—(Oct. 4, 1991)

176 AD2d 1229, 576 NYS2d 724

FACTS: DRT Construction Company, Inc. (DRT) sought approval from zoning and planning boards to construct 700 residences, including multiple family dwellings, two commercial plazas and a nursing home on a 288 acre parcel of land. Andrew Lenkel (Lenkel) is president of the Mapleleaf Homeowners Association (Association) which opposed the construction plans. The association distributed fliers in an effort to increase opposition to the development planned by DRT. One flier said, "Now is the time to act and . . . preserve the beauty and peaceful life of Amherst from profit hungry land abusers." The fliers identified DRT as the referenced developer.

Another flier cited engineering reports that suggested the land was not suitable for building and stated "yet this project is still being pushed by profit-hungry developers to whom your life and mine is of no concern instead they worship profit at any cost to others."

A third flier contained a cartoon described by the court as follows: "[It] depicted three men with Hitler moustaches on a bulldozer running over a deer calling for help. The men were waving an ax, a hatchet and a shovel and one had money coming out of his pockets."

DRT brings this action for defamation. Lenkel and the Association deny that the fliers are defamatory.

ISSUE: Do the statements in the fliers constitute defamation?

DECISION: No, judgment for Lenkel and the Association; complaint dismissed.

REASONING: To constitute defamation a statement must be one of fact and capable of being proven true or false. The statements in the fliers were opinion on a subject of public controversy. Such statements are protected speech and do not constitute defamation. The statement "money hungry land abusers" does not contain a statement of fact that can be proven true or false.

Cartoons by their nature are "rhetorical hyperbole or exaggerated statements of opinion." The cartoon in this case reflects the opinion of Lenkel and the Association of the impact development will have on the town of Amherst.

Case No. 7

DEFAMATION

<u>Huggins v. Povitch</u>

Supreme Court, New York County

1996 WL 515498 (1996)

FACTS: Plaintiff is a night club owner and the former spouse of actress and singer Melba Moore. Defendant is Maury Povitch, the host and star of the Maury Povitch Show, a television talk show. In this action plaintiff is suing defendant for defamation based on comments Moore made while a guest on the show.

Plaintiff married Melba Moore in 1976. He thereafter became her personal manager and started a business producing records. They had a daughter together in 1977. Plaintiff began divorce proceedings in Pennsylvania in 1990 and thereafter was awarded the divorce. Ms. Moore sought to void the Pennsylvania divorce and obtain a divorce in New York instead. In 1993 the parties executed a settlement agreement negating the Pennsylvania divorce. The settlement also contained a confidentiality provision which read in relevant part as follows:

> The terms and provisions of this Agreement shall remain private and confidential. Neither party shall publicly criticize, demean, malign or otherwise comment disparagingly or negatively about the other party.

A New York divorce was granted in 1993 incorporating the settlement agreement.

Thereafter Ms. Moore began issuing press releases and talking to the media about Huggins, her marriage, divorce and present financial status. Articles appeared in the National Enquirer, the New York Post and the Daily News. She was interviewed on television shows by Sally Jesse Raphael, Joan Rivers and Les Brown, plus numerous radio shows.

Ms. Moore also contacted the Povich Show. That show aired a segment entitled "Riches to Rags via Divorce" in 1994 which featured an interview with Melba Moore and two other divorced women and a man opposed to the concept of alimony or maintenance. Rounding out the panel was a divorce lawyer and a divorce counselor. The discussion was described as "spirited and argumentative." During the show Ms. Moore talked about Higgins, her marriage and the divorce. She generally blamed plaintiff for her poor financial situation and her resort to welfare.

Plaintiff had notified the show of the non-disclosure provision of Moore's and plaintiff's agreement, seeking to stop Moore from appearing as a guest. The show nonetheless aired the segment. Povich repeatedly stated during the broadcast that Moore was appearing despite a gag order and that her statements represented only one side of the case and that plaintiff denied Moore's allegations.

An example of the comments to which plaintiff objected are:

1) "My husband is a multi-millionaire . . . I can't prove that but as part of the partnership I should share in something.MAURY POVICH: And you feel you're sharing in nothing?MELBA MOORE: I don't feel it, I know it."

2) "[T]here would be times when my husband would have hundreds of dollars in his pocket and I had to take the subway, my daughter and myself. And we have a Rolls-Royce in the garage, and he would say the car is not available. I understand now that was psychological, eating me into the point where, either get used to it or get mad, I think he wanted me to divorce him."

3) "I can't afford an attorney." [Because plaintiff was withholding money from her.

FIRST ISSUE: Does statement number one above constitute defamation?

DECISION: No.

REASONING: Statements that are opinions and not assertions of fact do not support a defamation claim. Only statements alleging facts are capable of being proven false and therefore properly the subject of a defamation action. When determining whether statements constitute fact or opinion, the court should consider such factors as: 1) whether the particular language used has a precise meaning that is readily understood; 2) whether the statements are capable of being proven true or false; and 3) whether the context of the communication and surrounding circumstances suggest that the statements are likely to be opinion and not fact.

The forum and context of Ms. Moore's statement indicate they are her subjective opinion about the emotionally charged topic of her divorce and its financial consequences. The comments were made as part of the give and take of a television talk show. The talk show format provides a forum for expression of opinion. The introduction to the segment indicated that Ms. Moore was involved in a "knock-down, drag-out legal battle" with plaintiff. The camera showed a stack of legal papers representing the various litigations spawned by the termination of the marriage. It is obvious to the viewer that hotly contested matters are about to be discussed and that Moore's remarks are likely to reflect a certain personal bias that should not be taken as objective fact.

SECOND ISSUE: Does statement number two constitute defamation?

DECISION: No.

REASONING: In this statement Moore surmises about plaintiff's motivation for certain conduct. Statements as to motivation are speculative and not readily verifiable. They do not support a defamation action.

THIRD ISSUE: Does statement number three constitute defamation?

DECISION: No.

REASONING: This statement is not about plaintiff but rather about Moore's ability or inability to afford counsel. Since it does not involve plaintiff it cannot support his defamation action. Based on the above, plaintiff's lawsuit seeking damages for defamation is dismissed.

Case No. 8

INTENTIONAL INFLICTION OF EMOTIONAL DISTRESS

<u>Shannon v. MTA Metro-North Railroad</u>

Appellate Division, First Department

269 AD2d 218, 704 NYS2d 208 (2000)

FACTS: Plaintiff was an employee of defendant railroad company. Other defendants included some of plaintiff's co-workers. The complaint alleged that defendants intentionally and maliciously engaged in a pattern of harassment, intimidation, humiliation and abuse, causing plaintiff unjustified demotions, suspension, lost pay and psychological and emotional harm over a period of years.

ISSUE: Are the allegations sufficient, if proven, to establish intentional infliction of emotional distress?

DECISION: Yes.

REASONING: Where severe mental pain or anguish is inflicted through a deliberate and malicious campaign of harassment or intimidation, a remedy is available in the form of an action for intentional infliction of emotional distress.

To constitute the tort, extreme and outrageous behavior is required. The extreme and outrageous nature of the conduct may arise not only from what is done but also from abuse by the defendant of some relationship or position which gives the defendant actual or apparent power to damage the plaintiff's interests including professional standing. Plaintiff's allegations suggest an ongoing campaign of abuse of an employer/employee relationship which caused plaintiff significant loss and damage.

Case No. 9

INTENTIONAL INFLICTION OF EMOTIONAL DISTRESS

<u>Ferguson v. City of New York</u>

Appellate Division, First Department

273 AD2d 103, 709 NYS2d 90 (2000)

FACTS: Plaintiff was an inmate in a jail and apparently Jewish. Defendant was a guard at the jail. Defendant allegedly played an audiocassette within earshot of plaintiff that contained anti-Semitic statements. Evidence established that plaintiff was not playing the tape with the intent of causing plaintiff emotional distress but rather for his fellow officers to hear. Plaintiff could have avoided hearing the tape by moving to the back of the cell but chose not to.

ISSUE: Do the facts as alleged constitute intentional infliction of emotional distress?

DECISION: No.

REASONING: Although the relationship between the parties as captor-captive is intimidating, defendants acts were not so extreme and outrageous to establish a cause of action for intentional infliction of emotional distress.

The court added, "However, nothing in this decision is to condone the actions of defendant in playing an anti-Semitic tape in a penal institution so that it could be overheard by prisoners and others."

Summary judgment for the guard was granted.

Case No. 10

INTENTIONAL INFLICTION OF EMOTIONAL DISTRESS

Seltzer v. Bayer

Appellate Division, First Department

272 NYS2d 263, 709 NYS2d 21 (2000)

FACTS: This case involves a dispute between neighbors in Manhattan. Apparently as an outgrowth of the dispute, plaintiff claims that defendant engaged in numerous acts of vandalism including dumping a pile of cement on the sidewalk in front of plaintiff's house, tossing lighted cigarettes into plaintiff's backyard, throwing eggs on his front steps and threatening once to paint a swastika on plaintiff's house.

ISSUE: Do these acts constitute intentional infliction of emotional distress?

DECISION: No.

REASONING: To constitute the tort of intentional infliction of emotional distress, the conduct involved must be "so outrageous in character and so extreme in degree as to go beyond all possible bounds of decency and to be regarded as atrocious and utterly intolerable in a civilized community." The threshold of outrageousness is so difficult to reach that, of the intentional infliction of emotional distress claims considered by the Court of Appeals, every one has failed because the alleged conduct was not sufficiently outrageous. Those few claims of intentional infliction of emotional distress that have been upheld by lower courts were supported by allegations detailing a longstanding campaign of deliberate, systemic and malicious harassment of the plaintiff.

Here plaintiff alleges three incidents of littering and a particularly nasty remark. "Noxious and deplorable though this conduct may be, these incidents do not rise to the level of outrageousness of the kind of deliberate and malicious campaign of harassment or intimidation needed to establish the tort."

Case No. 11

INVASION OF PRIVACY

Shields v. Gross

Court of Appeals

58 N.Y.2d 338, 461 N.Y.S.2d 254 (1983)

FACTS: Plaintiff Brooke Shields (Shields), the well-known model and actress, modeled nude in a bathtub for the defendant, photographer Gary Gross (Gross), in 1975 when Shields was ten years old. Before Gross took the pictures, Shields' mother signed two "unrestricted" consent forms authorizing the photographer to use the pictures without any · limitations.

The photographs were financed by Playboy Press and intended for use in a publication entitled *Sugar and Spice*. The pictures were used by the photographer in that magazine as well as in other publications, and in larger- than-life displays in a store on Fifth Avenue in New York City. In addition, Shields used them in a book she prepared about herself.

In 1980 Shields learned that Gross had sold the pictures to numerous magazines. Displeased with the repeated use of the photos Shields brought an action against Gross for violation of her right of privacy. She sought compensation for the damage to her reputation and a court order (injunction) barring Gross from further use of the pictures. Gross denied that his actions constituted invasion of privacy and claimed the consent forms signed by Shields' mother provided the necessary consent for his continued use of the photographs.

ISSUE: Does an unrestricted consent form signed by a parent on behalf of a child bar the child from obtaining damages for the tort of invasion of privacy?

DECISION: Yes, judgment for Gross.

REASONING: In New York State the tort of invasion of privacy consists of using a person's name or picture for trade or advertising purposes without that person's prior written approval. Concerning minors (persons under the age of 18), New York law authorizes a parent or guardian to grant the necessary written approval. Such approval by a parent is binding on the minor and cannot be disaffirmed.

The uses for which a photographer is authorized to use photographs of a person can be restricted by the wording of the consent form. The photographer's permissible use of the photos is limited by the restrictions in the written consent.

Because Shields' mother signed the unrestricted consent form, Gross did not violate Shields' right of privacy by submitting the photos to numerous magazines.

* * * QUESTIONS * * *
(See back of text for answers)

1) Assume Brooke Shields' mother did not intend to give the photographer the right to use the photographs indefinitely. How could she have restricted the photographer's use of the photos?

2) What interests are protected by the tort of invasion of privacy?

Case No. 12

INVASION OF PRIVACY

<u>Gallon v. Hustler Magazine, Inc.</u>

Federal District Court, Southern District of New York

732 F.Supp 322 (1990)

FACTS: In the spring of 1982 plaintiff Sabrina Gallon (Gallon) was photographed nude by Waldo Ramsey (Ramsey), with whom she shared an apartment and had an intimate relationship. Late in 1982 their relationship ended after Gallon was physically and sexually abused in an incident where she had been held against her will for two days. With regard to the nude photographs, Gallon did not sign any release.

Defendant Hustler Magazine Inc. (Hustler) published in October 1983 one of the nude photographs of Gallon taken by Ramsey. Hustler alleged that it had both a properly signed release from Gallon and a verification process aimed at uncovering fraudulent releases. Gallon alleged that the release was fraudulent and is suing for invasion of privacy.

Hustler's verification process did not provide for any independent confirmation of the model's signature, such as requiring it be notarized, or requiring her social security number or driver's license number. Additionally, Hustler's research department failed to follow its own procedures in validating the release submitted by Ramsey.

ISSUE: Is the publication of a nude photograph in Hustler magazine an invasion of privacy where the photographer gave Hustler a written release but Hustler failed to verify its authenticity and it had not been signed by the model?

DECISION: Yes, judgment for Gallon.

REASONING: In New York State, an invasion of privacy includes the use of a person's name, picture, or other likeness for commercial purposes without permission.

In this case, the court noted that "the publication of a photograph of someone in the nude is a highly sensitive matter" and that Hustler acted with reckless disregard to verifying information submitted to it for publication. Gallon was awarded $30,000 for the "resulting persistent mental anguish" caused by this invasion of her privacy.

Case No. 13

INVASION OF PRIVACY

Joseph and Ida Finger v. Omni Publications International, Ltd.

Court of Appeals

77 N.Y.2d 138, 564 N.Y.S.2d 1014 (1990)

FACTS: Omni Publications International, Ltd. (Omni) publishes a monthly magazine entitled *Omni*. The June 1988 edition contained an article entitled "Caffeine and Fast Sperm", about research at the University of Pennsylvania School of Medicine. The article suggested that in vitro fertilization rates could be enhanced by exposing the sperm to high concentrations of caffeine. A photograph used in conjunction with the article portrayed Joseph and Ida Finger (Fingers) with their six attractive and apparently healthy children. The caption under the picture read:

> "Want a big family? Maybe your sperm needs a cup of Java in the morning. Tests reveal that caffeine-spritzed sperm swim faster, which may increase the chances for in vitro fertilization."

The article did not mention the Fingers by name. The Fingers did not use in vitro fertilization to conceive their children, nor did they participate in the caffeine study, nor did they give permission to Omni to use the picture. They sued Omni for invasion of privacy. Omni claimed that since in vitro fertilization is a newsworthy topic, the magazine was legally entitled to use the Fingers' picture without their consent.

ISSUE: Does the newsworthy exception to privacy rights encompass the publication of a picture of a family without their permission in conjunction with an article about an in vitro fertilization study, where the family did not participate in the study or in in vitro fertilization?

DECISION: Yes, judgment for Omni.

REASONING: By statute, New York prohibits the unconsensual use of one's picture or name for trade or advertising purposes. Publication of newsworthy events or matters of public interest are excepted. The newsworthy exception is liberally construed and includes reports of political happenings, social trends, matters of consumer interest such as the fashion world, and matters of scientific and biological interest. Publication without permission of a picture illustrating a matter of public interest is not prohibited as long as the picture has some relationship to the article.

Although the Fingers in this case claim the connection between their family's picture and the in vitro study is too tenuous to be considered a relationship, the connection is sufficient to relieve Omni from liability for invasion of privacy. The theme of fertility is reasonably related to a large family. Said the court,

"That the article also discussed in vitro fertilization as being enhanced by 'caffeine-spritzed sperm' does no more than discuss a specific aspect of fertilization and does not detract from the relationship between the photograph and the article."

NOTE: The facts in the case of <u>Y.G. and L.G. v. The Jewish, Hospital of St. Louis,</u> 795 S.W.2d 488 (Missouri Court of Appeals, 1990) are related but the outcome was different. The plaintiff wife was five months pregnant with triplets which she conceived through in vitro fertilization. The hospital that sponsored the in vitro program invited all participants to a social function to celebrate the program's fifth anniversary. Plaintiff had not disclosed to her friends or family her participation in the program and did not want to attend the anniversary celebration if it was to be publicized in any way. The hospital assured her and her husband that the function would not be publicized. Despite the assurance, a television station televised the event. Plaintiffs sued the hospital and television station for invasion of privacy. They moved to dismiss on the ground that in vitro fertilization was of legitimate public interest. The court denied the motions to dismiss and stated:

"The in vitro program and its success may well have been matters of public interest, but the identity of the plaintiffs participating in the program was, we conclude, a private matter . . . . The in vitro fertilization program participation was certainly not a matter of public record nor did it become of public concern due to any of the ordinary incidents of public concern."

* * * QUESTIONS * * *
(See back of text for answers)

1) The court in this case held in favor of the magazine. Make an argument that would support a decision in favor of the Fingers.

2) Good arguments exist in both sides of many cases. Who resolves the issues presented in a case?

3) Suppose a plaintiff was arrested by mistake and charged with robbery. The local television station filmed the arrest and televised it. Can plaintiff sue successfully for invasion of privacy?

Case No. 14

INVASION OF PRIVACY
<u>Messenger v. Gruner & Jahr Printing and Publishing</u>
New York Court of Appeals
94 NY2d 436, 706 NYS2d 52 (2000)

FACTS: Plaintiff is a 14 year old aspiring model. She posed for a series of photographs to appear in Young and Modern, a magazine for teenage girls published by defendant Gruner & Jahr Printing. Plaintiff consented to the photo shoot, but her parents did not provide written consent. The magazine used the photos to illustrate the "Love Crisis" column. Plaintiff sues for invasion of privacy.

The column began with a letter to the editor from a 14-year old girl identified only as "Mortified." She wrote that she became drunk at a party and then had sex with her 18 year old boyfriend and two of his friends. The editor responded that Mortified should avoid similar situations in the future, and advised her to be tested for pregnancy and sexually transmitted diseases. Above the column, in bold type, is a quotation saying, "I got trashed and had sex with three guys." Three full-color photos of plaintiff illustrate the column. One shows her hiding her face with three young men gloating in the background. The captions are: 1) "Wake up and face the facts; You made a pretty big mistake;" and 2) "Don't try to hide — just ditch him and his buds;" and 3) "Afraid you're pregnant? See a doctor."

Defendant claims it is not liable for invasion of privacy because the photos were used to illustrate a newsworthy column, the pictures had a direct relationship to the article, and the column was not an advertisement in disguise. Plaintiff conceded those facts but argued that the "newsworthy" exception did not apply because the column and pictures, when viewed together, created the false impression that plaintiff was the author of the letter.

ISSUE: Where a photograph that complements a newsworthy magazine story portrays the person in the photo in a false light and is used without written permission, is the magazine liable for invasion of privacy?

DECISION: No, judgment for defendant magazine.

REASONING: Precedents make clear that, where a picture illustrates an article on a matter of public interest, the newsworthy exception bars recovery for invasion of privacy. The courts interpret this exception broadly. The exception does not apply where there is no real relationship between the photo and the article, or the article is an advertisement in disguise.

Newsworthiness includes not only descriptions of actual events but also articles not constituting hard news. Qualifying stories may include political happenings, social trends or any subject of public interest. Whether a piece is newsworthy depends solely on the content of the article and not the publisher's motive to increase circulation.

The newsworthy exception applies even when the use of the picture in conjunction with an article could reasonably be viewed as falsifying or fictionalizing plaintiff's relation to the article. An example in a prior case involved a husband and wife whose picture with their six children was used to illustrate an article about caffeine-aided in vitro fertilization. The couple had not conceived any of their children through in vitro fertilization and they had not participated in the caffeine-aided fertility study. That notwithstanding, the couple's lawsuit for invasion of privacy was dismissed because the article was newsworthy, the picture was reasonably related to the article, and the story was not an advertisement in disguise.

In this case the "Love Crisis" column was newsworthy since it is informative and educational regarding teenage sex, alcohol abuse and pregnancy, all matters of public concern. The photo being of a female the same age as the writer had a direct connection with the article. There is no allegation the article was an advertisement in disguise.

Case No. 15

INVASION OF PRIVACY/CYBERSQUATTING DOMAIN NAMES

Diller v. Steurken

Supreme Court, New York County

185 M2d 274, 712 NYS2d 311 (2000)

FACTS: Plaintiff Barry Diller is the chairman and chief executive officer of USAi, a media and e-commerce company. Defendant collected the names of many celebrities, registered their names as internet domains, and then attempted to sell them to the celebrities at a substantial profit. One of the internet domain names defendant registered was "barrydiller.com". From June 1, 1999 through June 22 defendant's site contained numerous uses of Barry Diller's name and picture. Defendant never asked Diller for permission to use his name or picture.

One June 10 plaintiff wrote to defendant demanding removal from defendant's site all references to Barry Diller. Plaintiff also demanded that defendant transfer the domain name "barrydiller.com" to plaintiff. In response defendant removed plaintiff's picture but did not remove the name and offered to sell the domain name "barrydiller.com" to the plaintiffs for ten million dollars ($10,000,000).

Plaintiff filed suit alleging violation of his right to privacy. In July defendant removed all reference to Barry Diller from its site and stopped offering the domain name for sale, but did not transfer the domain name to plaintiff. Defendant failed to serve an answer in the lawsuit and a default judgment was granted. Plaintiff now seeks a court order to enjoin defendant from using "barrydiller.com" and requiring defendant to transfer the domain name to plaintiff.'

FIRST ISSUE: Is plaintiff entitled to an injunction barring defendant from using the domain name "barrydiller.com"?

DECISION: Yes.

REASONING: An injunction (a court order prohibiting someone from doing some specified act) is the appropriate remedy under New York law when a defendant violates the privacy of a plaintiff.

SECOND ISSUE: Is plaintiff entitled to a court order requiring defendant to transfer to plaintiff the domain name "barrydiller.com"?

DECISION: Yes.

REASONING: A federal law was enacted in November, 1999 called the Anticybersquatting Consumer Protection Act[1] in response to concerns over the proliferation of cybersquatting, that is, the practice of deliberately and in bad faith registering an internet domain name 'in violation of the rights of trademark owners[2]. The remedies for violations occurring after the effective date include money damages and transfer of the domain name to the trademark owner. For violations that occurred before the effective date, as in this case, the sole remedy is transfer of the domain name to the trademark owner.

---

[1] 15 USC § 1051 et seq.

[2] See <u>Virtual Works, Inc. v. Volkswagen of America, Inc.</u>, 200 WL 50988__F3d __ (4th Cir., 2001)

Case No. 16

INVASION OF PRIVACY/STATUTE OF LIMITATIONS
<u>Leary v. Punzi</u>

Supreme Court, Suffolk County
179 M2d 1025, 687 NYS2d 551 (1999)

FACTS: Plaintiff was a former dancer for defendant Long Island Ballet Center. She began the lawsuit on June 30, 1998 and alleges invasion of privacy. Specifically, plaintiff asserts that she was fired by defendant and thereafter, without her permission, an article appeared in a local newspaper on October 2, 1996 identifying her as defendant's manager. In addition plaintiff was identified on defendant's website as a contact person. Her name was removed from the website on July 13, 1997.

Defendant seeks dismissal of plaintiff's action based on the statute of frauds. A cause of action for invasion of privacy must be brought within one year from the alleged violation.

ISSUE: Is plaintiff's lawsuit barred by the statute of limitations?

DECISION: Yes for the newspaper article; no for the website.

REASONING: The newspaper article was published on October 2, 1996, more than a year before this lawsuit was commenced. Therefore any claim relating to that article is untimely. Plaintiff's action as it relates to the newspaper article is dismissed. Concerning the website, the invasion of privacy continued until plaintiff's name and picture were removed on July 13, 1997. Since that date was less than a year before the commencement of this lawsuit, the motion to dismiss with respect to the internet site was denied.

* * * QUESTIONS * * *
(See back of text for answers)

1) What is the statute of limitations?

2) What is the policy reason for having a statute of limitations?

Case No. 17

INTERFERENCE WITH CONTRACTUAL RELATIONS

<u>Click Model Management, Inc. v. Rachel Willis and Christy Turlington</u>

Appellate Division, First Department

561 N.Y.S.2d 781 (1990)

FACTS: Rachel Williams (Williams) is an internationally known model who was represented by Click Model Management, Inc. (Click), a modeling agency. Christy Turlington (Turlington), another internationally known model and a friend of Williams, is represented by Ford Models, Inc. (Ford), an agency that competes with Click.

While Williams and Turlington were on a fashion shoot together, Williams complained to Turlington about the commissions Click was paying her and the modeling jobs she was assigned. Turlington responded, "You ought to come over to Ford." Sometime thereafter, Williams and Turlington worked together at a Calvin Klein show in New York. While together, they placed a call to Ford. Turlington told a Ford employee that Williams wanted to make an appointment to speak with someone at Ford. Turlington then handed the phone to Williams, who made an appointment. Thereafter, Williams left Click and joined Ford.

Click, unhappy about losing Williams, sued Turlington for interference with contractual relations.

ISSUE: Do the facts establish a cause of action for interference with contractual relations?

DECISION: No, judgment for Turlington.

REASONING: To establish a claim for interference with contractual relations, also known as tortious interference with contractual relations, Click was required to prove the following:

> "(1) the existence of a valid contract between Click and Williams; (2) Turlington's knowledge of that contract; (3) Turlington's intentional procuring of the breach of that contract; and (4) damages."

Turlington's conduct does not evidence an intent to procure a breach of contract. Rather, it appears she wished to help a friend who was dissatisfied with Click's services, a dissatisfaction that Turlington did not induce or encourage.

* * * QUESTION * * *
(See back of text for answer)

1)   Can Click successfully sue Williams for breach of contract?

Case No. 18

INTERFERENCE WITH CONTRACTUAL RELATIONS

<u>Rapp Boxx, Inc. v. MTV, Inc.</u>

Appellate Division, First Department

226 AD2d 324, 642 NYS2d 228 (1st Dept, 1996)

FACTS: Plaintiff planned to produce a series of rap music shows. Defendant Lover had contracted to host the series. Thereafter defendant voluntarily and without inducement from defendant MTV canceled his contract with plaintiff. Lover thereafter independently solicited and initiated discussions with MTV for a position as a host on a rap show that competed with plaintiff's show.

ISSUE: Is MTV liable for interference with contractual relations?

DECISION: No.

REASONING: No evidence existed to establish that MTV intentionally induced a breach of Lover's contract with plaintiff. Instead the evidence establishes that Lover voluntarily repudiated his contract with plaintiff and initiated discussions with MTV to host its rap music show. Without evidence that defendant intentionally induced Lover to breach its contract with plaintiff, MTV is not liable for interference with contractual relations.

Case No. 19

WRONGFUL INDUCEMENT OF A BREACH OF CONTRACT

Gold Medal Farms, Inc. v. Rutland County Co-operative Creamery, Inc., et al

Appellate Division, Third Department

9 A.D.2d 473, 195 N.Y.S.2d 179 (1959)

FACTS: Plaintiff Gold Medal Farms, Inc. (Gold Medal) entered a contract with Defendant Rutland County Co-Operative Creamery, Inc. (Rutland), an association of milk producers that received milk from its members and arranged for its sale. The contract between Gold Medal and Rutland provided that Rutland would sell to Gold Medal all the milk Rutland handled for its members during a one year period at an agreed price.

For the first six months of the contract the parties satisfied their obligations. Meanwhile Vermont Milk and Creamery, Inc. (Vermont), which knew about the contract between Rutland and Gold Medal, made an offer to Rutland to purchase the milk at a price substantially higher than the price being paid by Gold Medal. Thereafter, Rutland notified Gold Medal that Rutland would not deliver any more milk to Gold Medal. Rutland then entered into a contract to sell the milk to Vermont. Gold Medal sued Vermont for inducement of a breach of contract.

ISSUE: Where an offeror makes an offer knowing that the offeree, in order to accept the offer, would have to breach a contract with a third party, is the offeror liable to the third party for the tort of wrongful interference with a contractual relationship if the offeree breaks the contract with the third party?

DECISION: Yes, judgment for Gold Medal.

REASONING: Wrongful inducement of a breach of contract occurs when a valid contract exists, the defendant knows of the existence of the contract, and intentionally attempts to persuade one party to the contract to terminate it.

Here Vermont knew of Rutland's contract with Gold Medal. Vermont nonetheless made a financially attractive offer to Rutland which Rutland could not accept without breaching its contract with Gold Medal. Such conduct constitutes the tort of wrongful inducement of a breach of contract.

* * * QUESTIONS * * *
(See back of text for answers)

1) Assume Vermont's offer to purchase milk from Rutland provided that sales to Vermont would not begin until termination of the one year contract between Rutland and Gold Medal. Would Vermont be liable for wrongful inducement of a breach of contract?

2) Assume Vermont did not know of the contract between Gold Medal and Rutland. Would Vermont be liable for wrongful inducement of a breach of contract?

3) What competing interests are involved with the tort of wrongful inducement of a breach of contract?

Case No. 20

INTERFERENCE WITH CONTRACTUAL RELATIONS

<u>Greenberg, Inc. v. Sir-Tech Software, Inc.</u>

Appellate Division, Third Department

245 AD2d 1004, 667 NYS2d 83 (1997)

FACTS: Plaintiff is the creator of the computer game known as Wizardry. In 1981 plaintiff granted defendant an exclusive license to manufacture and market the game and related products. The contract provided for graduated royalty payments to plaintiff and a requirement that all Wizardry games and related products be copyrighted in the name of both plaintiff and defendant. Defendant thereafter marketed the Wizardry products. Defendant entered a contract with the game's designer, David W. Bradley, for delivery of a new Wizardry game named "Crusaders of the Dark Savant" (hereinafter "Crusaders") on or before September 1, 1991. The game was intended to be sold during the lucrative Christmas selling season.

The relationship between plaintiff and defendant soured. In this lawsuit plaintiff is suing defendant promoter and Bradley for trademark and copyright infringement, an accounting, and fraud.

Defendant promoter counter-sued plaintiff for interference with contractual relations claiming that Bradley was distracted by the lawsuit and thus unable to timely complete Crusaders. As a result the Christmas selling season was missed resulting in loss of sales and its investment in promotional materials totaling $950,000. Defendant failed to produce any evidence from Bradley that his progress on Crusaders was in fact impeded by plaintiff's lawsuit against him. A series of correspondence between defendant promoter and Bradley spanning August 1991 through August 1992 detail Bradley's lack of progress on the Crusaders project. They make no reference to the lawsuit.

ISSUE: Is plaintiff liable for interfering with defendant promoter's contract with Bradley?

DECISION: No.

REASONING: To establish a cause of action for tortious interference with a contract, a plaintiff must establish: 1) it had a contract; 2) the defendant knew of the contract; 3) the defendant intentionally induced a breach of the contract; 4) the defendant's actions were in fact a substantial factor in causing the breach; and 5) the plaintiff suffered damages.

The defendant in this case failed to establish that plaintiff, by bringing its lawsuit against defendant and Bradley, intended to interfere with defendant's contract with Bradley. Defendant also failed to prove that plaintiff's lawsuit in fact interfered with Bradley's performance of his contract with defendant to produce Crusaders.

CHAPTER 5

Negligence and Strict Liability

The intentional torts discussed in Chapter 6 all involve acts that the tortfeasor (the one committing the tort) intended to commit. In this chapter, we examine the tort of negligence, which involves acts that depart from a reasonable standard of care and therefore create an unreasonable risk of harm to others. Negligence suits are probably the most prevalent type of lawsuits brought against businesses today. It is therefore essential that businesspersons understand their potential liability for negligent acts. In the concluding pages of this chapter, we also look at another basis for liability in tort—*strict liability*. Under this tort doctrine, liability does not depend on the actor's negligence or intent to harm, but on the breach of an absolute duty to make something safe.

Negligence

In contrast to intentional torts, in torts involving **negligence,** the tortfeasor neither wishes to bring about the consequences of the act nor believes that they will occur. The actor's conduct merely creates a risk of such consequences. If no risk is created, there is no negligence. Moreover, the risk must be foreseeable; that is, it must be such that a reasonable person engaging in the same activity would anticipate the risk and guard against it. In determining what is reasonable conduct, courts consider the nature of the possible harm. Creating a very slight risk of a dangerous explosion might be unreasonable, whereas creating a distinct possibility of someone's burning his or her fingers on a stove might be reasonable.

Many of the actions discussed in the chapter on intentional torts constitute negligence if the element of intent is missing (or cannot be proved). Suppose that Juarez walks up to Natsuyo and intentionally shoves her. Natsuyo falls and breaks her arm as a result. In this situation, Juarez has committed an intentional tort (battery). If Juarez carelessly bumps into Natsuyo, however, and she falls and breaks her arm as a result, Juarez's action constitutes negligence. In either situation, Juarez has committed a tort.

To succeed in a negligence action, the plaintiff must prove each of the following:

1. That the defendant owed a duty of care to the plaintiff.
2. That the defendant breached that duty.
3. That the plaintiff suffered a legally recognizable injury.
4. That the defendant's breach caused the plaintiff's injury.

We discuss here each of these four elements of negligence.

The Duty of Care and Its Breach

Central to the tort of negligence is the concept of a **duty of care.** This concept arises from the notion that if we are to live in society with other people, some actions can be tolerated and some cannot, and some actions are reasonable and some are not. The basic principle underlying the duty of care is that people are free to act as they please so long as their actions do not infringe on the interests of others.

When someone fails to comply with the duty to exercise reasonable care, a potentially tortious act may have been committed. Failure to live up to a standard of care may be an act (setting fire to a building) or an omission (neglecting to put out a campfire). It may be a careless act or a carefully performed but nevertheless dangerous act that results in injury. Courts consider the nature of the act (whether it is outrageous or commonplace), the manner in which the act is performed (heedlessly versus cautiously), and the nature of the injury (whether it is serious or slight) in determining whether the duty of care has been breached.

The Reasonable Person Standard Tort law measures duty by the **reasonable person standard.** In determining whether a duty of care has been breached, for example, the courts ask how a reasonable person would have acted in the same circumstances. The reasonable person standard is said to be (though in an absolute sense it cannot be) objective. It is not necessarily how a particular person *would* act. It is society's judgment of how an ordinarily prudent person *should* act. If the so-called reasonable person existed, he or she would be careful, conscientious, even tempered, and honest. That individuals are required to exercise a reasonable standard of care in their activities is a pervasive concept in business law, and many of the issues discussed in subsequent chapters of this text have to do with this duty.

In negligence cases, the degree of care to be exercised varies, depending on the defendant's occupation or profession, her or his relationship with the plaintiff, and other factors. Generally, whether an action constitutes a breach of the duty of care is determined on a case-by-case basis. The outcome depends on how the judge (or jury, if it is a jury trial) decides a reasonable person in the position of the defendant would act in the particular circumstances of the case. In the following subsections, we examine the degree of care typically expected of landowners and professionals.

The Duty of Landowners Landowners are expected to exercise reasonable care to protect individuals coming onto their property from harm. In some jurisdictions, landowners may even have a duty to protect trespassers against certain risks. Landowners who rent or lease premises to tenants are expected to exercise reasonable care to ensure that the tenants

and their guests are not harmed in common areas, such as stairways, entryways, and laundry rooms (see Chapter 48).

Duty to Warn Business Invitees of Risks. Retailers and other firms that explicitly or implicitly invite persons to come onto their premises are usually charged with a duty to exercise reasonable care to protect these **business invitees.** For example, if you entered a supermarket, slipped on a wet floor, and sustained injuries as a result, the owner of the supermarket would be liable for damages if, when you slipped, there was no sign warning that the floor was wet. A court would hold that the business owner was negligent because the owner failed to exercise a reasonable degree of care in protecting the store's customers against foreseeable risks about which the owner knew or *should have known.* That a patron might slip on the wet floor and be injured as a result was a foreseeable risk, and the owner should have taken care to avoid this risk or warn the customer of it.[1]

Obvious Risks Provide an Exception. Some risks, of course, are so obvious that an owner need not warn of them. For example, a business owner does not need to warn customers to open a door before attempting to walk through it. Other risks, however, even though they may seem obvious to a business owner, may not be so in the eyes of another, such as a child. For example, a hardware store owner may not think it is necessary to warn customers that, if climbed, a stepladder leaning against the back wall of the store could fall down and harm them. It is possible, though, that a child could tip the ladder over while climbing it and be hurt as a result.

The issue in the following case was whether the obviousness of the existence of wet napkins on the floor of a nightclub obviated the owner's duty to its customers to maintain the premises in a safe condition.

---

1. A business owner can warn of a risk in a number of ways; for example, to warn of a hole in the business's parking lot, the owner could place a sign, traffic cone, sawhorse, board, or the like near the hole.

C A S E 5.1 Izquierdo v. Gyroscope, Inc.
District Court of Appeal of Florida, Fourth District, 2007. 946 So.2d 115.

● **Background and Facts** Giorgio's Grill in Hollywood, Florida, is a restaurant that becomes a nightclub after hours. At those times, traditionally, as Giorgio's manager knew, the wait staff and

CASE CONTINUES

CASE 5.1 CONTINUED customers threw paper napkins into the air as the music played. The napkins landed on the floor, but no one picked them up. If they became too deep, customers pushed them to the side. Because drinks were occasionally spilled, sometimes the napkins were wet. One night, Jane Izquierdo went to Giorgio's to meet a friend. She had been to the club five or six times and knew of the napkin-throwing tradition. She had one drink and went to the restroom. On her return, she slipped and fell, breaking her leg. After surgery, she relied on a wheelchair for three months and continued to suffer pain. She filed a suit in a Florida state court against Gyroscope, Inc., the owner of Giorgio's, alleging negligence. A jury returned a verdict in favor of the defendant, and Izquierdo filed a motion for a new trial, which the court denied. She appealed to a state intermediate appellate court.

● **Decision and Rationale** The state intermediate appellate court reversed the lower court's decision, concluding that "the trial court abused its discretion" in denying Izquierdo's motion. The appellate court remanded the case for a new trial. The court reasoned that "the uncontroverted evidence shows at least some negligence on the part of the restaurant." The court emphasized, "[I]mportantly, the manager of the restaurant admitted that permitting the wet napkins to remain on the floor was a hazardous condition." Izquierdo testified that she slipped, fell down on a wet floor, and found napkins on her shoes. "The inference that the wet napkins on the floor caused her fall clearly was the only reasonable inference which could be drawn from the facts." Izquierdo knew of the napkin-throwing tradition, and the existence of napkins on the floor was obvious, but these circumstances "merely discharge[d] the landowner's duty to warn. It does not discharge the landowner's duty to maintain the premises in a reasonably safe condition."

● **What If the Facts Were Different?** *Should the result in this case have been different if, in all the years that the napkin-throwing tradition existed, no one had ever fallen on the napkins before Izquierdo? Why or why not?*

● **The Legal Environment Dimension** *Does a plaintiff's knowledge of a dangerous condition erase a defendant's potential liability for negligently permitting the dangerous condition to exist? Explain.*

PREVENTING LEGAL DISPUTES It can sometimes be difficult for business owners to determine whether risks are obvious. Because the law imposes liability on business owners who fail to discover hidden dangers on the premises and protect patrons from being injured, it is advisable to post warnings of any potential risks on the property. Businesspersons should train their employees to be on the lookout for possibly dangerous conditions on the premises at all times and to notify a superior immediately if they notice something unsafe. Making the business premises as safe as possible for all persons who might be there, including children, elderly persons, and individuals with disabilities, is one of the best ways to prevent potential legal disputes.

The Duty of Professionals If an individual has knowledge or skill superior to that of an ordinary person, the individual's conduct must be consistent with that status. Professionals—including physicians, dentists, architects, engineers, accountants, and lawyers, among others—are required to have a standard minimum level of special knowledge and ability. Therefore, in determining what constitutes reasonable care in the case of professionals, the court takes their training and expertise into account. In other words, an accountant cannot defend against a lawsuit for negligence by stating, "But I was not familiar with that general principle of accounting."

If a professional violates his or her duty of care toward a client, the client may bring a suit against the professional, alleging **malpractice,** which is essentially professional negligence. For example, a patient might sue a physician for *medical malpractice.* A client might sue an attorney for *legal malpractice.* The liability of professionals will be examined in further detail in Chapter 51.

No Duty to Rescue Although the law requires individuals to act reasonably and responsibly in their relations with one another, if a person fails to come to the aid of a stranger in peril, that person will not be considered negligent under tort law. Assume that you are walking down a city street and see a pedestrian about to step directly in front of an oncoming bus. You realize that the person has not seen the bus and is unaware of the danger. Do you have a legal duty to warn that individual? No. Although most people would probably concede that, in this situation, the observer has an *ethical* duty to warn the other, tort law does not impose a general duty to rescue others in peril. Duties may be imposed in regard to certain types of peril, however. For example, most states require a motorist involved in an automobile accident to stop and render aid. Failure to do so is both a tort and a crime.

The Injury Requirement and Damages

To recover damages (receive compensation), the plaintiff in a tort lawsuit must prove that she or he suffered a *legally recognizable* injury. In other words, the plaintiff must have suffered some loss, harm, wrong, or invasion of a protected interest. This is true in lawsuits for intentional torts as well as lawsuits for negligence. Essentially, the purpose of tort law is to compensate for legally recognized harms and injuries resulting from wrongful acts. If no harm or injury results from a given negligent action, there is nothing to compensate—and no tort exists.

For example, if you carelessly bump into a passerby, who stumbles and falls as a result, you may be liable in tort if the passerby is injured in the fall. If the person is unharmed, however, there normally can be no suit for damages because no injury was suffered. Although the passerby might be angry and suffer emotional distress, few courts recognize negligently inflicted emotional distress as a tort unless it results in some physical disturbance or dysfunction.

Compensatory damages are the norm in negligence cases. Occasionally, though, a court will award punitive damages if the defendant's conduct was grossly negligent, meaning that the defendant intentionally failed to perform a duty with reckless disregard of the consequences to others.

Causation

Another element necessary to the tort of negligence—and intentional torts as well—is *causation*. If a person breaches a duty of care and someone suffers injury, the wrongful activity must have caused the harm for a tort to have been committed.

Causation in Fact and Proximate Cause

In deciding whether the requirement of causation is met, the court must address two questions:

1. *Is there causation in fact?* Did the injury occur because of the defendant's act, or would it have occurred anyway? If an injury would not have occurred without the defendant's act, then there is causation in fact. **Causation in fact** can usually be determined by use of the *but for* test: "but for" the wrongful act, the injury would not have occurred. This test determines whether there was an actual cause-and-effect relationship between the act and the injury suffered. In theory, causation in fact is limitless. One could claim, for example, that "but for" the creation of the world, a particular injury would not have occurred. Thus, as a practical matter, the law has to establish limits, and it does so through the concept of proximate cause.

2. *Was the act the proximate, or legal, cause of the injury?* **Proximate cause,** or *legal cause,* exists when the connection between an act and an injury is strong enough to justify imposing liability. Consider an example. Ackerman carelessly leaves a campfire burning. The fire not only burns down the forest but also sets off an explosion in a nearby chemical plant that spills chemicals into a river, killing all the fish for a hundred miles downstream and ruining the economy of a tourist resort. Should Ackerman be liable to the resort owners? To the tourists whose vacations were ruined? These are questions of proximate cause that a court must decide.

Both questions must be answered in the affirmative for liability in tort to arise. If a defendant's action constitutes causation in fact but a court decides that the action is not the proximate cause of the plaintiff's injury, the causation requirement has not been met—and the defendant normally will not be liable to the plaintiff.

Foreseeability Questions of proximate cause are linked to the concept of foreseeability because it would be unfair to impose liability on a defendant unless the defendant's actions created a foreseeable risk of injury. Probably the most cited case on the concept of foreseeability and proximate cause is the *Palsgraf* case. The question before the court was as follows: Does the defendant's duty of care extend only to those who may be injured as a result of a foreseeable risk, or does it extend also to persons whose injuries could not reasonably be foreseen?

C A S E 5.2 Palsgraf v. Long Island Railroad Co.
Court of Appeals of New York, 1928. 248 N.Y. 339, 162 N.E. 99.

● **Background and Facts** The plaintiff, Helen Palsgraf, was waiting for a train on a station platform. A man carrying a package was rushing to catch a train that was moving away from a platform across the tracks from Palsgraf. As the man attempted to jump aboard the moving train, he seemed unsteady and about to fall. A railroad guard on the car reached forward to grab him, and another guard on the platform pushed him from behind to help him board the train. In the process, the man's package, which (unknown to the railroad guards) contained fireworks, fell on the railroad tracks and exploded. There was nothing about the package to indicate its contents. The repercussions of the explosion caused scales at the other end of the train platform to fall on Palsgraf, causing injuries for which she sued the railroad company. At the trial, the jury found that the railroad guards had been negligent in their conduct. The railroad company appealed. The appellate court affirmed the trial court's judgment, and the railroad company appealed to New York's highest state court.

● **Decision and Rationale** The New York Court of Appeals dismissed Palsgraf's complaint. The conduct of the railroad employees may have been negligent toward the man with the package, but it was not negligent in relation to Palsgraf, who was standing far away. The railroad was not negligent toward her because her injury had not been foreseeable. "Nothing in the situation gave notice * * * of peril to persons thus removed. * * * [No] hazard was apparent to the eye of ordinary vigilance * * * with reference to her." The court stated the principle as "the risk reasonably to be perceived defines the duty to be obeyed." To rule otherwise "would entail liability for any and all consequences, however novel or extraordinary."

● **Impact of This Case on Today's Law** *The* Palsgraf *case established foreseeability as the test for proximate cause. Today, the courts continue to apply this test in determining proximate cause—and thus tort liability for injuries. Generally, if the victim of a harm or the consequences of a harm done are unforeseeable, there is no proximate cause.*

● **The Global Dimension** *What would be the advantages and disadvantages of a universal principle of proximate cause applied everywhere by all courts in all relevant cases? Discuss.*

Defenses to Negligence

The basic defenses to liability in negligence cases are (1) assumption of risk, (2) superseding cause, and (3) contributory and comparative negligence. Additionally, defendants often defend against negligence claims by asserting that the plaintiffs failed to prove the existence of one or more of the required elements for negligence.

Assumption of Risk

A plaintiff who voluntarily enters into a risky situation, knowing the risk involved, will not be allowed to recover. This is the defense of **assumption of risk.** The requirements of this defense are (1) knowledge of the risk and (2) voluntary assumption of the risk. This

defense is frequently asserted when the plaintiff is injured during recreational activities that involve known risk, such as skiing and parachuting.

The risk can be assumed by express agreement, or the assumption of risk can be implied by the plaintiff's knowledge of the risk and subsequent conduct. For example, a driver entering an automobile race knows there is a risk of being injured or killed in a crash. The driver has assumed the risk of injury. Of course, the plaintiff does not assume a risk different from or greater than the risk normally carried by the activity. In our example, the race driver assumes the risk of being injured in the race but not the risk that the banking in the curves of the racetrack will give way during the race because of a construction defect.

Risks are not deemed to be assumed in situations involving emergencies. Neither are they assumed when a statute protects a class of people from harm and a member of the class is injured by the harm. For example, courts have generally held that an employee cannot assume the risk of an employer's violation of safety statutes passed for the benefit of employees.

In the following case, a ball kicked by a player practicing on a nearby field injured a man who was attending his son's soccer tournament. The question before the court was whether a bystander who was not watching a soccer match at the time of injury had nevertheless assumed the risk of being struck by a wayward ball.

C A S E **5.3** **Sutton v. Eastern New York Youth Soccer Association, Inc.**
New York Supreme Court, Appellate Division, Third Department, 2004.
8 A.D.3d 855, 779 N.Y.S.2d 149.

● **Background and Facts** On May 30, 1999, James Sutton's son, a member of the Latham Circle Soccer Club, was participating in a Highland Soccer Club Tournament at Maalyck Park in Glenville, New York. Sutton attended as a spectator. After watching his son's second game from the sidelines, Sutton walked to the end of the field to a tent that his son's team had put up thirty to forty yards behind the goal line to provide shade for the players when they were not engaged on the field. Half a dozen players from the Guilderland Soccer Club were on the field warming up for the next game. In the tent, while taking a sandwich from a cooler, Sutton was struck in the chest and knocked off his feet by a ball kicked from the field by a Guilderland player, Ian Goss. Sutton filed a suit in a New York state court against the Eastern New York Soccer Association and others sponsoring or participating in the tournament, as well as Goss, seeking to recover damages for knee injuries he sustained as a result of the accident. The court found that Sutton had assumed the risk of being struck by a soccer ball, issued a summary judgment in favor of all of the defendants, and dismissed the complaint. Sutton appealed this order to a state intermediate appellate court.

● **Decision and Rationale** The state intermediate appellate court affirmed the order of the lower court. "The doctrine of assumption of risk can apply not only to participants of sporting events, but to spectators and bystanders who are not actively engaged in watching the event at the time of their injury. Indeed, the spectator at a sporting event, no less than the participant, accepts the dangers that [are inherent] in it so far as they are obvious and necessary." This "tournament involved hundreds of players with teams playing at various times on at least five fields and plaintiff had been at the tournament all morning, surrounded by this activity." Sutton argued that the "defendants unreasonably enhanced the risk of injury *   *   * by essentially inviting him to stand at the end of the field through their placement of the team tent." The court reasoned, however, that "just as the owner of a baseball park is not responsible for the spectator who leaves his or her seat and walks through a potentially more hazardous zone to reach a bathroom or concession stand, thereby assuming the open and obvious risk of being hit by a ball, defendants here cannot be held responsible for the risk assumed by plaintiff when he, aware that players were active on the field, left the sidelines and stood in the tent positioned in the arguably more dangerous zone behind the goal line." Also, Sutton "was familiar with the game of soccer, having admittedly been a frequent spectator of the game for over 14 years."

● **The Legal Environment Dimension** *What is the basis underlying the defense of assumption of risk, and how does that basis support the court's decision in the* Sutton *case?*

● **What If the Facts Were Different?** *Had the plaintiffs prevailed, how might the sites for soccer matches be different today?*

Superseding Cause

An unforeseeable intervening event may break the causal connection between a wrongful act and an injury to another. If so, the intervening event acts as a *superseding cause*—that is, it relieves a defendant of

liability for injuries caused by the intervening event. For example, Derrick, while riding his bicycle, negligently hits Julie, who is walking on the sidewalk. As a result of the impact, Julie falls and fractures her hip. While she is waiting for help to arrive, a small aircraft crashes nearby and explodes, and some of the fiery debris hits her, causing her to sustain severe burns. Derrick will be liable for the damages caused by Julie's fractured hip, but normally he will not be liable for the injuries caused by the plane crash—because the risk of a plane crashing nearby and injuring Julie was not foreseeable.

Contributory and Comparative Negligence

All individuals are expected to exercise a reasonable degree of care in looking out for themselves. In the past, under the common law doctrine of **contributory negligence,** a plaintiff who was also negligent (failed to exercise a reasonable degree of care) could not recover anything from the defendant. Under this rule, no matter how insignificant the plaintiff's negligence was relative to the defendant's negligence, the plaintiff would be precluded from recovering any damages. Today, only a few jurisdictions still hold to this doctrine.

In the majority of states, the doctrine of contributory negligence has been replaced by a **comparative negligence** standard. The comparative negligence standard enables both the plaintiff's and the defendant's negligence to be computed and the liability for damages distributed accordingly. Some jurisdictions have adopted a "pure" form of comparative negligence that allows the plaintiff to recover damages even if her or his fault is greater than that of the defendant. Many states' comparative negligence statutes, however, contain a "50 percent" rule, under which the plaintiff recovers nothing if she or he was more than 50 percent at fault. Under this rule, a plaintiff who is 35 percent at fault could recover 65 percent of his or her damages, but a plaintiff who is 65 percent (over 50 percent) at fault could recover nothing.

Special Negligence Doctrines and Statutes

A number of special doctrines and statutes relating to negligence are also important. We examine a few of them here.

Res Ipsa Loquitur

Generally, in lawsuits involving negligence, the plaintiff has the burden of proving that the defendant was negligent. In certain situations, however, the courts may presume that negligence has occurred, in which case the burden of proof rests on the defendant—that is, the defendant must prove that he or she was *not* negligent. The presumption of the defendant's negligence is known as the doctrine of **res ipsa loquitur,**[2] which translates as "the facts speak for themselves."

This doctrine is applied only when the event creating the damage or injury is one that ordinarily does not occur in the absence of negligence. Suppose that a person undergoes abdominal surgery and following the surgery has nerve damage in her spine near the area of the operation. In this situation, the person can sue the surgeon under a theory of *res ipsa loquitur,* because the injury would not have occurred in the absence of the surgeon's negligence.[3] For the doctrine of *res ipsa loquitur* to apply, the event must have been within the defendant's power to control, and it must not have been due to any voluntary action or contribution on the part of the plaintiff.

Negligence *Per Se*

Certain conduct, whether it consists of an action or a failure to act, may be treated as **negligence *per se*** ("in or of itself"). Negligence *per se* may occur if an individual violates a statute or an ordinance providing for a criminal penalty and that violation causes another to be injured. The injured person must prove (1) that the statute clearly sets out what standard of conduct is expected, when and where it is expected, and of whom it is expected; (2) that he or she is in the class intended to be protected by the statute; and (3) that the statute was designed to prevent the type of injury that he or she suffered. The standard of conduct required by the statute is the duty that the defendant owes to the plaintiff, and a violation of the statute is the breach of that duty.

For example, a statute provides that anyone who operates a motor vehicle on a public highway and fails to give full time and attention to the operation of that vehicle is guilty of inattentive driving. After an accident involving two motor vehicles, one of the drivers is cited for and later found guilty of violating the inattentive driver statute. If the other driver was injured and subsequently files a lawsuit, a court could consider the violation of the statute to constitute negligence *per se*. The statute sets forth a standard of attentive driving specifically to protect the safety of the traveling public.[4]

2. Pronounced *rihz ihp*-suh *low*-kwuh-duhr.
3. See, for example, *Gubbins v. Hurson,* 885 A.2d 269 (D.C. 2005).
4. See, for example, *Wright v. Moore,* 931 A.2d 405 (Del.Supr. 2007).

"Danger Invites Rescue" Doctrine

Under the "danger invites rescue" doctrine, a person who is injured while going to someone else's rescue can sue the person who caused the dangerous situation. The original wrongdoer is liable not only for the injuries to the person who was placed in danger, but also for injuries to an individual attempting a rescue. The idea is that the rescuer should not be held liable for any damages because he or she did not cause the danger and because danger invites rescue. For example, Ludlam, while driving down a street, fails to see a stop sign because he is trying to end a squabble between his two young children in the car's backseat. Salter, on the curb near the stop sign, realizes that Ludlam is about to hit a pedestrian walking across the street at the intersection. Salter runs into the street to push the pedestrian out of the way, and Ludlam's vehicle hits Salter instead. Ludlam will be liable for Salter's injury as the rescuer, as well as for any injuries the other pedestrian (or any bystanders) may have sustained.

Special Negligence Statutes

A number of states have enacted statutes prescribing duties and responsibilities in certain circumstances. For example, most states now have what are called **Good Samaritan statutes.**[5] Under these statutes, persons who are aided voluntarily by others cannot turn around and sue the "Good Samaritans" for negligence. These laws were passed largely to protect physicians and other medical personnel who volunteer their services for free in emergency situations to those in need, such as individuals hurt in car accidents.[6]

Many states have also passed **dram shop acts,**[7] under which a tavern owner or bartender may be held liable for injuries caused by a person who became intoxicated while drinking at the bar or who was already intoxicated when served by the bartender. Some states' statutes also impose liability on *social hosts* (persons hosting parties) for injuries caused by guests who became intoxicated at the hosts' homes. Under these statutes, it is unnecessary to prove that the tavern owner, bartender, or social host was negligent. Sometimes, the definition of a "social host" is broadly fashioned. For example, in a New York case, the court held that the father of a minor who hosted a "bring-your-own-keg" party could be held liable for injuries caused by an intoxicated guest.[8]

Strict Liability

Another category of torts is called **strict liability,** or *liability without fault.* Intentional torts and torts of negligence involve acts that depart from a reasonable standard of care and cause injuries. Under the doctrine of strict liability, a person who engages in certain activities can be held responsible for any harm that results to others even if the person used the utmost care.

Development of Strict Liability

The modern concept of strict liability traces its origins, in part, to the 1868 English case of *Rylands v. Fletcher.*[9] In the coal-mining area of Lancashire, England, the Rylands, who were mill owners, had constructed a reservoir on their land. Water from the reservoir broke through a filled-in shaft of an abandoned coal mine nearby and flooded the connecting passageways in an active coal mine owned by Fletcher. Fletcher sued the Rylands, and the court held that the defendants (the Rylands) were liable, even though the circumstances did not fit within existing tort liability theories. The court held that a "person who for his own purposes brings on his land and collects and keeps there anything likely to do mischief if it escapes . . . is *prima facie* [on initial examination] answerable for all the damage which is the natural consequence of its escape."

British courts liberally applied the doctrine that emerged from the *Rylands v. Fletcher* case. Initially, few U.S. courts accepted this doctrine, presumably because the courts were worried about its effect on the expansion of American business. Today, however, the doctrine of strict liability is the norm rather than the exception.

---

5. These laws derive their name from the Good Samaritan story in the Bible. In the story, a traveler who had been robbed and beaten lay along the roadside, ignored by those passing by. Eventually, a man from the region of Samaria (the "Good Samaritan") stopped to render assistance to the injured person.

6. See, for example, the discussions of various state statutes in *Chamley v. Khokha,* 730 N.W.2d 864 (N.D. 2007); and *Mueller v. McMillian Warner Insurance Co.,* 2006 WI 54, 290 Wis.2d 571, 714 N.W.2d 183 (2006).

7. Historically, a dram was a small unit of liquid, and spirits were sold in drams. Thus, a dram shop was a place where liquor was sold in drams.

8. *Rust v. Reyer,* 91 N.Y.2d 355, 693 N.E.2d 1074, 670 N.Y.S.2d 822 (1998).

9. 3 L.R.–E & I App. [Law Reports, English & Irish Appeal Cases] (H.L. [House of Lords] 1868).

Abnormally Dangerous Activities

Strict liability for damages proximately caused by an abnormally dangerous, or ultrahazardous, activity is one application of strict liability. Courts apply the doctrine of strict liability in these situations because of the extreme risk of the activity. Abnormally dangerous activities are those that involve a high risk of serious harm to persons or property that cannot be completely guarded against by the exercise of reasonable care—activities such as blasting or storing explosives. Even if blasting with dynamite is performed with all reasonable care, there is still a risk of injury. Balancing that risk against the potential for harm, it seems reasonable to ask the person engaged in the activity to pay for injuries caused by that activity. Although there is no fault, there is still responsibility because of the dangerous nature of the undertaking.

Other Applications of Strict Liability

Persons who keep wild animals are strictly liable for any harm inflicted by the animals. The basis for applying strict liability is that wild animals, should they escape from confinement, pose a serious risk of harm to persons in the vicinity. An owner of domestic animals (such as dogs, cats, cows, or sheep) may be strictly liable for harm caused by those animals if the owner knew, or should have known, that the animals were dangerous or had a propensity to harm others.

A significant application of strict liability is in the area of product liability—liability of manufacturers and sellers for harmful or defective products. Liability here is a matter of social policy and is based on two factors: (1) the manufacturing company can better bear the cost of injury because it can spread the cost throughout society by increasing prices of goods, and (2) the manufacturing company is making a profit from its activities and therefore should bear the cost of injury as an operating expense. We will discuss product liability in greater detail in Chapter 23. Strict liability is also applied in certain types of *bailments* (a bailment exists when goods are transferred temporarily into the care of another—see Chapter 47).

REVIEWING Negligence and Strict Liability

Alaina Sweeney went to Ragged Mountain Ski Resort in New Hampshire with a friend. Alaina went snow tubing down a snow-tube run designed exclusively for snow tubers. There were no Ragged Mountain employees present in the snow-tube area to instruct Alaina on the proper use of a snow tube. On her fourth run down the trail, Alaina crossed over the center line between snow-tube lanes, collided with another snow tuber, and was injured. Alaina filed a negligence action against Ragged Mountain seeking compensation for the injuries that she sustained. Two years earlier, the New Hampshire state legislature had enacted a statute that prohibited a person who participates in the sport of skiing from suing a ski-area operator for injuries caused by the risks inherent in skiing. Using the information presented in the chapter, answer the following questions.

1. What defense will Ragged Mountain probably assert?
2. The central question in this case is whether the state statute establishing that skiers assume the risks inherent in the sport bars Alaina's suit. What would your decision be on this issue? Why?
3. Suppose that the court concludes that the statute applies only to skiing and does not apply to snow tubing. Will Alaina's lawsuit be successful? Explain.
4. Now suppose that the jury concludes that Alaina was partly at fault for the accident. Under what theory might her damages be reduced in proportion to the degree to which her actions contributed to the accident and her resulting injuries?

TERMS AND CONCEPTS

assumption of risk 138

business invitee 135

causation in fact 137

comparative negligence 140

contributory negligence 140

dram shop act 141

duty of care 134

Good Samaritan statute 141

malpractice 136

negligence 134

negligence *per se* 140

proximate cause 137

reasonable person standard 135

res ipsa loquitur 140

strict liability 141

QUESTIONS AND CASE PROBLEMS

7-1. Shannon's physician gives her some medication and tells her not to drive after she takes it, as the medication induces drowsiness. In spite of the doctor's warning, Shannon decides to drive while medicated. Owing to her lack of alertness, she fails to stop at a traffic light and crashes into another vehicle, causing a passenger to be injured. Is Shannon liable for the tort of negligence? Explain.

7-2. QUESTION WITH SAMPLE ANSWER

Ruth carelessly parks her car on a steep hill, leaving the car in neutral and failing to engage the parking brake. The car rolls down the hill and knocks down an electric line. The sparks from the broken line ignite a grass fire. The fire spreads until it reaches a barn one mile away. The barn houses dynamite, and the burning barn explodes, causing part of the roof to fall on and injure Jim, a passing motorist. Which element of negligence is of the greatest concern here? What legal doctrine resolves this issue? Will Jim be able to recover damages from Ruth?

- For a sample answer to Question 7–2,
  go to Appendix C at the end of this text.

7-3. Danny and Marion Klein were injured when part of a fireworks display went astray and exploded near them. They sued Pyrodyne Corp., the pyrotechnic company that was hired to set up and discharge the fireworks, alleging, among other things, that the company should be strictly liable for damages caused by the fireworks display. Will the court agree with the Kleins? What factors will the court consider in making its decision? Discuss fully.

7-4. CASE PROBLEM WITH SAMPLE ANSWER

New Hampshire International Speedway, Inc., owned the New Hampshire International Speedway, a racetrack next to Route 106 in Loudon, New Hampshire. In August 1998, on the weekend before the Winston Cup race, Speedway opened part of its parking facility to recreational vehicles (RVs). Speedway voluntarily positioned its employee Frederick Neergaard at the entrance to the parking area as a security guard and to direct traffic. Leslie Wheeler, who was planning to attend the race, drove an RV south on Route 106 toward Speedway. Meanwhile, Dennis Carignan was also driving south on Route 106 on a motorcycle, on which Mary Carignan was a passenger. As Wheeler approached the parking area, he saw Neergaard signaling him to turn left, which he began to do. At the same time, Carignan attempted to pass the RV on its left side, and the two vehicles collided. Mary sustained an injury to her right knee, lacerations on her ankle, and a broken hip. She sued Speedway and others for negligence. Which element of negligence is at the center of this dispute? How is a court likely to rule in this case, and why? [*Carignan v. New Hampshire International Speedway, Inc.*, 858 A.2d 536 (N.H. 2004)]

- To view a sample answer for Problem 7–4, go to this book's Web site at www.cengage. com/blaw/jentz, select "Chapter 7," and click on "Case Problem with Sample Answer."

7-5. Negligence. In July 2004, Emellie Anderson hired Kenneth Whitten, a licensed building contractor, to construct a two-story addition to her home. The bottom floor was to be a garage and the second floor a home office. In August, the parties signed a second contract under which Whitten agreed to rebuild a deck and railing attached to the house and to further improve the office. A later inspection revealed gaps in the siding on the new garage, nails protruding from incomplete framing, improper support for a stairway to the office, and gaps in its plywood flooring. One post supporting the deck was cracked; another was too short. Concrete had not been poured underneath the old posts. A section of railing was missing, and what was installed was warped, with gaps at the joints. Anderson filed a suit in a Connecticut state court against Whitten, alleging that his work was "substandard, not to code, unsafe and not done in a [workmanlike] manner." Anderson claimed that she would have to pay someone else to repair all of the work. Does Whitten's "work" satisfy the requirements for a claim grounded in negligence? Should Anderson's complaint be dismissed, or should she be awarded damages? Explain. [*Anderson v. Whitten*, 100 Conn.App. 730, 918 A.2d 1056 (2007)]

7-6. Defenses to Negligence. Neal Peterson's entire family skied, and Peterson started skiing at the age of two. In 2000, at the age of eleven, Peterson was in his fourth year as a member of a ski race team. One morning in February, Peterson was practicing his skills and was coming down a slope so fast that his skis were not touching the ground. At that point, Peterson collided with David Donahue. Donahue, a forty-three-year-old advanced skier, was skating (skiing slowly) across the slope toward the parking lot. Peterson and Donahue knew that falls or collisions and accidents and injuries were possible with skiing. Donahue saw Peterson "split seconds" before the impact, which knocked Donahue out of his skis and down the slope ten or twelve feet. When Donahue saw Peterson lying motionless nearby, he immediately sought help. To recover for his injuries, Peterson filed a suit in a Minnesota state court against Donahue, alleging negligence. Based on these facts, which defense to a claim of negligence is Donahue most likely to assert? How is the court likely to apply that defense and rule on Peterson's claim? Why? [*Peterson* ex rel. *Peterson v. Donahue*, 733 N.W.2d 790 (Minn. App. 2007)]

7-7. A QUESTION OF ETHICS

Donald and Gloria Bowden hosted a late afternoon cookout at their home in South Carolina, inviting mostly business acquaintances. Justin Parks, who was nineteen years old, attended the party. Alcoholic beverages were available to all of the guests, even those who, like Parks, were not minors but were underage. Parks consumed alcohol at the party and left with other guests. One of these guests detained Parks at the guest's home to give Parks time to "sober up." Parks then drove himself from this guest's home and was killed in a one-car accident. At the time of his death, he had a blood alcohol content of 0.291 percent, which exceeded the state's limit for driving a motor vehicle. Linda Marcum, Parks's mother, filed a suit in a South Carolina state court against the Bowdens and others, alleging that they were negligent. *[Marcum v. Bowden, 372 S.C. 452, 643 S.E.2d 85 (2007)]*

(a) Considering the principles discussed in this chapter, what are arguments in favor of, and opposed to, holding social hosts liable in this situation? Explain.

(b) The states vary widely in assessing liability and imposing sanctions in the circumstances described in this problem. Broadly, in other words, justice is not equal for parents and other social hosts who serve alcoholic beverages to underage individuals. Why?

7-8. VIDEO QUESTION

Go to this text's Web site at **www.cengage. com/blaw/jentz**, and select "Chapter 7." Click on "Video Questions" and view the video titled *Jaws.* Then answer the following questions.

(a) In the video, the mayor (Murray Hamilton) and a few other men try to persuade Chief Brody (Roy Scheider) not to close the town's beaches. If Brody keeps the beaches open and a swimmer is injured or killed because he failed to warn swimmers about the potential shark danger, has Brody committed the tort of negligence? Explain.

(b) Can Chief Brody be held liable for any injuries or deaths to swimmers under the doctrine of strict liability? Why or why not?

(c) Suppose that Chief Brody goes against the mayor's instructions and warns townspeople to stay off the beach. Nevertheless, several swimmers do not heed his warning and are injured as a result. What defense or defenses could Brody raise under these circumstances if he is sued for negligence?

LAW ON THE WEB

For updated links to resources available on the Web, as well as a variety of other materials, visit this text's Web site at

www.cengage.com/blaw/jentz

You can find cases and articles on torts, including business torts, in the tort law library at the Internet Law Library's Web site. Go to

www.lawguru.com/ilawlib

Legal Research Exercises on the Web

Go to **www.cengage.com/blaw/jentz**, the Web site that accompanies this text. Select "Chapter 7" and click on "Internet Exercises." There you will find the following Internet research exercises that you can perform to learn more about the topics covered in this chapter.

Internet Exercise 7–1: Legal Perspective
 Negligence and the *Titanic*

Internet Exercise 7–2: Management Perspective
 The Duty to Warn

Case No. 23

NEGLIGENCE/BREACH OF DUTY

Palsgraf v. The Long Island Railroad Company

Court of Appeals

248 N.Y. 339, 162 N.E. 99 (1928)

FACTS: While waiting for a train to Rockaway Beach, plaintiff Helen Palsgraf (Palsgraf) was injured by an explosion in a train station of the defendant Long Island Railroad Company (the Railroad).

As a train was beginning to pull out of the station, a man carrying a package approximately 15 inches long and wrapped in newspaper attempted to board the moving train. The man appeared unsteady to a guard on the train who reached to help the man board. Another guard on the platform pushed the man from behind. This pulling and pushing caused him to drop the package. It contained fireworks, which exploded when the package fell. The explosion caused scales at the other end of the platform to fall, striking Palsgraf and injuring her. Palsgraf contended that the guards were negligent and sued the Railroad for her injuries. The Railroad denied that the guards breached any duty owed to Palsgraf.

ISSUE: Under the circumstances of this case, did the Railroad breach a duty owed to Palsgraf?

DECISION: No, judgment for the Railroad.

REASONING: For a defendant to be liable for negligence a duty of care must exist and the defendant must have violated it. The court in this case identified the rule for determining whether a duty of care exists as follows: "The risk reasonably to be perceived defines the duty to be obeyed . . . ." Since the guards had no way of knowing the contents of the package they could not have foreseen from their acts the risk of injury to Palsgraf. Therefore no duty existed by the Railroad to Palsgraf and no duty was violated.

* * * QUESTIONS * * *
(See back of text for answers)

1) The law requires an employer to compensate a person who is injured by the acts of a negligent employee. In this case Palsgraf sued the Railroad as the employer of the guards. What is the reasoning for this rule?

2) Would the result in this case be different if the man's package had been clearly labeled as containing explosives?

3) If Palsgraf were to sue the man with the package for negligence should she be successful?

Case No. 24

NEGLIGENCE/FORESEEABILITY

Martinez v. Santoro d/b/a McDonald's Restaurant

Appellate Division, Second Department

273 AD2d 448, 710 NYS2d 374 (2000)

FACTS: Plaintiff was standing near the door of a McDonald's restaurant. She was knocked down by a panhandler who was opening the door to the restaurant. She sued the restaurant claiming it breached its duty to maintain the premises in a reasonably safe manner.

ISSUE: Did the restaurant breach a duty it owed to plaintiff?

DECISION: No.

REASONING: A party who owns or is in possession of real property is under a duty to exercise reasonable care to maintain that property in a safe condition. This duty requires that the owner of possessor protect members of the public from the reasonably foreseeable acts of third persons (someone other than the party injured and the owner or tenant of the property). However there is no legal duty to protect against an occurrence that is unusual and would not suggest itself to a reasonably careful and prudent person.

The incident between the panhandler and the plaintiff was unexpected and unforeseeable. Even a reasonably careful and prudent person would not have anticipated the encounter and thus could not protect against it.

Case No. 25

NEGLIGENCE/BREACH OF DUTY

Merrill v. The State of New York

Court of Claims

110 Misc.2d 260, 442 N.Y.S.2d 352 (1981)

FACTS: Plaintiff Theophane Merrill and his wife Virginia, both deaf, attended the New York State Fair in Syracuse, New York, with their two children on September 3, 1977. They drove to the fair from their home in Rochester. When they reached the fairgrounds, at about 1:30 p.m., the parking lots were full. At the direction of a state trooper they parked their car near the fairgrounds on a grassy median of Interstate Route 690. The median, which had been used for parking for the state fair in prior years, was in the middle of three lanes of eastbound traffic and two lanes of westbound traffic. The speed limit on Route 690 was 55 m.p.h.

To reach the fairgrounds from the median pedestrians had to cross the three lanes of eastbound traffic.

The Merrills reached the fairgrounds safely and remained at the fair until midnight. After leaving the fairgrounds they crossed the three lanes of traffic to the median but then had difficulty finding their car. The state trooper who had directed them earlier was not present. The median had no street lights. The Merrills, trying to find their car, walked back and forth single file along the median, on the yellow line that identified the edge of the lane of highway. While their backs faced oncoming traffic a car hit Theophane Merrill, cutting off part of his right arm. At the moment he was hit, Merrill was slightly to the right of the yellow line in a lane of traveled highway.

No signs along the median warned drivers of pedestrian traffic.

Merrill sued the State of New York for negligence, seeking compensation for his injuries.

ISSUE: Did the State of New York breach a duty of care by directing fairgoers to park in the median of an interstate highway?

DECISION: Yes, judgment for Merrill.

REASONING: Directing cars to park on a state highway created a foreseeable risk of injury to the fairgoers. The state, having created such a risk, had a duty to protect against the foreseeable injury. It failed to meet this responsibility. Fairgoers had to cross three lanes of highway traffic, the highway was not lighted, no trooper was present to direct traffic, and no warning signs for drivers were installed. The state's conduct thus constituted negligence. The state was therefore liable to Merrill who was injured by the negligence.

The court acknowledged that Merrill was acting negligently at the time he was hit. By walking on the portion of the highway used by cars with his back to traffic Merrill was exposing himself to the foreseeable risk of injury from an oncoming car.

Applying the rule of comparative negligence, 10% of the liability for the accident was allocated to him.

NOTE: The operator of the car that hit Merrill was also found to be negligent. The driver paid a portion of the damages awarded to Merrill pursuant to an out-of-court settlement.

* * * QUESTIONS * * *
(See back of text for answers)

1) What actions might the state have taken to avoid liability in this case?

2) Would the outcome have been different if Merrill was not deaf? Why or why not?

Case No. 26

NEGLIGENCE

Pappalardo v. New York Health & Racquet Club

Appellate Division, First Department

718 NYS2d 287 (2000)

FACTS: Defendant New York Health & Racquet Club ("HRC") operates a health and fitness center on three floors in a building on 13th Street in New York City. Plaintiff was a member of HRC. While working out there with his friend Cheryl Joseph on January 21, 1996 he was injured while using a leg curl machine located in a room on the second floor of the building. The machine was one in a circuit of approximately ten exercise machines which ran parallel to a large window overlooking East 13th Street. The window was approximately five feet high and eight feet wide, with the bottom edge less than 18 inches above the floor.

The machine is operated by using one's legs to lift weights while laying face-down. The machine was situated so that the user faced the window. The testimony concerning the distance between the machine and the window varied and ranged from 18 inches to three feet. Plaintiff and Ms. Joseph testified that the space was not sufficient to constitute an aisle or walkway.

After completing one set of repetitions on the machine, plaintiff dismounted and stepped aside to enable Ms. Joseph to begin exercising on it. Seeking to stretch his hamstrings, plaintiff moved to the area near the window, standing almost directly in front of the machine occupied by Ms. Joseph, with his back to the window. Plaintiff then noticed that his shoelace was untied and, while he "stepped back to tie the shoe", either bending over or squatting, the glass behind him shattered and he fell to the pavement below, suffering injuries.

Plaintiff claimed defendants violated their duty to maintain reasonably safe premises, and further that the doctrine of res ipsa loquitur applies thereby shifting the burden to defendants to refute the inference of negligence.

FIRST ISSUE: Did plaintiff prove that HRC violated its duty to maintain the property in a reasonably safe condition?

DECISION: No.

REASONING: One who owns or occupies premises has a duty to maintain the property in a reasonably safe condition to protect against injury to users of the premises. However, to recover damages a plaintiff must first establish that the landlord created or had actual or constructive notice of the hazardous condition that precipitated the injury.

To constitute constructive notice a defect must be visible and apparent and it must exist for a sufficient length of time prior to the accident to permit the owner's employees to discover and remedy it.

Plaintiff in this case has provided no proof that defendant installed the window (thus defendant did not create the problem) or had knowledge of a defect. Further, there is no indication that the defect was visible or apparent so as to constitute constructive notice. SECOND ISSUE: Does the doctrine of res ipsa loquitur apply in this case?

DECISION: No.

REASONING: When the doctrine of res ipsa loquitur applies, an inference of negligence can be drawn by the trier of fact (the jury or, if there is no jury, the judge) from the very occurrence of an accident and defendant's relationship to it. Stated differently, if all the requirements are met, a plaintiff may rely on circumstantial evidence when the cause of the accident is unknown. A plaintiff seeking to invoke the doctrine must prove the following:

> 1) The accident would not ordinarily have occurred in the absence of negligence;
>
> 2) The instrumentality causing the accident is in the sole control of the defendants; and
>
> 3) The accident was not caused in whole or part by any voluntary act or contribution by plaintiff. The plaintiff in this case has failed to establish the third element of the doctrine as he acknowledges that his buttocks brushed against the glass as the window simultaneously exploded. As a result the doctrine is inapplicable to the facts in this case.

The court thus granted summary judgment in favor of defendant.

Case No. 27

NEGLIGENCE/PROXIMATE CAUSE AND
COMPARATIVE NEGLIGENCE

<u>Gross v. Waldbaum, Inc.</u>

New York City Civil Court

102 Misc.2d 175, 423 N.Y.S.2d 123 (1979)

FACTS: Plaintiff Zita Gross (Gross) was in the checkout line at a Waldbaum's grocery store in Brooklyn. She had been waiting in line for about five to seven minutes during which time she noticed that the grocery cart of the shopper in front of her was overloaded with groceries. While Gross was still in line a large soda bottle fell from the cart in front of her, landed on her foot and caused injuries. The bottle had fallen from the "baby seat" portion of the cart through a hole that existed because the protective flap in the baby seat area was missing. The shopper from whose cart the bottle fell was not identified.

Gross sued defendant Waldbaum Inc. (Waldbaum's) for negligence to recover for her injuries. Waldbaum's argued that the failure to provide a protective flap was not negligent, and even if it were, the proximate cause of Gross' injuries was the overcrowded condition of the cart from which the bottle fell, and not the absence of a protective flap.

FIRST ISSUE: If a grocery store provides for customer use a cart with a missing protective flap on the baby seat portion of the cart, is the store acting negligently?

DECISION: Yes.

REASONING: A defendant is liable in negligence when it breaches a duty of care. Waldbaum's was aware that customers often fill shopping carts to the brim with groceries, including the baby seat space. Accordingly, a cart with an opening from which food could fall creates a foreseeable risk of injury to customers and thus creates a duty of care.

SECOND ISSUE: If a grocery store customer overloads a cart so that food falls through a gap created by the absence of a protective flap, and as a result someone is injured from the falling food, does the customer's act of overloading the cart break the causal relationship between the absence of the flap and the injury?

DECISION: No.

REASONING: The existence of an intervening act does not break the cause-and- effect relationship between a negligent act and injury if the injury could reasonably have been foreseen as a consequence of the negligent act. Although the injury in this case might not have occurred had the shopper with the defective cart not overloaded it, the type of injury that Gross sustained was a foreseeable result of Waldbaum's negligence.

THIRD ISSUE: Was Gross negligent in any way that contributed to the accident?

DECISION: Yes.

REASONING: Gross observed the overloaded condition of the cart in front of her for several minutes while she was in line waiting to check out. She should have foreseen the risk of food falling from the cart and causing injury. She could have avoided the risk by standing a safe distance behind the cart. Her failure to take precautions against the foreseeable risk of injury constituted negligence.

FOURTH ISSUE: Does Gross's negligence bar her from recovering for her injuries?

DECISION: No.

REASONING: New York follows the rule of comparative negligence. That rule provides that, where both the plaintiff and the defendant were negligent in contributing to the cause of an accident, an allocation of liability is made between the two parties. The plaintiff is entitled to recover that percentage of his/her loss equal to the percentage of liability attributed to defendant.

FIFTH ISSUE: How should the responsibility for the accident be apportioned between Gross and Waldbaum's?

DECISION: 80% to Waldbaum's; 20% to Gross.

REASONING: None given. The court exercised its discretion based on the facts and determined this allocation was the fairest.

*** QUESTIONS ***
(See back of text for answers)

1) Why was the injury that resulted from a missing protective flap on a grocery cart foreseeable?

2) Why was the shopper's act of overloading the cart not an intervening force that would break the causal connection between Waldbaum's negligence and Gross's injury, thereby relieving Waldbaum's of liability?

3) New York is one of a growing number of states that has adopted the rule of comparative negligence. How would the decision in this case have been affected if New York had followed instead the rule of contributory negligence?

4) Do you agree with the allocation of liability in this case (80% to Waldbaum's; 20% to Gross)?

Case No. 28

NEGLIGENCE/ABSENCE OF A DUTY

Kosok v. Young Men's Christian Association

Appellate Division, First Department

24 A.D.2d 113, 264 N.Y.S.2d 123 (1965)

FACTS: Plaintiff Karl Kosok (Kosok) attended a summer camp sponsored by the defendant, Y.M.C.A. in Orange County, New York. The camp schedule included a rest period immediately following lunch. During this period the older campers were required to stay close to their cabins and engage only in quiet activity. For the younger campers bed rest was required.

One day during the rest period Kosok, then 12 years old, was invited into a cabin of 15-year-olds. Inside, the boys had rigged a galvanized pail to the end of fishing line attached to a fishing rod and raised the pail above the entrance way to the cabin by reeling in the line. When Kosok entered the cabin the 15-year-olds let out the line causing the pail to drop and hit Kosok, resulting in injuries. Kosok sued the Y.M.C.A. camp claiming it was negligent by breaching a duty to supervise the activities of the boys during the rest period.

The total number of campers in attendance at the camp was 200; the number of counselors was 33. Camp regulations did not require counselors of the 15- year-old boys to remain in the cabin during rest periods. Such counselors frequently were absent from the cabins during rest period but usually were on the cabin porch or nearby. At the time of the pail incident no counselor was present in the cabin.

ISSUE: Did the camp owe a duty to the campers to have a counselor in each cabin throughout the entire rest period?

DECISION: No, judgment for the camp.

REASONING: A duty to supervise arises when the camp is put on notice of potentially dangerous activity. Had noise or some other telltale hint emanated from the cabin a duty to supervise the events would result. No such noise or other warning event occurred in this case. Also, constant supervision at a summer camp is neither possible nor desirable. A certain amount of rough and/or boisterous play is common at summer camps and should not be suppressed unless it becomes dangerous.

* * * QUESTIONS * * *
(See back of text for answers)

1) Assume the campers in the cabin with the rigged pail did the same stunt during the rest period on the day immediately after Kosok was injured and that a second camper was injured as a result. Assume further that no counselor was on duty in the cabin at

the time the second camper was injured. If the second injured camper sued the camp for negligence, might the decision of the court be different? Why or why not?

2) Assume the following additional facts: the camp was located 25 miles from a maximum-security prison; an inmate in the prison escaped one summer morning; the prison officials called the camp director to inform her of the escape; the escaped inmate entered an unattended cabin at the camp during rest period on the day following the escape and kidnapped one of the campers. The camper was rescued several days later but had been beaten by the inmate and suffered severe injuries. If the camper sued the camp for his injuries based on negligence, would the camp be liable for the injuries? Why or why not?

Case No. 29

NEGLIGENCE/FAILURE TO WARN

Herman v. State of New York

Court of Appeals

63 N.Y.2d 822, 482 N.Y.S.2d 248 (1984)

FACTS: On a warm summer day Plaintiff Glen Herman (Herman) and three friends were swimming at Jones Beach. While doing a surface dive Herman struck his head on a sand bar which resulted in serious permanent injuries. (A sand bar is a ridge of sand built up to or near the surface of a body of water by the water's currents.) The sand bar was not visible from the surface. Herman had swum at the same spot six times earlier that summer and on numerous occasions in previous summers.

Jones Beach, located on the Atlantic Ocean, is owned and operated by the State of New York. Herman sued the State claiming it was negligent by not warning swimmers of the existence or the possible existence of sand bars. The State denied knowledge of the sand bar prior to Herman's accident and denied that it had a duty to warn of sand bars of which it was not aware.

During the prior twenty-four years three other swimmers had suffered similar injuries from hitting sand bars at Jones Beach. Over the years millions of bathers had swum at Jones Beach without injury by sand bars. Sand bars by their nature constantly shift from place to place.

ISSUE: Does the operator of a beach have a duty to warn of the possible existence of sand bars under the facts of this case?

DECISION: No, judgment for the State of New York.

REASONING: A property owner can be liable in negligence for failing to warn of a dangerous condition where the property owner has notice of the condition and the unreasonable risks it creates. A property owner has no duty to warn of dangerous conditions of which she has no notice. In this case the mere fact that the ocean created natural shifting sand bars did not place the operator of the beach on notice that a dangerous sand bar condition existed at Jones Beach. Since millions of people swam at the beach without incident, the fact that three similar injuries occurred over 24 years did not place the state on notice of a dangerous condition. Because the State as operator of the beach did not have notice of a danger it had no duty to warn patrons and thus was not negligent for failing to warn.

* * * QUESTIONS * * *
(See back of text for answers)

1) Should the operators of Jones Beach have foreseen the presence of sand bars and the associated risk to swimmers? Why or why not?

2) Assume Herman was swimming on a hot Saturday in July at approximately 2:00 p.m. in a part of the beach identified as a public swimming area. No lifeguard was on duty. Herman suffered a cramp and yelled for help. No one came to his rescue. Due to the cramp he was unable to stay afloat or swim to shore, and drowned. If Herman's parents sued New York State as owner and operator of Jones Beach, claiming Herman's death was the result of negligence, would they be successful in proving the state was negligent? Why or why not?

3) Assume the operators of the beach knew that a ship had exploded and sunk near the beach, scattering debris over a portion of the swimming area. What action should the operators take to avoid liability for negligence to swimmers?

Case No. 30

NEGLIGENCE/FORSEEABILITY

Endres v. Mingles Restaurant, Ltd.

Appellate Division, First Department

271 AD2d 207, 706 NYS2d 32 (2000)

FACTS: Defendant restaurant served jello-based drinks in paper cups. The testimony of plaintiff, the bar owner, and another witness established that customers routinely discard the cups onto the floor. The restaurant promoted dancing on its premises. Plaintiff, while dancing at the restaurant, slipped and fell on an unidentified substance. Plaintiff sued the restaurant for her injuries. The restaurant claimed plaintiff fell because she was dropped by her dance partner.

ISSUE: Was defendant sufficiently aware of the dangerous condition created by the presence of discarded cups on its dance floor to support a finding of negligence liability against defendant?

DECISION: Yes, judgment for plaintiff.

REASONING: A party in possession of real property owes to its customers a duty to exercise reasonable care to maintain the property in a safe condition. When an unsafe condition is reoccurring, the owner or occupier of the premises is on constructive notice of the hazardous condition.

Cups on a dance floor constitute an unsafe condition because the restaurant can foresee that someone might trip and fall. The testimony established that the presence on the dance floor of the discarded cups was a recurring circumstance. The restaurant thus had constructive notice of the hazardous condition that caused plaintiff's injury. Failure to correct it constitutes negligence. There is no legal duty to protect against an occurrence that is unusual and therefore not foreseeable by a reasonably careful person.

Case No. 31

NEGLIGENCE/THE RULES OF COMPARATIVE
AND CONTRIBUTORY NEGLIGENCE

<u>Maddox v. The City of New York, et al.</u>

Appellate Division, Second Department

108 A.D.2d 42, 487 N.Y.S.2d 354 (1985)

FACTS: Plaintiff Elliot Maddox (Maddox) was center fielder for the New York Yankees. On June 13, 1975, he played in a night game against the Chicago White Sox at Shea Stadium in New York City. During the ninth inning he slipped and fell. He subsequently sued New York City, which maintained the stadium, for his injuries. At the time of the accident the field was, in Maddox's words, "awfully wet" with "some mud" and "some standing water." Maddox had caught a ball in right center field and was throwing it to the infield.

At that moment his left foot hit a wet spot while his right foot was stuck in a mud puddle, causing his right knee to buckle. Maddox was injured as a result.

Maddox sued the city claiming it was negligent in the maintenance, design, and construction of the stadium. He admitted he had played on wet fields in the past.

ISSUE: Is the City of New York liable for a baseball player's injuries incurred during a baseball game at Shea Stadium?

DECISION: No, not according to the law in New York at the time this case was decided; judgment for the City of New York.

REASONING: Players in athletic events assume the risk of injury normally associated with a sport. Thus, when an athlete suffers an injury as a result of an activity normally associated with the game, he or she is at least partially responsible for the resulting injuries. In this case, the fact that the field was wet was obvious, as was the risk associated with playing on a wet field. Therefore, Maddox assumed the risk of the injury he incurred.

When Maddox's injury occurred (June 13, 1975), New York followed the rule of contributory negligence, which provided that a plaintiff who assumed a risk or whose negligence contributed to an accident was barred from recovering any part of the damages suffered even if another person's negligence contributed to the accident. That rule was applied in this case.

On September 1, 1975 New York abolished the rule of contributory negligence and adopted instead the rule of comparative negligence. Under that rule, assumption of risk or negligence by a plaintiff does not bar the plaintiff from recovery. Instead, the amount of damages otherwise recoverable are reduced by the proportionate share of culpability for the accident attributed to plaintiff.

* * * QUESTIONS * * *
(See back of text for answers)

1) How would the result be different if the case were decided today and the injury resulted from Maddox's tripping on a hole in the playing field?

2) Which rule—comparative negligence or contributory negligence—do you think is fairer and why?

Case No. 32

NEGLIGENCE/MALPRACTICE

King v. Jordan

Appellate Division, Third Department

265 AD2d 619, 696 NYS2d 280 (1999)

FACTS: Plaintiff detected a lump in her right breast in April, 1990 and consulted with defendant doctor. He performed a biopsy which revealed the presence of cancer. Defendant then recommended a right modified radical mastectomy (removal of the afflicted breast) and the procedure was performed on April 23, 1990. In this malpractice action plaintiff claims defendant was negligent for failing to inform plaintiff of an alternative to the removal of her breast, namely the surgical procedure known as lumpectomy. A jury awarded plaintiff $925,000 and defendant appeals.

Plaintiff and her husband testified that defendant never discussed the possibility of performing a lumpectomy instead of a mastectomy, but defendant did tell plaintiff that other surgeons might handle her treatment differently.

Plaintiff further testified that had she known about the possibility of a lumpectomy she would have opted for it rather than go through life "maimed". Plaintiff's medical expert, a surgical oncologist experienced in breast cancer treatment, opined that a lumpectomy was a reasonable treatment option, that plaintiff did not have to lose her breast to be adequately treated for her cancer, and that defendant's failure to discuss the option of a lumpectomy under the circumstances represented a departure from accepted medical practice.

Defendant's records indicate that he and plaintiff discussed the reasons for the modified radical mastectomy and "possible complications and the alternatives to surgery."

FIRST ISSUE: Was the evidence sufficient to support the finding of malpractice by the doctor?

DECISION: Yes.

REASONING: A doctor has a duty to obtain informed consent from a patient for any surgical procedure. To establish lack of informed consent, a plaintiff must prove: 1) defendant failed to disclose alternatives that would have been disclosed by a reasonable medical practitioner; 2) a reasonably prudent person in plaintiff's position would not have undergone the treatment had the person been fully informed; and 3) the lack of informed consent was a proximate cause of plaintiff's injury.

After reviewing the trial evidence the court found sufficient support for the verdict.

ADDITIONAL FACTS: Concerning damages, $500,000 was awarded for past pain and suffering, $300,000 for future pain and suffering, and $125,000 for plaintiff's husband for loss of consortium.

The evidence established that plaintiff had a difficult recovery enduring weeks of pain followed by continuing emotional distress. She testified that the surgery left her with an ugly scar which makes her feel very self-conscious. She relayed difficulties associated with wearing a prosthesis. She no longer sunbathes or enjoys clothes shopping. She avoids many normal activities that couples customarily do such as going out to restaurants. She no longer dresses in front of her husband. She described feeling "less than a woman" and testified that the mastectomy has hampered intimate relations with her husband.

SECOND ISSUE: Were the damages awarded excessive?

DECISION: No.

REASONING: Based on the evidence, the amount of the jury's awards to plaintiff for past and future pain and suffering, and to her husband for loss of consortium, are reasonable.

* * * QUESTIONS * * *
(See back of text for answers)

1) What differentiates malpractice from negligence?

2) Why does the law require informed consent prior to a doctor performing a surgical procedure?

Case No. 33

NEGLIGENCE/DAMAGES

<u>Nelson v. The State of New York</u>

Court of Claims

431 N.Y.S.2d 955 (1980)

FACTS: Plaintiff Kenneth Nelson (Nelson) was in a car accident near Waterloo, New York. Both he and his wife were injured. The cause of the accident was the State's negligence in failing to correct an engineering problem in the road and Nelson's negligence in driving 1 to 2 feet left of the center line. Nelson and his wife sued the state seeking compensation for their injuries. The court allocated the negligence as follows: 90% to the State; 10% to Nelson. Nelson's wife suffered brain injuries and was left in a vegetative state with no hope of improvement.

FIRST ISSUE: What amount and type of damages is Nelson's wife entitled to collect from the state?

DECISION: Pain and suffering, as well as lost earnings in the total amount of $512,466.63.

REASONING: A person who is injured by another's negligence is entitled to compensation for the injuries. Two categories of loss for which compensation can be awarded are wages lost due to the injured party's inability to work, and pain and suffering experienced as a result of the injury.

The amount Mrs. Nelson should recover for pain and suffering. was difficult to determine. Her injuries left her unable to talk. Due to Mrs. Nelson's loss of certain brain functions it was not clear whether she could feel pain after the accident. However, for a period of time after the accident and before she slipped into a vegetative state, she was observed periodically moaning from pain and also scratching a rash that developed on her legs. The court concluded this was sufficient evidence that Mrs. Nelson experienced pain and awarded her $350,000.00 for pain and suffering.

To determine the amount Mrs. Nelson should recover for lost earnings, the court examined both income already lost and anticipated future lost earnings. To calculate already lost earnings, the court prorated her annual salary ($5357.00) over the number of lost weeks of work (121). Mrs. Nelson was thus awarded $12,466.63. To calculate an appropriate amount to compensate for loss of future income, the court considered her life expectancy and prospects for advancement. The court concluded that $150,000.00 was appropriate compensation for loss of future wages.

ADDITIONAL FACTS: Kenneth Nelson's injuries from the accident consisted of fractures to four ribs, lacerations to the left knee joint, a mild concussion and lacerations to his left chest and arm. For a while he needed the assistance of a walker in order to walk. Later, he progressed to crutches, and at the time of trial he walked unassisted. He continued to experience periodic pain in his right hip but did not claim the pain would be permanent.

SECOND ISSUE: What amount and type of damages was Kenneth Nelson entitled to collect?

DECISION: Nelson was entitled to reimbursement for medical bills for himself and his wife, plus pain and suffering and loss of consortium for himself. The total amount of his damages was $711,666.03 reduced by 10%, Nelson's proportionate share of culpability.

REASONING: Nelson's medical bills totaled $2862.40. To compensate him for his pain and suffering, the court awarded him $13,000.00.

When a spouse is injured and can no longer provide support, love, companionship, affection, and sexual relations, the noninjured spouse is entitled to compensation for this loss. Loss of consortium, also called loss of services, is the term used to refer to this loss. To determine the proper sum of money to award, the court considered the effect of the wife's total disability on the family relationship over the period of her life expectancy, the economic value of her services over that period of time, and the age of the Nelsons' three children (7, 9 and 11). The court awarded $200,000.00 for this loss. Nelson was entitled to compensation for the doctor and hospital bills associated with his wife's injuries.

Nelson had spent $125,804.03 for his wife's care prior to the trial. He was awarded compensation for this amount. Because of his wife's vegetative state, Nelson would continue to incur additional medical expenses for future care through her life expectancy. In determining the proper amount to award the court considered that the cost of medical care would inevitably increase. Nelson was awarded $370,000.00 for his wife's future medical expenses.

* * * QUESTIONS * * *
(See back of text for answers)

1) What factors should a jury consider when making a decision on how much money to award for pain and suffering?

2) In addition to the factors considered by the court to determine an appropriate award for loss of consortium, what other factors might be considered in this or a different case?

3) In the New York State legislature, bills have been proposed which would place a cap (maximum) on the amount of money an injured party could recover for pain and suffering in a negligence action. What are the arguments for and against such a bill?

Case No. 34

STRICT PRODUCTS LIABILITY

Chandler v. Hodge and Hammond, Inc.

Supreme Court, Bronx County

111 Misc. 2d 433, 444 N.Y.S.2d 398 (1981)

FACTS: Plaintiff James R. Chandler, Sr. (Chandler) was employed as a labor foreman in the construction of a five-mile strip of New Jersey Highway Route 15 in Sparta, New Jersey. In the course of his employment Chandler used a machine shovel to dig a trench. The machine was manufactured by Northwest Engineering Co. (Northwest). It had been sold to Chandler's employer by defendant Hodge & Hammond, Inc. (H & H), a sales representative for Northwest. (A sales representative is someone who promotes the sale of a company's product and who is usually an independent contractor rather than an employee.)

While working at the construction site on April 18, 1972, Chandler released the brake mechanism on the shovel. As a result of a design defect the machine then started moving forward toward Chandler. He ran to escape but was overtaken by it and killed instantly.

This lawsuit was brought by Chandler's wife, seeking damages for Chandler's death based on numerous legal theories including strict products liability. H & H denied liability on the grounds that it had no control over the design, manufacture or installation of the machine, and therefore should not be responsible for the consequences of a defect in the design.

ISSUE: Is a seller of a machine who had no involvement with the design, manufacture or installation of the machine liable in strict products liability to a user of the machine who was injured due to a design defect?

DECISION: Yes, judgment for Chandler.

REASONING: Strict products liability provides that any party in the chain of distribution of a defective product will be liable for injuries caused by the defect even though the party sued exercised all possible care in its relationship with the product. The law has seen fit to develop a basis for liability that is not dependent on fault or negligence. Instead, it is based on public policy that the financial burden of accidental injuries caused by defective products should be borne by those who market or manufacture the product as a cost of doing business. In this case, H & H participated in the marketing and distribution of the product and is thus liable to Chandler, who was mortally injured by the product, even though H & H did not cause the defect that led to Chandler's death.

NOTE: Assuming the product was defective when it left the manufacturer, the manufacturer would also be liable in strict products liability since it too was in the chain of distribution.

*** QUESTION ***
(See back of text for answer)

1) What are the public policy reasons for establishing a basis of liability without fault such as strict products liability?

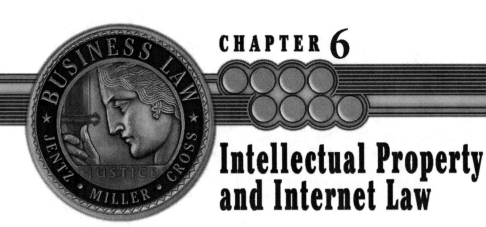

CHAPTER 6

Intellectual Property and Internet Law

Most people think of wealth in terms of houses, land, cars, stocks, and bonds. Wealth, however, also includes **intellectual property,** which consists of the products that result from intellectual, creative processes. Although it is an abstract term for an abstract concept, intellectual property is nonetheless wholly familiar to virtually everyone. *Trademarks, service marks, copyrights,* and *patents* are all forms of intellectual property. The book you are reading is copyrighted. The software you use, the movies you see, and the music you listen to are all forms of intellectual property. We provide a comprehensive synopsis of these forms of intellectual property, as

well as intellectual property that consists of *trade secrets,* in *Concept Summary 6.1* on page 165. In this chapter, we examine each of these forms in some detail.

Intellectual property has taken on increasing significance globally as well as in the United States. Today, the value of the world's intellectual property probably exceeds the value of physical property, such as machines and houses. For many U.S. companies, ownership rights in intangible intellectual property are more important to their prosperity than are their tangible assets. As you will read in this chapter, a pressing issue for businesspersons today is how to protect these valuable rights in the online world.

The need to protect creative works was voiced by the framers of the U.S. Constitution over two hundred years ago: Article I, Section 8, of the U.S. Constitution authorized Congress "[t]o promote the Progress of Science and useful Arts, by securing for limited Times to Authors and Inventors the exclusive Right to their respective Writings and Discoveries." Laws protecting patents, trademarks, and copyrights are explicitly designed to protect and reward inventive and artistic creativity. Although intellectual property law limits the economic freedom of some individuals, it does so to protect the freedom of others to enjoy the fruits of their labors—in the form of profits.

Trademarks and Related Property

A **trademark** is a distinctive mark, motto, device, or implement that a manufacturer stamps, prints, or otherwise affixes to the goods it produces so that they can be identified on the market and their origins made known. In other words, a trademark is a source indicator. At common law, the person who used a symbol or

mark to identify a business or product was protected in the use of that trademark. Clearly, by using another's trademark, a business could lead consumers to believe that its goods were made by the other business. The law seeks to avoid this kind of confusion. In this section, we examine various aspects of the law governing trademarks.

In the following classic case concerning Coca-Cola, the defendants argued that the Coca-Cola trademark was entitled to no protection under the law because the term did not accurately represent the product.

C A S E **6.1** The Coca-Cola Co. v. The Koke Co. of America

Supreme Court of the United States, 1920. 254 U.S. 143, 41 S.Ct. 113, 65 L.Ed. 189.
www.findlaw.com/casecode/supreme.html[a]

● **Company Profile** John Pemberton, an Atlanta pharmacist, invented a caramel-colored, carbonated soft drink in 1886. His bookkeeper, Frank Robinson, named the beverage Coca-Cola after two of the ingredients, coca leaves and kola nuts. Asa Candler bought the Coca-Cola Company (**www.cocacolacompany.com**) in 1891, and within seven years, he made the soft drink available in all of the United States, as well as in parts of Canada and Mexico. Candler continued to sell Coke aggressively and to open up new markets, reaching Europe before 1910. In doing so, however, he attracted numerous competitors, some of which tried to capitalize directly on the Coke name.

● **Background and Facts** The Coca-Cola Company sought to enjoin (prevent) the Koke Company of America and other beverage companies from, among other things, using the word *Koke* for their products. The Koke Company of America and other beverage companies contended that the Coca-Cola trademark was a fraudulent representation and that Coca-Cola was therefore not entitled to any help from the courts. The Koke Company and the other defendants alleged that the Coca-Cola Company, by its use of the Coca-Cola name, represented that the beverage contained cocaine (from coca leaves), which it no longer did. The trial court granted the injunction against the Koke Company, but the appellate court reversed the lower court's ruling. Coca-Cola then appealed to the United States Supreme Court.

● **Decision and Rationale** The United States Supreme Court upheld the district court's decision. The Court acknowledged that before 1900 Coca-Cola's goodwill was enhanced by the presence of a small amount of cocaine, but that the cocaine had long been eliminated from the drink.[b] The Court underscored that Coca-Cola was not "a medicine" and that its attraction did not lie in producing "a toxic effect." Since 1900 sales had greatly increased. The name had come to characterize a well-known beverage to be had almost anywhere "rather than a compound of particular substances." The Court noted that before this suit was brought Coca-Cola had advertised that the public would not find cocaine in Coca-Cola. "It would be going too far to deny the plaintiff relief against a palpable fraud because possibly here and there an ignorant person might call for the drink with the hope for incipient cocaine intoxication."

● **Impact of This Case on Today's Law** *In this early case, the United States Supreme Court made it clear that trademarks and trade names (and nicknames for those marks and names, such as the nickname "Coke" for "Coca-Cola") that are in common use receive protection under the common law. This holding is significant historically because it is the predecessor to the federal statute later passed to protect trademark rights—the Lanham Act of 1946, to be discussed next. In many ways, this act represented a codification of common law principles governing trademarks.*

● **What If the Facts Were Different?** *Suppose that Coca-Cola had been trying to make the public believe that its product contained cocaine. Would the result in this case likely have been different? Why or why not?*

---

a. This is the "U.S. Supreme Court Opinions" page within the Web site of the "FindLaw Internet Legal Resources" database. This page provides several options for accessing an opinion. Because you know the citation for this case, you can go to the "Citation Search" box, type in the appropriate volume and page numbers for the *United States Reports* ("254" and "143," respectively, for the *Coca-Cola* case), and click on "get it."

b. In reality, until 1903 the amount of active cocaine in each bottle of Coke was equivalent to one "line" of cocaine.

Statutory Protection of Trademarks

Statutory protection of trademarks and related property is provided at the federal level by the Lanham Act of 1946.[1] The Lanham Act was enacted, in part, to protect manufacturers from losing business to rival companies that used confusingly similar trademarks. The Lanham Act incorporates the common law of trademarks and provides remedies for owners of trademarks who wish to enforce their claims in federal court. Many states also have trademark statutes.

Trademark Dilution In 1995, Congress amended the Lanham Act by passing the Federal Trademark Dilution Act,[2] which extended the protection available to trademark owners by allowing them to bring a suit in federal court for trademark **dilution.** Until the passage of this amendment, federal trademark law prohibited only the unauthorized use of the same mark on competing—or on noncompeting but "related"—goods or services when such use would likely confuse consumers as to the origin of those goods and services. Trademark dilution laws protect "distinctive" or "famous" trademarks (such as Jergens, McDonald's, Dell, and Apple) from certain unauthorized uses even when the use is on noncompeting goods or is unlikely to confuse. More than half of the states have also enacted trademark dilution laws.

Use of a Similar Mark May Constitute Trademark Dilution A famous mark may be diluted not only by the use of an *identical* mark but also by the use of a *similar* mark. In 2003, however, the United States Supreme Court ruled that to constitute dilution, the similar mark must reduce the value of the famous mark or lessen its ability to identify goods and services. Therefore, lingerie maker Victoria's Secret could not establish a dilution claim against a small adult store named "Victor's Little Secret" because there was not enough evidence that Victoria's Secret's mark would be diminished in value.[3]

A similar mark is more likely to lessen the value of a famous mark when the companies using the marks provide related goods or compete against each other in the same market. For example, a woman was operat-

ing a coffee shop under the name "Sambuck's Coffeehouse" in Astoria, Oregon, even though she knew that "Starbucks" is one of the largest coffee chains in the nation. When Starbucks Corporation filed a dilution lawsuit, the federal court ruled that use of the "Sambuck's" mark constituted trademark dilution because it created confusion for consumers. Not only was there a "high degree" of similarity between the marks, but also both companies provided coffee-related services and marketed their services through "stand-alone" retail stores. Therefore, the use of the similar mark (Sambuck's) reduced the value of the famous mark (Starbucks).[4]

Trademark Registration

Trademarks may be registered with the state or with the federal government. To register for protection under federal trademark law, a person must file an application with the U.S. Patent and Trademark Office in Washington, D.C. Under current law, a mark can be registered (1) if it is currently in commerce or (2) if the applicant intends to put it into commerce within six months.

In special circumstances, the six-month period can be extended by thirty months, giving the applicant a total of three years from the date of notice of trademark approval to make use of the mark and file the required use statement. Registration is postponed until the mark is actually used. Nonetheless, during this waiting period, any applicant can legally protect his or her trademark against a third party who previously has neither used the mark nor filed an application for it. Registration is renewable between the fifth and sixth years after the initial registration and every ten years thereafter (every twenty years for those trademarks registered before 1990).

Trademark Infringement

Registration of a trademark with the U.S. Patent and Trademark Office gives notice on a nationwide basis that the trademark belongs exclusively to the registrant. The registrant is also allowed to use the symbol ® to indicate that the mark has been registered. Whenever that trademark is copied to a substantial degree or used in its entirety by another, intentionally or unintentionally, the trademark has been *infringed* (used without authorization). To sue for trademark infringement, a person need not have registered the

---

1. 15 U.S.C. Sections 1051–1128.
2. 15 U.S.C. Section 1125.
3. *Moseley v. V Secret Catalogue, Inc.*, 537 U.S. 418, 123 S.Ct. 1115, 155 L.Ed.2d 1 (2003). (A different case involving Victoria's Secret's trademark is presented as Case 8.2 on the following two pages.)

---

4. *Starbucks Corp. v. Lundberg*, 2005 WL 3183858 (D.Or. 2005).

trademark, but registration does furnish proof of the date of inception of the trademark's use.

When a trademark has been infringed, the owner has a cause of action against the infringer. Under the Lanham Act, a trademark owner that successfully proves infringement can recover actual damages, plus the profits that the infringer wrongfully received from the unauthorized use of the mark. In addition, the court may grant an *injunction* to prevent further infringement and has the authority to order that any goods bearing the unauthorized trademark be destroyed.

A central objective of the Lanham Act is to reduce the likelihood that consumers will be confused by similar marks. For that reason, only those trademarks that are deemed sufficiently distinctive from all competing trademarks will be protected.

Distinctiveness of Mark

A trademark must be sufficiently distinct to enable consumers to identify the manufacturer of the goods easily and to distinguish between those goods and competing products.

Strong Marks Fanciful, arbitrary, or suggestive trademarks are generally considered to be the most distinctive (strongest) trademarks. Marks that are fanciful, arbitrary, or suggestive are protected as inherently distinctive without demonstrating secondary meaning. These marks receive automatic protection because they serve to identify a particular product's source, as opposed to describing the product itself.

Fanciful trademarks include invented words, such as "Xerox" for one manufacturer's copiers and "Kodak" for another company's photographic products. Arbitrary trademarks are those that use common words in an uncommon way that is nondescriptive, such as "English Leather" used as a name for an aftershave lotion (and not for leather processed in England). Suggestive trademarks imply something about a product without describing the product directly. For example, the trademark "Dairy Queen" suggests an association between the products and milk, but it does not directly describe ice cream.

Secondary Meaning Descriptive terms, geographic terms, and personal names are not inherently distinctive and do not receive protection under the law until they acquire a secondary meaning. A secondary meaning may arise when customers begin to associate a specific term or phrase (such as London Fog) with specific trademarked items (coats with "London Fog" labels). Whether a secondary meaning becomes attached to a term or name usually depends on how extensively the product is advertised, the market for the product, the number of sales, and other factors.

Once a secondary meaning is attached to a term or name, a trademark is considered distinctive and is protected. The United States Supreme Court has held that even a color can qualify for trademark protection, once customers associate that color with the product.[5] In 2006, a federal court held that trademark law protects the particular color schemes used by the sports teams of four state universities, including Ohio State University and Louisiana State University.[6]

At issue in the following case was whether a certain mark was suggestive or descriptive.

---

5. *Qualitex Co. v. Jacobson Products Co.,* 514 U.S. 159, 115 S.Ct. 1300, 131 L.Ed.2d 248 (1995).
6. *Board of Supervisors of Louisiana State University v. Smack Apparel Co.,* 438 F.Supp.2d 653 (E.D.La. 2006).

C A S E **6.2** **Menashe v. V Secret Catalogue, Inc.**
United States District Court, Southern District of New York, 2006. 409 F.Supp.2d 412.

● **Background and Facts** In autumn 2002, Victoria's Secret Stores, Inc., and its affiliated companies, including V Secret Catalogue, Inc., began to develop a panty collection to be named "SEXY LITTLE THINGS." In spring 2004, Ronit Menashe, a publicist, and Audrey Quock, a fashion model and actress, began to plan a line of women's underwear also called "SEXY LITTLE THINGS." Menashe and Quock designed their line, negotiated for its manufacture, registered the domain name **www.sexylittlethings.com**, and filed an intent-to-use (ITU) application with the U.S. Patent and Trademark Office (USPTO). In July, Victoria's Secret's collection appeared in its stores in Ohio, Michigan, and California, and, in less than three months, was prominently displayed in all its stores, in its catalogues, and on its Web site. By mid-November, more than 13 million units of the line had

CASE 6.2 CONTINUED been sold, accounting for 4 percent of the company's sales for the year. When the firm applied to register "SEXY LITTLE THINGS" with the USPTO, it learned of Menashe and Quock's ITU application. The firm warned the pair that their use of the phrase constituted trademark infringement. Menashe and Quock filed a suit in a federal district court against V Secret Catalogue and others, asking the court to, among other things, declare "noninfringement of the trademark."

● **Decision and Rationale** The court concluded that "SEXY LITTLE THINGS" was a suggestive mark that Victoria's Secret used in commerce prior to the time the plaintiffs filed their ITU application. For this reason, Victoria's Secret had "priority in the Mark," and Menashe and Quock were not entitled to a judgment of "noninfringement." The court explained that "to merit trademark protection, a mark must be capable of distinguishing the products it marks from those of others." A descriptive term conveys an immediate idea of the ingredients, qualities, or characteristics of the goods. In contrast, a suggestive term requires imagination, thought, and perception to reach a conclusion as to the nature of the goods. Suggestive marks are automatically protected because they are inherently distinctive; that is, their intrinsic nature serves to identify a particular source of a product. Descriptive marks are not inherently distinctive and may only be protected on a showing of secondary meaning—that is, that the purchasing public associates the mark with a particular source. In this case, the court held that the mark "SEXY LITTLE THINGS" was suggestive because it calls to mind the phrase "sexy little things" popularly used to refer to attractive young women. The court observed that because of this suggestive nature, the mark prompts the purchaser to mentally associate the lingerie with its targeted twenty- to thirty-year-old consumers. Courts have classified marks that both describe the product and evoke other associations as inherently distinctive. In addition, the court reasoned that Victoria's Secret's use of the mark does not deprive competitors of ways to describe their lingerie products. "Indeed, Victoria's Secret's own descriptions of its lingerie in its catalogues and Web site illustrate that there are numerous ways to describe provocative underwear."

● **The E-Commerce Dimension** *If Victoria's Secret had just used the label "Sexy Little Things" on its Web site for online-only sales of this line of underwear, would the outcome of this case have been any different? Why or why not?*

● **The Legal Environment Dimension** *Why is it important to allow those who have applied for trademark protection—in this case, ITU applicants Menashe and Quock—to defend preemptively against the use of the mark by another party? (Hint: Why were Menashe and Quock seeking a court declaration of "noninfringement of a trademark"?)*

Generic Terms Generic terms that refer to an entire class of products, such as *bicycle* and *computer,* receive no protection, even if they acquire secondary meanings. A particularly thorny problem arises when a trademark acquires generic use. For example, *aspirin* and *thermos* were originally the names of trademarked products, but today the words are used generically. Other examples are *escalator, trampoline, raisin bran, dry ice, lanolin, linoleum, nylon,* and *corn flakes.*

Sometimes, a company's use of a particular generic phrase or mark becomes so closely associated with that company that the firm claims it should be protected under trademark law. In one case, for example, America Online, Inc. (AOL), sued AT&T Corporation, claiming that AT&T's use of "You Have Mail" on its WorldNet Service infringed AOL's trademark rights in the same phrase. The court ruled, how-

ever, that because each of the three words in the phrase was a generic term, the phrase as a whole was generic. Although the phrase had become widely associated with AOL's e-mail notification service, and thus might have acquired a secondary meaning, this issue was of no significance in the case. The court stated that it would not consider whether the mark had acquired any secondary meaning because "generic marks with secondary meaning are still not entitled to protection."[7]

Trade Dress

The term **trade dress** refers to the image and overall appearance of a product. Trade dress is a broad concept and can include either all or part of the total

---

7. *America Online, Inc. v. AT&T Corp.,* 243 F.3d 812 (4th Cir. 2001).

image or overall impression created by a product or its packaging. For example, the distinctive decor, menu, layout, and style of service of a particular restaurant may be regarded as trade dress. Trade dress can also include the layout and appearance of a catalogue, the use of a lighthouse as part of the design of a golf hole, the fish shape of a cracker, or the G-shaped design of a Gucci watch.

Basically, trade dress is subject to the same protection as trademarks. In cases involving trade dress infringement, as in trademark infringement cases, a major consideration is whether consumers are likely to be confused by the allegedly infringing use.

Service, Certification, and Collective Marks

A **service mark** is essentially a trademark that is used to distinguish the *services* (rather than the products) of one person or company from those of another. For example, each airline has a particular mark or symbol associated with its name. Titles and character names used in radio and television are frequently registered as service marks.

Other marks protected by law include certification marks and collective marks. A **certification mark** is used by one or more persons, other than the owner, to certify the region, materials, mode of manufacture, quality, or other characteristic of specific goods or services. When used by members of a cooperative, association, or other organization, it is referred to as a **collective mark.** Examples of certification marks are the phrases "Good Housekeeping Seal of Approval" and "UL Tested." Collective marks appear at the ends of motion picture credits to indicate the various associations and organizations that participated in the making of the films. The union marks found on the tags of certain products are also collective marks.

Counterfeit Goods

Counterfeit goods copy or otherwise imitate trademarked goods but are not genuine. The importation of goods that bear a counterfeit (fake) trademark poses a growing problem for U.S. businesses, consumers, and law enforcement. In addition to having negative financial effects on legitimate businesses, sales of certain counterfeit goods, such as pharmaceuticals and nutritional supplements, can present serious public health risks. It is estimated that nearly 7 percent of the goods imported into the United States from abroad are counterfeit.

Stop Counterfeiting in Manufactured Goods Act In 2006, Congress enacted the Stop Counterfeiting in Manufactured Goods Act[8] (SCMGA) to combat the growing problem of counterfeit goods. The act makes it a crime to intentionally traffic in or attempt to traffic in counterfeit goods or services, or to knowingly use a counterfeit mark on or in connection with goods or services. Prior to this act, the law did not prohibit the creation or shipment of counterfeit labels that were not attached to any product.[9] Therefore, counterfeiters would make labels and packaging bearing another's trademark, ship the labels to another location, and then affix them to an inferior product to deceive buyers. The SCMGA has closed this loophole by making it a crime to knowingly traffic in or attempt to traffic in counterfeit labels, stickers, packaging, and the like, regardless of whether the item is attached to any goods.

Penalties for Counterfeiting Persons found guilty of violating the SCMGA may be fined up to $2 million or imprisoned for up to ten years (or more if they are repeat offenders). If a court finds that the statute was violated, it must order the defendant to forfeit the counterfeit products (which are then destroyed), as well as any property used in the commission of the crime. The defendant must also pay restitution to the trademark holder or victim in an amount equal to the victim's actual loss. For example, in one case the defendant pleaded guilty to conspiring with others to import cigarette-rolling papers from Mexico that were falsely marked as "Zig-Zags" and sell them in the United States. The court sentenced the defendant to prison and ordered him to pay $566,267 in restitution. On appeal, the court affirmed the prison sentence but reversed the restitution because the amount exceeded the amount of actual loss suffered by the legitimate sellers of Zig-Zag rolling papers.[10]

Trade Names

Trademarks apply to *products*. The term **trade name** is used to indicate part or all of a business's name, whether the business is a sole proprietorship, a partner-

---

8. Pub. L. No. 109-181 (2006), which amended 18 U.S.C. Sections 2318–2320.
9. See, for example, *United States v. Giles*, 213 F.3d 1247 (10th Cir. 2000).
10. For a case discussing the appropriate measure of restitution, see *United States v. Beydoun*, 469 F.3d 102 (5th Cir. 2006).

ship, or a corporation. Generally, a trade name is directly related to a business and its goodwill. A trade name may be protected as a trademark if the trade name is also the name of the company's trademarked product—for example, Coca-Cola. Unless also used as a trademark or service mark, a trade name cannot be registered with the federal government. Trade names are protected under the common law, but only if they are unusual or fancifully used. The word *Safeway*, for example, was sufficiently fanciful to obtain protection as a trade name for a grocery chain.[11]

Cyber Marks

In cyberspace, trademarks are sometimes referred to as **cyber marks.** We turn now to a discussion of various trademark issues that are unique to cyberspace, such as domain names and cybersquatting, and how new laws and the courts are addressing these issues.

Domain Names

Conflicts over rights to domain names first emerged as e-commerce expanded on a worldwide scale and have reemerged in the last ten years. By using the same, or a similar, domain name, parties have attempted to profit from the goodwill of a competitor, sell pornography, offer for sale another party's domain name, and otherwise infringe on others' trademarks. A **domain name** is the core part of an Internet address—for example, "westlaw.com." It includes at least two parts. Every domain name ends with a generic top level domain (TLD), which is the part of the name to the right of the period. The TLD typically indicates the type of entity that operates the site. For example, *com* is an abbreviation for *commercial*, and *edu* is short for *education*. Although originally there were only six possible TLDs, several more generic TLDs are now available, some of which are not restricted to a particular type of entity (see Exhibit 6–1 on the following page for a list of generic TLDs and their uses).

The second level domain (SLD), which is the part of the name to the left of the period, is chosen by the business entity or individual registering the domain name. Competition among firms with similar names and products for SLDs has caused numerous disputes

over domain name rights. The Internet Corporation for Assigned Names and Numbers (ICANN), a nonprofit corporation, oversees the distribution of domain names. ICANN also facilitates the settlement of domain name disputes and operates an online arbitration system. In recent years, however, ICANN has been criticized for failing to keep up with the sheer volume of complaints involving domain names and accusations of cybersquatting. **Cybersquatting** occurs when a person registers a domain name that is the same as, or confusingly similar to, the trademark of another and then offers to sell the domain name back to the trademark owner.

Anticybersquatting Legislation

During the 1990s, cybersquatting led to so much litigation that Congress passed the Anticybersquatting Consumer Protection Act of 1999[12] (ACPA), which amended the Lanham Act—the federal law protecting trademarks discussed earlier. The ACPA makes it illegal for a person to "register, traffic in, or use" a domain name (1) if the name is identical or confusingly similar to the trademark of another and (2) if the one registering, trafficking in, or using the domain name has a "bad faith intent" to profit from that trademark.

The act does not define what constitutes bad faith. Instead, it lists several factors that courts can consider in deciding whether bad faith exists. For example, courts focus on the trademark rights of the other person and whether the alleged cybersquatter intended to divert consumers in a way that could harm the goodwill represented by the trademark. Courts also consider whether the alleged cybersquatter offered to transfer or sell the domain name to the trademark owner, or intended to use the domain name to offer goods and services.

The Ongoing Problem of Cybersquatting
The ACPA was intended to stamp out cybersquatting, but it continues to present a problem for businesses today, largely because, as mentioned, more TLDs are available and many more companies are registering domain names. Indeed, domain name registrars have proliferated. These companies charge a fee to businesses and individuals to register new names and to renew annual registrations (often through automated software). Many of these companies also buy and sell

---

11. *Safeway Stores v. Suburban Foods,* 130 F.Supp. 249 (E.D.Va. 1955).

12. 15 U.S.C. Section 1129.

EXHIBIT 6–1 ● **Existing Generic Top Level Domain Names**

.aero	Reserved for members of the air-transportation industry.
.asia	Restricted to the Pan-Asia and Asia Pacific community.
.biz	For businesses.
.cat	Reserved for the Catalan linguistic and cultural community.
.com	Originally intended for commercial organizations, but is now unrestricted in the United States.
.coop	Restricted to cooperative associations.
.edu	For postsecondary educational establishments.
.gov	Reserved for government agencies in the United States.
.info	For informational sites, but is unrestricted.
.int	Reserved for international organizations established by treaty.
.jobs	Reserved for human resource managers.
.mil	For the U.S. military.
.mobi	Reserved for consumers and providers of mobile products and services.
.museum	Reserved for museums.
.name	Reserved for individuals and families.
.net	Originally intended for network infrastructures, but is now unrestricted.
.org	Originally intended for noncommercial organizations, but is now unrestricted.
.pro	Restricted to certain credentialed professionals.
.tel	For business services involving connections between a telephone network and the Internet.
.travel	Reserved for the travel industry.

expired domain names. Although all domain name registrars are supposed to relay information about these transactions to ICANN and the other companies that keep a master list of domain names, this does not always occur. The speed at which domain names change hands and the difficulty in tracking mass automated registrations have created an environment in which cybersquatting can flourish.

Cybersquatters have also developed new tactics, such as typosquatting, or registering a name that is a misspelling of a popular brand, such as hotmai.com or myspac.com. Because many Internet users are not perfect typists, Web pages using these misspelled names get a lot of traffic. More traffic generally means increased profit (advertisers often pay Web sites based on the number of unique visits, or hits), which in turn provides incentive for more cybersquatters. Also, if the misspelling is significant, the trademark owner may have difficulty proving that the name is identical or confusingly similar to the trademark of another, as the ACPA requires.

Cybersquatting is costly for businesses, which must attempt to register all variations of a name to protect their domain name rights from would-be cybersquatters. Large corporations may have to register thousands of domain names across the globe just to protect their basic brands and trademarks.

Applicability of the ACPA and Sanctions under the Act The ACPA applies to all domain name registrations. Successful plaintiffs in suits brought under the act can collect actual damages and profits, or they can elect to receive statutory damages ranging from $1,000 to $100,000.

Although some companies have been successful suing under the ACPA, there are roadblocks to succeeding in such lawsuits. Some domain name registrars offer privacy services that hide the true owners of Web sites, making it difficult for trademark owners to identify cybersquatters. Thus, before a trademark owner can bring a suit, he or she has to ask the court for a subpoena to discover the identity of the owner of the infringing Web site. Because of the high costs of court proceedings, discovery, and even arbitration, many disputes over cybersquatting are settled out of court. Some companies have found that simply purchasing the domain name from the cybersquatter is the least expensive solution.

Meta Tags

Search engines compile their results by looking through a Web site's key-word field. **Meta tags,** or key words, may be inserted into this field to increase the likelihood that a site will be included in search engine results, even though the site may have nothing to do with the inserted words. Using this same technique, one site may appropriate the key words of other sites with more frequent hits so that the appropriating site will appear in the same search engine results as the more popular sites. Using another's trademark in a meta tag without the owner's permission, however, normally constitutes trademark infringement.

Some uses of another's trademark as a meta tag may be permissible if the use is reasonably necessary and does not suggest that the owner authorized or sponsored the use. For example, Terri Welles, a former model who had been "Playmate of the Year" in *Playboy* magazine, established a Web site that used the terms *Playboy* and *Playmate* as meta tags. Playboy Enterprises, Inc. (PEI), which publishes *Playboy,* filed a suit seeking to prevent Welles from using these meta tags. The court determined that Welles's use of PEI's meta tags to direct users to her Web site was permissible because it did not suggest sponsorship and there were no descriptive substitutes for the terms *Playboy* and *Playmate.*[13]

Dilution in the Online World

As discussed earlier, trademark *dilution* occurs when a trademark is used, without authorization, in a way that diminishes the distinctive quality of the mark. Unlike trademark infringement, a claim of dilution does not require proof that consumers are likely to be confused by a connection between the unauthorized use and the mark. For this reason, the products involved need not be similar. In the first case alleging dilution on the Web, a court precluded the use of "candyland.com" as the URL for an adult site. The successful lawsuit was brought by the company that manufactures the "Candyland" children's game and owns the "Candyland" mark.[14]

Licensing

One way to make use of another's trademark or other form of intellectual property, while avoiding litigation, is to obtain a license to do so. A license in this context is essentially an agreement, or contract, permitting the use of a trademark, copyright, patent, or trade secret for certain purposes. The party that owns the intellectual property rights and issues the license is the *licensor,*

and the party obtaining the license is the *licensee.* A licensor might, for example, allow the licensee to use the trademark as part of its company name, or as part of its domain name, but not otherwise use the mark on any products or services. Often, selling a license to an infringer is an inexpensive solution to the problem, at least when compared with the costs associated with litigation.

Note, however, that under modern law a licensor of trademarks has a duty to maintain some form of control over the nature and quality of goods or services sold under the mark. If the license does not include any provisions to protect the quality of goods or services provided under the trademark, then the courts may conclude that the licensor has abandoned the trademark and lost her or his trademark rights.[15] To avoid such problems, licensing agreements normally include detailed provisions that protect the trademark owners' rights.

PREVENTING LEGAL DISPUTES

To avoid litigation, anyone signing a licensing contract should consult with an attorney to make sure that the specific wording in the contract is very clear as to what rights are or are not being conveyed. Moreover, to prevent misunderstandings over the scope of the rights being acquired, the licensee should determine whether any other parties hold licenses to use that particular intellectual property and the extent of those rights.

Patents

A **patent** is a grant from the government that gives an inventor the right to exclude others from making, using, and selling an invention for a period of twenty years from the date of filing the application for a patent. Patents for designs, as opposed to inventions, are given for a fourteen-year period. The applicant must demonstrate to the satisfaction of the U.S. Patent and Trademark Office that the invention, discovery,

---

13. *Playboy Enterprises, Inc. v. Welles,* 279 F.3d 796 (9th Cir. 2002). See also *Rhino Sports, Inc. v. Sport Court, Inc.,* ___ F.Supp.2d ___ (D.Ariz. 2007).
14. *Hasbro, Inc. v. Internet Entertainment Group, Ltd.,* 1996 WL 84853 (W.D.Wash. 1996).

15. This is referred to as a *naked license,* and a trademark owner who fails to exercise adequate control over the mark is estopped, or prevented, from asserting his or her rights. See, for example, *Barcamerica International USA Trust v. Tyfield Importers, Inc.,* 289 F.3d 589 (9th Cir. 2002); and *Exxon Corp. v. Oxxford Clothes, Inc.,* 109 F.3d 1070 (5th Cir. 1997).

process, or design is novel, useful, and not obvious in light of current technology.

In contrast to patent law in many other countries, in the United States the first person to invent a product or process gets the patent rights rather than the first person to file for a patent on that product or process. Because it can be difficult to prove who invented an item first, however, the first person to file an application is often deemed the first to invent (unless the inventor has detailed prior research notes or other evidence). An inventor can publish the invention or offer it for sale prior to filing a patent application but must apply for a patent within one year of doing so or forfeit the patent rights. The period of patent protection begins on the date the patent application is filed, rather than when the patent is issued, which may sometimes be years later. After the patent period ends (either fourteen or twenty years later), the product or process enters the public domain, and anyone can make, sell, or use the invention without paying the patent holder.

Searchable Patent Databases

A significant development relating to patents is the availability online of the world's patent databases. The Web site of the U.S. Patent and Trademark Office (see the *Law on the Web* section at the end of this chapter for its URL) provides searchable databases covering U.S. patents granted since 1976. The Web site of the European Patent Office (its URL is also in the *Law on the Web* section) provides online access to 50 million patent documents in more than seventy nations through a searchable network of databases. Businesses use these searchable databases in many ways. Because patents are valuable assets, businesses may need to perform patent searches to list or inventory their assets. Patent searches may also be conducted to study trends and patterns in a specific technology or to gather information about competitors in the industry.

In addition, a business might search patent databases to develop a business strategy in a particular market or to evaluate a job applicant's contributions to a technology. Although online databases are accessible to anyone, businesspersons might consider hiring a specialist to perform advanced patent searches.

What Is Patentable?

Under federal law, "[w]hoever invents or discovers any new and useful process, machine, manufacture, or composition of matter, or any new and useful improvement thereof, may obtain a patent therefor, subject to the conditions and requirements of this title."[16] Thus, to be patentable, the item must be novel and not obvious.

In sum, almost anything is patentable, except (1) the laws of nature,[17] (2) natural phenomena, and (3) abstract ideas (including algorithms[18]). Even artistic methods, certain works of art, and the structure of storylines are patentable, provided that they are novel and not obvious. Plants that are reproduced asexually (by means other than from seed), such as hybrid or genetically engineered plants, are patentable in the United States, as are genetically engineered (or cloned) microorganisms and animals.

In the following case, the focus was on the application of the test for proving whether a patent claim is "obvious."

---

16. 35 U.S.C. 101.

17. Note that in 2006, several justices of the United States Supreme Court indicated that they believed a process to diagnose vitamin deficiencies should not be patentable, because allowing a patent would improperly give a monopoly over a scientific relationship, or law of nature. Nevertheless, the majority of the Supreme Court allowed the patent to stand. *Laboratory Corporation of America Holdings v. Metabolite Laboratories, Inc.*, 548 U.S. 124, 126 S.Ct. 2921, 165 L.Ed.2d 399 (2006).

18. An *algorithm* is a step-by-step procedure, formula, or set of instructions for accomplishing a specific task—such as the set of rules used by a search engine to rank the listings contained within its index in response to a particular query.

C A S E 6.3 KSR International Co. v. Teleflex, Inc.
Supreme Court of the United States, 2007. __ U.S. __, 127 S.Ct. 1727, 167 L.Ed.2d 705.

● **Background and Facts** Teleflex, Inc., sued KSR International Company for patent infringement. Teleflex holds the exclusive license to a patent for a device developed by Steven J. Engelgau. The patent issued is entitled "Adjustable Pedal with Electronic Throttle Control." In brief, the Engelgau patent combines an electronic sensor with an adjustable automobile pedal so that the pedal's position can be transmitted to a computer that controls the throttle in the vehicle's engine. KSR contended that the patent in question could not create a claim because the subject matter was obvious. During the trial, the district court found that several existing patents involving electronic pedal sensors for computer-

CASE 6.3 CONTINUED controlled throttles basically covered all of the important aspects of the Engelgau patent. On appeal, the U.S. Court of Appeals for the Federal Circuit reversed the district court ruling. KSR appealed to the United States Supreme Court.

● **Decision and Rationale** The United States Supreme Court reversed the judgment of the court of appeals and remanded the case. The Court pointed out that in many previous decisions it had held "that a patent for a combination which only unites old elements with no change in their respective functions * * * obviously withdraws what is already known into the field of its monopoly and diminishes the resources available to skillful [persons]. * * * If a technique has been used to improve one device, and a person of ordinary skill in the art would recognize that it would improve similar devices in the same way, using the technique is obvious unless its actual application is beyond his or her skill." In essence, the Court saw little difference between what existed in the "teachings" of previously filed patents and the adjustable electronic pedal disclosed in the Engelgau patent.

● **The Legal Environment Dimension** *If a person of ordinary skill can implement a predictable variation of another's patented invention, does the Court's opinion indicate that the item is likely not to be patentable? Explain.*

● **The Ethical Dimension** *Based on the Court's reasoning, what other factors should be considered when determining the obviousness of a patent?*

Patents for Software At one time, it was difficult for developers and manufacturers of software to obtain patent protection because many software products simply automate procedures that can be performed manually. In other words, it was thought that computer programs did not meet the "novel" and "not obvious" requirements previously mentioned. Also, the basis for software is often a mathematical equation or formula, which is not patentable. In 1981, however, the United States Supreme Court held that it is possible to obtain a patent for a *process* that incorporates a computer program—providing, of course, that the process itself is patentable.[19] Subsequently, many patents have been issued for software-related inventions.

Patents for Business Processes In 1998, in a landmark case, *State Street Bank & Trust Co. v. Signature Financial Group, Inc.,*[20] the U.S. Court of Appeals for the Federal Circuit ruled that business processes were patentable. After this decision, numerous technology firms applied for business process patents. Walker Digital applied for a business process patent for its "Dutch auction" system, which allowed consumers to make offers for airline tickets on the Internet and led to the creation of Priceline.com. Amazon.com obtained a business process patent for

its "one-click" ordering system, a method of processing credit-card orders securely. Indeed, after the *State Street* decision, the number of Internet-related patents issued by the U.S. Patent and Trademark Office increased dramatically.

Patent Infringement

If a firm makes, uses, or sells another's patented design, product, or process without the patent owner's permission, the tort of patent infringement occurs. Patent infringement may arise even though the patent owner has not put the patented product into commerce. Patent infringement may also occur even though not all features or parts of a product are identical to those used in the patented invention, provided that the features are equivalent. (With respect to a patented process, however, all steps or their equivalent must be copied for infringement to exist.)

Note that, as a general rule, under U.S. law no patent infringement occurs when a patented product is made and sold in another country. In 2007, this issue came before the United States Supreme Court in a patent infringement case that AT&T Corporation had brought against Microsoft Corporation. AT&T holds a patent on a device used to digitally encode, compress, and process recorded speech. Microsoft's Windows operating system, as Microsoft admitted, incorporated software code that infringed on AT&T's patent. The only question

---

19. *Diamond v. Diehr,* 450 U.S. 175, 101 S.Ct. 1048, 67 L.Ed.2d 155 (1981).
20. 149 F.3d 1368 (Fed.Cir. 1998).

before the Supreme Court was whether Microsoft's liability extended to computers made in another country. The Court held that it did not. Microsoft was liable only for infringement in the United States and not for the Windows-based computers sold in foreign locations. The Court reasoned that Microsoft had not "supplied" the software for the computers but had only electronically transmitted a master copy, which the foreign manufacturers then copied and loaded onto the computers.[21]

Remedies for Patent Infringement

If a patent is infringed, the patent holder may sue for relief in federal court. The patent holder can seek an injunction against the infringer and can also request damages for royalties and lost profits. In some cases, the court may grant the winning party reimbursement for attorneys' fees and costs. If the court determines that the infringement was willful, the court can triple the amount of damages awarded (treble damages).

In the past, permanent injunctions were routinely granted to prevent future infringement. In 2006, however, the United States Supreme Court ruled that patent holders are not automatically entitled to a permanent injunction against future infringing activities—the courts have discretion to decide whether equity requires it. According to the Supreme Court, a patent holder must prove that it has suffered irreparable injury and that the public interest would not be disserved by a permanent injunction.[22]

This decision gives courts discretion to decide what is equitable in the circumstances and allows them to consider what is in the public interest rather than just the interests of the parties. For example, in the first case applying this rule, a court found that although Microsoft had infringed on the patent of a small software company, the latter was not entitled to an injunction. According to the court, the small company was not irreparably harmed and could be adequately compensated by damages. Also, the public might suffer negative effects from an injunction because the infringement involved part of Microsoft's widely used Office suite software.[23]

PREVENTING LEGAL DISPUTES

Litigation over whether a patent has been infringed is typically expensive and often requires a team of experts to investigate and analyze the commercial, technical, and legal aspects of the case. Because of these costs, a businessperson facing patent infringement litigation—either as the patent holder or as the alleged infringer—should carefully evaluate the evidence as well as the various settlement options. If both sides appear to have good arguments as to whether the patent was infringed or whether it was valid, it may be in a firm's best interest to settle the case. This is particularly true if the firm is not certain that the court would grant an injunction.

Similarly, if the patented technology is not commercially significant to one's business, it might be best to consider a nonexclusive license as a means of resolving the dispute. This option is more important for patent holders now that injunctions may be harder to obtain. Settlement may be as simple as an agreement that one party will stop making, using, or selling the patented product or process, or it may involve monetary compensation for past activities and/or licensing for future activities.

Copyrights

A **copyright** is an intangible property right granted by federal statute to the author or originator of a literary or artistic production of a specified type. Today, copyrights are governed by the Copyright Act of 1976,[24] as amended. Works created after January 1, 1978, are automatically given statutory copyright protection for the life of the author plus 70 years. For copyrights owned by publishing houses, the copyright expires 95 years from the date of publication or 120 years from the date of creation, whichever is first. For works by more than one author, the copyright expires 70 years after the death of the last surviving author.

These time periods reflect the extensions of the length of copyright protection enacted by Congress in the Copyright Term Extension Act of 1998.[25] Critics challenged this act as overstepping the bounds of Congress's power and violating the constitutional

---

21. *Microsoft Corp. v. AT&T Corp.*, ___ U.S. ___, 127 S.Ct. 1746, 167 L.Ed.2d 737 (2007).

22. *eBay, Inc. v. MercExchange, LLC,* 547 U.S. 388, 126 S.Ct. 1837, 164 L.Ed.2d 641 (2006).

23. *Z4 Technologies, Inc. v. Microsoft Corp.*, 434 F.Supp.2d 437 (E.D.Tex. 2006).

24. 17 U.S.C. Sections 101 *et seq.*

25. 17 U.S.C. Section 302.

requirement that copyrights endure for only a limited time. In 2003, however, the United States Supreme Court upheld the act in *Eldred v. Ashcroft*.[26] This holding obviously favored copyright holders by preventing copyrighted works from the 1920s and 1930s from losing protection and falling into the public domain for an additional two decades.

Copyrights can be registered with the U.S. Copyright Office in Washington, D.C. A copyright owner no longer needs to place the symbol © or the term *Copr.* or *Copyright* on the work to have the work protected against infringement. Chances are that if somebody created it, somebody owns it.

What Is Protected Expression?

Works that are copyrightable include books, records, films, artworks, architectural plans, menus, music videos, product packaging, and computer software. To be protected, a work must be "fixed in a durable medium" from which it can be perceived, reproduced, or communicated. Protection is automatic. Registration is not required.

To obtain protection under the Copyright Act, a work must be original and fall into one of the following categories:

1. Literary works (including newspaper and magazine articles, computer and training manuals, catalogues, brochures, and print advertisements).
2. Musical works and accompanying words (including advertising jingles).
3. Dramatic works and accompanying music.
4. Pantomimes and choreographic works (including ballets and other forms of dance).
5. Pictorial, graphic, and sculptural works (including cartoons, maps, posters, statues, and even stuffed animals).
6. Motion pictures and other audiovisual works (including multimedia works).
7. Sound recordings.
8. Architectural works.

Section 102 Exclusions Section 102 of the Copyright Act specifically excludes copyright protection for any "idea, procedure, process, system, method of operation, concept, principle, or discovery, regardless of the form in which it is described, explained, illustrated, or embodied." Note that it is not possible to copyright an *idea*. The underlying ideas embodied in a work may be freely used by others. What is copyrightable is the

particular way in which an idea is expressed. Whenever an idea and an expression are inseparable, the expression cannot be copyrighted. Generally, anything that is not an original expression will not qualify for copyright protection. Facts widely known to the public are not copyrightable. Page numbers are not copyrightable because they follow a sequence known to everyone. Mathematical calculations are not copyrightable.

Compilations of Facts Unlike ideas, *compilations* of facts are copyrightable. Under Section 103 of the Copyright Act a compilation is "a work formed by the collection and assembling of preexisting materials or data that are selected, coordinated, or arranged in such a way that the resulting work as a whole constitutes an original work of authorship." The key requirement in the copyrightability of a compilation is originality. If the facts are selected, coordinated, or arranged in an original way, they can qualify for copyright protection. Therefore, the white pages of a telephone directory do not qualify for copyright protection because the facts (names, addresses, and telephone numbers) are listed in alphabetical order rather than being selected, coordinated, or arranged in an original way.[27] The Yellow Pages of a telephone directory, in contrast, can qualify for copyright protection.[28] Similarly, a compilation of information about yachts listed for sale may qualify for copyright protection.[29]

Copyright Infringement

Whenever the form or expression of an idea is copied, an infringement of copyright has occurred. The reproduction does not have to be exactly the same as the original, nor does it have to reproduce the original in its entirety. If a substantial part of the original is reproduced, the copyright has been infringed.

Damages for Copyright Infringement Those who infringe copyrights may be liable for damages or criminal penalties. These range from actual damages or statutory damages, imposed at the court's discretion, to criminal proceedings for willful violations. Actual damages are based on the harm caused to the copyright holder by the infringement, while

---

26. 537 U.S. 186, 123 S.Ct. 769, 154 L.Ed.2d 683 (2003).

27. *Feist Publications, Inc. v. Rural Telephone Service Co.*, 499 U.S. 340, 111 S.Ct. 1282, 113 L.Ed.2d 358 (1991).
28. *Bellsouth Advertising & Publishing Corp. v. Donnelley Information Publishing, Inc.*, 999 F.2d 1436 (11th Cir. 1993).
29. *BUC International Corp. v. International Yacht Council, Ltd.*, 489 F.3d 1129 (11th Cir. 2007).

statutory damages, not to exceed $150,000, are provided for under the Copyright Act. Criminal proceedings may result in fines and/or imprisonment.

The "Fair Use" Exception An exception to liability for copyright infringement is made under the "fair use" doctrine. In certain circumstances, a person or organization can reproduce copyrighted material without paying royalties (fees paid to the copyright holder for the privilege of reproducing the copyrighted material). Section 107 of the Copyright Act provides as follows:

> [T]he fair use of a copyrighted work, including such use by reproduction in copies or phonorecords or by any other means specified by [Section 106 of the Copyright Act], for purposes such as criticism, comment, news reporting, teaching (including multiple copies for classroom use), scholarship, or research, is not an infringement of copyright. In determining whether the use made of a work in any particular case is a fair use the factors to be considered shall include–
>
> (1) the purpose and character of the use, including whether such use is of a commercial nature or is for nonprofit educational purposes;
>
> (2) the nature of the copyrighted work;
>
> (3) the amount and substantiality of the portion used in relation to the copyrighted work as a whole; and
>
> (4) the effect of the use upon the potential market for or value of the copyrighted work.

Because these guidelines are very broad, the courts determine whether a particular use is fair on a case-by-case basis. Thus, anyone reproducing copyrighted material may still be committing a violation. In determining whether a use is fair, courts have often considered the fourth factor to be the most important.

In the following case, the owner of copyrighted music had issued a license to the manufacturer of karaoke devices to reproduce the sound recordings, but had not given its permission to reprint the song lyrics. The issue was whether the manufacturer should pay additional fees to display the lyrics at the same time as the music was playing. The manufacturer claimed, in part, that its use of the lyrics was educational and therefore did not constitute copyright infringement under the fair use exception.

C A S E 6.4 Leadsinger, Inc. v. BMG Music Publishing
United States Court of Appeals, Ninth Circuit, 2008. 512 F.3d 522.
www.ca9.uscourts.gov[a]

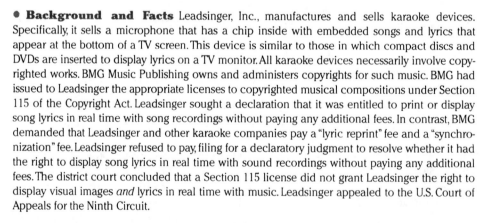

● **Background and Facts** Leadsinger, Inc., manufactures and sells karaoke devices. Specifically, it sells a microphone that has a chip inside with embedded songs and lyrics that appear at the bottom of a TV screen. This device is similar to those in which compact discs and DVDs are inserted to display lyrics on a TV monitor. All karaoke devices necessarily involve copyrighted works. BMG Music Publishing owns and administers copyrights for such music. BMG had issued to Leadsinger the appropriate licenses to copyrighted musical compositions under Section 115 of the Copyright Act. Leadsinger sought a declaration that it was entitled to print or display song lyrics in real time with song recordings without paying any additional fees. In contrast, BMG demanded that Leadsinger and other karaoke companies pay a "lyric reprint" fee and a "synchronization" fee. Leadsinger refused to pay, filing for a declaratory judgment to resolve whether it had the right to display song lyrics in real time with sound recordings without paying any additional fees. The district court concluded that a Section 115 license did not grant Leadsinger the right to display visual images *and* lyrics in real time with music. Leadsinger appealed to the U.S. Court of Appeals for the Ninth Circuit.

● **Decision and Rationale** The U.S. Court of Appeals for the Ninth Circuit affirmed the district court's decision to dismiss Leadsinger's complaint without the possibility of amending it. The court pointed out that a copyright holder has a right to control "the synchronization of musical compositions with the content of audiovisual works." Consequently, courts have required parties to obtain synchronization licenses from copyright holders. Moreover, "lyrics are copyrightable as a literary work and, therefore, enjoy separate protection under the Copyright Act." Leadsinger's microchip that stores visual images and visual representations of lyrics falls within the definition

---

a. Click on "Opinions." When that page opens, click on "2008" and then on "January." Scroll down to "01/02/08." Find the case name and click on it to access the opinion.

CASE 6.4 CONTINUED of an audiovisual work. Leadsinger could not avail itself of the fair use doctrine simply by arguing that karaoke devices help teach singing.

● **The Global Dimension** *Could Leadsinger have attempted to show that its karaoke programs were used extensively abroad to help others learn English? If successful in this line of reasoning, might Leadsinger have prevailed on appeal? Explain your answer.*

● **The Legal Environment Dimension** *What was the underlying basis of Leadsinger's attempt to avoid paying additional licensing fees to BMG?*

Copyright Protection for Software

In 1980, Congress passed the Computer Software Copyright Act, which amended the Copyright Act of 1976 to include computer programs in the list of creative works protected by federal copyright law.[30] The 1980 statute, which classifies computer programs as "literary works," defines a computer program as a "set of statements or instructions to be used directly or indirectly in a computer in order to bring about a certain result."

The unique nature of computer programs, however, has created problems for the courts in applying and interpreting the 1980 act. Generally, the courts have held that copyright protection extends not only to those parts of a computer program that can be read by humans, such as the "high-level" language of a source code, but also to the binary-language object code, which is readable only by the computer.[31] Additionally, such elements as the overall structure, sequence, and organization of a program have been deemed copyrightable, but generally not the "look and feel" of computer programs.[32] The "look and feel" of computer programs refers to their general appearance, command structure, video images, menus, windows, and other screen displays.

Copyrights in Digital Information

Copyright law is probably the most important form of intellectual property protection on the Internet. This is because much of the material on the Internet consists of works of authorship (including multimedia presentations, software, and database information), which are the traditional focus of copyright law. Copyright law is also important because the nature of the Internet requires that data be "copied" to be transferred online. Traditionally, many of the controversies arising in this area of the law have involved copies.

The Copyright Act of 1976

When Congress drafted the principal U.S. law governing copyrights, the Copyright Act of 1976, cyberspace did not exist for most of us. At that time, the primary threat to copyright owners was from persons making unauthorized *tangible* copies of works. Because of the nature of cyberspace, however, one of the early controversies was determining at what point an intangible, electronic "copy" of a work has been made. The courts have held that loading a file or program into a computer's random access memory, or RAM, constitutes the making of a "copy" for purposes of copyright law.[33] RAM is a portion of a computer's memory into which a file, for example, is loaded so that it can be accessed. Thus, a copyright is infringed when a party downloads software into RAM without owning the software or otherwise having a right to download it.[34] Today, technology has vastly increased the potential for copyright infringement. For a discussion of whether search engines that use thumbnail images of copyrighted materials are liable for infringement, see this chapter's *Insight into E-Commerce* feature on pages 160 and 161.

Further Developments in Copyright Law

In the last fifteen years, Congress has enacted legislation designed specifically to protect copyright holders in a digital age. Particularly significant are the No

---

30. Pub. L. No. 96-517 (1980), amending 17 U.S.C. Sections 101, 117.
31. See *Stern Electronics, Inc. v. Kaufman,* 669 F.2d 852 (2d Cir. 1982); and *Apple Computer, Inc. v. Franklin Computer Corp.,* 714 F.2d 1240 (3d Cir. 1983).
32. *Whelan Associates, Inc. v. Jaslow Dental Laboratory, Inc.,* 797 F.2d 1222 (3d Cir. 1986).

33. *MAI Systems Corp. v. Peak Computer, Inc.,* 991 F.2d 511 (9th Cir. 1993).
34. *DSC Communications Corp. v. Pulse Communications, Inc.,* 170 F.3d 1354 (Fed. Cir. 1999).

INSIGHT INTO E-COMMERCE
Search Engines versus Copyright Owners

Since their humble beginnings more than a decade ago, search engines have become ubiquitous in the e-commerce world. Every day, millions of consumers use search engines to locate various products on the Web. A major legal question arises, however, when the results of a search include copyrighted intellectual property, such as books, downloadable software, movies and other videos, and images. Can the owner of the search engine that returned these results be held liable for copyright infringement?

The Betamax Doctrine

The basic rule that has governed issues relating to the application of new technology for uses that might include copyright infringement was set out more than two decades ago by the United States Supreme Court in the landmark case *Sony Corporation of America v. Universal City Studios.*[a] The case involved the then new technology of the videocassette recorder (VCR), which was available in two formats—VHS and Betamax. Owners of copyrighted television programs, concerned that VCR owners were using the equipment to copy TV programs, brought a suit against a VCR manufacturer, claiming that it was liable for its customers' copyright infringement. The Supreme Court, however, in what became known as the

Betamax doctrine, held that the manufacturer was not liable for creating a technology that certain customers might use for copyright infringing purposes, as long as that technology was capable of substantial noninfringing uses. Legal scholars believe that the Betamax doctrine has allowed for the development of many other technologies that are capable of both infringing and noninfringing uses—including CD-ROM burners, DVRs, TiVo, Apple's iPod, and even the personal computer.

As discussed later in the text, twenty years after the *Sony* case, organizations and companies in the music and film industries brought a copyright infringement suit against Grokster, Morpheus, and KaZaA, the makers of file-sharing software that allowed millions of individuals to copy copyrighted music. In that case, the Supreme Court did find that there was ample evidence that the software makers had taken steps to promote copyright infringement, but significantly the Court did not overturn the Betamax doctrine. The Court did not specify what steps are necessary to impose liability on the provider of a technology, however.[b]

Does Providing Thumbnail Images Violate Copyright Law?

Just as VCRs and file-sharing technology raised new issues of copyright infringement, so does today's search engine technology. In response to a search

---

a. 464 U.S. 417, 104 S.Ct. 774, 78 L.Ed.2d 574 (1984).

b. *Metro-Goldwyn-Mayer Studios, Inc. v. Grokster, Ltd.,* 545 U.S. 913, 125 S.Ct. 2764, 162 L.Ed.2d 781 (2005).

Electronic Theft Act of 1997[35] and the Digital Millennium Copyright Act of 1998.[36]

The No Electronic Theft Act Prior to 1997, criminal penalties could be imposed under copyright law only if unauthorized copies were exchanged for financial gain. Yet much piracy of copyrighted materials was "altruistic" in nature; that is, unauthorized copies were made and distributed not for financial gain but simply for reasons of generosity—to share the copies with others. To combat altruistic piracy and for other reasons, Congress passed the No Electronic Theft (NET) Act of 1997.

NET extended criminal liability for the piracy of copyrighted materials to persons who exchange unauthorized copies of copyrighted works, such as software, even though they realize no profit from the exchange. The act also altered the traditional "fair use" doctrine by imposing penalties on those who make unauthorized electronic copies of books, magazines, movies, or music for *personal* use. The criminal penalties for violating the act are relatively severe; they include fines as high as $250,000 and incarceration for up to five years.

The Digital Millennium Copyright Act of 1998 The passage of the Digital Millennium Copyright Act (DMCA) of 1998 gave significant protection to owners of copyrights in digital information.[37]

---

35. Pub. L. No. 105-147 (1997). Codified at 17 U.S.C. Sections 101, 506; 18 U.S.C. Sections 2311, 2319, 2319A, 2320; and 28 U.S.C. Sections 994 and 1498.

36. 17 U.S.C. Sections 512, 1201–1205, 1301–1332; and 28 U.S.C. Section 4001.

37. This act implemented the World Intellectual Property Organization Copyright Treaty of 1996, which will be discussed later in this chapter.

request, numerous search engines show thumbnail images of books, album covers, and copyrighted photographs. Arriba Soft Corporation (now ditto.com), for example, operated a search engine that displayed its results in the form of thumbnail pictures. It obtained its database of photographs by copying images from other Web sites. When professional photographer Leslie Kelly discovered that his copyrighted photographs were part of Arriba's database, he brought a suit for copyright infringement. Arriba prevailed, as the Ninth Circuit Court of Appeals ruled that its thumbnails were a fair use under the Copyright Act.[c]

A recent innovation enables search engines to search specifically for images. Google Image Search, for example, stores thumbnail images of its search results on Google's servers. The thumbnail images are reduced, lower-resolution versions of full-size images stored on third party computers. In 2005, *Perfect 10*, a men's magazine that features high-resolution photographs of topless and nude women, brought a suit to enjoin Google from caching and displaying its photographs as thumbnails. *Perfect 10* argued that because Google "created the audience" for its sites and indexes, Google should be liable for whatever infringements occurred on those sites. The magazine also contended that Google had directly infringed *Perfect 10*'s copyrights by in-line linking and framing images published on other sites. (The case was combined with a similar suit brought against Amazon.com for its A9 search engine.) Once again,

however, as in its *Arriba* decision, the Ninth Circuit Court of Appeals held that the thumbnails constituted a fair use. Pointing out the public benefit that search engines provide, the court said that until *Perfect 10* gave Google specific URLs for infringing images, Google had no duty to act and could not be held liable. The court further held that Google could not "supervise or control" the third party Web sites linked to its search results.[d] In sum, the court refused to hold the creators of image search technology liable for users' infringement because the technology is capable of both infringing and noninfringing uses—just as the Betamax doctrine protected VCR manufacturers from liability for users' infringement.

CRITICAL THINKING

INSIGHT INTO TECHNOLOGY

What has changed in the world of technology since the Betamax doctrine was enunciated? Does the fact that more and more intellectual property is being digitized and made available online alter the reasoning underlying the Betamax doctrine?

---

c. *Kelly v. Arriba Soft Corporation*, 336 F.3d 811 (9th Cir. 2003).

d. *Perfect 10, Inc. v. Amazon.com, Inc.*, 487 F.3d 701 (9th Cir. 2007).

Among other things, the act established civil and criminal penalties for anyone who circumvents (bypasses, or gets around—by using a special decryption program, for example) encryption software or other technological antipiracy protection. Also prohibited are the manufacture, import, sale, and distribution of devices or services for circumvention.

The DMCA provides for exceptions to fit the needs of libraries, scientists, universities, and others. In general, the law does not restrict the "fair use" of circumvention methods for educational and other noncommercial purposes. For example, circumvention is allowed to test computer security, to conduct encryption research, to protect personal privacy, and to enable parents to monitor their children's use of the Internet. The exceptions are to be reconsidered every three years.

The DMCA also limits the liability of Internet service providers (ISPs). Under the act, an ISP is not liable for any copyright infringement by its customer *unless* the ISP is aware of the subscriber's violation. An ISP may be held liable only if it fails to take action to shut the subscriber down after learning of the violation. A copyright holder must act promptly, however, by pursuing a claim in court, or the subscriber has the right to be restored to online access.

MP3 and File-Sharing Technology

Soon after the Internet became popular, a few enterprising programmers created software to compress large data files, particularly those associated with music. The reduced file sizes make transmitting music over the Internet feasible. The most widely known compression and decompression system is MP3, which enables music fans to download songs or entire CDs onto their computers or onto portable listening devices, such as Rio or iPod. The MP3 system also made it possible for music fans to access other music fans' files by engaging in file-sharing via the Internet.

Peer-to-Peer (P2P) Networking File-sharing via the Internet is accomplished through what is called **peer-to-peer (P2P) networking.** The concept is simple. Rather than going through a central Web server, P2P uses numerous personal computers (PCs) that are connected to the Internet. Files stored on one PC can be accessed by others who are members of the same network. Sometimes this is called a **distributed network** because parts of the network are distributed all over the country or the world. File-sharing offers an unlimited number of uses for distributed networks. For example, thousands of researchers allow their home computers' computing power to be simultaneously accessed through file-sharing software so that very large mathematical problems can be solved quickly. Additionally, persons scattered throughout the country or the world can work together on the same project by using file-sharing programs.

Sharing Stored Music Files When file-sharing is used to download others' stored music files, copyright issues arise. Recording artists and their labels stand to lose large amounts of royalties and revenues if relatively few CDs are purchased and then made available on distributed networks, from which everyone can get them for free. The issue of file-sharing infringement has been the subject of an ongoing debate for some time.

For example, in the highly publicized case of *A&M Records, Inc. v. Napster, Inc.,*[38] several firms in the recording industry sued Napster, Inc., the owner of the then popular Napster Web site. The Napster site provided registered users with free software that enabled them to transfer exact copies of the contents of MP3 files from one computer to another via the Internet. Napster also maintained centralized search indices so that users could locate specific titles or artists' recordings on the computers of other members. The firms argued that Napster should be liable for contributory

and vicarious[39] (indirect) copyright infringement because it assisted others in obtaining copies of copyrighted music without the copyright owners' permission. The federal district court agreed, and the U.S. Court of Appeals for the Ninth Circuit affirmed, holding Napster liable for violating copyright laws. The court reasoned that Napster was liable for its users' infringement because the technology that Napster had used was centralized and gave it "the ability to locate infringing material listed on its search indices and the right to terminate users' access to the system."

After the *Napster* decision, the recording industry filed and won numerous lawsuits against companies that distribute online file-sharing software. The courts held these companies liable based on two theories: contributory infringement, which applies if the company had reason to know about a user's infringement and failed to stop it, and vicarious liability, which exists if the company was able to control the users' activities and stood to benefit financially from their infringement.

The Evolution of File-Sharing Technologies In the wake of the *Napster* decision, other companies developed new technologies that allow P2P network users to share stored music files, without paying a fee, more quickly and efficiently than ever. Software such as Morpheus, KaZaA, and LimeWire, for example, provides users with an interface that is similar to a Web browser.[40] Companies need not locate songs for users on other members' computers. Instead, the software automatically annotates files with descriptive information so that the music can easily be categorized and cross-referenced (by artist and title, for instance). When a user performs a search, the software is able to locate a list of peers that have the file available for downloading. Also, to expedite the P2P transfer, the software distributes the download task over the entire list of peers simultaneously. By downloading even one file, the user becomes a point of distribution for that file, which is then automatically shared with others on the network.

Because the file-sharing software was decentralized and did not use search indices that would enable the companies to locate infringing material, they had

---

38. 239 F.3d 1004 (9th Cir. 2001).

39. *Vicarious (indirect) liability* exists when one person is subject to liability for another's actions. A common example occurs in the employment context, when an employer is held vicariously liable by third parties for torts committed by employees in the course of their employment.
40. Note that in 2005, KaZaA entered into a settlement agreement with four major music companies that had alleged copyright infringement. KaZaA agreed to offer only legitimate, fee-based music downloads in the future.

no ability to supervise or control which music (or other media files) their users exchanged. In addition, it was difficult for courts to apply the traditional doctrines of contributory and vicarious liability to these new technologies.

The Supreme Court's *Grokster* Decision

In 2005, the United States Supreme Court expanded the liability of file-sharing companies in its decision in *Metro-Goldwyn-Mayer Studios, Inc. v. Grokster, Ltd.*[41] In that case, organizations in the music and film industry (the plaintiffs) sued several companies that distribute file-sharing software used in P2P networks, including Grokster, Ltd., and StreamCast Networks, Inc. (the defendants). The plaintiffs claimed that the defendants were contributorily and vicariously liable for the infringement of their end users. The Supreme Court held that "one who distributes a device [software] with the object of promoting its use to infringe the copyright, as shown by clear expression or other affirmative steps taken to foster infringement, is liable for the resulting acts of infringement by third parties."

Although the Supreme Court did not specify what kind of affirmative steps are necessary to establish liability, it did note that there was ample evidence that the defendants had acted with the intent to cause copyright violations. (Grokster, Ltd., later settled this dispute out of court and stopped distributing its software.) Essentially, this means that file-sharing companies that have taken affirmative steps to promote copyright infringement can be held secondarily liable for millions of infringing acts that their users commit daily. Because the Court did not define exactly what is necessary to impose liability, however, a substantial amount of legal uncertainty remains concerning this issue. Although some file-sharing companies have been shut down, illegal file-sharing—and lawsuits against file-sharing companies and the individuals who use them—has continued in the years since this decision.

Trade Secrets

The law of trade secrets protects some business processes and information that are not, or cannot be, patented, copyrighted, or trademarked against appropriation by competitors. **Trade secrets** include customer lists, plans, research and development, pricing information, marketing methods, production techniques, and

generally anything that makes an individual company unique and that would have value to a competitor.

Unlike copyright and trademark protection, protection of trade secrets extends both to ideas and to their expression. (For this reason, and because a trade secret involves no registration or filing requirements, trade secret protection may be well suited for software.) Of course, the secret formula, method, or other information must be disclosed to some persons, particularly to key employees. Businesses generally attempt to protect their trade secrets by having all employees who use the process or information agree in their contracts, or in confidentiality agreements, never to divulge it. (See the *Business Application* feature on the next page.)

State and Federal Law on Trade Secrets

Under Section 757 of the *Restatement of Torts,* "One who discloses or uses another's trade secret, without a privilege to do so, is liable to the other if (1) he [or she] discovered the secret by improper means, or (2) his [or her] disclosure or use constitutes a breach of confidence reposed in him [or her] by the other in disclosing the secret to him [or her]." The theft of confidential business data by industrial espionage, as when a business taps into a competitor's computer, is a theft of trade secrets without any contractual violation and is actionable in itself.

Until thirty years ago, virtually all law with respect to trade secrets was common law. In an effort to reduce the unpredictability of the common law in this area, a model act, the Uniform Trade Secrets Act, was presented to the states for adoption in 1979. Parts of the act have been adopted in more than thirty states. Typically, a state that has adopted parts of the act has adopted only those parts that encompass its own existing common law. Additionally, in 1996 Congress passed the Economic Espionage Act,[42] which made the theft of trade secrets a federal crime. We will examine the provisions and significance of this act in Chapter 9, in the context of crimes related to business.

Trade Secrets in Cyberspace

New computer technology is undercutting a business firm's ability to protect its confidential information, including trade secrets.[43] For example, a dishonest

---

41. 545 U.S. 913, 125 S.Ct. 2764, 162 L.Ed.2d 781 (2005).

42. 18 U.S.C. Sections 1831–1839.

43. Note that in at least one case, a court has held that customers' e-mail addresses may constitute trade secrets. See *T-N-T Motorsports, Inc. v. Hennessey Motorsports, Inc.,* 965 S.W.2d 18 (Tex.App.—Houston [1 Dist.] 1998); rehearing overruled (1998); petition dismissed (1998).

MANAGEMENT FACES A LEGAL ISSUE

Most successful businesses have trade secrets. The law protects trade secrets indefinitely provided that the information is not generally known, is kept secret, and has commercial value. Sometimes, of course, a business needs to disclose secret information to a party in the course of conducting business. For example, a company may need to engage a consultant to revamp a computer system or hire a marketing firm to implement a sales program. In addition, the company may also wish to expand its operations and will need a foreign agent or distributor. All of these individuals or firms may need access to some of the company's trade secrets. One way to protect against the unauthorized disclosure of such information is through *confidentiality agreements*. In such an agreement, one party promises not to divulge information about the other party's activities to anyone else and not to use the other party's confidential information for his or her own benefit. Most confidentiality agreements are included in licensing and employment contracts. The legal question is whether the courts will uphold such an agreement if a business claims it has been violated.

WHAT THE COURTS SAY

The courts are divided on the validity of confidentiality agreements, particularly in employment contracts. At issue is often whether the trade secrets described in the confidentiality agreement are truly "secrets." If they are generally known outside the employer's business, the courts normally will not enforce the agreement. When a clear argument can be made that such secrets are truly secret, a court normally will enforce a confidentiality agreement. For example, consider an insurance company. An employee signed both a confidentiality agreement and a *noncompete clause* (see Chapter 13). Just before quitting, that employee copied her employer's proprietary sales, marketing, and product information sheets. She then used them while working for her new employer. She also solicited former clients to move their business to her new employer's firm.

An appellate court upheld an injunction preventing this employee from using, divulging, disclosing, or communicating trade secrets and confidential information derived from her former employer.[a]

In the technology sector, confidentiality agreements are widespread for obvious reasons. One case involved a complicated system for testing flash memory cards, like those used in digital cameras and MP3 music players. An employee copied project documents he had authored and transmitted them to a third party for the purpose of using those documents to launch his own independent business. This employee had signed an explicit confidentiality agreement. At trial, one of his defenses was that his former employer had not used reasonable efforts to maintain secrecy because some employees were uncertain how to apply the company's procedures for handling confidential and trade secret documents. The court was unimpressed. The former employee was prevented from using those trade secrets.[b]

Employers often attempt to protect trade secrets by requiring potential employees to sign noncompete agreements. If the employer would suffer irreparable harm from the former employee's accepting employment with a competitor, the court will often uphold such agreements.[c]

IMPLICATIONS FOR MANAGERS

Most companies should require their employees to sign a confidentiality agreement to protect trade secrets. That is not enough, though. A company should have formal written procedures that apply to the selection and retention of documents relating to valuable trade secrets. If these documents exist only on hard drives, the firm should put an encryption system in place and limit access to the files that contain trade secrets.

---
a. *Freeman v. Brown Hiller, Inc.,* ___ S.W.3d ___, 2008 WL 868252. (Ark.App. 2008).
b. *Verigy US, Inc. v. Mayder,* ___ F.Supp.2d ___, 2008 WL 564634 (N.D.Cal. 2008).
c. *Gleeson v. Preferred Sourcing, LLC,* 883 N.E.2d 164 (Ind.App. 2008).

CONCEPT SUMMARY 6.1
Forms of Intellectual Property

	Definition	How Acquired	Duration	Remedy for Infringement
PATENT	A grant from the government that gives an inventor exclusive rights to an invention.	By filing a patent application with the U.S. Patent and Trademark Office and receiving its approval.	Twenty years from the date of the application; for design patents, fourteen years.	Monetary damages, including royalties and lost profits, *plus* attorneys' fees. Damages may be tripled for intentional infringements.
COPYRIGHT	The right of an author or originator of a literary or artistic work, or other production that falls within a specified category, to have the exclusive use of that work for a given period of time.	Automatic (once the work or creation is fixed in a durable medium). Only the *expression* of an idea (and not the idea itself) can be protected by copyright.	For authors: the life of the author plus 70 years. For publishers: 95 years after the date of publication or 120 years after creation.	Actual damages plus profits received by the party who infringed or statutory damages under the Copyright Act, *plus* costs and attorneys' fees in either situation.
TRADEMARK (SERVICE MARK AND TRADE DRESS)	Any distinctive word, name, symbol, or device (image or appearance), or combination thereof, that an entity uses to distinguish its goods or services from those of others. The owner has the exclusive right to use that mark or trade dress.	1. At common law, ownership created by use of the mark. 2. Registration with the appropriate federal or state office gives notice and is permitted if the mark is currently in use or will be within the next six months.	Unlimited, as long as it is in use. To continue notice by registration, the owner must renew by filing between the fifth and sixth years, and thereafter, every ten years.	1. Injunction prohibiting the future use of the mark. 2. Actual damages plus profits received by the party who infringed (can be increased under the Lanham Act). 3. Destruction of articles that infringed. 4. *Plus* costs and attorneys' fees.
TRADE SECRET	Any information that a business possesses and that gives the business an advantage over competitors (including formulas, lists, patterns, plans, processes, and programs).	Through the originality and development of the information and processes that constitute the business secret and are unknown to others.	Unlimited, so long as not revealed to others. Once revealed to others, it is no longer a trade secret.	Monetary damages for misappropriation (the Uniform Trade Secrets Act also permits punitive damages if willful), *plus* costs and attorneys' fees.

employee could e-mail trade secrets in a company's computer to a competitor or a future employer. If e-mail is not an option, the employee might walk out with the information on a flash pen drive.

International Protection for Intellectual Property

For many years, the United States has been a party to various international agreements relating to intellectual property rights. For example, the Paris Convention of 1883, to which about 170 countries are signatory, allows parties in one country to file for patent and trademark protection in any of the other member countries. Other international agreements in this area include the Berne Convention, the TRIPS agreement, and the Madrid Protocol.

The Berne Convention

Under the Berne Convention (an international copyright agreement) of 1886, as amended, if an American writes a book, every country that has signed the convention must recognize the American author's copyright in the book. Also, if a citizen of a country that has not signed the convention first publishes a book in one of the 170 countries that have signed, all other countries that have signed the convention must recognize that author's copyright. Copyright notice is not needed to gain protection under the Berne Convention for works published after March 1, 1989.

The laws of many countries, as well as international laws, are being updated to reflect changes in technology and the expansion of the Internet. Copyright holders and other owners of intellectual property generally agree that changes in the law are needed to stop the increasing international piracy of their property. The World Intellectual Property Organization (WIPO) Copyright Treaty of 1996, a special agreement under the Berne Convention, attempts to update international law governing copyright protection to include more safeguards against copyright infringement via the Internet. The United States signed the WIPO treaty in 1996 and implemented its terms in the Digital Millennium Copyright Act of 1998, which was discussed earlier in this chapter.

The Berne Convention and other international agreements have given some protection to intellectual property on a global level. Another significant worldwide agreement to increase such protection is the Trade-Related Aspects of Intellectual Property Rights agreement—or, more simply, the TRIPS agreement.

The TRIPS Agreement

Representatives from more than one hundred nations signed the TRIPS agreement in 1994. It was one of several documents that were annexed to the agreement that created the World Trade Organization, or WTO, in 1995. The TRIPS agreement established, for the first time, standards for the international protection of intellectual property rights, including patents, trademarks, and copyrights for movies, computer programs, books, and music. The TRIPS agreement provides that each member country must include in its domestic laws broad intellectual property rights and effective remedies (including civil and criminal penalties) for violations of those rights.

Members Cannot Discriminate against Foreign Intellectual Property Owners

Generally, the TRIPS agreement forbids member nations from discriminating against foreign owners of intellectual property rights (in the administration, regulation, or adjudication of such rights). In other words, a member nation cannot give its own nationals (citizens) favorable treatment without offering the same treatment to nationals of all member countries. For instance, if a U.S. software manufacturer brings a suit for the infringement of intellectual property rights under a member nation's national laws, the U.S. manufacturer is entitled to receive the same treatment as a domestic manufacturer. Each member nation must also ensure that legal procedures are available for parties who wish to bring actions for infringement of intellectual property rights. Additionally, a related document established a mechanism for settling disputes among member nations.

Covers All Types of Intellectual Property

Particular provisions of the TRIPS agreement relate to patent, trademark, and copyright protection for intellectual property. The agreement specifically provides copyright protection for computer programs by stating that compilations of data, databases, and other materials are "intellectual creations" and are to be protected as copyrightable works. Other provisions relate to trade secrets and the rental of computer programs and cinematographic works.

The Madrid Protocol

In the past, one of the difficulties in protecting U.S. trademarks internationally was the time and expense involved in applying for trademark registration in foreign countries. The filing fees and procedures for trademark registration vary significantly among individual countries. The Madrid Protocol, which President George W. Bush signed into law in 2003, may help to resolve these problems. The Madrid Protocol is an international treaty that has been signed by seventy-three countries. Under its provisions, a U.S. company wishing to register its trademark abroad can submit a single application and designate other member countries in which the U.S. company would like to register its mark. The treaty is designed to reduce the costs of international trademark protection by more than 60 percent, according to proponents.

Although the Madrid Protocol may simplify and reduce the cost of trademark registration in foreign countries, it remains to be seen whether it will provide significant benefits to trademark owners. Even assuming that the registration process will be easier, there is still the issue of whether member countries will enforce the law and protect the mark.

REVIEWING Intellectual Property and Internet Law

Two computer science majors, Trent and Xavier, have an idea for a new video game, which they propose to call "Hallowed." They form a business and begin developing their idea. Several months later, Trent and Xavier run into a problem with their design and consult with a friend, Brad, who is an expert in designing computer source codes. After the software is completed but before Hallowed is marketed, a video game called "Halo 2" is released for both the Xbox and Game Cube systems. Halo 2 uses source codes similar to those of Hallowed and imitates Hallowed's overall look and feel, although not all the features are alike. Using the information presented in the chapter, answer the following questions.

1. Would the name "Hallowed" receive protection as a trademark or as trade dress?

2. If Trent and Xavier had obtained a business process patent on Hallowed, would the release of Halo 2 infringe on their patent? Why or why not?

3. Based only on the facts described above, could Trent and Xavier sue the makers of Halo 2 for copyright infringement? Why or why not?

4. Suppose that Trent and Xavier discover that Brad took the idea of Hallowed and sold it to the company that produced Halo 2. Which type of intellectual property issue does this raise?

TERMS AND CONCEPTS

certification mark
collective mark
copyright
cyber mark

cybersquatting
dilution
distributed network
domain name
intellectual property
meta tag
patent

peer-to-peer (P2P)
   networking
service mark
trade dress
trade name
trade secret
trademark

QUESTIONS AND CASE PROBLEMS

8–1. Professor Wise is teaching a summer seminar in business torts at State University. Several times during the course, he makes copies of relevant sections from business law texts and distributes them to his students. Wise does not realize that the daughter of one of the textbook authors is a member of his seminar. She tells her father about Wise's copying activities, which have taken place without her father's or his publisher's permission. Her father sues Wise for copyright infringement. Wise claims protection under the fair use doctrine. Who will prevail? Explain.

8–2. QUESTION WITH SAMPLE ANSWER

In which of the following situations would a court likely hold Ursula liable for copyright infringement?

(a) Ursula goes to the library and photocopies ten pages from a scholarly journal relating to a topic on which she is writing a term paper.

(b) Ursula makes blouses, dresses, and other clothes and sells them in her small shop. She advertises some of the outfits as Guest items, hoping that customers might mistakenly assume that they were made by Guess, the well-known clothing manufacturer.

(c) Ursula teaches Latin American history at a small university. She has a VCR and frequently tapes television programs relating to Latin America. She then takes the videos to her classroom so that her students can watch them.

• For a sample answer to Question 8–2, go to Appendix C at the end of this text.

8–3. Domain Name Disputes. In 1999, Steve and Pierce Thumann and their father, Fred, created Spider Webs, Ltd., a partnership, to, according to Steve, "develop Internet address names." Spider Webs registered nearly two thousand Internet domain names at an average cost of $70 each, including the names of cities, the names of buildings, names related to a business or trade (such as air-conditioning or plumbing), and the names of famous companies. It offered many of the names for sale on its Web site and through eBay.com. Spider Webs registered the domain name "ERNESTANDJULIOGALLO.COM" in Spider Webs' name. E. & J. Gallo Winery filed a suit against Spider Webs, alleging, in part, violations of the Anticybersquatting Consumer Protection Act (ACPA). Gallo asked the court for, among other things, statutory damages. Gallo also sought to have the domain name at issue transferred to Gallo. During the suit, Spider Webs published anticorporate articles and negative opinions about Gallo, as well as discussions of the suit and of the risks associated with alcohol use, at the URL ERNESTANDJULIOGALLO.COM. Should the court rule in Gallo's favor? Why or why not? [*E. & J. Gallo Winery v. Spider Webs, Ltd.,* 129 F.Supp.2d 1033 (S.D.Tex. 2001)]

8–4. CASE PROBLEM WITH SAMPLE ANSWER

Gateway, Inc., sells computers, computer products, computer peripherals, and computer accessories throughout the world. By 1988, Gateway had begun its first national advertising campaign using black-and-white cows and black-and-white cow spots. By 1991, black-and-white cows and spots had become Gateway's symbol. The next year, Gateway registered a black-and-white cow-spots design in association with computers and computer peripherals as its trademark. Companion Products, Inc. (CPI), sells stuffed animals trademarked as "Stretch Pets." Stretch Pets have an animal's head and an elastic body that can wrap around the edges of computer monitors, computer cases, or televisions. CPI produces sixteen Stretch Pets, including a polar bear, a moose, several dogs, and a penguin. One of CPI's top-selling products is a black-and-white cow that CPI identifies as "Cody Cow," which was first sold in 1999. Gateway filed a suit in a federal district court against CPI, alleging trade dress infringement and related claims. What is trade dress? What is the major factor in cases involving trade dress infringement? Does that factor exist in this case? Explain. [*Gateway, Inc. v. Companion Products, Inc.,* 384 F.3d 503 (8th Cir. 2004)]

• To view a sample answer for Problem 8–4, go to this book's Web site at **www.cengage. com/blaw/jentz**, select "Chapter 8," and click on "Case Problem with Sample Answer."

8–5. Patent Infringement. As a cattle rancher in Nebraska, Gerald Gohl used handheld searchlights to find and help calving animals (animals giving birth) in harsh blizzard conditions. Gohl thought that it would be more helpful to have a portable searchlight mounted on the outside of a vehicle and remotely controlled. He and Al Gebhardt developed and patented practical applications of this idea—the Golight and the wireless, remote-controlled Radio Ray, which could rotate 360 degrees—and formed Golight, Inc., to make and market these products. In 1997, Wal-Mart Stores, Inc., began selling a portable, wireless, remote-controlled searchlight that was identical to the Radio Ray except for a stop piece that prevented the light from rotating more than 351 degrees. Golight sent Wal-Mart a letter claiming that its device infringed Golight's patent. Wal-Mart sold its remaining inventory of the devices and stopped carrying the product. Golight filed a suit in a federal district court against Wal-Mart, alleging patent infringement. How should the court rule? Explain. [*Golight, Inc. v. Wal-Mart Stores, Inc.,* 355 F.3d 1327 (Fed.Cir. 2004)]

8–6. Copyright Infringement. Bridgeport Music, Inc., is in the business of publishing music and exploiting musical composition copyrights. Westbound Records, Inc., is in the business of recording and distributing sound recordings. Bridgeport and Westbound own the composition and recording copyrights to "Get Off Your Ass and Jam" by George Clinton, Jr., and the Funkadelics. The recording "Get Off" opens with a three-note solo guitar riff that lasts four seconds. The rap song "100 Miles and Runnin'" contains a two-second sample from the guitar solo, at a lower pitch, looped and extended to sixteen beats, in five places in the song, with each looped segment lasting about seven seconds. "100 Miles" was included in the sound track of the movie *I Got the Hook Up,* which was distributed by No Limit Films. Bridgeport, Westbound, and others filed a suit in a federal district court against No Limit and others, alleging copyright infringement. Does a musician commit copyright infringement when he or she copies any part—even as little as two seconds—of a copyrighted sound recording without the permission of the copyright's owner? If so, how can an artist legally incorporate a riff from another's work in his or her own recording? Discuss. [*Bridgeport Music, Inc. v. Dimension Films,* 410 F.3d 792 (6th Cir. 2005)]

8–7. Trade Secrets. Briefing.com offers Internet-based analyses of investment opportunities to investors. Richard Green is the company's president. One of Briefing.com's competitors is StreetAccount, LLC (limited liability company), whose owners include Gregory Jones and Cynthia Dietzmann. Jones worked for Briefing.com for six years until he quit in March 2003 and was a member of its board of directors until April 2003. Dietzmann worked for Briefing.com for seven years until she quit in March 2003. As Briefing.com employees, Jones and Dietzmann had access to confidential business data. For instance, Dietzmann developed a list of contacts through which Briefing.com obtained market information to display online. When Dietzmann quit, however, she did not return all of the contact information to the company. Briefing.com and Green filed a suit in a federal district court against Jones, Dietzmann, and StreetAccount, alleging that they appropriated these data and other "trade secrets" to form a competing business. What are trade secrets? Why are they protected? Under what circumstances is a party liable at common law for their appropriation? How should these principles apply in this case? [*Briefing.com v. Jones,* 2006 WY 16, 126 P.3d 928 (2006)]

8–8. Trademarks. In 1969, Jack Masquelier, a professor of pharmacology, discovered a chemical antioxidant made from the bark of a French pine tree. The substance supposedly assists in nutritional distribution and blood circulation. Horphag Research, Ltd., began to sell the product under the name Pycnogenol, which Horphag registered as a trademark in 1993.

Pycnogenol became one of the fifteen best-selling herbal supplements in the United States. In 1999, through the Web site **healthierlife.com**, Larry Garcia began to sell Masquelier's Original OPCs, a supplement derived from grape pits. Claiming that this product was the "true Pycnogenol," Garcia used the mark as a meta tag and a generic term, attributing the results of research on Horphag's product to Masquelier's and altering quotations from scientific literature to substitute the name of Masquelier's product for Horphag's. Customers who purchased Garcia's product contacted Horphag about it, only to learn that they had not bought Horphag's product. Others called Horphag to ask whether Garcia "was selling . . . real Pycnogenol." Horphag filed a suit in a federal district court against Garcia, alleging, among other things, that he was diluting Horphag's mark. What is trademark dilution? Did it occur here? Explain. [*Horphag Research, Ltd. v. Garcia,* 475 F.3d 1029 (9th Cir. 2007)]

8–9. A QUESTION OF ETHICS
Custom Copies, Inc., in Gainesville, Florida, is a copy shop that, on request, reproduces and distributes, for profit, material published and owned by others. One of the copy shop's primary activities is the preparation and sale of coursepacks, which contain compilations of readings for college courses. For a particular coursepack, a teacher selects the readings and delivers a syllabus to the copy shop, which obtains the materials from a library, copies them, and then binds and sells the copies. Blackwell Publishing, Inc., in Malden, Massachusetts, publishes books and journals in medicine and other fields and owns the copyrights to these publications. Blackwell and others filed a suit in a federal district court against Custom Copies, alleging copyright infringement for its "routine and systematic reproduction of materials from plaintiffs' publications, without seeking permission," to compile coursepacks for classes at the University of Florida. The plaintiffs asked the court to issue an injunction and award them damages, as well the profit from the infringement. The defendant filed a motion to dismiss the complaint. [Blackwell Publishing, Inc. v. Custom Copies, Inc., ___ F.Supp.2d ___ (N.D.Fla. 2006)]

(a) Custom Copies argued in part that it did not "distribute" the coursepacks. Does a copy shop violate copyright law if it only copies materials for coursepacks? Does the copying fall under the "fair use" exception? Should the court grant the defendant's motion? Why or why not?

(b) What is the potential impact of creating and selling copies of a book or journal without the permission of, and the payment of royalties or a fee to, the copyright owner? Explain.

8-10. VIDEO QUESTION

Go to this text's Web site at **www.cengage. com/blaw/jentz** and select "Chapter 8." Click on "Video Questions" and view the video titled *The Jerk*. Then answer the following questions.

(a) In the video, Navin (Steve Martin) creates a special handle for Mr. Fox's (Bill Macy's) glasses. Can Navin obtain a patent or a copyright protecting his invention? Explain your answer.

(b) Suppose that after Navin legally protects his idea, Fox steals it and decides to develop it for himself, without Navin's permission. Has Fox committed infringement? If so, what kind—trademark, patent, or copyright?

(c) Suppose that after Navin legally protects his idea, he realizes he doesn't have the funds to mass-produce the glasses' special handle. Navin therefore agrees to allow Fox to manufacture the product. Has Navin granted Fox a license? Explain.

(d) Assume that Navin is able to manufacture his invention. What might Navin do to ensure that his product is identifiable and can be distinguished from other products on the market?

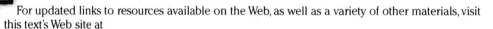

LAW ON THE WEB

For updated links to resources available on the Web, as well as a variety of other materials, visit this text's Web site at

www.cengage.com/blaw/jentz

An excellent overview of the laws governing various forms of intellectual property is available at FindLaw's Web site. Go to

profs.lp.findlaw.com

You can find answers to frequently asked questions (FAQs) about patents, trademarks, and copyrights—and links to registration forms, statutes, international patent and trademark offices, and numerous other resources—at the Web site of the U.S. Patent and Trademark Office. Go to

www.uspto.gov

To perform patent searches and to access information on the patenting process, go to

www.bustpatents.com

You can also access the European Patent Office's Web site at

www.epo.org

For information on copyrights, go to the U.S. Copyright Office at

www.copyright/gov

You can find extensive information on copyright law—including United States Supreme Court decisions in this area and the texts of the Berne Convention and other international treaties on copyright issues—at the Web site of the Legal Information Institute at Cornell University's School of Law. Go to

www.law.cornell.edu/wex/index.php/Copyright

Legal Research Exercises on the Web

Go to **www.cengage.com/blaw/jentz**, the Web site that accompanies this text. Select "Chapter 8" and click on "Internet Exercises." There you will find the following Internet research exercises that you can perform to learn more about the topics covered in this chapter.

Internet Exercise 8–1: Legal Perspective
Unwarranted Legal Threats

Internet Exercise 8–2: Management Perspective
Protecting Intellectual Property across Borders

Internet Exercise 8–3: Technological Perspective
File-Sharing

Case No. 21

DISCLOSURE AND MISAPPROPRIATION OF TRADE SECRETS

Chemfab Corporation v. Integrated Liner Technologies, Inc.
Appellate Division, 3rd Department

263 AD2d 788, 693 NYSd 752 (3rd Dept, 1999)

FACTS: Locite Corporation was the employer of several defendants, who were laid off in June, 1993. One month later those defendants created defendant corporation for the purpose of manufacturing a product called septa, the same business Locite conducted. Soon thereafter defendant began selling septa to La-Pha-Pak, a German company that had been a significant customer of Locite. Information distributed through trade shows and conferences identified La-Pha-Pak as a septa buyer. Locite's successor in interest [a company that bought Locite], Chemfab Corporation, sued defendants claiming the identity of La-Pha-Pak as a purchaser of septa was a trade secret.

ISSUE: Do defendants' actions constitute misappropriation of Locite's trade secrets?

DECISION: No, judgment for defendants.

REASONING: A trade secret is information treated as confidential used in a business that enables it to obtain an advantage over competitors who do not know or use that information. In this case, La-Pha-Pak's identity as a potential customer for septa was readily available through trade shows and conferences.

Case No. 22

TRADEMARK INFRINGEMENT

<u>Gallina v. Giacalone</u>

Supreme Court, Kings County

171 M2d 645, 655 NYS2d 317 (1997)

FACTS: In 1959 defendant Paul Giacalone adopted the stage name Paul DeMaya and created a musical doo-wop group named The Fireflies. The group performed together for four years and had two hit records entitled, "You Were Mine" and "I Can't Say Goodbye", both composed by defendant. Although the group broke up, royalties continued to be generated from record sales and radio air play of the group's recordings.

Thirty years later in 1992 defendant was asked defendant to audition three musicians, the plaintiffs herein, in an effort to reconstitute the Fireflies. Defendant agreed. They gave one performance together and defendant then decided he did not wish to continue to perform with them. Plaintiffs nonetheless continued to pursue singing engagements for the Fireflies and performed under that name. In advertisements, posters and appearances plaintiffs claimed they would perform "their smash hits of You Were Mine and I Can't Say Goodbye." Plaintiffs also claimed in an interview with a widely read daily newspaper in New York City that defendant withdrew from the Fireflies and plaintiffs had acquired a trademark for the name. In response defendant repeatedly communicated with journals, concert and event sponsors and radio stations that he and not plaintiffs represent the Fireflies. He further warned that he would sue any entity that permitted plaintiffs to bill or call themselves or perform under the name of The Fireflies.

In this action plaintiffs seek to enjoin defendant's actions, and defendant seeks to enjoin the plaintiffs from using the name The Fireflies.

ISSUE: Which of the parties can perform under the name "The Fireflies"?

DECISION: The defendant.

REASONING: The law of trademarks and service mark protection furthers two goals: 1) protection of consumers from false and misleading representations concerning the source, quality and identity of a product; and 2) protection of the rights of the owner of the trade or service mark to have his or her product or service identified by a distinct name or label.

For nearly 100 years courts in this country have protected From predatory encroachment by rival entertainers the rights of a musical group to its name.

Defendant was a founding member of The Fireflies in 1959. He wrote the group's two most famous songs which plaintiffs describe as "smash hits". From 1962 until the present defendant has been recognized by the record industry as the sole person qualified to represent the Fireflies.

Plaintiffs did not arrive on the scene until 33 years after The Fireflies were first formed and plaintiffs performed only once under the name. They have undertaken a course of conduct to expropriate the group's name and to mislead the public into believing that they are the original Fireflies. Plaintiff's publicity efforts show that they are deceptive and misleading, attempting to take credit for the group's "smash hits".

Quoting from precedent the court stated, "Where the apparent purpose [of misappropriating a name] is to reap where one has not sown, or to gather where one has not planted, or to build upon or profit from, the name, reputation, good will or work of another, such actions will be enjoyed as unfair competition."[1]

Even unregistered marks are protected under federal law when their use is likely to cause confusion or to deceive as to origin.[2] Likewise New York state law protects trademarks against the likelihood of injury to business reputation or of dilution of the distinctive quality of a trade mark whether or not the mark is registered.[3] Injunctive relief is authorized to prevent an entity from adopting a name for trade purposes that would deceive or mislead the public as to the connection of such entity with any other entity.[4]

---

[1] Apple Corps Ltd. v. Adirondack Group, 124 M2d 351, 476 NYS2d 716

[2] Federal Lanham Act, 15 USC § 1125 (a)

[3] New York General Business Law § 368-d

[4] New York General Business Law § 133

CHAPTER 7

Criminal Law and Cyber Crime

The law imposes various sanctions in attempting to ensure that individuals engaging in business in our society can compete and flourish. These sanctions include those imposed by civil law, such as damages for various types of tortious conduct (discussed in Chapters 6 and 7); damages for breach of contract (to be discussed in Chapter 18; and the equitable remedies discussed in Chapters 1 and 18. Additional sanctions are imposed under criminal law. Indeed, many statutes regulating business provide for criminal as well as civil penalties. Therefore, criminal law joins civil law as an important element in the legal environment of business.

In this chapter, after explaining some essential differences between criminal law and civil law, we look at how crimes are classified and at the elements that must be present for criminal liability to exist. We then examine the various categories of crimes, the defenses that can be raised to avoid criminal liability, and the rules of criminal procedure. We conclude the chapter with a discussion of crimes that occur in cyberspace, which are often referred to as *cyber crime*. Generally, cyber crime refers more to the way in which particular crimes are committed than to a new category of crimes.

Civil Law and Criminal Law

Recall from Chapter 1 that *civil law* pertains to the duties that exist between persons or between persons and their governments. Criminal law, in contrast, has to do with crime. A **crime** can be defined as a wrong against society proclaimed in a statute and punishable by a fine and/or imprisonment—or, in some cases, death. As mentioned in Chapter 1, because crimes are *offenses against society as a whole,* they are prosecuted by a public official, such as a district attorney (D.A.) or an attorney general (A.G.), not by the victims. Once a crime has been reported, the D.A. typically has the discretion to decide whether to file criminal charges and also determines to what extent to pursue the prosecution or carry out additional investigation.

Major Differences between Civil Law and Criminal Law

Because the state has extensive resources at its disposal when prosecuting criminal cases, there are numerous procedural safeguards to protect the rights of defendants. We look here at one of these safeguards—the higher burden of proof that applies in a criminal case—as well as the harsher sanctions for criminal acts compared with civil wrongs. Exhibit 7–1 on the following page summarizes these and other key differences between civil law and criminal law.

Burden of Proof In a civil case, the plaintiff usually must prove his or her case by a *preponderance of the evidence.* Under this standard, the plaintiff must convince the court that based on the evidence presented by both parties, it is more likely than not that the plaintiff's allegation is true.

In a criminal case, in contrast, the state must prove its case **beyond a reasonable doubt.** If the jury views the evidence in the case as reasonably permitting either a guilty or a not guilty verdict, then the jury's verdict must be not guilty. In other words, the government (prosecutor) must prove beyond a reasonable doubt that the defendant has committed every essential element of the offense with which she or he is charged. If the jurors are not convinced of the defendant's guilt beyond a reasonable doubt, they must find the defendant not guilty. Note also that in a criminal

EXHIBIT 7-1 • Key Differences between Civil Law and Criminal Law

Issue	Civil Law	Criminal Law
Party who brings suit	Person who suffered harm.	The state.
Wrongful act	Causing harm to a person or to a person's property.	Violating a statute that prohibits some type of activity.
Burden of proof	Preponderance of the evidence.	Beyond a reasonable doubt.
Verdict	Three-fourths majority (typically).	Unanimous.
Remedy	Damages to compensate for the harm or a decree to achieve an equitable result.	Punishment (fine, imprisonment, or death).

case, the jury's verdict normally must be unanimous—agreed to by all members of the jury—to convict the defendant. (In a civil trial by jury, in contrast, typically only three-fourths of the jurors need to agree.)

Criminal Sanctions The sanctions imposed on criminal wrongdoers are also harsher than those that are applied in civil cases. Remember from Chapters 6 and 7 that the purpose of tort law is to enable a person harmed by the wrongful act of another to obtain compensation from the wrongdoer, rather than to punish the wrongdoer. In contrast, criminal sanctions are designed to punish those who commit crimes and to deter others from committing similar acts in the future. Criminal sanctions include fines as well as the much harsher penalty of the loss of one's liberty by incarceration in a jail or prison. Most criminal sanctions also involve probation and sometimes require performance of community service, completion of an educational or treatment program, or payment of restitution. The harshest criminal sanction is, of course, the death penalty.

Civil Liability for Criminal Acts

Some torts, such as assault and battery, provide a basis for a criminal prosecution as well as a civil action in tort. Suppose that Jonas is walking down the street, minding his own business, when a person attacks him. In the ensuing struggle, the attacker stabs Jonas several times, seriously injuring him. A police officer restrains and arrests the wrongdoer. In this situation, the attacker may be subject both to criminal prosecution by the state and to a tort lawsuit brought by Jonas to obtain compensation for his injuries. Exhibit 7-2 illustrates how the same wrongful act can result in

both a civil (tort) action and a criminal action against the wrongdoer.

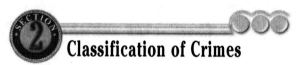

Classification of Crimes

Depending on their degree of seriousness, crimes are classified as felonies or misdemeanors.

Felonies

Felonies are serious crimes punishable by death or by imprisonment in a federal or state penitentiary for one year or longer.[1] The Model Penal Code[2] provides for four degrees of felony:

1. Capital offenses, for which the maximum penalty is death.
2. First degree felonies, punishable by a maximum penalty of life imprisonment.
3. Second degree felonies, punishable by a maximum of ten years' imprisonment.
4. Third degree felonies, punishable by up to five years' imprisonment.

Although criminal laws vary from state to state, some general rules apply when grading crimes by

---

1. Some states, such as North Carolina, consider felonies to be punishable by incarceration for at least two years.

2. The American Law Institute issued the Official Draft of the Model Penal Code in 1962. The Model Penal Code contains four parts: (1) general provisions, (2) definitions of special crimes, (3) provisions concerning treatment and corrections, and (4) provisions on the organization of corrections. The Model Penal Code is not a uniform code, however. Because of our federal structure of government, each state has developed its own set of laws governing criminal acts. Thus, types of crimes and prescribed punishments may differ from one jurisdiction to another.

EXHIBIT 7-2 • Civil (Tort) Lawsuit and Criminal Prosecution for the Same Act

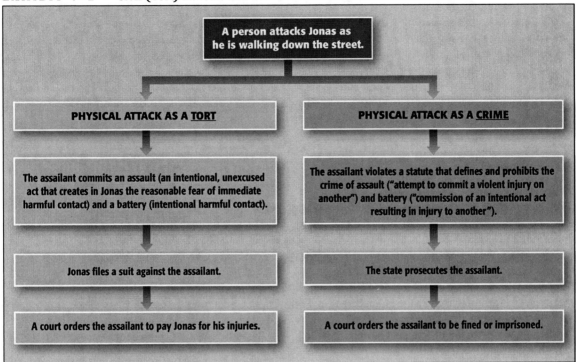

A person attacks Jonas as he is walking down the street.

PHYSICAL ATTACK AS A TORT

The assailant commits an assault (an intentional, unexcused act that creates in Jonas the reasonable fear of immediate harmful contact) and a battery (intentional harmful contact).

Jonas files a suit against the assailant.

A court orders the assailant to pay Jonas for his injuries.

PHYSICAL ATTACK AS A CRIME

The assailant violates a statute that defines and prohibits the crime of assault ("attempt to commit a violent injury on another") and battery ("commission of an intentional act resulting in injury to another").

The state prosecutes the assailant.

A court orders the assailant to be fined or imprisoned.

degree. For example, most jurisdictions punish a burglary that involves a forced entry into a home at night more harshly than a burglary that takes place during the day and involves a nonresidential building or structure. A homicide—the taking of another's life—is classified according to the degree of intent involved.

For example, first degree murder requires that the homicide be premeditated and deliberate, as opposed to a spontaneous act of violence. When no premeditation or deliberation is present but the offender acts with *malice aforethought* (that is, with wanton disregard for the consequences of his or her actions for the victim), the homicide is classified as second degree murder. A homicide that is committed without malice toward the victim is known as *manslaughter. Voluntary manslaughter* occurs when the intent to kill may be present, as in a crime committed in the heat of passion, but malice is lacking. A homicide is classified as *involuntary manslaughter* when it results from an act of negligence (such as when a drunk driver causes the death of another person) and there is no intent to kill.

Misdemeanors and Petty Offenses

Under federal law as well as under the law of most states, any crime that is not a felony is considered a **misdemeanor.** Misdemeanors are less serious crimes

punishable by a fine or by incarceration for up to one year. Disorderly conduct and trespass are common misdemeanors. In most jurisdictions, **petty offenses** are considered to be a subset of misdemeanors. Petty offenses are minor violations, such as disturbing the peace and violating building codes. Even for petty offenses, however, a guilty party can be put in jail for a few days, fined, or both, depending on state law.

Whether a crime is a felony or a misdemeanor can determine in which court the case is tried and, in some states, whether the defendant has a right to a jury trial. Many states have several classes of misdemeanors. For example, in Illinois, misdemeanors are either Class A (confinement for up to a year), Class B (not more than six months), or Class C (not more than thirty days).

Criminal Liability

Two elements must exist for a person to be convicted of a crime: (1) the performance of a prohibited act and (2) a specified state of mind, or intent, on the part of the actor. Additionally, to establish criminal liability, there must be a *concurrence* between the act and the intent. In other words, these two elements must occur together.

For example, a woman intends to kill her husband by poisoning him. On the day she plans to do so, she is driving her husband home from work and swerves to avoid hitting a cat crossing the road. As a result, the car crashes into a tree, killing her husband. Even though she had planned to murder her husband, the woman would not be guilty of murder in this situation because the two elements did not occur together. The woman had not intended to kill her husband by driving the car into a tree.

The Criminal Act

Every criminal statute prohibits certain behavior. Most crimes require an act of *commission*—that is, a person must *do* something in order to be accused of a crime. In criminal law, a prohibited act is referred to as the **actus reus,**[3] or guilty act. In some instances, an act of omission can be a crime, but only when a person has a legal duty to perform the omitted act, such as filing a tax return. For example, in 2005 the federal government criminally prosecuted a former winner of the reality TV show *Survivor* for failing to report more than $1 million in winnings.

The *guilty act* requirement is based on one of the premises of criminal law—that a person should be punished for harm done to society. For a crime to exist, the guilty act must cause some harm to a person or to property. Thinking about killing someone or about stealing a car may be morally wrong, but the thoughts do no harm until they are translated into action. Of course, a person can be punished for *attempting* murder or robbery, but normally only if substantial steps toward the criminal objective have been taken.

State of Mind

A wrongful mental state (**mens rea**)[4] is also typically required to establish criminal liability. The required mental state, or intent, is indicated in the applicable statute or law. Murder, for example, involves the guilty act of killing another human being, and the guilty mental state is the desire, or intent, to take another's life. For theft, the guilty act is the taking of another person's property, and the mental state involves both the awareness that the property belongs to another and the desire to deprive the owner of it.

A guilty mental state can be attributed to acts of negligence or recklessness as well. *Criminal negligence* involves the mental state in which the defendant deviates from the standard of care that a reasonable person would use under the same circumstances. The defendant is accused of taking an unjustified, substantial, and foreseeable risk that resulted in harm. Under the Model Penal Code, a defendant is negligent even if she or he was not actually aware of the risk but *should have been aware* of it.[5] A defendant is criminally reckless if he or she consciously disregards a substantial and unjustifiable risk.

Corporate Criminal Liability

As will be discussed in Chapter 38, a corporation is a legal entity created under the laws of a state. At one time, it was thought that a corporation could not incur criminal liability because, although a corporation is a legal person, it can act only through its agents (corporate directors, officers, and employees). Therefore, the corporate entity itself could not "intend" to commit a crime. Over time, this view has changed. Obviously, corporations cannot be imprisoned, but they can be fined or denied certain legal privileges (such as a license).

Liability of the Corporate Entity Today, corporations are normally liable for the crimes committed by their agents and employees within the course and scope of their employment.[6] For such criminal liability to be imposed, the prosecutor normally must show that the corporation could have prevented the act or that there was authorized consent to, or knowledge of, the act by persons in supervisory positions within the corporation. In addition, corporations can be criminally liable for failing to perform specific duties imposed by law (such as duties under environmental laws or securities laws).

Liability of Corporate Officers and Directors Corporate directors and officers are personally liable for the crimes they commit, regardless of whether the crimes were committed for their private benefit or on the corporation's behalf. Additionally, corporate directors and officers may be held liable for the actions of employees under their supervision. Under the *responsible corporate officer* doctrine, a court may impose criminal liability on a corporate officer regardless of whether he or she participated in, directed, or even knew about a given criminal violation.

---

3. Pronounced *ak*-tuhs *ray*-uhs.
4. Pronounced *mehns ray*-uh.

5. Model Penal Code Section 2.02(2)(d).
6. See Model Penal Code Section 2.07.

PREVENTING LEGAL DISPUTES Because corporate officers and directors can be held liable for the crimes of their subordinates, the former should always be aware of any criminal statutes relevant to their particular industry or trade. In addition, firms would be wise to train their employees in how to comply with the multitude of applicable laws, particularly environmental laws and health and safety regulations, which frequently involve criminal sanctions.

Types of Crimes

Numerous actions are designated as criminal. Federal, state, and local laws provide for the classification and punishment of hundreds of thousands of different criminal acts. Generally, though, criminal acts can be grouped into five broad categories: violent crime (crimes against persons), property crime, public order crime, white-collar crime, and organized crime. Cyber crime—which consists of crimes committed in cyberspace with the use of computers—is, as mentioned earlier in this chapter, less a category of crime than a new way to commit crime. We will examine cyber crime later in this chapter.

Violent Crime

Certain crimes are called *violent crimes,* or crimes against persons, because they cause others to suffer harm or death. Murder is a violent crime. So is sexual assault, or rape. Assault and battery, which were discussed in Chapter 6 in the context of tort law, are also classified as violent crimes. **Robbery**—defined as the taking of money, personal property, or any other article of value from a person by means of force or fear—is also a violent crime. Typically, states have more severe penalties for *aggravated robbery*—robbery with the use of a deadly weapon.

Each of these violent crimes is further classified by degree, depending on the circumstances surrounding the criminal act. These circumstances include the intent of the person committing the crime, whether a weapon was used, and (for crimes other than murder) the level of pain and suffering experienced by the victim.

Property Crime

The most common type of criminal activity is property crime, or those crimes in which the goal of the offender is some form of economic gain or the damaging of property. Robbery is a form of property crime, as well as a violent crime, because the offender seeks to gain the property of another. We look here at a number of other crimes that fall within the general category of property crime.

Burglary Traditionally, **burglary** was defined as breaking and entering the dwelling of another at night with the intent to commit a felony. Originally, the definition was aimed at protecting an individual's home and its occupants. Most state statutes have eliminated some of the requirements found in the common law definition. The time of day at which the breaking and entering occurs, for example, is usually immaterial. State statutes frequently omit the element of breaking, and some states do not require that the building be a dwelling. When a deadly weapon is used in a burglary, the perpetrator can be charged with *aggravated burglary* and punished more severely.

Larceny Under the common law, the crime of **larceny** involved the unlawful taking and carrying away of someone else's personal property with the intent to permanently deprive the owner of possession. Put simply, larceny is stealing or theft. Whereas robbery involves force or fear, larceny does not. Therefore, picking pockets is larceny, not robbery. Similarly, taking company products and supplies home for personal use, if one is not authorized to do so, is larceny. (Note that a person who commits larceny generally can also be sued under tort law because the act of taking possession of another's property involves a trespass to personal property.)

Most states have expanded the definition of property that is subject to larceny statutes. Stealing computer programs may constitute larceny even though the "property" consists of magnetic impulses. Stealing computer time may also be considered larceny. So, too, may the theft of natural gas or Internet and television cable service. Trade secrets can be subject to larceny statutes.

The common law distinguishes between grand and petit larceny depending on the value of the property taken. Many states have abolished this distinction, but in those that have not, grand larceny (or theft of an item worth above a certain amount) is a felony and petit larceny is a misdemeanor.

Arson The willful and malicious burning of a building (and, in some states, personal property) owned by another is the crime of **arson.** At common law, arson applied only to burning down another person's house. The law was designed to protect human life. Today, arson statutes have been extended to cover the destruction of any building, regardless of ownership, by fire or explosion.

Every state has a special statute that covers the act of burning a building for the purpose of collecting insurance. If Shaw owns an insured apartment building that is falling apart and sets fire to it himself or pays someone else to do so, he is guilty not only of arson but also of defrauding the insurer, which is an attempted larceny. Of course, the insurer need not pay the claim when insurance fraud is proved.

Receiving Stolen Goods It is a crime to receive stolen goods. The recipient of such goods need not know the true identity of the owner or the thief. All that is necessary is that the recipient knows or should know that the goods are stolen, which implies an intent to deprive the owner of those goods.

Forgery The fraudulent making or altering of any writing (including electronic records) in a way that changes the legal rights and liabilities of another is **forgery.** If, without authorization, Severson signs Bennett's name to the back of a check made out to Bennett, Severson is committing forgery. Forgery also includes changing trademarks, falsifying public records, counterfeiting, and altering a legal document.

Obtaining Goods by False Pretenses It is a criminal act to obtain goods by false pretenses, such as buying groceries with a check knowing that one has insufficient funds to cover it. Using another's credit-card number to obtain goods is an additional example of obtaining goods by false pretenses. Statutes dealing with such illegal activities vary widely from state to state.

Public Order Crime

Historically, societies have always outlawed activities that are considered contrary to public values and morals. Today, the most common public order crimes include public drunkenness, prostitution, gambling, and illegal drug use. These crimes are sometimes referred to as *victimless crimes* because they normally harm only the offender. From a broader perspective, however, they are deemed detrimental to society as a

whole because they may create an environment that gives rise to property and violent crimes.

White-Collar Crime

Crimes occurring in the business context are popularly referred to as white-collar crimes. Although there is no official definition of **white-collar crime,** the term is commonly used to mean an illegal act or series of acts committed by an individual or business entity using some nonviolent means to obtain a personal or business advantage. Usually, this kind of crime takes place in the course of a legitimate business occupation. Corporate crimes fall into this category. Certain property crimes, such as larceny and forgery, may also be white-collar crimes if they occur within the business context. The crimes discussed next normally occur only in the business environment.

Embezzlement When a person entrusted with another person's property or funds fraudulently appropriates that property or those funds, **embezzlement** occurs. Typically, embezzlement is carried out by an employee who steals funds. Banks are particularly prone to this problem, but embezzlement can occur in any firm. In a number of businesses, corporate officers or accountants have fraudulently converted funds for their own benefit and then "jimmied" the books to cover up their crime. Embezzlement is not larceny because the wrongdoer does not *physically* take the property from the possession of another, and it is not robbery because no force or fear is used.

It does not matter whether the accused takes the funds from the victim or from a third person. If the financial officer of a large corporation pockets a certain number of checks from third parties that were given to her to deposit into the corporate account, she is embezzling. Frequently, an embezzler takes a relatively small amount at one time but does so repeatedly over a long period. This might be done by underreporting income or deposits and embezzling the remaining amount, for example, or by creating fictitious persons or accounts and writing checks to them from the corporate account.

Practically speaking, an embezzler who returns what has been taken may not be prosecuted because the owner is unwilling to take the time to make a complaint, cooperate with the state's investigative efforts, and appear in court. Also, the owner may not want the crime to become public knowledge. Nevertheless, the intent to return the embezzled property is not a defense to the crime of embezzlement.

When an employer collects withholding taxes from his or her employees yet fails to remit these funds to the state, does such an action constitute a form of embezzlement? This was the primary issue in the following case.

C A S E **7.1** **George v. Commonwealth of Virginia**
Court of Appeals of Virginia, 2008. 51 Va.App. 137, 655 S.E.2d 43.
www.courts.state.va.us/wpcap.htm[a]

● **Background and Facts** Dr. Francis H. George owned and operated a medical practice in Luray, Virginia. From 2001 to 2004, George employed numerous individuals, including nursing assistants, nurse practitioners, and a pediatrician. George withheld funds from his employees' salaries, funds that represented state income taxes owed to the commonwealth[b] of Virginia. George placed these funds in the same banking account that he used to pay his personal and business expenses. During this period, George failed to file withholding tax returns required by state law. Moreover, he did not remit the withheld funds to the state. At trial, a jury convicted George on four counts of embezzlement. George appealed to the state intermediate appellate court claiming, among other things, that the evidence was insufficient to sustain the convictions because the state did not prove that he was entrusted with the property of another.

● **Decision and Rationale** The Court of Appeals of Virginia denied George's appeal to set aside his conviction. The evidence clearly established that George used for his own benefit funds that he held in trust for the state. Thus, he was guilty of embezzlement. "To sustain a conviction of embezzlement, the Commonwealth must prove that the accused wrongfully appropriated to his or her own benefit property entrusted or delivered to the accused with the intent to deprive the owner thereof." George contended that the withheld funds amounted to nothing more than a debt he owed the Commonwealth; therefore, he did not commit embezzlement. The appellate court pointed out that the withholding taxes that George had collected and maintained in his possession were in fact in trust for the Commonwealth. George "neither remitted the withheld funds to the Commonwealth nor maintained them for its benefit. In fact, [George] continued to use the money as though it were his own."

● **What If the Facts Were Different?** *Assume that George had actually kept a separate account for taxes withheld from his employees' salaries, but he simply failed to remit them to the state. Would the court have ruled differently? If so, in what way?*

● **The Ethical Dimension** *Does an employer ever have a valid reason for failing to remit withholding taxes to the state? Why or why not?*

---

a. Scroll down and click on case "0332064" for January 15, 2008, to access this opinion.
b. In addition to Virginia, three other states designate themselves as commonwealths—Kentucky, Massachusetts, and Pennsylvania. The term *commonwealth* dates to the fifteenth century when it meant "common well-being."

Mail and Wire Fraud One of the most potent weapons against white-collar criminals is the Mail Fraud Act of 1990.[7] Under this act, it is a federal crime to use the mails to defraud the public. Illegal use of the mails must involve (1) mailing or causing someone else to mail a writing—something written, printed, or photocopied—for the purpose of executing a scheme to defraud and (2) contemplating or organizing a scheme to defraud by false pretenses. If, for example, Johnson advertises by mail the sale of a cure for cancer that he knows to be fraudulent because it has no medical validity, he can be prosecuted for fraudulent use of the mails.

Federal law also makes it a crime (wire fraud) to use wire, radio, or television transmissions to defraud.[8]

---

7. 18 U.S.C. Sections 1341–1342.
8. 18 U.S.C. Section 1343.

Violators may be fined up to $1,000, imprisoned for up to twenty years, or both. If the violation affects a financial institution, the violator may be fined up to $1 million, imprisoned for up to thirty years, or both.

The following case involved charges of mail fraud stemming from the use of telemarketing to solicit funds that were misrepresented as going to support charities. The question for the court was whether the prosecution could offer proof of the telemarketers' commission rate when no one had lied about it.

C A S E **7.2** **United States v. Lyons**
United States Court of Appeals, Ninth Circuit, 2007. 472 F.3d 1055.

● **Background and Facts** In 1994, in California, Gabriel Sanchez formed the First Church of Life (FCL), which had no congregation, services, or place of worship. Timothy Lyons, Sanchez's friend, formed a fund-raising company called North American Acquisitions (NAA). Through FCL, Sanchez and Lyons set up six charities—AIDS Research Association, Children's Assistance Foundation, Cops and Sheriffs of America, Handicapped Youth Services, U.S. Firefighters, and U.S. Veterans League. NAA hired telemarketers to solicit donations on the charities' behalf. Over time, more than $6 million was raised, of which less than $5,000 was actually spent on charitable causes. The telemarketers kept 80 percent of the donated funds as commissions, and NAA took 10 percent. Most of the rest of the funds went to Sanchez, who spent it on himself. In 2002, Lyons and Sanchez were charged in a federal district court with mail fraud and other crimes. Throughout the trial, the prosecution referred to the high commissions paid to the telemarketers. The defendants were convicted, and each was sentenced to fifteen years in prison. They asked the U.S. Court of Appeals for the Ninth Circuit to overturn their convictions, asserting that the prosecution had used the high cost of fund-raising as evidence of fraud even though the defendants had not lied about the cost.

● **Decision and Rationale** The U.S. Court of Appeals for the Ninth Circuit upheld the convictions. The defendants' "undoing was not that the commissions were large but that their charitable web was a scam. Donors were told their contributions went to specific charitable activities when, in reality, almost no money did." The court acknowledged that a failure to reveal the high cost of fund-raising to potential donors does not establish fraud. "The mere fact that a telemarketer keeps [80 percent] of contributions it solicits cannot be the basis of a fraud conviction, and neither can the fact that a telemarketer fails to volunteer this information to would-be donors." But when "nondisclosure is accompanied by intentionally misleading statements designed to deceive the listener," the high cost of fund-raising may be introduced as evidence of fraud. "The State may vigorously enforce its antifraud laws to prohibit professional fundraisers from obtaining money on false pretenses or by making false statements." Here, in addition to the proof of the telemarketers' commissions, the prosecution offered evidence of Lyons and Sanchez's specific misrepresentations and omissions regarding the defendants' use of the donated funds. All of this "evidence underscored the fact that virtually none of the money that ended up in the bank accounts of the six FCL charities went to any charitable activities at all, let alone the specific charitable activities mentioned in the telemarketers' calls. * * * Admission of evidence regarding the fundraising costs was essential to understanding the overall scheme and the shell game of the multiple charities."

● **The Ethical Dimension** *It may have been legal in this case, but was it ethical for the prosecution to repeatedly emphasize the size of the telemarketers' commissions? Why or why not?*

● **The Legal Environment Dimension** *In what circumstance would the prosecution be prevented from introducing evidence of high fund-raising costs? Explain.*

Bribery The crime of bribery involves offering to give something of value to a person in an attempt to influence that person, who is usually, but not always, a public official, to act in a way that serves a private interest. Three types of bribery are considered crimes: bribery of public officials, commercial bribery, and bribery of foreign officials. As an element of the crime of bribery, intent must be present and proved. The bribe itself can be anything the recipient considers to be valuable. Realize that the *crime of bribery occurs when the bribe is offered*—it is not required that the bribe be accepted. *Accepting a bribe* is a separate crime.

Commercial bribery involves corrupt dealings between private persons or businesses. Typically, people make commercial bribes to obtain proprietary information, cover up an inferior product, or secure new business. Industrial espionage sometimes involves commercial bribes. For example, a person in one firm may offer an employee in a competing firm some type of payoff in exchange for trade secrets or pricing schedules. So-called kickbacks, or payoffs for special favors or services, are a form of commercial bribery in some situations.

Bribing foreign officials to obtain favorable business contracts is a crime. This crime was discussed in detail in Chapter 5, along with the Foreign Corrupt Practices Act of 1977, which was passed to curb the use of bribery by U.S. businesspersons in securing foreign contracts.

Bankruptcy Fraud Federal bankruptcy law (see Chapter 30) allows individuals and businesses to be relieved of oppressive debt through bankruptcy proceedings. Numerous white-collar crimes may be committed during the many phases of a bankruptcy action. A creditor, for example, may file a false claim against the debtor, which is a crime. Also, a debtor may fraudulently transfer assets to favored parties before or after the petition for bankruptcy is filed. For instance, a company-owned automobile may be "sold" at a bargain price to a trusted friend or relative. Closely related to the crime of fraudulent transfer of property is the crime of fraudulent concealment of property, such as the hiding of gold coins.

Insider Trading An individual who obtains "inside information" about the plans of a publicly listed corporation can often make stock-trading profits by purchasing or selling corporate securities based on this information. *Insider trading* is a violation of securities law and will be considered more fully in Chapter 41.

Basically, securities law prohibits a person who possesses inside information and has a duty not to disclose it to outsiders from trading on that information. He or she may not profit from the purchase or sale of securities based on inside information until the information is made available to the public.

The Theft of Trade Secrets As discussed in Chapter 8, trade secrets constitute a form of intellectual property that for many businesses can be extremely valuable. The Economic Espionage Act of 1996[9] makes the theft of trade secrets a federal crime. The act also makes it a federal crime to buy or possess another person's trade secrets, knowing that the trade secrets were stolen or otherwise acquired without the owner's authorization.

Violations of the act can result in steep penalties. The act provides that an individual who violates the act can be imprisoned for up to ten years and fined up to $500,000. If a corporation or other organization violates the act, it can be fined up to $5 million. Additionally, the law provides that any property acquired as a result of the violation, such as airplanes and automobiles, and any property used in the commission of the violation, such as computers and other electronic devices, is subject to criminal forfeiture—meaning that the government can take the property. A theft of trade secrets conducted via the Internet, for example, could result in the forfeiture of every computer or other device used to commit or facilitate the violation as well as any assets gained.

Organized Crime

White-collar crime takes place within the confines of the legitimate business world. Organized crime, in contrast, operates *illegitimately* by, among other things, providing illegal goods and services. Traditionally, the preferred markets for organized crime have been gambling, prostitution, illegal narcotics, and loan sharking (lending funds at higher-than-legal interest rates), along with more recent ventures into counterfeiting and credit-card scams.

Money Laundering The profits from organized crime and illegal activities amount to billions of dollars a year, particularly the profits from illegal drug transactions and, to a lesser extent, from racketeering, prostitution, and gambling. Under federal law, banks,

---

9. 18 U.S.C. Sections 1831–1839.

savings and loan associations, and other financial institutions are required to report currency transactions involving more than $10,000. Consequently, those who engage in illegal activities face difficulties in depositing their cash profits from illegal transactions.

As an alternative to storing cash from illegal transactions in a safe-deposit box, wrongdoers and racketeers have invented ways to launder "dirty" money to make it "clean." This **money laundering** is done through legitimate businesses. Assume that Harris, a successful drug dealer, becomes a partner with a restaurateur. Little by little, the restaurant shows increasing profits. As a partner in the restaurant, Harris is able to report the "profits" of the restaurant as legitimate income on which he pays federal and state taxes. He can then spend those funds without worrying that his lifestyle may exceed the level possible with his reported income.

RICO In 1970, in an effort to curb the entry of organized crime into the legitimate business world, Congress passed the Racketeer Influenced and Corrupt Organizations Act (RICO) as part of the Organized Crime Control Act.[10] The statute makes it a federal crime to (1) use income obtained from racketeering activity to purchase any interest in an enterprise, (2) acquire or maintain an interest in an enterprise through racketeering activity, (3) conduct or participate in the affairs of an enterprise through racketeering activity, or (4) conspire to do any of the preceding activities.

The broad language of RICO has allowed it to be applied in cases that have little or nothing to do with organized crime. In fact, today the statute is used to attack white-collar crimes more often than organized crime. In addition, RICO creates civil as well as criminal liability.

Criminal Provisions RICO incorporates by reference twenty-six separate types of federal crimes and nine types of state felonies—including many business-related crimes, such as bribery, embezzlement, forgery, mail and wire fraud, and securities fraud.[11] For purposes of RICO, a "pattern of racketeering activity" requires a person to commit at least two of these

offenses. Any individual who is found guilty is subject to a fine of up to $25,000 per violation, imprisonment for up to twenty years, or both. Additionally, the statute provides that those who violate RICO may be required to forfeit (give up) any assets, in the form of property or cash, that were acquired as a result of the illegal activity or that were "involved in" or an "instrumentality of" the activity.

Civil Liability In the event of a RICO violation, the government can seek civil penalties, including the divestiture of a defendant's interest in a business (called forfeiture) or the dissolution of the business. Moreover, in some cases, the statute allows private individuals to sue violators and potentially recover three times their actual losses (treble damages), plus attorneys' fees, for business injuries caused by a violation of the statute. This is perhaps the most controversial aspect of RICO and one that continues to cause debate in the nation's federal courts.

The prospect of receiving treble damages in civil RICO lawsuits has given plaintiffs financial incentive to pursue businesses and employers for violations. For example, Mohawk Industries, Inc., one of the largest carpeting manufacturers in the United States, was sued by a group of its employees for RICO violations. The employees claimed Mohawk conspired with recruiting agencies to hire and harbor illegal immigrants in an effort to keep labor costs low. The employees argued that Mohawk's pattern of illegal hiring expanded Mohawk's hourly workforce and resulted in lower wages for the plaintiffs. Mohawk filed a motion to dismiss, arguing that its conduct had not violated RICO. In 2006, however, a federal appellate court ruled that the plaintiffs had presented sufficient evidence of racketeering activity and remanded the case for a trial.[12] (See *Concept Summary 7.1* for a review of the different types of crimes.)

Defenses to Criminal Liability

In certain circumstances, the law may allow a person to be excused from criminal liability because she or he lacks the required mental state. Criminal defen-

---

10. 18 U.S.C. Sections 1961–1968.
11. See 18 U.S.C. Section 1961(1)(A). The crimes listed in this section include murder, kidnapping, gambling, arson, robbery, bribery, extortion, money laundering, securities fraud, counterfeiting, dealing in obscene matter, dealing in controlled substances (illegal drugs), and a number of others.

12. *Williams v. Mohawk Industries, Inc.*, 465 F.3d 1277 (11th Cir. 2006); *cert.* denied, ___ U.S. ___, 127 S.Ct. 1381, 167 L.Ed.2d 174 (2007). For another example, see *Trollinger v. Tyson Foods, Inc.*, 2007 WL 1574275 (E.D.Tenn. 2007).

CONCEPT SUMMARY 7.1
Types of Crimes

Crime Category	Definition and Examples
VIOLENT CRIME	*Definition*: Crime that causes others to suffer harm or death.
	Examples: Murder, assault and battery, sexual assault (rape), and robbery.
PROPERTY CRIME	*Definition*: Crime in which the goal of the offender is some form of economic gain or the damaging of property; the most common form of crime.
	Examples: Burglary, larceny, arson, receiving stolen goods, forgery, and obtaining goods by false pretenses.
PUBLIC ORDER CRIME	*Definition*: Crime that is contrary to public values and morals.
	Examples: Public drunkenness, prostitution, gambling, and illegal drug use.
WHITE-COLLAR CRIME	*Definition*: An illegal act or series of acts committed by an individual or business entity using some nonviolent means to obtain a personal or business advantage; usually committed in the course of a legitimate occupation.
	Examples: Embezzlement, mail and wire fraud, bribery, bankruptcy fraud, insider trading, and the theft of trade secrets.
ORGANIZED CRIME	*Definition*: A form of crime conducted by groups operating illegitimately to satisfy the public's demand for illegal goods and services (such as gambling and illegal narcotics).
	Examples:
	1. *Money laundering*—The establishment of legitimate enterprises through which "dirty" money (obtained through criminal activities, such as illegal drug trafficking) can be "laundered" (made to appear to be legitimate income).
	2. *RICO*—The Racketeer Influenced and Corrupt Organizations Act (RICO) of 1970 makes it a federal crime to (a) use income obtained from racketeering activity to purchase any interest in an enterprise, (b) acquire or maintain an interest in an enterprise through racketeering activity, (c) conduct or participate in the affairs of an enterprise through racketeering activity, or (d) conspire to do any of the preceding activities. RICO provides for both civil and criminal liability.

dants may also be relieved of criminal liability if they can show that their criminal actions were justified, given the circumstances. Among the most important defenses to criminal liability are infancy, intoxication, insanity, mistake, consent, duress, justifiable use of force, necessity, entrapment, and the statute of limitations. Additionally, in some cases defendants are given *immunity* from prosecution and thus are relieved, at least in part, of criminal liability for their actions. We look next at each of these defenses.

Note that procedural violations (such as obtaining evidence without a valid search warrant) may also operate as defenses. Evidence obtained in violation of a defendant's constitutional rights may not be admit-

ted in court. If the evidence is suppressed, then there may be no basis for prosecuting the defendant.

Infancy

The term *infant*, as used in the law, refers to any person who has not yet reached the age of majority (see Chapter 13). At common law, children under the age of seven could not commit a crime, and it was presumed that children between the ages of seven and fourteen were incapable of committing crimes because of their incapacity to appreciate right and wrong. Today, most state courts no longer presume that children are incapable of criminal conduct, but may evaluate the particular child's state of mind. In all states, certain courts handle cases involving children who allegedly have violated the law. Courts that handle juvenile cases may also have jurisdiction over additional matters. In most states, a child may be treated as an adult and tried in a regular court if she or he is above a certain age (usually fourteen) and is charged with a felony, such as rape or murder.

Intoxication

The law recognizes two types of intoxication, whether from drugs or from alcohol: involuntary and voluntary. *Involuntary intoxication* occurs when a person either is physically forced to ingest or inject an intoxicating substance or is unaware that such a substance contains drugs or alcohol. Involuntary intoxication is a defense to a crime if its effect was to make a person incapable of understanding that the act committed was wrong or incapable of obeying the law. Voluntary intoxication is rarely a defense, but it may be effective in cases in which the defendant was so *extremely* intoxicated as to negate the state of mind that a crime requires.

Insanity

Just as a child may be incapable of the state of mind required to commit a crime, so also may a person who suffers from a mental illness. Thus, insanity may be a defense to a criminal charge. The courts have had difficulty deciding what the test for legal insanity should be, however, and psychiatrists as well as lawyers are critical of the tests used. Almost all federal courts and some states use the relatively liberal standard set forth in the Model Penal Code:

> A person is not responsible for criminal conduct if at the time of such conduct as a result of mental disease or defect he or she lacks substantial capacity either to appreciate the wrongfulness of his [or her] conduct or to conform his [or her] conduct to the requirements of the law.

Some states use the *M'Naghten* test,[13] under which a criminal defendant is not responsible if, at the time of the offense, he or she did not know the nature and quality of the act or did not know that the act was wrong. Other states use the irresistible-impulse test. A person operating under an irresistible impulse may know an act is wrong but cannot refrain from doing it. Under any of these tests, proving insanity is extremely

difficult. For this reason, the insanity defense is rarely used and usually is not successful.

Mistake

Everyone has heard the saying "Ignorance of the law is no excuse." Ordinarily, ignorance of the law or a mistaken idea about what the law requires is not a valid defense. In some states, however, that rule has been modified. People who claim that they honestly did not know that they were breaking a law may have a valid defense if (1) the law was not published or reasonably made known to the public or (2) the people relied on an official statement of the law that was erroneous.

A *mistake of fact*, as opposed to a *mistake of law*, operates as a defense if it negates the mental state necessary to commit a crime. If, for example, Oliver Wheaton mistakenly walks off with Julie Tyson's briefcase because he thinks it is his, there is no theft. Theft requires knowledge that the property belongs to another. (If Wheaton's act causes Tyson to incur damages, however, Wheaton may be subject to liability for trespass to personal property or conversion, torts that were discussed in Chapter 6.)

Consent

What if a victim consents to a crime or even encourages the person intending a criminal act to commit it? **Consent** is not a defense to most crimes. The law forbids murder, prostitution, and drug use whether the victim consents or not. Consent may serve as a defense, however, in certain situations when it negates an element of the alleged criminal offense. Because crimes against property, such as burglary and larceny, usually require that the defendant intended to take someone else's property, the fact that the owner gave the defendant permission to take it will operate as a defense. Consent or forgiveness given after a crime has been committed is never a defense, although it can affect the likelihood of prosecution.

Duress

Duress exists when the *wrongful threat* of one person induces another person to perform an act that he or she would not otherwise have performed. In such a situation, duress is said to negate the mental state necessary to commit a crime because the defendant was forced or compelled to commit the act. Duress can be used as a defense to most crimes except murder.

---

13. A rule derived from *M'Naghten's* Case, 8 Eng. Rep. 718 (1843).

Duress excuses a crime only when another's unlawful threat of serious bodily injury or death reasonably causes the defendant to do a criminal act. In addition, there must have been no opportunity for the defendant to escape or avoid the threatened danger.[14] Essentially, to successfully assert duress as a defense, the defendant must reasonably believe in the immediate danger, and the jury (or judge) must conclude that the defendant's belief was reasonable.

Justifiable Use of Force

Probably the best-known defense to criminal liability is **self-defense.** Other situations, however, also justify the use of force: the defense of one's dwelling, the defense of other property, and the prevention of a crime. In all of these situations, it is important to distinguish between deadly and nondeadly force. *Deadly force* is likely to result in death or serious bodily harm. *Nondeadly force* is force that reasonably appears necessary to prevent the imminent use of criminal force.

Generally speaking, people can use the amount of nondeadly force that seems necessary to protect themselves, their dwellings, or other property, or to prevent the commission of a crime. Deadly force can be used in self-defense only when the defender *reasonably believes* that imminent death or grievous bodily harm will otherwise result and has no other means of escaping or avoiding the situation. Deadly force normally can be used to defend a dwelling only if the unlawful entry is violent and the person believes deadly force is necessary to prevent imminent death or great bodily harm. In some jurisdictions, however, deadly force can also be used if the person believes it is necessary to prevent the commission of a felony in the dwelling. Many states are expanding the situations in which the use of deadly force can be justified—see this chapter's *Emerging Trends* feature on pages 184 and 185.

Necessity

Sometimes, criminal defendants can be relieved of liability by showing that a criminal act was necessary to prevent an even greater harm. According to the Model Penal Code, the defense of **necessity** is justifiable if "the harm or evil sought to be avoided by such conduct is greater than that sought to be prevented by the law defining the offense charged."[15] For example, in

one case a convicted felon was threatened by an acquaintance with a gun. The felon grabbed the gun and fled the scene, but subsequently he was arrested under a statute that prohibits convicted felons from possessing firearms. In this situation, the necessity defense succeeded because the defendant's crime avoided a "greater evil."[16]

Entrapment

Entrapment is a defense designed to prevent police officers or other government agents from enticing persons to commit crimes in order to later prosecute them for criminal acts. In the typical entrapment case, an undercover agent *suggests* that a crime be committed and somehow pressures or induces an individual to commit it. The agent then arrests the individual for the crime. For entrapment to be considered a defense, both the suggestion and the inducement must take place. The defense is not intended to prevent law enforcement agents from setting a trap for an unwary criminal; rather, the intent is to prevent them from pushing the individual into it. The crucial issue is whether the person who committed a crime was predisposed to commit the illegal act or did so because the agent induced it.

Statute of Limitations

With some exceptions, such as the crime of murder, statutes of limitations apply to crimes just as they do to civil wrongs. In other words, the state must initiate criminal prosecution within a certain number of years. If a criminal action is brought after the statutory time period has expired, the accused person can raise the statute of limitations as a defense. The running of the time period in a statute of limitations may be tolled—that is, suspended or stopped temporarily—if the defendant is a minor or is not in the jurisdiction. When the defendant reaches the age of majority or returns to the jurisdiction, the statute revives—that is, its time period begins to run or to run again.

Immunity

At times, the state may wish to obtain information from a person accused of a crime. Accused persons are understandably reluctant to give information if it will be used to prosecute them, and they cannot be forced to do so. The privilege against self-incrimination is

---

14. See, for example, *State v. Heinemann*, 282 Conn. 281, 920 A.2d 278 (2007).

15. Model Penal Code Section 3.02.

16. *United States v. Paolello*, 951 F.2d 537 (3d Cir. 1991).

Stand-Your-Ground Laws

Traditionally, the justifiable use of force, or self-defense, doctrine required prosecutors to distinguish between deadly and nondeadly force. In general, state laws have allowed individuals to use the amount of nondeadly force that is necessary to protect themselves, their dwellings, or other property, or to prevent the commission of a crime.

The Duty-to-Retreat Doctrine

In the past, most states allowed deadly force to be used in self-defense only if the individual reasonably believed that imminent death or bodily harm would otherwise result. Additionally, the attacker had to be using unlawful force, and the defender had to have no other possible response or alternative way out of the life-threatening situation.[a] Today, many states, particularly in the Northeast, still have "duty-to-retreat" laws on their statute books. Under these laws, when a person's home is invaded or

a. *State v. Sandoval,* 342 Or. 506, 156 P.3d 60 (2007).

an assailant approaches, the person is required to retreat unless her or his life is in danger. Juries have sometimes been reluctant to apply the duty-to-retreat doctrine, however. In a famous case in the 1980s, Bernard Goetz shot and injured four young men who asked him for money while he was riding the subway in New York City. The jury found that Goetz had reasonably believed that he was in danger of being physically attacked.[b]

Stand-Your-Ground Legislation on the Increase

Whereas the duty-to-retreat doctrine attempts to reduce the likelihood that deadly—or even nondeadly—force will be used in defense of one's person or home, today several states are taking a very different approach and expanding the occasions when deadly

b. *People v. Goetz,* 506 N.Y.S.2d 18, 497 N.E.2d 41 (1986). See also *People v. Douglas,* 29 A.D.3d 47, 809 N.Y.S.2d 36 (2006); and *State v. Augustin,* 101 Haw. 127, 63 P.3d 1097 (2002).

force can be used in self-defense. Because such laws allow or even encourage the defender to stay and use force, they are known as "stand-your-ground" laws.

On October 1, 2005, for example, Florida enacted a statute that allows the use of deadly force to prevent the commission of a "forcible felony," including not only murder but also such crimes as robbery, carjacking, and sexual battery.[c] The law applies to both homes and vehicles. Under this statute, Floridians may use deadly force without having to prove that they feared for their safety. In other words, a Florida resident now has the right to shoot an intruder in his or her home or a would-be carjacker even if there is no physical threat to the owner's safety. The law prohibits the arrest, detention, or prosecution of individuals covered by the law and also prohibits civil suits against them.

Since the Florida statute was enacted, Alabama, Alaska, Arizona, Georgia, Indiana, Kentucky, Louisiana,

c. Florida Statutes Section 776.012.

---

guaranteed by the Fifth Amendment to the U.S. Constitution, which reads, in part, "nor shall [any person] be compelled in any criminal case to be a witness against himself." In cases in which the state wishes to obtain information from a person accused of a crime, the state can grant *immunity* from prosecution or agree to prosecute for a less serious offense in exchange for the information. Once immunity is given, the person now has an absolute privilege against self-incrimination and therefore can no longer refuse to testify on Fifth Amendment grounds.

Often, a grant of immunity from prosecution for a serious crime is part of the **plea bargaining** between the defending and prosecuting attorneys. The defendant may be convicted of a lesser offense, while the state uses the defendant's testimony to prosecute accomplices for serious crimes carrying heavy penalties.

Criminal Procedures

Criminal law brings the force of the state, with all of its resources, to bear against the individual. Criminal procedures are designed to protect the constitutional rights of individuals and to prevent the arbitrary use of power on the part of the government.

The U.S. Constitution provides specific safeguards for those accused of crimes. The United States Supreme Court has ruled that most of these safeguards apply not only in federal court but also in state courts by virtue of the due process clause of the Fourteenth Amendment. These protections include the following:

1. The Fourth Amendment protection from unreasonable searches and seizures.

Michigan, Mississippi, Missouri, Montana, Oklahoma, Pennsylvania, South Dakota, Washington, and Wyoming have passed or are considering passing similar laws. Utah already had a "stand-your-ground" law.[d] Louisiana's statute, which mimics the Florida statute, was passed after Hurricane Katrina devastated New Orleans. In Louisiana, there is now a presumption of innocence for anyone who uses deadly force when threatened with violence in his or her home, car, or place of business.

North Carolina's stand-your-ground statute is typical. It states that "(a) A lawful occupant within a home or other place of residence is justified in using any degree of force that the occupant reasonably believes is necessary, including deadly force, against an intruder to prevent a forcible entry into the home or residence or to terminate the intruder's unlawful entry (i) if the occupant reasonably apprehends that the intruder may kill or inflict serious bodily harm to the occupant or others in the home or residence, or (ii) if the occupant reasonably believes that the intruder intends to commit a felony in the home or residence. (b) A lawful occupant within a home or other place of residence does not have a duty to retreat from an intruder in the circumstances described in this section."[e]

Although the media sometimes describe stand-your-ground laws as "new," these statutes are actually based on a centuries-old precedent. The laws are a throwback to the "castle" doctrine, which was derived from English common law in the 1700s, when a person's home was considered to be his or her castle.[f]

IMPLICATIONS FOR THE BUSINESSPERSON

1. States that have enacted stand-your-ground laws often include

places of business as well as homes and vehicles. Consequently, businesspersons in those states can be less concerned about the duty-to-retreat doctrine.

2. Presumably, business liability insurance will eventually be less costly in stand-your-ground states.

FOR CRITICAL ANALYSIS

1. Those who oppose stand-your-ground laws argue that they encourage vigilantism and preemptive shootings. Do you agree? Explain.

2. "A person's home is his or her castle." Does this traditional saying justify the use of deadly force against an intruder under all circumstances? Why or why not?

RELEVANT WEB SITES

To locate information on the Web concerning the issues discussed in this feature, go to this text's Web site at **www.cengage.com/blaw/jentz**, select "Chapter 9," and click on "Emerging Trends."

---

d. Utah Code Ann. 76-2-402 and 76-2-407.

e. North Carolina General Statutes Ann. 14–51.1.

f. One reference to the castle doctrine can be found in William Blackstone, *Commentaries on the Laws of England*, Book 4, Chapter 16.

---

2. The Fourth Amendment requirement that no warrant for a search or an arrest be issued without probable cause.

3. The Fifth Amendment requirement that no one be deprived of "life, liberty, or property without due process of law."

4. The Fifth Amendment prohibition against **double jeopardy** (trying someone twice for the same criminal offense).[17]

5. The Fifth Amendment requirement that no person be required to be a witness against (incriminate) himself or herself.

6. The Sixth Amendment guarantees of a speedy trial, a trial by jury, a public trial, the right to confront witnesses, and the right to a lawyer at various stages in some proceedings.

7. The Eighth Amendment prohibitions against excessive bail and fines and cruel and unusual punishment.

---

17. The prohibition against double jeopardy means that once a criminal defendant is found not guilty of a particular crime, the government may not reindict the person and retry him or her for the same crime. The prohibition does not preclude a *civil* lawsuit against the same person by the crime victim to recover damages. For example, a person found not guilty of assault and battery in a criminal case may be sued by the victim in a civil tort case for damages. Additionally, a state's prosecution of a crime will not prevent a separate federal prosecution of the same crime, and vice versa. For example, a defendant found not guilty of violating a state law can be tried in federal court for the same act, if the act is also defined as a crime under federal law.

The Exclusionary Rule

Under what is known as the **exclusionary rule,** all evidence obtained in violation of the constitutional rights spelled out in the Fourth, Fifth, and Sixth Amendments generally is not admissible at trial. All evidence derived from the illegally obtained evidence is known as the "fruit of the poisonous tree," and such evidence normally must also be excluded from the trial proceedings. For example, if a confession is obtained after an illegal arrest, the arrest is the "poisonous tree," and the confession, if "tainted" by the arrest, is the "fruit."

As you will read shortly, under the *Miranda* rule, suspects must be advised of certain constitutional rights when they are arrested. For example, the Sixth Amendment right to counsel is one of the rights of which a suspect must be advised when she or he is arrested. In many cases, a statement that a criminal suspect makes in the absence of counsel is not admissible at trial unless the suspect has knowingly and voluntarily waived this right.

Purpose of the Exclusionary Rule The purpose of the exclusionary rule is to deter police from conducting warrantless searches and from engaging in other misconduct. The rule is sometimes criticized because it can lead to injustice. Many a defendant has "gotten off on a technicality" because law enforcement personnel failed to observe procedural requirements based on the above-mentioned constitutional amendments. Even though a defendant may be obviously guilty, if the evidence of that guilt was obtained improperly (without a valid search warrant, for example), it cannot be used against the defendant in court.

Exceptions to the Exclusionary Rule Over the last several decades, the United States Supreme Court has diminished the scope of the exclusionary rule by creating some exceptions to its applicability. For example, if illegally obtained evidence would have been discovered "inevitably" and obtained by the police using lawful means, the evidence will be admissible at trial.[18] The Court has also created a "good faith" exception to the exclusionary rule.[19] Under this exception, if the police officer who used a technically incorrect search warrant form to obtain evidence was acting in good faith, the evidence will be admissible. Additionally, the courts can exercise a certain amount of discretion in determining whether evidence has been obtained improperly—a possibility that somewhat balances the scales.

The *Miranda* Rule

In regard to criminal procedure, one of the questions many courts faced in the 1950s and 1960s was not whether suspects had constitutional rights—that was not in doubt—but how and when those rights could be exercised. Could the right to be silent (under the Fifth Amendment's prohibition against self-incrimination) be exercised during pretrial interrogation proceedings or only during the trial? Were confessions obtained from suspects admissible in court if the suspects had not been advised of their right to remain silent and other constitutional rights?

To clarify these issues, the United States Supreme Court issued a landmark decision in 1966 in *Miranda v. Arizona,* which we present here. Today, the procedural rights required by the Court in this case are familiar to virtually every American.

---

18. *Nix v. Williams,* 467 U.S. 431, 104 S.Ct. 2501, 81 L.Ed.2d 377 (1984).
19. *Massachusetts v. Sheppard,* 468 U.S. 981, 104 S.Ct. 3424, 82 L.Ed.2d 737 (1984).

C A S E **7.3** **Miranda v. Arizona**
Supreme Court of the United States, 1966. 384 U.S. 436, 86 S.Ct. 1602, 16 L.Ed.2d 694.

● **Background and Facts** On March 13, 1963, Ernesto Miranda was arrested at his home for the kidnapping and rape of an eighteen-year-old woman. Miranda was taken to a Phoenix, Arizona, police station and questioned by two officers. Two hours later, the officers emerged from the interrogation room with a written confession signed by Miranda. A paragraph at the top of the confession stated that the confession had been made voluntarily, without threats or promises of immunity, and "with full knowledge of my legal rights, understanding any statement I make may be used against me." Miranda was at no time advised that he had a right to remain silent and a right to have a lawyer present. The confession was admitted into evidence at the trial, and Miranda was convicted and sentenced to prison for twenty to thirty years. Miranda appealed the decision, claiming that he had not been informed of his constitutional rights. The Supreme Court of Arizona held that Miranda's constitutional rights had not been violated and affirmed his conviction. The *Miranda* case was subsequently reviewed by the United States Supreme Court.

● **Decision and Rationale** The United States Supreme Court reversed Miranda's conviction, holding that he could not be convicted of the crime on the basis of his confession because his confession was inadmissible as evidence. The Court ruled that for any statement made by a defendant to be admissible, the defendant must be informed of certain constitutional rights before a police interrogation. These are (1) that he or she has a right to remain silent; (2) that anything said can and will be used against the individual in court (to warn a person in custody of "the consequences of forgoing" the right to remain silent); (3) that he or she has the right to have an attorney present during questioning; and (4) that if the individual cannot afford an attorney, one will be appointed. If the accused waives his or her rights to remain silent and to have counsel present, the government must be able to demonstrate that the waiver was made knowingly and intelligently.

● **Impact of This Case on Today's Law** *Police officers routinely advise suspects of their "Miranda rights" on arrest. When Ernesto Miranda himself was later murdered, the suspected murderer was "read his Miranda rights." Despite significant criticisms and later attempts to overrule the Miranda decision through legislation, the requirements stated in this case continue to provide the benchmark by which criminal procedures are judged today.*

● **The Legal Environment Dimension** *The goal of the Miranda decision was to prevent the police from using "grilling" tactics to elicit "forced" confessions. Today, camcorders are so small and cheap that all interrogations, even at the scene of a crime, can be digitally recorded. Does this mean that the Miranda rights are less important? Why or why not?*

Exceptions to the *Miranda* Rule As part of a continuing attempt to balance the rights of accused persons against the rights of society, the Supreme Court has made a number of exceptions to the *Miranda* ruling. For example, the Court has recognized a "public safety" exception, holding that certain statements—such as statements concerning the location of a weapon—are admissible even if the defendant was not given *Miranda* warnings.[20] The Court has also clarified that, in certain circumstances, a defendant's confession need not be excluded as evidence even if the police failed to inform the defendant of his or her *Miranda* rights.[21] If other, legally obtained evidence admitted at trial is strong enough to justify the conviction without the confession, then the fact that the confession was obtained illegally can, in effect, be ignored.[22]

The Supreme Court has also ruled that a suspect must unequivocally and assertively request to exercise her or his right to counsel in order to stop police questioning. Saying, "Maybe I should talk to a lawyer" during an interrogation after being taken into custody

is not enough. The Court held that police officers are not required to decipher the suspect's intentions in such situations.[23]

Criminal Process

As mentioned earlier in this chapter, a criminal prosecution differs significantly from a civil case in several respects. These differences reflect the desire to safeguard the rights of the individual against the state. Exhibit 7–3 on the next page summarizes the major steps in processing a criminal case. We now discuss three phases of the criminal process—arrest, indictment or information, and trial—in more detail.

Arrest Before a warrant for arrest can be issued, there must be probable cause for believing that the individual in question has committed a crime. As discussed in Chapter 4, *probable cause* can be defined as a substantial likelihood that the person has committed or is about to commit a crime. Note that probable cause involves a likelihood, not just a possibility. Arrests can be made without a warrant if there is no time to get one, but the action of the arresting officer is still judged by the standard of probable cause.

20. *New York v. Quarles,* 467 U.S. 649, 104 S.Ct. 2626, 81 L.Ed.2d 550 (1984).

21. *Moran v. Burbine,* 475 U.S. 412, 106 S.Ct. 1135, 89 L.Ed.2d 410 (1986).

22. *Arizona v. Fulminante,* 499 U.S. 279, 111 S.Ct. 1246, 113 L.Ed.2d 302 (1991).

23. *Davis v. United States,* 512 U.S. 452, 114 S.Ct. 2350, 129 L.Ed.2d 362 (1994).

EXHIBIT 7-3 • Major Procedural Steps in a Criminal Case

ARREST
Police officer takes suspect into custody. Most arrests are made without a warrant. After the arrest, the officer searches the suspect, who is then taken to the police station.

BOOKING
At the police station, the suspect is searched again, photographed, fingerprinted, and allowed at least one telephone call. After the booking, charges are reviewed, and if they are not dropped, a complaint is filed, and a magistrate (judge) reviews the case for probable cause.

INITIAL APPEARANCE
The defendant appears before the judge, who informs the defendant of the charges and of his or her rights. If the defendant requests a lawyer and cannot afford one, a lawyer is appointed. The judge sets bail (conditions under which a suspect can obtain release pending disposition of the case).

GRAND JURY
A grand jury determines if there is probable cause to believe that the defendant committed the crime. The federal government and about half of the states require grand jury indictments for at least some felonies.

PRELIMINARY HEARING
In a court proceeding, a prosecutor presents evidence, and the judge determines if there is probable cause to hold the defendant over for trial.

INDICTMENT
An *indictment* is a written document issued by the grand jury to formally charge the defendant with a crime.

INFORMATION
An *information* is a formal criminal charge, or criminal complaint, made by the prosecutor.

ARRAIGNMENT
The defendant is brought before the court, informed of the charges, and asked to enter a plea.

PLEA BARGAIN
A *plea bargain* is a prosecutor's promise to make concessions (or promise to seek concessions) in return for a defendant's guilty plea. Concessions may include a reduced charge or a lesser sentence.

GUILTY PLEA
In many jurisdictions, most cases that reach the arraignment stage do not go to trial but are resolved by a guilty plea, often as a result of a plea bargain. The judge sets the case for sentencing.

TRIAL
Trials can be either jury trials or bench trials. (In a bench trial, there is no jury, and the judge decides questions of fact as well as questions of law.) If the verdict is "guilty," the judge sets a date for the sentencing. Everyone convicted of a crime has the right to an appeal.

Indictment or Information Individuals must be formally charged with having committed specific crimes before they can be brought to trial. If issued by a grand jury, such a charge is called an **indictment.**[24] A **grand jury** does not determine the guilt or innocence of an accused party; rather, its function is to hear the state's evidence and to determine whether a reasonable basis (probable cause) exists for believing that a crime has been committed and that a trial ought to be held.

Usually, grand juries are called in cases involving serious crimes, such as murder. For lesser crimes, an individual may be formally charged with a crime by an **information,** or criminal complaint. An information will be issued by a government prosecutor if the prosecutor determines that there is sufficient evidence to justify bringing the individual to trial.

Trial At a criminal trial, the accused person does not have to prove anything; the entire burden of proof is on the prosecutor (the state). As discussed at the beginning of this chapter, the burden of proof is higher in a criminal case than in a civil case. The prosecution must show that, based on all the evidence, the defendant's guilt is established *beyond a reasonable doubt.* If there is reasonable doubt as to whether a criminal defendant did, in fact, commit the crime with which she or he has been charged, then the verdict must be "not guilty." Note that giving a verdict of "not guilty" is not the same as stating that the defendant is innocent; it merely means that not enough evidence was properly presented to the court to prove guilt beyond a reasonable doubt.

Courts have complex rules about what types of evidence may be presented and how the evidence may be brought out in criminal cases, especially in jury trials. These rules are designed to ensure that evidence presented at trials is relevant, reliable, and not prejudicial toward the defendant.

Federal Sentencing Guidelines

In 1984, Congress passed the Sentencing Reform Act. This act created the U.S. Sentencing Commission, which was charged with the task of standardizing sentences for *federal* crimes. The commission's guidelines, which became effective in 1987, established a range of possible penalties for each federal crime and required the judge to select a sentence from within that range. In other words, the guidelines originally established a mandatory system because judges were not allowed to deviate from the specified sentencing range. Some federal judges felt uneasy about imposing the long prison sentences required by the guidelines on certain criminal defendants, particularly first-time offenders and those convicted in illegal substances cases involving small quantities of drugs.[25]

Shift Away from Mandatory Sentencing In 2005, the Supreme Court held that certain provisions of the federal sentencing guidelines were unconstitutional.[26] The case involved Freddie Booker, who was arrested with 92.5 grams of crack cocaine in his possession. Booker admitted to police that he had sold an additional 566 grams of crack cocaine, but he was never charged with, or tried for, possessing this additional quantity. Nevertheless, under the federal sentencing guidelines the judge was required to sentence Booker to twenty-two years in prison. Ultimately, the Supreme Court ruled that this sentence was unconstitutional because a jury did not find beyond a reasonable doubt that Booker had possessed the additional 566 grams of crack.

Essentially, the Supreme Court's ruling changed the federal sentencing guidelines from mandatory to advisory. Depending on the circumstances of the case, a federal trial judge may now depart from the guidelines if she or he believes that it is reasonable to do so.

Increased Penalties for Certain Criminal Violations It is important for businesspersons to understand that the sentencing guidelines still exist and provide for enhanced punishment for certain types of crimes. The U.S. Sentencing Commission recommends stiff sentences for many white-collar crimes, including mail and wire fraud, commercial bribery and kickbacks, and money laundering. Enhanced penalties are also suggested for violations of the Sarbanes-Oxley Act (discussed in Chapter 5).[27]

---

24. Pronounced in-*dyte*-ment.

25. See, for example, *United States v. Angelos,* 347 F.Supp.2d 1227 (D. Utah 2004).

26. *United States v. Booker,* 543 U.S. 220, 125 S.Ct. 738, 160 L.Ed.2d 621 (2005).

27. As required by the Sarbanes-Oxley Act of 2002, the U.S. Sentencing Commission revised its guidelines in 2003 to impose stiffer penalties for corporate securities fraud—see Chapter 41.

In addition, the commission recommends increased penalties for criminal violations of employment laws (see Chapters 33 and 34), securities laws (see Chapter 41), and antitrust laws (see Chapter 46). The guidelines set forth a number of factors that judges should take into consideration when imposing a sentence for a specified crime. These factors include the defendant company's history of past violations, management's cooperation with federal investigators, and the extent to which the firm has undertaken specific programs and procedures to prevent criminal activities by its employees.

Cyber Crime

Some years ago, the American Bar Association defined **computer crime** as any act that is directed against computers and computer parts, that uses computers as instruments of crime, or that involves computers and constitutes abuse. Today, because much of the crime committed with the use of computers occurs in cyberspace, many computer crimes fall under the broad label of **cyber crime.** Here we look at several types of activity that constitute cyber crimes against persons or property. Other cyber crimes will be discussed in later chapters as they relate to particular topics, such as banking or consumer law.

Cyber Theft

In cyberspace, thieves are not subject to the physical limitations of the "real" world. A thief can steal data stored in a networked computer with Internet access from anywhere on the globe. Only the speed of the connection and the thief's computer equipment limit the quantity of data that can be stolen.

Financial Crimes Computer networks also provide opportunities for employees to commit crimes that can involve serious economic losses. For example, employees of a company's accounting department can transfer funds among accounts with little effort and often with less risk than would be involved in transactions evidenced by paperwork.

Generally, the dependence of businesses on computer operations has left firms vulnerable to sabotage, fraud, embezzlement, and the theft of proprietary data, such as trade secrets or other intellectual property. As noted in Chapter 8, the piracy of intellectual property

via the Internet is one of the most serious legal challenges facing lawmakers and the courts today.

Identity Theft A form of cyber theft that has become particularly troublesome in recent years is **identity theft.** Identity theft occurs when the wrongdoer steals a form of identification—such as a name, date of birth, or Social Security number—and uses the information to access the victim's financial resources. This crime existed to a certain extent before the widespread use of the Internet. Thieves would "steal" calling-card numbers by watching people using public telephones, or they would rifle through garbage to find bank account or credit-card numbers. The identity thieves would then use the calling-card or credit-card numbers or would withdraw funds from the victims' accounts. The Internet, however, has turned identity theft into perhaps the fastest-growing financial crime in the United States. The Internet provides those who steal information offline with an easy medium for using items such as stolen credit-card numbers while remaining protected by anonymity.

Three federal statutes deal specifically with identity theft. The Identity Theft and Assumption Deterrence Act of 1998[28] made identity theft a federal crime and directed the U.S. Sentencing Commission to incorporate the crime into its sentencing guidelines. The Fair and Accurate Credit Transactions Act of 2003[29] gives victims of identity theft certain rights in working with creditors and credit bureaus to remove negative information from their credit reports. This act will be discussed in detail in Chapter 44 in the context of consumer law. The Identity Theft Penalty Enhancement Act of 2004[30] authorized more severe penalties in aggravated cases in which the identity theft was committed in connection with the thief's employment or with other serious crimes (such as terrorism or firearms or immigration offenses).

Hacking

Persons who use one computer to break into another are sometimes referred to as **hackers.** Hackers who break into computers without authorization often commit cyber theft. Sometimes, however, their principal aim is to prove how smart they are by gaining access to others' password-protected computers and

---

28. 18 U.S.C. Section 1028.
29. 15 U.S.C. Sections 1681 *et seq.*
30. 18 U.S.C. Section 1028A.

causing random data errors or making toll telephone calls for free.[31]

Cyberterrorism Hackers who, rather than trying to gain attention, strive to remain undetected so that they can exploit computers for a serious impact are called **cyberterrorists.** Just as "real" terrorists destroyed the World Trade Center towers and a portion of the Pentagon on September 11, 2001, cyberterrorists might explode "logic bombs" to shut down central computers. Such activities obviously can pose a danger to national security.

The Threat to Business Activities Any business may be targeted by cyberterrorists as well as hackers. The goals of a hacking operation might include a wholesale theft of data, such as a merchant's customer files, or the monitoring of a computer to discover a business firm's plans and transactions. A cyberterrorist might also want to insert false codes or data. For example, the processing control system of a food manufacturer could be changed to alter the levels of ingredients so that consumers of the food would become ill.

A cyberterrorist attack on a major financial institution, such as the New York Stock Exchange or a large bank, could leave securities or money markets in flux and seriously affect the daily lives of millions of citizens. Similarly, any prolonged disruption of computer, cable, satellite, or telecommunications systems due to the actions of expert hackers would have serious repercussions on business operations—and national security—on a global level. Computer viruses are another tool that can be used by cyberterrorists to cripple communications networks.

Spam

As discussed in Chapter 6, spamming (sending bulk unsolicited e-mail) has become a major problem for businesses. A few states, such as Maryland and Virginia, have passed laws that make spamming a crime.[32] Under the Virginia statute, it is a crime against property to use a computer or computer network "with the intent to falsify or forge electronic mail transmission information or other routing information in any man-

ner." Attempting to send spam to more than 2,500 recipients in a twenty-four-hour period is a felony. The Virginia law also includes provisions authorizing the forfeiture of assets obtained through an illegal spamming operation. The Maryland law is similar in that it prohibits spamming that falsely identifies the sender, the routing information, or the subject. Under the Maryland law, however, the number of spam messages required to convict a person of the offense is much lower. Sending only ten illegal messages in twenty-four hours violates the statute, and the more spam sent, the more severe the punishment will be, up to a maximum of ten years in prison and a $25,000 fine.

In 2006, a Virginia appellate court upheld the first felony conviction for criminal spamming in the United States against Jeremy Jaynes, who until his arrest was the eighth most prolific spammer in the world. Jaynes, a resident of North Carolina, had sent more than ten thousand junk messages a day using sixteen Internet connections and a number of aliases (such as Gaven Stubberfield). Because he had sent some of the messages through servers in Virginia, the court found that Virginia had jurisdiction over Jaynes. He was convicted of three counts of felony spamming and sentenced to nine years in prison.

Prosecuting Cyber Crime

The "location" of cyber crime (cyberspace) has raised new issues in the investigation of crimes and the prosecution of offenders. A threshold issue is, of course, jurisdiction. A person who commits an act against a business in California, where the act is a cyber crime, might never have set foot in California but might instead reside in New York, or even in Canada, where the act may not be a crime. If the crime was committed via e-mail, the question arises as to whether the e-mail would constitute sufficient "minimum contacts" (see Chapter 2) for the victim's state to exercise jurisdiction over the perpetrator.

Identifying the wrongdoer can also be difficult. Cyber criminals do not leave physical traces, such as fingerprints or DNA samples, as evidence of their crimes. Even electronic "footprints" can be hard to find and follow. For example, e-mail may be sent through a remailer, an online service that guarantees that a message cannot be traced to its source.

For these reasons, laws written to protect physical property often are difficult to apply in cyberspace. Nonetheless, governments at both the state and the federal level have taken significant steps toward

---

31. The total cost of crime on the Internet is estimated to be several billion dollars annually, but two-thirds of that total is said to consist of unpaid-for long-distance calls.

32. See, for example, Maryland Code, Criminal Law, Section 3-805.1, and Virginia Code Ann. Sections 18.2–152.3:1.

controlling cyber crime, both by applying existing criminal statutes and by enacting new laws that specifically address wrongs committed in cyberspace.

The Computer Fraud and Abuse Act

Perhaps the most significant federal statute specifically addressing cyber crime is the Counterfeit Access Device and Computer Fraud and Abuse Act of 1984 (commonly known as the Computer Fraud and Abuse Act, or CFAA).[33] Among other things, this act provides that a person who accesses a computer online, without authority, to obtain classified, restricted, or protected data (or attempts to do so) is subject to criminal prosecution. Such data could include financial and credit records, medical records, legal files, military and national security files, and other confidential information in government or private computers. The crime has two elements: accessing a computer without authority and taking the data.

This theft is a felony if it is committed for a commercial purpose or for private financial gain, or if the value of the stolen data (or computer time) exceeds $5,000.

---

33. 18 U.S.C. Section 1030.

Penalties include fines and imprisonment for up to twenty years. A victim of computer theft can also bring a civil suit against the violator to obtain damages, an injunction, and other relief.

PREVENTING
LEGAL DISPUTES

Although outside hackers are a threat to businesses, employees, former employees, and other "insiders" are responsible for most computer abuse, including breaches of information security. Therefore, businesspersons need to be cautious about which employees have access to computer data and to give employees access only to information that they need to know. Another important preventive measure is to have employees agree, in a written contract, not to disclose confidential information during or after employment without the employer's consent. Business owners should also make sure that they use the latest methods available to secure their computer systems, including firewalls and encryption techniques, for example.

REVIEWING Criminal Law and Cyber Crime

Edward Hanousek worked for Pacific & Arctic Railway and Navigation Company (P&A) as a roadmaster of the White Pass & Yukon Railroad in Alaska. Hanousek was responsible "for every detail of the safe and efficient maintenance and construction of track, structures and marine facilities of the entire railroad," including special projects. One project was a rock quarry, known as "6-mile," above the Skagway River. Next to the quarry, and just beneath the surface, ran a high-pressure oil pipeline owned by Pacific & Arctic Pipeline, Inc., P&A's sister company. When the quarry's backhoe operator punctured the pipeline, an estimated 1,000 to 5,000 gallons of oil were discharged into the river. Hanousek was charged with negligently discharging a harmful quantity of oil into a navigable water of the United States in violation of the criminal provisions of the Clean Water Act (CWA). Using the information presented in the chapter, answer the following questions.

1. Did Hanousek have the required mental state (*mens rea*) to be convicted of a crime? Why or why not?
2. Which theory discussed in the chapter would enable a court to hold Hanousek criminally liable for violating the statute regardless of whether he participated in, directed, or even knew about the specific violation?
3. Could the quarry's backhoe operator who punctured the pipeline also be charged with a crime in this situation? Explain.
4. Suppose that at trial, Hanousek argued that he could not be convicted because he was not aware of the requirements of the CWA. Would this defense be successful? Why or why not?

TERMS AND CONCEPTS

actus reus

arson

beyond a reasonable doubt

burglary

computer crime

consent

crime

cyber crime

cyberterrorist

double jeopardy

duress

embezzlement

entrapment

exclusionary rule

felony

forgery

grand jury

hacker

identity theft

indictment

information

larceny

mens rea

misdemeanor

money laundering

necessity

petty offense

plea bargaining

robbery

self-defense

white-collar crime

QUESTIONS AND CASE PROBLEMS

9–1. The following situations are similar (in all of them, Juanita's laptop computer is stolen), yet three different crimes are described. Identify the three crimes, noting the differences among them.

(a) While passing Juanita's house one night, Sarah sees a laptop computer left unattended on Juanita's lawn. Sarah takes the laptop, carries it home, and tells everyone she owns it.

(b) While passing Juanita's house one night, Sarah sees Juanita outside with a laptop computer. Holding Juanita at gunpoint, Sarah forces her to give up the computer. Then Sarah runs away with it.

(c) While passing Juanita's house one night, Sarah sees a laptop computer on a desk inside. Sarah breaks the front-door lock, enters, and leaves with the computer.

9–2. Which, if any, of the following crimes necessarily involves illegal activity on the part of more than one person?

(a) Bribery.
(b) Forgery.
(c) Embezzlement.
(d) Larceny.
(e) Receiving stolen property.

9–3. QUESTION WITH SAMPLE ANSWER

Armington, while robbing a drugstore, shot and seriously injured a drugstore clerk, Jennings. Subsequently, in a criminal trial, Armington was con-victed of armed robbery and assault and battery. Jennings later brought a civil tort suit against Armington for damages. Armington contended that he could not be tried again for the same crime, as that would constitute double jeopardy, which is prohibited by the Fifth Amendment to the Constitution. Is Armington correct? Explain.

• **For a sample answer to Question 9–3, go to Appendix C at the end of this text.**

9–4. Rafael stops Laura on a busy street and offers to sell her an expensive wristwatch for a fraction of its value. After some questioning by Laura, Rafael admits that the watch is stolen property, although he says he was not the thief. Laura pays for and receives the wristwatch. Has Laura committed any crime? Has Rafael? Explain.

9–5. Theft of Trade Secrets. Four Pillars Enterprise Co. is a Taiwanese company owned by Pin Yen Yang. Avery Dennison, Inc., a U.S. corporation, is one of Four Pillars' chief competitors in the manufacture of adhesives. In 1989, Victor Lee, an Avery employee, met Yang and Yang's daughter Hwei Chen. They agreed to pay Lee $25,000 a year to serve as a consultant to Four Pillars. Over the next eight years, Lee supplied the Yangs with confidential Avery reports, including information that Four Pillars used to make a new adhesive that had been developed by Avery. The Federal Bureau of Investigation (FBI) confronted Lee, and he agreed to cooperate in an operation to catch the Yangs. When Lee next met the Yangs, he showed them documents provided by the FBI. The documents bore "confidential" stamps, and Lee said that they were Avery's confidential property. The FBI arrested the Yangs with the documents in their possession. The Yangs and Four Pillars were charged with, among other crimes, the attempted theft of trade secrets. The defendants argued in part that it was impossible for them to have committed this crime because the documents were not actually trade secrets. Should the court acquit them? Why or why not? [*United States v. Yang*, 281 F.3d 534 (6th Cir. 2002)]

9–6. CASE PROBLEM WITH SAMPLE ANSWER

The Sixth Amendment secures to a defendant who faces possible imprisonment the right to counsel at all critical stages of the criminal process, including the arraignment and the trial. In 1996, Felipe Tovar, a twenty-one-year-old college student, was arrested in Ames, Iowa, for operating a motor vehicle while under the influence of alcohol (OWI). Tovar was informed of his right to apply for court-appointed counsel and waived it. At his arraignment, he pleaded guilty. Six weeks later, he appeared for sentencing, again waived his right to counsel, and was sentenced to two days' imprisonment. In 1998, Tovar was convicted of OWI again, and in 2000, he was charged with OWI for a third time. In Iowa, a third OWI offense is a felony. Tovar asked the court not to use his first OWI conviction to enhance the third OWI charge. He argued that his 1996 waiver of counsel was not "intelligent" because the court did not make him aware of "the dangers and disadvantages of self-representation." What determines whether a person's choice in any situation is "intelligent"? What should determine whether a defendant's waiver of counsel is "intelligent" at critical stages of a criminal proceeding? [*Iowa v. Tovar*, 541 U.S. 77, 124 S.Ct. 1379, 158 L.Ed.2d 209 (2004)]

- **To view a sample answer for Problem 9–6, go to this book's Web site at www.cengage.com/blaw/jentz, select "Chapter 9," and click on "Case Problem with Sample Answer."**

9–7. Larceny. In February 2001, a homeowner hired Jimmy Smith, a contractor claiming to employ a crew of thirty workers, to build a garage. The homeowner paid Smith $7,950 and agreed to make additional payments as needed to complete the project, up to $15,900. Smith promised to start the next day and finish within eight weeks. Nearly a month passed with no work, while Smith lied to the homeowner that materials were on "back order." During a second month, footings were created for the foundation, and a subcontractor poured the concrete slab, but Smith did not return the homeowner's phone calls. After eight weeks, the homeowner confronted Smith, who promised to complete the job, worked on the site that day until lunch, and never returned. Three months later, the homeowner again confronted Smith, who promised to "pay [him] off" later that day but did not do so. In March 2002, the state of Georgia filed criminal charges against Smith. While his trial was pending, he promised to pay the homeowner "next week" but again failed to refund any of the funds paid. The value of the labor performed before Smith abandoned the project was between $800 and $1,000, the value of the materials

was $367, and the subcontractor was paid $2,270. Did Smith commit larceny? Explain. [*Smith v. State of Georgia*, 592 S.E.2d 871 (Ga. App. 2004)]

9–8. Trial. Robert Michels met Allison Formal through an online dating Web site in 2002. Michels represented himself as the retired chief executive officer of a large company that he had sold for millions of dollars. In January 2003, Michels proposed that he and Formal create a *limited liability company* (a special form of business organization discussed in Chapter 37)—Formal Properties Trust, LLC—to "channel their investments in real estate." Formal agreed to contribute $100,000 to the company and wrote two $50,000 checks to "Michels and Associates, LLC." Six months later, Michels told Formal that their LLC had been formed in Delaware. Later, Formal asked Michels about her investments. He responded evasively, and she demanded that an independent accountant review the firm's records. Michels refused. Formal contacted the police. Michels was charged in a Virginia state court with obtaining funds by false pretenses. The Delaware secretary of state verified, in two certified documents, that "Formal Properties Trust, L.L.C." and "Michels and Associates, L.L.C." did not exist in Delaware. Did the admission of the Delaware secretary of state's certified documents at Michels's trial violate his rights under the Sixth Amendment? Why or why not? [*Michels v. Commonwealth of Virginia*, 47 Va. App. 461, 624 S.E.2d 675 (2006)]

9–9. White-Collar Crime. Helm Instruction Co. in Maumee, Ohio, makes custom electrical control systems. Helm hired Patrick Walsh in September 1998 to work as comptroller. Walsh soon developed a close relationship with Richard Wilhelm, Helm's president, who granted Walsh's request to hire Shari Price as Walsh's assistant. Wilhelm was not aware that Walsh and Price were engaged in an extramarital affair. Over the next five years, Walsh and Price spent more than $200,000 of Helm's money on themselves. Among other things, Walsh drew unauthorized checks on Helm's accounts to pay his personal credit-card bills and issued to Price and himself unauthorized salary increases, overtime payments, and tuition reimbursement payments, altering Helm's records to hide the payments. After an investigation, Helm officials confronted Walsh. He denied the affair with Price, claimed that his unauthorized use of Helm's funds was an "interest-free loan," and argued that it was less of a burden on the company to pay his credit-card bills than to give him the salary increases to which he felt he was entitled. Did Walsh commit a crime? If so, what crime did he commit? Discuss. [*State v. Walsh*, 113 Ohio App.3d 1515, 866 N.E.2d 513 (6 Dist. 2007)]

9–10. A QUESTION OF ETHICS

A troublesome issue concerning the constitutional privilege against self-incrimination is the extent to which law enforcement officers may use trickery during an interrogation to induce a suspect to incriminate himself or herself. For example, in one case two officers questioned Charles McFarland, who was incarcerated in a state prison, about his connection to a handgun that had been used to shoot two other officers. McFarland was advised of his rights but was not asked whether he was willing to waive those rights. Instead, to induce McFarland to speak, the officers deceived him into believing that "[n]obody is going to give you charges." McFarland made incriminating admissions and was indicted for possessing a handgun as a convicted felon. *[United States v. McFarland, 424 F. Supp. 2d 427 (N.D.N.Y. 2006)]*

(a) Review Case 9.3, *Miranda v. Arizona,* on pages 186 and 187 in this chapter. Should McFarland's statements be suppressed—that is, not be treated as admissible evidence at trial—because he was not asked whether he was willing to waive his rights prior to making his self-incriminating statements? Does the *Miranda* rule apply to McFarland's situation?

(b) Do you think that it is fair for the police to resort to trickery and deception to bring those who have committed crimes to justice? Why or why not? What rights or public policies must be balanced in deciding this issue?

9–11. VIDEO QUESTION

Go to this text's Web site at **www.cengage. com/blaw/jentz** and select "Chapter 9." Click on "Video Questions" and view the video titled *Casino.* Then answer the following questions.

(a) In the video, a casino manager, Ace (Robert DeNiro), discusses how politicians "won their 'comp life' when they got elected." "Comps" are the free gifts that casinos give to high-stakes gamblers to keep their business. If an elected official accepts comps, is he or she committing a crime? If so, what type of crime? Explain your answers.

(b) Assume that Ace committed a crime by giving politicians comps. Can the casino, Tangiers Corp., be held liable for that crime? Why or why not? How could a court punish the corporation?

(c) Suppose that the Federal Bureau of Investigation wants to search the premises of Tangiers for evidence of criminal activity. If casino management refuses to consent to the search, what constitutional safeguards and criminal procedures, if any, protect Tangiers?

LAW ON THE WEB

For updated links to resources available on the Web, as well as a variety of other materials, visit this text's Web site at

www.cengage.com/blaw/jentz

The Bureau of Justice Statistics in the U.S. Department of Justice offers an impressive collection of statistics on crime at the following Web site:

ojp.usdoj.gov/bjs

For summaries of famous criminal cases and documents relating to these trials, go to the Web site of truTV (formerly Court TV) at

www.trutv.com/sitemap/index.html

Many state criminal codes are now online. To find your state's code, go to the following home page and select "States" under the link to "Cases & Codes":

www.findlaw.com

You can learn about some of the constitutional questions raised by various criminal laws and procedures by going to the Web site of the American Civil Liberties Union at

www.aclu.org

The following Web site, which is maintained by the U.S. Department of Justice, offers information ranging from the various types of cyber crime to a description of how they are being prosecuted:

www.cybercrime.gov

Legal Research Exercises on the Web

Go to **www.cengage.com/blaw/jentz**, the Web site that accompanies this text. Select "Chapter 9" and click on "Internet Exercises." There you will find the following Internet research exercises that you can perform to learn more about the topics covered in this chapter.

Internet Exercise 9–1: Legal Perspective
Revisiting *Miranda*

Internet Exercise 9–2: Management Perspective
Hackers

Internet Exercise 9–3: International Perspective
Fighting Cyber Crime Worldwide

Ethics and Torts and Crimes

Ethical and legal concepts are often closely intertwined. This is because the common law, as it evolved in England and then in America, reflects society's values and customs. This connection between law and ethics is clearly evident in the area of tort law, which provides remedies for harms caused by actions that society has deemed wrongful. Criminal law is also rooted in common law concepts of right and wrong behavior, although common law concepts governing criminal acts are now expressed in, or replaced by, federal, state, and local criminal statutes. The number of torts and crimes has continued to expand as new ways to commit wrongs have been discovered.

The laws governing torts, crimes, and intellectual property—the areas of law covered in this unit—constitute an important part of the legal environment of business. In each of these areas, new legal (and ethical) challenges have emerged as a result of developments in technology. Today, we are witnessing some of the challenges posed by the use of new communications networks, particularly the Internet. In this *Focus on Ethics* feature, we look at the ethical dimensions of selected topics discussed in the preceding chapters, including some issues that are unique to the cyber age.

Privacy Rights in an Online World

Privacy rights are protected under constitutional law, tort law, and various federal and state statutes. How to protect privacy rights in the online world, though, has been a recurring problem over the past ten years. One difficulty is that individuals today often are not even aware that information about their personal lives and preferences is being collected by Internet companies and other online users. Nor do they know how that information will be used. "Cookies" installed in computers may allow users' Web movements to be tracked. Google now offers a Gmail service that automatically scans and saves information about its users. Persons who purchase goods from online merchants or auctions inevitably must reveal some personal information, often including their credit-card numbers.

The Increased Value of Personal Information

One of the major concerns of consumers in recent years has been the increasing value of personal information for online marketers, who are willing to pay a high price to those who collect and sell them such information. Because of these concerns—and the possibility of lawsuits based on privacy laws—businesses marketing goods online need to exercise care. Today, many online businesses create and post on their Web sites a privacy policy disclosing how any information obtained from their customers will be used.

The Duty of Care and Personal Information

Selling data can bolster a company's profits, which may satisfy the firm's duty to its owners, but when the information is personal, its sale may violate an ethical or legal duty. In what circumstances might a party who sells information about someone else have a duty to that other party with respect to the sale of the information?

The courts have found that private investigators owe a duty not to disclose private information about a person without a legitimate reason. In one case, for example, a man contacted an Internet-based investigation and information service and requested information about Amy Boyer. The man provided his name, address, and phone number and paid the fee online using his credit card. In return, the company provided him with Boyer's home address, birth date, Social Security number, and work address. The man then drove to Boyer's workplace and fatally shot her. The police subsequently discovered that the man maintained a Web site where he referred to stalking and killing Boyer. Boyer's mother filed a suit against the online information service for disclosing her daughter's private information without investigating the reason for the request. The state supreme court found that because the threats of stalking and identity theft were sufficiently foreseeable, the company had a duty to exercise reasonable care in disclosing a third person's personal information to a client.[1]

In another case, a man hired a licensed private investigator to follow his ex-girlfriend. The woman complained to the police that the investigator was stalking her, and criminal charges were filed against the investigator. The court concluded that the private detective had a duty to exercise reasonable care in disclosing the woman's personal information to the client (her former boyfriend). Because the private detective refused to testify as

---

1. *Remsburg v. Docusearch, Inc.,* 149 N.H. 148, 816 A.2d 1001 (2003).

(Continued)

to why he was hired to follow the woman, the court found that the investigator's conduct was not for a legitimate purpose.[2]

Privacy Rights in the Workplace

Another area of concern today is the extent to which employees' privacy rights should be protected in the workplace. Traditionally, employees have been afforded a certain "zone of privacy" in the workplace. For example, the courts have concluded that employees have a reasonable expectation of privacy with respect to personal items contained in their desks or in their lockers. Should this zone of privacy extend to personal e-mail sent via the employer's computer system? This question and others relating to employee privacy rights in today's cyber age will be discussed in greater detail in Chapter 33, in the context of employment law.

Should Civil Liberties Be Sacrificed to Control Crime and Terrorist Activities in the Cyber Age?

In an era when criminal conspirators and terrorists use the Internet to communicate and even to recruit new members, an issue that has come to the forefront is whether it is possible to control many types of crime and terrorist activities without sacrificing some civil liberties. Governments in certain countries, such as Russia, have succeeded in controlling online criminal communications to some extent by monitoring the e-mail and other electronic transmissions of users of specific Internet service providers. In the United States, however, any government attempt to monitor Internet use to detect criminal conspiracies or terrorist activities does not sit well with the American people. The traditional attitude has been that civil liberties must be safeguarded to the greatest extent feasible.

After the terrorist attacks in September 2001, Congress enacted legislation—including the USA Patriot Act mentioned in Chapter 4—that gave law enforcement personnel more authority to conduct electronic surveillance, such as monitoring Web sites and e-mail exchanges. For a time, it seemed that the terrorist attacks might have made Americans more willing to trade off some of their civil liberties for greater national security. Today, though, many complain that this legislation has gone too far in curbing traditional civil liberties guaranteed by the U.S. Constitution. As terrorists find more ways of using the Internet for their purposes, determining the degree to which individuals should sacrifice personal freedoms in exchange for greater protection will likely become even more difficult.

Global Companies and Censorship Issues—Google China

Doing business on a global level can sometimes involve serious ethical challenges. Consider the ethical firestorm that erupted when Google, Inc., decided to market "Google China." This version of Google's widely used search engine was especially tailored to the Chinese government's censorship requirements. To date, the Chinese government has maintained strict control over the flow of information in that country. The government's goal is to stop the flow of what it considers to be "harmful information." Web sites that offer pornography, criticism of the government, or information on sensitive topics, such as the Tiananmen Square massacre in 1989, are censored—that is, they cannot be accessed by Web users. Government agencies enforce the censorship and encourage citizens to inform on one another. Thousands of Web sites are shut down each year, and the sites' operators are subject to potential imprisonment.

Google's code of conduct opens with the company's informal motto: "Don't be evil." Yet critics question whether Google is following this motto. Human rights groups have come out strongly against Google's decision, maintaining that the company is seeking profits in a lucrative marketplace at the expense of assisting the Chinese Communist Party in suppressing free speech. In February 2006, Tom Lantos, who was the only Holocaust survivor serving in Congress until his death in 2008, stated that the "sickening collaboration" of Google and three other Web companies (Cisco Systems, Microsoft Corporation, and Yahoo!, Inc.) with the Chinese government was "decapitating the voice of dissidents" in that nation.[3]

Google's Response

Google defends its actions by pointing out that its Chinese search engine at least lets users know which sites are being censored. Google China

---

2. *Miller v. Blackden,* 154 N.H. 448, 913 A.2d 742 (2006).

3. As quoted in Tom Ziller, Jr., "Web Firms Questioned on Dealings in China," *The New York Times,* February 16, 2006.

includes the links to censored sites, but when a user tries to access a link, the program states that it is not accessible. Google claims that its approach is essentially the "lesser of two evils": if U.S. companies did not cooperate with the Chinese government, Chinese residents would have less user-friendly Internet access. Moreover, Google asserts that providing Internet access, even if censored, is a step toward more open access in the future because technology is, in itself, a revolutionary force.

The Chinese Government's Defense

The Chinese government insists that in restricting access to certain Web sites, it is merely following the lead of other national governments, which also impose controls on information access. As an example, it cites France, which bans access to any Web sites selling or portraying Nazi paraphernalia. The United States itself prohibits the dissemination of certain types of materials, such as child pornography, over the Internet. Furthermore, the U.S. government monitors Web sites and e-mail communications to protect against terrorist threats. How, ask Chinese officials, can other nations point their fingers at China for engaging in a common international practice?

Do Gun Makers Have a Duty to Warn?

One of the issues facing today's courts is how tort law principles apply to harms caused by guns. Across the nation, many plaintiffs have filed negligence actions against gun manufacturers, claiming that gun makers have a duty to warn users of their products of the dangers associated with gun use. Would it be fair to impose such a requirement on gun manufacturers? Some say no, because such dangers are "open and obvious." (Recall from Chapter 7 that, generally, there is no duty to warn of open and obvious dangers.) Others contend that warnings could prevent numerous gun accidents.

State courts addressing this issue have generally ruled that manufacturers have no duty to warn users of the obvious risks associated with gun use. For example, New York's highest court has held that a gun manufacturer's duty of care does not extend to those who are injured by the illegal use of handguns.[4]

FOCUS on ETHICS

Trademark Protection versus Free Speech Rights

Another legal issue involving questions of fairness pits the rights of trademark owners against the right to free speech. The issue—so-called cybergriping—is unique to the cyber age. Cybergripers are individuals who complain in cyberspace about corporate products, services, or activities. For a trademark owner, the issue becomes particularly thorny when cybergriping sites add the word *sucks* or *stinks* or some other disparaging term to the trademark owner's domain name. These sites, sometimes referred to collectively as "sucks" sites, are established solely for the purpose of criticizing the products or services sold by the trademark owner.

A number of companies have sued the owners of such sites for trademark infringement in the hope that a court or an arbitrating panel will order the site owner to cease using the domain name. To date, however, companies have had little success pursuing this alternative. In one case, for example, Bally Total Fitness Holding Corporation sued Andrew Faber, who had established a "Bally sucks" site for the purpose of criticizing Bally's health clubs and business practices. Bally claimed that Faber had infringed on its trademark. The court did not agree, holding that the "speech"—consumer commentary—on Faber's Web site was protected by the First Amendment. In short, Bally could not look to trademark law for a remedy against cyber critics.[5]

The courts have been reluctant to hold that the use of a business's domain name in a "sucks" site infringes on the trademark owner's rights. After all, one of the primary reasons trademarks are protected under U.S. law is to prevent customers from becoming confused about the origin of the goods for sale—and a cybergriping site certainly does not create such confusion. Furthermore, U.S. courts give extensive protection to free speech rights, including the right to express opinions about companies and their products.[6] Nevertheless, when a site's domain name is confusingly similar to a competitor's trade name and the site is used to

---

5. *Bally Total Fitness Holding Corp. v. Faber,* 29 F.Supp.2d 1161 (C.D.Cal. 1998).
6. Many businesses have concluded that although they cannot control what people say about them, they can make it more difficult for it to be said. Today, businesses commonly register such insulting domain names before the cybergripers themselves can register them.

---

4. *Hamilton v. Beretta U.S.A. Corp.,* 96 N.Y.2d 222, 750 N.E.2d 1055, 727 N.Y.S.2d 7 (2001).

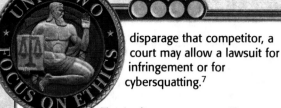

disparage that competitor, a court may allow a lawsuit for infringement or for cybersquatting.[7]

Trade Secrets versus Free Speech Rights

Another ongoing issue with ethical dimensions is the point at which free speech rights come into conflict with the right of copyright holders to protect their property by using encryption technology. This issue came before the California Supreme Court in the case of *DVD Copy Control Association v. Bunner*.[8] Trade associations in the movie industry (the plaintiffs) sued an Internet Web site operator (the defendant) who had posted the code of a computer program that cracked technology used to encrypt DVDs. This posed a significant threat to the plaintiffs because, by using the code-cracking software, users would be able to duplicate the copyrighted movies stored on the DVDs.

In their suit, the plaintiffs claimed that the defendant had misappropriated trade secrets. The defendant argued that software programs designed to break encryption programs were a form of constitutionally protected speech. When the case reached the California Supreme Court, the court held that although the First Amendment applies to

---

7. See, for example, *Sunlight Saunas, Inc. v. Sundance Sauna, Inc.*, 427 F.Supp.2d 1032 (D.Kan. 2006).
8. 31 Cal.4th 864, 75 P.3d 1, 4 Cal.Rptr.3d 69 (2003). But see also *O'Grady v. Superior Court*, 139 Cal.App.4th 1423, 44 Cal.Rptr.3d 72 (2006), in which a state appellate court distinguished the situation from the *Bunner* case and held that Apple, Inc., could prevent an online publisher from disclosing confidential information about the company's impending product.

computer code, computer code is not a form of "pure speech" and the courts can therefore protect it to a lesser extent. The court reinstated the trial court's order that enjoined (prevented) the defendant from continuing to post the code.

DISCUSSION QUESTIONS

1. Some observers maintain that privacy rights are quickly becoming a thing of the past. In your opinion, is it possible to protect privacy rights in today's online world?

2. Many argue that the federal government should not be allowed to monitor the Internet activities and e-mail exchanges of its citizens without obtaining a warrant. Yet others maintain that in some situations, when time is of the essence, such monitoring may be necessary to keep Americans safe from terrorism. Where should the line be drawn between justifiable and unjustifiable governmental interference with American citizens' civil liberties?

3. Do companies, such as Google, that do business on a global level have an ethical duty to foreign citizens not to suppress free speech, or is it acceptable to censor the information that they provide in other nations at the request of a foreign government?

4. In your opinion, should gun manufacturers have a duty to warn gun users of the dangers of using guns? Would such a warning be effective in preventing gun-related accidents?

5. Generally, do you believe that the law has struck a fair balance between the rights of intellectual property owners and the rights of the public?

Nature and Terminology

The noted legal scholar Roscoe Pound once said that "[t]he social order rests upon the stability and predictability of conduct, of which keeping promises is a large item."[1] Contract law deals with, among other things, the formation and keeping of promises. A **promise** is a person's assurance that the person will or will not do something.

Like other types of law, contract law reflects our social values, interests, and expectations at a given point in time. It shows, for example, to what extent our society allows people to make promises or commitments that are legally binding. It distinguishes between promises that create only *moral* obligations (such as a promise to take a friend to lunch) and promises that are legally binding (such as a promise to pay for merchandise purchased). Contract law also demonstrates which excuses our society accepts for breaking certain types of promises. In addition, it indicates which promises are considered to be contrary to public policy— against the interests of society as a whole—and therefore legally invalid. When the person making a promise is a child or is mentally incompetent, for example, a question will arise as to whether the promise should be enforced. Resolving such questions is the essence of contract law.

---

1. R. Pound, *Jurisprudence*, Vol. 3 (St. Paul, Minn.: West Publishing Co., 1959), p. 162.

 **An Overview of Contract Law**

Before we look at the numerous rules that courts use to determine whether a particular promise will be enforced, it is necessary to understand some fundamental concepts of contract law. In this section, we describe the sources and general function of contract law. We also provide the definition of a contract and introduce the objective theory of contracts.

Sources of Contract Law

The common law governs all contracts except when it has been modified or replaced by statutory law, such as the Uniform Commercial Code (UCC),[2] or by administrative agency regulations. Contracts relating to services, real estate, employment, and insurance, for example, generally are governed by the common law of contracts.

Contracts for the sale and lease of goods, however, are governed by the UCC—to the extent that the UCC has modified general contract law. The relationship between general contract law and the law governing sales and leases of goods will be explored in detail in Chapter 20. In the discussion of general contract law that follows, we indicate in footnotes the areas in which the UCC has significantly altered common law contract principles.

The Function of Contract Law

The law encourages competent parties to form contracts for lawful objectives. Indeed, no aspect of modern life is entirely free of contractual relationships. Even ordinary consumers in their daily activities

---

2. See Chapters 1 and 20 for further discussions of the significance and coverage of the UCC. The UCC is presented in Appendix C at the end of this book.

acquire rights and obligations based on contract law. You acquire rights and obligations, for example, when you purchase an iPod or when you borrow funds to buy a house. Contract law is designed to provide stability and predictability, as well as certainty, for both buyers and sellers in the marketplace.

Contract law deals with, among other things, the formation and enforcement of agreements between parties (in Latin, *pacta sunt servanda*—"agreements shall be kept"). By supplying procedures for enforcing private contractual agreements, contract law provides an essential condition for the existence of a market economy. Without a legal framework of reasonably assured expectations within which to make long-run plans, businesspersons would be able to rely only on the good faith of others. Duty and good faith are usually sufficient to obtain compliance with a promise, but when price changes or adverse economic factors make compliance costly, these elements may not be enough. Contract law is necessary to ensure compliance with a promise or to entitle the innocent party to some form of relief.

Definition of a Contract

A **contract** is "a promise or a set of promises for the breach of which the law gives a remedy, or the performance of which the law in some way recognizes as a duty."[3] Put simply, a contract is a legally binding agreement between two or more parties who agree to perform or to refrain from performing some act now or in the future. Generally, contract disputes arise when there is a promise of future performance. If the contractual promise is not fulfilled, the party who made it is subject to the sanctions of a court (see Chapter 18). That party may be required to pay damages for failing to perform the contractual promise; in limited instances, the party may be required to perform the promised act.

The Objective Theory of Contracts

In determining whether a contract has been formed, the element of intent is of prime importance. In contract law, intent is determined by what is called the

---

3. *Restatement (Second) of Contracts,* Section 1. The *Restatement of the Law of Contracts* is a nonstatutory, authoritative exposition of the common law of contracts compiled by the American Law Institute in 1932. The *Restatement,* which is now in its second edition (a third edition is being drafted), will be referred to throughout the following chapters on contract law.

objective theory of contracts, not by the personal or subjective intent, or belief, of a party. The theory is that a party's intention to enter into a legally binding agreement, or contract, is judged by outward, objective facts as interpreted by a *reasonable* person, rather than by the party's own secret, subjective intentions. Objective facts include (1) what the party said when entering into the contract, (2) how the party acted or appeared (intent may be manifested by conduct as well as by oral or written words), and (3) the circumstances surrounding the transaction. We will look further at the objective theory of contracts in Chapter 11, in the context of contract formation.

Elements of a Contract

The many topics that will be discussed in the following chapters on contract law require an understanding of the basic elements of a valid contract and the way in which a contract is created. The topics to be covered in this unit on contracts also require an understanding of the types of circumstances in which even legally valid contracts will not be enforced.

Requirements of a Valid Contract

The following list briefly describes the four requirements that must be met before a valid contract exists. If any of these elements is lacking, no contract will have been formed. (Each requirement will be explained more fully in subsequent chapters.)

1. *Agreement.* An agreement to form a contract includes an *offer* and an *acceptance.* One party must offer to enter into a legal agreement, and another party must accept the terms of the offer.
2. *Consideration.* Any promises made by the parties to the contract must be supported by legally sufficient and bargained-for *consideration* (something of value received or promised, such as money, to convince a person to make a deal).
3. *Contractual capacity.* Both parties entering into the contract must have the contractual *capacity* to do so; the law must recognize them as possessing characteristics that qualify them as competent parties.
4. *Legality.* The contract's purpose must be to accomplish some goal that is legal and not against public policy.

Defenses to the Enforceability of a Contract

Even if all of the above-listed requirements are satisfied, a contract may be unenforceable if the following requirements are not met. These requirements typically are raised as *defenses* to the enforceability of an otherwise valid contract.

1. *Genuineness of assent, or voluntary consent.* The apparent consent of both parties must be genuine, or voluntary. For example, if a contract was formed as a result of fraud, undue influence, mistake, or duress, the contract may not be enforceable.
2. *Form.* The contract must be in whatever form the law requires; for example, some contracts must be in writing to be enforceable.

Types of Contracts

There are many types of contracts. In this section, you will learn that contracts can be categorized based on legal distinctions as to formation, performance, and enforceability.

Contract Formation

As you can see in Exhibit 8–1, three classifications, or categories, of contracts are based on how and when a contract is formed. We explain each of these types of contracts in the following subsections.

Bilateral versus Unilateral Contracts

Every contract involves at least two parties. The **offeror** is the party making the offer. The **offeree** is the party to whom the offer is made. Whether the contract is classified as *bilateral* or *unilateral* depends on what the offeree must do to accept the offer and bind the offeror to a contract.

Bilateral Contracts. If the offeree can accept simply by promising to perform, the contract is a **bilateral contract.** Hence, a bilateral contract is a "promise for a promise." No performance, such as payment of funds or delivery of goods, need take place for a bilateral contract to be formed. The contract comes into existence at the moment the promises are exchanged.

For example, Javier offers to buy Ann's digital camcorder for $200. Javier tells Ann that he will give her the funds for the camcorder next Friday when he gets paid. Ann accepts Javier's offer and promises to give him the camcorder when he pays her on Friday. Javier and Ann have formed a bilateral contract.

Unilateral Contracts. If the offer is phrased so that the offeree can accept the offer only by completing the contract performance, the contract is a **unilateral contract.** Hence, a unilateral contract is a "promise for an act."[4] In other words, the time of contract formation in a unilateral contract is not the moment when promises are exchanged but the moment when the contract is *performed.* A classic example of a unilateral contract is as follows: O'Malley says to Parker, "If you carry this package across the Brooklyn Bridge, I'll give you $20."

---

4. Clearly, a contract cannot be "one sided," because, by definition, an agreement implies the existence of two or more parties. Therefore, the phrase *unilateral contract,* if read literally, is a contradiction in terms. As traditionally used in contract law, however, the phrase refers to the kind of contract that results when only one promise is being made (the promise made by the offeror in return for the offeree's performance).

EXHIBIT 8–1 • **Classifications Based on Contract Formation**

CONTRACT FORMATION		
BILATERAL A promise for a promise	**FORMAL** Requires a special form for creation	**EXPRESS** Formed by words
UNILATERAL A promise for an act	**INFORMAL** Requires no special form for creation	**IMPLIED IN FACT** Formed at least in part by the parties' conduct

Only on Parker's complete crossing with the package does she fully accept O'Malley's offer to pay $20. If she chooses not to undertake the walk, there are no legal consequences.

Contests, lotteries, and other competitions involving prizes are examples of offers to form unilateral contracts. If a person complies with the rules of the contest—such as by submitting the right lottery number at the right place and time—a unilateral contract is formed, binding the organization offering the prize to a contract to perform as promised in the offer.

Can a school's, or an employer's, letter of tentative acceptance to a prospective student, or a possible employee, qualify as a unilateral contract? That was the issue in the following case.

 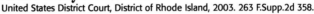

CASE 8.1 Ardito v. City of Providence
United States District Court, District of Rhode Island, 2003. 263 F.Supp.2d 358.

● **Background and Facts** In 2001, the city of Providence, Rhode Island, decided to begin hiring police officers to fill vacancies in its police department. Because only individuals who had graduated from the Providence Police Academy were eligible, the city also decided to conduct two training sessions, the "60th and 61st Police Academies." To be admitted, an applicant had to pass a series of tests and be deemed qualified by members of the department after an interview. The applicants judged most qualified were sent a letter informing them that they had been selected to attend the academy if they successfully completed a medical checkup and a psychological examination. The letter for the applicants to the 61st Academy, dated October 15, stated that it was "a conditional offer of employment." Meanwhile, a new chief of police, Dean Esserman, decided to revise the selection process, which caused some of those who had received the letter to be rejected. Derek Ardito and thirteen other newly rejected applicants—who had all completed the examinations—filed a suit in a federal district court against the city, seeking a halt to the 61st Academy unless they were allowed to attend. They alleged that, among other things, the city was in breach of contract.

● **Decision and Rationale** The court held that the October 15 letter was a unilateral offer that the plaintiffs had accepted, and issued an injunction to prohibit the city from conducting the 61st Police Academy unless the plaintiffs were included. The court found the October 15 letter to be "a classic example of an offer to enter into a unilateral contract. The October 15 letter expressly stated that it was a 'conditional offer of employment' and the message that it conveyed was that the recipient would be admitted into the 61st Academy if he or she successfully completed the medical and psychological examinations." The court contrasted the letter with "notices sent to applicants by the City at earlier stages of the selection process. Those notices merely informed applicants that they had completed a step in the process and remained eligible to be considered for admission into the Academy. Unlike the October 15 letter, the prior notices did not purport to extend a 'conditional offer' of admission." The court concluded that "the plaintiffs accepted the City's offer of admission into the Academy by satisfying the specified conditions. Each of the plaintiffs submitted to and passed lengthy and intrusive medical and psychological examinations."

● **What If the Facts Were Different?** *Suppose that the October 15 letter had used the phrase "potential offer of employment" instead of using the word "conditional." Would the court in this case still have considered the letter to be a unilateral contract? Why or why not?*

● **The Legal Environment Dimension** *Why did the court order the city to stop the 61st Police Academy unless the plaintiffs were included?*

A Problem with Unilateral Contracts. A problem arises in unilateral contracts when the **promisor** (the one making the promise) attempts to *revoke* (cancel) the offer after the **promisee** (the one to whom the promise was made) has begun performance but before the act has been completed. The promisee can accept the offer only on full performance, and under traditional contract principles, an offer may be revoked at any time before the offer is accepted. The present-day view, however, is that an offer to form a unilateral contract becomes irrevocable—cannot be revoked—once performance has begun. Thus, even though the offer has not yet been accepted, the offeror is prohibited from revoking it for a reasonable time period.

For instance, in the earlier example involving the Brooklyn Bridge, suppose that Parker is walking across the bridge and has only three yards to go when O'Malley calls out to her, "I revoke my offer." Under traditional contract law, O'Malley's revocation would terminate the offer. Under the modern view of unilateral contracts, however, O'Malley will not be able to revoke his offer because Parker has undertaken performance and walked all but three yards of the bridge. In these circumstances, Parker can finish crossing the bridge and bind O'Malley to the contract.

Formal versus Informal Contracts Another classification system divides contracts into formal contracts and informal contracts. **Formal contracts** are contracts that require a special form or method of creation (formation) to be enforceable. *Contracts under seal* are a type of formal contract that involves a formalized writing with a special seal attached.[5] In the past, the seals were often made of wax and impressed on the paper document. Today, the significance of the seal in contract law has lessened, though standard-form contracts still sometimes include a place for a seal next to the signature lines. *Letters of credit,* which are frequently used in international sales contracts, are another type of formal contract. As will be discussed in Chapter 22, letters of credit are agreements to pay contingent on the purchaser's receipt of invoices and bills of lading (documents evidencing receipt of, and title to, goods shipped).

---

5. The contract under seal has been almost entirely abolished under such provisions as UCC 2–203 (Section 2–203 of the Uniform Commercial Code). In sales of real estate, however, it is still common to use a seal (or an acceptable substitute).

Informal contracts (also called *simple contracts*) include all other contracts. No special form is required (except for certain types of contracts that must be in writing), as the contracts are usually based on their substance rather than their form. Typically, business-persons put their contracts in writing to ensure that there is some proof of a contract's existence should problems arise.

Express versus Implied-in-Fact Contracts
Contracts may also be categorized as *express* or *implied* by the conduct of the parties. We look here at the differences between these two types of contracts.

Express Contracts. In an **express contract,** the terms of the agreement are fully and explicitly stated in words, oral or written. A signed lease for an apartment or a house is an express written contract. If a classmate calls you on the phone and agrees to buy your textbook from last semester for $45, an express oral contract has been made.

Implied-in-Fact Contracts. A contract that is implied from the conduct of the parties is called an **implied-in-fact contract** or an *implied contract.* This type of contract differs from an express contract in that the *conduct* of the parties, rather than their words, creates and defines the terms of the contract. (Note that a contract may be a mixture of an express contract and an implied-in-fact contract. In other words, a contract may contain some express terms, while others are implied.)

Requirements for Implied-in-Fact Contracts. For an implied-in-fact contract to arise, certain requirements must be met. Normally, if the following conditions exist, a court will hold that an implied contract was formed:

1. The plaintiff furnished some service or property.
2. The plaintiff expected to be paid for that service or property, and the defendant knew or should have known that payment was expected.
3. The defendant had a chance to reject the services or property and did not.

For example, you need an accountant to complete your tax return this year. You look through the Yellow Pages and find an accountant with an office in your neighborhood. You drop by the firm's office, explain your problem to an accountant, and learn what fees will be charged. The next day you return and give her administrative assistant all the necessary information and documents, such as canceled checks and W-2 forms. You then walk out the door without saying anything expressly to the accountant. In this situation, you have entered into an implied-in-fact contract to pay the accountant the usual and reasonable fees for her services. The contract is implied by your conduct and by hers. She expects to be paid for completing your tax return, and by bringing in the records she will need to do the work, you have implied an intent to pay her.

During the construction of a home, the homeowner often requests that the builder make changes in the original specifications. When do these changes form part of an implied-in-fact contract for which the homeowner is liable to the builder for any extra expenses? That was the issue in the following case.

C A S E **8.2** **Uhrhahn Construction & Design, Inc. v. Hopkins**
Court of Appeals of Utah, 2008. 179 P.3d 808.

● **Background and Facts** Uhrhahn Construction & Design, Inc., was hired by Lamar and Joan Hopkins for several projects in the building of their home. Each project was based on a cost estimate and specifications. The proposals accepted by the Hopkinses each said that any changes in the signed contracts would be done only "upon written orders." When work was in progress, the Hopkinses made several requests for changes. There was no written record of these changes, but the work was performed and paid for by the Hopkinses. This dispute arose from the couple's request that Uhrhahn use Durisol blocks rather than cinder blocks in some construction. The original proposal specified cinder blocks, but the Hopkinses told Uhrhahn that the change should be made as Durisol blocks were "easier to install than traditional cinder block and would take half the time." The homeowners said the total cost would be the same. Uhrhahn orally agreed to the change but then discovered that Durisol blocks were more complicated to use than cinder blocks, and Uhrhahn demanded extra payment. The Hopkinses refused to pay, claiming the cost should be the same. Uhrhahn sued. The trial court held for Uhrhahn, finding that the Durisol blocks were more costly to install. The Hopkinses appealed.

● **Decision and Rationale** The Utah appeals court affirmed the decision of the trial court, finding that there was a valid contract between the parties and that both parties had agreed to oral changes in the contract. All of the elements of a contract existed: offer and acceptance, competent parties, and consideration. The terms were clearly specified in the proposals accepted by the Hopkinses. Uhrhahn promised to perform work in exchange for payment. While the contract stated that any changes would be in writing, both parties waived that term in the contract when they agreed to some changes in the work performed. As often happens in construction, changes were requested that were outside the contract. The builder did the work, and the buyer accepted the work and paid for it. Such oral modification of the original contract creates an enforceable contract, and payment is due for the extra work. This is an implied-in-fact contract. The Hopkinses requested Uhrhahn to perform certain work. Uhrhahn expected to be compensated for the work, and the Hopkinses knew, or should have known, that Uhrhahn would be paid for this work that was outside the specifications of the original contract.

● **What If the Facts Were Different?** *Suppose that the Hopkinses and Uhrhahn had not agreed to deviate from the contract on previous occasions, and that the Hopkinses had not paid for any additional work performed by Uhrhahn. How might this have changed the court's ruling in this case?*

● **The E-Commerce Dimension** *Would the outcome have been different if the parties had communicated by e-mail for all details regarding changes in the work performed? Explain.*

Contract Performance

Contracts are also classified according to the degree to which they have been performed. A contract that has been fully performed on both sides is called an **executed contract.** A contract that has not been fully performed by the parties is called an **executory contract.** If one party has fully performed but the other has not, the contract is said to be executed on the one side and executory on the other, but the contract is still classified as executory.

Assume that you agree to buy ten tons of coal from the Northern Coal Company. Further assume that Northern has delivered the coal to your steel mill, where it is now being burned. At this point, the contract is executed on the part of Northern and executory on your part. After you pay Northern for the coal, the contract will be executed on both sides.

Contract Enforceability

A **valid contract** has the elements necessary to entitle at least one of the parties to enforce it in court. Those elements, as mentioned earlier, consist of (1) an agreement consisting of an offer and an acceptance of that offer, (2) supported by legally sufficient consideration, (3) made by parties who have the legal capacity to enter into the contract, and (4) made for a legal purpose. As you can see in Exhibit 8–2, valid contracts may be enforceable, voidable, or unenforceable. Additionally, a contract may be referred to as a *void contract.* We look next at the meaning of the terms *voidable, unenforceable,* and *void* in relation to contract enforceability.

Voidable Contracts A **voidable contract** is a valid contract but one that can be avoided at the option of one or both of the parties. The party having the option can elect either to avoid any duty to perform or to *ratify* (make valid) the contract. If the contract is avoided, both parties are released from it. If it is ratified, both parties must fully perform their respective legal obligations.

As you will read in Chapter 13, contracts made by minors, insane persons, and intoxicated persons may be voidable. For example, contracts made by minors generally are voidable at the option of the minor (with certain exceptions). Additionally, contracts entered into under fraudulent conditions are voidable at the option of the defrauded party. Contracts entered into under legally defined duress or undue influence are also voidable (see Chapter 14).

Unenforceable Contracts An **unenforceable contract** is one that cannot be enforced because of certain legal defenses against it. It is not unenforceable because a party failed to satisfy a legal requirement of the contract; rather, it is a valid contract rendered unenforceable by some statute or law. For example, certain contracts must be in writing (see Chapter 15), and if they are not, they will not be enforceable except in certain exceptional circumstances.

Void Contracts A **void contract** is no contract at all. The terms *void* and *contract* are contradictory. A void contract produces no legal obligations on any of the parties. For example, a contract can be void because one of the parties was adjudged by a court to

EXHIBIT 8–2 • **Enforceable, Voidable, Unenforceable, and Void Contracts**

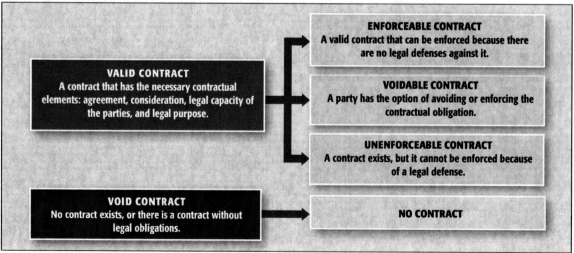

be legally insane (and thus lacked the legal capacity to enter into a contract—see Chapter 13) or because the purpose of the contract was illegal. To review the various types of contracts, see *Concept Summary 8.1.*

Quasi Contracts

Quasi contracts, or contracts *implied in law,* are not actual contracts. Express contracts and implied-in-fact contracts are actual contracts formed by the words or actions of the parties. Quasi contracts, in contrast, are fictional contracts created by courts and imposed on parties in the interests of fairness and justice. Quasi contracts are therefore equitable, rather than contractual, in nature.

Usually, quasi contracts are imposed to avoid the *unjust enrichment* of one party at the expense of another. The doctrine of unjust enrichment is based on the theory that individuals should not be allowed to profit or enrich themselves inequitably at the expense of others. When the court imposes a quasi contract, a plaintiff may recover in **quantum meruit,**[6] a Latin phrase meaning "as much as he or she deserves." *Quantum meruit* essentially describes the extent of compensation owed under a contract implied in law.

Suppose that a vacationing physician is driving down the highway and finds Potter lying unconscious on the side of the road. The physician renders medical aid that saves Potter's life. Although the injured, unconscious Potter did not solicit the medical aid and was not aware that the aid had been rendered, Potter received a valuable benefit, and the requirements for a quasi contract were fulfilled. In such a situation, the law will impose a quasi contract, and Potter normally will have to pay the physician for the reasonable value of the medical services rendered.

Limitations on Quasi-Contractual Recovery

Although quasi contracts exist to prevent unjust enrichment, the party obtaining the enrichment is not held liable for the fair value in some situations.

6. Pronounced *kwahn*-tuhm *mehr*-oo-wit.

CONCEPT SUMMARY 8.1
Types of Contracts

Aspect	Definition
FORMATION	1. *Bilateral*—A promise for a promise.
	2. *Unilateral*—A promise for an act (acceptance is the completed performance of the act).
	3. *Formal*—Requires a special form for creation.
	4. *Informal*—Requires no special form for creation.
	5. *Express*—Formed by words (oral, written, or a combination).
	6. *Implied in fact*—Formed by the conduct of the parties.
PERFORMANCE	1. *Executed*—A fully performed contract.
	2. *Executory*—A contract not fully performed.
ENFORCEABILITY	1. *Valid*—The contract has the necessary contractual elements: agreement (offer and acceptance), consideration, legal capacity of the parties, and legal purpose.
	2. *Voidable*—One party has the option of avoiding or enforcing the contractual obligation.
	3. *Unenforceable*—A contract exists, but it cannot be enforced because of a legal defense.
	4. *Void*—No contract exists, or there is a contract without legal obligations.

Basically, a party who has conferred a benefit on someone else unnecessarily or as a result of misconduct or negligence cannot invoke the principle of quasi contract. The enrichment in those situations will not be considered "unjust."

For example, you take your car to the local car wash and ask to have it run through the washer and to have the gas tank filled. While it is being washed, you go to a nearby shopping center for two hours. In the meantime, one of the workers at the car wash has mistaken your car for the one that he is supposed to hand wax. When you come back, you are presented with a bill for a full tank of gas, a wash job, and a hand wax. Clearly, a benefit has been conferred on you. But this benefit has been conferred because of a mistake by the car wash employee. You have not been *unjustly* enriched under these circumstances. People normally cannot be forced to pay for benefits "thrust" on them.

When an Actual Contract Exists

The doctrine of quasi contract generally cannot be used when there is an *actual contract* that covers the matter in controversy. For example, Bateman contracts with Cameron to deliver a furnace to a building owned by Jones. Bateman delivers the furnace, but Cameron never pays Bateman. Jones has been unjustly enriched in this situation, to be sure. Bateman, however, cannot recover from Jones in quasi contract because Bateman had an actual contract with Cameron. Bateman already has a remedy—he can sue for breach of contract to recover the price of the furnace from Cameron. The court does not need to impose a quasi contract in this situation to achieve justice.

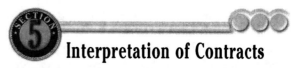

Interpretation of Contracts

Sometimes, parties agree that a contract has been formed but disagree on its meaning or legal effect. One reason this may happen is that one of the parties is not familiar with the legal terminology used in the contract. To an extent, *plain language* laws (enacted by the federal government and a majority of the states) have helped to avoid this difficulty. Sometimes, though, a dispute may arise over the meaning of a contract simply because the rights or obligations under the contract are not expressed clearly—no matter how "plain" the language used.

In this section, we look at some common law rules of contract interpretation. These rules, which have evolved over time, provide the courts with guidelines for deciding disputes over how contract terms or provisions should be interpreted. Exhibit 8–3 provides a brief graphic summary of how these rules are applied.

PREVENTING LEGAL DISPUTES

To avoid disputes over contract interpretation, business managers should make sure that their intentions are clearly expressed in their contracts. Careful drafting of contracts not only helps prevent potential disputes over the meaning of certain terms but may also be crucial if the firm brings or needs to defend against a lawsuit for breach of contract. By using simple, clear language and avoiding legalese, managers take a major step toward avoiding contract disputes.

EXHIBIT 8–3 • **Rules of Contract Interpretation**

WRITTEN CONTRACT

PLAIN MEANING RULE
If a court determines that the terms of the contract are clear from the written document alone, the plain meaning rule will apply, and the contract will be enforced according to what it clearly states.

OTHER RULES OF INTERPRETATION
If a court finds that there is a need to determine the parties' intentions from the terms of the contract, the court will apply a number of well-established rules of interpretation. For example, one rule of interpretation states that specific wording will be given greater weight than general wording.

The Plain Meaning Rule

When a contract's writing is clear and unequivocal, a court will enforce it according to its obvious terms. The meaning of the terms must be determined from *the face of the instrument*—from the written document alone. This is sometimes referred to as the *plain meaning rule.*

Under this rule, if a contract's words appear to be clear and unambiguous, a court cannot consider *extrinsic evidence*—that is, any evidence not contained in the document itself. If a contract's terms are unclear or ambiguous, however, extrinsic evidence may be admissible to clarify the meaning of the contract. The admissibility of such evidence can significantly affect the court's interpretation of ambiguous contractual provisions and thus the outcome of litigation. The following case illustrates these points.

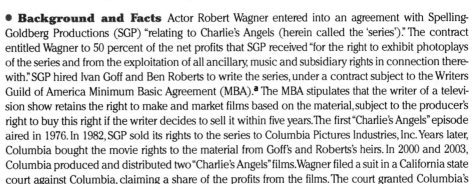

C A S E **8.3** **Wagner v. Columbia Pictures Industries, Inc.**
California Court of Appeal, Second District, Division 7, 2007.
146 Cal.App.4th 586, 52 Cal.Rptr.3d 898.

● **Background and Facts** Actor Robert Wagner entered into an agreement with Spelling-Goldberg Productions (SGP) "relating to Charlie's Angels (herein called the 'series')." The contract entitled Wagner to 50 percent of the net profits that SGP received "for the right to exhibit photoplays of the series and from the exploitation of all ancillary, music and subsidiary rights in connection therewith." SGP hired Ivan Goff and Ben Roberts to write the series, under a contract subject to the Writers Guild of America Minimum Basic Agreement (MBA).[a] The MBA stipulates that the writer of a television show retains the right to make and market films based on the material, subject to the producer's right to buy this right if the writer decides to sell it within five years. The first "Charlie's Angels" episode aired in 1976. In 1982, SGP sold its rights to the series to Columbia Pictures Industries, Inc. Years later, Columbia bought the movie rights to the material from Goff's and Roberts's heirs. In 2000 and 2003, Columbia produced and distributed two "Charlie's Angels" films. Wagner filed a suit in a California state court against Columbia, claiming a share of the profits from the films. The court granted Columbia's motion for summary judgment. Wagner appealed to a state intermediate appellate court.

● **Decision and Rationale** The state intermediate appellate court affirmed the lower court's judgment. The contract "unambiguously" stated the conditions under which the parties were to share the films' profits, and those conditions had not occurred. Wagner offered evidence to show that a previous contract with SGP had been intended to give him half of the net profits from a property titled "Love Song" received from all sources without limitation as to source or time. Wagner argued that the "Charlie's Angels" agreement used identical language in its profits provision, which thus should be interpreted to give him the same share. The court stated that an "agreement is the writing itself." Extrinsic evidence is not admissible "to show intention independent of an unambiguous written instrument." In this case, even if the parties intended Wagner to share in the profits from all sources, "they did not say so in their contract." Under the language of the contract, Wagner was entitled to share in the profits from the exercise of the movie rights to "Charlie's Angels" if those rights were exploited as "ancillary" or "subsidiary" to the primary "right to exhibit photoplays of the series" but not if those rights were acquired separately. SGP's contract with Goff and Roberts was subject to the MBA, under which the writers kept the movie rights, which the producer could buy if the writers opted to sell them within five years. SGP did not acquire the movie rights to "Charlie's Angels" by exercising this right within the five-year period. Columbia obtained those rights independently more than five years later.

● **What If the Facts Were Different?** *How might the result in this case have been different if the court had admitted Wagner's evidence of the "Love Song" contract?*

● **The Legal Environment Dimension** *Under what circumstance would Wagner's evidence of the "Love Song" contract have been irrelevant and yet he would still have been entitled to a share of the profits from the "Charlie's Angels" movies?*

a. The Writers Guild of America is an association of screen and television writers that negotiates industrywide agreements with motion picture and television producers.

Other Rules of Interpretation

Generally, a court will interpret the language to give effect to the parties' intent as *expressed in their contract*. This is the primary purpose of the rules of interpretation—to determine the parties' intent from the language used in their agreement and to give effect to that intent. A court normally will not make or remake a contract, nor will it interpret the language according to what the parties *claim* their intent was when they made it. The courts use the following rules in interpreting contractual terms:

1. Insofar as possible, a reasonable, lawful, and effective meaning will be given to all of a contract's terms.
2. A contract will be interpreted as a whole; individual, specific clauses will be considered subordinate to the contract's general intent. All writings that are a part of the same transaction will be interpreted together.
3. Terms that were the subject of separate negotiation will be given greater consideration than standardized terms and terms that were not negotiated separately.
4. A word will be given its ordinary, commonly accepted meaning, and a technical word or term will be given its technical meaning, unless the parties clearly intended something else.[7]
5. Specific and exact wording will be given greater consideration than general language.
6. Written or typewritten terms will prevail over preprinted ones.
7. Because a contract should be drafted in clear and unambiguous language, a party who uses ambiguous expressions is held to be responsible for the ambiguities. Thus, when the language has more than one meaning, it will be interpreted against the party who drafted the contract.
8. Evidence of trade usage, prior dealing, and course of performance may be admitted to clarify the meaning of an ambiguously worded contract (these terms will be defined and discussed in Chapter 20). When considering custom and usage, a court will look at what is common to the particular business or industry and to the locale where the contract was made or is to be performed.

---

7. See, for example, *Citizens Communications Co. v. Trustmark Insurance,* 303 F.Supp.2d 197 (2004).

REVIEWING Nature and Terminology

Grant Borman, who was engaged in a construction project, leased a crane from Allied Equipment and hired Crosstown Trucking Company to deliver the crane to the construction site. Crosstown, while the crane was in its possession and without permission from either Borman or Allied Equipment, used the crane to install a transformer for a utility company, which paid Crosstown for the job. Crosstown then delivered the crane to Borman's construction site at the appointed time of delivery. When Allied Equipment learned of the unauthorized use of the crane by Crosstown, it sued Crosstown for damages, seeking to recover the rental value of Crosstown's use of the crane. Using the information presented in the chapter, answer the following questions.

1. What are the four requirements of a valid contract?
2. Did Crosstown have a valid contract with Borman concerning the use of the crane? If so, was it a bilateral or a unilateral contract? Explain.
3. What are the requirements of an implied-in-fact contract? Can Allied Equipment obtain damages from Crosstown based on an implied-in-fact contract? Why or why not?
4. Should a court impose a quasi contract on the parties in this situation to allow Allied to recover damages from Crosstown? Why or why not?

TERMS AND CONCEPTS

bilateral contract

contract

executed contract

executory contract

express contract

formal contract

implied-in-fact contract

informal contract

objective theory of contracts

offeree

offeror

promise

promisee

promisor

quantum meruit

quasi contract

unenforceable contract

unilateral contract

valid contract

void contract

voidable contract

QUESTIONS AND CASE PROBLEMS

10-1. Suppose that Everett McCleskey, a local businessperson, is a good friend of Al Miller, the owner of a local candy store. Every day on his lunch hour, McCleskey goes into Miller's candy store and spends about five minutes looking at the candy. After examining Miller's candy and talking with Miller, McCleskey usually buys one or two candy bars. One afternoon, McCleskey goes into Miller's candy shop, looks at the candy, and picks up a $1 candy bar. Seeing that Miller is very busy, he waves the candy bar at Miller without saying a word and walks out. Is there a contract? If so, classify it within the categories presented in this chapter.

10-2. QUESTION WITH SAMPLE ANSWER

Janine was hospitalized with severe abdominal pain and placed in an intensive care unit. Her doctor told the hospital personnel to order around-the-clock nursing care for Janine. At the hospital's request, a nursing services firm, Nursing Services Unlimited, provided two weeks of in-hospital care and, after Janine was sent home, an additional two weeks of at-home care. During the at-home period of care, Janine was fully aware that she was receiving the benefit of the nursing services. Nursing Services later billed Janine $4,000 for the nursing care, but Janine refused to pay on the ground that she had never contracted for the services, either orally or in writing. In view of the fact that no express contract was ever formed, can Nursing Services recover the $4,000 from Janine? If so, under what legal theory? Discuss.

• For a sample answer to Question 10–2, go to Appendix C at the end of this text.

10-3. Burger Baby restaurants engaged Air Advertising to fly an advertisement above the Connecticut beaches. The advertisement offered $1,000 to any person who could swim from the Connecticut beaches to Long Island across Long Island Sound in less than a day. At 10:00 A.M. on Saturday, October 10, Air Advertising's pilot flew a sign above the Connecticut beaches that read, "Swim across the Sound and Burger Baby pays $1,000." On seeing the sign, Davison dived in. About four hours later, when he was about halfway across the Sound, Air Advertising flew another sign over the Sound that read, "Burger Baby revokes." Davison completed the swim in another six hours. Is there a contract between Davison and Burger Baby? Can Davison recover anything?

10-4. Bilateral versus Unilateral Contracts. D.L. Peoples Group (D.L.) placed an ad in a Missouri newspaper to recruit admissions representatives, who were hired to recruit Missouri residents to attend D.L.'s college in Florida. Donald Hawley responded to the ad, his interviewer recommended him for the job, and he signed, in Missouri, an "Admissions Representative Agreement," which was mailed to D.L.'s president, who signed it in his office in Florida. The agreement provided, in part, that Hawley would devote exclusive time and effort to the business in his assigned territory in Missouri and that D.L. would pay Hawley a commission if he successfully recruited students for the school. While attempting to make one of his first calls on his new job, Hawley was accidentally shot and killed. On the basis of his death, a claim was filed in Florida for workers' compensation. (Under Florida law, when an accident occurs outside Florida, workers' compensation benefits are payable only if the employment contract was made in Florida.) Was this admissions representative agreement a bilateral or a unilateral contract? What are the consequences of the distinction in this case? Explain. [*D.L. Peoples Group, Inc. v. Hawley*, 804 So.2d 561 (Fla.App. 1 Dist. 2002)]

10-5. Interpretation of Contracts. East Mill Associates (EMA) was developing residential "units" in East

Brunswick, New Jersey, within the service area of the East Brunswick Sewerage Authority (EBSA). The sewer system required an upgrade to the Ryder's Lane Pumping Station to accommodate the new units. EMA agreed to pay "fifty-five percent (55%) of the total cost" of the upgrade. At the time, the estimated cost to EMA was $150,000 to $200,000. Impediments to the project arose, however, substantially increasing the cost. Among other things, the pumping station had to be moved to accommodate a widened road nearby. The upgrade was delayed for almost three years. When it was completed, EBSA asked EMA for $340,022.12, which represented 55 percent of the total cost. EMA did not pay. EBSA filed a suit in a New Jersey state court against EMA for breach of contract. What rule should the court apply to interpret the parties' contract? How should that rule be applied? Why? [*East Brunswick Sewerage Authority v. East Mill Associates, Inc.*, 365 N.J.Super. 120, 838 A.2d 494 (A.D. 2004)]

10-6. CASE PROBLEM WITH SAMPLE ANSWER

In December 2000, Nextel South Corp., a communications firm, contacted R.A. Clark Consulting, Ltd., an executive search company, about finding an employment manager for Nextel's call center in Atlanta, Georgia. Over the next six months, Clark screened, evaluated, and interviewed more than three hundred candidates. Clark provided Nextel with more than fifteen candidate summaries, including one for Dan Sax. Nextel hired Sax for the position at an annual salary of $75,000. Sax started work on June 25, 2001, took two weeks' vacation, and quit on July 31 in the middle of a project. Clark spent the next six weeks looking for a replacement, until Nextel asked Clark to stop. Clark billed Nextel for its services, but Nextel refused to pay, asserting, among other things, that the parties had not signed an agreement. Nextel's typical agreement specified payment to an employment agency of 20 percent of an employee's annual salary. Clark filed a suit in a Georgia state court against Nextel to recover in *quantum meruit*. What is *quantum meruit*? What should Clark have to show to recover on this basis? Should the court rule in Clark's favor? Explain. [*Nextel South Corp. v. R.A. Clark Consulting, Ltd.*, 266 Ga.App. 85, 596 S.E.2d 416 (2004)]

- **To view a sample answer for Problem 10–6, go to this book's Web site at www.cengage. com/blaw/jentz, select "Chapter 10," and click on "Case Problem with Sample Answer."**

10-7. Contract Enforceability. California's Subdivision Map Act (SMA) prohibits the sale of real property until a map of its subdivision is filed with, and approved by, the appropriate state agency. In November 2004, Black Hills Investments, Inc., entered into two contracts with Albertson's, Inc., to buy two parcels of property in a shopping center development. Each contract required that "all governmental approvals relating to any lot split [or] sub-

division" be obtained before the sale but permitted Albertson's to waive this condition. Black Hills made a $133,000 deposit on the purchase. A few weeks later, before the sales were complete, Albertson's filed with a local state agency a map that subdivided the shopping center into four parcels, including the two that Black Hills had agreed to buy. In January 2005, Black Hills objected to concessions that Albertson's had made to a buyer of one of the other parcels, told Albertson's that it was terminating its deal, and asked for a return of its deposit. Albertson's refused. Black Hills filed a suit in a California state court against Albertson's, arguing that the contracts were void. Are these contracts valid, voidable, unenforceable, or void? Explain. [*Black Hills Investments, Inc. v. Albertson's, Inc.*, 146 Cal.App.4th 883, 53 Cal.Rptr.3d 263 (4 Dist. 2007)]

10-8. A QUESTION OF ETHICS

International Business Machines Corp. (IBM) hired Niels Jensen in 2000 as a software sales representative. In 2001, IBM presented a new "Software Sales Incentive Plan" (SIP) at a conference for its sales employees. A brochure given to the attendees stated, "[T]here are no caps to your earnings; the more you sell, * * * the more earnings for you." The brochure outlined how the plan worked and referred the employees to the "Sales Incentives" section of IBM's corporate intranet for more details. Jensen was given a "quota letter" that said he would be paid $75,000 as a base salary and, if he attained his quota, an additional $75,000 as incentive pay. In September, Jensen closed a deal with the U.S. Department of the Treasury's Internal Revenue Service that was worth over $24 million to IBM. Relying on the SIP brochure, Jensen estimated his commission to be $2.6 million. IBM paid him less than $500,000, however. Jensen filed a suit in a federal district court against IBM, contending that the SIP brochure and quota letter constituted a unilateral offer that became a binding contract when Jensen closed the sale. In view of these facts, consider the following questions. [Jensen v. International Business Machines Corp., 454 F.3d 382 (4th Cir. 2006)]

(a) Would it be fair to the employer in this case to hold that the SIP brochure and the quota letter created a unilateral contract if IBM did not intend to create such a contract? Would it be fair to the employee to hold that no contract was created? Explain.

(b) The "Sales Incentives" section of IBM's intranet included a clause providing that "[m]anagement will decide if an adjustment to the payment is appropriate" when an employee closes a large transaction. Jensen's quota letter stated, "[The SIP] program does not constitute a promise by IBM to make any distributions under it. IBM reserves the right to adjust the program terms or to cancel or otherwise modify the program at any time." How do these statements affect your answers to the above questions? From an ethical perspective, would it be fair to hold that a contract exists despite these statements?

10-9. VIDEO QUESTION

Go to this text's Web site at **www.cengage. com/blaw/jentz** and select "Chapter 10." Click on "Video Questions" and view the video titled *Bowfinger*. Then answer the following questions.

(a) In the video, Renfro (Robert Downey, Jr.) says to Bowfinger (Steve Martin), "You bring me this script and Kit Ramsey and you've got yourself a 'go' picture." Assume for the purposes of this question that their agreement is a contract. Is the contract bilateral or unilateral? Is it express or implied? Is it formal or informal? Is it executed or executory? Explain your answers.

(b) What criteria would a court rely on to interpret the terms of the contract?

(c) Recall from the video that the contract between Bowfinger and the producer was oral. Suppose that a statute requires contracts of this type to be in writing. In that situation, would the contract be void, voidable, or unenforceable? Explain.

LAW ON THE WEB

For updated links to resources available on the Web, as well as a variety of other materials, visit this text's Web site at

www.cengage.com/blaw/jentz

The 'Lectric Law Library provides information about contract law, including a definition of a contract and the elements required for a contract. Go to

www.lectlaw.com/def/c123.htm

You can keep abreast of recent and planned revisions of the *Restatements of the Law*, including the *Restatement (Second) of Contracts,* by accessing the American Law Institute's Web site at

www.ali.org

Legal Research Exercises on the Web

Go to **www.cengage.com/blaw/jentz**, the Web site that accompanies this text. Select "Chapter 10" and click on "Internet Exercises." There you will find the following Internet research exercises that you can perform to learn more about the topics covered in this chapter.

Internet Exercise 10–1: Legal Perspective
Contracts and Contract Provisions

Internet Exercise 10–2: Management Perspective
Implied Employment Contracts

Internet Exercise 10–3: Historical Perspective
Contracts in Ancient Mesopotamia

Contracts: Classification of Contracts

Case No. 35

EXPRESS AND IMPLIED CONTRACTS

Trimmer v. Van Bomel

Supreme Court, New York County

107 Misc.2d 201, 434 N.Y.S.2d 82 (1980)

FACTS: Plaintiff Leonard Trimmer (Trimmer) was a travel tour operator and man of modest means. On a tour he was managing he met Defendant Catherine Van Bomel (Van Bomel), a wealthy widow with assets in excess of forty million dollars. A relationship blossomed between them and led to an arrangement in which Van Bomel supported Trimmer in a luxurious fashion and he devoted all of his time and attention to her. He traveled with her on trips, accompanied her to parties and the theater, and went with her to lunch and dinner engagements. The relationship survived five years, during which she spent money on him lavishly, dressing him in clothes made in Italy and London, buying him two Pontiacs and a Jaguar, paying his travel expenses and providing him with a monthly allowance.

For reasons unknown, the relationship terminated. Trimmer thereafter sought money from Van Bomel to maintain the lifestyle to which he had become accustomed. When she refused to pay him he began this action claiming breach of implied and express contracts. He argued that a duty on Van Bomel's part to pay for his support should be implied from the services he provided and the fact he forfeited his travel tour operator's job. With regard to the express contract, Trimmer claimed that he and Van Bomel had talked about her setting aside for Trimmer enough money to enable him to live the rest of his life "in the sumptuous style" he had maintained during his association with her.

FIRST ISSUE: Does a valid express contract exist between the parties obligating Van Bomel to provide for Trimmer's support indefinitely?

DECISION: No.

REASONING: For a contract to be enforceable the terms must be definite. Even if Trimmer were able to prove the alleged express agreement, the terms were too vague to be enforceable. The terms that were indefinite included the amount of money Van Bomel would pay and the time when payment would be due.

SECOND ISSUE: Where two parties are companions for a period of time and one party contributes substantially to the support of the other, does an implied contract exist requiring the party who contributed to the support of the other to continue to support that other person indefinitely?

DECISION: No, judgment for Van Bomel.

REASONING: An implied obligation to compensate arises from those acts for which one customarily expects to pay. The services rendered by Trimmer were of the type that are ordinarily performed by one person for another as a sign of caring and affection without the expectation of pay. Therefore, no agreement to pay for the services provided by Van Bomel can be implied. Trimmer's claim based on implied contract was therefore rejected.

NOTE: Unmarried persons living together in New York may form express contracts with each other for domestic services in return for payment, and such contracts are enforceable. No requirement exists that such contracts be in writing. Before such a contract can be enforced, its existence must be proved. Further, if part of the consideration for the contract is sexual relations, the contract will be illegal and therefore void.

* * * QUESTIONS * * *
(See back of text for answers)

1) What is an express contract and how does it differ from an implied contract?

2) Assume Trimmer and Van Bomel had an express agreement requiring her to support him indefinitely. If, when they terminated their relationship, she refused to pay, how could Trimmer prove the existence of the agreement?

Case No. 36

EXPRESS, IMPLIED, AND QUASI CONTRACTS

<u>Soderholm v. Kosty</u>

Justice Court, Village of Horseheads, Chemung County

177 Misc.2d 403, 676 N.Y.S.2d 850 (1998)

FACTS: Kurt Soderholm and Stephanie R. Kosty, both students at Corning Community College, lived together as a couple from September 1994 until their eventual break-up in December 1995. A reconciliation attempt failed. During the period of their relationship the couple incurred various expenses related to running a household such as rent, utilities, car payments, magazines, schoolbooks, movie rentals, and gasoline. Soderholm and Kosty had agreed to split the rent equally and did not address how to allocate other expenses.

Soderholm claimed that both parties did not contribute equally to the expenses. He substantiated these claims with detailed notes he kept regarding many of the expenses he incurred for their mutual benefit during the term of their relationship. Additionally he documented some of the expenses through checkbook entries, for example, $770.25 for Kosty's share of the rent and $647.43 for Kosty's car payments in four of the sixteen months of their cohabitation. Other entries documented other expenses that seemingly were for the sole benefit of Kosty. As a result Soderholm is suing Kosty for $2,500 in expenses claiming breach of implied and express contract. Additionally, Solderholm seeks reimbursement under the theory of quasi contract.

FIRST ISSUE: Does an implied contract exist between Soderholm and Kosty obligating Kosty to reimburse Solderholm for expenses incurred during the term of their relationship?

DECISION: No

REASONING: An implied contract to share various expenses will not be found where parties are involved in a close relationship. Instead the expenses incurred for one another are viewed by the law as customarily given out of a sense of love, caring, and affection without an expectation of repayment.

SECOND ISSUE: Does an express contract exist between Soderholm and Kosty obligating Kosty to reimburse Solderholm for expenses incurred during their relationship?

DECISION: Yes but only for Kosty's share of the rent.

REASONING: An express contract between unmarried people living together is enforceable provided its existence can be proven. The express agreement between Soderholm and Kosty to share rent equally was thus enforceable. Soderholm failed to prove the existence of an express contract with Kosty other than for the equal payment of rent. The detailed notes he kept regarding expenses were in his own handwriting, not initialed by Kosty, and so were rejected by the court as self-serving. Additionally Kosty proved that Solderholm often used Kosty's vehicle and that Kosty had paid for numerous dinners, movies, groceries, and clothes for Soderholm.

THIRD ISSUE: Does a quasi contract exist obligating Kosty to reimburse Solderholm for the expenses paid by Solderholm for Kosty's sole benefit?

DECISION: No

REASONING: To prove the existence of a quasi-contract Solderholm must prove that Kosty was enriched at Soderholm's expense and that equity and good conscience would require a return of the money or property constituting the enrichment. Recognizing the "give and take" in any relationship and the financial contributions made by Kosty for such expenses as food and entertainment, the court held that "equity and good conscience " do not cry out for any financial adjustment between the parties.

Case No. 37

QUANTUM MERUIT

Rollerston-Daines v. Estate of Hopiak

Appellate Division, Third Department

263 A.D.2d 883, 694 N.Y.S.2d 225 (1999)

FACTS: Nature photographer Michael J. Hopiak died in September 1994. In April 1995, Barrie Rolleston-Daines (Daines), friend and colleague of the deceased submitted a proposal to the administrators of Hopiak's estate that she create an exhibition of Hopiak's art as a living legacy of his work. The proposal required that she do all the work necessary in sorting, arranging and identifying approximately 26,000 slides for the exhibit at a cost of $25,000. Daines estimated that the task would require approximately 1433 hours of her time.

The administrators agreed to negotiate a contract with her. In anticipation of the contract, the administrators advanced $6000 to Daines in September 1995 to begin the project and an additional $2000 in December, 1995. Daines worked on the project for five months.   In January 1996 the project was canceled with no contract between Daines and the administrators having been entered.

Daines claims that she spent approximately 608 hours reviewing and cataloging 14,646 of the approximately 26,000 slides.   She contended that she should receive $50 an hour for her services ($30,400) under the theory of quantum meruit. As proof she submitted an affidavit of a respected professional photographer stating that services of Daines' professional caliber were worth $50 an hour. Concerning the number of hours she worked, Daines did not keep accurate records and so was unable to give a clear account of the work she had performed. The trial court rejected her claim of $50 an hour because the expert never inspected or evaluated her work and her records were unreliable.

The trial court determined that a rate of $15 an hour was reasonable compensation. Daines appealed.

ISSUE: When an individual renders services where an express or implied contract for those services does not exist, what is the proper measure for determining damages in quasi contract?

DECISION: Quantum meruit, a Latin phrase for "as much as he deserves".

REASONING: If a quasi contract exists, a plaintiff may recover in quantum meruit. The appeals court here found that a quasi contract did exist. The court noted that Daines, in her original proposal, identified the number of hours the project would require and the total pay she sought. Based on these figures the court determined Daines was entitled to the reasonable value of her services at an hourly rate of $17.45 ($25,000 project price divided by 1433).

3) Assume the following events occurred on the following days. Does a contract exist and if so on what day was it created?

December 1—Jerry received a letter from Dale in which Dale offered to sell to Jerry a motorcycle for $600.00.

December 2—Dale mailed a letter revoking the offer to sell the motorcycle.

December 3—Jerry mailed an acceptance of Dale's offer.

December 4—Jerry received Dale's letter of revocation.

CHAPTER 9

Agreement

An essential element for contract formation is **agreement**—the parties must agree on the terms of the contract and manifest to each other their **mutual assent** (agreement) to the same bargain. Ordinarily, agreement is evidenced by two events: an *offer* and an *acceptance*. One party offers a certain bargain to another party, who then accepts that bargain. The agreement does not necessarily have to be in writing. Both parties, however, must manifest their assent to the same bargain. Once an agreement is reached, if the other elements of a contract are present (consideration, capacity, and legality—discussed in subsequent chapters), a valid contract is formed, generally creating enforceable rights and duties between the parties.

Note that not all agreements are contracts. John and Kevin may agree to play golf on a certain day, but a court would not hold that their agreement is an enforceable contract. A *contractual* agreement arises only when the terms of the agreement impose legally enforceable obligations on the parties.

In today's world, contracts are frequently formed via the Internet. For a discussion of online offers and acceptances, see Chapter 19, which is devoted entirely to the subject of electronic contracts, or e-contracts.

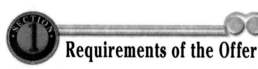

Requirements of the Offer

As mentioned in Chapter 10, the parties to a contract are the *offeror*, the one who makes an offer or proposal to another party, and the *offeree*, the one to whom the offer or proposal is made. An **offer** is a promise or commitment to do or refrain from doing some specified thing in the future. Under the common law, three elements are necessary for an offer to be effective:

1. The offeror must have a serious intention to become bound by the offer.
2. The terms of the offer must be reasonably certain, or definite, so that the parties and the court can ascertain the terms of the contract.
3. The offer must be communicated to the offeree.

Once an effective offer has been made, the offeree has the power to accept the offer. If the offeree accepts, an agreement is formed (and thus a contract arises, if other essential elements are present). The requirements for traditional offers apply to online offers as well, as you will read in Chapter 19.

Intention

The first requirement for an effective offer is a serious intent on the part of the offeror. Serious intent is not determined by the *subjective* intentions, beliefs, and assumptions of the offeror. As discussed in Chapter 10, courts generally adhere to the *objective theory of contracts* in determining whether a contract has been formed. Under this theory, a party's words and conduct are held to mean whatever a reasonable person in the offeree's position would think they meant. The court will give words their usual meanings even if "it were proved by twenty bishops that [the] party . . . intended something else."[1]

---

1. Judge Learned Hand in *Hotchkiss v. National City Bank of New York*, 200 F. 287 (2d Cir. 1911), aff'd 231 U.S. 50, 34 S.Ct. 20, 58 L.Ed. 115 (1913).

Offers made in obvious anger, jest, or undue excitement do not meet the intent test because a reasonable person would realize that a serious offer was not being made. Because these offers are not effective, an offeree's acceptance does not create an agreement. Suppose that you and three classmates ride to school each day in Davina's new automobile, which has a market value of $20,000. One cold morning, the four of you get into the car, but Davina cannot get the car started. She yells in anger, "I'll sell this car to anyone for $500!" You drop $500 in her lap. Given these facts, a reasonable person, taking into consideration Davina's frustration and the obvious difference in worth between the market value of the car and the proposed purchase price, would declare that her offer was not made with serious intent and that you did not have an agreement.

The concept of intention can be further clarified through an examination of the types of expressions and statements that are *not* offers. We look at these expressions and statements in the subsections that follow. In the classic case of *Lucy v. Zehmer*, presented here, the court considered whether an offer made "after a few drinks" met the serious-intent requirement.

CASE 9.1 Lucy v. Zehmer

Supreme Court of Appeals of Virginia, 1954. 196 Va. 493, 84 S.E.2d 516.

● **Background and Facts** W. O. Lucy and J. C. Lucy, the plaintiffs, filed a suit against A. H. Zehmer and Ida Zehmer, the defendants, to compel the Zehmers to transfer title of their property, known as the Ferguson Farm, to the Lucys for $50,000, as the Zehmers had allegedly agreed to do. Lucy had known Zehmer for fifteen or twenty years and for the last eight years or so had been anxious to buy the Ferguson Farm from Zehmer. One night, Lucy stopped in to visit the Zehmers in the combination restaurant, filling station, and motor court they operated. While there, Lucy tried to buy the Ferguson Farm once again. This time he tried a new approach. According to the trial court transcript, Lucy said to Zehmer, "I bet you wouldn't take $50,000 for that place." Zehmer replied, "Yes, I would too; you wouldn't give fifty." Throughout the evening, the conversation returned to the sale of the Ferguson Farm for $50,000. At the same time, the parties continued to drink whiskey and engage in light conversation. Eventually, Lucy enticed Zehmer to write up an agreement to the effect that the Zehmers would sell the Ferguson Farm to Lucy for $50,000 complete. Later, Lucy sued Zehmer to compel him to go through with the sale. Zehmer argued that he had been drunk and that the offer had been made in jest and hence was unenforceable. The trial court agreed with Zehmer, and Lucy appealed.

● **Decision and Rationale** The Supreme Court of Appeals of Virginia reversed the ruling of the lower court. The state supreme court ordered the Zehmers to carry through with the sale. The court noted that Lucy attempted to testify in detail as to what was said and done the night of the transaction. "Zehmer was not intoxicated to the extent of being unable to comprehend the nature and consequences of the instrument he executed, and hence that instrument is not to be invalidated on that ground." The court found that the execution of the agreement was a serious business transaction, as evidenced by a number of circumstances. These included the discussion of the contract for forty minutes or more before it was signed, its rewriting to reflect Mrs. Zehmer's interest, the discussion of what was to be included in the sale, the provision for an examination of the title, the completeness of the instrument, and Lucy's taking possession of the agreement without Zehmer's request that he give it back. As the court explained, "We must look to the outward expression of a person as manifesting his intention rather than to his secret and unexpressed intention."

● **Impact of This Case on Today's Law** *This is a classic case in contract law because it illustrates so clearly the objective theory of contracts with respect to determining whether a serious offer was intended. Today, the courts continue to apply the objective theory of contracts and routinely cite* Lucy v. Zehmer *as a significant precedent in this area.*

CASE CONTINUES

CASE 9.1 CONTINUED ● **What If the Facts Were Different?** *Suppose that the day after Lucy signed the purchase agreement for the farm, he decided that he didn't want it after all, and Zehmer sued Lucy to perform the contract. Would this change in the facts alter the court's decision that Lucy and Zehmer had created an enforceable contract? Why or why not?*

Expressions of Opinion An expression of opinion is not an offer. It does not indicate an intention to enter into a binding agreement. Consider an example. Hawkins took his son to McGee, a physician, and asked McGee to operate on the son's hand. McGee said that the boy would be in the hospital three or four days and that the hand would *probably* heal a few days later. The son's hand did not heal for a month, but the father did not win a suit for breach of contract. The court held that McGee had not made an offer to heal the son's hand in a few days. He had merely expressed an opinion as to when the hand would heal.[2]

Statements of Future Intent A statement of an *intention* to do something in the future is not an offer. If Arif says, "I *plan* to sell my stock in Novation, Inc., for $150 per share," a contract is not created if John "accepts" and tenders the $150 per share for the stock. Arif has merely expressed his intention to enter into a future contract for the sale of the stock. If John accepts and tenders the $150 per share, no contract is formed because a reasonable person would conclude that Arif was only *thinking about* selling his stock, not *promising* to sell it.

Preliminary Negotiations A request or invitation to negotiate is not an offer. It only expresses a willingness to discuss the possibility of entering into a contract. Statements such as "Will you sell Blythe Estate?" or "I wouldn't sell my car for less than $5,000" are examples. A reasonable person in the offeree's position would not conclude that these statements indicated an intention to enter into a binding obligation. Likewise, when the government or private firms require construction work, they invite contractors to submit bids. The *invitation* to submit bids is not an offer, and a contractor does not bind the government or private firm by submitting a bid. (The bids that the contractors submit are offers, however, and the government or private firm can bind the contractor by accepting the bid.)

Agreements to Agree Traditionally, agreements to agree—that is, agreements to agree to the material terms of a contract at some future date—were not considered to be binding contracts. The modern view, however, is that agreements to agree may be enforceable agreements (contracts) if it is clear that the parties intended to be bound by the agreements. In other words, under the modern view the emphasis is on the parties' intent rather than on form.

For example, after a person was injured and nearly drowned on a water ride at Six Flags Amusement Park, Six Flags, Inc., filed a lawsuit against the manufacturer that designed the particular ride. The defendant manufacturer claimed that there was no binding contract between the parties, only preliminary negotiations that were never formalized into a construction contract. The court, however, held that a faxed document specifying the details of the water ride, along with the parties' subsequent actions (beginning construction and handwriting notes on the fax), was sufficient to show an intent to be bound. Because of the court's finding, the manufacturer was required to provide insurance for the water ride at Six Flags, and its insurer was required to defend Six Flags in the personal-injury lawsuit that arose out of the incident.[3]

Increasingly, the courts are holding that a preliminary agreement constitutes a binding contract if the parties have agreed on all essential terms and no disputed issues remain to be resolved.[4] In contrast, if the parties agree on certain major terms but leave other terms open for further negotiation, a preliminary agreement is binding only in the sense that the parties have committed themselves to negotiate the unde-

---

2. *Hawkins v. McGee*, 84 N.H. 114, 146 A. 641 (1929).

3. *Six Flags, Inc. v. Steadfast Insurance Co.*, 474 F.Supp.2d 201 (D.Mass. 2007).

4. See, for example, *Tractebel Energy Marketing, Inc. v. AEP Power Marketing, Inc.*, 487 F.3d 89 (2d Cir. 2007); and *Florine On Call, Ltd. v. Fluorogas Limited*, No. 01-CV-186 (W.D.Tex. 2002), contract issue affirmed on appeal at 380 F.3d 849 (5th Cir. 2004). A significant precedent in this area is *Texaco, Inc. v. Pennzoil Co.*, 729 S.W.2d 768 (Tex.App.—Houston [1st Dist.] 1987, writ ref'd n.r.e.). (Generally, a complete Texas Court of Appeals citation includes the writ-of-error history showing the Texas Supreme Court's disposition of the case. In this case, *writ ref'd n.r.e.* is an abbreviation for "writ refused, no reversible error," which means that Texas's highest court refused to grant the appellant's request to review the case, because the court did not think there was any reversible error.)

cided terms in good faith in an effort to reach a final agreement.[5]

In the following case, the dispute was over an agreement to settle a case during a trial. One party claimed that the agreement formed via e-mail was binding, and the other party claimed it was merely an agreement to agree, or an agreement to work out the terms of a settlement in the future. Can an exchange of e-mails create a complete and unambiguous agreement? That was the question the court had to address in this case.

---

5. See, for example, *MBH, Inc. v. John Otte Oil & Propane, Inc.*, 727 N.W.2d 238 (Neb.App. 2007); and *Barrand v. Whataburger, Inc.*, 214 S.W.3d 122 (Tex.App.—Corpus Christi 2006).

C A S E 9.2 Basis Technology Corp. v. Amazon.com, Inc.
Appeals Court of Massachusetts, 2008. 71 Mass.App.Ct. 29, 878 N.E.2d 952.
www.malawyersweekly.com/macoa.cfm[a]

● **Background and Facts** Basis Technology Corporation created software and provided technical services for Amazon.com, Inc.'s, Japanese-language Web site. The agreement between the two companies allowed for separately negotiated contracts for additional services that Basis might provide to Amazon. At the end of 1999, Basis and Amazon entered into stock-purchase agreements. Later, Amazon objected to certain actions related to the securities that Basis sold. Basis sued Amazon for various claims involving these securities and for nonpayment of services performed by Basis that were not included in the original agreement. During the trial, the two parties appeared to reach an agreement to settle out of court via a series of e-mail exchanges outlining the settlement. When Amazon reneged, Basis served a motion to enforce the proposed settlement. The trial judge entered judgment against Amazon, which appealed.

● **Decision and Rationale** The Appeals Court of Massachusetts affirmed the trial court's finding that Amazon intended to be bound by the terms of the March 23 e-mail. The court examined the evidence consisting of e-mails between the two parties. It pointed out that in open court and on the record, counsel "reported the result of the settlement without specification of the terms." Amazon claimed that the e-mail terms were not complete and definite enough to form an agreement. The court noted, nonetheless, that "provisions are not ambiguous simply because the parties have developed different interpretations of them." In the exchange of e-mails, the essential business terms were indeed resolved. Afterwards, the parties were simply proceeding to record the settlement terms, not to create them. The e-mails constituted a complete and unambiguous statement of the parties' desire to be bound by the settlement terms.

● **What If the Facts Were Different?** *Assume that the attorneys for both sides had simply had a phone conversation that included all of the terms to which they actually agreed in their e-mail exchanges. Would the court have ruled differently? Why or why not?*

● **The Ethical Dimension** *Under what circumstances could Amazon justify its "about-face" after having agreed in an e-mail to the settlement terms?*

---

a. In the search box on the right, enter "71 Mass.App.Ct. 29" and click on "Search." On the resulting page, click on the case name to access the court's opinion.

PREVENTING LEGAL DISPUTES

To avoid potential legal disputes, businesspersons should be cautious when drafting a memorandum outlining a preliminary agreement or understanding with another party. If all the major terms are included, a court might hold that the agreement is binding even though it was intended to be only a tentative agreement. One approach to avoid being bound to the terms of a preliminary agreement is to include in the writing not only the points on which the parties agree, but also the points of disagreement. Alternatively, a person might add a disclaimer to the memorandum stating that, although the parties anticipate entering into a contract in the future, neither party intends to be legally bound to the terms that were discussed. That way, the other party cannot claim that an agreement on all the essential terms has already been reached.

Advertisements In general, advertisements—including representations made in mail-order catalogues, price lists, and circulars—are treated not as offers to contract but as invitations to negotiate. Suppose that Loeser advertises a used paving machine. The ad is mailed to hundreds of firms and reads, "Used Loeser Construction Co. paving machine. Builds curbs and finishes cement work all in one process. Price: $42,350." If Star Paving calls Loeser and says, "We accept your offer," no contract is formed. Any reasonable person would conclude that Loeser was not promising to sell the paving machine but rather was soliciting offers to buy it. If such an ad were held to constitute a legal offer, and fifty people accepted the offer, there would be no way for Loeser to perform all fifty of the resulting contracts. He would have to breach forty-nine contracts. Obviously, the law seeks to avoid such unfairness.

Price lists are another form of invitation to negotiate or trade. A seller's price list is not an offer to sell at that price; it merely invites the buyer to offer to buy at that price. In fact, the seller usually puts "prices subject to change" on the price list. Only in rare circumstances will a price quotation be construed as an offer.[6]

Although most advertisements and the like are treated as invitations to negotiate, this does not mean that an advertisement can never be an offer. On some occasions, courts have construed advertisements to be offers because the ads contained definite terms that invited acceptance (such as an ad offering a reward for the return of a lost dog).[7]

The plaintiff in the following case argued that an ad on a Web site constituted an offer, which he accepted.

---

6. See, for example, *Nordyne, Inc. v. International Controls & Measurements Corp.*, 262 F.3d 843 (8th Cir. 2001).

7. The classic example is *Lefkowitz v. Great Minneapolis Surplus Store, Inc.*, 251 Minn. 188, 86 N.W.2d 689 (1957).

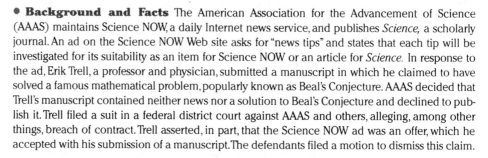

C A S E 9.3   **Trell v. American Association for the Advancement of Science**
United States District Court, Western District of New York, 2007. __ F.Supp.2d __.

● **Background and Facts** The American Association for the Advancement of Science (AAAS) maintains Science NOW, a daily Internet news service, and publishes *Science,* a scholarly journal. An ad on the Science NOW Web site asks for "news tips" and states that each tip will be investigated for its suitability as an item for Science NOW or an article for *Science.* In response to the ad, Erik Trell, a professor and physician, submitted a manuscript in which he claimed to have solved a famous mathematical problem, popularly known as Beal's Conjecture. AAAS decided that Trell's manuscript contained neither news nor a solution to Beal's Conjecture and declined to publish it. Trell filed a suit in a federal district court against AAAS and others, alleging, among other things, breach of contract. Trell asserted, in part, that the Science NOW ad was an offer, which he accepted with his submission of a manuscript. The defendants filed a motion to dismiss this claim.

● **Decision and Rationale** The court granted the defendants' motion and dismissed the plaintiff's complaint. The appellate court found that the advertisement for "news tips" on the Science NOW Web site could not be construed as an offer. Rather, "statements that urge the general public to take some action in response thereto" are commonly characterized as advertisements: "Advertisements are not offers—they invite offers. Likewise, responses to advertisements are not acceptances—they are offers." Just because the advertisement was soliciting ideas (news tips) rather than goods makes little difference. The use of the Internet to advertise the offer also does not change the outcome. Science NOW's ad for news tips was not an offer but an invitation for offers.

● **The Ethical Dimension** *Besides breach of contract, Trell charged the defendants with fraud, misappropriation of property, breach of fiduciary duty, unfair competition, conversion, and conspiracy with intent to defraud. What might have been Trell's motivation for all of these charges? Is this a reasonable basis for a lawsuit? Discuss.*

● **The E-Commerce Dimension** *Should the court have made an exception to the rule applied in this case because the ad was posted on the Internet? Why or why not?*

Auctions In an auction, a seller "offers" goods for sale through an auctioneer, but this is not an offer to form a contract. Rather, it is an invitation asking bidders to submit offers. In the context of an auction, a bidder is the offeror, and the auctioneer is the offeree. The offer is accepted when the auctioneer strikes the hammer. Before the fall of the hammer, a bidder may revoke (take back) her or his bid, or the auctioneer may reject that bid or all bids. Typically, an auctioneer will reject a bid that is below the price the seller is willing to accept.

When the auctioneer accepts a higher bid, he or she rejects all previous bids. Because rejection terminates an offer (as will be discussed later), those bids represent offers that have been terminated. Thus, if the highest bidder withdraws his or her bid before the hammer falls, none of the previous bids is reinstated. If the bid is not withdrawn or rejected, the contract is formed when the auctioneer announces, "Going once, going twice, sold!" (or something similar) and lets the hammer fall.

Traditionally, auctions have been referred to as either "with reserve" or "without reserve." In an auction with reserve, the seller (through the auctioneer) may withdraw the goods at any time before the auctioneer closes the sale by announcement or by the fall of the hammer. All auctions are assumed to be auctions with reserve unless the terms of the auction are explicitly stated to be *without reserve*. In an auction without reserve, the goods cannot be withdrawn by the seller and must be sold to the highest bidder. In auctions with reserve, the seller may reserve the right to confirm or reject the sale even after "the hammer has fallen." In this situation, the seller is obligated to notify those attending the auction that sales of goods made during the auction are not final until confirmed by the seller.[8]

Definiteness of Terms

The second requirement for an effective offer involves the definiteness of its terms. An offer must have terms that are reasonably definite so that, if it is accepted and a contract formed, a court can determine if a breach has occurred and can provide an appropriate remedy. The specific terms required depend, of course, on the type of contract. Generally, a contract must include the following terms, either expressed in the contract or capable of being reasonably inferred from it:

1. The identification of the parties.
2. The identification of the object or subject matter of the contract (also the quantity, when appropri-

ate), including the work to be performed, with specific identification of such items as goods, services, and land.
3. The consideration to be paid.
4. The time of payment, delivery, or performance.

An offer may invite an acceptance to be worded in such specific terms that the contract is made definite. Suppose that Marcus Business Machines contacts your corporation and offers to sell "from one to ten MacCool copying machines for $1,600 each; state number desired in acceptance." Your corporation agrees to buy two copiers. Because the quantity is specified in the acceptance, the terms are definite, and the contract is enforceable.

Courts sometimes are willing to supply a missing term in a contract when the parties have clearly manifested an intent to form a contract. If, in contrast, the parties have attempted to deal with a particular term of the contract but their expression of intent is too vague or uncertain to be given any precise meaning, the court will not supply a "reasonable" term because to do so might conflict with the intent of the parties. In other words, the court will not rewrite the contract.[9]

Communication

A third requirement for an effective offer is communication—the offer must be communicated to the offeree. Ordinarily, one cannot agree to a bargain without knowing that it exists. Suppose that Estrich advertises a reward for the return of his lost dog. Hoban, not knowing of the reward, finds the dog and returns it to Estrich. Hoban cannot recover the reward because she did not know it had been offered.[10]

Termination of the Offer

The communication of an effective offer to an offeree gives the offeree the power to transform the offer into a binding, legal obligation (a contract) by an acceptance. This power of acceptance, however, does not

---

8. These rules apply under both the common law of contracts and the Uniform Commercial Code (UCC)—see UCC 2–328.

9. See Chapter 20 and UCC 2–204. Article 2 of the UCC specifies different rules relating to the definiteness of terms used in a contract for the sale of goods. In essence, Article 2 modifies general contract law by requiring less specificity.

10. A few states allow recovery of the reward, but not on contract principles. Because Estrich wanted his dog to be returned and Hoban returned it, these few states would allow Hoban to recover on the basis that it would be unfair to deny her the reward just because she did not know it had been offered.

continue forever. It can be terminated either by action of the parties or by operation of law.

Termination by Action of the Parties

An offer can be terminated by action of the parties in any of three ways: by revocation, by rejection, or by counteroffer.

Revocation of the Offer by the Offeror

The offeror's act of withdrawing (revoking) an offer is known as **revocation.** Unless an offer is irrevocable (discussed shortly), the offeror usually can revoke the offer (even if he or she has promised to keep it open) as long as the revocation is communicated to the offeree before the offeree accepts. Revocation may be accomplished by express repudiation of the offer (for example, with a statement such as "I withdraw my previous offer of October 17") or by performance of acts that are inconsistent with the existence of the offer and are made known to the offeree (for example, selling the offered property to another person in the presence of the offeree).

In most states, a revocation becomes effective when the offeree or the offeree's agent (a person acting on behalf of the offeree) actually receives it. Therefore, if a letter revoking an offer is mailed on April 1 and arrives on April 3, the revocation becomes effective on April 3.

An offer made to the general public can be revoked in the same manner that the offer was originally communicated. Suppose that a department store offers a $10,000 reward to anyone providing information leading to the apprehension of the persons who burglarized the store's downtown branch. The offer is published in three local papers and four papers in neighboring communities. To revoke the offer, the store must publish the revocation in all seven of the papers in which it published the offer. The revocation is then accessible to the general public, even if some particular offeree does not know about it.

Irrevocable Offers

Although most offers are revocable, some can be made irrevocable—that is, they cannot be revoked, or canceled. An option contract involves one type of irrevocable offer. Increasingly, courts also refuse to allow an offeror to revoke an offer when the offeree has changed position because of justifiable reliance on the offer. (In some circumstances, "firm offers" made by merchants may also be considered irrevocable—see the discussion of the "merchant's firm offer" in Chapter 20.)

Option Contract. An **option contract** is created when an offeror promises to hold an offer open for a specified period of time in return for a payment (consideration) given by the offeree. An option contract takes away the offeror's power to revoke the offer for the period of time specified in the option. If no time is specified, then a reasonable period of time is implied. Suppose that you are in the business of writing movie scripts. Your agent contacts the head of development at New Line Cinema and offers to sell New Line your latest movie script. New Line likes your script and agrees to pay you $25,000 for a six-month option. In this situation, you (through your agent) are the offeror, and New Line is the offeree. You cannot revoke your offer to sell New Line your script for the next six months. If after six months no contract has been formed, however, New Line loses the $25,000, and you are free to sell the script to another movie studio.

Real Estate Option Contracts. Option contracts are also frequently used in conjunction with the sale or lease of real estate. For example, you might agree with a landowner to lease a home and include in the lease contract a clause stating that you will pay $9,000 for an option to purchase the home within a specified period of time. If you decide not to purchase the home after the specified period has lapsed, you forfeit the $9,000, and the landlord is free to sell the property to another buyer.

Additionally, contracts to lease business premises often include options to renew the leases at certain intervals, such as after five years. Typically, a lease contract containing a renewal option requires notification—that is, the person leasing the premises must notify the property owner of his or her intention to exercise the renewal option within a certain number of days or months before the current lease expires.

Detrimental Reliance and Promissory Estoppel. When the offeree justifiably relies on an offer to her or his detriment, the court may hold that this *detrimental reliance* makes the offer irrevocable. For example, Sue Fox has rented commercial property from Luis Rivera for the past thirty-three years under a series of five-year leases. As their seventh lease nears its end, Fox tells Rivera that she is going to look at other, less expensive properties as possible sites for her business. Wanting Fox to remain a tenant, Rivera promises to reduce the rent in their next lease. In reliance on the promise, Fox continues to occupy and do business on Rivera's property and does not look at other sites. When they sit down to negotiate a new lease, however, Rivera says he has changed his mind and will increase the rent. Can he effectively revoke his promise?

Normally, he cannot, because Fox has been relying on his promise to reduce the rent. Had the promise not been made, she would have relocated her business. This is a case of detrimental reliance on a promise, which therefore cannot be revoked. In this situation, the doctrine of **promissory estoppel** comes into play. To **estop** means to bar, impede, or preclude someone from doing something. Thus, promissory estoppel means that the promisor (the offeror) is barred from revoking the offer, in this situation because the offeree has already changed her actions in reliance on the offer. We look again at the doctrine of promissory estoppel in Chapter 12 in the context of consideration.

Detrimental Reliance and Partial Performance.
Detrimental reliance can also occur when an offeree partially performs in response to an offer to form a unilateral contract. As discussed in Chapter 10, an offer to form a unilateral contract invites acceptance only by full performance; merely promising to perform does not constitute acceptance. Injustice can result if an offeree expends time and funds in partial performance, only to have the offeror revoke the offer before performance can be completed. Many courts will not allow the offeror to revoke the offer after the offeree has performed some substantial part of his or her duties.[11] In effect, partial performance renders the offer irrevocable, giving the original offeree reasonable time to complete performance. Of course, once the performance is complete, a unilateral contract exists.

Rejection of the Offer by the Offeree If the offeree rejects the offer, the offer is terminated. Any subsequent attempt by the offeree to accept will be construed as a new offer, giving the original offeror (now the offeree) the power of acceptance. A rejection is ordinarily accomplished by words or conduct indicating an intent not to accept the offer. As with a revocation, a rejection of an offer is effective only when it is actually received by the offeror or the offeror's agent.

Note that merely inquiring about an offer does not constitute rejection. Suppose that a friend offers to buy your PlayStation 3 for $300, and you respond, "Is that your best offer?" or "Will you pay me $375 for it?" A reasonable person would conclude that you did not reject the offer but merely made an inquiry for further consideration of the offer. You can still accept and bind your friend to the $300 purchase price. When the

offeree merely inquires as to the firmness of the offer, there is no reason to presume that he or she intends to reject it.

Counteroffer by the Offeree A **counteroffer** is a rejection of the original offer and the simultaneous making of a new offer. Suppose that Burke offers to sell his home to Lang for $270,000. Lang responds, "Your price is too high. I'll offer to purchase your house for $250,000." Lang's response is called a counteroffer because it rejects Burke's offer to sell at $270,000 and creates a new offer by Lang to purchase the home at a price of $250,000.

At common law, the **mirror image rule** requires the offeree's acceptance to match the offeror's offer exactly—to mirror the offer. Any change in, or addition to, the terms of the original offer automatically terminates that offer and substitutes the counteroffer. The counteroffer, of course, need not be accepted; but if the original offeror does accept the terms of the counteroffer, a valid contract is created.[12]

Termination by Operation of Law

The power of the offeree to transform the offer into a binding, legal obligation can be terminated by operation of law through the occurrence of any of the following events:

1. Lapse of time.
2. Destruction of the specific subject matter of the offer.
3. Death or incompetence of the offeror or the offeree.
4. Supervening illegality of the proposed contract.

Lapse of Time An offer terminates automatically by law when the period of time *specified in the offer* has passed. For example, Alejandro offers to sell his camper to Kelly if she accepts within twenty days. Kelly must accept within the twenty-day period or the offer will lapse (terminate). The time period specified in an offer normally begins to run when the offer is actually received by the offeree, not when it is formed or sent. If the offer states that it will be left open until a particular date, then the offer will terminate at midnight on that day. When the offer is delayed (through the

---

11. *Restatement (Second) of Contracts*, Section 45.

12. The mirror image rule has been greatly modified in regard to sales contracts. Section 2–207 of the UCC provides that a contract is formed if the offeree makes a definite expression of acceptance (such as signing the form in the appropriate location), even though the terms of the acceptance modify or add to the terms of the original offer (see Chapter 20).

misdelivery of mail, for example), the period begins to run from the date the offeree would have received the offer, but only if the offeree knows or should know that the offer is delayed.[13]

If the offer does not specify a time for acceptance, the offer terminates at the end of a *reasonable* period of time. What constitutes a reasonable period of time depends on the subject matter of the contract, business and market conditions, and other relevant circumstances. An offer to sell farm produce, for example, will terminate sooner than an offer to sell farm equipment because farm produce is perishable and subject to greater fluctuations in market value.

Destruction of the Subject Matter An offer is automatically terminated if the specific subject matter of the offer is destroyed before the offer is accepted.[14] If Johnson offers to sell his prize greyhound to Rizzo, for example, but the dog dies before Rizzo can accept, the offer is automatically terminated. Johnson does not have to tell Rizzo that the animal has died for the offer to terminate.

Death or Incompetence of the Offeror or Offeree An offeree's power of acceptance is terminated when the offeror or offeree dies or is deprived of legal capacity to enter into the proposed contract. A revocable offer is personal to both parties and cannot pass to the heirs, guardian, or estate of either. Furthermore, this rule applies whether or not the other party had notice of the death or incompetence. If the offer is irrevocable, however, the death of the offeror or offeree does not terminate the offer.[15]

Supervening Illegality of the Proposed Contract A statute or court decision that makes an offer illegal automatically terminates the offer.[16] For example, Lee offers to lend Kim $10,000 at an annual interest rate of 12 percent. Before Kim can accept the offer, a law is enacted that prohibits interest rates higher than 10 percent. Lee's offer is automatically terminated. (If the statute is enacted after Kim accepts the offer, a valid contract is formed, but the contract may still be unenforceable—see Chapter 13.) *Concept Summary 9.1* provides a review of the ways in which an offer can be terminated.

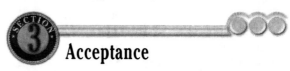

Acceptance

Acceptance is a voluntary act by the offeree that shows assent (agreement) to the terms of an offer. The offeree's act may consist of words or conduct. The acceptance must be unequivocal and must be communicated to the offeror.

Unequivocal Acceptance

To exercise the power of acceptance effectively, the offeree must accept unequivocally. This is the *mirror image rule* previously discussed. If the acceptance is subject to new conditions or if the terms of the acceptance change the original offer, the acceptance may be deemed a counteroffer that implicitly rejects the original offer.

An acceptance may be unequivocal even though the offeree expresses dissatisfaction with the contract. For example, "I accept the offer, but I wish I could have gotten a better price" is an effective acceptance. So, too, is "I accept, but can you shave the price?" In contrast, the statement "I accept the offer but only if I can pay on ninety days' credit" is not an unequivocal acceptance and operates as a counteroffer, rejecting the original offer.

Certain terms, when added to an acceptance, will not qualify the acceptance sufficiently to constitute rejection of the offer. Suppose that in response to an offer to sell a piano, the offeree replies, "I accept; please send a written contract." The offeree is requesting a written contract but is not making it a condition for acceptance. Therefore, the acceptance is effective without the written contract. If the offeree replies, "I accept if you send a written contract," however, the acceptance is expressly conditioned on the request for a writing, and the statement is not an acceptance but a counteroffer. (Notice how important each word is!)[17]

---

13. *Restatement (Second) of Contracts*, Section 49.

14. *Restatement (Second) of Contracts*, Section 36.

15. *Restatement (Second) of Contracts*, Section 48. If the offer is such that it can be accepted by the performance of a series of acts, and those acts began before the offeror died, the offeree's power of acceptance is not terminated.

16. *Restatement (Second) of Contracts*, Section 36.

17. As noted in footnote 12, in regard to sales contracts, the UCC provides that an acceptance may still be valid even if some terms are added. The new terms are simply treated as proposed additions to the contract.

CONCEPT SUMMARY 9.1
Methods by Which an Offer Can Be Terminated

BY ACTION OF THE PARTIES	1. *Revocation*—Unless the offer is irrevocable, it can be revoked at any time before acceptance without liability. Revocation is not effective until received by the offeree or the offeree's agent. Some offers, such as a merchant's firm offer and option contracts, are irrevocable. Also, in some situations, an offeree's detrimental reliance and/or partial performance will cause a court to rule that the offeror cannot revoke the offer.
	2. *Rejection*—Accomplished by words or actions that demonstrate a clear intent not to accept the offer; not effective until received by the offeror or the offeror's agent.
	3. *Counteroffer*—A rejection of the original offer and the making of a new offer.
BY OPERATION OF LAW	1. *Lapse of time*—The offer terminates (a) at the end of the time period specified in the offer or (b) if no time period is stated in the offer, at the end of a reasonable time period.
	2. *Destruction of the subject matter*—When the specific subject matter of the offer is destroyed before the offer is accepted, the offer automatically terminates.
	3. *Death or incompetence of the offeror or offeree*—If the offeror or offeree dies or becomes incompetent, this terminates the offer (unless the offer is irrevocable).
	4. *Supervening illegality*—When a statute or court decision makes the proposed contract illegal, the offer automatically terminates.

Silence as Acceptance

Ordinarily, silence cannot constitute acceptance, even if the offeror states, "By your silence and inaction, you will be deemed to have accepted this offer." This general rule applies because an offeree should not be obligated to act affirmatively to reject an offer when no consideration has passed to the offeree to impose such a duty.

In some instances, however, the offeree does have a duty to speak. In these situations, her or his silence or inaction will operate as an acceptance. For example, silence may be an acceptance when an offeree takes the benefit of offered services even though he or she had an opportunity to reject them and knew that they were offered with the expectation of compensation. Suppose that Sayre watches while a stranger rakes his leaves, even though the stranger has not been asked to rake the yard. Sayre knows the stranger expects to be paid and does nothing to stop her. Here, his silence constitutes an acceptance, and an implied-in-fact contract is created (see Chapter 10). He is bound to pay a reasonable value for the stranger's work.

Silence can also operate as acceptance when the offeree has had prior dealings with the offeror. Suppose that a business routinely receives shipments from a certain supplier and always notifies that supplier when defective goods are rejected. In this situation, silence regarding a shipment will constitute acceptance.

Communication of Acceptance

Whether the offeror must be notified of the acceptance depends on the nature of the contract. In a bilateral contract, communication of acceptance is necessary because acceptance is in the form of a promise (not performance) and the contract is formed when the promise is made (rather than when the act is performed). The offeree must communicate the acceptance to the offeror. Communication of acceptance is not necessary, however, if the offer dispenses with the requirement. Additionally, if the offer can be accepted by silence, no communication is necessary.

Because a unilateral contract calls for the full performance of some act, acceptance is usually evident, and notification is therefore unnecessary. Nevertheless, exceptions do exist, such as when the offeror requests notice of acceptance or has no way of determining whether the requested act has been performed. In addition, sometimes the law requires notice of acceptance, and thus notice is necessary.[18]

Mode and Timeliness of Acceptance

Acceptance in bilateral contracts must be timely. The general rule is that acceptance in a bilateral contract is timely if it is made before the offer is terminated. Problems may arise, though, when the parties involved are not dealing face to face. In such situations, the offeree should use an authorized mode of communication.

Acceptance takes effect, thus completing formation of the contract, at the time the offeree sends or delivers the communication via the mode expressly or impliedly authorized by the offeror. This is the so-called **mailbox rule,** which the majority of courts follow. Under this rule, if the authorized mode of communication is the mail, then an acceptance becomes valid when it is dispatched (placed in the control of the U.S. Postal Service)—*not* when it is received by the offeror.

The mailbox rule was created to prevent the confusion that arises when an offeror sends a letter of revocation but, before it arrives, the offeree sends a letter of acceptance. Thus, whereas a revocation becomes effective only when it is *received* by the offeree, an acceptance becomes effective on *dispatch* (when sent, even if it is never received), provided that an *authorized* means of communication is used.

The mailbox rule does not apply to instantaneous forms of communication, such as when the parties are dealing face to face, by telephone, or by fax. There is still some uncertainty in the courts as to whether e-mail should be considered an instantaneous form of communication to which the mailbox rule does not apply. If the parties have agreed to conduct transactions electronically and if the Uniform Electronic Transactions Act (to be discussed in Chapter 19) applies, then e-mail is considered sent when it either leaves control of the sender or is received by the recip-

ient. This rule takes the place of the mailbox rule when the Uniform Electronic Transactions Act applies but essentially allows an e-mail acceptance to become effective when sent (as it would if sent by U.S. mail).

Authorized Means of Acceptance A means of communicating acceptance can be expressly authorized—that is, expressly stipulated in the offer— or impliedly authorized by the facts and circumstances surrounding the situation or by law.[19] An acceptance sent by means not expressly or impliedly authorized normally is not effective until it is received by the offeror.

When an offeror specifies how acceptance should be made (for example, by overnight delivery), *express authorization* is said to exist, and the contract is not formed unless the offeree uses that specified mode of acceptance. Moreover, both offeror and offeree are bound in contract the moment this means of acceptance is employed. For example, Shaylee & Perkins, a Massachusetts firm, offers to sell a container of antique furniture to Leaham's Antiques in Colorado. The offer states that Leaham's must accept the offer via FedEx overnight delivery. The acceptance is effective (and a binding contract is formed) the moment that Leaham's gives the overnight envelope containing the acceptance to the FedEx driver.

When the Preferred Means of Acceptance Is Not Indicated. Most offerors do not expressly specify the means by which the offeree is to accept. When the offeror does not specify expressly that the offeree is to accept by a certain means, or that the acceptance will be effective only when received, acceptance of an offer may be made by any medium that is *reasonable under the circumstances.*[20]

Whether a mode of acceptance is reasonable depends on what would reasonably be expected by parties in the position of the contracting parties. Courts look at prevailing business usages and other surrounding circumstances such as the method of communica-

---

18. Under UCC 2–206(1)(b), an order or other offer to buy goods for prompt shipment may be treated as an offer contemplating either a bilateral or a unilateral contract and may be accepted by either a promise to ship (bilateral contract) or actual shipment (unilateral contract). If the offer is accepted by actual shipment of the goods, the buyer must be notified of the acceptance within a reasonable period of time, or the buyer may treat the offer as having lapsed before acceptance [UCC 2–206(2)]. See also Chapter 20.

19. *Restatement (Second) of Contracts*, Section 30, provides that an offer invites acceptance "by any medium reasonable in the circumstances," unless the offer is specific about the means of acceptance. Under Section 65, a medium is reasonable if it is one used by the offeror or one customary in similar transactions, unless the offeree knows of circumstances that would argue against the reasonableness of a particular medium (the need for speed because of rapid price changes, for example).

20. *Restatement (Second) of Contracts*, Section 30. This is also the rule under UCC 2–206(1)(a).

tion the parties have used in the past and the means that were used to convey the offer. The offeror's choice of a particular means in making the offer implies that the offeree is authorized to use the same *or a faster* means for acceptance. Suppose that two parties have been negotiating a deal via fax and then the offeror sends a formal contract offer by priority mail without specifying the means of acceptance. In that situation, the offeree's acceptance by priority mail or by fax is impliedly authorized.

When the Authorized Means of Acceptance Is Not Used. An acceptance sent by means not expressly or impliedly authorized normally is not effective *until it is received by the offeror.* Suppose that Frank Cochran is interested in buying a house from Ray Nunez. Cochran faxes an offer to Nunez that clearly specifies acceptance by fax. Nunez has to be out of town for a few days, however, and doesn't have access to a fax machine. Therefore, Nunez sends his acceptance to Cochran via FedEx instead of by fax. In this situation, the acceptance is not effective (and no contract is formed) until Cochran receives the FedEx delivery. The use of an alternative method does not render the acceptance ineffective if the substituted method performs the same function or serves the same purpose as the authorized method.[21]

Exceptions The following are three basic exceptions to the rule that a contract is formed when an acceptance is sent by authorized means:

1. If the offeree's acceptance is not properly dispatched, in most states it will not be effective until it is received by the offeror. For example, if an offeree types in the recipient's e-mail address incorrectly when accepting an offer via e-mail, or if the offeree faxes an acceptance to the wrong telephone number, it will not be effective until received by the offeror. If U.S. mail is the authorized means for acceptance, the offeree's letter must be properly addressed and have the correct postage. Nonetheless, if the acceptance is timely sent and timely received, despite the offeree's carelessness in sending it, it may still be considered to have been effective on dispatch.[22]
2. If the offer stipulates when acceptance will be effective, then the offer will not be effective until the

time specified. The offeror has the power to control the offer and can stipulate both the means by which the offer is accepted and the precise time that an acceptance will be effective. For example, an offer might state that acceptance will not be effective until it is received by the offeror, or it might make acceptance effective twenty-four hours after being shipped via DHL delivery.
3. Sometimes, an offeree sends a rejection first, then later changes his or her mind and sends an acceptance. Obviously, this chain of events could cause confusion and even detriment to the offeror, depending on whether the rejection or the acceptance arrived first. In such situations, the law cancels the rule of acceptance on dispatch, and the first communication received by the offeror determines whether a contract is formed. If the rejection arrives first, there is no contract.[23]

For a review of the effective time of acceptance, see *Concept Summary 9.2* on the next page.

Technology and Acceptance Rules

Clearly, some of the traditional rules governing acceptance do not seem to apply to an age in which acceptances are commonly delivered via e-mail, fax, or other delivery system, such as FedEx or DHL. For example, when accepting an online offer, the mailbox rule does not apply to online acceptances, which typically are communicated instantaneously to the offeror. Nonetheless, the traditional rules—and the principles that underlie those rules—provide a basis for understanding what constitutes a valid acceptance in today's online environment. This is because, as in other areas of the law, much of the law governing online offers and acceptances has been adapted from traditional law to a new context.

Although online offers are not significantly different from traditional offers contained in paper documents, online acceptances have posed some unusual problems for the court. These problems, as well as other aspects of e-contracting, will be discussed in detail in Chapter 19.

---

21. See, for example, *Osprey, L.L.C. v. Kelly Moore Paint Co.,* 984 P.2d 194 (Okla. 1999).
22. *Restatement (Second) of Contracts,* Section 67.

---

23. *Restatement (Second) of Contracts,* Section 40.

CONCEPT SUMMARY 9.2
Effective Time of Acceptance

Acceptance	Time Effective
BY AUTHORIZED MEANS OF COMMUNICATION	Effective at the time communication is sent (deposited in a mailbox or delivered to a courier service) via the mode expressly or impliedly authorized by the offeror (mailbox rule). *Exceptions:* 1. If the acceptance is not properly dispatched, it will not be effective until received by the offeror. 2. If the offeror specifically conditioned the offer on receipt of acceptance, it will not be effective until received by the offeror. 3. If acceptance is sent after rejection, whichever is received first is given effect.
BY UNAUTHORIZED MEANS OF COMMUNICATION	Effective on receipt of acceptance by the offeror (if timely received, it is considered to have been effective on dispatch).

REVIEWING Agreement

Shane Durbin wanted to have a recording studio custom-built in his home. He sent invitations to a number of local contractors to submit bids on the project. Rory Amstel submitted the lowest bid, which was $20,000 less than any of the other bids Durbin received. Durbin called Amstel to ascertain the type and quality of the materials that were included in the bid and to find out if he could substitute a superior brand of acoustic tiles for the same bid price. Amstel said he would have to check into the price difference. The parties also discussed a possible start date for construction. Two weeks later, Durbin changed his mind and decided not to go forward with his plan to build a recording studio. Amstel filed a suit against Durbin for breach of contract. Using the information presented in the chapter, answer the following questions.

1. Did Amstel's bid meet the requirements of an offer? Explain.
2. Was there an acceptance of the offer? Why or why not?
3. Suppose that the court determines that the parties did not reach an agreement. Further suppose that Amstel, in anticipation of building Durbin's studio, had purchased materials and refused other jobs so that he would have time in his schedule for Durbin's project. Under what theory discussed in the chapter might Amstel attempt to recover these costs?
4. How is an offer terminated? Assuming that Durbin did not inform Amstel that he was rejecting the offer, was the offer terminated at any time described here? Explain.

TERMS AND CONCEPTS

acceptance

agreement

counteroffer

estop

mailbox rule

mirror image rule

mutual assent

offer

option contract

promissory estoppel

revocation

QUESTIONS AND CASE PROBLEMS

11-1. Ball writes to Sullivan and inquires how much Sullivan is asking for a specific forty-acre tract of land Sullivan owns. In a letter received by Ball, Sullivan states, "I will not take less than $60,000 for the forty-acre tract as specified." Ball immediately sends Sullivan a telegram stating, "I accept your offer for $60,000 for the forty-acre tract as specified." Discuss whether Ball can hold Sullivan to a contract for the sale of the land.

11-2. QUESTION WITH SAMPLE ANSWER

Schmidt, operating a sole proprietorship, has a large piece of used farm equipment for sale. He offers to sell the equipment to Barry for $10,000. Discuss the legal effects of the following events on the offer:

(a) Schmidt dies prior to Barry's acceptance, and at the time he accepts, Barry is unaware of Schmidt's death.

(b) The night before Barry accepts, fire destroys the equipment.

(c) Barry pays $100 for a thirty-day option to purchase the equipment. During this period, Schmidt dies, and later Barry accepts the offer, knowing of Schmidt's death.

(d) Barry pays $100 for a thirty-day option to purchase the equipment. During this period, Barry dies, and Barry's estate accepts Schmidt's offer within the stipulated time period.

- **For a sample answer to Question 11-2, go to Appendix C at the end of this text.**

11-3. Perez sees an advertisement in the newspaper indicating that the ABC Corp. is offering for sale a two-volume set of books, *How to Make Repairs around the House*, for $39.95. All Perez has to do is send in a card requesting delivery of the books for a thirty-day trial period. If he does not ship the books back within thirty days of delivery, ABC will bill him for $39.95. Discuss whether Perez and ABC have a contract under either of the following circumstances:

(a) Perez sends in the card and receives the books in the U.S. mail. He uses the books to make repairs and fails to return them within thirty days.

(b) Perez does not send in the card, but ABC sends him the books anyway through the U.S. mail. Perez uses the books and fails to return them within thirty days.

11-4. On Thursday, Dennis mailed a letter to Tanya's office offering to sell his car to her for $3,000. On Saturday, having changed his mind, Dennis sent a fax to Tanya's office revoking his offer. Tanya did not go to her office over the weekend and thus did not learn about the revocation until Monday morning, just a few minutes after she had mailed a letter of acceptance to Dennis. When Tanya demanded that Dennis sell his car to her as promised, Dennis claimed that no contract existed because he had revoked his offer prior to Tanya's acceptance. Is Dennis correct? Explain.

11-5. Definiteness of Terms. Southwick Homes, Ltd., develops and markets residential subdivisions. William McLinden and Ronald Coco are the primary owners of Southwick Homes. Coco is also the president of Mutual Development Co. Whiteco Industries, Inc., wanted to develop lots and sell homes in Schulien Woods, a subdivision in Crown Point, Indiana. In September 1996, Whiteco sent McLinden a letter enlisting Southwick Homes to be the project manager for developing and marketing the finished lots (lots where roads had been built and on which utility installation and connections to water and sewer lines were complete); the letter set out the roles and expectations of each of the parties, including the terms of payment. In October 1997, Whiteco sent Coco a letter naming Mutual Development the developer and general contractor for the houses to be built on the finished lots. A few months later, Coco told McLinden that he would not share in the profits from the construction of the houses. McLinden and others filed a suit in an Indiana state court against Coco and others, claiming, in part, a breach of fiduciary duty. The defendants responded that the letter to McLinden lacked such essential terms as to render it unenforceable. What terms must an agreement include to be an enforceable contract? Did the letter sent to McLinden include these terms? In whose favor should the court rule? Explain. [*McLinden v. Coco*, 765 N.E.2d 606 (Ind. App. 2002)]

11-6. CASE PROBLEM WITH SAMPLE ANSWER

The Pittsburgh Board of Public Education in Pittsburgh, Pennsylvania, as required by state law, keeps lists of eligible teachers in order of their rank or standing. According to an "Eligibility List" form made available to applicants, no one may be hired to teach whose name is not within the top 10 percent of the names on the list. In 1996, Anna Reed was in the top 10 percent. She was not hired that year, although four other applicants who placed lower on the list—and not within the top 10 percent—were hired. In 1997 and 1998, Reed was again in the top 10 percent, but she was not hired until 1999. Reed filed a suit in a federal district court against the board and others. She argued, in part, that the state's requirement that the board keep a list constituted an offer, which she accepted by participating in the process to be placed on that list. She claimed that the board breached this contract by hiring applicants who ranked lower than she did. The case was transferred to a Pennsylvania state court. What are the requirements of an offer? Do the circumstances in this case meet those requirements? Why or why not? [*Reed v. Pittsburgh Board of Public Education*, 862 A.2d 131 (Pa.Cmwlth. 2004)]

- **To view a sample answer for Problem 11-6, go to this book's Web site at www.cengage. com/blaw/jentz, select "Chapter 11," and click on "Case Problem with Sample Answer."**

11-7. Intention. Music that is distributed on compact discs and similar media generates income in the form of "mechanical" royalties. Music that is publicly performed, such as when a song is played on a radio, included in a movie or commercial, or sampled in another song, produces "performance" royalties. Each of these types of royalties is divided between the songwriter and the song's publisher. Vincent Cusano is a musician and songwriter who performed under the name "Vinnie Vincent" as a guitarist with the group KISS in the early 1980s. Cusano co-wrote three songs entitled "Killer," "I Love It Loud," and "I Still Love You" that KISS recorded and released in 1982 on an album titled *Creatures of the Night*. Cusano left KISS in 1984. Eight years later, Cusano sold to Horipro Entertainment Group "one hundred (100%) percent undivided interest" of his rights in the songs "other than Songwriter's share of performance income." Later, Cusano filed a suit in a federal district court against Horipro, claiming, among other things, that he never intended to sell the writer's share of the mechanical royalties. Horipro filed a motion for summary judgment. Should the court grant the motion? Explain. [*Cusano v. Horipro Entertainment Group*, 301 F.Supp.2d 272 (S.D.N.Y. 2004)]

11-8. Agreement. In 2000, David and Sandra Harless leased 2.3 acres of real property at 2801 River Road S.E. in Winnabow, North Carolina, to their son-in-law and daughter, Tony and Jeanie Connor. The Connors planned to operate a "general store/variety store" on the premises. They agreed to lease the property for sixty months with an option to renew for an additional sixty months. The lease included an option to buy the property for "fair market value at the time of such purchase (based on at least two appraisals)." In March 2003, Tony told David that the Connors wanted to buy the property. In May, Tony gave David an appraisal that estimated the property's value at $140,000. In July, the Connors presented a second appraisal that determined the value to be $160,000. The Connors offered $150,000. The Harlesses replied that "under no circumstances would they ever agree to sell their old store building and approximately 2.5 acres to their daughter . . . and their son-in-law." The Connors filed a suit in a North Carolina state court against the Harlesses, alleging breach of contract. Did these parties have a contract to sell the property? If so, what were its terms? If not, why not? [*Connor v. Harless*, 176 N.C.App. 402, 626 S.E.2d 755 (2006)]

11-9. Offer. In August 2000, in California, Terry Reigelsperger sought treatment for pain in his lower back from chiropractor James Siller. Reigelsperger felt better after the treatment and did not intend to return for more, although he did not mention this to Siller. Before leaving the office, Reigelsperger signed an "informed consent" form that read, in part, "I intend this consent form to cover the entire course of treatment for my present condition and for any future condition(s) for which I seek treatment." He also signed an agreement that required the parties to submit to arbitration "any dispute as to medical malpractice. . . . This agreement is intended to bind the patient and the health care provider . . . who now or in the future treat[s] the patient." Two years later, Reigelsperger sought treatment from Siller for a different condition relating to his cervical spine and shoulder. Claiming malpractice with respect to the second treatment, Reigelsperger filed a suit in a California state court against Siller. Siller asked the court to order the dispute to be submitted to arbitration. Did Reigelsperger's lack of intent to return to Siller after his first treatment affect the enforceability of the arbitration agreement and consent form? Why or why not? [*Reigelsperger v. Siller*, 40 Cal.4th 574, 150 P.3d 764, 53 Cal.Rptr.3d 887 (2007)]

11-10. A QUESTION OF ETHICS

In 1980, Kenneth McMillan and his associate in a dental practice obtained life insurance policies that designated each the beneficiary of the other. They set up automatic withdrawals from their bank accounts to pay the premiums. Later, Laurence Hibbard joined the practice, which was renamed Bentley, McMillan and Hibbard, P.C. (professional corporation), or BMH. When the three terminated their business relationship in 2003, McMillan sold his BMH stock to Hibbard. But Hibbard did not pay, and McMillan obtained a judgment against him for $52,972.74. When Hibbard still did not pay, McMillan offered him a choice. In lieu of paying the judgment, Hibbard could take over the premiums on Bentley's insurance policy or "cash" it in. Either way, the policy's proceeds

would be used to pay off loans against the policy—which McMillan had arranged—and Hibbard would accept responsibility for any unpaid amount. Hibbard signed the agreement but did not make a choice between the two options. McMillan filed a suit in a Georgia state court against Hibbard, seeking reimbursement for the premiums paid since their agreement. [Hibbard v. McMillan, *284 Ga.App. 753, 645 S.E.2d 356 (2007)*]

(a) McMillan asked the court to award him attorneys' fees because Hibbard had been "stubbornly litigious," forcing McMillan to litigate to enforce their agreement. Should the court grant this request? Are there any circumstances in which Hibbard's failure to choose between McMillan's options would be justified? Explain.

(b) Generally, parties are entitled to contract on their own terms without the courts' intervention. Under the principles discussed in this chapter, what are some of the limits to this freedom? Do any of these limits apply to the agreement between McMillan and Hibbard? Why or why not?

11-11. VIDEO QUESTION

Go to this text's Web site at **www.cengage. com/blaw/jentz** and select "Chapter 11." Click on "Video Questions" and view the video titled *Offer and Acceptance*. Then answer the following questions.

(a) On the video, Vinny indicates that he can't sell his car to Oscar for four thousand dollars and then says, "maybe five . . . ." Discuss whether Vinny has made an offer or a counteroffer.

(b) Oscar then says to Vinny, "Okay, I'll take it. But you gotta let me pay you four thousand now and the other thousand in two weeks." According to the chapter, do Oscar and Vinny have an agreement? Why or why not?

(c) When Maria later says to Vinny, "I'll take it," has she accepted an offer? Why or why not?

LAW ON THE WEB

For updated links to resources available on the Web, as well as a variety of other materials, visit this text's Web site at

www.cengage.com/blaw/jentz

To learn what kinds of clauses are included in typical contracts for certain goods and services, you can explore the collection of contract forms made available by FindLaw at

forms.lp.findlaw.com

Legal Research Exercises on the Web

Go to **www.cengage.com/blaw/jentz**, the Web site that accompanies this text. Select "Chapter 11" and click on "Internet Exercises." There you will find the following Internet research exercises that you can perform to learn more about the topics covered in this chapter.

Internet Exercise 11–1: Legal Perspective
Contract Terms

Internet Exercise 11–2: Management Perspective
Sample Contracts

Internet Exercise 11–3: Ethical Perspective
Offers and Advertisements

Contracts: Offer and Acceptance

Case No. 38

DEFINITENESS/AGREEMENTS TO AGREE

<u>**Joseph Martin, Jr., Delicatessen, Inc. v. Schumacker**</u>

Court of Appeals

52 N.Y.2d 105, 436 N.Y.S.2d 247 (1981)

FACTS: In 1973 Defendant Henry Schumacker (Schumacker) leased a store to Plaintiff Joseph Martin, Jr., Delicatessen, Inc. (Delicatessen) for a five-year term at an initial rent of $500.00 per month. According to the terms of the written lease, the rent increased over the five year term to $650.00 per month. A renewal clause in the contract stated, "The tenant may renew this lease for an additional period of five years at annual rentals to be agreed upon . . ."

At the end of the first five year term Delicatessen sought to renew the lease. Landlord agreed to renew but required a starting rent of $900.00 per month. Delicatessen hired a professional appraiser who determined that the fair market rental value for the store was approximately $550.00 per month.

In this action Delicatessen seeks to compel landlord to extend the lease for a rent of $550.00 per month or whatever amount the court determined was reasonable. Landlord denied it was obligated to rent at the fair market value and sought to evict Delicatessen.

ISSUE: Is a lease that states it can be renewed "at annual rentals to be agreed upon" sufficiently definite to be enforceable when the parties cannot agree on the amount of the rent?

DECISION: No, judgment against Delicatessen.

REASONING: "Agreements to agree" are unenforceable for lack of definiteness when material terms are left open for future negotiations. If the parties substantially agree on the indefinite terms their agreement will be enforceable. Where the parties cannot agree, as was the situation in this case, the court will not guess what the parties intended nor impose fair market value or reasonableness as a standard to clarify the open term. Instead the agreement is unenforceable due to indefiniteness. The requirement of definiteness could have been satisfied by identifying a method for determining the amount of the new rent even though the actual amount of rent was not stated. The parties in this case failed to provide such a method.

* * * QUESTIONS * * *
(See back of text for answers)

1) What provision could the parties have included in the original lease to avoid the problem in this case?

2) Why are courts hesitant to enforce contracts that leave important terms such as the price undefined?

3) Compare the common law requirement of definiteness with the UCC requirement of definiteness.

Case No. 39

OFFER AND ACCEPTANCE/ DEFINITENESS

Maffea V. Ippolito

Appellate Division, Second Department

247 A.D.2d 366, 668 N.Y.S.2d 653 (1998)

FACTS: In April 1995 Michael Ippolito purchased a winning New York State lottery ticket valued at 7.5 million dollars. Patrick Maffea, a relative of Ipploito, sued Ippolito for one-half of the winnings. Maffea claimed that at a family gathering nine years prior to Ippolito hitting the jackpot, Maffea and Ippolito entered an oral contract stating that if either of them ever won the lottery, they would share the proceeds equally. Maffea claimed the agreement included all tickets the parties would purchase in the future but did not produce any proof that Ippolito assented to the terms of the alleged agreement.

ISSUE: Did an enforceable contract exist between Ippolito and Maffea where no evidence existed of Ippolito's agreement to the alleged terms?

DECISION: No

REASONING: For a contract to exist there must be a valid offer and acceptance. In this case the alleged agreement was unenforceable because Maffea failed to present any reliable evidence of acceptance on the part of Ippolito.

Case No. 40

OFFER AND ACCEPTANCE DEFINITENESS

S.S.I. Investors, Ltd. v. Korea Tungsten Mining Co., Ltd.

Court of Appeals

55 N.Y.2d 934, 449 N.Y.S.2d 173 (1982)

FACTS: Defendant Korea Tungsten Mining Co., Ltd. (Mining Co.) wanted to sell certain real estate it owned in midtown Manhattan. Mining Co. requested bids from interested buyers and agreed to sell to the highest bidder. Plaintiff S.S.I. Investors, Ltd. (S.S.I.) submitted a sealed bid for the purchase of Mining Co.'s real property. The bid was as follows: "The total price of Five Hundred Fifty-Six thousand dollars ($556,000.00) and/or One dollar ($1.00) more than the highest bid you have received ...".

The highest bid aside from S.S.I.'s was $750,000.00. Mining Co. accepted the $750,000.00 bid.

S.S.I. claimed that it was the highest bidder based on its "one dollar more" bid. It brought this action for specific performance seeking a court order requiring Mining Co. to sell the property to S.S.I.

ISSUE: Does a bid which states a price of one dollar more than the next highest bid constitute a valid offer?

DECISION: No, judgment against S.S.I.

REASONING: For an offer to be valid it must be definite and certain. S.S.I.'s bid was too indefinite to constitute a valid offer. The bid proposed two possible prices and did not specify which alternative was intended to be the price offered. No determining modifier such as "whichever is higher" was included. Further, the "one dollar more" option was indefinite because the amount of the other bids was not known.

In some circumstances an otherwise indefinite bid can be made sufficiently definite by reference to an external document. To determine in this case, however, that the "one dollar more" bid could be made definite by reference to the other bids would frustrate the process of sealed bidding. The "very essence of sealed competitive bidding is the submission of independent, self-contained bids . . . to give effect to this or any other similar bidding practice . . . would be to recognize means whereby effective sealed competitive bidding could be wholly frustrated."

*** QUESTIONS ***
(See back of text for answers)

1) Who was the offeror in this case and who was the offeree?

2) At an auction who is the offeror—the bidder or the auctioneer?

Case No. 41

OFFER AND ACCEPTANCE

Donaldson Acoustics Co., Inc. v. Nab Construction Corporation

Appellate Division, Second Department

709 N.Y.S.2d 107 (2000), 273 AD2d 192

FACTS: Donaldson Acoustics Co., Inc. (Donaldson) alleged that it entered an agreement with general contractor Nab Construction Corporation (Nab) to do ceiling and plaster work in the renovation of a subway station. Nab initially accepted Donaldson's bid and, as is customary, forwarded a proposed contract to Donaldson. Donaldson did not immediately sign the proposed agreement and continued to negotiate its terms, as several critical issues relating to the nature of the ceiling work had yet to be resolved. After an eleven-month delay, Donaldson executed the contract and forwarded it to Nab with some significant modifications. Nab rejected the modifications and subsequently hired a different subcontractor to complete the work.

Donaldson initiated this lawsuit against Nab for breach of contract. Nab contends that Donaldson's offer to do the proposed work was never accepted. The trial court granted Nab's motion for summary judgment dismissing the claim and Donaldson appealed.

ISSUE: When an offeree, in response to an offer, makes significant modifications to the written offer, does the response constitute an acceptance?

DECISION: No

REASONING: For a contract to exist, the offeree must unequivocally accept the terms of the offer. If the response to the offer adds new conditions or changes material terms it is a counteroffer and not an acceptance. In this case the material modifications in Donaldson's response rendered it a counteroffer and not an acceptance.

Case No. 42

CONTRACTS/ACCEPTANCE

John William Costello Associates, Inc. v. Standard Metals Corp.

Appellate Division, First Department

99 A.D.2d 717, 472 N.Y.S.2d 324 (1984)

FACTS: John William Costello Associates, Inc. (Costello) is an employment agency. Its president, Edward Nottage (Nottage), wrote to Boris Gresov (Gresov), the president of Standard Metals Corporation (Standard), suggesting that Gresov might want to interview a client of Costello as a prospective employee. Soon thereafter Nottage received a phone call from Gresov's assistant, Mary Di Rienzo (Di Rienzo), who expressed an interest in the client. Nottage informed her that, if the client was hired, Costello's fee would be 30% of the client's first year salary. In due time a phone interview was scheduled between Costello's client and Gresov. Costello sent a letter confirming the interview and the 30% fee. Standard did not sign a written contract with Costello agreeing to the 30% fee.

Standard hired Costello's client and Costello sent Standard a bill for 30% of the client's first-year salary. Standard refused to pay, arguing that it never agreed to pay a 30% fee.

ISSUE: Where a written offer is submitted and no written acceptance is received, and the offeree utilizes the benefit proposed in the offer, does a contract exist?

DECISION: Yes, judgment for Costello.

REASONING: An acceptance of a written offer does not have to be in writing or even expressed. The acceptance can take the form of conduct or acquiescence. In this case, Standard did not reject the offer. Instead, it accepted the benefits of Costello's services by interviewing and ultimately hiring Costello's client. This conduct constitutes an acceptance of Costello's offer to refer a potential employee in exchange for a 30% fee if the person was hired.

* * * QUESTION * * *
(See back of text for answer)

1) How might Costello have avoided the problem in this case?

Case No. 43

CONTRACTS/ACCEPTANCE BY CONDUCT

Rudolph & Beer. LLP v. Roberts

Appellate Division, First Department

260 A.D.2d 274, 688 N.Y.S.2d 553 (1999)

FACTS: Inato Roberts (Roberts) asked Rudolph & Beer (Beer), a law firm, to represent him in negotiations with the City of New York on a contract to construct an auto racing facility on Staten Island.

Beer proposed a retainer and fee arrangement in a letter dated July 16, 1995. The arrangement included payment to Beer of 10% of the gross receipts from the project and an hourly fee of $100 plus expenses. The proposal further stated that all fees were deferred until the project produced revenue. Additionally an arbitration clause stated that all disputes between the parties would be arbitrated in accordance with the rules of the American Arbitration Association. Roberts never signed the agreement.

Per the retainer and fee proposal, Roberts' business, Autodrome Inc., was incorporated in July 1995. The partners in the law firm became officers, partners, and equity owners in the newly formed corporation per the retainer document. Concerned that the venture would not be profitable, Beer proposed a buyout to Roberts. In the proposed buyout letter, Beer made references to the June retainer and fee arrangement and indicated that the firm had been relying "upon this agreement since coming on board as your counsel...." Additionally Beer included billing records with the buyout offer to facilitate Roberts' calculating the value of the proposed buyout.

Roberts discharged Beer as attorney in November 1995. When the parties failed to agree on compensation Beer sued Roberts for quantum meruit at its normal fee of $250 per hour. Beer contended that the retainer and fee agreement with the arbitration clause, at a proposed an hourly fee of $100, was unenforceable because Roberts never signed it. The trial court agreed and Roberts appealed claiming the arbitration clause in the retainer and fee proposal was enforceable.

ISSUE: Does an enforceable arbitration agreement exist between Roberts and Beer notwithstanding Roberts did not sign Beer's retainer and fee proposal that included the arbitration clause?

DECISION: Yes

REASONING: While the law requires that an agreement to arbitrate be in writing to be enforceable, a signature by the party seeking enforcement (Roberts) is not required provided the conduct of the party who proposed the agreement (Beer) evidenced an intent to be bound by it. In this case Beer sought to deny Roberts the benefits of the arbitration clause because Roberts did not sign it. However, Beer treated the unsigned agreement as governing the relationship between the parties. This was evidenced by the following: 1) the proposed buyout letter referencing the June retainer/ fee arrangement; 2) Beer's statement in the letter referring to himself as an officer of Autodrome Inc., and 3) Beer's letter stating he had relied on the agreement since "coming on board" as counsel. The letter also included billing records that were consistent with the terms of the retainer and fee proposal. Finally, Roberts's actions were consistent with the terms of the document demonstrating intent to be bound by its terms.

As a result, the appellate court dismissed the case and referred it to arbitration.

Case No. 44

ACCEPTANCE IN A SPECIFIED MANNER/

LEMON LAW/PUNITIVE DAMAGES

<u>Cintron v. Tony Royal Quality Used Cars, Inc.</u>

New York City Civil Court

132 Misc.2d 75, 503 N.Y.S.2d 230 (1986)

FACTS: Plaintiff Hector Cintron (Cintron) purchased a used 1978 Chevrolet Malibu for a price of $3039 from defendant Tony Royal Quality Used Cars, Inc. (Royal). The purchase order was a printed form provided by Royal. Above the line for the buyer's signature appeared the words, "This contract to be effective only when approved by the General Manager." While the purchase order contained a description of the 1978 Malibu, the purchase price, and the signature of Cintron, it did not contain the signature of the General Manager on the line reserved for the signature.

Cintron took delivery of the vehicle but was not provided with a proper New York State Certificate of Title or a written warranty as required by the "lemon law". Problems with the vehicle developed and Cintron returned it to Royal for repairs within the warranty period provided by the lemon law. Royal failed to make the needed repairs, in violation of the lemon law, and Cintron is now suing for the return of his purchase price and for punitive damages.

FIRST ISSUE: Did an enforceable contract exist between Cintron and Royal for the purchase of the automobile?

DECISION: No, Cintron was entitled to a full refund of the purchase price.

REASONING: In order for a contract to exist, there must be a valid offer and an acceptance. In this case Cintron created a valid offer by signing the preprinted order form drafted by Royal. However, Royal never accepted in the manner required by the contract, that is, the signature of the General Manager.

An offer can be revoked at any time prior to acceptance. The court found that when Royal refused to repair the vehicle, Cintron withdrew his offer. Hence, even though Cintron had taken delivery of the vehicle, no contract existed.

SECOND ISSUE: Is Cintron entitled to recover punitive damages from Royal even though a valid contract did not exist?

DECISION: Yes.

REASONING: When awarding punitive damages the court considers the "moral culpability of the defendant." Because Royal blatantly violated various sections of New York law involving certificates of title and the lemon law, and refused to repair the vehicle as required by law, the court awarded Cintron punitive damages even though a valid contract did not exist. The court noted that Royal's actions were a "total disregard of the public policy of this state. . . as to amount to gross, wanton and willful fraud."

Case No. 45

ACCEPTANCE

<u>1020 Park Avenue, Inc. v. Raynor</u>

New York City Civil Court

97 Misc.2d 288, 411 N.Y.S.2d 172 (1978)

FACTS: Defendant Richard Raynor (Raynor) rented a suite of offices from Plaintiff corporation named 1020 Park Avenue, Inc. (Landlord). Two terms of the lease relevant to this lawsuit were as follows: (1) The lease expired on June 30, 1978, unless the lease was renewed; and (2) Raynor had an option to renew the lease. To exercise the option he had to give written notice at least one year prior to expiration of the lease. Raynor properly gave the Landlord notice of his intention to renew more than a year before the lease expired.

Sometime after Raynor sent the renewal notice to Landlord and prior to the last day to renew the lease had he not already done so, Raynor wrote a letter to Landlord suggesting the rent should be lowered and stating that he, Raynor, "will have to give very careful consideration to renewing my lease". When the first lease term expired on June 30, 1978, Raynor continued to occupy the suite of offices. Landlord began a lawsuit to evict Raynor, claiming the second letter Raynor sent, stating he was reconsidering renewal, revoked Raynor's exercise of the option to renew the lease.

ISSUE: Can the exercise of an option to renew a lease be revoked?

DECISION: No, judgment for Raynor.

REASONING: An offer, once accepted, ripens into a contract. The acceptance cannot generally be revoked thereafter. An option in a lease is an offer by the landlord to renew the lease. When a tenant accepts the offer by exercising the option to renew, a contract for a new lease term is created, preventing the offeree from thereafter withdrawing the acceptance. Raynor's exercise of the option constituted an acceptance of the Landlord's offer to renew the lease and created a contract to extend the lease. The subsequent letter could not revoke that acceptance; hence, the Landlord cannot evict Raynor.

* * * QUESTIONS * * *
(See back of text for answers)

1)   Under what circumstances can an acceptance be revoked?

2)   Under what circumstances can an offeror revoke an offer?

3)   Why can the offeror withdraw an offer any time before acceptance but the offeree cannot normally withdraw an acceptance?

Case No. 46

OFFER AND ACCEPTANCE/REPUDIATION

<u>Camrex Contractors Marine Ltd. v. Reliance Marine Applicators, Inc.</u>

Federal Court, Eastern District of New York

579 F.Supp. 1420 (1984)

FACTS: Plaintiff corporation was in the business of maintaining ships' surfaces by grit blasting and coating them. Defendant corporation sought to hire plaintiff to service two ships. On October 27, 1978, Plaintiff sent to defendant by telex an offer to service the surface of two ships for $1.47 per square foot. Included in plaintiff's telex was a detailed statement of the work plaintiff would perform, as well as proposed schedules for the work and payment. In response, defendant sent a telex the same date with a counterproposal of $1.46 per square foot.

Also on the same day plaintiff wired back, agreeing to the price of $1.46 for one ship and asking $1.47 for the other ship, and proposing a price of $1.37 to service areas of the ships not previously mentioned. Defendant responded on October 30 saying: "With . . . reference to your telex of October 27, 1978 . . . we accept your offer as noted in our two aforementioned telexes. However regarding your request of $1.37 . . . we reserve the right to discuss same with you to a mutual satisfactory agreement when you visit us this weekend."

On November 3 plaintiff started work on one ship. Two days later, defendant informed plaintiff by telex that it was changing the contract and that it would pay $1,000,000 lump sum for the work on both ships. This arrangement would result in less money being paid to plaintiff. Plaintiff agreed to the new terms after determining they were "commercially viable".

Plaintiff wired defendant, "We accept your offer of 1,000,000 dollars ...". Defendant responded on the same day, "Reference . . . your recent offer . . . we accept."

Plaintiff finished the work then commenced this action for breach of contract.

FIRST ISSUE: Did the exchange of telexes on October 27 create a contract?

DECISION: Yes.

REASONING: An offer is a manifestation of willingness to enter into a bargain. A counteroffer is a proposed substitute bargain that terminates the original offer and continues the negotiations. Acceptance of an offer is a manifestation of assent to the terms of an offer.

In this case, the parties' conduct and expressions displayed a mutual intent to reach a binding agreement. Plaintiff's original telex, by its specificity in prices, schedules, inclusions, and exclusions, evidenced an intent to make an offer that could, upon acceptance, create a contract. Defendant's response, seeking to change the price, constituted a counteroffer. Plaintiff's response proposing another price change constituted yet another counteroffer. Defendant's response agreeing to plaintiff's counteroffer constituted an acceptance.

The fact that the parties failed to agree on a price for the extra work does not prevent a contract from arising. All the terms of a contract need not be finalized with complete certainty for a contract to be enforceable. When the parties come to agreement on the essential terms of a contract and performance has begun with an understanding that agreement on unsettled matters will follow, the contract will be enforceable although the open terms exist, provided some objective method of determining the open terms is available. Here, expert testimony on industry price standards would be an acceptable method for determining the price for the extra work if the parties could not agree.

SECOND ISSUE: Does the November exchange of telexes changing the price from a per-square-foot to a lump-sum basis constitute a modification of the contract?

DECISION: Yes, judgment for defendant.

REASONING: When one party to a contract refuses to perform the contract he thereby repudiates it. The other party can rescind the contract and seek a remedy for breach. If, however, that party chooses not to rescind and instead continues to insist on performance, such insistence may constitute a waiver of the repudiation and a forfeiture of the right to rescind. In this case defendant's insistence on the $1,000,000 lump-sum price after a contract had been made with a square-foot-price calculation may well have constituted a repudiation of the contract. Such a repudiation would have entitled plaintiff to discontinue its own performance and seek damages. However, plaintiff lost that opportunity by agreeing to the changed terms.

THIRD ISSUE: Was the modification to the contract enforceable even without consideration?

DECISION: Yes.

REASONING: A modification of a contract contained in a writing signed by the party against whom the modification is sought to be enforced does not need consideration under New York law. Here, the telexes constituted the necessary signed writings.

* * * QUESTIONS * * *
(See back of text for answers)

1) Assume defendant rejected the counteroffer of $1.46 per square foot for one ship and $1.47 for the other. Assume further that plaintiff then sent a telex stating "We accept your offer of $1.46." Would a contract then exist between the parties?

2) Assume plaintiff sent fliers to various shipyards and marinas announcing the availability for sale of ship maintenance equipment and stating the price. Do the fliers constitute an offer?

Case No. 47

OFFER/EFFECTIVE DATE

<u>Trevor v. Wood</u>

Court of Appeals

36 N.Y. 306 (1867)

FACTS: On January 30, 1860, Plaintiff Trevor & Colgate (Trevor) telegraphed from New York Defendant John Wood & Co. (Wood) in New Orleans, expressing an interest in buying One Hundred Thousand Mexican dollars. On January 31, Wood telegraphed an offer to deliver Fifty Thousand Mexican dollars at a specified price. On the same date Trevor responded by telegraph, "Your offer Fifty Thousand Mexicans, at seven and one-quarter, accepted; send more if you can." Additionally both Trevor and Wood sent letters on January 31 stating the same information contained in the telegrams. On February 1 Trevor sent another telegram reaffirming its acceptance of the previous day.

Neither the January 31 nor the February 1 telegram reached Wood until February 4 because of a problem with part of the telegraph line. Trevor did not know of the problem until February 4 when he was notified by the telegraph company. On February 3, Wood sent and Trevor received a telegram stating, "No answer to our dispatch—dollars are sold."

Trevor sued Wood for breach of contract claiming a valid contract existed between the parties as of January 31 and that Trevor was entitled to damages for breach of contract. Wood claimed no contract was ever created because Wood had not received the telegraphed acceptance.

ISSUE: Is a telegraphed acceptance effective when it is sent or when it is received?

DECISION: When it is sent; judgment for Trevor.

REASONING: To create a contract, both a valid offer and an acceptance must exist. Communication of an acceptance when dealing person to person gives the offeror immediate knowledge of the offeree's acceptance. When distance exists between the offeror and the offeree, the acceptance is effective when sent.

The January 31 telegram, when dispatched, effectively established Trevor's acceptance of Wood's offer to sell.

* * * QUESTIONS * * *
(See back of text for answers)

1) When is an offer effective?

2) When is a revocation of an offer effective?

3) Assume the following events occurred on the following days. Does a contract exist and if so on what day was it created?

December 1—Jerry received a letter from Dale in which Dale offered to sell to Jerry a motorcycle for $600.00.

December 2—Dale mailed a letter revoking the offer to sell the motorcycle.

December 3—Jerry mailed an acceptance of Dale's offer.

December 4—Jerry received Dale's letter of revocation.

Consideration

The fact that a promise has been made does not mean the promise can or will be enforced. Under Roman law, a promise was not enforceable without some sort of *causa*—that is, a reason for making the promise that was also deemed to be a sufficient reason for enforcing it. Under the common law, a primary basis for the enforcement of promises is consideration. **Consideration** is usually defined as the value (such as cash) given in return for a promise (such as the promise to sell a stamp collection on receipt of payment) or in return for a performance.

Elements of Consideration

Often, consideration is broken down into two parts: (1) something of *legally sufficient value* must be given in exchange for the promise; and (2) usually, there must be a *bargained-for* exchange.

Legal Value

The "something of legally sufficient value" may consist of (1) a promise to do something that one has no prior legal duty to do, (2) the performance of an action that one is otherwise not obligated to undertake, or (3) the refraining from an action that one has a legal right to undertake (called a **forbearance**). Consideration in bilateral contracts normally consists of a promise in return for a promise, as explained in Chapter 10. For example, suppose that in a contract for the sale of goods, the seller promises to ship specific goods to the buyer, and the buyer promises to pay for those goods when they are received. Each of these promises constitutes consideration for the contract.

In contrast, unilateral contracts involve a promise in return for a performance. Suppose that Anita says to her neighbor, "When you finish painting the garage, I will pay you $100." Anita's neighbor paints the garage. The act of painting the garage is the consideration that creates Anita's contractual obligation to pay her neighbor $100.

What if, in return for a promise to pay, a person refrains from pursuing harmful habits (a forbearance), such as the use of tobacco and alcohol? Does such forbearance constitute legally sufficient consideration? This was the issue before the court in the following case, which is one of the classics in contract law with respect to consideration.

C A S E **10.1 Hamer v. Sidway**
Court of Appeals of New York, Second Division, 1891. 124 N.Y. 538, 27 N.E. 256.

● **Background and Facts** William E. Story, Sr., was the uncle of William E. Story II. In the presence of family members and guests invited to a family gathering, the elder Story promised to pay his nephew $5,000 ($72,000 in today's dollars) if he would refrain from drinking, using tobacco, swearing, and playing cards or billiards for money until he reached the age of twenty-one. (Note that in 1869, when this contract was formed, it was legal in New York to drink and play cards for money prior to the

CASE 10.1 CONTINUED age of twenty-one.) The nephew agreed and fully performed his part of the bargain. When he reached the age of twenty-one, he wrote and told his uncle that he had kept his part of the agreement and was therefore entitled to $5,000. The uncle replied that he was pleased with his nephew's performance, writing, "I have no doubt but you have, for which you shall have five thousand dollars, as I promised you. I had the money in the bank the day you was twenty-one years old that I intend for you, and you shall have the money certain. . . . P.S. You can consider this money on interest." The nephew received his uncle's letter and thereafter consented that the money should remain with his uncle according to the terms and conditions of the letter. The uncle died about twelve years later without having paid his nephew any part of the $5,000 and interest. The executor of the uncle's estate (Franklin Sidway, the defendant in this action) claimed that there had been no valid consideration for the promise and therefore refused to pay the $5,000 (plus interest) to Louisa Hamer, a third party to whom the nephew had transferred his rights in the note. The court reviewed the case to determine whether the nephew had given valid consideration under the law.

● **Decision and Rationale** The Court of Appeals of New York disagreed with Sidway. The court ruled that the nephew had provided legally sufficient consideration by giving up smoking, drinking alcohol, swearing, and playing cards or billiards for money until he became twenty-one and was therefore entitled to the money. Sidway argued that the nephew had suffered no detriment, because what he had done was in his own best interest. The court pointed out that "in general a waiver of any legal right at the request of another party is a sufficient consideration for a promise." In this case, the court noted that "the promisee used tobacco, occasionally drank liquor, and he had a legal right to do so. That right he abandoned for a period of years upon the strength of the promise of [his uncle] that for such forbearance he would give him $5,000. * * * It is of no moment whether such performance actually proved a benefit to the promisor."

● **Impact of This Case on Today's Law** *Although this case was decided more than a century ago, the principles enunciated in the case remain applicable to contracts formed today, including online contracts. For a contract to be valid and binding, consideration must be given, and that consideration must be something of legally sufficient value.*

● **What If the Facts Were Different?** *If the nephew had not had a legal right to engage in the behavior that he agreed to forgo, would the result in this case have been different? Explain.*

Bargained-for Exchange

The second element of consideration is that it must provide the basis for the bargain struck between the contracting parties. The promise given by the promisor (offeror) must induce the promisee (offeree) to offer a return promise, a performance, or a forbearance, and the promisee's promise, performance, or forbearance must induce the promisor to make the promise.

This element of bargained-for exchange distinguishes contracts from gifts. Suppose that Paloma says to her son, "In consideration of the fact that you are not as wealthy as your brothers, I will pay you $5,000." The fact that the word *consideration* is used does not, by itself, mean that consideration has been given. Indeed, this is not an enforceable promise because the son does not have to do anything in order to receive the promised $5,000.[1] The son need not give Paloma something of legal value in return for her promise, and the promised $5,000 does not involve a bargained-for exchange. Rather, Paloma has simply stated her motive for giving her son a gift.

Does asking a bank for change for a $50 or $100 bill initiate a bargained-for exchange? The bank in the following case argued that obtaining change is not a contractual transaction because there is no consideration.

---

1. See *Fink v. Cox*, 18 Johns. 145, 9 Am.Dec. 191 (N.Y. 1820).

C A S E 10.2 Barfield v. Commerce Bank, N.A.[a]

United States Court of Appeals, Tenth Circuit, 2007. 484 F.3d 1276.
www.kscourts.org/ca10[b]

● **Background and Facts** Chris Barfield, an African American man, entered a branch of Commerce Bank, N.A., in Wichita, Kansas, and requested change for a $50 bill. He was refused change on the ground that he did not have an account with the bank. The next day, Chris Barfield's father, James Barfield, asked a white friend, John Polson, to make the same request at the bank. The teller gave Polson change without asking whether he had an account. A few minutes later, James Barfield entered the bank, asked for change for a $100 bill, and was told that he could not be given change unless he was an account holder. The Barfields filed a suit in a federal district court against Commerce Bank, alleging discrimination on the basis of race in the impairment of their ability to contract. The court granted the bank's motion to dismiss the suit for failure to state a claim. The Barfields appealed this ruling to the U.S. Court of Appeals for the Tenth Circuit.

● **Decision and Rationale** The reviewing court reversed the lower court's dismissal of the plaintiffs' complaint and remanded the case "for further proceedings in accordance with this opinion." The court pointed out that whenever a merchant denies service or refuses to engage in business with a customer attempting to contract with that merchant, there is a violation of federal law. In any event, every contract must be supported by consideration to be enforceable. "Consideration is defined as some right, interest, profit, or benefit accruing to one party, or some forbearance, detriment, loss, or responsibility, given, suffered, or undertaken by the other." In the transaction proposed by the Barfields, "they would give up something of value (a large-denomination bill) in exchange for something they valued more (smaller-denomination bills). It is hard to see why this is not a contract. * * * Consideration does not need to have quantifiable financial value * * * ." The consideration that the bank would have obtained through this exchange would have been increased goodwill and perhaps a future client. There is consideration in an exchange of paper money as there can be in any other bargained-for exchange.

● **The Ethical Dimension** *In most circumstances, parties are free to make whatever promises they wish, but only those promises made with consideration will be enforced as contracts. What is the purpose of this requirement?*

● **The Legal Environment Dimension** *The courts generally do not weigh the sufficiency of consideration according to the comparative economic value of what is exchanged. Should they? Why or why not?*

---

a. *N.A.* is an abbreviation for National Association.
b. In the first paragraph, click on "plaintiff/defendant case name." In the result, scroll through the list to the name of the case and click on it to access the opinion. Washburn University School of Law Library in Topeka, Kansas, maintains this Web site.

Adequacy of Consideration

Legal sufficiency of consideration involves the requirement that consideration be something of legally sufficient value in the eyes of the law. Adequacy of consideration involves "how much" consideration is given. Essentially, adequacy of consideration concerns the fairness of the bargain.

Courts Typically Will Not Consider Adequacy

On the surface, when the items exchanged are of unequal value, fairness would appear to be an issue. In general, however, a court will not question the adequacy of consideration based solely on the comparative value of the things exchanged. In other words, the determination of whether consideration exists does not depend on a comparison of the values of the things exchanged. Something need not be of direct economic or financial value to be considered legally sufficient consideration. In many situations, the exchange of promises and potential benefits is deemed sufficient as consideration.

Under the doctrine of freedom of contract, courts leave it up to the parties to decide what something is worth, and the parties are normally free to make bad bargains. If people could sue merely because they had entered into an unwise contract, the courts would be overloaded with frivolous suits.

Evidence of Grossly Inadequate Consideration

When there is a gross disparity in the amount or value of the consideration exchanged, the inadequate consideration may raise a red flag for a court to look more closely at the bargain. This is because shockingly inadequate consideration can indicate that fraud, duress, or undue influence was involved or that the element of bargained-for exchange was lacking.

Judges are uneasy about enforcing unequal bargains, and it is the courts' task to police contracts and make sure that there was not some defect in a contract's formation that negates mutual assent. If an elderly person sells her Mercedes-Benz convertible to her neighbor for $5,000 even though it is worth well over $50,000, the disparity in value may indicate that the sale involved undue influence or fraud. When the consideration is grossly inadequate, a court may also declare the contract unenforceable because it is unconscionable,[2] which generally means that the contract is so one sided under the circumstances as to be clearly unfair.[3] (*Unconscionability* will be discussed further in Chapter 13.)

Agreements That Lack Consideration

Sometimes, one of the parties (or both parties) to an agreement may think that consideration has been exchanged when in fact it has not. Here, we look at some situations in which the parties' promises or actions do not qualify as contractual consideration.

Preexisting Duty

Under most circumstances, a promise to do what one already has a legal duty to do does not constitute legally sufficient consideration.[4] The preexisting legal duty may be imposed by law or may arise out of a previous contract. A sheriff, for example, cannot collect a reward for providing information leading to the capture of a criminal if the sheriff already has a legal duty to capture the criminal.

Likewise, if a party is already bound by contract to perform a certain duty, that duty cannot serve as consideration for a second contract.[5] For example, Bauman-Bache, Inc., begins construction on a seven-story office building and after three months demands an extra $75,000 on its contract. If the extra $75,000 is not paid, the contractor will stop working. The owner of the land, finding no one else to complete the construction, agrees to pay the extra $75,000. The agreement is unenforceable because it is not supported by legally sufficient consideration; Bauman-Bache was bound by a preexisting contract to complete the building.

Unforeseen Difficulties The rule regarding preexisting duty is meant to prevent extortion and the so-called holdup game. What happens, though, when an honest contractor who has contracted with a landowner to construct a building runs into extraordinary difficulties that were totally unforeseen at the time the contract was formed? In the interests of fairness and equity, the courts sometimes allow exceptions to the preexisting duty rule. In the example just mentioned, if the landowner agrees to pay extra compensation to the contractor for overcoming unforeseen difficulties, the court may refrain from applying the preexisting duty rule and enforce the agreement. When the "unforeseen difficulties" that give rise to a contract modification involve the types of risks ordinarily assumed in business, however, the courts will usually assert the preexisting duty rule.[6]

---

2. Pronounced un-*kon*-shun-uh-bul.

3. See, for example, *Rissett v. W. B. Doner & Co.*, 293 F.3d 164 (4th Cir. 2002).

4. See *Foakes v. Beer*, 9 App.Cas. 605 (1884); and *Cobern v. Whatmusic Holdings, Ltd.*, 2003 WL 22073940 (Chan.Div. 2003).

5. See, for example, *Braude & Margulies, P.C. v. Fireman's Fund Insurance Co.*, 468 F.Supp.2d 190 (D.D.C. 2007).

6. Note that under Article 2 of the Uniform Commercial Code (UCC), an agreement modifying a contract needs no consideration to be binding. See UCC 2–209(1).

Rescission and New Contract The law recognizes that two parties can mutually agree to rescind, or cancel, their contract, at least to the extent that it is executory (still to be carried out). **Rescission**[7] is the unmaking of a contract so as to return the parties to the positions they occupied before the contract was made. Sometimes, parties rescind a contract and make a new contract at the same time. When this occurs, it is often difficult to determine whether there was consideration for the new contract, or whether the parties had a preexisting duty under the previous contract. If a court finds there was a preexisting duty, then the new contract will be invalid because there was no consideration.

Past Consideration

Promises made in return for actions or events that have already taken place are unenforceable. These promises lack consideration in that the element of bargained-for exchange is missing. In short, you can bargain for something to take place now or in the future but not for something that has already taken place. **Past consideration** is no consideration.

Suppose that Elsie, a real estate agent, does her friend Judy a favor by selling Judy's house and not charging any commission. Later, Judy says to Elsie, "In return for your generous act, I will pay you $3,000." This promise is made in return for past consideration and is thus unenforceable; in effect, Judy is stating her intention to give Elsie a gift.

Does prior employment constitute valid consideration for a *covenant not to compete* clause (or a *noncompete agreement*—see Chapter 13)? That was the issue in the following case.

---

7. Pronounced reh-*sih*-zhen.

C A S E **10.3** **Access Organics, Inc. v. Hernandez**
Supreme Court of Montana, 2008. 341 Mont. 73, 175 P.3d 899.

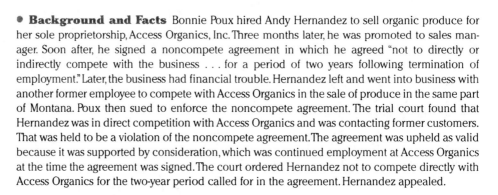

● **Background and Facts** Bonnie Poux hired Andy Hernandez to sell organic produce for her sole proprietorship, Access Organics, Inc. Three months later, he was promoted to sales manager. Soon after, he signed a noncompete agreement in which he agreed "not to directly or indirectly compete with the business . . . for a period of two years following termination of employment." Later, the business had financial trouble. Hernandez left and went into business with another former employee to compete with Access Organics in the sale of produce in the same part of Montana. Poux then sued to enforce the noncompete agreement. The trial court found that Hernandez was in direct competition with Access Organics and was contacting former customers. That was held to be a violation of the noncompete agreement. The agreement was upheld as valid because it was supported by consideration, which was continued employment at Access Organics at the time the agreement was signed. The court ordered Hernandez not to compete directly with Access Organics for the two-year period called for in the agreement. Hernandez appealed.

● **Decision and Rationale** The Montana Supreme Court reversed the decision, holding that agreements not to compete are restraints of trade that are not favored unless certain conditions are met. The court stated that although noncompete contracts are upheld in some circumstances, the agreement in this case failed for lack of consideration. If the noncompete agreement had been a part of the original employment bargain, then there might have been a bargained-for exchange. Here, Hernandez was simply told to sign the agreement when he was already working for Access Organics. His prior employment would not be consideration, because past consideration is not sufficient to support a promise. This was an "afterthought agreement" that could have been valid had it been supported by a pay increase or some other new benefit, but it was not. Hernandez received no new benefit from the agreement. Because the agreement was unsupported by consideration, it did not create an enforceable contract.

● **The Ethical Dimension** *Unless employees have access to trade secrets or other proprietary information, is it ethical to require them to sign noncompete agreements as a condition of employment? Explain your answer.*

CASE 10.3 CONTINUED ● **The Legal Environment Dimension** *How could Access Organics have obtained a non-compete agreement from Hernandez that would have been enforceable?*

Illusory Promises

If the terms of the contract express such uncertainty of performance that the promisor has not definitely promised to do anything, the promise is said to be *illusory*—without consideration and unenforceable. A promise is illusory when it fails to bind the promisor. For example, a corporate president says to her employees, "All of you have worked hard, and if profits continue to remain high, a 10 percent bonus at the end of the year will be given—if management thinks it is warranted." The employees continue to work hard, and profits remain high, but no bonus is given. This is an *illusory promise*, or no promise at all, because performance depends solely on the discretion of the president (the management). There is no bargained-for consideration, only a declaration that management may or may not do something in the future. The president is not obligated (incurs no detriment) now or later.

Option-to-Cancel Clauses Option-to-cancel clauses in term contracts sometimes present problems in regard to consideration. When the promisor has the option to cancel the contract before performance has begun, then the promise is illusory. Suppose that Abe contracts to hire Chris for one year at $5,000 per month, reserving the right to cancel the contract at any time. On close examination of these words, you can see that Abe has not actually agreed to hire Chris, as Abe could cancel without liability before Chris started performance. This contract is therefore illusory. But if Abe had instead reserved the right to cancel the contract at any time *after* Chris has begun performance by giving Chris *thirty days' notice,* the promise would not be illusory. Abe, by saying that he will give Chris thirty days' notice, is relinquishing the opportunity (legal right) to hire someone else instead of Chris for a thirty-day period. If Chris works for one month, at the end of which Abe gives him thirty days' notice, Chris has an enforceable claim for $10,000 in salary.[8]

Requirements Contracts and Output Contracts Problems with consideration may also arise in other types of contracts because of uncertainty of performance.[9] Uncertain performance is characteristic of requirements and output contracts, for example. In a *requirements contract,* a buyer and a seller agree that the buyer will purchase from the seller all of the goods of a designated type that the buyer needs, or requires. In an *output contract,* the buyer and seller agree that the buyer will purchase from the seller all of what the seller produces, or the seller's output. These types of contracts will be discussed further in Chapter 20. *Concept Summary 10.1* on the next page provides a convenient summary of the main aspects of consideration.

Settlement of Claims

Businesspersons or others can settle legal claims in several ways, and it is important to understand the nature of consideration given in these kinds of settlement agreements, or contracts. In an *accord and satisfaction,* which is a common means of settling a claim, a debtor offers to pay a lesser amount than the creditor purports to be owed. Other common methods used to settle claims include a *release* and a *covenant not to sue.*

Accord and Satisfaction

The concept of **accord and satisfaction** involves a debtor's offer of payment and a creditor's acceptance of a lesser amount than the creditor originally claimed was owed. The *accord* is the agreement under which one of the parties undertakes to give or perform—and the other to accept, in satisfaction of a claim—something other than that on which the parties originally agreed. *Satisfaction* takes place when the accord is executed. A basic rule is that there can be no satisfaction unless there is first an accord. For accord and satisfaction to occur, the amount of the debt *must be in dispute.*

---

8. For another example, see *Vanegas v. American Energy Services,* 224 S.W.3d 544 (Tex. App.—Eastland 2007).

9. See, for example, *Johnson Controls, Inc. v. TRW Vehicle Safety Systems,* 491 F.Supp.2d 707 (E.D.Mich. 2007).

ELEMENTS OF CONSIDERATION	Consideration is the value given in exchange for a promise. A contract cannot be formed without sufficient consideration. Consideration is often broken down into two elements: 1. *Legal value*—Something of legally sufficient value must be given in exchange for a promise. This may consist of a promise, a performance, or a forbearance. 2. *Bargained-for exchange*—There must be a bargained-for exchange.
ADEQUACY OF CONSIDERATION	Adequacy of consideration relates to how much consideration is given and whether a fair bargain was reached. Courts will inquire into the adequacy of consideration (if the consideration is legally sufficient) only when fraud, undue influence, duress, or the lack of a bargained-for exchange may be involved.
AGREEMENTS THAT LACK CONSIDERATION	Consideration is lacking in the following situations: 1. *Preexisting duty*—Consideration is not legally sufficient if one is either by law or by contract under a *preexisting duty* to perform the action being offered as consideration for a new contract. 2. *Past consideration*—Actions or events that have already taken place do not constitute legally sufficient consideration. 3. *Illusory promises*—When the nature or extent of performance is too uncertain, the promise is rendered illusory and unenforceable.

Liquidated Debts If a debt is *liquidated,* accord and satisfaction cannot take place. A liquidated debt is one whose amount has been ascertained, fixed, agreed on, settled, or exactly determined. For example, if Kwan signs an installment loan contract with her banker in which she agrees to pay a specified rate of interest on a specified amount of borrowed funds at monthly intervals for two years, that is a liquidated debt. The total obligation is precisely known to both parties, and reasonable persons cannot dispute the amount owed.

Suppose that Kwan has missed her last two payments on the loan and the creditor demands that she pay the overdue debt. Kwan makes a partial payment and states that she believes this payment is all she should have to pay and that the debt will be satisfied if the creditor accepts the payment. In the majority of states, acceptance of a lesser sum than the entire amount of a liquidated debt is *not* satisfaction, and the balance of the debt is still legally owed. The rationale for this rule is that the debtor has not given any consideration to satisfy the obligation of paying the balance to the creditor—because the debtor has a preexisting legal obligation to pay the entire debt.

Unliquidated Debts An *unliquidated debt* is the opposite of a liquidated debt. Here, reasonable persons may differ over the amount owed. It is not settled,

fixed, agreed on, ascertained, or determined, and thus acceptance of the payment of a lesser amount operates as satisfaction, or discharge, of the debt. For example, Devereaux goes to the dentist's office and the dentist tells him that he needs three special types of gold inlays. The price is not discussed, and there is no standard fee for this type of procedure. Devereaux has the work done and leaves the office. At the end of the month, the dentist sends him a bill for $3,000.

Devereaux, believing that this amount grossly exceeds what a reasonable person would believe the debt owed should be, sends a check for $2,000. On the back of the check he writes, "payment in full for three gold inlays." The dentist cashes the check. Because the situation involves an unliquidated debt—the amount has not been agreed on—the payment accepted by the dentist normally will eradicate the debt. One argument to support this rule is that the parties give up a legal right to contest the amount in dispute, and thus consideration is given.

Release

A **release** is a contract in which one party forfeits the right to pursue a legal claim against the other party. It bars any further recovery beyond the terms stated in the release. For example, your car is damaged in an automobile accident caused by Donovan's negligence. Donovan offers to give you $1,000 if you will release him from further liability resulting from the accident. You believe that this amount will cover your damages, so you agree and sign the release. Later, you discover that it will cost $1,500 to repair your car. Can you collect the balance from Donovan?

The answer is normally no; you are limited to the $1,000 specified in the release because the release represents a valid contract. You and Donovan both agreed to the bargain, and sufficient consideration was present. The consideration was the legal detriment you suffered (by releasing Donovan from liability, you forfeited your right to sue to recover damages in exchange for $1,000).

Clearly, you are better off if you know the extent of your injuries or damages before signing a release. Releases will generally be binding if they are (1) given in good faith, (2) stated in a signed writing (which is required in many states), and (3) accompanied by consideration.[10]

Covenant Not to Sue

A **covenant not to sue** is an agreement to substitute a contractual obligation for some other type of legal action based on a valid claim. Unlike a release, a covenant not to sue does not always bar further recovery. Suppose (continuing the earlier example) that you agree with Donovan not to sue for damages in a tort action if he will pay for the damage to your car. If Donovan fails to pay, you can bring an action against him for breach of contract.

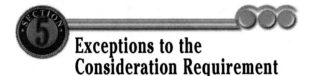

Exceptions to the Consideration Requirement

There are some exceptions to the rule that only promises supported by consideration are enforceable. The following types of promises may be enforced despite the lack of consideration:

1. Promises that induce detrimental reliance, under the doctrine of promissory estoppel.
2. Promises to pay debts that are barred by a statute of limitations.
3. Promises to make charitable contributions.

Promissory Estoppel

As discussed in Chapter 11, under the doctrine of *promissory estoppel* (also called *detrimental reliance*), a person who has reasonably and substantially relied on the promise of another may be able to obtain some measure of recovery. This doctrine is applied in a wide variety of contexts in which a promise is otherwise unenforceable, such as when a promise is not supported by consideration. Under this doctrine, a court may enforce an otherwise unenforceable promise to avoid the injustice that would otherwise result.

Requirements to State a Claim for Promissory Estoppel For the doctrine to be applied, the following elements are required:

1. There must be a clear and definite promise.
2. The promisor should have expected that the promisee would rely on the promise.
3. The promisee reasonably relied on the promise by acting or refraining from some act.
4. The promisee's reliance was definite and resulted in substantial detriment.
5. Enforcement of the promise is necessary to avoid injustice.

If these requirements are met, a promise may be enforced even though it is not supported by consideration.[11] In essence, the promisor will be *estopped* (prevented) from asserting the lack of consideration as a defense.

Application of the Doctrine Promissory estoppel was originally applied to situations involving gifts (I promise to pay you $350 a week so that you will not have to work) and donations to charities (I promise to contribute $50,000 a year toward the orphanage). Later, courts began to apply the doctrine to avoid inequity or hardship in other situations, including business transactions.

For example, the Air Force has opened the bidding process for construction of a new building at Elmendorf Air Force Base in Anchorage, Alaska. A general contractor, Vern Hickel, anxious to get the job, contacts eight different subcontractors to find the lowest price on electrical work. Bussell, an electrical subcontractor, tells Hickel that he will do the electrical portion of the project for $477,498. Hickel reasonably relies on this amount when he submits his primary bid for the entire project to the Air Force and wins the contract. After the bidding is over, Bussell realizes that he made

---

10. Under the UCC, a written, signed waiver or renunciation by an aggrieved party discharges any further liability for a breach, even without consideration.

11. *Restatement (Second) of Contracts*, Section 90.

CONTEMPORARY LEGAL DEBATES
Promissory Estoppel and Employment Contracts

Today, approximately 85 percent of American workers have the legal status of "employees at will." Under this common law employment doctrine, which applies in all states except Montana, an employer may fire an employee for any reason or no reason. The at-will doctrine, however, does not apply to any employee who has an employment contract or who falls under the protection of a state or federal statute—which is, of course, a large number of employees. Even when an employee is subject to the employment-at-will doctrine, the courts sometimes make exceptions to the doctrine based on tort theory or contract principles or on the ground that a termination violates an established public policy (see Chapter 33).

These exceptions to the at-will doctrine, however, apply only when a current employee's employment is *terminated.* Should they also apply when a company fails to *hire* a job candidate after promising to do so? For example, a job candidate, relying on a company's offer of employment, quits his or her existing job, moves to another city, and rents or buys housing in the new location. Then the company decides not to hire the candidate after all. Given the candidate's detrimental reliance on the company's job offer, should the company be prevented from revoking its offer under the doctrine of promissory estoppel? This question has come before a number of courts. As yet, however, the courts have not reached a consensus on the issue. Some jurisdictions allow the doctrine of promissory estoppel to be applied, but others do not.

Promissory Estoppel Should Not Be Applied

Many jurisdictions believe that reliance on a prospective employer's promise of at-will employment is unreasonable as a matter of law. Courts in these jurisdictions reason that a job applicant should know that, even if she or he is hired, the employer could terminate the employment at any time for any reason without liability. According to these courts, it would be contrary to reason to allow someone who has not yet begun work to recover damages under a theory of promissory estoppel, given that the same person's job could be terminated without liability one day after beginning work.

Consider a case example. Arlie Thompson had worked for nine years at a hospital as a technician assistant when she was laid off. A year later, the same hospital offered her a clerical position, which she accepted. She was measured for a new uniform, given a security badge, and provided with the password for the computer system. Thompson, who was then working at another job, quit the other position in reliance on the hospital's job offer. Shortly thereafter, the hospital asked her to take a test. When she failed the test, the hospital refused to hire her. Thompson filed a suit claiming that the doctrine of promissory estoppel should prevent the hospital from revoking its offer. The court, however, held that the hospital's promise of employment was not sufficiently "clear and definite" for that doctrine to be applied.[a]

a. *Thompson v. Bridgeport Hospital,* 2001 WL 823130 (Conn.Super. 2001). See also *Lower v. Electronic Data Systems Corp.,* 494 F.Supp.2d 770 (S.D. Ohio 2007); and *Rice v. NN, Inc., Ball & Roller Division,* 210 S.W.3d 536 (Tenn.Ct.App. 2006).

---

a mistake and refuses to perform the electrical work for Hickel for $477,498. Hickel has to hire another subcontractor at a substantially higher cost to complete the electrical work.

Under the doctrine of promissory estoppel, Hickel can sue Bussell for the cost difference because he detrimentally relied on Bussell's bid even though there was no consideration for Bussell's promise to do the work for $477,498.[12] (See this chapter's *Contemporary Legal*

Debates feature for a discussion of promissory estoppel and promises of employment.)

Promises to Pay Debts Barred by a Statute of Limitations

Statutes of limitations in all states require a creditor to sue within a specified period to recover a debt. If the creditor fails to sue in time, recovery of the debt is barred by the statute of limitations. A debtor who promises to pay a previous debt even though recovery is barred by the statute of limitations makes an enforceable promise. *The promise needs no consideration.* (Some states, however, require that it be in writing.) In effect, the promise extends the limitations period, and

---

12. See *Alaska Bussell Electric Co. v. Vern Hickel Construction Co.,* 688 P.2d 576 (1984); also see *Commerce Bancorp, Inc. v. BK International Insurance Brokers, Ltd.,* 490 F.Supp.2d 556 (D.N.J. 2007).

Promissory Estoppel Should Be Applied

A number of other jurisdictions, however, have held that a person can recover damages incurred as a result of resigning from a former job in reliance on an offer of at-will employment. These jurisdictions have determined that when a prospective employer knows or should know that a promise of employment will induce the future employee to leave his or her current job, the employer should be responsible for the prospective employee's damages. After all, without the offer from the prospective employer, the prospective employee would have continued to work in his or her prior position.

This approach is reflected in a case from 2007 involving Thomas Frey. In 1999, Frey was working for a firm at which he had substantial benefits and would have been entitled to stock options. Then Andrew Taitz of Workhorse Custom Chassis, LLC, offered Frey a position, promising him a large bonus if the company's earnings exceeded $39.1 million by the end of 2002. In reliance on that promise, Frey left his job and took the position at Workhorse.

By the end of 2002, projections indicated that Workhorse's earnings would exceed the required level. Frey therefore believed that he was entitled to the bonus when he left the company in January 2003. In the spring of 2003, Frey asked for his bonus, but Taitz responded that because Frey no longer worked for the company, he was not entitled to the bonus. Frey filed a lawsuit against Workhorse, claiming, among other things, that he was entitled to damages under the doctrine of promissory estoppel

because he had left a lucrative and secure position to take the job at Workhorse.

Although Workhorse claimed at the trial that its 2002 earnings were only around $37.6 million, the audited financial statements it presented had been completed ten months late and were subject to a 5 percent margin of error. Workhorse also admitted that many employees would have received substantial bonuses if the earnings had exceeded $39.1 million. A jury found Frey's argument convincing and awarded him $648,220. Workhorse moved for a judgment as a matter of law and for a new trial, but the court ruled that Frey had presented enough evidence to support the jury's verdict.[b]

WHERE DO YOU STAND?

Some jurisdictions maintain that it is irrational to apply the doctrine of promissory estoppel to a promise of at-will employment, given that the employee could be fired after working for only one day on the job. Other jurisdictions conclude that the doctrine should apply because the employer should reasonably expect a job candidate in this situation to act in reliance on the promise. Does one of these two arguments have greater merit than the other? What is your position on this issue?

---

b. *Frey v. Workhorse Custom Chassis, LLC,* ___ F.Supp.2d ___ (S.D.Ind. 2007). For a case allowing a job candidate to recover damages from a prospective employer, see *Goff-Hamel v. Obstetricians & Gynecologists, P.C.,* 256 Neb. 19, 588 N.W.2d 798 (1999).

---

the creditor can sue to recover the entire debt or at least the amount promised. The promise can be implied if the debtor acknowledges the barred debt by making a partial payment.

Charitable Subscriptions

Subscriptions to religious, educational, and charitable institutions are promises to make gifts. Traditionally, these promises were unenforceable because they are not supported by legally sufficient consideration. A gift, after all, is the opposite of bargained-for consideration. The modern view, however, is to make exceptions to the general rule by applying the doctrine of promissory estoppel.

Suppose that a church solicits and receives pledges (commitments to contribute funds) from church members to erect a new church building. On the basis of these pledges, the church purchases land, hires architects, and makes other contracts that change its position. Because of the church's detrimental reliance, a court may enforce the pledges under the theory of promissory estoppel. Alternatively, a court may find consideration in the fact that each promise was made in reliance on the other promises of support or that the trustees, by accepting the subscriptions, impliedly promised to complete the proposed undertaking.

REVIEWING Consideration

John operates a motorcycle repair shop from his home but finds that his business is limited by the small size of his garage. Driving by a neighbor's property, he notices a for-sale sign on a large, metal-sided garage. John contacts the neighbor and offers to buy the building, hoping that it can be dismantled and moved to his own property. The neighbor accepts John's payment and makes a generous offer in return: if John will help him dismantle the garage, which will take a substantial amount of time, he will help John reassemble it after it has been transported to John's property. They agree to have the entire job completed within two weeks. John spends every day for a week working with his neighbor to disassemble the building. In his rush to acquire a larger workspace, he turns down several lucrative repair jobs. Once the disassembled building has been moved to John's property, however, the neighbor refuses to help John reassemble it as he originally promised. Using the information presented in the chapter, answer the following questions.

1. Are the basic elements of consideration present in the neighbor's promise to help John reassemble the garage? Why or why not?

2. Suppose that the neighbor starts to help John but then realizes that, because of the layout of John's property, putting the building back together will take much more work than dismantling it took. Under which principle discussed in the chapter might the neighbor be allowed to ask for additional compensation?

3. What if John's neighbor made his promise to help reassemble the garage at the time he and John were moving it to John's property, saying, "Since you helped me take it down, I will help you put it back up." Would John be able to enforce this promise? Why or why not?

4. Under what doctrine discussed in the chapter might John seek to recover the profits he lost when he declined to do repair work for one week?

TERMS AND CONCEPTS

accord and satisfaction

consideration
covenant not to sue
forbearance
past consideration

release
rescission

QUESTIONS AND CASE PROBLEMS

12–1. Tabor is a buyer of file cabinets manufactured by Martin. Martin's contract with Tabor calls for delivery of fifty file cabinets at $40 per cabinet in five equal installments. After delivery of two installments (twenty cabinets), Martin informs Tabor that because of inflation, Martin is losing money and will promise to deliver the remaining thirty cabinets only if Tabor will pay $50 per cabinet. Tabor agrees in writing to do so. Discuss whether Martin can legally collect the additional $100 on delivery to Tabor of the next installment of ten cabinets.

12–2. QUESTION WITH SAMPLE ANSWER

Bernstein owns a lot and wants to build a house according to a particular set of plans and specifications. She solicits bids from building contractors and receives three bids: one from Carlton for $160,000, one from Friend for $158,000, and one from Shade for $153,000. She accepts Shade's bid. One month after beginning construction of the house, Shade contacts Bernstein and informs her that because of inflation and a recent price hike for materials, he will not finish the house unless Bernstein agrees to pay an extra $13,000. Bernstein reluctantly agrees to pay the additional sum. After the house is finished, however, Bernstein refuses to pay the extra $13,000. Discuss whether Bernstein is legally required to pay this additional amount.

- **For a sample answer to Question 12–2, go to Appendix C at the end of this text.**

12–3. Daniel, a recent college graduate, is on his way home for the Christmas holidays from his new job. He gets caught in a snowstorm and is taken in by an elderly couple, who provide him with food and shelter. After the snowplows have cleared the road, Daniel proceeds home. Daniel's father, Fred, is most appreciative of the elderly couple's action and in a letter promises to pay them $500. The elderly couple, in need of funds, accept Fred's offer. Then, because of a dispute between Daniel and Fred, Fred refuses to pay the elderly couple the $500. Discuss whether the couple can hold Fred liable in contract for the services rendered to Daniel.

12–4. Costello hired Sagan to drive his racing car in a race. Sagan's friend Gideon promised to pay Sagan $3,000 if she won the race. Sagan won the race, but Gideon refused to pay the $3,000. Gideon contended that no legally binding contract had been formed because he had received no consideration from Sagan in exchange for his promise to pay the $3,000. Sagan sued Gideon for breach of contract, arguing that winning the race was the consideration given in exchange for Gideon's promise to pay the $3,000. What rule of law discussed in this chapter supports Gideon's claim?

12–5. Accord and Satisfaction. E. S. Herrick Co. grows and sells blueberries. Maine Wild Blueberry Co. agreed to buy all of Herrick's 1990 crop under a contract that left the price unliquidated. Herrick delivered the berries, but a dispute arose over the price. Maine Wild sent Herrick a check with a letter stating that the check was the "final settlement." Herrick cashed the check but filed a suit in a Maine state court against Maine Wild, on the ground of breach of contract, alleging that the buyer owed more. What will the court likely decide in this case? Why? [*E. S. Herrick Co. v. Maine Wild Blueberry Co.,* 670 A.2d 944 (Me. 1996)]

12–6. CASE PROBLEM WITH SAMPLE ANSWER

As a child, Martha Carr once visited her mother's 108-acre tract of unimproved land in Richland County, South Carolina. In 1968, Betty and Raymond Campbell leased the land. Carr, a resident of New York, was diagnosed as having schizophrenia and depression in 1986, was hospitalized five or six times, and subsequently took prescription drugs for the illnesses. In 1996, Carr inherited the Richland property and, two years later, contacted the Campbells about selling the land. Carr asked Betty about the value of the land, and Betty said that the county tax assessor had determined that the land's *agricultural value* was $54,000. The Campbells knew at the time that the county had assessed the total property value at $103,700 for tax purposes. A real estate appraiser found that the *real market value* of the property was $162,000. On August 6, Carr signed a contract to sell the land to the Campbells for $54,000. Believing the price to be unfair, however, Carr did not deliver the deed. The Campbells filed a suit in a South Carolina state court against Carr, seeking specific performance of the contract. At trial, an expert real estate appraiser testified that the real market value of the property was $162,000 at the time of the contract. Under what circumstances will a court examine the adequacy of consideration? Are those circumstances present in this case? Should the court enforce the contract between Carr and the Campbells? Explain. [*Campbell v. Carr,* 361 S.C. 258, 603 S.E.2d 625 (S.C. App. 2004)]

- **To view a sample answer for Problem 12–6, go to this book's Web site at www.cengage.com/blaw/jentz, select "Chapter 12," and click on "Case Problem with Sample Answer."**

12–7. Preexisting Duty. New England Rock Services, Inc., agreed to work as a subcontractor on a sewer project on which Empire Paving, Inc., was the general contractor. For drilling and blasting a certain amount of rock, Rock Services was to be paid $29 per cubic yard or on a time-and-materials basis, whichever was less. From the beginning, Rock Services encountered problems. The primary obstacle was a heavy concentration of water, which, according to the custom in the industry, Empire should have controlled but did not. Rock Services was compelled to use more costly and time-consuming methods than anticipated, and it was unable to complete the work on time. The subcontractor asked Empire to pay for the rest of the project on a time-and-materials basis. Empire signed a modification of the original agreement. On completion of the work, Empire refused to pay Rock Services the balance due under the modification. Rock Services filed a suit in a Connecticut state court against Empire. Empire claimed that the modification lacked consideration and was thus not valid and enforceable. Is Empire right? Why or why not? [*New England Rock Services, Inc. v. Empire Paving, Inc.,* 53 Conn. App. 771, 731 A.2d 784 (1999)]

12–8. Consideration. In 1995, Helikon Furniture Co. appointed Tom Gaede as an independent sales agent for the sale of its products in parts of Texas. The parties signed a one-year contract that specified, among other things, the commissions that Gaede would receive. Over a year later, although the parties had not signed a new contract, Gaede was still representing Helikon when it was acquired by a third party. Helikon's new management allowed Gaede to continue to perform for the same commissions and sent him a letter stating that it would make no changes in its sales representatives "for at least the next year." Three months later, in December 1997, the new managers sent Gaede a letter proposing new terms for a contract. Gaede continued to sell Helikon products until May 1997, when he received a letter effectively reducing the amount of his commissions. Gaede filed a suit in a Texas state court against Helikon, alleging breach of contract. Helikon argued, in part, that there was no contract because there was no consideration. In whose favor should the court rule, and why? [*Gaede v. SK Investments, Inc.*, 38 S.W.3d 753 (Tex. App.—Houston [14 Dist.] 2001)]

12-9. Settlement of Claims. In Gulf Shores, Alabama, Shoreline Towers Condominium Owners Association authorized Resort Development, Inc. (RDI), to manage Shoreline's property. On Shoreline's behalf, RDI obtained a property insurance policy from Zurich American Insurance Co. In October 1995, Hurricane Opal struck Gulf Shores. RDI filed claims with Zurich regarding damage to Shoreline's property. Zurich determined that the cost of the damage was $334,901. Zurich then subtracted an applicable $40,000 deductible and sent checks to RDI totaling $294,901. RDI disputed the amount. Zurich eventually agreed to issue a check for an additional $86,000 in return for RDI's signing a "Release of All Claims." Later, contending that the deductible had been incorrectly applied and that this was a breach of contract, among other things, Shoreline filed a suit against Zurich in a federal district court. How, if at all, should the agreement reached by RDI and Zurich affect Shoreline's claim? Explain. [*Shoreline Towers Condominium Owners Association, Inc. v. Zurich American Insurance Co.*, 196 F.Supp.2d 1210 (S.D. Ala. 2002)]

12-10. A QUESTION OF ETHICS

John Sasson and Emily Springer met in January 2002. John worked for the U.S. Army as an engineer. Emily was an attorney with a law firm. Six months later, John bought a townhouse in Randolph, New Jersey, and asked Emily to live with him. She agreed but retained the ownership of her home in Monmouth Beach. John paid the mortgage and the other expenses on the townhouse. He urged Emily to quit her job and work from "our house." In May 2003, Emily took John's advice and started her own law practice. In December, John made her the beneficiary of his $150,000 individual retirement account (IRA) and said that he would give her his 2002 BMW M3 car before the end of the next year. He proposed to her in September 2004, giving her a diamond engagement ring and promising to "take care of her" for the rest of her life. Less than a month later, John was critically injured by an accidental blow to his head during a basketball game and died. On behalf of John's estate, which was valued at $1.1 million, his brother Steven filed a complaint in a New Jersey state court to have Emily evicted from the townhouse. Given these facts, consider the following questions. [In re Estate of Sasson, 387 N.J.Super. 459, 904 A.2d 769 (App. Div. 2006)]

(a) Based on John's promise to "take care of her" for the rest of her life, Emily claimed that she was entitled to the townhouse, the BMW, and an additional portion of John's estate. Under what circumstances would such a promise constitute a valid, enforceable contract? Does John's promise meet these requirements? Why or why not?

(b) Whether or not John's promise is legally binding, is there an ethical basis on which it should be enforced? Is there an ethical basis for not enforcing it? Are there any circumstances under which a promise of support should be—or should not be—enforced? Discuss.

LAW ON THE WEB

For updated links to resources available on the Web, as well as a variety of other materials, visit this text's Web site at

www.cengage.com/blaw/jentz

To find recent cases on contract law, access Cornell University's School of Law site at

www.law.cornell.edu/wex/index.php/Contracts

Legal Research Exercises on the Web

Go to **www.cengage.com/blaw/jentz**, the Web site that accompanies this text. Select "Chapter 12" and click on "Internet Exercises." There you will find the following Internet research exercises that you can perform to learn more about the topics covered in this chapter.

Internet Exercise 12–1: Legal Perspective
Legal Value of Consideration

Internet Exercise 12–2: Management Perspective
Promissory Estoppel

Internet Exercise 12–3: International Perspective
Contract Consideration in Canada

Contracts: Consideration

Case No. 48

ADEQUACY OF CONSIDERATION

Kirshner v. Spinella

District Court, Suffolk County

73 Misc.2d 962, 343 N.Y.S.2d 298 (1973)

FACTS: Plaintiff Alfred Barry Kirshner (Kirshner) was the owner and operator of a teachers' employment service. Defendant Vincent Spinella (Spinella) was a teacher and a client of Kirshner. Spinella and Kirshner entered a contract that stated that if Kirshner assisted Spinella in locating a job, Spinella would pay Kirshner a specified fee. If Spinella obtained a position exclusively through his own efforts, he would not pay Kirshner anything. Spinella was required to notify Kirshner by registered mail of any positions for which he applied without Kirshner's assistance. The contract further provided that if Spinella breached the contract and Kirshner had to sue to collect his fee, he could recover his attorney's fees as well.

Spinella, without Kirshner's help, sought employment at a school on Fisher Island. Spinella failed to notify Kirshner of these efforts. Some time after Spinella applied, Kirshner, unaware that Spinella had applied, contacted the school and attempted to arrange an interview for Spinella, and refrained from referring any other of Kirshner's clients to that school. At the time Kirshner called the school on behalf of Spinella, Spinella had already been offered and accepted the job.

Kirshner claims Spinella owed Kirshner a fee. Spinella claimed Kirshner's services did not constitute consideration because Spinella had been offered the job before Kirshner contacted the school.

FIRST ISSUE: Does Kirshner's phone call and his refraining from referring other clients to the Fisher Island school opening constitute consideration for Spinella's promise to pay a fee?

DECISION: Yes, judgment for Kirshner.

REASONING: Consideration is required for a contract to be enforceable. The value of the things exchanged need not be equal nor near equal in value provided the parties agreed to the specified consideration. The court stated, ". . . the rule in this state is that even the slightest consideration is sufficient to support the most onerous obligation . . . It is for the parties to determine, at the time the contract is entered into, and not for the court when it is sought to be enforced, whether adequate consideration is provided for . . .".

Kirshner obtained information about the position at Fisher's Island School and arranged for an interview for Spinella. Although Spinella had already been offered the position, his failure to so notify Kirshner resulted in Kirshner's spending time and effort in attempting to arrange an interview.

SECOND ISSUE: Is Kirshner entitled to recover from Spinella money to cover the cost of Kirshner's attorney's fees incurred in pursuing this matter?

DECISION: Yes, judgment for Kirshner.

REASONING: Ordinarily, the successful party in a lawsuit cannot collect the cost of attorney's fees from the losing party. However, if a valid contract between the parties specifically states that attorney's fees are recoverable, that provision may be enforceable.

* * * QUESTIONS * * *
(See back of text for answers)

1) In order for a contract to be valid it must be supported by legally sufficient consideration. Compare the concept of sufficiency of consideration with adequacy of consideration.

2) Jane won four million dollars in the New York State lottery. As a result she offered to sell to her good friend John her one-month-old Pontiac for $5.00.

   a) Identify the consideration given by Jane and by John.

   b) Is the consideration legally sufficient?

   c) Is the consideration adequate?

Case No. 49

CONSIDERATION/FORBEARANCE

<u>Hamer v. Sidway</u>

Court of Appeals

124 N.Y. 538 (1891)

FACTS: On March 20, 1869, William E. Story, Sr. (Story) promised to pay his sixteen-year-old nephew William E. Story II (William), five thousand dollars if William would refrain from drinking, using tobacco, swearing and playing cards or billiards for money until he was twenty-one years old. On his twenty-first birthday, January 31, 1875, William informed Story by letter that he had performed his end of the agreement and requested the five thousand dollars. Story acknowledged William's right to the money in a letter dated February 6, 1875, but recommended he hold the money for safekeeping until William was older. William consented to this arrangement.

Story died twelve years later without having paid William the five thousand dollars. The Executor of Story's estate (Sidway) refused to pay the five thousand dollars, claiming that William did not give consideration for Story's promise to pay.

ISSUE: Did William's promise to refrain from drinking, using tobacco, swearing and playing cards or billiards for money constitute consideration for Story's promise to pay five thousand dollars?

DECISION: Yes; Story's estate must pay the five thousand dollars.

REASONING: Generally the waiver of a legal right that is bargained for by the other party to a contract is sufficient consideration. William's promise to refrain from engaging in activities that he had a legal right to engage in is forbearance and constitutes sufficient consideration to support the uncle's promise to pay five thousand dollars.

* * * QUESTIONS * * *
(See back of text for answers)

1) Assume an uncle promised to give his sixteen-year-old nephew five thousand dollars on the nephew's eighteenth birthday provided the nephew refrains from purchasing any alcoholic beverages until he reaches the age of eighteen. The nephew refrains from purchasing alcoholic beverages during the two-year period. Does the nephew have a contractual right to the money? Why or why not?

2) Assume a grandfather promised to give his grandson four hundred dollars as a birthday gift. If the grandfather fails to pay the money, does the grandson have a contractual right to enforce the promise?

Case No. 50

UNJUST ENRICHMENT/RULES OF CONSTRUCTION/BEST EFFORTS

<u>Strauss Paper Co., Inc. v. RSA Executive Search, Inc.</u>

Appellate Division, Second Department

260 A.D.2d 570, 688N.Y.S.2d 641 (1999)

FACTS: Strauss Paper Company (Strauss) entered into an agreement with RSA Executive Search (RSA) wherein RSA agreed to "find an ideal candidate for the senior sales management position" at Strauss. The agreement "guaranteed" the candidate and included a provision that the "entire fee will be earned upon placement completion". The agreement also provided that if the referral candidate resigned or was terminated within 180 days of hiring RSA would use its "best efforts to replace the candidate at no additional charge". The agreement did not define the term "best efforts".

Strauss hired one of the referral candidates and remitted one-half of the placement fee. Four months later Strauss terminated the referral candidate's employment. Strauss demanded the return of the portion of the placement fee it had previously paid. RSA did not return the portion of the fee it had been paid and claimed that the language in the contract entitled it to the full fee. RSA contended that the fee was collectable upon "placement," that it had fulfilled its obligation, and that, in any event, it was permitted to use its "best efforts" to find a suitable replacement candidate. The trial court disagreed and granted Strauss' motion for summary judgment alleging unjust enrichment. RSA appealed.

ISSUE: Is a contract that contains several ambiguous terms and a clause expressly providing that a party use its "best efforts" where the term "best efforts' is not defined, enforceable?

DECISION: No

REASONING: Strauss was entitled under the theory of unjust enrichment to recover the portion of the fee it had paid after terminating the referral candidate. When a contract contains unclear terms a court will apply various rules of interpretation to determine the intent of the parties. A contract will be interpreted as a whole with specific clauses interpreted in light of the general intention of the parties. Additionally, when a party uses an ambiguous term a court will strictly interpret that term against the drafting party. In this case the "guarantee" immediately preceded the 180-day probationary period and indicated that the fee would be paid on "placement completion", not simply "placement" as RSA contended. Applying the rules of interpretation as a whole and strict construction against the drafting party, Strauss' interpretation is reasonable in light of the circumstances. They were guaranteed a suitable candidate and the fee for such was not payable until the successful permanent placement was made. This did not occur, hence, they were entitled to a return of the partial payment.

Regarding the "best efforts" clause, the court noted that clear guidelines to are required to determine how to measure these efforts. Because this term was not defined in the contract the clause was unenforceable.

Case No. 51

ACCORD AND SATISFACTION

Century 21 Kaaterskill Realty v. Grasso

Appellate Division, Third Department

124 A.D.2d 316, 508 N.Y.S.2d 99 (1986)

FACTS: Defendant Savino Grasso (Grasso) owned real property he wanted to sell. He hired plaintiff Century 21 Kaaterskill Realty (Century 21) as the broker for the sale and agreed to pay Century 21 10% of the sale price as a commission. The property sold for $82,000.00 and Century 21 sought payment from Grasso of $8,200.00. Grasso's attorney sent a check to Century 21 for $6000.00 and included the following notation on it: "In full accord and satisfaction for any real estate commission claimed by Century 21 against . . . Grasso". An officer of Century 21 endorsed and deposited the check.

In this action, Century 21 sued for the unpaid balance of the commission—$2200.00. Grasso defended on the basis that an accord and satisfaction occurred when Century 21 deposited the check.

ISSUE: Where a creditor cashes a check presented by a debtor as full payment of the debt, the amount of which is not disputed (liquidated), can the creditor pursue the debtor for the difference between the amount of the check and the amount the debtor owes?

DECISION: Yes, judgment for Century 21.

REASONS: Accord and satisfaction applies only to a situation where a good- faith dispute exists about the amount owed by the debtor. Where, as here, the amount owed is not disputed, the debt will not be satisfied by payment of less than the amount the parties have agreed is owed.

* * * QUESTIONS * * *
(See back of text for answers)

1) What is an accord?

2) What is a satisfaction?

3) Why did an accord and satisfaction not result in this case?

4) Would the outcome of this case have been different if the parties had not agreed on the amount of the commission owed by Grasso to Century 21?

Case No. 52

ACCORD AND SATISFACTION

<u>Schnell v. Perlmon</u>

Court of Appeals

238 N.Y. 362, 144 N.E. 641 (1924)

FACTS: Plaintiff H. Schnell and Co. (Schnell) sold to defendant Sol Perlmon (Perlmon) ten carloads of spanish onions for an agreed price. When the shipments arrived a portion of the onions were rotted and decayed. A government food products official inspected the onions and in a written report confirmed the presence of the decay.

Perlmon paid for the onions but deducted $801.29 for the decayed portion. Payment was made by checks to which Perlmon attached letters informing Schnell that the checks were offered as payment in full. Schnell cashed the checks then sought payment of the $801.29 Perlmon had deducted.

FIRST ISSUE: Where a seller cashes a check presented by a buyer as full payment of a debt, the amount of which is disputed, can the seller pursue the buyer for the difference between the amount of the check and the amount the seller believes buyer owes?

DECISION: No.

REASONING: When the debtor offers as payment in full partial payment of a debt, the amount of which is disputed in good faith, and the creditor accepts the payment, the entire debt is deemed settled for the amount of the partial payment.

SECOND ISSUE: Was the debt in this case liquidated or unliquidated?

DECISION: Unliquidated; judgment for Perlmon.

REASONING: Normally, when the parties in a contract agree on a price, the amount of money owed is not in dispute. However, where a seller does not perform as required by the contract, the buyer has a good-faith basis to dispute the amount owed to the seller. In this case, the buyer proved that a portion of the onions delivered by seller were rotted and decayed. Buyer's letters accompanying his checks also informed seller that buyer disputed the claim. The amount of the obligation owed in this case by buyer was disputed in good faith and therefore unliquidated.

Perlmon had a claim against Schnell for damages for breach of contract. Perlmon subtracted from the money he owed Schnell the amount of the claim. Schnell kept the checks Perlmon sent. The result was an accord and satisfaction; all claims for any additional money were relinquished by the acceptance of the offered amount.

*** QUESTION ***
(See back of text for answer)

1) What facts gave rise to the accord and satisfaction in this case?

Case No. 53

ACCORD AND SATISFACTION

Horn Waterproofing Corp. v. Bushwick Iron and Steel Co., Inc.

Court of Appeals

66 N.Y.2d 321; 497 N.Y.S.2d 310 (1985)

FACTS: Plaintiff Horn Waterproofing Corp. (Horn) was hired by defendant Bushwick Iron and Steel Co., Inc. (Bushwick) to repair a leaking roof on a building owned by Bushwick. Horn worked on the roof for two days and then determined that, rather than repairs, a new roof was required. Horn billed Bushwick for $1080.00 for the two days of work.

Bushwick, disputing the amount of the bill, sent Horn a check for $500.00 and wrote the following on the back of it: "This check is accepted in full payment, settlement, satisfaction, release and discharge of any and all claims and/or demands of whatsoever kind and nature".

Horn, unwilling to accept $500.00 as payment in full, printed the following under Bushwick's notation, "Under Protest". Horn then endorsed and deposited the check. Thereafter, Horn began this lawsuit seeking the balance of the bill, $580.00. Defendant denied owing the money, claiming that Horn's deposit of the check constituted an accord and satisfaction.

ISSUE: Where a debtor makes a partial payment by check of a disputed bill and puts a notation on the check indicating the check is offered as payment in full, and the creditor adds to the check the words "under protest", does an accord and satisfaction exist?

DECISION: No.

REASONING: A creditor may retain the right to collect the balance of a disputed claim and avoid an accord and satisfaction by explicitly reserving such right in the endorsement of the check offered as payment in full of a debt. Use of expressions such as "under protest" or "without prejudice" are sufficient for this purpose.

Fairness requires that a creditor should be able to retain a partial payment made by the debtor without having to forfeit the right to whatever else is due. To hold otherwise would be unjust to creditors who would be in the unfair position of having to choose between forfeiting the partial payment or sacrificing the right to the balance of the debt.

* * * QUESTIONS * * *
(See back of text for answers)

1) Concerning the elements of an accord and satisfaction, how are the facts of this case similar to the facts of Schnell v. Perlmon?

2) In <u>Schnell</u>, the court determined an accord and satisfaction existed, while in this case the court determined an accord and satisfaction did not exist. What facts led to the different results?

Case No. 54

ACCORD AND SATISFACTION

Sullivan v. Conant Valley Associates, Ltd., et. al.

Supreme Court, Westchester County

148 Misc.2d 483 (1990), 560 NYS2d 617

FACTS: Plaintiff Joseph Sullivan (Sullivan), a plumbing contractor, did work on property owned by defendant Conant Valley Associates Ltd. (Conant) located in the Town of Pound Ridge early in 1989. A dispute arose between the parties over the amount owed by Conant. He tendered a check to Sullivan and placed the words "complete and final payment" at the top of the back of the check where Sullivan would endorse it. Sullivan scratched out the words, deposited the check for collection, and is now suing Conant for the higher amount he claims is due under the contract.

ISSUE: Where a debtor makes payment by check of a disputed bill and offers it as payment in full, and the creditor scratches out the reference to payment in full and thereafter cashes the check, has the creditor reserved the right to pursue a claim against the debtor for the additional money?

DECISION: No, judgment for Conant; complaint dismissed.

REASONING: A creditor can retain the right to collect the balance of a disputed debt by explicitly reserving such right in the endorsement of the check. Expressions such as "under protest", "without prejudice", or other similar phrases are sufficient for this purpose.

In this case, Sullivan merely scratched out the notation indicating payment in full and did not explicitly reserve his right to collect the balance he alleged was due. The court noted that "scratching out of final payment conditions on a check followed by endorsement and cashing is not the explicit and unambiguous reservation of rights required; further added words bespeaking reservation are necessary." As a result, Sullivan's cashing of the check constitutes a valid accord and satisfaction.

* * * QUESTION * * *
(See back of text for answer)

1) Jerry owed a disputed amount of money to Eileen. He sent her a check for $1800.00 marked "payment in full". Eileen claims an additional $1200.00 is due and wants to reserve the right to pursue Jerry for that money. Describe two different things Eileen can do to preserve her right to seek the additional $1200.00.

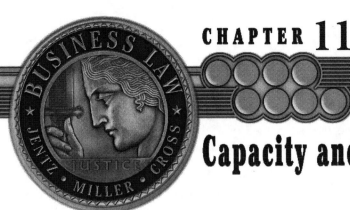

CHAPTER 11

Capacity and Legality

In addition to agreement and consideration, for a contract to be deemed valid the parties to the contract must have **contractual capacity**—the legal ability to enter into a contractual relationship. Courts generally presume the existence of contractual capacity, but in some situations, such as those involving mentally incompetent persons or minors, capacity is lacking or may be questionable. Similarly, contracts calling for the performance of an illegal act are illegal and thus void—they are not contracts at all. In this chapter, we examine contractual capacity and some aspects of illegal bargains.

Realize that capacity and legality are not inherently related other than that they are both contract requirements. We treat these topics in one chapter merely for convenience and reasons of space.

Contractual Capacity

Historically, the law has given special protection to those who bargain with the inexperience of youth or those who lack the degree of mental competence required by law. A person who has been determined by a court to be mentally incompetent, for example, cannot form a legally binding contract with another party. In other situations, a party may have the capacity to enter into a valid contract but also have the right to avoid liability under it. For example, minors—or *infants,* as they are commonly referred to in legal terminology—usually are not legally bound by contracts. In this section, we look at the effect of youth, intoxication, and mental incompetence on contractual capacity.

Minors

Today, in virtually all states, the **age of majority** (when a person is no longer a minor) for contractual purposes is eighteen years.[1] In addition, some states pro-

vide for the termination of minority on marriage. Minority status may also be terminated by a minor's **emancipation,** which occurs when a child's parent or legal guardian relinquishes the legal right to exercise control over the child. Normally, minors who leave home to support themselves are considered emancipated. Several jurisdictions permit minors to petition a court for emancipation themselves. For business purposes, a minor may petition a court to be treated as an adult.

The general rule is that a minor can enter into any contract that an adult can, provided that the contract is not one prohibited by law for minors (for example, the sale of tobacco or alcoholic beverages). A contract entered into by a minor, however, is voidable at the option of that minor, subject to certain exceptions. To exercise the option to avoid a contract, a minor need only manifest an intention not to be bound by it. The minor "avoids" the contract by disaffirming it.

A Minor's Right to Disaffirm The legal avoidance, or setting aside, of a contractual obligation is referred to as **disaffirmance.** To disaffirm, a minor must express his or her intent, through words or conduct, not to be bound to the contract. The minor must disaffirm the entire contract, not merely a portion of it.

---

1. The age of majority may still be twenty-one for other purposes, such as the purchase and consumption of alcohol.

For example, the minor cannot decide to keep part of the goods purchased under a contract and return the remaining goods.

A contract can ordinarily be disaffirmed at any time during minority[2] or for a reasonable period after reaching majority. What constitutes a "reasonable" time may vary. Two months would probably be considered reasonable, but except in unusual circumstances, a court may not find it reasonable to wait a year or more after coming of age to disaffirm. If an individual fails to disaffirm an executed contract within a reasonable time after reaching the age of majority, a court will likely hold that the contract has been ratified (*ratification* will be discussed shortly).

Note that an adult who enters into a contract with a minor cannot avoid his or her contractual duties on the ground that the minor can do so. Unless the minor exercises the option to disaffirm the contract, the adult party normally is bound by it.

A Minor's Obligations on Disaffirmance

Although all states' laws permit minors to disaffirm contracts (with certain exceptions), states differ on the extent of a minor's obligations on disaffirmance.

Majority Rule. Courts in a majority of states hold that the minor need only return the goods (or other consideration) subject to the contract, provided the goods are in the minor's possession or control. Suppose that Jim Garrison, a seventeen-year-old, purchases a computer from Radio Shack. While transporting the computer to his home, Garrison negligently drops it, breaking the plastic casing. The next day, he returns the computer to Radio Shack and disaffirms the contract. Under the majority view, this return fulfills Garrison's duty even though the computer is now damaged. Garrison is entitled to receive a refund of the purchase price (if paid in cash) or to be relieved of any further obligations under a credit agreement.

Minority Rule. An increasing number of states, either by statute or by court decision, place an additional duty on the minor—the duty to restore the adult party to the position that she or he held before the contract was made. Consider an example. Sixteen-year-old Joseph Dodson bought a pickup truck for $4,900 from a used-car dealer. Although the truck developed mechanical problems nine months later, Dodson con-

tinued to drive it until the engine blew up and the truck stopped running. Then Dodson disaffirmed the contract and attempted to return the truck to the dealer for a full refund of the purchase price. When the dealer refused to accept the pickup or refund the money, Dodson filed a lawsuit. Ultimately, the Tennessee Supreme Court allowed Dodson to disaffirm the contract but required him to compensate the seller for the depreciated value—not the purchase price—of the pickup.[3] This case illustrates the trend among today's courts to hold a minor responsible for damage, ordinary wear and tear, and depreciation of goods that the minor used prior to disaffirmance.

Exceptions to a Minor's Right to Disaffirm State courts and legislatures have carved out several exceptions to the minor's right to disaffirm. Some contracts cannot be avoided simply as a matter of law, on the ground of public policy. For example, marriage contracts and contracts to enlist in the armed services fall into this category. Other contracts may not be disaffirmed for other reasons, including those discussed here.

Misrepresentation of Age. Suppose that a minor tells a seller that she is twenty-one years old when she is really seventeen. Ordinarily, the minor can disaffirm the contract even though she has misrepresented her age. In many jurisdictions, however, a minor who has misrepresented his or her age can be bound by a contract, at least under certain circumstances. First, several states have enacted statutes for precisely this purpose. In these states, misrepresentation of age is enough to prohibit disaffirmance. Other statutes prohibit disaffirmance by a minor who has engaged in business as an adult. Second, some courts refuse to allow minors to disaffirm executed (fully performed) contracts unless they can return the consideration received. The combination of the minors' misrepresentation and their unjust enrichment has persuaded these courts to *estop* (prevent) minors from asserting contractual incapacity.

Contracts for Necessaries. A minor who enters into a contract for necessaries may disaffirm the contract but remains liable for the reasonable value of the goods. **Necessaries** are items that fulfill basic needs, such as food, clothing, shelter, and medical services, at a level of value required to maintain the minor's stan-

---

2. In some states, however, a minor who enters into a contract for the sale of land cannot disaffirm the contract until she or he reaches the age of majority.

3. *Dodson v. Shrader*, 824 S.W.2d 545 (Tenn.Sup.Ct. 1992) is a seminal case on this subject. See also *Restatement (Third) of Restitution*, Sections 16 and 33 (2004).

dard of living or financial and social status. Thus, what will be considered a necessary for one person may be a luxury for another. Additionally, what is considered a necessary depends on whether the minor is under the care or control of his or her parents, who are required by law to provide necessaries for the minor. If a minor's parents provide him or her with shelter, for example, then a contract to lease shelter (such as an apartment) normally will not be classified as a contract for necessaries.

Generally, then, for a contract to qualify as a contract for necessaries, (1) the item contracted for must be necessary for the minor's subsistence, (2) the value

of the necessary item must be up to a level required to maintain the minor's standard of living or financial and social status, and (3) the minor must not be under the care of a parent or guardian who is required to supply this item. Unless these three criteria are met, the minor can disaffirm the contract *without* being liable for the reasonable value of the goods used.

The issue in the following case was whether, under the doctrine of necessaries, a medical service provider could collect from a minor the cost of emergency services rendered to the minor when his mother did not pay.

C A S E 11.1 Yale Diagnostic Radiology v. Estate of Harun Fountain
Supreme Court of Connecticut, 2004. 267 Conn. 351, 838 A.2d 179.

● **Background and Facts** In March 1996, Harun Fountain was shot in the back of the head at point-blank range by a playmate. Fountain required extensive lifesaving medical services from a variety of providers, including Yale Diagnostic Radiology. Yale billed Fountain's mother, Vernetta Turner-Tucker, for the cost of its services ($17,694), but she did not pay. Instead, in January 2001, Turner-Tucker filed for bankruptcy (see Chapter 30), and all of her debts, including the amount owed to Yale, were discharged. Meanwhile, she filed a suit in a Connecticut state court against the boy who shot Fountain and obtained funds for Fountain's medical care. These funds were deposited in an account, which is sometimes referred to as an "estate," established on Fountain's behalf. Yale filed a suit against Fountain's estate, asking the court to order the estate to pay Yale's bill, but the court ruled against Yale. Yale appealed to a state intermediate appellate court, which reversed this ruling and ordered the payment. The estate appealed to the state supreme court.

● **Decision and Rationale** The Connecticut Supreme Court affirmed the judgment of the lower court. Yale could collect from Fountain's estate for the cost of its services under the doctrine of necessaries. The state supreme court explained that "Connecticut has long recognized the common-law rule that a minor child's contracts are voidable" but "a minor may not avoid a contract for goods or services necessary for his health." The court reasoned that this principle is based on the theory of quasi contract. "Thus, when a medical service provider renders necessary medical care to an injured minor, two contracts arise: the primary contract between the provider and the minor's parents; and an implied-in-law contract between the provider and the minor himself. The primary contract between the provider and the parents is based on the parents' duty to pay for their children's necessary expenses * * * . The secondary implied-in-law contract between the medical services provider and the minor arises from equitable considerations, including the law's disfavor of unjust enrichment. Therefore, where necessary medical services are rendered to a minor whose parents do not pay for them, equity and justice demand that a secondary implied-in-law contract arise between the medical services provider and the minor who has received the benefits of those services."

● **What If the Facts Were Different?** *What might have happened in future cases if the court had held that there was no implied-in-law contract between Fountain and Yale Diagnostic Radiology?*

● **The Ethical Dimension** *How does the result in this case encourage payment on contracts for necessaries?*

Insurance and Loans. Traditionally, insurance has not been viewed as a necessary, so minors can ordinarily disaffirm their insurance contracts and recover all premiums paid. Some jurisdictions, though, prohibit the right to disaffirm insurance contracts—for example, when minors contract for life insurance on their own lives. Financial loans are seldom considered to be necessaries.

Ratification In contract law, **ratification** is the act of accepting and giving legal force to an obligation that previously was not enforceable. A minor who has reached the age of majority can ratify a contract expressly or impliedly. *Express* ratification takes place when the individual, on reaching the age of majority, states orally or in writing that he or she intends to be bound by the contract. *Implied* ratification takes place when the minor, on reaching the age of majority, indicates an intent to abide by the contract.

Suppose that Lin enters into a contract to sell her laptop to Arturo, a minor. If, on reaching the age of majority, Arturo writes a letter to Lin stating that he still agrees to buy the laptop, he has *expressly* ratified the contract. If, instead, Arturo takes possession of the laptop as a minor and continues to use it well after reaching the age of majority, he has *impliedly* ratified the contract.

If a minor fails to disaffirm a contract within a reasonable time after reaching the age of majority, then the court must determine whether the conduct constitutes ratification or disaffirmance. Generally, a contract that is *executed* (fully performed by both parties) is presumed to be ratified. A contract that is still *executory* (not yet fully performed by both parties) normally is considered to be disaffirmed.

Parents' Liability As a general rule, parents are not liable for contracts made by minor children acting on their own. This is why businesses ordinarily require parents to cosign any contract made with a minor. The parents then become personally obligated under the contract even if their child avoids liability.

Normally, minors are personally liable for their own torts. The parents of the minor can *also* be held liable in certain situations. In some states, parents may be liable if they failed to exercise proper parental control over the minor child when they knew or should have known that this lack of control posed an unreasonable risk of harm to others. Suppose that parents allow their eleven-year-old child to drive a car on public roads. If the child drives negligently and causes someone else to be injured, the parents may be held liable for the minor's tort (negligence). Other states have enacted statutes that impose liability on parents for certain tortious acts, such as those that are willful or grossly negligent, that their children commit. *Concept Summary 11.1* reviews the rules relating to contracts by minors.

Intoxication

Intoxication is a condition in which a person's normal capacity to act or think is inhibited by alcohol or some other drug.[4] A contract entered into by an intoxicated person can be either voidable or valid (and thus

---

4. Note that if an alcoholic makes a contract while sober, there is no lack of capacity. See *Wright v. Fisher*, 32 N.W. 605 (Mich. 1887).

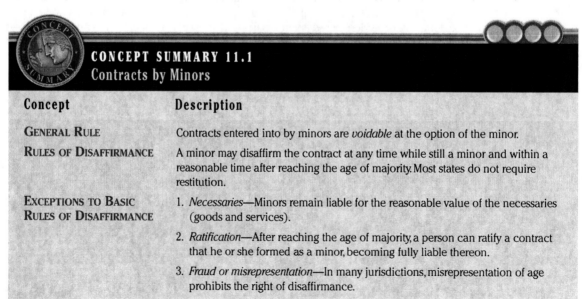

CONCEPT SUMMARY 11.1
Contracts by Minors

Concept	Description
GENERAL RULE	Contracts entered into by minors are *voidable* at the option of the minor.
RULES OF DISAFFIRMANCE	A minor may disaffirm the contract at any time while still a minor and within a reasonable time after reaching the age of majority. Most states do not require restitution.
EXCEPTIONS TO BASIC RULES OF DISAFFIRMANCE	1. *Necessaries*—Minors remain liable for the reasonable value of the necessaries (goods and services).
	2. *Ratification*—After reaching the age of majority, a person can ratify a contract that he or she formed as a minor, becoming fully liable thereon.
	3. *Fraud or misrepresentation*—In many jurisdictions, misrepresentation of age prohibits the right of disaffirmance.

enforceable). If the person was sufficiently intoxicated to lack mental capacity, then the contract may be voidable even if the intoxication was purely voluntary. For the contract to be voidable, however, the person must prove that the intoxication impaired her or his reason and judgment so severely that she or he did not comprehend the legal consequences of entering into the contract.

If, despite intoxication, the person understood the legal consequences of the agreement, the contract will be enforceable. The fact that the terms of the contract are foolish or obviously favor the other party does not make the contract voidable (unless the other party *fraudulently* induced the person to become intoxicated).

As a practical matter, courts rarely permit contracts to be avoided on the ground of intoxication because it is difficult to determine whether a party was sufficiently intoxicated to lack contractual capacity. Many courts prefer to look at objective indications of agreement when dealing with intoxicated parties.[5]

Disaffirmance If a contract is voidable because of a person's intoxication, that person has the option of disaffirming it while intoxicated and for a reasonable time after becoming sober—the same option available to a minor. To avoid the contract in most states, the person claiming intoxication must be able to return all consideration received—except in contracts involving necessaries. Contracts for necessaries are voidable, but

5. See, for example, Case 9.1 *(Lucy v. Zehmer)* in Chapter 9.

the intoxicated person is liable in quasi contract for the reasonable value of the consideration received.

Ratification An intoxicated person, after becoming sober, may ratify a contract expressly or impliedly, just as a minor may do on reaching majority. Implied ratification occurs when a person enters into a contract while intoxicated and fails to disaffirm the contract within a *reasonable* time after becoming sober. Acts or conduct inconsistent with an intent to disaffirm—such as the continued use of property purchased under a voidable contract—will also ratify the contract. See *Concept Summary 11.2* for a review of the rules relating to contracts by intoxicated persons.

Mental Incompetence

Contracts made by mentally incompetent persons can be void, voidable, or valid. We look here at the circumstances that determine which of these classifications apply.

When the Contract Will Be Void If a court has previously determined that a person is mentally incompetent and has appointed a guardian to represent the individual, any contract made by the mentally incompetent person is *void*—no contract exists. Only the guardian can enter into binding legal obligations on the incompetent person's behalf.

When the Contract Will Be Voidable If a court has not previously judged a person to be mentally incompetent but in fact the person was

---

CONCEPT SUMMARY 11.2
Contracts by Intoxicated Persons

Concept	Description
GENERAL RULES	If a person was sufficiently intoxicated to lack the mental capacity to comprehend the legal consequences of entering into the contract, the contract may be *voidable* at the option of the intoxicated person. If, despite intoxication, the person understood these legal consequences, the contract will be enforceable.
DISAFFIRMANCE	An intoxicated person may disaffirm the contract at any time while intoxicated and for a reasonable time after becoming sober but must make full restitution. Contracts for necessaries are voidable, but the intoxicated person is liable for the reasonable value of the goods or services.
RATIFICATION	After becoming sober, a person can ratify a contract that she or he formed while intoxicated, becoming fully liable thereon.

incompetent at the time the contract was formed, the contract may be voidable. A contract is *voidable* if the person did not know he or she was entering into the contract or lacked the mental capacity to comprehend its nature, purpose, and consequences. Only the mentally incompetent person has the option to avoid the contract, not the other party. The contract may then be disaffirmed or ratified (if the person regains mental competence). Like intoxicated persons, mentally incompetent persons must return any consideration and pay for the reasonable value of any necessaries they receive.

For example, Milo, who had not been previously declared incompetent by a judge, agrees to sell twenty lots in a prime residential neighborhood to Anastof. At the time of entering the contract, Milo is mentally incompetent and is confused over which lots he is selling and how much they are worth. As a result, he contracts to sell the properties for substantially less than their market value. If the court finds that Milo was unable to understand the nature and consequences of the contract, Milo can avoid the sale, provided that he returns any consideration he received.

When the Contract Will Be Valid A contract entered into by a mentally incompetent person (whom a court has not previously declared incompetent) may also be *valid* if the person had capacity *at the time the contract was formed.* A person may be able to understand the nature and effect of entering into a certain contract yet simultaneously lack capacity to engage in other activities. If so, the contract will be valid because the person does not lack contractual

capacity.[6] Similarly, an otherwise mentally incompetent person may have a *lucid interval*—a temporary restoration of sufficient intelligence, judgment, and will—during which she or he will be considered to have full legal capacity. See *Concept Summary 11.3* for a review of the rules relating to contracts entered into by mentally incompetent persons.

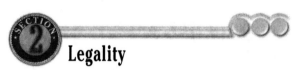

Legality

For a contract to be valid and enforceable, it must be formed for a legal purpose. A contract to do something that is prohibited by federal or state statutory law is illegal and, as such, void from the outset and thus unenforceable. Also, a contract that calls for a tortious act or an action contrary to public policy is illegal and unenforceable. It is important to note that a contract or a clause in a contract may be illegal even in the absence of a specific statute prohibiting the action promised by the contract.

Contracts Contrary to Statute

Statutes often prescribe the terms of contracts. We now examine several ways in which contracts may be contrary to statute and thus illegal.

---

6. Modern courts no longer require a person to be completely irrational to disaffirm contracts on the basis of mental incompetence. A contract may be voidable if, by reason of a mental illness or defect, an individual was unable to act reasonably with respect to the transaction and the other party had reason to know of the condition.

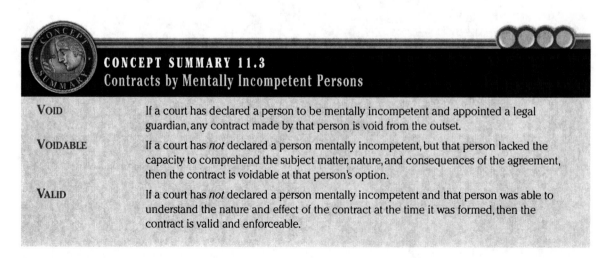

CONCEPT SUMMARY 11.3
Contracts by Mentally Incompetent Persons

VOID	If a court has declared a person to be mentally incompetent and appointed a legal guardian, any contract made by that person is void from the outset.
VOIDABLE	If a court has *not* declared a person mentally incompetent, but that person lacked the capacity to comprehend the subject matter, nature, and consequences of the agreement, then the contract is voidable at that person's option.
VALID	If a court has *not* declared a person mentally incompetent and that person was able to understand the nature and effect of the contract at the time it was formed, then the contract is valid and enforceable.

Contracts to Commit a Crime Any contract to commit a crime is a contract in violation of a statute. Thus, a contract to sell an illegal drug (the sale of which is prohibited by statute) is not enforceable, and a contract to provide inside information regarding the sale of securities is unenforceable (violations of securities laws will be discussed in Chapter 41). Should the object or performance of the contract be rendered illegal by statute *after* the contract has been entered into, the contract is considered to be discharged by law. (See the discussion of impossibility or impracticability of performance in Chapter 17.)

Usury Virtually every state has a statute that sets the maximum rate of interest that can be charged for different types of transactions, including ordinary loans. A lender who makes a loan at an interest rate above the lawful maximum commits **usury.** The maximum rate of interest varies from state to state, as do the consequences for lenders who make usurious loans. Some states allow the lender to recover only the principal of a loan along with interest up to the legal maximum. In effect, the lender is denied recovery of the excess interest. In other states, the lender can recover the principal amount of the loan but no interest.

Although usury statutes place a ceiling on allowable rates of interest, exceptions have been made to facilitate business transactions. For example, many states exempt corporate loans from the usury laws, and nearly all states allow higher-interest-rate loans for borrowers who could not otherwise obtain funds.

Gambling All states have statutes that regulate gambling—defined as any scheme that involves a distribution of property by chance among persons who have paid a valuable consideration for the opportunity (chance) to receive the property. Gambling is the creation of risk for the purpose of assuming it. Traditionally, state statutes have deemed gambling contracts to be illegal and thus void.

In several states, however, including Louisiana, Michigan, Nevada, and New Jersey, casino gambling is lawful. In other states, certain forms of gambling are legal. California, for example, has not defined draw poker as a crime, although criminal statutes prohibit numerous other types of gambling games. A number of states allow gambling at horse races, and the majority of the states have legalized state-operated lotteries, as well as lotteries (such as bingo) conducted for charitable purposes. Many states also allow gambling on Indian reservations.

Sometimes, it is difficult to distinguish a gambling contract from the risk sharing inherent in almost all contracts. In one case, five co-workers each received a free lottery ticket from a customer and agreed to split the winnings if one of the tickets turned out to be the winning one. At first glance, this may seem entirely legal. The court, however, noted that the oral contract in this case "was an exchange of promises to share winnings from the parties' individually owned lottery tickets upon the happening of the uncertain event" that one of the tickets would win. Consequently, concluded the court, the agreement at issue was "founded on a gambling consideration" and therefore was void.[7]

Online Gambling A significant issue today is how gambling laws can be applied in the Internet context. Because state laws pertaining to gambling differ, online gambling raises a number of unique issues. For example, if a state does not allow casino gambling or offtrack betting, what can the state government do if its residents place bets online? Also, where does the actual act of gambling occur? Suppose that a resident of New York places bets via the Internet at a gambling site located in Antigua. Is the actual act of "gambling" taking place in New York or in Antigua? According to a New York court in one case, "if the person engaged in gambling is located in New York, then New York is the location where the gambling occurred."[8] Other states' courts may take a different view, however.

Another issue is whether entering into contracts that involve gambling on sports teams that do not really exist—fantasy sports—is a form of gambling. For a discussion of this issue, see this chapter's *Contemporary Legal Debates* feature on pages 252 and 253.

Sabbath (Sunday) Laws Statutes referred to as Sabbath (Sunday) laws prohibit the formation or performance of certain contracts on a Sunday. These statutes, which date back to colonial times, are often called blue laws. **Blue laws** get their name from the blue paper on which New Haven, Connecticut, printed its town ordinance in 1781 that prohibited work and required businesses to close on Sunday. According to a few state and local laws, all contracts entered into on a Sunday are illegal. Laws in other states or municipalities prohibit only the sale of certain types of merchandise, such as alcoholic beverages, on a Sunday.

---

7. *Dickerson v. Deno,* 770 So.2d 63 (Ala. 2000).
8. *United States v. Cohen,* 260 F.3d. 68 (2d Cir. 2001).

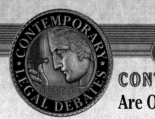

CONTEMPORARY LEGAL DEBATES
Are Online Fantasy Sports Gambling?

As many as 20 million adults in the United States play some form of fantasy sports via the Internet. A fantasy sport is a game in which participants, often called owners, build teams composed of real-life players from different real-life teams. A fantasy team then competes against the fantasy teams belonging to other "owners." At the end of each week, the statistical performances of all the real-life players are translated into points, and the points of all the players on an owner's fantasy team are totaled. Although a wide variety of fantasy games are available, most participants play fantasy football. On many fantasy sports sites, participants pay a fee in order to play and use the site's facilities, such as statistical tracking and message boards; at the end of the season, prizes ranging from T-shirts to flat-screen televisions are awarded to the winners.

In other instances, the participants in fantasy sports gamble directly on the outcome. In a fantasy football league, for example, each participant-owner adds a given amount to the pot and then "drafts" his or her fantasy team from actual National Football League players. At the end of the football season, each owner's points are totaled, and the owner with the most points wins the pot.

Congress Weighs In

As online gambling has expanded, Congress has attempted to regulate it. In late 2006, a federal law went into effect that makes it illegal for credit-card companies and banks to engage in transactions with Internet gambling companies.[a] Although the law does not prohibit individuals from placing online bets, in effect it makes it almost impossible for them to do so by preventing them from obtaining financing for online gambling. At first glance, the legislation appears comprehensive, but it specifically exempts Internet wagers on horse racing, state lotteries, and fantasy sports. Hence, one could argue that Congress has determined that fantasy sports do not constitute a prohibited Internet gambling activity.

Testing the Gambling Aspect in Court

Thus far, the courts have had the opportunity to rule only on whether the pay-to-play fantasy sports sites that charge an entrance fee and offer prizes to the winners are running gambling operations. Charles Humphrey brought a lawsuit against Viacom, ESPN, *The Sporting News*, and other hosts of such fantasy sports sites under a New Jersey statute that allows the recovery of gambling losses. Humphrey claimed that the fantasy sports leagues were games of chance, not games of skill, because events beyond the participants' control could determine the

---

a. Security and Accountability for Every Port Act, Public L. No. 109-347, Sections 5361–5367, 120 Stat. 1884 (2006). (A version of the Unlawful Internet Gambling Enforcement Act of 2006 was incorporated into this statute as Title VIII.)

In most states with such statutes, contracts that were entered into on a Sunday can be ratified during a weekday. Also, if a contract that was entered into on a Sunday has been fully performed (executed), normally it cannot be rescinded (canceled). When the date of performance of a contract ends on Sunday, the general view is that the contract is performable on the next business day, and therefore it is not illegal. Many states do not enforce Sunday laws, and some state courts have held these laws to be unconstitutional because they interfere with the freedom of religion.

Licensing Statutes All states require that members of certain professions or occupations obtain licenses allowing them to practice. Physicians, lawyers, real estate brokers, architects, electricians, and stockbrokers are but a few of the people who must be licensed. Some licenses are obtained only after extensive schooling and examinations, which indicate to the public that a special skill has been acquired. Others require only that the particular person be of good moral character and pay a fee.

Generally, business licenses provide a means of regulating and taxing certain enterprises and protecting the public against actions that could threaten the general welfare. For example, in nearly all states, a stockbroker must be licensed and must file a bond with the state to protect the public from fraudulent stock transactions. Similarly, a plumber must be licensed and bonded to protect the public against incompetent plumbers and to protect the public health. Only per-

outcome—for example, a star quarterback might be injured. He also pointed out that in the offline world, federal law prohibits any games of chance, such as sweepstakes or drawings, that require entrants to submit consideration in order to play. *Consideration* has been defined as the purchase of a product or the payment of money. For these reasons, he argued, the entrance fees constituted gambling losses that could be recovered.

The federal district court that heard the case ruled against Humphrey, mostly on procedural grounds, but the court did conclude that as a matter of law the entrance fees did not constitute "bets" or "wagers" because the fees are paid unconditionally, the prizes offered are for a fixed amount and certain to be awarded, and the defendants do not compete for the prizes.[b] The court also observed that if a combination of entrance fees and prizes constituted gambling, a host of contests ranging from golf tournaments to track meets to spelling bees and beauty contests would be gambling operations—a conclusion that the court deemed "patently absurd."[c] Note, however, that the case involved only pay-to-play sites. The court did not have to address the question of whether fantasy sports sites that enable participants to contibute to a pot in the hopes of winning it at the end of the season constitute gambling sites.

••

WHERE DO YOU STAND?

Determining what is and what is not gambling does not always lend itself to an easy answer. If you buy a mutual fund that consists of a broad array of stocks and your purpose is to enhance your standard of living during your retirement, no one considers that gambling. In contrast, if you are a day trader—buying and selling stocks during a one-day period—you are clearly "betting" that the stocks you buy in the morning and then sell in the evening will have gone up in value. Should day trading be deemed gambling and therefore illegal? Where do you draw the line between what is and what is not gambling in our society?

---

b. *Humphrey v. Viacom, Inc.,* ___ F.Supp.2d ___ , 2007 WL1797648 (D.N.J. 2007).
c. In reaching this conclusion, the federal district court cited portions of an Arizona Supreme Court ruling, *State v. American Holiday Association, Inc.,* 151 Ariz. 312, 727 P.2d 807 (1986).

---

sons or businesses possessing the qualifications and complying with the conditions required by statute are entitled to licenses.

When a person enters into a contract with an unlicensed individual, the contract may still be enforceable, depending on the nature of the licensing statute. Some states expressly provide that the lack of a license in certain occupations bars the enforcement of work-related contracts. If the statute does not expressly declare this, one must look to the underlying purpose of the licensing requirements for a particular occupation. If the purpose is to protect the public from unauthorized practitioners, a contract involving an unlicensed individual normally is illegal and unenforceable. If the underlying purpose of the statute is to raise government revenues, however, a contract entered into with an unlicensed practitioner generally is enforceable—although the unlicensed person is usually fined.

Contracts Contrary to Public Policy

Although contracts involve private parties, some are not enforceable because of the negative impact they would have on society. Examples include a contract to commit an immoral act, such as selling a child, and a contract that prohibits marriage. We look here at certain types of business contracts that are often said to be *contrary to public policy.*

Contracts in Restraint of Trade Contracts in restraint of trade (anticompetitive agreements) usually adversely affect the public policy that favors competition in the economy. Typically, such contracts also violate one or more federal or state statutes.[9] An exception is recognized when the restraint is reasonable and is contained in an ancillary (secondary, or subordinate) clause in a contract. Many such exceptions involve a type of restraint called a **covenant not to compete,** or a *restrictive covenant.*

Covenants Not to Compete and the Sale of an Ongoing Business. Covenants (promises) not to compete are often contained as ancillary clauses in contracts concerning the sale of an ongoing business. A covenant not to compete is created when a seller agrees not to open a new store in a certain geographic area surrounding the existing store. Such agreements enable the seller to sell, and the purchaser to buy, the goodwill and reputation of an ongoing business. If, for example, a well-known merchant sells her store and opens a competing business a block away, many customers will likely do business at the merchant's new store. This, in turn, renders less valuable the good name and reputation purchased for a price by the new owner of the old store. If a covenant not to compete is not ancillary to a sales agreement, however, it is void, because it unreasonably restrains trade and is contrary to public policy.

Covenants Not to Compete in Employment Contracts. Agreements not to compete (sometimes referred to as *noncompete agreements*) can also be contained in employment contracts. People in middle- or upper-level management positions commonly agree not to work for competitors or not to start competing businesses for a specified period of time after termination of employment. Such agreements are legal in most states so long as the specified period of time (of restraint) is not excessive in duration and the geographic restriction is reasonable. What constitutes a reasonable time period may be shorter in the online environment than in conventional employment contracts because the restrictions apply worldwide. (For a further discussion of this issue, see this chapter's *Business Application* feature on page 256.)

To be reasonable, a restriction on competition must protect a legitimate business interest and must not be any greater than necessary to protect that interest.[10] In the following case, the court had to decide whether it was reasonable for an employer's noncompete agreement to restrict a former employee from competing "in any area of business" in which the employer was engaged.

---

9. Federal statutes include the Sherman Antitrust Act, the Clayton Act, and the Federal Trade Commission Act (see Chapter 46).

10. See, for example, *Gould & Lamb, LLC v. D'Alusio,* 949 So.2d 1212 (Fla.App. 2007). See also *Moore v. Midwest Distribution, Inc.,* 76 Ark.App. 397, 65 S.W.3d 490 (2002).

C A S E **11.2 Stultz v. Safety and Compliance Management, Inc.**
Court of Appeals of Georgia, 2007. 285 Ga.App. 799, 648 S.E.2d 129.

● **Background and Facts** Safety and Compliance Management, Inc. (S&C), in Rossville, Georgia, provides alcohol- and drug-testing services in multiple states. In February 2002, S&C hired Angela Burgess. Her job duties included providing customer service, ensuring that specimens were properly retrieved from clients and transported to the testing lab, contacting clients, and managing the office. Burgess signed a covenant not to compete "in any area of business conducted by Safety and Compliance Management . . . for a two-year period . . . beginning at the termination of employment." In May 2004, Burgess quit her job to work at Rossville Medical Center (RMC) as a medical assistant. RMC provides medical services, including occupational medicine, medical physicals, and workers' compensation injury treatment. RMC also offers alcohol- and drug-testing services. Burgess's duties included setting patient appointments, taking patient medical histories, checking vital signs, performing urinalysis testing, administering injections, conducting alcohol-breath tests, and collecting specimens for drug testing. S&C filed a suit in a Georgia state court against Burgess and others (including a defendant named Stultz), alleging, among other things, that she had violated the noncompete agreement. The court issued a summary judgment in S&C's favor. Burgess appealed to a state intermediate appellate court.

● **Decision and Rationale** The appellate court reversed the judgment of the lower court. The reviewing court pointed out that noncompete clauses in employment contracts cannot

CASE 11.2 CONTINUED impose an unreasonable restraint of trade. "A three-element test of duration, territorial coverage, and scope of activity has evolved as a helpful tool in examining the reasonableness of the particular factual setting to which it is applied." The noncompete clause in Burgess's employment contract stated that she would "not compete in any area of business conducted by [her employer]." This agreement, concluded the court, was intended to prevent any type of competing activity whatsoever. The covenant not to compete was "overly broad and indefinite." Therefore, it was unenforceable.

● **The Ethical Dimension** *To determine the enforceability of a covenant not to compete, the courts balance the rights of an employer against those of a former employee. What are these rights? How did S&C's covenant not to compete tip the balance in the employer's favor?*

● **The Global Dimension** *Should an employer be permitted to restrict a former employee from engaging in a competing business on a global level? Why or why not?*

Enforcement Problems. The laws governing the enforceability of covenants not to compete vary significantly from state to state. In some states, such as Texas, such a covenant will not be enforced unless the employee has received some benefit in return for signing the noncompete agreement. This is true even if the covenant is reasonable as to time and area. If the employee receives no benefit, the covenant will be deemed void. California prohibits the enforcement of covenants not to compete altogether.

If a covenant is found to be unreasonable in time or geographic area, courts in some jurisdictions may convert the terms into reasonable ones and then enforce the reformed covenant. A court normally will engage in this kind of rewriting of the terms only in rare situations, however, when it is necessary to prevent undue burdens or hardships.

Unconscionable Contracts or Clauses
Ordinarily, a court does not look at the fairness or equity of a contract. For example, the courts generally do not inquire into the adequacy of consideration (as discussed in Chapter 12). Persons are assumed to be reasonably intelligent, and the courts will not come to their aid just because they have made an unwise or foolish bargain. In certain circumstances, however, bargains are so oppressive that the courts relieve innocent parties of part or all of their duties. Such bargains are deemed **unconscionable** because they are so unscrupulous or grossly unfair as to be "void of conscience."[11] A contract can be unconscionable on

either procedural or substantive grounds, as discussed in the following subsections and illustrated graphically in Exhibit 11–1 on page 311.

Procedural Unconscionability. *Procedural* unconscionability has to do with how a term becomes part of a contract and involves factors that make it difficult for a party to know or understand the contract terms—for example, inconspicuous print, unintelligible language ("legalese"), or the lack of an opportunity to read the contract or to ask questions about its meaning. Procedural unconscionability may also occur when there is such disparity in bargaining power between the two parties that the weaker party's consent is not voluntary. Contracts entered into because of one party's vastly superior bargaining power may be deemed unconscionable. These situations often involve an **adhesion contract,** which is a contract written exclusively by one party (the dominant party, usually the seller or creditor) and presented to the other (the adhering party, usually the buyer or borrower) on a take-it-or-leave-it basis.[12] In other words, the adhering party has no opportunity to negotiate the terms of the contract. Standard-form contracts are often adhesion contracts.

Substantive Unconscionability. *Substantive* unconscionability characterizes those contracts, or portions of contracts, that are oppressive or overly harsh. Courts generally focus on provisions that deprive one party of the benefits of the agreement or leave that party without a remedy for nonperformance by the other. For example, a person with little income and with only a

---

11. The Uniform Commercial Code incorporated the concept of unconscionability in Sections 2–302 and 2A–108. These provisions, which apply to contracts for the sale or lease of goods, will be discussed in Chapter 20.

12. For a classic case involving an adhesion contract, see *Henningsen v. Bloomfield Motors, Inc.,* 32 N.J. 358, 161 A.2d 69 (1960).

MANAGEMENT FACES A LEGAL ISSUE

For some companies today, particularly those in high-tech industries, trade secrets are their most valuable assets. Often, to prevent departing employees from disclosing trade secrets to competing employers, business owners and managers have their key employees sign covenants not to compete. In such a covenant, the employee typically agrees not to set up a competing business or work for a competitor in a specified geographic area for a certain period of time. Generally, the time and geographic restrictions must be reasonable. A serious issue facing management today is whether time and space restrictions that have been deemed reasonable in the past serve as a guide to what might constitute reasonable restrictions in today's changing legal landscape, which includes the Internet environment.

WHAT THE COURTS SAY

There is little case law to guide management on this issue. One case involved Mark Schlack, who worked as a Web site manager for EarthWeb, Inc., in New York. Schlack signed a covenant stating that, on termination of his employment, he would not work for any competing company for one year. When he resigned and accepted an offer from a company in Massachusetts to design a Web site, EarthWeb sued to enforce the covenant not to compete. The court refused to enforce the covenant, in part because there was no evidence that Schlack had misappropriated any of EarthWeb's trade secrets or clients. The court also stated that because the Internet lacks physical borders, a covenant prohibiting an employee from working for a competitor anywhere in the world for one year is excessive in duration.[a]

In a later case, a federal district court enforced a one-year noncompete agreement against the founder of a law-related Web site business even though no geographic restriction was included in the agreement. According to the court, "Although there is no geographic limitation on the provision, this is nonetheless reasonable in light of the national, and indeed international, nature of Internet business."[b]

The sale of an Internet-only business involves literally the full worldwide scope of the Internet itself. In a relatively recent case, a company selling vitamins over the Internet was sold for more than $2 million. The purchase agreement contained a noncompete clause. For four years after the sale, the seller was prohibited from engaging in the sale of nutritional and health products via the Internet. The court pointed out that the seller was still able to engage in his former business by other means using non-Internet markets. The seller also remained free to sell other types of products on the Internet. Notwithstanding the noncompete agreement, the seller created at least two other Internet sites from which he sold health products and vitamins. The court held for the buyer of the Internet-only business and enjoined (prevented) the seller from violating the noncompete agreement.[c]

IMPLICATIONS FOR MANAGERS

Management in high-tech companies should avoid overreaching in terms of time and geographic restrictions in noncompete agreements. Additionally, when considering the reasonability of time and place restrictions, the courts tend to balance time restrictions against other factors, such as geographic restrictions. Because for Web-based work the geographic restriction can be worldwide in scope, the time restriction should be narrowed considerably to compensate for the extensive geographic restriction.

a. *EarthWeb, Inc. v. Schlack,* 71 F.Supp.2d 299 (S.D.N.Y. 1999).

b. *West Publishing Corp. v. Stanley,* 2004 WL 73590 (D.N.D. 2004).

c. *MyVitaNet.com v. Kowalski,* __ F.Supp.2d __, 2008 WL 203008 (S.D. Ohio 2008).

---

fourth-grade education agrees to purchase a refrigerator for $4,000 and signs a two-year installment contract. The same type of refrigerator usually sells for $900 on the market. Some courts have held this type of contract to be unconscionable because the contract terms are so oppressive as to "shock the conscience" of the court.[13]

Substantive unconscionability can arise in a wide variety of business contexts. For example, a contract clause that gives the business entity free access to the courts but requires the other party to arbitrate any dispute with the firm may be unconscionable.[14] Similarly, an arbitration clause in a credit-card agreement that prevents credit cardholders from obtaining relief for abusive

13. See, for example, *Jones v. Star Credit Corp.,* 59 Misc.2d 189, 298 N.Y.S.2d 264 (1969). This case will be presented in Chapter 20 as Case 20.3.

14. See, for example, *Wisconsin Auto Loans, Inc. v. Jones,* 290 Wis.2d 514, 714 N.W.2d 155 (2006).

EXHIBIT 11-1 • Unconscionability

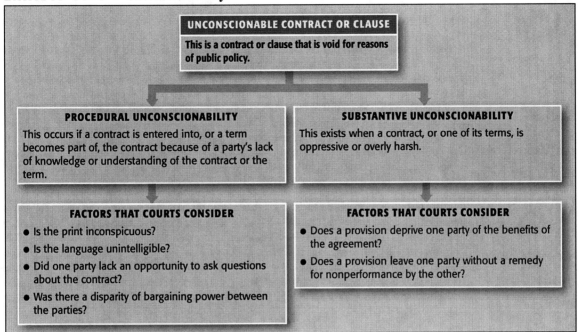

UNCONSCIONABLE CONTRACT OR CLAUSE

This is a contract or clause that is void for reasons of public policy.

PROCEDURAL UNCONSCIONABILITY

This occurs if a contract is entered into, or a term becomes part of, the contract because of a party's lack of knowledge or understanding of the contract or the term.

FACTORS THAT COURTS CONSIDER

- Is the print inconspicuous?
- Is the language unintelligible?
- Did one party lack an opportunity to ask questions about the contract?
- Was there a disparity of bargaining power between the parties?

SUBSTANTIVE UNCONSCIONABILITY

This exists when a contract, or one of its terms, is oppressive or overly harsh.

FACTORS THAT COURTS CONSIDER

- Does a provision deprive one party of the benefits of the agreement?
- Does a provision leave one party without a remedy for nonperformance by the other?

debt-collection practices under consumer law may be unconscionable.[15] Contracts drafted by insurance companies and cell phone providers have been struck down as substantively unconscionable when they included provisions that were overly harsh or one sided.[16]

Exculpatory Clauses Closely related to the concept of unconscionability are **exculpatory clauses**—clauses that release a party from liability in the event of monetary or physical injury *no matter who is at fault.* Indeed, courts sometimes refuse to enforce such clauses on the ground that they are unconscionable. For example, an employer requires its employees to sign a contract containing a provision that shields the employer from liability for any injuries to those employees. In that situation, a court would usually hold the exculpatory clause to be contrary to public policy.[17]

Exculpatory clauses found in rental agreements for commercial property are frequently held to be contrary to public policy, and such clauses are almost always unenforceable in residential property leases.

Although courts view exculpatory clauses with disfavor, they do enforce such clauses when they do not contravene public policy, are not ambiguous, and do not claim to protect parties from liability for intentional misconduct. Businesses such as health clubs, racetracks, amusement parks, skiing facilities, horse-rental operations, golf-cart concessions, and skydiving organizations frequently use exculpatory clauses to limit their liability for patrons' injuries. Because these services are not essential, the firms offering them are sometimes considered to have no relative advantage in bargaining strength, and anyone contracting for their services is considered to do so voluntarily.

Sometimes, a company includes an indemnification provision in its contracts with *independent contractors* (see Chapter 31). Such a provision, or clause, removes any responsibility on the company's part for accidents that happen to the independent contractor while working for the company. When is such a provision against public policy? This was the main question in the following case.

---

15. See, for example, *Coady v. Cross County Bank*, 2007 WI App 26, 299 Wis.2d 420, 729 N.W.2d 732 (2007).

16. See, for example, *Gatton v. T-Mobile USA, Inc.*, 152 Cal.App.4th 571, 61 Cal.Rptr.3d 344 (2007); *Kinkel v. Cingular Wireless, LLC*, 223 Ill.2d 1, 857 N.E.2d 250, 306 Ill.Dec. 157 (2006); and *Aul v. Golden Rule Insurance Co.*, 2007 WI App 165, 737 N.W.2d 24 (2007).

17. For a case with similar facts, see *Little Rock & Fort Smith Railway Co. v. Eubanks*, 48 Ark. 460, 3 S.W. 808 (1887). Today, this type of exculpatory clause may also be illegal on the basis of a violation of a state workers' compensation law.

CASE 11.3 Speedway SuperAmerica, LLC v. Erwin
Court of Appeals of Kentucky, 2008. 250 S.W.3d 339.

● **Background and Facts** Speedway SuperAmerica, LLC, hired Sebert Erwin to provide "General Contracting" for five years, but reserved the right to end the contract at any time. The contract contained an *indemnification* clause. Under that clause, Erwin promised to "hold harmless" Speedway for anything that happened to him while working for the company. One day, Erwin was told to report to a Speedway gas station in another city and help remove a walk-in freezer. When he was helping load it on a truck, he fell and was injured. Erwin sued Speedway for damages resulting from the injury he suffered. Speedway counterclaimed, seeking enforcement of the contract's indemnification clause. Erwin moved to dismiss the counterclaim on the grounds that the indemnification clause was invalid and unenforceable because it was against public policy. The trial court held for Erwin. Speedway appealed.

● **Decision and Rationale** The appeals court affirmed the trial court's ruling, holding that the indemnification clause was contrary to public policy and could not be enforced. The contract was one sided because it was between a chain of convenience stores and a single worker. While such contracts are not always against public policy, they are when there is no bargaining between parties of similar strength. Here, the situation involved one worker with an eighth-grade education contracting with a large company; the bargaining powers were clearly unequal. Erwin was called an independent contractor despite not having control over his work. The contract stated that he agreed to defend the owner and hold it harmless in the event of any negligence. As an independent contractor rather than an employee, Erwin had no right to workers' compensation or other benefits that an employee normally would be due (see Chapter 31 for a full discussion of the distinction between employees and independent contractors). The contract was the equivalent of an exculpatory clause, releasing the employer from any liability regardless of fault. It could not be enforced.

● **What If the Facts Were Different?** *Suppose that Erwin worked for another company as a mover and his employer had sent him to help Speedway move the freezer. Suppose further that the indemnification clause was in a contract signed between Speedway and Erwin's employer. Would that clause be valid? Explain your answer.*

● **The Ethical Dimension** *What benefit was there for Speedway to impose such a clause on Erwin?*

Discriminatory Contracts Contracts in which a party promises to discriminate on the basis of race, color, national origin, religion, gender, age, or disability are contrary to both statute and public policy. They are also unenforceable.[18] For example, if a property owner promises in a contract not to sell the property to a member of a particular race, the contract is unenforceable. The public policy underlying these prohibitions is very strong, and the courts are quick to invalidate discriminatory contracts. Exhibit 11–2 illustrates the types of contracts that may be illegal because they are contrary to statute or public policy.

Effect of Illegality

In general, an illegal contract is void—that is, the contract is deemed never to have existed, and the courts will not aid either party. In most illegal contracts, both parties are considered to be ***in pari delicto***[19] (equally at fault). In such cases, the contract is void. If the contract is executory, neither party can enforce it. If it has been executed, there can be neither contractual nor quasi-contractual recovery.

That one wrongdoer who is a party to an illegal contract is unjustly enriched at the expense of the other is of no concern to the law—except under certain special circumstances that will be discussed below. The major justification for this hands-off atti-

---

18. The major federal statute prohibiting discrimination is the Civil Rights Act of 1964, 42 U.S.C. Sections 2000e–2000e-17. For a discussion of this act and other acts prohibiting discrimination in the employment context, see Chapter 34.

19. Pronounced in *pah*-ree deh-*lick*-tow.

EXHIBIT 11–2 • Contract Legality

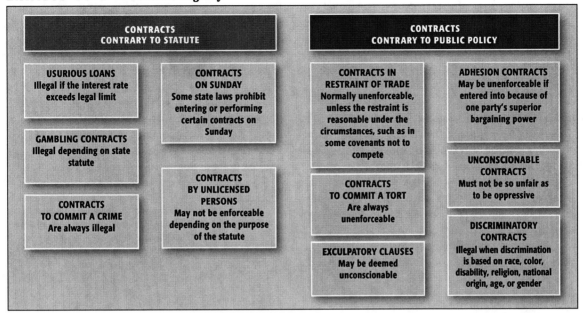

CONTRACTS CONTRARY TO STATUTE		CONTRACTS CONTRARY TO PUBLIC POLICY	
USURIOUS LOANS Illegal if the interest rate exceeds legal limit	**CONTRACTS ON SUNDAY** Some state laws prohibit entering or performing certain contracts on Sunday	**CONTRACTS IN RESTRAINT OF TRADE** Normally unenforceable, unless the restraint is reasonable under the circumstances, such as in some covenants not to compete	**ADHESION CONTRACTS** May be unenforceable if entered into because of one party's superior bargaining power
GAMBLING CONTRACTS Illegal depending on state statute	**CONTRACTS BY UNLICENSED PERSONS** May not be enforceable depending on the purpose of the statute	**CONTRACTS TO COMMIT A TORT** Are always unenforceable	**UNCONSCIONABLE CONTRACTS** Must not be so unfair as to be oppressive
CONTRACTS TO COMMIT A CRIME Are always illegal		**EXCULPATORY CLAUSES** May be deemed unconscionable	**DISCRIMINATORY CONTRACTS** Illegal when discrimination is based on race, color, disability, religion, national origin, age, or gender

tude is that it is improper to place the machinery of justice at the disposal of a plaintiff who has broken the law by entering into an illegal bargain. Another justification is the hoped-for deterrent effect of this general hands-off rule. A plaintiff who suffers loss because of an illegal bargain should presumably be deterred from entering into similar illegal bargains.

Exceptions to the General Rule There are some exceptions to the general rule that neither party to an illegal bargain can sue for breach and that neither party can recover for performance rendered.

Justifiable Ignorance of the Facts. When one of the parties is relatively innocent, that party can often recover any benefits conferred in a partially executed contract. In this situation, the courts will not enforce the contract but will allow the parties to return to their original positions. An innocent party who has fully performed under the contract may sometimes enforce the contract against the guilty party. For example, a trucking company contracts with Gillespie to carry goods to a specific destination for a normal fee of $5,000. The trucker delivers the goods and later finds out that the contents of the shipped crates were illegal. Although the law specifies that the shipment, use, and sale of the goods were illegal, the trucker, being an innocent party, can still legally collect the $5,000 from Gillespie.

Members of Protected Classes. When a statute is clearly designed to protect a certain class of people, a member of that class can enforce a contract in violation of the statute even though the other party cannot. For example, flight attendants and pilots are subject to a federal statute that prohibits them from flying more than a certain number of hours every month. If an attendant or a pilot exceeds the maximum, the airline must nonetheless pay for those extra hours of service.

State statutes often regulate the sale of insurance. If an insurance company violates a statute when selling insurance, the purchaser can nevertheless enforce the policy and recover from the insurer.

Withdrawal from an Illegal Agreement. If an agreement has been only partly carried out and the illegal portion of the bargain has not yet been performed, the party rendering performance can withdraw from the contract and recover the performance or its value. For example, Sam and Jim decide to wager (illegally) on the outcome of a boxing match. Each deposits money with a stakeholder, who agrees to pay the winner of the bet. At this point, each party has performed part of the agreement, but the illegal element of the agreement will not occur until the funds are paid to the winner. Before such payment occurs, either party is entitled to withdraw from the bargain by giving notice of repudiation to the stakeholder.

Contract Illegal through Fraud, Duress, or Undue Influence. Often, one party to an illegal contract is more at fault than the other. When a party has been induced to enter into an illegal bargain by fraud, duress, or undue influence on the part of the other party to the agreement, that party will be allowed to recover for the performance or its value.

Severable, or Divisible, Contracts

A contract that is *severable,* or divisible, consists of distinct parts that can be performed separately, with separate consideration provided for each part. In contrast, a contract is *indivisible* when the parties intend that complete performance by each party will be essential, even if the contract contains a number of seemingly separate provisions.

If a contract is divisible into legal and illegal portions, a court may enforce the legal portion but not the illegal one, so long as the illegal portion does not affect the essence of the bargain.[20] This approach is consistent with the courts' basic policy of enforcing the legal intentions of the contracting parties whenever possible. For example, Cole signs an employment contract that includes an overly broad and thus illegal covenant not to compete. In that situation, the court might allow the employment contract to be enforceable but reform the unreasonably broad covenant by converting its terms into reasonable ones. Alternatively, the court could declare the covenant illegal (and thus void) and enforce the remaining employment terms.

---

[20]. The United States Supreme Court has held that under the Federal Arbitration Act, arbitration clauses are severable from the underlying contract. See *Buckeye Check Cashing, Inc. v. Cardegna,* 546 U.S. 440, 126 S.Ct. 1204, 163 L.Ed.2d 1038 (2006), which was presented as Case 2.2 in Chapter 2.

REVIEWING Capacity and Legality

Renee Beaver started racing go-karts competitively in 1997, when she was fourteen. Many of the races required her to sign an exculpatory clause to participate, which she or her parents regularly signed. In 2000, she participated in the annual Elkhart Grand Prix, a series of races in Elkhart, Indiana. During the event in which she drove, a piece of foam padding used as a course barrier was torn from its base and ended up on the track. A portion of the padding struck Beaver in the head, and another portion was thrown into oncoming traffic, causing a multikart collision during which she sustained severe injuries. Beaver filed an action against the race organizers for negligence. The organizers could not locate the exculpatory clause that Beaver was supposed to have signed. Race organizers argued that she must have signed one to enter the race, but even if she had not signed one, her actions showed her intent to be bound by its terms. Using the information presented in the chapter, answer the following questions.

1. Did Beaver have the contractual capacity to enter a contract with an exculpatory clause? Why or why not?
2. Assuming that Beaver did, in fact, sign the exculpatory clause, did she later disaffirm or ratify the contract? Explain.
3. Now assume that Beaver had stated that she was eighteen years old at the time that she signed the exculpatory clause. How might this affect Beaver's ability to disaffirm or ratify the contract?
4. If Beaver did not actually sign the exculpatory clause, could a court conclude that she impliedly accepted its terms by participating in the race? Why or why not?

TERMS AND CONCEPTS

adhesion contract

age of majority

blue laws

contractual capacity

covenant not to compete

disaffirmance

emancipation

exculpatory clause

in pari delicto

necessaries

ratification

unconscionable

usury

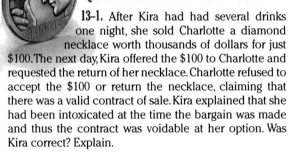

QUESTIONS AND CASE PROBLEMS

13-1. After Kira had had several drinks one night, she sold Charlotte a diamond necklace worth thousands of dollars for just $100. The next day, Kira offered the $100 to Charlotte and requested the return of her necklace. Charlotte refused to accept the $100 or return the necklace, claiming that there was a valid contract of sale. Kira explained that she had been intoxicated at the time the bargain was made and thus the contract was voidable at her option. Was Kira correct? Explain.

13-2. QUESTION WITH SAMPLE ANSWER

A famous New York City hotel, Hotel Lux, is noted for its food as well as its luxury accommodations. Hotel Lux contracts with a famous chef, Chef Perlee, to become its head chef at $6,000 per month. The contract states that should Perlee leave the employment of Hotel Lux for any reason, he will not work as a chef for any hotel or restaurant in New York, New Jersey, or Pennsylvania for a period of one year. During the first six months of the contract, Hotel Lux heavily advertises Perlee as its head chef, and business at the hotel is excellent. Then a dispute arises between the hotel management and Perlee, and Perlee terminates his employment. One month later, he is hired by a famous New Jersey restaurant just across the New York state line. Hotel Lux learns of Perlee's employment through a large advertisement in a New York City newspaper. It seeks to enjoin (prevent) Perlee from working in that restaurant as a chef for one year. Discuss how successful Hotel Lux will be in its action.

- **For a sample answer to Question 13–2, go to Appendix C at the end of this text.**

13-3. Joanne is a seventy-five-year-old widow who survives on her husband's small pension. Joanne has become increasingly forgetful, and her family worries that she may have Alzheimer's disease (a brain disorder that seriously affects a person's ability to carry out daily

activities). No physician has diagnosed her, however, and no court has ruled on Joanne's legal competence. One day while she is out shopping, Joanne stops by a store that is having a sale on pianos and enters into a fifteen-year installment contract to buy a grand piano. When the piano arrives the next day, Joanne seems confused and repeatedly asks the deliveryperson why a piano is being delivered. Joanne claims that she does not recall buying a piano. Explain whether this contract is void, voidable, or valid. Can Joanne avoid her contractual obligation to buy the piano? If so, how?

13-4. Covenants Not to Compete. In 1993, Mutual Service Casualty Insurance Co. and its affiliates (collectively, MSI) hired Thomas Brass as an insurance agent. Three years later, Brass entered into a career agent's contract with MSI. This contract contained provisions regarding Brass's activities after termination. These provisions stated that, for a period of not less than one year, Brass could not solicit any MSI customers to "lapse, cancel, or replace" any insurance contract in force with MSI in an effort to take that business to a competitor. If he did, MSI could at any time refuse to pay the commissions that it otherwise owed him. The contract also restricted Brass from working for American National Insurance Co. for three years after termination. In 1998, Brass quit MSI and immediately went to work for American National, soliciting MSI customers. MSI filed a suit in a Wisconsin state court against Brass, claiming that he had violated the noncompete terms of his MSI contract. Should the court enforce the covenant not to compete? Why or why not? [*Mutual Service Casualty Insurance Co. v. Brass*, 2001 WI App 92, 242 Wis.2d 733, 625 N.W.2d 648 (2001)]

13-5. Unconscionability. Frank Rodziewicz was driving a Volvo tractor-trailer on Interstate 90 in Lake County, Indiana, when he struck a concrete barrier. His tractor-trailer became stuck on the barrier, and the Indiana State Police contacted Waffco Heavy Duty Towing, Inc., to assist in the recovery of the truck. Before beginning work,

Waffco told Rodziewicz that it would cost $275 to tow the truck. There was no discussion of labor or any other costs. Rodziewicz told Waffco to take the truck to a local Volvo dealership. Within a few minutes, Waffco pulled the truck off the barrier and towed it to Waffco's nearby towing yard. Rodziewicz was soon notified that, in addition to the $275 towing fee, he would have to pay $4,070 in labor costs and that Waffco would not release the truck until payment was made. Rodziewicz paid the total amount. Disputing the labor charge, however, he filed a suit in an Indiana state court against Waffco, alleging, in part, breach of contract. Was the towing contract unconscionable? Would it make a difference if the parties had discussed the labor charge before the tow? Explain. [*Rodziewicz v. Waffco Heavy Duty Towing, Inc.*, 763 N.E.2d 491 (Ind.App. 2002)]

13–6. CASE PROBLEM WITH SAMPLE ANSWER

Millennium Club, Inc., operates a tavern in South Bend, Indiana. In January 2003, Pamela Avila and other minors gained admission by misrepresenting themselves to be at least twenty-one years old. According to the club's representatives, the minors used false driver's licenses, "fraudulent transfer of a stamp used to gain admission by another patron or other means of false identification." To gain access, the minors also signed affidavits falsely attesting to the fact that they were aged twenty-one or older. When the state filed criminal charges against the club, the club filed a suit in an Indiana state court against Avila and more than two hundred others, charging that they had misrepresented their ages and seeking damages of $3,000 each. The minors filed a motion to dismiss the complaint. Should the court grant the motion? What are the competing policy interests in this case? If the club was not careful in checking minors' identification, should it be allowed to recover? If the club reasonably relied on the minors' representations, should the minors be allowed to avoid liability? Discuss. [*Millennium Club, Inc. v. Avila*, 809 N.E.2d 906 (Ind.App. 2004)]

- To view a sample answer for Problem 13–6, go to this book's Web site at www.cengage. com/blaw/jentz, select "Chapter 13," and click on "Case Problem with Sample Answer."

13–7. Covenant Not to Compete. Gary Forsee was an executive officer with responsibility for the U.S. operations of BellSouth Corp., a company providing global telecommunications services. Under a covenant not to compete, Forsee agreed that for a period of eighteen months after termination from employment, he would not "provide services . . . in competition with [BellSouth] . . . to any person or entity which provides products or services identical or similar to products and services provided by [BellSouth] . . . within the territory." *Territory* was defined to include the geographic area in which

Forsee provided services to BellSouth. The *services* included "management, strategic planning, business planning, administration, or other participation in or providing advice with respect to the communications services business." Forsee announced his intent to resign and accept a position as chief executive officer of Sprint Corp., a competitor of BellSouth. BellSouth filed a suit in a Georgia state court against Forsee, claiming, in part, that his acceptance of employment with Sprint would violate the covenant not to compete. Is the covenant legal? Should it be enforced? Why or why not? [*BellSouth Corp. v. Forsee*, 265 Ga.App. 589, 595 S.E.2d 99 (2004)]

13–8. Licensing Statutes. Under California law, a contract to manage a professional boxer must be in writing, and the manager must be licensed by the State Athletic Commission. Marco Antonio Barrera is a professional boxer and two-time world champion. In May 2003, José Castillo, who was not licensed by the state, orally agreed to assume Barrera's management. He "understood" that he would be paid in accord with the "practice in the professional boxing industry, but in no case less than ten percent (10%) of the gross revenue" that Barrera generated as a boxer and through endorsements. Among other accomplishments, Castillo negotiated an exclusive promotion contract for Barrera with Golden Boy Promotions, Inc., which is owned and operated by Oscar De La Hoya. Castillo also helped Barrera settle three lawsuits and resolve unrelated tax problems so that Barrera could continue boxing. Castillo did not train Barrera, pick his opponents, or arrange his fights, however. When Barrera abruptly stopped communicating with Castillo, Castillo filed a suit in a California state court against Barrera and others, alleging breach of contract. Under what circumstances is a contract with an unlicensed practitioner enforceable? Is the alleged contract in this case enforceable? Why or why not? [*Castillo v. Barrera*, 146 Cal.App.4th 1317, 53 Cal.Rptr.3d 494 (2 Dist. 2007)]

13–9. A QUESTION OF ETHICS

Dow AgroSciences, LLC (DAS), makes and sells agricultural seed products. In 2000, Timothy Glenn, a DAS sales manager, signed a covenant not to compete. He agreed that for two years from the date of his termination, he would not "engage in or contribute my knowledge to any work or activity involving an area of technology or business that is then competitive with a technology or business with respect to which I had access to Confidential Information during the five years immediately prior to such termination." Working with DAS business, operations, and research and development personnel, and being a member of high-level teams, Glenn had access to confidential DAS information, including agreements with DAS's business partners, marketing plans, litigation details, product secrets, new product development, future plans, and pricing strategies. In 2006, Glenn resigned to work for Pioneer Hi-Bred International, Inc., a DAS competitor. DAS filed a suit in an Indiana state court against Glenn, asking that he be enjoined from accepting any "position that would call on him to use confidential DAS information." [Glenn v. Dow AgroSciences, LLC, 861 N.E.2d 1 (Ind.App. 2007)]

(a) Generally, what interests are served by enforcing covenants not to compete? What interests are served by refusing to enforce them?

(b) What argument could be made in support of reforming (and then enforcing) illegal covenants not to compete? What argument could be made against this practice?

(c) How should the court rule in this case? Why?

13–10. VIDEO QUESTION

Go to this text's Web site at **www.cengage.com/blaw/jentz** and select "Chapter 13." Click on "Video Questions" and view the video titled *The Money Pit.* Then answer the following questions.

(a) Assume that a valid contract exists between Walter (Tom Hanks) and the plumber. Recall from the video that the plumber had at least two drinks before agreeing to take on the plumbing job. If the plumber was intoxicated, is the contract voidable? Why or why not?

(b) Suppose that state law requires plumbers in Walter's state to have a plumber's license and that this plumber does not have a license. Would the contract be enforceable? Why or why not?

(c) In the video, the plumber suggests that Walter has been "turned down by every other plumber in the valley." Although the plumber does not even look at the house's plumbing, he agrees to do the repairs if Walter gives him a check for $5,000 right away "before he changes his mind." If Walter later seeks to void the contract because it is contrary to public policy, what should he argue?

LAW ON THE WEB

For updated links to resources available on the Web, as well as a variety of other materials, visit this text's Web site at

www.cengage.com/blaw/jentz

For a table that includes links to every state's statutory provisions governing the emancipation of minors, go to

topics.law.cornell.edu/wex/table_emancipation

For more information on restrictive covenants in employment contracts, you can access an article written by attorneys at Loose Brown & Associates, P.C., at

www.loosebrown.com/articles/art009.pdf

Legal Research Exercises on the Web

Go to **www.cengage.com/blaw/jentz**, the Web site that accompanies this text. Select "Chapter 13" and click on "Internet Exercises." There you will find the following Internet research exercises that you can perform to learn more about the topics covered in this chapter.

Internet Exercise 13–1: Legal Perspective
Covenants Not to Compete

Internet Exercise 13–2: Management Perspective
Minors and the Law

Internet Exercise 13–3: Social Perspective
Online Gambling

Contracts: Contractual Capacity

Case No. 55

CONTRACTUAL CAPACITY/MINORS

Rodriguez v. Northern Auto Auction, Inc.

Appellate Term, Second Department

22 N.Y.S.2d 107 (1962)

FACTS: Plaintiff Anna Rodriguez (Rodriguez) purchased a car from Defendant Northern Auto Auction, Inc. (Northern Auto). At the time of the purchase Rodriguez was a minor. Some time after she purchased the car and within the legally permissible time to disaffirm, Rodriguez notified Northern she no longer wanted the car. In this lawsuit she sought to return the car and obtain reimbursement of the purchase price.

FIRST ISSUE: Is a minor entitled to disaffirm a contract?

DECISION: Yes.

REASONING: A minor is generally entitled to disaffirm contracts to which minor is a party.

SECOND ISSUE: Is a party who avoids a contract for the purchase of a car on the basis of minority entitled to reimbursement of all money paid for, the car?

DECISION: No, but the minor may be entitled to receive a portion of the money paid.

REASONING: When a minor disaffirms a contract for the sale of a car, the minor is liable to the seller for any deterioration of the car that occurred when the minor used it. The minor is entitled to reimbursement of the money paid in excess of the deterioration.

* * * QUESTIONS * * *
(See back of text for answers)

1) What are the public policy reasons for the special status the law affords to minors which allows them to disaffirm their contracts?

2) During what period of time can a minor disaffirm a contract?

Case No. 56

MINORITY/RIGHT TO DISAFFIRM/RESTITUTION

Fisher d/b/a Syosset Employment Services v. Cattani

District Court, Nassau County

53 Misc.2d 221, 278 N.Y.S.2d 420 (1966)

FACTS: In September, 1962, Plaintiff Syosset Employment Services (Syosset) contracted with Defendant Elaine Cattani (Cattani) to secure employment for her for a fee. Cattani at the time was a minor. Syosset found Cattani a job. She resigned after one month and notified Syosset in November, 1962, while still a minor, that she was disaffirming her contract with the employment agency. When the contract with Syosset was originally made Cattani paid $45.00 which was one-third of the total fee required by the contract. Syosset sued Cattani for the balance of the fee. In the lawsuit Syosset claimed Cattani could not disaffirm the contract.

FIRST ISSUE: Can a minor disaffirm a contract?

DECISION: Yes.

REASONING: Generally a minor has the right to disaffirm contracts. The reason for this rule is the minor's lack of business experience and judgment.

SECOND ISSUE: Is a minor who disaffirms a contract with an employment agency required to pay the unpaid balance of the employment agency's fee?

DECISION: No, judgment for Cattani.

REASONING: The court gave no reasoning for its decision.

NOTE: Cattani did not request a refund of the initial $45.00 payment. The court did not order Syosset to refund that money.

* * * QUESTION * * *
(See back of text for answer)

1) How might the employment service have avoided the problem in this case?

Case No. 57

CONTRACTUAL CAPACITY

Scott Eden Management v. Andrew M. Kavovit

Supreme Court, Westchester County

563 N.Y.S.2d 1001 (1990)

FACTS: Andrew M. Kavovit (Kavovit) was a child actor. When he was 12 years old, he entered a contract with Scott Eden Management (Eden) by which Eden was hired as Kavovit's exclusive manager. Eden's contractual responsibilities included the supervision and promotion of Kavovit's acting career. In return, Eden was entitled to a commission of 15% of Kavovit's gross pay.

At Eden's direction, Kavovit signed numerous contracts, the most lucrative of which was a role on "As the World Turns", a long-running television soap opera.

Thereafter Kavovit disaffirmed the management contract. Eden sued Kavovit seeking commissions on money Kavovit made after the disaffirmance from contracts he entered during the term of the contract with Eden.

ISSUE: Is Kavovit entitled to disaffirm the contract with Eden?

DECISION: Yes.

REASONING: A minor has an absolute right to disaffirm. This right is firmly entrenched in the law, dating back as early as the 15th century.

ISSUE 2: Where an actor who is a minor disaffirms a contract with his personal manager, is the minor obligated to pay commissions earned on contracts entered during the term of the contract with the manager?

DECISION 2: Yes, judgment for Eden.

REASONING 2: When a minor disaffirms a contract, a court may require the minor to restore the other contracting party to its position prior to entering the contract. The court would thus order the minor to return any contractual benefits the minor has received.

Much of the work of a personal manager such as Eden is in negotiating contracts. Kavovit will continue, after the disaffirmance, to receive the benefits of the contracts arranged by Eden. If Kavovit is not obligated to pay Eden commissions on that income, Kavovit would be in a superior position for having canceled the contract. Such a result would be unfair.

To ensure Kavovit continues to pay, the court required Kavovit to submit periodic statements to Eden identifying the sources and amount of Kavovit's income, and also to permit Eden to inspect Kavovit's income records on an annual basis.

Contracts: Illegal Contracts

Case No. 58

ILLEGALITY/COMMISSION OF A CRIME

<u>Braustein v. Jason Tarantella, Inc.</u>

Appellate Division, Second Department

87 A.D.2d 203, 450 N.Y.S.2d 862 (1982)

FACTS: Jason Tarantella, Inc. (Tarantella) produced a film entitled "Fulfilling Young Cups", rated X. Tarantella had a contract with a distributor in which Tarantella gave the distributor the right to market the film and the distributor agreed to pay Tarantella a specified amount. The distributor failed to pay Tarantella. In this lawsuit Tarantella sought payment from the distributor.

The film was produced in New York State. While it was being shown in Hempstead, New York, Tarantella was charged with obscenity for its part in the production and marketing of the film. Tarantella pleaded guilty to first degree obscenity, a felony, and was fined $10,000.00.

ISSUE: Will the courts enforce a contract for the distribution of an illegal product?

DECISION: No, judgment against Tarantella.

REASONING: If the performance of a contract requires criminal acts, the contract is void and unenforceable. Distribution of obscene material is a criminal act. Since the contract between Tarantella and the distributor involved the distribution of an obscene film, the contract is void. The court stated, "To permit a recovery in this case would provide an incentive for the further production of obscene films in New York in violation of this state's penal statutes. Long-settled public policy closes the door of our courts to those who sued to collect the rewards of corruption. That the distributors may profit as a result by not having to share with the producers the ill- gotten money acquired through the distribution of the obscene film is not the issue."

NOTE: Not all pornography nor X-rated movies are obscene. Only those that are obscene are illegal. The distinction between obscenity and legal pornography is not clearly defined in the law.

* * * QUESTIONS * * *
(See back of text for answers)

1)   What is obscenity?

2)   What is pornography?

Case No. 59

ILLEGALITY/LACK OF REQUIRED LICENSE

East Coast Moving & Storage, Inc. v. Flappin

New York City Civil Court

355 N.Y.S.2d 525 (1974)

FACTS: Defendant Mark Flappin (Flappin), responding to an advertisement in New York Magazine, contacted Crockett's Movers and Storage Company (Crocketts) seeking an estimate of the cost to move his belongings to a new apartment. He was given an estimate of $100.00 and agreed to hire Crocketts.

For unknown reasons Crocketts requested another moving company, Plaintiff East Coast Moving & Storage, Inc. (East Coast Moving), to move Flappin. On the day of the move East Coast Moving's employees arrived several hours later than the appointed time. They took 15 hours to complete the move and sought $385.00 in payment from Flappin. He refused to pay and East Coast Moving began this action for payment. Flappin counterclaimed for $200.00, the cost of goods lost and damaged by East Coast Moving during the move.

New York City law requires moving companies that do business in New York City to be licensed. East Coast Moving did not have the license.

FIRST ISSUE: Is an unlicensed mover entitled to enforce a contract for payment for moving services?

DECISION: No, judgment for Flappin.

REASONING: If a statute requires a person to obtain a license before engaging in a business and the purpose of the license is to protect the public, contracts made by a person engaging in the business without the license are void. The purpose of the licensing law for movers was to protect the public. Fraudulent behavior in the moving industry was a frequent problem in New York City. Such behavior included movers deliberately getting lost while traveling to customers' new residence and then charging customers on a per-hour basis, including the hours the movers were "lost", and offering to move customers at a low price and then charging substantially more. The low estimates lured customers away from doing business with the licensed movers, whose higher estimates more accurately reflected the final price. The licensing law sought to protect customers and licensed dealers from such unfair practices.

SECOND ISSUE: Is Flappin entitled to the $200.00 he sought in his counterclaim?

DECISION: Yes, judgment for Flappin.

REASONING: Credible testimony at trial established that East Coast Moving was negligent in losing and damaging Flappin's possessions.

* * * QUESTIONS * * *
(See back of text for answers)

1) Assume the purpose of the movers' license was merely revenue raising. Would the result of the case have been different and if so, in what way?

2) The case did not describe the evidence presented by Flappin to prove East Coast Moving's liability for the lost and damaged furniture. What evidence might Flappin have presented for this purpose?

Case No. 60

AGREEMENT NOT TO COMPETE

<u>Sung v. Ramirez</u>

Supreme Court, Queens County

121 Misc.2d 313, 467 N.Y.S.2d 486 (1983)

FACTS: Plaintiff Foyer Key Sung (Sung) purchased from Defendant Juan Ramirez (Ramirez) a deli-grocery known as The Broadway Store for $27,000.00. The sales contract contained an agreement not to compete, which stated, "And the Transferor covenants and agrees to and with the Transferee not to re-establish, reopen, be engaged in, nor in any manner whatsoever become interested, directly or indirectly, either as employee, as owners, as partners, as agent or as stockholders, director or officer of the corporation, or otherwise, in any business, trade or occupation similar to the one hereby sold, within the County of Richmond for 5 years."

Nine months later Ramirez leased a building he owned to one Raphael Diaz. The lease stated that the building would be used as a deli-grocery. The building was 2-1/2 blocks from The Broadway Store. Once Diaz opened the deli-grocery, The Broadway Store's weekly gross revenues decreased by about $4,000.00. Sung attributed the decrease to the opening of Diaz' deli-grocery. Sung claimed Ramirez' lease with Diaz violated Ramirez' agreement not to compete and sued Ramirez for breach of contract. Ramirez denied that the lease violated the contract.

FIRST ISSUE: Is a promise not to compete with a deli-grocery valid when it covers a county-wide area and lasts for five years?

DECISION: Yes, with modification of the applicable territory.

REASONING: A promise not to compete made by a seller of a business to the buyer is enforceable provided it is no more restrictive than is reasonably necessary to protect the good will purchased by the buyer. The agreement not to compete signed by Ramirez barred him from operating or acquiring an interest in a competing business in Richmond County, which encompasses all of Staten Island. The five-year period was not unreasonable. The county-wide territory appeared to the court, however, to be too broad. The court concluded it had the authority to reduce the geographical area and enforce the agreement as so modified. In this case the 2-1/2 blocks which separated the deli- groceries were within what would be a reasonable geographical area within which to restrict Ramirez from competition. Therefore, the promise not to compete was valid in the circumstances of this case.

SECOND ISSUE: Does the seller of a business violate a promise not to compete by leasing a building to tenants whose business competes with the business sold by the seller?

DECISION: No.

REASONING: Ramirez did not open the competing business, nor did he become an employee, officer, shareholder, owner, or agent of the competing business, nor did he have an interest in the competing deli-grocery. Ramirez was entitled to rental payments regardless of the success or failure of Diaz' business. Ramirez did not receive a share of the profits nor did he participate in the promotion of the business. Therefore, Ramirez did not violate the agreement not to compete.

* * * QUESTIONS * * *
(See back of text for answers)

1) What are the public policy reasons restricting the enforceability of contracts in restraint of trade?

2) Why was the designation of territory too broad?

Case No. 61

AGREEMENTS NOT TO COMPETE

Savannah Bank, N.A. v. Savings Bank of the Fingerlakes

Appellate Division, Fourth Department

261 A.D.2d 917, 691 N.Y.S.2d 227 (1999)

FACTS: Savannah Bank, N.A. (Savannah) sued Savings Bank of the Fingerlakes (Fingerlakes) for, among other things, misappropriation of trade secrets and interference with a contractual relationship. The lawsuit resulted when two commercial loan officers left Savannah and began working for Fingerlakes. The loan officers had signed a restrictive covenant that they would not accept employment at a competing bank located within a 25-mile radius of Savannah for a year following the termination of their employment. Fingerlakes was successful in showing the information in question was readily ascertainable through sources outside the business and therefore no trade secrets or confidential customer lists were misappropriated.

FIRST ISSUE: Was the restrictive covenant signed by the loan officers enforceable?

DECISION: No

REASONING: An agreement not to compete in an employment contract is enforceable only if: 1) the restriction is no greater than is required for the protection of the legitimate interests of the employer; 2) the agreement does not impose an undue hardship on the employee; 3) the agreement is not harmful to the general public. Additionally, restrictive covenants are enforceable only if they protect trade secrets or confidential information or in cases where "unique or extraordinary" services are provided by the employee in question.

In this case Fingerlakes was successful in showing that no trade secrets or confidential customers lists were misappropriated. Although both employees were "knowledgeable and experienced," the appellate court agreed with the findings of the lower court that the services provided by the employees in question were not "unique or extraordinary". Therefore, the restrictive covenant was unenforceable.

SECOND ISSUE: Can Savannah successfully pursue a claim of interference with a contractual relationship against Fingerlakes where the claim for interference is based on an unenforceable contract?

DECISION: No

REASONING: An element of a claim for interference with a contractual relationship is that a valid contract exist. Since the parties in this case lacked such an agreement, the tort claim for interference cannot be sustained.

Case No. 62

ILLEGALITY

Hartogs v. Employers Mutual Liability Insurance Company of Wisconsin

Supreme Court, New York County

89 Misc.2d 468, 391 N.Y.S.2d 262 (1977)

FACTS: Plaintiff Renatus Hartogs (Hartogs), a psychiatrist, purchased malpractice insurance from Defendant Employers Mutual Liability Insurance Company of Wisconsin (the Insurance Company). The policy obligated the Insurance Company to pay for an attorney to defend Hartogs in the event he was sued for malpractice, and to pay any judgment awarded against him for malpractice.

A lesbian patient sued Hartogs for malpractice. Under the guise of medical therapy, supposedly to treat the patient's lesbianism, Hartogs administered multiple doses of "fornication therapy." Hartogs later admitted that he knew such treatment was a violation of professional ethics and not within acceptable medical standards.

The Insurance Company refused to pay Hartogs' lawyer to defend the malpractice action. Hartogs sued the Insurance Company to enforce its contractual obligation to pay.

ISSUE: Is the insurance contract enforceable under the circumstances of this case?

DECISION: No, judgment for the Insurance Company.

REASONING: Courts will not enforce contracts that promote immoral and unconscionable purposes. Hartogs' actions were both immoral and unconscionable. As a matter of public policy, the court therefore refused to enforce the Insurance Company's contractual obligations to defend him in a lawsuit based on such action.

* * * QUESTIONS * * *
(See back of text for answers)

1) What is malpractice?

2) Was the contract between Hartogs and the Insurance Company illegal?

3) If the contract was not illegal, why did the court refuse to enforce the contract?

Case No. 63

UNCONSCIONABLE/ADHESION CONTRACTS

Harwood v. Lincoln Square Apartments Section Five, Inc.

New York City Civil Court

78 Misc.2d 1097, 359 N.Y.S.2d 387 (1974)

FACTS: Plaintiff Herbert Harwood (Harwood) is a tenant of Defendant landlord Lincoln Square Apartments Section Five, Inc. (Square Apartments). During six weeks of summer 1973, the central air conditioning system supplied by Square Apartments did not operate. Harwood in this action sought reimbursement for money he spent to rent an air conditioning unit for his apartment for the six-week period. The written lease between Harwood and Square Apartments specified that Square Apartments would provide air conditioning and further that "interruption or curtailment of any service or services shall not . . . entitle tenant to any . . . abatement of rent nor subject landlord to any liability for damages or otherwise."

ISSUE: Does a disclaimer of liability for failure to provide air conditioning contained in a lease relieve the landlord of liability for failure to provide air conditioning during a six-week period in the summer?

DECISION: No, judgment for Harwood.

REASONING: While a court will not normally modify the terms of a contract, it will do so if the terms are unfair and the result of gross inequality of bargaining power. Square Apartments failed to perform an important obligation under the lease—furnishing air conditioning. The tenant, through his rent payments, paid for the six weeks of air conditioning although he did not receive it. To be consistent with prevailing notions of justice, one should not be forced to give something for nothing. The number of available apartments in Manhattan was limited. As a result, standardized lease forms unreasonably favorable to landlords were frequently used. Tenants, when provided with such a lease, were unable to bargain for reasonable terms. The term in issue in this case is unconscionable and therefore unenforceable.

* * * QUESTIONS * * *
(See back of text for answers)

1) What terminology, if included in the contract between Harwood and Square Apartments, would have eliminated the landlord's alleged defense that the contract, by its terms, relieved it from liability?

2) Does the court's refusal to enforce the contract term in issue violate the landlord's right of freedom of contract?

3) What is an adhesion contract?

Case No. 64

ADHESION CONTRACT

St. John's Episcopal Hospital v. McAdoo

New York City Civil Court

94 Misc.2d 967, 405 N.Y.S.2d 935 (1978)

FACTS: Mrs. McAdoo was separated from her husband, Defendant Charles McAdoo (McAdoo), and was pregnant with a child that was not his. During the pregnancy Mrs. McAdoo needed emergency surgery for a problem related to the pregnancy. She therefore went to Plaintiff St. John's Episcopal Hospital (Hospital), where she was joined by her husband. The Hospital required McAdoo to sign a contract. Based on Mrs. McAdoo's appearance and mental state at the time, McAdoo believed his wife was near death. He signed the contract without carefully reading it.

Less than an hour after arriving at the Hospital, Mrs. McAdoo underwent emergency surgery. She recovered and was discharged eight days later. After bringing his wife to the Hospital on the night of the emergency, McAdoo did not visit her and had no other contact with her following the emergency.

The contract that McAdoo signed was a standard form contract prepared by the Hospital. Its terms included a paragraph entitled "Assignment of Insurance Benefits". This title was written in bold print. The last sentence of the paragraph read, "I understand that I am financially responsible to the hospital for charges not covered by my group insurance plan."

The Hospital sought payment from McAdoo for his wife's hospital bill based on the contract that he signed. McAdoo refused to pay.

ISSUE: Is the agreement signed by McAdoo valid and enforceable?

DECISION: No, judgment for McAdoo.

REASONING: While competent adults are normally held responsible for their contractual obligations even if they fail to read the terms, circumstances exist where requiring adherence to a contract would be grossly unfair. Under the circumstances of this case, the contract was one of adhesion and therefore unenforceable. At the time McAdoo signed the contract he was understandably preoccupied by his wife's medical emergency. It was reasonable for McAdoo to conclude under the circumstances that he had no choice but to sign the form. Also, the contract term requiring him to pay the bill was misleading. The provision imposing liability was inserted in a paragraph containing the unrelated heading "Assignment of Insurance Benefits". The Hospital should have been well aware of the anxiety experienced by the families of emergency room patients and have prepared a clearer contract.

* * * QUESTIONS * * *
(See back of text for answers)

1) How could the Hospital have strengthened its position in this case?

2) What is the policy behind the rule that contractual obligations are binding even on parties who fail to read the terms of their written contracts?

Case No. 65

UNCONSCIONABLE CONTRACTS

BGW Associates, Inc. v. Valley Broadcasting Co.

Federal District Court, Southern District of New York

532 F.Supp. 1112 (1981)

FACTS: Plaintiff BGW Associates, Inc. (BGW) is a corporation engaged in consulting services to the radio and television industries. The defendant, Valley Broadcasting Company (Valley), wanted to operate a television channel. BGW and Valley entered a contract that required BGW to provide consulting services to Valley for which Valley agreed to pay BGW $25,000.00. Thereafter Valley was successful in securing a license to operate a television channel.

After completing their performance on the first contract, the parties entered a second contract which required BGW to provide additional consulting services for three years, in return for which Valley would pay a total of $216,000.00 plus expenses. Both parties performed for about fourteen months. Thereafter, Valley informed BGW in writing it refused to continue to perform the contract. BGW sued for the remaining money due on the contract. Valley defended on the basis the contract was unconscionable and therefore unenforceable. Specifically, Valley claimed: a) BGW had an unfair advantage when the contract was negotiated because Valley was inexperienced in the television industry; and b) BGW exploited that advantage by obtaining for itself a very high consulting fee.

Although the principals of Valley had no prior experience in the television industry, its president and another officer were both successful attorneys.

ISSUE: Is the contract between BGW and Valley unconscionable?

DECISION: No, judgment for BGW.

REASONING: A court may refuse to enforce a contract that is unconscionable. The elements of an unconscionable contract include: a) the absence of meaningful choice by one contracting party, often the result of gross disparity in bargaining power, and b) contract terms that are unreasonably favorable to the other party. Concerning disparity of bargaining power, both parties here were knowledgeable business persons. Although Valley's principals may not nave been knowledgeable about the television industry and therefore considered themselves to be in need of BGW's services, the resulting bargaining advantage for BGW is not so significant as to be unconscionable.

Concerning the requirement of grossly unfavorable terms, Valley did not prove the contract price in this case was sufficiently unfair. The court noted that high fees in the broadcast industry were not unusual.

* * * QUESTIONS * * *
(See back of text for answers)

1) Why are the concepts of adhesion and unconscionability generally not applicable to the contracts of experienced business people?

2) What options does the court have for treating an unconscionable contract?

Case No. 66

EXCULPATORY CLAUSE

Gross v. Sweet

Court of Appeals

49 N.Y.2d 102, 424 N.Y.S.2d 365 (1979)

FACTS: Plaintiff Bruce Gross (Gross) was a student at a parachute training school owned and operated by Defendant William Sweet (Sweet). As a prerequisite for admission to the course, Gross signed a form entitled "Responsibility Release" which read as follows:

> I, the undersigned, hereby and by these covenants, do waive any and all claims that I, my heirs, and/or assignees may have against Nathaniel Sweet, the Stormville Parachute Center, the Jumpmaster and the Pilot who shall operate the aircraft when used for the purpose of parachute jumping for any personal injuries or property damage that I may sustain or which may arise out of my learning, practicing or actually jumping from an aircraft. I also assume full responsibility for any damage that I may do or cause while participating in this sport.

During Gross' first practice jump he was seriously injured. He sued Sweet for negligence in failing to provide adequate training, and failing to sufficiently warn Gross of the dangers of parachute jumping. Sweet denied liability, claiming the responsibility release signed by Gross released Sweet from any liability for negligence.

ISSUE: Does the responsibility release relieve Sweet from liability for negligence?

DECISION: No.

REASONING: Contract terms that seek to free a person from the consequences of that person's own negligence are not favored by the law. If the exculpatory clause applies by its terms to gross negligence, it is unenforceable. Concerning ordinary negligence, an exculpatory clause will be enforced only if the clause clearly and conspicuously states that the limitation of liability applies to negligence.

A release like the one in this case, which does not mention negligence, serves only to emphasize that a person who signs it cannot sue for injuries resulting from the ordinary risks of the activity undertaken. Such a release, however, does not prevent a lawsuit for injuries resulting from negligence.

* * * QUESTIONS * * *
(See back of text for answers)

1) What is an exculpatory clause?

2) How could Sweet strengthen his position in another similar lawsuit?

Case No. 67

EXCULPATORY CLAUSE

Public Service Mutual Insurance Company v.
Royal Burglar and Fire Alarm Inc.

New York City Civil Court

394 N.Y.S.2d 524 (1977)

FACTS: Defendant Royal Burglar and Fire Alarm Inc. (Royal) was in the business of renting burglar alarm systems. A customer signed a contract to rent a system from Royal. Royal agreed in a written contract to maintain the system and to repair and replace parts as needed. The contract contained a clause that relieved Royal from liability for damages arising from its own negligence. This limitation was printed in large, bold print and was clearly stated.

During the term of the lease the alarm malfunctioned. The customer called Royal who negligently replaced the malfunctioning alarm with another malfunctioning alarm. The following day the property on which the alarm was located was burglarized. The alarm failed to operate and the burglars stole $712.75 worth of property. The customer was compensated for the loss by its insurance company, Plaintiff Public Service Mutual Insurance Company (Insurance Company). In this action Insurance Company sought to collect from Royal the money paid to the customer on the grounds that Royal acted negligently by not verifying that the second system it installed worked properly. Royal claimed the exculpatory clause freed it from liability for negligence.

ISSUE: Is the contract provision seeking to free Royal from liability for its own negligence enforceable?

DECISION: Yes.

REASONING: Generally, parties to a contract can exempt or limit their liability for losses resulting from their own negligence, absent a statute to the contrary. The exculpatory clause in the contract between the customer and Royal was conspicuously presented in large, bold print and the language was clear. Under these circumstances a clause limiting a party's liability for negligence is enforceable.

* * * QUESTIONS * * *
(See back of text for answers)

1) The reasoning in this case suggests statutes may exist which preclude parties from inserting exculpatory clauses into certain types of contracts. What are some examples of contracts that are prohibited by New York statutes from including exculpatory clauses?

2) If an exculpatory clause is inserted into a contract in violation of a statute, is the clause enforceable?

Case No. 68

EXCULPATORY CLAUSE

DeVito v. New York University College of Dentistry

Supreme Court, New York County

145 Misc.2d 144, 544 N.Y.S.2d 109 (1989)

FACTS: Plaintiff Carmen DeVito (DeVito) received various dental treatments at a clinic operated by defendant New York University College of Dentistry (University). In exchange for reduced fees, DeVito agreed to be treated by dental school students and was required to sign the following release:

> "In consideration of the reduced rates given me by New York University, I hereby release and agree to save harmless New York University, its doctors, and students, from any and all liability arising out of, or in connection with, any injuries or damages which I may sustain while on its premises, or as a result of any treatment in its infirmaries."

DeVito was injured during the treatments and sued University for malpractice (negligence in the performance of professional duties). University claimed the release barred DeVito's claim.

ISSUE: Does the release relieve University from liability for malpractice?

DECISION: No.

REASONING: Contract terms that are designed to exculpate persons from their own negligence are carefully scrutinized by the courts. They consider the relationship between the parties and whether enforcement of the exculpatory clause would be in the public interest. The court also examines the wording of the release to determine if the terms are clear and understandable to a lay person.

For an exculpatory clause to relieve the defendant of liability for negligence, its terms must be so "clear, explicit, and unambiguous that it appears certain that the limitation of liability is intended to cover negligence ...". Although the word "negligence" is not indispensable, its use is strongly favored. If the word "negligence" is not present, other words clearly referring to the concept of fault must exist. Open-ended phrases, like "any and all claims" or "any and all responsibility or liability of any nature whatsoever", are insufficient.

In this case, the wording of the release did not specifically mention negligence, is otherwise ambiguous, and would not be understood by a lay person to release the University from liability for malpractice.

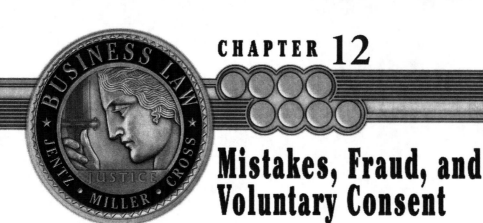

CHAPTER 12

Mistakes, Fraud, and Voluntary Consent

An otherwise valid contract may still be unenforceable if the parties have not genuinely agreed to its terms. As mentioned in Chapter 10, lack of genuineness of assent, or voluntary consent, can be used as a defense to the contract's enforceability. Voluntary consent may be lacking because of a mistake, misrepresentation, undue influence, or duress—in other words, because there is no true "meeting of the minds." Generally, a party who demonstrates that he or she did not truly agree to the terms of a contract can choose either to carry out the contract or to rescind (cancel) it and thus avoid the entire transaction. In this chapter, we examine the kinds of factors that may indicate a lack of voluntary consent.

Mistakes

We all make mistakes, so it is not surprising that mistakes are made when contracts are formed. In certain circumstances, contract law allows a contract to be avoided on the basis of mistake. It is important to distinguish between *mistakes of fact* and *mistakes of value or quality*. Only a mistake of fact makes a contract voidable.

Mistakes of Fact

Mistakes of fact occur in two forms—*bilateral* and *unilateral*. A bilateral, or mutual, mistake is made by *both* of the contracting parties. A unilateral mistake is made by only *one* of the parties. We look next at these two types of mistakes and illustrate them graphically in Exhibit 12–1.

Bilateral (Mutual) Mistakes of Fact A bilateral, or mutual, mistake occurs when both parties are mistaken as to an existing *material fact*—that is, a fact important to the subject matter of the contract. It is a "mutual misunderstanding concerning a basic assumption on which the contract was made."[1] When a

bilateral mistake occurs, normally the contract is voidable by the adversely affected party and can be rescinded, or canceled. For example, Gilbert contracts to sell Magellan three tracts of undeveloped land for $6 million on the basis of a surveyor's report showing the layout and acreage. After agreeing to the price, the parties discover that the surveyor made an error and that the tracts actually contain 10 percent more acreage than reported. In this situation, Gilbert can seek rescission (cancellation) of the contract based on mutual mistake. The same result—rescission—would occur if both parties had mistakenly believed that the tracts of land were adjoining but they were not.[2]

A word or term in a contract may be subject to more than one reasonable interpretation. If the parties to the contract attach materially different meanings to the term, a court may allow the contract to be rescinded because there has been no true "meeting of the minds."[3] The classic example is *Raffles v. Wichelhaus,*[4] a case decided by an English court in 1864. Wichelhaus agreed to buy a shipment of Surat

---

1. *Restatement (Second) of Contracts*, Section 152.

2. See, for example, *Rawson v. UMLIC VP, LLC*, 933 So.2d 1206 (Fla.App. 2006).
3. The only way for a court to find out the meaning that each party attached to the contract term is to allow the parties to introduce *parol evidence*, which is basically oral testimony about the terms of their agreement. Parol evidence will be discussed in Chapter 15.
4. 159 Eng.Rep. 375 (1864).

EXHIBIT 12-1 • **Mistakes of Fact**

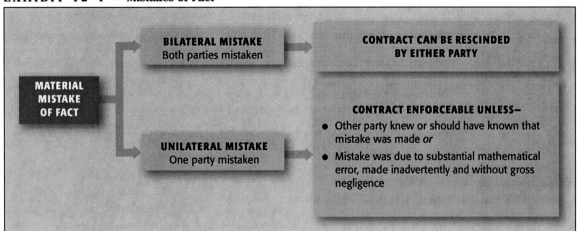

cotton from Raffles, "to arrive 'Peerless' from Bombay." There were two ships named *Peerless* sailing from Bombay, India, however. Wichelhaus was referring to the *Peerless* that sailed in October; Raffles meant a different *Peerless* that sailed in December. When Raffles tried to deliver the goods in December, Wichelhaus refused to accept them, and a lawsuit followed. The court held in favor of Wichelhaus, concluding that a mutual mistake had been made because the parties had attached materially different meanings to an essential term of the contract.

In the following case, the court had to grapple with a question of mutual mistake that was perhaps not what it seemed to be.

C A S E 12.1 Inkel v. Pride Chevrolet-Pontiac, Inc.
Supreme Court of Vermont, 2008. 945 A.2d 855.

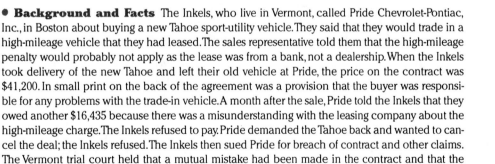

• **Background and Facts** The Inkels, who live in Vermont, called Pride Chevrolet-Pontiac, Inc., in Boston about buying a new Tahoe sport-utility vehicle. They said that they would trade in a high-mileage vehicle that they had leased. The sales representative told them that the high-mileage penalty would probably not apply as the lease was from a bank, not a dealership. When the Inkels took delivery of the new Tahoe and left their old vehicle at Pride, the price on the contract was $41,200. In small print on the back of the agreement was a provision that the buyer was responsible for any problems with the trade-in vehicle. A month after the sale, Pride told the Inkels that they owed another $16,435 because there was a misunderstanding with the leasing company about the high-mileage charge. The Inkels refused to pay. Pride demanded the Tahoe back and wanted to cancel the deal; the Inkels refused. The Inkels then sued Pride for breach of contract and other claims. The Vermont trial court held that a mutual mistake had been made in the contract and that the Inkels should have agreed to undo the deal. The court granted summary judgment for Pride, ordering the Inkels to pay damages. They appealed.

• **Decision and Rationale** The Supreme Court of Vermont reversed in favor of the Inkels, holding that it was not clear that there was a mutual mistake and that Pride may have engaged in consumer fraud. A mutual mistake means both parties were ignorant of the same facts. Pride knew the terms of its contract, and the Inkels knew their vehicle was high mileage. It appears that either Pride was hiding the truth about what would happen due to the high mileage on the trade-in vehicle, or the Inkels were trying to take advantage of Pride's ignorance about the extra payoff needed to their bank for their high-mileage vehicle. Even if there was a mutual mistake, which

CASE CONTINUES

CASE 12.1 CONTINUED should be determined at trial, it was not clear that Pride offered to rescind the contract when it said the Inkels could return the vehicle. The terms of a return were never made clear.

● **The Ethical Dimension** *Some car dealerships are notorious for dubious sales practices. If a Pride sales representative led the Inkels to believe that the dealership did not care about the extra miles on the trade-in, should it be willing to incur the loss? Why or why not?*

● **The Legal Environment Dimension** *If a car dealership wants a quality reputation, how can it avoid the kind of problem that arose in this case?*

Unilateral Mistakes of Fact A unilateral mistake occurs when only one of the contracting parties is mistaken about a material fact. Generally, a unilateral mistake does not afford the mistaken party any right to relief from the contract. Normally, the contract is enforceable. For example, DeVinck intends to sell his motor home for $32,500. When he learns that Benson is interested in buying a used motor home, DeVinck faxes Benson an offer to sell the vehicle to him. When typing the fax, however, DeVinck mistakenly keys in the price of $23,500. Benson immediately sends DeVinck a fax accepting DeVinck's offer. Even though DeVinck intended to sell his motor home for $32,500, his unilateral mistake falls on him. He is bound in contract to sell the motor home to Benson for $23,500.

There are at least two exceptions to this general rule.[5] First, if the *other* party to the contract knows or should have known that a mistake of fact was made, the contract may not be enforceable. In the above example, if Benson knew that DeVinck intended to sell his motor home for $32,500, then DeVinck's unilateral mistake (stating $23,500 in his offer) can render the resulting contract unenforceable.

The second exception arises when a unilateral mistake of fact was due to a mathematical mistake in addition, subtraction, division, or multiplication and was made inadvertently and without gross (extreme) negligence. The clerical error must be readily provable, though. For example, in preparing a bid a contractor itemized the estimated cost of each portion of the project, but made a mistake in addition when totaling the estimated costs, resulting in a total significantly lower than the correct total. Because the clerical error can be easily ascertained, a court may allow any contract resulting from the bid to be rescinded. Alternatively, a court may reform the contract to reflect the accurate total.

Mistakes of Value

If a mistake concerns the future market value or quality of the object of the contract, the mistake is one of *value,* and the contract normally is enforceable. Mistakes of value can be bilateral or unilateral; but either way, they do not serve as a basis for avoiding a contract. Suppose that Hari buys a violin from Bev for $250. Although the violin is very old, neither party believes that it is extremely valuable. Later, however, an antiques dealer informs the parties that the violin is rare and worth thousands of dollars. Although both parties were mistaken, the mistake is not a mistake of *fact* that warrants contract rescission. This would be true even if, at the time of contracting, only Bev believed the violin was not particularly valuable (a unilateral mistake) and Hari thought it was rare and worth more than $250.

The reason that mistakes of value or quality have no legal significance is that value is variable. Depending on the time, place, and other circumstances, the same item may be worth considerably different amounts. When parties form a contract, their agreement establishes the value of the object of their transaction—for the moment. Each party is considered to have assumed the risk that the value will change in the future or prove to be different from what he or she thought. Without this rule, almost any party who did not receive what she or he considered a fair bargain could argue mistake.

Fraudulent Misrepresentation

Although fraud is a tort (see Chapter 6), it also affects the authenticity of the innocent party's consent to the contract. When an innocent party is fraudulently induced to enter into a contract, the contract normally can be avoided because that party has not *voluntarily*

---

5. The *Restatement (Second) of Contracts,* Section 153, liberalizes the general rule to take into account the modern trend of allowing avoidance even though only one party has been mistaken.

consented to its terms.[6] Ordinarily, the innocent party can either rescind (cancel) the contract and be restored to her or his original position or enforce the contract and seek damages for any injuries resulting from the fraud.

Generally, fraudulent misrepresentation refers only to misrepresentation that is consciously false and is intended to mislead another. The person making the fraudulent misrepresentation knows or believes that the assertion is false or knows that she or he does not have a basis (stated or implied) for the assertion.[7] Typically, fraudulent misrepresentation consists of the following elements:

1. A misrepresentation of a material fact must occur.
2. There must be an intent to deceive.
3. The innocent party must justifiably rely on the misrepresentation.

With its anonymity and rapidly changing technology, the online world is a hospitable environment for fraudulent misrepresentation. In 2006, for example, users of an online dating service sued Yahoo!, Inc., for fraudulent misrepresentation in connection with personal ads posted online. The plaintiffs claimed that Yahoo was deliberately creating false profiles and sending them to subscribers as "potential new matches." Although Yahoo insisted that it was immune from such suits under the Communications Decency Act of 1996 (see the in-depth discussion in Chapter 6), the court held that the company was not entitled to immunity because Yahoo itself had provided the content.[8] Another source of fraudulent misrepresentation on the Web is "click fraud," the topic of this chapter's *Insight into Ethics* feature on pages 270 and 271.

---

6. *Restatement (Second) of Contracts*, Sections 163 and 164.
7. *Restatement (Second) of Contracts*, Section 162.
8. *Anthony v. Yahoo!, Inc.*, 421 F.Supp.2d 1257 (N.D.Cal. 2006).

Misrepresentation Has Occurred

The first element of proving fraud is to show that misrepresentation of a material fact has occurred. This misrepresentation can occur by words or actions. For example, the statement "This sculpture was created by Michelangelo" is a misrepresentation of fact if another artist sculpted the statue. Similarly, suppose that Swan tells the owner of an art gallery that she is interested in buying only paintings by a particular artist. The owner immediately leads Swan over to six individual paintings. Here, the gallery owner, without saying a word, has represented by his conduct that the six paintings are works of that artist. If Swan buys one of the paintings and it turns out to have been painted by another artist, she can sue the gallery owner for fraud. The identity of the artist would be a material fact in the formation of either contract.

Statements of opinion and representations of future facts (predictions) are generally not subject to claims of fraud. Every person is expected to exercise care and judgment when entering into contracts, and the law will not come to the aid of one who simply makes an unwise bargain. Statements such as "This land will be worth twice as much next year" or "This car will last for years and years" are statements of opinion, not fact. Contracting parties should recognize them as such and not rely on them. An opinion is usually subject to contrary or conflicting views; a fact is objective and verifiable. Thus, a seller of goods is allowed to use *puffery* to sell his or her wares without liability for fraud.

In certain cases, however, particularly when a naïve purchaser relies on a so-called expert's opinion, the innocent party may be entitled to rescission or reformation. (*Reformation* is an equitable remedy granted by a court in which the terms of a contract are altered to reflect the true intentions of the parties—see Chapter 18.) The issue in the following case was whether the statements made by instructors at a dance school to one of the school's students qualified as statements of opinion or statements of fact.

C A S E **12.2 Vokes v. Arthur Murray, Inc.**
District Court of Appeal of Florida, Second District, 1968. 212 So.2d 906.

● **Company Profile** Arthur Murray, founder of Arthur Murray, Inc. (**www.arthurmurray.com**), began teaching people how to dance in 1919. At the time, social dancing was becoming increasingly popular among young people, in part because so many adults were shocked by the new "jazz dancing." Across America, young people wanted to learn the new steps—the turkey trot, the fox-trot,

CASE 12.2 CONTINUED the kangaroo dip, the chicken scratch, the bunny hug, the grizzly bear, and others. By the 1930s, Murray's instructors were giving lessons on cruise ships, in tourist hotels, and to the employees of New York stores during the employees' lunch breaks. In 1937, Murray founded the Arthur Murray Studios, a chain of franchised dance schools. During the 1950s, Murray sponsored a television show—*The Arthur Murray Party*—to attract students to the schools. Murray retired in 1964, estimating that he had taught more than 20 million people how to dance.

● **Background and Facts** Audrey E. Vokes, a widow without family, wished to become "an accomplished dancer" and to find "a new interest in life." In 1961, she was invited to attend a "dance party" at J. P. Davenport's "School of Dancing," an Arthur Murray, Inc., franchise. Vokes went to the school and received elaborate praise from her instructor for her grace, poise, and potential as "an excellent dancer." The instructor sold her eight half-hour dance lessons for $14.50 each, to be utilized within one calendar month. Subsequently, over a period of less than sixteen months, Vokes bought a total of fourteen dance courses, which amounted to 2,302 hours of dancing lessons at Davenport's school, for a total cash outlay of $31,090.45 (in 2008, this would amount to nearly $140,000). When it became clear to Vokes that she did not, in fact, have the potential to be an excellent dancer, she filed a suit against the school, alleging fraudulent misrepresentation. When the trial court dismissed her complaint, she appealed.

● **Decision and Rationale** The state intermediate appellate court reinstated the complaint and remanded the case to the trial court to allow Vokes to prove her case. The appellate court held that Vokes could avoid the contract because it was procured by false representations that she had a promising career in dancing. The court acknowledged that ordinarily, to be grounds for rescission, a misrepresentation must be one of fact rather than of opinion. "A statement of a party having * * * superior knowledge may be regarded as a statement of fact although it would be considered as opinion if the parties were dealing on equal terms. It could be reasonably supposed here that defendants had 'superior knowledge' as to whether plaintiff had 'dance potential.'"

● **Impact of This Case on Today's Law** *This case has become a classic in contract law because it clearly illustrates an important principle. The general rule—that a misrepresentation must be one of fact rather than one of opinion to be actionable—does not apply in certain situations, such as when one party misrepresents something about which he or she possesses superior knowledge (Vokes's dancing ability, in this case).*

● **The Ethical Dimension** *If one of Vokes's fellow students, rather than her instructor, had praised her ability and encouraged her to buy more lessons, should the result in this case have been different? Explain.*

Misrepresentation by Concealment Misrepresentation can also take place when a party takes specific action to conceal a fact that is material to the contract.[9] Suppose that Rakas contracts to buy a new car from Bustamonte, a dealer in new automobiles. The car has been used as a demonstration model for prospective customers to test-drive, but Bustamonte has turned back the odometer. Rakas cannot tell from the odometer reading that the car has been driven nearly one thousand miles, and Bustamonte does not tell Rakas the distance the car has actually been driven. Bustamonte's concealment constitutes misrepresentation by conduct.

As another example, suppose that Cummings contracts to purchase a racehorse from Garner. The horse is blind in one eye, but when Garner shows the horse, he skillfully conceals this fact by keeping the horse's head turned so that Cummings does not see the defect. The concealment constitutes fraud.

Misrepresentation of Law Misrepresentation of law *ordinarily* does not entitle a party to relief from a contract. For example, Camara has a parcel of property that she is trying to sell to Pye. Camara knows that a local ordinance prohibits building anything higher

---

9. *Restatement (Second) of Contracts*, Section 160.

than three stories on the property. Nonetheless, she tells Pye, "You can build a condominium fifty stories high if you want to." Pye buys the land and later discovers that Camara's statement was false. Normally, Pye cannot avoid the contract because at common law people are assumed to know state and local ordinances. Additionally, a layperson should not rely on a statement made by a nonlawyer about a point of law.

Exceptions to this rule occur, however, when the misrepresenting party is in a profession that is known to require greater knowledge of the law than the average citizen possesses. The courts are recognizing an increasing number of such professions. For example, the courts recognize that clients expect their real estate brokers to know the law governing real estate sales and land use. If Camara, in the preceding example, had been a lawyer or a real estate broker, her misrepresentation of the area's zoning status would probably have constituted fraud.

Misrepresentation by Silence Ordinarily, neither party to a contract has a duty to come forward and disclose facts. Therefore, a contract cannot be set aside because certain pertinent information is not volunteered. Suppose that you are selling a car that has been in an accident and has been repaired. You do not need to volunteer this information to a potential buyer. If, however, the purchaser asks you if the car has had extensive bodywork and you lie, you have committed a fraudulent misrepresentation.

Exceptions. Exceptions to the general rule do exist. Generally, if the seller knows of a serious potential problem that could not reasonably be suspected by the buyer, the seller may have a duty to speak. For example, if a city fails to disclose to bidders subsoil conditions that will cause great expense in constructing a sewer system, the city is guilty of fraud. Normally, the seller must disclose only "latent" defects—that is, defects that could not readily be discovered. Thus, termites in a house may not be a latent defect because a buyer could normally discover their presence through a termite inspection.

When the parties are in a *fiduciary relationship* (one of trust, such as the relationship between business partners or between attorneys and their clients— see Chapter 31), there is a duty to disclose material facts; failure to do so may constitute fraud.[10] Statutes provide still other exceptions to the general rule of

nondisclosure. The Truth-in-Lending Act, for example, requires disclosure of certain facts in financial transactions (see Chapter 44).

Duty to Prospective Employees. A duty to disclose information may also arise in an employment context when the employer either misrepresents or conceals information from a prospective employee during the hiring process. Courts have held employers liable for fraudulent misrepresentation about a company's financial health during hiring interviews. In one case, for example, applicants for jobs at the El-Jay Division asked about El-Jay's future. The employer represented during interviews that business was growing, that sales were up, and that the future looked promising. In reality, company management had already planned to close the El-Jay facility. In the subsequent trial, the court stated that the employer could be held liable for either failing to disclose material facts or making representations that were misleading because they were in the nature of "half-truth."[11]

In another case, the employer was found liable for fraud because it failed to disclose a potential takeover of the company. Representatives from a brokerage firm approached Philip McConkey, a former New York Giants professional football player, and offered him a position with their company. Because McConkey had heard rumors that the firm was going to be acquired by another firm, he asked about a possible takeover. He was assured on several occasions that the company was absolutely not going to be sold to another firm. When it was sold a few months later, McConkey was fired. He filed a lawsuit and won a substantial damages award based on the company's fraudulent misrepresentation.[12]

Intent to Deceive

The second element of fraud is knowledge on the part of the misrepresenting party that facts have been falsely represented. This element, normally called ***scienter***,[13] or "guilty knowledge," signifies that there was an *intent to deceive*. *Scienter* clearly exists if a party knows a fact is not as stated. *Scienter* also exists if a

---

10. *Restatement (Second) of Contracts,* Sections 161 and 173.

11. *Meade v. Cedarapids, Inc.,* 164 F.3d 1218 (9th Cir. 1999).

12. *McConkey v. Aon Corp.,* 354 N.J.Super. 25, 804 A.2d 572 (2002). Note that a number of subsequent cases have disputed this court's calculation of damages in situations involving fraudulent misreprestation. See, for example, *Goldstein v. Miles,* 859 A.2d 313 (Md.App. 2004); and *Horton v. Ross University School of Medicine,* 2006 WL 1128705 (D.N.J. 2006).

13. Pronounced sy-*en*-ter.

party makes a statement that he or she believes is not true or makes a statement recklessly, without regard to whether it is true or false. Finally, this element is met if a party says or implies that a statement is made on some basis, such as personal knowledge or personal investigation, when it is not.

Assume that Meese, a securities broker, offers to sell BIM stock to Packer. Meese assures Packer that BIM shares are blue-chip securities—that is, they are stable, entail limited risk, and yield a good return on investment over time. In fact, Meese knows nothing about the quality of BIM stock and does not believe that what he is saying is true. Meese's statement is thus a misrepresentation. If Packer is induced by Meese's intentional misrepresentation of a material fact to enter into a contract to buy the stock, normally he can avoid his obligations under the contract.

Innocent Misrepresentation If a person makes a statement that she or he believes to be true but that actually misrepresents material facts, the person is guilty only of an **innocent misrepresentation,** not of fraud. When an innocent misrepresentation occurs, the aggrieved party can rescind the contract but usually cannot seek damages. For example, Parris tells Roberta that a tract of land contains 250 acres. Parris is mistaken—the tract contains only 215 acres—but Parris had no knowledge of the mistake. Roberta relies on the statement and contracts to buy the land. Even though the misrepresentation is innocent, Roberta can avoid the contract if the misrepresentation is material.

Negligent Misrepresentation Sometimes, a party will make a misrepresentation through carelessness, believing the statement is true. If a person fails to exercise reasonable care in uncovering or disclosing the facts or does not use the skill and competence that her or his business or profession requires, it could constitute **negligent misrepresentation.** For example, an operator of a weight scale certifies the weight of Sneed's commodity, even though the scale's accuracy has not been checked in more than a year.

In virtually all states, such negligent misrepresentation is equal to *scienter,* or knowingly making a misrepresentation. In effect, negligent misrepresentation is treated as fraudulent misrepresentation, even though the implied covenant of good faith and fair dealing, which requires honesty and the observance of reasonable standards of fair dealing between contracting parties (see Chapter 22). Additionally, when Web site owners purposefully inflate the number of clicks so that they can charge more for advertising, they can be sued for, among other things, unjust enrichment.

Indeed, in the past few years, both Google and Yahoo have been the defendants in click fraud suits, several of which have been settled for amounts reaching tens of millions of dollars.[b] Google now uses filtering software so that it does not count repetitive clicks that presumably come from Internet robots.

Click Fraud's Close Cousin—Lead Fraud

Closely related to click fraud is lead fraud. "Leads" in this context are simply the names of individuals who have expressed an interest in purchasing a certain product, such as insurance. NetQuote, for example, is a lead-generating site for insurance companies. Users can submit requests on NetQuote's Web page, and NetQuote then sells these "qualified" leads to insurance companies. NetQuote now has brought a fraud claim against MostChoice, a competitor, charging that MostChoice had an employee submit hundreds of fraudulent requests through the NetQuote system.[c] NetQuote maintains that when it submitted these leads to its insurance company clients, the conversion rate— the percentage of leads that actually purchase insurance—dropped dramatically, thereby reducing the value of the leads to the insurance companies.

CRITICAL THINKING
INSIGHT INTO TECHNOLOGY

"As long as each click on an ad link on the Web triggers a commission that has to be paid, we will be facing a financial formula that gives rise to unethical behavior." Do you think that technology will some day be able to distinguish between bona fide clicks by truly interested parties and bogus clicks? Why or why not?

b. See, for example, *Checkmate Strategic Group, Inc. v. Yahoo!, Inc.,* No. 2:05-CV-04588-CAS-FMO (C.D.Cal. preliminary settlement approved June 28, 2006); *Bradley v. Google, Inc.,* 2006 WL3798134 (N.D.Cal. 2006, voluntarily dismissed after a settlement in 2007); and *Lane's Gifts and Collectibles, LLC v. Yahoo! Inc.,* No. CV-2005-52-1 (Ark.Cir.Ct. complaint filed February 17, 2005).

c. *NetQuote, Inc. v. Byrd,* 504 F.Supp.2d 1126 (D.Colo. 2007). This case has not yet been fully resolved.

the misrepresentation was not purposeful. In negligent misrepresentation, culpable ignorance of the truth supplies the intention to mislead, even if the defendant can claim, "I didn't know."

Reliance on the Misrepresentation

The third element of fraud is reasonably *justifiable reliance* on the misrepresentation of fact. The deceived party must have a justifiable reason for relying on the misrepresentation, and the misrepresentation must be an important factor (but not necessarily the sole factor) in inducing that party to enter into the contract. Suppose that to rent a car, an eighteen-year-old misrepresents his age and presents a false driver's license listing his age as twenty-two. In that situation, the car-rental agency would be justified in relying on this misrepresentation (provided that the proof of identity was not clearly false).[14]

Reliance is not justified if the innocent party knows the true facts or relies on obviously extravagant statements. If a used-car dealer tells you, "This old Cadillac will get fifty miles to the gallon," you normally will not be justified in relying on the statement. Or suppose that Kovich, a bank director, induces Mallory, a co-director, to sign a guaranty that the bank's assets will satisfy its liabilities, stating, "We have plenty of assets to satisfy our creditors." If Mallory knows the true facts, he will not be justified in relying on Kovich's statement. If, however, Mallory does not know the true facts *and has no way of discovering them,* he may be justified in relying on Kovich's statement.

The same rule applies to defects in property sold. If the defects are of the kind that would be obvious on inspection, the buyer cannot justifiably rely on the seller's representations. If the defects are hidden or latent (that is, not apparent on the surface), the buyer is justified in relying on the seller's statements.

Injury to the Innocent Party

Most courts do not require a showing of injury when the action is to rescind (cancel) the contract. These courts hold that because rescission returns the parties to the positions they held before the contract was

14. See, for example, *Fogel v. Enterprise Leasing Co. of Chicago,* 353 Ill.App.3d 165, 817 N.E.2d 1135, 288 Ill.Dec. 485 (2004).

made, a showing of injury to the innocent party is unnecessary.

For a person to recover damages caused by fraud, proof of an injury is universally required. The measure of damages is ordinarily equal to the property's value had it been delivered as represented, less the actual price paid for the property. Additionally, because fraud actions necessarily involve wrongful conduct, courts may also award *punitive damages,* or *exemplary damages.*[15] As discussed in Chapter 6, punitive damages are damages intended to punish the defendant and are granted to a plaintiff over and above the proved, actual compensation for the loss. Because of the potential for punitive damages, which normally are not available in contract actions, plaintiffs prefer to include a claim for fraudulent misrepresentation in their contract disputes.

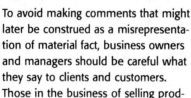

PREVENTING LEGAL DISPUTES

To avoid making comments that might later be construed as a misrepresentation of material fact, business owners and managers should be careful what they say to clients and customers. Those in the business of selling products or services should assume that all customers are naïve and are relying on the seller's representations. Instruct employees to phrase their comments so that customers understand that any statements that are not factual are the employee's opinion. If someone asks a question that is beyond the employee's knowledge, it is better to say that he or she does not know than to guess and have the customer rely on a representation that turns out to be false. This can be particularly important when the questions concern topics such as compatibility or speed of electronic and digital goods, software, or related services.

Businesspersons should also be prudent about what they say when interviewing potential employees. They should not speculate on the financial health of the firm or exaggerate the company's future prospects. Exercising caution in one's statements to others in a business context is the best way to avoid potential legal actions for fraudulent misrepresentation.

Undue Influence

Undue influence arises from special kinds of relationships in which one party can greatly influence another party, thus overcoming that party's free will. A contract entered into under excessive or undue influence lacks voluntary consent and is therefore voidable.[16]

How Undue Influence May Occur

As mentioned, undue influence arises from relationships in which one party may dominate another party, thus unfairly influencing him or her. Minors and elderly people, for example, are often under the influence of guardians (persons who are legally responsible for another). If a guardian induces a young or elderly ward (the person whom the guardian looks after) to enter into a contract that benefits the guardian, undue influence may have been exerted. Undue influence can arise from a number of confidential or fiduciary relationships: attorney-client, physician-patient, guardianward, parent-child, husband-wife, or trustee-beneficiary.

The essential feature of undue influence is that the party being taken advantage of does not, in reality, exercise free will in entering into a contract. Just because a person is elderly or suffers from some physical or mental impairment, however, does not mean that she or he was the victim of undue influence—there must be clear and convincing evidence that the person did not act out of her or his free will.[17] Similarly, the existence of a confidential relationship alone is insufficient to prove undue influence.[18]

To determine whether undue influence has been exerted, a court must ask, "To what extent was the transaction induced by domination of the mind or emotions of the person in question?" It follows, then, that the mental state of the person in question will often demonstrate to what extent the persuasion from the outside influence was "unfair."

The Presumption of Undue Influence

When the principal in a confidential relationship benefits from that relationship, a presumption of undue influence arises. In a relationship of trust and confidence,

---

15. See, for example, *McIver v. Bondy's Ford, Inc.,* 963 So.2d 136 (Ala. App. 2007); and *Alexander v. Meduna,* 47 P.3d 206 (Wyo. 2002).

16. *Restatement (Second) of Contracts,* Section 177.
17. See, for example, *Bailey v. Turnbow,* 273 Va. 262, 639 S.E.2d 291 (2007); and *Hooten v. Jensen,* 94 Ark. App. 130, 227 S.W.3d 431 (2006).
18. See, for example, *Landers v. Sgouros,* 224 S.W.3d 651 (Mo. App. 2007); and *Ware v. Ware,* 161 P.3d 1188 (Alaska 2007).

such as that between an attorney and a client, the dominant party (the attorney) must exercise the utmost good faith in dealing with the other party. When a contract enriches the dominant party, the court will often *presume* that the contract was made under undue influence. For example, if a guardian enters into a contract on behalf of the ward that financially benefits the guardian and the ward challenges the contract, a presumption arises that the guardian has taken advantage of the ward. To rebut (refute) this presumption successfully, the guardian has to show that full disclosure was made to the ward, that consideration was adequate, and that the ward received, if available, independent and competent advice before completing the transaction. Unless the presumption can be rebutted, the contract will be rescinded (canceled).

Duress

Consent to the terms of a contract is not voluntary if one of the parties is *forced* into the agreement. Recall from Chapter 9 that forcing a party to do something, including entering into a contract, through fear created by threats is legally defined as *duress*. In addition, blackmail or extortion to induce consent to a contract constitutes duress. Duress is both a defense to the enforcement of a contract and a ground for the rescission of a contract.

The Threatened Act Must Be Wrongful or Illegal

To establish duress, there must be proof of a threat to do something that the threatening party has no right to do. The threatened act must be legally or morally wrongful and must render the person incapable of exercising free will. Suppose that Joan accidentally crashes into Olin's car, which is stopped at a red traffic light. Joan has no automobile insurance, but she has substantial assets. At the scene of the accident, Olin claims to have suffered whiplash and tells Joan he will agree not to file a lawsuit against her if she pays him $5,000. Joan initially refuses, but after an argument, Olin says, "If you don't pay me $5,000 immediately, I'm going to sue you for $25,000." Joan then gives Olin a check for $5,000 to avoid the lawsuit. The next day, Joan stops payment on the check. When Olin later sues to enforce their oral settlement agreement for $5,000, Joan claims duress as a defense

to its enforcement. In this situation, because Olin had a right to sue Joan, threatening to sue her will not constitute duress. A court would not consider the threat of a civil suit to constitute duress.

Economic Duress

Economic need generally is not sufficient to constitute duress, even when one party exacts a very high price for an item that the other party needs. If the party exacting the price also creates the need, however, *economic duress* may be found.

For example, the Internal Revenue Service (IRS) assesses a large tax and penalty against Weller. Weller retains Eyman, the accountant who prepared the tax returns on which the assessment was based, to challenge the assessment. Two days before the deadline for filing a reply with the IRS, Eyman declines to represent Weller unless he signs a very high contingency-fee agreement for the services. This agreement would be unenforceable. Although Eyman has threatened only to withdraw his services, something that he is legally entitled to do, he is responsible for delaying the withdrawal until the last days before the deadline. Because it would be impossible at that late date to obtain adequate representation elsewhere, Weller would be forced either to sign the contract or to lose his right to challenge the IRS assessment.

Adhesion Contracts and Unconscionability

Questions concerning genuineness of assent may arise when the terms of a contract are dictated by a party with overwhelming bargaining power and the signer must agree to those terms or go without the commodity or service in question. As explained in Chapter 13, such contracts, which are written *exclusively* by one party and presented to the other party on a take-it-or-leave-it basis, are often referred to as *adhesion contracts*. These contracts often use standard forms, which give the adhering party no opportunity to negotiate the contract terms.

Standard-Form Contracts

Standard-form contracts often contain fine-print provisions that shift a risk naturally borne by one party to the other. A variety of businesses use such contracts. Life insurance policies, residential leases, loan agreements, and employment agency contracts are often standard-form contracts. To avoid enforcement of the contract or of a particular clause, the aggrieved party must show that the parties had substantially unequal bargaining positions and that enforcement would be manifestly unfair or oppressive. If the required showing is made, the contract or particular term is deemed *unconscionable* and is not enforced.

Adhesion contracts are standard in the retail automobile industry. The following case arose out of an arbitration clause in such a contract between an auto dealership and its customer.

C A S E   **12.3   Simpson v. MSA of Myrtle Beach, Inc.**
Supreme Court of South Carolina, 2007. 373 S.C. 14, 644 S.E.2d 663.
www.findlaw.com/11stategov/sc/scca.html[a]

● **Background and Facts** MSA of Myrtle Beach, Inc., in South Carolina does business as Addy's Harbor Dodge (Addy), a car dealership. Sherry Simpson signed a contract with Addy to trade in her 2001 Toyota 4Runner for a new 2004 Dodge Caravan. Directly above the signature line on the first page of the contract, a signee was instructed in bold type to "SEE ADDITIONAL TERMS AND CONDITIONS ON OPPOSITE PAGE." The additional terms and conditions contained an arbitration clause, which provided, among other things, that "in no event shall the arbitrator be authorized to award punitive, exemplary, double, or treble damages (or any other damages which are punitive in nature or effect) against either party." Six months later, Simpson filed a suit in a South Carolina state court against Addy, claiming that the dealer had misrepresented the trade-in value of her vehicle, artificially increased the purchase price, and failed to provide all rebates promised, in violation of state statutes. Addy filed a motion to compel arbitration. Simpson responded that the arbitration clause was unconscionable and unenforceable. The court denied Addy's motion. Addy appealed to the South Carolina Supreme Court.

● **Decision and Rationale** The state supreme court affirmed the lower court's denial of Addy's motion to compel arbitration. The reviewing court pointed out that unconscionability involves the absence of meaningful choice due to one-sided contract provisions. The "absence of meaningful choice on the part of one party generally speaks to the fundamental fairness of the bargaining process in the contract at issue." The court further pointed out that the arbitration clause was printed in very small type and embedded in one paragraph out of the sixteen included on a single page. Thus, the arbitration clause was inconspicuous. "The general rule is that courts will not enforce a contract which is violative of public policy, statutory law, or provisions of the Constitution." The state supreme court found that the arbitration clause was both unconscionable and unenforceable. The terms limiting Simpson's remedies were oppressive and one sided.

● **The Ethical Dimension** *Could the court have severed the unconscionable portions of the arbitration clause and otherwise allowed arbitration to proceed? Why or why not?*

● **The Legal Environment Dimension** *The dealer's contract also provided that Addy did not have to submit to arbitration any claims it might have against Simpson for "monies owed" and that these claims "shall not be stayed pending the outcome of arbitration." Is this provision unconscionable? Discuss.*

---

a. In the "2007" section, click on "March." In the result, click on the number next to the name of the case to access the opinion.

Unconscionability and the Courts

Technically, unconscionability under Section 2–302 of the Uniform Commercial Code (UCC) applies only to contracts for the sale of goods. Many courts, however, have broadened the concept and applied it in other situations.

Although unconscionability was discussed in Chapter 13, it is important to note here that the UCC gives courts a great degree of discretion to invalidate or strike down a contract or clause as being unconscionable. As a result, some states have not adopted Section 2–302 of the UCC. In those states, the legislature and the courts prefer to rely on traditional notions of fraud, undue influence, and duress. (See *Concept Summary 12.1* for a review of all of the factors that may indicate a lack of voluntary consent.)

CONCEPT SUMMARY 12.1
Voluntary Consent

Problems of Assent	Rule
MISTAKES	1. *Unilateral*—Generally, the mistaken party is bound by the contract, unless the other party knows or should have known of the mistake, or in some states, the mistake is an inadvertent mathematical error in addition, subtraction, and the like that is committed without gross negligence.
	2. *Bilateral (mutual)*—If both parties are mistaken about a material fact, such as the identity of the subject matter, either party can avoid the contract. If the mistake relates to the value or quality of the subject matter, either party can enforce the contract.
FRAUDULENT MISREPRESENTATION	Three elements are necessary to establish fraudulent misrepresentation:
	1. A misrepresentation of a material fact has occurred.
	2. There has been an intent to deceive.
	3. The innocent party has justifiably relied on the misrepresentation.
UNDUE INFLUENCE/DURESS	1. *Undue influence*—Arises from special relationships, such as fiduciary relationships, in which one party's free will has been overcome by the undue influence of another. Usually, the contract is voidable.
	2. *Duress*—Defined as forcing a party to enter into a contract under fear of threat—for example, the threat of violence or economic pressure. The party forced to enter into the contract can rescind the contract.
ADHESION CONTRACTS AND UNCONSCIONABILITY	Concerns one-sided bargains in which one party has substantially superior bargaining power and can dictate the terms of a contract. Unconscionability typically occurs as a result of the following:
	1. Standard-form contracts in which a fine-print provision purports to shift a risk normally borne by one party to the other (for example, a liability disclaimer).
	2. Take-it-or-leave-it adhesion contracts in which the buyer has no choice but to agree to the seller's dictated terms if the buyer is to procure certain goods or services.

REVIEWING Mistakes, Fraud, and Voluntary Consent

Chelene had been a caregiver for Marta's eighty-year-old mother, Janis, for nine years. Shortly before Janis passed away, Chelene convinced her to buy Chelene's house for Marta. The elderly woman died before the papers were signed, however. Four months later, Marta used her inheritance to buy Chelene's house without having it inspected. The house was built in the 1950s, and Chelene said it was in "perfect condition." Nevertheless, one year after the purchase, the basement started leaking. Marta had the paneling removed from the basement walls and discovered that the walls were bowed inward and cracked. Marta then had a civil engineer inspect the basement walls, and he found that the cracks had been caulked and painted over before the paneling was installed. He

REVIEWING CONTINUES

REVIEWING Mistakes, Fraud, and Voluntary Consent, Continued

concluded that the "wall failure" had existed "for at least thirty years" and that the basement walls were "structurally unsound." Using the information presented in the chapter, answer the following questions.

1. Can Marta obtain rescission of the contract based on undue influence? If the sale to Janis had been completed before her death, could Janis have obtained rescission based on undue influence? Explain.

2. Can Marta sue Chelene for fraudulent misrepresentation? Why or why not? What element(s) might be lacking?

3. Now assume that Chelene knew that the basement walls were cracked and bowed and that she had hired someone to install paneling prior to offering to sell the house. Did she have a duty to disclose this defect to Marta? Could a court find that Chelene's silence in this situation constituted misrepresentation? Explain.

4. If Chelene knew about the problem with the walls but did not know that the house was structurally unsound, could she be liable for negligent misrepresentation? Why or why not?

5. Can Marta avoid the contract on the ground that both parties made a mistake about the condition of the house? Explain.

TERMS AND CONCEPTS

innocent misrepresentation   *scienter*
negligent misrepresentation

QUESTIONS AND CASE PROBLEMS

14-1. Juan is an elderly man who lives with his nephew, Samuel. Juan is totally dependent on Samuel's support. Samuel tells Juan that unless he transfers a tract of land he owns to Samuel for a price 35 percent below its market value, Samuel will no longer support and take care of him. Juan enters into the contract. Discuss fully whether Juan can set aside this contract.

14-2. QUESTION WITH SAMPLE ANSWER

Grano owns a forty-room motel on Highway 100. Tanner is interested in purchasing the motel. During the course of negotiations, Grano tells Tanner that the motel netted $30,000 during the previous year and that it will net at least $45,000 the next year. The motel books, which Grano turns over to Tanner before the purchase, clearly show that Grano's motel netted only $15,000 the previous year. Also, Grano fails to tell Tanner that a bypass to Highway 100 is being planned that will redirect most traffic away from the front of the motel. Tanner purchases the motel. During the first year under Tanner's operation, the motel nets only $18,000. At this time, Tanner learns of the previous low profitability of the motel and the planned bypass. Tanner wants his money back from Grano. Discuss fully Tanner's probable success in getting his money back.

- **For a sample answer to Question 14–2, go to Appendix C at the end of this text.**

14-3. Discuss whether either of the following contracts will be unenforceable on the ground that voluntary consent is lacking:

(a) Simmons finds a stone in his pasture that he believes to be quartz. Jenson, who also believes that the stone is quartz, contracts to purchase it for $10. Just before delivery, the stone is discovered to be a diamond worth $1,000.

(b) Jacoby's barn is burned to the ground. He accuses Goldman's son of arson and threatens to have the prosecutor bring a criminal action unless Goldman agrees to pay him $5,000. Goldman agrees to pay.

14-4. Lund offered to sell Steck his car and told Steck that the car had been driven only 25,000 miles and had never been in an accident. Steck hired Carvallo, a mechanic, to appraise the condition of the car, and Carvallo said that the car probably had at least 50,000 miles on it and most likely had been in an accident. In spite of this information, Steck still thought the car would be a good buy for the price, so he purchased it. Later, when the car developed numerous mechanical problems, Steck sought to rescind the contract on the basis of Lund's fraudulent misrepresentation of the auto's condition. Will Steck be able to rescind his contract? Explain.

14-5. Fraudulent Misrepresentation. In 1987, United Parcel Service Co. and United Parcel Service of America, Inc. (together known as UPS), decided to change the parcel delivery business from relying on contract carriers to establishing its own airline. During the transition, which took sixteen months, UPS hired 811 pilots. At the time, UPS expressed a desire to hire pilots who remained throughout that period with its contract carriers, which included Orion Air. A UPS representative met with more than fifty Orion pilots and made promises of future employment. John Rickert, a captain with Orion, was one of the pilots. Orion ceased operation after the UPS transition, and UPS did not hire Rickert, who obtained employment about six months later as a second officer with American Airlines, but at a lower salary. Rickert filed a suit in a Kentucky state court against UPS, claiming, in part, fraud based on the promises made by the UPS representative. UPS filed a motion for a directed verdict. What are the elements for a cause of action based on fraudulent misrepresentation? In whose favor should the court rule in this case, and why? [*United Parcel Service, Inc. v. Rickert,* 996 S.W.2d 464 (Ky. 1999)]

14-6. Negligent Misrepresentation. Cleveland Chiropractic College (CCC) promised prospective students that CCC would provide clinical training and experience—a critical part of a chiropractic education and a requirement for graduation and obtaining a license to practice. Specifically, CCC expressly promised that it would provide an ample variety of patients. CCC knew, however, that it did not have the ability to provide sufficient patients, as evidenced by its report to the Council on Chiropractic Education, an accreditation body through which chiropractic colleges monitor and certify themselves. In that report, CCC said that patient recruitment was the "joint responsibility" of the college and the student. During the 1990s, most of the "patients" that students saw were healthy persons whom the students recruited to be stand-in patients. After graduating and obtaining licenses to practice, Michael Troknya and nineteen others filed a

suit in a federal district court against CCC, alleging, among other things, negligent misrepresentation. What are the elements of this cause of action? Are they satisfied in this case? Why or why not? [*Troknya v. Cleveland Chiropractic Clinic,* 280 F.3d 1200 (8th Cir. 2002)]

14-7. CASE PROBLEM WITH SAMPLE ANSWER

The law firm of Traystman, Coric and Keramidas represented Andrew Daigle in a divorce in Norwich, Connecticut. Scott McGowan, an attorney with the firm, handled the two-day trial. After the first day of the trial, McGowan told Daigle to sign a promissory note in the amount of $26,973, which represented the amount that Daigle then owed to the firm, or McGowan would withdraw from the case, and Daigle would be forced to get another attorney or to continue the trial by himself. Daigle said that he wanted another attorney, Martin Rutchik, to see the note. McGowan urged Daigle to sign it and assured him that a copy would be sent to Rutchik. Feeling that he had no other choice, Daigle signed the note. When he did not pay, the law firm filed a suit in a Connecticut state court against him. Daigle asserted that the note was unenforceable because he had signed it under duress. What are the requirements for the use of duress as a defense to a contract? Are the requirements met here? What might the law firm argue in response to Daigle's assertion? Explain. [*Traystman, Coric and Keramidas v. Daigle,* 84 Conn.App. 843, 855 A.2d 996 (2004)]

- **To view a sample answer for Problem 14–7, go to this book's Web site at www.cengage. com/blaw/jentz, select "Chapter 14," and click on "Case Problem with Sample Answer."**

14-8. Fraudulent Misrepresentation. According to the student handbook at Cleveland Chiropractic College (CCC) in Missouri, *academic misconduct* includes "selling . . . any copy of any material intended to be used as an instrument of academic evaluation in advance of its initial administration." Leonard Verni was enrolled at CCC in Dr. Aleksandr Makarov's dermatology class. Before the first examination, Verni was reported to be selling copies of the test. CCC investigated and concluded that Verni had committed academic misconduct. He was dismissed from CCC, which informed him of his right to an appeal. According to the handbook, at the hearing on appeal a student could have an attorney or other adviser, present witnesses' testimony and other evidence, and "question any testimony . . . against him/her." At his hearing, however, Verni did not bring his attorney, present evidence on his behalf, or question any adverse witnesses. When the dismissal was upheld, Verni filed a suit in a Missouri state court against CCC and others, claiming, in part, fraudulent misrepresentation. Verni argued that because he "relied" on the handbook's "representation" that CCC would follow its appeal procedure, he was unable to properly refute the charges against him. Can Verni succeed with this argument? Explain. [*Verni v. Cleveland Chiropractic College*, 212 S.W.3d 150 (Mo. 2007)]

14-9. A QUESTION OF ETHICS

On behalf of BRJM, LLC, Nicolas Kepple offered Howard Engelsen $210,000 for a parcel of land known as lot five on the north side of Barnes Road in Stonington, Connecticut. Engelsen's company, Output Systems, Inc., owned the land. Engelsen had the lot surveyed and obtained an appraisal. The appraiser valued the property at $277,000, after determining that it was 3.0 acres and thus could not be subdivided because it did not meet the town's minimum legal requirement of 3.7 acres for subdivision. Engelsen responded to Kepple's offer with a counteroffer of $230,000, which Kepple accepted. On May 3, 2002, the parties signed a contract. When Engelsen refused to go through with the deal, BRJM filed a suit in a Connecticut state court against Output, seeking specific performance and other relief. The defendant asserted the defense of mutual mistake on at least two grounds. [BRJM, LLC v. Output Systems, Inc., 100 Conn. App. 143, 917 A.2d 605 (2007)]

(a) In the counteroffer, Engelsen asked Kepple to remove from their contract a clause requiring written confirmation of the availability of a "free split," which meant that the property could be subdivided without the town's prior approval. Kepple agreed. After signing the contract, Kepple learned that the property was not entitled to a free split. Would this circumstance qualify as a mistake on which the defendant could avoid the contract? Why or why not?

(b) After signing the contract, Engelsen obtained a second appraisal that established the size of lot five as 3.71 acres, which meant that it could be subdivided, and valued the property at $490,000. Can the defendant avoid the contract on the basis of a mistake in the first appraisal? Explain.

14-10. VIDEO QUESTION

Go to this text's Web site at **www.cengage. com/blaw/jentz** and select "Chapter 14." Click on "Video Questions" and view the video titled *Mistake*. Then answer the following questions.

(a) What kind of mistake is involved in the dispute shown in the video (mutual or unilateral, mistake of fact or mistake of value)?

(b) According to the chapter, in what two situations would the supermarket be able to rescind a contract to sell peppers to Melnick at the incorrectly advertised price?

(c) Does it matter if the price that was advertised was a reasonable price for the peppers? Why or why not?

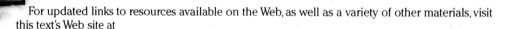

LAW ON THE WEB

For updated links to resources available on the Web, as well as a variety of other materials, visit this text's Web site at

www.cengage.com/blaw/jentz

For a discussion of fraudulent misrepresentation, go to the Web site of attorney Owen Katz at

www.katzlawoffice.com/misrep.html

For a collection of leading cases on contract law, including cases involving topics covered in this chapter, go to

www.lectlaw.com/files/lws49.htm

Legal Research Exercises on the Web

Go to **www.cengage.com/blaw/jentz**, the Web site that accompanies this text. Select "Chapter 14" and click on "Internet Exercises." There you will find the following Internet research exercises that you can perform to learn more about the topics covered in this chapter.

Internet Exercise 14–1: Legal Perspective
Negligent Misrepresentation and *Scienter*

Internet Exercise 14–2: Management Perspective
Fraudulent Misrepresentation

Internet Exercise 14–3: Economic Perspective
Economic Duress

Contracts: Genuine Assent

Case No. 69

FRAUD

Rodas v. Manitaras. et. al.

Appellate Division, First Department

159 A.D.2d 341, 552 N.Y.S.2d 618 (1990)

FACTS: In November 1987, plaintiff Paul Rodas (Rodas) purchased a restaurant business from defendant Oyster House, Inc. (Oyster House). During the negotiations, Oyster House falsely represented that the income of the business was $20,000 per week. Rodas asked to examine the records of the business but Oyster House refused. The contract of sale contained a disclaimer stating that Rodas was making the purchase based upon his business judgment and not upon any representation made by Oyster House.

In this lawsuit, Rodas is seeking to rescind the contract for sale, claiming that Oyster House falsely represented that the income from the business was $20,000 per week.

ISSUE: Where a buyer of a business expressly disclaims reliance on representations made by the seller and later learns that statements made by the seller are false, is the buyer entitled to rescind the contract based on fraud?

DECISION: No, judgment for defendant; Rodas cannot rescind.

REASONING: To prove fraud, the plaintiff must show that a misrepresentation of a material fact was made by the defendant, it was made with knowledge of its falsity and with an intent to induce the plaintiff to rely, plaintiff reasonably relies and suffers injury as a result. Although Rodas relied on the information provided by Oyster House, Rodas' reliance was not reasonable. He should have examined the restaurant's records himself.

* * * QUESTION * * *
(See back of text for answer)

1) What could Rodas have done to avoid this problem?

Case No. 70

ECONOMIC DURESS

<u>Austin Instrument, Inc. v. Loral Corporation</u>

Court of Appeals

29 N.Y.2d 124, 324 N.Y.S.2d 22 (1971)

FACTS: Defendant Loral Corporation (Loral) had a contract with the Navy in which Loral was required to manufacture radar sets by a specific date. In return the Navy was to pay Loral $6 million. The radar sets were highly sophisticated and had to be made consistent with the strictest engineering standards.

The contract provided that, in the event Loral was late in delivering the radar sets, Loral would be required to pay to the Navy as damages a substantial amount of money specified in the contract. Further, late delivery would entitle the Navy to cancel the contract.

In order to produce the radar sets, Loral needed to purchase from suppliers certain component parts. Loral contracted with Plaintiff Austin Instrument, Inc. (Austin) for the purchase of many of those parts.

During the course of manufacturing the radar sets, Loral was awarded a second contract from the Navy for the production of more radar sets. Loral sought bids on this second contract from several suppliers of the component parts. Austin threatened to discontinue performance on the first contract unless Loral agreed to the following: (a) purchase from Austin all the component parts on the second contract; and (b) increase the price paid to Austin under the first contract.

In response to Austin's threat, Loral attempted to replace Austin as the supplier. It contacted all other suppliers whose products, facilities, techniques and performance had been previously inspected by Loral and found to be satisfactory. None could supply the parts in time for Loral to meet the deadline of the first contract. As a result, Loral agreed to Austin's demands, as it was concerned that if it were late in delivering the radar sets, the Navy would seek substantial damages and cancel the contract. Further, Loral did a substantial amount of business with the government and it feared the loss of future contracts if it defaulted on this one.

After Austin completed final delivery to Loral, Austin sued Loral for money still due on the second contract. Loral, in response, sued Austin to recover the price increases on the first contract. Loral's action was based on economic duress.

ISSUE: Where a party to a contract agrees to pay the other party additional money to avoid threatened economic harm, is the party able to avoid its promise to pay the additional amount based on economic duress?

DECISION: Yes, judgment for Loral.

REASONING: A contract is voidable on the grounds of economic duress when one party threatens to breach a contract by not delivering goods required by the contract, the nonbreaching party cannot obtain the goods from another source, and the non breaching party would not be adequately compensated by recovery of damages for breach of contract.

The facts of this case establish economic duress. Loral feared its lucrative relationship and future contracts with the government would be jeopardized if it were unable to deliver the radar sets on time. Loral was also concerned about the contract provision that required it to pay substantial damages in the event of late delivery. No other supplier could provide the goods within a time frame to meet Loral's commitments to the Navy.

Under these circumstances, Austin's threat to withhold delivery constituted economic duress. Loral was thus entitled to avoid its promise to Austin to pay more than the contract price and to recover the payments it made to Austin that constituted the price increases.

* * * QUESTIONS * * *
(See back of text for answers)

1) What similarities and dissimilarities exist between economic duress and physical duress?

2) If other suppliers had been able to deliver the goods on time to Loral, would the defense of economic duress apply to Loral?

Case No. 71

MUTUAL MISTAKE

Leasco Corp. v. Taussig

United States Court of Appeals, Second Circuit

473 F2d 777 (1972)

FACTS: Plaintiff Leasco Corp. (Leasco) purchased in 1969 two businesses engaged in civil engineering and consulting. Defendant Peter Taussig (Taussig), a civil engineer and lawyer, was hired by Leasco as vice president of one of these new civil engineering businesses. One of his assignments included the investigation of another engineering company that Leasco was interested in purchasing. The name of that firm was McCreary-Koretsky Engineers, Inc. (McCreary). A subsidiary of Leasco known as MKI did purchase McCreary's assets and Taussig became McCreary's vice president. His duties included acting as the liaison officer between MKI and Leasco.

The civil engineering and consulting business is known for "serious income fluctuations." By late 1970 Leasco had become disenchanted with the engineering business for that reason and sought to sell its various civil engineering companies. Taussig expressed an interest in purchasing MKI and negotiations between Taussig and Leasco were undertaken. A purchase price of $625,000.00 was agreed upon based in large part upon a projected 1971 pre-tax earning for MKI of $200,000.00. A written purchase and sale contract was signed by Taussig and Leasco on February 26, 1971, and the closing was scheduled for May 28, 1971.

The February 1971 financial statement for MKI, received by Taussig on March 12, 1971, disclosed a net loss. Upon investigation Taussig discovered the loss resulted from a design error on a job performed by MKI involving the Fruitvale Bridge in San Francisco. Due to the error the bridge, which was more than half completed when the error was discovered, had to be almost completely rebuilt. Thus, the financial statements for March and April 1971 continued to show losses for MKI.

On May 28, 1971, the scheduled closing date for the sale of MKI, Leasco tendered MKI to Taussig. Due to the losses disclosed in the financial statements, Taussig refused to go through with the sale. Within two weeks Leasco began this action against Taussig for breach of contract. Taussig defended the lawsuit by claiming he could avoid the contract due to mutual mistake about the projected earnings of MKI.

ISSUE: Where a buyer and seller of a business determine the purchase-sale price based on projected earnings, and those projected earnings do not materialize, can the buyer avoid the contract based on mutual mistake?

DECISION: No, judgment for Leasco.

REASONING: Where both parties assume a certain set of facts to exist and contract on the faith of that assumption, they can be relieved from their obligations if the assumption is erroneous. However, when parties to a contract know at the time they contract that doubt exists as to the existence of a fact, its failure to materialize does not amount to a mutual mistake for which the contract can be avoided. In this case, the parties projected earnings for 1971 of $200,000.00. Neither could have been certain at the time the contract was entered that such projections would materialize. Both parties knew the civil engineering business was an extremely risky one. Thus, the failure of MKI to earn $200,000.00 or any profit in 1971 does not amount to a mutual mistake that would justify avoiding the contract.

*** QUESTIONS ***
(See back of text for answers)

1) With regard to the enforceability of a contract, what is the difference between: (a) a situation where two contracting parties reasonably assume the truth of facts that turn out to be false; and (b) a situation where the parties rely on a projected fact which they know may or may not be true and it turns out to be false?

2) How could Taussig have avoided the problem in this case?

Case No. 72

SPECIFIC PERFORMANCE/MUTUAL MISTAKE

Ryan v. Boucher, et al

Appellate Division, Third Department

144 A.D.2d 144, 534 N.Y.S.2d 473 (1988)

FACTS: Plaintiff James Ryan (Ryan) entered a contract with defendant Gerald Boucher (Boucher) to purchase a parcel of real estate. The contract contained a description of the property that did not include the number of acres. The southern boundary was described in the contract as follows: ". . . on the south by tree line base of hill, . . .".

Ryan believed, based on the contract description of the south boundary line, that he was purchasing 23 1/2 acres. Boucher claimed the property described in the contract was only 16 1/2 acres. The variation was due to the parties' differing interpretation of the south boundary line.

Photographic evidence submitted by Ryan showed only one tree line and it supported Ryan's claim of 23 1/2 acres. Boucher identified a different growth of trees as the southern boundary line. The court described Boucher's claimed boundary as "little more than a patch of brush."

Ryan sued for specific performance seeking 23 1/2 acres.

ISSUE: Do the facts support Boucher's claim of a mutual mistake as to the southern boundary?

DECISION: No, judgment for Ryan, specific performance granted.

REASONING: When both parties to a contract are mistaken as to a material fact, the contract is voidable by either party. The mistaken fact must be mutual and based on a reasonable assumption made by each party. Additionally, the mistake must exist at the time the contract was entered and must be material.

The evidence submitted by Ryan clearly showed the southern boundary to be the line of mature trees and not the "patch of brush". The boundary line was a material fact in this case. The court held that Boucher could not reasonably have relied on the "patch of brush" being the boundary.

* * * QUESTION * * *
(See back of text for answer)

1) When a mutual mistake occurs, either party to the contract is entitled to rescind it. What is recission?

Case No. 73

MUTUAL MISTAKE/RELEASES

Mangini v. McClurg

Court of Appeals

24 N.Y.2d 556, 301 N.Y.S.2d 508 (1969)

FACTS: On February 26, 1963, plaintiff Deborah Mangini (Mangini), then about 18 years old, was a passenger in the front seat of a car that collided with one driven by defendant Howard McClurg (McClurg). As a result of the collision, Mangini "was thrown to the floor of the car striking her face on the dashboard and injuring her knees and her lower back". On the day of the accident she was examined by a Dr. Harrington. She complained to him of "pain and tenderness of the lumbar spine with pain radiating down the posterior left thigh". Dr. Harrington attributed the pain to a lower back injury. She was examined by him again in April, at which time he confirmed his diagnosis of a back injury.

In May 1963, Mangini was examined by a second doctor, a Dr. Schlesinger. She complained that the lower back pain had become more severe. He diagnosed the condition as a back injury. She was examined by a third doctor, a Dr. Magovem. He concluded the injured part of Mangini's body was the back and the injury would leave "no permanency." Thus, all three doctors who examined Mangini prior to settling the case identified the injury resulting from the accident as one to the lower back.

Mangini decided to settle her claim and hired a lawyer. A settlement of $1000.00 plus medical expenses of $198.28 was agreed upon. On July 1, 1963 Mangini signed a general release releasing McClurg from "any and all claims for personal injuries, medical expenses, loss of wages as a result of an automobile accident on February 26, 1963."

Six months after the settlement Mangini experienced an increase in pain in the area of her left hip. She went to a Dr. Gazeley, who determined she had injured her hip in the accident. This particular hip injury, by its nature, takes at least six months to develop and thus could not have been discovered at the time of the settlement. As a result of the hip problem Mangini was apparently in extreme pain, required extensive surgery, and suffered permanent injury. She began this lawsuit against McClurg claiming $110,000.00 in damages. McClurg denied liability on the basis that Mangini released him from liability upon payment of the settlement money and signing of the release.

ISSUE: Where a releasor signs a general release as part of the settlement of a lawsuit, is the releasor barred from suing the releasee for additional damages for an injury of which the releasor did not know and could not have known at the time she signed the release?

DECISION: No, Mangini is not prevented by the release from suing McClurg.

REASONING: A release is a valid contract and cannot be set aside unless, as with most contracts, duress, illegality, fraud or mutual mistake exists. Unknown injuries, as opposed to unknown consequences of known injuries, can amount to mutual mistake.

If, following the signing of a release, unknown consequences of a known injury result, the release will not be set aside. If, however, following the signing of a release, injuries caused by an accident appear for the first time, and the parties were unaware of the injury at the time of signing the release, the release may be voidable on the basis of mutual mistake concerning the identity of the injuries suffered. However, even in such case, the release will be upheld if the releasee can show the releasor intended to release the releasee for unknown injuries. Such an intention might be proven by showing the parties had discussed the consequences of later discovering an injury more severe than medical examination suggested, by showing that the parties believed the releasee's liability was doubtful, or by showing the releasor was anxious for an early settlement at whatever risk.

In this case Mangini, at the time she signed the release, reasonably believed, based on three doctors' diagnoses, that the pain in her lower back area resulted from a lower back injury, not from a separate and then unknown hip injury. McClurg was under the same impression. Nothing in the facts of this case suggest Mangini intended to release McClurg from unknown injuries. Thus, the release may be set aside based on mutual mistake and Mangini can sue for her losses attributed to the hip injury.

* * * QUESTIONS * * *
(See back of text for answers)

1) The release in this case was set aside due to a mutual mistake. Identify the fact about which the parties were mistaken.

2) As stated in the case, releases are valid contracts. Identify the consideration exchanged by Mangini and McClurg.

3) How might the decision in this case have been different if Mangini's pain were caused by the back injury instead of a hip injury?

Case No. 74

RELEASES/ABSENCE OF MUTUAL MISTAKE

Marchello v. Lennox Hill Hospital

Appellate Division, First Department

107 A.D.2d 566, 438 N.Y.S.2d 305 (1985)

FACTS: In April 1971, plaintiff Maureen Marchello (Marchello) suffered second degree burns on her right leg as a result of the negligent application of hot compresses administered by defendant Lennox Hill Hospital (Lennox) during a cardiac catheterization procedure. Marchello sued Lennox in 1974 for damages. She subsequently settled the suit for $3,500.00 and signed a general release.

In 1978 Marchello began this action against Lennox for a right footdrop condition (a dropping of a foot from paralysis of the anterior leg muscles) that allegedly developed as a result of the cardiac catheterization procedure administered in 1971. An expert witness, Dr. Lawrence Kaplan, concluded that the footdrop condition "was undoubtedly related" to burns that resulted from the use of the hot compresses during the 1971 procedure.

Marchello sought to rescind the general release she signed after settling the first action. She claimed that the settlement of the first suit was the result of mutual mistake, that is, both parties believed that the footdrop was the result of the catheterization procedure rather than the negligent application of the hot compresses. Lennox claimed the release was valid and sought a court order dismissing the complaint.

ISSUE: When a releasor signs a general release and subsequently an unknown consequence of a known injury reveals itself, should the release be deemed inapplicable to the unknown consequence on the theory of mutual mistake?

DECISION: No, complaint dismissed.

REASONING: In resolving issues of mutual mistake relating to the execution of a release settling an action for personal injuries, "a mistaken belief as to the nonexistence of a presently existing injury is a prerequisite to avoidance of a release." If the injury was known at the time the release was signed and the mistaken fact was the consequences of the known injury, the release cannot be avoided and will preclude an action based on such consequences.

Marchello's footdrop condition was the consequence of a known injury (burns from the hot compresses) and not the result of an unknown injury. Hence, the release was valid and barred Marchello from pursuing this action for damages.

* * * QUESTIONS * * *
(See back of text for answers)

1) With regard to the injuries at issue, why was the release in this case enforceable and the release in <u>Mangini v. McClurg</u> unenforceable?

2) The release in both <u>Mangini v. McClurg</u> and <u>Marchello v. Lennox Hill Hospital</u> were general releases. Assume that, rather than general releases, the releases specifically stated they related to only a known consequence of a known injury. How, if at all, would the outcome of the cases have been affected?

Case No. 75

UNILATERAL MISTAKE

Balabon-Gordon Company v. Brighton Sewer District No. 2

Appellate Division, Fourth Department

41 A.D.2d 246, 342 N.Y.S.2d 435 (1973)

FACTS: Defendant Brighton Sewer District No. 2 (Sewer District) sought bids for the construction of two sewage treatment plants. Bids were submitted for the following jobs: general construction, plumbing, heating, and electrical work.

Plaintiff Balabon-Gordon Company (Balabon) was the lowest bidder on the general construction contract for both plants. Its total bid of $2,249,700.00 was $530,300.00 below the next lowest bidder. Balabon also bid on the plumbing contract and was the highest bidder for that job. Its bid for the plumbing contract was $376,230.00 higher than the lowest bid which was $687,770.00.

When Sewer District discovered the discrepancies in the bid it immediately notified Balabon, which reexamined its work sheets and determined that it had incorrectly interpreted the Sewer District's specifications for the work. As a result, Balabon included the cost of several pieces of mechanical equipment in the bid for the plumbing contract that should have been included in the bid for the general construction. The bid Balabon submitted to perform the general construction contract should therefore have been significantly higher and the bid for the plumbing work correspondingly lower.

Because of the mistake, Balabon attempted to withdraw its bid. The Sewer District claimed Balabon could not withdraw the bid because New York law provides that a bid submitted for a municipal construction project is irrevocable for 45 days following submission.

ISSUE: Where a construction company submits a bid that is artificially low due to incorrect interpretation of the job specifications, can the construction company withdraw its bid?

DECISION: Yes, judgment for Balabon.

REASONING: Ordinarily a unilateral mistake will not excuse a party from performing a contract or permit rescission of an irrevocable bid. The court stated, however, where the nonmistaken party had reason to know of the mistake, "(I)f the mistake concerns a material matter in an executory contract under circumstances where relief to the bidder results in no damage to the municipality but enforcement results in serious harm to the bidder, rescission will be granted."

Balabon's bid on the general construction portion of the bidding was more than 20% lower than the second lowest bidder. That discrepancy and Sewer District's immediate notification thereof to Balabon suggests that Balabon's mistake was recognized by Sewer District. Allowing Balabon to withdraw would result in no damage to Sewer District but would expose Balabon to a burdensome loss by having to do the work for a price much lower than intended.

Notwithstanding the above, if the error made by Balabon was an error in judgment in estimating the requirements or costs necessary to fulfill the contracts, withdrawal would not be permitted. That type of mistake involves business risks from which relief will not be granted. If, on the other hand, the error is a mathematical or clerical one, a bid can normally be withdrawn. The mistake made in this case was not strictly mathematical or clerical, but neither did it involve business risk-taking. Balabon's bid was not his intended bid because Balabon misinterpreted the specifications. Under these circumstances Balabon was permitted to withdraw the bid.

* * * QUESTIONS * * *
(See back of text for answers)

1) How does the error made in this case differ from a mathematical or clerical error?

2) How does the error made by Balabon differ from the type of mistake for which a bidder would not be able to withdraw its bid?

CHAPTER 13

The Statute of Frauds—Writing Requirement

As discussed in Chapter 14, a contract that is otherwise valid may still be unenforceable if the parties have not voluntarily consented to its terms. An otherwise valid contract may also be unenforceable for another reason—because it is not in the proper form. For example, certain types of contracts are required to be in writing or evidenced by a memorandum, note, or electronic record. The writing requirement does not mean that an agreement must be a formal written contract. All that is necessary is some written proof that a contract exists, such as an e-mail exchange evidencing the agreement. Under what is called the **Statute of Frauds,** certain agreements are required by law to be in writing. If there is no written evidence of the contract, it may not be enforceable.

In this chapter, we examine the kinds of contracts that require a writing under the Statute of Frauds and some exceptions to the writing requirement. We also discuss the *parol evidence rule,* which courts follow when determining whether evidence that is extraneous, or external, to written contracts may be admissible at trial. Though not inherently related to the Statute of Frauds, the parol evidence rule has general application in contract law. We cover these topics within one chapter primarily for reasons of convenience and space.

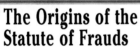

The Origins of the Statute of Frauds

At early common law, parties to a contract were not allowed to testify. This led to the practice of hiring third party witnesses. As early as the seventeenth century, the English recognized the many problems presented by this practice and enacted a statute to help deal with it. The statute, passed by the English Parliament in 1677, was known as "An Act for the Prevention of Frauds and Perjuries." The act established that certain types of contracts, to be enforceable, had to be evidenced by a writing and signed by the party against whom enforcement was sought.

Today, every state has a statute, modeled after the English act, that stipulates what types of contracts must be in writing or evidenced by a writing. Although the statutes vary slightly from state to state, all states require certain types of contracts to be in writing or evidenced by a written (or electronic) memorandum signed by the party against whom enforcement is sought, unless certain exceptions apply. (These exceptions will be discussed later in this chapter.) In this text, we refer to these statutes collectively as the Statute of Frauds. The actual name of the Statute of Frauds is misleading because it neither applies to fraud nor invalidates any type of contract. Rather, it denies *enforceability* to certain contracts that do not comply with its requirements.

Contracts That Fall within the Statute of Frauds

The following types of contracts are said to fall "within" or "under" the Statute of Frauds and therefore are required to be in writing or evidenced by a written memorandum or record:

1. Contracts involving interests in land.
2. Contracts that cannot by their terms be performed within one year from the day after the date of formation.

3. Collateral, or secondary, contracts, such as promises to answer for the debt or duty of another and promises by the administrator or executor of an estate to pay a debt of the estate personally—that is, out of her or his own pocket.
4. Promises made in consideration of marriage.
5. Under the Uniform Commercial Code (UCC), contracts for the sale of goods priced at $500 or more.[1]

Contracts Involving Interests in Land

A contract calling for the sale of land is not enforceable unless it is in writing or evidenced by a written memorandum. Land is *real property* and includes all physical objects that are permanently attached to the soil, such as buildings, fences, trees, and the soil itself (see Chapter 47). The Statute of Frauds operates as a *defense* to the enforcement of an oral contract for the sale of land. For example, if Sam contracts orally to sell Blackacre to Betty but later decides not to sell, under most circumstances Betty cannot enforce the contract.

The Statute of Frauds also requires written evidence of contracts for the transfer of other interests in land. For example, mortgage agreements and leases (see Chapter 48) normally must be written, although most state laws provide for the enforcement of short-term oral leases. Similarly, an agreement that includes an option to purchase real property must be in writing for the option to be enforced.[2]

The One-Year Rule

A contract that cannot, *by its own terms*, be performed within one year *from the day after* the contract is formed must be in writing to be enforceable.[3] Suppose that Superior University forms a contract with Kimi San stating that San will teach three courses in history during the coming academic year (September 15 through June 15). If the contract is formed in March, it must be in writing to be enforceable—because it cannot be performed within one year. If the contract is not formed until July, however, it will not have to be in writing to be enforceable—because it can be performed within one year.

The test for determining whether an oral contract is enforceable under the one-year rule of the Statute of Frauds is whether performance is *possible* within one year from the day after the date of contract formation—not whether the agreement is *likely* to be performed within one year. When performance of a contract is objectively impossible during the one-year period, the oral contract will be unenforceable. Exhibit 13–1 illustrates graphically the application of the one-year rule.

---

1. Although in 2003 it was proposed that this amount be changed from $500 to $5,000, no state has yet adopted this higher dollar threshold (see Chapter 20).

2. See, for example, *Michel v. Bush,* 146 Ohio App.3d 208, 765 N.E.2d 911 (2001); and *Stickney v. Tullis-Vermillion,* 165 Ohio App.3d 480, 847 N.E.2d 29 (2006).

3. *Restatement (Second) of Contracts,* Section 130.

EXHIBIT 13-1 • The One-Year Rule

Under the Statute of Frauds, contracts that by their terms are impossible to perform within one year from the day after the date of contract formation must be in writing to be enforceable. Put another way, if it is at all possible to perform an oral contract within one year from the day after the contract is made, the contract will fall outside the Statute of Frauds and be enforceable.

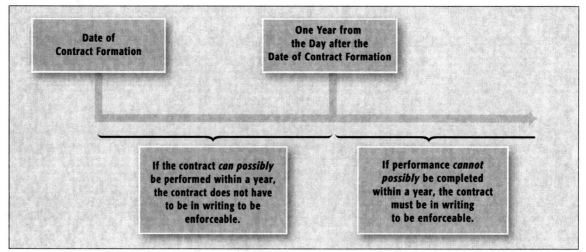

Suppose that Bankers Life orally contracts to lend $40,000 to Janet Lawrence "as long as Lawrence and Associates operates its financial consulting firm in Omaha, Nebraska." The contract does not fall within the Statute of Frauds—no writing is required—because Lawrence and Associates could go out of business in one year or less. In this event, the contract would be fully performed within one year.[4] Similarly, an oral contract for lifetime employment does not fall within the Statute of Frauds. Because an employee

who is hired "for life" can die within a year, the courts reason that the contract can be performed within one year.[5]

In the following case, an employee argued that her employer's oral promise to pay her a certain amount as a bonus in installments over 107 months was removed from the Statute of Frauds because the total sum could have been paid within one year.

---

4. See *Warner v. Texas & Pacific Railroad Co.*, 164 U.S. 418, 17 S.Ct. 147, 41 L.Ed. 495 (1896).

5. See, for example, *Gavengno v. TLT Construction Corp.*, 67 Mass.App.Ct. 1102, 851 N.E.2d 1133 (2006); *Czapla v. Commerz Futures, LLC*, 114 F.Supp.2d 715 (N.D.Ill. 2000); and *Doherty v. Doherty Insurance Agency, Inc.*, 878 F.2d 546 (1st Cir. 1989).

C A S E **13.1** **Sawyer v. Mills**
Court of Appeals of Kentucky, 2007. __ S.W.3d __.

● **Background and Facts** Barbara Sawyer was a paralegal in Melbourne Mills's law firm. Mills had promised Sawyer that he would reward her for assisting in instituting class-action lawsuits. The parties, however, never specified the amount of the bonus nor when it would be paid to Sawyer. After Mills's firm received a substantial settlement in a class-action suit, Sawyer and her husband met with Mills. Sawyer's husband secretly recorded the conversation. The tape recording confirmed that Mills agreed to pay Sawyer a bonus of $1 million, plus the cost of a luxury car. The total amount was to be paid in monthly installments of $10,000. Mills agreed to sign a writing verifying the terms, but he never did. Sawyer received a total of $165,000, and then the payments stopped. Sawyer sued. Mills filed a motion for summary judgment prior to trial, arguing that Sawyer's claims were barred by the Statute of Frauds. The trial proceeded, nonetheless, and the jury returned a verdict in favor of Sawyer for $900,000. Mills filed a motion for a judgment notwithstanding the verdict, again arguing that the agreement between him and Sawyer was barred by the Statute of Frauds. The trial court agreed and granted the motion.

● **Decision and Rationale** The appellate court affirmed the lower court's judgment notwithstanding the verdict. The reviewing court pointed out that Sawyer claimed the Statute of Frauds was not applicable "because the agreement was capable of being performed within one year." But the oral agreement would have taken over one hundred months to be completed. Sawyer countered with the argument that, in spite of the parties not contemplating performance in less than one year, the agreement *could* have been performed in less than one year. The court pointed out that the secret tape recording "clearly shows that Mills never intended to pay Sawyer the bonus as a lump sum and Sawyer is recorded agreeing to the monthly payments. The parties never contemplated that the bonus would be paid within one year." The Statute of Frauds barred Sawyer's claim against Mills because she produced no writing.

● **What If the Facts Were Different?** *Would an oral agreement between Sawyer and Mills to begin the bonus's installment payments on a certain date—July 1, 2008, for example—and complete them no later than fifteen months from that date have been outside the one-year rule of the Statute of Frauds? Explain.*

● **The Legal Environment Dimension** *Sawyer contended that the writing requirement of the Statute of Frauds was met through the combination of the recording of the parties' conversation and the checks Mills signed to Sawyer totaling $165,000. Obviously, the court did not agree. Why not?*

Collateral Promises

A **collateral promise,** or secondary promise, is one that is ancillary (subsidiary) to a principal transaction or primary contractual relationship. In other words, a collateral promise is one made by a third party to assume the debts or obligations of a primary party to a contract if that party does not perform. Any collateral promise of this nature falls under the Statute of Frauds and therefore must be in writing to be enforceable. To understand this concept, it is important to distinguish between primary and secondary promises and obligations.

Primary versus Secondary Obligations

As a general rule, a contract in which a party assumes a primary obligation does not need to be in writing to be enforceable. Suppose that Bancroft forms an oral contract with Harmony's Floral Boutique to send his mother a dozen roses for Mother's Day. Bancroft's oral contract with Harmony's provides that he will pay for the roses when he receives the bill for the flowers. Bancroft is a direct party to this contract and has incurred a *primary* obligation under the contract. Because he is a party to the contract and has a primary obligation to Harmony's, this contract does not fall under the Statute of Frauds and does not have to be in writing to be enforceable. If Bancroft fails to pay the florist and the florist sues him for payment, Bancroft cannot raise the Statute of Frauds as a defense.

In contrast, a contract in which a party assumes a secondary obligation does have to be in writing to be enforceable. Now suppose that Bancroft's mother borrows $10,000 from the International Trust Company on a promissory note payable six months later. Bancroft

promises the bank officer handling the loan that he will pay the $10,000 *only if his mother does not pay the loan on time.* Bancroft, in this situation, becomes what is known as a *guarantor* on the loan—that is, he is guaranteeing to the bank that he will pay back the loan if his mother fails to do so—and has incurred a *secondary* obligation. This kind of collateral promise, in which the guarantor states that he or she will become responsible only if the primary party does not perform, must be in writing to be enforceable. Exhibit 13–2 illustrates the concept of a collateral promise. (We will return to the concept of guaranty and the distinction between primary and secondary obligations in Chapter 28, in the context of creditors' rights.)

An Exception—The "Main Purpose" Rule

An oral promise to answer for the debt of another is covered by the Statute of Frauds *unless* the guarantor's main purpose in incurring a secondary obligation is to secure a personal benefit. This type of contract need not be in writing.[6] The assumption is that a court can infer from the circumstances of a particular case whether the "leading objective" of the promisor was to secure a personal benefit and thus, in effect, to answer for her or his own debt.

Consider an example. Braswell contracts with Custom Manufacturing Company to have some machines custom-made for Braswell's factory. She promises Newform Supply, Custom's supplier, that if Newform continues to deliver the materials to Custom for the production of the custom-made machines, she will guarantee payment. This promise need not be in writing, even though the effect may be to pay the debt

---

6. *Restatement (Second) of Contracts,* Section 116.

EXHIBIT 13–2 • Collateral Promises

A collateral (secondary) promise is one made by a third party (C, in this exhibit) to a creditor (B, in this exhibit) to pay the debt of another (A, in this exhibit), who is primarily obligated to pay the debt. Under the Statute of Frauds, collateral promises must be in writing to be enforceable.

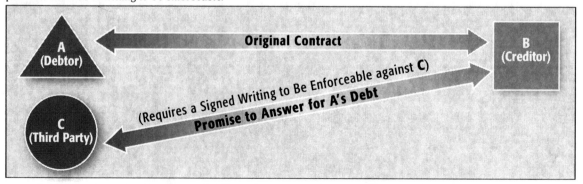

of another. This is because Braswell's main purpose in forming the contract is to secure a benefit for herself.

Another typical application of the main purpose rule occurs when one creditor guarantees a debtor's debt to another creditor to prevent litigation. This allows the debtor to remain in business long enough to generate profits sufficient to pay both creditors.

Promises Made in Consideration of Marriage

A unilateral promise to make a monetary payment or to give property in consideration of a promise to marry must be in writing. If Baumann promises to pay Villard $10,000 if Villard promises to marry Baumann's daughter, the promise must be in writing. The same rule applies to **prenuptial agreements**—agreements made before marriage that define each partner's ownership rights in the other partner's property. A couple might make such an agreement if, for example, a prospective wife wishes to limit the amount her prospective husband can obtain if the marriage ends in divorce. Prenuptial agreements must be in writing to be enforceable.[7]

Consideration Generally Required Generally, courts tend to give more credence to prenuptial agreements that are accompanied by consideration. For example, Maureen, who has few assets, and Kaiser, who has a net worth of $300 million, plan to marry. Kaiser has several children, and he wants them to receive most of his wealth on his death. The couple form a prenuptial agreement in which Kaiser promises to give Maureen $100,000 a year for the rest of her life should they divorce. Kaiser offers to give Maureen $500,000 if she consents to the agreement. If Maureen consents to the agreement and accepts the $500,000, very likely a court will hold this to be a valid prenuptial agreement should it ever be contested.

Courts have used the same reasoning to require adequate consideration in *postnuptial agreements* (agreements entered into after the marriage that define each spouse's rights). Suppose that one year after a couple married, they entered into an agreement concerning the division of marital assets in the event of divorce. The husband, a medical student, agreed to give the wife one-half of his future earnings if he insti-

gated a divorce. The wife, in turn, promised not to return to her dental career, which she had given up when they married, and not to leave the marriage. Is the agreement enforceable? According to many states' courts, the answer is no. Because the wife in this situation had already given up her career to stay at home and tend to the household, this promise was based on past consideration, which is no consideration. Also, because the parties were not having marital difficulties at the time, she was not giving up anything by promising to stay in the marriage.[8]

Must Be Voluntarily Entered In some circumstances, a prenuptial agreement will not be enforceable even if it is in writing. For example, an agreement is not enforceable if the party against whom enforcement is sought proves that he or she did not sign the agreement voluntarily. (For a further discussion of this topic, see this chapter's *Contemporary Legal Debates* feature on pages 284 and 285.)

Contracts for the Sale of Goods

The Uniform Commercial Code (UCC) includes Statute of Frauds provisions that require written evidence of a contract for the sale of goods priced at $500 or more (see Chapter 20). A writing that will satisfy the UCC requirement need only state the quantity term; other terms agreed on can be omitted or even stated imprecisely in the writing, as long as they adequately reflect both parties' intentions. A written memorandum or series of communications evidencing a contract will suffice. The contract will not be enforceable, however, for any quantity greater than that set forth in the writing. In addition, the writing must have been signed by the person to be charged—that is, by the person who refuses to perform or the one being sued. Beyond these two requirements, the writing normally need not designate the buyer or the seller, the terms of payment, or the price. Requirements of the Statute of Frauds under the UCC will be discussed in more detail in Chapter 20.

Exceptions to the Applicability of the Statute of Frauds

Exceptions to the applicability of the Statute of Frauds are made in certain circumstances. We look here at these exceptions.

---

7. To add certainty to the enforceability of prenuptial agreements, the National Conference of Commissioners on Uniform State Laws issued the Uniform Prenuptial Agreements Act (UPAA) in 1983. The act provides that a prenuptial agreement must be in writing to be enforceable and that the agreement becomes effective when the parties marry.

8. See, for example, *Bratton v. Bratton,* 136 S.W.3d 595 (Tenn. 2004).

CONTEMPORARY LEGAL DEBATES
Prenuptial Agreements and Advice of Counsel

The drafting and signing of prenuptial agreements are often at odds with the very concept of marriage. After all, the parties purport to be in love with each other and desirous of sharing all aspects of their lives. Under these circumstances, the thought of involving lawyers in the negotiation of a prenuptial agreement seems inappropriate. Nonetheless, prenuptial agreements are drafted and entered into every day. Cases occasionally come before the courts in which a party to a prenuptial agreement claims that the agreement should not be enforced because he or she was not advised to consult his or her own attorney before signing the agreement.

Some Jurisdictions Require Independent Counsel

In a growing number of jurisdictions, courts regard the advice of independent counsel as a significant factor in determining whether a party signed a prenuptial agreement voluntarily. In other words, if a prospective spouse did not have the advice of her or his own attorney before signing the agreement, that could indicate that the agreement was not signed voluntarily. In one case, for example, a woman challenged the enforceability of a prenuptial agreement on the ground that her husband's lawyer, who was hired to draft the agreement, did not advise her to have it reviewed by her own attorney. The Supreme Court of North Dakota held that the agreement could in fact be unenforceable for this reason.[a] In a subsequent case involving similar facts, the Supreme Court of North Dakota reiterated that "adequate legal representation will often be the best evidence that a spouse signed the agreement knowledgeably and voluntarily."[b]

Many courts have been particularly suspicious of prenuptial agreements involving a waiver by the future wife of all spousal support in the event of marriage and divorce. The reasoning has been that any prenuptial support waiver might undermine the permanency of the marital relationship, which would be contrary to public policy.

Other Jurisdictions Do Not Require Independent Counsel

Other jurisdictions take a different approach. For example, in a highly publicized case involving baseball player Barry Bonds, the California Supreme Court held that a prenuptial agreement was enforceable even though Bonds's wife was not advised to obtain independent counsel before signing it. The wife, who was Swedish and had little knowledge of English, later stated that she had not understood that by signing the agreement, she would forfeit any right to the earnings and property

a. *Estate of Lutz,* 563 N.W.2d 90 (N.Dak. 1997).
b. See *Binek v. Binek,* 673 N.W.2d 594 (N.Dak. 2004).

Partial Performance In cases involving contracts relating to the transfer of interests in land, a court may grant *specific performance* (performance of the contract according to its precise terms) of an oral contract that has been partially performed. For instance, when the purchaser has paid part of the price, taken possession of the property, and made permanent improvements to it, the parties clearly cannot be returned to the positions they occupied before the contract was formed. Whether a court will enforce an oral contract pertaining to land due to partial performance is usually determined by the degree of injury that would otherwise result. The party seeking performance must have reasonably relied on the contract (and on the other party's continuing agreement) and so changed her or his position that injustice can be avoided only by specific enforcement.[9]

Under the UCC, an oral contract for the sale of goods is enforceable to the extent that a seller accepts payment or a buyer accepts delivery of the goods (see Chapter 20 for a fuller discussion of this exception).[10] The existence and extent of a contract to supply computer kiosks for use in school cafeterias were in dispute in the following case.

9. *Restatement (Second) of Contracts,* Section 129.
10. UCC 2–201(3)(c).

acquisitions of the parties during their marriage. The court, however, held that the agreement was enforceable. The court concluded that the evidence indicated that the wife had consented to the terms of the agreement.[c]

In another case, just days before the wedding, a man drove his future wife to his attorney's office and asked her to sign a prenuptial agreement as a precondition of their marriage. The agreement provided that each spouse waived his or her rights to the other spouse's property. The attorney advised the woman to obtain independent counsel and gave her an opportunity to review the document before signing it, but she did neither. After her husband's death, she claimed that the agreement was invalid because she had not signed it voluntarily. She stated that she had been very embarrassed by the scene in the attorney's office when she signed the agreement and had just wanted to "get it over with." Nonetheless, the court held that the agreement was valid. The court declared that while the husband's actions were "certainly not laudatory" and could be "fairly characterized as surprise tactics," they did not negate the "voluntary nature of the execution."[d]

In a more recent case, the Connecticut Supreme Court rejected a trial court's conclusion that the ex-wife had had insufficient time to digest and understand the disclosure on the day she signed the agreement. The appellate court ruled that "it is the party's responsibility to delay the signing of an agreement that is not understood."[e]

WHERE DO YOU STAND?

Some observers argue that enforcing prenuptial agreements when both parties did not have the advice of independent counsel unduly burdens the financially weaker party to the marriage, customarily the woman. Others contend that allowing financially successful future spouses to protect their assets encourages more marriages to take place.

Clearly, the courts are divided on the issue of whether prenuptial agreements should be upheld despite the lack of independent counsel by both parties. Should the advice of independent counsel be a requirement for a valid prenuptial agreement? What is your position on this issue?

---

c. *In re Marriage of Bonds,* 24 Cal.4th 1, 5 P.3d 815, 99 Cal.Rptr.2d 252 (2000).
d. *In re Estate of Ingmand,* 2001 WL 855406 (Iowa App. 2001).

e. *Friezo v. Friezo,* 281 Conn. 166, 914 A.2d 533 (2007).

C A S E **13.2** **School-Link Technologies, Inc. v. Applied Resources, Inc.**
United States District Court, District of Kansas, 2007. 471 F.Supp.2d 1101.

● **Background and Facts** Applied Resources, Inc. (ARI), makes computer hardware for point-of-sale systems—kiosks consisting of computers encased in chassis on which card readers or other payment devices are mounted. School-Link Technologies, Inc. (SLT), sells food-service technology to schools. In August 2003, the New York City Department of Education (NYCDOE) asked SLT to propose a cafeteria payment system that included kiosks. SLT asked ARI to participate in a pilot project, orally promising ARI that it would be the exclusive supplier of as many as 1,500 kiosks if the NYCDOE awarded the contract to SLT. ARI agreed. SLT intended to cut ARI out of the deal, however, and told the NYCDOE that SLT would be making its own kiosks. Meanwhile, SLT paid ARI in advance for a certain number of goods but insisted on onerous terms for a written contract to which ARI would not agree. ARI suspended production of the prepaid items and refused to

CASE CONTINUES

CASE 13.2 CONTINUED refund more than $55,000 that SLT had paid. SLT filed a suit in a federal district court against ARI. ARI responded with, among other things, a counterclaim for breach of contract, asserting that SLT failed to use ARI as an exclusive supplier as promised. ARI sought the expenses it incurred for the pilot project and the amount of profit that it would have realized on the entire deal. SLT filed a motion for summary judgment on this claim.

● **Decision and Rationale** The district court denied SLT's motion for summary judgment on ARI's counterclaim for breach of contract "with respect to goods which SLT already received and accepted, [that is], the goods for the pilot program with the NYCDOE." The court acknowledged that, according to the Uniform Commercial Code, a contract for a sale of goods for a price of $500 or more generally must be in writing and must be signed by the party against whom enforcement is sought. The court reasoned that "because the NYCDOE contract undisputedly involved the sale of goods in excess of $500, the parties' oral contract that ARI would be the exclusive supplier of kiosks for the project is not enforceable in the absence of an applicable exception to this general rule." Under the partial performance exception to the rule, an oral contract for a sale of goods for more than $500 that would otherwise be unenforceable for the lack of a writing is enforceable to the extent that the seller delivers the goods and the buyer accepts them. In that situation, the performance serves as a substitute for the required writing. Thus, in this case, the court concluded that the alleged oral contract between SLT and ARI, to the effect that ARI would be the exclusive supplier of kiosks for SLT's contract with NYCDOE, was enforceable to the extent that ARI had delivered the kiosks for the pilot project and SLT had accepted them. The court added, however, that "the remaining aspect of that claim is barred by the Statute of Frauds."

● **The Ethical Dimension** *Are there additional theories on which ARI's request for relief could be based in this case? What common thread underlies these theories?*

● **The Legal Environment Dimension** *Could ARI have successfully asserted a claim against SLT based on fraudulent misrepresentation? Explain.*

Admissions In some states, if a party against whom enforcement of an oral contract is sought "admits" in pleadings, testimony, or otherwise in court that a contract for sale was made, the contract will be enforceable.[11] A contract subject to the UCC will be enforceable, but only to the extent of the quantity admitted.[12] Thus, if the president of Ashley Corporation admits under oath that an oral agreement was made with Com Best to buy certain business equipment for $10,000, the agreement will be enforceable, but only to the extent it is admitted.

Promissory Estoppel In some states, an oral contract that would otherwise be unenforceable under the Statute of Frauds may be enforced under the doctrine of promissory estoppel, based on detrimental reliance. Recall from Chapter 12 that if a promisor makes a promise on which the promisee justifiably relies to his or her detriment, a court may *estop* (prevent) the promisor from denying that a contract exists. Section 139 of the *Restatement (Second) of Contracts* provides that in these circumstances, an oral promise can be enforceable notwithstanding the Statute of Frauds if the reliance was foreseeable to the person making the promise and if injustice can be avoided only by enforcing the promise. (Note the similarities between this exception and the doctrine of partial performance discussed above: both require reasonable reliance and operate to estop a party from claiming that no contract exists.)

Special Exceptions under the UCC Special exceptions to the applicability of the Statute of Frauds apply to sales contracts. Oral contracts for customized goods may be enforced in certain circumstances. Another exception has to do with oral contracts *between merchants* that have been confirmed in a written memorandum. These exceptions and those mentioned above will be examined in greater detail in Chapter 20, when we discuss the UCC provisions regarding the Statute of Frauds. Exhibit 13–3 graphically summarizes the types of contracts that fall under the Statute of Frauds and the various exceptions that apply.

---

11. *Restatement (Second) of Contracts*, Section 133.
12. UCC 2–201(3)(b).

EXHIBIT 13–3 • **Contracts Subject to the Statute of Frauds**

Contracts for the sale of goods priced at $500 or more[a]	Contracts involving interests in land	Contracts that cannot be performed within one year	Contracts containing collateral promises
EXCEPTIONS • Memorandum • Customized goods • Admission (quantity) • Partial performance • Merchants confirm in writing	**EXCEPTIONS** • Memorandum • Partial performance • Admission[b] • Promissory estoppel[b]	**EXCEPTIONS** • Memorandum • Admission[b] • Promissory estoppel[b]	**EXCEPTIONS** • Memorandum • Main purpose rule • Admission[b] • Promissory estoppel[b]

a. Under a 2003 amendment to the UCC that has not been adopted by any state, a contract for a sale of goods must involve goods priced at $5,000 or more (this dollar threshold may increase in the future) to be subject to the writing requirement of the Statute of Frauds. This amendment also exempts contracts for the sale of goods from the one-year rule.

b. Some states follow Section 133 (on admissions) and Section 139 (on promissory estoppel) of the *Restatement (Second) of Contracts*.

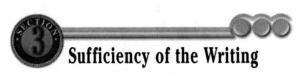

Sufficiency of the Writing

The Statute of Frauds and the UCC require either a written contract or a memorandum (written evidence of the oral contract) signed by the party against whom enforcement is sought, unless there is a legally recognized exception. The signature need not be placed at the end of the document but can be anywhere in the writing. It can be an initial rather than the full name. Indeed, it can even be some form of electronic signature, such as a person's name keyed in at the bottom of an e-mail message.[13] (For a discussion of electronic signatures, see Chapter 19.)

What Constitutes a Writing?

A writing can consist of any order confirmation, invoice, sales slip, check, fax, or e-mail—or such items in combination. The written contract need not consist of a single document to constitute an enforceable contract. One document may incorporate another document by expressly referring to it. Several documents may form a single contract if they are physically attached, such as by staple, paper clip, or glue. Several documents may form a single contract even if they are only placed in the same envelope.

Suppose that Simpson orally agrees to sell some land next to a shopping mall to Terro Properties. Simpson gives Terro an unsigned memo that contains a legal description of the property, and Terro gives Simpson an unsigned first draft of their contract. Simpson sends Terro a signed letter that refers to the memo and to the first and final drafts of the contract. Terro sends Simpson an unsigned copy of the final draft of the contract with a signed check stapled to it. Together, the documents can constitute a writing sufficient to satisfy the Statute of Frauds and bind both parties to the terms of the contract as evidenced by the writings.

What Must Be Contained in the Writing?

A memorandum or note evidencing the oral contract need only contain the essential terms of the contract, not every term. There must, of course, also be some indication that the parties voluntarily agreed to the terms. A faxed memo of the terms of an agreement could be sufficient if it shows that there was a meeting of the minds and that the faxed terms were not just part of the preliminary negotiations.[14]

As mentioned earlier, under the UCC, a writing evidencing a contract for the sale of goods need only state the quantity and be signed by the party to be

---

13. See, for example, *Rosenfeld v. Zerneck*, 4 Misc.3d 193, 776 N.Y.S.2d 458 (N.Y.Sup. 2004); and *Lamle v. Mattel, Inc.*, 394 F.3d 1355 (Fed.Cir. 2005).

14. See, for example, *Coca-Cola Co. v. Babyback's International, Inc.*, 841 N.E.2d 557 (Ind.App. 2006).

charged. Under most state Statute of Frauds provisions, the writing must also name the parties and identify the subject matter, the consideration, and the essential terms with reasonable certainty. In addition, contracts for the sale of land often are required to state the price and describe the property with sufficient clarity to allow them to be determined without reference to outside sources.

Note that because only the party against whom enforcement is sought must have signed the writing, a contract may be enforceable by one of its parties but not by the other. For example, Rock orally agrees to buy Betty Devlin's lake house and lot for $150,000. Devlin writes Rock a letter confirming the sale by identifying the parties and the essential terms of the sales contract—price, method of payment, and legal address—and signs the letter. Devlin has made a written memorandum of the oral land contract. Because she signed the letter, she normally can be held to the oral contract by Rock. Devlin cannot enforce the contract against Rock, however, because he has not signed or entered into a written contract or memorandum and can assert the Statute of Frauds as a defense.

The Parol Evidence Rule

Sometimes, a written contract does not include—or contradicts—an oral understanding reached by the parties before or at the time of contracting. For exam-

ple, Laura is about to lease an apartment. As she is signing the lease, she asks the landlord whether cats are allowed in the building. The landlord says that they are and that Laura can keep her cat in the apartment. The lease that Laura actually signs, however, contains a provision prohibiting pets. Later, a dispute arises between Laura and the landlord over whether the landlord agreed that Laura could have a cat in the apartment. Will Laura be able to introduce evidence at trial to show that, at the time the written contract was formed, the landlord orally agreed that she could have a cat, or will the written contract absolutely control?

In determining the outcome of contract disputes such as the one between Laura and her landlord, the courts look to a common law rule governing the admissibility in court of oral evidence, or *parol evidence*. Under the **parol evidence rule,** if a court finds that the parties intended their written contract to be a complete and final statement of their agreement, then it will not allow either party to present parol evidence (testimony or other evidence of communications between the parties that is not contained in the contract itself).[15]

Did a football team's agreement with its fans to sell "stadium builder licenses" (SBLs) for seats represent the parties' entire contract, or could an SBL brochure vary the agreement? That was the question in the following case.

---

15. *Restatement (Second) of Contracts,* Section 213.

C A S E 13.3 Yocca v. Pittsburgh Steelers Sports, Inc.
Supreme Court of Pennsylvania, 2004. 578 Pa. 479, 854 A.2d 425.

● **Company Profile** Pittsburgh Steelers Sports, Inc., is the operating company for the National Football League's (NFL's) Pittsburgh Steelers (**www.steelers.com**). Art Rooney founded the company, which his family still owns. The team began in 1933 as the Pittsburgh Pirates, named after the baseball team. One of the star players in the early years was Byron "Whizzer" White, who led the NFL in rushing in 1938. White became a justice of the United States Supreme Court in 1962. Renamed in a contest sponsored by the *Pittsburgh Post-Gazette* in 1940, the Steelers had winning seasons only eight times in their first forty years. In the 1970s and 1980, the Steelers won the Super Bowl four times, adding a fifth title in 2006. Groundbreaking for a new stadium took place in 1999.

● **Background and Facts** In October 1998, Pittsburgh Steelers Sports, Inc., and others (collectively, the Steelers) sent Ronald Yocca a brochure that advertised a new stadium to be built for the Pittsburgh Steelers football team. The brochure publicized the opportunity to buy stadium builder licenses (SBLs), which grant the right to buy annual season tickets to the games. Prices varied depending on the seats' locations, which were indicated by small diagrams. Yocca applied for an SBL, listing his seating preferences. The Steelers sent him a letter notifying him of the section in which his seat was located. A diagram included with the letter detailed the parameters of the sec-

CASE 13.3 CONTINUED tion, but it differed from the brochure's diagrams. The Steelers also sent Yocca documents setting out the terms of the SBL and requiring his signature. These documents included an integration clause[a] that read, "This Agreement contains the entire agreement of the parties." Yocca signed the documents, and the Steelers told him the specific location of his seat. When he arrived at the stadium, however, the seat was not where he expected it to be. Yocca and other SBL buyers filed a suit in a Pennsylvania state court against the Steelers, alleging, among other things, breach of contract. The court ordered the dismissal of the complaint. The plaintiffs appealed to a state intermediate appellate court, which reversed this order. The defendants appealed to the state supreme court.

● **Decision and Rationale** The Pennsylvania Supreme Court reversed the lower court's judgment. The state supreme court held that the SBL documents constituted the parties' entire contract and under the parol evidence rule could not be supplemented by previous negotiations or agreements. Because the plaintiffs based their complaint on the claim that the defendants violated the terms of the brochure, and the brochure was not part of the contract, the complaint was properly dismissed. The court explained, "The SBL Brochure did not represent a promise by the Steelers to sell SBLs to Appellees. Rather, the Brochure was merely an offer by the Steelers to sell Appellees the right to be assigned an unspecified seat in an unspecified section of the new stadium and the right to receive a contract to buy an SBL for that later-assigned seat. *   *   * The SBL Agreement clearly represented the parties' contract concerning the sale of SBLs. Unlike the SBL Brochure, the SBL Agreement reflected a promise by the Steelers to actually sell Appellees a specific number of SBL seats in a specified section. Furthermore, the SBL Agreement *   *   * explicitly stated that it represented the parties' entire contract regarding the sale of SBLs."

● **What If the Facts Were Different?** *Suppose that the Steelers had not sent Yocca a diagram with the letter notifying him of his seat's section and that the SBL documents had not included an integration clause. Would the result have been different?*

● **The Legal Environment Dimension** *Could Yocca and the other plaintiffs have plausibly argued that the terms of the SBL brochure must have been integrated within the SBL agreement because those terms were needed to define and describe the section assignments to which the agreement referred? Explain.*

---

a. An *integration clause* is a provision stating that all of the terms of the parties' agreement are included in the written contract. Integrated contracts will be discussed later in this chapter.

Exceptions to the Parol Evidence Rule

Because of the rigidity of the parol evidence rule, the courts have created the following exceptions:

1. *Contracts subsequently modified.* Evidence of any *subsequent modification* (oral or written) of a written contract can be introduced into court. Keep in mind that the oral modifications may not be enforceable if they come under the Statute of Frauds—for example, if they increase the price of the goods for sale to $500 or more or increase the term for performance to more than one year. Also, oral modifications will not be enforceable if the original contract provides that any modification must be in writing.[16]

2. *Voidable or void contracts.* Oral evidence can be introduced in all cases to show that the contract was voidable or void (for example, induced by mistake, fraud, or misrepresentation). The reason is simple: if deception led one of the parties to agree to the terms of a written contract, oral evidence attesting to the fraud should not be excluded. Courts frown on bad faith and are quick to allow such evidence when it establishes fraud.

3. *Contracts containing ambiguous terms.* When the terms of a written contract are ambiguous and require interpretation, evidence is admissible to show the meaning of the terms.

4. *Incomplete contracts.* When the written contract is incomplete in that it lacks one or more of the essential terms, the courts allow evidence to "fill in the gaps."

---

16. UCC 2–209(2), (3).

5. *Prior dealing, course of performance, or usage of trade.* Under the UCC, evidence can be introduced to explain or supplement a written contract by showing a prior dealing, course of performance, or usage of trade.[17] These terms will be discussed in further detail in Chapter 20, in the context of sales contracts. Here, it is sufficient to say that when buyers and sellers deal with each other over extended periods of time, certain customary practices develop. These practices are often overlooked in the writing of the contract, so courts allow the introduction of evidence to show how the parties have acted in the past. Usage of trade—practices and customs generally followed in a particular industry—can also shed light on the meaning of certain contract provisions, and thus evidence of trade usage may be admissible.

6. *Contracts subject to an orally agreed-on condition precedent.* As you will read in Chapter 17, sometimes the parties agree that a condition must be fulfilled before a party is required to perform the contract. This is called a *condition precedent.* If the parties have orally agreed on a condition precedent and the condition does not conflict with the terms of a written agreement, then a court may allow parol evidence to prove the oral condition. The parol evidence rule does not apply here because the existence of the entire written contract is subject to an orally agreed-on condition. Proof of the condition does not alter or modify the written terms but affects the *enforceability* of the written contract.

For example, a city leases property for an airport from a helicopter business and the lease is renewable every five years. During the second five-year lease, a dispute arises, and the parties go to mediation. They enter into a settlement memorandum under which they agree to amend the lease agreement subject to the approval of the city council. The city amends the lease, but the business refuses to sign it, contending that the council has not given its approval. In this situation, the council's approval is a condition precedent to the formation of the settlement memorandum contract. Therefore, the parol evidence rule does not apply, and oral evidence is admissible to show that no agreement exists as to the terms of the settlement.[18]

7. *Contracts with an obvious or gross clerical (or typographic) error that clearly would not represent the agreement of the parties.* Parol evidence is admissible to correct an obvious typographic error. Suppose that Bazza agrees to lease 1,000 square feet of office space from Stone Enterprises at the current monthly rate of $3 per square foot. The signed written lease provides for a monthly lease payment of $300 rather than the $3,000 agreed to by the parties. Because the error is obvious, Stone Enterprises would be allowed to admit parol evidence to correct the mistake.

Integrated Contracts

The key in determining whether evidence will be allowed basically depends on whether the written contract is intended to be a complete and final statement of the terms of the agreement. If it is so intended, it is referred to as an **integrated contract,** and extraneous evidence (evidence derived from sources outside the contract itself) is excluded.

An integrated contract can be either completely or partially integrated. If it contains all of the terms of the parties' agreement, then it is completely integrated. If it contains only some of the terms that the parties agreed on and not others, it is partially integrated. If the contract is only partially integrated, evidence of consistent additional terms is admissible to supplement the written agreement.[19] Note that for both complete and partially integrated contracts, courts exclude any evidence that *contradicts* the writing and allow parol evidence only to add to the terms of a partially integrated contract. Exhibit 13–4 illustrates the relationship between integrated contracts and the parol evidence rule.

The Statute of Frauds in the International Context

As you will read in Chapter 20, the Convention on Contracts for the International Sale of Goods (CISG) provides rules that govern international sales contracts between citizens of countries that have ratified the convention (agreement). Article 11 of the CISG does not incorporate any Statute of Frauds provisions. Rather, it states that a "contract for sale need not be

---

17. UCC 1–205, 2–202.

18. *Castroville Airport, Inc. v. City of Castroville,* 974 S.W.2d 207 (Tex.App.—San Antonio 1998).

19. *Restatement (Second) of Contracts,* Section 216; and UCC 2–202.

EXHIBIT 13–4 • **Parol Evidence Rule**

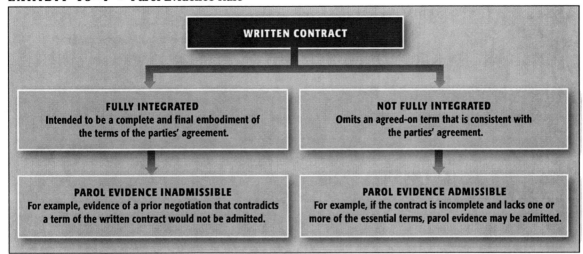

WRITTEN CONTRACT

FULLY INTEGRATED
Intended to be a complete and final embodiment of the terms of the parties' agreement.

NOT FULLY INTEGRATED
Omits an agreed-on term that is consistent with the parties' agreement.

PAROL EVIDENCE INADMISSIBLE
For example, evidence of a prior negotiation that contradicts a term of the written contract would not be admitted.

PAROL EVIDENCE ADMISSIBLE
For example, if the contract is incomplete and lacks one or more of the essential terms, parol evidence may be admitted.

concluded in or evidenced by writing and is not subject to any other requirements as to form."

Article 11 accords with the legal customs of most nations, which no longer require contracts to meet certain formal or writing requirements to be enforceable. Ironically, even England, the nation that created the original Statute of Frauds in 1677, has repealed all of it except the provisions relating to collateral promises and to transfers of interests in land. Many other countries that once had such statutes have also repealed all or parts of them. Some countries, such as France, have never required certain types of contracts to be in writing.

REVIEWING The Statute of Frauds—Writing Requirement

Charter Golf, Inc., manufactures and sells golf apparel and supplies. Ken Odin had worked as a Charter sales representative for six months when he was offered a position with a competing firm. Charter's president, Jerry Montieth, offered Odin a 10 percent commission "for the rest of his life" if Ken would turn down the offer and stay on with Charter. He also promised that Odin would not be fired unless he was dishonest. Odin turned down the competitor's offer and stayed with Charter. Three years later, Charter fired Odin for no reason. Odin sued, alleging breach of contract. Using the information presented in the chapter, answer the following questions.

1. Would a court likely decide that Odin's employment contract falls within the Statute of Frauds? Why or why not?
2. Assume that the court does find that the contract falls within the Statute of Frauds and that the state in which the court sits recognizes every exception to the Statute of Frauds discussed in the chapter. What exception provides Odin with the best chance of enforcing the oral contract in this situation?
3. Now suppose that Montieth had taken out a pencil, written "10 percent for life" on the back of a register receipt, and handed it to Odin. Would this satisfy the Statute of Frauds? Why or why not?
4. Assume that Odin had signed a written employment contract at the time he was hired to work for Charter, but it was not completely integrated. Would a court allow Odin to present parol evidence of Montieth's subsequent promises?

TERMS AND CONCEPTS

collateral promise

integrated contract
parol evidence rule

prenuptial agreement
Statute of Frauds

QUESTIONS AND CASE PROBLEMS

15-1. On May 1, by telephone, Yu offers to hire Benson to perform personal services. On May 5, Benson returns Yu's call and accepts the offer. Discuss fully whether this contract falls under the Statute of Frauds in the following circumstances:

(a) The contract calls for Benson to be employed for one year, with the right to begin performance immediately.

(b) The contract calls for Benson to be employed for nine months, with performance of services to begin on September 1.

(c) The contract calls for Benson to submit a written research report, with a deadline of two years for submission.

15-2. QUESTION WITH SAMPLE ANSWER

Mallory promises a local hardware store that she will pay for a lawn mower that her brother is purchasing on credit if the brother fails to pay the debt. Must this promise be in writing to be enforceable? Why or why not?

• **For a sample answer to Question 15–2, go to Appendix C at the end of this text.**

15-3. On January 1, Damon, for consideration, orally promised to pay Gary $300 a month for as long as Gary lived, with the payments to be made on the first day of every month. Damon made the payments regularly for nine months and then made no further payments. Gary claimed that Damon had breached the oral contract and sued Damon for damages. Damon contended that the contract was unenforceable because, under the Statute of Frauds, contracts that cannot be performed within one year must be in writing. Discuss whether Damon will succeed in this defense.

15-4. Jeremy took his mother on a special holiday to Mountain Air Resort. Jeremy was a frequent patron of the resort and was well known by its manager. The resort required each of its patrons to make a large deposit to ensure payment of the room rental. Jeremy asked the manager to waive the requirement for his mother and

told the manager that if his mother for any reason failed to pay the resort for her stay there, he would cover the bill. Relying on Jeremy's promise, the manager waived the deposit requirement for Jeremy's mother. After she returned home from her holiday, Jeremy's mother refused to pay the resort bill. The resort manager tried to collect the sum from Jeremy, but Jeremy also refused to pay, stating that his promise was not enforceable under the Statute of Frauds. Is Jeremy correct? Explain.

15-5. Oral Contracts. Robert Pinto, doing business as Pinto Associates, hired Richard MacDonald as an independent contractor in March 1992. The parties orally agreed on the terms of employment, including payment to MacDonald of a share of the company's income, but they did not put anything in writing. In March 1995, MacDonald quit. Pinto then told MacDonald that he was entitled to $9,602.17—25 percent of the difference between the accounts receivable and the accounts payable as of MacDonald's last day. MacDonald disagreed and demanded more than $83,500—25 percent of the revenue from all invoices, less the cost of materials and outside processing, for each of the years that he worked for Pinto. Pinto refused. MacDonald filed a suit in a Connecticut state court against Pinto, alleging breach of contract. In Pinto's response and at the trial, he testified that the parties had an oral contract under which MacDonald was entitled to 25 percent of the difference between accounts receivable and payable as of the date of MacDonald's termination. Did the parties have an enforceable contract? What should the court rule, and why? [*MacDonald v. Pinto*, 62 Conn.App. 317, 771 A.2d 156 (2001)]

15-6. Interests in Land. Sierra Bravo, Inc., and Shelby's, Inc., entered into a written "Waste Disposal Agreement" under which Shelby's allowed Sierra to deposit on Shelby's land waste products, deleterious (harmful) materials, and debris removed by Sierra in the construction of a highway. Later, Shelby's asked Sierra why it had not constructed a waterway and a building pad suitable for a commercial building on the property, as they had orally agreed. Sierra denied any such agreement. Shelby's filed a suit in a Missouri state court against Sierra, alleging breach of contract. Sierra contended that any oral agreement was unenforceable under the Statute of Frauds. Sierra argued that because the right to *remove* minerals from land is considered a contract for the sale of an interest in land to which the Statute of Frauds applies, the Statute of Frauds should apply to the right to *deposit* soil on another person's property. How should the court rule, and why? [*Shelby's, Inc. v. Sierra Bravo, Inc.,* 68 S.W.3d 604 (Mo.App. S.D. 2002)]

15–7. CASE PROBLEM WITH SAMPLE ANSWER

Novell, Inc., owned the source code for DR DOS, a computer operating system that Microsoft Corp. targeted with allegedly anticompetitive practices in the early 1990s. Novell worried that if it filed a suit, Microsoft would retaliate with further alleged unfair practices. Consequently, Novell sold DR DOS to Canopy Group, Inc., a Utah corporation. The purposes of the sale were to obligate Canopy to bring an action against Microsoft and to allow Novell to share in the recovery without revealing its role. Novell and Canopy signed two documents—a contract of sale, obligating Canopy to pay $400,000 for rights to the source code, and a temporary license, obligating Canopy to pay at least $600,000 in royalties, which included a percentage of any recovery from the suit. Canopy settled the dispute with Microsoft, deducted its expenses, and paid Novell the remainder of what was due. Novell filed a suit in a Utah state court against Canopy, alleging breach of contract for Canopy's deduction of expenses. Canopy responded that it could show that the parties had an oral agreement on this point. On what basis might the court refuse to consider this evidence? Is that the appropriate course in this case? Explain. [*Novell, Inc. v. Canopy Group, Inc.,* 2004 UT App 162, 92 P.3d 768 (2004)]
- **To view a sample answer for Problem 15–7, go to this book's Web site at www.cengage. com/blaw/jentz, select "Chapter 15," and click on "Case Problem with Sample Answer."**

15–8. The Parol Evidence Rule. Carlin Krieg owned a dairy farm in St. Joe, Indiana, that was appraised at $154,000 in December 1997. In August 1999, Krieg told Donald Hieber that he intended to sell the farm for $106,000. Hieber offered to buy it. Krieg also told Hieber that he wanted to retain a "right of residency" for life in the farm. In October, Krieg and Hieber executed a purchase agreement that provided Krieg "shall transfer full and complete possession" of the farm "subject to [his] right of residency." The agreement also contained an integration clause that stated "there are no conditions, representations, warranties or agreements not stated in this instrument." In November 2000, the house was burned in a fire, rendering it uninhabitable. Hieber filed an insurance claim for the damage and received the proceeds, but he did not fix the house. Krieg filed a suit in an Indiana state court against Hieber, alleging breach of

contract. Is there any basis on which the court can consider evidence regarding the parties' negotiations prior to their agreement for the sale of the farm? Explain. [*Krieg v. Hieber,* 802 N.E.2d 938 (Ind.App. 2004)]

15–9. Contract for a Sale of Goods. Milton Blankenship agreed in writing to buy 15 acres of Ella Mae Henry's junkyard property for $15,000 per acre with a ten-year option to buy the remaining 28.32 acres. Blankenship orally agreed to (1) begin operating a car skeleton processing plant within six to fifteen months; (2) buy as many car skeletons generated by the yard as Clifford Henry wanted to sell him, at a certain premium over the market price; and (3) allow all junk vehicles on the property to remain until they were processed at the new plant. Blankenship never operated such a plant, never bought any vehicles from the yard, and demanded that all vehicles be removed from the property. To obtain the remaining 28.32 acres, Blankenship filed a suit in a Georgia state court against Henry, who responded with a counterclaim for breach of contract. Under oath during discovery, Henry testified that their oral agreement allowed him to sell "as many of the car skeletons generated by the Henry junkyard" as he wished, and Blankenship testified that he had agreed to buy as many skeletons as Henry was willing to sell. Does the Statute of Frauds undercut or support Henry's counterclaim? Explain. [*Henry v. Blankenship,* 284 Ga.App. 578, 644 S.E.2d 419 (2007)]

15–10. A QUESTION OF ETHICS

William Williams is an attorney in Birmingham, Alabama. In 1997, Robert Shelborne asked Williams to represent him in a deal in London, England, from which Shelborne expected to receive $31 million. Shelborne agreed to pay Williams a fee of $1 million. Their overseas contact was Robert Tundy, who said that he was with the "Presidency" in London. Tundy said that a tax of $100,010 would have to be paid for Shelborne to receive the $31 million. Shelborne asked James Parker, a former co-worker, to lend him $50,000. Shelborne signed a note agreeing to pay Parker $100,000 within seventy-two hours. Parker, Shelborne, and Williams wired the $50,000 to an account at Chase Manhattan Bank. They never heard from Tundy again. No $31 million was transferred to Shelborne, who soon disappeared. Williams then learned that no "Presidency" existed in London. Whenever Parker asked Williams about the note, Williams assured him that he would be paid. On Parker's behalf, Williams filed a suit in an Alabama state court against Shelborne, seeking the amount due on the note and damages. The court entered a judgment against the defendant for $200,000, but there were no assets from which to collect it. [Parker v. Williams, 977 So.2d 476 (Ala. 2007)]

(a) Parker filed a suit in an Alabama state court against Williams, alleging, among other things, breach of contract. Parker offered as evidence a tape recording of a phone conversation in which Williams guaranteed Shelborne's loan. Is the court likely to rule in Parker's favor on the contract claim? Why or why not?

(b) In response to Parker's suit, Williams filed a counterclaim, seeking unpaid attorneys' fees relating to the suit that Williams filed against Shelborne on Parker's behalf. The court ruled against Williams on this claim. He appealed to the Alabama Supreme Court but failed to supply a transcript of the trial on his counterclaim, as it was his duty to do. Is the appellate court likely to rule in his favor? Why or why not?

(c) The sham deal at the center of this case is known to law enforcement authorities as advance fee fraud, commonly referred to as a "419 scam." Induced by a promise of a transfer of funds from an overpaid contract or some other suspect source, a victim may be asked to pay a tax or other fee first. Among the parties attracted by the 419 scam in this case, who, if anyone, behaved ethically? Discuss.

LAW ON THE WEB

For updated links to resources available on the Web, as well as a variety of other materials, visit this text's Web site at

www.cengage.com/blaw/jentz

The online version of UCC Section 2–201 on the Statute of Frauds includes links to definitions of certain terms used in the section. To access this site, go to

www.law.cornell.edu/ucc/2/2-201.html

To read a summary of cases concerning whether the exchange of e-mails satisfies the writing requirements of the Statute of Frauds, go to

www.internetlibrary.com/topics/statute_frauds.cfm

Wikipedia provides an interesting discussion of the history and current applicability of the Statute of Frauds, both internationally and in the United States, at

en.wikipedia.org/wiki/Statute_of_frauds

Legal Research Exercises on the Web

Go to **www.cengage.com/blaw/jentz**, the Web site that accompanies this text. Select "Chapter 15" and click on "Internet Exercises." There you will find the following Internet research exercises that you can perform to learn more about the topics covered in this chapter.

Internet Exercise 15–1: Legal Perspective
Promissory Estoppel and the Statute of Frauds

Internet Exercise 15–2: Management Perspective
"Get It in Writing"

Internet Exercise 15–3: Historical Perspective
The English Act for the Prevention of Frauds and Perjuries

Contracts: Writing, Form, Interpretation

Case No. 76

STATUTE OF FRAUDS/QUASI-CONTRACT

Farash v. Sykes Datatronics, Inc.

Court of Appeals

59 N.Y.2d 500, 465 N.Y.S.2d 917 (1983)

FACTS: Plaintiff Max M. Farash (Farash), a building developer, entered an oral agreement to lease building space with Plaintiff Sykes Datatronics, Inc. (Sykes), a company that manufactures computer-related products. The term of the oral lease was more than a year. Prior to entering the lease, Farash had begun renovating the building. To accommodate Sykes' needs, Farash agreed to accelerate the renovation schedule and modify the renovation plans according to Sykes' specifications.

For unidentified reasons, the parties never signed a written contract and Sykes never occupied the building. Farash sued Sykes to recover lost rent and the value of the renovation work.

FIRST ISSUE: Where parties enter an oral contract that cannot be completed within a year from when it is made and one party thereafter fails to perform the contract, can the other enforce the contract by seeking damages?

DECISION: No, judgment for Sykes.

REASONING: The Statute of Frauds requires a writing for the enforcement of an agreement that cannot be completed within a year from when it was made. The lease in this case was oral and for a period longer than one year.

SECOND ISSUE: Is Farash entitled to collect from Sykes, under the theory of quasi-contract, the value of the renovation work performed in the space that Sykes had orally promised to lease?

DECISION: Yes, judgment for Farash.

REASONING: The renovation work was accelerated and modified by Farash in reliance upon Sykes' promise to rent the space. The doctrine of quasi-contract imposes an obligation to do justice in a situation, where, as here, an enforceable agreement does not exist. Farash expended money to satisfy Sykes' special needs in reliance on Sykes' oral promises to rent the space. Farash would not have changed its renovation plans had Sykes not made the promise. The fact that Sykes did not benefit from the work does not diminish Farash's right to damages based on quasi-contract.

NOTE: The court in this case did not discuss the part performance exception to the Statute of Frauds. That exception provides that, under some circumstances where an oral contract which requires a writing is performed in part, a court of equity may enforce the contract notwithstanding the absence of a writing. For the exception to apply, the part performance must unequivocally refer to the agreement and injustice must result from nonenforcement.

* * * QUESTIONS * * *
(See back of text for answers)

1) If the lease in this case had been for a period of less than one year, would the Statute of Frauds have been an obstacle to a lawsuit by Farash for the lost rent?

2) If the contract between Farash and Sykes involved a sale of the building from Farash to Sykes instead of a lease, and the contract required the transfer of title to the property to occur within three months from the date the contract was made, would a writing be required to enforce the contract?

Case No. 77

IMPLIED CONTRACTS AND

STATUTE OF FRAUDS/SUFFICIENCY OF WRITING

<u>Valentino v. H.F. Davis</u>

Appellate Division, Third Department

270 A.D.2d 635, 703 N.Y.S.2d 609 (2000)

FACTS: John Valentino (Valentino) is in the business of breeding and raising horses. Jonathon H. F. Davis (Davis) is a veterinarian who operates Milfer Farm Inc. in the Town of Unadilla, Chenango County. Valentino and Davis decided to breed their horses and exchanged several drafts of agreements regarding the boarding, breeding, and care of Valentino's mares with Davis' stallions. Additionally, the draft proposals addressed the care and ownership of any future foals (young horses) for a three-year period at Milfer Farm. The parties were unable to agree on the terms and as a result no written agreement was executed. Evidence showed that the parties intended, had they been able to reach an agreement, to have a formal contract prepared by an attorney and signed by the parties.

While the parties were still negotiating, Valentino delivered twenty mares and unweaned foals to Milfer Farms. Per agreement, Davis cared for the mares and foals over the next four months, and was successful in breeding many of the mares. Thereafter, Valentino removed all his horses from Milfer Farms claiming that they were overgrazed and maintained in overcrowded stalls leading to sickness, and in some cases, death. Valentino kept the foals later born to mares as a result of breeding during this four-month period.

Valentino sued Davis for breach of contract. The trial court determined that no written agreement had been entered but held that there were triable issues of fact regarding the existence of an enforceable oral or implied-in-fact contract. Davis appealed.

FIRST ISSUE: Where parties exchange draft proposals for a prospective agreement, and it is clear that the parties intended to draft a formal written contract once an oral agreement was reached, will the draft proposals satisfy the writing requirement of the Statute of Frauds?

DECISION: No

REASONING: A contract that by its terms cannot be performed within one year of making is unenforceable under the Statute of Frauds unless it is in writing. In this case the proposed contract was for a period of three years, hence it is unenforceable unless reduced to writing. Valentino claimed that the exchange of written proposals constituted a sufficient writing to satisfy the Statute of Frauds. The court rejected this argument because the evidence and testimony clearly indicated an intention by the parties to reduce

—

their agreement to a formal writing prepared by an attorney. Since no writing was ever executed, the writing requirement of the Statute of Frauds was not satisfied.

SECOND ISSUE: Does an implied-in-fact contract exist from the conduct of the parties where the parties clearly intended to be bound only by the terms of a formal written agreement?

DECISION: No

REASONING: Valentino contended that an implied-in-fact agreement existed for a three year period because Davis partially performed by caring for Valentino's mares and unweaned foals in addition to facilitating the breeding process during a four month period. However, Valentino acknowledged that the parties intended that any long term agreement be reduced to writing. For this reason, the court denied the existence of an implied-in-fact contract noting that "a contract may not be implied in fact from the conduct of the parties where it appears that they intended to be bound only by a formal written agreement".

Case No. 78

STATUTE OF FRAUDS/ONE-YEAR RULE

Paul v. Emil Ascher, Inc.

Supreme Court, Nassau County

NYLJ, April 29, 1985, p. 16, col. 2m

FACTS: Plaintiff Charles Paul (Paul) was a composer who specialized in background music for, among other projects, soap operas. He wrote the theme for "As the World Turns" and "Love of Life". Defendant Emil Ascher, Inc. (Ascher) was a music publisher. Paul and Ascher had a composer/publisher relationship for more than forty years. Between 1939 and 1959 Paul and Ascher entered into written agreements regarding four compositions, in which Paul transferred to Ascher the right to copyright the works. In return, Ascher agreed in the written contracts to pay Paul 10% of the list price for each copy of sheet music for the songs Ascher sold and 50% of net income received by Ascher in exchange for the right to perform the work.

Paul in this lawsuit claimed that Ascher orally agreed to pay Paul 50% of the money Ascher received from both the sale of the sheet music and the sale of the right to perform the work. For unknown reasons Paul took no action to enforce the alleged agreement for twenty years. Ascher denied liability for more than 10% of the list price of the sheet music, the amount specified in the written contract.

ISSUE: Can a party seeking to modify a written contract by evidence of an oral agreement made prior to the time the written contract was signed, introduce evidence in an attempt to prove the oral agreement?

DECISION: No, judgment for Ascher.

REASONING: The Statute of Frauds provides that an agreement that cannot be performed within a year from the date it was made is unenforceable unless it is in writing. An agreement to divide copyright royalties is effective for the full term of the copyright unless the agreement states otherwise. Ascher's copyright on the four songs was valid for a minimum of fourteen years and a maximum of twenty-eight. Because the alleged oral agreement to pay Paul 50% of all proceeds could not be completed within a year from when it was made, and because it was not in writing, Paul cannot introduce evidence seeking to prove the oral agreement.

NOTE: The parol evidence rule might present another obstacle to Paul's lawsuit. The court did not discuss this issue.

The duration of a copyright changed when the Copyright Law was revised in 1978. Prior to the revisions, the duration of a copyright was fourteen years and could be renewed once for a second fourteen year period. Under the new law, a copyright lasts for the life of the author of the copyrighted work plus fifty years.

Case No. 79

STATUTE OF FRAUDS

P.J. Carlin Construction Company v. Whiffen Electric Company, Inc.

Appellate Division, First Department

66 A.D.2d 684, 411 N.Y.S.2d 27 (1978)

FACTS: Plaintiff P.J. Carlin Construction Company (Carlin) submitted a bid for the construction of Greenwich High School. According to Carlin, before it submitted its bid, it had a telephone conversation with defendant Whiffen Electric Company, Inc. (Whiffen) in which Whiffen agreed to perform the necessary electrical work for Carlin on the school construction project for $941,200.00. Carlin further claimed Whiffen agreed to guarantee all labor, materials, and equipment for two years. Carlin was awarded the contract to build the high school.

A few weeks later Carlin sent Whiffen a written contract incorporating the terms of their alleged agreement. Whiffen refused to sign it and thereafter refused to perform any of the electrical work. Carlin sued Whiffen for breach of contract. Whiffen claimed that the alleged agreement between them was subject to the Statute of Frauds, and since Whiffen had not signed any writings, the agreement was unenforceable. Whiffen did admit that the electrical work in question could have been performed within one year from when the contract was allegedly made.

ISSUE: Does the Statute of Frauds require a writing to enforce a contract to perform electrical work where the electrical work could be completed within a year from when the contract was made and the labor, materials, and equipment were guaranteed for two years?

DECISION: No.

REASONING: As provided by the Statute of Frauds, a contract that, by its terms, cannot be performed within one year from the date it is made is unenforceable unless a written memorandum of the contract exists and is signed by the nonperforming party. While Whiffen guaranteed its work, materials and equipment for two years, such guarantee was not considered by the Court to be a promise to perform in the future. The electrical work by Whiffen's admission could have been fully performed within a year from when the contract was made. Therefore, a writing to enforce the agreement was not necessary.

NOTE: The Appellate Division in this case addressed the issue of whether the Statute of Frauds constituted a bar to Carlin's claim that a contract existed between it and Whiffen. Because the court concluded the Statute of Frauds was not a bar, it referred the case back to the court with original jurisdiction for determination of the other issues in the case.

* * * QUESTIONS * * *
(See back of text for answers)

1) The guarantee allegedly made by Whiffen provided that all labor, materials, and equipment would be guaranteed to be free from defects for two years. Why did the court reject Whiffen's argument that the Statute of Frauds required a writing?

2) The Note following this case indicates the issue of the Statute of Frauds was addressed before other issues were reviewed. Why should the Statute of Frauds be treated in this way?

Case No. 80

STATUTE OF FRAUDS/ONE YEAR RULE/COLLATERAL PROMISES

<u>Nakamura v. Fujii</u>

Appellate Division, First Department

253 A.D.2d 387, 677 N.Y.S.2d 113 (1998)

FACTS: Masaki and Isako Fujii (Fujii) informed Mikio Nakamura (Nakamura) that Fujii was unable to afford college tuition for his two daughters. Nakamura agreed to pay the tuition expenses in exchange for Fujii's promise to repay Nakamura "on demand". Nakamura issued several checks to the University of Southern California totaling approximately $101,000.

Nakamura contends that the repayment obligations were confirmed during several meetings with Fujii. Fujii later refused to pay and Nakamura sued for breach of contract. Fujii claimed, among other things, that the oral repayment agreement was unenforceable under the Statute of Frauds because it could not be performed within one year and it was a collateral promise.

The trial court granted Fujii's motion to dismiss and Nakamura appealed.

FIRST ISSUE: Does the Statute of Frauds require a writing to enforce a contract to pay "certain tuition invoices" with repayment due on demand?

DECISION: No

REASONING: An agreement that cannot by its terms be performed within one year of its making must be in writing to be enforceable. In this case the money was due on demand. Because specific terms mandating payment at a specified time were absent from the agreement, it could possibly be performed within one year and so did not require a writing to be enforceable.

The court also noted that the Statute of Frauds does not apply where "the performance...depends on a contingency which may or may not happen within one year". In this case the daughters could have left USC within one year.

SECOND ISSUE: Is a promise by parents to a third party to pay the tuition costs of their children a promise to answer for the debt of another requiring a writing under the Statute of Frauds?

DECISION: No

REASONING: A collateral or secondary promise is one made by a third party to assume the debts or obligations of a primary party to the contract if that party does not pay. Such a promise must be in writing to be enforceable under the Statute of Frauds.

In this case Fujii's daughters did not owe any money to Nakamura. Therefore Fujii's agreement to repay the tuition costs was not a contract to pay the debts of their daughters in the event that they failed to pay. It was a primary promise made directly and exclusively by Fujii to Nakamura. As a result, the promise to pay did not require a writing to be enforceable under the Statute of Frauds.

Case No. 81

STATUTE OF FRAUDS/QUANTUM MERUIT/DAMAGES

<u>Frank v. Feiss</u>

Appellate Division, Second Department

266 A.D.2d 825, 698 N.Y.S.2d 363 (1999)

FACTS: John Frank (Frank) entered into an oral home improvement contract with Grant and Sandra Feiss (Feiss) for their property located in Cattaraugus County at a contract price of $58,835.00. Feiss paid Frank $37,589.00. Because of a dispute, Frank never completed the project. Frank later sued Feiss for breach of contract claiming that he had substantially performed and was entitled to money damages and a lien against the property. Feiss contends that Frank had not substantially performed and that the contract was unenforceable because it was not in writing as required by a New York law relating specifically to home improvement contracts. The trial court agreed with Frank and Feiss appealed.

FIRST ISSUE: Did an enforceable home improvement contract exist between Frank and Feiss?

DECISION: No

REASONING: Under New York law, certain home improvement contracts must be in writing to be enforceable. Failure to meet the requirements of the statute bars recover for breach of contract. Frank is not entitled to recover damages for breach under the statute, as the contract was not in writing.

SECOND ISSUE: Can Frank recover damages under the theory of quantum meruit?

DECISION: Yes

REASONING: Where no contract exists and one party has conferred a benefit on another party who knowingly accepts the benefit, equity requires the receiving party to pay the reasonable value of the services provided based on quasi contract.

THIRD ISSUE: How are damages in quantum meruit calculated?

DECISION: The trial court measured Frank's damages as the contract price minus the cost of completing the unfinished work and the cost of repairing improperly performed work.

REASONING: The appellate court held that Frank had completed 90% of the work properly and was entitled to the reasonable value of his labor and services. In this case that amounted to 90% of the contract price less any payments made by Feiss.

Case No. 82

STATUTE OF FRAUDS

PART PERFORMANCE/PROMISSORY ESTOPPEL

<u>Steele v. Delverde S.R.L.</u>

Appellate Division, First Department

242 A.D.2d 414, 662 N.Y.S.2d 30 (1997)

FACTS: John H. Steele (Steele) entered an oral agreement with Delverde S.R.L. (Delverde) pursuant to which Steele was to be Delverde's exclusive agent in the United States for the sale of various Delverde food products manufactured in Italy for a period of two years. No written agreement existed. During the period of negotiations with Delverde, Steele engaged in various preliminary activities in anticipation of successfully securing the Delverde account while simultaneously rejecting several of Delverde's draft agreements. Thereafter Steele learned that Delverde had entered into an exclusive agency agreement with another party. Steele sued Delverde claiming breach of contract.

Delverde sought dismissal of the claim arguing that a contract that could not be performed within one year of its making was unenforceable under the Statute of Frauds unless it is in writing. Steele contended that the oral contract was enforceable because the doctrines of part performance and promissory estoppel. The trial court agreed with Steele and Delverde appealed.

FIRST ISSUE: Does the doctrine of part performance eliminate the need for a written agreement under the Statute of Frauds?

DECISION: No, judgment for defendant.

REASONING: In order for the doctrine of part performance to apply as an exception to the Statute of Frauds, it must be shown that the partially performed oral contract unequivocally refers to the alleged agreement. The court rejected the part performance doctrine in this case and held that any actions taken on Steele's part in anticipation of securing the Delverde account did not unequivocally refer to the alleged agreement but instead were merely "preparatory steps in the expectation of a future agreement".

While the hopes of securing an agreement may provide motivation for Steele's conduct, it was not enough to remove the agreement from the Statute of Frauds.

SECOND ISSUE: Does the doctrine of promissory estoppel eliminate the need for a written agreement under the Statute of Frauds?

DECISION: No, judgment for defendant.

REASONING: The doctrine of promissory estoppel applies where a party can show that a clear promise was made that was reasonably relied upon resulting in injury, and where refusal to enforce the promise would be unconscionable. As a general rule an oral promise will not be enforced on this ground unless it would be unconscionable to deny it. In this case, the court held that even if all the allegations made by Steele were true they did not "rise to the level of reliance and unconscionability" to invoke the doctrine of promissory estoppel.

Case No. 83

PAROL EVIDENCE RULE

Mitchill v. Lath

Court of Appeals

247 N.Y. 377, 160 N.E. 646 (1928)

FACTS: Plaintiff Katherine C. Mitchill (Mitchill) contracted to purchase from Defendant Charles Lath (Lath) a farm for $8,400.00 in Fall 1923. Mitchill alleged that Lath orally agreed to move an "unsightly" icehouse Lath owned that was located across the street on a different parcel of land. The removal was to be completed in Spring, 1924.

When the contract for sale was drafted it did not mention the icehouse or the alleged agreement to remove it. The writing identified in detail the contractual duties of the parties and contained clearly stated terms and conditions usually found in contracts for the sale of land.

The parties performed their various duties with the exception of removal of the icehouse. In this action Mitchill sought to compel Lath to remove it. Lath defended, asserting the parol evidence rule precluded Mitchill from proving the alleged agreement to remove the icehouse.

ISSUE: When parties enter a written contract that establishes in detail the terms of the agreement, can a party to the contract introduce parol evidence that will add to the provisions of the written agreement?

DECISION: No, complaint dismissed; decision for Lath.

REASONING: According to the parol evidence rule, evidence of an oral agreement made prior to written contract cannot be introduced to contradict or modify the terms of a written contract complete on its face. Instead, such a written contract is assumed to contain the entire agreement between the parties. In this case the written contract "shows a full and complete agreement, setting forth in detail the obligations of each party." The parol evidence rule thus bars introduction of oral evidence that would alter or modify such a complete written contract.

* * * QUESTIONS * * *
(See back of text for answers)

1) Identify several exceptions to the parol evidence rule.

2) Assume that Mitchill did not see the icehouse until after she had signed the contract. Assume further that she discovered it before title and money were transferred. She voiced her objections to Lath and they orally agreed to increase the purchase price by $200.00 in return for Lath removing the objectionable structure. If Lath thereafter refused to remove the icehouse would the parol evidence rule prevent Mitchill from proving Lath's promise to do so?

Case No. 84

PAROL EVIDENCE RULE

Battista v. Radesi

Appellate Division, Fourth Department

112 A.D.2d 42, 491 N.Y.S.2d 81 (1985)

FACTS: Richard L. Radesi (Radesi) obtained from wine wholesaler Raffaele Battista (Battista) an exclusive distributorship of Geleso wines in western New York. Radesi received 1000 cases of wine from Battista and signed an invoice which contained Radesi and Battista's names and addresses, the date, payment terms of "net 45 days" (payment due 45 days after delivery), a thorough description and price breakdown of each type of wine delivered in the shipment, and identified a price of $18,808.75.

Several months later, Battista, having received only $500 from Radesi since the invoice was signed, began this action for the balance due. Radesi contends that they had agreed payment would not be due until Radesi had sold the entire inventory of 1000 cases. He seeks dismissal of Battista's suit. Battista asserts that the parol evidence rule precludes Radesi from introducing evidence of the alleged agreement concerning payment after sale because it contradicts the written contract.

ISSUE: When parties enter into a contract that is evidenced by a signed invoice that contains the names and addresses of the parties, the quantity, a description of the goods, payment terms, and price, can a party to the contract introduce parol evidence that modifies the payment terms?

DECISION: No, judgment for Battista; Radesi must pay regardless of his sales.

REASONING: The parol evidence rule applies to written contracts intended by the parties to be the final expression of their agreement. The rule prohibits the introduction of evidence of oral agreements made prior to signing the written contract that would contradict its terms.

The court determined that the invoice was a complete expression of Radesi and Battista's agreement and therefore barred Radesi's testimony of an alleged oral agreement that no payments would be due until the entire inventory was sold.

Case No. 85

PAROL EVIDENCE RULE

Potler, as Trustee in Bankruptcy for
Underwater Advisors Corp. v. MCP Facilities Corp.

Federal District Court, Eastern District of New York

471 F. Supp. 1344 (1979)

FACTS: Plaintiff Underwater Advisors Corp. (UAC) was hired to apply a coat of anticorrosive paint to underwater piles (beams driven into the ground to support a wall, bridge or like structure). Defendant MCP Facilities Corp. (MCP) manufactured paint for use underwater.

UAC alleged it had conversations and correspondence with MCP concerning the suitability of Steelmate, a paint manufactured by MCP, for underwater painting. UAC further alleged that MCP represented that Steelmate would meet the job requirements.

UAC submitted a purchase order for 450 gallons of Steelmate. The purchase order did not refer to the representations made by MCP. The order did contain payment terms that contradicted themselves and did not contain a clause stating that the order was intended to be the complete contract between the parties.

After MCP delivered the paint UAC discovered it did not adhere to the surface of the piles. UAC was thus forced to discontinue performance. As a result, UAC lost the profit it would have made on the job and incurred various expenses. It sued MCP for these damages and attempted to prove that the representations allegedly made by MCP concerning the suitability of the paint for the job were untrue. MCP in its defense invoked the parol evidence rule.

MCP claimed the purchase order, which did not refer to the alleged representations, was a "complete and exclusive statement of the terms of the contract" preventing evidence of any prior oral agreements or representations.

ISSUE: Where a buyer submits to a seller a purchase order that does not contain an integration clause and has contradictory terms, can the buyer introduce evidence of an oral agreement which would modify the written order?

DECISION: Yes.

REASONING: According to the parol evidence rule, evidence of an agreement not included in a written statement of the terms of a contract cannot be used to modify the contract if the writing contains a complete and exclusive statement of the contract terms. In this case, the existence of the contradictory and confusing terms in the order suggests it was not intended as the final and complete embodiment of the contract between the parties. Further, the absence of a clause stating that the order was intended as the complete and exclusive contract between the parties suggests further that the order did not contain the entire agreement between the parties. Therefore, UAC was not barred by the parol evidence rule from introducing evidence concerning the representations made by MCP.

* * * QUESTION * * *
(See back of text for answer)

1)   What is the purpose of the parol evidence rule?

CHAPTER 14

Third Party Rights

O nce it has been determined that a valid and legally enforceable contract exists, attention can turn to the rights and duties of the parties to the contract. A contract is a private agreement between the parties who have entered into it, and traditionally these parties alone have rights and liabilities under the contract. This principle is referred to as **privity of contract.**

A *third party*—one who is not a direct party to a particular contract—normally does not have rights under that contract.

There are exceptions to the rule of privity of contract. For example, privity of contract between a seller and a buyer is no longer a requirement to recover damages under product liability laws (see Chapter 23). In this chapter, we look at two other exceptions. One

exception allows a party to a contract to transfer the rights or duties arising from the contract to another person through an *assignment* (of rights) or a *delegation* (of duties). The other exception involves a *third party beneficiary contract*—a contract in which the parties to the contract intend that the contract benefit a third party.

Assignments and Delegations

In a bilateral contract, the two parties have corresponding rights and duties. One party has a *right* to require the other to perform some task, and the other has a *duty* to perform it. The transfer of contractual *rights* to a third party is known as an **assignment.** The transfer of contractual *duties* to a third party is known as a **delegation.** An assignment or a delegation occurs *after* the original contract was made.

Assignments

Assignments are important because they are involved in many types of business financing. Banks, for example, frequently assign their rights to receive payments under their loan contracts to other firms, which pay for those rights. If you obtain a loan from your local bank to purchase a car, you may later receive in the mail a notice from your bank stating that it has transferred (assigned) its rights to receive payments on the

loan to another firm and that, when the time comes to repay your loan, you must make the payments to that other firm.

Financial institutions that make *mortgage loans* (loans to enable prospective home buyers to purchase land or a home) often assign their rights to collect the mortgage payments to a third party, such as GMAC Mortgage Corporation. Following the assignment, the home buyers are notified that they must make future payments *not* to the bank that loaned them the funds but to the third party. Millions of dollars change hands daily in the business world in the form of assignments of rights in contracts. If it were not possible to transfer (assign) contractual rights, many businesses could not continue to operate.

Terminology In an assignment, the party assigning the rights to a third party is known as the **assignor,** and the party receiving the rights is the **assignee.** Other traditional terms used to describe the parties in assignment relationships are **obligee** (the person to whom a duty, or obligation, is owed) and **obligor** (the person who is obligated to perform the duty).

The Effect of an Assignment When rights under a contract are assigned unconditionally, the rights of the assignor are extinguished.[1] The third party (the assignee) has a right to demand performance from the other original party to the contract. The assignee takes only those rights that the assignor originally had, however.

For example, Brower is obligated by contract to pay Horton $1,000. In this situation, Brower is the obligor because she owes an obligation, or duty, to Horton. Horton is the obligee, the one to whom the obligation, or duty, is owed. Now suppose that Horton assigns his right to receive the $1,000 to Kuhn. Horton is the assignor, and Kuhn is the assignee. Kuhn now becomes the obligee because Brower owes Kuhn the $1,000. Here, a valid assignment of a debt exists. Kuhn (the assignee-obligee) is entitled to enforce payment in court if Brower (the obligor) does not pay him the $1,000. These concepts are illustrated in Exhibit 14–1.

Rights Assigned Are Subject to the Same Defenses The assignee's rights are subject to the defenses that the obligor has against the assignor. Assume that in the preceding scenario, Brower owed Horton the $1,000 under a contract in which Brower agreed to buy Horton's MacBook laptop. Brower, in deciding to purchase the laptop, relied on Horton's fraudulent misrepresentation that the computer had a 160 gigabyte hard drive. When Brower discovers that the computer has only an 80 gigabyte hard drive, she tells Horton that she is going to return the laptop to him and cancel the contract. Even though Horton has assigned his "right" to receive the $1,000 to Kuhn, Brower need not pay Kuhn the $1,000—Brower can raise the defense of Horton's fraudulent misrepresentation to avoid payment.

Form of the Assignment In general, an assignment can take any form, oral or written. Naturally, it is more difficult to prove that an oral assignment occurred, so it is practical to put all assignments in writing. Of course, assignments covered by the Statute of Frauds must be in writing to be enforceable. For example, an assignment of an interest in land must be in writing to be enforceable. In addition, most states require contracts for the assignment of wages to be in writing.[2]

The circumstances in the following case illustrate some of the problems that can arise with oral assignments. The case also stands for the principle that an assignment, like any contract, must have consideration—in this case, a dance center's assumption of a choreographer's legal and financial duties associated with her choreography.

---

1. *Restatement (Second) of Contracts*, Section 317.

2. See, for example, California Labor Code Section 300. There are other assignments that must be in writing as well.

EXHIBIT 14–1 • Assignment Relationships

In the assignment relationship illustrated here, Horton assigns his *rights* under a contract that he made with Brower to a third party, Kuhn. Horton thus becomes the *assignor* and Kuhn the *assignee* of the contractual rights. Brower, the *obligor* (the party owing performance under the contract), now owes performance to Kuhn instead of Horton. Horton's original contract rights are extinguished after assignment.

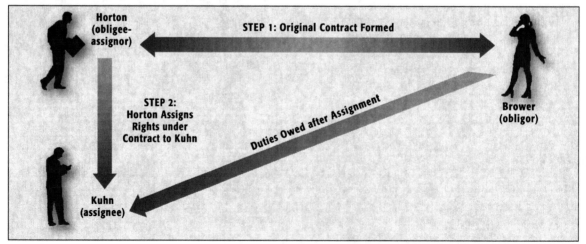

Horton (obligee-assignor)

STEP 1: Original Contract Formed

Brower (obligor)

STEP 2: Horton Assigns Rights under Contract to Kuhn

Duties Owed after Assignment

Kuhn (assignee)

CASE 14.1 Martha Graham School and Dance Foundation, Inc. v.
Martha Graham Center of Contemporary Dance, Inc.
United States Court of Appeals, Second Circuit, 2004. 380 F.3d 624.

● **Background and Facts** Martha Graham's career as a dancer, dance instructor, and chore-ographer began in the first third of the twentieth century. In the 1920s, she started a dance company and a dance school and choreographed works on commission. In the 1940s, she funded the Martha Graham Center of Contemporary Dance, Inc. (the Center). She sold her school to the Martha Graham School of Contemporary Dance, Inc. (the School), in 1956. By 1980, the Center encompassed the School. In 1989, two years before her death, Graham executed a will in which she gave Ronald Protas, the Center's general director, "any rights or interests" in "dance works, musical scores [and] scenery sets." After her death, Protas asserted ownership of all of Graham's dances and related property. In 1999, the Center's board removed Protas and, due to financial problems, suspended operations. Meanwhile, Protas founded the Martha Graham School and Dance Foundation, Inc., and began licensing Graham's dances. When the School reopened in 2001, Protas and his foundation filed a suit in a federal district court against the Center and others to enjoin their use of, among other things, seventy of the dances. The Center responded, in part, that Graham had assigned the dances to it. The court ruled that twenty-one of the dances had been assigned to the Center. The plaintiffs appealed to the U.S. Court of Appeals for the Second Circuit.

● **Decision and Rationale** The U.S. Court of Appeals for the Second Circuit affirmed the lower court's judgment on this issue, "commend[ing] the District Court for its careful rulings on the many issues in this complicated case." The appellate court held that Graham had received consideration for her assignment of certain dances (she benefited by being relieved of various administrative duties), and although the assignment had been oral, it had been reliably proved by written testimony. Evidence that Graham had assigned all of her pre-1956 dances to the Center were two letters from Lee Leatherman, the Center's executive administrator at the time. The letters, written in 1968 and 1971, indicated that "recently Miss Graham assigned performing rights to all of her works to the Martha Graham Center of Contemporary Dance, Inc.," and that "Martha has assigned all rights to all of her works to the Martha Graham Center, Inc." In addition, Jeannette Roosevelt, former president of the Center's board of directors, testified that Graham had given the dances to the Center prior to 1965 or 1966, when she joined the board. There was additional evidence that the Center had acted as the owner of the dances by entering into contracts with other parties, and that Graham was aware of this and did not object. Other evidence showed that the Center received royalties for the dances and treated them as its assets.

● **What If the Facts Were Different?** Suppose that Graham had not benefited from the Center's assumption of the duties associated with her choreography. Would the alleged assignment have been valid? Why or why not?

● **The E-Commerce Dimension** If Graham's dances had existed as part of a database available only over the Internet, would the principles applied in this case, and the way in which they were applied, have been different? Why or why not?

Rights That Cannot Be Assigned

As a general rule, all rights can be assigned. Exceptions are made, however, under certain circumstances. Some of these exceptions are described next.

When a Statute Expressly Prohibits Assignment.
When a statute expressly prohibits assignment of a particular right, that right cannot be assigned. For example, Quincy is an employee of Specialty Computer, Inc. Specialty Computer is an employer under workers' compensation statutes in this state, and thus Quincy is a covered employee. Quincy is injured on the job and begins to collect monthly workers' compensation checks (see Chapter 33 for a discussion of workers' compensation laws). In need of a loan, Quincy borrows from Draper, assigning to Draper all of her future

workers' compensation benefits. A state statute prohibits the assignment of future workers' compensation benefits, however, and thus such rights cannot be assigned.

When a Contract Is Personal in Nature. When a contract is for personal services, the rights under the contract normally cannot be assigned unless all that remains is a monetary payment.[3] Suppose that Brower signs a contract to be a tutor for Horton's children. Horton then attempts to assign to Kuhn his right to Brower's services. Kuhn cannot enforce the contract against Brower. Kuhn's children may be more difficult to tutor than Horton's; thus, if Horton could assign his rights to Brower's services to Kuhn, it would change the nature of Brower's obligation. Because personal services are unique to the person rendering them, rights to receive personal services are likewise unique and cannot be assigned.

When an Assignment Will Significantly Change the Risk or Duties of the Obligor. A right cannot be assigned if the assignment will significantly increase or alter the risks to or the duties of the obligor (the party owing performance under the contract).[4] Assume that Horton has a hotel, and to insure it, he takes out a policy with Southeast Insurance. The policy insures against fire, theft, floods, and vandalism. Horton attempts to assign the insurance policy to Kuhn, who also owns a hotel. The assignment is ineffective because it substantially alters Southeast Insurance's *duty of performance.* An insurance company evaluates the particular risk of a certain party and tailors its policy to fit that risk. If the policy is assigned to a third party, the insurance risk is materially altered because the insurance company may have no information on the third party. Therefore, the assignment will not operate to give Kuhn any rights against Southeast Insurance.

When the Contract Prohibits Assignment. When a contract specifically stipulates that a right cannot be assigned, then *ordinarily* the right cannot be assigned. Whether an antiassignment clause is effective depends, in part, on how it is phrased. A contract that states that any assignment is void effectively prohibits any assignment. Note that restraints on the power to assign operate only against the parties themselves. They do not prohibit an assignment by

operation of law, such as an assignment pursuant to bankruptcy or death.

The general rule that a contract can prohibit assignment has several exceptions.

1. A contract cannot prevent an assignment of the right to receive monetary payments. This exception exists to encourage the free flow of funds and credit in modern business settings.
2. The assignment of rights in real estate often cannot be prohibited because such a prohibition is contrary to public policy in most states. Prohibitions of this kind are called restraints against **alienation** (transfer of land ownership).
3. The assignment of *negotiable instruments* (see Chapter 24) cannot be prohibited.
4. In a contract for the sale of goods, the right to receive damages for breach of contract or payment of an account owed may be assigned even though the sales contract prohibits such an assignment.[5]

Notice of Assignment Once a valid assignment of rights has been made, the assignee (the third party to whom the rights have been assigned) should notify the obligor (the one owing performance) of the assignment. For instance, in the previously discussed example, when Horton assigns to Kuhn his right to receive the $1,000 from Brower, Kuhn should notify Brower, the obligor, of the assignment. Giving notice is not legally necessary to establish the validity of the assignment: an assignment is effective immediately, whether or not notice is given. Two major problems arise, however, when notice of the assignment is not given to the obligor.

1. If the assignor assigns the same right to two different persons, the question arises as to which one has priority—that is, which one has the right to the performance by the obligor. Although the rule most often observed in the United States is that the first assignment in time is the first in right, some states follow the English rule, which basically gives priority to the first assignee who gives notice.
2. Until the obligor has notice of an assignment, the obligor can discharge his or her obligation by performance to the assignor (the obligee), and performance by the obligor to the assignor (obligee) constitutes a discharge to the assignee. Once the obligor receives proper notice, however, only performance to the assignee can discharge the

---

3. *Restatement (Second) of Contracts,* Sections 317 and 318.
4. Section 2–210(2) of the Uniform Commercial Code (UCC).

5. UCC 2–210(2).

obligor's obligations. In the Horton-Brower-Kuhn example, assume that Brower, the obligor, is not notified of Horton's assignment of his rights to Kuhn. Brower subsequently pays Horton the $1,000. Although the assignment was valid, Brower's payment to Horton discharges the debt. Kuhn's failure to give notice to Brower of the assignment has caused Kuhn to lose the right to collect the cash from Brower. If, however, Kuhn had given Brower notice of the assignment, Brower's payment to Horton would not have discharged the debt, and Kuhn would have had a legal right to require payment from Brower.

In a business context, the importance of notifying the obligor (the party that is obligated to perform the duty) of an assignment cannot be overemphasized. Providing notice of assignment, though not legally required, is one of the best ways to avoid potential legal disputes over assignments. Whether the businessperson is the assignee or the assignor, she or he should inform the obligor of the assignment. As already described, an assignee who does not give notice may lose the right to performance, but failure to notify the obligor may have repercussions for the assignor as well.

Consider what would happen if no notice is given by either the assignor or the assignee, and the obligor performs the duty for the assignor. In this situation, the assignee, to whom the right to receive performance was assigned, can sue the assignor for breach of contract. The assignor will also likely be involved in litigation if he or she has assigned a right to two different parties, which can happen when assigning rights that overlap somewhat (such as rights to receive profits from a given enterprise). Assignments of rights are extremely useful in business, but to prevent legal problems, businesspersons should be careful to assign the same rights only once and should always give the obligor notice of the assignment.

Delegations

Just as a party can transfer rights through an assignment, a party can also transfer duties. Duties are not assigned, however; they are *delegated*. Normally, a delegation of duties does not relieve the party making the delegation (the **delegator**) of the obligation to perform in the event that the party to whom the duty has been delegated (the **delegatee**) fails to perform. No special form is required to create a valid delegation of duties. As long as the delegator expresses an intention to make the delegation, it is effective; the delegator need not even use the word *delegate*. Exhibit 14–2 illustrates delegation relationships.

EXHIBIT 14–2 • **Delegation Relationships**

In the delegation relationship illustrated here, Brower delegates her *duties* under a contract that she made with Horton to a third party, Kuhn. Brower thus becomes the *delegator* and Kuhn the *delegatee* of the contractual duties. Kuhn now owes performance of the contractual duties to Horton. Note that a delegation of duties normally does not relieve the delegator (Brower) of liability if the delegatee (Kuhn) fails to perform the contractual duties.

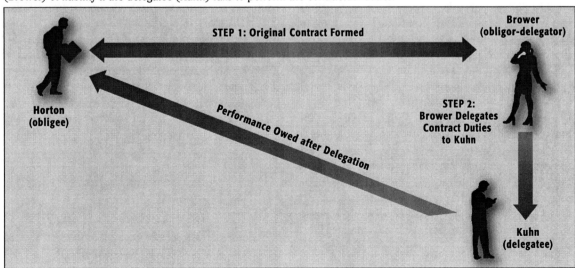

Duties That Cannot Be Delegated As a general rule, any duty can be delegated. There are, however, some exceptions to this rule. Delegation is prohibited in the circumstances discussed next.

When the Duties Are Personal in Nature. When special trust has been placed in the obligor or when performance depends on the personal skill or talents of the *obligor* (the person contractually obligated to perform), contractual duties cannot be delegated. For example, Horton, who is impressed with Brower's ability to perform veterinary surgery, contracts with Brower to have Brower perform surgery on Horton's prize-winning stallion in July. Brower later decides that she would rather spend the summer at the beach, so she delegates her duties under the contract to Kuhn, who is also a competent veterinary surgeon. The delegation is not effective without Horton's consent, no matter how competent Kuhn is, because the contract is for *personal* performance.

In contrast, nonpersonal duties may be delegated. Assume that Brower contracts with Horton to pick up and deliver heavy construction machinery to Horton's property. Brower delegates this duty to Kuhn, who is in the business of delivering heavy machinery. This delegation is effective because the performance required is of a *routine* and *nonpersonal* nature.

When Performance by a Third Party Will Vary Materially from That Expected by the Obligee. When performance by a third party will vary materially from that expected by the obligee (the one to whom performance is owed) under the contract, contractual duties cannot be delegated. Suppose that Alex Payton is a wealthy philanthropist who recently established a charitable foundation. Payton has known Brent Murdoch for twenty years and knows that Murdoch shares his beliefs on many humanitarian issues. He contracts with Murdoch to be in charge of allocating funds among various charitable causes. Six months later, Murdoch is experiencing health problems and delegates his duties to Drew Cole. Payton does not approve of Cole as a replacement. In this situation, Payton can claim the delegation was not effective because it *materially altered his expectations* under the contract. Payton had reasonable expectations about the types of charities to which Murdoch would give the foundation's funds, and substituting Cole's performance materially changes those expectations.

When the Contract Prohibits Delegation. When the contract expressly prohibits delegation by including an *antidelegation clause*, the duties cannot be delegated. For example, R.W. Stern Company contracts with Jan Pearson, a certified public accountant, to perform its annual audits for the next five years. If the contract prohibits delegation, then Pearson cannot delegate her duty to perform the audit to another accountant at the same firm. In some situations, however, when the duties are completely impersonal in nature, courts have held that the duties can be delegated notwithstanding an antidelegation clause.

Effect of a Delegation If a delegation of duties is enforceable, the obligee (the one to whom performance is owed) must accept performance from the delegatee (the one to whom the duties have been delegated). Consider again the example in which Brower delegates to Kuhn the duty to pick up and deliver heavy construction machinery to Horton's property. In that situation, Horton (the obligee) must accept performance from Kuhn (the delegatee) because the delegation was effective. The obligee can legally refuse performance from the delegatee only if the duty is one that cannot be delegated.

As noted, a valid delegation of duties does not relieve the delegator of obligations under the contract.[6] Thus, in the above example, if Kuhn (the delegatee) fails to perform, Brower (the delegator) is still liable to Horton (the obligee). The obligee can also hold the delegatee liable if the delegatee made a promise of performance that will directly benefit the obligee. In this situation, there is an "assumption of duty" on the part of the delegatee, and breach of this duty makes the delegatee liable to the obligee. For example, if Kuhn (the delegatee) promises Brower (the delegator), in a contract, to pick up and deliver the construction equipment to Horton's property but fails to do so, Horton (the obligee) can sue Brower, Kuhn, or both. Although there are many exceptions, the general rule today is that the obligee can sue both the delegatee and the delegator. *Concept Summary 14.1* outlines the basic principles of the laws governing assignments and delegations.

---

6. See, for example, *Mehul's Investment Corp. v. ABC Advisors, Inc.*, 130 F.Supp.2d 700 (D.Md. 2001).

CONCEPT SUMMARY 14.1
Assignments and Delegations

WHICH RIGHTS CAN BE ASSIGNED, AND WHICH DUTIES CAN BE DELEGATED?	All rights can be assigned *unless:*	All duties can be delegated *unless:*
	1. A statute expressly prohibits assignment.	1. Performance depends on the obligor's personal skills or talents.
	2. The contract is for personal services.	2. Special trust has been placed in the obligor.
	3. The assignment will materially alter the obligor's risk or duties.	3. Performance by a third party will materially vary from that expected by the obligee.
	4. The contract prohibits assignment.	4. The contract prohibits delegation.
WHAT IF THE CONTRACT PROHIBITS ASSIGNMENT OR DELEGATION?	No rights can be assigned *except:*	Generally, no duties can be delegated.
	1. Rights to receive funds.	
	2. Ownership rights in real estate.	
	3. Rights to negotiable instruments.	
	4. Rights to sales contract payments or damages for breach of a sales contract.	
WHAT IS THE EFFECT ON THE ORIGINAL PARTY'S RIGHTS?	On a valid assignment, effective immediately, the original party (assignor) no longer has any rights under the contract.	On a valid delegation, if the delegatee fails to perform, the original party (delegator) is liable to the obligee (who may also hold the delegatee liable).

Assignment of "All Rights"

When a contract provides for an "assignment of all rights," this wording may create both an assignment of rights and a delegation of duties.[7] Therefore, when general words are used (for example, "I assign the contract" or "I assign all my rights under the contract"), the contract normally is construed as implying both an assignment of the assignor's rights and a delegation of any duties of performance owed by the assignor under the contract being assigned. Thus, the assignor remains liable if the assignee fails to perform the contractual obligations.

Third Party Beneficiaries

Another exception to the doctrine of privity of contract arises when the original parties to the contract intend at the time of contracting that the contract perfor-

mance directly benefit a third person. In this situation, the third person becomes a **third party beneficiary** of the contract. As an **intended beneficiary** of the contract, the third party has legal rights and can sue the promisor directly for breach of the contract.

Who, though, is the promisor? In a bilateral contract, both parties to the contract are promisors because they both make promises that can be enforced. To determine the identity of the promisor in a third party beneficiary contract, the court will ask which party made the promise that benefits the third party—that person is the promisor. Allowing a third party to sue the promisor directly in effect circumvents the "middle person" (the promisee) and thus reduces the burden on the courts. Otherwise, the third party would sue the promisee, who would then sue the promisor.

Types of Intended Beneficiaries

At one time, third party beneficiaries had no legal rights in contracts. Over time, however, the concept developed that a third party for whose benefit a contract was formed (an intended beneficiary) could sue

---

7. *Restatement (Second) of Contracts*, Section 328; UCC 2–210(3), (4).

the promisor to have the contract enforced. In a classic case decided in 1859, *Lawrence v. Fox,*[8] the court permitted a third party beneficiary to bring suit directly against a promisor. This case established the rule that a *creditor beneficiary* can sue the promisor directly. A creditor beneficiary is one who benefits from a contract in which one party (the promisor) promises another party (the promisee) to pay a debt that the promisee owes to a third party (the creditor beneficiary). As an intended beneficiary, the creditor beneficiary can sue the promisor directly to enforce the contract and obtain payment on the debt.

Another type of intended beneficiary is a *donee beneficiary.* When a contract is made for the express purpose of giving a *gift* to a third party, the third party (the donee beneficiary) can sue the promisor directly to enforce the promise.[9] The most common donee beneficiary contract is a life insurance contract. For example, Akins (the promisee) pays premiums to Standard Life, a life insurance company, and Standard Life (the promisor) promises to pay a certain amount on Akins's death to anyone Akins designates as a beneficiary. The designated beneficiary is a donee beneficiary under the life insurance policy and can enforce the promise made by the insurance company to pay her or him on Akins's death.

As the law concerning third party beneficiaries evolved, numerous cases arose in which the third party beneficiary did not fit readily into either the creditor beneficiary or the donee beneficiary category. Thus, the modern view, and the one adopted by the *Restatement (Second) of Contracts,* does not draw such clear lines between the types of intended beneficiaries. Today, courts frequently distinguish only between *intended beneficiaries* (who can sue to enforce contracts made for their benefit) and *incidental beneficiaries* (who cannot sue, as will be discussed shortly).

The Vesting of an Intended Beneficiary's Rights

An intended third party beneficiary cannot enforce a contract against the original parties until the rights of the third party have *vested,* which means the rights have taken effect and cannot be taken away. Until these rights have vested, the original parties to the contract—the promisor and the promisee—can modify or rescind the contract without the consent of the third party.

When do the rights of third parties vest? The majority of courts hold that the rights vest when any of the following occurs:

1. The third party materially changes his or her position in justifiable reliance on the promise.
2. The third party brings a lawsuit on the promise.
3. The third party demonstrates her or his consent to the promise at the request of the promisor or promisee.[10]

If the contract expressly reserves to the contracting parties the right to cancel, rescind, or modify the contract, the rights of the third party beneficiary are subject to any changes that result. If the original contract reserves the right to revoke the promise or change the beneficiary, the vesting of the third party's rights does not terminate that power.[11] For example, in most life insurance contracts, the policyholder reserves the right to change the designated beneficiary.

Intended versus Incidental Beneficiaries

The benefit that an **incidental beneficiary** receives from a contract between two parties is unintentional. Because the benefit is *unintentional,* an incidental beneficiary cannot sue to enforce the contract.

Determining Whether a Third Party Is an Intended or an Incidental Beneficiary In determining whether a third party beneficiary is an intended or an incidental beneficiary, the courts focus on the intent, as expressed in the contract language and implied by the surrounding circumstances. No single test is available to embrace all possible situations in which a third party is an intended beneficiary. One factor that courts consider is whether a reasonable person in the position of the beneficiary would believe that the promisee intended to confer on the beneficiary the right to enforce the contract. The courts also look at other factors. For example, if performance is to be rendered directly to the third party or the contract expressly designates the third party as a beneficiary, this strongly indicates that the third party is an *intended* beneficiary. Exhibit 14–3 graphically illustrates the distinction between intended beneficiaries and incidental beneficiaries.

---

8. 20 N.Y. 268 (1859).

9. *Seaver v. Ransom,* 224 N.Y. 233, 120 N.E. 639 (1918).

10. *Restatement (Second) of Contracts,* Section 311.

11. Defenses against third party beneficiaries are given in the *Restatement (Second) of Contracts,* Section 309.

EXHIBIT 14-3 ● **Third Party Beneficiaries**

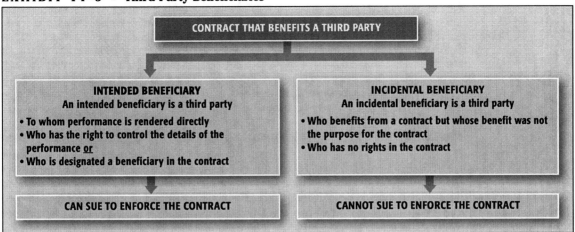

CONTRACT THAT BENEFITS A THIRD PARTY

INTENDED BENEFICIARY
An intended beneficiary is a third party
- To whom performance is rendered directly
- Who has the right to control the details of the performance **or**
- Who is designated a beneficiary in the contract

CAN SUE TO ENFORCE THE CONTRACT

INCIDENTAL BENEFICIARY
An incidental beneficiary is a third party
- Who benefits from a contract but whose benefit was not the purpose for the contract
- Who has no rights in the contract

CANNOT SUE TO ENFORCE THE CONTRACT

In the following case, a subcontractor claimed to be an intended beneficiary of the general contractor's contractual promise to obtain property insurance after the construction of an addition to a building was completed. The case illustrates how resolving the issue of whether a beneficiary is intended or incidental can have serious consequences for the beneficiary's liability.

C A S E 14.2 Midwestern Indemnity Co. v. Systems Builders, Inc.
Court of Appeals of Indiana, 2004. 801 N.E.2d 661.

● **Background and Facts** Action Steel, Inc., entered into a contract with Systems Builders, Inc., a general contractor, to construct an addition to a commercial building in Indianapolis, Indiana. The contract provided that Action Steel would obtain, after the addition's completion, insurance which "shall include the interest of . . . subcontractors." The parties would then "waive all rights against . . . any of their subcontractors." Varco-Pruden Building, a subcontractor, designed the addition, which was completed in the summer of 1995. Action Steel obtained an insurance policy from Midwestern Indemnity Co. In January 1996, a snowstorm hit the Indianapolis area and the new addition collapsed. Midwestern paid more than $1.3 million to Action Steel for the loss. Because Midwestern paid for the loss, it stood in Action Steel's place in a suit filed in an Indiana state court against Varco-Pruden and others to recover this amount. Varco-Pruden filed a motion for summary judgment, arguing, in part, that it was a third party beneficiary of the waiver clause in the contract between Action Steel and Systems Builders. The court issued a summary judgment in favor of Varco-Pruden on this point. Midwestern appealed to a state intermediate appellate court, arguing that Varco-Pruden was not a third party beneficiary of the contract.

● **Decision and Rationale** The state intermediate appellate court affirmed the lower court's judgment. One who is not a party to a contract can enforce the contract as a third party beneficiary if (1) the contracting parties intended to benefit the third party; (2) the contract imposed a duty on one of the parties in favor of the third party; and (3) the performance of the terms of the contract rendered a direct benefit to the third party. According to the appellate court, a "plain reading" of the construction contract indicated that Action Steel intended to benefit Varco-Pruden. Under the contract's terms, when Action Steel bought property insurance after the project was complete, Action Steel intended that subcontractors, such as Varco-Pruden, would benefit from the waiver clause. The contract provided that the insurance "shall include the interest of * * * subcontractors." Furthermore, the contract imposed a duty on Action Steel, providing that

CASE CONTINUES

CASE 14.2 CONTINUED if it acquired insurance after the completion of the project, it "shall * * * waive all rights against * * * any of [the parties'] subcontractors." Finally, the court concluded that the performance of these clauses in the contract rendered a direct benefit—Action Steel's waiver—to Varco-Pruden.

● **What If the Facts Were Different?** *If the collapse of the building had been due to the negligence of a subcontractor, how might that party argue successfully against recovery?*

● **The Legal Environment Dimension** *For what reasons did the state intermediate appellate court uphold the lower court's summary judgment?*

Examples of Incidental Third Party Beneficiaries The benefit that an *incidental beneficiary* receives from a contract between two parties is unintentional, which is why he or she cannot enforce a contract. Any beneficiary who is not deemed an intended beneficiary is considered incidental.

For example, in one case, spectators at a Mike Tyson boxing match in which Tyson was disqualified for biting his opponent's ear sued Tyson and the fight's promoters for a refund on the basis of breach of contract. The spectators claimed that they had standing to sue the defendants as third party beneficiaries of the contract between Tyson and the fight's promoters. The court, however, held that the spectators did not have standing to sue because they were not in contractual privity with any of the defendants. Furthermore, any

benefits they received from the contract were incidental to the contract. The court noted that the spectators got what they paid for: "the right to view whatever event transpired."[12]

In the following case, a national beauty pageant organization and one of its state affiliates agreed that the national organization would accept the winner of the state contest as a competitor in the national pageant. When the state winner was asked to resign her title, she filed a suit to enforce the agreement to have herself declared a contestant in the national pageant. The national organization argued that she was an incidental, not an intended, beneficiary of the agreement.

---

12. *Castillo v. Tyson*, 268 A.D.2d 336, 701 N.Y.S.2d 423 (Sup.Ct.App.Div. 2000). See also *Bowers v. Federation Internationale de l'Automobile*, 489 F.3d 316 (7th Cir. 2007).

C A S E 14.3 Revels v. Miss America Organization
Court of Appeals of North Carolina, 2007. 182 N.C.App. 334, 641 S.E.2d 721.
www.aoc.state.nc.us/www/public/html/opinions.htm[a]

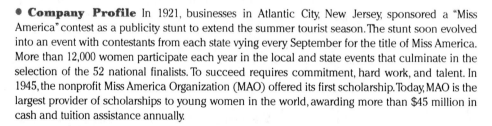

● **Company Profile** In 1921, businesses in Atlantic City, New Jersey, sponsored a "Miss America" contest as a publicity stunt to extend the summer tourist season. The stunt soon evolved into an event with contestants from each state vying every September for the title of Miss America. More than 12,000 women participate each year in the local and state events that culminate in the selection of the 52 national finalists. To succeed requires commitment, hard work, and talent. In 1945, the nonprofit Miss America Organization (MAO) offered its first scholarship. Today, MAO is the largest provider of scholarships to young women in the world, awarding more than $45 million in cash and tuition assistance annually.

● **Background and Facts** Miss North Carolina Pageant Organization, Inc. (MNCPO), is a franchisee of Miss America Organization (MAO). Under the "Miss America Organization Official Franchise Agreement," MNCPO conducts a public contest (the "State Finals") to select Miss North Carolina and to prepare Miss North Carolina for participation in the Miss America pageant (the "National Finals").[b] In return, MAO "accept[s] the winner of the State Finals . . . as a contestant in the National Finals." On June 22, 2002, MNCPO designated Rebekah Revels "Miss North Carolina 2002." On July 19, MAO received an anonymous e-mail (which was later determined to have been

---

a. In the "Court of Appeals Opinions" section, click on "2007." In the result, scroll to the "20 March 2007" section and click on the name of the case to access the opinion. The North Carolina Administrative Office of the Courts maintains this Web site.
b. A *franchise* is an arrangement by which the owner of a trademark, or other intellectual property, licenses the use of the mark to another party under specific conditions.

CASE 14.3 CONTINUED sent by Revels's ex-boyfriend), implying that she had formerly cohabited with a "male non-relative" and that nude photos of her existed. Revels confirmed the existence of the photos. On July 22, MAO and MNCPO asked Revels to resign as Miss North Carolina and told her that if she refused, she would be excluded from competing in the National Finals. On July 23, she resigned. She then filed a suit in a North Carolina state court against MAO, MNCPO, and others, asserting, among other things, breach of contract. The court issued a summary judgment in MAO's favor. Revels appealed this judgment to a state intermediate appellate court.

● **Decision and Rationale** The appellate court affirmed the lower court's judgment in favor of MAO. Revels contended that there was sufficient evidence that she was a third party beneficiary under the franchise agreement between MAO and MNCPO. The reviewing court held that "in order to establish a claim as a third-party beneficiary, plaintiff must show (1) that a contract exists between two persons or entities; (2) that the contract is valid and enforceable; and (3) that the contract was executed for the direct, and not intentional, benefit of the third party." But, the court pointed out, Revels was an incidental beneficiary of the agreement between MAO and MNCPO. Although the agreement provided that MAO would accept the winner of the State Finals as a contestant in the National Finals, this did not establish that the two organizations intended to make the winner a direct beneficiary of the agreement. Thus, Revels was an incidental beneficiary and could not maintain an action against MAO based on the agreement.

● **The Global Dimension** *If the agreement between MAO and MNCPO had involved a third party—an international pageant organization—would this have been a basis for concluding that Revels was a third party intended beneficiary? Why or why not?*

● **The E-Commerce Dimension** *How might Revels's third party status with respect to the agreement between MAO and MNCPO have been affected if the contracting parties had conducted their business online? Explain.*

REVIEWING Third Party Rights

Myrtle Jackson owns several commercial buildings that she leases to businesses, one of which is a restaurant. The lease states that tenants are responsible for securing all necessary insurance policies but the landlord is obligated to keep the buildings in good repair. The owner of the restaurant, Joe McCall, tells his restaurant manager to purchase insurance, but the manager never does so. Jackson tells her son-in-law, Rob Dunn, to perform any necessary maintenance for the buildings. Dunn knows that the ceiling in the restaurant needs repair but fails to do anything about it. One day a customer, Ian Faught, is dining in the restaurant when a chunk of the ceiling falls on his head and fractures his skull. Faught files suit against the restaurant and discovers that there is no insurance policy in effect. Faught then files suit against Jackson, arguing that he is an intended third party beneficiary of the lease provision requiring insurance and thus can sue Jackson for failing to enforce the lease (which requires the restaurant to carry insurance). Using the information presented in the chapter, answer the following questions.

1. Can Jackson delegate her duty to maintain the buildings to Dunn? Why or why not?
2. Who can be held liable for Dunn's failure to fix the ceiling, Jackson or Dunn?
3. Was Faught an intended third party beneficiary of the lease between Jackson and McCall? Why or why not?
4. Suppose that Jackson tells Dan Stryker, a local builder to whom she owes $50,000, that he can collect the rents from the buildings' tenants until the debt is satisfied. Is this a valid assignment? Why or why not?

TERMS AND CONCEPTS

alienation
assignee
assignment

assignor
delegatee
delegation
delegator
incidental beneficiary
intended beneficiary

obligee
obligor
privity of contract
third party beneficiary

QUESTIONS AND CASE PROBLEMS

16-1. Alexander has been accepted as a freshman at a college two hundred miles from his home for the fall semester. Alexander's wealthy uncle, Michael, decides to give Alexander a car for Christmas. In November, Michael makes a contract with Jackson Auto Sales to purchase a new car for $18,000 to be delivered to Alexander just before the Christmas holidays, in mid-December. The title to the car is to be in Alexander's name. Michael pays the full purchase price, calls Alexander and tells him about the gift, and takes off for a six-month vacation in Europe. Is Alexander an intended third party beneficiary of the contract between Michael and Jackson Auto Sales? Suppose that Jackson Auto Sales never delivers the car to Alexander. Does Alexander have the right to sue Jackson Auto Sales for breaching its contract with Michael? Explain.

16-2. QUESTION WITH SAMPLE ANSWER

Five years ago, Hensley purchased a house. At that time, being unable to pay the full purchase price, she borrowed funds from Thrift Savings and Loan, which in turn took a mortgage at 6.5 interest on the house. The mortgage contract did not prohibit the assignment of the mortgage. Then Hensley secured a new job in another city and sold the house to Sylvia. The purchase price included payment to Hensley of the value of her equity and the assumption of the mortgage debt still owed to Thrift. At the time the contract between Hensley and Sylvia was made, Thrift did not know about or consent to the sale. On the basis of these facts, if Sylvia defaults in making the house payments to Thrift, what are Thrift's rights? Discuss.

- **For a sample answer to Question 16–2,
  go to Appendix C at the end of this text.**

16-3. Marsala, a college student, signs a one-year lease agreement that runs from September 1 to August 31. The lease agreement specifies that the lease cannot be assigned without the landlord's consent. In late May, Marsala decides not to go to summer school and assigns the balance of the lease (three months) to a close friend, Fred. The landlord objects to the assignment and denies Fred access to the apartment. Marsala claims that Fred is financially sound and should be allowed the full rights and privileges of an assignee. Discuss fully who is correct, the landlord or Marsala.

16-4. Inez has a specific set of plans to build a sailboat. The plans are detailed, and any boatbuilder can construct the boat. Inez secures bids, and the low bid is made by the Whale of a Boat Corp. Inez contracts with Whale to build the boat for $4,000. Whale then receives unexpected business from elsewhere. To meet the delivery date in the contract with Inez, Whale delegates its obligation to build the boat, without Inez's consent, to Quick Brothers, a reputable boatbuilder. When the boat is ready for delivery, Inez learns of the delegation and refuses to accept delivery, even though the boat is built to her specifications. Discuss fully whether Inez is obligated to accept and pay for the boat. Would your answer be any different if Inez had not had a specific set of plans but had instead contracted with Whale to design and build a sailboat for $4,000? Explain.

16-5. Notice of Assignment. As the building services manager for Fulton County, Georgia, Steve Fullard oversaw custodial services. Fullard determined which services to contract for, received the bids, and recommended the selection of a vendor. After the selection of Total Quality Maintenance of Georgia (TQM) on a particular contract, Fullard supervised TQM's performance and received and processed its invoices. Later, TQM assigned its unpaid invoices to American Factors of Nashville, Inc., which forwarded copies to Fullard with a statement rubber-stamped on each invoice. The statement began with the word "NOTICE" and the name, address, and phone number of American Factors. It also said, "Remittance to other than American Factors of Nashville, Inc., does not constitute payment of this Invoice." Included with each invoice was a certification by TQM's president that the invoice had been assigned to American Factors. Nevertheless, the county paid TQM on these invoices, and American

Factors filed a suit in a Georgia state court against the county, claiming that it still owed American Factors. Did the county have sufficient notice of TQM's assignment? Can the county be required to pay the same invoice twice? Why or why not? [*Fulton County v. American Factors of Nashville, Inc.*, 551 S.E.2d 781 (Ga.App. 2001)]

16-6. Third Party Beneficiary. Acciai Speciali Terni USA, Inc. (AST), hired a carrier to ship steel sheets and coils from Italy to the United States on the *M/V Berane.* The ship's receipt for the goods included a forum-selection clause, which stated that any dispute would be "decided in the country where the carrier has his principal place of business." The receipt also contained a "Himalaya" clause, which extended "every right, exemption from liability, defense and immunity" that the carrier enjoyed to those acting on the carrier's behalf. Transcom Terminals, Ltd., was the U.S. stevedore—that is, Transcom off-loaded the vessel and stored the cargo for eventual delivery to AST. Finding the cargo damaged, AST filed a suit in a federal district court against Transcom and others, charging, among other things, negligence in the off-loading. Transcom filed a motion to dismiss on the basis of the forum-selection clause. Transcom argued that it was an intended third party beneficiary of this provision through the Himalaya clause. Is Transcom correct? What should the court rule? Explain. [*Acciai Speciali Terni USA, Inc. v. M/V Berane*, 181 F.Supp.2d 458 (D.Md. 2002)]

16-7. CASE PROBLEM WITH SAMPLE ANSWER

The National Collegiate Athletic Association (NCAA) regulates intercollegiate amateur athletics among the more than 1,200 colleges and universities with whom it contracts. Among other things, the NCAA maintains rules of eligibility for student participation in intercollegiate athletic events. Jeremy Bloom, a high school football and track star, was recruited to play football at the University of Colorado (CU). Before enrolling, he competed in Olympic and professional World Cup skiing events, becoming the World Cup champion in freestyle moguls. During the Olympics, Bloom appeared on MTV and was offered other paid entertainment opportunities, including a chance to host a show on Nickelodeon. Bloom was also paid to endorse certain ski equipment and contracted to model clothing for Tommy Hilfiger. On Bloom's behalf, CU asked the NCAA to waive its rules restricting student-athlete endorsement and media activities. The NCAA refused, and Bloom quit the activities to play football for CU. He filed a suit in a Colorado state court against the NCAA, however, asserting breach of contract on the ground that its rules permitted these activities if they were needed to support a professional athletic career. The NCAA responded that Bloom did not have standing to pursue this claim. What contract has allegedly been breached in this case? Is Bloom a party to this contract? If not, is he a third party beneficiary of it, and if so, is his status intended or inci-

dental? Explain. [*Bloom v. National Collegiate Athletic Association*, 93 P.3d 621 (Colo.App. 2004)]

- To view a sample answer for Problem 16–7, go to this book's Web site at www.cengage. com/blaw/jentz, select "Chapter 16," and click on "Case Problem with Sample Answer."

16-8. Third Party Beneficiary. National Association for Stock Car Auto Racing, Inc. (NASCAR), sanctions stock car races. NASCAR and Sprint Nextel Corp. agreed that Sprint would become the Official Series Sponsor of the NASCAR Nextel Cup Series in 2004. The agreement granted sponsorship exclusivity to Sprint and contained a list of "Competitors" who were barred from sponsoring Series events. Excepted were existing sponsorships: in "Driver and Car Owner Agreements" between NASCAR and the cars' owners, NASCAR promised to "preserve and protect" those sponsorships, which could continue and be renewed at the owner's option despite Sprint's exclusivity. RCR Team #31, LLC, owns the #31 Car in the Series. Cingular Wireless, LLC (a Sprint competitor), had been #31 Car's primary sponsor since 2001. In 2007, Cingular changed its name to AT&T Mobility, LLC, and proposed a new paint scheme for the #31 Car that called for the Cingular logo to remain on the hood while the AT&T logo would be added on the rear quarter panel. NASCAR rejected the proposal. AT&T filed a suit in a federal district court against NASCAR, claiming, in part, that NASCAR was in breach of its "Driver and Car Owner Agreement" with RCR. Can AT&T maintain an action against NASCAR based on this agreement? Explain. [*AT&T Mobility, LLC v. National Association for Stock Car Auto Racing, Inc.*, 494 F.3d 1356 (11th Cir. 2007)]

16-9. A QUESTION OF ETHICS

In 1984, James Grigg's mother was killed in a car accident. Royal Insurance Co. of America agreed to pay Grigg a number of monthly payments and two lump-sum payments of $50,000 due May 1, 1995, and May 1, 2005. Royal contracted with Safeco Life Insurance Co. to make the payments. In 1997, Grigg assigned the 2005 payment of $50,000 to Howard Foley for $10,000. Neither Grigg nor Foley notified Safeco or Royal. Four years later, Grigg offered to sell Settlement Capital Corp. (SCC) his interest in the 2005 payment. On SCC's request, an Idaho state court approved the transfer. Foley later notified Safeco of his interest in the payment, and in 2005, the court approved an arrangement by which Foley and SCC would share the $50,000. Shortly before the 2005 payment was made, however, it was revealed that Grigg had also tried to sell his interest to Canco Credit Union, whose manager, Timothy Johnson, paid Grigg for it. Later, Johnson assigned the interest to Robert Chris, who used it as collateral for a loan from Canco. Foley filed a suit in an Idaho state court against Grigg, asking the court to determine who, among these parties, was entitled to the 2005 payment. [Foley v. Grigg, 144 Idaho 530, 164 P.3d 180 (2007)]

(a) If the court applies the rule most often observed in the United States, who is likely to be awarded the $50,000? If the court applies the English rule, who will have priority to the payment?

(b) Regardless of the legal principles to be applied, is there a violation of ethics in these circumstances? Explain.

16–10. VIDEO QUESTION

Go to this text's Web site at **www.cengage.com/blaw/jentz** and select "Chapter 16." Click on "Video Questions" and view the video titled *Third Party Beneficiaries*. Then answer the following questions.

(a) Discuss whether a valid contract was formed when Oscar and Vinny bet on the outcome of a football game. Would Vinny be able to enforce the contract in court?

(b) Is the Fresh Air Fund an incidental or intended beneficiary? Why?

(c) Can Maria sue to enforce Vinny's promise to donate Oscar's winnings to the Fresh Air Fund?

LAW ON THE WEB

For updated links to resources available on the Web, as well as a variety of other materials, visit this text's Web site at

www.cengage.com/blaw/jentz

You can find a summary of the law governing assignments, as well as "SmartAgreement" forms that you can use for various types of contracts, including assignments, at

www.smartagreements.com

Legal Research Exercises on the Web

Go to **www.cengage.com/blaw/jentz**, the Web site that accompanies this text. Select "Chapter 16" and click on "Internet Exercises." There you will find the following Internet research exercises that you can perform to learn more about the topics covered in this chapter.

Internet Exercise 16–1: Legal Perspective
New York's Leading Decisions

Internet Exercise 16–2: Management Perspective
Professional Liability to Third Parties

Contracts: Third Party Rights

Case No. 86

PRIVITY, THIRD PARTY BENEFICIARIES

Ralston Purina Company v. Arthur G. McKee & Company, et al.

Appellate Division, Fourth Department

158 A.D.2d 969, 551 N.Y.S.2d 720 (1990)

FACTS: Plaintiff Ralston Purina Company (Ralston) entered into a contract with defendant Arthur G. McKee & Company (McKee) in which McKee agreed to build a pet food plant. Another defendant, Industrial First Inc. (Industrial), a subcontractor of McKee's, was responsible for the construction of the roof for the plant.

The contract between McKee and Industrial extended to Ralston all warranties Industrial made to McKee, and contained an agreement by Industrial to indemnify Ralston for damages arising out of its construction of the roof.

Various problems with the roof developed soon after completion. Ralston sued Industrial for negligence in the construction of the roof and for breach of contract. Industrial claimed that Ralston could not sue it for breach because Industrial and Ralston were not in privity of contract.

ISSUE: When two parties expressly agree to extend the benefits of their contract to a third party who is not an original party to the contract, can the third party sue to enforce the contract?

DECISION: Yes.

REASONING: Generally, only parties to a contract have rights, duties, and liabilities under that contract and only they can sue to enforce it. These parties are said to be in privity of a contract. One exception to the requirement of privity is a third party beneficiary, that is, a third person who the parties to the contract intend to benefit.

In this case, the agreement between Industrial and McKee obligated Industrial to extend its warranties to Ralston and indemnify Ralston. This demonstrated that Ralston was an intended beneficiary. Hence, Ralston can sue Industrial for breach of contract.

* * * QUESTIONS * * *
(See back of text for answers)

1) What is another exception to the requirement of privity to enforce a contract?

2) How does a third party beneficiary contract differ from an assignment of rights or a delegation of duties?

Case No. 87

THIRD PARTY BENEFICIARIES

<u>Castillo v. Tyson</u>

Appellate Division, First Department

268 A.D.2d 336, 701 N.Y.S.2d 423 (2000)

FACTS: This case involves the boxing match in which Mike Tyson was disqualified for biting his opponent's ear. Damian Castillo (Castillo) and other boxing fans brought a class action suit against Tyson, fight promoters, and fight telecasters for refund of money paid to view that fight.

The class action was based on the claim that fans who "paid to view" were entitled to a "legitimate heavyweight title fight" fought per governing boxing commission rules and regulations. Plaintiffs claim that they are third-party beneficiaries of Tyson's contracts to promote and televise the fight. Plaintiffs contend that, pursuant to boxing rules, the fight should have ended in either a technical knockout or a 12 round decision, and not in a disqualification. Plaintiffs are suing under numerous legal theories including breach of contract, breach of the implied covenant of good faith and fair dealing, unjust enrichment, breach of warranty, and others. The trial court granted the defendants motion to dismiss for failure to state a cause of action and Castillo appealed.

ISSUE: Are fans that pay to view a sporting event third party beneficiaries of the various contracts entered to promote the event?

DECISION: No, affirmed.

REASONING: Plaintiffs were not in privity of contract with any of the named defendants. The court rejected their claim of third party beneficiary status as "contrived" presumably because plaintiffs were not intended beneficiaries of the contracts to promote the fight.

Additionally, the court noted that disqualification of a boxer is a possible outcome per the rules of the sport. Thus breach of implied covenant of good faith and fair dealing did not occur. Regarding the claim of unjust enrichment, the court held that fight fans paid for "the right to view whatever transpired," and that is what they received. The court thus rejected the claim of unjust enrichment.

Case No. 88

THIRD PARTY BENEFICIARIES

<u>**Conklin v. City of Saratoga Springs**</u>

Appellate Division, Third Department

267 A.D.2d 841, 699 N.Y.S.2d 820 (1999)

FACTS: In June 1995 the City of Saratoga Springs (Saratoga Springs) awarded an $80,000 grant to Shelters of Saratoga, Incorporated, (Shelters) to subsidize the construction of a homeless shelter on land belonging to the city. The written contract required the city to transfer title to the property to Shelters upon completion of construction provided the shelter was built by December 31, 1996. Payment of the grant money was likewise conditional upon completion of construction by that date.

Shelters contracted with Bruce Conklin (Conklin) for the construction of the shelter. The work was not completed until June 1997, six months after the completion date specified in the contract between Saratoga Springs and Shelter. Saratoga Springs refused to transfer to Shelter the grant money or title to the property. As a result Shelter was unable to pay Conklin. Conklin in turn sued Saratoga Springs for breach of contract as a third party beneficiary. The trial court granted Saratoga Spring's motion to dismiss and Conklin appealed.

ISSUE: Where two parties enter a contract and do not expressly or impliedly extend the benefits of the contract to a third party, can the third party sue to enforce the contract?

DECISON: No, judgment for Saratoga Springs.

REASONING: Conklin's claim was properly dismissed because only parties to a contract can sue to enforce its terms. These parties are said to be in privity of contract. An exception to this requirement of privity is a third party beneficiary, that is, a third party who the original parties to the contract intended to benefit. The intent of the parties in privity can be either express or implied.

The contract between Shelters and Saratoga Springs did not contain an express term that identified Conklin as an intended third party beneficiary. Further, the contract did not otherwise infer an intention to extend any benefit to Conklin or give him a right to enforce its terms. As a result Conklin does not qualify as a third party beneficiary and cannot sue to enforce the terms of the agreement.

CHAPTER 15

Performance and Discharge

Just as rules are necessary to determine when a legally enforceable contract exists, so also are they required to determine when one of the parties can justifiably say, "I have fully performed, so I am now discharged from my obligations under this contract." The legal environment of business requires the identification of some point at which the parties can reasonably know that their duties are at an end.

The most common way to **discharge,** or terminate, one's contractual duties is by the **performance** of those duties. For example, a buyer and seller have a contract for the sale of a 2010 Lexus for $39,000. This contract will be discharged by performance when the buyer pays $39,000 to the seller and the seller transfers possession of the Lexus to the buyer.

The duty to perform under a contract may be *conditioned* on the occurrence or nonoccurrence of a certain event, or the duty may be *absolute*. In the first part of this chapter, we look at conditions of performance and the degree of performance required. We then examine some other ways in which a contract can be discharged, including discharge by agreement of the parties and discharge by operation of law.

Conditions

In most contracts, promises of performance are not expressly conditioned or qualified. Instead, they are *absolute promises*. They must be performed, or the parties promising the acts will be in breach of contract. In some situations, however, performance is contingent on the occurrence or nonoccurrence of a certain event. A **condition** is a possible future event, the occurrence or nonoccurrence of which will trigger the performance of a legal obligation or terminate an existing obligation under a contract.[1] If this condition is not satisfied, the obligations of the parties are discharged. Suppose that Alfonso offers to purchase a painting from Jerome only if an independent appraisal

indicates that it is worth at least $10,000. Jerome accepts Alfonso's offer. Their obligations (promises) are conditioned on the outcome of the appraisal. Should the condition not be satisfied (for example, if the appraiser deems the value of the painting to be only $5,000), the parties' obligations to each other are discharged and cannot be enforced.

Three types of conditions can be present in contracts: conditions *precedent,* conditions *subsequent,* and *concurrent* conditions. Conditions are also classified as *express* or *implied*.

Conditions Precedent

A condition that must be fulfilled before a party's performance can be required is called a **condition precedent.** The condition precedes the absolute duty to perform, as in the Jerome-Alfonso example just discussed. Real estate contracts frequently are conditioned on the buyer's ability to obtain financing. For example, Fisher promises to buy Calvin's house if Salvation Bank approves Fisher's mortgage application.

---

1. The *Restatement (Second) of Contracts,* Section 224, defines a condition as "an event, not certain to occur, which must occur, unless its nonoccurrence is excused, before performance under a contract becomes due."

The Fisher-Calvin contract is therefore subject to a condition precedent—the bank's approval of Fisher's mortgage application. If the bank does not approve the application, the contract will fail because the condition precedent was not met. Insurance contracts frequently specify that certain conditions, such as passing a physical examination, must be met before the insurance company will be obligated to perform under the contract.

Conditions Subsequent

When a condition operates to terminate a party's absolute promise to perform, it is called a **condition subsequent.** The condition follows, or is subsequent to, the arising of an absolute duty to perform. If the condition occurs, the party's duty to perform is discharged. For example, imagine that a law firm hires Koker, a recent law school graduate and newly licensed attorney. Their contract provides that the firm's obligation to continue employing Koker is discharged if Koker fails to maintain her license to practice law. This is a condition subsequent because a failure to maintain the license would discharge a duty that has already arisen.

Generally, conditions precedent are common; conditions subsequent are rare. The *Restatement (Second) of Contracts* does not use the terms *condition subsequent* and *condition precedent* but refers to both simply as conditions.[2]

Concurrent Conditions

When each party's performance is conditioned on the other party's performance or tender of performance (offer to perform), there are **concurrent conditions.** Concurrent conditions occur only when the contract calls for the parties to perform their respective duties *simultaneously*. For example, if a buyer promises to pay for goods when the seller delivers them, each party's promise to perform is mutually dependent. The buyer's duty to pay for the goods does not become absolute until the seller either delivers or tenders the goods. Likewise, the seller's duty to deliver the goods does not become absolute until the buyer tenders or actually makes payment. Therefore, neither can recover from the other for breach without first tendering performance.

Express and Implied-in-Fact Conditions

Conditions can also be classified as express or implied in fact. *Express conditions* are provided for by the parties' agreement. Although no particular words are necessary, express conditions are normally prefaced by the words *if, provided, after,* or *when.*

Conditions *implied in fact* are similar to express conditions in that they are understood to be part of the agreement, but they are not found in the express language of the agreement. Courts may imply conditions from the purpose of the contract or from the intent of the parties. Conditions are often implied when they are necessarily inherent in the actual performance of the contract.

Suppose that a clause in an automobile insurance policy states that, if involved in an accident, the insured must cooperate with the insurance company in the investigation, settlement, or defense of any claim or lawsuit. Alejandro Alvarado signs the contract and is later involved in an accident from which a negligence lawsuit against him arises. Alvarado knows that the insurance company is representing him in the suit; yet he fails to cooperate in his defense and does not appear in court on the date of the trial. The court enters a judgment against him, which prejudices the rights of the insurance company. In this situation, a court could find that the cooperation clause is a condition precedent to coverage under the policy because it was inherent in the actual performance of the contract. If so, because Alvarado did not cooperate with the insurer, he will not be covered under the policy, and the insurance company will not be liable for the damages awarded.[3]

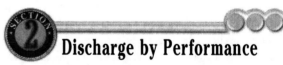

Discharge by Performance

The great majority of contracts are discharged by performance. The contract comes to an end when both parties fulfill their respective duties by performing the acts they have promised. Performance can also be accomplished by *tender*. **Tender** is an unconditional offer to perform by a person who is ready, willing, and able to do so. Therefore, a seller who places goods at the disposal of a buyer has tendered delivery and can demand payment. A buyer who offers to pay for goods

---

2. *Restatement (Second) of Contracts*, Section 224.

3. *Progressive County Mutual Insurance Co. v. Trevino*, 202 S.W.3d 811 (Tex.App.—San Antonio 2006).

has tendered payment and can demand delivery of the goods. Once performance has been tendered, the party making the tender has done everything possible to carry out the terms of the contract. If the other party then refuses to perform, the party making the tender can sue for breach of contract.

Types of Performance

There are two basic types of performance—*complete performance* and *substantial performance.* A contract may stipulate that performance must meet the personal satisfaction of either the contracting party or a third party. Such a provision must be considered in determining whether the performance rendered satisfies the contract.

Complete Performance When a party performs exactly as agreed, there is no question as to whether the contract has been performed. When a party's performance is perfect, it is said to be complete.

Normally, conditions expressly stated in a contract must be fully satisfied for complete performance to take place. For example, most construction contracts require the builder to meet certain specifications. If the specifications are conditions, complete performance is required to avoid material breach (*material breach* will be discussed shortly). If the conditions are met, the other party to the contract must then fulfill her or his obligation to pay the builder. If the specifications are not conditions and if the builder, without the other party's permission, fails to comply with the specifications, performance is not complete. What effect does such a failure have on the other party's obligation to pay? The answer is part of the doctrine of *substantial performance.*

Substantial Performance A party who in good faith performs substantially all of the terms of a con-

tract can enforce the contract against the other party under the doctrine of substantial performance. Note that good faith is required. Intentionally failing to comply with the terms is a breach of the contract.

Confers Most of the Benefits Promised. Generally, to qualify as substantial, the performance must not vary greatly from the performance promised in the contract, and it must create substantially the same benefits as those promised in the contract. If the omission, variance, or defect in performance is unimportant and can easily be compensated for by awarding damages, a court is likely to hold that the contract has been substantially performed.

Courts decide whether the performance was substantial on a case-by-case basis, examining all of the facts of the particular situation. For example, in a construction contract, a court would look at the intended purpose of the structure and the expense required to bring the structure into complete compliance with the contract. Thus, the exact point at which performance is considered substantial varies.

Entitles the Other Party to Damages. Because substantial performance is not perfect, the other party is entitled to damages to compensate for the failure to comply with the contract. The measure of the damages is the cost to bring the object of the contract into compliance with its terms, if that cost is reasonable under the circumstances. If the cost is unreasonable, the measure of damages is the difference in value between the performance that was rendered and the performance that would have been rendered if the contract had been performed completely.

The following classic case emphasizes that there is no exact formula for deciding when a contract has been substantially performed.

C A S E   15.1   Jacob & Youngs v. Kent
Court of Appeals of New York, 1921. 230 N.Y. 239, 129 N.E. 889.

● **Background and Facts** The plaintiff, Jacob & Youngs, was a builder that had contracted with the defendant, George Kent, to construct a country residence for the defendant. A specification in the building contract required that "all wrought-iron pipe must be well galvanized, lap welded pipe of the grade known as 'standard pipe' of Reading manufacture." The plaintiff installed substantially similar pipe that was not of Reading manufacture. When the defendant became aware of the difference, he ordered the plaintiff to remove all of the plumbing and replace it with

CASE CONTINUES

CASE 15.1 CONTINUED the Reading type. To do so would have required removing finished walls that encased the plumbing—an expensive and difficult task. The plaintiff explained that the plumbing was of the same quality, appearance, value, and cost as Reading pipe. When the defendant refused to pay the plaintiff the $3,483.46 still owed for the work, the plaintiff sued to compel payment. The trial court ruled in favor of the defendant. The plaintiff appealed, and the appellate court reversed the trial court's decision. The defendant then appealed to the Court of Appeals of New York, the state's highest court.

● **Decision and Rationale** The Court of Appeals of New York held that the plaintiff had substantially performed the contract and affirmed the state intermediate appellate court's decision. The state's highest court explained, "The courts never say that one who makes a contract fills the measure of his duty by less than full performance. They do say, however, that an omission, both trivial and innocent, will sometimes be atoned for by allowance of the resulting damage, and will not always be the breach of a condition. *   *   * The question is one of degree *   *   * . We must weigh the purpose to be served, the desire to be gratified, the excuse for deviation from the letter, [and] the cruelty of enforced adherence." As for adjusting the contract price, "the measure of the allowance is not the cost of replacement, *   *   * but the difference in value" (the cost to complete). The builder was entitled to the amount owed to it, less the difference in value between the specified and substituted pipe (which the court stated would be "nominal or nothing").

● **Impact of This Case on Today's Law** *At the time of the* Jacob & Youngs *case, some courts did not apply the doctrine of substantial performance to disputes involving breaches of contract. This landmark decision contributed to a developing trend toward equity and fairness in those circumstances. Today, an unintentional and trivial omission or deviation from the terms of a contract will not prevent its enforcement but will permit an adjustment in the value of its performance.*

● **The Legal Environment Dimension** *A requirement of substantial performance is good faith. Do you think that Jacob & Youngs substantially performed all of the terms of the contract in good faith? Why or why not?*

Performance to the Satisfaction of Another Contracts often state that completed work must personally satisfy one of the parties or a third person. The question then is whether this satisfaction becomes a condition precedent, requiring actual personal satisfaction or approval for discharge, or whether the test of satisfaction is an absolute promise requiring such performance as would satisfy a *reasonable person* (substantial performance).

When the subject matter of the contract is *personal*, a contract to be performed to the satisfaction of one of the parties is conditioned, and performance must actually satisfy that party. For example, contracts for portraits, works of art, and tailoring are considered personal. Therefore, only the personal satisfaction of the party fulfills the condition—unless a court finds the party is expressing dissatisfaction only to avoid payment or otherwise is not acting in good faith.

Most other contracts need to be performed only to the satisfaction of a reasonable person unless they *expressly state otherwise*. When such contracts require performance to the satisfaction of a third party (for example, "to the satisfaction of Robert Ames, the supervising engineer"), the courts are divided. A majority of courts require the work to be satisfactory to a reasonable person, but some courts hold that the personal satisfaction of the third party designated in the contract (Robert Ames, in this example) must be met. Again, the personal judgment must be made honestly, or the condition will be excused.

Material Breach of Contract

A **breach of contract** is the nonperformance of a contractual duty. The breach is *material* when performance is not at least substantial.[4] If there is a material

---

4. *Restatement (Second) of Contracts,* Section 241.

breach, then the nonbreaching party is excused from the performance of contractual duties and can sue for damages resulting from the breach. If the breach is *minor* (not material), the nonbreaching party's duty to perform can sometimes be suspended until the breach has been remedied, but the duty to perform is not entirely excused. Once the minor breach has been cured, the nonbreaching party must resume performance of the contractual obligations undertaken.

Any breach entitles the nonbreaching party to sue for damages, but only a material breach discharges the nonbreaching party from the contract. The policy underlying these rules allows contracts to go forward when only minor problems occur but allows them to be terminated if major difficulties arise.

Under what circumstances is an employer excused from further performance under a contract with an employee? That was the question in the following case.

C A S E **15.2 Shah v. Cover-It, Inc.**
Appellate Court of Connecticut, 2004. 86 Conn.App. 71, 859 A.2d 959.

● **Background and Facts** In November 1997, Cover-It, Inc., hired Khalid Shah to work as its structural engineering manager. Shah agreed to work a flexible schedule of thirty-five hours per week. In exchange, he would receive an annual salary of $70,000 for five years, a 2 percent commission on the sales of products that he designed, three weeks of paid vacation after one year, a company car, time off to attend to prior professional obligations, and certain other benefits. Either party could terminate the contract with ninety days' written notice, but if Cover-It terminated it, Shah would receive monthly payments for the rest of the five-year term.[a] In June 1998, Shah went on vacation and did not return until September. In mid-October, Brian Goldwitz, Cover-It's owner and president, terminated Shah's contract. Shah filed a suit in a Connecticut state court against Cover-It and others. The court determined that Shah had breached the contract and rendered a judgment in the defendants' favor. Shah appealed to a state intermediate appellate court.

● **Decision and Rationale** The state intermediate appellate court affirmed the judgment of the lower court. The appellate court held that Shah had materially breached his contract with Cover-It and that this breach excused Cover-It from further performance of its contractual duties, specifically the payment to Shah of ninety days' salary and other amounts according to the contract's schedule. The court said, "The standards of materiality are to be applied in the light of the facts of each case in such a way as to further the purpose of securing for each party his expectation of an exchange of performances." In this case, among other things, Shah "took a ten-week vacation, which exceeded the time authorized." He then reported for work only two or three days per week and spent long periods of time surfing the Internet and reviewing Web sites that were unrelated to his professional duties. After the company asked Shah to document his attendance by using a time clock, he simply marked his time sheets with a "P" rather than actually clocking in. Finally, when Goldwitz asked about the completion time for certain projects, Shah responded that he was not sure but that he would take his time in completing them.

● **What If the Facts Were Different?** *Suppose that during his ten-week absence Shah was fulfilling prior professional obligations and that on his return he met Cover-It's hours and timekeeping requirements. Further suppose that Shah responded to Goldwitz's questions about his projects with reasonable estimates. Would the outcome of the case have been different? Why or why not?*

● **The E-Commerce Dimension** *If Shah had worked for Cover-It from his home by telecommuting over the Internet and other employees were therefore not aware of his conduct, would he have been in breach of his contract? Explain.*

---

a. The contract provided that for up to two years of service, Shah would be paid $20,000 per year; for three years of service, $30,000 per year; and for four years of service, $40,000 per year.

Anticipatory Repudiation

Before either party to a contract has a duty to perform, one of the parties may refuse to carry out his or her contractual obligations. This is called **anticipatory repudiation**[5] of the contract. When anticipatory repudiation occurs, it is treated as a material breach of contract, and the nonbreaching party is permitted to bring an action for damages immediately, even though the scheduled time for performance under the contract may still be in the future. Until the nonbreaching party treats an early repudiation as a breach, however, the repudiating party can retract her or his anticipatory repudiation by proper notice and restore the parties to their original obligations.[6]

Rationale for Treating Repudiation as Breach An anticipatory repudiation is treated as a present, material breach for two reasons. First, the nonbreaching party should not be required to remain ready and willing to perform when the other party has already repudiated the contract. Second, the nonbreaching party should have the opportunity to seek a similar contract elsewhere and may have a duty to do so to minimize his or her loss.[7]

Anticipatory Repudiation and Market Prices Quite often, anticipatory repudiation occurs when performance of the contract would be extremely unfavorable to one of the parties because of a sharp fluctuation in market prices. For example, Martin Corporation contracts to manufacture and sell ten thousand personal computers to ComAge, a retailer of computer equipment that has five hundred outlet stores. Delivery is to be made six months from the date of the contract. The contract price is based on Martin's present costs of purchasing inventory parts from others. One month later, three inventory suppliers raise their prices to Martin.

Based on these higher prices, Martin stands to lose $500,000 if it sells the computers to ComAge at the contract price. Martin immediately writes to ComAge, stating that it cannot deliver the ten thousand computers at the contract price. Martin's letter is an anticipa-tory repudiation of the contract. ComAge has the option of treating the repudiation as a material breach of contract and proceeding immediately to pursue remedies, even though the actual contract delivery date is still five months away.

Time for Performance

If no time for performance is stated in the contract, a *reasonable time* is implied.[8] If a specific time is stated, the parties must usually perform by that time. Unless time is expressly stated to be vital, however, a delay in performance will not destroy the performing party's right to payment.[9] When time is expressly stated to be "of the essence" or vital, the parties normally must per-form within the stated time period because the time element becomes a condition.

Discharge by Agreement

Any contract can be discharged by agreement of the parties. The agreement can be contained in the origi-nal contract, or the parties can form a new contract for the express purpose of discharging the original contract.

Discharge by Rescission

As mentioned in previous chapters, *rescission* is the process by which a contract is canceled or terminated and the parties are returned to the positions they occu-pied prior to forming it. For **mutual rescission** to take place, the parties must make another agreement that also satisfies the legal requirements for a contract. There must be an *offer,* an *acceptance,* and *consideration.* Ordinarily, if the parties agree to rescind the original contract, their promises not to perform the acts stipu-lated in the original contract will be legal consideration for the second contract (the rescission).

Agreements to rescind most executory contracts (in which neither party has performed) are enforce-able, even if the agreement is made orally and even if the original agreement was in writing. Agreements to rescind contracts involving transfers of realty, however, must be evidenced by a writing. An exception applies under the Uniform Commercial Code (UCC) to agree-ments rescinding a contract for the sale of goods,

---

5. *Restatement (Second) of Contracts,* Section 253; Section 2–610 of the Uniform Commercial Code (UCC).

6. See UCC 2–611.

7. The doctrine of anticipatory repudiation first arose in the landmark case of *Hochster v. De La Tour,* 2 Ellis and Blackburn Reports 678 (1853), when an English court recognized the delay and expense inherent in a rule requiring a nonbreaching party to wait until the time of perfor-mance before suing on an anticipatory repudiation.

8. See UCC 2–204.

9. See, for example, *Manganaro Corp. v. Hitt Contracting, Inc.,* 193 F.Supp.2d 88 (D.D.C. 2002).

regardless of price, when the contract requires a written rescission.[10]

When one party has fully performed, an agreement to cancel the original contract normally will not be enforceable. Because the performing party has received no consideration for the promise to call off the original bargain, additional consideration is necessary to support a rescission contract.

Discharge by Novation

A contractual obligation may also be discharged through novation. A **novation** occurs when both of the parties to a contract agree to substitute a third party for one of the original parties. The requirements of a novation are as follows:

1. A previous valid obligation.
2. An agreement by all the parties to a new contract.
3. The extinguishing of the old obligation (discharge of the prior party).
4. A new contract that is valid.

For example, Union Corporation contracts to sell its pharmaceutical division to British Pharmaceuticals, Ltd. Before the transfer is completed, Union, British Pharmaceuticals, and a third company, Otis Chemicals, execute a new agreement to transfer all of British Pharmaceuticals' rights and duties in the transaction to Otis Chemicals. As long as the new contract is supported by consideration, the novation will discharge the original contract (between Union and British Pharmaceuticals) and replace it with the new contract (between Union and Otis Chemicals).

A novation expressly or impliedly revokes and discharges a prior contract.[11] The parties involved may expressly state in the new contract that the old contract is now discharged. If the parties do not expressly discharge the old contract, it will be impliedly discharged if the new contract's terms are inconsistent with the old contract's terms.

Discharge by Substituted Agreement

A *compromise,* or settlement agreement, that arises out of a genuine dispute over the obligations under an existing contract will be recognized at law. Such an

agreement will be substituted as a new contract, and it will either expressly or impliedly revoke and discharge the obligations under any prior contract. In contrast to a novation, a substituted agreement does not involve a third party. Rather, the two original parties to the contract form a different agreement to substitute for the original one.

Discharge by Accord and Satisfaction

For a contract to be discharged by accord and satisfaction, the parties must agree to accept performance that is different from the performance originally promised. As discussed in Chapter 12, an *accord* is a contract to perform some act to satisfy an existing contractual duty that is not yet discharged.[12] A *satisfaction* is the performance of the accord agreement. An accord and its satisfaction discharge the original contractual obligation.

Once the accord has been made, the original obligation is merely suspended. The obligor (the one owing the obligation) can discharge the obligation by performing either the obligation agreed to in the accord or the original obligation. If the obligor refuses to perform the accord, the obligee (the one to whom performance is owed) can bring an action on the original obligation or seek a decree compelling specific performance on the accord.

Suppose that Frazer has a judgment against Ling for $8,000. Later, both parties agree that the judgment can be satisfied by Ling's transfer of his automobile to Frazer. This agreement to accept the auto in lieu of $8,000 in cash is the accord. If Ling transfers the car to Frazer, the accord is fully performed, and the debt is discharged. If Ling refuses to transfer the car, the accord is breached. Because the original obligation is merely suspended, Frazer can sue Ling to enforce the original judgment for $8,000 in cash or bring an action for breach of the accord.

Discharge by Operation of Law

Under certain circumstances, contractual duties may be discharged by operation of law. These circumstances include material alteration of the contract, the running of the statute of limitations, bankruptcy, and the impossibility or impracticability of performance.

---

10. UCC 2–209(2), (4).
11. It is this immediate discharge of the prior contract that distinguishes a novation from both an accord and satisfaction, discussed in a later subsection, and an assignment of all rights, discussed in Chapter 16. In an *assignment of all rights*, the original party to the contract (the assignor) remains liable under the original contract if the assignee fails to perform the contractual obligations. In contrast, in a novation, the original party's obligations are completely discharged.

12. *Restatement (Second) of Contracts,* Section 281.

Alteration of the Contract

To discourage parties from altering written contracts, the law operates to allow an innocent party to be discharged when the other party has materially altered a written contract without consent. For example, contract terms such as quantity or price might be changed without the knowledge or consent of all parties. If so, the party who was not involved in the alteration can treat the contract as discharged or terminated.[13]

Statutes of Limitations

As mentioned earlier in this text, statutes of limitations restrict the period during which a party can sue on a particular cause of action. After the applicable limitations period has passed, a suit can no longer be brought. For example, the limitations period for bringing suits for breach of oral contracts is usually two to three years; for written contracts, four to five years; and for recovery of amounts awarded in judgments, ten to twenty years, depending on state law. Lawsuits for breach of a contract for the sale of goods generally must be brought within four years after the breach occurs.[14] By their original agreement, the parties can reduce this four-year period to not less than one year, but they cannot agree to extend it.

Bankruptcy

A proceeding in bankruptcy attempts to allocate the assets the debtor owns to the creditors in a fair and equitable fashion. Once the assets have been allocated, the debtor receives a **discharge in bankruptcy.** A discharge in bankruptcy will ordinarily bar enforcement of most of the debtor's contracts by the creditors. Partial payment of a debt *after* discharge in bankruptcy will not revive the debt. (Bankruptcy will be discussed in detail in Chapter 30.)

---

13. The contract is voidable, and the innocent party can also treat the contract as in effect, either on the original terms or on the terms as altered. For example, a buyer who discovers that a seller altered the quantity of goods in a sales contract from 100 to 1,000 by secretly inserting a zero can purchase either 100 or 1,000 of the items.

14. Section 2–725 of the UCC contains this four-year limitation period. A cause of action in sales contracts generally accrues when the breach occurs, regardless of the aggrieved party's lack of knowledge of the breach. For example, a breach of warranty normally occurs when the seller delivers the goods to the buyer.

Impossibility or Impracticability of Performance

After a contract has been made, supervening events (such as a fire) may make performance impossible in an objective sense. This is known as **impossibility of performance** and can discharge a contract.[15] Performance may also become so difficult or costly due to some unforeseen event that a court will consider it commercially unfeasible, or impracticable.

Objective Impossibility of Performance
Objective impossibility ("It can't be done") must be distinguished from *subjective impossibility* ("I'm sorry, I simply can't do it"). For example, subjective impossibility occurs when a party cannot deliver goods on time because of freight car shortages or cannot make payment on time because the bank is closed. In effect, in each of these situations the party is saying, "It is impossible for *me* to perform," not "It is impossible for *anyone* to perform." Accordingly, such excuses do not discharge a contract, and the nonperforming party is normally held in breach of contract.

Note that to justify not performing the contract, the supervening event must have been unforeseeable at the time of the contract. Parties are supposed to consider foreseeable events, such as floods in a flood zone, at the time of contracting and allocate those risks accordingly through insurance and other means. Three basic types of situations, however, may qualify as grounds for the discharge of contractual obligations based on impossibility of performance:[16]

1. *When one of the parties to a personal contract dies or becomes incapacitated prior to performance.* For example, Fred, a famous dancer, contracts with Ethereal Dancing Guild to play a leading role in its new ballet. Before the ballet can be performed, Fred becomes ill and dies. His personal performance was essential to the completion of the contract. Thus, his death discharges the contract and his estate's liability for his nonperformance.

2. *When the specific subject matter of the contract is destroyed.* For example, A-1 Farm Equipment agrees to sell Gudgel the green tractor on its lot and promises to have it ready for Gudgel to pick up on

---

15. *Restatement (Second) of Contracts,* Section 261.

16. *Restatement (Second) of Contracts,* Sections 262–266; UCC 2–615.

Saturday. On Friday night, however, a truck veers off the nearby highway and smashes into the tractor, destroying it beyond repair. Because the contract was for this specific tractor, A-1's performance is rendered impossible owing to the accident.

3. *When a change in law renders performance illegal.* For example, a contract to build an apartment building becomes impossible to perform when the zoning laws are changed to prohibit the construction of residential rental property at the planned location. A contract to paint a bridge using lead paint becomes impossible when the government passes new regulations forbidding the use of lead paint on bridges.[17]

Temporary Impossibility An occurrence or event that makes performance temporarily impossible operates to suspend performance until the impossibility ceases. Then, ordinarily, the parties must perform the contract as originally planned. If, however, the lapse of time and the change in circumstances surrounding the contract make it substantially more burdensome for the parties to perform the promised acts, the contract is discharged.

The leading case on the subject, *Autry v. Republic Productions,*[18] involved an actor (Gene Autry) who was drafted into the army in 1942. Being drafted rendered the actor's contract temporarily impossible to perform, and it was suspended until the end of the war. When the actor got out of the army, the purchasing power of the dollar had so diminished that performance of the contract would have been substantially burdensome to him. Therefore, the contract was discharged.

A more recent example involves a contract entered into shortly before Hurricane Katrina hit Louisiana. On August 22, 2005, Keefe Hurwitz contracted to sell his home in Madisonville, Louisiana, to Wesley and Gwendolyn Payne for a price of $241,500. On August 26—just four days after the parties signed the contract—Hurricane Katrina made landfall and caused extensive property damage to the house. The cost of repairs was estimated at $60,000, and Hurwitz would have to make the repairs before the *closing date* (see Chapter 48). Hurwitz did not have the funds and refused to pay $60,000 for the repairs only to sell the property to the Paynes for the previously agreed-on price of $241,500. The Paynes filed a lawsuit to enforce the contract. Hurwitz claimed that Hurricane Katrina had made it impossible for him to perform and had discharged his duties under the contract. The court, however, ruled that Hurricane Katrina had only caused a temporary impossibility. Hurwitz was required to pay for the necessary repairs and to perform the contract as written. In other words, he could not obtain a higher purchase price to offset the cost of the repairs.[19]

Commercial Impracticability When a supervening event does not render performance objectively impossible, but does make it much more difficult or expensive to perform, the courts may excuse the parties' obligations under the contract. For someone to invoke the doctrine of **commercial impracticability** successfully, however, the anticipated performance must become significantly more difficult or costly than originally contemplated at the time the contract was formed.[20]

The added burden of performing not only must be extreme but also *must not have been known by the parties when the contract was made.* In one case, for example, the court allowed a party to rescind a contract for the sale of land because of a potential problem with contaminated groundwater under the land. The court found that "the potential for substantial and unbargained-for" liability made contract performance economically impracticable. Interestingly, the court in that case also noted that the possibility of "environmental degradation with consequences extending well beyond the parties' land sale" was just as important to its decision as the economic considerations.[21]

The contract dispute in the following case arose out of the cancellation of a wedding reception due to a power failure. Is a power failure sufficient to invoke the doctrine of commercial impracticability?

---

17. *M. J. Paquet, Inc. v. New Jersey Department of Transportation,* 171 N.J. 378, 794 A.2d 141 (2002).

18. 30 Cal.2d 144, 180 P.2d 888 (1947).

19. *Payne v. Hurwitz,* 978 So.2d 1000 (La.App. 2008).

20. *Restatement (Second) of Contracts,* Section 264.

21. *Cape-France Enterprises v. Estate of Peed,* 305 Mont. 513, 29 P.3d 1011 (2001).

CASE 15.3 Facto v. Pantagis

Superior Court of New Jersey, Appellate Division, 2007. 390 N.J.Super. 227, 915 A.2d 59.
lawlibrary.rutgers.edu/search.shtml[a]

● **Background and Facts** Leo and Elizabeth Facto contracted with Snuffy Pantagis Enterprises, Inc., for the use of Pantagis Renaissance, a banquet hall in Scotch Plains, New Jersey, for a wedding reception in August 2002. The Factos paid the $10,578 price in advance. The contract excused Pantagis from performance "if it is prevented from doing so by an act of God (for example, flood, power failure, etc.), or other unforeseen events or circumstances." Soon after the reception began, there was a power failure. The lights and the air-conditioning shut off. The band hired for the reception refused to play without electricity to power their instruments, and the lack of lighting prevented the photographer and videographer from taking pictures. The temperature was in the 90s, the humidity was high, and the guests quickly became uncomfortable. Three hours later, after a fight between a guest and a Pantagis employee, the emergency lights began to fade, and the police evacuated the hall. The Factos filed a suit in a New Jersey state court against Pantagis, alleging breach of contract, among other things. The Factos sought to recover their prepayment, plus amounts paid to the band, the photographer, and the videographer. The court concluded that Pantagis did not breach the contract and dismissed the complaint. The Factos appealed to a state intermediate appellate court.

● **Decision and Rationale** The state intermediate appellate court agreed that the power failure relieved Pantagis of its contractual obligation, but held that Pantagis's inability to perform also relieved the Factos of their obligation. The court reversed the dismissal and remanded the case for an award to the Factos of the amount of their prepayment less the value of the services they received. The appellate court did not attribute any significance to the contract's reference to a power failure as "an act of God." The court reasoned that "even if a power failure caused by circumstances other than a natural event [was] not considered to be 'an act of God,' it still would constitute an unforeseen event or circumstance that would excuse performance." Of course, a power failure is not absolutely unforeseeable during hot summer months. But "absolute unforeseeability of a condition is not a prerequisite to the defense of impracticability." It is "the destruction or * * * deterioration of a specific thing necessary for the performance of the contract [that] makes performance impracticable." In this case, the power failure was area-wide and beyond the control of Pantagis, which was prevented from performing its contract. Because Pantagis was not in breach, however, did not mean that the Factos could not recover the amount they prepaid for the reception. When "one party to a contract is excused from performance as a result of an unforeseen event that makes performance impracticable, the other party is also generally excused from performance." Therefore, the power failure that relieved Pantagis of its obligation to the Factos also relieved the Factos of their obligation to Pantagis.

● **The Ethical Dimension** *Should Pantagis have offered to reschedule the reception? Would this have absolved Pantagis of the obligation to refund the Factos' prepayment? Explain.*

● **The Legal Environment Dimension** *Does a power failure always constitute the kind of unexpected occurrence that relieves a party of the duty to perform a contract? In what circumstances might a power failure have no effect on a contract? (Hint: Is electricity always necessary for the performance of a contract?)*

---

a. In the "Search by party name" section, select the "Appellate Division," type "Pantagis" in the "First Name:" box, and click on "Submit Form." In the result, click on the "click here to get this case" link to access the opinion. The Rutgers University School of Law in Camden, New Jersey, maintains this Web site.

Frustration of Purpose A theory closely allied with the doctrine of commercial impracticability is the doctrine of **frustration of purpose.** In principle, a contract will be discharged if supervening circumstances make it impossible to attain the purpose both parties had in mind when making the contract. As with commercial impracticability and impossibility, the supervening event must not have been reasonably

EXHIBIT 15–1 • Contract Discharge

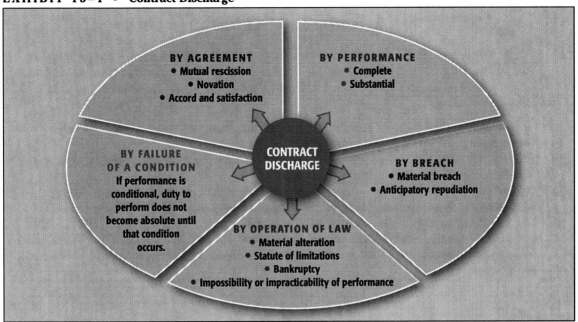

foreseeable at the time of the contracting. In contrast to impracticability, which usually involves an event that increases the cost or difficulty of performance, frustration of purpose typically involves an event that decreases the value of what a party receives under the contract.

Because many problems are foreseeable by contracting parties and value is subjective, courts rarely excuse contract performance on this basis. For example, in one case, New Beginnings was searching for a new location for its drug rehabilitation center. After receiving preliminary approval for the use of a particular building from the city zoning official, New Beginnings signed a three-year lease on the property. Then opposition from the community developed, and the city denied New Beginnings a permit to use the property for a rehab center. New Beginnings appealed the decision and eventually received a permit from the city, but by then the state was threatening to rescind all state contracts with New Beginnings if it moved into that location. Because New Beginnings would lose its funding if it actually moved onto the property, the value of the leased building was practically worthless. Nevertheless, the court refused to excuse New Beginnings from the lease contract on the ground of frustration of purpose because the situation was reasonably foreseeable.[22]

See Exhibit 15–1 for a summary of the ways in which a contract may be discharged.

---

22. *Adbar, L.C. v. New Beginnings C-Star,* 103 S.W.3d 799 (Mo.App. 2003).

REVIEWING Performance and Discharge

Val's Foods signs a contract to buy 1,500 pounds of basil from Sun Farms, a small organic herb grower, as long as an independent organization inspects the crop and certifies that it contains no pesticide or herbicide residue. Val's has a contract with several restaurant chains to supply pesto and intends to use Sun Farms' basil in the pesto to fulfill these contracts. While Sun Farms is preparing to harvest the basil, an unexpected hailstorm destroys half the crop. Sun Farms attempts to

REVIEWING CONTINUES

REVIEWING Performance and Discharge, Continued

purchase additional basil from other farms, but it is late in the season and the price is twice the normal market price. Sun Farms is too small to absorb this cost and immediately notifies Val's that it will not fulfill the contract. Using the information presented in the chapter, answer the following questions.

1. Suppose that the basil does not pass the chemical-residue inspection. Which concept discussed in the chapter might allow Val's to refuse to perform the contract in this situation?
2. Under which legal theory or theories might Sun Farms claim that its obligation under the contract has been discharged by operation of law? Discuss fully.
3. Suppose that Sun Farms contacts every basil grower in the country and buys the last remaining chemical-free basil anywhere. Nevertheless, Sun Farms is able to ship only 1,475 pounds to Val's. Would this fulfill Sun Farms' obligations to Val's? Why or why not?
4. Now suppose that Sun Farms sells its operations to Happy Valley Farms. As a part of the sale, all three parties agree that Happy Valley will provide the basil as stated under the original contract. What is this type of agreement called?

TERMS AND CONCEPTS

anticipatory repudiation
breach of contract
commercial impracticability

concurrent conditions
condition
condition precedent
condition subsequent
discharge
discharge in bankruptcy

frustration of purpose
impossibility of performance
mutual rescission
novation
performance
tender

QUESTIONS AND CASE PROBLEMS

17-1. The Caplans own a real estate lot, and they contract with Faithful Construction, Inc., to build a house on it for $360,000. The specifications list "all plumbing bowls and fixtures . . . to be Crane brand." The Caplans leave on vacation, and during their absence Faithful is unable to buy and install Crane plumbing fixtures. Instead, Faithful installs Kohler brand fixtures, an equivalent in the industry. On completion of the building contract, the Caplans inspect the work, discover the substitution, and refuse to accept the house, claiming Faithful has breached the conditions set forth in the specifications. Discuss fully the Caplans' claim.

17-2. QUESTION WITH SAMPLE ANSWER

Junior owes creditor Iba $1,000, which is due and payable on June 1. Junior has been in a car accident, has missed a great deal of work, and consequently will not have the funds on June 1. Junior's father, Fred, offers to pay Iba $1,100 in four equal installments if Iba will discharge Junior from any further liability on the debt. Iba accepts. Is this transaction a novation or an accord and satisfaction? Explain.

- For a sample answer to Question 17–2, go to Appendix C at the end of this text.

17-3. ABC Clothiers, Inc., has a contract with Taylor & Sons, a retailer, to deliver one thousand summer suits to Taylor's place of business on or before May 1. On April 1, Taylor senior receives a letter from ABC informing him that ABC will not be able to make the delivery as scheduled. Taylor is very upset, as he had planned a big ad campaign. He wants to file a suit against ABC immediately (on April 2). Taylor's son Tom tells his father that filing a lawsuit is not proper until ABC actually fails to deliver the suits on May 1. Discuss fully who is correct, Taylor or Tom.

17-4. In the following situations, certain events take place after the contracts are formed. Discuss which of these contracts are discharged because the events render the contracts impossible to perform.

(a) Jimenez, a famous singer, contracts to perform in your nightclub. He dies prior to performance.

(b) Raglione contracts to sell you her land. Just before title is to be transferred, she dies.

(c) Oppenheim contracts to sell you one thousand bushels of apples from her orchard in the state of Washington. Because of a severe frost, she is unable to deliver the apples.

(d) Maxwell contracts to lease a service station for ten years. His principal income is from the sale of gasoline. Because of an oil embargo by foreign oil-producing nations, gasoline is rationed, cutting sharply into Maxwell's gasoline sales. He cannot make his lease payments.

17-5. Heublein, Inc., makes wines and distilled spirits. Tarrant Distributors, Inc., agreed to distribute Heublein brands. When problems arose, the parties entered mediation. Under a settlement agreement, Heublein agreed to pay Tarrant the amount of its "net loss" as determined by Coopers & Lybrand, an accounting firm, according to a specified formula. The parties agreed that Coopers & Lybrand's calculation would be "final and binding." Heublein disagreed with Coopers & Lybrand's calculation, however, and refused to pay. The parties asked a court to rule on the dispute. Heublein argued that the settlement agreement included an implied condition precedent that Coopers & Lybrand would correctly apply the specified formula before Heublein would be obligated to pay. Tarrant pointed to the clause stating that the calculation would be "final and binding." With whom will the court agree, and why?

17-6. Performance. In May 1996, O'Brien-Shiepe Funeral Home, Inc., in Hempstead, New York, hired Teramo & Co. to build an addition to O'Brien's funeral home. The parties' contract did not specify a date for the completion of the work. The city of Hempstead issued a building permit for the project on June 14, and Teramo began work about two weeks later. There was some delay in construction because O'Brien asked that no construction be done during funeral services, but by the end of March 1997, the work was substantially complete. The city of Hempstead issued a "Certificate of Completion" on April 15. During the construction, O'Brien made periodic payments to Teramo, but there was a balance due of $17,950, which O'Brien did not pay. To recover this amount, Teramo filed a suit in a New York state court against O'Brien. O'Brien filed a counterclaim to recover lost profits for business allegedly lost due to the time Teramo took to build the addition and for $6,180 spent to correct problems caused by poor craftsmanship. Which, if any, party is entitled to an award in this case? Explain. [*Teramo & Co. v. O'Brien-Shiepe Funeral Home, Inc.,* 725 N.Y.S.2d 87 (A.D. 2 Dept. 2001)]

17-7. Substantial Performance. Adolf and Ida Krueger contracted with Pisani Construction, Inc., to erect a metal building as an addition to an existing structure. The two structures were to share a common wall, and the frames and panel heights of the new building were to match those of the existing structure. Shortly before completion of the project, however, it was apparent that the roofline of the new building was approximately three inches higher than that of the existing structure. Pisani modified the ridge caps of the buildings to blend the rooflines. The discrepancy had other consequences, however, including misalignment of the gutters and windows of the two buildings, which resulted in an icing problem in the winter. The Kruegers occupied the new structure but refused to make the last payment under the contract. Pisani filed a suit in a Connecticut state court to collect. Did Pisani substantially perform its obligations? Should the Kruegers be ordered to pay? Why or why not? [*Pisani Construction, Inc. v. Krueger,* 68 Conn. App. 361, 791 A.2d 634 (2002)]

17-8. CASE PROBLEM WITH SAMPLE ANSWER

Train operators and other railroad personnel use signaling systems to ensure safe train travel. Reading Blue Mountain & Northern Railroad Co. (RBMN) and Norfolk Southern Railway Co. entered into a contract for the maintenance of a signaling system that serviced a stretch of track near Jim Thorpe, Pennsylvania. The system included a series of poles, similar to telephone poles, suspending wires above the tracks. The contract provided that "the intent of the parties is to maintain the existing . . . facilities" and split the cost equally. In December 2002, a severe storm severed the wires and destroyed most of the poles. RBMN and Norfolk discussed replacing the old system, which they agreed was antiquated, inefficient, dangerous to rebuild, and expensive, but they could not agree on an alternative. Norfolk installed an entirely new system and filed a suit in a federal district court against RBMN to recover half of the cost. RBMN filed a motion for summary judgment, asserting, in part, the doctrine of frustration of purpose. What is this doctrine? Does it apply in this case? How should the court rule on RBMN's motion? Explain. [*Norfolk Southern Railway Co. v. Reading Blue Mountain & Northern Railroad Co.,* 346 F.Supp.2d 720 (M.D.Pa. 2004)]

- **To view a sample answer for Problem 17–8, go to this book's Web site at www.cengage. com/blaw/jentz, select "Chapter 17," and click on "Case Problem with Sample Answer."**

17-9. Material Breach. Kermit Johnson formed FB&I Building Products, Inc., in Watertown, South Dakota, to sell building materials. In December 1998, FB&I contracted with Superior Truss & Components in Minneota, Minnesota, "to exclusively sell Superior's open-faced wall panels, floor panels, roof trusses and other miscellaneous products." In March 2000, FB&I agreed to exclusively sell Component Manufacturing Co.'s building products in Colorado. Two months later, Superior learned of FB&I's deal with Component and terminated its contract with FB&I. That contract provided that on cancellation, "FB&I

will be entitled to retain the customers that they continue to sell and service with Superior products." Superior refused to honor this provision. Between the cancellation of FB&I's contract and 2004, Superior made $2,327,528 in sales to FB&I customers without paying a commission. FB&I filed a suit in a South Dakota state court against Superior, alleging, in part, breach of contract and seeking the unpaid commissions. Superior insisted that FB&I had materially breached their contract, excusing Superior from performing. In whose favor should the court rule and why? [*FB&I Building Products, Inc. v. Superior Truss & Components, a Division of Banks Lumber, Inc.*, 2007 SD 13, 727 N.W.2d 474 (2007)]

17–10. A QUESTION OF ETHICS

King County, Washington, hired Frank Coluccio Construction Co. (FCCC) to act as general contractor for a public works project involving the construction of a small utility tunnel under the Duwamish Waterway. FCCC hired Donald B. Murphy Contractors, Inc. (DBM), as a subcontractor. DBM was responsible for constructing an access shaft at the eastern end of the tunnel. Problems arose during construction, including a "blow-in" of the access shaft that caused it to fill with water, soil, and debris. FCCC and DBM incurred substantial expenses from the repairs and delays. Under the project contract, King County was supposed to buy an insurance policy to "insure against physical loss or damage by perils included under an 'All-Risk' Builder's Risk policy." Any claim under this policy was to be filed through the insured. King County, which had general property damage insurance, did not obtain an all-risk builder's risk policy. For the losses attributable to the blow-in, FCCC and DBM submitted builder's risk claims, which the county denied. FCCC filed a suit in a Washington state court against King County, alleging, among other claims, breach of contract. [Frank Coluccio Construction Co. v. King County, 136 Wash.App. 751, 150 P.3d 1147 (Div. 1 2007)]

(a) King County's property damage policy specifically excluded, at the county's request, coverage of tunnels. The county drafted its contract with FCCC to require the all-risk builder's risk policy and authorize itself to "sponsor" claims. When FCCC and DBM filed their claims, the county secretly colluded with its property damage insurer to deny payment. What do these facts indicate about the county's ethics and legal liability in this situation?

(b) Could DBM, as a third party to the contract between King County and FCCC, maintain an action on the contract against King County? Discuss.

(c) All-risk insurance is a promise to pay on the "fortuitous" happening of a loss or damage from any cause except those that are specifically excluded. Payment usually is not made on a loss that, at the time the insurance was obtained, the claimant subjectively knew would occur. If a loss results from faulty workmanship on the part of a contractor, should the obligation to pay under an all-risk policy be discharged? Explain.

LAW ON THE WEB

For updated links to resources available on the Web, as well as a variety of other materials, visit this text's Web site at

www.cengage.com/blaw/jentz

For a summary of how contracts may be discharged and other principles of contract law, go to

www.rnoon.com/law_for_laymen/contracts/performance.html

Legal Research Exercises on the Web

Go to **www.cengage.com/blaw/jentz**, the Web site that accompanies this text. Select "Chapter 17" and click on "Internet Exercises." There you will find the following Internet research exercises that you can perform to learn more about the topics covered in this chapter.

Internet Exercise 17–1: Legal Perspective
Anticipatory Repudiation

Internet Exercise 17–2: Management Perspective
Commercial Impracticability

Contracts: Discharge of Contracts

Case No. 89

IMPOSSIBILITY OF PERFORMANCE

City of New York v. Local 333, Marine Division International Longshoreman's Association and Moran Towing and Transportation Company, Inc.

Appellate Division, First Department

79 A.D.2d 410, 437 N.Y.S.2d 98 (1981)

FACTS: Defendant Moran Towing and Transportation Co., Inc. (Moran) was in the business of providing towing services for barges. Moran entered a contract with Plaintiff City of New York (City) to furnish towing services to barges of the Department of Sanitation (Sanitation) in the port of New York from July 1, 1978, through June 30, 1979. On April 1, 1979 (during the contract period) Local 333, United Marine Division, International Longshoremen's Association (the Union), went on strike against thirty marine towing companies, including Moran. During the strike Moran was unable to provide towing services to Sanitation.

In this lawsuit the City is suing Moran for several million dollars as damages for breach of contract, based on Moran's failure to provide towing services during the strike. Moran defended on the basis the strike made performance impossible and thus Moran should be excused from performance without liability.

The contract did not include a provision addressing liability in the event of a strike. It did state that if Moran did not perform its contractual duties the City could perform instead and Moran would be liable for any additional expenses incurred by the City as a result.

ISSUE: Does a strike amount to "impossibility of performance" thereby relieving a contracting party of its failure to perform a contract?

DECISION: Not necessarily; more evidence is required for a decision.

REASONING: The rule identifying when a circumstance will make performance of a contract impossible has been stated as follows: "It applies where, since the formation of the contract, there has supervened an event or circumstance of such a character that reasonable [people] in the position of the parties would not have made the contract, or would not have made it without inserting some appropriate provision, if they had known or anticipated what was going to happen." A strike may be such a supervening event, thus excusing the struck employer from contract performance. However, if the strike was foreseeable, it would not excuse the employer from performance and she would be liable for resulting damages.

In this case, the court had insufficient facts about the circumstances surrounding the strike to determine if it should have been foreseen. Relevant facts that were available included the following: maritime strikes occur "quite frequently"; the strike involved in this case was portwide; in a 1970 strike the Union permitted towing services to be furnished to Sanitation; although the contract included a provision stating Moran would be liable for additional expenses caused in the event of Moran's failure to perform, the provision is unclear as to whether it applies to a strike situation. For a determination of whether the strike in this case was foreseeable, the plaintiff could request a hearing on that issue.

NOTE: Moran could have avoided this situation by inserting in the contract a provision that excused it from performance and liability in the event of a strike. Such provisions are commonplace in contracts for the sale of services where the employees of the service provider are unionized.

* * * QUESTIONS * * *
(See back of text for answers)

1) Assume that, at the time Moran and the City of New York entered their contract, Moran's employees were formally complaining to Moran about their wages and threatening to strike. How might this fact affect the decision of the judge that will decide whether the strike excused Moran from performance on the basis of impossibility of performance?

2) Assume a famous ballet dancer contracted with the Eastman Theatre of Rochester to perform on June 1. One week prior to that date the dancer was in a car accident and broke his leg. As a result, he notified the theater he would not be able to perform on June 1. Will the dancer be liable to the theater for damages for breach?

3) Assume Alex, a student at SUNY Potsdam, accumulated a bill on his MasterCard of $2800.00. He lost his part-time job and was unable to make his monthly payments on the bill. If MasterCard sued Alex for nonpayment, would he be excused from liability on the basis of impossibility of performance?

Case No. 90

IMPOSSIBILITY OF PERFORMANCE

Kenyon & Eckhardt, Inc. v. 808 Third Avenue Co.

Appellate Division, First Department

87 A.D.2d 507, 443 N.Y.S.2d 163 (1981)

FACTS: Plaintiff Kenyon & Eckhardt, Inc. (Kenyon) signed a lease with Defendant 808 Third Avenue Co. (808 Third Avenue) to rent eleven floors of a 34-story building designed but not yet constructed. At least four of the eleven floors leased by Kenyon exceeded the maximum building height permitted by law. At the time it entered the lease with Kenyon, 808 Third Avenue was seeking government approval to build all 34 stories. The lease provided that, in the event such approval was not obtained, the space to be rented to Kenyon would be recalculated "to reflect any such change proportionately."

The approval for the added height was denied. As a result 808 Third Avenue sought to terminate the lease. Kenyon claims the lease was still valid although the space to be rented would be altered consistent with the terms of the lease. Kenyon sued 808 Third Avenue to enforce the lease. In response 808 Third Avenue claimed impossibility of performance.

ISSUE: Where performance under a lease becomes impossible due to foreseeable circumstances and the lease provides an alternative course of performance in the event performance becomes impossible, can the party whose performance has become impossible avoid liability for nonperformance on the basis of impossibility of performance?

DECISION: No, judgment for Kenyon.

REASONING: The lease addresses specifically the circumstances that led to 808 Third Avenue's inability to perform and provides a way to handle the situation without terminating the contract. Since both parties agreed to the lease and since performance of the contract was possible, the contract will be enforced.

* * * QUESTION * * *
(See back of text for answer)

1) Assume the lease between Kenyon and 808 Third Avenue did not state what would happen in the event government approval for the extra floors was denied. What effect would this have on 808's claim of impossibility of performance?

Case No. 91

FRUSTRATION OF PURPOSE/RESCISSION

Sure Fire Transport Corporation v. Garsite Products, Inc.

Supreme Court, Kings County

NYLJ, August 21, 1984, p. 11, col. 3b

FACTS: On May 10, 1983, Plaintiff Sure Fire Transport Corporation (Sure Fire) entered a contract with Defendant Garsite Products, Inc. (Garsite) in which Garsite agreed to expand a fuel tank owned by Sure Fire so that it could carry 6500 gallons of fuel rather than 5500 gallons. The contract price for the service was approximately $8,000.00.

Prior to June 22, 1983, Garsite had completed half of the expansion job. On or about that date, an explosion of unknown causes occurred at Garsite's place of business and damaged Sure Fire's fuel tank. As a result, the tank was rendered unsafe for transporting fuel, a fact that was confirmed by a consulting engineer whose specialty was in petroleum handling and transportation. At the time of the explosion, Garsite had completed about half the work required to expand the tank according to the contract. After the explosion, Sure Fire instructed Garsite not to do any more work because of the damaged and unsafe condition of the tank. When Sure Fire refused to pay, Garsite filed a lien (security interest) against property of Sure Fire. In response, Sure Fire sought a court order stating that it was not obligated to pay Garsite and cancelling the lien. In return, Garsite sought a court order requiring Sure Fire to pay for Garsite's services.

FIRST ISSUE: Where the benefit anticipated by a party from performance of a contract is no longer possible due to the occurrence of an unforeseeable event, is the party entitled to rescind the contract?

DECISION: Yes.

REASONING: The doctrine of frustration of purpose applies in this case. Frustration of purpose provides that where, as a result of unforeseeable events, performance would no longer provide the benefit which induced the party to enter the contract, that party can rescind. Here the explosion was an unforeseeable event that damaged the fuel tank rendering it dangerous for transporting fuel. Since Sure Fire would no longer use it for transporting fuel, Sure Fire's purpose in expanding the tank's fuel-carrying capabilities had been frustrated (eliminated). Sure Fire thus rightly rescinded the contract by directing Garsite to discontinue its performance.

SECOND ISSUE: When a contract is rescinded due to frustration of purpose, is a party who has partly performed prior to the occurrence of the event that caused the frustration entitled to compensation for the services performed?

DECISION: Yes. In this case, Garsite is entitled to $4,000.00, the value of the work done up to the time Garsite was instructed by Sure Fire to discontinue the work.

REASONING: When rescinding a contract, the rescinding party must put the other party in the same position it was in before the contract was made. Sure Fire is thus obligated to pay Garsite for the work completed prior to the rescission. Since half of the manhours required for the job had been performed at the time of the explosion, Garsite is entitled to half the price. However, because Sure Fire rightly rescinded the contract, Garsite was not entitled to payment for the work performed after Sure Fire rescinded.

* * * QUESTION * * *
(See back of text for answer)

1) How do the doctrines of frustration of purpose and impossibility of performance differ?

Case No. 92

ANTICIPATORY BREACH

<u>Tenavision, Inc. v. Neuman</u>

Court of Appeals

45 N.Y.2d 145, 408 N.Y.S.2d 36 (1978)

FACTS: Plaintiff Tenavision, Inc. (Tenavision) entered a contract with Defendant James Square Nursing Home (Nursing Home), located in Syracuse. Tenavision agreed to lease to Nursing Home 144 television sets, in return for which the Nursing Home agreed to pay a specified amount of rent.

Prior to the date scheduled for delivery of the televisions, an employee of Tenavision made several calls to the Nursing Home to make final delivery arrangements. At that time the purchasing agent for the Nursing Home advised Tenavision's employee that the Nursing Home no longer wished to rent the television sets and would refuse to accept delivery of them. Tenavision thereafter discontinued its performance under the contract and sued the Nursing Home for damages for breach of contract. The Nursing Home claimed it did not owe Tenavision any money because Tenavision failed to tender delivery of the television sets.

ISSUE: Where a buyer notifies a seller with whom the buyer has a contract for the purchase of goods that the buyer will not accept the goods if and when they are delivered, must the seller nonetheless tender delivery of the goods in order to establish a claim for damages for breach of contract?

DECISION: No, judgment for Tenavision.

REASONING: Ordinarily, to collect damages for breach of contract a seller must tender the goods required by the contract. However, an anticipatory repudiation of a contract by a buyer eliminates the need for further performance by a seller. An anticipatory repudiation occurs whenever one party to a contract makes an "overt communication of intention" not to perform the contract. In this case, the Nursing Home made such a communication. Its purchasing agent advised Tenavision before the time of delivery that the sets were no longer needed and that delivery of them would be refused. Thus Tenavision's failure to tender delivery does not prevent it from collecting damages for breach of contract.

* * * QUESTIONS * * *
(See back of text for answers)

1) What differentiates an anticipatory breach from any other kind of breach?

2) Referring to <u>1020 Park Avenue, Inc. v. Raynor</u> reviewed in the section on Offer and Acceptance in this book, Raynor accepted an offer to renew a lease. Thereafter, he apparently had second thoughts about the amount of rent and wrote a letter to the landlord stating he "will have to give very careful consideration to renegotiating my lease." Would this letter constitute an anticipatory repudiation?

CHAPTER 16

Breach of Contract and Remedies

When one party breaches a contract, the other party—the nonbreaching party—can choose one or more of several remedies. A *remedy* is the relief provided for an innocent party when the other party has breached the contract. It is the means employed to enforce a right or to redress an injury.

The most common remedies available to a nonbreaching party include damages, rescission and restitution, specific performance, and reformation. As discussed in Chapter 1, a distinction is made between *remedies at law* and *remedies in equity.* Today, the remedy at law is normally monetary damages, which are discussed in the first part of this chapter. Equitable remedies include rescission and restitution,

specific performance, and reformation, all of which will be examined later in the chapter. Usually, a court will not award an equitable remedy unless the remedy at law is inadequate. Special legal doctrines and concepts relating to remedies will be discussed in the final pages of this chapter.

Damages

A breach of contract entitles the nonbreaching party to sue for monetary damages. As discussed in Chapter 6, damages are designed to compensate a party for harm suffered as a result of another's wrongful act. In the context of contract law, damages compensate the nonbreaching party for the loss of the bargain. Often, courts say that innocent parties are to be placed in the position they would have occupied had the contract been fully performed.[1]

Realize at the outset, though, that collecting damages through a court judgment requires litigation, which can be expensive and time consuming. Also keep in mind that court judgments are often difficult to enforce, particularly if the breaching party does not have sufficient assets to pay the damages awarded (as

discussed in Chapter 3). For these reasons, the majority of actions for damages (or other remedies) are settled by the parties before trial.

Types of Damages

There are basically four broad categories of damages:

1. Compensatory (to cover direct losses and costs).
2. Consequential (to cover indirect and foreseeable losses).
3. Punitive (to punish and deter wrongdoing).
4. Nominal (to recognize wrongdoing when no monetary loss is shown).

Compensatory and punitive damages were discussed in Chapter 6 in the context of tort law. Here, we look at these types of damages, as well as consequential and nominal damages, in the context of contract law.

Compensatory Damages Damages compensating the nonbreaching party for the *loss of the bargain* are known as *compensatory damages.* These

---

1. *Restatement (Second) of Contracts,* Section 347; Section 1–106(1) of the Uniform Commercial Code (UCC).

damages compensate the injured party only for damages actually sustained and proved to have arisen directly from the loss of the bargain caused by the breach of contract. They simply replace what was lost because of the wrong or damage and, for this reason, are often said to "make the person whole."

The standard measure of compensatory damages is the difference between the value of the breaching party's promised performance under the contract and the value of her or his actual performance. This amount is reduced by any loss that the injured party has avoided, however.

To illustrate: Wilcox contracts to perform certain services exclusively for Hernandez during the month of March for $4,000. Hernandez cancels the contract and is in breach. Wilcox is able to find another job during the month of March but can earn only $3,000. He can sue Hernandez for breach and recover $1,000 as compensatory damages. Wilcox can also recover from Hernandez the amount that he spent to find the other job. Expenses that are caused directly by a breach of contract—such as those incurred to obtain performance from another source—are known as **incidental damages.**

The measurement of compensatory damages varies by type of contract. Certain types of contracts deserve special mention. They are contracts for the sale of goods and for the sale of land.

Sale of Goods. In a contract for the sale of goods, the usual measure of compensatory damages is an amount equal to the difference between the contract price and the market price.[2] Suppose that Chrylon Corporation contracts to buy ten model UTS network servers from an XEXO Corporation dealer for $8,000 each. The dealer, however, fails to deliver the ten servers to Chrylon. The market price of the servers at the time the buyer learns of the breach is $8,150. Therefore, Chrylon's measure of damages is $1,500 (10 × $150) plus any incidental damages (expenses) caused by the breach. In a situation in which the buyer breaches and the seller has not yet produced the goods, compensatory damages normally equal lost profits on the sale, not the difference between the contract price and the market price.

Sale of Land. Ordinarily, because each parcel of land is unique, the remedy for a seller's breach of a contract for a sale of real estate is specific performance—that is, the buyer is awarded the parcel of property for which she or he bargained (*specific performance* is discussed more fully later in this chapter). When this remedy is unavailable (for example, when the seller has sold the property to someone else), or when the buyer has breached, the measure of damages is ordinarily the same as in contracts for the sale of goods—that is, the difference between the contract price and the market price of the land. The majority of states follow this rule.

A minority of states follow a different rule when the seller breaches the contract and the breach is not deliberate.[3] When the breach was not willful, these states limit the prospective buyer's damages to a refund of any down payment made plus any expenses incurred (such as fees for title searches, attorneys, and escrows). This rule effectively returns purchasers to the positions they occupied prior to the sale, rather than giving them the benefit of the bargain.

Construction Contracts. The measure of damages in a building or construction contract varies depending on which party breaches and when the breach occurs. The owner can breach at three different stages of the construction:

1. Before performance has begun.
2. During performance.
3. After performance has been completed.

If the owner breaches *before performance has begun,* the contractor can recover only the profits that would have been made on the contract (that is, the total contract price less the cost of materials and labor). If the owner breaches *during performance,* the contractor can recover the profits plus the costs incurred in partially constructing the building. If the owner breaches *after the construction has been completed,* the contractor can recover the entire contract price, plus interest.

When the construction contractor breaches the contract either by failing to undertake construction or by stopping work partway through the project, the mea-

---

2. In other words, the amount is the difference between the contract price and the market price at the time and place at which the goods were to be delivered or tendered. See UCC 2–708 and 2–713.

---

3. "Deliberate" breaches include the seller's failure to convey the land because the market price has gone up. "Nondeliberate" breaches include the seller's failure to convey the land because of a problem with the title, such as the discovery of an unknown *easement* that gives another a right of use over the property (see Chapter 48).

EXHIBIT 16–1 • Measurement of Damages—Breach of Construction Contracts

Party in Breach	Time of Breach	Measurement of Damage
Owner	Before construction has begun.	Profits (contract price less cost of materials and labor).
Owner	During construction.	Profits, plus costs incurred up to time of breach.
Owner	After construction is completed.	Contract price, plus interest.
Contractor	Before construction has begun.	Cost above contract price to complete work.
Contractor	Before construction is completed.	Generally, all costs incurred by owner to complete work.

sure of damages is the cost of completion, which includes reasonable compensation for any delay in performance. If the contractor finishes late, the measure of damages is the loss of use. These rules concerning the measurement of damages in breached construction contracts are summarized in Exhibit 16–1.

Construction Contracts and Economic Waste. If the contractor substantially performs, a court may use the cost-of-completion formula, but only if requiring completion will not entail unreasonable economic waste. *Economic waste* occurs when the cost of repairing or completing the performance as required by the contract greatly outweighs the benefit to the owner. For example, a contractor discovers that it will cost $20,000 to move a large coral rock eleven inches as specified in the contract. Because changing the rock's position will alter the appearance of the project only a trifle, a court would likely conclude that full completion would involve economic waste. Thus, the contractor will not be required to pay the full $20,000 to complete performance.

Consequential Damages Foreseeable damages that result from a party's breach of contract are called **consequential damages,** or *special damages.*

They differ from compensatory damages in that they are caused by special circumstances beyond the contract itself. They flow from the consequences, or results, of a breach.

For example, when a seller fails to deliver goods, knowing that the buyer is planning to use or resell those goods immediately, consequential damages are awarded for the loss of profits from the planned resale. (The buyer will also recover compensatory damages for the difference between the contract price and the market price of the goods.)

To recover consequential damages, the breaching party must know (or have reason to know) that special circumstances will cause the nonbreaching party to suffer an additional loss. This rule was enunciated in the classic case of *Hadley v. Baxendale,* which is presented next. In reading this decision, it is helpful to understand that in the mid-1800s in England large flour mills customarily kept more than one crankshaft on hand in the event that the main crankshaft broke and had to be repaired. It is against this background that the parties in the case presented here argued their respective positions on whether the damages resulting from the loss of profits while the crankshaft was repaired were reasonably foreseeable.

 C A S E **16.1 Hadley v. Baxendale**
Court of Exchequer, 1854. 156 Eng.Rep. 145.

• **Background and Facts** The Hadleys (the plaintiffs) ran a flour mill in Gloucester. The crankshaft attached to the steam engine in the mill broke, causing the mill to shut down. The shaft had to be sent to a foundry located in Greenwich so that the new shaft could be made to fit the other parts of the engine. Baxendale, the defendant, was a common carrier that transported the

CASE CONTINUES

CASE 16.1 CONTINUED shaft from Gloucester to Greenwich. The freight charges were collected in advance, and Baxendale promised to deliver the shaft the following day. It was not delivered for a number of days, however. As a consequence, the mill was closed for several days. The Hadleys sued to recover the profits lost during that time. Baxendale contended that the loss of profits was "too remote" to be recoverable. The court held for the plaintiffs, and the jury was allowed to take into consideration the lost profits. The defendant appealed.

● **Decision and Rationale** The Court of Exchequer ordered a new trial. The court explained that if an injury is outside the usual course of events, it must be shown that the breaching party had reason to foresee the injury. According to the court, to collect consequential damages the plaintiffs in this case would have to have given express notice of the special circumstances that caused the loss of profits. The court reasoned that "special circumstances were here never communicated by the plaintiffs to the defendants. It follows, therefore, that the loss of profits here cannot reasonably be considered such a consequence of the breach of contract as could have been fairly and reasonably contemplated by both the parties when they made this contract."

● **Impact of This Case on Today's Law** *This case established the rule that when damages are awarded, compensation is given only for those injuries that the defendant could reasonably have foreseen as a probable result of the usual course of events following a breach. Today, the rule enunciated by the court in this case still applies. To recover consequential damages, the plaintiff must show that the defendant had reason to know or foresee that a particular loss or injury would occur.*

● **The E-Commerce Dimension** *If a Web merchant loses business due to a computer system's failure that can be attributed to malfunctioning software, can the merchant recover the lost profits from the software maker? Explain.*

PREVENTING LEGAL DISPUTES

Business owners and managers should realize that it is sometimes impossible to prevent contract disputes. They should also understand that collecting damages through a court judgment requires litigation, which can be expensive and time consuming. Furthermore, court judgments are often difficult to enforce, particularly if the breaching party does not have sufficient assets to pay the damages awarded.[4]

For these reasons, parties generally choose to settle their contract disputes before trial rather than litigate in hopes of being awarded—and being able to collect—damages (or other remedies). In sum, there is wisdom in the old saying, "a bird in the hand is worth two in the bush."

---

4. Courts dispose of cases, after trials, by entering judgments. A judgment may order the losing party to pay monetary damages to the winning party. Collecting a judgment, however, can pose problems. For example, the judgment debtor may be insolvent (unable to pay his or her bills when they come due) or have only a small net worth, or exemption laws may prevent a creditor from seizing the debtor's assets to satisfy a debt (see Chapter 30).

Punitive Damages Punitive, or exemplary, damages generally are not recoverable in contract law, even for an intentional breach of contract. Because punitive damages are designed to punish a wrongdoer and set an example to deter similar conduct in the future, they have no legitimate place in contract law. A contract is simply a civil relationship between the parties, so breaching a contract is not a crime; nor does it necessarily harm society (as torts do). Thus, a court will not award punitive damages but will compensate one party for the loss of the bargain—no more and no less.

In a few situations, however, when a person's actions constitute both a breach of contract and a tort, punitive damages may be available. For example, some parties, such as an engineer and her client, may establish by contract a certain reasonable standard or duty of care. Failure to live up to that standard is a breach of contract, and the act itself may constitute negligence. Similarly, some intentional torts, such as fraud, may be tied to a breach of the terms of a contract and enable the injured party to seek punitive damages. Additionally, when an insurance company exhibits bad faith in failing to settle a claim on behalf of the insured party, courts may award punitive damages. Overall, though, punitive damages are almost never available in contract disputes.

Nominal Damages When no actual damage or financial loss results from a breach of contract and only a technical injury is involved, the court may award **nominal damages** to the innocent party. Awards of nominal damages are often small, such as one dollar, but they do establish that the defendant acted wrongfully. Most lawsuits for nominal damages are brought as a matter of principle under the theory that a breach has occurred and some damages must be imposed regardless of actual loss.

Suppose that Jackson contracts to buy potatoes from Stanley at fifty cents a pound. Stanley breaches the contract and does not deliver the potatoes. In the meantime, the price of potatoes has fallen. Jackson is able to buy them in the open market at half the price he contracted for with Stanley. He is clearly better off because of Stanley's breach. Thus, because Jackson sustained only a technical injury and suffered no monetary loss, he is likely to be awarded only nominal damages if he brings a suit for breach of contract.

Mitigation of Damages

In most situations, when a breach of contract occurs, the innocent injured party is held to a duty to mitigate, or reduce, the damages that he or she suffers. Under this doctrine of **mitigation of damages,** the duty owed depends on the nature of the contract.

For example, some states require a landlord to use reasonable means to find a new tenant if a tenant abandons the premises and fails to pay rent. If an acceptable tenant is found, the landlord is required to lease the premises to this tenant to mitigate the damages recoverable from the former tenant. The former tenant is still liable for the difference between the amount of the rent under the original lease and the rent received from the new tenant. If the landlord has not taken the reasonable steps necessary to find a new tenant, a court will likely reduce any award made by the amount of rent the landlord could have received had such reasonable means been used.

In the majority of states, a person whose employment has been wrongfully terminated owes a duty to mitigate the damages suffered because of the employer's breach of the employment contract. In other words, a wrongfully terminated employee has a duty to take a similar job if one is available. If the employee fails to do this, the damages awarded will be equivalent to the person's salary less the income he or she would have received in a similar job obtained by reasonable means. The employer has the burden of proving that such a job existed and that the employee could have been hired. Normally, the employee is under no duty to take a job of a different type and rank, however.

Whether a tenant farmer acceptably attempted to mitigate his damages on his landlord's breach of their lease was at issue in the following case.

C A S E **16.2 Hanson v. Boeder**
Supreme Court of North Dakota, 2007. 2007 ND 20, 727 N.W.2d 280.
www.ndcourts.com/court/opinions.htm[a]

● **Background and Facts** In 1998, Paul Hanson signed a five-year lease to farm 1,350 acres of Donald Boeder's land in Steele County, North Dakota, for $50 per acre beginning with the 1999 crop year. Under the lease, Hanson could use grain bins with a capacity of 93,000 bushels and two machine sheds on the property. The rent was $67,515 per year, with half due on April 1 and the balance due on November 1. In 2003, Boeder and Hanson renewed the lease for a second five-year period. During both terms, Boeder and Hanson disagreed about Hanson's farming practices, but during the second term, their disagreement escalated. In August 2005, Boeder told Hanson that their lease was over. Boeder also told Hanson not to till the land in the fall because it had been leased to a new tenant who wanted to do it himself. Hanson continued to work Boeder's land, however, while running ads in the local newspapers for other farmland to rent. Unable to find other land, Hanson filed a suit in a North Dakota state court against Boeder for breach of contract, asking the court to assess damages. The court awarded Hanson $315,194.26 to cover his lost profits,

---

a. Click on the "By ND citation" link. In the result, click on "2007" and then the name of the case to access the opinion. The North Dakota Supreme Court maintains this Web site.

CASE CONTINUES

CASE 16.2 CONTINUED the lost use of the bins and sheds, and the value of the fall tillage. Boeder appealed to the North Dakota Supreme Court, arguing, in part, that Hanson failed to mitigate his damages.

● **Decision and Rationale** The Supreme Court of North Dakota affirmed the lower court's award of damages to Hanson. The state supreme court explained that normally, "for the breach of an obligation arising from contract, the measure of damages * * * is the amount which will compensate the party aggrieved for all the detriment proximately caused thereby or which in the ordinary course of things would be likely to result therefrom." The court recognized that "a person injured by the wrongful acts of another has a duty to mitigate or minimize the damages and must protect himself if he can do so with reasonable exertion or at trifling expense, and can recover from the delinquent party only such damages as he could not, with reasonable effort, have avoided." In this case, Hanson had not been aware of any farmland available for lease, and he had run ads in the local newspapers seeking other farmland to rent. That Hanson was unsuccessful affected the amount of his recovery, but it did not point to a failure to mitigate his damages.

● **The Ethical Dimension** *During the trial, Boeder tried to retract his repudiation of the lease to allow Hanson to continue farming for the rest of the lease term. Should the court have considered this an acceptable substitute to mitigate Hanson's damages? Why or why not?*

● **The Legal Environment Dimension** *Hanson initially asked the lower court to enforce the contract and requested damages only "in the alternative"—that is, only if specific performance was not available (pleading in the alternative is discussed later in this chapter). Could the court have awarded Hanson specific performance of the lease in this case? Should that relief have been granted? Explain.*

Liquidated Damages Provisions

A **liquidated damages** provision in a contract specifies that a certain dollar amount is to be paid in the event of a *future* default or breach of contract. (*Liquidated* means determined, settled, or fixed.) For example, a provision requiring a construction contractor to pay $300 for every day he or she is late in completing the project is a liquidated damages provision. Liquidated damages provisions are frequently used in construction contracts because it is difficult to estimate the amount of damages that would be caused by a delay in completion. They are also common in contracts for the sale of goods.[5]

Liquidated damages differ from penalties. A **penalty** specifies a certain amount to be paid in the event of a default or breach of contract and is designed to penalize the breaching party. Liquidated damages provisions normally are enforceable. In contrast, if a court finds that a provision calls for a penalty, the agreement as to the amount will not be enforced, and recovery will be limited to actual damages. To determine if a particular provision is for liquidated damages or for a penalty, the court asks two questions:

1. When the contract was entered into, was it apparent that damages would be difficult to estimate in the event of a breach?
2. Was the amount set as damages a reasonable estimate and not excessive?[6]

If the answers to both questions are yes, the provision normally will be enforced. If either answer is no, the provision normally will not be enforced. For example, in a case involving a sophisticated business contract to lease computer equipment, the court held that a liquidated damages provision that valued the computer equipment at more than four times its market value was a reasonable estimate. According to the court, the amount of actual damages was difficult to ascertain at the time the contract was formed because of the "speculative nature of the value of computers at termination of lease schedules."[7]

---

5. Section 2–718(1) of the UCC specifically authorizes the use of liquidated damages provisions.

6. *Restatement (Second) of Contracts*, Section 356(1).

7. *Winthrop Resources Corp. v. Eaton Hydraulics, Inc.*, 361 F.3d 465 (8th Cir. 2004).

Rescission and Restitution

As discussed in Chapter 17, *rescission* is essentially an action to undo, or terminate, a contract—to return the contracting parties to the positions they occupied prior to the transaction.[8] When fraud, a mistake, duress, undue influence, misrepresentation, or lack of capacity to contract is present, unilateral rescission is available. Rescission may also be available by statute.[9] The failure of one party to perform entitles the other party to rescind the contract. The rescinding party must give prompt notice to the breaching party.

Restitution

Generally, to rescind a contract, both parties must make **restitution** to each other by returning goods, property, or funds previously conveyed.[10] If the physical property or goods can be returned, they must be. If the goods or property have been consumed, restitution must be made in an equivalent dollar amount.

Essentially, restitution involves the plaintiff's recapture of a benefit conferred on the defendant through which the defendant has been unjustly enriched. For example, Katie pays $10,000 to Bob in return for Bob's promise to design a house for her. The next day, Bob calls Katie and tells her that he has taken a position with a large architectural firm in another state and cannot design the house. Katie decides to hire another architect that afternoon. Katie can obtain restitution of the $10,000.

Restitution Is Not Limited to Rescission Cases

Restitution may be appropriate when a contract is rescinded, but the right to restitution is not limited to rescission cases. Because an award of restitution basically gives back or returns something to its rightful owner, this remedy may be sought in actions for breach of contract, tort actions, and other types of actions. For example, restitution can be obtained when funds or property has been transferred by mistake or because of fraud or incapacity. Restitution may also be available in situations involving embezzlement, conversion, theft, copyright infringement, or misconduct by a party in a confidential or other special relationship.

Specific Performance

The equitable remedy of **specific performance** calls for the performance of the act promised in the contract. This remedy is often attractive to a nonbreaching party because it provides the exact bargain promised in the contract. It also avoids some of the problems inherent in a suit for damages. First, the nonbreaching party need not worry about collecting the judgment (see Chapter 3 for a discussion of the difficulties of enforcing court judgments). Second, the nonbreaching party need not look around for another contract. Third, the actual performance may be more valuable than the monetary damages.

Normally, however, specific performance will not be granted unless the party's legal remedy (monetary damages) is inadequate.[11] For this reason, contracts for the sale of goods rarely qualify for specific performance. The legal remedy—monetary damages—is ordinarily adequate in such situations because substantially identical goods can be bought or sold in the market. Only if the goods are unique will a court grant specific performance. For example, paintings, sculptures, or rare books or coins are so unique that monetary damages will not enable a buyer to obtain substantially identical substitutes in the market.

Sale of Land

A court may grant specific performance to a buyer in an action for a breach of contract involving the sale of land. In this situation, the legal remedy of monetary damages may not compensate the buyer adequately because every parcel of land is unique: the same land in the same location obviously cannot be obtained elsewhere. Only when specific performance is unavailable (for example, when the seller has sold the property to someone else) will monetary damages be awarded instead.

Is specific performance warranted when one of the parties has substantially—but not *fully*—performed under the contract? That was the question in the following case.

---

8. The rescission discussed here is *unilateral* rescission, in which only one party wants to undo the contract. In mutual rescission, both parties agree to undo the contract (see Chapter 17). Mutual rescission discharges the contract; unilateral rescission is generally available as a remedy for breach of contract.

9. The Federal Trade Commission and many states have rules or statutes allowing consumers to unilaterally rescind contracts made at home with door-to-door salespersons. Rescission is allowed within three days for any reason or for no reason at all. See, for example, California Civil Code Section 1689.5.

10. *Restatement (Second) of Contracts*, Section 370.

11. *Restatement (Second) of Contracts*, Section 359.

C A S E 16.3 Stainbrook v. Low
Court of Appeals of Indiana, 2006. 842 N.E.2d 386.

● **Background and Facts** In April 2004, Howard Stainbrook agreed to sell to Trent Low forty acres of land in Jennings County, Indiana, for $45,000. Thirty-two of the acres were wooded and eight were tillable. Under the agreement, Low was to pay for a survey of the property and other costs, including a tax payment due in November. Low gave Stainbrook a check for $1,000 to show his intent to fulfill the contract. They agreed to close the deal on May 11, and Low made financial arrangements to meet his obligations. On May 8, a tractor rolled over on Stainbrook, and he died. Howard's son David became the executor of Stainbrook's estate. David asked Low to withdraw his offer to buy the forty acres. Low refused and filed a suit against David in an Indiana state court, seeking to enforce the contract. The court ordered specific performance. David appealed to a state intermediate appellate court, arguing, among other things, that his father's contract with Low was "ambiguous and inequitable."

● **Decision and Rationale** The state intermediate appellate court held that specific performance was an appropriate remedy in this case and affirmed the lower court's order. Stainbrook's son, David, the executor of the estate, argued that specific performance was not appropriate because Low did not prove full and complete performance for his part of the contract. The court pointed out that while Low did not pay the November 2004 property taxes, he offered to make the tax payment, and David refused his offer. In reality, in this case, "specific performance is an appropriate remedy to a party who has *substantially* performed under the terms of the contract." In addition, David's contention that the agreement was unfair was not convincing to the court. Stainbrook, although old, was competent at the time of the making of the contract. He consulted a lawyer regarding the agreement, and he insisted on several handwritten changes to the contract that benefited his own interest.

● **The Ethical Dimension** *Should a party who seeks specific performance of a contract be required to prove that he or she has performed, substantially performed, or offered to perform his or her contract obligations? Why or why not?*

● **The Global Dimension** *Suppose that Stainbrook and Low had been citizens and residents of other countries. Would the location of the land that was the subject of their contract have been sufficient to support the Indiana state court's jurisdiction and award in this case? Discuss.*

Contracts for Personal Services

Personal-service contracts require one party to work personally for another party. Courts normally refuse to grant specific performance of personal-service contracts because to order a party to perform personal services against his or her will amounts to a type of involuntary servitude.[12]

Moreover, the courts do not want to have to monitor a service contract if supervision would be difficult—as it would be if the contract required the exercise of personal judgment or talent. For example, if you contracted with a brain surgeon to perform brain surgery on you and the surgeon refused to perform, the court would not compel (and you certainly would not want) the surgeon to perform under those circumstances. A court cannot assure meaningful performance in such a situation.[13] If a contract is not deemed personal, the remedy at law of monetary damages may be adequate if substantially identical service (for example, lawn mowing) is available from other persons.

---

12. Involuntary servitude, or slavery, is contrary to the public policy expressed in the Thirteenth Amendment to the U.S. Constitution. A court can, however, enter an order (injunction) prohibiting a person who breached a personal-service contract from engaging in similar contracts for a period of time in the future.

13. Similarly, courts often refuse to order specific performance of construction contracts because courts are not set up to operate as construction supervisors or engineers.

Reformation

Reformation is an equitable remedy used when the parties have *imperfectly* expressed their agreement in writing. Reformation allows a court to rewrite the contract to reflect the parties' true intentions.

When Fraud or Mutual Mistake Is Present

Courts order reformation most often when fraud or mutual mistake (for example, a clerical error) is present. Typically, a party seeks reformation so that some other remedy may then be pursued. For example, if Keshan contracts to buy a certain parcel of land from Malboa but their contract mistakenly refers to a parcel of land different from the one being sold, the contract does not reflect the parties' intentions. Accordingly, a court can reform the contract so that it conforms to the parties' intentions and accurately refers to the parcel of land being sold. Keshan can then, if necessary, show that Malboa has breached the contract as reformed. She can at that time request an order for specific performance.

Oral Contracts and Covenants Not to Compete

Courts also frequently reform contracts in two other situations. The first involves two parties who have made a binding oral contract. They further agree to put the oral contract in writing, but in doing so, they make an error in stating the terms. Normally, a court will allow into evidence the correct terms of the oral contract, thereby reforming the written contract.

The second situation occurs when the parties have executed a written covenant not to compete (dis-cussed in Chapter 13). If the covenant is for a valid and legitimate purpose (such as the sale of a business) but the area or time restraints of the covenant are unreasonable, some courts will reform the restraints by making them reasonable and will enforce the entire contract as reformed. Other courts, however, will throw out the entire restrictive covenant as illegal.

Exhibit 16–2 graphically summarizes the remedies, including reformation, that are available to the non-breaching party.

Recovery Based on Quasi Contract

Recall from Chapter 10 that quasi contract is not a true contract but rather a fictional contract that is imposed on the parties to prevent unjust enrichment. Hence, quasi contract provides a basis for relief when no enforceable contract exists. The legal obligation arises because the law considers that the party accepting the benefits has made an implied promise to pay for them. Generally, when one party has conferred a benefit on another party, justice requires the party receiving the benefit to pay the reasonable value for it. The party conferring the benefit can recover in *quantum meruit*, which means "as much as he or she deserves" (see Chapter 10).

When Quasi Contracts Are Used

In addition to being used when there is no actual contract or agreement between the parties, quasi contract may be available when the parties have a contract, but it is unenforceable for some reason. Quasi-contractual recovery is often granted when one party has partially

EXHIBIT 16–2 • **Remedies for Breach of Contract**

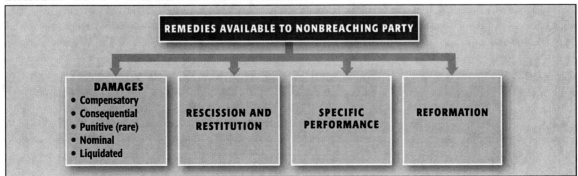

performed under a contract that is unenforceable. It provides an alternative to suing for damages and allows the party to recover the reasonable value of the partial performance, measured in some cases according to the benefit received and in others according to the detriment suffered.

Suppose that Watson contracts to build two oil derricks for Energy Industries. The derricks are to be built over a period of three years, but the parties do not make a written contract. The Statute of Frauds will thus bar the enforcement of the contract.[14] After Watson completes one derrick, Energy Industries informs him that it will not pay for the derrick. Watson can sue Energy Industries under the theory of quasi contract.

The Requirements of Quasi Contract

To recover under the theory of quasi contract, the party seeking recovery must show the following:

1. The party has conferred a benefit on the other party.
2. The party conferred the benefit with the reasonable expectation of being paid.

---

14. Contracts that by their terms cannot be performed within one year must be in writing to be enforceable (see Chapter 15).

3. The party did not act as a volunteer in conferring the benefit.
4. The party receiving the benefit would be unjustly enriched by retaining the benefit without paying for it.

In the example just given, Watson can sue in quasi contract because all of the conditions for quasi-contractual recovery have been fulfilled. Watson conferred a benefit on Energy Industries with the reasonable expectation of being paid. The derrick conferred an obvious benefit on Energy Industries. Allowing Energy Industries to retain the derrick without paying Watson would enrich the company unjustly. Therefore, Watson should be able to recover in *quantum meruit* the reasonable value of the oil derrick, which is ordinarily equal to its fair market value. (*Concept Summary 16.1* reviews all of the equitable remedies, including quasi contract, that may be available in the event that a contract is breached.)

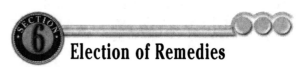

Election of Remedies

In many cases, a nonbreaching party has several remedies available. When the remedies are inconsistent with one another, the common law of contracts

---

CONCEPT SUMMARY 16.1
Equitable Remedies

Remedy	Description
RESCISSION AND RESTITUTION	1. *Rescission*—A remedy whereby a contract is canceled and the parties are restored to the original positions that they occupied prior to the transaction. 2. *Restitution*—When a contract is rescinded, both parties must make restitution to each other by returning the goods, property, or funds previously conveyed.
SPECIFIC PERFORMANCE	An equitable remedy calling for the performance of the act promised in the contract. Only available when monetary damages would be inadequate—such as in contracts for the sale of land or unique goods—and never available in personal-service contracts.
REFORMATION	An equitable remedy allowing a contract to be "reformed," or rewritten, to reflect the parties' true intentions. Available when an agreement is imperfectly expressed in writing, such as when a mutual mistake has occurred.
RECOVERY BASED ON QUASI CONTRACT	An equitable theory under which a party who confers a benefit on another with the reasonable expectation of being paid can seek a court order for the fair market value of the benefit conferred.

requires the party to choose which remedy to pursue. This is called *election of remedies*.

The Purpose of the Doctrine

The purpose of the doctrine of election of remedies is to prevent double recovery. Suppose that McCarthy agrees in writing to sell his land to Tally. Then McCarthy changes his mind and repudiates the contract. Tally can sue for compensatory damages *or* for specific performance. If Tally could seek compensatory damages in addition to specific performance, she would recover twice for the same breach of contract. The doctrine of election of remedies requires Tally to choose the remedy she wants, and it eliminates any possibility of double recovery. In other words, the election doctrine represents the legal embodiment of the adage "You can't have your cake and eat it, too."

The doctrine has often been applied in a rigid and technical manner, leading to some harsh results. For example, Beacham is fraudulently induced to buy a parcel of land for $150,000. He spends an additional $10,000 moving onto the land and then discovers the fraud. Instead of suing for damages, Beacham sues to rescind the contract. The court allows Beacham to recover the purchase price of $150,000 in restitution, but not the additional $10,000 in moving expenses (because the seller did not receive this payment, he or she will not be required to return it). So Beacham suffers a net loss of $10,000 on the transaction. If Beacham had elected to sue for damages instead of seeking the remedy of rescission and restitution, he could have recovered the $10,000 as well as the $150,000.

The UCC's Rejection of the Doctrine

Because of the many problems associated with the doctrine of election of remedies, the UCC expressly rejects it.[15] As will be discussed in Chapter 22, remedies under the Uniform Commercial Code (UCC) are not exclusive but are cumulative in nature and include all the available remedies for breach of contract.

Pleading in the Alternative

Although the nonbreaching party must ultimately elect which remedy to pursue, modern court procedures do allow plaintiffs to plead their cases "in the alternative" (pleadings were discussed in Chapter 3).

---

15. See UCC 2–703 and 2–711.

In other words, when the plaintiff originally files a lawsuit, he or she can ask the court to order either rescission (and restitution) or damages, for example. Then, as the case progresses to trial, the party can elect the remedy that is most beneficial or appropriate, or the judge can order one remedy and not another. This process still prevents double recovery because the party can be awarded only one of the remedies that was requested.

Waiver of Breach

Under certain circumstances, a nonbreaching party may be willing to accept a defective performance of the contract. This knowing relinquishment of a legal right (that is, the right to require satisfactory and full performance) is called a **waiver.**

Consequences of a Waiver of Breach

When a waiver of a breach of contract occurs, the party waiving the breach cannot take any later action on it. In effect, the waiver erases the past breach; the contract continues as if the breach had never occurred. Of course, the waiver of breach of contract extends only to the matter waived and not to the whole contract.

Reasons for Waiving a Breach

Businesspersons often waive breaches of contract to get whatever benefit is still possible out of the contract. For example, a seller contracts with a buyer to deliver to the buyer ten thousand tons of coal on or before November 1. The contract calls for the buyer to pay by November 10 for coal delivered. Because of a coal miners' strike, coal is hard to find. The seller breaches the contract by not tendering delivery until November 5. The buyer will likely choose to waive the seller's breach, accept delivery of the coal, and pay as contracted.

Waiver of Breach and Subsequent Breaches

Ordinarily, the waiver by a contracting party will not operate to waive subsequent, additional, or future breaches of contract. This is always true when the subsequent breaches are unrelated to the first breach. For example, an owner who waives the right to sue for late completion of a stage of construction does not waive the right to sue for failure to comply with engineering specifications on the same job. A waiver will be extended to subsequent defective performance, however, if a reasonable person would conclude that similar defective performance in the future will be acceptable. Therefore, a *pattern of conduct* that waives a number of successive breaches will operate as a continued waiver. To change this result, the nonbreaching party should give notice to the breaching party that full performance will be required in the future.

The party who has rendered defective or less-than-full performance remains liable for the damages caused by the breach of contract. In effect, the waiver operates to keep the contract going. The waiver prevents the nonbreaching party from calling the contract to an end or rescinding the contract. The contract continues, but the nonbreaching party can recover damages caused by the defective or less-than-full performance.

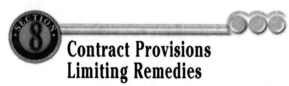

Contract Provisions Limiting Remedies

A contract may include provisions stating that no damages can be recovered for certain types of breaches or that damages will be limited to a maximum amount. The contract may also provide that the only remedy for breach is replacement, repair, or refund of the purchase price. Provisions stating that no damages can be recov-

ered are called *exculpatory clauses* (see Chapter 13). Provisions that affect the availability of certain remedies are called *limitation-of-liability clauses.*

The UCC Allows Sales Contracts to Limit Remedies

The UCC provides that in a contract for the sale of goods, remedies can be limited. We will examine the UCC provisions on limited remedies in Chapter 22, in the context of the remedies available on the breach of a contract for the sale or lease of goods.[16]

Enforceability of Limitation-of-Liability Clauses

Whether a limitation-of-liability clause in a contract will be enforced depends on the type of breach that is excused by the provision. For example, a provision excluding liability for fraudulent or intentional injury will not be enforced. Likewise, a clause excluding liability for illegal acts or violations of law will not be enforced.

A clause excluding liability for negligence may be enforced in certain situations, however. When an exculpatory clause for negligence is contained in a contract made between parties who have roughly equal bargaining positions, the clause usually will be enforced.[17]

---

16. See UCC 2–719(1).

17. See, for example, *Asch Webhosting, Inc. v. Adelphia Business Solutions Investment, LLC,* __ F.Supp.2d __ (D.N.J. 2007); and *Lucier v. Williams,* 366 N.J.Super. 485, 841 A.2d 907 (2004).

REVIEWING Breach of Contract and Remedies

Kyle Bruno enters a contract with X Entertainment to be a stuntman in a movie. Bruno is widely known as the best motorcycle stuntman in the business, and the movie to be produced, *Xtreme Riders,* has numerous scenes involving high-speed freestyle street-bike stunts. Filming is set to begin August 1 and end by December 1 so that the film can be released the following summer. Both parties to the contract have stipulated that the filming must end on time to capture the profits from the summer movie market. The contract states that Bruno will be paid 10 percent of the net proceeds from the movie for his stunts. The contract also includes a liquidated damages provision, which specifies that if Bruno breaches the contract, he will owe X Entertainment $1 million. In addition, the contract includes a limitation-of-liability clause stating that if Bruno is injured during filming, X Entertainment's

REVIEWING Breach of Contract and Remedies, Continued

liability is limited to nominal damages. Using the information presented in the chapter, answer the following questions.

1. One day, while Bruno is preparing for a difficult stunt, he gets into an argument with the director and refuses to perform any stunts at all. Can X Entertainment seek specific performance of the contract? Why or why not?

2. Suppose that while performing a high-speed wheelie on a motorcycle, Bruno is injured by the intentionally reckless act of an X Entertainment employee. Will a court be likely to enforce the limitation-of-liability clause? Why or why not?

3. What factors would a court consider to determine whether the $1 million liquidated damages provision constitutes valid damages or is a penalty?

4. Suppose that the contract had no liquidated damages provision (or the court refused to enforce it) and X Entertainment breached the contract. The breach caused the release of the film to be delayed until the fall. Could Bruno seek consequential (special) damages for lost profits from the summer movie market in that situation? Explain.

TERMS AND CONCEPTS

consequential damages

incidental damages

liquidated damages

mitigation of damages

nominal damages

penalty

reformation

restitution

specific performance

waiver

QUESTIONS AND CASE PROBLEMS

18-1. Cohen contracts to sell his house and lot to Windsor for $100,000. The terms of the contract call for Windsor to pay 10 percent of the purchase price as a deposit toward the purchase price, or a down payment. The terms further stipulate that if the buyer breaches the contract, Cohen will retain the deposit as liquidated damages. Windsor pays the deposit, but because her expected financing of the $90,000 balance falls through, she breaches the contract. Two weeks later Cohen sells the house and lot to Ballard for $105,000. Windsor demands her $10,000 back, but Cohen refuses, claiming that Windsor's breach and the contract terms entitle him to keep the deposit. Discuss who is correct.

18-2. QUESTION WITH SAMPLE ANSWER

In which of the following situations would specific performance be an appropriate remedy? Discuss fully.

(a) Thompson contracts to sell her house and lot to Cousteau. Then, on finding another buyer willing to pay a higher purchase price, she refuses to deed the property to Cousteau.

(b) Amy contracts to sing and dance in Fred's nightclub for one month, beginning May 1. She then refuses to perform.

(c) Hoffman contracts to buy a rare coin owned by Erikson, who is breaking up his coin collection. At the last minute, Erikson decides to keep his collection intact and refuses to deliver the coin to Hoffman.

(d) ABC Corp. has three shareholders: Panozzo, who owns 48 percent of the stock; Chang, who owns another 48 percent; and Ryan, who owns 4 percent. Ryan contracts to sell her 4 percent to Chang. Later, Ryan refuses to transfer the shares to Chang.

• For a sample answer to Question 18–2, go to Appendix C at the end of this text.

18-3. Ken owns and operates a famous candy store and makes most of the candy sold in the store. Business is particularly heavy during the Christmas season. Ken contracts with Sweet, Inc., to purchase ten thousand pounds of sugar to be delivered on or before November 15. Ken has informed Sweet that this particular order is to be used for the Christmas season business. Because of problems at the refinery, the sugar is not tendered to Ken until December 10, at which time Ken refuses it as being too late. Ken has been unable to purchase the quantity of sugar needed to meet his Christmas orders and has had to turn down numerous regular customers, some of whom have indicated that they will purchase candy elsewhere in the future. The sugar Ken has been able to purchase has cost him 10 cents per pound above the price contracted for with Sweet. Ken sues Sweet for breach of contract, claiming as damages the higher price paid for sugar from others, lost profits from this year's lost Christmas sales, future lost profits from customers who have indicated that they will discontinue doing business with him, and punitive damages for failure to meet the contracted delivery date. Sweet claims Ken is limited to compensatory damages only. Discuss who is correct, and why.

18-4. Mitigation of Damages. William West, an engineer, worked for Bechtel Corp., an organization of about 150 engineering and construction companies, which is headquartered in San Francisco, California, and operates worldwide. Except for a two-month period in 1985, Bechtel employed West on long-term assignments or short-term projects for thirty years. In October 1997, West was offered a position on a project with Saudi Arabian Bechtel Co. (SABCO), which West understood would be for two years. In November, however, West was terminated for what he believed was his "age and lack of display of energy." After his return to California, West received numerous offers from Bechtel for work that suited his abilities and met his salary expectations, but he did not accept any of them and did not look for other work. Three months later, he filed a suit in a California state court against Bechtel, alleging, in part, breach of contract and seeking the salary he would have earned during two years with SABCO. Bechtel responded, in part, that, even if there had been a breach, West had failed to mitigate his damages. Is Bechtel correct? Discuss. [*West v. Bechtel Corp.*, 96 Cal.App.4th 966, 117 Cal.Rptr.2d 647 (1 Dist. 2002)]

18-5. Liquidated Damages versus Penalties. Every homeowner in the Putnam County, Indiana, subdivision of Stardust Hills must be a member of the Stardust Hills Owners Association, Inc., and must pay annual dues of $200 for the maintenance of common areas and other community services. Under the association's rules, dues paid more than ten days late "shall bear a delinquent fee at a rate of $2.00 per day." Phyllis Gaddis owned a Stardust Hills lot on which she failed to pay the dues. Late fees began to accrue. Nearly two months later, the association filed a suit in an Indiana state court to collect the unpaid dues and the late fees. Gaddis argued in response that the delinquent fee was an unenforceable penalty. What questions should be considered in determining the status of this fee? Should the association's rule regarding assessment of the fee be enforced? Explain. [*Gaddis v. Stardust Hills Owners Association, Inc.*, 804 N.E.2d 231 (Ind.App. 2004)]

18-6. CASE PROBLEM WITH SAMPLE ANSWER
Tyna Ek met Russell Peterson in Seattle, Washington. Peterson persuaded Ek to buy a boat that he had once owned, the *O'Hana Kai*, which was in Juneau, Alaska. Ek paid $43,000 for the boat, and in January 2000, the parties entered into a contract. In the contract, Peterson agreed to make the vessel seaworthy so that within one month it could be transported to Seattle, where he would pay its moorage costs. He would also renovate the boat at his own expense in return for a portion of the profit on its resale in 2001. At the time of the resale, Ek would recover her costs, after which she would reimburse Peterson for his expenses. Ek loaned Peterson her cell phone so that they could communicate while he prepared the vessel for the trip to Seattle. In March, Peterson, who was still in Alaska, borrowed $4,000 from Ek. Two months later, Ek began to receive unanticipated, unauthorized bills for vessel parts and moorage, the use of her phone, and charges on her credit card. She went to Juneau to take possession of the boat. Peterson moved it to Petersburg, Alaska, where he registered it under a false name, and then to Taku Harbor, where the police seized it. Ek filed a suit in an Alaska state court against Peterson, alleging breach of contract and seeking damages. If the court finds in Ek's favor, what should her damages include? Discuss. [*Peterson v. Ek*, 93 P.3d 458 (Alaska 2004)]

- To view a sample answer for Problem 18–6, go to this book's Web site at www.cengage. com/blaw/jentz, select "Chapter 18," and click on "Case Problem with Sample Answer."

18-7. Waiver of Breach. In May 1998, RDP Royal Palm Hotel, L.P., contracted with Clark Construction Group, Inc., to build the Royal Palms Crowne Plaza Resort in Miami Beach, Florida. The deadline for "substantial completion" was February 28, 2000, but RDP could ask for changes, and the date would be adjusted accordingly. During construction, Clark faced many setbacks, including a buried seawall, contaminated soil, the unforeseen deterioration of the existing hotel, and RDP's issue of hundreds of change orders. Clark requested extensions of the deadline, and RDP agreed, but the parties never specified a date. After the original deadline passed, RDP continued to issue change orders, Clark continued to perform, and RDP accepted the work. In March 2002, when the resort was substantially complete, RDP stopped paying Clark. Clark stopped working. RDP hired another contractor to finish the resort, which opened in May. RDP filed a suit in a federal district court against Clark, alleging, among other things, breach of contract for the two-year delay in the resort's completion. In whose favor should the court rule, and why? Discuss. [*RDP Royal Palm Hotel, L.P. v. Clark Construction Group, Inc.,* __ F.3d __ (11th Cir. 2006)]

18–8. Remedies. On July 7, 2000, Frances Morelli agreed to sell to Judith Bucklin a house at 126 Lakedell Drive in Warwick, Rhode Island, for $77,000. Bucklin made a deposit on the house. The closing at which the parties would exchange the deed for the price was scheduled for September 1. The agreement did not state that "time is of the essence," but it did provide, in "Paragraph 10," that "[i]f Seller is unable to [convey good, clear, insurable, and marketable title], Buyer shall have the option to: (a) accept such title as Seller is able to convey without abatement or reduction of the Purchase Price, or (b) cancel this Agreement and receive a return of all Deposits." An examination of the public records revealed that the house did not have marketable title. Wishing to be flexible, Bucklin offered Morelli time to resolve the problem, and the closing did not occur as scheduled. Morelli decided "the deal is over" and offered to return the deposit. Bucklin refused and, in mid-October, decided to exercise her option under Paragraph 10(a). She notified Morelli, who did not respond. Bucklin filed a suit in a Rhode Island state court against Morelli. In whose favor should the court rule? Should damages be awarded? If not, what is the appropriate remedy? Why? [*Bucklin v. Morelli,* 912 A.2d 931 (R.I. 2007)]

18–9. A QUESTION OF ETHICS

In 2004, Tamara Cohen, a real estate broker, began showing property in Manhattan to Steven Galistinos, who represented comedian Jerry Seinfeld and his wife, Jessica. According to Cohen, she told Galistinos that her commission would be 5 or 6 percent, and he agreed. According to Galistinos, there was no such agreement. Cohen spoke with Maximillan Sanchez, another broker, about a townhouse owned by Ray and Harriet Mayeri. According to Cohen, Sanchez said that the commission would be 6 percent, which they agreed to split equally. Sanchez later acknowledged that they agreed to split the fee, but claimed that they did not discuss a specific amount. On a Friday in February 2005, Cohen showed the townhouse to Jessica. According to Cohen, she told Jessica that the commission would be 6 percent, with the Seinfelds paying half, and Jessica agreed. According to Jessica, there was no such conversa-

tion. Later that day, Galistinos asked Cohen to arrange for the Seinfelds to see the premises again. Cohen told Galistinos that her religious beliefs prevented her from showing property on Friday evenings or Saturdays before sundown. She suggested the following Monday or Tuesday, but Galistinos said that Jerry would not be available and asked her to contact Carolyn Liebling, Jerry's business manager. Cohen left Liebling a message. Over the weekend, the Seinfelds toured the building on their own and agreed to buy the property for $3.95 million. Despite repeated attempts, they were unable to contact Cohen. [Cohen v. Seinfeld, 15 Misc.3d 1118(A), 839 N.Y.S.2d 432 (Sup. 2007)]

(a) The contract between the Seinfelds and the Mayeris stated that the sellers would pay Sanchez's fee and the "buyers will pay buyer's real estate broker's fees." The Mayeris paid Sanchez $118,500, which is 3 percent of $3.95 million. The Seinfelds refused to pay Cohen. She filed a suit in a New York state court against them, asserting, among other things, breach of contract. Should the court order the Seinfelds to pay Cohen? If so, is she entitled to a full commission even though she was not available to show the townhouse when the Seinfelds wanted to see it? Explain.

(b) What obligation do parties involved in business deals owe to each other with respect to their religious beliefs? How might the situation in this case have been avoided?

18–10. VIDEO QUESTION

Go to this text's Web site at **www.cengage.com/blaw/jentz** and select "Chapter 18." Click on "Video Questions" and view the video titled *Midnight Run.* Then answer the following questions.

(a) In the video, Eddie (Joe Pantoliano) and Jack (Robert De Niro) negotiate a contract for Jack to find the Duke, a mob accountant who embezzled funds, and bring him back for trial. Assume that the contract is valid. If Jack breaches the contract by failing to bring in the Duke, what kinds of remedies, if any, can Eddie seek? Explain your answer.

(b) Would the equitable remedy of specific performance be available to either Jack or Eddie in the event of a breach? Why or why not?

(c) Now assume that the contract between Eddie and Jack is unenforceable. Nevertheless, Jack performs his side of the bargain (brings in the Duke). Does Jack have any legal recourse in this situation? Why or why not?

LAW ON THE WEB

For updated links to resources available on the Web, as well as a variety of other materials, visit this text's Web site at

www.cengage.com/blaw/jentz

For a summary of how contracts may be breached and other information on contract law, go to Lawyers.com's Web page at

contracts.lawyers.com

The following sites offer information on contract law, including breach of contract and remedies:

www.nolo.com

www.law.cornell.edu/wex/index.php/Contracts

Legal Research Exercises on the Web

Go to **www.cengage.com/blaw/jentz**, the Web site that accompanies this text. Select "Chapter 18" and click on "Internet Exercises." There you will find the following Internet research exercises that you can perform to learn more about the topics covered in this chapter.

Internet Exercise 18–1: Legal Perspective
Contract Damages and Contract Theory

Internet Exercise 18–2: Management Perspective
The Duty to Mitigate

Contracts: Breach of Contract and Remedies

Case No. 93

DAMAGES FOR BREACH OF CONTRACT/CONSEQUENTIAL DAMAGES

Harbor Hill Lithographing Corporation v. Dittler Brothers, Inc.

Supreme Court, Nassau County

348 N.Y.S.2d 920 (1973), 76 Misc. 2d 145

FACTS: Plaintiff Harbor Hill Lithographing Corporation (Harbor Hill) was in the business of arranging for the development of printed materials for its clients. It entered a contract with client Barnell Loft, Inc. (Barnell) to publish an advertising brochure for Barnell. Harbor Hill in turn entered a written contract with defendant Dittler Brothers, Inc. (Dittler), a printer, for the printing of the Barnell brochure. Dittler failed to deliver the printed brochure by the date required in Dittler's contract with Harbor Hill. As a result Harbor Hill could not deliver the brochures to Barnell on the date required by Harbor Hill's contract with Barnell. Barnell therefore refused to accept or pay for the brochures.

Harbor Hill sued Dittler for breach of contract. A jury trial was held. Dittler was found liable for breach and Harbor Hill was awarded a sum of money that did not include its lost profits on its contract with Barnell.

In this proceeding, Harbor Hill sought to recover as consequential damages the profits it would have made on its contract with Barnell had the brochure been delivered on time. Dittler denied liability claiming it did not know Harbor Hill intended to sell the brochures to Barnell and therefore could not have foreseen Harbor Hill's lost profits.

FIRST ISSUE: Where a printer contracts to print brochures for a customer and the brochures are obviously intended for a client of the customer, if the printer fails to provide the ordered brochures on time, should the printer be charged with knowledge that its customer would lose the profits it would have made from the sale of the brochure?

DECISION: Yes, Harbor Hill is entitled to collect from Dittler the profits Harbor Hill lost as a result of Dittler's breach.

REASONING: To be recoverable in a breach of contract case, consequential damages suffered by the nonbreaching party must have been foreseeable to the breaching party. Where a party sells goods to a buyer who is in the business of reselling them, intent to resell and the probability of associated profits are deemed foreseeable to the seller. Here, Harbor Hill was known to be in the business of reselling printed brochures. The brochure in issue was individualized, promoting Harbor Hill's customer. Also, Harbor Hill had informed Dittler that it was under deadline pressure to deliver the brochure to Barnell. Dittler thus had sufficient information to determine that, by breaching its printing contract with Harbor Hill, the latter would lose profits it would have made on the resale of the brochures.

ADDITIONAL FACTS: As a result of Harbor Hill's inability to deliver the brochures to Barnell on time, Barnell apparently ceased doing business with Harbor Hill. The latter's lawsuit against Dittler therefore also sought damages representing the lost profits Harbor Hill might have made in the future from other contracts with Barnell.

SECOND ISSUE: Is loss of possible future profits recoverable as damages for breach of contract?

DECISION: No, judgment for Dittler.

REASONING: The amount of future profits Harbor Hill might have made on future contracts with Barnell is too speculative a figure to support a recovery for damages for breach of contract.

* * * QUESTIONS * * *
(See back of text for answers)

1) What is the law's objective in granting a remedy for breach of contract?

2) If Dittler Brothers did not know and had no reason to know that Harbor Hill intended to sell the brochures to a customer, would Dittler Brothers have been liable for the resale profits lost by Harbor Hill?

3) Assume that Dittler Brothers notified Harbor Hill three weeks before the date the brochures were due that it could not perform by the due date (anticipatory breach). Assume also that Harbor Hill, with the three weeks' notice, could have had the brochures printed by a different company and still delivered the brochures to its customer by the deadline. If Harbor Hill failed to utilize the services of the second printer, could it nonetheless recover lost resale profits from Dittler?

Case No. 94

DAMAGES FOR BREACH OF CONTRACT

<u>Neri v. Retail Marine Corporation</u>

Court of Appeals

30 N.Y.2d 393, 334 N.Y.S.2d 165 (1972)

FACTS: Plaintiff Anthony Neri (Neri) contracted to purchase from defendant Retail Marine Corporation (Marine) a boat for $12,587.40. Neri gave Marine $4,250.00 as a deposit. Six days later Neri's attorney sent Marine a letter rescinding the contract because Neri discovered he had to undergo surgery and hospitalization. Meanwhile, Marine had ordered and received from the manufacturer the boat ordered by Neri. Four months after Neri cancelled the contract, Marine was able to sell the boat to another buyer for the same price Neri had contracted to pay.

Neri seeks in this action to recover his deposit. Marine asserted a counterclaim, seeking the profit it would have made on the sale to Neri.

At the trial Marine proved its profit on the sale to Neri would have been $2,579.00 and that it spent $674.00 during the four months between Neri's cancellation and the second sale for storage, insurance, upkeep, and finance charges on the boat.

FIRST ISSUE: Is a seller, who has an unlimited supply of standard-priced goods, entitled to collect as damages, from a customer who breaches a contract to purchase one of the goods, the profit the seller would have made on the cancelled sale?

DECISION: Yes.

REASONING: Where a seller such as Marine has an unlimited supply of standard- priced goods and a party who contracts to buy one of the goods cancels the contract, the seller loses the profit it would have made on the sale. This is true even if a subsequent buyer purchases the unit since the seller would have been able to sell a second unit to that second buyer even if the first buyer had not cancelled.

SECOND ISSUE: Is Marine entitled to collect from Neri the $674.00 Marine spent for insurance, storage, upkeep, and interest charges?

DECISION: Yes.

REASONING: A seller's right to collect lost profits is not the only item of damages a seller can collect from a breaching buyer. A seller is also entitled to collect incidental damages. The money spent by Marine for insurance, storage, upkeep, and interest charges constitutes incidental damage incurred solely because of Neri's breach. Neri was entitled to the return of $997.00 of his $4,250.00 deposit. Marine was entitled to retain its lost profits of $2,579.00 plus the expense of $674.00.

* * * QUESTIONS * * *
(See back of text for answers)

1) Assume the company that manufactured the boat in this case went out of business and discontinued manufacturing boats. As a result Marine could not have ordered any additional boats of the type it ordered for Neri. How would Marine's damages be calculated in this situation?

2) Assume in the above example Marine found the second buyer the same day Neri cancelled the contract. As a result Marine expended no money for insurance, storage, upkeep and interest for the boat. What damages, if any, would Marine be entitled to recover?

Case No. 95

CONTRACTS/DAMAGES FOR BREACH

North American Foreign Trading Corp. v. Direct Mail Specialist a/k/a DMS, Inc.

United States District Court, Southern District of New York (1988)

697 F. Supp 163

FACTS: Plaintiff North American Foreign Trading Corp. (North American) contracted to sell to defendant Direct Mail Specialist a/k/a DMS, Inc. (DMS) 164,968 blackjack games at $12.00 per game in monthly installments of 15,000 games. After five months DMS requested North American to delay delivery to enable DMS to absorb its inventory. North American refused and DMS then canceled the contract. North American attempted to resell the goods and was eventually able to do so. In this lawsuit it seeks from DMS, in addition to other damages, interest on the unpaid contract price from the time of the breach until the resale.

ISSUE: Where a buyer breaches a contract by refusing to accept delivery, is the seller entitled to collect from the buyer interest on the purchase price for the period between the breach and resale?

DECISION: Yes.

REASONING: Damages for breach of contract are designed to put the nonbreaching party in the same position it would have been in had there been no breach. Money has a time value. Where buyer's breach causes seller to lose the use of the money for a period of time, seller suffers a loss equal to the money's time value. To put the seller in the position it would have been in had the buyer fully performed, an award of interest is necessary.

* * * QUESTION * * *
(See back of text for answers)

1) Which of the following expenses would an aggrieved seller be entitled to collect as damages from a breaching buyer?

   a) The cost to store the goods until the seller was able to resell them.

   b) The full contract price, regardless of resale.

   c) Where the resale is done by auction, the cost to advertise the auction and the auctioneer's fee.

Case No. 96

BREACH OF CONTRACT/DISCLAIMERS/DAMAGES

<u>Griffin-Ameil v. Frank Terris Orchestras</u>

City Court, City of Yonkers

178 Misc.2d 71, 677 N.Y.S.2d 908 (1998)

FACTS: Nearly a year in advance of their wedding Bridget Griffin-Amiel (Amiel) and Michael Amiel began planning the event. Frank Terris Orchestras (Terris) is in the business of providing musicians and singers for many types of functions including weddings. Through its advertising Terris encourages prospective couples to attend its "wedding showcase" featuring several different orchestras and singers from which each couple can choose. Michael and Bridget attended several of the Terris Showcases in an effort to find the perfect wedding singer and orchestra. Of particular importance to them was the singer. After observing several showcases the couple fell in love with the melodious voice of Paul Rich. Eventually Amiel and Terris contracted for a five-piece orchestra and singers Paul Rich and Gloria Carpenter for $3275.00. Amiel paid a deposit of $1275.00.

Amiel's fondness and specific desire for singer Paul Rich was evident from discussions that took place at the time of booking. The contract contained the following disclaimer, "Terris agrees to provide the musical services set forth above but shall be free without liability to cease services (due) to act(s) of God or circumstances beyond its control".

On the day of the wedding, the orchestra showed up with singers Gloria Carpenter and Tony Avena, a substitute for Paul Rich who the couple had never heard sing. While adequate, Tony Avena was not the equal of Rich. Amiel demanded a 50% refund, $1637.50. Terris agreed to refund $1000 but refused any additional amount based on the disclaimer in the contract. Amiel then began this lawsuit seeking the return of the full contract price minus the $1000 refund.

FIRST ISSUE: Is the contract disclaimer in this case valid?

DECISION: No, it is unconscionable.

REASONING: The contract disclaimer, in the words of the court, was "null and void as striking at the heart of the bargain contracted for". Amiel contracted for Paul Rich to perform at her wedding and this disclaimer would frustrate that term. Enforcing this disclaimer would encourage Terris to promise its most popular singer to all its clients and then send a lesser substitute and risk no punishment.

SECOND ISSUE: Where two parties enter a personal service contract for an orchestra and a specific singer, is the provider of that service liable for breach of contract if it provides a substitute singer?

DECISION: Yes

REASONING: Terris agreed to provide Amiel with an orchestra and a specified pair of singers, Paul Rich and Gloria Carpenter. Amiel painstakingly selected Paul Rich, Terris guaranteed that Rich would be present, and Amiel emphasized how important Paul Rich would be to set the right mood for her special event. As a result, Terris breached its contract with Amiel.

The court awarded Amiel damages of one half of the purchase price, $1637.50. Additionally, Amiel was awarded $500 for "disappointment, humiliation and annoyance suffered". In addition the court awarded treble damages under a New York State statute prohibiting deceptive practices and then reduced the treble damages to $1000, the maximum allowable under the statute.

Case No. 97

ARBITRATION CLAUSE RENDERING ARBITRATION FINAL

Fotiadis v. Fiveson

District Court, Nassau County

181 Misc.2d 820, 695 N.Y.S.2d 490

FACTS: Gina Fotiadis (Fotiadis) received a gift for membership in On Line Fitness Club (Fitness) from a friend Sandy Fiveson (Fiveson). Fiveson paid $500 to Fitness for the membership. Apparently the relationship between Fotiadis and Fiveson soured. For reasons not specified in this suit, Fotiadis is suing Fiveson for $25 and Fitness to recover the $500 membership fee.

Previous to this suit, Fotiadis had sued Fitness on the television program "Peoples Court". In doing so the parties agreed to waive their rights to sue in any court based on the same facts and claims. This waiver was contained in an agreement to arbitrate required by the television show. In the case, Judge Sheindlin (Judge Judy's husband) dismissed Fotiadis' claim and paid both parties a $250 fee for their televised appearance. Fiveson was not a party to the televised arbitration.

ISSUE: When parties agree to arbitrate their claim on a television show and waive their right to sue in any court based on the same facts, can the party nonetheless sue in court based on the same set of claims?

DECISION: No

REASONING: When parties agree to arbitrate their claims in a judicial or non-judicial setting, they customarily agree to accept the arbitrator's decision as final and waive their rights to sue in court on the same facts or claims. In this case Fotiadis waved her right to sue by agreeing to have the claim arbitrated on the TV show The Peoples Court.

Additionally, the court ruled that Fiveson, who was not a party to the televised arbitration, was entitled to a full refund of $500 from Fitness as Fotiadis had cancelled her membership with Fitness and Fiveson had not waived her rights to sue.

NOTE: The court took judicial notice of the number of claims filed by Fotiadis and her mother between 1990 and 1999. Fotiadis filed nineteen claims and her mother eight. The court held that Fotiadis had abused judicial process and small claims procedures and barred her from the use small claims courts without first obtaining the permission of a judge.

Case No. 98

DAMAGES FOR BREACH OF CONSTRUCTION CONTRACT

American Standard, Inc. vs. Schectman

Appellate Division, Fourth Department

80 A.D.2d 318; 439 N.Y.S.2d 529 (1981)

FACTS: Plaintiff American Standard, Inc. (Standard) operated a pig iron manufacturing plant on a 26-acre parcel of land in Tonawanda, New York on the Niagara River. Standard decided to discontinue manufacturing, demolish the plant, return the land to its natural state, and sell it as a vacant lot. Standard entered a contract with defendant Harold Schectman (Schectman), a demolition and excavation contractor. Standard agreed to transfer to Schectman ownership of various buildings, other structures, and numerous pieces of equipment that had been used as part of the manufacturing plant. In return, Schectman was to pay Standard $275,000.00, remove the equipment, demolish the structures, including their underground foundations, and grade the property.

Schectman removed the equipment and buildings but failed to remove the subsurface structure foundations. Standard sued for breach of contract. At the trial, the jury decided that Schectman had not substantially performed and awarded Standard $90,000.00, the cost to complete the work left unfinished by Schectman. Schectman appealed, claiming the measure of damages should be the decrease in the value of the property caused by his failure to perform, which he claimed was only $3,000.00.

ISSUE: What is the proper measure of damages in this case: (a) the cost to complete the work left undone by the defendant; or (b) the decrease in value of the land resulting from defendant's failure to perform?

DECISION: The cost to complete the work; judgment for Standard.

REASONING: In the usual case where a contractor has failed to perform in part or in whole, the appropriate measure of damages is the reasonable cost to complete the unfinished work. Where the contractor has substantially performed in good faith but defects exist and the correction of the defects would result in economic waste, the measure of damages is calculated differently. In this case, the court determined Schectman failed to perform a substantial part of what he promised to do. Therefore, the measure of damages is the cost to complete the job.

* * * QUESTIONS * * *
(See back of text for answers)

1) What is substantial performance?

2) What is the usual measure of damages in a construction contract where the construction company fails to fully perform?

Case No. 99

SUBSTANTIAL PERFORMANCE

<u>**Reale v. Linder**</u>

District Court, Nassau County

135 Misc.2d 317, 514 N.Y.S.2d 1004 (1987)

FACTS: Plaintiff Orlando Reale (Reale) entered into a contract with defendant Thomas Linder (Linder) for the construction of a 12 x 12 addition to Linder's home and for other construction work. The contract price was $22,500.

Reale finished the work but Linder refused to pay the balance owed of $5855.00 and Reale sued. Linder contended that the work was defective and in violation of state and local building codes, and countersued for damages. Reale, as part of his claim for the unpaid balance due and in defense of the counterclaim, asserted that he had substantially performed the contract.

At trial Linder proved: 1) the crawl space beneath the addition was only 11 to 14 inches high, 4 to 7 inches less than required by law; 2) that no "frame inspection" was made because the construction was "closed up" (finished) before a building department representative could inspect it, thereby preventing determination of whether the frame, rafters, and headers complied with approved building plans and New York State fire and building codes; and 3) the cathedral ceiling on the addition lacked proper ventilation. Reale admitted to these and other problems. He also admitted to disguising certain problems to prevent their discovery, and to making false representations in an effort to secure a certificate of occupancy, and to making structural changes from town-approved plans without town approval. The cost to repair the problems so that the construction would satisfy building codes would be $15,000.00.

ISSUE: Where a contractor completes the work required by the contract but deviates from the specifications in such a way that the work does not comply with state and local building codes, has the contractor substantially performed?

DECISION: No, judgment for Linder; Reale is not entitled to the unpaid balance; Linder is entitled to $15,000.00.

REASONING: For a performance of a contract to qualify as substantial, it cannot deviate significantly from the performance promised and the deviation must not be willful or intentional. By definition, substantial performance is less than full performance, but the deviation from full performance is not substantial. When a party to a contract substantially performs, the other party is entitled to damages for the incomplete performance and must perform its own contractual obligation. If a party's performance is less than substantial, the breach is considered material. The nonbreaching party in such a case is entitled to damages and is excused from its own performance.

In this case, the court determined that Reale's performance was not substantial because the work failed to meet building code requirements. His claim for $5855.00 was thus dismissed. Linder is entitled to damages of $15,000.00, the cost to correct Reale's performance.

* * * QUESTION * * *
(See back of text for answer)

1)   What is the objective of the doctrine of substantial performance?

Case No. 100

SUBSTANTIAL PERFORMANCE

<u>**Windjammer Homes, Inc. v. Lieberman**</u>

Appellate Division, Second Department

278 AD2d 411, 711 NYS2d 362

FACTS: In December 1994, Windjammer Homes Inc. (Windjammer) entered into a contract with Bruce Lieberman (Lieberman), to build a home in the Town of Southampton. Of the $157,670.80 alleged contract price, $56,900.00 remained unpaid by Lieberman based on the claim that Windjammer had not substantially performed the contract. Windjammer sued Lieberman for failure to pay. Evidence showed that Windjammer failed to complete between 14% and 43% of the contract and that the overall quality and workmanship was below industry standards.

ISSUE: Where a contractor completes work that is well below industry standards and fails to complete between approximately 14% and 43%* of the contract, has the contractor substantially performed?

DECISION: No

REASONING: When parties to a contract perform as agreed, no question arises as to whether the contract has been performed.

An incomplete performance that nonetheless provides the non-breaching party with the essential benefits of the agreement constitutes substantial performance. When a party substantially performs it may sue to have the terms of the contract enforced. In such circumstances, the performing party still remains liable for the damages suffered by the non-breaching party.

When a party has not substantially performed it has materially breached the contract and the non-breaching party is excused from performance. However, the non-breaching party may remain liable, under the theory of quasi contract, for the reasonable value of services performed less the cost to complete the job.

In this case the appellate court held that Windjammer did not substantially perform given that the overall workmanship was below industry standards and the work was between 14% and 43% incomplete. Because Windjammer did not substantially perform, it could not recover the balance of the contract price.

*While these numbers cover a wide range, the court record did not explain how they were determined. The appellate court accepted them as accurate.

Case No. 101

DAMAGES FOR SUBSTANTIAL PERFORMANCE IN A CONSTRUCTION CONTRACT/ECONOMIC WASTE

Jacob & Youngs, Inc. v. Kent

Court of Appeals

230 N.Y. 239, 129 N.E. 889 (1921)

FACTS: Plaintiff Jacob & Youngs, Inc. (Jacob) contracted to build a home for defendant George E. Kent (Kent) for approximately $77,000.00. One of the plumbing specifications in the contract required that the pipe be of the grade known as "standard pipe of Reading manufacture." In March 1915, Kent learned that some of the pipe was not Reading but instead was made by other manufacturers. Kent demanded that the pipe be replaced to conform to contract specifications. Some of the pipe was exposed and accessible in the basement but most of it was encased in the walls and thus not reasonably accessible. Replacement of the pipe would therefore have required demolition of various parts of the structure at considerable expense.

Jacob did not replace the pipe and in this action sought to recover the unpaid balance of the contract price, $3,483.46. Jacob was able to demonstrate that its use of the wrong pipe was neither willful nor fraudulent but rather was the result of an oversight. Additionally Jacob proved that no difference existed in quality, appearance, and market value between the Reading brand specified in the contract and the brands that were installed.

ISSUE: Where a contractor completes the building of a home but deviates from the contract requirements, albeit in an insignificant way, and the cost to correct the work so that it conforms with the contract would be substantial, is the measure of damages the cost to correct the work so that it conforms with the contract requirements or the difference in value?

DECISION: The difference in value; judgment for Jacob.

REASONING: When a contractor deviates from the required performance yet substantially performs, the contractor is entitled to the contract price less damages for the improper performance. The usual measure of damages is the cost of completion. If, however, the cost of completion would result in economic waste, that is, the benefit gained would be slight compared to the cost, the proper measure of damages is the difference in value of the building as constructed and the value if the building had been built consistent with contract specifications. In this case Jacob had substantially performed. To require Jacob to demolish substantial parts of the structure in order to replace pipe with new pipe of the same general quality would far exceed the value, if any, added to the structure and thus would constitute economic waste.

The amount of damages in this case measured by the difference in value "would be either nominal or nothing."

* * * QUESTION * * *
(See back of text for answer)

1)   Why was the cost of completion not the appropriate measure of damages in this case?

Case No. 102

LIQUIDATED DAMAGES/UNCONSCIONABILITY

<u>Spring Valley Garden Associates v. Earle</u>

County Court, Rockland County

112 Misc.2d 786, 447 N.Y.S.2d 629 (1982)

FACTS: Plaintiff Spring Valley Garden Associates (Spring Valley) is the owner of property that is leased to tenants for residential purposes. Defendant Felmin Earle (Earle) was a tenant in an apartment owned by Spring Valley.

In November 198 1, Earle paid her rent with a check that bounced. By the time Spring Valley deposited the check and learned that it would not clear, more than ten days from the rent due date had passed. A provision in the lease required Earle to pay a service fee of $50.00 for rent not paid within ten days of the due date. Spring Valley refused to accept Earle's second payment for November rent unless it included the $50.00 late fee. Earle refused to pay the late fee. Therefore, Spring Valley brought this action to evict Earle.

ISSUE: Is a clause in a lease enforceable where the clause requires a late fee of $50.00 when payment of the monthly rent of $405 is made more than ten days late?

DECISION: No, judgment for Earle.

REASONING: A clause in a contract that identifies an amount of money to be paid in the event of a breach is called a liquidated damage clause. Where a liquidated damage clause in a contract requires payment by the breaching party of a sum of money disproportionate to the loss suffered by the nonbreaching party, the clause will be unenforceable. The amount of the late fee in this case was grossly disproportionate to any loss suffered by the landlord as a result of Earle's late payment. The fee was therefore a penalty and not liquidated damage and as such was unenforceable.

Another basis to invalidate the clause was unconscionability. A lease is a contract for a necessity of life (living space). The clause resulted in an excessive economic benefit for the landlord, it was drafted by the landlord, and apparently the landlord was not willing to negotiate the terms of the lease it had prepared. Thus the clause is unconscionable and, as such, invalid.

* * * QUESTIONS * * *
(See back of text for answers)

1) Under what circumstances is a liquidated damage clause enforceable?

2) Why might parties choose to include a liquidated damage clause in their contract?

Case No. 103

LIQUIDATED DAMAGE CLAUSE/A SUM CERTAIN

The Stock Shop, Inc. v. Bozell and Jacobs, Inc.

Supreme Court, New York County

NYLJ, November 27,1984, p. 6, col. 1m

FACTS: In November and December 1979, plaintiff The Stock Shop, Inc. (Stock Shop) submitted to defendant Bozell and Jacobs, Inc. (Bozell) 697 photographs for possible use by Bozell in a slide show it was preparing for a client. Bozell agreed to rent 40 photographs and return the others to the Stock Shop. Of the 40 that were rented, Bozell never returned 39. The Stock Shop sued Bozell for $1,500.00 for each lost photograph, based on a clause in the rental agreement that read: "The monetary damage for loss or damage of an original color . . . photograph shall be determined by the value of each photograph. Recipient agrees, however, that the reasonable minimum value of such . . . damaged photographs . . . shall be no less than fifteen hundred ($1,500.00) dollars." The Stock Shop claimed this clause was a valid liquidated damage clause and sought in this action a judgment of $1,500.00 for each of the 39 unreturned photographs. Defendant claimed $1,500.00 per photograph exceeded the value of the photographs and the clause was thus a penalty and unenforceable.

ISSUE: Is a clause in a contract stating the amount of damages in case of breach will be determined on a case-by-case basis but identifying a minimum amount of money the breaching party will be required to pay in any event an enforceable liquidated damage clause?

DECISION: No.

REASONING: Parties to a contract may set damages in advance of a breach by including in their contract a liquidated damage clause. Such a clause is enforceable provided the amount identified as damages: (a) is reasonable in relation to the anticipated or actual harm caused by the breach; and (b) is a sum certain.

Concerning the reasonableness of the amount, it is possible the photographs in issue may never have generated any revenue, may be neither unique nor novel, may be easily duplicated by the photographer, and may vary in nature and quality. Thus the $1,500.00 amount may exceed the actual loss to the photographer by the loss of the photograph. Concerning the need for a sum certain as liquidated damages, the purpose of a liquidated damage clause is to settle the amount of damages in advance of a breach. Here, the clause failed to state a sum certain. The $1,500.00 figure per photo is a minimum amount only; the clause provides the Stock Shop with the opportunity to prove a greater value for the lost photos. "The clause would allow the plaintiff to have his cake and eat it too."

* * * QUESTION * * *
(See back of text for answer)

1) Assume a town contracted with a construction company for the repair of a toll bridge. The contract required that the work be completed by September 1. It further stated that, in the event the construction company did not complete the work by that date, it would pay the town $500.00 for each day beyond September 1 that the work was not completed. During the course of the repair work the bridge was closed to traffic. Revenues from the bridge toll customarily yielded between $400.00 and $900.00 a day. Would the liquidated damage clause be enforceable?

CHAPTER 17

E-Contracts and E-Signatures

The basic principles of contract law that were covered in previous chapters evolved over an extended period of time. Certainly, they were formed long before cyberspace and electronic contracting became realities. Therefore, new legal theories, new adaptations of existing laws, and new laws are needed to govern **e-contracts,** or contracts entered into electronically. To date, however, most courts have adapted traditional contract law

principles and, when applicable, provisions of the Uniform Commercial Code (UCC) to cases involving e-contract disputes. Although an e-contract has the same basic requirements to be valid—agreement, consideration, capacity, and legality—certain aspects of forming e-contracts are unique, such as the method by which the offer and acceptance are communicated.

In the first part of this chapter, we look at how traditional laws

are being applied to contracts formed online. We then examine some new laws that have been enacted to apply in situations that are not readily encompassed by the traditional laws governing contracts. For example, traditional laws governing signature and writing requirements are not easily adapted to contracts formed in the online environment. Thus, new laws have been created to address these issues.

Online Contract Formation

Today, numerous contracts are being formed online. Although these contracts are being generated through a new medium, the age-old problems attending contract formation still exist. Disputes concerning contracts formed online continue to center around contract terms and whether the parties voluntarily assented to those terms.

Note that online contracts may be formed not only for the sale of goods and services but also for the purpose of *licensing*. The "sale" of software generally involves a license, or a right to use the software, rather than the passage of title (ownership rights) from the seller to the buyer. For example, Galynn wants to obtain software that will allow her to work on spreadsheets on her BlackBerry. She goes online and purchases GridMagic. During the transaction, she has to click on several on-screen "I agree" boxes to indicate that she understands that she is purchasing only the right to use the software and will not obtain any own-

ership rights. After she agrees to these terms (the licensing agreement), she can download the software to her BlackBerry. Although in this chapter we typically refer to the offeror and offeree as a *seller* and a *buyer,* in many transactions these parties would be more accurately described as a *licensor* and a *licensee.*

Online Offers

Sellers doing business via the Internet can protect themselves against contract disputes and legal liability by creating offers that clearly spell out the terms that will govern their transactions if the offers are accepted. Significant terms should be conspicuous and easy to view.

Displaying the Offer The seller's Web site should include a hypertext link to a page containing the full contract so that potential buyers are made aware of the terms to which they are assenting. The contract generally must be displayed online in a readable format such as a twelve-point typeface. For example, Netquip sells a variety of heavy equipment, such as trucks and trailers, online at its Web site. Netquip must include its full pricing schedule on the Web site with explanations of all complex provisions. In addition, the terms of the sale (such as any warranties and Netquip's refund policy) must be fully disclosed.

Is an online contract enforceable if the offeror requires an offeree to scroll down or print the contract to read its terms, which are otherwise readily accessible and clear? That was the question in the following case.

C A S E **17.1** Feldman v. Google, Inc.
United States District Court, Eastern District of Pennsylvania, 2007. 513 F.Supp.2d 229.

● **Company Profile** In the mid-1990s, Larry Page and Sergey Brin, Stanford University graduate students in computer science, began work on an Internet search engine called "BackRub." Renamed "Google" after the mathematical term for a 1 followed by 100 zeros, the engine was made available in 1998. In less than a year, the service was acquiring major clients, receiving achievement awards, being included on many "Top Web Site" lists, and handling millions of queries per day. By 2000, Google had become the world's largest search engine. According to Google, Inc.'s Web site at **www.google.com**, its mission is to organize the world's information and make it universally accessible and useful. The company's revenue derives from keyword-targeted advertising.

● **Background and Facts** In Google, Inc.'s AdWords program, when an Internet user searches on **www.google.com** using key words that an advertiser has identified, an ad appears. If the user clicks on it, Google charges the advertiser. Google requires an advertiser to agree to certain terms before placing an ad. These terms—set out in a preamble and seven paragraphs—are displayed online in a window with a scroll bar. A link to a printer-friendly version of the terms is at the top of the window. At the bottom of the page, viewable without scrolling, are the words, "Yes, I agree to the above terms and conditions," and a box on which an advertiser must click to proceed. Among the terms, a forum-selection clause provides that any dispute over the program is to be "adjudicated in Santa Clara County, California." Lawrence Feldman, a lawyer, participated in the program by selecting key words, including "Vioxx," "Bextra," and "Celebrex," to trigger a showing of his ad to potential clients. In a subsequent suit between Feldman and Google in a federal district court in Pennsylvania, Feldman claimed that at least 20 percent of the clicks for which he was charged $100,000 between January 2003 and January 2006 were fraudulent.[a] Feldman filed a motion for summary judgment. Google asked the court to transfer the case to a court in Santa Clara County, California.

● **Decision and Rationale** The court denied Feldman's motion for summary judgment and granted Google's motion to transfer the case. The court held that "the requirements of an express contract for reasonable notice of terms and mutual assent are satisfied" in this situation. Feldman and Google were bound to the terms. The court pointed out that the contract at issue was a click-wrap agreement (or *click-on agreement*, to be discussed shortly in this chapter) that appeared on an Internet Web page. "Even though they are electronic, click-wrap agreements are considered to be writings because they are printable and storable. * * * Absent a showing of fraud, failure to read an enforceable click-wrap agreement, as with any binding contract, will not excuse compliance with its terms." By clicking "Yes," Feldman agreed to all of the terms. Without clicking the "Yes" button, Feldman could not have engaged in an agreement with the defendant.

● **The Ethical Dimension** *With respect to click fraud, which was the heart of Feldman's claim in this case, what circumstances might suggest unethical behavior by Google?*

● **The E-Commerce Dimension** *Under what different facts might the court have held that the plaintiff did not have reasonable notice of the terms of the agreement and thus did not assent to them?*

---

a. Feldman was alleging that *click fraud* had taken place. Click fraud occurs when someone, such as a competitor or a prankster with no interest in an advertiser's goods or services, clicks repeatedly on an ad, driving up the ad's cost to the advertiser without generating a sale. For more on click fraud, see the *Insight into Ethics* feature on pages 270 and 271.

Provisions to Include An important rule to keep in mind is that the offeror controls the offer and thus the resulting contract. Therefore, the seller should anticipate the terms that he or she wants to include in a contract and provide for them in the offer. At a minimum, an online offer should include the following provisions:

1. A clause that clearly indicates what constitutes the buyer's agreement to the terms of the offer, such as a box containing the words "I accept" that the buyer can click on to indicate acceptance. (Mechanisms for accepting online offers are discussed in detail later in the chapter.)
2. A provision specifying how payment for the goods and of any applicable taxes must be made.
3. A statement of the seller's refund and return policies.
4. Disclaimers of liability for certain uses of the goods. For example, an online seller of business forms may add a disclaimer that the seller does not accept responsibility for the buyer's reliance on the forms rather than on an attorney's advice.
5. A provision specifying the remedies available to the buyer if the goods are found to be defective or if the contract is otherwise breached. Any limitation of remedies should be clearly spelled out.
6. A statement indicating how the seller will use the information gathered about the buyer.
7. Provisions relating to dispute settlement, such as an arbitration clause or a *forum-selection clause* (discussed next).

Dispute-Settlement Provisions Online offers frequently include provisions relating to dispute settlement. An arbitration clause might be included, indicating that any dispute arising under the contract will be arbitrated in a specified forum. Many online contracts also contain a **forum-selection clause,** which indicates the forum, or place (such as the court or jurisdiction), for the resolution of any dispute arising under the contract. These clauses can help online sellers avoid having to appear in court in many distant jurisdictions when customers are dissatisfied with their purchases.

Suppose that a California buyer purchases defective goods sold online by a company located in New York. Unable to obtain a refund or adequate replacement goods from the seller, the California buyer files a suit against the seller in a California state court. If the New York seller meets the "minimum-contacts" requirement (discussed in Chapter 2) for the California court to exercise jurisdiction over the dispute, the New York seller will need to travel to California—or at least hire an attorney in California—to defend against the lawsuit. Forum-selection clauses in online contracts offer a way for sellers to avoid this problem. Forum-selection clauses are also routinely included in contracts for the international sale of goods (see Chapter 20).

Online Acceptances

The *Restatement (Second) of Contracts*—a compilation of common law contract principles—states that parties may agree to a contract "by written or spoken words or by other action or by failure to act."[1] Similarly, Section 2–204 of the UCC states that any contract for the sale of goods "may be made in any manner sufficient to show agreement, including conduct by both parties which recognizes the existence of such a contract."

Click-On Agreements The courts have used these provisions to conclude that a binding contract can be created by conduct, including the act of clicking on a box indicating "I accept" or "I agree" to accept an online offer. When an online buyer indicates his or her assent to be bound by the terms of the offer by clicking on some on-screen prompt, a **click-on agreement** (sometimes referred to as a *click-on license* or *click-wrap agreement*) is formed. Exhibit 17–1 on the following page shows a portion of a click-on agreement that accompanies a package of software made and marketed by Microsoft.

Generally, the law does not require that all of the parties to a contract must actually have read all of its terms for the contract to be effective. Clicking on a button or box that states "I agree" to certain terms can be enough. The terms may be contained on a Web site through which the buyer is obtaining goods or services, or they may appear on a computer screen when software is loaded from a CD-ROM or DVD or downloaded from the Internet.

In the following case, the court considered the enforceability of a click-wrap software licensing agreement that included a forum-selection clause.

---

1. *Restatement (Second) of Contracts,* Section 19.

EXHIBIT 17-1 • A Click-On Agreement

This exhibit illustrates an online offer to form a contract. To accept the offer, the user simply scrolls down the page and clicks on the "Accept" box.

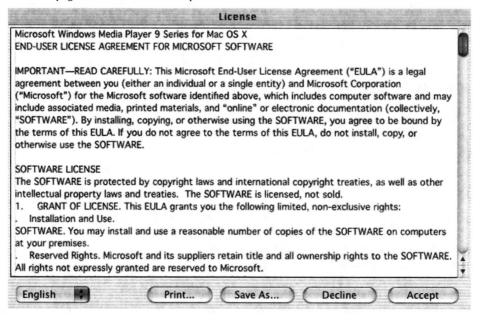

C A S E **17.2** **Mortgage Plus, Inc. v. DocMagic, Inc.**
United States District Court, District of Kansas, 2004. __ F.Supp.2d __.

● **Background and Facts** In 1997, Mortgage Plus, Inc., a mortgage lender in Kansas, asked DocMagic, Inc., a California firm, for software to prepare and manage loan documents and for document preparation services. DocMagic sent Mortgage Plus a CD-ROM containing the software, which had to be loaded onto a computer. Before it could be installed, however, a window displayed a "Software License and User Agreement" on the screen. The agreement asked, "Do you accept all terms of the preceding License Agreement? If you choose No, Setup will close." A click on a "Yes" button was needed to continue. The agreement also included a clause designating California as the venue for the resolution of any disputes. To prepare loan documents, the software asked for certain information, which it used to create a worksheet. The worksheet was e-mailed to DocMagic, which completed the documents and returned them via e-mail. Over the next six years, Mortgage Plus borrowers filed claims against the firm, alleging that the firm had made mistakes that cost the borrowers $150,000 to resolve. Mortgage Plus filed a suit in a federal district court against DocMagic, alleging that its software failed to produce documents that met certain legal requirements. The defendant filed a motion to transfer the suit to a federal court in California based on the clause in the click-on agreement.

● **Decision and Rationale** The court concluded that the software licensing agreement was a valid contract because a user had to agree to its terms before the software could be installed and used. The forum-selection clause was thus enforceable, and the court ordered the suit to be transferred to a federal district court in California. Mortgage Plus argued that the parties had negotiated and entered into a contract before DocMagic shipped the software and that the forum-selection clause was a later, improper attempt to modify this contract. The court, however, found no evidence of this purported "original contractual agreement." Mortgage Plus then argued that it was not aware of, and thus did not accept, the licensing agreement, claiming that "a clickwrap agreement consisting of a window entitled 'Software Licensing Agreement' appearing prior to installation of software cannot be construed as a legally binding contract." The court rejected this argument and explained, "The software required users to accept the terms by clicking through a series of screens before they could access and subsequently install the software." Because

CASE 17.2 CONTINUED Mortgage Plus had a choice as to whether to download the software and utilize the related services, "installation and use of the software with the attached license constituted an affirmative acceptance of the license terms."

● **What If the Facts Were Different?** *Suppose that the individual who clicked on the "Yes" button and installed the software was not authorized to do so. Would the result have been different?*

● **The E-Commerce Dimension** *If DocMagic had e-mailed the forum-selection clause to Mortgage Plus and Mortgage Plus had not responded, could the "silence" be construed as an acceptance of the clause? Explain your answer.*

Shrink-Wrap Agreements In many ways, click-on agreements are the Internet equivalents of *shrink-wrap agreements* (or *shrink-wrap licenses,* as they are sometimes called). A **shrink-wrap agreement** is an agreement whose terms are expressed inside a box in which the goods are packaged. (The term *shrink-wrap* refers to the plastic that covers the box.) Usually, the party who opens the box is told that she or he agrees to the terms by keeping whatever is in the box.

Similarly, when the purchaser opens a software package, he or she agrees to abide by the terms of the limited license agreement. Suppose that Garcia orders a new computer from a national company, which ships the computer to Garcia. Along with the computer, the box contains an agreement setting forth the terms of the sale, including what remedies are available. The document also states that Garcia's retention of the computer for longer than thirty days will be construed as an acceptance of the terms.

In most instances, a shrink-wrap agreement is not between a retailer and a buyer, but between the manufacturer of the hardware or software and the ultimate buyer-user of the product. The terms generally concern warranties, remedies, and other issues associated with the use of the product.

Shrink-Wrap Agreements—Enforceable Contract Terms. In many cases, the courts have treated the terms of shrink-wrap agreements as just as enforceable as the terms of other contracts. These courts reason that by including the terms with the product, the seller proposes a contract that the buyer can accept by using the product after having an opportunity to read the terms. Thus, a buyer's failure to object to terms contained within a shrink-wrapped software package (or an online offer) may constitute an acceptance of the terms by conduct.[2] Additionally, it seems practical from a business's point of view to enclose a full statement of the legal terms of a sale with the product rather than to

read the statement over the phone, for example, when a buyer calls in an order for the product.

Shrink-Wrap Terms That May Not Be Enforced. Nevertheless, the courts have not enforced all of the terms included in shrink-wrap agreements. One important consideration is whether the parties form their contract before or after the seller communicates the terms of the shrink-wrap agreement to the buyer. If a court finds that the buyer learned of the shrink-wrap terms *after* the parties entered into a contract, the court may conclude that those terms were proposals for additional terms and were not part of the contract unless the buyer expressly agreed to them.[3]

Businesspersons should be aware that courts have sometimes refused to enforce shrink-wrap terms on the ground that the parties did not expressly agree to the terms at the time of entering into the contract. To ensure that contract terms are enforceable, businesspersons should consider avoiding shrink-wrap terms altogether, particularly in transactions with consumers. By structuring an offer as a click-on agreement, they can prevent many potential problems that have arisen with shrink-wrap agreements.

If the purchase transaction cannot take place online, then they should consider whether it is feasible to require the buyer to register the goods online after receipt. If the goods being sold include software, for example, then a seller can require a buyer to register the purchase online. At that time, the buyer can be informed of all the contract terms and be required to click on a box to show her or his agreement to those terms. As long as a buyer has to indicate her or his assent to the terms in some fashion, the courts generally will uphold the terms.

---

2. For a leading case on this issue, see *ProCD, Inc. v. Zeidenberg,* 86 F.3d 1447 (7th Cir. 1996).

3. See, for example, *Klocek v. Gateway, Inc.,* 104 F.Supp.2d 1332 (D.Kans. 2000).

Browse-Wrap Terms Like the terms of a click-on agreement, **browse-wrap terms** can occur in a transaction conducted over the Internet. Unlike a click-on agreement, however, browse-wrap terms do not require an Internet user to assent to the terms before, say, downloading or using certain software. In other words, a person can install the software without clicking "I agree" to the terms of a license. Offerors of browse-wrap terms generally assert that the terms are binding without the user's active consent.

Critics contend that browse-wrap terms are not enforceable because they do not satisfy the basic elements of contract formation. Some argue that a user must at least be presented with the terms before indicating agreement in order to form a valid online contract. With respect to a browse-wrap term, this would require that a user navigate past it and agree to it before being able to obtain whatever is being sold.

For example, Netscape Communications Corporation provided free downloadable software called "SmartDownload" on its Web site to those who indicated, by clicking on a designated box, that they wished to obtain it. On the Web site's download page was a reference to a license agreement that was visible only by scrolling to the next screen. In other words, the user did not have to agree to the terms of the license before downloading the software. One of the terms in the license required all disputes to be submitted to arbitration in California. When a group of users filed a lawsuit against Netscape in New York, however, the court held that the arbitration clause in the browse-wrap license agreement was unenforceable because users were not required to indicate their assent to the agreement.[4]

E-Signatures

In many instances, a contract cannot be enforced unless it is signed by the party against whom enforcement is sought. In the days when many people could not write, documents were signed with an "X." Then handwritten signatures became common, followed by typed signatures, printed signatures, and, most recently, digital signatures that are transmitted electronically. Throughout the evolution of signature technology, the question of what constitutes a valid signature has arisen frequently, and with good rea-

son—without some consensus on what constitutes a valid signature, little business or legal work could be accomplished. In this section, we look at how electronic signatures, or *e-signatures,* can be created and verified on e-contracts, as well as how the parties can enter into agreements that prevent disputes concerning e-signatures.

E-Signature Technologies

Today, numerous technologies allow electronic documents to be signed. An **e-signature** has been defined as "an electronic sound, symbol, or process attached to or logically associated with a record and executed or adopted by a person with the intent to sign the record."[5] Thus, e-signatures include encrypted digital signatures, names (intended as signatures) at the ends of e-mail messages, and "clicks" on a Web page if the click includes the identification of the person. Various forms of e-signatures have been—or are now being—developed, but most e-signatures used today fall into one of two categories, *digitized handwritten signatures* and *public-key infrastructure–based digital signatures.*

Digitized Handwritten Signatures A digitized signature is a graphical image of a handwritten signature that is often created using a digital pen and pad, such as an ePad, and special software. For security reasons, the strokes of a person's signature can be measured by software to authenticate the person signing (this is referred to as *signature dynamics*).

Examples of digitized signatures are abundant. When United Parcel Service (UPS) delivers a package to your office, for example, the delivery person asks you to sign a digital pad to verify receipt. Similarly, when you pick up a prescription, some pharmacies ask you to sign an electronic pad to confirm that the pharmacist has informed you of the potential side effects of the prescribed medications.

Public-Key Infrastructure Digital Signatures In a public-key infrastructure (such as an *asymmetric cryptosystem*), two mathematically linked but different keys are generated—a private signing key and a public validation key. A digital signature is created when the signer uses the private key to create a unique mark on an electronic document. With the

---

4. *Specht v. Netscape Communications Corp.,* 306 F.3d 17 (2d Cir. 2002).

5. This definition is from the Uniform Electronic Transactions Act, which will be discussed later in this chapter.

appropriate software, the recipient of the document can use the public key to verify the identity of the signer. A **cybernotary**—a legally recognized certification authority—issues the key pair, identifies the owner of the keys, and certifies the validity of the public key. The cybernotary also serves as a repository for public keys.

State Laws Governing E-Signatures

Most states have laws governing e-signatures. The problem is that state e-signature laws are not uniform. Some states—California is a notable example—prohibit many types of documents from being signed with e-signatures, whereas other states are more permissive. Additionally, some states recognize only digital signatures as valid, while others permit other types of e-signatures.

In an attempt to create more uniformity among the states, in 1999 the National Conference of Commissioners on Uniform State Laws and the American Law Institute promulgated the Uniform Electronic Transactions Act (UETA). To date, the UETA has been adopted, at least in part, by forty-eight states. Among other things, the UETA declares that a signature may not be denied legal effect or enforceability solely because it is in electronic form.[6] (The provisions of the UETA will be discussed in more detail shortly.)

Federal Law on E-Signatures and E-Documents

In 2000, Congress enacted the Electronic Signatures in Global and National Commerce Act (E-SIGN Act),[7] which provides that no contract, record, or signature may be "denied legal effect" solely because it is in electronic form. In other words, under this law, an electronic signature is as valid as a signature on paper, and an e-document can be as enforceable as a paper one.

For an e-signature to be enforceable, the contracting parties must have agreed to use electronic signatures. For an electronic document to be valid, it must be in a form that can be retained and accurately reproduced.

The E-SIGN Act does not apply to all types of documents, however. Contracts and documents that are exempt include court papers, divorce decrees, evictions, foreclosures, health-insurance terminations, prenuptial agreements, and wills. Also, the only agreements governed by the UCC that fall under this law are those covered by Articles 2 and 2A and UCC 1–107 and 1–206. Despite these limitations, the E-SIGN Act significantly expanded the possibilities for contracting online. For a discussion of e-signature laws and e-commerce issues worldwide, see this chapter's *Insight into the Global Environment* feature on page 347.

In the case that follows, the court applied a variety of contract principles to determine the legal effect of an exchange of e-mails, plus a phone call.

---

6. Many states have also included a similar provision in their versions of the UCC.

7. 15 U.S.C. Sections 7001 *et seq.*

C A S E **17.3** **Amber Chemical, Inc. v. Reilly Industries, Inc.**
United States District Court, Eastern District of California, 2007. __ F.Supp.2d __.

● **Background and Facts** Amber Chemical, Inc., a California corporation, sells chemicals to oil companies and agricultural businesses. In the fall of each year, Amber agreed to buy a minimum quantity of potassium chloride from Reilly Industries, Inc., an Indiana firm, at a price set by Reilly. Based on this price, Amber entered into contracts with its own customers. Amber then submitted periodic purchase orders to Reilly to process. In the fall of 2003, through e-mails between Reilly employee Brett Wilhelm and Amber employee Bob Brister, Reilly agreed to sell potassium chloride throughout 2004 for $122.50 per ton as long as the quantity of Amber's purchases met or exceeded the quantity of its purchases in 2003. In a phone call from Wilhelm, Brister orally confirmed that Amber would buy as much or more as it had the previous year. In mid-March 2004, Reilly sold its potassium chloride business, and the shipments to Amber stopped. In a suit between the parties in a federal district court, Amber alleged breach of contract. Reilly filed a motion for

CASE CONTINUES

CASE 17.3 CONTINUED summary judgment, claiming that the parties did not have a written contract, as the Statute of Frauds required. Amber responded by asserting the doctrine of promissory estoppel.

● **Decision and Rationale** The court denied Reilly's motion for summary judgment. "In sum, viewing the evidence in the light most favorable to [Amber, a] contract was formed; * * * and unconscionable injury occurred." The court acknowledged that the transaction between Amber and Reilly involved a sale of goods for a price of $500 or more and thus was subject to the writing requirement of the Statute of Frauds. The court interpreted Wilhelm's e-mail as an invitation to negotiate—to "discuss this proposal" and "work out a contract"—not an offer. Similarly, Brister's e-mailed reply to "please work the contract up" did not constitute an acceptance. And no written contract was otherwise prepared. Amber contended, however, that Reilly made a promise on which Amber relied to its detriment. The court concluded that the e-mails and phone call between Brister and Wilhelm "resulted in a two-way promise, pursuant to which Reilly promised to provide Amber a firm price for 2004, in exchange for Amber's commitment * * * to purchase at least as much potassium chloride as it had in 2003." Also, Wilhelm knew that Amber would use Reilly's price to enter into contracts to supply its own customers, and "it is undisputed that Amber suffered financial damages as a result of the alleged breach, because Amber purchased potassium chloride from other sources at unfavorable prices" to supply those customers after the shipments from Reilly stopped.

● **The Legal Environment Dimension** *Under the Uniform Commercial Code, a contract for a sale of goods normally must state a quantity so that a court will have a basis for determining a remedy. Here, Amber's alleged oral contract did not include a specific quantity. On what basis, then, could the court in this case determine a remedy?*

● **The E-Commerce Dimension** *Reilly included with each shipment a standard invoice stating that it constituted the parties' entire agreement and that its "Standard Terms" could be modified only in a writing signed by the parties. This, Reilly asserted, made those terms "a complete expression of the parties' agreement." Should the court agree with Reilly and apply the* parol evidence rule *(see Chapter 15)? If so, what would be its effect? If not, why not?*

Partnering Agreements

One way that online sellers and buyers can prevent disputes over signatures, as well as disputes over the terms and conditions of their e-contracts, is to form partnering agreements. In a **partnering agreement,** a seller and a buyer who frequently do business with each other agree in advance on the terms and conditions that will apply to all transactions subsequently conducted electronically. The partnering agreement can also establish special access and identification codes to be used by the parties when transacting business electronically.

A partnering agreement reduces the likelihood that disputes will arise under the contract because the buyer and the seller have agreed in advance to the terms and conditions that will accompany each sale. Furthermore, if a dispute does arise, a court or arbitration forum will be able to refer to the partnering agreement when determining the parties' intent with respect to subsequent contracts. Of course, even with a partnering agreement, fraud remains a possi-

bility. If an unauthorized person uses a purchaser's designated access number and identification code, it may be some time before the problem is discovered.[8]

The Uniform Electronic Transactions Act

As noted earlier, the Uniform Electronic Transactions Act (UETA) was promulgated in 1999. It represented one of the first comprehensive efforts to create uniform laws pertaining to e-commerce.

The primary purpose of the UETA is to remove barriers to e-commerce by giving the same legal effect to electronic records and signatures as is given to paper documents and signatures. As mentioned earlier, the UETA broadly defines an *e-signature* as "an electronic

---

8. See, for example, *AET, Inc. v. C5 Communications, LLC,* ___ F.Supp.2d ___ (S.D.Tex. 2007).

Today, most e-commerce conducted on a worldwide basis involves buyers, sellers, and enablers from the United States. Not surprisingly, then, U.S. law is often used to resolve legal issues related to global e-commerce. The preeminence of U.S. law in this area is likely to be challenged in the future, however, as Internet use continues to expand around the globe. Already, several international organizations have created their own codes of conduct, rules, and regulations for global Internet transactions. We examine a selection of them here.

A United Nations Convention

An important step toward creating international rules for Internet transactions was taken in 2005, when the United Nations Convention on the Use of Electronic Communications in International Contracts was completed. This convention will go into effect as soon as enough countries ratify it, which may have happened by the time you read this. A major goal of the convention is to improve commercial certainty by determining an Internet user's location for legal purposes. The convention also establishes standards for creating functional equivalence between electronic communciations and paper documents. Like the E-SIGN Act discussed in the text, the convention provides that e-signatures should be treated as the equivalent of signatures on paper documents. The drafters also attempted to codify the proper use of automated message systems for contract formation.

Choice of Court

Another recent treaty that will help to foster international trade is the Convention on the Choice of Court Agreements, completed by the Hague Conference on Private International Law on June 30, 2005. Although this convention does not specifically address e-commerce and applies only to business-to-business transactions, not business-to-consumer transactions, it will provide more certainty regarding jurisdiction and recognition of judgments by other nations' courts. Such matters are important to both offline and online transactions, so the convention should enhance e-commerce as well.

The Choice of Court Convention was designed to promote international trade and investment by providing more certainty in resolving international contract disputes. It governs business agreements that designate a single court, or the courts of a single country, to be the forum for resolving disputes. One of its goals is to offer parties entering into international trade contracts a balanced choice between litigation and arbitration when selecting a method of settling disputes. In this sense, the convention is similar to the United Nations Convention on the Recognition and Enforcement of Foreign Arbitral Awards of 1958, commonly referred to as the New York Arbitration Convention (see Chapter 2 for further discussion of this convention).

Fighting International Cyber Crime

Unfortunately, cyber crime has expanded along with the Internet, but steps are beginning to be taken to combat cyber crime on an international basis. At the beginning of this decade, the Council of Europe created the Cyber-Crime Convention, which has been signed by thirty nations including the United States. This treaty provides mechanisms for international cooperation in the battle against Internet-related crime. It prohibits the unauthorized access of an Internet computer system, the unauthorized interception of Internet data, Internet fraud and forgery, and copyright infringement through the use of the Internet.

CRITICAL THINKING
INSIGHT INTO POLITICS
There are about two hundred sovereign nations in the world today, but only thirty have signed the Cyber-Crime Convention. Why do you think so many nations' governments have been reluctant to be bound by the convention?

---

sound, symbol, or process attached to or logically associated with a record and executed or adopted by a person with the intent to sign the record."[9] A **record** is "information that is inscribed on a tangible medium or that is stored in an electronic or other medium and is retrievable in perceivable [visual] form."[10]

---

9. UETA 102(8).

10. UETA 102(15).

The Scope and Applicability of the UETA

The UETA does not create new rules for electronic contracts but rather establishes that records, signatures, and contracts may not be denied enforceability solely due to their electronic form. The UETA does not apply to all writings and signatures but only to electronic records and electronic signatures *relating to a transaction*. A *transaction* is defined as an interaction between two or more people relating to business, commercial, or governmental activities.[11]

The act specifically does *not* apply to wills or testamentary trusts (see Chapter 50) or to transactions governed by the UCC (other than those covered in Articles 2 and 2A).[12] In addition, the provisions of the UETA allow the states to exclude its application to other areas of law.

As described earlier, Congress passed the E-SIGN Act in 2000, a year after the UETA was presented to the states for adoption. Thus, a significant issue is whether and to what extent the federal E-SIGN Act preempts the UETA as adopted by the states.

The Federal E-SIGN Act and the UETA

The E-SIGN Act refers explicitly to the UETA and provides that if a state has enacted the uniform version of the UETA, it is not preempted by the E-SIGN Act.[13] In other words, if the state has enacted the UETA without modification, state law will govern. The problem is that many states have enacted nonuniform (modified) versions of the UETA, largely for the purpose of excluding other areas of state law from the UETA's terms. The E-SIGN Act specifies that those exclusions will be preempted to the extent that they are inconsistent with the E-SIGN Act's provisions.

The E-SIGN Act, however, explicitly allows the states to enact alternative procedures or requirements for the use or acceptance of electronic records or electronic signatures. Generally, however, the procedures or requirements must be consistent with the provisions of the E-SIGN Act, and the state must not give greater legal status or effect to one specific type of technology. Additionally, if a state enacted alternative procedures or requirements *after* the E-SIGN Act was adopted, the state law must specifically refer to the E-SIGN Act. The relationship between the UETA and the E-SIGN Act is illustrated in Exhibit 17–2.

Highlights of the UETA

We look next at selected provisions of the UETA. Our discussion is, of course, based on the act's uniform provisions. Keep in mind that the states that have enacted the UETA may have adopted slightly different versions.

The Parties Must Agree to Conduct Transactions Electronically The UETA will not apply to a transaction unless each of the parties has previously agreed to conduct transactions by electronic means. The agreement need not be explicit, however, and it may be implied by the conduct of the parties and the surrounding circumstances.[14] In the comments that accompany the UETA, the drafters stated that it may be reasonable to infer that a person who gives out a business card with an e-mail address on it has consented to transact business electronically.[15] The party's agreement may also be inferred from a letter or other writing, as well as from some verbal communication. Nothing in the UETA requires that the agreement to conduct transactions electronically be made electronically.

Note, however, that some courts have required that the parties' agreement to conduct transactions electronically be clear and unambiguous. For example, in one Louisiana case, the fact that the parties had *negotiated* the terms of previous contracts via e-mail was not sufficient evidence (by itself) to show that the parties had *agreed* to transact business electronically.[16]

A person who has previously agreed to an electronic transaction can withdraw his or her consent and refuse to conduct further business electronically. Additionally, the act expressly gives parties the power to vary the UETA's provisions by contract. In other words, *parties can opt out of some or all of the terms of the UETA*. If the parties do not opt out of the terms of the UETA, however, the UETA will govern their electronic transactions.

Attribution In the context of electronic transactions, the term *attribution* refers to the procedures that may be used to ensure that the person sending an electronic record is the same person whose e-signature accompanies the record. Under the UETA, if an electronic record or signature was the act of a particular person, the record or signature may be attrib-

---

11. UETA 2(12) and 3.
12. UETA 3(b).
13. 15 U.S.C. Section 7002(2)(A)(i).

---

14. UETA 5(b).
15. UETA 5, Comment 4B.
16. See, for example, *EPCO Carbondioxide Products, Inc. v. Bank One, N.A.*, ___ F.Supp.2d ___ (W.D.La. 2007).

EXHIBIT 17-2 • The E-SIGN Act and the UETA

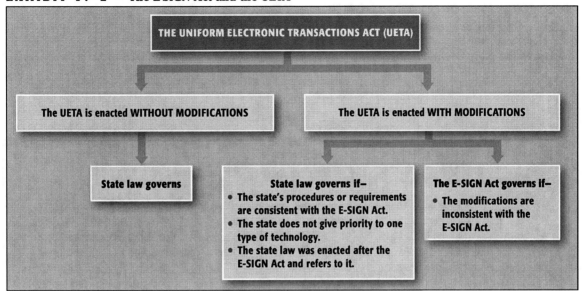

uted to that person. If a person types her or his name at the bottom of an e-mail purchase order, that name will qualify as a "signature" and be attributed to the person whose name appears. Just as in paper contracts, one may use any relevant evidence to prove that the record or signature is or is not the act of the person.[17]

Note that even if an individual's name does not appear on a record (a voice-mail message, for example), the UETA states that the effect of the record is to be determined from the context and surrounding circumstances. In other words, a record may have legal effect even if no one has signed it. For instance, a fax that contains a letterhead identifying the sender may, depending on the circumstances, be attributed to that sender.

Notarization If existing state law requires a document to be notarized, the UETA provides that this requirement is satisfied by the electronic signature of a notary public or other person authorized to verify signatures. For example, if a person intends to accept an offer to purchase real estate via e-mail, the requirement is satisfied if a notary public is present to verify the person's identity and affix an electronic signature to the e-mail acceptance.

The Effect of Errors Section 10 of the UETA encourages, but does not require, the use of security

procedures (such as encryption) to verify changes to electronic documents and to correct errors. If the parties have agreed to a security procedure and one party fails to detect an error because of not following the procedure, the other party can legally avoid the effect of the change or error. If the parties have not agreed to use a security procedure, then other state laws (including contract law governing mistakes—see Chapter 14) will determine the effect of the error on the parties' agreement.

To avoid the effect of errors, a party must promptly notify the other party of the error and of her or his intent not to be bound by the error. In addition, the party must take reasonable steps to return any benefit or consideration received. Parties cannot avoid a transaction from which they have benefited.

Timing Section 15 of the UETA sets forth provisions relating to the sending and receiving of electronic records. These provisions apply unless the parties agree to different terms. Under Section 15, an electronic record is considered *sent* when it is properly directed to the intended recipient in a form readable by the recipient's computer system. Once the electronic record leaves the control of the sender or comes under the control of the recipient, the UETA deems it to have been sent. An electronic record is considered *received* when it enters the recipient's processing system in a readable form—*even if no individual is aware of its receipt.*

17. UETA 9.

Additionally, the UETA provides that, unless otherwise agreed, an electronic record is to be sent from or received at the party's principal place of business. If a party has no place of business, the provision then authorizes the place of sending or receipt to be the party's residence. If a party has multiple places of business, the record should be sent from or received at the location that has the closest relationship to the underlying transaction.

REVIEWING E-Contracts and E-Signatures

Ted and Betty Hyatt live in California, a state that has extensive statutory protection for consumers. The Hyatts decided to buy a computer so that they could use e-mail to stay in touch with their grandchildren, who live in another state. Over the phone, they ordered a computer from CompuEdge, Inc. When the box arrived, it was sealed with a brightly colored sticker warning that the terms enclosed within the box would govern the sale unless the customer returned the computer within thirty days. Among those terms was a clause that required any disputes to be resolved in a Tennessee state court. The Hyatts then signed up for Internet service through CyberTool, an Internet service provider. They downloaded CyberTool's software and clicked on the "quick install" box that allowed them to bypass CyberTool's "Terms of Service" page. It was possible to read this page by scrolling to the next screen, but the Hyatts did not realize this. The terms included a clause that stated that all disputes were to be submitted to a Virginia state court. As soon as the Hyatts attempted to e-mail their grandchildren, they experienced problems using CyberTool's e-mail service, which continually stated that the network was busy. They also were unable to receive the photos sent by their grandchildren. Using the information presented in the chapter, answer the following questions.

1. Did the Hyatts accept the list of contract terms included in the computer box? Why or why not? What is the name used for this type of e-contract?
2. What type of agreement did the Hyatts form with CyberTool?
3. Suppose that the Hyatts experienced trouble with the computer's components after they had used the computer for two months. What factors will a court consider in deciding whether to enforce the forum-selection clause? Would a court be likely to enforce the clause in this contract? Why or why not?
4. Are the Hyatts bound by the contract terms specified on CyberTool's "Terms of Service" page that they did not read? Which of the required elements for contract formation might the Hyatts' claim lack? How might a court rule on this issue?

TERMS AND CONCEPTS

cybernotary

e-contract

e-signature

forum-selection clause

browse-wrap terms

click-on agreement

partnering agreement

record

shrink-wrap agreement

QUESTIONS AND CASE PROBLEMS

19-1. Paul is a financial analyst for King Investments, Inc., a brokerage firm. He uses the Internet to investigate the background and activities of companies that might be good investments for King's customers. While visiting the Web site of Business Research, Inc., Paul sees on his screen a message that reads, "Welcome to businessresearch.com. By visiting our site, you have been entered as a subscriber to our e-publication, *Companies Unlimited.* This publication will be sent to you daily at a cost of $7.50 per week. An invoice will be included with *Companies Unlimited* every four weeks. You may cancel your subscription at any time." Has Paul entered into an enforceable contract to pay for *Companies Unlimited?* Why or why not?

19-2. QUESTION WITH SAMPLE ANSWER

Anne is a reporter for *Daily Business Journal,* a print publication consulted by investors and other businesspersons. She often uses the Internet to conduct research for the articles that she writes for the publication. While visiting the Web site of Cyberspace Investments Corp., Anne reads a pop-up window that states, "Our business newsletter, *E-Commerce Weekly,* is available at a one-year subscription rate of $5 per issue. To subscribe, enter your e-mail address below and click 'SUBSCRIBE.' By subscribing, you agree to the terms of the subscriber's agreement. To read this agreement, click 'AGREEMENT.' " Anne enters her e-mail address, but does not click on "AGREEMENT" to read the terms. Has Anne entered into an enforceable contract to pay for *E-Commerce Weekly?* Explain.

* **For a sample answer to Question 19–2, go to Appendix C at the end of this text.**

19-3. Bob, a sales representative for Central Computer Co., occasionally uses the Internet to obtain information about his customers and to look for new sales leads. While visiting the Web site of Marketing World, Inc., Bob is presented with an on-screen message that offers, "To improve your ability to make deals, read our monthly online magazine, *Sales Genius,* available at a subscription rate of $15 a month. To subscribe, fill in your name, company name, and e-mail address below, and click 'YES!' By clicking 'YES!' you agree to the terms of the subscription contract. To read this contract, click 'TERMS.' " Among those terms is a clause that allows Marketing World to charge interest for subscription bills not paid within a certain time. The terms also prohibit subscribers from copying or distributing part or all of *Sales Genius* in any form. Bob subscribes without reading the terms. Marketing World later files a suit against Bob based on his failure to pay for his subscription. Should the court hold that Bob is obligated to pay interest on the amount? Explain.

19-4. Browse-Wrap Terms. Ticketmaster Corp. operates a Web site that allows customers to buy tickets to concerts, ball games, and other events. On the site's home page are instructions and an index to internal pages (one page per event). Each event page provides basic information (a short description of the event, with the date, time, place, and price) and a description of how to order tickets over the Internet, by telephone, by mail, or in person. The home page contains—if a customer scrolls to the bottom—"terms and conditions" that proscribe, among other things, linking to Ticketmaster's internal pages. A customer need not view these terms to go to an event page. Tickets.Com, Inc., operates a Web site that also publicizes special events. Tickets.Com's site includes links to Ticketmaster's internal events pages. These links bypass Ticketmaster's home page. Ticketmaster filed a suit in a federal district court against Tickets.Com, alleging, in part, breach of contract on the ground that Tickets.Com's linking violated Ticketmaster's terms and conditions. Tickets.Com filed a motion to dismiss. Was Tickets.Com bound by the terms and conditions posted on Ticketmaster's home page? Why or why not? How should the court rule on the motion? [*Ticketmaster Corp. v. Tickets.Com, Inc.,* __ F.Supp.2d __ (C.D.Cal. 2000)]

19-5. Shrink-Wrap Agreements. 1-A Equipment Co. signed a sales order to lease Accware 10 User NT software, which is made and marketed by ICode, Inc. Just above the signature line, the order stated: "Thank you for your order. No returns or refunds will be issued for software license and/or services. All sales are final. Please read the End User License and Service Agreement." The software was delivered in a sealed envelope inside a box. On the outside of the envelope, an "End User Agreement" provided, in part, "BY OPENING THIS PACKAGING, CLICKING YOUR ACCEPTANCE OF THE AGREEMENT DURING DOWNLOAD OR INSTALLATION OF THIS PRODUCT, OR BY USING ANY PART OF THIS PRODUCT, YOU AGREE TO BE LEGALLY BOUND BY THE TERMS OF THE AGREEMENT. . . . This agreement will be governed by the laws in force in the Commonwealth of Virginia . . . and exclusive venue for any litigation shall be in Virginia." Later, dissatisfied with the software, 1-A filed a suit in a Massachusetts state court against ICode, alleging breach of contract and misrepresentation. ICode asked the court to dismiss the case on the basis of the "End User Agreement." Is the agreement enforceable? Should the court dismiss the suit? Why or why not? [*1-A Equipment Co. v. ICode, Inc.,* __ N.E.2d __ (Mass.Dist. 2000)]

19-6. Click-On Agreements. America Online, Inc. (AOL), provided e-mail service to Walter Hughes and other members under a click-on agreement titled "Terms of Service." This agreement consisted of three parts: a "Member Agreement," "Community Guidelines," and a "Privacy Policy." The Member Agreement included a forum-selection clause that read, "You expressly agree that exclusive jurisdiction for any claim or dispute with AOL or relating in any way to your membership or your use of AOL resides in the courts of Virginia." When Officer Thomas McMenamon of the Methuen, Massachusetts, Police Department received threatening e-mail sent from an AOL account, he requested and obtained from AOL Hughes's name and other personal information. Hughes filed a suit in a federal district court against AOL, which filed a motion to dismiss on the basis of the forum-selection clause. Considering that the clause was a click-on provision, is it enforceable? Explain. [*Hughes v. McMenamon*, 204 F.Supp.2d 178 (D.Mass. 2002)]

19–7. CASE PROBLEM WITH SAMPLE ANSWER

Stewart Lamle invented "Farook," a board game similar to "Tic Tac Toe." In May 1996, Lamle began negotiating with Mattel, Inc., to license Farook for distribution outside the United States. On June 11, 1997, the parties met and agreed on many terms, including a three-year duration, the geographic scope of the agreement, a schedule for payment, and a royalty percentage. On June 26, Mike Bucher, a Mattel employee, sent Lamle an e-mail titled "Farook Deal" that repeated these terms and added that they "ha[ve] been agreed [to] . . . by . . . Mattel subject to contract. . . . Best regards Mike Bucher." Lamle faxed Mattel a more formal draft of the terms, but Mattel did not sign it. Mattel displayed Farook at its Pre-Toy Fair in August. After the fair, Mattel sent Lamle a fax saying that it no longer wished to license his game. Lamle filed a suit in a federal district court against Mattel, asserting, in part, breach of contract. One of the issues was whether the parties had entered into a contract. Could Bucher's name on the June 26 e-mail be considered a valid signature under the Uniform Electronic Transactions Act (UETA)? Could it be considered a valid signature outside the UETA? Why or why not? [*Lamle v. Mattel, Inc.*, 394 F.3d 1355 (Fed.Cir. 2005)]

- **To view a sample answer for Problem 19–7, go to this book's Web site at www.cengage. com/blaw/jentz, select "Chapter 19," and click on "Case Problem with Sample Answer."**

19–8. Shrink-Wrap Agreements and Browse-Wrap Terms. Mary DeFontes bought a computer and a service contract from Dell Computers Corp. DeFontes was charged $950.51, of which $13.51 was identified on the invoice as "tax." This amount was paid to the state of Rhode Island. DeFontes and other Dell customers filed a suit in a Rhode Island state court against Dell, claiming that Dell was overcharging its customers by collecting a tax on service contracts and transportation costs. Dell asked the court to order DeFontes to submit the dispute to arbitration. Dell cited its "Terms and Conditions Agreement," which provides, in part, that by accepting delivery of Dell's products or services, a customer agrees to submit any dispute to arbitration. Customers can view this agreement through an *inconspicuous* link at the bottom of Dell's Web site, and Dell encloses a copy with each order when it is shipped. Dell argued that DeFontes accepted these terms by failing to return her purchase within thirty

days, although the agreement did not state this. Is DeFontes bound to the "Terms and Conditions Agreement"? Should the court grant Dell's request? Why or why not? [*DeFontes v. Dell Computers Corp.*, ___ A.2d ___ (R.I. 2004)]

19–9. Online Acceptances. Internet Archive (IA) is devoted to preserving a record of resources on the Internet for future generations. IA uses the "Wayback Machine" to automatically browse Web sites and reproduce their contents in an archive. IA does not ask the owners' permission before copying their material but will remove it on request. Suzanne Shell, a resident of Colorado, owns **www.profane-justice.org**, which is dedicated to providing information to individuals accused of child abuse or neglect. The site warns, "IF YOU COPY OR DISTRIBUTE ANYTHING ON THIS SITE YOU ARE ENTERING INTO A CONTRACT." The terms, which can be accessed only by clicking on a link, include, among other charges, a fee of $5,000 for each page copied "in advance of printing." Neither the warning nor the terms require a user to indicate assent. When Shell discovered that the Wayback Machine had copied the contents of her site—approximately eighty-seven times between May 1999 and October 2004—she asked IA to remove the copies from its archive and pay her $100,000. IA removed the copies and filed a suit in a federal district court against Shell, who responded, in part, with a counterclaim for breach of contract. IA filed a motion to dismiss this claim. Did IA contract with Shell? Explain. [*Internet Archive v. Shell*, 505 F.Supp.2d 755 (D.Colo. 2007)]

19–10. A QUESTION OF ETHICS

In 2000 and 2001, Dewayne Hubbert, Elden Craft, Chris Grout, and Rhonda Byington bought computers from Dell Corp. through its Web site. Before buying, Hubbert and the others configured their own computers. To make a purchase, each buyer completed forms on five Web pages. On each page, Dell's "Terms and Conditions of Sale" were accessible by clicking on a blue hyperlink. A statement on three of the pages read, "All sales are subject to Dell's Term[s] and Conditions of Sale," but a buyer was not required to click an assent to the terms to complete a purchase. The terms were also printed on the backs of the invoices and on separate documents contained in the shipping boxes with the computers. Among those terms was a "Binding Arbitration" clause. The computers contained Pentium 4 microprocessors, which Dell advertised as the fastest, most powerful Intel Pentium processor available. In 2002, Hubbert and the others filed a suit in an Illinois state court against Dell, alleging that this marketing was false, misleading, and deceptive. The plaintiffs claimed that the Pentium 4 microprocessor was slower and less powerful, and provided less performance, than either a Pentium III or an AMD Athlon, and at a greater cost. Dell asked the court to compel arbitration. [Hubbert v. Dell Corp., 359 Ill.App.3d 976, 835 N.E.2d 113, 296 Ill.Dec. 258 (5 Dist. 2005)]

(a) Should the court enforce the arbitration clause in this case? If you were the judge, how would you rule on this issue?

(b) In your opinion, do shrink-wrap, click-on, and browse-wrap terms impose too great a burden on purchasers? Why or why not?

(c) An ongoing complaint about shrink-wrap, click-on, and browse-wrap terms is that sellers (often large corporations) draft them and buyers (typically individual consumers) do not read them. Should purchasers be bound in contract by terms that they have not even read? Why or why not?

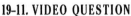

19-11. VIDEO QUESTION

Go to this text's Web site at **www.cengage. com/blaw/jentz** and select "Chapter 19." Click on "Video Questions" and view the video titled *E-Contracts: Agreeing Online.* Then answer the following questions.

(a) According to the instructor in the video, what is the key factor in determining whether a particular term in an online agreement is enforceable?

(b) Suppose that you click on "I accept" in order to download software from the Internet. You do not read the terms of the agreement before accepting it, even though you know that such agreements often contain forum-selection and arbitration clauses. The software later causes irreparable harm to your computer system, and you want to sue. When you go to the Web site and view the agreement, however, you discover that a choice-of-law clause in the contract specifies that the law of Nigeria controls. Is this term enforceable? Is it a term that should be reasonably expected in an online contract?

(c) Does it matter what the term actually says if it is a type of term that one could reasonably expect to be in the contract? What arguments can be made for and against enforcing a choice-of-law clause in an online contract?

LAW ON THE WEB

For updated links to resources available on the Web, as well as a variety of other materials, visit this text's Web site at

www.cengage.com/blaw/jentz

You can access the UCC, including Article 2, at the Web site of Cornell University Law School. Go to

www.law.cornell.edu/ucc/ucc.table.html

The Web site of the National Conference of Commissioners on Uniform State Laws provides the draft and final versions of the UETA, lists the states that have adopted it, and offers information on why states should adopt it, at

www.nccusl.org

Legal Research Exercises on the Web

Go to **www.cengage.com/blaw/jentz**, the Web site that accompanies this text. Select "Chapter 19" and click on "Internet Exercises." There you will find the following Internet research exercises that you can perform to learn more about the topics covered in this chapter.

Internet Exercise 19–1: Legal Perspective
E-Contract Formation

Internet Exercise 19–2: Management Perspective
E-Signatures

Contract Law and the Application of Ethics

Generally, as you read in Chapter 5, a responsible business manager will evaluate a business transaction on the basis of three criteria—legality, profitability, and ethics. But what does acting ethically mean in the area of contracts? If an individual with whom you enter into a contract fails to look after her or his own interests, is that your fault? Should you be doing something about it? If the contract happens to be to your advantage and to the other party's detriment, do you have a responsibility to correct the situation?

Suppose that your neighbor puts a "For sale" sign on her car, offering to sell it for $6,000. You learn that she is moving to another state and needs the extra cash to help finance the move. You know that she could easily get $10,000 for the car, and you are considering purchasing it and then reselling it at a profit. But you also discover that your neighbor is completely unaware that she has priced the car significantly below its *Blue Book* value. Are you ethically obligated to tell her that she is essentially giving away $4,000 if she sells you the car for only $6,000?

This kind of situation, transplanted into the world of commercial transactions, raises an obvious question: At what point should the sophisticated businessperson cease looking after his or her own economic welfare and become "his brother's keeper," so to speak?

Freedom of Contract and Freedom from Contract

The answer to the question just raised is not simple. On the one hand, a common ethical assumption in our society is that individuals should be held responsible for the consequences of their own actions, including their contractual promises. This principle is expressed in the legal concept of freedom of contract. On the other hand, another common assumption in our society is that individuals should not harm one another by their actions. This is the basis of both tort law and criminal law.

In the area of contract law, ethical behavior often involves balancing these principles. In the above example, if you purchased the car and your neighbor later learned its true value and sued you for the difference, very likely no court of law would find that the contract should be rescinded. At times, however, courts will hold that the principle of

freedom *of* contract should give way to the principle of freedom *from* contract, a doctrine based on the assumption that people should not be harmed by the actions of others. We look next at some examples of situations in which parties to contracts may be excused from performance under their contracts to prevent injustice.

Impossibility of Performance The doctrine of impossibility of performance is based to some extent on the ethical question of whether one party should suffer economic loss when it is impossible to perform a contract. The rule that one is "bound by his or her contracts" is not followed when performance becomes impossible. This doctrine, however, is applied only when the parties themselves did not consciously assume the risk of the events that rendered performance impossible. Furthermore, this doctrine rests on the assumption that the party claiming the defense of impossibility has acted ethically.

A contract is discharged, for example, if it calls for the delivery of a particular car and, through no fault of either party, this car is stolen and completely demolished in an accident. Yet the doctrine would not excuse performance if the party agreeing to sell the car caused its destruction by her or his negligence.

Before the late nineteenth century, courts were reluctant to discharge a contract even when performance was literally impossible. Just as society's ethics changes with the passage of time, however, the law also changes to reflect society's new perceptions of ethical behavior.[1] Today, courts are much more willing to discharge a contract when its performance has become literally impossible. Holding a party in breach of contract, when performance has become impossible through no fault of that party, no longer coincides with society's notions of fairness.

Unconscionability The doctrine of unconscionability is a good example of how the law attempts to enforce ethical behavior. Under this doctrine, a contract may be deemed to be so unfair to one party as to be unenforceable—even though that party voluntarily agreed to the contract's terms.

---

1. A leading English case in which the court held that a defendant was discharged from the duty to perform due to impossibility of performance is *Taylor v. Caldwell*, 122 Eng.Rep. 309 (K.B. [King's Bench] 1863).

Unconscionable action, like unethical action, defies precise definition. Information about the particular facts and specific circumstances surrounding the contract is essential. For example, a court might find that a contract made with a marginally literate consumer was unfair and unenforceable but might uphold the same contract made with a major business firm.

Section 2–302 of the Uniform Commercial Code, which incorporates the common law concept of unconscionability, similarly does not define the concept with any precision. Rather, it leaves it to the courts to determine when a contract is so one sided and unfair to one party as to be unconscionable and thus unenforceable.

Usually, courts will do all that they can to save contracts rather than render them unenforceable. Only in extreme situations, as when a contract or clause is so one sided as to "shock the conscience" of the court, will a court hold a contract or contractual clause unconscionable.

Exculpatory Clauses In some situations, courts have also refused to enforce exculpatory clauses on the ground that they are unconscionable or contrary to public policy. An *exculpatory clause* attempts to excuse a party from liability in the event of monetary or physical injury, no matter who is at fault. In some situations, such clauses are upheld. For example, a health club can require its members to sign a clause releasing the club from any liability for injuries the members might incur while using the club's equipment and facilities. The law permits parties to assume, by express agreement, the risks inherent in certain activities. In such situations, exculpatory clauses make it possible for a firm's owner to stay in business—by shifting some of the liability risks from the business to the customer.

Nonetheless, some jurisdictions take a dubious view of exculpatory clauses, particularly when the agreement is between parties with unequal bargaining power, such as a landlord and a tenant or an employer and an employee. An exculpatory clause that attempts to exempt an employer from *all* liability for negligence toward its employees frequently is held to be against public policy and thus void.[2] The courts reason that disparity in bargaining power and economic necessity force the employee to accept the employer's terms.

Covenants Not to Compete

In today's complicated, technological business world, knowledge learned on the job, including trade secrets, has become a valuable commodity. To prevent this knowledge from falling into the hands of competitors, more and more employers are requiring their employees to sign covenants not to compete. The increasing number of lawsuits over noncompete clauses in employment contracts has caused many courts to reconsider the reasonableness of these covenants.

Should Courts Reform Unreasonable Noncompete Covenants? In a number of jurisdictions, if a court finds that a restraint in a noncompete covenant is not reasonable in light of the circumstances, it will reform the unreasonable provision and then enforce it. For example, a court might rewrite an unreasonable restriction by reducing the time period during which a former employee cannot compete from three years to one year, and then enforce the reformed agreement.[3]

Other jurisdictions are not so "employer friendly" and refuse to enforce unreasonable covenants. As one observer noted, the farther west you go from the Mississippi River, the harder it is to enforce a covenant not to compete. Under California law, covenants not to compete are illegal, and other western states tend to regard such covenants with suspicion. For example, the Washington Supreme Court has refused to reform noncompete covenants that are unreasonable and lacking in consideration.[4] Courts in Arizona and Texas have reached similar conclusions.[5]

Some commentators argue that when the courts modify and then enforce unreasonable covenants, this only encourages employers to continue to create unreasonable covenants—for two reasons: (1) most noncompete covenants are never challenged in court, and (2) if a covenant is

---

2. See, for example, *City of Santa Barbara v. Superior Court,* 62 Cal.Rptr.3d 527, 161 P.3d 1095 (2007); and *Health Net of California, Inc. v. Department of Health Services,* 113 Cal.App.4th 224, 6 Cal.Rptr.3d 235 (2003).

---

3. See, for example, *Estee Lauder Companies, Inc. v. Batra,* 430 F.Supp.2d 158 (S.D.N.Y. 2006); *National Café Services, Ltd. v. Podaras,* 148 S.W.3d 194 (Tex.App.–Waco 2004); *Pathfinder Communications Corp. v. Macy,* 795 N.E.2d 1103 (Ind.App. 2003); and *Health Care Enterprises, Inc. v. Levy,* 715 So.2d 341 (Fla.App.4th 1998).
4. See, for example, *Labriola v. Pollard Group, Inc.,* 152 Wash.2d 828, 100 P.3d 791 (2004).
5. *Hardy v. Mann Frankfort Stein & Lipp Advisors, Inc.* ___ S.W.3d ___ (Tex.App.–Houston [1 Dist.] 2007); and *Varsity Gold, Inc. v. Porzio,* 202 Ariz. 355, 45 P.3d 352 (2002).

(Continued)

contested, the worst that can happen is that the court will modify, and then enforce, the covenant.

Do Noncompete Covenants Stifle Innovation? One of the reasons that the courts usually look closely at covenants not to compete and evaluate them on a case-by-case basis is the strong public policy favoring competition in this country. Even so, claim some scholars, covenants not to compete, regardless of their "reasonability," may stifle competition and innovation.

Consider, for example, the argument put forth by Ronald Gilson, a Stanford University professor of law and business. He contends that California's prohibition on covenants not to compete may help to explain why technological innovation and economic growth have skyrocketed in California's Silicon Valley, while technological development along Massachusetts's Route 128 has languished. According to Gilson, "The different legal rules governing postemployment covenants not to compete in California and Massachusetts help explain the difference in employee job mobility and therefore the knowledge transfer that [is] a critical factor in explaining the differential performance of Silicon Valley and Route 128."[6] For this and for other reasons, some scholars contend that covenants not to compete may not survive the cyber age.[7] Certainly, such covenants present new types of challenges for the courts in deciding what restrictions are reasonable in the context of the Internet.[8]

Oral Contracts and Promissory Estoppel

Oral contracts are made every day. Many—if not most—of them are carried out, and no problems arise. Occasionally, however, oral contracts are not performed, and one party decides to sue the other. Sometimes, to prevent injustice, the courts will enforce oral contracts under the theory of promissory estoppel if detrimental reliance can be shown. The court may even use this theory to

---

6. Ronald J. Gilson, "The Legal Infrastructure of High Technology Industrial Districts: Silicon Valley, Route 128, and Covenants Not to Compete," 575 *New York University Law Review* 579 (June 1999).

7. See, for example, Robert C. Welsh, Larry C. Drapkin, and Samantha C. Grant, "Are Noncompete Clauses Kaput?" *The National Law Journal,* August 14, 2000, pp. B13–B14.

8. For an example of a dispute in the Internet context, see *EarthWeb v. Schlack,* 71 F. Supp.2d 299 (S.D.N.Y. 1999).

remove a contract from the Statute of Frauds—that is, render the oral contract enforceable.

In addition, ethical standards certainly underlie the doctrine of *promissory estoppel,* under which a person who has reasonably relied on the promise of another to his or her detriment can often obtain some measure of recovery. Essentially, promissory estoppel allows a variety of promises to be enforced even though they lack what is formally regarded as consideration.

An oral promise made by an insurance agent to a business owner, for example, may be binding if the owner relies on that promise to her or his detriment. Employees who rely to their detriment on an employer's promise may be able to recover under the doctrine of promissory estoppel. A contractor who, when bidding for a job, relies on a subcontractor's promise to perform certain construction work at a certain price may be able to recover, on the basis of promissory estoppel, any damages sustained because of the subcontractor's failure to perform. These are but a few of the many examples in which the courts, in the interests of fairness and justice, have estopped a promisor from denying that a contract existed.

Oral Contracts and the Statute of Frauds

As you learned in Chapter 15, the Statute of Frauds was originally enacted in England in 1677. The act was intended to prevent harm to innocent parties by requiring written evidence of agreements concerning important transactions.

Until the Statute of Frauds was passed, the English courts had enforced oral contracts on the strength of oral testimony by witnesses. Under these conditions, it was not too difficult to evade justice by procuring "convincing" witnesses to support the claim that a contract had been created and then breached. The possibility of fraud in such actions was enhanced by the fact that seventeenth-century English courts did not allow oral testimony to be given by the parties to a lawsuit—or by any parties with an interest in the litigation, such as husbands or wives. Defense against actions for breach of contract was thus limited to written evidence or the testimony of third parties.

Detrimental Reliance Under the Statute of Frauds, if a contract is oral when it is required to be in writing, it will not, as a rule, be enforced by the courts. An exception to this rule is made if a party has reasonably relied, to his or her detriment, on the oral contract. Enforcing an oral contract on the basis of a party's reliance arguably undercuts the essence of the Statute of Frauds. The reason that such an exception is made is to prevent the statute—which was created to prevent injustice—from being used to promote injustice. Nevertheless, this use of the doctrine is controversial—as is the Statute of Frauds itself.

Criticisms of the Statute of Frauds Since its inception more than three hundred years ago, the statute has been criticized by some because, although it was created to protect the innocent, it can also be used as a technical defense by a party breaching a genuine, mutually agreed-on oral contract—if the contract falls within the Statute of Frauds. For this reason, some legal scholars believe the act has caused more injustice than it has prevented. Thus, exceptions are sometimes made—such as under the doctrine of promissory estoppel—to prevent unfairness and inequity. Generally, the courts are slow to apply the statute if doing so will result in obvious injustice. In some instances, this has required a good deal of inventiveness on the part of the courts.

DISCUSSION QUESTIONS

1. Suppose that you contract to purchase steel at a fixed price per ton. Before the contract is performed, a lengthy steelworkers' strike causes the price of steel to triple from the price specified in the contract. If you demand that the supplier fulfill the contract, the supplier will go out of business. What are your ethical obligations in this situation? What are your legal rights?

2. Many countries have no Statute of Frauds, and even England, the country that created the original act, has repealed it. Should the United States do likewise? What are some of the costs and benefits to society of the Statute of Frauds?

3. In determining whether an exculpatory clause should be enforced, why does it matter whether the contract containing the clause involves essential services (such as transportation) or nonessential services (such as skiing or other leisure-time activities)?

4. Employers often include covenants not to compete in employment contracts to protect their trade secrets. What effect, if any, will the growth in e-commerce have on the reasonability of covenants not to compete?

CHAPTER 18

Ethics and Business Decision Making

All of the following businesspersons have been in the news recently:

- Dennis Kozlowski (former chairman and chief executive officer of Tyco International).
- Mark H. Swartz (former chief financial officer of Tyco International).
- Jeffrey Skilling (former chief executive officer of Enron Corporation).
- Bernard Ebbers (former chief executive officer of WorldCom).

What do these individuals have in common? They are all in prison, and some may stay there until they die. They were all convicted of various crimes ranging from overseeing revenue exaggeration in order to increase stock prices to personal use of millions of dollars of public company funds. Not only did they break the law, but they also clearly violated even the minimum ethical principles that a civil society expects to be followed. Other officers and directors of the companies mentioned in the preceding list cost shareholders billions of dollars. In the case of those companies that had to enter bankruptcy, such as Enron Corporation, tens of thousands of employees lost their jobs.

Acting ethically in a business context is not child's play; it can mean billions of dollars—up or down—for corporations, shareholders, and employees. In the wake of the recent scandals, Congress attempted to prevent similar unethical business behavior in the future by passing stricter legislation in the form of the Sarbanes-Oxley Act of 2002, which will be explained in detail in Chapters 41 and 51. This act generally imposed more reporting requirements on corporations in an effort to deter unethical behavior and encourage accountability.

Business Ethics

As you might imagine, business ethics is derived from the concept of ethics. **Ethics** can be defined as the study of what constitutes right or wrong behavior. It is a branch of philosophy focusing on morality and the way moral principles are derived. Ethics has to do with the fairness, justness, rightness, or wrongness of an action.

What Is Business Ethics?

Business ethics focuses on what is right and wrong behavior in the business world. It has to do with how businesses apply moral and ethical principles to situations that arise in the workplace. Because business decision makers must often address more complex ethical issues in the workplace than they face in their personal lives, business ethics is more complicated than personal ethics.

Why Is Business Ethics Important?

For an answer to the question of why business ethics is so important, reread the list at the beginning of this chapter. All of the individuals who are sitting behind bars could have avoided their fates. Had they engaged in ethical decision making throughout their business careers, they would never have followed their different paths to criminal behavior. The corporations, shareholders, and employees who suffered because of those individuals' unethical and criminal behavior certainly paid a high price. Thus, an in-depth understanding of business ethics is important to the long-run viability of any corporation today. It is also important to the well-being of individual officers and directors and to the firm's employees. Finally, unethical corporate decision making can negatively affect suppliers, consumers, the community, and society as a whole.

At the end of every unit in this book, you will be exposed to a series of ethical issues in features called *Focus on Ethics*. In each of these unit-ending features, we expand on the concepts of business ethics that we present in this chapter.

Common Reasons Why Ethical Problems Occur

Not that many years ago, the popular painkiller Vioxx was recalled because its long-term use increased the risk of heart attack and stroke. Little by little, evidence surfaced that the drug's maker, Merck & Company, knew about these dangers yet allowed Vioxx to remain on the market. Merck's failure to recall the drug earlier could potentially have adversely affected the health of thousands of patients. In addition, Merck has undergone investigations by both Congress and the U.S. Department of Justice. Merck was facing thousands of lawsuits, years of litigation, and millions of dollars in attorneys' fees and settlements when it agreed, in November 2007, to settle all outstanding cases concerning Vioxx for $4.85 billion. How did a major corporation manage to make so many missteps? The answer is simply that certain officers and employees of Merck felt that it was not necessary to reveal the results of studies that might have decreased sales of Vioxx.

In other words, the common thread among the ethical problems that occur in business is the desire to increase sales (or not lose them), thereby increasing profits and, for the corporation, increasing market value. In most situations, though, ethically wrong behavior by a corporation turns out to be costly to everyone concerned. Just ask the shareholders of Merck (and, of course, Enron, WorldCom, and Tyco).

Short-Run Profit Maximization Some people argue that a corporation's only goal should be profit maximization, which will be reflected in a higher market value. When all firms strictly adhere to the goal of profit maximization, resources tend to flow to where they are most highly valued by society. Ultimately, profit maximization, in theory, leads to the most efficient allocation of scarce resources.

Corporate executives and employees have to distinguish, though, between *short-run* and *long-run* profit maximization. In the short run, the employees of Merck & Company may have increased profits because of the continuing sales of Vioxx. In the long run, though, because of lawsuits, large settlements, and bad publicity, profits have suffered. Thus, business ethics is consistent only with long-run profit maximization.

Determining Society's Rules—The Role of Corporate Influence Another possible cause of bad business ethics has to do with corporations' role in influencing the law. Corporations may use lobbyists to persuade government agencies not to institute new regulations that would increase the corporations' costs and reduce their profits. Once regulatory rules are promulgated, corporations may undertake actions to reduce their impact. One way to do this is to make it known that members of regulatory agencies will always have jobs waiting for them when they leave the agencies. This revolving door, as it is commonly called, has existed as long as there have been regulatory agencies at the state and federal levels of government.

The Importance of Ethical Leadership

Talking about ethical business decision making is meaningless if management does not set standards. Furthermore, managers must apply the same standards to themselves as they do to the employees of the company.

Attitude of Top Management One of the most important ways to create and maintain an ethical workplace is for top management to demonstrate its commitment to ethical decision making. A manager who is not totally committed to an ethical workplace rarely succeeds in creating one. Management's behavior, more than anything else, sets the ethical tone of a firm. Employees take their cues from management. For example, an employee who observes a manager cheating on her expense account quickly learns that such behavior is acceptable.

Managers who set unrealistic production or sales goals increase the probability that employees will act unethically. If a sales quota can be met only through high-pressure, unethical sales tactics, employees will try to act "in the best interest of the company" and will continue to behave unethically.

A manager who looks the other way when she or he knows about an employee's unethical behavior also sets an example—one indicating that ethical transgressions will be accepted. Managers have found that discharging even one employee for ethical reasons has a tremendous impact as a deterrent to unethical behavior in the workplace.

Behavior of Owners and Managers

Business owners and managers sometimes take more active roles in fostering unethical and illegal conduct.

This may indicate to their co-owners, co-managers, employees, and others that unethical business behavior will be tolerated. The following case illustrates how business owners' misbehavior can have negative consequences for themselves and their business. Not only can a court sanction the business owners and managers, but it can also issue an injunction that prevents them from engaging in similar patterns of conduct in the future.

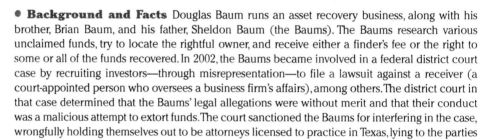

C A S E **18.1** **Baum v. Blue Moon Ventures, LLC**
United States Court of Appeals, Fifth Circuit, 2008. 513 F.3d 181.

● **Background and Facts** Douglas Baum runs an asset recovery business, along with his brother, Brian Baum, and his father, Sheldon Baum (the Baums). The Baums research various unclaimed funds, try to locate the rightful owner, and receive either a finder's fee or the right to some or all of the funds recovered. In 2002, the Baums became involved in a federal district court case by recruiting investors—through misrepresentation—to file a lawsuit against a receiver (a court-appointed person who oversees a business firm's affairs), among others. The district court in that case determined that the Baums' legal allegations were without merit and that their conduct was a malicious attempt to extort funds. The court sanctioned the Baums for interfering in the case, wrongfully holding themselves out to be attorneys licensed to practice in Texas, lying to the parties and the court, and generally abusing the judicial system.

    The district court also issued a permanent injunction against all three Baums to prohibit them from filing claims related to the same case in Texas state courts without the express permission of Judge Lynn Hughes (the district court judge). In June 2005, the Baums entered an appearance in the bankruptcy proceeding (bankruptcy will be discussed in Chapter 30) involving Danny Hilal and Blue Moon Ventures, LLC. Blue Moon's primary business was purchasing real property at foreclosure sales and leasing those properties to residential tenants. Sheldon Baum claimed to be a creditor in the bankruptcy, but he would not identify his claim. Brian Baum misled the parties and the court about being a licensed attorney in Texas. Douglas Baum participated by posting a fake notice stating that the Internal Revenue Service might foreclose on some property to collect unpaid taxes. The bankruptcy court concluded that this was a continuation of a pattern of malicious conduct and forwarded a memo on the case to the district court that had imposed the sanctions on the Baums. The district court, after conducting two hearings and listening to testimony from all of the Baums, also found that the Baums had continued in their abusive practices. The district court therefore modified and expanded its injunction to include the filing of any claim in any federal or state court or agency in Texas. Douglas Baum filed an appeal, claiming that the court had exceeded its power and arguing that the injunction would impede his business.

● **Decision and Rationale** The U.S. Court of Appeals for the Fifth Circuit upheld the modified prefiling injunction as it applied to all filings in Texas state courts, in lower federal courts located in Texas, and in administrative agencies in Texas. In contrast, the court struck down those portions of the injunction that required the Baums to obtain Judge Hughes's permission prior to filing a claim in any court or agency located outside the state of Texas, or prior to filing in any federal appellate court. The appellate court accepted that a district court has jurisdiction to impose prefiling injunctions to deter abusive and harassing litigation. "Federal courts have both the inherent power and the Constitutional obligation to protect their jurisdiction from conduct [that] impairs their ability to carry out [their] functions." It further stated that federal courts have the power to prevent plaintiffs from future filings when those plaintiffs consistently abuse the court system and harass their opponents. Nevertheless, the district court "had abused its discretion" with its

CASE 18.1 CONTINUED broad extension of the prefiling injunction, and therefore, those requirements were not upheld. Furthermore, the appellate court noted that "those [other] courts or agencies are capable of taking appropriate action on their own."

● **The Legal Environment Dimension** *What might the Baums have done to avoid the sanctions that were imposed on them in this case?*

● **The Ethical Dimension** *Are there situations in which a business owner's conduct would be more reprehensible than the Baums' behavior in this case? Explain.*

Approaches to Ethical Reasoning

Each individual, when faced with a particular ethical dilemma, engages in **ethical reasoning**—that is, a reasoning process in which the individual examines the situation at hand in light of his or her moral convictions or ethical standards. Businesspersons do likewise when making decisions with ethical implications.

How do business decision makers decide whether a given action is the "right" one for their firms? What ethical standards should be applied? Broadly speaking, ethical reasoning relating to business traditionally has been characterized by two fundamental approaches. One approach defines ethical behavior in terms of duty, which also implies certain rights. The other approach determines what is ethical in terms of the consequences, or outcome, of any given action. We examine each of these approaches here.

In addition to the two basic ethical approaches, a few theories have been developed that specifically address the social responsibility of corporations. Because these theories also influence today's business decision makers, we conclude this section with a short discussion of the different views of corporate social responsibility.

Duty-Based Ethics

Duty-based ethical standards often are derived from revealed truths, such as religious precepts. They can also be derived through philosophical reasoning.

Religious Ethical Standards In the Judeo-Christian tradition, which is the dominant religious tradition in the United States, the Ten Commandments of the Old Testament establish fundamental rules for moral action. Other religions have their own sources of revealed truth. Religious rules generally are absolute with respect to the behavior of their adherents. For example, the commandment "Thou shalt not steal" is an absolute mandate for a person who believes that the Ten Commandments reflect revealed truth. Even a benevolent motive for stealing (such as Robin Hood's) cannot justify the act because the act itself is inherently immoral and thus wrong.

Kantian Ethics Duty-based ethical standards may also be derived solely from philosophical reasoning. The German philosopher Immanuel Kant (1724–1804), for example, identified some general guiding principles for moral behavior based on what he believed to be the fundamental nature of human beings. Kant believed that human beings are qualitatively different from other physical objects and are endowed with moral integrity and the capacity to reason and conduct their affairs rationally. Therefore, a person's thoughts and actions should be respected. When human beings are treated merely as a means to an end, they are being treated as the equivalent of objects and are being denied their basic humanity.

A central theme in Kantian ethics is that individuals should evaluate their actions in light of the consequences that would follow if *everyone* in society acted in the same way. This **categorical imperative** can be applied to any action. For example, suppose that you are deciding whether to cheat on an examination. If you have adopted Kant's categorical imperative, you will decide *not* to cheat because if everyone cheated, the examination (and the entire education system) would be meaningless.

The Principle of Rights Because a duty cannot exist without a corresponding right, duty-based ethical standards imply that human beings have basic rights. The principle that human beings have certain fundamental rights (to life, freedom, and the pursuit of happiness, for example) is deeply embedded in Western culture. As discussed in Chapter 1, the natural law tradition embraces the concept that certain actions (such as killing another person) are morally wrong because they are contrary to nature (the natural desire to continue living). Those who adhere to this **principle of rights,** or "rights theory," believe that a key factor in determining whether a business decision is ethical is how that decision affects the rights of others. These others include the firm's owners, its employees, the consumers of its products or services, its suppliers, the community in which it does business, and society as a whole.

A potential dilemma for those who support rights theory, however, is that they may disagree on which rights are most important. When considering all those affected by a business decision, for example, how much weight should be given to employees relative to shareholders, customers relative to the community, or employees relative to society as a whole?

In general, rights theorists believe that whichever right is stronger in a particular circumstance takes precedence. Suppose that a firm can either keep a plant open, saving the jobs of twelve workers, or shut the plant down and avoid contaminating a river with pollutants that would endanger the health of thousands of people. In this situation, a rights theorist can easily choose which group to favor. (Not all choices are so clear-cut, however.)

Outcome-Based Ethics: Utilitarianism

"The greatest good for the greatest number" is a paraphrase of the major premise of the utilitarian approach to ethics. **Utilitarianism** is a philosophical theory developed by Jeremy Bentham (1748–1832) and modified by John Stuart Mill (1806–1873)—both British philosophers. In contrast to duty-based ethics, utilitarianism is outcome oriented. It focuses on the consequences of an action, not on the nature of the action itself or on any set of preestablished moral values or religious beliefs.

Under a utilitarian model of ethics, an action is morally correct, or "right," when, among the people it affects, it produces the greatest amount of good for the greatest number. When an action affects the majority adversely, it is morally wrong. Applying the utilitarian theory thus requires (1) a determination of which individuals will be affected by the action in question; (2) a **cost-benefit analysis,** which involves an assessment of the negative and positive effects of alternative actions on these individuals; and (3) a choice among alternative actions that will produce maximum socie-

tal utility (the greatest positive net benefits for the greatest number of individuals).

Corporate Social Responsibility

For many years, groups concerned with civil rights, employee safety and welfare, consumer protection, environmental preservation, and other causes have pressured corporate America to behave in a responsible manner with respect to these causes. Thus was born the concept of **corporate social responsibility**—the idea that those who run corporations can and should act ethically and be accountable to society for their actions. Just what constitutes corporate social responsibility has been debated for some time, however, and there are a number of different theories today.

Stakeholder Approach One view of corporate social responsibility stresses that corporations have a duty not just to shareholders, but also to other groups affected by corporate decisions (stakeholders). Under this approach, a corporation would consider the impact of its decision on the firm's employees, customers, creditors, suppliers, and the community in which the corporation operates. The reasoning behind this "stakeholder view" is that in some circumstances, one or more of these other groups may have a greater stake in company decisions than the shareholders do. Although this may be true, it is often difficult to decide which group's interests should receive greater weight if the interests conflict (see the earlier discussion of conflicting rights).

Corporate Citizenship Another theory of social responsibility argues that corporations should behave as good citizens by promoting goals that society deems worthwhile and taking positive steps toward solving social problems. The idea is that because business controls so much of the wealth and power of this country, business in turn has a responsibility to society to use that wealth and power in socially beneficial ways. Under a corporate citizenship view, companies are judged on how much they donate to social causes, as well as how they conduct their operations with respect to employment discrimination, human rights, environmental concerns, and similar issues.

In the following case, a corporation's board of directors did not seem to doubt the priority of the firm's responsibilities. Focused solely on the profits delivered into the hands of the shareholders, the board failed to check the actions of the firm's chief executive officer (CEO) and, in fact, appeared to condone the CEO's misconduct. If the board had applied a different set of priorities, the shareholders might have been in a better financial position, however. A regulatory agency soon found the situation "troubling" and imposed a restric-

tion on the firm. The board protested. The protest reminded the court of "the old saw about the child who murders his parents and then asks for mercy because he is an orphan."

C A S E   18.2   Fog Cutter Capital Group, Inc. v. Securities and Exchange Commission
United States Court of Appeals, District of Columbia Circuit, 2007. 474 F.3d 822.

● **Background and Facts** The National Association of Securities Dealers (NASD) operates the Nasdaq, an electronic securities exchange, on which Fog Cutter Capital Group was listed.[a] Andrew Wiederhorn had founded Fog Cutter in 1997 to manage a restaurant chain and make other investments. With family members, Wiederhorn controlled more than 50 percent of Fog Cutter's stock. The firm agreed that if Wiederhorn was terminated "for cause," he was entitled only to his salary through the date of termination. If terminated "without cause," he would be owed three times his $350,000 annual salary, three times his largest annual bonus from the previous three years, and any unpaid salary and bonus. "Cause" included the conviction of a felony. In 2001, Wiederhorn became the target of an investigation into the collapse of Capital Consultants, LLC. Fog Cutter then redefined "cause" in his termination agreement to cover only a felony involving Fog Cutter. In June 2004, Wiederhorn agreed to plead guilty to two felonies, serve eighteen months in prison, pay a $25,000 fine, and pay $2 million to Capital Consultants. The day before he entered his plea, Fog Cutter agreed that while he was in prison, he would keep his title, responsibilities, salary, bonuses, and other benefits. It also agreed to a $2 million "leave of absence payment." In July, the NASD delisted Fog Cutter from the Nasdaq. Fog Cutter appealed this decision to the Securities and Exchange Commission (SEC), which dismissed the appeal. Fog Cutter petitioned the U.S. Court of Appeals for the District of Columbia Circuit for review.

● **Decision and Rationale** The U.S. Court of Appeals for the District of Columbia Circuit denied Fog Cutter's petition for review of the SEC's decision. The NASD was concerned with the integrity and the public's perception of the Nasdaq exchange in light of Wiederhorn's legal troubles and the Fog Cutter board's acceptance of his demands. The appellate court was unconvinced by Fog Cutter's complaint that the SEC had failed to take into account the company's sound business reasons for acting as it did. The court looked at the deal that Fog Cutter made with Wiederhorn that cost the company almost $5 million during a year in which it reported a $4 million loss. In short, "the decision was in accordance with NASD rules giving the organization broad discretion to determine whether the public interest requires delisting securities in light of events at a company. The rule is obviously consistent with [the law], and NASD's decision did not burden competition."

● ***The Ethical Dimension*** *Should the court have given more consideration to the fact that Fog Cutter was not convicted of a violation of the law? Why or why not?*

● ***The Global Dimension*** *What does the decision in this case suggest to foreign investors who may be considering investments in securities listed on U.S. exchanges?*

---

a. Securities (stocks and bonds) can be bought and sold through national exchanges. Whether a security is listed on an exchange is subject to the discretion of the organization that operates it. The Securities and Exchange Commission oversees the securities exchanges (see Chapter 41).

Creating Ethical Codes of Conduct

One of the most effective ways to set a tone of ethical behavior within an organization is to create an ethical

code of conduct. A well-written code of ethics explicitly states a company's ethical priorities and demonstrates the company's commitment to ethical behavior.

Business owners wishing to avoid disputes over ethical violations must focus on creating a written ethical code that is clear and understandable (in plain English). The code should establish specific procedures that employees can follow if they have questions or complaints. It should assure employees that their jobs will be secure and that they will not face reprisals if they do file a complaint. Business owners should also explain to employees why these ethics policies are important to the company. A well-written code might include examples to clarify what the company considers to be acceptable and unacceptable conduct.

Providing Ethics Training to Employees
For an ethical code to be effective, its provisions must be clearly communicated to employees. Most large companies have implemented ethics training programs in which management discusses with employees on a face-to-face basis the firm's policies and the importance of ethical conduct. Some firms hold periodic ethics seminars during which employees can openly discuss any ethical problems that they may be experiencing and learn how the firm's ethical policies apply to those specific problems. Smaller firms should also offer some form of ethics training to employees, because this is one factor that courts will consider if the firm is later accused of an ethics violation.

The Sarbanes-Oxley Act and Web-Based Reporting Systems The Sarbanes-Oxley Act of 2002[1] requires that companies set up confidential systems so that employees and others can "raise red flags" about suspected illegal or unethical auditing and accounting practices.

Some companies have created online reporting systems to accomplish this goal. In one such system, employees can click on an icon on their computers that anonymously links them with Ethicspoint, an organization based in Portland, Oregon. Through Ethicspoint, employees can report suspicious accounting practices, sexual harassment, and other possibly unethical behavior. Ethicspoint, in turn, alerts management personnel or the audit committee at the designated company to the

potential problem. Those who have used the system say that it is less inhibiting than calling a company's toll-free number.

How the Law Influences Business Ethics

Although business ethics and the law are closely related, they are not always identical. Here, we examine some situations in which what is legal and what is ethical may not be the same.

The Moral Minimum

Compliance with the law is normally regarded as the **moral minimum**—the minimum acceptable standard for ethical business behavior. In many corporate scandals, had most of the businesspersons involved simply followed the law, they would not have gotten into trouble. Note, though, that in the interest of preserving personal freedom, as well as for practical reasons, the law does not—and cannot—codify all ethical requirements. As they make business decisions, businesspersons must remember that just because an action is legal does not necessarily make it ethical. Look at Exhibit 18–1. Here, you see that there is an intersection between what is ethical and what is legal. Businesspersons should attempt to operate in the area where what is legal and what is ethical intersect.

EXHIBIT 18–1• The Intersection of What Is Legal and What Is Ethical

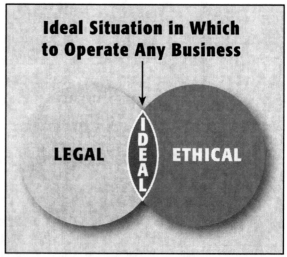

---

1. 15 U.S.C. Sections 7201 *et seq.* This act will be discussed in Chapters 41 and 51.

Excessive Executive Pay As just mentioned, business behavior that is legal may still be unethical. Consider executive pay. There is no law that specifies what public corporations can pay their officers. Consequently, "executive-pay scandals" do not have to do with executives breaking the law. Rather, such scandals have to do with the ethical underpinnings of executive-pay scales that can exceed millions of dollars. Such high pay for executives may appear unethical when their companies are not making very high profits (or are even suffering losses) and their share prices are falling.

Even this subject, though, does not lend itself to a black-and-white ethical analysis. As with many other things, there is a market for executives that operates according to supply and demand. Sometimes, corporate boards decide to offer executives very large compensation packages in order either to entice them to come to work for the company or to keep them from leaving for another corporation. There is no simple formula for determining the ethical level of compensation for a given executive in a given company. If a law were passed that limited executive compensation to, say, twenty times the salary of the lowest-paid worker in the company, there would be fewer individuals willing to undergo the stress and long hours associated with running major companies.

Determining the Legality of a Given Action It may seem that determining the legality of a given action should be simple. Either something is legal or it is not. In fact, one of the major challenges businesspersons face is that the legality of a particular action is not always clear. In part, this is because there are so many laws regulating business that it is increasingly possible to violate one of them without realizing it. The law also contains numerous "gray areas," making it difficult to predict with certainty how a court will apply a given law to a particular action.

Determining whether a planned action is legal thus requires that decision makers keep abreast of the law. Normally, large business firms have attorneys on their staffs to assist them in making key decisions. Small firms must also seek legal advice before making important business decisions because the consequences of just one violation of a regulatory rule may be costly.

Ignorance of the law will not excuse a business owner or manager from liability for violating a statute or regulation. In one case, Riverdale Mills Corporation was held liable when an employee attempted to board a plane with two cans of flammable hazardous material from Riverdale in his luggage. The court found that even though the employer was unaware of the employee's actions—and the employee was ignorant of the illegality of his actions—Riverdale had violated Federal Aviation Administration (FAA) regulations.[2]

The Law Cannot Control All Business Behavior

Congress, the regulatory agencies, and state and local governments do not have perfect knowledge. Often they only discover the negative impact of corporate activities after the fact. The same can be true of corporate executives. They do not always know the full impact of their actions. When asbestos was used for insulation, for example, the corporations that supplied it did not know that it was capable of causing a rare type of cancer.

At other times, though, the law is not ambiguous. Nevertheless, it may still be unable to control business behavior—at least initially.

Breaking the Law—Backdating Stock Options Stock options are a device that potentially rewards hard work. Publicly held corporations offer stock options to employees at the current price of the company's stock on the day that the options are granted. If at a later time the market price of the stock has gone up, an employee can exercise the stock options and reap the difference between the price of the options and the current market price.

In 2006 and 2007, it was revealed that a number of large corporations had backdated stock options. If stock options are granted and the price of the company's stock subsequently falls or does not rise very much, the value of the stock options is essentially zero. One way around this problem is to go back and change the date on which the stock options were granted to the employee. In other words, the date of the stock options is simply moved back to a day when the stock had a lower price than it has currently, thereby making the options valuable again.

Backdating is illegal if companies do not follow proper accounting procedures and the disclosure rules of the Securities and Exchange Commission (SEC). It is also illegal if the company misrepresents the authorization for, or falsifies records relating to, the

---

2. *Riverdale Mills Corp. v. FAA*, 417 F.Supp.2d 167 (D.Mass. 2006).

backdating. For example, in February 2007, the former chief executive officer of Brocade Communications Systems, Inc., Gregory L. Reyes, Jr., was sentenced to twenty-one months in prison, plus a $15 million fine for "tampering" with records of stock option grants. At least a dozen other business executives face similar charges.

The backdating scandal is another example of unethical behavior resulting in long-run profit reduction. As of 2008, at least 250 public companies had disclosed that they had undertaken internal investigations to discover if backdating had occurred without following proper procedures. The companies involved faced more than 125 shareholder lawsuits and as many SEC investigations, plus fifty-eight U.S. Department of Justice investigations and even six criminal cases.

Misleading Regulators—The Case of OxyContin In 1996, the pharmaceutical company Purdue Pharma, LP, started marketing a "wonder" narcotic painkiller called OxyContin. This powerful, long-lasting drug provides pain relief for twelve hours. Just a few years after its introduction, Purdue Pharma's annual sales of the drug reached $1 billion.

The company's executives initially contended that OxyContin, because of its time-release formulation, posed no risk for serious abuse or addiction. Quickly, though, experienced drug abusers and even teenagers discovered that chewing on an OxyContin tablet or crushing one and snorting the powder produced a powerful high, comparable to that of heroin. By 2000, large parts of the United States were experiencing increases in addiction and crime related to OxyContin.

In reality, the company and three of its executives had fraudulently marketed OxyContin for over six years as a drug unlikely to lead to abuse. Internal company documents showed that even before OxyContin was marketed, executives recognized that if physicians knew that the drug could be abused and become addictive, they would be less likely to prescribe it. Consequently, the company simply kept the information secret.

On May 10, 2007, Purdue Pharma and three former executives pleaded guilty to criminal charges that they had misled regulators, patients, and physicians about OxyContin's risks of addiction. Purdue Pharma agreed to pay $600 million in fines and other payments. The three ex-executives agreed to pay $34.5 million in fines. Once again, company executives engaged in unethical reasoning because they wanted to maximize profits in the short run, rather than engaging in behavior that would lead to profit maximization in the long run.

"Gray Areas" in the Law

In many situations, business firms can predict with a fair amount of certainty whether a given action is legal. For instance, firing an employee solely because of that person's race or gender clearly violates federal laws prohibiting employment discrimination. In some situations, though, the legality of a particular action may be less clear.

Suppose that a firm decides to launch a new advertising campaign. How far can the firm go in making claims for its products or services? Federal and state laws prohibit firms from engaging in "deceptive advertising." At the federal level, the test for deceptive advertising normally used by the Federal Trade Commission is whether an advertising claim would deceive a "reasonable consumer."[3] At what point, though, would a reasonable consumer be deceived by a particular ad?

In addition, many rules of law require a court to determine what is "foreseeable" or "reasonable" in a particular situation. Because a business has no way of predicting how a specific court will decide these issues, decision makers need to proceed with caution and evaluate an action and its consequences from an ethical perspective. The same problem often occurs in cases involving the Internet because it is often unclear how a court will apply existing laws in the context of cyberspace. Generally, if a company can demonstrate that it acted in good faith and responsibly in the circumstances, it has a better chance of successfully defending its action in court or before an administrative law judge.

The following case shows that businesses and their customers have different expectations with respect to the standard of care regarding the handling of personal information. The case also illustrates that the legal standards in this area may be inconsistent and vague.

---

3. See Chapter 44 for a discussion of the Federal Trade Commission's role in regulating deceptive trade practices, including misleading advertising.

C A S E **18.3** **Guin v. Brazos Higher Education Service Corp.**
United States District Court, District of Minnesota, 2006. __ F.Supp.2d __.

● **Background and Facts** Brazos Higher Education Service Corporation, which is based in Waco, Texas, makes and services student loans. Brazos issued a laptop computer to its employee John Wright, who worked from an office in his home in Silver Spring, Maryland, analyzing loan information. Wright used the laptop to store borrowers' personal information. In September 2004, Wright's home was burglarized and the laptop was stolen. Based on Federal Trade Commission (FTC) guidelines and California state law (which requires notice to all resident borrowers), Brazos sent a letter to all of its 550,000 customers. The letter stated that "some personal information associated with your student loan, including your name, address, Social Security number and loan balance, may have been inappropriately accessed by [a] third party." The letter urged borrowers to place "a free 90-day security alert" on their credit bureau files and review FTC consumer assistance materials. Brazos set up a call center to answer further questions and track any reports of identity theft. Stacy Guin, a Brazos customer, filed a suit in a federal district court against Brazos, alleging negligence. Brazos filed a motion for summary judgment.

● **Decision and Rationale** The court granted the defendant's motion for summary judgment and dismissed the case. Brazos may have owed Guin a duty of care, but neither Brazos nor Wright breached that duty. Wright had followed Brazos's written security procedures, which was all that the law requires. The court acknowledged that Brazos had a duty to protect the security and confidentiality of its customers' personal information. Under the Gramm-Leach-Bliley (GLB) Act, a financial institution must "develop, implement, and maintain a comprehensive written information security program that * * * contains administrative, technical, and physical safeguards that are appropriate to * * * the sensitivity of any customer information." Guin argued that Brazos breached this duty by (1) "providing Wright with [personal information] that he did not need for the task at hand," (2) "permitting Wright to continue keeping [personal information] in an unattended, insecure personal residence," and (3) "allowing Wright to keep [personal information] on his laptop unencrypted." The court disagreed. Brazos had established written security policies and other mandated safeguards for its customers' personal information. Brazos gave Wright access to the information because Wright needed it to analyze loan portfolios. Besides, the GLB Act does not prohibit someone from working with sensitive data on a laptop computer in a home office or require that the data be encrypted.

● **What If the Facts Were Different?** *Suppose that Wright had not been a financial analyst and his duties for Brazos had not included reviewing confidential loan data. How might the opinion of the court have been different?*

● **The Ethical Dimension** *Do businesses have an ethical duty to use enhanced security measures to protect confidential customer information? Why or why not? Does the fact that Brazos allowed its employees to store customers' unencrypted personal information on a laptop outside the office violate any ethical duty?*

Making Ethical Business Decisions

As Dean Krehmeyer, executive director of the Business Roundtable's Institute for Corporate Ethics, once said, "Evidence strongly suggests being ethical—doing the right thing—pays." Instilling ethical business decision making into the fabric of a business organization is no small task, even if ethics "pays." The job is to get people to understand that they have to think more broadly about how their decisions will affect employees, shareholders, customers, and even the community. Great companies, such as Enron and the accounting firm

Arthur Andersen, were brought down by the unethical behavior of a few. A two-hundred-year-old British investment banking firm, Barings Bank, was destroyed by the actions of one employee and a few of his friends. Clearly, ensuring that all employees get on the ethical business decision-making "bandwagon" is crucial in today's fast-paced world.

The George S. May International Company has provided six basic guidelines to help corporate employees judge their actions. Each employee—no matter what his or her level in the organization—should evaluate his or her actions using the following six guidelines:

1. *The law.* Is the action you are considering legal? If you do not know the laws governing the action, then find out. Ignorance of the law is no excuse.
2. *Rules and procedures.* Are you following the internal rules and procedures that have already been laid out by your company? They have been developed to avoid problems. Is what you are planning to do consistent with your company's policies and procedures? If not, stop.
3. *Values.* Laws and internal company policies reinforce society's values. You might wish to ask yourself whether you are attempting to find a loophole in the law or in your company's policies. Next, you have to ask yourself whether you are following the "spirit" of the law as well as the letter of the law or the internal policy.
4. *Conscience.* If you have any feeling of guilt, let your conscience be your guide. Alternatively, ask yourself whether you would be happy to be interviewed by a national news magazine about the actions you are going to take.
5. *Promises.* Every business organization is based on trust. Your customers believe that your company will do what it is supposed to do. The same is true for your suppliers and employees. Will your actions live up to the commitments you have made to others, both inside the business and outside?
6. *Heroes.* We all have heroes who are role models for us. Is what you are planning on doing an action that your hero would take? If not, how would your hero act? That is how you should be acting.

Business Ethics on a Global Level

Given the various cultures and religions throughout the world, conflicts in ethics frequently arise between foreign and U.S. businesspersons. For example, in certain countries the consumption of alcohol and specific foods is forbidden for religious reasons. Under such circumstances, it would be thoughtless and imprudent for a U.S. businessperson to invite a local business contact out for a drink.

The role played by women in other countries may also present some difficult ethical problems for firms doing business internationally. Equal employment opportunity is a fundamental public policy in the United States, and Title VII of the Civil Rights Act of 1964 prohibits discrimination against women in the employment context (see Chapter 34). Some other countries, however, offer little protection for women against gender discrimination in the workplace, including sexual harassment.

We look here at how the employment practices that affect workers in other countries, particularly developing countries, have created some especially difficult ethical problems for U.S. sellers of goods manufactured in foreign nations. We also examine some of the ethical ramifications of laws prohibiting bribery and the expansion of ethics programs in the global community.

Monitoring the Employment Practices of Foreign Suppliers

Many U.S. businesses now contract with companies in developing nations to produce goods, such as shoes and clothing, because the wage rates in those nations are significantly lower than those in the United States. Yet what if a foreign company hires women and children at below-minimum-wage rates, for example, or requires its employees to work long hours in a workplace full of health hazards? What if the company's supervisors routinely engage in workplace conduct that is offensive to women?

Given today's global communications network, few companies can assume that their actions in other nations will go unnoticed by "corporate watch" groups that discover and publicize unethical corporate behavior. As a result, U.S. businesses today usually take steps to avoid such adverse publicity—either by refusing to deal with certain suppliers or by arranging to monitor their suppliers' workplaces to make sure that the employees are not being mistreated.

The Foreign Corrupt Practices Act

Another ethical problem in international business dealings has to do with the legitimacy of certain side payments to government officials. In the United States, the majority of contracts are formed within the private sector. In many foreign countries, however, government officials make the decisions on most major construction and manufacturing contracts because of extensive government regulation and control over trade and industry. Side payments to government officials in exchange for favorable business contracts are not unusual in such countries, nor are they considered to be unethical. In the past, U.S. corporations doing business in these nations largely followed the dictum, "When in Rome, do as the Romans do."

In the 1970s, however, the U.S. press uncovered a number of business scandals involving large side payments by U.S. corporations to foreign representatives for the purpose of securing advantageous international trade contracts. In response to this unethical behavior, in 1977 Congress passed the Foreign Corrupt Practices Act (FCPA), which prohibits U.S. businesspersons from bribing foreign officials to secure beneficial contracts. (For a discussion of how a German corporation ran afoul of Germany's anti-bribery laws, see this chapter's *Insight into the Global Environment* feature on the following page.)

Prohibition against the Bribery of Foreign Officials The first part of the FCPA applies to all U.S. companies and their directors, officers, shareholders, employees, and agents. This part prohibits the bribery of most officials of foreign governments if the purpose of the payment is to get the official to act in his or her official capacity to provide business opportunities.

The FCPA does not prohibit payment of substantial sums to minor officials whose duties are ministerial. These payments are often referred to as "grease," or facilitating payments. They are meant to accelerate the performance of administrative services that might otherwise be carried out at a slow pace. Thus, for example, if a firm makes a payment to a minor official to speed up an import licensing process, the firm has not violated the FCPA. Generally, the act, as amended, permits payments to foreign officials if such payments are lawful within the foreign country. The act also does not prohibit payments to private foreign companies or other third parties unless the U.S. firm knows that the payments will be passed on to a foreign government in violation of the FCPA.

Accounting Requirements In the past, bribes were often concealed in corporate financial records. Thus, the second part of the FCPA is directed toward accountants. All companies must keep detailed records that "accurately and fairly" reflect their financial activities. In addition, all companies must have accounting systems that provide "reasonable assurance" that all transactions entered into by the companies are accounted for and legal. These requirements assist in detecting illegal bribes. The FCPA further prohibits any person from making false statements to accountants or false entries in any record or account.

Penalties for Violations In 1988, the FCPA was amended to provide that business firms that violate the act may be fined up to $2 million. Individual officers or directors who violate the FCPA may be fined up to $100,000 (the fine cannot be paid by the company) and may be imprisoned for up to five years.

Breach of Trust Issues Hit Major German Corporations

Whether you call it immoral, unethical, illegal, or a breach of trust, bribery by any name is wrong. In recent years, officers and managing directors at several major German corporations have been investigated, arrested, and fined for bribery. One German firm that has faced numerous charges is Siemens, a venerable corporation that was founded in 1847. Siemens built the first long-distance telegraph line in Europe from Berlin to Frankfurt in 1849. Today, the company, which its almost 500,000 workers like to call the House of Siemens, has operations in communications, radar, traffic control, and cell phones.

Corruption Charges Are Not New

When global competition intensified in the 1980s and 1990s, Siemens began to face fierce competition from multinational giants such as General Electric. To maintain the company's cash flow and sales dominance, some of Siemens's managers started bribing potential clients—usually government agencies—to generate new business. In the early 1990s, the German government investigated Siemens's activities and convicted nine of the company's managers on bribery charges. The judge in the case wondered why the managers kept referring to the company as the "House of Siemens"—a name that, in the judge's view, implies "that the firm rises above the muck of ordinary business; it conveys a sense of moral exemption and entitlement." Of course, part of Siemens's problem may have been the somewhat ambiguous approach to bribery taken by German law. Bribes paid to foreign officials were tax deductible in Germany until 1999.

Unethical Actions Continue

Apparently, Siemens did not learn its lesson, for complaints about its behavior continued. In the early 2000s, Swiss authorities began an investigation that continued for a year and a half. The allegations of corruption did not trouble Heinrich von Pierer, Siemens's chair, however, or spur him to look into his managers' behavior. Instead, he stated simply, "I'm aware that our organization is hard to understand for outsiders. The job of board members is primarily strategic. Going over the books is the responsibility of others." Several years later, the company finally disclosed that about $600 million in "suspicious transactions" (read "bribes") had been discovered.

By 2007, von Pierer had resigned, and the chief executive officer decided not to ask for a new contract. In the meantime, a German court had convicted two former Siemens executives of bribery and fined the company about $50 million.

Once again, ambiguities in German law entered the case. One former Siemens executive told the court that he did indeed authorize millions of dollars of bribes to win contracts from an Italian electric company. He insisted, though, that he did not break any laws and that the payments were not illegal because German law only forbids payments to "civil servants." The executive contended that the payments he made to the Italian company's managers were made to representatives of a private-sector company, not to "civil servants." German prosecutors had to admit that the legal definition of what constitutes a civil servant allows room for interpretation.

Bribing the Union

Siemens executives may not have restricted their activities to bribing "civil servants" or private-sector managers. One Siemens executive, Johannes Feldmayer, has been arrested on a special type of bribery charge. He has been accused of bribing the head of a workers' organization, a type of independent labor union. Apparently, Siemens wanted a counterweight to IG Metall, the most powerful German union, and Feldmayer allegedly oversaw the transfer of some $45 million to the independent union to facilitate this. Earlier, another major German corporation, Volkswagen (VW), faced similar charges of making illegal payments to the head of its workers' council. Peter Harz, formerly VW's head of labor relations, pleaded guilty to the charges and paid a fine of about $750,000.

CRITICAL THINKING
INSIGHT INTO POLITICS

Clearly, the corporate culture at Siemens, at least in the last few decades, did not distinguish among actions that were both ethical and legal, actions that were unethical but perhaps legal, and actions that were both unethical and illegal. What could top management at that company have done to instill a different corporate culture that would have resulted in a different outcome?

REVIEWING Ethics and Business Decision Making

Isabel Arnett was promoted to chief executive officer (CEO) of Tamik, Inc., a pharmaceutical company that manufactures a vaccine called Kafluk, which supposedly provides some defense against bird flu. The company began marketing Kafluk throughout Asia. After numerous media reports that bird flu could soon become a worldwide epidemic, the demand for Kafluk increased, sales soared, and Tamik earned record profits. Tamik's CEO, Arnett, then began receiving disturbing reports from Southeast Asia that in some patients, Kafluk had caused psychiatric disturbances, including severe hallucinations, and heart and lung problems. Arnett was informed that six children in Japan had committed suicide by jumping out of windows after receiving the vaccine. To cover up the story and prevent negative publicity, Arnett instructed Tamik's partners in Asia to offer cash to the Japanese families whose children had died in exchange for their silence. Arnett also refused to authorize additional research within the company to study the potential side effects of Kafluk. Using the information presented in the chapter, answer the following questions.

1. This scenario illustrates one of the main reasons why ethical problems occur in business. What is that reason?
2. Would a person who adheres to the principle of rights consider it ethical for Arnett not to disclose potential safety concerns and to refuse to perform additional research on Kafluk? Why or why not?
3. If Kafluk prevented fifty Asian people who were infected with bird flu from dying, would Arnett's conduct in this situation be ethical under a utilitarian model of ethics? Why or why not?
4. Did Tamik or Arnett violate the Foreign Corrupt Practices Act in this scenario? Why or why not?

TERMS AND CONCEPTS

business ethics
categorical imperative

corporate social
   responsibility
cost-benefit analysis
ethical reasoning
ethics

moral minimum
principle of rights
utilitarianism

QUESTIONS AND CASE PROBLEMS

5–1. Some business ethicists maintain that whereas personal ethics has to do with "right" or "wrong" behavior, business ethics is concerned with "appropriate" behavior. In other words, ethical behavior in business has less to do with moral principles than with what society deems to be appropriate behavior in the business context. Do you agree with this distinction? Do personal and business ethics ever

overlap? Should personal ethics play any role in business ethical decision making?

5-2. QUESTION WITH SAMPLE ANSWER

If a firm engages in "ethical" behavior solely for the purpose of gaining profits from the good-will it generates, the "ethical" behavior is essentially a means toward a self-serving end (profits and the accumulation of wealth). In this situation, is the firm acting unethically in any way? Should motive or conduct carry greater weight on the ethical scales in this situation?

- **For a sample answer to Question 5–2, go to Appendix C at the end of this text.**

5–3. Susan Whitehead serves on the city planning commission. The city is planning to build a new subway system, and Susan's brother-in-law, Jerry, who owns the Custom Transportation Co., has submitted the lowest bid for the system. Susan knows that Jerry could complete the job for the estimated amount, but she also knows that once Jerry finishes this job, he will probably sell his company and retire. Susan is concerned that Custom Transportation's subsequent management might not be as easy to work with if revisions need to be made on the subway system after its completion. She is torn as to whether she should tell the city about the potential changes in Custom Transportation's management. If the city knew about the instability of Custom Transportation, it might prefer to give the contract to one of Jerry's competitors, whose bid was only slightly higher than Jerry's. Does Susan have an ethical obligation to disclose the information about Jerry to the city planning commission? How would you apply duty-based ethical standards to this question? What might be the outcome of a utilitarian analysis? Discuss fully.

5–4. Assume that you are a high-level manager for a shoe manufacturer. You know that your firm could increase its profit margin by producing shoes in Indonesia, where you could hire women for $40 a month to assemble them. You also know, however, that human rights advocates recently accused a competing shoe manufacturer of engaging in exploitative labor practices because the manufacturer sold shoes made by Indonesian women working for similarly low wages. You personally do not believe that paying $40 a month to Indonesian women is unethical because you know that in their impoverished country, $40 a month is a better-than-average wage rate. Assuming that the decision is yours to make, should you have the shoes manufactured in Indonesia and make higher profits for your company? Or should you avoid the risk of negative publicity and the consequences of that publicity for the firm's reputation and subsequent profits? Are there other alternatives? Discuss fully.

5–5. Shokun Steel Co. owns many steel plants. One of its plants is much older than the others. Equipment at the old plant is outdated and inefficient, and the costs of production at that plant are now twice as high as at any of Shokun's other plants. Shokun cannot increase the price of its steel because of competition, both domestic and international. The plant employs more than a thousand workers; it is located in Twin Firs, Pennsylvania, which has a population of about forty-five thousand. Shokun is contemplating whether to close the plant. What factors should the firm consider in making its decision? Will the

firm violate any ethical duties if it closes the plant? Analyze these questions from the two basic perspectives on ethical reasoning discussed in this chapter.

5–6. CASE PROBLEM WITH SAMPLE ANSWER

Eden Electrical, Ltd., owned twenty-five appliance stores throughout Israel, at least some of which sold refrigerators made by Amana Co. Eden bought the appliances from Amana's Israeli distributor, Pan El A/Yesh Shem, which approached Eden about taking over the distributorship. Eden representatives met with Amana executives. The executives made assurances about Amana's good faith, its hope of having a long-term business relationship with Eden, and its willingness to have Eden become its exclusive distributor in Israel. Eden signed a distributorship agreement and paid Amana $2.4 million. Amana failed to deliver this amount in inventory to Eden, continued selling refrigerators to other entities for the Israeli market, and represented to others that it was still looking for a long-term distributor. Less than three months after signing the agreement with Eden, Amana terminated it, without explanation. Eden filed a suit in a federal district court against Amana, alleging fraud. The court awarded Eden $12.1 million in damages. Is this amount warranted? Why or why not? How does this case illustrate why business ethics is important? [*Eden Electrical, Ltd. v. Amana Co.*, 370 F.3d 824 (8th Cir. 2004)]

- **To view a sample answer for Problem 5–6, go to this book's Web site at www.cengage. com/blaw/jentz, select "Chapter 5," and click on "Case Problem with Sample Answer."**

5–7. Ethical Conduct. Richard Fraser was an "exclusive career insurance agent" under a contract with Nationwide Mutual Insurance Co. Fraser leased computer hardware and software from Nationwide for his business. During a dispute between Nationwide and the Nationwide Insurance Independent Contractors Association, an organization representing Fraser and other exclusive career agents, Fraser prepared a letter to Nationwide's competitors asking whether they were interested in acquiring the represented agents' policyholders. Nationwide obtained a copy of the letter and searched its electronic file server for e-mail indicating that the letter had been sent. It found a stored e-mail that Fraser had sent to a co-worker indicating that the letter had been sent to at least one competitor. The e-mail was retrieved from the co-worker's file of already received and discarded messages stored on the server. When Nationwide canceled its contract with Fraser, he filed a suit in a federal district court against the firm, alleging, among other things, violations of various federal laws that prohibit the interception of electronic communications during transmission. In whose favor should the court rule, and why? Did Nationwide act ethically in retrieving the e-mail? Explain. [*Fraser v. Nationwide Mutual Insurance Co.*, 352 F.3d 107 (3d Cir. 2004)]

5–8. Ethical Conduct. Unable to pay more than $1.2 billion in debt, Big Rivers Electric Corp. filed a petition to declare bankruptcy in a federal bankruptcy court in September 1996. Big Rivers' creditors included Bank of New York (BONY), Chase Manhattan Bank, Mapco Equities, and others. The court appointed J. Baxter Schilling to work as a "disinterested" (neutral) party with Big Rivers and the creditors to resolve their disputes and set an hourly fee as Schilling's compensation. Schilling told Chase, BONY, and Mapco that he wanted them to pay him an additional percentage fee based on the "success" he attained in finding "new value" to pay Big Rivers' debts. Without such a deal, he told them, he would not perform his mediation duties. Chase agreed; the others disputed the deal, but no one told the court. In October 1998, Schilling asked the court for nearly $4.5 million in compensation, including the hourly fees, which totaled about $531,000, and the percentage fees. Big Rivers and others asked the court to deny Schilling any fees on the basis that he had improperly negotiated "secret side agreements." How did Schilling violate his duties as a "disinterested" party? Should he be denied compensation? Why or why not? [*In re Big Rivers Electric Corp.*, 355 F.3d 415 (6th Cir. 2004)]

5–9. Ethical Conduct. Ernest Price suffered from sickle-cell anemia. In 1997, Price asked Dr. Ann Houston, his physician, to prescribe OxyContin, a strong narcotic, for the pain. Over the next several years, Price saw at least ten different physicians at ten different clinics in two cities, and used seven pharmacies in three cities, to obtain and fill simultaneous prescriptions for OxyContin. In March 2001, when Houston learned of these activities, she refused to write more prescriptions for Price. As other physicians became aware of Price's actions, they also stopped writing his prescriptions. Price filed a suit in a Mississippi state court against Purdue Pharma Co. and other producers and distributors of OxyContin, as well as his physicians and the pharmacies that had filled the prescriptions. Price alleged negligence, among other things, claiming that OxyContin's addictive nature caused him injury and that this was the defendants' fault. The defendants argued that Price's claim should be dismissed because it arose from his own wrongdoing. Who should be held *legally* liable? Should any of the parties be considered *ethically* responsible? Why or why not? [*Price v. Purdue Pharma Co.*, 920 So.2d 479 (Miss. 2006)]

5–10. Ethical Leadership. In 1999, Andrew Fastow, chief financial officer of Enron Corp., asked Merrill Lynch, an investment firm, to participate in a bogus sale of three barges so that Enron could record earnings of $12.5 million from the sale. Through a third entity, Fastow bought the barges back within six months and paid Merrill for its participation. Five Merrill employees were convicted of conspiracy to commit wire fraud, in part, on an "honest services" theory. Under this theory, an employee deprives

his or her employer of "honest services" when the employee promotes his or her own interests, rather than the interests of the employer. Four of the employees appealed to the U.S. Court of Appeals for the Fifth Circuit, arguing that this charge did not apply to the conduct in which they engaged. The court agreed, reasoning that the barge deal was conducted to benefit Enron, not to enrich the Merrill employees at Enron's expense. Meanwhile, Kevin Howard, chief financial officer of Enron Broadband Services (EBS), engaged in "Project Braveheart," which enabled EBS to show earnings of $111 million in 2000 and 2001. Braveheart involved the sale of an interest in the future revenue of a video-on-demand venture to nCube, a small technology firm, which was paid for its help when EBS bought the interest back. Howard was convicted of wire fraud, in part, on the "honest services" theory. He filed a motion to vacate his conviction on the same basis that the Merrill employees had argued. Did Howard act unethically? Explain. Should the court grant his motion? Discuss. [*United States v. Howard*, 471 F.Supp.2d 772 (S.D.Tex. 2007)]

5–11. A QUESTION OF ETHICS

Steven Soderbergh is the Academy Award–winning director of Erin Brockovich, Traffic, *and many other films. CleanFlicks, LLC, filed a suit in a federal district court against Soderbergh, fifteen other directors, and the Directors Guild of America. The plaintiff asked the court to rule that it had the right to sell DVDs of the defendants' films altered without the defendants' consent to delete scenes of "sex, nudity, profanity and gory violence." CleanFlicks sold or rented the edited DVDs under the slogan "It's About Choice" to consumers, sometimes indirectly through retailers. It would not sell to retailers that made unauthorized copies of the edited films. The defendants, with DreamWorks, LLC, and seven other movie studios that own the copyrights to the films, filed a counterclaim against CleanFlicks and others engaged in the same business, alleging copyright infringement. Those filing the counterclaim asked the court to enjoin (prevent) CleanFlicks and the others from making and marketing altered versions of the films. [CleanFlicks of Colorado, LLC v. Soderbergh, 433 F.Supp.2d 1236 (D.Colo. 2006)]*

(a) Movie studios often edit their films to conform to content and other standards and sell the edited versions to network television and other commercial buyers. In this case, however, the studios objected when CleanFlicks edited the films and sold the altered versions directly to consumers. Similarly, CleanFlicks made unauthorized copies of the studios' DVDs to edit the films, but objected to others' making unauthorized copies of the altered versions. Is there anything unethical about these apparently contradictory positions? Why or why not?

(b) CleanFlicks and its competitors asserted, among other things, that they were making "fair use" of the studios' copyrighted works. They argued that by their actions "they are criticizing the objectionable content commonly found in current movies and that they are providing more socially acceptable alternatives to enable families to view the films together, without exposing children to the presumed harmful effects emanating from the objectionable content." If you were the judge, how would you view this argument? Is a court the appropriate forum for making determinations of public or social policy? Explain.

5–12. VIDEO QUESTION

Go to this text's Web site at **www.cengage. com/blaw/jentz** and select "Chapter 5." Click on "Video Questions" and view the video titled *Ethics:*

Business Ethics an Oxymoron? Then answer the following questions.

(a) According to the instructor in the video, what is the primary reason that businesses act ethically?

(b) Which of the two approaches to ethical reasoning that were discussed in the chapter seems to have had more influence on the instructor in the discussion of how business activities are related to societies? Explain your answer.

(c) The instructor asserts that "in the end, it is the unethical behavior that becomes costly, and conversely ethical behavior creates its own competitive advantage." Do you agree with this statement? Why or why not?

LAW ON THE WEB

For updated links to resources available on the Web, as well as a variety of other materials, visit this text's Web site at

www.cengage.com/blaw/jentz

You can find articles on issues relating to shareholders and corporate accountability at the Corporate Governance Web site. Go to

www.corpgov.net

For an example of an online group that focuses on corporate activities from the perspective of corporate social responsibility, go to

www.corpwatch.org

Global Exchange offers information on global business activities, including some of the ethical issues stemming from those activities, at

www.globalexchange.org

Legal Research Exercises on the Web

Go to **www.cengage.com/blaw/jentz**, the Web site that accompanies this text. Select "Chapter 5" and click on "Internet Exercises." There you will find the following Internet research exercises that you can perform to learn more about the topics covered in this chapter.

Internet Exercise 5–1: Legal Perspective
                        Ethics in Business

Internet Exercise 5–2: Management Perspective
                        Environmental Self-Audits

Ethics and the Legal Environment of Business

In Chapter 5, we examined the importance of ethical standards in the business context. We also offered suggestions on how business decision makers can create an ethical workplace. Certainly, it is not wrong for a businessperson to try to increase his or her firm's profits. But there are limits, both ethical and legal, to how far businesspersons can go. In preparing for a career in business, you will find that a background in business ethics and a commitment to ethical behavior are just as important as a knowledge of the specific laws that are covered in this text. Of course, no textbook can give an answer to each and every ethical question that arises in the business environment. Nor can it anticipate the types of ethical questions that will arise in the future, as technology and globalization continue to transform the workplace and business relationships.

The most we can do is examine the types of ethical issues that businesspersons have faced in the past and that they are facing today. In the *Focus on Ethics* sections in this book, we provide examples of specific ethical issues that have arisen in various areas of business activity.

In this initial *Focus on Ethics* feature, we look first at the relationship between business ethics and business law. We then examine various obstacles to ethical behavior in the business context. We conclude the feature by exploring the parameters of corporate social responsibility through a discussion of whether corporations have an ethical duty to the community or society at large.

Business Ethics and Business Law

Business ethics and business law are closely intertwined because ultimately the law rests on social beliefs about right and wrong behavior in the business world. Thus, businesspersons, by complying with the law, are acting ethically. Mere legal compliance (the "moral minimum" in terms of business ethics), however, is often not enough. This is because the law does not—and cannot—provide the answers for all ethical questions.

In the business world, numerous actions may be unethical but not necessarily illegal. Consider an example. Suppose that a pharmaceutical company is banned from marketing a particular drug in the United States because of the drug's possible adverse side effects. Yet no law prohibits the company from selling the drug in foreign markets—even though some consumers in those markets may suffer serious health problems as a result of using the drug. At issue here is not whether it would be legal to market the drug in other countries but whether it would be *ethical* to do so. In other words, the law has its limits—it cannot make all ethical decisions for us. Rather, the law assumes that those in business will behave ethically in their day-to-day dealings. If they do not, the courts will not come to their assistance.

Obstacles to Ethical Business Behavior

People sometimes behave unethically in the business context, just as they do in their private lives. Some businesspersons knowingly engage in unethical behavior because they think that they can "get away with it"—that no one will ever learn of their unethical actions. Examples of this kind of unethical behavior include padding expense accounts, casting doubts on the integrity of a rival co-worker to gain a job promotion, and stealing company supplies or equipment. Obviously, these acts are unethical, and some of them are illegal as well. In some situations, however, businesspersons who would choose to act ethically may be deterred from doing so because of situational circumstances or external pressures.

Ethics and the Corporate Environment Individuals in their personal lives normally are free to decide ethical issues as they wish and to follow through on those decisions. In the business world, and particularly in the corporate environment, rarely is such a decision made by *one* person. If you are an officer or a manager of a large company, for example, you will find that the decision as to what is right or wrong for the company is not totally yours to make. Your input may weigh in the decision, but ultimately a corporate decision is a collective undertaking.

Additionally, collective decision making, because it places emphasis on consensus and unity of opinion, tends to hinder individual ethical assertiveness. Suppose that a director has ethical concerns about a planned corporate venture that promises to be highly profitable. If the other directors have no such misgivings, the director who does may be swayed by the others' enthusiasm for the project and downplay her or his own criticisms.

Furthermore, just as no one person makes a collective decision, so no one person (normally) is held accountable for the decision. The corporate

(Continued)

515

enterprise thus tends to shield corporate personnel from both individual exposure to the consequences of their decisions (such as direct experience with someone who suffers harm from a corporate product) and personal accountability for those decisions.

Ethics and Management Much unethical business behavior occurs simply because management does not always make clear what ethical standards and behaviors are expected of the firm's employees. Although most firms now issue ethical policies or codes of conduct, these policies and codes are not always effective in creating an ethical workplace. At times, this is because the firm's ethical policies are not communicated clearly to employees or do not bear on the real ethical issues confronting decision makers. Additionally, particularly in a large corporation, unethical behavior in one corporate department may simply escape the attention of the officers in control of the corporation or those responsible for implementing and monitoring the company's ethics program.

Unethical behavior may also occur when corporate management, by its own conduct, indicates that ethical considerations take a back seat. If management makes no attempt to deter unethical behavior—through reprimands or employment terminations, for example—it will be obvious to employees that management is not all that serious about ethics. Likewise, if a company gives promotions or salary increases to those who clearly use unethical tactics to increase the firm's profits, then employees who do not resort to such tactics will be at a disadvantage. An employee in this situation may decide that because "everyone else does it," he or she might as well do it, too.

Of course, an even stronger encouragement to unethical behavior occurs when employers engage in blatantly unethical or illegal conduct and expect their employees to do so as well. An employee in this situation faces two options, neither of which is satisfactory: participate in the conduct or "blow the whistle" on (inform authorities of) the employer's actions—and, of course, risk being fired. (See Chapter 33 for a more detailed discussion of this ethical dilemma and its consequences for employees.)

Corporate Social Responsibility

As discussed in Chapter 5, just what constitutes corporate social responsibility has been debated for some time. In particular, questions arise concerning a corporation's ethical obligations to its community and to society as a whole.

A Corporation's Duty to the Community In some circumstances, the community in which a business enterprise is located is greatly affected by corporate decisions and therefore may be considered a stakeholder. Assume, for example, that a company employs two thousand workers at one of its plants. If the company decides that it would be profitable to close the plant, the employees—and the community—would suffer as a result. To be considered ethical in that situation (and, in some circumstances, to comply with laws governing plant shutdowns), a corporation must take both employees' needs and community needs into consideration when making such a decision.

Another ethical question sometimes arises when a firm moves into a community. Does the company have an obligation to evaluate first how its presence will affect that community (even though the community is not a stakeholder yet)? This question has surfaced in regard to the expansion of Wal-Mart Stores, Inc., into smaller communities. Generally, most people in such communities welcome the lower prices and wider array of goods that Wal-Mart offers relative to other, smaller stores in the area. A vocal minority of people in some communities, however, claim that smaller stores often find it impossible to compete with Wal-Mart's prices and thus are forced to go out of business. Many of these smaller stores have existed for years and, according to Wal-Mart's critics, enhance the quality of community life. These critics claim that it is unethical of Wal-Mart to disregard a town's interest in the quality and character of its community life.

In addition to expanding, Wal-Mart has been consolidating some of its smaller stores into large "superstores." As it consolidates, Wal-Mart is closing stores in some of the very towns in which it drove its smaller competitors out of business. This development raises yet another ethical question: Does a store such as Wal-Mart have an obligation to continue operations in a community once it has driven its competitors out of business?

A Corporation's Duty to Society Perhaps the most disputed area of corporate social responsibility is the nature of a corporation's duty to society at large. Those who contend that corporations should first and foremost attend to the goal of profit maximization would argue that it is by generating profits that a firm can best contribute to society.

Society benefits by profit-making activities because profits can only be realized when a firm markets products or services that are desired by society. These products and services enhance the standard of living, and the profits accumulated by successful business firms generate national wealth. Our laws and court decisions promoting trade and commerce reflect the public policy that the fruits of commerce (wealth) are desirable and good. Because our society values wealth as an ethical goal, corporations, by contributing to that wealth, automatically are acting ethically.

Those arguing for profit maximization as a corporate goal also point out that it would be inappropriate to use the power of the corporate business world to further society's goals by promoting social causes. Determinations as to what exactly is in society's best interest involve questions that are essentially political, and therefore the public, through the political process, should have a say in making those determinations. Thus, the legislature—not the corporate boardroom—is the appropriate forum for such decisions.

Critics of the profit-maximization view believe that corporations should become actively engaged in seeking and furthering solutions to social problems. Because so much of the wealth and power of this country is controlled by business, business in turn has a responsibility to society to use that wealth and power in socially beneficial ways. Corporations should therefore promote human rights, strive for equal treatment of minorities and women in the workplace, take steps to preserve the environment, and generally not profit from activities that society has deemed unethical. The critics also point out that it is ethically irresponsible to leave decisions concerning social welfare up to the government, because many social needs are not being met sufficiently through the political process.

It Pays to Be Ethical

Most corporations today have learned that it pays to be ethically responsible—even if this means less profit in the short run (and it often does). Today's corporations are subject to more intensive scrutiny—by both government agencies and the public—than corporations of the past. "Corporate watch" groups monitor the activities of U.S. corporations, including activities conducted in foreign countries. Through

the Internet, complaints about a corporation's practices can easily be disseminated to a worldwide audience. Similarly, dissatisfied customers and employees can voice their complaints about corporate policies, products, or services in Internet chat rooms and other online forums. Thus, if a corporation fails to conduct its operations ethically or to respond quickly to an ethical crisis, its goodwill and reputation (and future profits) will likely suffer as a result.

There are other reasons as well for a corporation to behave ethically. For example, companies that demonstrate a commitment to ethical behavior—by implementing ethical programs, complying with environmental regulations, and promptly investigating product complaints, for example—often receive more lenient treatment from government agencies and the courts. Additionally, investors may shy away from a corporation's stock if the corporation is perceived to be socially irresponsible. Finally, unethical (and/or illegal) corporate behavior may result in government action, such as new laws imposing further requirements on corporate entities.

DISCUSSION QUESTIONS

1. What might be some other deterrents to ethical behavior in the business context, besides those discussed in this *Focus on Ethics* feature?

2. Can you think of a situation in which a business firm may be acting ethically but not in a socially responsible manner? Explain.

3. Why are consumers and the public generally more concerned with ethical and socially responsible business behavior today than they were, say, fifty years ago?

4. Suppose that an automobile manufacturing company has to choose between two alternatives: contributing $1 million annually to the United Way or reinvesting the $1 million in the company. In terms of ethics and social responsibility, which is the "better" choice?

5. Have Internet chat rooms and online forums affected corporate decision makers' willingness to consider the community and public interest when making choices? Are corporate decision makers more apt to make ethical choices in the cyber age? Explain.

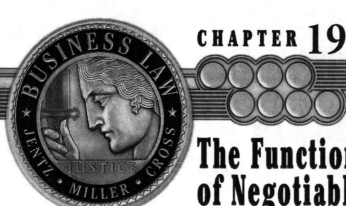

CHAPTER 19

The Function and Creation of Negotiable Instruments

A **negotiable instrument** is a signed writing (or record) that contains an unconditional promise or order to pay an exact amount of money, either on demand or at a specific future time. The checks you write to pay for groceries, rent, your monthly car payment, insurance premiums, and other items are negotiable instruments.

Most commercial transactions that take place in the modern business world would be inconceivable without negotiable instruments. A negotiable instrument can function as a substitute for cash or as an extension of credit. For example, when a buyer writes a check to pay for goods, the check serves as a substitute for cash. When a buyer gives a seller a promissory note in which the buyer promises to pay the seller the purchase price within sixty days, the seller has essentially extended credit to the buyer for a sixty-day period. For a negotiable instrument to operate *practically* as either a substitute for cash or a credit device, or both, it is essential that the instrument be *easily transferable without danger of being uncollectible.* This is a fundamental function of negotiable instruments. Each rule described in the following pages can be examined in light of this function.

The law governing negotiable instruments grew out of commercial necessity. In the medieval world, merchants engaging in foreign trade used *bills of exchange* to finance and conduct their affairs, rather than risk transporting gold or coins. Because the English king's courts of those times did not recognize the validity of these bills of exchange, the merchants developed their own set of rules, which were enforced by "fair" or "borough" courts. Eventually, the decisions of these courts became a distinct set of laws known as the *Lex Mercatoria* (Law Merchant). The Law Merchant was codified in England in the Bills of Exchange Act of 1882. In 1896, in the United States, the National Conference of Commissioners on Uniform State Laws (NCCUSL) drafted the Uniform Negotiable Instruments Law. This law was the forerunner of Article 3 of the Uniform Commercial Code (UCC).

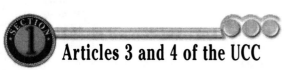

Articles 3 and 4 of the UCC

Negotiable instruments are governed by Articles 3 and 4 of the UCC. In this chapter and in Chapters 25 and 26, we will focus on the law as established by Article 3. You will learn about the different types of negotiable instruments, the requirements that all negotiable instruments must meet, the process of *negotiation* (transferring an instrument from one party to another), and the responsibilities of parties to negotiable instruments. Note that UCC 3–104(b) defines an *instrument* as a "negotiable instrument." For that reason, whenever the term *instrument* is used in this book, it refers to a negotiable instrument. Article 4 governs bank deposits and collections as well as bank-customer relationships—topics that we will examine in Chapter 27.

The 1990 Revision of Articles 3 and 4

In 1990, a revised version of Article 3 was issued for adoption by the states. Many of the changes to Article 3 simply clarified old sections; some, however, significantly altered the former provisions. As of this writing, all of the states except New York and South Carolina have adopted the revised article. Therefore, all references to Article 3 in this chapter and in the following chapters are to the *revised* Article 3. When the revisions to Article 3 have made important changes in the law, however, we discuss the previous law in footnotes. Article 4 was also revised in 1990. In part, these changes were necessary because the changes in Article 3 affected Article 4 provisions. The revised Articles 3 and 4 are included in their entirety in Appendix C.

The 2002 Amendments to Articles 3 and 4

In 2002, the NCCUSL and the American Law Institute approved a number of amendments to Articles 3 and 4 of the UCC. One of the purposes of the amendments was to update the law with respect to e-commerce. For example, the amended versions of the articles implement the policy of the Uniform Electronic Transactions Act (see Chapter 19) by removing unnecessary obstacles to electronic communications. Additionally, the word *writing* has been replaced with the term *record* throughout the articles. Other amendments relate to such topics as telephone-generated checks and the payment and discharge of negotiable instruments.

Most states have not yet adopted these amendments. Therefore, in this text we provide footnotes discussing the amendments only if they will significantly alter existing law. Keep in mind, however, that even when the changes are not substantive, some section numbers may change slightly once a state has adopted the amendments to Article 3 (subsection 9 may become subsection 12, for example).

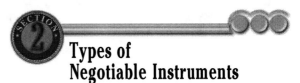

Types of Negotiable Instruments

The UCC specifies four types of negotiable instruments: *drafts, checks, notes,* and *certificates of deposit* (CDs). These instruments, which are summarized briefly in Exhibit 19–1, are frequently divided into the two classifications that we will discuss in the following subsections: *orders to pay* (drafts and checks) and *promises to pay* (promissory notes and CDs).

Negotiable instruments may also be classified as either demand instruments or time instruments. A *demand instrument* is payable on demand—that is, it is payable immediately after it is issued and thereafter for

EXHIBIT 19–1 • **Basic Types of Negotiable Instruments**

Instruments	Characteristics	Parties
ORDERS TO PAY		
Draft	An order by one person to another person or to bearer [UCC 3–104(e)].	*Drawer*—The person who signs or makes the order to pay [UCC 3–103(a)(3)].
Check	A draft drawn on a bank and payable on demand [UCC 3–104(f)].[a] (With certain types of checks, such as cashier's checks, the bank is both the drawer and the drawee—see Chapter 27 for details.)	*Drawee*—The person to whom the order to pay is made [UCC 3–103(a)(2)]. *Payee*—The person to whom payment is ordered.
PROMISES TO PAY		
Promissory note	A promise by one party to pay money to another party or to bearer [UCC 3–104(e)].	*Maker*—The person who promises to pay [UCC 3–103(a)(5)].
Certificate of deposit	A note made by a bank acknowledging a deposit of funds made payable to the holder of the note [UCC 3–104(j)].	*Payee*—The person to whom the promise is made.

a. Under UCC 4–105(1), banks include savings banks, savings and loan associations, credit unions, and trust companies.

a reasonable period of time.[1] **Issue** is "the first delivery of an instrument by the maker or drawer . . . for the purpose of giving rights on the instrument to any person" [UCC 3–105]. All checks are demand instruments because, by definition, they must be payable on demand. A *time instrument* is payable at a future date.

Drafts and Checks (Orders to Pay)

A **draft** is an unconditional written order that involves *three parties*. The party creating the draft (the **drawer**) orders another party (the **drawee**) to pay money, usually to a third party (the **payee**). The most common type of draft is a check.

Time Drafts and Sight Drafts A *time draft* is payable at a definite future time. A *sight draft* (or demand draft) is payable on sight—that is, when it is presented for payment. A sight draft may be payable on acceptance. **Acceptance** is the drawee's written promise to pay the draft when it comes due. An instrument is usually accepted by writing the word *accepted* across the face of the instrument, followed by the date of acceptance and the signature of the drawee. A draft

can be both a time and a sight draft; such a draft is payable at a stated time after sight.

Exhibit 19–2 shows a typical time draft. For the drawee to be obligated to honor the order, the drawee must be obligated to the drawer either by agreement or through a debtor-creditor relationship. For example, on January 16, Ourtown Real Estate orders $1,000 worth of office supplies from Eastman Supply Company, with payment due April 16. Also on January 16, Ourtown sends Eastman a draft drawn on its account with the First National Bank of Whiteacre as payment. In this scenario, the drawer is Ourtown, the drawee is Ourtown's bank (First National Bank of Whiteacre), and the payee is Eastman Supply Company. First National Bank is obligated to honor the draft because of its account agreement with Ourtown Real Estate.

Trade Acceptances A trade acceptance is a type of draft that is frequently used in the sale of goods. In a **trade acceptance,** the seller of the goods is both the drawer and the payee. Essentially, the draft orders the buyer to pay a specified amount to the seller, usually at a stated time in the future.

For example, Midwestern Style Fabrics sells $50,000 worth of fabric to D&F Clothiers, Inc., each spring on terms requiring payment to be made in ninety days. One year, Midwestern Style needs cash, so it draws a *trade acceptance* that orders D&F to pay $50,000 to the order of Midwestern Style Fabrics ninety days hence. Midwestern Style presents the draft to D&F, which

---

1. "A promise or order is 'payable on demand' if it (i) states that it is payable on demand or at sight, or otherwise indicates that it is payable at the will of the holder, or (ii) does not state any time of payment" [UCC 3–108(a)]. The UCC defines a *holder* as "the person in possession if a negotiable instrument is payable either to bearer or to an identified person [who] is the person in possession" [see UCC 1–201(21)(A)]. The term *bearer* will be defined later in this chapter.

EXHIBIT 19–2 • A Typical Time Draft

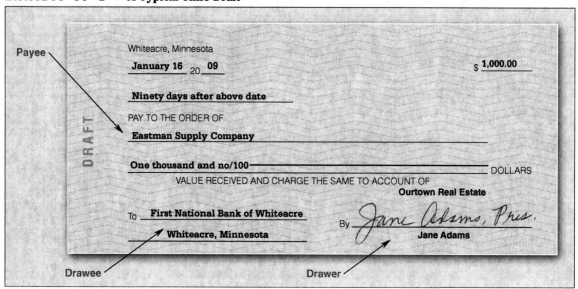

accepts the draft by signing and dating the face of the instrument. D&F then returns the draft to Midwestern Style Fabrics. D&F's acceptance creates an enforceable promise to pay the draft when it comes due in ninety days. Midwestern Style can now obtain the cash it needs by selling the trade acceptance in the *commercial money market* (a financial market for short-term borrowing that businesses use). Trade acceptances are the standard credit instruments in sales transactions (see Exhibit 19–3).

When the draft orders the buyer's bank to pay, it is called a banker's acceptance. A **banker's acceptance** is commonly used in international trade.

Checks As mentioned, the most commonly used type of draft is a **check.** The writer of the check is the drawer, the bank on which the check is drawn is the drawee, and the person to whom the check is made payable is the payee. As mentioned earlier, checks are demand instruments because they are payable on demand. (Do other countries always consider checks to be negotiable instruments? For a discussion of this issue, see this chapter's *Insight into the Global Environment* feature on the next page.)

Checks will be discussed more fully in Chapter 27, but it should be noted here that with certain types of checks, such as *cashier's checks,* the bank is both the drawer and the drawee. The bank customer purchases a cashier's check from the bank—that is, pays the bank the amount of the check—and indicates to whom the check should be made payable. The bank, not the customer, is the drawer of the check, as well as the drawee. The idea behind a cashier's check is that it functions

the same as cash, so there is no question of whether the check will be paid—the bank has committed itself to paying the stated amount on demand.

Promissory Notes and CDs (Promises to Pay)

A **promissory note** is a written promise made by one person (the **maker** of the promise to pay) to another (usually a payee). A promissory note, which is often referred to simply as a *note,* can be made payable at a definite time or on demand. It can name a specific payee or merely be payable to bearer (*bearer instruments* are discussed later in this chapter). For example, on April 30, Laurence and Margaret Roberts sign a writing unconditionally promising to pay "to the order of" the First National Bank of Whiteacre $3,000 (with 8 percent interest) on or before June 29. This writing is a promissory note. A typical promissory note is shown in Exhibit 19–4 on page 523.

Promissory notes are used in a variety of credit transactions. Often a promissory note will carry the name of the transaction involved. For example, suppose that a note is secured by personal property, such as an automobile. This type of note is referred to as a *collateral note* because the property pledged as security for the satisfaction of the debt is called *collateral.*[2]

---

2. To minimize the risk of loss when making a loan, a creditor often requires the debtor to provide some *collateral,* or security, beyond a promise that the debt will be repaid. When this security takes the form of personal property (such as a motor vehicle), the creditor has an interest in the property known as a *security interest.* Security interests will be discussed in detail in Chapter 29.

EXHIBIT 19–3 • **A Typical Trade Acceptance**

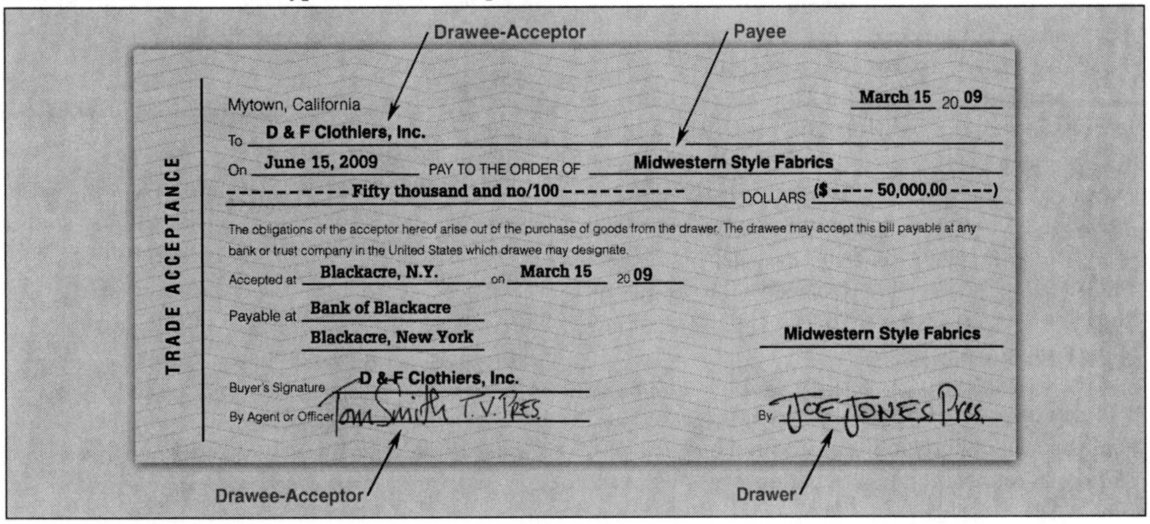

A note payable in installments, such as installment payments for a large-screen television over a twelve-month period, is called an *installment note*.

A **certificate of deposit (CD)** is a type of note. A CD is issued when a party deposits funds with a bank, and the bank promises to repay the funds, with interest, on a certain date [UCC 3–104(j)]. The bank is the maker of the note, and the depositor is the payee. For example, on February 15, Sara Levin deposits $5,000 with the First National Bank of Whiteacre. The bank promises to repay the $5,000, plus 3.25 percent annual interest, on August 15.

Certificates of deposit in small denominations (for amounts up to $100,000) are often sold by savings and loan associations, savings banks, commercial banks, and credit unions. Certificates of deposit for amounts greater than $100,000 are referred to as large or jumbo CDs. Exhibit 19–5 shows a typical small CD.

Requirements for Negotiability

For an instrument to be negotiable, it must meet the following requirements:

1. Be in writing.
2. Be signed by the maker or the drawer.
3. Be an unconditional promise or order to pay.
4. State a fixed amount of money.
5. Be payable on demand or at a definite time.
6. Be payable to order or to bearer, unless it is a check.

EXHIBIT 19-4 • A Typical Promissory Note

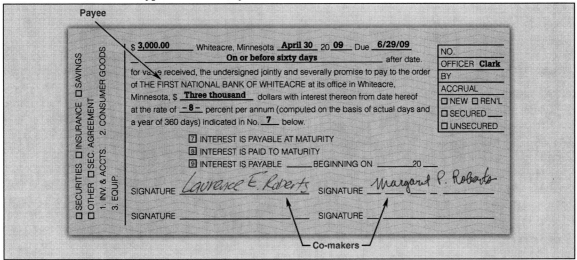

Written Form

Negotiable instruments normally must be in written form.[3] Clearly, an oral promise can create the danger

---

[3]. UCC Section 3–104, which defines negotiable instruments, does not explicitly require a writing. The writing requirement comes from the UCC's definitions of an *order* (as a written instruction) and a *promise* (as a written undertaking) [UCC 3–103(a)(6), (9)]. Note, however, that since the widespread adoption of the Uniform Electronic Transactions Act (UETA), discussed in Chapter 19, an electronic record may be sufficient evidence of a written instruction to constitute a negotiable instrument (see UETA Section 16). Additionally, a handful of states have adopted the 2002 amendments to Article 3 of the UCC, which, as explained earlier, were issued explicitly to authorize electronic records. Thus, these states allow electronic negotiable instruments.

of fraud or make it difficult to determine liability. The writing must be on material that lends itself to *permanence*. Promises carved in blocks of ice or inscribed in the sand or on other impermanent surfaces would not qualify as negotiable instruments. The UCC nevertheless gives considerable leeway as to what can be a negotiable instrument. Checks and notes have been written on napkins, menus, tablecloths, shirts, and a variety of other materials.

The writing must also have *portability*. Although the UCC does not explicitly state this requirement, if an instrument is not movable, it obviously cannot meet the requirement that it be freely transferable. Suppose that Cullen writes on the side of a cow, "I, Cullen, promise to pay to Merrill or her order $500 on demand."

EXHIBIT 19-5 • A Typical Small Certificate of Deposit

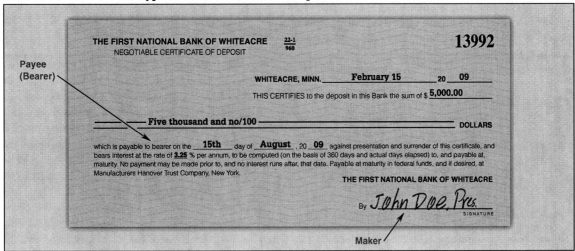

Technically, this meets the requirements of a negotiable instrument, but because a cow cannot easily be transferred in the ordinary course of business, the "instrument" is nonnegotiable.

Signatures

For an instrument to be negotiable, it must be signed by (1) the maker if it is a note or a certificate of deposit or (2) the drawer if it is a draft or a check [UCC 3–103(a)(3),(5)]. If a person signs an instrument as an authorized *agent* for the maker or drawer, the maker or drawer has effectively signed the instrument [UCC 3–402]. (Agents' signatures will be discussed in Chapter 26.)

Signature Requirements The UCC grants extreme latitude in regard to what constitutes a signature. UCC 1–201(39) provides that a **signature** may include "any symbol executed or adopted by a party with present intention to authenticate a writing." UCC 3–401(b) expands on this by stating that a "signature may be made (i) manually or by means of a device or machine, and (ii) by the use of any name, including a trade or assumed name, or by a word, mark, or symbol executed or adopted by a person with present intention to authenticate a writing." Thus, initials, an X (if the writing is also signed by a witness), or a thumbprint will suffice as a signature. A trade name or an assumed name is also sufficient. Signatures that are placed onto instruments by means of rubber stamps are permitted and frequently used in the business world. If necessary, parol evidence (discussed in Chapter 15) is admissible to identify the signer. When the signer is identified, the signature becomes effective.

There are virtually no limitations on the manner in which a signature can be made, but one should be careful about receiving an instrument that has been signed in an unusual way. Furthermore, an unusual signature clearly decreases the *marketability* of an instrument because it creates uncertainty.

Placement of the Signature The location of the signature on the document is unimportant, although the usual place is the lower right-hand corner. A *handwritten* statement on the body of the instrument, such as "I, Kammie Orlik, promise to pay Janel Tan," is sufficient to act as a signature.

Unconditional Promise or Order to Pay

The terms of the promise or order must be included in the writing on the face of a negotiable instrument. The terms must also be *unconditional*—that is, they cannot be conditioned on the occurrence or nonoccurrence of some other event or agreement [UCC 3–104(a)].

Promise or Order For an instrument to be negotiable, it must contain an express promise or order to pay. A mere acknowledgment of the debt, such as an I.O.U. ("I owe you"), might logically *imply* a promise, but it is not sufficient under the UCC. This is because the UCC requires that a promise be an *affirmative* (express) undertaking [UCC 3–103(a)(9)]. If such words as "to be paid on demand" or "due on demand" are added to an I.O.U., however, the need for an express promise is satisfied. Thus, if a buyer executes a promissory note using the words "I promise to pay $1,000 to the order of the seller for the purchase of X goods," then this requirement for a negotiable instrument is satisfied.

A certificate of deposit is exceptional in this respect. No express promise is required in a CD because the bank's acknowledgment of the deposit and the other terms of the instrument clearly indicate a promise by the bank to repay the sum of money [UCC 3–104(j)].

An *order* is associated with three-party instruments, such as trade acceptances, checks, and drafts. An order directs a third party to pay the instrument as drawn. In the typical check, for example, the word *pay* (to the order of a payee) is a command to the drawee bank to pay the check when presented, and thus it is an order. A command, such as "pay," is mandatory even if it is accompanied by courteous words, as in "Please pay" or "Kindly pay." Generally, the language used must indicate that a command, or order, is being given. Stating "I wish you would pay" does not fulfill this requirement. An order may be addressed to one person or to more than one person, either jointly ("to A *and* B") or alternatively ("to A *or* B") [UCC 3–103(a)(6)].

Unconditionality of the Promise or Order A negotiable instrument's utility as a substitute for cash or as a credit device would be dramatically reduced if it had conditional promises attached to it. Investigating the conditional promises would be time consuming and expensive, and therefore the transferability of the negotiable instrument would be greatly restricted. Suppose that Granados promises in a note to pay McGraw $10,000 only if a certain ship reaches port. No one could safely purchase the promissory note without first investigating whether the ship had arrived. Even then, the facts disclosed by the investigation might be incorrect. To avoid such problems, the UCC provides that only instruments with *unconditional* promises or orders can be negotiable [UCC 3–104(a)].

A promise or order is conditional (and *not* negotiable) if it states (1) an express condition to payment, (2) that the promise or order is subject to or governed by another writing, or (3) that the rights or obligations with respect to the promise or order are stated in another writing. A mere *reference* to another writing, however, does not of itself make the promise or order conditional [UCC 3–106(a)]. For example, including the phrase "as per contract" or "This debt arises from the sale of goods X and Y" does not render an instrument nonnegotiable.

Payment Out of a Particular Fund. Similarly, a statement in the instrument that payment can be made only out of a particular fund or source will not render the instrument nonnegotiable [UCC 3–106(b)(ii)]. Thus, for example, terms in a note that include the condition that payment will be made out of the proceeds of next year's cotton crop will not make the note nonnegotiable. (The payee of such a note, however, may find the note commercially unacceptable and refuse to take it.)

Note Secured by a Mortgage. Finally, a simple statement in an otherwise negotiable note indicating that the note is secured by a mortgage does not destroy its negotiability [UCC 3–106(b)(i)]. Actually, such a statement might even make the note more acceptable in commerce. Realize, though, that the statement that a note is secured by a mortgage must not stipulate that the maker's promise to pay is *subject to* the terms and conditions of the mortgage [UCC 3–106(a)(ii)].

 As when drafting contracts, businesspersons should use clear language when creating negotiable instruments to avoid potential misunderstandings. **PREVENTING LEGAL DISPUTES** To create an order instrument, generally the language used must indicate that a command, or order, is being given. Business owners and managers can be polite (and say "Please pay") if they like, provided that they include a clear command. Also, businesspersons should make certain that they do not use any words that could be interpreted as making the promise conditional. They should not refer to any terms in another document or contract controlling the instrument. If in doubt, they need to contact an attorney.

A Fixed Amount of Money

Negotiable instruments must state with certainty a fixed amount of money, with or without interest or other charges described in the promise or order, to be paid at the time the instrument is payable [UCC 3–104(a)]. This requirement ensures that the value of the instrument can be determined with clarity and certainty.

Fixed Amount The term *fixed amount* means that the amount must be ascertainable from the face of the instrument. Interest may be stated as a fixed or variable rate. A demand note payable with 10 percent interest meets the requirement of a fixed amount because its amount can be determined at the time it is payable [UCC 3–104(a)].

The rate of interest may also be determined with reference to information that is not contained in the instrument if that information is readily ascertainable by reference to a formula or a source described in the instrument [UCC 3–112(b)]. For example, an instrument that is payable at the *legal rate of interest* (a rate of interest fixed by statute) is negotiable. Mortgage notes tied to a variable rate of interest (a rate that fluctuates as a result of market conditions) can also be negotiable.

Payable in Money UCC 3–104(a) provides that a fixed amount is to be *payable in money.* The UCC defines money as "a medium of exchange authorized or adopted by a domestic or foreign government as a part of its currency" [UCC 1–201(24)].

Suppose that the maker of a note promises "to pay on demand $1,000 in U.S. gold." Because gold is not a medium of exchange adopted by the U.S. government, the note is not payable in money. The same result occurs if the maker promises "to pay $1,000 and fifty magnums of 1994 Chateau Lafite-Rothschild wine" because the instrument is not payable *entirely* in money. An instrument payable in government bonds or in shares of IBM stock is not negotiable because neither is a medium of exchange recognized by the U.S. government. The statement "Payable in $1,000 U.S. currency or an equivalent value in gold" renders the instrument nonnegotiable because the maker reserved the option of paying in money *or* gold. Any instrument payable in the United States with a face amount stated in a foreign currency can be paid in the foreign money or in the equivalent in U.S. dollars [UCC 3–107].

Payable on Demand or at a Definite Time

A negotiable instrument must "be payable on demand or at a definite time" [UCC 3–104(a)(2)]. Clearly, to ascertain the value of a negotiable instrument, it is essential to know when the maker, drawee, or *acceptor* is required to pay (an **acceptor** is a drawee who has accepted, or agreed to pay, an instrument when it is presented later for payment). It is also necessary to know when the obligations of secondary parties, such as *indorsers*,[4] will arise. Furthermore, it is necessary to know when an instrument is due in order to calculate when the statute of limitations may apply [UCC 3–118(a)]. Finally, with an interest-bearing instrument, it is necessary to know the exact interval during which

the interest will accrue to determine the instrument's value at the present time.

Payable on Demand Instruments that are payable on demand include those that contain the words "Payable at sight" or "Payable upon presentment." When a person takes the instrument to the appropriate party for payment or acceptance, *presentment* occurs. **Presentment** means a demand made by or on behalf of a person entitled to enforce an instrument to either pay or accept the instrument [UCC 3–501].

The very nature of the instrument may indicate that it is payable on demand. For example, a check, by definition, is payable on demand [UCC 3–104(f)]. If no time for payment is specified and the person responsible for payment must pay on the instrument's presentment, the instrument is payable on demand [UCC 3–108(a)].

At the center of the dispute in the following case was a note that required payments in monthly installments beginning several months before the note was executed. Was this a demand note?

---

4. We should note that because the UCC uses the spelling *indorse* (*indorsement*, and the like), rather than the more common spelling *endorse* (*endorsement*, and the like), we adopt the UCC's spelling here and in other chapters in this text. Indorsers will be discussed in Chapter 25.

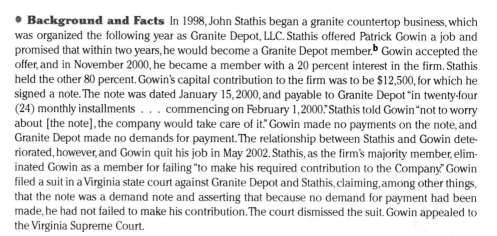

C A S E 19.1 Gowin v. Granite Depot, LLC [a]

Supreme Court of Virginia, 2006. 272 Va. 246, 634 S.E.2d 714.

● **Background and Facts** In 1998, John Stathis began a granite countertop business, which was organized the following year as Granite Depot, LLC. Stathis offered Patrick Gowin a job and promised that within two years, he would become a Granite Depot member.[b] Gowin accepted the offer, and in November 2000, he became a member with a 20 percent interest in the firm. Stathis held the other 80 percent. Gowin's capital contribution to the firm was to be $12,500, for which he signed a note. The note was dated January 15, 2000, and payable to Granite Depot "in twenty-four (24) monthly installments . . . commencing on February 1, 2000." Stathis told Gowin "not to worry about [the note], the company would take care of it." Gowin made no payments on the note, and Granite Depot made no demands for payment. The relationship between Stathis and Gowin deteriorated, however, and Gowin quit his job in May 2002. Stathis, as the firm's majority member, eliminated Gowin as a member for failing "to make his required contribution to the Company." Gowin filed a suit in a Virginia state court against Granite Depot and Stathis, claiming, among other things, that the note was a demand note and asserting that because no demand for payment had been made, he had not failed to make his contribution. The court dismissed the suit. Gowin appealed to the Virginia Supreme Court.

● **Decision and Rationale** The state supreme court reversed the lower court's judgment and remanded the case for further proceedings. The reviewing court held that the note was a demand note and agreed with Gowin that because no demand for payment had been made, his obligation to make a payment had not arisen. The termination of his membership in Granite Depot was thus improper, and Gowin was still a member of the firm. The state supreme court emphasized

---

a. An *LLC* is a limited liability company, which is a form of business organization discussed in detail in Chapter 37.
b. A member in an LLC has many of the same rights as a partner in a partnership but is not personally liable for the obligations of the firm. See Chapters 36 and 37.

CASE 19.1 CONTINUED that the note was dated January 15, 2000, with its first payment due on February 1, but that it was not signed until November, "making compliance with the stated dates impossible." The parties agreed that the payment dates were not correct, but no one contended that this mistake invalidated the note. The court reasoned that the note effectively did not state a date for its payment and was therefore a demand note under UCC 3–108(a). According to UCC 3–304(a)(1) and (3), a demand note does not become overdue until the day after demand is made or the note has been outstanding for an "unreasonably long [time]," whichever occurs first. Under the circumstances in this case, the note never became overdue because payment was never demanded.

● **The Ethical Dimension** *Did the statement "not to worry, the company will take care of it," which was made about the $12,500 note, imply that the company did not require a capital contribution by Gowin? Why might the company have made such a statement?*

● **The Legal Environment Dimension** *Why is a note with no stated time for payment considered a demand note rather than an unenforceable note?*

Payable at a Definite Time If an instrument is not payable on demand, to be negotiable it must be payable at a definite time. An instrument is payable at a definite time if it states that it is payable (1) on a specified date, (2) within a definite period of time (such as thirty days) after being presented for payment, or (3) on a date or time readily ascertainable at the time the promise or order is issued [UCC 3–108(b)]. The maker or drawee is under no obligation to pay until the specified time.

When an instrument is payable by the maker or drawer *on or before* a stated date, it is clearly payable at a definite time. The maker or drawer has the *option* of paying before the stated maturity date, but the holder can still rely on payment being made by the maturity date. The option to pay early does not violate the definite-time requirement. For example, John gives Ernesto an instrument dated May 1, 2009, that indicates on its face that it is payable *on or before* May 1, 2010. This instrument satisfies the definite-time requirement.

In contrast, an instrument that is undated and made payable "one month after date" is clearly nonnegotiable. There is no way to determine the maturity date from the face of the instrument. Whether the time period is a month or a year, if the date is uncertain, the instrument is not payable at a definite time. Thus, an instrument that states, "One year after the death of my grandfather, Jeremy Adams, I promise to pay to the order of Lucy Harmon $5,000. [Signed] Jacqueline Wells," is nonnegotiable.

Acceleration Clause An **acceleration clause** allows a payee or other holder of a time instrument to demand payment of the entire amount due, with interest, if a certain event occurs, such as a default in payment of an installment when due. (Under the UCC, a **holder** is any person in possession of a negotiable instrument that is payable either to the bearer or to an identified person that is the person in possession [UCC 1–201(20)].)

Assume that Martin lends $1,000 to Ruth, who makes a negotiable note promising to pay $100 per month for eleven months. The note contains an acceleration provision that permits Martin or any holder to immediately demand all the payments plus the interest owed to date if Ruth fails to pay an installment in any given month. If, for example, Ruth fails to make the third payment and Martin accelerates the unpaid balance, the note will be due and payable in full. Ruth will owe Martin the remaining principal plus any unpaid interest to that date.

Under the UCC, instruments that include acceleration clauses are negotiable, regardless of the reason for the acceleration, because (1) the exact value of the instrument can be ascertained and (2) the instrument will be payable on a specified date if the event allowing acceleration does not occur [UCC 3–108(b)(ii)]. Thus, the specified date is the outside limit used to determine the value of the instrument.

In the following case, the question was whether a party entitled to installment payments on a promissory note that contained an acceleration clause waived the right to exercise this provision when the party accepted late payments from the maker.

CASE **19.2** **Foundation Property Investments, LLC v. CTP, LLC**
Court of Appeals of Kansas, 2007. 37 Kan.App.2d 890, 159 P.3d 1042.
www.kscourts.org/Cases-and-Opinions/opinions[a]

● **Background and Facts** In April 2004, CTP, LLC, bought a truck stop in South Hutchinson, Kansas. As part of the deal, CTP borrowed $96,000 from Foundation Property Investments, LLC. The loan was evidenced by a promissory note, which provided that CTP was to make monthly payments of $673.54 between June 1, 2004, and June 1, 2009. The note stated that on default in any payment, "the whole amount then unpaid shall become immediately due and payable at the option of the holder without notice." CTP paid the first four installments on or before the due dates, but beginning in October 2004, CTP paid the next ten installments late. In July 2005, citing the late payments, Foundation demanded full payment of the note by the end of the month. CTP responded that the parties' course of dealing permitted payments to be made beyond their due dates. Foundation filed a suit in a Kansas state court against CTP to collect the note's full amount. CTP asserted that Foundation had waived its right to accelerate the note by its acceptance of late payments. The court determined that Foundation was entitled to payment of the note in full, plus interest and attorneys' fees and costs, for a total of $110,975.58, and issued a summary judgment in Foundation's favor. CTP appealed to a state intermediate appellate court.

● **Decision and Rationale** The appellate court reversed the lower court's ruling and remanded the case with instructions to enter a judgment in CTP's favor. The plaintiff argued at trial that the provisions of the acceleration clause in the note should be strictly construed against CTP. The reviewing court looked, nonetheless, to the plaintiff's actions. *Course of dealing* is defined as "a sequence of previous conduct between the parties to a particular transaction which is fairly to be regarded as a establishing a common basis of understanding for interpreting their expressions and other conduct." The reviewing court pointed out that Foundation Property Investments never objected to CTP's late payments during the nine-month period. The action of accepting late payments "was inconsistent with [Foundation's] claim or right to receive prompt payments. Accordingly, the trial court incorrectly determined that Foundation's conduct did not constitute a wavier of its right of acceleration." The acceptance of late payments did constitute a waiver. CTP was not required to pay the note in full, plus interest and attorneys' fees and costs.

● **The E-Commerce Dimension** *If Foundation had sent CTP an e-mail threatening to accelerate the note each time CTP's payment was late, would this have been sufficient to support the holder's eventual demand for full payment? Why or why not?*

● **The Global Dimension** *Suppose that Foundation was an entity based outside the United States. Could it have successfully claimed, in attempting to enforce the acceleration clause, that it had not given CTP notice because it had not been aware of Kansas law? Discuss.*

a. In the menu at the left, click on "Search by Docket Number." In the result, in the right column, click on "96000–96999." On the next page, scroll to "96697" and click on the number to access the opinion. The Kansas courts, Washburn University School of Law Library, and University of Kansas School of Law Library maintain this Web site.

Extension Clause The reverse of an acceleration clause is an **extension clause,** which allows the date of maturity to be extended into the future [UCC 3–108(b)(iii), (iv)]. To keep the instrument negotiable, the interval of the extension must be specified if the right to extend the time of payment is given to the maker or the drawer of the instrument. If, however, the holder of the instrument can extend the time of payment, the extended maturity date need not be specified.

Suppose that Alek executes a note that reads, "The maker has the right to postpone the time of payment of this note beyond its definite maturity date of January 1, 2010. This extension, however, shall be for no more than a reasonable time." A note with this language is not negotiable because it does not satisfy the definite-time requirement. The right to extend is the maker's, and the maker has not indicated when the note will become due after the extension.

In contrast, suppose that Alek's note reads, "The holder of this note at the date of maturity, January 1, 2010, can extend the time of payment until the following June 1 or later, if the holder so wishes." This note is a negotiable instrument. The length of the extension does not have to be specified because the option to extend is solely that of the holder. After January 1, 2010, the note is, in effect, a demand instrument.

Payable to Order or to Bearer

Because one of the functions of a negotiable instrument is to serve as a substitute for cash, freedom to transfer is essential. To ensure a proper transfer, the instrument must be "payable to order or to bearer" at the time it is issued or first comes into the possession of the holder [UCC 3–104(a)(1)]. An instrument is not negotiable unless it meets this requirement.

Order Instruments An **order instrument** is an instrument that is payable (1) "to the order of an identified person" or (2) "to an identified person or order" [UCC 3–109(b)]. An identified person is the person "to whom the instrument is initially payable" as determined by the intent of the maker or drawer [UCC 3–110(a)]. The identified person, in turn, may transfer the instrument to whomever he or she wishes. Thus, the maker or drawer is agreeing to pay either the person specified on the instrument or whomever that person might designate. In this way, the instrument retains its transferability. Suppose that an instrument states, "Payable to the order of James Crawford" or "Pay to James Crawford or order." Clearly, the maker or drawer has indicated that payment will be made to Crawford or to whomever Crawford designates. The instrument is negotiable.

Except for bearer instruments (explained in the following subsection), the person specified must be named with *certainty* because the transfer of an order instrument requires an indorsement. An **indorsement** is a signature placed on an instrument, such as on the back of a check, generally for the purpose of transferring one's ownership rights in the instrument. Indorsements will be discussed at length in Chapter 25.

If an instrument states, "Payable to the order of my nicest cousin," the instrument is nonnegotiable because a holder could not be sure that the person who indorsed the instrument was actually the "nicest cousin" who was supposed to have indorsed it.

Bearer Instruments A **bearer instrument** is an instrument that does not designate a specific payee

[UCC 3–109(a)]. The term **bearer** refers to a person in possession of an instrument that is payable to bearer or indorsed in blank (with a signature only, as will be discussed in Chapter 25) [UCC 1–201(5), 3–109(a), 3–109(c)]. This means that the maker or drawer agrees to pay anyone who presents the instrument for payment. Any instrument containing terms such as the following is a bearer instrument:

1. "Payable to the order of bearer."
2. "Payable to Simon Reed or bearer."
3. "Payable to bearer."
4. "Pay cash."
5. "Pay to the order of cash."

In addition, an instrument that "indicates that it is not payable to an identified person" is a bearer instrument [UCC 3–109(a)(3)]. Thus, an instrument that is "payable to X" can be negotiated as a bearer instrument, as though it were payable to cash. The UCC does not accept an instrument issued to a nonexistent organization as payable to bearer, however [UCC 3–109, Comment 2]. Therefore, an instrument "payable to the order of the Camrod Company," if no such company exists, is not a bearer instrument or an order instrument and, in fact, does not qualify as a negotiable instrument. (See *Concept Summary 19.1* on the following page for a convenient summary of the basic rules governing negotiability.)

Factors Not Affecting Negotiability

Certain ambiguities or omissions will not affect the negotiability of an instrument. Article 3's rules for interpreting ambiguous terms include the following:

1. Unless the date of an instrument is necessary to determine a definite time for payment, the fact that an instrument is undated does not affect its negotiability. A typical example is an undated check, which is still negotiable. If a check is not dated, under the UCC its date is the date of its issue, meaning the date on which the drawer first delivers the check to another person to give that person rights on the check [UCC 3–113(b)].
2. Antedating or postdating an instrument does not affect its negotiability [UCC 3–113(a)]. *Antedating* occurs when a party puts a date on an instrument that precedes the actual calendar date. *Postdating*

CONCEPT SUMMARY 19.1
Requirements for Negotiability

Requirements	Basic Rules
MUST BE IN WRITING UCC 3–103(6),(9)	A writing can be on anything that is readily transferable and that has a degree of permanence.
MUST BE SIGNED BY THE MAKER OR DRAWER UCC 1–201(39) UCC 3–103(a)(3),(5) UCC 3–401(b) UCC 3–402	1. The signature can be anywhere on the face of the instrument. 2. It can be in any form (such as a word, mark, or rubber stamp) that purports to be a signature and authenticates the writing. 3. A signature may be made in a representative capacity.
MUST BE A DEFINITE PROMISE OR ORDER UCC 3–103(a)(6),(9) UCC 3–104(a)	1. A promise must be more than a mere acknowledgment of a debt. 2. The words "I/We promise" or "Pay" meet this criterion.
MUST BE UNCONDITIONAL UCC 3–106	1. Payment cannot be expressly conditional on the occurrence of an event. 2. Payment cannot be made subject to or governed by another agreement.
MUST BE AN ORDER OR PROMISE TO PAY A FIXED AMOUNT UCC 3–104(a) UCC 3–107 UCC 3–112(b)	An amount may be considered a fixed sum even if payable in installments, with a fixed or variable rate of interest, or at a foreign exchange rate.
MUST BE PAYABLE IN MONEY UCC 3–104(a)	1. Any medium of exchange recognized as the currency of a government is money. 2. The maker or drawer cannot retain the option to pay the instrument in money *or* something else.
MUST BE PAYABLE ON DEMAND OR AT A DEFINITE TIME UCC 3–104(a)(2) UCC 3–108(a),(b),(c)	1. Any instrument that is payable on sight, presentment, or issue or that does not state any time for payment is a demand instrument. 2. An instrument is still payable at a definite time, even if it is payable on or before a stated date or within a fixed period after sight or if the drawer or maker has the option to extend the time for a definite period. 3. Acceleration clauses do not affect the negotiability of the instrument.
MUST BE PAYABLE TO ORDER OR TO BEARER UCC 3–104(a)(1) UCC 3–109 UCC 3–110(a)	1. An order instrument must identify the payee with reasonable certainty. 2. An instrument whose terms intend payment to no particular person is payable to bearer.

occurs when a party puts a date on an instrument that is after the actual date. Suppose that Crenshaw draws a check on his account at First Bank, payable to Sung Imports. Crenshaw postdates the check by fifteen days. Sung Imports can immediately negotiate the check, and, unless Crenshaw tells First Bank otherwise, the bank can charge the amount of the check to Crenshaw's account [UCC 4–401(c)].

3. Handwritten terms outweigh typewritten and printed terms (preprinted terms on forms, for example), and typewritten terms outweigh printed terms

[UCC 3–114]. For example, if your check is printed "Pay to the order of," and in handwriting you insert in the blank "Anita Delgado or bearer," the check is a bearer instrument.

4. Words outweigh figures unless the words are ambiguous [UCC 3–114]. This rule becomes important when the numerical amount and the written amount on a check differ. Suppose that Paruzzo issues a check payable to Cheaper Appliance Company. For the amount, she fills in the number "$100" but writes out the words "One thousand and 00/100" dollars. The check is payable in the amount of $1,000.

5. When an instrument simply states "with interest" and does not specify a particular interest rate, the interest rate is the judgment rate of interest (a rate of interest fixed by statute that is applied to a monetary judgment awarded by a court until the judgment is paid or terminated) [UCC 3–112(b)].

6. A check is negotiable even if there is a notation on it stating that it is "nonnegotiable" or "not governed by Article 3." Any other instrument, however, can be made nonnegotiable by the maker's or drawer's conspicuously noting on it that it is "nonnegotiable" or "not governed by Article 3" [UCC 3–104(d)].

REVIEWING The Function and Creation of Negotiable Instruments

Robert Durbin, a student, borrowed funds from a bank for his education and signed a promissory note for its repayment. The bank lent the funds under a federal program designed to assist students at postsecondary institutions. Under this program, repayment ordinarily begins nine to twelve months after the student borrower fails to carry at least one-half of the normal full-time course load at his or her school. The federal government guarantees that the note will be fully repaid. If the student defaults on the repayment, the lender presents the current balance—principal, interest, and costs—to the government. When the government pays the balance, it becomes the lender, and the borrower owes the government directly. After Durbin defaulted on his note, the government paid the lender the balance due and took possession of the note. Durbin then refused to pay the government, claiming that the government was not the holder of the note. The government filed a suit in a federal district court against Durbin to collect the amount due. Using the information presented in the chapter, answer the following questions.

1. Using the categories discussed in the chapter, what type of negotiable instrument was the note that Durbin signed (an order to pay or a promise to pay)? Explain.
2. Suppose that the note did not state a specific interest rate but instead referred to a statute that established the maximum interest rate for government-guaranteed school loans. Would the note fail to meet the requirements for negotiability in that situation? Why or why not?
3. How does a party who is not named by a negotiable instrument (in this situation, the government) obtain a right to enforce the instrument?
4. Suppose that in court, Durbin argues that because the school closed down before he could finish his education, there was a failure of consideration: he did not get something of value in exchange for his promise to pay. Assuming that the government is a holder of the promissory note, would this argument likely be successful against it? Why or why not?

TERMS AND CONCEPTS

acceleration clause

acceptance

acceptor

banker's acceptance

bearer

bearer instrument

certificate of deposit (CD)

check

draft

drawee

drawer

extension clause

holder

indorsement

issue

maker

negotiable instrument

order instrument

payee

presentment

promissory note

signature

trade acceptance

QUESTIONS AND CASE PROBLEMS

24–1. Sabrina Runyan writes the following note on a sheet of paper: "I, the undersigned, do hereby acknowledge that I owe Leo Woo one thousand dollars, with interest, payable out of the proceeds of the sale of my horse, Lightning, next month. Payment is to be made on or before six months from date." Discuss specifically why this is not a negotiable instrument.

24–2. QUESTION WITH SAMPLE ANSWER

Juan Sanchez writes the following note on the back of an envelope: "I, Juan Sanchez, promise to pay Kathy Martin or bearer $500 on demand." Is this a negotiable instrument? Discuss fully.

• **For a sample answer to Question 24–2, go to Appendix C at the end of this text.**

24–3. A college student, Austin Keynes, wished to purchase a new entertainment system from Friedman Electronics, Inc. Because Keynes did not have the cash to pay for the entertainment system, he offered to sign a note promising to pay $150 per month for the next six months. Friedman Electronics, eager to sell the system to Keynes, agreed to accept the promissory note, which read, "I, Austin Keynes, promise to pay to Friedman Electronics or its order the sum of $150 per month for the next six months." The note was signed by Austin Keynes. About a week later, Friedman Electronics, which was badly in need of cash, signed the back of the note and sold it to the First National Bank of Halston. Give the specific designation of each of the three parties on this note.

24–4. Adam's checks are imprinted with the words "Pay to the order of" followed by a blank. Adam fills in an amount on one of the checks and signs it, but he does not write anything in the blank following the "Pay to the order of"

language. Adam gives this check to Beth. On another check, Adam writes in the blank "Carl or bearer." Which, if either, of these checks is a bearer instrument, and why?

24–5. Negotiability. In October 1998, Somerset Valley Bank notified Alfred Hauser, president of Hauser Co., that the bank had begun to receive what appeared to be Hauser Co. payroll checks. None of the payees were Hauser Co. employees, however, and Hauser had not written the checks or authorized anyone to sign them on his behalf. Automatic Data Processing, Inc., provided payroll services for Hauser Co. and used a facsimile signature on all its payroll checks. Hauser told the bank not to cash the checks. In early 1999, Robert Triffin, who deals in negotiable instruments, bought eighteen of the checks, totaling more than $8,800, from various check-cashing agencies. The agencies stated that they had cashed the checks expecting the bank to pay them. Each check was payable to a bearer for a fixed amount, on demand, and did not state any undertaking by the person promising payment other than the payment of money. Each check bore a facsimile drawer's signature stamp identical to Hauser Co.'s authorized stamp. Each check had been returned to an agency marked "stolen check" and stamped "do not present again." When the bank refused to cash the checks, Triffin filed a suit in a New Jersey state court against Hauser Co. Were the checks negotiable instruments? Why or why not? [*Triffin v. Somerset Valley Bank*, 343 N.J.Super. 73, 777 A.2d 993 (2001)]

24–6. Negotiability. In October 1996, Robert Hildebrandt contracted with Harvey and Nancy Anderson to find a tenant for the Andersons' used-car lot. The Andersons agreed to pay Hildebrandt "a commission equal in amount to five percent up to first three years of lease." On December 12, Paramount Automotive, Inc., agreed to lease the premises for three years at $7,500 per month, and the Andersons

532

signed a promissory note, which stated that they would pay Hildebrandt $13,500, plus interest, in consecutive monthly installments of $485 until the total sum was paid. The note contained an acceleration clause. In a separate agreement, Paramount promised to pay $485 of its monthly rent directly to Hildebrandt. Less than a year later, Paramount stopped making payments to all parties. To enforce the note, Hildebrandt filed a suit in an Oregon state court against the Andersons. One issue in the case was whether the note was a negotiable instrument. The Andersons claimed that it was not, because it was not "unconditional," arguing that their obligation to make payments on the note was conditioned on their receipt of rent from Paramount. Are the Andersons correct? Explain. [*Hildebrandt v. Anderson,* 180 Or.App. 192, 42 P.3d 355 (2002)]

24–7. CASE PROBLEM WITH SAMPLE ANSWER

In July 1981, Southeast Bank in Miami, Florida, issued five cashier's checks, totaling $450,000, to five payees, including Roberto Sanchez. Two months later, in Colombia, South America, Sanchez gave the checks to Juan Diaz. In 1991, Southeast failed. Under federal law, notice must be mailed to a failed bank's depositors, who then have eighteen months to file a claim for their funds. Under an "Assistance Agreement," First Union National Bank agreed to assume Southeast's liability for outstanding cashier's checks and other items. First Union received funds to pay these items but was required to return the funds if, within eighteen months after Southeast's closing, payment for any item had been not claimed. In 1996, in Colombia, Diaz gave the five cashier's checks that he had received from Sanchez to John Acevedo in payment of a debt. In 2001, Acevedo tendered these checks to First Union for payment. Does First Union have to pay? Would it make any difference if the required notice had not been mailed? Why or why not? [*Acevedo v. First Union National Bank,* 357 F.3d 1244 (11th Cir. 2004)]

- **To view a sample answer for Problem 24–7, go to this book's Web site at www.cengage. com/blaw/jentz, select "Chapter 24," and click on "Case Problem with Sample Answer."**

24–8. Negotiability. In September 2001, Cory Babcock and Honest Air Conditioning & Heating, Inc., bought a new 2001 Chevrolet Corvette from Cox Chevrolet in Sarasota, Florida. Their retail installment sales contract (RISC) required monthly payments until $52,516.20 was paid. The RISC imposed many other conditions on the buyers and seller with respect to the payment for, and handling of, the Corvette. Cox assigned the RISC to General Motors Acceptance Corp. (GMAC). In August 2002, the buyers sold the car to Florida Auto Brokers, which agreed to pay the balance due on the RISC. The check to GMAC for this amount was dishonored for insufficient funds, however, after the vehicle's title had

been forwarded. GMAC filed a suit in a Florida state court against Honest Air and Babcock, seeking $35,815.26 as damages for breach of contract. The defendants argued that the RISC was a negotiable instrument. A ruling in their favor on this point would reduce any damages due GMAC to less than the Corvette's current value. What are the requirements for an instrument to be negotiable? Does the RISC qualify? Explain. [*General Motors Acceptance Corp. v. Honest Air Conditioning & Heating, Inc.,* 933 So.2d 34 (Fla.App. 2 Dist. 2006)]

24–9. A QUESTION OF ETHICS

In November 2000, Monay Jones signed a promissory note in favor of a mortgage company in the amount of $261,250, using the deed to her home in Denver, Colorado, as collateral. Fifth Third Bank soon became the holder of the note. After Jones defaulted on the payment, in September 2001 she and the bank agreed to raise the note's balance to $280,231.23. She again defaulted. In November, the bank received a check from a third party as payment on Jones's note. It was the bank's policy to refuse personal checks in payoff of large debts. The bank representative who worked on Jones's account noted receipt of the check in the bank's records and forwarded it to the "payoff department." A week later, the bank discovered that the check had been lost without having been posted to Jones's account or submitted for payment. The bank notified Jones, and both parties searched, without success, for a copy of the check or evidence of the identity of its maker, the drawee bank, or the amount. In late 2002, the bank filed a suit in a Colorado state court to foreclose on Jones's home. She insisted that the note had been paid in full by a cashier's check issued by an Arkansas bank at the request of her deceased aunt. [*Fifth Third Bank v. Jones,* 168 P.3d 1 (Colo.App. 2007)]

(a) What evidence supports a finding that Jones gave the bank a check? Does it seem more likely that the check was a cashier's check or a personal check? Would it be fair for a court to find that the check had paid the note in full?

(b) Under UCC 3–310, if a cashier's check or other certified check "is taken for an obligation, the obligation is discharged." The bank argued that it had not "taken [Jones's check] for an obligation" because the bank's internal administrative actions were still pending when the check was lost. Would it be fair for the court to rule in the bank's favor based on this argument? Why or why not?

24–10. VIDEO QUESTION

Go to this text's Web site at **www.cengage/ com/blaw/jentz** and select "Chapter 24." Click on "Video Questions" and view the video titled *Negotiable Instruments*. Then answer the following questions.

(a) Who is the maker of the promissory note discussed in the video?

(b) Is the note in the video payable on demand or at a definite time?

(c) Does the note contain an unconditional promise or order to pay?

(d) If the note does not meet the requirements of negotiability, can Onyx assign the note (assignment was discussed in Chapter 16) to the bank in exchange for cash?

LAW ON THE WEB

For updated links to resources available on the Web, as well as a variety of other materials, visit this text's Web site at

www.cengage.com/blaw/jentz

The National Conference of Commissioners on Uniform State Laws, in association with the University of Pennsylvania Law School, now offers an official site for in-process and final drafts of uniform and model acts. For an index of final acts, including UCC Articles 3 and 4, go to

www.law.upenn.edu/bll/archives/ulc/ulc_final.htm

Cornell University's Legal Information Institute offers online access to the UCC, as well as to UCC articles as enacted by particular states and proposed revisions to articles, at

www.law.cornell.edu/ucc/ucc.table.html

Legal Research Exercises on the Web

Go to **www.cengage.com/blaw/jentz**, the Web site that accompanies this text. Select "Chapter 24" and click on "Internet Exercises." There you will find the following Internet research exercises that you can perform to learn more about the topics covered in this chapter.

Internet Exercise 24–1: Legal Perspective
Overview of Negotiable Instruments

Internet Exercise 24–2: Management Perspective
Banks and Bank Accounts

CHAPTER 20

Transferability and Holder in Due Course

Once issued, a negotiable instrument can be transferred to others by *assignment* or by *negotiation*. Recall from Chapter 16 that an assignment is a transfer of rights under a contract. Under general contract principles, a transfer by assignment to an assignee gives the assignee only those rights that the assignor possessed. Any defenses that can be raised against an assignor can normally be raised against the assignee. This same principle applies when a negotiable instrument, such as a promissory note, is transferred by assignment to an assignee.

Under the Uniform Commercial Code (UCC), **negotiation** is the transfer of an instrument in such form that the transferee (the person to whom the instrument is transferred) becomes a *holder* [UCC 3–201(a)]. A holder receives, at the very least, the rights of the previous possessor [UCC 3–203(b), 3–305]. Unlike an assignment, a transfer by negotiation can make it possible for a holder to receive *more* rights in the instrument than the prior possessor had [UCC 3–305]. A holder who receives greater rights is known as a *holder in due course,* a concept we discuss in this chapter. First, though, we look at the requirements for negotiation and examine the various types of *indorsements* that are used when order instruments are negotiated.

Negotiation

There are two methods of negotiating an instrument so that the receiver becomes a holder. The method used depends on whether the instrument is an *order instrument* or a *bearer instrument*.

Negotiating Order Instruments

An order instrument contains the name of a payee capable of indorsing, as in "Pay to the order of Elliot Goodseal." If an instrument is an order instrument, it is negotiated by delivery with any necessary indorsements (*indorsements* will be discussed shortly). For example, the Carrington Corporation issues a payroll check "to the order of Elliot Goodseal." Goodseal takes the check to the bank, signs his name on the back (an indorsement), gives it to the teller (a delivery), and receives cash. Goodseal has negotiated the check to the bank [UCC 3–201(b)].

Negotiating order instruments requires both delivery and indorsement. If Goodseal had taken the check to the bank and delivered it to the teller without signing it, the transfer would not qualify as a negotiation. In that situation, the transfer would be treated as an assignment, and the bank would become an assignee rather than a holder.

Negotiating Bearer Instruments

If an instrument is payable to bearer, it is negotiated by delivery—that is, by transfer into another person's possession. Indorsement is not necessary [UCC 3–201(b)]. The use of bearer instruments thus involves a greater risk of loss or theft than the use of order instruments.

Assume that Alonzo Cruz writes a check payable to "cash," thus creating a bearer instrument. Cruz then hands the check to Blaine Parrington (a delivery). Parrington puts the check in his wallet, which is subsequently stolen. The thief now has possession of the check. At this point, the thief has no rights in the check.

If the thief "delivers" the check to an innocent third person, however, negotiation will be complete. All rights to the check will pass *absolutely* to that third person, and Parrington will lose all right to recover the proceeds of the check from that person [UCC 3–306]. Of course, Parrington can recover his funds from the thief if the thief can be found.

Indorsements

As just described, an indorsement is required whenever an order instrument is negotiated. An *indorsement* is a signature with or without additional words or statements. It is most often written on the back of the instrument itself. If there is no room on the instrument, the indorsement can be written on a separate piece of paper, called an **allonge**,[1] and affixed to the instrument. A paper affixed to a negotiable instrument is part of the instrument [UCC 3–204(a)].

A person who transfers a note or a draft by signing (indorsing) it and delivering it to another person is an **indorser.** The person to whom the check is indorsed and delivered is the **indorsee.** Suppose that Luisa Parks receives a graduation check for $100. She can transfer the check to her mother (or to anyone) by signing it on the back. Luisa is an indorser. If Luisa indorses the check by writing "Pay to Aretha Parks," Aretha Parks is the indorsee.

We examine here four categories of indorsements: blank indorsements, special indorsements, qualified indorsements, and restrictive indorsements.

Blank Indorsements

A **blank indorsement** specifies no particular indorsee and can consist of a mere signature [UCC 3–205(b)]. Hence, a check payable "to the order of Mark Deitsch" can be indorsed in blank simply by writing Deitsch's signature on the back of the check. Exhibit 20–1 shows a blank indorsement.

EXHIBIT 20–1 • A Blank Indorsement

> *Mark Deitsch*

An instrument payable to order and indorsed in blank becomes a bearer instrument and can be negotiated by delivery alone [UCC 3–205(b)]. In other words, as will be discussed later, a blank indorsement converts an order instrument to a bearer instrument, which anybody can cash. Suppose that Rita Chou indorses in blank a check payable to her order and then loses it on the street. If Coker finds the check, he can sell it to Duncan for value without indorsing it. This constitutes a negotiation because Coker has made delivery of a bearer instrument (which was an order instrument until it was indorsed in blank).

Special Indorsements

A **special indorsement** identifies the person to whom the indorser intends to make the instrument payable; that is, it names the indorsee [UCC 3–205(a)]. For example, words such as "Pay to the order of Russell Clay" or "Pay to Russell Clay," followed by the signature of the indorser, are sufficient. When an instrument is indorsed in this way, it is an order instrument.

To avoid the risk of loss from theft, a holder may convert a blank indorsement to a special indorsement. This changes the bearer instrument back to an order instrument. A holder may "convert a blank indorsement that consists only of a signature into a special indorsement by writing, above the signature of the indorser, words identifying the person to whom the instrument is made payable" [UCC 3–205(c)].

For example, a check is made payable to Hal Cohen. He signs his name on the back of the check—a blank indorsement—and negotiates the check to William Hunter. Hunter is not able to cash the check immediately but wants to avoid any risk should he lose the check. He therefore writes "Pay to William Hunter" above Cohen's blank indorsement. In this manner, Hunter has converted Cohen's blank indorsement into a special indorsement. Further negotiation now requires William Hunter's indorsement, plus delivery. Exhibit 20–2 shows a special indorsement.

EXHIBIT 20–2 • A Special Indorsement

> *Pay to William Hunter*
> *Hal Cohen*

---

1. Pronounced uh-*lohnj.*

Qualified Indorsements

Generally, an indorser, *merely by indorsing*, impliedly promises to pay the holder, or any subsequent indorser, the amount of the instrument in the event that the drawer or maker defaults on the payment [UCC 3–415(a)]. Usually, then, indorsements are *unqualified indorsements*. In other words, the indorser is guaranteeing payment of the instrument in addition to transferring title to it. An indorser who does not wish to be liable on an instrument can use a **qualified indorsement** to disclaim this liability [UCC 3–415(b)]. The notation "without recourse" is commonly used to create a qualified indorsement.

Suppose that a check is made payable to the order of Sarah Jacobs. Sarah wants to negotiate the check to Allison Jong but does not want to assume liability for the check's payment. Sarah could create a qualified indorsement by indorsing the check as follows: "Pay to Allison Jong, without recourse, [signed] Sarah Jacobs" (see Exhibit 20–3).

EXHIBIT 20-3 • A Qualified Indorsement

Pay to Allison Jong,
without recourse
Sarah Jacobs

The Effect of Qualified Indorsements

Qualified indorsements are often used by persons acting in a representative capacity. For example, insurance agents sometimes receive checks payable to them that are really intended as payment to the insurance company. The agent is merely indorsing the payment through to the insurance company and should not be required to make good on a check if it is later dishonored. The "without recourse" indorsement relieves the agent from any liability on the check. If the instrument is dishonored, the holder cannot obtain recovery from the agent who indorsed "without recourse" unless the indorser has breached one of the transfer warranties that will be discussed in Chapter 26. These warranties relate to good title, authorized signature, no material alteration, and other requirements.

Special versus Blank Qualified Indorsements

A qualified indorsement ("without recourse") can be accompanied by either a special indorsement or a blank indorsement. A special qualified indorsement includes the name of the indorsee as well as the words "without recourse," as in Exhibit 20–3. The special indorsement makes the instrument an order instrument, and it requires an indorsement, plus delivery, for negotiation. A blank qualified indorsement makes the instrument a bearer instrument, and only delivery is required for negotiation. In either situation, the instrument still transfers title to the indorsee and can be further negotiated.

Restrictive Indorsements

A **restrictive indorsement** requires the indorsee to comply with certain instructions regarding the funds involved but does not prohibit further negotiation of the instrument [UCC 3–206(a)]. Restrictive indorsements come in many forms, some of which we discuss here.

Indorsements Prohibiting Further Indorsement An indorsement such as "Pay to Julie Thrush only, [signed] Thomas Fasulo" does not destroy negotiability. Thrush can negotiate the paper to a holder just as if it had read "Pay to Julie Thrush, [signed] Thomas Fasulo" [UCC 3–206(a)]. If the holder gives value, this type of restrictive indorsement has the same legal effect as a special indorsement.

Conditional Indorsements When payment depends on the occurrence of some event specified in the indorsement, the instrument has a conditional indorsement [UCC 3–204(a)]. For example, Ken Barton indorses a check as follows: "Pay to Lars Johansen if he completes the renovation of my kitchen by June 1, 2009, [signed] Ken Barton." Article 3 states that an indorsement conditioning the right to receive payment "does not affect the right of the indorsee to enforce the instrument" [UCC 3–206(b)]. A person paying or taking an instrument for value (*taking for value* will be discussed later in the chapter) can disregard the condition without liability.

A conditional indorsement (on the back of the instrument) does not prevent further negotiation of the instrument. If conditional language appears on the *face* (front) of an instrument, however, the instrument is not negotiable because it does not meet the requirement that a negotiable instrument must contain an unconditional promise to pay.

Indorsements for Deposit or Collection A common type of restrictive indorsement makes the indorsee (almost always a bank) a collecting agent of the indorser [UCC 3–206(c)]. Exhibit 20–4 illustrates this type of indorsement on a check payable and issued to Marcel Dumont. In particular, the indorsements "For deposit only" and "For collection only" have the effect of locking the instrument into the bank collection process. Only a bank can acquire the rights of a holder following one of these indorsements until the item has been specially indorsed by a bank to a person who is not a bank [UCC 3–206(c), 4–201(b)]. A bank's liability for payment of an instrument with a restrictive indorsement of this kind will be discussed in Chapter 27.

EXHIBIT 20–4 • "For Deposit Only" and "For Collection Only" Indorsements

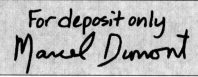

Trust (Agency) Indorsements Indorsements to persons who are to hold or use the funds for the benefit of the indorser or a third party are called **trust indorsements** (also known as *agency indorsements*) [UCC 3–206(d), (e)]. Assume that Ralph Zimmer asks his accountant, Stephanie Contento, to pay some bills for him while he is out of the country. He indorses a check, drawn by a friend, to Stephanie Contento "as agent for Ralph Zimmer." This trust (agency) indorsement obligates Contento to use the funds from the friend's check only for the benefit of Zimmer.

The result of a trust indorsement is that legal rights in the instrument are transferred to the original indorsee. To the extent that the original indorsee pays or applies the proceeds consistently with the indorsement (for example, in an indorsement stating "Pay to Ellen Cook in trust for Roger Callahan"), the indorsee is a holder and can become a holder in due course (a status that will be described shortly). Sample trust (agency) indorsements are shown in Exhibit 20–5.

EXHIBIT 20–5 • Trust (Agency) Indorsements

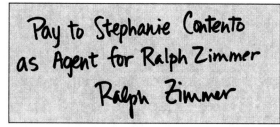

The fiduciary restrictions—restrictions mandated by a relationship involving trust and loyalty—on the instrument do not reach beyond the original indorsee [UCC 3–206(d), (e)]. Any subsequent purchaser can qualify as a holder in due course unless he or she has actual notice that the instrument was negotiated in breach of a fiduciary duty. For a synopsis of the various indorsements and the consequences of using each type, see *Concept Summary 20.1* on page 536.

How Indorsements Can Convert Order Instruments to Bearer Instruments and Vice Versa

As we saw earlier, order instruments and bearer instruments are negotiated differently. The method used for negotiation depends on the character of the instrument *at the time the negotiation takes place*. Indorsement can convert an order instrument into a bearer instrument. For example, a check originally payable to "cash" but subsequently indorsed with the words "Pay to Arnold" must be negotiated as an order instrument (by indorsement and delivery), even though it was previously a bearer instrument [UCC 3–205(a)].

As mentioned earlier, an instrument payable to the order of a named payee and indorsed in blank becomes a bearer instrument [UCC 3–205(b)]. For example, a check made payable to the order of Jessie Arnold is issued to Arnold, and Arnold indorses it by signing her name on the back. The instrument, which is now a bearer instrument, can be negotiated by delivery without indorsement. Arnold can negotiate the check to whomever she wishes merely by delivery, and that person can negotiate by delivery without indorsement. If Arnold loses the check after she indorses it, anyone who finds the check can negotiate it further.

Similarly, a bearer instrument can be converted into an order instrument through indorsement. Suppose that Arnold takes the check that she indorsed in blank (now a bearer instrument) and negotiates it, by delivery, to Jonas Tolling. Tolling indorses the check "Pay to Mark Hyatt, [signed] Jonas Tolling." By adding this special indorsement, Tolling has converted the check into an order instrument. The check can be further negotiated only by indorsement (by Mark Hyatt) and delivery [UCC 3–205(b)]. Exhibit 20–6 illustrates how an indorsement can convert an order instrument into a bearer instrument and vice versa.

Miscellaneous Indorsement Problems

Of course, a significant problem occurs when an indorsement is forged or unauthorized. The UCC rules concerning unauthorized or forged signatures and indorsements will be discussed in Chapter 26 in the context of signature liability. These rules will be examined again in Chapter 27 in the context of the bank's liability for payment of an instrument containing an unauthorized signature. Here we look at some other difficulties that may arise with indorsements.

Misspelled Names

An indorsement should be identical to the name that appears on the instrument. A payee or indorsee whose name is misspelled can indorse with the misspelled name, the correct name, or both [UCC 3–204(d)]. For example, if Marie Ellison receives a check payable to the order of Mary Ellison, she can indorse the check either "Marie Ellison" or "Mary Ellison." The usual practice is to indorse with the name as it appears on the instrument followed by the correct name.

Instruments Payable to Entities

A negotiable instrument can be drawn payable to an entity such as an estate, a partnership, or an organization. In this situation, an authorized representative of the entity can negotiate the instrument. For example, a check may read "Pay to the order of the Red Cross." An authorized representative of the Red Cross can negotiate this check. Similarly, negotiable paper can be payable to a public officer. For example, checks reading "Pay to the order of the County Tax Collector" or "Pay to the order of Larry White, Receiver of Taxes" can be negotiated by whoever holds the office [UCC 3–110(c)].

Alternative or Joint Payees

An instrument payable to two or more persons *in the alternative* (for example, "Pay to the order of Ying or Mifflin") requires the indorsement of only one of the payees [UCC 3–110(d)]. If, however, an instrument is made payable to two or more persons *jointly* (for

EXHIBIT 20–6 • **Converting an Order Instrument to a Bearer Instrument and Vice Versa**

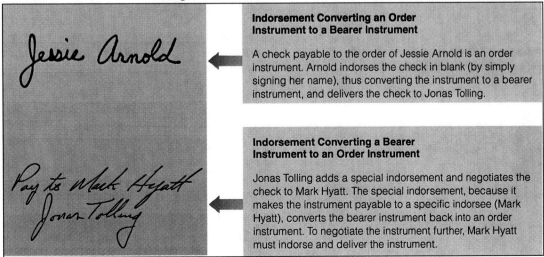

Indorsement Converting an Order Instrument to a Bearer Instrument

A check payable to the order of Jessie Arnold is an order instrument. Arnold indorses the check in blank (by simply signing her name), thus converting the instrument to a bearer instrument, and delivers the check to Jonas Tolling.

Indorsement Converting a Bearer Instrument to an Order Instrument

Jonas Tolling adds a special indorsement and negotiates the check to Mark Hyatt. The special indorsement, because it makes the instrument payable to a specific indorsee (Mark Hyatt), converts the bearer instrument back into an order instrument. To negotiate the instrument further, Mark Hyatt must indorse and deliver the instrument.

CONCEPT SUMMARY 20.1
Types of Indorsements and Their Effect

Type of Indorsement	Description	Examples	Legal Effect
BLANK INDORSEMENTS	Indorser does not identify the person to whom the instrument is payable; can consist of a mere signature.	"Elana Guiterrez" "Mark Deitsch"	Creates a bearer instrument, which can be negotiated by delivery alone.
SPECIAL INDORSEMENTS	Indorser identifies the person to whom the instrument is payable.	"Pay to the order of Russell Clay" "Pay to William Hunter"	Creates an order instrument; negotiation requires delivery and indorsement.
QUALIFIED INDORSEMENTS	Indorser includes words indicating that he or she is not guaranteeing or assuming liability for payment.	"Without recourse, Elana Guitterez" (blank qualified indorsement) "Pay to Allison Jong without recourse, Sarah Jacobs" (special qualified indorsement, which creates an order instrument)	Relieves indorser of any liability for payment of the instrument; frequently used by agents or others acting on behalf of another.
RESTRICTIVE INDORSEMENTS	Indorser includes specific instructions regarding the funds involved or states a condition to the right of the indorsee to receive payment.	"For deposit only" "For collection only"	Only a bank can become a holder of instruments that are indorsed for deposit or collection.
		"Pay to Stephanie Contento as agent for Ralph Zimmer" "Pay to Ellen Cook in trust for Roger Callahan"	In a trust indorsement, the third party agent or trustee has the rights of a holder but has fiduciary duties to use the funds consistently with the indorsement.

example, "Pay to the order of Bridgette and Tony Van Horn"), all of the payees' indorsements are necessary for negotiation.

Alternative Payees Presumed If the Instrument Is Ambiguous If an instrument payable to two or more persons does not clearly indi-

cate whether it is payable in the alternative or payable jointly, then "the instrument is payable to the persons alternatively" [UCC 3–110(d)]. The same principles apply to special indorsements that identify more than one person to whom the indorser intends to make the instrument payable [UCC 3–205(a)]. These principles were applied in the following case.

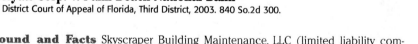

C A S E **20.1** **Hyatt Corp. v. Palm Beach National Bank**
District Court of Appeal of Florida, Third District, 2003. 840 So.2d 300.

● **Background and Facts** Skyscraper Building Maintenance, LLC (limited liability company—see Chapter 37), contracted with Hyatt Corporation to perform maintenance services for certain hotels owned and operated by Hyatt in Florida. Under an agreement with Skyscraper, J&D Financial Corporation asked Hyatt to make checks for the services payable to Skyscraper and J&D. Of the many checks issued by Hyatt to the two payees, Palm Beach National Bank negotiated

CASE 20.1 CONTINUED two that were indorsed only by Skyscraper. These two checks were made payable to "J&D Financial Corp. Skyscraper Building Maint." Parties listed in this manner are referred to as "stacked payees." J&D filed a suit in a Florida state court against Hyatt, the bank, and others, seeking, among other things, full repayment of the two checks. J&D and Hyatt asserted that the checks were payable jointly, requiring indorsement by both payees. The bank argued that the checks were payable to J&D and Skyscraper alternatively and thus negotiable on only one payee's indorsement. The court issued a summary judgment in the bank's favor. J&D and Hyatt appealed to a state intermediate appellate court.

● **Decision and Rationale** The state intermediate appellate court affirmed the lower court's judgment, holding that the bank properly negotiated the checks even though they were indorsed by only one of the two payees. The appellate court pointed out that UCC 3–110(d) provides, "If an instrument payable to two or more persons is ambiguous as to whether it is payable to the persons alternatively, the instrument is payable to the persons alternatively." The court acknowledged that under the previous version of this provision, "if an ambiguity existed as to whether multiple payees were intended as joint or alternative payees, they were deemed joint payees," but noted that the statute had been amended and the amendment "reverses the prior rule." The court concluded that when a check lists two payees without the use of the word *and* or *or*, the nature of the payees, as to whether they are alternative or joint, is ambiguous. "Therefore, the UCC amendment prevails and they are to be treated as alternative payees, thus requiring only one of the payees' signatures." In other words, a check payable to stacked payees is payable alternatively. "Consequently," the court stated, "the bank could negotiate the check when it was endorsed by only one of the two payees, thereby escaping liability."

● **The Legal Environment Dimension** *Other than negotiation, what is the significance of the UCC provision at issue in this case?*

● **The Ethical Dimension** *If an instrument made payable to two persons without specifying and or or (a stacked-payee designation) was considered unambiguous and payable jointly before the amendment of this provision of the UCC, should that same payee designation be considered unambiguous after the amendment? Explain.*

Suspension of the Drawer's Obligation

When a drawer gives one alternative or joint payee a check, the drawer's obligation on the check to other payees is suspended [UCC 3–310(b)(1)]. The payee who has possession of the check holds it for the benefit of all of the payees.

On the check's negotiation, is the drawer obliged to ensure that the funds are disbursed between the payees? In the following case, one of the parties—a payee on a "co-payable" check—contended in effect that a drawer has such a duty.

C A S E **20.2 Graves v. Johnson**
Court of Appeals of Indiana, 2007. 862 N.E.2d 716.

● **Background and Facts** Vernon and Shirley Graves owned a commercial building and the property on which it was located in Kokomo, Indiana. The Graveses leased the premises to John and Tamara Johnson, who operated Johnson's Towing & Recovery on the property. The Johnsons insured the property and their business through Westport Insurance Company. A fire destroyed the building in November 2003. Westport hired Claims Management Services, Inc. (CMS), to investigate and pay the claim. On CMS's behalf, Robert Davis met with Vernon, who was acting as the rebuilding contractor, and agreed that Westport would pay $98,000 in three "progress payments" with the

CASE CONTINUES

CASE 20.2 CONTINUED checks to be "co-payable" to Johnson's Towing and Vernon. Westport issued two checks, for $30,000 and $29,000, respectively, and delivered them to Vernon, who deposited them into his account. A third check for $68,037.42 was tendered to the Johnsons. They did not remit the funds to the Graveses, however, who subsequently filed a suit in an Indiana state court against the Johnsons and Westport.[a] The court entered a summary judgment in Westport's favor. The Graveses appealed to a state intermediate appellate court.

● **Decision and Rationale** The state intermediate appellate court affirmed the judgment of the lower court. The reviewing court pointed out that when there are joint payees to a check, "payment to and possession by one joint payee is constructive possession by the other joint payee." Thereafter, the obligations of the check's issuer are suspended with respect to the other joint payee. Any underlying debt for which the check constitutes a discharge is extinguished even when a jointly payable check is sent to just one co-payee and that co-payee embezzles the funds, as occurred in this case. The insurance company's tender of the last check to the Johnsons suspended the insurance company's obligation to both payees.

● **The Ethical Dimension** *Does a drawer who acts as Westport did—consulting with, and delivering the first two checks to, the Graveses—create an ethical obligation with respect to the delivery of the third check? Why or why not?*

● **The Legal Environment Dimension** *Is there a method, other than payment, that would have discharged Westport's obligation as the drawer of the check? Explain.*

***

a. The Johnsons filed for bankruptcy, which automatically suspended the Graveses' suit against them.

***

SECTION 4
Holder versus Holder in Due Course

The rules contained in Article 3 of the UCC govern a party's right to payment of a check, draft, note, or certificate of deposit.[2] Problems arise when a holder seeking payment of a negotiable instrument learns that a defense to payment exists or that another party has a prior claim to the instrument. In such situations, it becomes important for the person seeking payment to have the rights of a *holder in due course* (HDC). An HDC takes a negotiable instrument free of all claims and most defenses of other parties.

Status of an Ordinary Holder

As pointed out in Chapter 24, the UCC defines a *holder* as "the person in possession of a negotiable instrument

***

2. The rights and liabilities on checks, drafts, notes, and certificates of deposit are determined under Article 3 of the UCC. Other kinds of documents, such as stock certificates, bills of lading, and other documents of title, meet the requirements of negotiable instruments, but the rights and liabilities of the parties on these documents are covered by Articles 7 and 8 of the UCC. See Chapter 47, on bailments, for information about Article 7.

that is payable either to bearer or to an identified person that is the person in possession" [UCC 1–201(21)(A)]. An ordinary holder obtains only those rights that the transferor had in the instrument. In this respect, a holder has the same status as an assignee (see Chapter 16). A holder normally is subject to the same defenses that could be asserted against the transferor, just as an assignee is subject to the defenses that could be asserted against the assignor.

Status of a Holder in Due Course (HDC)

In contrast, a **holder in due course (HDC)** is a holder who, by meeting certain acquisition requirements (to be discussed shortly), takes an instrument free of most of the defenses and claims to which the transferor was subject. Stated another way, an HDC can normally acquire a higher level of immunity than can an ordinary holder in regard to defenses against payment on the instrument or ownership claims to the instrument by other parties.

An example will help to clarify the distinction between the rights of an ordinary holder and the rights of an HDC. Debby Morrison signs a $10,000 note payable to Alex Jerrod in payment for goods. Jerrod negotiates the note to Beverly Larson, who promises to pay Jerrod for it in thirty days. During the next month, Larson learns that Jerrod has breached his contract with Morrison by delivering defective goods and that, for this reason, Morrison will not honor the $10,000 note. Whether Larson can hold Morrison liable on the note depends on whether Larson has met the requirements for HDC status. If Larson has met these requirements and thus has HDC status, she is entitled to payment on the note. If Larson has not met these requirements, she has the status of an ordinary holder, and Morrison's defense against payment to Jerrod will also be effective against Larson.

Requirements for HDC Status

The basic requirements for attaining HDC status are set forth in UCC 3–302. An HDC must first be a holder of a negotiable instrument and must have taken the instrument (1) for value; (2) in good faith; and (3) without notice that it is overdue, that it has been dishonored, that any person has a defense against it or a claim to it, or that the instrument contains unauthorized signatures or alterations or is so irregular or incomplete as to call into question its authenticity. We now examine each of these requirements.

Taking for Value

An HDC must have given value for the instrument [UCC 3–302(a)(2)(i), 3–303]. A person who receives an instrument as a gift or inherits it has *not* met the requirement of value. In these situations, the person normally becomes an ordinary holder and does not possess the rights of an HDC.

How an Instrument Is Taken for Value Under UCC 3–303(a), a holder takes an instrument for value if the holder has done any of the following:

1. Performed the promise for which the instrument was issued or transferred.
2. Acquired a security interest or other lien in the instrument (other than a lien obtained by a judicial proceeding).[3]
3. Taken the instrument in payment of, or as security for, an **antecedent** (preexisting) **claim.** For example, Zon owes Dwyer $2,000 on a past-due account. If Zon negotiates a $2,000 note signed by Gordon to

Dwyer and Dwyer accepts it to discharge the overdue account balance, Dwyer has given value for the instrument.
4. Given a negotiable instrument as payment. Suppose that Martin has issued a $5,000 negotiable promissory note to Paulene. The note is due six months from the date issued. Paulene needs funds and does not want to wait until the maturity date to collect. She negotiates the note to her friend Kristen, who pays her $2,000 in cash and writes her a check—a negotiable instrument—for the balance of $3,000. Kristen has given full value for the note by paying $2,000 in cash and issuing Paulene the check for $3,000.
5. Given an irrevocable commitment (such as a letter of credit described in Chapter 22 on page 417) as payment.

The Concept of Value in Negotiable Instruments Law The concept of value in the law of negotiable instruments is not the same as the concept of consideration in the law of contracts. An executory promise (a promise to give value in the future) is clearly valid consideration to support a contract [UCC 1–201(44)]. In contrast, it normally does not constitute sufficient value to make the promisor an HDC. UCC 3–303(a)(1) provides that a holder takes the instrument for value only to the extent that the promise has been performed. Therefore, if the holder plans to pay for the instrument later or plans to perform the required services at some future date, the holder has not yet given value. In that situation, the holder is not yet an HDC.

In the Morrison-Jerrod-Larson example presented earlier, Larson is not an HDC because she did not take the instrument (Morrison's note) for value—she has not yet paid Jerrod for the note. Thus, Morrison's defense of breach of contract is valid against Larson as well as against Jerrod. If Larson had paid Jerrod for the note at the time of transfer (which would mean she had given value for the instrument), she would be an HDC. As an HDC, she could hold Morrison liable on the note even though Morrison has a valid defense against Jerrod on the basis of breach of contract. Exhibit 20–7 on page 544 illustrates these concepts.

Exceptions In a few situations, the holder may pay for the instrument but does not acquire HDC status. For example, when the instrument is purchased at a judicial sale, such as a bankruptcy or creditor's sale, the holder will not be an HDC. Similarly, if the instrument is acquired as a result of taking over a trust or estate (as administrator), or as part of a corporate purchase

---

3. Security interests will be discussed in Chapter 29. Other liens will be discussed in Chapter 28.

EXHIBIT 20-7 • Taking for Value

By exchanging defective goods for the note, Jerrod breached his contract with Morrison. Morrison could assert this defense if Jerrod presented the note to her for payment. Jerrod exchanged the note for Larson's promise to pay in thirty days, however. Because Larson did not take the note for value, she is not a holder in due course. Thus, Morrison can assert against Larson the defense of Jerrod's breach when Larson submits the note to Morrison for payment. If Larson had taken the note for value, Morrison could not assert that defense and would be liable to pay the note.

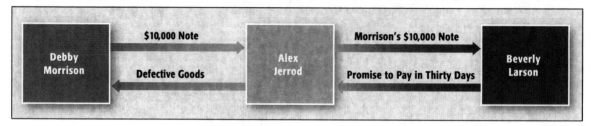

of assets, the holder will have only the rights of an ordinary holder [UCC 3–302(c)].

Taking in Good Faith

The second requirement for HDC status is that the holder take the instrument in *good faith* [UCC 3–302(a)(2)(ii)]. Under Article 3, *good faith* is defined as "honesty in fact and the observance of reasonable commercial standards of fair dealing" [UCC 3–103(a)(4)].[4] The good faith requirement applies

4. Before the revision of Article 3, the applicable definition of *good faith* was "honesty in fact in the conduct or transaction concerned" [UCC 1–201(19)].

only to the *holder*. It is immaterial whether the transferor acted in good faith. Thus, a person who in good faith takes a negotiable instrument from a thief may become an HDC.

The good faith requirement means that the purchaser, when acquiring the instrument, must honestly believe that it is not defective. If a person purchases a $10,000 note for $300 from a stranger on a street corner, the issue of good faith can be raised on the grounds of both the suspicious circumstances and the grossly inadequate consideration (value). In the following case, the court had to deal with the meaning of accepting a check in good faith.

C A S E **20.3 Georg v. Metro Fixtures Contractors, Inc.**
Supreme Court of Colorado, 2008. 178 P.3d 1209.

● **Background and Facts** Clinton Georg employed Cassandra Demery as a bookkeeper at his business, Freestyle, until he discovered she had embezzled more than $200,000 and had failed to pay $240,000 in state and federal taxes owed by Freestyle. Georg fired Demery and said that if she did not repay the embezzled funds, he would notify the authorities. Demery went to work for Metro Fixtures, a company owned by her parents, as a bookkeeper. She wrote a check to Freestyle for $189,000 out of Metro's account and deposited it to Freestyle's checking account. She told Georg it was a loan to her from her family to repay him. Georg used the funds to pay his back taxes. Two years later, Metro discovered Demery's theft and sued Georg and Freestyle for *conversion* (see Chapter 6), as Demery had no authority to take the funds. The trial court held that Freestyle was a holder in due course and granted summary judgment. Metro appealed. The appeals court reversed, holding that because Demery deposited the check directly into Freestyle's account, Freestyle could not have been a holder in due course as it never had actual possession of the check. Georg and Freestyle appealed.

● **Decision and Rationale** Colorado's highest court reversed the appellate court's decision, finding that the payee, Freestyle, was a holder in due course based on its constructive posses-

CASE 20.3 CONTINUED sion of the check. Even though Metro did not authorize Demery to issue the check for $189,000, she had authority to issue checks for Metro. Georg had no reason to know that Demery had lied when she said her parents, who owned the company, had loaned her the funds. Freestyle took the check in good faith. The UCC intends to protect the party least able to protect itself. So, as in this case, when two innocent parties suffer because of wrongdoing, the loss falls on the party who has created the circumstances that enabled the third party to engage in wrongdoing. Metro gave Demery authority to write checks on its account, so it bears the loss.

● **What If the Facts Were Different?** *Suppose that Demery had gone to work for a company with which she had no relationship and stole funds from it to pay Georg. Would Georg then be the more innocent party? Why or why not?*

● **The Ethical Dimension** *Was it right for Georg to let the loss fall on Metro, and was it reasonable for him to believe that Demery's parents had loaned her the funds? Explain your answer.*

Taking without Notice

The final requirement for HDC status concerns notice of defects. A person cannot be a HDC if she or he knows or has reason to know that the instrument is defective in any one of the following ways [UCC 3–302(a)]:

1. It is overdue.
2. It has been dishonored.
3. It is part of a series of which at least one instrument has an uncured (uncorrected) default.
4. The instrument contains an unauthorized signature or has been altered.
5. There is a defense against the instrument or a claim to the instrument.
6. The instrument is so incomplete or irrregular as to call into question its authenticity.[5]

What Constitutes Notice? Notice of a defective instrument is given whenever the holder (1) has actual knowledge of the defect; (2) has received a notice of the defect (such as a letter from a bank identifying the serial numbers of stolen checks); or (3) has reason to know that a defect exists, given all the facts and circumstances known at the time in question [UCC 1–201(25)]. The holder must also have received the notice "at a time and in a manner that gives a reasonable opportunity to act on it" [UCC 3–302(f)]. A purchaser's knowledge of certain facts, such as insolvency proceedings against the maker or drawer of the instrument, does not constitute notice that the instrument is defective [UCC 3–302(b)].

Overdue Instruments What constitutes notice that an instrument is overdue depends on whether it is a demand instrument (payable on demand) or a time instrument (payable at a definite time).

Demand Instruments. A purchaser has notice that a *demand instrument* is overdue if he or she either takes the instrument knowing that demand has been made or takes the instrument an unreasonable length of time after its date. For a check, a "reasonable time" is ninety days after the date of the check. For all other demand instruments, what will be considered a reasonable time depends on the circumstances [UCC 3–304(a)].

Time Instruments. Normally, a *time instrument* is overdue on the day after its due date; hence, anyone who takes a time instrument after the due date is on notice that it is overdue [UCC 3–304(b)].[6] Thus, if a promissory note due on May 15 is purchased on May 16, the purchaser will be an ordinary holder, not an HDC. If an instrument states that it is "Payable in thirty days," counting begins the day after the instrument is dated. For example, a note dated December 1 that is payable in thirty days is due by midnight on December 31. If the payment date falls on a Sunday or holiday, the instrument is payable on the next business day.

A series of notes issued at the same time with successive maturity dates is overdue when any note in the series is overdue. This serves to notify prospective purchasers that they cannot qualify as HDCs [UCC 3–302(a)(2)(iii)].

---

5. Section 302(1)(c) of the unrevised Article 3 provided that HDC protection is lost if a holder has notice that an instrument is overdue or has been dishonored or if there is a claim to or a defense against it.

6. A time instrument also becomes overdue the day after an accelerated due date, unless the purchaser has no reason to know that the due date has been accelerated [UCC 3–302(a)(2)(iii), 3–304(b)(3)].

If the principal is to be paid in installments, the default or nonpayment of any one installment will make the instrument overdue and provide notice to prospective purchasers of the default. The instrument will remain overdue until the default is cured [UCC 3–304(b)(1)]. An instrument does not become overdue if there is a default on a payment of interest only [UCC 3–304(c)]. Most installment notes provide that any payment shall be applied first to interest and the balance to the principal. This serves as notice that any installment payment for less than the full amount results in a default on an installment payment toward the principal.

Dishonored Instruments An instrument is *dishonored* when the party to whom the instrument is presented refuses to pay it. If a holder knows or has reason to know that an instrument has been dishonored, the holder is on notice and cannot claim HDC status [UCC 3–302(a)(2)]. Thus, a person who takes a check clearly stamped "insufficient funds" is put on notice.

For example, Gonzalez holds a demand note dated September 1 on Apex, Inc., a local business firm. On September 17, she demands payment, and Apex refuses (that is, dishonors the instrument). On September 22, Gonzalez negotiates the note to Brenner, a purchaser who lives in another state. Brenner does not know, and has no reason to know, that the note has been dishonored. Because Brenner is *not* put on notice, Brenner can become an HDC.

Notice of Claims or Defenses A holder cannot become an HDC if he or she has notice of any claim to the instrument or defense against it [UCC 3–302(a)(2)(v),(vi)]. Knowledge of claims or defenses can be imputed (attributed) to the purchaser if these claims or defenses are apparent on the face of the instrument or if the purchaser otherwise had reason to know of them from facts surrounding the transaction.[7]

Knowledge of a Defense. It stands to reason that a purchaser cannot be an HDC if she or he knows that a party to an instrument has a defense that entitles that party to avoid the obligation. For example, a potential purchaser who knows that the maker of a note has breached the underlying contract with the payee cannot thereafter purchase the note as an HDC.

Knowledge of one defense precludes a holder from asserting HDC status in regard to all other defenses. For example, Litton, knowing that the note he has taken has a forged indorsement, presents it to the maker for payment. The maker refuses to pay on the ground of breach of the underlying contract. The maker can assert this defense against Litton even though Litton had no knowledge of the breach, because Litton's knowledge of the forgery alone prevents him from being an HDC in *all* circumstances.

Knowledge of Wrongful Negotiation by a Fiduciary. Knowledge that a fiduciary has wrongfully negotiated an instrument is sufficient notice of a claim against the instrument to preclude HDC status. Suppose that O'Banion, a university trustee, improperly writes a check on the university trust account to pay a personal debt. Lewis knows that the check has been improperly drawn on university funds, but she accepts it anyway. Lewis cannot claim to be an HDC. When a purchaser knows that a fiduciary is acting in breach of duty, HDC status is denied [UCC 3–307(b)].

Incomplete Instruments A purchaser cannot become an HDC of an instrument so incomplete on its face that an element of negotiability is lacking (for example, the amount is not filled in) [UCC 3–302(a)(1)]. Minor omissions (such as the omission of the date—see Chapter 24) are permissible because these do not call into question the validity of the instrument [UCC 3–113(b)].

Similarly, when a person accepts an instrument that has been completed without knowing that it was incomplete when issued, the person can take it as an HDC [UCC 3–115(b), 3–302(a)(1)]. Even if an instrument that is originally incomplete is later completed in an unauthorized manner, an HDC can still enforce the instrument as completed [UCC 3–407(c)].

To illustrate: Peyton asks Brittany to buy a textbook for him when she goes to the campus bookstore. Peyton writes a check payable to the campus store, leaves the amount blank, and tells Brittany to fill in the price of the textbook. The cost of the textbook is $85. If Brittany fills in the check for $150 before she gets to the bookstore, the bookstore cashier sees only a properly completed instrument. Therefore, because the

---

7. If an instrument contains a statement required by a statute or an administrative rule to the effect that the rights of a holder or transferee are subject to the claims or defenses that the issuer could assert against the original payee, the instrument is negotiable, but there cannot be an HDC of the instrument. See UCC 3–106(d) and the discussion of federal limitations on HDC rights in Chapter 26.

bookstore had no notice that the check was incomplete when it was issued, the bookstore can take the check for $150 and become an HDC. (Material alterations will be discussed in Chapter 26.)

Irregular Instruments Any irregularity on the face of an instrument (such as an obvious forgery or alteration) that calls into question its validity or ownership, or that creates an ambiguity as to the party to pay, will bar HDC status. A difference between the handwriting used in the body of a check and that used in the signature will not in and of itself make an instrument irregular. Antedating or postdating a check or stating the amount in digits but failing to write out the numbers normally will not make a check irregular [UCC 3–113(a)].[8] Visible evidence of forgery of a maker's or drawer's signature, however, will disqualify a purchaser from HDC status. Conversely, a good forgery of a signature or a careful alteration can go undetected by reasonable examination; therefore, the purchaser can qualify as an HDC [UCC 3–302(a)(1)].

Losses that result from well-crafted forgeries usually fall on the party to whom the forger transferred the instrument (assuming, of course, that the forger cannot be found). This means that a bank that accepts checks for deposit despite apparent evidence on the faces of the checks that they were irregular will bear the loss if the checks later turn out to be forged.[9]

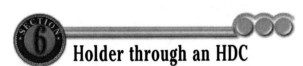

Holder through an HDC

A person who does not qualify as an HDC but who derives his or her title through an HDC can acquire the rights and privileges of an HDC. This rule, which is called the **shelter principle,** is set out in UCC 3–203(b):

> Transfer of an instrument, whether or not the transfer is a negotiation, vests in the transferee any right of the trans-

feror to enforce the instrument, including any right as a holder in due course, but the transferee cannot acquire rights of a holder in due course by a transfer, directly or indirectly, from a holder in due course if the transferee engaged in fraud or illegality affecting the instrument.

The Purpose of the Shelter Principle

The shelter principle extends the benefits of HDC status and is designed to aid the HDC in readily disposing of the instrument. Anyone, no matter how far removed from an HDC, who can ultimately trace her or his title back to an HDC comes within the shelter principle. Normally, a person who acquires an instrument from an HDC or from someone with HDC rights receives HDC rights on the legal theory that the transferee of an instrument receives at least the rights that the transferor had. By extending the benefits of HDC status, the shelter principle promotes the marketability and free transferability of negotiable instruments.

Limitations on the Shelter Principle

Nevertheless, there are some limitations on the shelter principle. Certain persons who formerly held instruments cannot improve their positions by later reacquiring the instruments from HDCs [UCC 3–203(b)]. Therefore, if a holder was a party to fraud or illegality affecting the instrument or if, as a prior holder, he or she had notice of a claim or defense against the instrument, that holder is not allowed to improve his or her status by repurchasing the instrument from a later HDC.

To illustrate: Matthew and Carla collaborate to defraud Lorena. Lorena is induced to give Carla a negotiable note payable to Carla's order. Carla then specially indorses the note for value to Larry, an HDC. Matthew and Carla split the proceeds. Larry negotiates the note to Stuart, another HDC. Stuart then negotiates the note for value to Matthew. Matthew, even though he obtained the note through an HDC, is not a holder through an HDC, because he participated in the original fraud and can never acquire HDC rights in this note.

See *Concept Summary 20.2* on the following page for a review of the requirements for HDC status.

---

8. Note that some courts have held that the postdating of a check may raise substantial suspicions about its authenticity, particularly if it is a commercial check. See, for example, *Bay Shore Check Cashing Corp. v. Landscapes by North East Construction Corp.*, 776 N.Y.S.2d 742 (N.Y.Dist. 2004).

9. See, for example, *Firstar Bank, N.A. v. First Star Title Agency, Inc.*, 2004 WL 1906851 (Ohio App. 2004).

CONCEPT SUMMARY 20.2
Rules and Requirements for HDC Status

Basic Requirements	Rules
MUST BE A *HOLDER*	A *holder* is defined as a person in possession of an instrument "if the instrument is payable to bearer or, in the cases of an instrument payable to an identified person, if the identified person is in possession" [UCC 1–201(20)].
MUST TAKE *FOR VALUE*	A holder gives *value* by doing any of the following [UCC 3–303]: 1. Performing the promise for which the instrument was issued or transferred. 2. Acquiring a security interest or other lien in the instrument (other than a lien obtained by a judicial proceeding). 3. Taking the instrument in payment of, or as security for, an antecedent debt. 4. Giving a negotiable instrument as payment. 5. Giving an irrevocable commitment as payment.
MUST TAKE IN *GOOD FAITH*	*Good faith* is defined for purposes of revised Article 3 as "honesty in fact and the observance of reasonable commercial standards of fair dealing" [UCC 3–103(a)(4)].
MUST TAKE *WITHOUT NOTICE*	A holder must not be *on notice* that the instrument is defective in any of the following ways [UCC 3–302, 3–304]: 1. The instrument is overdue. 2. The instrument has been dishonored. 3. There is an uncured (uncorrected) default with respect to another instrument issued as part of the same series. 4. The instrument contains an unauthorized signature or has been altered. 5. There is a defense against the instrument or a claim to the instrument. 6. The instrument is so irregular or incomplete as to call into question its authenticity.
SHELTER PRINCIPLE— HOLDER THROUGH A HOLDER IN DUE COURSE	A holder who cannot qualify as an HDC has the rights of an HDC if he or she derives title through an HDC [UCC 3–203(b)].

REVIEWING Transferability and Holder in Due Course

The Brown family owns several companies, including the J. H. Stevedoring Company and Penn Warehousing and Distribution, Inc. Many aspects of the companies' operations and management are intertwined. Dennis Bishop began working for J. H. and Penn in 1999. By 2008, Bishop was financial controller at J. H., where he was responsible for approving invoices for payment and reconciling the corporate checkbook. In December 2008, Bishop began stealing from Penn and J. H. by writing checks on the corporate accounts and using the funds for his own benefit (committing the crime of embezzlement). Several members of the Brown family signed the checks for Bishop without hesitation because he was a longtime, trusted employee. Over the next two years, Bishop embezzled $1,209,436, of which $670,632 was used to buy horses from the Fasig-Tipton Company and Fasig-Tipton

REVIEWING Transferability and Holder in Due Course, Continued

Midlantic, Inc., with Penn and J. H. checks made payable to those firms. When Bishop's fraud was revealed, J. H. and Penn filed a suit in a federal district court against the Fasig-Tipton firms (the defendants) to recover the amounts of the checks made payable to them. Using the information presented in the chapter, answer the following questions.

1. What method was most likely used to negotiate the instruments described here?
2. Suppose that all of the checks issued to the defendants were made payable to "Fasig-Tipton Co., Fasig-Tipton Midlantic, Inc." Under the Uniform Commercial Code, were the instruments payable jointly or in the alternative? Why is this significant?
3. Do the defendants in this situation (the two Fasig-Tipton firms) meet the requirements of an HDC? Why or why not?
4. In whose favor should the court rule and why?

TERMS AND CONCEPTS

allonge
antecedent claim

blank indorsement
holder in due course (HDC)
indorsee
indorser
negotiation

qualified indorsement
restrictive indorsement
shelter principle
special indorsement
trust indorsement

QUESTIONS AND CASE PROBLEMS

25–1. A check drawn by Cullen for $500 is made payable to the order of Jordan and issued to Jordan. Jordan owes his landlord $500 in rent and transfers the check to his landlord with the following indorsement: "For rent paid, [signed] Jordan." Jordan's landlord has contracted to have Deborah do some landscaping on the property. When Deborah insists on immediate payment, the landlord transfers the check to Deborah without indorsement. Later, to pay for some palm trees purchased from Better-Garden Nursery, Deborah transfers the check with the following indorsement: "Pay to Better-Garden Nursery, without recourse, [signed] Deborah." Better-Garden Nursery sends the check to its bank indorsed "For deposit only, [signed] Better-Garden Nursery."

(a) Classify each of these indorsements.
(b) Was the transfer from Jordan's landlord to Deborah, without indorsement, an assignment or a negotiation? Explain.

25–2. QUESTION WITH SAMPLE ANSWER

Celine issues a ninety-day negotiable promissory note payable to the order of Hayden. The amount of the note is left blank, pending a determination of the amount that Hayden will need to purchase a used car for Celine. Celine authorizes any amount not to exceed $2,000. Hayden, without authority, fills in the note in the amount of $5,000 and thirty days later sells the note to First National Bank of Oklahoma for $4,850. Hayden does not buy the car and leaves the state. First National Bank has no knowledge that the instrument was incomplete when issued or that Hayden had no authority to complete the instrument in the amount of $5,000.

(a) Does the bank qualify as a holder in due course? If so, for what amount? Explain.
(b) If Hayden had sold the note to a stranger in a bar for $500, would the stranger qualify as a holder in due course? Explain.

- **For a sample answer to Question 25–2, go to Appendix C at the end of this text.**

25–3. Through negotiation, Emilio has received from dishonest payees two checks with the following histories:

(a) The drawer issued a check to the payee for $9. The payee cleverly altered the numeral on the check from $9 to $90 and the written word from "nine" to "ninety."

(b) The drawer issued a check to the payee without filling in the amount. The drawer authorized the payee to fill in the amount for no more than $90. The payee filled in the amount of $900.

Discuss whether Emilio, by giving value to the payees, can qualify as a holder in due course of these checks.

25–4. Bertram writes a check for $200 payable to "cash." He puts the check in his pocket and drives to the bank to cash the check. As he gets out of his car in the bank's parking lot, the check slips out of his pocket and falls to the pavement. Jerrod walks by moments later, picks up the check, and later that day delivers it to Amber, to whom he owes $200. Amber indorses the check "For deposit only, [signed] Amber Dowel" and deposits it into her checking account. In light of these circumstances, answer the following questions:

(a) Is the check a bearer instrument or an order instrument?

(b) Did Jerrod's delivery of the check to Amber constitute a valid negotiation? Why or why not?

(c) What type of indorsement did Amber make?

(d) Does Bertram have a right to recover the $200 from Amber? Explain.

25–5. Transfer of Instruments. In July 1988, Chester Crow executed a promissory note payable "to the order of THE FIRST NATIONAL BANK OF SHREVEPORT or BEARER" in the amount of $21,578.42 at an interest rate of 3 percent per year above the "prime rate in effect at The First National Bank of Shreveport" in Shreveport, Louisiana, until paid. The note was a standard preprinted promissory note. In 1999, Credit Recoveries, Inc., filed a suit in a Louisiana state court against Crow, alleging that he owed $7,222.57 on the note, plus interest. Crow responded that the debt represented by the note had been canceled by the bank in September 1994. He also contended that, in any event, to collect on the note Credit Recoveries had to prove its legitimate ownership of it. When no evidence of ownership was forthcoming, Crow filed a motion to dismiss the suit. Is the note an order instrument or a bearer instrument? How might it have been transferred to Credit Recoveries? With this in mind, should the court dismiss the suit on the basis of Crow's contention? [*Credit Recoveries, Inc. v. Crow,* 862 So.2d 1146 (La.App. 2 Cir. 2003)]

25–6. Alternative or Joint Payees. Hartford Mutual Insurance Co. issued a check for $60,150 payable to "Andrew Michael Bogdan, Jr., Crystal Bogdan, Oceanmark Bank FSB, Goodman-Gable-Gould Company." The check was to pay a claim related to the Bogdans' commercial property. Besides the Bogdans, the payees were the mortgage holder (Oceanmark) and the insurance agent who adjusted the claim. The Bogdans and the agent indorsed the check and cashed it at Provident Bank of Maryland. Meanwhile, Oceanmark sold the mortgage to Pelican National Bank, which asked Provident to pay it the amount of the check. Provident refused. Pelican filed a suit in a Maryland state court against Provident, arguing that the check had been improperly negotiated. Was this check payable jointly or in the alternative? Whose indorsements were required to cash it? In whose favor should the court rule? Explain. [*Pelican National Bank v. Provident Bank of Maryland,* 381 Md. 327, 849 A.2d 475 (2004)]

25–7. CASE PROBLEM WITH SAMPLE ANSWER

In February 2001, New York Linen Co., a party rental company, agreed to buy 550 chairs from Elite Products. On delivery of the chairs, New York Linen issued a check (dated February 27) for $13,300 to Elite. Elite's owner, Meir Shmeltzer, transferred the check to General Credit Corp., a company in the business of buying instruments from payees for cash. Meanwhile, after recounting the chairs, New York Linen discovered that delivery was not complete and stopped payment of the check. The next day, New York Linen drafted a second check, reflecting an adjusted payment of $11,275, and delivered it to Elite. A notation on the second check indicated that it was a replacement for the first check. When the first check was dishonored, General Credit filed a suit in a New York state court against New York Linen to recover the amount. New York Linen argued in part that General Credit was not a holder in due course because of the notation on the second check. In whose favor should the court rule? Why? [*General Credit Corp. v. New York Linen Co.,* __ Misc.2d __ (N.Y. City Civ.Ct. 2002)]

- **To view a sample answer for Problem 25–7, go to this book's Web site at www.cengage. com/blaw/jentz, select "Chapter 25," and click on "Case Problem with Sample Answer."**

25–8. Holder in Due Course. Robert Triffin bought a number of dishonored checks from McCall's Liquor Corp., Community Check Cashing II, LLC (CCC), and other licensed check-cashing businesses in New Jersey. Seventeen of the checks had been dishonored as counterfeit. In an attempt to recover on the items, Triffin met with the drawer, Automatic Data Processing, Inc. (ADP). At the meeting, Triffin said that he knew the checks were counterfeit. When ADP refused to pay, Triffin filed suits in New Jersey state courts to collect, asserting claims totaling $11,021.33. With each complaint were copies of assignment agreements corresponding to each check. Each agreement stated, among other things, that the seller was a holder in due course (HDC) and had assigned its rights in the check to Triffin. ADP had not previously seen these agreements. A private investigator determined that the forms attached to the McCall's and CCC checks had not been signed by their sellers but that

Triffin had scanned the signatures into his computer and pasted them onto the agreements. ADP claimed fraud. Does Triffin qualify as an HDC? If not, did he acquire the rights of an HDC under the shelter principle? As for the fraud claim, which element of fraud would ADP be least likely to prove? [*Triffin v. Automatic Data Processing, Inc.,* 394 N.J.Super. 237, 926 A.2d 362 (App.Div. 2007)]

25-9. A QUESTION OF ETHICS

As an assistant comptroller for Interior Crafts, Inc., in Chicago, Illinois, Todd Leparski was authorized to receive checks from Interior's customers and deposit the checks into Interior's account. Between October 2000 and February 2001, Leparski stole more than $500,000 from Interior by indorsing the checks "Interior Crafts—For Deposit Only" but depositing some of them into his own account at Marquette Bank through an automated teller machine owned by Pan American Bank. Marquette alerted Interior, which was able to recover about $250,000 from Leparski. Interior also recovered $250,000 under its policy with American Insurance Co. To collect the rest of the missing funds, Interior filed a suit in an Illinois state court against Leparski and the banks. The court ruled in favor of Interior, and Pan American appealed to a state intermediate appellate court. [Interior Crafts, Inc. v. Leparski, 366 Ill.App.3d 1148, 853 N.E.2d 1244, 304 Ill.Dec. 878 (3 Dist. 2006)]

(a) What type of indorsement is "Interior Crafts—For Deposit Only"? What is the obligation of a party that receives a check with this indorsement? Does the fact that Interior authorized Leparski to indorse its checks but not to deposit those checks into his own account absolve Pan American of liability? Explain.

(b) From an ethical perspective, how might a business firm such as Interior discourage an employee's thievery such as Leparski's acts in this case? Discuss.

25-10. VIDEO QUESTION

Go to this text's Web site at **www.cengage. com/blaw/jentz** and select "Chapter 25." Click on "Video Questions" and view the video titled *Negotiability & Transferability: Indorsing Checks.* Then answer the following questions.

(a) According to the instructor in the video, what are the two reasons why banks generally require a person to indorse a check that is made out to cash (a bearer instrument), even when the check is signed in the presence of the teller?

(b) Suppose that your friend makes out a check payable to cash, signs it, and hands it to you. You take the check to your bank and indorse the check with your name and the words "without recourse." What type of indorsement is this? How does this indorsement affect the bank's rights?

(c) Now suppose that you go to your bank and write a check on your account payable to cash for $500. The teller gives you the cash without asking you to indorse the check. After you leave, the teller slips the check into his pocket. Later, the teller delivers it (without an indorsement) to his friend Carol in payment for a gambling debt. Carol takes your check to her bank, indorses it, and deposits the money. Discuss whether Carol is a holder in due course.

LAW ON THE WEB

For updated links to resources available on the Web, as well as a variety of other materials, visit this text's Web site at

www.cengage.com/blaw/jentz

To find information on the UCC, including the Article 3 provisions discussed in this chapter, refer to the Web sites listed in the *Law on the Web* section in Chapter 24.

Legal Research Exercises on the Web

Go to **www.cengage.com/blaw/jentz**, the Web site that accompanies this text. Select "Chapter 25" and click on "Internet Exercises." There you will find the following Internet research exercises that you can perform to learn more about the topics covered in this chapter.

Internet Exercise 25–1: Legal Perspective
                Electronic Negotiable Instruments

Internet Exercise 25–2: Management Perspective
                Holder in Due Course

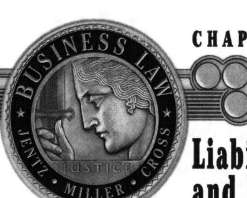

CHAPTER 21

Liability, Defenses, and Discharge

Two kinds of liability are associated with negotiable instruments: signature liability and warranty liability. *Signature liability* relates to signatures on instruments. Those who sign negotiable instruments are potentially liable for payment of the amount stated on the instrument. *Warranty liability,* in contrast, extends to both signers and nonsigners. A breach of warranty can occur when the instrument is transferred or presented for payment.

Note that the focus is on liability on the *instrument itself or on warranties connected with the transfer or presentment of the instrument* as opposed to liability on any underlying contract. Suppose that Donna agrees to buy one thousand compact discs from Luis and issues a check to Luis in payment. The liability discussed in this chapter does not relate directly to the contract (for instance, whether the compact discs are of proper quality or fit for the purpose for which they are intended). The liability discussed here is the liability arising in connection with the *check* (such as what recourse Luis will have if Donna's bank refuses to pay the check due to insufficient funds in Donna's account or Donna's order to her bank to stop payment on the check).

The first part of this chapter covers the liability of the parties who sign instruments—for example, drawers of drafts and checks, makers of notes and certificates of deposit, and indorsers. It also covers the liability of accommodation parties and the warranty liability of those who transfer instruments and present instruments for payment. The chapter then examines the defenses that can be raised to avoid liability on an instrument. The final section in the chapter looks at some of the ways in which parties can be *discharged* from liability on negotiable instruments.

Signature Liability

The key to liability on a negotiable instrument is a signature. As discussed in Chapter 24, the Uniform Commercial Code (UCC) broadly defines a signature as any name, word, mark, or symbol executed or adopted by a person with the present intention to authenticate a writing [UCC 1–209(39), 3–401(b)]. A signature can be made manually or by use of any device or machine.

The general rule is as follows: "A person is not liable on an instrument unless (i) the person signed the instrument, or (ii) the person is represented by an agent or representative who signed the instrument and the signature is binding on the represented person"

[UCC 3–401(a)]. Essentially, this means that every person, except a qualified indorser,[1] who signs a negotiable instrument is either primarily or secondarily liable for payment of that instrument when it comes due. The following subsections discuss these two types of liability, as well as the conditions that must be met before liability can arise.

Primary Liability

A person who is primarily liable on a negotiable instrument is absolutely required to pay the instrument—unless, of course, he or she has a valid defense to

---

1. A qualified indorser—one who indorses "without recourse"—undertakes no obligation to pay [UCC 3–415(b)]. A qualified indorser merely assumes warranty liability, which will be discussed later in this chapter.

payment. Liability is immediate when the instrument is signed or issued. No action by the holder of the instrument is required. *Makers* and *acceptors* are primarily liable [UCC 3–412, 3–413].

Makers The maker of a promissory note promises to pay the instrument according to its terms. It is the maker's promise to pay that renders the instrument negotiable. If the instrument was incomplete when the maker signed it, the maker is obligated to pay it according to either its stated terms or terms that were agreed on and later filled in to complete the instrument [UCC 3–115, 3–407, 3–412]. For example, Tristan executes a preprinted promissory note to Sharon, without filling in the due-date blank. If Sharon does not complete the form by adding the date, the note will be payable on demand. If Sharon subsequently writes in a due date that Tristan authorized, the note is payable on the stated due date. In either situation, Tristan (the maker) is obligated to pay the note.

Acceptors An *acceptor* is a drawee that promises to pay an instrument when it is presented later for payment, as mentioned in Chapter 24. When a drawee *accepts* a draft (usually by writing "accepted" across its face), the drawee becomes primarily liable to all subsequent holders of the instrument. In other words, the drawee's acceptance is a promise to pay that places the drawee in virtually the same position as the maker of a promissory note [UCC 3–413]. A drawee that refuses to accept a draft that requires the drawee's acceptance (such as a trade acceptance) has dishonored the instrument. (**Dishonor** of an instrument occurs when payment or acceptance of the instrument, whichever is required, is refused even though the instrument is presented in a timely and proper manner.)

Acceptance of a check is called *certification,* as will be discussed in Chapter 27. Certification is not necessary on checks, and a bank is under no obligation to certify checks. If it does certify a check, however, the drawee bank occupies the position of an acceptor and is primarily liable on the check to any holder [UCC 3–409(d)].

Secondary Liability

Drawers and *indorsers* have secondary liability. On a negotiable instrument, secondary liability is similar to the liability of a guarantor in a simple contract (described in Chapter 28) in the sense that it is *contingent liability.* In other words, a drawer or an indorser will be liable only if the party that is responsible for paying the instrument refuses to do so (dishonors the instrument). With respect to drafts and checks, a drawer's secondary liability does not arise until the drawee fails to pay or to accept the instrument, whichever is required. In regard to notes, an indorser's secondary liability does not arise until the maker, who is primarily liable, has defaulted on the instrument [UCC 3–412, 3–415].

Dishonor of an instrument thus triggers the liability of parties who are secondarily liable on the instrument—that is, the drawer and *unqualified* indorsers. Suppose that Lamar writes a check for $1,000 on her account at Western Bank payable to the order of Carerra. Carerra indorses and delivers the check, for value, to Deere. Deere deposits the check into his account at Universal Bank, but the bank returns the check to Deere marked "insufficient funds," thus dishonoring the check. The question for Deere is whether the drawer (Lamar) or the indorser (Carerra) can be held liable on the check after the bank has dishonored it. The answer to the question depends on whether certain conditions for secondary liability have been satisfied.

Parties who are secondarily liable on a negotiable instrument promise to pay on that instrument *only if* the following events occur:[2]

1. The instrument is properly and timely presented.
2. The instrument is dishonored.
3. Timely notice of dishonor is given.[3]

Proper and Timely Presentment As discussed in Chapter 24, *presentment* is the formal demand for the payment or acceptance of a negotiable instrument. The UCC requires that a holder present the instrument to the appropriate party, in a timely fashion, and in a proper manner (providing reasonable identification if requested) [UCC 3–414(f), 3–415(e), 3–501]. The party to whom the instrument must be presented depends on the type of instrument involved. A note or certificate of deposit (CD) must be presented to the maker for payment. A draft is presented to the drawee for acceptance, payment, or both.

---

2. An instrument can be drafted to include a waiver of the presentment and notice of dishonor requirements [UCC 3–504]. Presume, for simplicity's sake, that such waivers have *not* been incorporated into the instruments described in this chapter.

3. Note that these requirements are necessary for a secondarily liable party to have *signature* liability on a negotiable instrument, but they are not necessary for a secondarily liable party to have *warranty* liability (to be discussed later in this chapter).

A check is presented to the drawee (bank) for payment [UCC 3–501(a), 3–502(b)].

Presentment can be made by any commercially reasonable means, including oral, written, or electronic communication [UCC 3–501(b)]. It can also be made at the place specified in the instrument. Ordinarily, presentment is effective when the demand for payment or acceptance is received (if presentment takes place after an established cutoff hour, however, it may be treated as occurring the next business day).

One of the most crucial criteria for proper presentment is timeliness [UCC 3–414(f), 3–415(e), 3–501(b)(4)]. Failure to present within a reasonable time is a common reason for improper presentment and can lead to the instrument's dishonor and potentially discharge parties from secondary liability. A reasonable time for presentment is determined by the nature of the instrument, any usage of banking or trade, and the facts of the particular case. If the instrument is payable on demand, the holder should present it for payment or acceptance within a reasonable time.

For domestic, uncertified checks, the UCC establishes a presumptively reasonable time period [UCC 3–414(f), 3–415(e)]. An ordinary check should be presented for payment within thirty days of its date or the date that it was indorsed. A drawer is *not* automatically discharged from liability for checks presented after thirty days, but the holder must be able to prove that the presentment after that time was reasonable.[4] The time for proper presentment for different types of instruments is shown in Exhibit 21–1.

Dishonor As mentioned earlier, an instrument is dishonored when payment or acceptance of the instrument is refused in spite of proper and timely presentment. An instrument is also dishonored when the required presentment is excused (as it would be, for example, if the maker had died) and the instrument is not properly accepted or paid [UCC 3–502(e), 3–504].

In certain situations, a delay in payment or a refusal to pay an instrument will *not* dishonor the instrument. When presentment is made after an established cutoff hour (not earlier than 2:00 P.M.), for instance, a bank can postpone payment until the following business day without dishonoring the instrument [UCC 3–501(b)(4)]. In addition, when the holder refuses to exhibit the instrument, to give reasonable identification, or to sign a receipt for the payment on the instrument, a bank's refusal to pay does not dishonor the instrument [UCC 3–501(b)(2)]. Returning an instrument because it lacks a proper indorsement also is not a dishonor [UCC 3–501(b)(3)(i)].

Proper Notice Once an instrument has been dishonored, proper notice must be given to secondary parties (drawers and indorsers) for them to be held liable. Notice may be given in any reasonable manner, including an oral, written, or electronic communication, as well as by writing or stamping on the instrument itself [UCC 3–503(b)].[5] If the party giving notice is a bank, it must give any necessary notice before its midnight deadline (midnight of the next banking day

---

4. For a seminal case in which a state's highest court held that presentment more than thirty days after the date of an uncertified check did not discharge the liability of the drawer, see *Grist v. Osgood*, 90 Nev. 165, 521 P.2d 368 (1974).

5. Note that written notice is preferable, as oral notice makes it possible for a secondary party to claim that notice was not received. Also, to give proper notice of the dishonor of a foreign draft (a draft drawn in one country and payable in another country), a formal notice called a *protest* is required [UCC 3–505(b)].

EXHIBIT 21–1 • Time for Proper Presentment

Type of Instrument	For Acceptance	For Payment
Time	On or before due date.	On due date.
Demand	Within a reasonable time (after date of issue or after secondary party becomes liable on the instrument).	Within a reasonable time.
Check	No stated time limit.	Within thirty days of its date, to hold drawer secondarily liable. Within thirty days of indorsement, to hold indorser secondarily liable.

after receipt) [UCC 3–503(c)]. If the party giving notice is not a bank, the party must give notice within thirty days following the day of dishonor or the day on which the person receives notice of dishonor [UCC 3–503(c)].

Accommodation Parties

An **accommodation party** is one who signs an instrument for the purpose of lending his or her name as credit to another party on the instrument [UCC 3–419(a)]. Requiring an accommodation party is one way to secure against nonpayment of a negotiable instrument. When one person (such as a parent) cosigns a promissory note with the maker (such as the parent's son or daughter), the cosigner is an accommodation party, and the maker is the accommodated party.

If the accommodation party signs on behalf of the *maker*, he or she is an *accommodation maker* and is primarily liable on the instrument.[6] For example, if Alex takes out a loan to purchase a car and his uncle cosigns the note, the uncle becomes primarily liable on the instrument. In other words, Alex's uncle is guaranteeing payment, and the bank can seek payment directly from the uncle.

If, however, the accommodation party signs on behalf of a *payee or other holder* (usually to make the instrument more marketable), she or he is an *accommodation indorser* and, as an indorser, is secondarily liable. Suppose that Frank Huston applies to Northeast Bank for a $20,000 loan to start a small business. Huston's lender (who has possession of the note) has Finch Smith, who has invested in Huston's business, sign the note. In this situation, Smith is an indorser and his liability is secondary; that is, the lender must pursue Huston first before seeking payment from Smith. If Smith ends up paying the amount due on the note, he has a right to reimbursement from Huston (the accommodated party) [UCC 3–419(e)].

Authorized Agents' Signatures

The general law of agency, covered in Chapters 31 and 32, applies to negotiable instruments. Questions often arise as to the liability on an instrument signed by an

agent. An **agent** is a person who agrees to represent or act for another, called the **principal.** Agents can sign negotiable instruments, just as they can sign contracts, and thereby bind their principals [UCC 3–401(a)(ii), 3–402(a)]. Without such a rule, all corporate commercial business would stop, as every corporation can and must act through its agents. Certain requirements must be met, however, before the principal becomes liable on the instrument. A basic requirement to hold the principal liable on the instrument is that the agent be *authorized* to sign the instrument on the principal's behalf.

Liability of the Principal Generally, an authorized agent binds a principal on an instrument if the agent *clearly names* the principal in the signature (by writing, mark, or some symbol). In this situation, the UCC presumes that the signature is authorized and genuine [UCC 3–308(a)]. The agent may or may not add his or her own name, but if the signature shows clearly that it is made on behalf of the principal, the agent is not liable on the instrument [UCC 3–402(b)(1)]. For example, either of the following signatures by Sandra Binney as agent for Bob Aronson will bind Aronson on the instrument:

1. Aronson, by Binney, agent.
2. Aronson.

If Binney (the agent) signs just her own name, however, she will be personally liable to a holder in due course who has no notice of her agency status. An agent can escape liability to ordinary holders if the agent proves that the original parties did not intend the agent to be liable on the instrument [UCC 3–402(a), (b)(2)].[7] In either situation, the principal is bound if the party entitled to enforce the instrument can prove the agency relationship.

Liability of the Agent An authorized agent may be held personally liable on a negotiable instrument in two other situations. An agent can be personally liable when the instrument is signed in both the agent's name and the principal's name but nothing on the instrument indicates the agency relationship. For instance, if Binney signs the instrument "Sandra Binney, Bob Aronson" or "Aronson, Binney," she may be held personally liable because it is not clear that there is an agency relationship. When the agent indicates agency

---

6. A 2002 amendment to UCC Article 3 expressly provides that an accommodation party is primarily liable if the party indicates on the instrument that he or she guarantees payment or "does not unambiguously indicate an intention to guarantee collection rather than payment" [Amended UCC 3–419(e)]. Recall from Chapter 24, however, that as yet only a few states have adopted the 2002 amendments to Article 3.

7. See UCC 3–402, Comment 1.

status in signing a negotiable instrument but fails to name the principal (for example, "Sandra Binney, agent"), the agent may also be liable [UCC 3–402(b)(2)]. Because the above forms of signing are ambiguous, however, parol evidence is admissible to prove the agency relationship.

An important exception to the rules on agent liability is made for checks that are signed by agents. If an agent signs his or her own name on a *check that is payable from the account of the principal,* and the principal is identified on the check, the agent will not be personally liable on the check [UCC 3–402(c)]. Suppose that Binney, who is *authorized* to draw checks on Aronson Company's account, signs a check that is preprinted with Aronson Company's name. The signature reads simply "Sandra Binney." In this situation, Binney will not be personally liable on the check.

Unauthorized Signatures

Unauthorized signatures arise in two situations—when a person forges another person's name on a negotiable instrument and when an agent who lacks the authority signs an instrument on behalf of a principal. The general rule is that an unauthorized signature is wholly inoperative and will not bind the person whose name is signed or forged. For example, Pablo finds Veronica's checkbook lying on the street, writes out a check to himself, and forges Veronica's signature. If a bank negligently fails to ascertain that Veronica's signature is not genuine and cashes the check for Pablo, the bank generally will be liable to Veronica for the amount. (The liability of banks for paying instruments with forged signatures will be discussed further in Chapter 27.)

If an agent lacks the authority to sign the principal's name or has exceeded the authority given by the principal, the signature does not bind the principal but will bind the "unauthorized signer" [UCC 3–403(a)]. Assume that Maya Campbell is the principal and Lena Shem is her agent. Shem, without authority, signs a promissory note as follows: "Maya Campbell, by Lena Shem, agent." Because Maya Campbell's "signature" is unauthorized, Campbell cannot be held liable, but Shem is liable to a holder of the note. This would be true even if Shem had signed the note "Maya Campbell," without indicating any agency relationship. In either situation, the unauthorized signer, Shem, is liable on the instrument.

Exceptions to the General Rule There are two exceptions to the general rule that an unautho-

rized signature will not bind the person whose name is signed:

1. When the person whose name is signed *ratifies* (affirms) the signature, he or she will be bound [UCC 3–403(a)]. For example, a principal can ratify an unauthorized signature made by an agent, either expressly (by affirming the validity of the signature) or impliedly (by other conduct, such as keeping any benefits received in the transaction or failing to repudiate the signature). The parties involved need not be principal and agent. Thus, a mother may ratify her daughter's signature forging the mother's name so that the daughter will not be prosecuted for forgery.

2. When the negligence of the person whose name was forged substantially contributed to the forgery, a court may not allow the person to deny the effectiveness of an unauthorized signature [UCC 3–115, 3–406, 4–401(d)(2)]. Assume that Rob, the owner of a business, leaves his signature stamp and a blank check on an office counter. An employee, using the stamp, fills in and cashes the check. Rob can be estopped (prevented), on the basis of his negligence, from denying liability for payment of the check [UCC 3–115, 3–406, 4–401(d)(2)]. Whatever loss occurs may be allocated, however, between certain parties on the basis of *comparative negligence* [UCC 3–406(b)]. If Rob, in this example, can demonstrate that the bank was negligent in paying the check, the bank may bear a portion of the loss. The liability of the parties in this type of situation will be discussed further in Chapter 27.

When the Holder Is a Holder in Due Course A person who forges a check or signs an instrument without authorization can be held personally liable for payment by a holder in due course, or HDC [UCC 3–403(a)]. This is true even if the name of the person signing the instrument without authorization does not appear on the instrument. If Michel Vuillard signs "Paul Richaud" without Richaud's authorization, Vuillard is personally liable just as if he had signed his own name. Vuillard's liability is limited, however, to persons who in good faith pay the instrument or take it for value. A holder who knew the signature was unauthorized would not qualify as an HDC and thus could not recover from Vuillard on the instrument. (The defenses that are effective against ordinary holders versus HDCs will be discussed in detail later in this chapter.)

PREVENTING LEGAL DISPUTES

Businesspersons should be aware that although an unauthorized signature on a negotiable instrument is ineffective against the person whose name was signed, the signer remains liable. While this rule may not be of great consequence with forgeries (because persons who commit forgery are likely to be difficult to locate and have limited financial resources), it can be very significant when dealing with unauthorized agents.

A corporate agent, for instance, may have exceeded her or his authority when signing on behalf of a corporation. If you accepted an instrument from this person in good faith and paid value for it, you should be able to collect from the unauthorized agent what you cannot collect from the corporation. Because persons acting on behalf of a corporation typically have access to financial resources, pursuing this avenue may be your best chance of obtaining payment in some situations.

Special Rules for Unauthorized Indorsements

Generally, when an indorsement is forged or unauthorized, the burden of loss falls on the first party to take the instrument with the forged or unauthorized indorsement. This general rule is premised on the concept that the first party to take an instrument is in the best position to prevent the loss.

For example, Jenny Nilson steals a check drawn on Universal Bank and payable to the order of Inga Leed. Nilson indorses the check "Inga Leed" and presents the check to Universal Bank for payment. The bank, without asking Nilson for identification, pays the check, and Nilson disappears. In this situation, Leed will not be liable on the check because her indorsement was forged. The bank will bear the loss, which it might have avoided if it had requested identification from Nilson.

This general rule has two important exceptions. These exceptions arise when an indorsement is made by an imposter or by a fictitious payee. We look at these two situations here.

Imposters An **imposter** is one who uses mail, Internet, telephone, or other means to induce a maker or drawer to issue an instrument in the name of an impersonated payee. If the maker or drawer believes

the imposter to be the named payee at the time of issue, the indorsement by the imposter is not treated as unauthorized when the instrument is transferred to an innocent party. This is because the maker or drawer *intended* the imposter to receive the instrument. In this situation, under the UCC's *imposter rule*, the imposter's indorsement will be effective—that is, not considered a forgery—insofar as the drawer or maker is concerned [UCC 3–404(a)].

Suppose that Kayla impersonates Donna and induces Edward to write a check payable to the order of Donna. Kayla, continuing to impersonate Donna, negotiates the check to First National Bank. In this situation, Kayla's signature will be considered effective, and Edward, as the drawer of the check, is liable for its amount to First National. (The state can still file criminal charges against Kayla for her conduct, of course.)

The comparative negligence standard mentioned previously also applies to situations involving imposters [UCC 3–404(d)]. Thus, if a bank fails to exercise ordinary care in cashing a check made out to an imposter, the drawer may be able to recover a portion of the loss from the bank.

Fictitious Payees When a person causes an instrument to be issued to a payee who will have *no interest* in the instrument, the payee is referred to as a **fictitious payee**. A fictitious payee can be a person or firm that does not truly exist, or it may be an identifiable party that will not acquire any interest in the instrument. Under the UCC's *fictitious payee rule*, the payee's indorsement is not treated as a forgery, and an innocent holder can hold the maker or drawer liable on the instrument [UCC 3–404(b), 3–405].

Situations involving fictitious payees most often arise when (1) a dishonest employee deceives the employer into signing an instrument payable to a party with no right to receive payment on the instrument or (2) a dishonest employee or agent has the authority to issue an instrument on behalf of the employer and issues a check to a party who has no interest in the instrument.

How a Fictitious Payee Can Be Created—An Example. Assume that Goldstar Aviation, Inc., gives its bookkeeper, Leslie Rose, general authority to issue company checks drawn on First State Bank so that Rose can pay employees' wages and other corporate bills. Rose decides to cheat Goldstar out of $10,000 by issuing a check payable to the Del Rey Company, a supplier of aircraft parts. Rose does not intend Del Rey to

receive any of the funds, nor is Del Rey entitled to the payment. Rose indorses the check in Del Rey's name and deposits the check in an account that she opened in West National Bank in the name "Del Rey Co." West National Bank accepts the check and collects payment from the drawee bank, First State Bank. First State Bank charges Goldstar's account $10,000. Rose transfers $10,000 out of the Del Rey account and closes the account. Goldstar discovers the fraud and demands that the account be recredited.

Who Bears the Loss? According to the UCC's fictitious payee rule, Rose's indorsement in the name of a payee with no interest in the instrument is "effective," so there is no "forgery" [UCC 3–404(b)(2)]. Under this provision, West National Bank is protected in paying on the check, and the drawee bank is protected in charging Goldstar's account. Thus, the employer-drawer, Goldstar, will bear the loss. Of course, Goldstar has recourse against Rose, if she has not absconded with the funds. Additionally, if Goldstar can prove that West National Bank's failure to exercise reasonable care contributed substantially to the loss, the bank may be required to bear a proportionate share of the loss under the UCC's comparative negligence standard [UCC 3–404(d)]. Thus, West National Bank could be liable for a portion of the loss if it failed to exercise ordinary care in its dealings with Rose.

Whether a dishonest employee actually signs the check or merely supplies his or her employer with names of fictitious creditors (or with true names of creditors having fictitious debts), the result is the same under the UCC. Assume that Dan Symes draws up the payroll list from which employees' salary checks are written. He fraudulently adds the name Penny Trip (a real person but a fictitious employee) to the payroll, thereby causing checks to be issued to her. Trip cashes the checks and shares the proceeds with Symes. Again, it is the employer-drawer who bears the loss. For a synopsis of the rules relating to signature liability, see *Concept Summary 21.1.*

Warranty Liability

In addition to the signature liability discussed in the preceding section, transferors make certain implied warranties regarding the instruments that they are negotiating. Liability under these warranties is not subject to the conditions of proper presentment, dishonor,

and notice of dishonor. These warranties arise even when a transferor does not indorse the instrument (as in delivery of a bearer instrument). Warranty liability is particularly important when a holder cannot hold a party liable on her or his signature.

Warranties fall into two categories: those that arise from the *transfer* of a negotiable instrument and those that arise on *presentment* [UCC 3–416, 3–417]. Both transfer and presentment warranties attempt to shift liability back to the wrongdoer or to the person who dealt face to face with the wrongdoer and thus was in the best position to prevent the wrongdoing.

Transfer Warranties

The UCC describes five **transfer warranties** [UCC 3–416]. For transfer warranties to arise, an instrument *must be transferred for consideration.* For example, Quality Products Corporation sells goods to Royal Retail Stores, Inc., and receives in payment Royal Retail's note. Quality then sells the note, for value, to Superior Finance Company. In this situation, the instrument has been transferred for consideration. One who transfers an instrument for consideration makes the following transfer warranties to all subsequent transferees and holders who take the instrument in good faith (with some exceptions, as will be noted shortly):

1. The transferor is entitled to enforce the instrument.
2. All signatures are authentic and authorized.
3. The instrument has not been altered.
4. The instrument is not subject to a defense or claim of any party that can be asserted against the transferor.
5. The transferor has no knowledge of any bankruptcy proceedings against the maker, the acceptor, or the drawer of the instrument.[8]

Parties to Whom Warranty Liability Extends The manner of transfer and the type of negotiation that are used determine how far and to

---

8. A 2002 amendment to UCC 3–416(a) adds a sixth warranty: "with respect to a remotely created consumer item, that the person on whose account the item is drawn authorized the issuance of the item in the amount for which the item is drawn." UCC 3–103(16) defines a "remotely created consumer item" as an item, such as a check, drawn on a consumer account, that is not created by the payor bank and does not contain the drawer's handwritten signature. Suppose that a telemarketer submits an instrument to a bank for payment, claiming that the consumer on whose account the instrument purports to be drawn authorized it over the phone. Under this amendment, a bank that accepts and pays the instrument warrants to the next bank in the collection chain that the consumer authorized the item in that amount.

CONCEPT SUMMARY 21.1
Signature Liability

Concept	Description

PRIMARY AND SECONDARY LIABILITY	Every party (except a qualified indorser) who signs a negotiable instrument is either primarily or secondarily liable for payment of the instrument when it comes due.
	
	1. *Primary liability*—Makers and acceptors are primarily liable [UCC 3–409, 3–412, 3–413].
	
	2. *Secondary liability*—Drawers and indorsers are secondarily liable [UCC 3–414, 3–415, 3–501, 3–502, 3–503]. Parties who are secondarily liable on an instrument promise to pay on that instrument only if the following events occur:
	  a. The instrument is properly and timely presented.
	  b. The instrument is dishonored.
	  c. Timely notice of dishonor is given.

ACCOMMODATION PARTIES	An *accommodation party* is one who signs an instrument for the purpose of lending his or her name as credit to another party on the instrument [UCC 3–419]. Accommodation *makers* are primarily liable; accommodation *indorsers* are secondarily liable.
AGENTS' SIGNATURES	An *agent* is a person who agrees to represent or act for another, called the *principal.* Agents can sign negotiable instruments and thereby bind their principals. Liability on the instrument depends on whether the agent is authorized and on whether the agent's representative capacity and the principal's identity are both indicated on the instrument [UCC 3–401, 3–402, 3–403]. Agents need not indicate their representative capacity on *checks*—provided the checks clearly identify the principal and are drawn on the principal's account.
UNAUTHORIZED SIGNATURES	An unauthorized signature is wholly inoperative as the signature of the person whose name is signed *unless:* 1. The person whose name is signed ratifies (affirms) it or is precluded from denying it [UCC 3–115, 3–403, 3–406, 4–401]. 2. The instrument has been negotiated to a holder in due course [UCC 3–403].
SPECIAL RULES FOR UNAUTHORIZED INDORSEMENTS	An unauthorized indorsement will not bind the maker or drawer of the instrument except in the following circumstances: 1. When an imposter induces the maker or drawer of an instrument to issue it to the imposter *(imposter rule)* [UCC 3–404(a)]. 2. When a person causes an instrument to be issued to a payee who will have *no interest* in the instrument *(fictitious payee rule)* [UCC 3–404(b), 3–405].

whom a transfer warranty will run. Transfer of an order instrument by indorsement and delivery extends warranty liability to any subsequent holder who takes the instrument in good faith. The warranties of a person who, for consideration, transfers *without indorsement* (by delivery of a bearer instrument), however, will extend only to the immediate transferee [UCC 3–416(a)].

Suppose that Wylie forges Kim's name as a maker of a promissory note. The note is made payable to Wylie. Wylie indorses the note in blank, negotiates it for consideration to Bret, and then leaves the country. Bret, without indorsement, delivers the note for consideration to Fern. Fern, also without indorsement, delivers the note for consideration to Rick. On Rick's presentment of the note to Kim, the forgery is discovered. Rick

CONCEPT SUMMARY 21.2
Transfer Warranty Liability for Transferors Who Receive Consideration

Transferors	Transferees to Whom Warranties Extend If Consideration Is Received
INDORSERS WHO RECEIVE CONSIDERATION	Five transfer warranties extend to *all* subsequent holders: 1. The transferor is entitled to enforce the instrument. 2. All signatures are authentic and authorized. 3. The instrument has not been altered. 4. The instrument is not subject to a defense or claim of any party that can be asserted against the transferor. 5. The transferor has no knowledge of insolvency proceedings against the maker, acceptor, or drawer of the instrument.
NONINDORSERS WHO RECEIVE CONSIDERATION	Same as for indorsers, but warranties extend *only* to the *immediate transferee*.

can hold Fern (the immediate transferor) liable for breach of the warranty that all signatures are genuine. Rick cannot hold Bret liable because Bret is not Rick's immediate transferor; rather, Bret is a prior nonindorsing transferor.

Note that if Wylie had added a special indorsement ("Payable to Bret") instead of a blank indorsement, the instrument would have remained an order instrument. In that situation, Bret would have had to indorse the instrument to negotiate it to Fern, and his transfer warranties would extend to all subsequent holders, including Rick. This example shows the importance of the distinction between transfer by indorsement and delivery (of an order instrument) and transfer by delivery only, without indorsement (of a bearer instrument). For a synopsis of the rules on transfer warranty liability, see *Concept Summary 21.2.*

Recovery for Breach of Warranty A transferee or holder who takes an instrument in good faith can sue on the basis of breach of a warranty as soon as he or she has reason to know of the breach [UCC 3–416(d)]. Notice of a claim for breach of warranty must be given to the warrantor within thirty days after the transferee or holder has reason to know of the breach and the identity of the warrantor, or the warrantor is not liable for any loss caused by a delay [UCC 3–416(c)]. The transferee or holder can recover damages for the breach in an amount equal to the loss suffered (but not more than the amount of the instrument), plus expenses and any loss of interest caused by the breach [UCC 3–416(b)].

These warranties can be disclaimed with respect to any instrument except a check [UCC 3–416(c)]. In the check-collection process, banks rely on these warranties. For all other instruments, the immediate parties can agree to a disclaimer, and an indorser can disclaim by including in the indorsement such words as "without warranties."

Presentment Warranties

Any person who presents an instrument for payment or acceptance makes the following **presentment warranties** to any other person who in good faith pays or accepts the instrument [UCC 3–417(a), (d)]:

1. The person obtaining payment or acceptance is entitled to enforce the instrument or is authorized to obtain payment or acceptance on behalf of a person who is entitled to enforce the instrument. (This is, in effect, a warranty that there are no missing or unauthorized indorsements.)
2. The instrument has not been altered.
3. The person obtaining payment or acceptance has no knowledge that the signature of the drawer of the instrument is unauthorized.[9]

These warranties are referred to as *presentment warranties* because they protect the person to whom the instrument is presented. The second and third war-

---

9. As discussed in footnote 8, the 2002 amendments to Article 3 of the UCC provide additional protection for "remotely created" consumer items, such as a check drawn on a personal account that the account holder authorized over the phone but did not physically sign.

ranties do not apply in certain circumstances (to certain parties). It is assumed, for example, that a drawer will recognize her or his own signature and that a maker or an acceptor will recognize whether an instrument has been materially altered.

Presentment warranties cannot be disclaimed with respect to checks, and a claim for breach must be given to the warrantor within thirty days after the claimant knows or has reason to know of the breach and the identity of the warrantor, or the warrantor is not liable for any loss caused by a delay [UCC 3–417(e)].

How should these warranties apply when two banks dispute whether a check was altered and its paper copy has been destroyed, leaving only its digital image? That was the question in the following case.

C A S E **21.1** **Wachovia Bank, N.A. v. Foster Bancshares, Inc.**
United States Court of Appeals, Seventh Circuit, 2006. 457 F.3d 619.

● **Background and Facts** Sunjin Choi deposited in her account at Foster Bank in Chicago, Illinois, a check for $133,026, on which she appeared to be the payee. The check was drawn on the account of MediaEdge, LLC, at Wachovia Bank, N.A., in Charlotte, North Carolina. Foster presented the check to Wachovia, which paid it and debited MediaEdge's account. Wachovia then made a digital copy of the check and destroyed the paper copy. The payee of the check as originally issued was not Choi, however, but CMP Media, Inc. Before MediaEdge learned that CMP had not received the check, Choi withdrew the funds from her account and disappeared. MediaEdge asked Wachovia to recredit its account. Wachovia filed a suit in a federal district court against Foster, seeking the amount of the check on the basis of the presentment warranty that an instrument has not been altered. The court issued a summary judgment in Wachovia's favor. Foster appealed to the U.S. Court of Appeals for the Seventh Circuit. Because only the digital copy of the check existed and there was no way to determine from it whether the paper copy had been altered, Foster argued that it should be assumed that the check was forged. Under that assumption, Wachovia, not Foster, would be liable for the loss. (Liability on a forged check will be discussed in detail in Chapter 27.)

● **Decision and Rationale** The U.S. Court of Appeals for the Seventh Circuit affirmed the lower court's judgment. "Changing the payee's name is the classic alteration. It can with modern technology be effected by forging a check rather than by altering an original check, but since this is a novel method, the presenting bank must do more than merely assert the possibility of it." The appellate court stated that a bank in which a check is deposited may reasonably suspect the payee's name has been altered even if there is no visible evidence such as traces of a chemical wash. "The size of the check may be a warning flag that induces the bank to delay making funds deposited by the check available for withdrawal." The court also emphasized what Foster did *not* prove: that keeping a paper copy of the check would have been "a reasonable method of determining whether the drawee bank or the presenting bank should be liable for the loss"; that the forgery of checks was a more common method of bank fraud than their alteration; that banks normally contract for a different allocation of liability than the UCC provides; or that Choi's *modus operandi* (usual method of operation) was to forge checks instead of to alter them. Here, the check deposited with Foster "was for a hefty $133,000, and there is no evidence that Choi had previously deposited large checks. We do not suggest that Foster was careless in deciding to make the money available for withdrawal when it did. But the uncertainties that the bank has made no effort to dispel counsel against [making the assumption] that it urges."

● **The E-Commerce Dimension** *How might the principles in this case have been applied if there had never been a paper copy of the check—if, for example, Choi's deposit and withdrawal of funds had occurred entirely online?*

● **The Legal Environment Dimension** *What is the practical basis for the warranty that a check presented for payment has not been altered since its issuance? (Hint: Presentment warranties often shift liability back to the party that was in the best position to prevent the wrongdoing.)*

Defenses

Depending on whether a holder or a holder in due course (HDC)—or a holder through an HDC—makes the demand for payment, certain defenses can bar collection from persons who would otherwise be liable on an instrument. There are two general categories of defenses—*universal defenses* and *personal defenses,* which are discussed below and summarized in Exhibit 21–2.

Universal Defenses

Universal defenses (also called *real defenses*) are valid against *all* holders, including HDCs and holders through HDCs. Universal defenses include those described in the following subsections.

Forgery Forgery of a maker's or drawer's signature cannot bind the person whose name is used unless that person ratifies (approves or validates) the signature or is precluded from denying it (because the forgery was made possible by the maker's or drawer's negligence, for example) [UCC 3–401(a), 3–403(a)]. Thus, when a person forges an instrument, the person whose name is forged has no liability to pay any holder or any HDC the value of the forged instrument.

Fraud in the Execution If a person is deceived into signing a negotiable instrument, believing that she or he is signing something other than a negotiable instrument (such as a receipt), *fraud in the execution* (or inception) is committed against the signer [UCC 3–305(a)(1)(iii)]. Suppose that Gerard, a salesperson, asks Javier, a customer, to sign a paper, which Gerard says is a receipt for the delivery of goods that Javier is picking up from the store. In fact, the paper is a promissory note, but Javier is unfamiliar with the English language and does not realize this. In this situation, even if the note is negotiated to an HDC, Javier has a valid defense against payment.

This defense cannot be raised, however, if a reasonable inquiry would have revealed the nature and terms of the instrument. Thus, the signer's age, experience, and intelligence are relevant because they frequently determine whether the signer should have understood the nature of the transaction before signing.

Material Alteration An alteration is *material* if it changes the contract terms between two parties *in any way.* Examples of material alterations include completing an instrument, adding words or numbers, or making any other unauthorized change that relates to a party's obligation [UCC 3–407(a)]. Any change in the amount, the date, or the rate of interest—even if the change is only one penny, one day, or 1 percent—is

EXHIBIT 21–2 • **Defenses against Liability on Negotiable Instruments**

UNIVERSAL (REAL) DEFENSES	PERSONAL (LIMITED) DEFENSES
Valid against all holders, including holders in due course	Valid against ordinary holders but not against holders in due course
1. Forgery. 2. Fraud in the execution. 3. Material alteration. 4. Discharge in bankruptcy. 5. Minority, if the contract is voidable. 6. Illegality, incapacity, or duress, if the contract is void under state law.	1. Breach of contract (including breach of contract warranties). 2. Lack or failure of consideration. 3. Fraud in the inducement. 4. Illegality, incapacity (other than minority), or duress, if the contract is voidable. 5. Previous payment or cancellation of the instrument. 6. Unauthorized completion of an incomplete instrument.

material. It is not a material alteration, however, to correct the maker's address, to draw a red line across the instrument to indicate that an auditor has checked it, or to correct the total final payment due when a mathematical error is discovered in the original computation. If the alteration is not material, any holder is entitled to enforce the instrument according to its original terms.

Material alteration is a *complete defense* against an ordinary holder but only a *partial defense* against an HDC. An ordinary holder can recover nothing on an instrument that has been materially altered [UCC 3–407(b)]. In contrast, when the holder is an HDC and an original term, such as the monetary amount payable, has been *altered,* the HDC can enforce the instrument against the maker or drawer according to the original terms but not for the altered amount [UCC 3–407(c)(i)]. If the instrument was originally incomplete and was later completed in an unauthorized manner, alteration can no longer be claimed as a defense against an HDC, and the HDC can enforce the instrument as completed [UCC 3–407(b), (c)]. This is because a drawer or maker who has issued an incomplete instrument normally will be held responsible for such an alteration, which could have been avoided by the exercise of greater care. If the alteration is readily apparent (such as a number changed on the face of a check), then obviously the holder has notice of some defect or defense and therefore cannot be an HDC [UCC 3–302(a)(1), (2)(iv)].

Is a note that allows for an extension of the time for payment materially altered when, on its expiration, its maker and payee execute a second note that the payee insists is only an extension of the time for payment but that in reality increases the balance due? That was the question in the following case.

C A S E **21.2** **Keesling v. T.E.K. Partners, LLC**
Indiana Court of Appeals, 2007. 861 N.E.2d 1246.

● **Background and Facts** In January 1998, two separate entities formed Heritage/M.G., LLC, in order to develop a residential neighborhood. A year and a half later, Heritage/M.G. borrowed $300,000 to partially finance the development. Final payment on the note was due on June 1, 2001. The signatories included Thomas McMullen, on behalf of Heritage/M.G., and Larry and Vivian Keesling. Heritage/M.G. did not complete the payments by the original deadline. By January 3, 2002, the balance was just below $50,000. Without the knowledge or consent of the Keeslings, Heritage/M.G. borrowed another $102,000 on which no payments were ever made. The original lenders assigned both the first and the second note to T.E.K. Partners, LLC. The trial court concluded that T.E.K. Partners was entitled to a judgment of $375,905.07. The Keeslings appealed.

● **Decision and Rationale** The Indiana Court of Appeals reversed the trial court's judgment against the Keeslings. The reviewing court agreed with T.E.K. Partners that a guarantee is a promise to answer for the debt, default, or miscarriage of another person. It is an "agreement collateral to the debt itself and represents a conditional promise whereby the guarantor promises to pay only if the principal debtor fails to pay." Nonetheless, "when parties cause material alteration of an underlying obligation without the consent of the guarantor, the guarantor is discharged from future liability." In this case, the change increased the risk of loss to the guarantor. Initially, the Keeslings guaranteed the original note; they were accommodation parties. McMullen, on behalf of Heritage/M.G., executed the second note for $102,000 without consulting the accommodation parties (the Keeslings). This "second note not only added new debt but increased the total principle draws beyond the $300,000 face amount of the original note." This second note constituted a material alteration of the original obligation. The Keeslings were discharged from their personal liability on the original note. "And they have no liability for the additional sums advanced under the second note, which they did not sign."

● **What If the Facts Were Different?** *If the court had affirmed the judgment in favor of T.E.K. Partners, against whom might the Keeslings have had a right of recourse?*

● **The Legal Environment Dimension** *What might the parties who executed the second note have done at the time to avoid the outcome in this case?*

Discharge in Bankruptcy Discharge in bankruptcy (see Chapter 30) is an absolute defense on any instrument regardless of the status of the holder [UCC 3–305(a)(1)(iv)]. This defense exists because the purpose of bankruptcy is to finally settle all of the insolvent party's debts.

Minority Minority, or infancy, is a universal defense only to the extent that state law recognizes it as a defense to a simple contract. Because state laws on minority vary, so do determinations of whether minority is a universal defense against an HDC [UCC 3–305(a)(1)(i)]. (See Chapter 13 for further discussion of the contractual liability of minors.)

Illegality Certain types of illegality constitute universal defenses, whereas others are personal defenses. If a statute provides that an illegal transaction is void, then the defense is universal—that is, absolute against both an ordinary holder and an HDC. If the law merely makes the instrument voidable, then the illegality is a personal defense against an ordinary holder, but not against an HDC [UCC 3–305(a)(1)(ii)]. Note that courts sometimes treat the word *void* in a statute as meaning *voidable* to protect an HDC.

Mental Incapacity If a court has declared a person to be mentally incompetent, then any instrument issued by that person is void. The instrument is void *ab initio* (from the beginning) and unenforceable by any holder or HDC [UCC 3–305(a)(1)(ii)]. Mental incapacity in these circumstances is a universal defense. If a court has not declared a person to be mentally incompetent, then mental incapacity operates as a personal defense against ordinary holders but not HDCs.

Extreme Duress When a person signs and issues a negotiable instrument under such extreme duress as an immediate threat of force or violence (for example, at gunpoint), the instrument is void and unenforceable by any holder or HDC [UCC 3–305(a)(1)(ii)]. (Ordinary duress is a personal, rather than a universal, defense.)

Personal Defenses

Personal defenses, such as those described next, are used to avoid payment to an ordinary holder of a negotiable instrument, but not to an HDC or a holder through an HDC.

Breach of Contract or Breach of Warranty When there is a breach of the underlying contract for which the negotiable instrument was issued, the maker of a note can refuse to pay it, or the drawer of a check can stop payment. Breach of warranty can also be claimed as a defense to liability on the instrument.

For example, Elias purchases two dozen pairs of athletic shoes from De Soto. The shoes are to be delivered in six weeks. Elias gives De Soto a promissory note for $1,000, which is the price of the shoes. The shoes arrive, but many of them are stained, and the soles of several pairs are coming apart. Elias has a defense to liability on the note on the basis of breach of contract and breach of warranty. (Recall from Chapter 23 that a seller impliedly promises that the goods being sold are at least merchantable.) If, however, the note is no longer in the hands of the payee-seller (De Soto) but is presented for payment by an HDC, the maker-buyer (Elias) will not be able to plead breach of contract or warranty as a defense against liability on the note.

Lack or Failure of Consideration The absence of consideration may be a successful defense in some instances [UCC 3–303(b), 3–305(a)(2)]. Suppose that Tony gives Cleo, as a gift, a note that states, "I promise to pay you $100,000," and Cleo accepts the note. No consideration is given in return for Tony's promise, and a court will not enforce the promise.

Similarly, if delivery of goods becomes impossible, a party who has issued a draft or note under the contract has a defense for not paying it. Thus, in the hypothetical athletic-shoe transaction described previously, if delivery of the shoes became impossible due to their loss in an accident, De Soto could not subsequently enforce Elias's promise to pay the $1,000 promissory note. If the note was in the hands of an HDC, however, Elias's defense would not be available against the HDC.

Fraud in the Inducement (Ordinary Fraud) A person who issues a negotiable instrument based on false statements by the other party will be able to avoid payment on that instrument, unless the holder is an HDC. To illustrate: Gerhard agrees to purchase Carla's used tractor for $26,500. Carla, knowing her statements to be false, tells Gerhard that the tractor is in good working order and that it has been used for only one harvest. In addition, she tells Gerhard that she owns the tractor free and clear of all claims. Gerhard pays Carla $4,500 in cash and issues a negotiable promissory note for the balance. As it turns out, Carla still owes the original seller $10,000 on the purchase of the tractor, and the tractor is subject to a valid security interest (discussed in Chapter 29). In addition, the tractor is three years old and has been used in three harvests.

In this situation, Gerhard can refuse to pay the note if it is held by an ordinary holder. If, however, Carla has negotiated the note to an HDC, Gerhard must pay the HDC. Of course, Gerhard can then sue Carla to recover the funds.

Illegality As mentioned, if a statute provides that an illegal transaction is void, a universal defense exists. If, however, the statute provides that an illegal transaction is voidable, the defense is personal. For example, a state may make gambling contracts illegal and void but be silent on the payment of gambling debts. Thus, an instrument given in payment of a gambling debt becomes voidable and is a personal defense.

Mental Incapacity As mentioned, if a maker or drawer has been declared by a court to be mentally incompetent, mental incapacity is a universal defense [UCC 3–305(a)(1)(ii)]. If a maker or drawer issues a negotiable instrument while mentally incompetent but before a formal court hearing has declared him or her to be so, however, the instrument is voidable. In this situation, mental incapacity can serve only as a personal defense.

Other Personal Defenses A number of other personal defenses can be used to avoid payment to an ordinary holder, but not an HDC, of a negotiable instrument, including the following:

1. Discharge by payment or cancellation [UCC 3–601(b), 3–602(a), 3–603, 3–604].
2. Unauthorized completion of an incomplete instrument [UCC 3–115, 3–302, 3–407, 4–401(d)(2)].
3. Nondelivery of the instrument [UCC 1–201(14), 3–105(b), 3–305(a)(2)].
4. Ordinary duress or undue influence rendering the contract voidable [UCC 3–305(a)(1)(ii)].

Federal Limitations on HDC Rights

The federal government limits HDC rights in certain circumstances because the HDC doctrine sometimes has harsh effects on consumers. Consider an example. A consumer purchases a used car under an express warranty from an automobile dealer. The consumer pays $5,000 down and signs a promissory note to the dealer for the remaining $10,000 due on the car. The dealer sells the bank this promissory note, which is a negotiable instrument, and the bank then becomes the creditor, to whom the consumer makes payments.

The car, however, does not perform as warranted. The consumer returns the car and requests a refund of the down payment and cancellation of the contract. Even if the dealer refunds the $5,000, however, under the traditional HDC rule, the consumer would normally still owe the remaining $10,000 because the consumer's claim of breach of warranty is a personal defense and the bank is an HDC.

Thus, the traditional HDC rule leaves consumers who have purchased defective products liable to HDCs. To protect consumers, in 1976 the Federal Trade Commission (FTC) issued Rule 433,[10] which effectively abolished the HDC doctrine in consumer credit transactions.

Requirements of FTC Rule 433 FTC Rule 433, entitled "Preservation of Consumers' Claims and Defenses," limits an HDC's rights in an instrument that evidences a debt arising out of a consumer credit transaction. The rule attempts to prevent a consumer from being required to make payment for a defective product to a third party (the bank, in the previous example) who is an HDC of a promissory note that formed part of the contract with the dealer who sold the defective good.

FTC Rule 433 applies to any seller of goods or services who takes or receives a consumer credit contract. The rule also applies to a seller who accepts as full or partial payment for a sale the proceeds of any purchase-money loan[11] made in connection with any consumer credit contract. Under this rule, these parties must include in the consumer credit contract the following provision:

NOTICE

ANY HOLDER OF THIS CONSUMER CREDIT CONTRACT IS SUBJECT TO ALL CLAIMS AND DEFENSES WHICH THE DEBTOR COULD ASSERT AGAINST THE SELLER OF GOODS OR SERVICES OBTAINED PURSUANT HERETO OR WITH THE PROCEEDS HEREOF. RECOVERY HEREUNDER BY THE DEBTOR SHALL NOT EXCEED AMOUNTS PAID BY THE DEBTOR HEREUNDER.

---

10. 16 C.F.R. Section 433.2. The rule was enacted in 1976 pursuant to the FTC's authority under the Federal Trade Commission Act, 15 U.S.C. Sections 41–58.

11. A *purchase-money loan* is one in which a seller or lessor advances funds to a buyer or lessee through a credit contract to purchase or lease the goods, as will be discussed in Chapter 29.

Effect of the Rule FTC Rule 433 allows a consumer who is a party to a consumer credit transaction to bring any defense she or he has against the seller of a product against a subsequent holder as well. In essence, the rule places an HDC of the instrument in the position of a contract assignee. The rule makes the buyer's duty to pay conditional on the seller's full performance of the contract. Both the seller and the creditor are responsible for the seller's misconduct. The rule also clearly reduces the degree of transferability of negotiable instruments resulting from consumer credit contracts. An instrument that contains this notice or a similar statement required by law may remain negotiable, but there cannot be an HDC of such an instrument [UCC 3–106(d)].

What if the seller does not include the notice in a promissory note and then sells the note to a third party, such as a bank? Although the seller has violated the rule, the bank has not. Because the FTC rule does not prohibit third parties from purchasing notes or credit contracts that do *not* contain the required rule, the third party does not become subject to the buyer's defenses against the seller. Thus, some consumers remain unprotected by the FTC rule.[12]

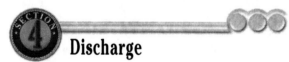

Discharge

Discharge from liability on an instrument can occur in several ways, including by payment, by cancellation, and, as previously discussed, by material alteration. Discharge can also occur if a party reacquires an instrument, if a holder impairs another party's right of recourse, or if a holder surrenders collateral without consent.

Discharge by Payment or Tender of Payment

All parties to a negotiable instrument will be discharged when the party primarily liable on it pays to a holder the amount due in full [UCC 3–602, 3–603].[13]

The liability of all parties is also discharged if the drawee of an unaccepted draft or check makes payment in good faith to the holder. Payment by any other party (for example, an indorser) discharges only the liability of that party and subsequent parties. The party making such a payment still has the right to recover on the instrument from any prior parties.[14]

A party will not be discharged when paying in bad faith to a holder who acquired the instrument by theft or who obtained the instrument from someone else who acquired it by theft (unless, of course, the person has the rights of an HDC) [UCC 3–602(b)(2)].

If a tender of payment is made to a person entitled to enforce the instrument and the tender is refused, indorsers and accommodation parties with a right of recourse against the party making the tender are discharged to the extent of the amount of the tender [UCC 3–603(b)]. If a tender of payment of an amount due on an instrument is made to a person entitled to enforce the instrument, the obligor's obligation to pay interest after the due date on the amount tendered is discharged [UCC 3–603(c)].

Discharge by Cancellation or Surrender

Intentional cancellation of an instrument discharges the liability of all parties [UCC 3–604]. Intentionally writing "Paid" across the face of an instrument cancels it. Intentionally tearing up an instrument cancels it. If a holder intentionally crosses out a party's signature, that party's liability and the liability of subsequent indorsers who have already indorsed the instrument are discharged. Materially altering an instrument may discharge the liability of all parties, as previously discussed [UCC 3–407(b)]. (An HDC may be able to enforce a materially altered instrument against its maker or drawer according to the instrument's *original* terms, however.)

Destruction or mutilation of a negotiable instrument is considered cancellation only if it is done with the intention of eliminating obligation on the instrument [UCC 3–604(a)(i)]. Thus, if destruction or mutilation occurs by accident, the instrument is not discharged, and the original terms can be established by parol evidence [UCC 3–309]. A note's holder may

---

12. Under a 2002 amendment to UCC 3–305(e), a third party holder in possession of a note or other instrument that is required to include this notice would be subject to a buyer's defenses against a seller even if the instrument did not include the notice.

13. This is true even if the payment is made with knowledge of a claim to the instrument by another person unless the payor knows that "payment is prohibited by injunction or similar process of a court of competent jurisdiction" or, in most situations, "the party making payment accepted, from a person having a claim to the instrument, indemnity against loss resulting from refusal to pay the person entitled to enforce the instrument" [UCC 3–602(a), (b)(1)].

14. Under the 2002 amendment to UCC 3–602(b), when a party entitled to enforce an instrument transfers it without giving notice to the parties obligated to pay it, and one of those parties pays the transferor, that payment is effective. Suppose that Roberto borrows $5,000 from Consumer Finance Company on a note payable to the lender. Consumer Finance transfers the note to Delta Investment Corporation but continues to collect payments from Roberto. Under this amendment, those payments effectively discharge Roberto to the extent of their amount.

also discharge the obligation by surrendering the note to the person to be discharged [UCC 3–604(a)(i)].

Discharge by Reacquisition

A person who reacquires an instrument that he or she held previously discharges all intervening indorsers against subsequent holders who do not qualify as HDCs [UCC 3–207]. Of course, the person reacquiring the instrument may be liable to subsequent holders if the instrument is dishonored.

Discharge by Impairment of Recourse

Discharge can also occur when a party's right of recourse is impaired [UCC 3–605]. A *right of recourse* is a right to seek reimbursement. Ordinarily, when a holder collects the amount of an instrument from an indorser, the indorser has a right of recourse against prior indorsers, the maker or drawer, and accommodation parties. If the holder has adversely affected the indorser's right to seek reimbursement from these other parties, however, the indorser is not liable on the instrument (to the extent that the indorser's right of recourse is impaired). This occurs when, for example, the holder releases or agrees not to sue a party against whom the indorser has a right of recourse. It also occurs when a holder agrees to an extension of the instrument's due date or to some other material modification that results in a loss to the indorser with respect to the right of recourse [UCC 3–605(c), (d)].[15]

Discharge by Impairment of Collateral

Sometimes, a party to an instrument gives collateral as security that her or his performance will occur. When a holder "impairs the value" of that collateral without the consent of the parties who would benefit from the collateral in the event of nonpayment, those parties to the instrument are discharged to the extent of the impairment [UCC 3–605(e), (f)].

For example, Jerome and Myra sign a note as co-makers, putting up Jerome's property as collateral. The note is payable to Montessa. Montessa is required by law to file a financing statement with the state to put others on notice of her interest in Jerome's property as collateral for the note. If Montessa fails to file the statement and Jerome goes through bankruptcy—which results in his property's being sold to pay other debts and leaves him unable to pay anything on the note—Montessa has impaired the value of the collateral to Myra, who is discharged to the extent of that impairment.

In other words, when Jerome goes through bankruptcy, Montessa's earlier failure to file the statement prevents her from taking possession of the collateral, selling it, and crediting the amount owed on the note. Myra, as co-maker, is then responsible only for any remaining indebtedness, instead of the entire unpaid balance. Thus, Myra is discharged to the extent that the proceeds from the sale of the collateral would have discharged her liability on the note.

---

15. The 2002 amendments to UCC 3–605 essentially apply the principles of suretyship and guaranty (to be discussed in Chapter 28) to circumstances that involve the impairment of the right of recourse of "secondary obligors," which include indorsers and accommodation parties. One important difference from the principles of suretyship and guaranty, however, is that under amended UCC 3–605(a), the release of a principal obligor by a person entitled to enforce a check grants a complete discharge to an indorser of the check without requiring proof of harm.

REVIEWING Liability, Defenses, and Discharge

Nancy Mahar was the office manager at Golden Years Nursing Home, Inc. She was given a signature stamp to issue checks to the nursing home's employees for up to $100 as advances on their pay. The checks were drawn on Golden Years' account at First National Bank. Over a seven-year period, Mahar wrote a number of checks to employees exclusively for the purpose of embezzling funds for herself. She forged the employees' indorsements on the checks, signed her name as a second indorser, and deposited the checks in her personal account at Star Bank. The employees whose names were on the checks never actually requested them. When the scheme was uncovered,

REVIEWING CONTINUES

REVIEWING Liability, Defenses, and Discharge, Continued

Golden Years filed a suit against Mahar, Star Bank, and others to recover the funds. Using the information presented in the chapter, answer the following questions.

1. With regard to signature liability, which provision of the Uniform Commercial Code (UCC) discussed in this chapter applies to this scenario?
2. What is the rule set forth by that provision?
3. Under the UCC, which party, Golden Years or Star Bank, must bear the loss in this situation? Why?
4. Based on these facts, describe any transfer or presentment warranties that Mahar may have violated.

TERMS AND CONCEPTS

accommodation party
agent

dishonor
fictitious payee
imposter
personal defense

presentment warranty
principal
transfer warranty
universal defense

QUESTIONS AND CASE PROBLEMS

26–1. What are the exceptions to the rule that a bank will be liable for paying a check over an unauthorized indorsement?

26–2. Waldo makes out a negotiable promissory note payable to the order of Grace. Grace indorses the note by writing on it "Without recourse, Grace" and transfers the note for value to Adam. Adam, in need of cash, negotiates the note to Keith by indorsing it with the words "Pay to Keith, Adam." On the due date, Keith presents the note to Waldo for payment, only to learn that Waldo has filed for bankruptcy and will have all debts (including the note) discharged. Discuss fully whether Keith can hold Waldo, Grace, or Adam liable on the note.

26–3. QUESTION WITH SAMPLE ANSWER

Niles sold Kennedy a small motorboat for $1,500, maintaining to Kennedy that the boat was in excellent condition. Kennedy gave Niles a check for $1,500, which Niles indorsed and gave to Frazier for value. When Kennedy took the boat for a trial run, she discovered that the boat leaked, needed to be painted, and required a new motor. Kennedy stopped payment on her check, which had not yet been cashed. Niles has disap-

peared. Can Frazier recover from Kennedy as a holder in due course? Discuss.

• **For a sample answer to Question 26–3, go to Appendix C at the end of this text.**

26–4. Williams purchased a used car from Stein for $1,000. Williams paid for the car with a check (written in pencil) payable to Stein for $1,000. Stein, through careful erasures and alterations, changed the amount on the check to read $10,000 and negotiated the check to Boz. Boz took the check for value, in good faith, and without notice of the alteration and thus met the Uniform Commercial Code's requirements for the status of a holder in due course. Can Williams successfully raise the universal (real) defense of material alteration to avoid payment on the check? Explain.

26–5. Gil makes out a $900 negotiable promissory note payable to Ben. By special indorsement, Ben transfers the note for value to Jess. By blank indorsement, Jess transfers the note for value to Pam. By special indorsement, Pam transfers the note for value to Adrien. In need of cash, Adrien transfers the instrument for value by blank indorsement back to Jess. When told that Ben has left the country, Jess strikes out Ben's indorsement. Later she learns that Ben is a wealthy restaurant owner in

Baltimore and that Gil is financially unable to pay the note. Jess contends that, as a holder in due course, she can hold Ben, Pam, or Adrien liable on the note. Discuss fully Jess's contentions.

26–6. Unauthorized Indorsements. Telemedia Publications, Inc., publishes *Cablecast* magazine, a weekly guide to the listings of the cable television programming in Baton Rouge, Louisiana. Cablecast hired Jennifer Pennington as a temporary employee. Pennington's duties included indorsing subscription checks received in the mail with the Cablecast deposit stamp, preparing the deposit slip, and taking the checks to be deposited to City National Bank. John McGregor, the manager of Cablecast, soon noticed shortages in revenues coming into Cablecast. When he learned that Pennington had taken checks payable to Cablecast and deposited them into her personal account at Premier Bank, N.A., he confronted her. She admitted to taking $7,913.04 in Cablecast checks. Cablecast filed a suit in a Louisiana state court against Premier Bank. The bank responded in part that Cablecast was solely responsible for losses caused by the fraudulent indorsements of its employees. At trial, Cablecast failed to prove that Premier Bank had not acted in good faith or that it had not exercised ordinary care in its handling of the checks. What rule should the court apply here? Why? [*Cablecast Magazine v. Premier Bank, N.A.*, 729 So.2d 1165 (La.App. 1 Cir. 1999)]

26–7. Agents' Signatures. Robert Helmer and Percy Helmer, Jr., were authorized signatories on the corporate checking account of Event Marketing, Inc. The Helmers signed a check drawn on Event Marketing's account and issued to Rumarson Technologies, Inc. (RTI), in the amount of $24,965. The check was signed on July 13, 1998, but dated August 14. When RTI presented the check for payment, it was dishonored due to insufficient funds. RTI filed a suit in a Georgia state court against the Helmers to collect the amount of the check. Claiming that the Helmers were personally liable on Event Marketing's check, RTI filed a motion for summary judgment. Can an authorized signatory on a corporate account be held personally liable for corporate checks returned for insufficient funds? Are the Helmers liable in this case? Discuss. [*Helmer v. Rumarson Technologies, Inc.*, 245 Ga.App. 598, 538 S.E.2d 504 (2000)]

26–8. Defenses. On September 13, 1979, Barbara Shearer and Barbara Couvion signed a note for $22,500, with interest at 11 percent, payable in monthly installments of $232.25 to Edgar House and Paul Cook. House and Cook assigned the note to Southside Bank in Kansas City, Missouri. In 1997, the note was assigned to Midstates Resources Corp., which assigned the note to The Cadle Co. in 2000. According to the payment history that Midstates gave to Cadle, the interest rate on the note was 12 percent. A Cadle employee noticed the discrepancy and recalculated the payments at 11 percent. When Shearer and Couvion refused to make further payments

on the note, Cadle filed a suit in a Missouri state court against them to collect. Couvion and Shearer responded that they had made timely payments on the note, that Cadle and the previous holders had failed to accurately apply the payments to the reduction of principal and interest, and that the note "is either paid in full and satisfied or very close to being paid in full and satisfied." Is the makers' answer sufficient to support a verdict in their favor? If so, on what ground? If not, why not? [*The Cadle Co. v. Shearer*, 69 S.W.3d 122 (Mo.App.W.D. 2002)]

26–9. CASE PROBLEM WITH SAMPLE ANSWER

Ameripay, LLC, is a payroll services company that, among other things, issues payroll checks to the employees of its clients. In July 2002, Nu Tribe Radio Networks, Inc. (NTRN), based in New York City, hired Ameripay. Under their agreement, Ameripay set up an account on NTRN's behalf at Commerce Bank. NTRN agreed to deposit funds in the account to cover its payroll obligations. Arthur Piacentini, an owner of Ameripay, was an authorized signatory on the account. On the checks, NTRN was the only identified company, and Piacentini's signature appeared without indicating his status. At the end of the month, four NTRN employees cashed their payroll checks, which Piacentini had signed, at A-1 Check Cashing Emporium, Inc. The checks were returned dishonored. Ameripay had stopped their payment because it had not received the funds from NTRN. A-1 assigned its interest in the checks to Robert Triffin, who filed a suit in a New Jersey state court against Ameripay. What principles determine who, between a principal and an agent, is liable for the amount of an unpaid instrument? How do those principles apply in this case? Is Ameripay liable? Why or why not? [*Triffin v. Ameripay, LLC*, 368 N.J.Super. 587, 847 A.2d 628 (App.Div. 2004)]

- To view a sample answer for Problem 26–9, go to this book's Web site at <u>www.cengage.com/blaw/jentz</u>, select "Chapter 26," and click on "Case Problem with Sample Answer."

26–10. Accommodation Parties. Donald Goosic, a building contractor in Nebraska, did business as "Homestead" builders. To construct a house on "spec" (without a preconstruction buyer), Donald obtained materials from Sack Lumber Co. on an open account. When Donald "got behind in his payments," his wife, Frances, cosigned a note payable to Sack for $43,000, the outstanding balance on the account. Donald made payments on the note until he obtained a discharge of his debts in a bankruptcy proceeding to which Frances was not a party. Less than a year later, Sack filed a suit in a Nebraska state court against Frances to collect on the note. She contended that she was an accommodation party, not a maker, and thus was not liable because the applicable statute of limitations had run. She testified that Donald "made more debt than . . . money" and that she was "paying the bills out of [her] income." The Goosics' most recent tax returns showed only losses relating to Homestead. Under the Uniform Commercial Code, a person receiving only an indirect benefit from a transaction can qualify as an accommodation party. How would you rule on this question of fact? Why? [*Sack Lumber Co. v. Goosic*, 15 Neb. App. 529, 732 N.W.2d 690 (2007)]

26-11. A QUESTION OF ETHICS

Clarence Morgan, Jr., owned Easy Way Automotive, a car dealership in D'Lo, Mississippi. Easy Way sold a truck to Loyd Barnard, who signed a note for the amount of the price payable to Trustmark National Bank in six months. Before the note came due, Barnard returned the truck to Easy Way, which sold it to another buyer. Using some of the proceeds from the second sale, Easy Way sent a check to Trustmark to pay Barnard's note. Meanwhile, Barnard obtained another truck from Easy Way, financed through another six-month note payable to Trustmark. After eight of these deals, some of which involved more than one truck, an Easy Way check to Trustmark was dishonored. In a suit in a Mississippi state court, Trustmark sought to recover the amounts of two of the notes from Barnard. Trustmark had not secured titles to two of the trucks covered by the notes, however, and this complicated Barnard's efforts to reclaim the vehicles from the later buyers. [Trustmark National Bank v. Barnard, 930 So.2d 1281 (Miss. App. 2006)]

(a) On what basis might Barnard be liable on the Trustmark notes? Would he be primarily or secondarily liable? Could this liability be discharged on the theory that Barnard's right of recourse had been impaired when Trustmark did not secure titles to the trucks covered by the notes? Explain.

(b) Easy Way's account had been subject to other recent overdrafts, and a week after the check to Trustmark was returned for insufficient funds, Morgan committed suicide. At the same time, Barnard was unable to obtain a mortgage because the unpaid notes affected his credit rating. How do the circumstances of this case underscore the importance of practicing business ethics?

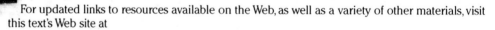

LAW ON THE WEB

For updated links to resources available on the Web, as well as a variety of other materials, visit this text's Web site at

www.cengage.com/blaw/jentz

To find information on the UCC, including the Article 3 provisions discussed in this chapter, refer to the Web sites listed in the *Law on the Web* section in Chapter 24.

Legal Research Exercises on the Web

Go to **www.cengage.com/blaw/jentz,** the Web site that accompanies this text. Select "Chapter 26" and click on "Internet Exercises." There you will find the following Internet research exercises that you can perform to learn more about the topics covered in this chapter.

Internet Exercise 26–1: Legal Perspective
Fictitious Payees

Internet Exercise 26–2: Management Perspective
FTC Rule 433

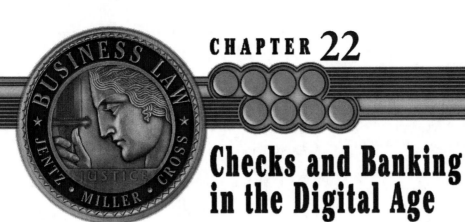

CHAPTER 22

Checks and Banking in the Digital Age

Checks are the most common type of negotiable instruments governed by the Uniform Commercial Code (UCC). Although debit cards now account for more retail payments than checks, commercial checks remain an integral part of the U.S. economic system. Issues relating to checks are governed by Articles 3 and 4 of the UCC. As noted in the preceding chapters, Article 3 establishes the requirements that all negotiable instruments, including checks, must meet.

Article 3 also sets forth the rights and responsibilities of parties to negotiable instruments. Article 4 establishes a framework for deposit and checking agreements between a bank and its customers. Article 4 also governs the relationships of banks with one another as they process checks for payment. A check therefore may fall within the scope of Article 3 and yet be subject to the provisions of Article 4 while in the course of collection. If a conflict arises between Article 3 and

Article 4, Article 4 controls [UCC 4–102(a)].

In this chapter, we first identify the legal characteristics of checks and the legal duties and liabilities that arise when a check is issued. Then we examine the collection process. Increasingly, credit cards, debit cards, and other devices and methods for transferring funds electronically are being used to pay for goods and services. In the latter part of this chapter, we look at the law governing electronic fund transfers.

Checks

A **check** is a special type of draft that is drawn on a bank, ordering the bank to pay a fixed amount of money on demand [UCC 3–104(f)]. Article 4 defines a *bank* as "a person engaged in the business of banking, including a savings bank, savings and loan association, credit union or trust company" [UCC 4–105(1)].[1] If any other nonbank institution (such as a brokerage firm) handles a check for payment or for collection, the check is not covered by Article 4.

Recall from the preceding chapters that a person who writes a check is called the *drawer*. The drawer is

usually a depositor in the bank on which the check is drawn. The person to whom the check is payable is the *payee*. The bank or financial institution on which the check is drawn is the *drawee*. Thus, if Anne Tomas writes a check on her checking account to pay her college tuition, she is the drawer, her bank is the drawee, and her college is the payee.

Between the time a check is drawn and the time it reaches the drawee, the effectiveness of the check may be altered by some event—for example, the drawer may die or order payment not to be made, or the account on which the check is drawn may be depleted. To avoid this problem, a payee may insist on payment by an instrument that has already been accepted by the drawee. Such an instrument may be a cashier's check, a traveler's check, or a certified check.

Cashier's Checks

Checks are usually three-party instruments, but on some checks, the bank serves as both the drawer *and* the drawee. For example, when a bank draws a check on itself, the check is called a **cashier's check** and is

---

1. The unrevised Article 4 does not define the term *bank*, except to distinguish among banks that deposit, collect, and pay instruments. The term was generally considered to include only commercial banks, which at the time the unrevised Article 4 was written were the only banks that could offer checking accounts. Revised Article 4's definition makes it clear that other depository institutions now have the authority to issue and otherwise deal with checks.

a negotiable instrument on issue (see Exhibit 22–1) [UCC 3–104(g)]. Normally, a cashier's check indicates a specific payee. In effect, with a cashier's check, the bank assumes responsibility for paying the check, thus making the check more readily acceptable in commerce.

For example, Blake needs to pay a moving company $7,000 for moving his household goods to a new home in another state. The moving company requests payment in the form of a cashier's check. Blake goes to a bank (he need not have an account at the bank) and purchases a cashier's check, payable to the moving company, in the amount of $7,000. Blake has to pay the bank the $7,000 for the check, plus a small service fee. He then gives the check to the moving company.

Cashier's checks are sometimes used in the business community as nearly the equivalent of cash. Except in very limited circumstances, the issuing bank must honor its cashier's checks when they are presented for payment. If a bank wrongfully dishonors a cashier's check, a holder can recover from the bank all expenses incurred, interest, and consequential damages [UCC 3–411]. This same rule applies if a bank wrongfully dishonors a certified check (to be discussed shortly) or a teller's check. (A **teller's check** is usually drawn by a bank on another bank; when drawn on a nonbank, it is payable at or through a bank [UCC 3–104(h)].) For example, when a credit union issues a check to withdraw funds from its account at another financial institution, and the teller at the credit union signs the check, it is a teller's check.)

Traveler's Checks

A **traveler's check** is an instrument that is payable on demand, drawn on or payable at a financial institution (such as a bank), and designated as a traveler's check. The issuing institution is directly obligated to accept and pay its traveler's check according to the check's terms. Traveler's checks are designed as a safe substitute for cash when a person is on vacation or traveling and are issued for a fixed amount, such as $20, $50, or $100. The purchaser is required to sign the check at the time it is purchased and again at the time it is used [UCC 3–104(i)]. Most major banks today do not issue traveler's checks; rather, they purchase and issue American Express traveler's checks for their customers (see Exhibit 22–2).

Certified Checks

A **certified check** is a check that has been *accepted* by the bank on which it is drawn [UCC 3–409(d)]. When a drawee bank agrees to certify a check, it immediately charges the drawer's account with the amount of the check and transfers those funds to its own certified-check account. In effect, the bank is agreeing in advance to accept that check when it is presented for payment and to make payment from those funds reserved in the certified-check account.

EXHIBIT 22–1 • **A Cashier's Check**

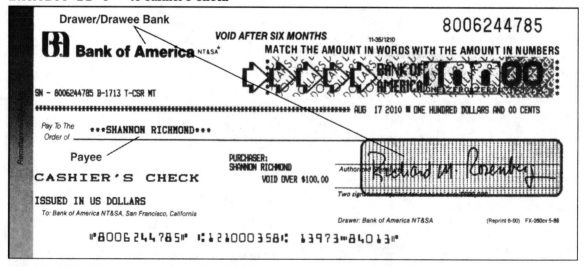

*The abbreviation *NT&SA* stands for National Trust and Savings Association. The Bank of America NT&SA is a subsidiary of Bank of America Corporation, which is engaged in financial services, insurance, investment management, and other businesses.

EXHIBIT 22-2 • An American Express Traveler's Check

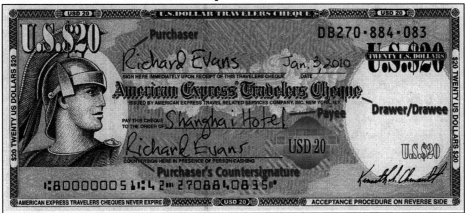

Essentially, certification prevents the bank from denying liability. It is a promise that sufficient funds are on deposit and *have been set aside* to cover the check.

To certify a check, the bank writes or stamps the word *certified* on the face of the check and typically writes the amount that it will pay.[2] Either the drawer or the holder (payee) of a check can request certification, but the drawee bank is not required to certify a check. A bank's refusal to certify a check is not a dishonor of the check [UCC 3–409(d)]. Once a check is certified, the drawer and any prior indorsers are completely discharged from liability on the check [UCC 3–414(c), 3–415(d)]. Only the certifying bank is required to pay the instrument.

The Bank-Customer Relationship

The bank-customer relationship begins when the customer opens a checking account and deposits funds that the bank will use to pay for checks written by the customer. The rights and duties of the bank and the customer are contractual and depend on the nature of the transaction. Essentially, three types of relationships come into being, as discussed next.

Creditor-Debtor Relationship

A creditor-debtor relationship is created between a customer and a bank when, for example, the customer

makes cash deposits into a checking account. When a customer makes a deposit, the customer becomes a creditor, and the bank a debtor, for the amount deposited.

Agency Relationship

An agency relationship also arises between the customer and the bank when the customer writes a check on his or her account. In effect, the customer is ordering the bank to pay the amount specified on the check to the holder when the holder presents the check to the bank for payment. In this situation, the bank becomes the customer's agent and is obligated to honor the customer's request. Similarly, if the customer deposits a check into his or her account, the bank, as the customer's agent, is obligated to collect payment on the check from the bank on which the check was drawn.

Contractual Relationship

Whenever a bank-customer relationship is established, certain contractual rights and duties arise. The rights and duties of the bank and the customer are contractual and depend on the nature of the transaction. The respective rights and duties of banks and their customers will be discussed in detail in the following pages.

Honoring Checks

When a banking institution provides checking services, it agrees to honor the checks written by its customers, with the usual stipulation that sufficient funds

---

2. If the certification does not state an amount, and the amount is later increased and the instrument negotiated to a holder in due course (HDC), the obligation of the certifying bank is the amount of the instrument when it was taken by the HDC [UCC 3–413(b)].

must be available in the account to pay each check. When a drawee bank *wrongfully* fails to honor a check, it is liable to its customer for damages resulting from its refusal to pay. The UCC does not attempt to specify the theory under which the customer may recover for wrongful dishonor; it merely states that the drawee is liable [UCC 4–402(b)].

The customer's agreement with the bank includes a general obligation to keep sufficient funds on deposit to cover all checks written. The customer is liable to the payee or to the holder of a check in a civil suit if a check is not honored. If intent to defraud can be proved, the customer can also be subject to criminal prosecution for writing a bad check.

When the bank properly dishonors a check for insufficient funds, it has no liability to the customer. The bank may rightfully refuse payment on a customer's check in other circumstances as well. We look here at the rights and duties of both the bank and its customers in relation to specific situations.

Overdrafts

When the bank receives an item properly payable from its customer's checking account but the account contains insufficient funds to cover the amount of the check, the bank has two options. It can either (1) dishonor the item or (2) pay the item and charge the customer's account, thus creating an **overdraft,** providing that the customer has authorized the payment and the payment does not violate any bank-customer agreement [UCC 4–401(a)].[3] The bank can subtract the difference from the customer's next deposit because the check carries with it an enforceable implied promise to reimburse the bank.

When a check "bounces," a holder can resubmit the check, hoping that at a later date sufficient funds will be available to pay it. The holder must notify any indorsers on the check of the first dishonor, however; otherwise, they will be discharged from their signature liability, as discussed in Chapter 26.

A bank can expressly agree with a customer to accept overdrafts through what is sometimes called an "overdraft protection agreement." If such an agreement is formed, any failure of the bank to honor a check because it would create an overdraft breaches this agreement and is treated as a wrongful dishonor [UCC 4–402(a), (b)].

3. When customers have a joint account, the bank cannot hold any customer on the account liable for payment of an overdraft unless that customer has signed the check or has benefited from the proceeds of the check [UCC 4–401(b)].

Postdated Checks

A bank may also charge a postdated check against a customer's account, unless the customer notifies the bank, in a timely manner, not to pay the check until the stated date. The notice of postdating must be given in time to allow the bank to act on the notice before committing itself to pay on the check. The UCC states that the bank should treat the notice like a stop-payment order (to be discussed shortly). If the bank fails to act on the customer's notice and charges the customer's account before the date on the postdated check, the bank may be liable for any damages incurred by the customer. Damages include those that result from the dishonor of checks that are subsequently presented for payment and are dishonored for insufficient funds [UCC 4–401(c)].

Stale Checks

Commercial banking practice regards a check that is presented for payment more than six months from its date as a **stale check.** A bank is not obligated to pay an uncertified check presented more than six months from its date [UCC 4–404]. When receiving a stale check for payment, the bank has the option of paying or not paying the check. If a bank pays a stale check in good faith without consulting the customer, the bank has the right to charge the customer's account for the amount of the check.

Death or Incompetence of a Customer

Neither the death nor the incompetence of a customer revokes a bank's authority to pay an item until the bank knows of the situation and has had reasonable time to act on the notice [UCC 4–405]. Thus, if, at the time a check is issued or its collection is undertaken, a bank does not know that the customer who wrote the check has been declared incompetent, the bank can pay the item without incurring liability. Even when a bank knows of the death of its customer, for ten days after the *date of death* it can pay or certify checks drawn on or before the date of death. Without this provision, banks would constantly be required to verify the continued life and competence of their drawers. An exception to the rule is made if a person claiming an interest in the account of the deceased customer, such as an heir or an executor of the estate (see Chapter 50), orders the bank to stop payment.

Stop-Payment Orders

A **stop-payment order** is an order by a customer to her or his bank not to pay a certain check.[4] Only a customer or a "person authorized to draw on the account" can order the bank not to pay the check when it is presented for payment [UCC 4–403(a)]. A customer has no right to stop payment on a check that has already been certified (or accepted) by a bank, however. Also, a stop-payment order must be received within a reasonable time and in a reasonable manner to permit the bank to act on it [UCC 4–403(a)]. Although a stop-payment order can be given orally, usually by phone, the order is binding on the bank for only fourteen calendar days unless confirmed in writing.[5] A written stop-payment order (see Exhibit 22–3) or an oral order confirmed in writing is effective for six months, at which time it must be renewed in writing [UCC 4–403(b)].

Bank's Liability for Wrongful Payment If the bank pays the check over the customer's properly instituted stop-payment order, the bank will be obligated to recredit the customer's account. In addition, if the bank's payment over a stop-payment order causes

---

4. Note that although this discussion focuses on checks, the right to stop payment is not limited to checks; it extends to any item payable by any bank. See Official Comment 3 to UCC 4–403.

5. Some states do not recognize oral stop-payment orders; the orders must be in writing.

subsequent checks written on the drawer's account to "bounce," the bank will be liable for the resultant costs the drawer incurs. The bank is liable only for the amount of the actual loss suffered by the drawer because of the wrongful payment, however [UCC 4–403(c)].

Assume that Toshio Murano orders one hundred cellular telephones from Advanced Communications, Inc., at $50 each. Murano pays in advance for the phones with a check for $5,000. Later that day, Advanced Communications tells Murano that it will not deliver the phones as arranged. Murano immediately calls the bank and stops payment on the check. Two days later, in spite of this stop-payment order, the bank inadvertently honors Murano's check to Advanced Communications for the undelivered phones. The bank will be liable to Murano for the full $5,000.

The result would be different, however, if Advanced Communications had delivered and Murano had accepted ninety-nine phones. Because Murano would have owed Advanced Communications $4,950 for the goods delivered, Murano's actual loss would be only $50. Consequently, the bank would be liable to Murano for only $50.

Customer's Liability for Wrongful Stop-Payment Order A stop-payment order has its risks for a customer. The drawer must have a *valid legal*

EXHIBIT 22–3 • A Stop-Payment Order

		Checking Account Stop-Payment Order
Bank of America		

To: Bank of America NT&SA
I want to stop payment on the following check(s).

ACCOUNT NUMBER: ☐☐☐☐☐☐☐ — ☐☐☐☐☐☐

BANK USE ONLY

TRANCODE:
☐ 21—ENTER STOP PAYMENT
(SEE OTHER SIDE TO REMOVE)

SPECIFIC STOP

*ENTER DOLLAR AMOUNT: _____ *CHECK NUMBER: _____

THE CHECK WAS SIGNED BY: _____
THE CHECK IS PAYABLE TO: _____
THE REASON FOR THIS STOP PAYMENT IS: _____

NON READS: _____
UNPROC. STMT HIST: _____
PRIOR STMT CYCLE: _____
HOLDS ON COOLS: _____
REJECTED CHKS: _____
LARGE ITEMS: _____
FEE COLLECTED: _____
DATE ACCEPTED: _____
TIME ACCEPTED: _____

STOP RANGE (Use for lost or stolen check(s) only.)

DOLLAR AMOUNT: 000

*ENTER STARTING CHECK NUMBER: _____ *END CHECK NUMBER: _____

THE REASON FOR THIS STOP PAYMENT IS: _____

I agree that this order (1) is effective only if the above check(s) has (have) not yet been cashed or paid against my account, (2) will end six months from the date it is delivered to you unless I renew it in writing, and (3) is not valid if the check(s) was (were) accepted on the strength of my Bank of America courtesy-check guarantee card by a merchant participating in that program. I also agree (1) to notify you immediately to cancel this order if the reason for the stop payment no longer exists or (2) that closing the account on which the check(s) is (are) drawn automatically cancels this order.

IF ANOTHER BRANCH OF THIS BANK OR ANOTHER PERSON OR ENTITY BECOMES A "HOLDER IN DUE COURSE" OF THE ABOVE CHECK, I UNDERSTAND THAT PAYMENT MAY BE ENFORCED AGAINST THE CHECK'S MAKER (SIGNER).

*I CERTIFY THE AMOUNT AND CHECK NUMBER(S) ABOVE ARE CORRECT.
☐ I have written a replacement check (number and date of check).

(Optional—please circle one: Mr., Ms., Mrs., Miss) CUSTOMER'S SIGNATURE X _____ DATE _____ *ground* for issuing such an order; otherwise, the holder can sue the drawer for payment. Moreover, defenses sufficient to refuse payment to a payee may not be valid grounds to prevent payment to a subsequent holder in due course [UCC 3–305, 3–306]. A person who wrongfully stops payment on a check not only will be liable to the payee for the amount of the check but also may be liable for consequential damages incurred by the payee as a result of the wrongful stop-payment order.

Checks Bearing Forged Signatures

When a bank pays a check on which the drawer's signature is forged, generally the bank suffers the loss.[6] A bank may be able to recover at least some of the loss from the customer, however, if the customer's negligence substantially contributed to the forgery. A bank may also obtain partial recovery from the forger of the check (if he or she can be found) or from the holder who presented the check for payment (if the holder knew that the signature was forged).

The General Rule A forged signature on a check has no legal effect as the signature of a drawer [UCC 3–403(a)]. For this reason, banks require a signature card from each customer who opens a checking account so that the bank can determine whether the signature on a customer's check is genuine. The general rule is that the bank must recredit the customer's account when it pays on a forged signature. (Note that banks today normally verify signatures only on checks that exceed a certain threshold, such as $1,000, $2,500, or some higher amount. Even though a bank sometimes incurs liability costs when it has paid forged checks, the costs involved in verifying the signature on every check signature would be much higher.)

Note that a bank may contractually shift to the customer the risk of forged checks created by the use of facsimile or other nonmanual signatures. For example, the contract might stipulate that the customer is solely responsible for maintaining security over any device affixing a signature. The contract might also provide that any nonmanual signature is effective as the customer's signature regardless of whether the person who affixed the signature was authorized to do so.[7]

Customer Negligence When a customer's negligence substantially contributes to a forgery, the bank normally will not be obligated to recredit the customer's account for the amount of the check [UCC 3–406(a)]. If negligence on the part of the bank (or other "person") paying the instrument or taking it for value or for collection substantially contributed to the customer's loss, however, the customer's liability may be reduced by the amount of the loss caused by the bank's negligence [UCC 3–406(b)].[8]

Suppose that CompuNet, Inc., uses a check-writing machine to write its payroll and business checks. A CompuNet employee uses the machine to create a check payable to himself for $10,000, and CompuNet's bank subsequently honors it. CompuNet requests the bank to recredit $10,000 to its account for incorrectly paying on a forged check. If the bank can show that CompuNet failed to take reasonable care in controlling access to the check-writing equipment, the bank will not be required to recredit its account for the amount of the forged check. If CompuNet can show that negligence on the part of the bank (or another person) contributed substantially to the loss, however, then CompuNet's liability may be reduced proportionately.

In the following case, an employee opened a bogus bank account and fraudulently deposited his employer's checks in it for years. The court had to determine if the bank should have requested written authorization from the company before opening the account.

---

6. Each year, check fraud costs banks many billions of dollars—more than the combined losses from credit-card fraud, theft from automated teller machines, and armed robberies.

7. *Lor-Mar/Toto, Inc. v. 1st Constitution Bank,* 376 N.J.Super. 520, 871 A.2d 110 (2005).

8. The unrevised Article 3 does not include a similar provision.

C A S E   22.1   Auto-Owners Insurance Co. v. Bank One
Supreme Court of Indiana, 2008. 879 N.E.2d 1086.

● **Background and Facts** Kenneth Wulf worked in the claims department of Auto-Owners Insurance Company for ten years. When the department received a check, a staff member would note it for the files and send it on to headquarters. Wulf opened a checking account at Bank One in the name of "Auto-Owners, Kenneth B. Wulf." Over eight years, he deposited $546,000 worth of

CASE 22.1 CONTINUED checks that he had stolen from Auto-Owners and had indorsed with a stamp that read "Auto-Owners Insurance Deposit Only." When the scam was finally discovered, Auto-Owners sued Bank One, contending that it had failed to exercise ordinary care in opening the account because it had not asked for documentation to show that Wulf was authorized to open an account in the name of Auto-Owners. The trial courts rejected that argument and granted summary judgment for Bank One. After an intermediate appellate court upheld the summary judgment, Auto-Owners appealed to the Indiana Supreme Court.

● **Decision and Rationale** Indiana's highest court affirmed the lower courts' decisions, finding that Bank One's conduct did not "substantially contribute" to bringing about the losses suffered by Auto-Owners. The bank breached no duty to the insurance company by opening Wulf's checking account. In such cases, the courts consider all of the facts surrounding the transactions that occurred. Here, the major reason for the losses suffered by Auto-Owners was its weak internal monitoring of its own files and the lack of controls in the handling of company checks. The bank did not worsen the situation by allowing Wulf to have a checking account.

● **The E-Commerce Dimension** *Would the situation have been different if Wulf had handled his account electronically rather than manually? Why or why not?*

● **The Legal Environment Dimension** *What reasonable steps could Auto-Owners have taken to prevent such internal fraud?*

Timely Examination of Bank Statements Required. Banks typically send or make available to their customers monthly statements detailing the activity of the customers' checking accounts. Banks are not obligated to include the original canceled checks themselves with the statement sent to the customer. If the bank does not send the canceled checks, however, it must provide the customer with information (check number, amount, and date of payment) on the statement that will allow the customer to reasonably identify each check that the bank has paid [UCC 4–406(a), (b)]. Sometimes, banks send photocopies of the canceled checks with the statement. If the bank retains the canceled checks, it must keep the checks—or legible copies of them—for seven years [UCC 4–406(b)]. The customer may obtain a canceled check (or a copy of the check) from the bank during this period of time.

The customer has a duty to promptly examine bank statements (and canceled checks or photocopies, if they are included with the statements) with reasonable care when the statements are received or made available to determine whether any payment was not authorized [UCC 4–406(c)]. The customer must report any alterations or forged signatures, including forged signatures of indorsers if discovered (to be discussed later). If the customer fails to fulfill this duty and the bank suffers a loss as a result, the customer will be liable for the loss [UCC 4–406(d)].

Consequences of Failing to Detect Forgeries. When a series of forgeries by the same wrongdoer has taken place, the UCC provides that the customer, to recover for all of the forged items, must have discovered and reported the first forged check to the bank within thirty calendar days of the receipt or availability of the bank statement (and canceled checks or copies, if they are included) [UCC 4–406(d)(2)]. Failure to notify the bank within this time period discharges the bank's liability for all forged checks that it pays prior to notification.

For example, Joseph Montanez, an employee and bookkeeper for Espresso Roma Corporation, used stolen computer software and blank checks to generate company checks on his home computer. The series of forged checks spanned a period of more than two years and totaled more than $330,000. When the bank statements containing the forged checks arrived in the mail, Montanez sorted through the statements and removed the checks so that the forgeries would go undetected. Eventually, Espresso Roma did discover the forgeries and asked the bank to recredit its account. The bank refused and litigation ensued. The court held that the bank was not liable for the forged checks because Espresso Roma failed to report the first forgeries within the UCC's time period of thirty days.[9]

---

9. *Espresso Roma Corp. v. Bank of America, N.A.*, 100 Cal.App.4th 525, 124 Cal.Rptr.2d 549 (2002).

When the Bank Is Also Negligent. In one situation, a bank customer can escape liability, at least in part, for failing to notify the bank of forged or altered checks within the required thirty-day period. If the customer can prove that the bank was also negligent—that is, that the bank failed to exercise ordinary care—then the bank will also be liable, and the loss will be allocated between the bank and the customer on the basis of comparative negligence [UCC 4–406(e)]. In other words, even though a customer may have been negligent, the bank may still have to recredit the customer's account for a portion of the loss if the bank failed to exercise ordinary care.

Section 3–103(a)(7) of the UCC defines *ordinary care* as the "observance of reasonable commercial standards, prevailing in the area in which [a] person is located, with respect to the business in which that person is engaged." As mentioned earlier, it is customary in the banking industry to manually examine signatures only on checks over a certain amount (such as $1,000, $2,500, or some higher amount). Thus, if a bank, in accordance with prevailing banking standards, fails to examine a signature on a particular check, the bank may or may not have breached its duty to exercise ordinary care.

Regardless of the degree of care exercised by the customer or the bank, the UCC places an absolute time limit on the liability of a bank for paying a check with a forged customer signature. A customer who fails to report her or his forged signature within one year from the date that the statement was made available for inspection loses the legal right to have the bank recredit her or his account [UCC 4–406(f)].

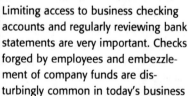

PREVENTING LEGAL DISPUTES

Limiting access to business checking accounts and regularly reviewing bank statements are very important. Checks forged by employees and embezzlement of company funds are disturbingly common in today's business world. One of the best ways to avoid significant losses due to forgery or embezzlement, and to prevent litigation over a bank's liability for forged items, is to keep a watchful eye on business accounts and always be on the lookout for suspicious transactions. Business owners and managers should limit the number of persons who have access to the bank accounts and bank statements of their business. Company checkbooks or signature stamps should never be left in public or unsecured areas. Passwords should be used to limit access to computerized check-writing software. Businesspersons should also review monthly bank statements in a timely fashion and report any discrepancies to the bank.

The UCC's rules pertaining to a series of forged checks are not flexible—by failing to report forgeries within thirty days of the first statement in which a forged item appears, the account holder loses the right to hold the bank liable. Businesspersons should be careful not to do anything that could be construed as negligence contributing to a forgery (or to a subsequent alteration of a check, to be discussed shortly).

Other Parties from Whom the Bank May Recover As noted earlier, a forged signature on a check has no legal effect as the signature of a drawer; a forged signature, however, is effective as the signature of the unauthorized signer [UCC 3–403(a)]. Therefore, when a bank pays a check on which the drawer's signature is forged, the bank has a right to recover from the party who forged the signature. The bank may also have a right to recover from a party (its customer or a collecting bank—to be discussed later in this chapter) who transferred a check bearing a forged drawer's signature and received payment (see the discussion of transfer warranties discussed in Chapter 26). This right is limited, however, in that the bank cannot recover from a person who took the check in good faith and for value or who in good faith changed position in reliance on the payment or acceptance [UCC 3–418(c)].

Checks Bearing Forged Indorsements

A bank that pays a customer's check bearing a forged indorsement must recredit the customer's account or be liable to the customer (drawer) for breach of contract. Suppose that Carlo issues a $500 check "to the order of Sophia." Marcello steals the check, forges Sophia's indorsement, and cashes the check. When the check reaches Carlo's bank, the bank pays it and debits Carlo's account. The bank must recredit Carlo's account for the $500 because it failed to carry out Carlo's order to pay "to the order of Sophia" [UCC 4–401(a)]. (Carlo's bank will in turn recover—under the principle of breach of warranty—from the bank that cashed the check [UCC 4–207(a)(2)].)

Eventually, *the loss usually falls on the first party to take the instrument bearing the forged indorsement* because, as discussed in Chapter 26, a forged indorsement does not transfer title. Thus, whoever takes an instrument with a forged indorsement cannot become a holder.

The customer, in any event, has a duty to report forged indorsements promptly on discovery or notice. Failure to report forged indorsements, whether discovered or not, within a three-year period after the forged items become available to the customer relieves the bank of liability [UCC 4–111].[10]

Altered Checks

The customer's instruction to the bank is to pay the exact amount on the face of the check to the holder. The bank has an implicit duty to examine checks before making final payments. If it fails to detect an alteration, it is liable to its customer for the loss because it did not pay as the customer ordered. The loss is the difference between the original amount of the check and the amount actually paid. Suppose that a check written for $11 is raised to $111. The customer's account will be charged $11 (the amount the customer ordered the bank to pay). The bank will normally be responsible for the $100 [UCC 4–401(d)(1)].

Customer Negligence As in a situation involving a forged drawer's signature, a customer's negligence can shift the loss when payment is made on an altered check (unless the bank was also negligent). A common example occurs when a person carelessly writes a check, leaving large gaps around the numbers and words where additional numbers and words can be inserted (see Exhibit 22–4).

Similarly, a person who signs a check and leaves the dollar amount for someone else to fill in is barred from protesting when the bank unknowingly and in good faith pays whatever amount is shown [UCC 4–401(d)(2)]. Finally, if the bank can trace its loss on successive altered checks to the customer's failure to discover the initial alteration, then the bank can reduce its liability for reimbursing the customer's account [UCC 4–406].[11] The law governing the customer's duty to examine monthly statements and canceled checks, and to discover and report alterations to the bank, is the same as that applied to a forged drawer's signature.

In every situation involving a forged drawer's signature or an alteration, a bank must observe reasonable commercial standards of care in paying on a customer's checks [UCC 4–406(e)]. The customer's contributory negligence can be asserted only if the bank has exercised ordinary care.

---

10. This is a general statute of limitations for all actions under Article 4; it provides that any lawsuit must be begun within three years of the time that the cause of action arises.

11. The bank's defense is the same whether the successive payments were made on a forged drawer's signature or on altered checks. The bank must prove that prompt notice would have prevented its loss. For example, notification might have alerted the bank not to pay further items or might have enabled it to catch the forger.

EXHIBIT 22–4 • **A Poorly Filled-Out Check**

Other Parties from Whom the Bank May Recover The bank is entitled to recover the amount of loss (including expenses and any loss of interest) from the transferor who, by presenting the check for payment, warrants that the check has not been altered.[12]

There are two exceptions, however. If the bank is the drawer (as it is on a cashier's check and a teller's check), it cannot recover on this ground from the presenting party if the party is a holder in due course (HDC) acting in good faith [UCC 3–417(a)(2), 4–208(a)(2)]. The reason is that an instrument's drawer is in a better position than an HDC to know whether the instrument has been altered.

Similarly, an HDC, acting in good faith in presenting a certified check for payment, does not warrant to the check's certifier that the check was not altered before the HDC acquired it [UCC 3–417(a)(2), 4–208(a)(2)]. Consider an example. Alan, the drawer, draws a check for $500 payable to Pam, the payee. Pam alters the amount to $5,000. National City Bank, the drawee, certifies the check for $5,000. Pam negotiates the check to Don, an HDC. The drawee bank pays Don $5,000. On discovering the mistake, the bank cannot recover from Don the $4,500 paid by mistake, even though the bank was not in a superior position to detect the alteration. This is in accord with the purpose of certification, which is to obtain the definite obligation of a bank to honor a definite instrument. For a synopsis of the rules governing the honoring of checks, see *Concept Summary 22.1*.

Accepting Deposits

A bank has a duty to its customer to accept the customer's deposits of cash and checks. When checks are deposited, the bank must make the funds represented by those checks available within certain time frames. A bank also has a duty to collect payment on any checks payable or indorsed to its customer and deposited by the customer into his or her account. Cash deposits made in U.S. currency are received into the customer's

account without being subject to further collection procedures.

Availability Schedule for Deposited Checks

The Expedited Funds Availability Act of 1987[13] and Regulation CC,[14] which was issued by the Federal Reserve Board of Governors (the *Federal Reserve System* will be discussed shortly) to implement the act, require that any local check deposited must be available for withdrawal by check or as cash within one business day from the date of deposit. A check is classified as a local check if the first bank to receive the check for payment and the bank on which the check is drawn are located in the same check-processing region (regions are designated by the Federal Reserve Board of Governors). For nonlocal checks, the funds must be available for withdrawal within not more than five business days. (Note that eventually, under the Check 21 Act discussed later in this chapter, a bank will have to credit a customer's account as soon as the bank receives the funds.)

In addition, the act requires the following:

1. That funds be available on the next business day for cash deposits and wire transfers, government checks, the first $100 of a day's check deposits, cashier's checks, certified checks, and checks for which the banks receiving and paying the checks are branches of the same institution.

2. That the first $100 of any deposit be available for cash withdrawal on the opening of the *next business day* after deposit. If a local check is deposited, the next $400 is to be available for withdrawal by no later than 5:00 P.M. on the next business day. If, for example, you deposit a local check for $500 on Monday, you can withdraw $100 in cash at the opening of the business day on Tuesday, and an additional $400 must be available for withdrawal by no later than 5:00 P.M. on Wednesday.

A different availability schedule applies to deposits made at *nonproprietary* automated teller machines (ATMs). These are ATMs that are not owned or operated by the bank receiving the deposits. Basically, a five-day hold is permitted on all deposits, including cash deposits, that are made at nonproprietary ATMs. Other exceptions also exist. For example, a banking

---

12. Usually, the party presenting an instrument for payment is the payee, a holder, a bank customer, or a collecting bank. A bank's customers include its account holders, which may include other banks [UCC 4–104(a)(5)]. As will be discussed later in this chapter, a *collecting bank* is any bank handling an item for collection except the bank on which the check is drawn [UCC 4–105(5)].

13. 12 U.S.C. Sections 4001–4010.
14. 12 C.F.R. Sections 229.1–229.42.

institution has eight days to make funds available in new accounts (those open less than thirty days) and has an extra four days on deposits that exceed $5,000 (except deposits of government and cashier's checks).

Interest-Bearing Accounts

Under the Truth-in-Savings Act (TISA) of 1991[15] and Regulation DD,[16] the act's implementing regulation, banks must pay interest based on the full balance of a

15. 12 U.S.C. Sections 4301–4313.
16. 12 C.F.R. Sections 230.1–230.9.

customer's interest-bearing account each day. For example, Vogel has an interest-bearing checking account with First National Bank. Vogel keeps a $500 balance in the account for most of the month but withdraws all but $50 the day before the bank posts the interest. The bank cannot pay interest on just the $50. The interest must be adjusted to account for the entire month, including those days when Vogel's balance was higher.

Before opening a deposit account, new customers must be provided certain information in a brochure, pamphlet, or other handout. The information, which

CONCEPT SUMMARY 22.1
Honoring Checks

Situation	Basic Rules
WRONGFUL DISHONOR [UCC 4–402]	The bank is liable to its customer for actual damages proved if it wrongfully dishonors a check due to mistake.
OVERDRAFT [UCC 4–401]	The bank has a right to charge a customer's account for any item properly payable, even if the charge results in an overdraft.
POSTDATED CHECK [UCC 4–401]	The bank may charge a postdated check against a customer's account, unless the customer notifies the bank of the postdating in time to allow the bank to act on the notice before the bank commits itself to pay on the check.
STALE CHECK [UCC 4–404]	The bank is not obligated to pay an uncertified check presented more than six months after its date, but the bank may do so in good faith without liability.
DEATH OR INCOMPETENCE OF A CUSTOMER [UCC 4–405]	So long as the bank does not know of the death or incompetence of a customer, the bank can pay an item without liability. Even with knowledge of a customer's death, a bank can honor or certify checks (in the absence of a stop-payment order) for ten days after the date of the customer's death.
STOP-PAYMENT ORDER [UCC 4–403]	The customer (or a "person authorized to draw on the account") must institute a stop-payment order in time for the bank to have a reasonable opportunity to act. Oral orders (if allowed) are binding for only fourteen days unless they are confirmed in writing. Written orders are effective for only six months, unless renewed in writing. The bank is liable for wrongful payment over a timely stop-payment order to the extent that the customer suffers a loss. A customer has no right to stop payment on a certified check or an accepted draft and can be held liable for stopping payment on any check without a valid legal ground.
FORGED SIGNATURE OR ALTERATION [UCC 4–406]	The customer has a duty to examine account statements with reasonable care on receipt and to notify the bank promptly of any unauthorized signatures or alterations. On a series of unauthorized signatures or alterations by the same wrongdoer, examination and report must be made within thirty calendar days of receipt of the first statement containing a forged or altered item. The customer's failure to comply with these rules releases the bank from liability unless the bank failed to exercise reasonable care; in that event, liability may be apportioned according to a comparative negligence standard. Regardless of care or lack of care, the customer is *estopped* (prevented) from holding the bank liable after one year for unauthorized customer signatures or alterations and after three years for unauthorized indorsements.

must also appear in all advertisements, includes the following:

1. The minimum balance required to open an account and to be paid interest.
2. The interest, stated in terms of the annual percentage yield on the account.
3. How interest is calculated.
4. Any fees, charges, and penalties and how they are calculated.

Also, under the TISA and Regulation DD, a customer's monthly statement must declare the interest earned on the account, any fees that were charged, how the fees were calculated, and the number of days that the statement covers.

The Traditional Collection Process

Usually, deposited checks involve parties who do business at different banks, but sometimes checks are written between customers of the same bank. Either situation brings into play the bank collection process as it operates within the statutory framework of Article 4 of the UCC. Note that the check-collection process described in the following subsections will be modified in the future as the banking industry implements the Check Clearing in the 21st Century Act,[17] also known as the Check 21 Act, which will be discussed shortly.

Designations of Banks Involved in the Collection Process The first bank to receive a check for payment is the **depositary bank.**[18] For example, when a person deposits a tax-refund check from the Internal Revenue Service into a personal checking account at the local bank, that bank is the depositary bank. The bank on which a check is drawn (the drawee bank) is called the **payor bank.** Any bank except the payor bank that handles a check during some phase of the collection process is a **collecting bank.** Any bank except the payor bank or the depositary bank to which an item is transferred in the course of this collection process is called an **intermediary bank.**

During the collection process, any bank can take on one or more of the various roles of depositary, payor, collecting, or intermediary bank. To illustrate: A buyer in New York writes a check on her New York bank and sends it to a seller in San Francisco. The seller deposits the check in her San Francisco bank account. The seller's bank is both a *depositary bank* and a *collecting bank.* The buyer's bank in New York is the *payor bank.* As the check travels from San Francisco to New York, any *collecting bank* handling the item in the collection process (other than the ones acting as depositary bank and payor bank) is also called an *intermediary bank.* Exhibit 22–5 illustrates how various banks function in the collection process.

Check Collection between Customers of the Same Bank An item that is payable by the depositary bank that receives it (which in this situation is also the payor bank) is called an "on-us item." If the bank does not dishonor the check by the opening of the second banking day following its receipt, the check is considered paid [UCC 4–215(e)(2)]. For example, Oswald and Martin both have checking accounts at First State Bank. On Monday morning, Martin deposits into his own checking account a $300 check from Oswald. That same day, the bank issues Martin a "provisional credit" for $300. When the bank opens on Wednesday, Oswald's check is considered honored, and Martin's provisional credit becomes a final payment.

Check Collection between Customers of Different Banks Once a depositary bank receives a check, it must arrange to present the check, either directly or through intermediary banks, to the appropriate payor bank. Each bank in the collection chain must pass the check on before midnight of the next banking day following its receipt [UCC 4–202(b)].[19] A "banking day" is any part of a day that the bank is open to carry on substantially all of its banking functions. Thus, if only a bank's drive-through facilities are open, a check deposited on Saturday would not trigger a bank's midnight deadline until the following Monday. When the check reaches the payor bank, that bank is liable for the face amount of the check, unless the payor bank dishonors the check or

---

17. 12 U.S.C. Sections 5001–5018.
18. All definitions in this section are found in UCC 4–105. The terms *depositary* and *depository* have different meanings in the banking context. A depository bank refers to a *physical place* (a bank or other institution) in which deposits or funds are held or stored.

---

19. A bank may take a "reasonably longer time" in certain circumstances, such as when the bank's computer system is down because of a power failure [UCC 4–202(b)].

EXHIBIT 22–5 • **The Traditional Check-Collection Process**

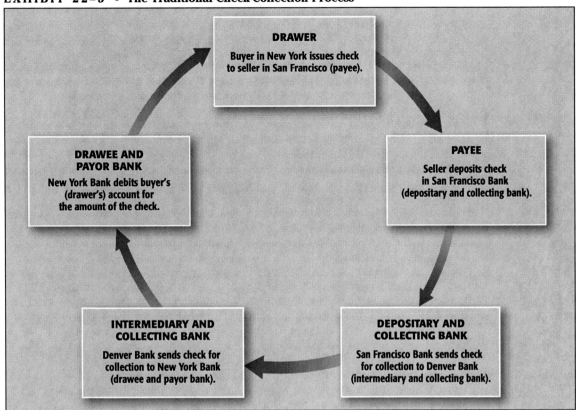

DRAWER

Buyer in New York issues check to seller in San Francisco (payee).

PAYEE

Seller deposits check in San Francisco Bank (depositary and collecting bank).

DEPOSITARY AND COLLECTING BANK

San Francisco Bank sends check for collection to Denver Bank (intermediary and collecting bank).

INTERMEDIARY AND COLLECTING BANK

Denver Bank sends check for collection to New York Bank (drawee and payor bank).

DRAWEE AND PAYOR BANK

New York Bank debits buyer's (drawer's) account for the amount of the check.

returns it by midnight of the next banking day following receipt [UCC 4–302].[20]

Because of this deadline and because banks need to maintain an even work flow in the many items they handle daily, the UCC permits what is called *deferred posting*. According to UCC 4–108, "a bank may fix an afternoon hour of 2:00 P.M. or later as a cutoff hour for

the handling of money and items and the making of entries on its books." Any checks received after that hour "may be treated as being received at the opening of the next banking day." Thus, if a bank's "cutoff hour" is 3:00 P.M., a check received by a payor bank at 4:00 P.M. on Monday will be deferred for posting until Tuesday. In this situation, the payor bank's deadline will be midnight Wednesday.

Does a delay of more than one month in a bank's notice to its customer that a check deposited in his account is counterfeit reduce the customer's liability for overdrafts in the account? That was the customer's contention in the following case.

---

20. Most checks are cleared by a computerized process, and communication and computer facilities may fail because of electrical outages, equipment malfunction, or other conditions. If such conditions arise and a bank fails to meet its midnight deadline, the bank is "excused" from liability if the bank has exercised "such diligence as the circumstances require" [UCC 4–109(d)].

C A S E **22.2 Bank One, N.A. v. Dunn**

Court of Appeal of Louisiana, Second Circuit, 2006. 927 So.2d 645.

• **Background and Facts** Floyd Dunn, a U.S. citizen, was hired to lobby in the United States for Zaire (now named the Democratic Republic of the Congo). After three years of efforts on Zaire's behalf, Dunn submitted a bill for $500,000. Instead of paying, Zaire agreed to trade computers to Dunn, who was to sell them to Nigeria for $32.1 million. "Senator Frank," who claimed to be

CASE CONTINUES

CASE 22.2 CONTINUED from Nigeria, told Dunn that he would receive his $32.1 million after he paid "back taxes" supposedly due to that country. Frank offered to facilitate the payments. Dunn gave Frank the number of his account at Bank One, N.A., in Shreveport, Louisiana. As part of the deal, on August 1, 2001, a check in the amount of $315,000 drawn on the account of Argenbright Security, Inc., at First Union National Bank of Georgia was deposited into Dunn's account—which had never held more than $5,000—and sent out for collection. Because it contained an incorrect routing number, its processing was delayed. Meanwhile, on Frank's instructions, Dunn wired $277,000 to an account at a Virginia bank. On September 24, the $315,000 check was returned to Bank One as counterfeit. Bank One filed a suit in a Louisiana state court against Dunn, alleging that he owed $281,019.11, the amount by which his account was overdrawn. The court issued a summary judgment in Bank One's favor. Dunn appealed to a state intermediate appellate court.

● **Decision and Rationale** The state intermediate appellate court affirmed the lower court's judgment. Even if Dunn had received notice of the counterfeit status of the check from Bank One before September 24, he would not have been able to collect the amount of the check from Argenbright Security. In the collection process, a bank is required to pass on a check before midnight of the next banking day following the check's receipt. The appellate court acknowledged that under UCC 4–202, the bank must "exercise ordinary care in sending a notice of dishonor after learning that the item has not been paid or accepted." The court explained that "notifying the customer of dishonor after the bank's midnight deadline may constitute the exercise of ordinary care if the bank took proper action within a reasonably longer time." Of course, the bank is liable for its failure to exercise ordinary care. In that situation, the measure of damages is the amount of the check "reduced by an amount that could not have been realized by the exercise of ordinary care." In other words, if a check could not have been collected even by the use of ordinary care, the recovery for a failure to exercise ordinary care is reduced by the amount of the uncollectible check. Thus, in this case, "Dunn's liability is not diminished because of Bank One's delay in notifying Dunn that the check was counterfeit. Even if Dunn had received earlier notice from Bank One that the check was counterfeit, he still had no recourse against Argenbright Security. The $315,000 was uncollectible against Argenbright Security."

● **The Ethical Dimension** *Does a bank have a duty to protect its customers from their own naïveté, as exemplified in this case by Dunn's trusting someone he did not know with his bank account information? Why or why not?*

● **The E-Commerce Dimension** *How would electronic check presentment (to be discussed shortly) have affected the timeliness of the events in this case and ultimately the outcome?*

How the Federal Reserve System Clears Checks The **Federal Reserve System** is a network of twelve district banks, which are located around the country and headed by the Federal Reserve Board of Governors. Most banks in the United States have Federal Reserve accounts. The Federal Reserve System has greatly simplified the check-collection process by acting as a **clearinghouse**—a system or a place where banks exchange checks and drafts drawn on each other and settle daily balances.

Suppose that Pamela Moy of Philadelphia writes a check to Jeanne Sutton of San Francisco. When Jeanne receives the check in the mail, she deposits it in her bank. Her bank then deposits the check in the Federal Reserve Bank of San Francisco, which transfers it to the Federal Reserve Bank of Philadelphia. That Federal Reserve bank then sends the check to Moy's bank, which deducts the amount of the check from Moy's account.

Electronic Check Presentment In the past, most checks were processed manually—the employees of each bank in the collection chain would physically handle each check that passed through the bank for collection or payment. Today, however, most checks are processed electronically. In contrast to manual check processing, which can take days, *electronic check presentment* can be done on the day of the deposit. With electronic check presentment, items may be encoded with information (such as the amount of the check) that can be read and processed by other banks' computers. In some situations, a check is retained at its place of deposit, and only its image or description is presented for payment under an electronic presentment agreement [UCC 4–110].[21]

A person who encodes information on an item after the item has been issued warrants to any subsequent bank or payor that the encoded information is correct [UCC 4–209]. This is also true for a person who retains an item while transmitting its image or information describing it as presentation for payment. This

person warrants that the retention and presentment of the item comply with a Federal Reserve or other agreement.

Regulation CC provides that a returned check must be encoded with the routing number of the depositary bank, the amount of the check, and other information and adds that this "does not affect a paying bank's responsibility to return a check within the deadlines required by the UCC." What happens when a payor bank fails to properly encode an item and thereby causes the check to be returned to the depositary bank after the required deadline? That was the question in the following case.

---

21. UCC 4–110 assumes that no bank will participate in an electronic presentment program without an express agreement (which is no longer true since Check 21 went into effect).

C A S E **22.3** **NBT Bank, N.A. v. First National Community Bank**
United States Court of Appeals, Third Circuit, 2004. 393 F.3d 404.

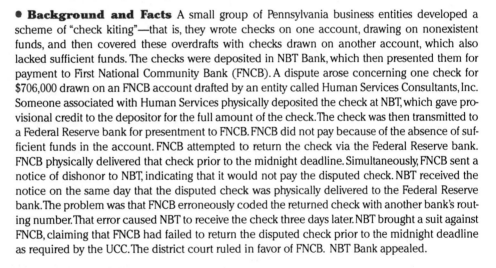

● **Background and Facts** A small group of Pennsylvania business entities developed a scheme of "check kiting"—that is, they wrote checks on one account, drawing on nonexistent funds, and then covered these overdrafts with checks drawn on another account, which also lacked sufficient funds. The checks were deposited in NBT Bank, which then presented them for payment to First National Community Bank (FNCB). A dispute arose concerning one check for $706,000 drawn on an FNCB account drafted by an entity called Human Services Consultants, Inc. Someone associated with Human Services physically deposited the check at NBT, which gave provisional credit to the depositor for the full amount of the check. The check was then transmitted to a Federal Reserve bank for presentment to FNCB. FNCB did not pay because of the absence of sufficient funds in the account. FNCB attempted to return the check via the Federal Reserve bank. FNCB physically delivered that check prior to the midnight deadline. Simultaneously, FNCB sent a notice of dishonor to NBT, indicating that it would not pay the disputed check. NBT received the notice on the same day that the disputed check was physically delivered to the Federal Reserve bank. The problem was that FNCB erroneously coded the returned check with another bank's routing number. That error caused NBT to receive the check three days later. NBT brought a suit against FNCB, claiming that FNCB had failed to return the disputed check prior to the midnight deadline as required by the UCC. The district court ruled in favor of FNCB. NBT Bank appealed.

● **Decision and Rationale** The Court of Appeals for the Third Circuit affirmed the district court's decision. The appellate court pointed out that Federal Reserve "Regulation CC" complemented, but did not replace, the requirements of Article 4 of the UCC. In other words, Federal Reserve regulations may vary the terms of the UCC. Regulation CC outlines the measure of damages when a bank fails to exercise ordinary care. These damages are calculated by the amount of the loss incurred, up to the amount of the check, reduced by the amount of the loss that the plaintiff bank would have incurred even if the defendant bank had exercised ordinary care. The plaintiff bank, NBT, suffered no loss as a result of FNCB's encoding error. Therefore, NBT could not recover from FNCB.

● **What If the Facts Were Different?** *How might the result in this case have been different if NBT had committed the encoding error and FNCB had suffered the loss?*

● **The Ethical Dimension** *If a bank warrants that the information it encoded on an item is correct and FNCB committed an error in encoding, then why did the court not hold FNCB liable for the amount of the check?*

Check Clearing and the Check 21 Act

In the traditional collection process, paper checks had to be physically transported before they could be cleared. To streamline this costly and time-consuming process and to improve the overall efficiency of the nation's payment system, Congress passed the Check Clearing in the 21st Century Act[22] (Check 21).

Purpose of Check 21 Prior to the implementation of Check 21, banks had to present the original paper check for payment in the absence of an agreement for presentment in some other form. Although the UCC authorizes banks to use other means of presentment, such as electronic presentment, a broadbased system of electronic presentment failed to develop because it required agreements among individual banks. Check 21 has changed this situation by creating a new negotiable instrument called a *substitute check*. Although the act did not require any bank to change its current check-collection practices, the creation of substitute checks will certainly facilitate the use of electronic check processing over time.

What Is a Substitute Check? A substitute check is a paper reproduction of the front and back of an original check that contains all of the same information required on checks for automated processing. Banks create a substitute check from a digital image of an original check. Every substitute check must include the following statement somewhere on it: "This a legal copy of your check. You can use it in the same way you would use the original check."

In essence, those financial institutions that exchange digital images of checks do not have to send the original paper checks. They can simply transmit the information electronically and replace the original checks with the paper reproductions—the substitute checks. Banks that do not exchange checks electronically are required to accept substitute checks in the same way that they accept original checks.

The Gradual Elimination of Paper Checks
Because financial institutions must accept substitute checks as if they were original checks, the original checks will no longer be needed and will probably be destroyed after their digital images are created. By eliminating the original check after a substitute check is created, the financial system can prevent the check from being paid twice. Also, eliminating original checks and retaining only digital images will reduce the expense of storage and retrieval. Nevertheless, at least for quite a while, not all checks will be converted to substitute checks. That means that if a bank returns canceled checks to deposit holders at the end of each month, some of those returned checks may be substitute checks, and some may be original canceled paper checks.

Since the passage of Check 21, financial institution customers cannot demand an original canceled check. Check 21 is a federal law and applies to all financial institutions, other businesses, and individuals in the United States. In other words, no customers can opt out of Check 21 and demand that their original canceled checks be returned with their monthly statements. Also, businesses and individuals must accept a substitute check as proof of payment because it is the legal equivalent of the original check.

Reduced "Float" Time Sometimes, individuals and businesses write checks even though they have insufficient funds in their accounts to cover those checks. Such check writers are relying on "float," or the time between when a check is written and when the amount is actually deducted from their account. When all checks had to be physically transported, the float time could be several days, but as Check 21 is implemented, the time required to process checks will be substantially reduced—and so will float time. Thus, account holders who plan to cover their checks after writing them may experience unexpected overdrafts.

Though consumers and businesses will no longer be able to rely on float time, they may benefit in another way from Check 21. The Expedited Funds Availability Act (mentioned earlier in this chapter) requires that the Federal Reserve Board revise the availability schedule for funds from deposited checks to correspond to reductions in check-processing time. Therefore, as the speed of check processing increases under Check 21, the Federal Reserve Board will reduce the maximum time that a bank can hold funds from deposited checks before making them available to the depositor. Thus, account holders will have faster access to their deposited funds.

Electronic Fund Transfers

The application of computer technology to banking, in the form of electronic fund transfer systems, has helped to relieve banking institutions of the burden of

---

22. 12 U.S.C. Section 5001, Pub. L. No. 108-100.

having to move mountains of paperwork to process fund transfers. An **electronic fund transfer (EFT)** is a transfer of funds made by the use of an electronic terminal, a telephone, a computer, or magnetic tape. The law governing EFTs depends on the type of transfer involved. Consumer fund transfers are governed by the Electronic Fund Transfer Act (EFTA) of 1978.[23] Commercial fund transfers are governed by Article 4A of the UCC.

The benefits of electronic banking are obvious. Automatic payments, direct deposits, and other fund transfers are now made electronically; no physical transfers of cash, checks, or other negotiable instruments are involved. Not surprisingly, though, electronic banking can also pose difficulties. For example, it is difficult to issue stop-payment orders with electronic banking. In addition, fewer records are available to prove or disprove that a transaction took place, and the possibilities for tampering with a person's private banking information have increased.

Types of EFT Systems

Most banks today offer EFT services to their customers. The following are the four most common types of EFT systems used by bank customers:

1. *Automated teller machines* (ATMs)—The machines are connected online to the bank's computers. A customer inserts a **debit card** (a plastic card, also called an *ATM card*) issued by the bank and keys in a *personal identification number* (PIN) to access her or his accounts and conduct banking transactions.
2. *Point-of-sale systems*—Online terminals allow consumers to transfer funds to merchants to pay for purchases using a debit card.
3. *Direct deposits and withdrawals*—Customers can authorize the bank to allow another party, such as the government or an employer, to make direct deposits into their accounts. Similarly, a customer can request the bank to make automatic payments to a third party at regular, recurrent intervals from the customer's funds (insurance premiums or loan payments, for example).
4. *Internet payment systems*—Many financial institutions permit their customers to access the institution's computer system via the Internet and direct a transfer of funds between accounts or pay a particular bill, such as a utility bill. Payments can be made on a onetime or a recurring basis.

Consumer Fund Transfers

The Electronic Fund Transfer Act (EFTA) provides a basic framework for the rights, liabilities, and responsibilities of users of EFT systems. Additionally, the act gave the Federal Reserve Board authority to issue rules and regulations to help implement the act's provisions. The Federal Reserve Board's implemental regulation is called **Regulation E.**

The EFTA governs financial institutions that offer electronic transfers of funds involving customer accounts. The types of accounts covered include checking accounts, savings accounts, and any other asset accounts established for personal, family, or household purposes. Telephone transfers are covered by the EFTA only if they are made in accordance with a prearranged plan under which periodic or recurring transfers are contemplated.

Disclosure Requirements The EFTA is essentially a disclosure law benefiting consumers. The act requires financial institutions to inform consumers of their rights and responsibilities, including those listed here, with respect to EFT systems.

1. If a customer's debit card is lost or stolen and used without her or his permission, the customer may be required to pay no more than $50. The customer, however, must notify the bank of the loss or theft within two days of learning about it. Otherwise, the customer's liability increases to $500. The customer may be liable for more than $500 if she or he does not report the unauthorized use within sixty days after it appears on the customer's statement.
2. The customer has sixty days to discover and notify the bank of any error on the monthly statement. The bank then has ten days to investigate and must report its conclusions to the customer in writing. If the bank takes longer than ten days to do so, it must return the disputed amount to the customer's account until it finds the error. If there is no error, however, the customer must return the funds to the bank.
3. The bank must furnish receipts for transactions made through computer terminals, but it is not obligated to do so for telephone transfers.
4. The bank must provide a monthly statement for every month in which there is an electronic transfer of funds. Otherwise, the bank must provide a statement every quarter. The statement must show the amount and date of the transfer, the names of the retailers or other third parties involved, the

---

23. 15 U.S.C. Sections 1693–1693r. The EFTA amended Title IX of the Consumer Credit Protection Act.

location or identification of the terminal, and the fees. Additionally, the statement must give an address and a phone number for inquiries and error notices.

5. Any preauthorized payment for utility bills and insurance premiums can be stopped three days before the scheduled transfer if the customer notifies the financial institution orally or in writing. (The institution may require the customer to provide written confirmation within fourteen days of an oral notification.) For other EFT transactions, however, the EFTA does not provide for the reversal of an electronic transfer of funds once the transfer has occurred.

Unauthorized Transfers Because of the vulnerability of EFT systems to fraudulent activities, the EFTA clearly defined what constitutes an unauthorized transfer. Under the act, a transfer is unauthorized if (1) it is initiated by a person who has no actual authority to initiate the transfer, (2) the consumer receives no benefit from it, and (3) the consumer did not furnish the person "with the card, code, or other means of access" to his or her account. Gaining unauthorized access to an EFT system constitutes a federal felony, and those convicted may be fined up to $10,000 and sentenced to as long as ten years in prison.

Violations and Damages Banks are held to strict compliance with the terms of the EFTA. If they fail to adhere to the letter of the law of the EFTA, they will be held liable for the violation. For a bank's violation of the EFTA, a consumer may recover both actual damages (including attorneys' fees and costs) and punitive damages of not less than $100 and not more than $1,000. In a class-action suit, the punitive-damages award can be up to $500,000 or 1 percent of the institution's net worth. (Unlike actual damages, punitive damages are assessed to punish a defendant or to deter similar wrongdoers.) Failure to investigate an error in good faith makes the bank liable for treble damages (three times the amount of damages). Even when a customer has sustained no actual damage, the bank may be liable for legal costs and punitive damages if it fails to follow the proper procedures outlined by the EFTA in regard to error resolution.

Commercial Fund Transfers

Funds are also transferred electronically "by wire" between commercial parties. In fact, the dollar volume of payments made via wire transfers is more than $1 trillion a day—an amount that far exceeds the dol-

lar volume of payments made by other means. The two major wire payment systems are the Federal Reserve wire transfer network (Fedwire) and the New York Clearing House Interbank Payments Systems (CHIPS).

Commercial wire transfers are governed by Article 4A of the UCC, which has been adopted by most of the states. Article 4A uses the term *funds transfer* rather than *wire transfer* to describe the overall payment transaction. The full text of Article 4A is presented in Appendix C.

As an example of the type of funds transfer covered by Article 4A, assume that American Industries, Inc., owes $5 million to Chandler Corporation. Instead of sending Chandler a check or some other instrument that would enable Chandler to obtain payment, American Industries tells its bank, North Bank, to credit $5 million to Chandler's account in South Bank. North Bank debits American Industries' North Bank account and wires $5 million to South Bank with instructions to credit $5 million to Chandler's South Bank account. In more complex transactions, additional banks would be involved.

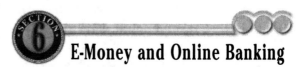

E-Money and Online Banking

New forms of electronic payments (e-payments) have the potential to replace *physical* cash—coins and paper currency—with *virtual* cash in the form of electronic impulses. This is the unique promise of **digital cash,** which consists of funds stored on microchips and other computer devices. Digital cash is increasingly being used to launder money, as discussed in this chapter's *Emerging Trends* feature on pages 520 and 521.

Various forms of electronic money, or **e-money,** are emerging. The simplest kind of e-money system uses *stored-value cards.* These are plastic cards embossed with magnetic strips containing magnetically encoded data. In some applications, a stored-value card can be used only to purchase specific goods and services offered by the card issuer.

Another form of e-money is the smart card. **Smart cards** are plastic cards containing computer microchips that can hold much more information than magnetic strips. A smart card carries and processes security programming. This capability gives smart cards a technical advantage over stored-value cards. The microprocessors on smart cards can also authenticate the validity of transactions. Retailers can program electronic cash registers to confirm the authenticity of a smart card by examining a unique digital signature stored on its microchip. (Digital signatures were discussed in Chapter 19.)

Online Banking Services

Increasingly, many bank customers are conducting at least part of their banking online. Today, most online bank customers use three kinds of services. One of the most popular is bill consolidation and payment. Another is transferring funds among accounts (which may often also be accomplished by phone or through an ATM). The third is applying for loans, which many banks permit customers to do via the Internet. Customers typically must appear in person to finalize the terms of a loan, however.

Two important banking activities generally are not yet available online: depositing and withdrawing funds. With smart cards, people could transfer funds on the Internet, thereby effectively transforming their personal computers into ATMs. Many observers believe that people will eventually be introduced to e-money and smart cards through online banking.

Since the late 1990s, several banks have operated exclusively on the Internet. These "virtual banks" have no physical branch offices. Because few individuals are equipped to send funds to virtual banks via smart-card technology, the virtual banks have accepted deposits through physical delivery systems, such as the U.S. Postal Service, FedEx, UPS, or DHL.

Regulatory Compliance

Banks have an interest in promoting the widespread use of online banking because it has significant potential for reducing costs and thus increasing profits. As in other areas of cyberspace, however, determining how laws apply to online banking activities can be difficult.

The Home Mortgage Disclosure Act[24] and the Community Reinvestment Act (CRA) of 1977,[25] for example, require a bank to define its market area and also to provide information about its deposits and loans. Under the CRA, banks establish market areas situated next to their branch offices. The banks map these areas using boundaries defined by counties or standard metropolitan areas and annually review the maps. The purpose of these requirements is to prevent discrimination in lending practices.

How does a successful "cyberbank" delineate its community? If, for example, Bank of Internet becomes a tremendous success, does it really have any physical communities? Will the Federal Reserve Board simply allow a written description of a cybercommunity for Internet customers? Such regulatory issues are new, challenging, and certain to become more complicated as Internet banking widens its scope internationally.

Privacy Protection

At the present time, it is not clear which, if any, laws apply to the security of e-money payment information and e-money issuers' financial records. This is partly because it is not clear whether e-money issuers fit within the traditional definition of a financial institution.

E-Money Payment Information The Federal Reserve has decided not to impose Regulation E, which governs certain electronic fund transfers, on e-money transactions. Federal laws prohibiting unauthorized access to electronic communications might apply, however. For example, the Electronic Communications Privacy Act of 1986[26] prohibits any person from knowingly divulging to any other person the contents of an electronic communication while that communication is in transmission or in electronic storage.

E-Money Issuers' Financial Records Under the Right to Financial Privacy Act of 1978,[27] before a financial institution may give financial information about you to a federal agency, you must explicitly consent. If you do not, a federal agency wishing to access your financial records normally must obtain a warrant. A digital cash issuer may be subject to this act if that issuer is deemed to be (1) a bank by virtue of its holding customer funds or (2) any entity that issues a physical card similar to a credit or debit card.

Consumer Financial Data In 1999, Congress passed the Financial Services Modernization Act,[28] also known as the Gramm-Leach-Bliley Act, in an attempt to delineate how financial institutions can treat customer data. In general, the act and its rules[29] place restrictions and obligations on financial institutions to protect consumer data and privacy. Every financial institution must provide its customers with information on its privacy policies and practices. No financial institution can disclose nonpublic personal information about a consumer to an unaffiliated third party unless the act's disclosure and opt-out requirements are met.

---

24. 12 U.S.C. Sections 2801–2810.
25. 12 U.S.C. Sections 2901–2908.
26. 18 U.S.C. Sections 2510–2521.
27. 12 U.S.C. Sections 3401 *et seq.*
28. 12 U.S.C. Sections 24a, 248b, 1820a, 1828b, and others.
29. 12 C.F.R. Part 40.

As Chapter 9 pointed out, criminals often engage in money laundering to make their illegitimate funds appear legitimate. Profits illegally obtained—through drug trafficking, for example—are processed through a series of financial transactions that conceals their criminal origin. For example, Colombian drug cartels have used some of their profits to buy the most advanced computers and programming available so that they can engage in digital money laundering using secret Web sites. At a typical encrypted private Web site operated by a drug cartel, black market money changers bid on cash in U.S. and other currencies and eventually enable it to be converted to Colombian pesos.

Investigators for the U.S. Treasury Department estimate that these private Web sites can launder as much as $3 billion per year. Although most countries have legislation against money laundering, it is estimated that worldwide more than $600 billion in drug-trafficking profits is laundered every year—an amount

equal to between 2 and 5 percent of the world's gross domestic product.[a]

Reporting Requirements for Cash Transfers

Under current law, U.S. financial institutions must report transactions or fund transfers involving more than $10,000 in cash.[b] In the past, to avoid running afoul of these reporting requirements, drug traffickers—and terrorist groups—had to move their cash a little at a time in numerous transactions or smuggle bundles of cash across borders. Now the advent of digital cash has given them new options.

---

a. This statistic was taken from the Web site of the U.S. Department of Justice, **www.usdoj.gov/dea/programs/money.htm**.
b. The Bank Secrecy Act of 1970, 18 U.S.C. Sections 1956–1957, as amended by the Money Laundering Control Act of 1986, 31 C.F.R. Section 103.22(a)(1); and as modified by Title III of the Patriot Act of 2001.

Laundering Money through Prepaid ATM Cards

Today, many drug traffickers, terrorist groups, and other criminals who must move large amounts of cash are turning to prepaid ATM cards. From a would-be money launderer's perspective, a prepaid ATM card offers several advantages over a standard ATM or debit card issued by a bank. Any bank-issued card is linked to the customer's bank account. Thus, using such a card creates a paper trail (albeit electronically) that can be easily traced.

In contrast, a prepaid ATM card has no link to a bank account. It is essentially a *stored-value card*. The purchaser simply pays a specific amount to the card provider, and that amount is loaded onto the card. The user can then access those funds anywhere in the world without having to provide identification or have a bank account. Students and travelers use prepaid ATM cards as a convenient and safe substitute for cash. So, too, do about 75 million

---

REVIEWING Checks and Banking in the Digital Age

RPM Pizza, Inc., issued a check for $96,000 to Systems Marketing for an advertising campaign. A few days later, RPM decided not to go through with the deal and placed a written stop-payment order on the check. RPM and Systems had no further contact for many months. Three weeks after the stop-payment order expired, however, Toby Rierson, an employee at Systems, cashed the check. Bank One Cambridge, RPM's bank, paid the check with funds from RPM's account. Because of the amount of the check, and because the check was more than six months old (stale), the signature on the check should have been specially verified according to standard banking procedures and Bank One's own policies, but it was not. RPM filed a suit in a federal district court against Bank One to recover the amount of the check. Using the information presented in the chapter, answer the following questions.

residents of the United States who do not have bank accounts.

More important for money laundering purposes is that prepaid ATM cards can be purchased anonymously at retail and check-cashing stores across the nation—businesses that are not yet subject to the government's reporting requirements. Thus, drug traffickers and terrorist groups can pay for the cards with large amounts of cash and then use the cards to move funds across the border—a much easier process than smuggling physical cash.

Using Virtual Gaming Currency to Launder Money

The growing popularity of virtual gaming has opened the door to cyber laundering—and provided money launderers with a new source of prepaid ATM cards. For years, gamers in virtual worlds have been selling their digital monies, goods, and properties for real-world compensation. Initally, players were able to convert their virtual dollars or credits to real-world cash only by selling them on online auction sites, such as eBay. Now, however, gamers can go to various Web sites and exchange their virtual currency for real-world ATM cards. In 2006, for example, the makers of Entropia Universe began offering prepaid ATM cards in exchange for virtual assets.

With these new types of ATM cards, a gamer can instantly convert his or her virtual-world assets into physical currency and withdraw "real" cash from any Versatel brand ATM in the world. This means that a person can generate and hold financial assets anonymously in the virtual world without having to report the proceeds to the government or pay taxes on them. More importantly, these assets can be purchased, transferred, and accessed from any place in the world and are completely unregulated and unreported. Once the funds are withdrawn from a virtual account, they are "clean" and cannot be traced to an identifiable source. Hence, the virtual world holds great appeal for those who wish to hide their assets from the government's view and transfer funds internationally without risking detection.

IMPLICATIONS FOR THE BUSINESSPERSON

1. Be aware that all banks are required to report any wire transfers of more than $10,000 to the U.S. Treasury.

2. Be prepared for increased government regulation of digital cash transactions.

FOR CRITICAL ANALYSIS

1. Should only banks and regulated financial institutions be allowed to issue ATM cards? Why or why not?

2. How else might the government regulate digital funds to reduce the potential for cyber laundering?

RELEVANT WEB SITES

To locate information on the Web concerning the issues discussed in this feature, go to this text's Web site at **www.cengage.com/blaw/jentz**, select "Chapter 27," and click on "Emerging Trends."

REVIEWING Checks and Banking in the Digital Age, Continued

1. How long is a written stop-payment order effective? What else could RPM have done to prevent this check from being cashed?
2. What would happen if it turned out that RPM did not have a legitimate reason for stopping payment on the check?
3. What are a bank's obligations with respect to stale checks? Should Bank One have contacted RPM before paying the check? Why or why not?
4. Assume that Rierson's indorsement on the check was a forgery. Would a court be likely to hold the bank liable for the amount of the check because it failed to verify the signature on the check? Why or why not?

TERMS AND CONCEPTS

cashier's check
certified check
check
clearinghouse
collecting bank

debit card
depositary bank
digital cash
electronic fund transfer (EFT)
e-money
Federal Reserve System
intermediary bank
overdraft

payor bank
Regulation E
smart card
stale check
stop-payment order
teller's check
traveler's check

QUESTIONS AND CASE PROBLEMS

27-1. Checks are usually three-party instruments. On what type of check, however, does a bank serve as both the drawer and the drawee? What type of check does a bank agree in advance to accept when the check is presented for payment?

27-2. QUESTION WITH SAMPLE ANSWER

Gary goes grocery shopping and carelessly leaves his checkbook in his shopping cart. His checkbook, with two blank checks remaining, is stolen by Dolores. On May 5, Dolores forges Gary's name on a check for $10 and cashes the check at Gary's bank, Citizens Bank of Middletown. Gary has not reported the loss of his blank checks to his bank. On June 1, Gary receives his monthly bank statement and copies of canceled checks from Citizens Bank, including the forged check, but he does not examine the canceled checks. On June 20, Dolores forges Gary's last check. This check is for $1,000 and is cashed at Eastern City Bank, a bank with which Dolores has previously done business. Eastern City Bank puts the check through the collection process, and Citizens Bank honors it. On July 1, on receipt of his bank statement and canceled checks covering June transactions, Gary discovers both forgeries and immediately notifies Citizens Bank. Dolores cannot be found. Gary claims that Citizens Bank must recredit his account for both checks, as his signature was forged. Discuss fully Gary's claim.

- **For a sample answer to Question 27–2, go to Appendix C at the end of this text.**

27-3. On January 5, Brian drafts a check for $3,000 drawn on Southern Marine Bank and payable to his assistant, Shanta. Brian puts last year's date on the check by mistake. On January 7, before Shanta has had a chance to go to the bank, Brian is killed in an automobile accident. Southern Marine Bank is aware of Brian's death. On January 10, Shanta presents the check to the bank, and the bank honors the check by payment to Shanta. Later, Brian's widow, Joyce, claims that because the bank knew of Brian's death and also because the check was by date over one year old, the bank acted wrongfully when it paid Shanta. Joyce, as executor of Brian's estate and sole heir by his will, demands that Southern Marine Bank recredit Brian's estate for the check paid to Shanta. Discuss fully Southern Marine's liability in light of Joyce's demand.

27-4. Yannuzzi has a checking account at Texas Bank. She frequently uses her access card to obtain cash from the bank's automated teller machines. She always withdraws $50 when she makes a withdrawal, but she never withdraws more than $50 in any one day. When she received the April statement on her account, she noticed that on April 13 two withdrawals for $50 each had been made from the account. Believing this to be a mistake, she went to her bank on May 10 to inform it of the error. A bank officer told her that the bank would investigate and advise her as to the result. On May 26, the bank officer called her and said that bank personnel were having trouble locating the error but would continue to try to find it. On June 20, the bank sent her a full written report telling her that no error had been made. Yannuzzi, unhappy with the bank's explanation, filed suit against the bank, alleging that it had violated the Electronic Fund Transfer Act. What was the outcome of the suit? Would it matter if the bank could show that on the day in question it deducted $50 from Yannuzzi's account to cover a check that cleared the bank on that day—a check that Yannuzzi had written to a local department store?

27-5. Forged Signatures. Visiting Nurses Association of Telfair County, Inc. (VNA), maintained a checking account at Security State Bank in Valdosta, Georgia. Wanda Williamson, a VNA clerk, was responsible for making VNA bank deposits, but she was not a signatory on the association's account. Over a four-year period, Williamson embezzled more than $250,000 from VNA by forging its indorsement on checks, cashing them at the bank, and keeping a portion of the proceeds. Williamson was arrested, convicted, sentenced to a prison term, and ordered to pay restitution. VNA filed a suit in a Georgia state court against the bank, alleging, among other things, negligence. The bank filed a motion for summary judgment on the ground that VNA was precluded by Section 4–406(f) of the Uniform Commercial Code from recovering on checks with forged indorsements. Should the court grant the motion? Explain. [*Security State Bank v. Visiting Nurses Association of Telfair County, Inc.*, 568 S.E.2d 491 (Ga.App. 2002)]

27–6. Forged Signatures. Cynthia Stafford worked as an administrative professional at Gerber & Gerber, P.C. (professional corporation), a law firm, for more than two years. During that time, she stole ten checks payable to Gerber & Gerber (G&G), which she indorsed in blank by forging one of the attorney's signatures. She then indorsed the forged checks in her name and deposited them in her account at Regions Bank. Over the same period, G&G deposited in its accounts at Regions Bank thousands of checks amounting to $300 million to $400 million. Each G&G check was indorsed with a rubber stamp for deposit into the G&G account. The thefts were made possible, in part, because G&G kept unindorsed checks in an open file accessible to all employees and Stafford was sometimes the person assigned to stamp the checks. When the thefts were discovered, G&G filed a suit in a Georgia state court against Regions Bank to recover the stolen funds, alleging, among other things, negligence. Regions Bank filed a motion for summary judgment. What principles apply to attribute liability between these parties? How should the court rule on the bank's motion? Explain. [*Gerber & Gerber, P.C. v. Regions Bank*, 266 Ga.App. 8, 596 S.E.2d 174 (2004)]

27–7. CASE PROBLEM WITH SAMPLE ANSWER

In December 1999, Jenny Triplett applied for a bookkeeping position with Spacemakers of America, Inc., in Atlanta, Georgia. Spacemakers hired Triplett and delegated to her all responsibility for maintaining the company checkbook and reconciling it with the monthly statements from SunTrust Bank. Triplett also handled invoices from vendors. Spacemakers' president, Dennis Rose, reviewed the invoices and signed the checks to pay them, but no other employee checked Triplett's work. By the end of her first full month of employment, Triplett had forged six checks totaling more than $22,000, all payable to Triple M Entertainment, which was not a Spacemakers vendor. By October 2000, Triplett had forged fifty-nine more checks, totaling more than $475,000. A SunTrust employee became suspicious of an item that required sight inspection under the bank's fraud detection standards, which exceeded those of other banks in the area. Triplett was arrested. Spacemakers filed a suit in a Georgia state court against SunTrust. The bank filed a motion for summary judgment. On what basis could the bank avoid liability? In whose favor should the court rule, and why?

[*Spacemakers of America, Inc. v. SunTrust Bank*, 271 Ga.App. 335, 609 S.E.2d 683 (2005)]

- **To view a sample answer for Problem 27–7, go to this book's Web site at www.cengage. com/blaw/jentz, select "Chapter 27," and click on "Case Problem with Sample Answer."**

27–8. Forged Indorsements. In 1994, Brian and Penny Grieme bought a house in Mandan, North Dakota. They borrowed for the purchase through a loan program financed by the North Dakota Housing Finance Agency (NDHFA). The Griemes obtained insurance for the house from Center Mutual Insurance Co. When a hailstorm damaged the house in 2001, Center Mutual determined that the loss was $4,378 and issued a check for that amount, drawn on Bremer Bank, N.A. The check's payees included Brian Grieme and the NDHFA. Grieme presented the check for payment to Wells Fargo Bank of Tempe, Arizona. The back of the check bore his signature and in hand-printed block letters the words "ND Housing Finance." The check was processed for collection and paid, and the canceled check was returned to Center Mutual. By the time the insurer learned that NDHFA's indorsement had been forged, the Griemes had canceled their policy, defaulted on their loan, and filed for bankruptcy. The NDHFA filed a suit in a North Dakota state court against Center Mutual for the amount of the check. Who is most likely to suffer the loss in this case? Why? [*State ex rel. North Dakota Housing Finance Agency v. Center Mutual Insurance Co.*, 720 N.W.2d 425 (N.Dak. 2006)]

27–9. A QUESTION OF ETHICS

From the 1960s, James Johnson served as Bradley Union's personal caretaker and assistant, and was authorized by Union to handle his banking transactions. Louise Johnson, James's wife, wrote checks on Union's checking account to pay his bills, normally signing the checks "Brad Union." Branch Banking & Trust Co. (BB&T) managed Union's account. In December 2000, on the basis of Union's deteriorating mental and physical condition, a North Carolina state court declared him incompetent. Douglas Maxwell was appointed as Union's guardian. Maxwell "froze" Union's checking account and asked BB&T for copies of the canceled checks, which were provided by July 2001. Maxwell believed that Union's signature on the checks had been forged. In August 2002, Maxwell contacted BB&T, which refused to recredit Union's account. Maxwell filed a suit on Union's behalf in a North Carolina state court against BB&T. [Union v. Branch Banking & Trust Co., 176 N.C.App. 711, 627 S.E.2d 276 (2006)]

(a) Before Maxwell's appointment, BB&T sent monthly statements and canceled checks to Union, and Johnson reviewed them, but no unauthorized signatures were ever reported. On whom can liability be imposed in the case of a forged drawer's signature on a check? What are the limits set by Section

4–406(f) of the Uniform Commercial Code? Should Johnson's position, Union's incompetence, or Maxwell's appointment affect the application of these principles? Explain.

(b) Why was this suit brought against BB&T? Is BB&T liable? If not, who is? Why? Regardless of any violations of the law, did anyone act unethically in this case? If so, who and why?

LAW ON THE WEB

For updated links to resources available on the Web, as well as a variety of other materials, visit this text's Web site at

www.cengage.com/blaw/jentz

You can obtain extensive information on banking regulation from the Federal Deposit Insurance Corporation (FDIC) at

www.fdic.gov

Additional information about banking can be obtained from the Federal Reserve System at

www.federalreserveonline.org

The American Bankers Association is the largest banking trade association in the United States. To learn more about the banking industry, go to

www.aba.com

Legal Research Exercises on the Web

Go to **www.cengage.com/blaw/jentz**, the Web site that accompanies this text. Select "Chapter 27" and click on "Internet Exercises." There you will find the following Internet research exercises that you can perform to learn more about the topics covered in this chapter.

Internet Exercise 27–1: Legal Perspective
Smart Cards

Internet Exercise 27–2: Management Perspective
Check Fraud

Negotiable Instruments

Articles 3 and 4 of the Uniform Commercial Code (UCC), which deal with negotiable instruments, constitute an important part of the law governing commercial transactions. These articles reflect several fundamental ethical principles. One principle is that individuals should be protected against harm caused by the misuse of negotiable instruments. Another basic principle—and one that underlies the entire concept of negotiable instruments—is that the laws governing the use of negotiable instruments should be practical and reasonable to encourage the free flow of commerce.

Here, we look first at some of the ethical implications of the concept of a holder in due course (HDC). We then examine some other ethical issues that frequently arise in relation to these instruments.

Ethics, the HDC Concept, and *Ort v. Fowler*

The drafters of Article 3 did not create the HDC concept out of thin air. Indeed, under the common law, courts had often restricted the extent to which defenses could successfully be raised against a good faith holder of a negotiable instrument. As an example, consider a classic 1884 case, *Ort v. Fowler.*[1]

Case Background Ort, a farmer, was working alone in his field one day, when he was approached by a stranger who claimed to be the statewide agent for a manufacturer of iron posts and wire fencing. The two men conversed for some time, and eventually the stranger persuaded the farmer to act as an area representative for the manufacturer. The stranger then completed two documents for Ort to sign, telling him that they were identical copies of an agreement in which Ort agreed to represent the manufacturer.

Because the farmer did not have his glasses with him and could read only with great difficulty, he asked the stranger to read the document to him. The stranger then purported to do so, not mentioning that the document was a promissory note. Both men signed each document. The stranger later negotiated the promissory note he had fraudulently obtained from Ort to a party that today we would refer to as an HDC. When this party

brought suit against him, Ort attempted to defend on the basis of fraud in the execution.

The Court's Decision The Kansas court deciding the issue entertained three possible views. One was that because Ort never *intended* to execute a note, he should not be held liable for doing so. A second view was that the jury should decide, as a question of fact, whether Ort was guilty of negligence under the circumstances. The third view was that because Ort possessed all of his faculties and was able to read the English language, signing a promissory note solely in reliance on a stranger's assurances that it was a different instrument constituted negligence.

This third view was the one adopted by the court in 1884. The court held that Ort's negligence had contributed to the fraud and that such negligence precluded Ort from raising fraud as a defense against payment on the note. Today, the UCC expresses essentially the same reasoning: fraud is a defense against an HDC only if the injured party signed the instrument "with neither knowledge nor a reasonable opportunity to learn of its character or its essential terms" [UCC 3–305(a)(1)(iii)].

The Reasoning Underlying the HDC Concept
Although it may not seem fair that an innocent victim should have to suffer the consequences of another's fraudulent act, the UCC assumes that it would be even less fair if an HDC could not collect payment. The reasoning behind this assumption is that an HDC, as a third party, is less likely to have been responsible for—or to have had an opportunity to protect against—the fraud in the underlying transaction.

In general, the HDC doctrine, like other sections of the UCC, reflects the philosophy that when two or more innocent parties are at risk, the burden should fall on the party that was in the best position to prevent the loss. For businesspersons, the HDC doctrine means that they should exercise caution when issuing and accepting commercial paper in order to protect against the risk of loss through fraud.

Good Faith in Negotiable Instruments Law

Clearly, the principle of good faith reflects ethical principles. The most notable application of the good

---

1. 31 Kan. 478, 2 P. 580 (1884).

(Continued)

faith requirement in negotiable instruments law is, of course, the HDC doctrine. Traditionally, to acquire the protected status of an HDC, a holder must have acquired an instrument in good faith. Yet other transactions subject to Articles 3 and 4 also require good faith—as, indeed, do all transactions governed by the UCC.

The Importance of Good Faith A party that acts in bad faith may be precluded from seeking shelter under UCC provisions that would otherwise apply. This point was emphasized by a Pennsylvania court's decision with respect to the fictitious payee rule. The bank in this case had accepted 882 payroll checks generated and indorsed by Dorothy Heck, a payroll clerk employed by Pavex, Inc. The checks were made payable to various current and former Pavex employees, indorsed by Heck with the payees' names, and deposited into Heck's personal checking account at her bank.

Although the indorsements on the checks that Heck deposited did not exactly match the names of the payees—as was required by the bank's policy—the bank allowed Heck to deposit the checks anyway. Because the bank failed to follow its own policy, the court held that the bank had acted in bad faith and could not assert the fictitious payee rule as a defense. The bank was therefore liable for approximately $170,000 of the $250,000 loss suffered by Pavex.[2]

A different court reached a very different result in another case when a dishonest insurance agent took 279 checks written to his employer, Brooks Insurance; indorsed them; and deposited them into his own bank account. The bank in this case had a policy that any checks written to a business entity should be deposited into an account with that business's name. Although the bank violated its own policy when it allowed the agent to deposit the checks into an account with a different name, the court decided that this was not enough to show bad faith. Even though the bank may have acted negligently, the court allowed the bank to assert the fictitious payee rule and avoid liability.[3]

How Should Good Faith Be Tested? There has long been a division of opinion as to how good faith should be measured or tested. At one end of the spectrum of views is the position that the test of good faith should be subjective in nature. In other words, as long as a person acts honestly, no matter how negligent or foolish the conduct may be, that person is acting in good faith. At the other end of the spectrum is the "objective" test of good faith. Under this test, honesty in itself is not enough. A party must also act reasonably under the circumstances. Whereas a fool might pass the subjective test, he or she would not meet the objective test.

Over time, the pendulum seems to have swung from one end of the spectrum to the other. When the UCC was initially drafted, the definition of *good faith* set forth in UCC 1–201(19) established a subjective test for good faith. It defined *good faith* as "honesty in fact in the conduct or transaction concerned." The only UCC article that incorporated a more objective test for good faith was Article 2. Section 2–103(1)(b) defined good faith as both honesty in fact *and* the observance of reasonable commercial standards of fair dealing in the trade. Under this test, a person who acts honestly in fact but does not observe reasonable commercial standards of fair dealing will not meet the good faith requirement.

This more objective measure of good faith has since been incorporated into other articles of the UCC, including Articles 3, 4, and 4A.

Criticisms of the Objective Standard Some critics claim that while the subjective test of "honesty in fact" is manageable, the objective test that requires the "observance of reasonable commercial standards" opens the door to potentially endless litigation. After all, it is difficult to determine what is commercially reasonable in a given context until you hear what others in that commercial situation have to say. Thus, parties to a dispute can nearly always make some kind of good faith argument, and any time the issue is raised, litigation can result.

How Good Faith Standards Can Affect HDC Status Whether the objective or the subjective standard of good faith is used has considerable impact on HDC status, as an example will illustrate. Mitchell was a farmer who operated a multistate farming operation on leased property. Runnells, a grain broker, had sold Mitchell's 2001 grain crop. Mitchell instructed Runnells to use the crop proceeds to draw checks payable to Mitchell's various landlords in fulfillment

---

2. *Pavex, Inc. v. York Federal Savings and Loan Association,* 716 A.2d 640 (Pa.Super.Ct. 1998).

3. *Continental Casualty Co. v. Fifth/Third Bank,* 418 F.Supp.2d 964 (N.D. Ohio 2006).

of his rent obligations. The checks totaled more than $153,000. The landlords accepted the checks in payment of the farmer's rent— completely unaware that Mitchell had already pledged the proceeds from the sale of his crops as collateral for a loan from Agriliance (security interests will be discussed in Chapter 29). Agriliance filed a lawsuit in a federal court against Runnells and the various landlords for conversion (wrongful taking of personal property—see Chapter 6).

According to the UCC, an HDC takes a negotiable instrument free of any claim to the instrument, including claims of prior secured parties. Thus, the outcome of the case depended on whether Runnells and the landlords were HDCs. Under the subjective standard, the landlords would be HDCs because they had taken the checks without actual knowledge of Agriliance's claim to the crop proceeds. The objective standard, however, dictated a different result. Because it is common for farmers to put their crops up as collateral for loans, the court held that reasonable commercial standards of fair dealing required Mitchell's creditors (Runnells and the landlords) to conduct a search of the public records. Such a search would have revealed the existence of Agriliance's prior secured claim. Runnells and the landlords in this case could not be HDCs because they failed to meet the objective element of good faith. The court, therefore, ruled that Agriliance was entitled to the crop proceeds.[4]

Efficiency versus Due Care

A major problem faced by today's banking institutions is how to verify customer signatures on the billions of checks that are processed by the banking system each month. If a bank fails to verify a signature on a check it receives for payment and the check turns out to be forged, the bank will normally be held liable to its customer for the amount paid. But how can banks possibly examine, item by item, each signature on every check that they pay?

The banks' solution to this problem is simply to not examine all signatures. Instead, computers are programmed to verify signatures only on checks exceeding a certain threshold amount, such as

$1,000 or $2,500 or perhaps some higher figure. Checks for less than the threshold amount are selected for signature verification only on a random basis. In other words, serious attention is restricted to serious matters. As a result, many, if not most, checks are paid without signature verification. This practice, which has become an acceptable standard in today's banking industry, is economically efficient for banks. Even though liability costs are sometimes incurred— when forged checks are paid—the total costs involved in verifying the authenticity of each and every signature would be far higher.

Some people have argued that banks using such procedures are not exercising due care in handling their customers' accounts. Under the UCC, banks are held to a standard of "ordinary care." At one time in the banking industry, ordinary care was generally interpreted to mean that a bank had a duty to inspect *all* signatures on checks. But what constitutes ordinary care in today's world? Does a bank exercise ordinary care if it follows the prevailing industry practice of examining signatures on only a few, randomly selected checks payable for under a certain amount? Or does ordinary care still mean that a bank should examine each signature?

DISCUSSION QUESTIONS

1. Because the UCC offers special protection to HDCs, innocent makers of notes or drawers of checks in fraudulent transactions often have no legal recourse. From an ethical standpoint, how could you justify to the "losers" in such situations the provisions of the UCC that fail to protect them? Can you think of a way in which such problems could be handled more fairly or ethically than they are under the UCC?

2. What do you think would result if the law was changed to allow personal defenses to be successfully raised against HDCs? Who would lose, and who would gain? How would such a change in the law affect the flow of commerce in this country?

3. Do you think that the UCC's provisions have struck an appropriate balance between the interests of banks and those of bank customers? Why or why not?

---

4. *Agriliance, L.L.C. v. Runnells Grain Elevator, Inc.,* 272 F.Supp.2d 800 (S.D. Iowa 2003).

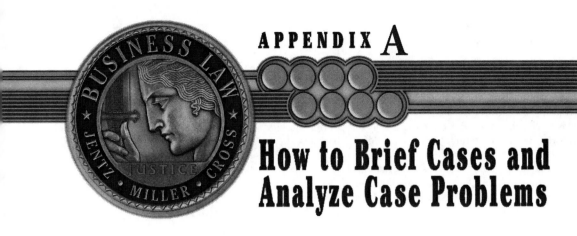

How to Brief Cases and Analyze Case Problems

How to Brief Cases

To fully understand the law with respect to business, you need to be able to read and understand court decisions. To make this task easier, you can use a method of case analysis that is called *briefing*. There is a fairly standard procedure that you can follow when you "brief" any court case. You must first read the case opinion carefully. When you feel you understand the case, you can prepare a brief of it.

Although the format of the brief may vary, typically it will present the essentials of the case under headings such as those listed below.

1. Citation. Give the full citation for the case, including the name of the case, the date it was decided, and the court that decided it.

2. Facts. Briefly indicate (a) the reasons for the lawsuit; (b) the identity and arguments of the plaintiff(s) and defendant(s), respectively; and (c) the lower court's decision—if appropriate.

3. Issue. Concisely phrase, in the form of a question, the essential issue before the court. (If more than one issue is involved, you may have two—or even more—questions here.)

4. Decision. Indicate here—with a "yes" or "no," if possible—the court's answer to the question (or questions) in the *Issue* section above.

5. Reason. Summarize as briefly as possible the reasons given by the court for its decision (or decisions) and the case or statutory law relied on by the court in arriving at its decision.

An Example of a Briefed Sample Court Case

As an example of the format used in briefing cases, we present here a briefed version of the sample court case that was presented in Exhibit 1–6 on pages 24 and 25.

BERGER V. CITY OF SEATTLE

United States Court of Appeals,
Ninth Circuit, 2008.
512 F.3d 582.

FACTS The Seattle Center is an entertainment "zone" in downtown Seattle, Washington, that attracts nearly ten million tourists each year. The center encompasses theaters, arenas, museums, exhibition halls, conference rooms, outdoor stadiums, and restaurants, and features street performers. Under the authority of the city, the center's director issued rules in 2002 to address safety concerns and other matters. Among other things, street performers were required to obtain permits and wear badges. After members of the public filed numerous complaints of threatening behavior by street performer and balloon artist Michael Berger, Seattle Center staff cited Berger for several rules violations. He filed a suit in a federal district court against the city and others, alleging, in part, that the rules violated his free speech rights under the First Amendment to the U.S. Constitution. The court issued a judgment in the plaintiff's favor. The city appealed to the U.S. Court of Appeals for the Ninth Circuit.

ISSUE Did the rules issued by the Seattle Center under the city's authority meet the requirements for valid restrictions on speech under the First Amendment?

DECISION Yes. The U.S. Court of Appeals for the Ninth Circuit reversed the decision of the lower court and remanded the case for further proceedings. "Such content neutral and narrowly tailored rules * * * must be upheld."

REASON The court concluded first that the rules requiring permits and badges were "content neutral." Time, place, and manner restrictions do not violate the First Amendment if they burden all expression equally and do not allow officials to treat different messages differently. In this case, the rules met this test and thus did not discriminate based on content. The court also concluded that the rules were "narrowly tailored" to "promote a substantial government interest that would be achieved less effectively" otherwise. With the rules, the city was trying to "reduce territorial disputes among performers, deter patron harassment, and facilitate the identification and apprehension of offending performers." This was pursuant to the valid governmental objective of protecting the safety and convenience of the other performers and the public generally. The public's complaints about Berger and others showed that unregulated street performances posed a threat to these interests. The court was "satisfied that the city's permit scheme was designed to further valid governmental objectives."

REVIEW OF SAMPLE COURT CASE

Here, we provide a review of the briefed version to indicate the kind of information that is contained in each section.

CITATION The name of the case is *Berger v. City of Seattle.* Berger is the plaintiff; the City of Seattle is the defendant. The U.S. Court of Appeals for the Ninth Circuit decided this case in 2008. The citation states that this case can be found in volume 512 of the *Federal Reporter, Third Series*, on page 582.

FACTS The *Facts* section identifies the plaintiff and the defendant, describes the events leading up to this suit, the allegations made by the plaintiff in the initial suit, and (because this case is an appellate court decision) the lower court's ruling and the party appealing. The party appealing's argument on appeal is also sometimes included here.

ISSUE The *Issue* section presents the central issue (or issues) decided by the court. In this case, the U.S. Court of Appeals for the Ninth Circuit considered whether certain rules imposed on street performers by local government authorities satisfied the requirements for valid restrictions on speech under the First Amendment to the U.S. Constitution.

DECISION The *Decision* section includes the court's decision on the issues before it. The decision reflects the opinion of the judge or justice hearing the case. Decisions by appellate courts are frequently phrased in reference to the lower court's decision. In other words, the appellate court may "affirm" the lower court's ruling or "reverse" it. Here, the court determined that Seattle's rules were "content neutral" and "narrowly tailored" to "promote a substantial government interest that would otherwise be achieved less effectively." The court found in favor of the city and reversed the lower court's ruling in the plaintiff's (Berger's) favor.

REASON The *Reason* section includes references to the relevant laws and legal principles that the court applied in coming to its conclusion in the case. The relevant law in the *Berger* case included the requirements under the First Amendment for evaluating the purpose and effect of government regulation with respect to expression. This section also explains the court's application of the law to the facts in this case.

ANALYZING CASE PROBLEMS

In addition to learning how to brief cases, students of business law and the legal environment also find it helpful to know how to analyze case problems. Part of the study of business law and the legal environment usually involves analyzing case problems, such as those included in this text at the end of each chapter.

For each case problem in this book, we provide the relevant background and facts of the lawsuit and the issue before the court. When you are assigned one of these problems, your job will be to determine how the court should decide the issue, and why. In other words, you will need to engage in legal analysis and reasoning. Here, we offer some suggestions on how to make this task less daunting. We begin by presenting a sample problem:

> While Janet Lawson, a famous pianist, was shopping in Quality Market, she slipped and fell on a wet floor in one of the aisles. The floor had recently been mopped by one of the store's employees, but there were no signs warning customers that the floor in that area was wet. As a result of the fall, Lawson injured her right arm and was unable to perform piano concerts for the next six months. Had she been able to perform the scheduled concerts, she would have earned approximately $60,000 over that period of time. Lawson sued Quality Market for this amount, plus another $10,000 in medical expenses. She claimed that the store's failure to warn customers of the wet floor constituted negligence and therefore the market was liable for her injuries. Will the court agree with Lawson? Discuss.

UNDERSTAND THE FACTS

This may sound obvious, but before you can analyze or apply the relevant law to a specific set of facts, you must clearly understand those facts. In other words, you should read through the case problem carefully—more than once, if necessary—to make sure you understand the identity of the plaintiff(s) and defendant(s) in the case and the progression of events that led to the lawsuit.

In the sample case problem just given, the identity of the parties is fairly obvious. Janet Lawson is the one bringing the suit; therefore, she is the plaintiff. Quality Market, against whom she is bringing the suit, is the defendant. Some of the case problems you may work on have multiple plaintiffs or defendants. Often, it is helpful to use abbreviations for the parties. To indicate a reference to a plaintiff, for example, the *pi* symbol—π—is often used, and a defendant is denoted by a *delta*—Δ—a triangle.

The events leading to the lawsuit are also fairly straightforward. Lawson slipped and fell on a wet floor, and she contends that Quality Market should be liable for her injuries because it was negligent in not posting a sign warning customers of the wet floor.

When you are working on case problems, realize that the facts should be accepted as they are given. For example, in our sample problem, it should be accepted that the floor was wet and that there was no sign. In other words, avoid making conjectures, such as "Maybe the floor wasn't too wet," or "Maybe an employee was getting a sign to put up," or "Maybe someone stole the sign." Questioning the facts as they are presented only adds confusion to your analysis.

LEGAL ANALYSIS AND REASONING

Once you understand the facts given in the case problem, you can begin to analyze the case. Recall from Chapter 1 that the IRAC method is a helpful tool to use in the legal analysis and reasoning process. IRAC is an acronym for Issue, Rule, Application, Conclusion. Applying this method to our sample problem would involve the following steps:

1. First, you need to decide what legal **issue** is involved in the case. In our sample case, the basic issue is whether Quality Market's failure to warn customers of the wet floor constituted negligence. As discussed in Chapter 6, negligence is a *tort*—a civil wrong. In a tort lawsuit, the plaintiff seeks to be compensated for another's wrongful act. A defendant will be deemed negligent if he or she breached a duty of care owed to the plaintiff and the breach of that duty caused the plaintiff to suffer harm.

2. Once you have identified the issue, the next step is to determine what **rule of law** applies to the issue. To make this determination, you will want to review carefully the text of the chapter in which the relevant rule of law for the problem appears. Our sample case problem involves the tort of negligence, which is covered in Chapter 6. The applicable rule of law is the tort law principle that business owners owe a duty to exer-

cise reasonable care to protect their customers ("business invitees"). Reasonable care, in this context, includes either removing—or warning customers of—*foreseeable* risks about which the owner *knew* or *should have known*. Business owners need not warn customers of "open and obvious" risks, however. If a business owner breaches this duty of care (fails to exercise the appropriate degree of care toward customers), and the breach of duty causes a customer to be injured, the business owner will be liable to the customer for the customer's injuries.

3. The next—and usually the most difficult—step in analyzing case problems is the **application** of the relevant rule of law to the specific facts of the case you are studying. In our sample problem, applying the tort law principle just discussed presents few difficulties. An employee of the store had mopped the floor in the aisle where Lawson slipped and fell, but no sign was present indicating that the floor was wet. That a customer might fall on a wet floor is clearly a foreseeable risk. Therefore, the failure to warn customers about the wet floor was a breach of the duty of care owed by the business owner to the store's customers.

4. Once you have completed Step 3 in the IRAC method, you should be ready to draw your **conclusion.** In our sample problem, Quality Market is liable to Lawson for her injuries, because the market's breach of its duty of care caused Lawson's injuries.

The fact patterns in the case problems presented in this text are not always as simple as those presented in our sample problem. Often, for example, a case has more than one plaintiff or defendant. A case may also involve more than one issue and have more than one applicable rule of law. Furthermore, in some case problems the facts may indicate that the general rule of law should not apply. For example, suppose that a store employee advised Lawson not to walk on the floor in the aisle because it was wet, but Lawson decided to walk on it anyway. This fact could alter the outcome of the case because the store could then raise the defense of *assumption of risk* (see Chapter 7). Nonetheless, a careful review of the chapter should always provide you with the knowledge you need to analyze the problem thoroughly and arrive at accurate conclusions.

APPENDIX B

The Constitution of the United States

PREAMBLE

We the People of the United States, in Order to form a more perfect Union, establish Justice, insure domestic Tranquility, provide for the common defence, promote the general Welfare, and secure the Blessings of Liberty to ourselves and our Posterity, do ordain and establish this Constitution for the United States of America.

ARTICLE I

Section 1. All legislative Powers herein granted shall be vested in a Congress of the United States, which shall consist of a Senate and House of Representatives.

Section 2. The House of Representatives shall be composed of Members chosen every second Year by the People of the several States, and the Electors in each State shall have the Qualifications requisite for Electors of the most numerous Branch of the State Legislature.

No Person shall be a Representative who shall not have attained to the Age of twenty five Years, and been seven Years a Citizen of the United States, and who shall not, when elected, be an Inhabitant of that State in which he shall be chosen.

Representatives and direct Taxes shall be apportioned among the several States which may be included within this Union, according to their respective Numbers, which shall be determined by adding to the whole Number of free Persons, including those bound to Service for a Term of Years, and excluding Indians not taxed, three fifths of all other Persons. The actual Enumeration shall be made within three Years after the first Meeting of the Congress of the United States, and within every subsequent Term of ten Years, in such Manner as they shall by Law direct. The Number of Representatives shall not exceed one for every thirty Thousand, but each State shall have at Least one Representative; and until such enumeration shall be made, the State of New Hampshire shall be entitled to chuse three, Massachusetts eight, Rhode Island and Providence Plantations one, Connecticut five, New York six, New Jersey four, Pennsylvania eight, Delaware one, Maryland six, Virginia ten, North Carolina five, South Carolina five, and Georgia three.

When vacancies happen in the Representation from any State, the Executive Authority thereof shall issue Writs of Election to fill such Vacancies.

The House of Representatives shall chuse their Speaker and other Officers; and shall have the sole Power of Impeachment.

Section 3. The Senate of the United States shall be composed of two Senators from each State, chosen by the Legislature thereof, for six Years; and each Senator shall have one Vote.

Immediately after they shall be assembled in Consequence of the first Election, they shall be divided as equally as may be into three Classes. The Seats of the Senators of the first Class shall be vacated at the Expiration of the second Year, of the second Class at the Expiration of the fourth Year, and of the third Class at the Expiration of the sixth Year, so that one third may be chosen every second Year; and if Vacancies happen by Resignation, or otherwise, during the Recess of the Legislature of any State, the Executive thereof may make temporary Appointments until the next Meeting of the Legislature, which shall then fill such Vacancies.

No Person shall be a Senator who shall not have attained to the Age of thirty Years, and been nine Years a Citizen of the United States, and who shall not, when elected, be an Inhabitant of that State for which he shall be chosen.

The Vice President of the United States shall be President of the Senate, but shall have no Vote, unless they be equally divided.

The Senate shall chuse their other Officers, and also a President pro tempore, in the Absence of the Vice President, or when he shall exercise the Office of President of the United States.

The Senate shall have the sole Power to try all Impeachments. When sitting for that Purpose, they shall be on Oath or Affirmation. When the President of the United States is tried, the Chief Justice shall preside: And no Person shall be convicted without the Concurrence of two thirds of the Members present.

Judgment in Cases of Impeachment shall not extend further than to removal from Office, and disqualification to hold and enjoy any Office of honor, Trust, or Profit under the United States: but the Party convicted shall nevertheless be liable and subject to Indictment, Trial, Judgment, and Punishment, according to Law.

Section 4. The Times, Places and Manner of holding Elections for Senators and Representatives, shall be prescribed in each State by the Legislature thereof; but the Congress may at any time by Law make or alter such Regulations, except as to the Places of chusing Senators.

The Congress shall assemble at least once in every Year, and such Meeting shall be on the first Monday in December, unless they shall by Law appoint a different Day.

Section 5. Each House shall be the Judge of the Elections, Returns, and Qualifications of its own Members, and a Majority of each shall constitute a Quorum to do Business; but a smaller Number may adjourn from day to day, and may be authorized to compel the Attendance of absent Members, in such Manner, and under such Penalties as each House may provide.

Each House may determine the Rules of its Proceedings, punish its Members for disorderly Behavior, and, with the Concurrence of two thirds, expel a Member.

Each House shall keep a Journal of its Proceedings, and from time to time publish the same, excepting such Parts as may in their Judgment require Secrecy; and the Yeas and Nays of the Members of either House on any question shall, at the Desire of one fifth of those Present, be entered on the Journal.

Neither House, during the Session of Congress, shall, without the Consent of the other, adjourn for more than three days, nor to any other Place than that in which the two Houses shall be sitting.

Section 6. The Senators and Representatives shall receive a Compensation for their Services, to be ascertained by Law, and paid out of the Treasury of the United States. They shall in all Cases, except Treason, Felony and Breach of the Peace, be privileged from Arrest during their Attendance at the Session of their respective Houses, and in going to and returning from the same; and for any Speech or Debate in either House, they shall not be questioned in any other Place.

No Senator or Representative shall, during the Time for which he was elected, be appointed to any civil Office under the Authority of the United States, which shall have been created, or the Emoluments whereof shall have been increased during such time; and no Person holding any Office under the United States, shall be a Member of either House during his Continuance in Office.

Section 7. All Bills for raising Revenue shall originate in the House of Representatives; but the Senate may propose or concur with Amendments as on other Bills.

Every Bill which shall have passed the House of Representatives and the Senate, shall, before it become a Law, be presented to the President of the United States; If he approve he shall sign it, but if not he shall return it, with his Objections to the House in which it shall have originated, who shall enter the Objections at large on their Journal, and proceed to reconsider it. If after such Reconsideration two thirds of that House shall agree to pass the Bill, it shall be sent together with the Objections, to the other House, by which it shall likewise be reconsidered, and if approved by two thirds of that House, it shall become a Law. But in all such Cases the Votes of both Houses shall be determined by Yeas and Nays, and the Names of the Persons voting for and against the Bill shall

be entered on the Journal of each House respectively. If any Bill shall not be returned by the President within ten Days (Sundays excepted) after it shall have been presented to him, the Same shall be a Law, in like Manner as if he had signed it, unless the Congress by their Adjournment prevent its Return in which Case it shall not be a Law.

Every Order, Resolution, or Vote, to which the Concurrence of the Senate and House of Representatives may be necessary (except on a question of Adjournment) shall be presented to the President of the United States; and before the Same shall take Effect, shall be approved by him, or being disapproved by him, shall be repassed by two thirds of the Senate and House of Representatives, according to the Rules and Limitations prescribed in the Case of a Bill.

Section 8. The Congress shall have Power To lay and collect Taxes, Duties, Imposts and Excises, to pay the Debts and provide for the common Defence and general Welfare of the United States; but all Duties, Imposts and Excises shall be uniform throughout the United States;

To borrow Money on the credit of the United States;

To regulate Commerce with foreign Nations, and among the several States, and with the Indian Tribes;

To establish an uniform Rule of Naturalization, and uniform Laws on the subject of Bankruptcies throughout the United States;

To coin Money, regulate the Value thereof, and of foreign Coin, and fix the Standard of Weights and Measures;

To provide for the Punishment of counterfeiting the Securities and current Coin of the United States;

To establish Post Offices and post Roads;

To promote the Progress of Science and useful Arts, by securing for limited Times to Authors and Inventors the exclusive Right to their respective Writings and Discoveries;

To constitute Tribunals inferior to the supreme Court;

To define and punish Piracies and Felonies committed on the high Seas, and Offenses against the Law of Nations;

To declare War, grant Letters of Marque and Reprisal, and make Rules concerning Captures on Land and Water;

To raise and support Armies, but no Appropriation of Money to that Use shall be for a longer Term than two Years;

To provide and maintain a Navy;

To make Rules for the Government and Regulation of the land and naval Forces;

To provide for calling forth the Militia to execute the Laws of the Union, suppress Insurrections and repel Invasions;

To provide for organizing, arming, and disciplining, the Militia, and for governing such Part of them as may be employed in the Service of the United States, reserving to the States respectively, the Appointment of the Officers, and the Authority of training the Militia according to the discipline prescribed by Congress;

To exercise exclusive Legislation in all Cases whatsoever, over such District (not exceeding ten Miles square) as may, by Cession of particular States, and the Acceptance of Congress, become the Seat of the Government of the United States, and to exercise like Authority over all Places purchased by the Consent of the Legislature of the State in which the Same shall be, for the Erection of Forts, Magazines, Arsenals, dock-Yards, and other needful Buildings;—And

To make all Laws which shall be necessary and proper for carrying into Execution the foregoing Powers, and all other Powers vested by this Constitution in the Government of the United States, or in any Department or Officer thereof.

Section 9. The Migration or Importation of such Persons as any of the States now existing shall think proper to admit, shall not be prohibited by the Congress prior to the Year one thousand eight hundred and eight, but a Tax or duty may be imposed on such Importation, not exceeding ten dollars for each Person.

The privilege of the Writ of Habeas Corpus shall not be suspended, unless when in Cases of Rebellion or Invasion the public Safety may require it.

No Bill of Attainder or ex post facto Law shall be passed.

No Capitation, or other direct, Tax shall be laid, unless in Proportion to the Census or Enumeration herein before directed to be taken.

No Tax or Duty shall be laid on Articles exported from any State.

No Preference shall be given by any Regulation of Commerce or Revenue to the Ports of one State over those of another: nor shall Vessels bound to, or from, one State be obliged to enter, clear, or pay Duties in another.

No Money shall be drawn from the Treasury, but in Consequence of Appropriations made by Law; and a regular Statement and Account of the Receipts and Expenditures of all public Money shall be published from time to time.

No Title of Nobility shall be granted by the United States: And no Person holding any Office of Profit or Trust under them, shall, without the Consent of the Congress, accept of any present, Emolument, Office, or Title, of any kind whatever, from any King, Prince, or foreign State.

Section 10. No State shall enter into any Treaty, Alliance, or Confederation; grant Letters of Marque and Reprisal; coin Money; emit Bills of Credit; make any Thing but gold and silver Coin a Tender in Payment of Debts; pass any Bill of Attainder, ex post facto Law, or Law impairing the Obligation of Contracts, or grant any Title of Nobility.

No State shall, without the Consent of the Congress, lay any Imposts or Duties on Imports or Exports, except what may be absolutely necessary for executing its inspection Laws: and the net Produce of all Duties and Imposts, laid by any State on Imports or Exports, shall be for the Use of the Treasury of the United States; and all such Laws shall be subject to the Revision and Controul of the Congress.

No State shall, without the Consent of Congress, lay any Duty of Tonnage, keep Troops, or Ships of War in time of Peace, enter into any Agreement or Compact with another State, or with a foreign Power, or engage in War, unless actually invaded, or in such imminent Danger as will not admit of delay.

ARTICLE II

Section 1. The executive Power shall be vested in a President of the United States of America. He shall hold his Office during the Term of four Years, and, together with the Vice President, chosen for the same Term, be elected, as follows:

Each State shall appoint, in such Manner as the Legislature thereof may direct, a Number of Electors, equal to the whole Number of Senators and Representatives to which the State may be entitled in the Congress; but no Senator or Representative, or Person holding an Office of Trust or Profit under the United States, shall be appointed an Elector.

The Electors shall meet in their respective States, and vote by Ballot for two Persons, of whom one at least shall not be an Inhabitant of the same State with themselves. And they shall make a List of all the Persons voted for, and of the Number of Votes for each; which List they shall sign and certify, and transmit sealed to the Seat of the Government of the United States, directed to the President of the Senate. The President of the Senate shall, in the Presence of the Senate and House of Representatives, open all the Certificates, and the Votes shall then be counted. The Person having the greatest Number of Votes shall be the President, if such Number be a Majority of the whole Number of Electors appointed; and if there be more than one who have such Majority, and have an equal Number of Votes, then the House of Representatives shall immediately chuse by Ballot one of them for President; and if no Person have a Majority, then from the five highest on the List the said House shall in like Manner chuse the President. But in chusing the President, the Votes shall be taken by States, the Representation from each State having one Vote; A quorum for this Purpose shall consist of a Member or Members from two thirds of the States, and a Majority of all the States shall be necessary to a Choice. In every Case, after the Choice of the President, the Person having the greater Number of Votes of the Electors shall be the Vice President. But if there should remain two or more who have equal Votes, the Senate shall chuse from them by Ballot the Vice President.

The Congress may determine the Time of chusing the Electors, and the Day on which they shall give their Votes; which Day shall be the same throughout the United States.

No person except a natural born Citizen, or a Citizen of the United States, at the time of the Adoption of this Constitution, shall be eligible to the Office of President; neither shall any Person be eligible to that Office who shall not have attained to the Age of thirty five Years, and been fourteen Years a Resident within the United States.

In Case of the Removal of the President from Office, or of his Death, Resignation or Inability to discharge the

Powers and Duties of the said Office, the same shall devolve on the Vice President, and the Congress may by Law provide for the Case of Removal, Death, Resignation or Inability, both of the President and Vice President, declaring what Officer shall then act as President, and such Officer shall act accordingly, until the Disability be removed, or a President shall be elected.

The President shall, at stated Times, receive for his Services, a Compensation, which shall neither be increased nor diminished during the Period for which he shall have been elected, and he shall not receive within that Period any other Emolument from the United States, or any of them.

Before he enter on the Execution of his Office, he shall take the following Oath or Affirmation: "I do solemnly swear (or affirm) that I will faithfully execute the Office of President of the United States, and will to the best of my Ability, preserve, protect and defend the Constitution of the United States."

Section 2. The President shall be Commander in Chief of the Army and Navy of the United States, and of the Militia of the several States, when called into the actual Service of the United States; he may require the Opinion, in writing, of the principal Officer in each of the executive Departments, upon any Subject relating to the Duties of their respective Offices, and he shall have Power to grant Reprieves and Pardons for Offenses against the United States, except in Cases of Impeachment.

He shall have Power, by and with the Advice and Consent of the Senate to make Treaties, provided two thirds of the Senators present concur; and he shall nominate, and by and with the Advice and Consent of the Senate, shall appoint Ambassadors, other public Ministers and Consuls, Judges of the supreme Court, and all other Officers of the United States, whose Appointments are not herein otherwise provided for, and which shall be established by Law; but the Congress may by Law vest the Appointment of such inferior Officers, as they think proper, in the President alone, in the Courts of Law, or in the Heads of Departments.

The President shall have Power to fill up all Vacancies that may happen during the Recess of the Senate, by granting Commissions which shall expire at the End of their next Session.

Section 3. He shall from time to time give to the Congress Information of the State of the Union, and recommend to their Consideration such Measures as he shall judge necessary and expedient; he may, on extraordinary Occasions, convene both Houses, or either of them, and in Case of Disagreement between them, with Respect to the Time of Adjournment, he may adjourn them to such Time as he shall think proper; he shall receive Ambassadors and other public Ministers; he shall take Care that the Laws be faithfully executed, and shall Commission all the Officers of the United States.

Section 4. The President, Vice President and all civil Officers of the United States, shall be removed from Office

on Impeachment for, and Conviction of, Treason, Bribery, or other high Crimes and Misdemeanors.

ARTICLE III

Section 1. The judicial Power of the United States, shall be vested in one supreme Court, and in such inferior Courts as the Congress may from time to time ordain and establish. The Judges, both of the supreme and inferior Courts, shall hold their Offices during good Behaviour, and shall, at stated Times, receive for their Services a Compensation, which shall not be diminished during their Continuance in Office.

Section 2. The judicial Power shall extend to all Cases, in Law and Equity, arising under this Constitution, the Laws of the United States, and Treaties made, or which shall be made, under their Authority;—to all Cases affecting Ambassadors, other public Ministers and Consuls;—to all Cases of admiralty and maritime Jurisdiction;—to Controversies to which the United States shall be a Party;—to Controversies between two or more States;—between a State and Citizens of another State;—between Citizens of different States;—between Citizens of the same State claiming Lands under Grants of different States, and between a State, or the Citizens thereof, and foreign States, Citizens or Subjects.

In all Cases affecting Ambassadors, other public Ministers and Consuls, and those in which a State shall be a Party, the supreme Court shall have original Jurisdiction. In all the other Cases before mentioned, the supreme Court shall have appellate Jurisdiction, both as to Law and Fact, with such Exceptions, and under such Regulations as the Congress shall make.

The Trial of all Crimes, except in Cases of Impeachment, shall be by Jury; and such Trial shall be held in the State where the said Crimes shall have been committed; but when not committed within any State, the Trial shall be at such Place or Places as the Congress may by Law have directed.

Section 3. Treason against the United States, shall consist only in levying War against them, or, in adhering to their Enemies, giving them Aid and Comfort. No Person shall be convicted of Treason unless on the Testimony of two Witnesses to the same overt Act, or on Confession in open Court.

The Congress shall have Power to declare the Punishment of Treason, but no Attainder of Treason shall work Corruption of Blood, or Forfeiture except during the Life of the Person attainted.

ARTICLE IV

Section 1. Full Faith and Credit shall be given in each State to the public Acts, Records, and judicial Proceedings of every other State. And the Congress may by general Laws prescribe the Manner in which such Acts, Records and Proceedings shall be proved, and the Effect thereof.

Section 2. The Citizens of each State shall be entitled to all Privileges and Immunities of Citizens in the several States.

A Person charged in any State with Treason, Felony, or other Crime, who shall flee from Justice, and be found in another State, shall on Demand of the executive Authority of the State from which he fled, be delivered up, to be removed to the State having Jurisdiction of the Crime.

No Person held to Service or Labour in one State, under the Laws thereof, escaping into another, shall, in Consequence of any Law or Regulation therein, be discharged from such Service or Labour, but shall be delivered up on Claim of the Party to whom such Service or Labour may be due.

Section 3. New States may be admitted by the Congress into this Union; but no new State shall be formed or erected within the Jurisdiction of any other State; nor any State be formed by the Junction of two or more States, or Parts of States, without the Consent of the Legislatures of the States concerned as well as of the Congress.

The Congress shall have Power to dispose of and make all needful Rules and Regulations respecting the Territory or other Property belonging to the United States; and nothing in this Constitution shall be so construed as to Prejudice any Claims of the United States, or of any particular State.

Section 4. The United States shall guarantee to every State in this Union a Republican Form of Government, and shall protect each of them against Invasion; and on Application of the Legislature, or of the Executive (when the Legislature cannot be convened) against domestic Violence.

Article V

The Congress, whenever two thirds of both Houses shall deem it necessary, shall propose Amendments to this Constitution, or, on the Application of the Legislatures of two thirds of the several States, shall call a Convention for proposing Amendments, which, in either Case, shall be valid to all Intents and Purposes, as part of this Constitution, when ratified by the Legislatures of three fourths of the several States, or by Conventions in three fourths thereof, as the one or the other Mode of Ratification may be proposed by the Congress; Provided that no Amendment which may be made prior to the Year One thousand eight hundred and eight shall in any Manner affect the first and fourth Clauses in the Ninth Section of the first Article; and that no State, without its Consent, shall be deprived of its equal Suffrage in the Senate.

Article VI

All Debts contracted and Engagements entered into, before the Adoption of this Constitution shall be as valid against the United States under this Constitution, as under the Confederation.

This Constitution, and the Laws of the United States which shall be made in Pursuance thereof; and all Treaties made, or which shall be made, under the Authority of the United States, shall be the supreme Law of the Land; and the Judges in every State shall be bound

thereby, any Thing in the Constitution or Laws of any State to the Contrary notwithstanding.

The Senators and Representatives before mentioned, and the Members of the several State Legislatures, and all executive and judicial Officers, both of the United States and of the several States, shall be bound by Oath or Affirmation, to support this Constitution; but no religious Test shall ever be required as a Qualification to any Office or public Trust under the United States.

Article VII

The Ratification of the Conventions of nine States shall be sufficient for the Establishment of this Constitution between the States so ratifying the Same.

Amendment I [1791]

Congress shall make no law respecting an establishment of religion, or prohibiting the free exercise thereof; or abridging the freedom of speech, or of the press; or the right of the people peaceably to assembly, and to petition the Government for a redress of grievances.

Amendment II [1791]

A well regulated Militia, being necessary to the security of a free State, the right of the people to keep and bear Arms, shall not be infringed.

Amendment III [1791]

No Soldier shall, in time of peace be quartered in any house, without the consent of the Owner, nor in time of war, but in a manner to be prescribed by law.

Amendment IV [1791]

The right of the people to be secure in their persons, houses, papers, and effects, against unreasonable searches and seizures, shall not be violated, and no Warrants shall issue, but upon probable cause, supported by Oath or affirmation, and particularly describing the place to be searched, and the persons or things to be seized.

Amendment V [1791]

No person shall be held to answer for a capital, or otherwise infamous crime, unless on a presentment or indictment of a Grand Jury, except in cases arising in the land or naval forces, or in the Militia, when in actual service in time of War or public danger; nor shall any person be subject for the same offence to be twice put in jeopardy of life or limb; nor shall be compelled in any criminal case to be a witness against himself, nor be deprived of life, liberty, or property, without due process of law; nor shall private property be taken for public use, without just compensation.

Amendment VI [1791]

In all criminal prosecutions, the accused shall enjoy the right to a speedy and public trial, by an impartial jury of the State and district wherein the crime shall have been committed, which district shall have been previously ascertained by law, and to be informed of the nature and cause of the accusation; to be confronted with the witnesses against him; to have compulsory process for obtaining witnesses in his favor, and to have the Assistance of Counsel for his defence.

AMENDMENT VII [1791]

In Suits at common law, where the value in controversy shall exceed twenty dollars, the right of trial by jury shall be preserved, and no fact tried by jury, shall be otherwise re-examined in any Court of the United States, than according to the rules of the common law.

AMENDMENT VIII [1791]

Excessive bail shall not be required, nor excessive fines imposed, nor cruel and unusual punishments inflicted.

AMENDMENT IX [1791]

The enumeration in the Constitution, of certain rights, shall not be construed to deny or disparage others retained by the people.

AMENDMENT X [1791]

The powers not delegated to the United States by the Constitution, nor prohibited by it to the States, are reserved to the States respectively, or to the people.

AMENDMENT XI [1798]

The Judicial power of the United States shall not be construed to extend to any suit in law or equity, commenced or prosecuted against one of the United States by Citizens of another State, or by Citizens or Subjects of any Foreign State.

AMENDMENT XII [1804]

The Electors shall meet in their respective states, and vote by ballot for President and Vice-President, one of whom, at least, shall not be an inhabitant of the same state with themselves; they shall name in their ballots the person voted for as President, and in distinct ballots the person voted for as Vice-President, and they shall make distinct lists of all persons voted for as President, and of all persons voted for as Vice-President, and of the number of votes for each, which lists they shall sign and certify, and transmit sealed to the seat of the government of the United States, directed to the President of the Senate;—The President of the Senate shall, in the presence of the Senate and House of Representatives, open all the certificates and the votes shall then be counted;—The person having the greatest number of votes for President, shall be the President, if such number be a majority of the whole number of Electors appointed; and if no person have such majority, then from the persons having the highest numbers not exceeding three on the list of those voted for as President, the House of Representatives shall choose immediately, by ballot, the President. But in choosing the President, the votes shall be taken by states, the represen-

tation from each state having one vote; a quorum for this purpose shall consist of a member or members from two-thirds of the states, and a majority of all states shall be necessary to a choice. And if the House of Representatives shall not choose a President whenever the right of choice shall devolve upon them, before the fourth day of March next following, then the Vice-President shall act as President, as in the case of the death or other constitutional disability of the President.—The person having the greatest number of votes as Vice-President, shall be the Vice-President, if such number be a majority of the whole number of Electors appointed, and if no person have a majority, then from the two highest numbers on the list, the Senate shall choose the Vice-President; a quorum for the purpose shall consist of two-thirds of the whole number of Senators, and a majority of the whole number shall be necessary to a choice. But no person constitutionally ineligible to the office of President shall be eligible to that of Vice-President of the United States.

AMENDMENT XIII [1865]

Section 1. Neither slavery nor involuntary servitude, except as a punishment for crime whereof the party shall have been duly convicted, shall exist within the United States, or any place subject to their jurisdiction.

Section 2. Congress shall have power to enforce this article by appropriate legislation.

AMENDMENT XIV [1868]

Section 1. All persons born or naturalized in the United States, and subject to the jurisdiction thereof, are citizens of the United States and of the State wherein they reside. No State shall make or enforce any law which shall abridge the privileges or immunities of citizens of the United States; nor shall any State deprive any person of life, liberty, or property, without due process of law; nor deny to any person within its jurisdiction the equal protection of the laws.

Section 2. Representatives shall be apportioned among the several States according to their respective numbers, counting the whole number of persons in each State, excluding Indians not taxed. But when the right to vote at any election for the choice of electors for President and Vice President of the United States, Representatives in Congress, the Executive and Judicial officers of a State, or the members of the Legislature thereof, is denied to any of the male inhabitants of such State, being twenty-one years of age, and citizens of the United States, or in any way abridged, except for participation in rebellion, or other crime, the basis of representation therein shall be reduced in the proportion which the number of such male citizens shall bear to the whole number of male citizens twenty-one years of age in such State.

Section 3. No person shall be a Senator or Representative in Congress, or elector of President and Vice President, or hold any office, civil or military, under the United States, or under any State, who having previously taken an oath, as a member of Congress, or as an officer of the United States, or as a member of any State legislature, or as an executive or judicial officer of any State, to support the Constitution of the United States, shall have engaged in insurrection or rebellion against the same, or given aid or comfort to the enemies thereof. But Congress may by a vote of two-thirds of each House, remove such disability.

Section 4. The validity of the public debt of the United States, authorized by law, including debts incurred for payment of pensions and bounties for services in suppressing insurrection or rebellion, shall not be questioned. But neither the United States nor any State shall assume or pay any debt or obligation incurred in aid of insurrection or rebellion against the United States, or any claim for the loss or emancipation of any slave; but all such debts, obligations and claims shall be held illegal and void.

Section 5. The Congress shall have power to enforce, by appropriate legislation, the provisions of this article.

AMENDMENT XV [1870]

Section 1. The right of citizens of the United States to vote shall not be denied or abridged by the United States or by any State on account of race, color, or previous condition of servitude.

Section 2. The Congress shall have power to enforce this article by appropriate legislation.

AMENDMENT XVI [1913]

The Congress shall have power to lay and collect taxes on incomes, from whatever source derived, without apportionment among the several States, and without regard to any census or enumeration.

AMENDMENT XVII [1913]

Section 1. The Senate of the United States shall be composed of two Senators from each State, elected by the people thereof, for six years; and each Senator shall have one vote. The electors in each State shall have the qualifications requisite for electors of the most numerous branch of the State legislatures.

Section 2. When vacancies happen in the representation of any State in the Senate, the executive authority of such State shall issue writs of election to fill such vacancies: *Provided,* That the legislature of any State may empower the executive thereof to make temporary appointments until the people fill the vacancies by election as the legislature may direct.

Section 3. This amendment shall not be so construed as to affect the election or term of any Senator chosen before it becomes valid as part of the Constitution.

AMENDMENT XVIII [1919]

Section 1. After one year from the ratification of this article the manufacture, sale, or transportation of intoxicating liquors within, the importation thereof into, or the exportation thereof from the United States and all territory subject to the jurisdiction thereof for beverage purposes is hereby prohibited.

Section 2. The Congress and the several States shall have concurrent power to enforce this article by appropriate legislation.

Section 3. This article shall be inoperative unless it shall have been ratified as an amendment to the Constitution by the legislatures of the several States, as provided in the Constitution, within seven years from the date of the submission hereof to the States by the Congress.

AMENDMENT XIX [1920]

Section 1. The right of citizens of the United States to vote shall not be denied or abridged by the United States or by any State on account of sex.

Section 2. Congress shall have power to enforce this article by appropriate legislation.

AMENDMENT XX [1933]

Section 1. The terms of the President and Vice President shall end at noon on the 20th day of January, and the terms of Senators and Representatives at noon on the 3d day of January, of the years in which such terms would have ended if this article had not been ratified; and the terms of their successors shall then begin.

Section 2. The Congress shall assemble at least once in every year, and such meeting shall begin at noon on the 3d day of January, unless they shall by law appoint a different day.

Section 3. If, at the time fixed for the beginning of the term of the President, the President elect shall have died, the Vice President elect shall become President. If the President shall not have been chosen before the time fixed for the beginning of his term, or if the President elect shall have failed to qualify, then the Vice President elect shall act as President until a President shall have qualified; and the Congress may by law provide for the case wherein neither a President elect nor a Vice President elect shall have qualified, declaring who shall then act as President, or the manner in which one who is to act shall be selected, and such person shall act accordingly until a President or Vice President shall have qualified.

Section 4. The Congress may by law provide for the case of the death of any of the persons from whom the House of Representatives may choose a President whenever the right of choice shall have devolved upon them, and for the case of the death of any of the persons from whom the Senate may choose a Vice President whenever the right of choice shall have devolved upon them.

Section 5. Sections 1 and 2 shall take effect on the 15th day of October following the ratification of this article.

Section 6. This article shall be inoperative unless it shall have been ratified as an amendment to the Constitution by the legislatures of three-fourths of the several States within seven years from the date of its submission.

AMENDMENT XXI [1933]

Section 1. The eighteenth article of amendment to the Constitution of the United States is hereby repealed.

Section 2. The transportation or importation into any State, Territory, or possession of the United States for delivery or use therein of intoxicating liquors, in violation of the laws thereof, is hereby prohibited.

Section 3. This article shall be inoperative unless it shall have been ratified as an amendment to the Constitution by conventions in the several States, as provided in the Constitution, within seven years from the date of the submission hereof to the States by the Congress.

AMENDMENT XXII [1951]

Section 1. No person shall be elected to the office of the President more than twice, and no person who has held the office of President, or acted as President, for more than two years of a term to which some other person was elected President shall be elected to the office of President more than once. But this Article shall not apply to any person holding the office of President when this Article was proposed by the Congress, and shall not prevent any person who may be holding the office of President, or acting as President, during the term within which this Article becomes operative from holding the office of President or acting as President during the remainder of such term.

Section 2. This article shall be inoperative unless it shall have been ratified as an amendment to the Constitution by the legislatures of three-fourths of the several States within seven years from the date of its submission to the States by the Congress.

AMENDMENT XXIII [1961]

Section 1. The District constituting the seat of Government of the United States shall appoint in such manner as the Congress may direct:

A number of electors of President and Vice President equal to the whole number of Senators and Representatives in Congress to which the District would be entitled if it were a State, but in no event more than the least populous state; they shall be in addition to those appointed by the states, but they shall be considered, for the purposes of the election of President and Vice President, to be electors appointed by a state; and they shall meet in the District and perform such duties as provided by the twelfth article of amendment.

Section 2. The Congress shall have power to enforce this article by appropriate legislation.

AMENDMENT XXIV [1964]

Section 1. The right of citizens of the United States to vote in any primary or other election for President or Vice President, for electors for President or Vice President, or for Senator or Representative in Congress, shall not be denied or abridged by the United States, or any State by reason of failure to pay any poll tax or other tax.

Section 2. The Congress shall have power to enforce this article by appropriate legislation.

AMENDMENT XXV [1967]

Section 1. In case of the removal of the President from office or of his death or resignation, the Vice President shall become President.

Section 2. Whenever there is a vacancy in the office of the Vice President, the President shall nominate a Vice President who shall take office upon confirmation by a majority vote of both Houses of Congress.

Section 3. Whenever the President transmits to the President pro tempore of the Senate and the Speaker of the House of Representatives his written declaration that he is unable to discharge the powers and duties of his office, and until he transmits to them a written declaration to the contrary, such powers and duties shall be discharged by the Vice President as Acting President.

Section 4. Whenever the Vice President and a majority of either the principal officers of the executive departments or of such other body as Congress may by law provide, transmit to the President pro tempore of the Senate and the Speaker of the House of Representatives their written declaration that the President is unable to discharge the powers and duties of his office, the Vice President shall immediately assume the powers and duties of the office as Acting President.

Thereafter, when the President transmits to the President pro tempore of the Senate and the Speaker of the House of Representatives his written declaration that no inability exists, he shall resume the powers and duties of his office unless the Vice President and a majority of either the principal officers of the executive department or of such other body as Congress may by law provide, transmit within four days to the President pro tempore of the Senate and the Speaker of the House of Representatives their written declaration that the President is unable to discharge the powers and duties of his office. Thereupon Congress shall decide the issue, assembling within forty-eight hours for that purpose if not in session. If the Congress, within twenty-one days after receipt of the latter written declaration, or, if Congress is not in session, within twenty-one days after Congress is required to assemble, determines by two-thirds vote of both Houses that the President is unable to discharge the powers and duties of his office, the Vice President shall continue to discharge the same as Acting President; otherwise, the President shall resume the powers and duties of his office.

AMENDMENT XXVI [1971]

Section 1. The right of citizens of the United States, who are eighteen years of age or older, to vote shall not be denied or abridged by the United States or by any State on account of age.

Section 2. The Congress shall have power to enforce this article by appropriate legislation.

AMENDMENT XXVII [1992]

No law, varying the compensation for the services of the Senators and Representatives, shall take effect, until an election of Representatives shall have intervened.

APPENDIX C

Sample Answers for End-of-Chapter Questions with Sample Answer

1–2A. QUESTION WITH SAMPLE ANSWER

At the time of the Nuremberg trials, "crimes against humanity" were new international crimes. The laws criminalized such acts as murder, extermination, enslavement, deportation, and other inhumane acts committed against any civilian population. These international laws derived their legitimacy from "natural law." Natural law, which is the oldest and one of the most significant schools of jurisprudence, holds that governments and legal systems should reflect the moral and ethical ideals that are inherent in human nature. Because natural law is universal and discoverable by reason, its adherents believe that all other law is derived from natural law. Natural law therefore supersedes laws created by humans (national, or "positive," law), and in a conflict between the two, national or positive law loses its legitimacy. The Nuremberg defendants asserted that they had been acting in accordance with German law. The judges dismissed these claims, reasoning that the defendants' acts were commonly regarded as crimes and that the accused must have known that the acts would be considered criminal. The judges clearly believed the tenets of natural law and expected that the defendants, too, should have been able to realize that their acts ran afoul of it. The fact that the "positivist law" of Germany at the time required them to commit these acts is irrelevant. Under natural law theory, the international court was justified in finding the defendants guilty of crimes against humanity.

2–2A. QUESTION WITH SAMPLE ANSWER

Trial courts, as explained in the text, are responsible for settling "questions of fact." Often, when parties bring a case to court there is a dispute as to what actually happened. Different witnesses have different versions of what they saw or heard, and there may be only indirect evidence of certain issues in dispute. During the trial, the judge and the jury (if it is a jury trial) listen to the witnesses and view the evidence firsthand. Thus, the trial court is in the best position to assess the credibility (truthfulness) of the witnesses and determine the weight that should be given to various items of evidence. At the end of the trial, the judge and the jury (if it is a jury trial)

decide what will be considered facts for the purposes of the case. Trial courts are best suited to this job, as they have the opportunity to observe the witnesses and evidence, and they regularly determine the reliability of certain evidence. Appellate courts, in contrast, see only the written record of the trial court proceedings and cannot evaluate the credibility of witnesses and the persuasiveness of evidence. For these reasons, appellate courts nearly always defer to trial courts' findings of fact. An appellate court can reverse a lower court's findings of fact, however, when so little evidence was presented at trial that no reasonable person could have reached the conclusion that the judge or jury reached.

3–2A. QUESTION WITH SAMPLE ANSWER

(a) After all of the pleadings (the complaint, answer, and any counterclaim and reply) have been filed, either party can file a motion for judgment on the pleadings. This may happen because it is clear from just the pleadings that the plaintiff has failed to state a cause of action. This motion is also appropriate when all the parties agree on the facts, and the only question remaining is how the law applies to those facts. The court may consider only those facts pleaded in the documents and stipulated (agreed to) by the parties. This is the difference between a motion for judgment on the pleadings and a motion for summary judgment (discussed below). In a motion for summary judgment, there may be some facts in dispute and the parties may supplement the pleadings with sworn statements and other materials.

(b) During the trial, at the conclusion of the plaintiff's case, the defendant may move for a directed verdict. If the defendant does this, he or she will argue to the court that the plaintiff presented inadequate evidence that he or she is entitled to the remedy being sought. In considering a motion for a directed verdict (federal courts use the term "motion for a judgment as a matter of law"), the judge looks at the evidence in the light most favorable to the plaintiff and grants the motion only if there is insufficient evidence to raise an issue of fact. These motions are rarely granted at this stage of a trial. At the end of the defendant's case, the parties have another opportunity to

610

move for a directed verdict. This time, either party can seek the motion. The motion will be granted only if there is no reasonable way to find for the party against whom the motion is made. In other words, if, after the defense's case is concluded, the plaintiff asks the court to direct a verdict against the defendant, the court will do so if no reasonable interpretation of the evidence would allow the defendant to win the case.

(c) As noted in part (a) of this answer, a motion for summary judgment is similar to a motion for a judgment on the pleadings in that it asks the court to grant a judgment without a trial. Either party can file a summary judgment motion when the only question is how the law applies to the facts in a case. When a court considers a motion for summary judgment, it can take into account evidence outside the pleadings. The evidence may consist of sworn statements by parties or witnesses as well as documents. The use of this additional evidence distinguishes the motion for summary judgment from the motion for judgment on the pleadings. Summary judgment motions will be granted only when there are no questions of fact that need to be decided and the only question is a question of law, which requires a judge's ruling. These motions can be made before or during a trial.

(d) If a losing party has previously moved for a directed verdict, that party can make a motion for a judgment *n.o.v.* (notwithstanding the verdict) after the jury issues its verdict. The standards for granting a judgment *n.o.v.* are the same as those for granting a motion to dismiss a case or a motion for a directed verdict. Essentially, the losing party argues that even if the evidence is viewed in the light most favorable to the other party, a reasonable jury could not have found in that party's favor. If the judge finds this contention to be correct or decides that the law requires the opposite result, the motion will be granted.

4–2A. QUESTION WITH SAMPLE ANSWER

As the text points out, Thomas has a constitutionally protected right to his religion and the free exercise of it. In denying his unemployment benefits, the state violated these rights. Employers are obligated to make reasonable accommodations for their employees' beliefs, right or wrong, that are openly and sincerely held. Thomas's beliefs were openly and sincerely held. By placing him in a department that made military goods, his employer effectively put him in a position of having to choose between his job and his religious principles. This unilateral decision on the part of the employer was the reason Thomas left his job and why the company was required to compensate Thomas for his resulting unemployment.

5–2A. QUESTION WITH SAMPLE ANSWER

This question essentially asks whether good behavior can ever be unethical. The answer to this question depends on which approach to ethical reasoning you are using. Under the outcome-based approach of utilitarianism, it is simply not possible for selfish motives to be unethical if they

result in good conduct. A good outcome is moral regardless of the nature of the action itself or the reason for the action. Under a duty-based approach, motive would be more relevant in assessing whether a firm's conduct was ethical. You would need to analyze the firm's conduct in terms of religious truths or to determine whether human beings were being treated with the inherent dignity that they deserve. Although a good motive would not justify a bad act to a religious ethicist, in this situation the actions were good and the motive was questionable (because the firm was simply seeking to increase its profit). Nevertheless, unless one's religion prohibited making a profit, the firm's actions would likely not be considered unethical. Applying Kantian ethics would require you to evaluate the firm's actions in light of what would happen if everyone in society acted that way (categorical imperative). Here, because the conduct was good, it would be positive for society if every firm acted that way. Hence, the profit-seeking motive would be irrelevant in a Kantian analysis. In a debate between motive and conduct, then, conduct is almost always given greater weight in evaluating ethics.

6–2A. QUESTION WITH SAMPLE ANSWER

To answer this question, you must first decide if there is a legal theory under which Harley may be able to recover. You may recall from your reading the intentional tort of "wrongful interference with a contractual relationship." To recover damages under this theory, Harley would need to show that he and Martha had a valid contract, that Lothar knew of this contractual relationship between Martha and Harley, and that Lothar intentionally convinced Martha to break her contract with Harley. Even though Lothar hoped that his advertisments would persuade Martha to break her contract with Harley, the question states that Martha's decision to change bakers was based solely on the advertising and not on anything else that Lothar did. Lothar's advertisements did not constitute a tort. Note, though, that while Harley cannot collect from Lothar for Martha's actions, he does have a cause of action against Martha for her breach of their contract.

7–2A. QUESTION WITH SAMPLE ANSWER

This is a causation question. You will recall from the chapter that four elements must be proved for a plaintiff to recover in a claim for negligence: that the defendant owed a duty of care, the defendant breached this duty, the plaintiff suffered a legally recognizable injury, and the defendant's breach of the duty of care caused the injury. Ruth did breach the duty of care that she owed Jim (and others in society) when she parked carelessly on the hill. Jim also clearly suffered an injury. The only remaining question, then, has to do with causation. Causation is broken down into two parts, causation in fact and proximate cause. In order for Jim to recover, he must prove that both kinds of causation existed in this case. Causation in fact is answered by the "but for" test and readily answered here.

Ruth's car set into motion a chain of events without which the barn would not have fallen down. Meeting the proximate cause test will be more difficult for Jim. Recall that proximate cause exists only when the connection between an act and an injury is strong enough to justify imposing liability. Careless parking on a hill creates a risk that a reasonable person can foresee could result in harm. The question here is whether the electric spark, the grass fire, the barn full of dynamite, and the roof falling in are *foreseeable* risks stemming from a poor parking job. In this case, it would be a question of fact for a jury to determine whether there were enough intervening events between Ruth's parking and Jim's injury to defeat Jim's claim.

8–2A. QUESTION WITH SAMPLE ANSWER

(a) Ursula will not be held liable for copyright infringement in this case because her photocopying pages for use in scholarly research falls squarely under the "fair use" exception to the Copyright Act.

(b) While Ursula's actions are improper, they could constitute trademark infringement, not copyright infringement. Copyrights are granted for literary and artistic productions; trademarks are distinctive marks created and used by manufacturers to differentiate their goods from those of their competitors. Trademark infringement occurs when a mark is copied to a substantial degree, intentionally or unintentionally.

(c) As with the answer to (a) above, Ursula's actions fall within the "fair use" doctrine of copyright law. Her use of the taped television shows for teaching is the exact type of use the exception is designed to cover.

9–3A. QUESTION WITH SAMPLE ANSWER

As you read in the text, some torts, including assault and battery, provide a basis for criminal prosecution as well as civil liability. This question aptly demonstrates this principle. Double jeopardy is a criminal law concept and does not constitute a defense against a civil lawsuit. The Fifth Amendment prohibition against double jeopardy means that once Armington has been tried and found guilty or not guilty for this assault, he may not be tried for it again. Nevertheless, Jennings may seek damages for his injuries in a civil lawsuit because Armington's prison sentence will do nothing to reimburse him for his medical bills and disability. Armington's guilty verdict has no bearing on the civil lawsuit. The criminal conviction, however, having been proved beyond a reasonable doubt, will likely improve Jennings's chances of recovering damages from Armington in a civil case. As you will recall, in a civil suit the plaintiff merely has to prove his or her case by a preponderance of the evidence. For Jennings, this burden of proof will probably be much easier to meet, given Armington's conviction.

10–2A. QUESTION WITH SAMPLE ANSWER

According to the question, Janine was apparently unconscious or otherwise unable to agree to a contract for the nursing services she received while she was in the hospital. As you read in the chapter, however, sometimes the law will create a fictional contract in order to prevent one party from unjustly receiving a benefit at the expense of another. This is known as a *quasi contract* and provides a basis for Nursing Services to recover the value of the services it provided while Janine was in the hospital. As for the at-home services that were provided to Janine, because Janine was aware that those services were being provided for her, Nursing Services can recover for those services under an implied-in-fact contract. Under this type of contract, the conduct of the parties creates and defines the terms. Janine's acceptance of the services constitutes her agreement to form a contract, and she will probably be required to pay Nursing Services in full.

11–2A. QUESTION WITH SAMPLE ANSWER

(a) Death of either the offeror or the offeree prior to acceptance automatically terminates a revocable offer. The basic legal reason is that the offer is personal to the parties and cannot be passed on to others, not even to the estate of the deceased. This rule applies even if the other party is unaware of the death. Thus, Schmidt's offer terminates on Schmidt's death, and Barry's later acceptance does not constitute a contract.

(b) An offer is automatically terminated by the destruction of the specific subject matter of the offer prior to acceptance. Thus, Barry's acceptance after the fire does not constitute a contract.

(c) When the offer is irrevocable, under an option contract, death of the offeror does not terminate the option contract, and the offeree can accept the offer to sell the equipment, binding the offeror's estate to performance. Performance is not personal to Schmidt, as the estate can transfer title to the equipment. Knowledge of the death is immaterial to the offeree's right of acceptance. Thus, Barry can hold Schmidt's estate to a contract for the purchase of the equipment.

(d) When the offer is irrevocable, under an option contract, death of the offeree also does not terminate the offer. Because the option is a separate contract, the contract survives and passes to the offeree's estate, which can exercise the option by acceptance within the option period. Thus, acceptance by Barry's estate binds Schmidt to a contract for the sale of the equipment.

12–2A. QUESTION WITH SAMPLE ANSWER

The legal issue deals with the preexisting duty rule, which basically states that a promise to do what one already has a legal or contractual duty to do does not constitute consideration, and thus the return promise is unenforceable. In this case, Shade was required contractually to build a house according to a specific set of plans for $53,000, and Bernstein's later agreement to pay an additional $3,000 for exactly what Shade was required to do for $53,000 is without consideration and unenforceable. One of the purposes of this general rule is to prevent commercial blackmail. There are four basic exceptions to this rule:

(a) If the duties of Shade are modified, for example, by changes made by Bernstein in the specifications, these changes can constitute consideration and bind Bernstein to pay the additional $3,000.

(b) Rescission and new contract theory could be applied, by which the old contract of $53,000 would mutually be canceled and a new contract for $56,000 would be made. Most courts would not apply this theory unless there was a clear intent to cancel the original contract. It appears here that the intent to cancel the $53,000 contract is lacking (there is merely an intent to modify), so this exception would not apply.

(c) A few states have statutes that allow any modification to be enforceable if it is in writing. The facts stated give no evidence that Bernstein's agreement to the additional $3,000 is in writing, but, if it is, Bernstein is bound in those states.

(d) The unforeseen difficulty or hardship rule could be argued. This rule, however, applies only to unknown risks not ordinarily assumed in business transactions. Because inflation and price rises are risks ordinarily assumed in business, this exception cannot be used by Shade.

13–2A. QUESTION WITH SAMPLE ANSWER

Contracts in restraint of trade are usually illegal and unenforceable. An exception to this rule applies to a covenant not to compete that is ancillary to certain types of business contracts in which some fair protection is deemed appropriate (such as in the sale of a business). The covenant, however, must be reasonable in terms of time and area to be legally enforceable. If either term is excessive, the court can declare that the restraint goes beyond what is necessary for reasonable protection. In this event, the court can either declare the covenant illegal or it can reform the covenant to make the terms of time and area reasonable and then enforce it. Suppose the court declares the covenant illegal and unenforceable. Because the covenant is ancillary and severable from the primary contract, the primary contract is not affected by such a ruling. In the case of Hotel Lux, the primary contract concerns employment; the covenant is ancillary and desirable for the protection of the hotel. The time period of one year may be considered reasonable for a chef with an international reputation. The reasonableness of the three-state area restriction may be questioned, however. If it is found to be reasonable, the covenant probably will be enforced. If it is not found to be reasonable, the court could declare the entire covenant illegal, allowing Perlee to be employed by any restaurant or hotel, including one in direct competition with Hotel Lux. Alternatively, the court could reform the covenant, making its terms reasonable for protecting Hotel Lux's normal customer market area.

14–2A. QUESTION WITH SAMPLE ANSWER

Four basic elements are necessary to prove fraud, thus rendering a contract voidable: (1) an intent to deceive, usually with knowledge of the falsity; (2) a misrepresentation of material facts; (3) a reliance by the innocent party on the misrepresentation; and (4) usually damage or injury caused by the misrepresentation. Statements of events to take place in the future or statements of opinions are generally not treated as representations of fact. Therefore, even though the prediction or opinion may turn out to be incorrect, a contract based on this type of statement would remain enforceable. Grano's statement that the motel would make at least $45,000 next year would probably be treated as a prediction or opinion; thus, one of the elements necessary to prove fraud—misrepresentation of facts—would be missing. The statement that the motel netted $30,000 last year is a deliberate falsehood (with intent and knowledge). Grano's defense will be that the books in Tanner's possession clearly indicated that the figure stated was untrue, and therefore Tanner cannot be said to have purchased the motel in reliance on the falsehood. If the innocent party, Tanner, knew the true facts, or should have known the true facts because they were available to him, Grano's argument will prevail.

Finally, the issue centers on Grano's duty to tell Tanner of the bypass. Ordinarily, neither party in a nonfiduciary relationship has a duty to disclose facts, even when the information might bear materially on the other's decision to enter into the contract. Exceptions are made, however, when the buyer cannot reasonably be expected to discover the information known by the seller, in which case fairness imposes a duty to speak on the seller. Here, the court can go either way. If the court decides there was no duty to disclose, deems the prediction of future profits to be opinion rather than a statement of fact, and also decides there was no justifiable reliance by Tanner because the books available to Tanner clearly indicated Grano's profit statement for the last year to be false, then Tanner cannot get his money back on the basis of fraud.

15–2A. QUESTION WITH SAMPLE ANSWER

In this situation, Mallory becomes what is known as a *guarantor* on the loan; that is, she guarantees to the hardware store that she will pay for the mower if her brother fails to do so. This kind of collateral promise, in which the guarantor states that he or she will become responsible *only* if the primary party does not perform, must be in writing to be enforceable. There is an exception, however. If the main purpose in accepting secondary liability is to secure a personal benefit—for example, if Mallory's brother bought the mower for her—the contract need not be in writing. The assumption is that a court can infer from the circumstances of the case whether the main purpose was to secure a personal benefit and thus, in effect, to answer for the guarantor's own debt.

16–2A. QUESTION WITH SAMPLE ANSWER

Thrift is a creditor beneficiary. To be a creditor beneficiary one must be the creditor in a previously established debtor-creditor relationship, and then the debtor's subsequent contract terms with a third party must confer a benefit on the creditor. The contract made between the debtor and third party is not made expressly for the benefit of the creditor (as is required for a donee beneficiary). Rather, it is made for the benefit of the contracting parties. In this case, the original mortgage contract created a debtor-creditor relationship between Hensley and Thrift. Hensley's contract of sale in which Sylvia agreed to assume the mortgage payments conferred a benefit on Thrift as to payment of the debt. The primary purpose of the contract was strictly to benefit the contracting parties. Hensley was to receive money for the sale of the house, and Sylvia was to receive the low mortgage interest rate. Thrift still has the house and lot as security for the loan, can hold Hensley personally liable for the mortgage note, and as a creditor beneficiary can hold Sylvia personally liable on the basis of her contract with Hensley to assume the mortgage.

17–2A. Question with Sample Answer

A novation exists when a new, valid contract expressly or impliedly discharges a prior contract by the substitution of a party. Accord and satisfaction exists when the parties agree that the original obligation can be discharged by a substituted performance. In this case, Fred's agreement with Iba to pay off Junior's debt for $1,100 (as compared to the $1,000 owed) is definitely a valid contract. The terms of the contract substitute Fred as the debtor for Junior, and Junior is definitely discharged from further liability. This agreement is a *novation*.

18–2A. Question with Sample Answer

Generally, the equitable remedy of specific performance will be granted only if two criteria are met: monetary damages (under the situation) must be inadequate as a remedy, and the subject matter of the contract must be unique.

(a) In the sale of land, the buyer's contract is for a specific piece of real property. The land under contract is unique, because no two pieces of real property have the same legal description. In addition, money damages would not compensate a buyer adequately, as the same land cannot be purchased elsewhere. Specific performance is an appropriate remedy.

(b) The basic criteria for specific performance do not apply well to personal-service contracts. If the identical service contracted for is readily available from others, the service is not unique, and monetary damages for nonperformance are adequate. If, however, the services are so personal that only the contract party can perform them, the contract meets the test of uniqueness; but the courts will refuse to decree specific performance if (1) the enforcement of specific performance requires involuntary servitude (prohibited by the Thirteenth Amendment to the U.S. Constitution), or (2) it is impractical to attempt to force meaningful performance by someone against his or her will. In the case of Amy and Fred, specific performance is not an appropriate remedy.

(c) A rare coin is unique, and monetary damages for breach are inadequate, as Hoffman cannot obtain a substantially identical substitute in the market. This is a typical case in which specific performance is an appropriate remedy.

(d) The key issue here is that this is a closely held corporation. Therefore, the stock is not available in the market, and the shares become unique. The uniqueness of these shares is enhanced by the fact that if Ryan sells her 4 percent of the shares to Chang, Chang will control the corporation. Because of this, monetary damages for Chang are totally inadequate as a remedy. Specific performance is an appropriate remedy.

19–2A. Question with Sample Answer

Anne has entered into an enforceable contract to subscribe to *E-Commerce Weekly*. In this problem, the offer to deliver, via e-mail, the newsletter was presented by the offeror with a statement of how to accept—by clicking on the "SUBSCRIBE" button. Consideration was in the promise to deliver the newsletter and in the price that the subscriber agreed to pay. The offeree had an opportunity to read the terms of the subscription agreement before making the contract. Whether she actually read those terms does not matter.

20–2A. Question with Sample Answer

The entire answer falls under UCC 2–206(1)(b), because the situation deals with a buyer's order to buy goods for prompt shipment. The law is that such an order or offer invites acceptance by a prompt promise to ship conforming goods. If the promise (acceptance) is sent by a medium reasonable under the circumstances, the acceptance is effective when sent. Therefore, a contract was formed on October 8, and it required Martin to ship 100 model Color-X television sets. Martin's shipment is nonconforming, and Flint is correct in claiming that Martin is in breach. Martin's claim would be valid if Martin had not sent its promise of shipment. The UCC provides that shipment of nonconforming goods constitutes an acceptance *unless* the seller seasonably notifies the buyer that such shipment is sent only as an accommodation. Thus, had a contract not been formed on October 8, the nonconforming shipment on the 28th would not be treated as an acceptance, and no contract would be in existence to breach.

21–2A. Question with Sample Answer

There is no question that the suit is in existence and identified to the contract. Nor do the facts indicate that there was an agreement as to when title or risk of loss would pass. Therefore, these situations deal with passage of title and risk of loss to goods that are "to be delivered" without physical movement of the goods by the seller and not represented by a document of title. The rules of law are that title passes to the buyer on the making of the contract, and risk of loss passes from a *merchant* seller to the buyer when the buyer *receives* the goods.

(a) In the case of the major creditor, title is with Sikora, and the major creditor cannot levy on the suit.

(b) The risk of loss on the suit destroyed by fire falls on Carson. Carson is a merchant, and because Sikora has not taken possession, Carson retains the risk of loss. This problem illustrates that title and risk of loss do not always pass from seller to buyer at the same time.

22–2A. QUESTION WITH SAMPLE ANSWER

Topken basically has the following remedies.

(a) Topken can identify the 500 washing machines to the contract and resell the goods [UCC 2–704].

(b) Topken can withhold delivery and proceed with other remedies [UCC 2–703].

(c) Topken can cancel the contract and proceed with other remedies [UCC 2–703 and 2–106(4)].

(d) Topken can resell the goods in a commercially reasonable manner (public or private sale with notice to Lorwin, holding Lorwin liable for any loss and retaining any profits) [UCC 2–706]. If Topken cannot resell after making a reasonable effort, Topken can sue for the purchase price [UCC 2–709 (1)(b)].

(e) Topken can sue Lorwin for breach of contract, recovering as damages the difference between the market price (at the time and place of tender) and the contract price, plus incidental damages [UCC 2–708].

The student should note the combination of remedies that would be most beneficial for Topken under the circumstances.

23–2A. QUESTION WITH SAMPLE ANSWER

If Colt can prove that all due care was exercised in the manufacture of the pistol, Colt cannot be held in an action based on negligence. Under the theory of strict liability in tort, however, Colt can be held liable regardless of the degree of care exercised. The doctrine of strict liability states that a merchant seller who sells a defective product that is unreasonably dangerous is liable for injuries caused by that product (even if all possible care in preparation and sale is exercised), provided that the product has not been substantially changed after the time of sale. Therefore, if Wayne can prove the pistol is defective, unreasonably dangerous, and caused him injury, Colt as a merchant is strictly liable, because there is no evidence that the pistol has been altered since the date of its manufacture.

24–2A. QUESTION WITH SAMPLE ANSWER

For an instrument to be negotiable, it must meet the following requirements:

(a) Be in writing.

(b) Be signed by the maker or drawer.

(c) Be an unconditional promise or order.

(d) State a fixed amount of money.

(e) Be payable on demand or at a definite time.

(f) Be payable to bearer or order (unless it is a check).

The instrument in this case meets the writing requirement in that it is handwritten and on something with a degree of permanence that is transferable. The instrument meets the requirement of being signed by the maker, as Juan Sanchez's signature (his name in his handwriting) appears in the body of the instrument. The instrument's payment is not conditional and contains Juan Sanchez's definite promise to pay. In addition, the sum of $100 is both a fixed amount and payable in money (U.S. currency). Because the instrument is payable on demand and to bearer (Kathy Martin or any holder), it is negotiable.

25–2A. QUESTION WITH SAMPLE ANSWER

(a) The bank does qualify as a holder in due course (HDC) for the amount of $5,000. To qualify as an HDC under UCC 3–302, one must take the instrument for value, in good faith, and without being put on notice that a defense exists against it, that it has been dishonored, or that it is overdue. In this situation the bank has given full value for the instrument—$4,850 ($5,000 – $150 discount). Therefore, the bank is entitled to be an HDC for the face value of the instrument ($5,000). In addition, the bank took the instrument in good faith and without notice of the original incompleteness of the instrument (completed when purchased by the bank) or the lack of authority of Hayden to complete the instrument in an amount over $2,000. The instrument was also taken before overdue (before the maturity date). Thus, First National Bank is an HDC.

(b) The sale to a stranger in a bar for $500 creates an entirely different situation. One of the requirements for the status of an HDC is that a holder take the instrument in good faith. *Good faith* is defined in the UCC as "honesty in fact in the conduct or transaction concerned" [UCC 1–201(19)]. Although the UCC does not provide clear guidelines to determine what is or is not good faith, both the amount paid (as compared to the face value of the instrument) and the circumstances under which the instrument is taken (as interpreted by a reasonable person) dictate whether the holder honestly believed the instrument was not defective when taken. In this case, taking a $5,000 note for $500 in a bar would raise a serious question of the stranger's good faith. Thus, the stranger would not qualify as a holder in due course.

26–3A. QUESTION WITH SAMPLE ANSWER

Frazier can recover the $1,500 from Kennedy if he is a holder in due course (HDC). He will be an HDC only if he, as a holder, took the check (a) for value, (b) in good faith, and (c) without notice that the check was overdue or dishonored or that a claim or defense against it exists. In this instance, Frazier qualifies for HDC status. First, he is a holder as the check was properly negotiated to him (by indorsement). Second, the facts indicate that he gave value. Third, there is nothing to indicate that he took the instrument in bad faith. Fourth, he was unaware of Niles's fraud (claim or defense), and he took the check before it was overdue (within thirty days of issue). Thus, Frazier is a holder in due course and can hold Kennedy liable.

27–2A. QUESTION WITH SAMPLE ANSWER

Citizens Bank will not have to recredit Gary's account for the $1,000 check and probably will not have to recredit his account for the first forged check for $100. Generally, a drawee bank is responsible for determining whether the signature of its customer is genuine, and when it pays on a forged customer's signature, the bank must recredit the customer's account [UCC 3–401, 4–406]. There are, however, exceptions to this general rule. First, when a customer's negligence substantially contributes to the making of an unauthorized signature (including a forgery), the drawee bank that pays the instrument in good faith will not be obligated to recredit the customer's account for the full amount of the check [UCC 3–406]. In addition, when a drawee bank sends to its customer a statement of account and canceled checks, the customer has a duty to exercise reasonable care and promptness in examining the statement to discover any forgeries and report them to the drawee bank. Failure of the customer to do so relieves the drawee from liability to the customer to the extent that the drawee bank suffers a loss [UCC 4–406(c)]. Therefore, Gary's negligence in allowing his checkbook to be stolen and his failure to report the theft or examine his May statement will preclude his recovery on the $100 check from the Citizens Bank. Under UCC 3–406(b) and 4–406(e), however, the bank could be liable to the extent that its negligence substantially contributes to the loss. Second, when a series of forgeries is committed by the same wrongdoer, the customer must discover and report the initial forgery within fourteen calendar days from the date that the statement of account and canceled checks (containing the initial forged check) are made available to the customer [UCC 4–406(d)(2)]. Failure to discover and report a forged check releases the drawee bank from liability for all additional forged checks in the series written after the thirty-day period. Therefore, Gary's failure to discover the May forged check by June 30 relieves the bank from liability for the June 20 check of $1,000.

28–2A. QUESTION WITH SAMPLE ANSWER

Three basic actions are available to Holiday:

(a) Attachment—a court-ordered seizure of nonexempt property prior to Holiday's reducing the debt to judgment. The grounds for granting the writ of attachment are limited, but in most states (when submitted), the writ is granted on introduction of evidence that a debtor intends to remove the property from the jurisdiction in which a judgment would be rendered. Holiday would have to post a bond and reduce its claim to judgment; then it could sell the attached property to satisfy the debt, returning any surplus to Kanahara.

(b) Writ of execution, on reducing the debt to judgment. The writ is an order issued by the clerk directing the sheriff or other officer of the court to seize (levy) nonexempt property of the debtor located within the court's jurisdiction. The property is then sold, and the proceeds are used to pay for the judgment and cost of sale, with any surplus going to the debtor (in this case, Kanahara).

(c) Garnishment of the wages owed to Kanahara by the Cross-Bar Packing Corp. Whenever a third person, the garnishee, owes a debt, such as wages, to the debtor, the creditor can proceed to have the court order the employer garnishee to turn over a percentage of the take-home pay (usually no more than 25 percent) to pay the debt. Garnishment actions are continuous in some states; in others, the action must be taken for each pay period.

Holiday can proceed with any one or a combination of these three actions. Because the property may be removed from the jurisdiction, and perhaps Kanahara himself may leave the jurisdiction (he may quit his job), prompt action is important.

29–3A. QUESTION WITH SAMPLE ANSWER

Generally, under Article 9, a secured party, on repossession of the collateral, has the right to keep it in full satisfaction of the debt (on proper notice and if no objection is received within twenty-one days) or to sell it or dispose of it, using the proceeds to cancel the debt. If the debtor has paid 60 percent of the cash price of a purchase-money security interest in consumer goods and has not after default signed a waiver of rights, the secured party cannot keep the collateral in full satisfaction of the debt. The secured party is forced to dispose of the collateral within ninety days [UCC 9–620(f)]. *Consumer goods* are defined as those used or bought primarily for personal, family, or household purposes [UCC 9–102(a)(23)]. In this case, Cummings has paid $400 ($100 down plus six $50 payments) of the $600 purchase price. Because the security interest is purchase money in consumer goods and the amount paid exceeds 60 percent of the price, Delgado cannot keep the repossessed set in full satisfaction of the debt. Therefore, Delgado has a duty to sell, lease, or otherwise dispose of the collateral and to apply the proceeds as prescribed in UCC 9–610.

30–3A. QUESTION WITH SAMPLE ANSWER

A trustee is given avoidance powers by the Bankruptcy Code. One situation in which the trustee can avoid transfers of property or payments by a debtor to a creditor is when such transfer constitutes a *preference.* A preference is a transfer of property or payment that favors one creditor over another. For a preference to exist, the debtor must be insolvent and must have made payment for a preexisting debt within ninety days of the filing of the petition in bankruptcy. The Code provides that the debtor is *presumed* to be insolvent during this ninety-day period. If the payment is made to an insider (and in this case payment was made to a close relative), the preference period is extended to one year, but the presumption of insolvency still applies only to the ninety-day period. In this case, the trustee has an excellent chance of having both payments declared preferences. The payment to Cool Springs was within ninety days of the filing of the petition, and it is doubtful that Cool Springs could overcome the presumption that Peaslee was insolvent at the time the payment was made. The $5,000 payment was made to an insider, Peaslee's father, and any payment made to an insider within one year of the petition of bankruptcy is a preference—as long as the debtor was insolvent at the time of payment. The facts indicate that Peaslee probably was insolvent at the time he paid his father. If he was not, the payment is not a preference, and the trustee's avoidance of the transfer would be improper.

31–2A. Question with Sample Answer

On creation of an agency, the agent owes certain fiduciary duties to the principal. Two such duties are the duty of loyalty and the duty to inform or notify. The duty of loyalty is a fundamental concept of the fiduciary relationship. The agent must act solely for the benefit of the principal, not in the agent's own interest or in the interest of another person. One of the principles invoked by this duty is that an agent employed to sell cannot become a purchaser without the principal's consent. When the agent is a partner, contracting to sell to another partner is equivalent to selling to oneself and is therefore a breach of the agent's duty. In addition, the agent has a duty to disclose to the principal any facts pertinent to the subject matter of the agency. Failure to disclose to Peter the knowledge of the shopping mall and the increased market value of the property also was a breach of Alice's fiduciary duties. When an agent breaches fiduciary duties owed to the principal by becoming a recipient of a contract, the contract is voidable at the election of the principal. Neither Carl nor Alice can hold Peter to the contract, and Alice's breach of fiduciary duties also allows Peter to terminate the agency relationship.

32–2A. Question with Sample Answer

As a general rule, a principal and third party are bound only to a contract made by the principal's agent within the scope of the agent's authority. An agent's authority to act can come from actual authority given to the agent (express or implied), apparent authority, or authority derived from an emergency. Express authority is directly given by the principal to the agent. Implied authority is deemed customary or inferred from the agent's position. Apparent authority is created when a principal gives a third person reason to believe the agent possesses authority not truly possessed. In this case, no express authority was given, and certainly no implied authority exists for a purchasing agent of goods to acquire realty. Moreover, A & B did nothing to lead Wilson to believe that Adams had authority to purchase land on its behalf. In addition, there was no emergency creating a need for Adams to purchase the land. Therefore, although Adams indicated

in the contract that she was an agent, she acted outside the scope of her authority. Because of this, the contract between Adams and Wilson is treated merely as an unaccepted offer. As such, neither Wilson nor A & B is bound unless A & B ratifies (accepts) the contract before Wilson withdraws (revokes) the offer. Ratification can take place only when the principal is aware of all material facts and makes some act of affirmation. If A & B affirms the contract before Wilson withdraws, A & B can enforce Adams's contract. If Wilson withdraws first, Adams's contract cannot be enforced by A & B.

33–2A. Question with Sample Answer

The Occupational Health and Safety Act (OSHA) requires employers to provide safe working conditions for employees. The act prohibits employers from discharging or discriminating against any employee who refuses to work when the employee believes in good faith that he or she will risk death or great bodily harm by undertaking the employment activity. Denton and Carlo had sufficient reason to believe that the maintenance job required of them by their employer involved great risk, and therefore, under OSHA, their discharge was wrongful. Denton and Carlo can turn to the Occupational Safety and Health Administration, which is part of the Department of Labor, for assistance.

34–2A. Question with Sample Answer

An employer can legally impose an educational requirement if the requirement is directly related to, and necessary for, performance of the job. In this situation, the employer is requiring a high school diploma as a condition of employment for its cleaning crew. A high school diploma is not related to, or necessary for, the competent performance of a job on a cleaning crew. Chinawa obviously comes under Title VII of the 1964 Civil Rights Act, as amended. Therefore, if someone were to challenge Chinawa's practices, a court would be likely to consider the disparate impact that the educational requirement had on Chinawa's hiring of minorities. Chinawa's educational requirement resulted in its hiring an all-white cleaning crew in an area in which 75 percent of the pool of qualified applicants were minorities. Therefore, Chinawa's educational requirement would likely be considered unintentional (disparate-impact) discrimination against minorities.

35–2A. Question with Sample Answer

The court would likely conclude that National Foods was responsible for the acts of harassment by the manager at the franchised restaurant, on the ground that the employees were the agents of National Foods. An agency relationship can be implied from the circumstances and conduct of the parties. The important question is the degree of control that a franchisor has over its franchisees. Whether it exercises that control is beside the point. Here, National Foods retained considerable control over the new hires and the franchisee's policies, as well as the right to terminate the franchise for violations. That its supervisors routinely approved the policies would not undercut National Foods' liability.

36–2A. QUESTION WITH SAMPLE ANSWER

(a) A limited partner's interest is assignable. In fact, assignment allows the assignee to become a substituted limited partner with the consent of the remaining partners. The assignment, however, does not dissolve the limited partnership.

(b) Bankruptcy of the limited partnership itself causes dissolution, but bankruptcy of one of the limited partners does not dissolve the partnership unless it causes the bankruptcy of the firm.

(c) The retirement, death, or insanity of a general partner dissolves the partnership unless the business can be continued by the remaining general partners. Because Dorinda was the only general partner, her death dissolves the limited partnership.

37–2A. QUESTION WITH SAMPLE ANSWER

Although a joint stock company has characteristics of a corporation, it is usually treated as a partnership. Therefore, although the joint stock company issues transferable shares of stock and is managed by directors and officers, the shareholders have personal liability. Unless the shareholders transfer their stock and ownership to a third party, not only are the joint stock company's assets available for damages caused by a breach, but the individual shareholders' estates are also subject to such liability. The business trust resembles and is treated like a corporation in many respects. One similarity is the limited liability of the beneficiaries. Unless by state law beneficiaries are treated as partners, making them liable to business trust creditors, Bateson Corp. can look to only business trust assets in the event of breach.

38–2A. QUESTION WITH SAMPLE ANSWER

(a) As a general rule, a promoter is personally liable for all preincorporation contracts made by the promoter. The basic theory behind such liability is that the promoter cannot be an agent for a nonexistent principal (a corporation not yet formed). It is immaterial whether the contracting party knows of the prospective existence of the corporation, and the general rule of promoter liability continues even after the corporation is formed. Three basic exceptions to promoter liability are:

(1) The promoter's contract with a third party can stipulate that the third party will look only to the new corporation, not to the promoter, for performance and liability.

(2) The third party can release the promoter from liability.

(3) After formation, the corporation can assume the contractual obligations and liability by *novation.*

(If it is by *adoption,* most courts hold that the promoter is still personally liable.)

Peterson is therefore personally liable on both contracts, because (1) neither Owens nor Babcock has released him from liability, (2) the corporation has not assumed contractual responsibility by novation, and (3) Peterson's contract with Babcock did not limit Babcock to holding only the corporation liable. (Peterson's liability was conditioned only on the corporation's formation, which did occur.)

(b) Incorporation in and of itself does not make the newly formed corporation liable for preincorporation contracts. Until the newly formed corporation assumes Peterson's contracts by novation (releasing Peterson from personal liability) or by adoption (undertaking to perform Peterson's contracts, which makes both the corporation and Peterson liable), Babcock cannot enforce Peterson's contract against the corporation.

39–2A. QUESTION WITH SAMPLE ANSWER

Directors are personally answerable to the corporation and the shareholders for breach of their duty to exercise reasonable care in conducting the affairs of the corporation. Reasonable care is defined as being the degree of care that a reasonably prudent person would use in the conduct of personal business affairs. When directors delegate the running of the corporate affairs to officers, the directors are expected to use reasonable care in the selection and supervision of such officers. Failure to do so will make the directors liable for negligence or mismanagement. A director who dissents to an action by the board is not personally liable for losses resulting from that action. Unless the dissent is entered into the board meeting minutes, however, the director is presumed to have assented. Therefore, the first issue in the case of AstroStar, Inc., is whether the board members failed to use reasonable care in the selection of the president. If so, and particularly if the board failed to provide a reasonable amount of supervision (and openly embezzled funds indicate that failure), the directors will be personally liable. This liability will include Eckhart unless she can prove that she dissented and that she tried to reasonably supervise the new president. Considering the facts in this case, it is questionable that Eckhart could prove this.

40–2A. QUESTION WITH SAMPLE ANSWER

Ajax apparently has given shareholder Alir notice of the meeting for approval of the merger. In addition, however, Ajax should have notified Alir of her right to dissent and of her right, should the merger be approved, to be paid a fair value for her shares. The law recognizes that a dissenting shareholder should not be forced to become an unwilling shareholder in a new corporation. If Alir adheres strictly to statutory procedures, she has appraisal rights for the Ajax shares she holds after approval of the merger. Alir's appraisal rights entitle her to be paid by Zeta the "fair value" of her shares. Fair value is the value of the shares on the day prior to the date on which the vote for merger is taken. This value must not reflect appreciation or depreciation of the stock in anticipation of the approval. If $20 is a true value (the market value on the day before the vote), Alir will receive $200,000 for her 10,000 Ajax shares.

41–2A. QUESTION WITH SAMPLE ANSWER

No. Under federal securities law, a stock split is exempt from registration requirements. This is because no *sale* of stock is involved. The existing shares are merely being split, and no consideration is received by the corporation for the additional shares created.

42–2A. QUESTION WITH SAMPLE ANSWER

A court might initially consider whether a member of a limited liability company (LLC) who has a material conflict of interest should be prohibited from dealing with matters of the LLC. Most likely, a court would conclude that a member—even a member with a conflict of interest—can vote to transfer LLC property, but must do so fairly. In this problem, the transfer of BP's sole asset by two of BP's members to themselves, disguised as Excel (a newly created LLC), represented a material conflict of interest. Not only did Amy and Carl engage in self-dealing, but in doing so, they increased their interests in Excel. This conflict did not prohibit Amy and Carl from voting to transfer BP's sole asset to Excel, however, so long as they dealt fairly with Dave. To judge the fairness, a court might consider the members' conduct, the end result, the purpose of the LLC, and the parties' expectations. Here, the transfer was arguably unfair in two respects. First, it was not an "arm's length transaction" because it did not occur on the open market. Second, the sale undercut BP's capacity to carry on its intended business (to own the property as a long-term investment). The court might still rule in favor of Amy and Carl if they could argue successfully that the transaction did not need to be, or could not be, at "arm's length" and that BP's investment capacity was not undercut.

43–2A. QUESTION WITH SAMPLE ANSWER

The court will consider first whether the agency followed the procedures prescribed in the Administrative Procedure Act (APA). Ordinarily, courts will not require agencies to use procedures beyond those of the APA. Courts will, however, compel agencies to follow their own rules. If an agency has adopted a rule granting extra procedures, the agency must provide those extra procedures, at least until the rule is formally rescinded. Ultimately, in this case, the court will most likely rule for the food producers.

44–3A. QUESTION WITH SAMPLE ANSWER

Yes. A regulation of the Federal Trade Commission (FTC) under Section 5 of the Federal Trade Commission Act makes it a violation for door-to-door sellers to fail to give consumers three days to cancel any sale. In addition, a number of state statutes require this three-day "cooling off" period to protect consumers from unscrupulous door-to-door sellers. Because the Gonchars sought to rescind the contract within the three-day period, Renowned Books was obligated to agree to cancel the contract. Its failure to allow rescission was in violation of the FTC regulation and of most state statutes.

45–2A. QUESTION WITH SAMPLE ANSWER

Fruitade has violated a number of federal environmental laws if such actions are being taken without a permit. First, because the dumping is in a navigable waterway, the River and Harbor Act of 1886, as amended, has been violated. Second, the Clean Water Act of 1972, as amended, has been violated. This act is designed to make the waters safe for swimming, to protect fish and wildlife, and to eliminate discharge of pollutants into the water. Both the crushed glass and the acid violate this act. Third, the Toxic Substances Control Act of 1976 was passed to regulate chemicals that are known to be toxic and could have an effect on human health and the environment. The acid in the cleaning fluid or compound could come under this act.

46–2A. QUESTION WITH SAMPLE ANSWER

Instant Foto has created a tying arrangement. To get Instant Foto's film, the purchaser is virtually required to also have the film developed by Instant Foto. The legality of a tying agreement depends on many factors, such as the purpose of the agreement and its likely effect on competition in the relevant markets (the market for the tying product and the market for the tied product). When the effect of the tying agreement is to substantially lessen competition, the agreement violates either the Sherman Act, Section 1, or the Clayton Act, Section 3. In this scenario, the fact that Instant Foto holds 50 percent of the film-sale market enables it to have a substantial effect on the film-processing market (the tied product). The combination substantially restricts the buyer's freedom of choice in processing the film and thus is illegal. Although Instant Foto might claim that the tie is required as a quality control, it is highly unlikely that only Instant Foto can provide such quality processing. Therefore, the business purpose is suspect, and the tie is a definite anticompetitive device.

47–2A. QUESTION WITH SAMPLE ANSWER

For Curtis to recover against the hotel, he must first prove that a bailment relationship was created between himself and the hotel as to the car or the fur coat, or both. For a bailment to exist, there must be a delivery of the personal property that gives the bailee exclusive possession of the property, and the bailee must knowingly accept the bailed property. If either element is lacking, there is no bailment relationship and no liability on the part of the bailee hotel. The facts clearly indicate that the bailee hotel took exclusive possession and control of Curtis's car, and it knowingly accepted the car when the attendant took the car from Curtis and parked it in the underground guarded garage, retaining the keys. Thus, a bailment was created as to the car, and, because a mutual benefit bailment was created, the hotel owes Curtis the duty to exercise reasonable care over the property to and to return the bailed car at the end of the bailment. Failure to return the car creates a presumption of negligence (lack of reasonable care), and unless the hotel can rebut this presumption, the hotel is liable to Curtis for the loss of the car. As to the fur coat, the hotel neither knew nor expected that the trunk contained an expensive fur coat. Thus, although the hotel knowingly took exclusive possession of the car, the hotel did not do so with the fur coat. (But for a regular coat and other items likely to be in the car, the hotel would be liable.) Because no bailment of the expensive fur coat was created, the hotel has no liability for its loss.

48–3A. QUESTION WITH SAMPLE ANSWER

Wilfredo understandably wants a general warranty deed, as this type of deed will give him the most extensive protection against any defects of title claimed against the property transferred. The general warranty would have Patricia warranting the following covenants:

(a) Covenant of seisin and right to convey—a warranty that the seller has good title and power to convey.

(b) Covenant against encumbrances—a guaranty by the seller that, unless stated, there are no outstanding encumbrances or liens against the property conveyed.

(c) Covenant of quiet possession—a warranty that the grantee's possession will not be disturbed by others claiming a prior legal right. Patricia, however, is conveying only ten feet along a property line that may not even be accurately surveyed. Patricia therefore does not wish to make these warranties. Consequently, she is offering a quitclaim deed, which does not convey any warranties but conveys only whatever interest, if any, the grantor owns. Although title is passed by the quitclaim deed, the quality of the title is not warranted.

Because Wilfredo really needs the property, it appears that he has three choices: he can accept the quitclaim deed; he can increase his offer price to obtain the general warranty deed he wants; or he can offer to have a title search made, which should satisfy both parties.

49–2A. QUESTION WITH SAMPLE ANSWER

Ajax will probably not be able to void the policy. Most life insurance policies contain what is called an incontestability clause. Such a clause provides that a policy cannot be contested for misstatements by the insured after the policy has been in effect for a given period, usually two years. Even though the application is part of the policy (attached to the policy), Patrick's innocent error in answering the question dealing with heart problems or ailments can no longer be contested by the insurer, as the incontestability clause is now in effect (three years have passed since the issuance of the policy). In addition, a misstatement about age is not grounds in and of itself for Ajax to avoid the policy. Ajax does, however, have the right to adjust premium payments to reflect the correct age or to reduce the amount of the insurance coverage accordingly. Thus, Ajax cannot escape liability on Patrick's death, but it can reduce the $50,000 coverage to account for the premiums that should have been paid for a person who is thirty-three years old, not thirty-two years old.

50–3A. QUESTION WITH SAMPLE ANSWER

(a) State laws vary on whether a will written and executed before marriage is revoked by the marriage. Some states declare that the will is revoked by a subsequent marriage only if a child is born out of that marriage. Under the Uniform Probate Code, a subsequent marriage does not revoke a will; however, the new spouse is entitled to share the estate as if the deceased has died intestate, and the balance passes under the will. In this case, if the will is revoked by marriage, Lisa will receive the entire estate, and Carol, as James's mother, will receive nothing. If the marriage does not revoke the will, Lisa will probably receive one-half the estate under the laws of intestacy, and the balance will go to Carol.

(b) At common law and under the Uniform Probate Code, divorce does not in and of itself revoke a will made and executed during a previous marriage. If the divorce is accompanied by a property settlement, most states revoke that portion of the will that disposed property to the former spouse. Although this matter is frequently controlled by statute, in the absence of such a statute, if Lisa received a property settlement on divorce, the will of James would be revoked and Mandis would recover the entire estate by the laws of intestacy.

(c) If a child is born after a will has been executed and the child is not provided for in the will, the law will allow the child to inherit as if the testator had died intestate. The philosophy is that unless the child is specifically excluded by the will, the child was intended to inherit and was omitted in error. Therefore, Claire would receive one-half of the estate in most states.

51–2A. QUESTION WITH SAMPLE ANSWER

Assuming that the court has abandoned the *Ultramares* rule, it is likely that the accounting firm of Goldman, Walters, Johnson & Co. will be held liable to Happydays State Bank for negligent preparation of financial statements. There are various policy reasons for holding accountants liable to third parties even in the absence of privity. The potential liability would make accountants more careful in the preparation of financial statements. Moreover, in some situations the accountants may be the only solvent defendants, and hence, unless liability is imposed on accountants, third parties who reasonably rely on financial statements may go unprotected. Accountants, rather than third parties, are in better positions to spread the risks. If third parties such as banks have to absorb the costs of bad loans made as a result of negligently prepared financial statements, then the cost of credit to the public in general will increase. In contrast, accountants are in a better position to spread the risk by purchasing liability insurance.

52–2A. QUESTION WITH SAMPLE ANSWER

Each system has its advantages and its disadvantages. In a common law system, the courts independently develop the rules governing certain areas of law, such as torts and contracts. This judge-made law exists in addition to the laws passed by a legislature. Judges must follow precedential decisions in their jurisdictions, but courts may modify or even overturn precedents when deemed necessary. Also, if there is no case law to guide a court, the court may create a new rule of law. In a civil law system, the only official source of law is a statutory code. Courts are required to interpret the code and apply the rules to individual cases, but courts may not depart from the code and develop their own laws. In theory, the law code will set forth all the principles needed for the legal system. Common law and civil law systems are not wholly distinct. For example, the United States has a common law system, but crimes are defined by statute as in civil law systems. Civil law systems may allow considerable room for judges to develop law: law codes cannot be so precise as to address every contested issue, so the judiciary must interpret the codes. There are also significant differences among common law countries. The judges of different common law nations have produced differing common law principles. The roles of judges and lawyers under the different systems should be taken into account. Among other factors that should be considered in establishing a business law system and in deciding what regulations to impose are the goals that the system and its regulations are intended to achieve and the expectations of those to whom both will apply, including foreign and domestic investors.

Glossary

A

Abandoned property Property with which the owner has voluntarily parted, with no intention of recovering it.

Abandonment In landlord-tenant law, a tenant's departure from leased premises completely, with no intention of returning before the end of the lease term.

Abatement A process by which legatees receive reduced benefits if the assets of an estate are insufficient to pay in full all general bequests provided for in the will.

Acceleration clause A clause in an installment contract that provides for all future payments to become due immediately on the failure to tender timely payments or on the occurrence of a specified event.

Acceptance (1) In contract law, the offeree's notification to the offeror that the offeree agrees to be bound by the terms of the offeror's proposal. Although historically the terms of acceptance had to be the mirror image of the terms of the offer, the Uniform Commercial Code provides that even modified terms of the offer in a definite expression of acceptance constitute a contract. (2) In negotiable instruments law, the drawee's signed agreement to pay a draft when presented.

Acceptor The person (the drawee) who accepts a draft and who agrees to be primarily responsible for its payment.

Accession Occurs when an individual adds value to personal property by either labor or materials. In some situations, a person may acquire ownership rights in another's property through accession.

Accommodation party A person who signs an instrument for the purpose of lending his or her name as credit to another party on the instrument.

Accord and satisfaction An agreement for payment (or other performance) between two parties, one of whom has a right of action against the other. After the payment has been accepted or other performance has been made, the "accord and satisfaction" is complete and the obligation is discharged.

Accredited investors In the context of securities offerings, "sophisticated" investors, such as banks, insur-ance companies, investment companies, the issuer's executive officers and directors, and persons whose income or net worth exceeds certain limits.

Acquittal A certification or declaration following a trial that the individual accused of a crime is innocent, or free from guilt, and is thus absolved of the charges.

Act of state doctrine A doctrine that provides that the judicial branch of one country will not examine the validity of public acts committed by a recognized foreign government within its own territory.

Actionable Capable of serving as the basis of a lawsuit.

Actual authority Authority of an agent that is express or implied.

Actual malice A condition that exists when a person makes a statement with either knowledge of its falsity or a reckless disregard for the truth. In a defamation suit, a statement made about a public figure normally must be made with actual malice for liability to be incurred.

Actus reus (pronounced *ak*-tus *ray*-uhs) A guilty (prohibited) act. The commission of a prohibited act is one of the two essential elements required for criminal liability, the other element being the intent to commit a crime.

Adequate protection doctrine In bankruptcy law, a doctrine that protects secured creditors from losing their security as a result of an automatic stay on legal proceedings by creditors against the debtor once the debtor petitions for bankruptcy relief. In certain circumstances, the bankruptcy court may provide adequate protection by requiring the debtor or trustee to pay the creditor or provide additional guaranties to protect the creditor against the losses suffered by the creditor as a result of the stay.

Adhesion contract A "standard-form" contract, such as that between a large retailer and a consumer, in which the stronger party dictates the terms.

Adjudication The process of resolving a dispute by presenting evidence and arguments before a neutral third party decision maker in a court or an administrative law proceeding.

Administrative agency A federal, state, or local government agency established to perform a specific function. Administrative agencies are authorized by legislative acts to make and enforce rules to administer and enforce the acts.

Administrative law The body of law created by administrative agencies (in the form of rules, regulations, orders, and decisions) in order to carry out their duties and responsibilities.

Administrative law judge (ALJ) One who presides over an administrative agency hearing and who has the power to administer oaths, take testimony, rule on questions of evidence, and make determinations of fact.

Administrative process The procedure used by administrative agencies in the administration of law.

Administrator One who is appointed by a court to handle the probate (disposition) of a person's estate if that person dies intestate (without a valid will) or if the executor named in the will cannot serve.

Adverse possession The acquisition of title to real property by occupying it openly, without the consent of the owner, for a period of time specified by a state statute. The occupation must be actual, open, notorious, exclusive, and in opposition to all others, including the owner.

Affidavit A written or printed voluntary statement of facts, confirmed by the oath or affirmation of the party making it and made before a person having the authority to administer the oath or affirmation.

Affirm To validate; to give legal force to. *See also* Ratification

Affirmative action Job-hiring policies that give special consideration to members of protected classes in an effort to overcome present effects of past discrimination.

Affirmative defense A response to a plaintiff's claim that does not deny the plaintiff's facts but attacks the plaintiff's legal right to bring an action. An example is the running of the statute of limitations.

After-acquired evidence A type of evidence submitted in support of an affirmative defense in employment discrimination cases. Evidence that, prior to the employer's discriminatory act, the employee engaged in misconduct sufficient to warrant dismissal had the employer known of it earlier.

After-acquired property Property of the debtor that is acquired after the execution of a security agreement.

Age of majority The age at which an individual is considered legally capable of conducting himself or herself responsibly. A person of this age is entitled to the full rights of citizenship, including the right to vote in elections. In contract law, one who is no longer an infant and can no longer disaffirm a contract.

Agency A relationship between two parties in which one party (the agent) agrees to represent or act for the other (the principal).

Agency by estoppel An agency that arises when a principal negligently allows an agent to exercise powers not granted to the agent, thus justifying others in believing that the agent possesses the requisite agency authority.

Agent A person who agrees to represent or act for another, called the principal.

Agreement A meeting of two or more minds in regard to the terms of a contract; usually broken down into two events—an offer by one party to form a contract, and an acceptance of the offer by the person to whom the offer is made.

Alien corporation A designation in the United States for a corporation formed in another country but doing business in the United States.

Alienation In real property law, the voluntary transfer of property from one person to another (as opposed to a transfer by operation of law).

Allegation A statement, claim, or assertion.

Allege To state, recite, assert, or charge.

Allonge (pronounced uh-*lohnj*) A piece of paper firmly attached to a negotiable instrument, on which transferees can make indorsements if there is no room left on the instrument itself.

Alternative dispute resolution (ADR) The resolution of disputes in ways other than those involved in the traditional judicial process. Negotiation, mediation, and arbitration are forms of ADR.

Amend To change through a formal procedure.

American Arbitration Association (AAA) The major organization offering arbitration services in the United States.

Analogy In logical reasoning, an assumption that if two things are similar in some respects, they will be similar in other respects also. Often used in legal reasoning to infer the appropriate application of legal principles in a case being decided by referring to previous cases involving different facts but considered to come within the policy underlying the rule.

Annuity An insurance policy that pays the insured fixed, periodic payments for life or for a term of years, as stipulated in the policy, after the insured reaches a specified age.

Annul To cancel; to make void.

Answer Procedurally, a defendant's response to the plaintiff's complaint.

Antecedent claim A preexisting claim. In negotiable instruments law, taking an instrument in satisfaction of an antecedent claim is taking the instrument for value—that is, for valid consideration.

Anticipatory repudiation An assertion or action by a party indicating that he or she will not perform an obligation that the party is contractually obligated to perform at a future time.

Antitrust law The body of federal and state laws and statutes protecting trade and commerce from unlawful restraints, price discrimination, price fixing, and monopolies. The principal federal antitrust statues are the Sherman Act of 1890, the Clayton Act of 1914, and the Federal Trade Commission Act of 1914.

Apparent authority Authority that is only apparent, not real. In agency law, a person may be deemed to have had the power to act as an agent for another party if the other party's manifestations to a third party led the third party to believe that an agency existed when, in fact, it did not.

Appeal　Resort to a superior court, such as an appellate court, to review the decision of an inferior court, such as a trial court or an administrative agency.

Appellant　The party who takes an appeal from one court to another.

Appellate court　A court having appellate jurisdiction.

Appellate jurisdiction　Jurisdiction that is exercised by reviewing courts, or appellate courts. Generally, cases can be brought before appellate courts only on appeal from an order or a judgment of a trial court or other lower court.

Appellee　The party against whom an appeal is taken—that is, the party who opposes setting aside or reversing the judgment.

Appraisal right　The right of a dissenting shareholder, if he or she objects to an extraordinary transaction of the corporation (such as a merger or consolidation), to have his or her shares appraised and to be paid the fair value of his or her shares by the corporation.

Appropriation　In tort law, the use by one person of another person's name, likeness, or other identifying characteristic without permission and for the benefit of the user.

Arbitrary and capricious test　A court reviewing an informal administrative agency action applies this test to determine whether or not that action was in clear error. The court gives wide discretion to the expertise of the agency and decides if the agency had sufficient factual information on which to base its action. If no clear error was made, then the agency's action stands.

Arbitration　The settling of a dispute by submitting it to a disinterested third party (other than a court), who renders a decision. The decision may or may not be legally binding.

Arbitration clause　A clause in a contract that provides that, in the event of a dispute, the parties will submit the dispute to arbitration rather than litigate the dispute in court.

Arraignment　A procedure in which an accused person is brought before the court to answer the criminal charges. The charge is read to the person, and he or she is asked to enter a plea—such as "guilty" or "not guilty."

Arson　The malicious burning of another's dwelling. Some statutes have expanded this to include any real property regardless of ownership and the destruction of property by other means—for example, by explosion.

Articles of incorporation　The document filed with the appropriate governmental agency, usually the secretary of state, when a business is incorporated; state statutes usually prescribe what kind of information must be contained in the articles of incorporation.

Articles of organization　The document filed with a designated state official by which a limited liability company is formed.

Articles of partnership　A written agreement that sets forth each partner's rights and obligations with respect to the partnership.

Artisan's lien　A possessory lien given to a person who has made improvements and added value to another person's personal property as security for payment for services performed.

Assault　Any word or action intended to make another person fearful of immediate physical harm; a reasonably believable threat.

Assignee　The person to whom contract rights are assigned.

Assignment　The act of transferring to another all or part of one's rights arising under a contract.

Assignor　The person who assigns contract rights.

Assumption of risk　A defense against negligence that can be used when the plaintiff is aware of a danger and voluntarily assumes the risk of injury from that danger.

Attachment　(1) In the context of secured transactions, the process by which a security interest in the property of another becomes enforceable. (2) In the context of judicial liens, a court-ordered seizure and taking into custody of property prior to the securing of a judgment for a past-due debt.

Attempted monopolization　Any actions by a firm to eliminate competition and gain monopoly power.

Authenticate　To sign a record, or with the intent to sign a record, to execute or to adopt an electronic sound, symbol, or the like to link with the record. A *record* is retrievable information inscribed on a tangible medium or stored in an electronic or other medium.

Authority　In agency law, the agent's permission to act on behalf of the principal. An agent's authority may be actual (express or implied) or apparent. *See also* Actual authority; Apparent authority

Authorization card　A card signed by an employee that gives a union permission to act on his or her behalf in negotiations with management. Unions typically use authorization cards as evidence of employee support during union organization.

Authorized means　In contract law, the means of acceptance authorized by the offeror.

Automatic stay　In bankruptcy proceedings, the suspension of virtually all litigation and other action by creditors against the debtor or the debtor's property; the stay is effective the moment the debtor files a petition in bankruptcy.

Award　In the context of litigation, the amount of money awarded to a plaintiff in a civil lawsuit as damages. In the context of arbitration, the arbitrator's decision.

B

Bailee　One to whom goods are entrusted by a bailor. Under the Uniform Commercial Code, a party who, by a bill of lading, warehouse receipt, or other document of title, acknowledges possession of goods and contracts.

Bailee's lien A possessory lien, or claim, that a bailee entitled to compensation can place on the bailed property to ensure that he or she will be paid for the services provided. The lien is effective as long as the bailee retains possession of the bailed goods and has not agreed to extend credit to the bailor. Sometimes referred to as an artisan's lien.

Bailment A situation in which the personal property of one person (a bailor) is entrusted to another (a bailee), who is obligated to return the bailed property to the bailor or dispose of it as directed.

Bailor One who entrusts goods to a bailee.

Bait-and-switch advertising Advertising a product at a very attractive price (the "bait") and then informing the consumer, once he or she is in the store, that the advertised product is either not available or is of poor quality; the customer is then urged to purchase ("switched" to) a more expensive item.

Banker's acceptance A negotiable instrument that is commonly used in international trade. A banker's acceptance is drawn by a creditor against the debtor, who pays the draft at maturity. The drawer creates a draft without designating a payee. The draft can pass through many parties' hands before a bank (drawee) accepts it, transforming the draft into a banker's acceptance. Acceptances can be purchased and sold in a way similar to securities.

Bankruptcy court A federal court of limited jurisdiction that handles only bankruptcy proceedings. Bankruptcy proceedings are governed by federal bankruptcy law.

Bargain A mutual undertaking, contract, or agreement between two parties; to negotiate over the terms of a purchase or contract.

Basis of the bargain In contract law, the affirmation of fact or promise on which the sale of goods is predicated, creating an express warranty.

Battery The unprivileged, intentional touching of another.

Bearer A person in the possession of an instrument payable to bearer or indorsed in blank.

Bearer instrument Any instrument that is not payable to a specific person, including instruments payable to the bearer or to "cash."

Beneficiary One to whom life insurance proceeds are payable or for whose benefit a trust has been established or property under a will has been transferred.

Bequest A gift by will of personal property (from the verb—to bequeath).

Beyond a reasonable doubt The standard used to determine the guilt or innocence of a person criminally charged. To be guilty of a crime, one must be proved guilty "beyond and to the exclusion of every reasonable doubt." A reasonable doubt is one that would cause a prudent person to hesitate before acting in matters important to him or her.

Bilateral contract A type of contract that arises when a promise is given in exchange for a return promise.

Bill of lading A document that serves both as evidence of the receipt of goods for shipment and as documentary evidence of title to the goods.

Bill of Rights The first ten amendments to the U.S. Constitution.

Binder A written, temporary insurance policy.

Binding authority Any source of law that a court must follow when deciding a case. Binding authorities include constitutions, statutes, and regulations that govern the issue being decided, as well as court decisions that are controlling precedents within the jurisdiction.

Blank indorsement An indorsement that specifies no particular indorsee and can consist of a mere signature. An order instrument that is indorsed in blank becomes a bearer instrument.

Blue laws State or local laws that prohibit the performance of certain types of commercial activities on Sunday.

Blue sky laws State laws that regulate the offer and sale of securities.

Bona fide Good faith. A bona fide obligation is one made in good faith—that is, sincerely and honestly.

Bona fide occupational qualification (BFOQ) Identifiable characteristics reasonably necessary to the normal operation of a particular business. These characteristics can include gender, national origin, and religion, but not race.

Bond A certificate that evidences a corporate (or government) debt. It is a security that involves no ownership interest in the issuing entity.

Bounty payment A reward (payment) given to a person or persons who perform a certain service— such as informing legal authorities of illegal actions.

Boycott A concerted refusal to do business with a particular person or entity in order to obtain concessions or to express displeasure with certain acts or practices of that person or business. *See also* Secondary boycott

Breach To violate a law, by an act or an omission, or to break a legal obligation that one owes to another person or to society.

Breach of contract The failure, without legal excuse, of a promisor to perform the obligations of a contract.

Bribery The offering, giving, receiving, or soliciting of anything of value with the aim of influencing an official action or an official's discharge of a legal or public duty or (with respect to commercial bribery) a business decision.

Brief A formal legal document submitted by the attorney for the appellant—or the appellee (in answer to the appellant's brief)—to an appellate court when a case is appealed. The appellant's brief outlines the facts and issues of the case, the judge's rulings or jury's findings that should be reversed or modified, the applicable law, and the arguments on the client's behalf.

Browse-wrap terms Terms and conditions of use that are presented to an Internet user at the time certain products, such as software, are being downloaded but that need not be agreed to (by clicking "I agree," for example) before being able to install or use the product.

Bureaucracy A large organization that is structured hierarchically to carry out specific functions.

Burglary The unlawful entry into a building with the intent to commit a felony. (Some state statutes expand this to include the intent to commit any crime.)

Business ethics Ethics in a business context; a consensus of what constitutes right or wrong behavior in the world of business and the application of moral principles to situations that arise in a business setting.

Business invitees Those people, such as customers or clients, who are invited onto business premises by the owner of those premises for business purposes.

Business judgment rule A rule that immunizes corporate management from liability for actions that result in corporate losses or damages if the actions are undertaken in good faith and are within both the power of the corporation and the authority of management to make.

Business necessity A defense to allegations of employment discrimination in which the employer demonstrates that an employment practice that discriminates against members of a protected class is related to job performance.

Business plan A document describing a company, its products, and its anticipated future performance. Creating a business plan is normally the first step in obtaining loans or venture-capital funds for a new business enterprise.

Business tort The wrongful interference with the business rights of another.

Business trust A voluntary form of business organization in which investors (trust beneficiaries) transfer cash or property to trustees in exchange for trust certificates that represent their investment shares. Management of the business and trust property is handled by the trustees for the use and benefit of the investors. The certificate holders have limited liability (are not responsible for the debts and obligations incurred by the trust) and share in the trust's profits.

Buyer in the ordinary course of business A buyer who, in good faith and without knowledge that the sale to him or her is in violation of the ownership rights or security interest of a third party in the goods, purchases goods in the ordinary course of business from a person in the business of selling goods of that kind.

Buyout price The amount payable to a partner on his or her dissociation from a partnership, based on the amount distributable to that partner if the firm were wound up on that date, and offset by any damages for wrongful dissociation.

Buy-sell agreement In the context of partnerships, an express agreement made at the time of partnership formation for one or more of the partners to buy out the other or others should the situation warrant—and thus provide for the smooth dissolution of the partnership.

Bylaws A set of governing rules adopted by a corporation or other association.

Bystander A spectator, witness, or person standing nearby when an event occurred and who did not engage in the business or act leading to the event.

C

C.I.F. or C.&F. Cost, insurance, and freight—or just cost and freight. A pricing term in a contract for the sale of goods requiring, among other things, that the seller place the goods in the possession of a carrier before risk passes to the buyer.

C.O.D. Cash on delivery. In sales transactions, a term meaning that the buyer will pay for the goods on delivery and before inspecting the goods.

Callable bond A bond that may be called in and the principal repaid at specified times or under conditions specified in the bond when it is issued.

Cancellation The act of nullifying, or making void. *See also* Rescission

Capital Accumulated goods, possessions, and assets used for the production of profits and wealth; the equity of owners in a business.

Carrier An individual or organization engaged in transporting passengers or goods for hire. *See also* Common carrier

Case law The rules of law announced in court decisions. Case law includes the aggregate of reported cases that interpret judicial precedents, statutes, regulations, and constitutional provisions.

Case on point A previous case involving factual circumstances and issues that are similar to the case before the court.

Cash surrender value The amount that the insurer has agreed to pay to the insured if a life insurance policy is canceled before the insured's death.

Cashier's check A check drawn by a bank on itself.

Categorical imperative A concept developed by the philosopher Immanuel Kant as an ethical guideline for behavior. In deciding whether an action is right or wrong, or desirable or undesirable, a person should evaluate the action in terms of what would happen if everybody else in the same situation, or category, acted the same way.

Causation in fact An act or omission without ("but for") which an event would not have occurred.

Cause of action A situation or set of facts sufficient to justify a right to sue.

Cease-and-desist order An administrative or judicial order prohibiting a person or business firm from conducting activities that an agency or court has deemed illegal.

Certificate of deposit (CD) A note of a bank in which a bank acknowledges a receipt of money from a party and promises to repay the money, with interest, to the party on a certain date.

Certificate of limited partnership The basic document filed with a designated state official by which a limited partnership is formed.

Certification mark A mark used by one or more persons, other than the owner, to certify the region, materials, mode of manufacture, quality, or accuracy of the owner's goods or services. When used by members of a cooperative, association, or other organization, such a mark is referred to as a collective mark. Examples of certification marks include the "Good Housekeeping Seal of Approval" and "UL Tested."

Certified check A check that has been accepted by the bank on which it is drawn. Essentially, the bank, by certifying (accepting) the check, promises to pay the check at the time the check is presented.

Certiorari *See* Writ of *certiorari*

Chain-style business franchise A franchise that operates under a franchisor's trade name and that is identified as a member of a select group of dealers that engage in the franchisor's business. The franchisee is generally required to follow standardized or prescribed methods of operation. Examples of this type of franchise are McDonald's and most other fast-food chains.

Chancellor An adviser to the king at the time of the early king's courts of England. Individuals petitioned the king for relief when they could not obtain an adequate remedy in a court of law, and these petitions were decided by the chancellor.

Charging order In partnership law, an order granted by a court to a judgment creditor that entitles the creditor to attach profits or assets of a partner on dissolution of the partnership.

Charitable trust A trust in which the property held by a trustee must be used for a charitable purpose, such as the advancement of health, education, or religion.

Chattel All forms of personal property.

Chattel paper Any writing or writings that show both a debt and the fact that the debt is secured by personal property. In many instances, chattel paper consists of a negotiable instrument coupled with a security agreement.

Check A draft drawn by a drawer ordering the drawee bank or financial institution to pay a certain amount of money to the holder on demand.

Checks and balances The national government is composed of three separate branches: the executive, the legislative, and the judicial branches. Each branch of the government exercises a check on the actions of the others.

Choice-of-language clause A clause in a contract designating the official language by which the contract will be interpreted in the event of a future disagreement over the contract's terms.

Choice-of-law clause A clause in a contract designating the law (such as the law of a particular state or nation) that will govern the contract.

Citation A reference to a publication in which a legal authority—such as a statute or a court decision—or other source can be found.

Civil law The branch of law dealing with the definition and enforcement of all private or public rights, as opposed to criminal matters.

Civil law system A system of law derived from that of the Roman Empire and based on a code rather than case law; the predominant system of law in the nations of continental Europe and the nations that were once their colonies. In the United States, Louisiana is the only state that has a civil law system.

Claim As a verb, to assert or demand. As a noun, a right to payment.

Clearinghouse A system or place where banks exchange checks and drafts drawn on each other and settle daily balances.

Click-on agreement An agreement that arises when a buyer, engaging in a transaction on a computer, indicates his or her assent to be bound by the terms of an offer by clicking on a button that says, for example, "I agree"; sometimes referred to as a *click-on license* or a *click-wrap agreement.*

Close corporation A corporation whose shareholders are limited to a small group of persons, often including only family members. The rights of shareholders of a close corporation usually are restricted regarding the transfer of shares to others.

Closed shop A firm that requires union membership by its workers as a condition of employment. The closed shop was made illegal by the Labor-Management Relations Act of 1947.

Closing The final step in the sale of real estate—also called settlement or closing escrow. The escrow agent coordinates the closing with the recording of deeds, the obtaining of title insurance, and other concurrent closing activities. A number of costs must be paid, in cash, at the time of closing, and they can range from several hundred to several thousand dollars, depending on the amount of the mortgage loan and other conditions of the sale.

Closing argument An argument made after the plaintiff and defendant have rested their cases. Closing arguments are made prior to the jury charges.

Codicil A written supplement or modification to a will. A codicil must be executed with the same formalities as a will.

Collateral Under Article 9 of the Uniform Commercial Code, the property subject to a security interest.

Collateral promise A secondary promise that is ancillary (subsidiary) to a principal transaction or primary contractual relationship, such as a promise made by one person to pay the debts of another if the latter fails to perform. A collateral promise normally must be in writing to be enforceable.

Collecting bank Any bank handling an item for collection, except the payor bank.

Collective bargaining The process by which labor and management negotiate the terms and conditions of employment, including working hours and workplace conditions.

Collective mark A mark used by members of a cooperative, association, or other organization to certify the region, materials, mode of manufacture, quality, or accuracy of the specific goods or services. Examples of collective marks include the labor union marks found on tags of certain products and the credits of movies, which indicate the various associations and organizations that participated in the making of the movies.

Comity A deference by which one nation gives effect to the laws and judicial decrees of another nation. This recognition is based primarily on respect.

Comment period A period of time following an administrative agency's publication or a notice of a proposed rule during which private parties may comment in writing on the agency proposal in an effort to influence agency policy. The agency takes any comments received into consideration when drafting the final version of the regulation.

Commerce clause The provision in Article I, Section 8, of the U.S. Constitution that gives Congress the power to regulate interstate commerce.

Commercial impracticability A doctrine under which a seller may be excused from performing a contract when (1) a contingency occurs, (2) the contingency's occurrence makes performance impracticable, and (3) the nonoccurrence of the contingency was a basic assumption on which the contract was made. Despite the fact that UCC 2–615 expressly frees only sellers under this doctrine, courts have not distinguished between buyers and sellers in applying it.

Commercial paper *See* Negotiable instrument

Commingle To mix together. To put funds or goods together into one mass so that the funds or goods are so mixed that they no longer have separate identities. In corporate law, if personal and corporate interests are commingled to the extent that the corporation has no separate identity, a court may "pierce the corporate veil" and expose the shareholders to personal liability.

Common area In landlord-tenant law, a portion of the premises over which the landlord retains control and maintenance responsibilities. Common areas may include stairs, lobbies, garages, hallways, and other areas in common use.

Common carrier A carrier that holds itself out or undertakes to carry persons or goods of all persons indifferently, or of all who choose to employ it.

Common law That body of law developed from custom or judicial decisions in English and U.S. courts, not attributable to a legislature.

Common stock Shares of ownership in a corporation that give the owner of the stock a proportionate interest in the corporation with regard to control, earnings, and net assets; shares of common stock are lowest in priority with respect to payment of dividends and distribution of the corporation's assets on dissolution.

Community property A form of concurrent ownership of property in which each spouse technically owns an undivided one-half interest in property acquired during the marriage. This form of joint ownership occurs in only a minority of states and Puerto Rico.

Comparative negligence A theory in tort law under which the liability for injuries resulting from negligent acts is shared by all parties who were negligent (including the injured party), on the basis of each person's proportionate negligence.

Compensatory damages A money award equivalent to the actual value of injuries or damages sustained by the aggrieved party.

Complaint The pleading made by a plaintiff alleging wrongdoing on the part of the defendant; the document that, when filed with a court, initiates a lawsuit.

Complete performance Performance of a contract strictly in accordance with the contract's terms.

Composition agreement *See* Creditors' composition agreement

Computer crime Any wrongful act that is directed against computers and computer parties, or wrongful use or abuse of computers or software.

Concentrated industry An industry in which a large percentage of market sales is controlled by either a single firm or a small number of firms.

Concurrent conditions Conditions in a contract that must occur or be performed at the same time; they are mutually dependent. No obligations arise until these conditions are simultaneously performed.

Concurrent jurisdiction Jurisdiction that exists when two different courts have the power to hear a case. For example, some cases can be heard in either a federal or a state court.

Concurrent ownership Joint ownership.

Concurring opinion A written opinion outlining the views of a judge or justice to make or emphasize a point that was not made or emphasized in the majority opinion.

Condemnation The process of taking private property for public use through the government's power of eminent domain.

Condition A possible future event, the occurrence or nonoccurrence of which will trigger the performance of a legal obligation or terminate an existing obligation under a contract.

Condition precedent A condition in a contract that must be met before a party's promise becomes absolute.

Condition subsequent A condition in a contract that operates to terminate a party's absolute promise to perform.

Confession of judgment The act of a debtor in permitting a judgment to be entered against him or her by a creditor, for an agreed sum, without the institution of legal proceedings.

Confiscation A government's taking of privately owned business or personal property without a proper public purpose or an award of just compensation.

Conforming goods Goods that conform to contract specifications.

Confusion The mixing together of goods belonging to two or more owners so that the separately owned goods cannot be identified.

Conglomerate merger A merger between firms that do not compete with each other because they are in different markets (as opposed to horizontal and vertical mergers).

Consent Voluntary agreement to a proposition or an act of another. A concurrence of wills.

Consequential damages Special damages that compensate for a loss that is not direct or immediate (for example, lost profits). The special damages must have been reasonably foreseeable at the time the breach or injury occurred in order for the plaintiff to collect them.

Consideration Generally, the value given in return for a promise or a performance. The consideration, which must be present to make the contract legally binding, must be something of legally sufficient value and bargained for.

Consignment A transaction in which an owner of goods (the consignor) delivers the goods to another (the consignee) for the consignee to sell. The consignee pays the consignor for the goods when they are sold by the consignee.

Consolidation A contractual and statutory process in which two or more corporations join to become a completely new corporation. The original corporations cease to exist, and the new corporation acquires all their assets and liabilities.

Constitutional law Law that is based on the U.S. Constitution and the constitutions of the various states.

Constructive condition A condition in a contract that is neither expressed nor implied by the contract but rather is imposed by law for reasons of justice.

Constructive delivery An act equivalent to the actual, physical delivery of property that cannot be physically delivered because of difficulty or impossibility; for example, the transfer of a key to a safe constructively delivers the contents of the safe.

Constructive discharge A termination of employment brought about by making an employee's working conditions so intolerable that the employee reasonably feels compelled to leave.

Constructive eviction A form of eviction that occurs when a landlord fails to perform adequately any of the undertakings (such as providing heat in the winter) required by the lease, thereby making the tenant's further use and enjoyment of the property exceedingly difficult or impossible.

Constructive trust An equitable trust that is imposed in the interests of fairness and justice when someone wrongfully holds legal title to property. A court may require the owner to hold the property in trust for the person or persons who rightfully should own the property.

Consumer credit Credit extended primarily for personal or household use.

Consumer-debtor An individual whose debts are primarily consumer debts (debts for purchases made primarily for personal or household use).

Consumer goods Goods that are primarily for personal or household use.

Consumer law The body of statutes, agency rules, and judicial decisions protecting consumers of goods and services from dangerous manufacturing techniques, mislabeling, unfair credit practices, deceptive advertising, and the like. Consumer laws provide remedies and protections that are not ordinarily available to merchants or to businesses.

Contingency fee An attorney's fee that is based on a percentage of the final award received by his or her client as a result of litigation.

Continuation statement A statement that, if filed within six months prior to the expiration date of the original financing statement, continues the perfection of the original security interest for another five years. The perfection of a security interest can be continued in the same manner indefinitely.

Contract An agreement that can be enforced in court; formed by two or more parties, each of whom agrees to perform or to refrain from performing some act now or in the future.

Contract implied in law *See* Quasi contract

Contract under seal A formal agreement in which the seal is a substitute for consideration. A court will not invalidate a contract under seal for lack of consideration.

Contractual capacity The threshold mental capacity required by the law for a party who enters into a contract to be bound by that contract.

Contribution *See* Right of contribution

Contributory negligence A theory in tort law under which a complaining party's own negligence contributed to or caused his or her injuries. Contributory negligence is an absolute bar to recovery in a minority of jurisdictions.

Conversion The wrongful taking, using, or retaining possession of personal property that belongs to another.

Convertible bond A bond that can be exchanged for a specified number of shares of common stock under certain conditions.

Conveyance The transfer of a title to land from one person to another by deed; a document (such as a deed) by which an interest in land is transferred from one person to another.

Conviction The outcome of a criminal trial in which the defendant has been found guilty of the crime.

Cooperative An association that is organized to provide an economic service to its members (or shareholders). An incorporated cooperative is a nonprofit corporation. It will make distributions of dividends, or profits, to its owners on the basis of their transactions with the cooperative rather than on the basis of the amount of capital they contributed. Examples of cooperatives are consumer purchasing cooperatives, credit cooperatives, and farmers' cooperatives.

Co-ownership Joint ownership.

Copyright The exclusive right of authors to publish, print, or sell an intellectual production for a statutory period of time. A copyright has the same monopolistic nature as a patent or trademark, but it differs in that it applies exclusively to works of art, literature, and other works of authorship, including computer programs.

Corporate governance The relationship between a corporation and its shareholders—specifically, a system that details the distribution of rights and responsibilities of those within the corporation and spells out the rules and procedures for making corporate decisions.

Corporate social responsibility The concept that corporations can and should act ethically and be accountable to society for their actions.

Corporation A legal entity formed in compliance with statutory requirements. The entity is distinct from its shareholders-owners.

Cosign The act of signing a document (such as a note promising to pay another in return for a loan or other benefit) jointly with another person and thereby assuming liability for performing what was promised in the document.

Cost-benefit analysis A decision-making technique that involves weighing the costs of a given action against the benefits of the action.

Co-surety A joint surety. One who assumes liability jointly with another surety for the payment of an obligation.

Counteradvertising New advertising that is undertaken pursuant to a Federal Trade Commission order for the purpose of correcting earlier false claims that were made about a product.

Counterclaim A claim made by a defendant in a civil lawsuit that in effect sues the plaintiff.

Counteroffer An offeree's response to an offer in which the offeree rejects the original offer and at the same time makes a new offer.

Course of dealing Prior conduct between parties to a contract that establishes a common basis for their understanding.

Course of performance The conduct that occurs under the terms of a particular agreement; such conduct indicates what the parties to an agreement intended it to mean.

Court of equity A court that decides controversies and administers justice according to the rules, principles, and precedents of equity.

Court of law A court in which the only remedies that could be granted were things of value, such as money damages. In the early English king's courts, courts of law were distinct from courts of equity.

Covenant against encumbrances A grantor's assurance that on land conveyed there are no encumbrances—that is, that no third parties have rights to or

interests in the land that would diminish its value to the grantee.

Covenant not to compete A contractual promise to refrain from competing with another party for a certain period of time (not excessive in duration) and within a reasonable geographic area. Although covenants not to compete restrain trade, they are commonly found in partnership agreements, business sale agreements, and employment contracts. If they are ancillary to such agreements, covenants not to compete will normally be enforced by the courts unless the time period or geographic area is deemed unreasonable.

Covenant not to sue An agreement to substitute a contractual obligation for some other type of legal action based on a valid claim.

Covenant of quiet enjoyment A promise by a grantor (or landlord) that the grantee (or tenant) will not be evicted or disturbed by the grantor or a person having a lien or superior title.

Covenant of the right to convey A grantor's assurance that he or she has sufficient capacity and title to convey the estate that he or she undertakes to convey by deed.

Covenant running with the land An executory promise made between a grantor and a grantee to which they and subsequent owners of the land are bound.

Cover A buyer or lessee's purchase on the open market of goods to substitute for those promised but never delivered by the seller. Under the Uniform Commercial Code, if the cost of cover exceeds the cost of the contract goods, the buyer or lessee can recover the difference, plus incidental and consequential damages.

Cram-down provision A provision of the Bankruptcy Code that allows a court to confirm a debtor's Chapter 11 reorganization plan even though only one class of creditors has accepted it. To exercise the court's right under this provision, the court must demonstrate that the plan does not discriminate unfairly against any creditors and is fair and equitable.

Creditor A person to whom a debt is owed by another person (the debtor).

Creditor beneficiary A third party beneficiary who has rights in a contract made by the debtor and a third person. The terms of the contract obligate the third person to pay the debt owed to the creditor. The creditor beneficiary can enforce the debt against either party.

Creditors' composition agreement An agreement formed between a debtor and his or her creditors in which the creditors agree to accept a lesser sum than that owed by the debtor in full satisfaction of the debt.

Crime A wrong against society proclaimed in a statute and, if committed, punishable by society through fines and/or imprisonment—and, in some cases, death.

Criminal act *See Actus reus*

Criminal intent *See Mens rea*

Criminal law Law that defines and governs actions that constitute crimes. Generally, criminal law has to do with wrongful actions committed against society for which society demands redress.

Cross-border pollution Pollution across national boundaries; air and water degradation in one nation resulting from pollution-causing activities in a neighboring country.

Cross-collateralization The use of an asset that is not the subject of a loan to collateralize that loan.

Cross-examination The questioning of an opposing witness during the trial.

Cumulative voting A method of shareholder voting designed to allow minority shareholders to be represented on the board of directors. With cumulative voting, the number of members of the board to be elected is multiplied by the total number of voting shares held. The result equals the number of votes a shareholder has, and this total can be cast for one or more nominees for director.

Cure Under the Uniform Commercial Code, the right of a party who tenders nonconforming performance to correct his or her performance within the contract period.

Cyber crime A crime that occurs online, in the virtual community of the Internet, as opposed to the physical world.

Cyber mark A trademark in cyberspace.

Cyber tort A tort committed via the Internet.

Cyberlaw An informal term used to refer to all laws governing electronic communications and transactions, particularly those conducted via the Internet.

Cybernotary A legally recognized authority that can certify the validity of digital signatures.

Cybersquatting The act of registering a domain name that is the same as, or confusingly similar to, the trademark of another and then offering to sell that domain name back to the trademark owner.

Cyberterrorist A hacker whose purpose is to exploit a target computer for a serious impact, such as the corruption of a program to sabotage a business.

D

Damages Money sought as a remedy for a breach of contract or for a tortious act.

Debenture bond A bond for which no specific assets of the corporation are pledged as backing; rather, the bond is backed by the general credit rating of the corporation, plus any assets that can be seized if the corporation allows the debentures to go into default.

Debit card A plastic card issued by a financial institution that allows the user to access his or her accounts online via automated teller machines.

Debtor Under Article 9 of the Uniform Commercial Code, a debtor is any party who owes payment or performance of a secured obligation, whether or not the party actually owns or has rights in the collateral.

Debtor in possession (DIP) In Chapter 11 bankruptcy proceedings, a debtor who is allowed to continue in possession of the estate in property (the business) and to continue business operations.

Deceptive advertising Advertising that misleads consumers, either by making unjustified claims concerning a product's performance or by omitting a material fact concerning the product's composition or performance.

Declaratory judgment A court's judgment on a justiciable controversy when the plaintiff is in doubt as to his or her legal rights; a binding adjudication of the rights and status of litigants even though no consequential relief is awarded.

Decree The judgment of a court of equity.

Deed A document by which title to property (usually real property) is passed.

Defalcation The misuse of funds.

Defamation Any published or publicly spoken false statement that causes injury to another's good name, reputation, or character.

Default The failure to observe a promise or discharge an obligation. The term is commonly used to mean the failure to pay a debt when it is due.

Default judgment A judgment entered by a court against a defendant who has failed to appear in court to answer or defend against the plaintiff's claim.

Defendant One against whom a lawsuit is brought; the accused person in a criminal proceeding.

Defense Reasons that a defendant offers in an action or suit as to why the plaintiff should not obtain what he or she is seeking.

Deficiency judgment A judgment against a debtor for the amount of a debt remaining unpaid after collateral has been repossessed and sold.

Delegatee One to whom contract duties are delegated by another, called the delegator.

Delegation The transfer of a contractual duty to a third party. The party delegating the duty (the delegator) to the third party (the delegatee) is still obliged to perform on the contract should the delegatee fail to perform.

Delegation doctrine A doctrine based on Article I, Section 8, of the U.S. Constitution, which has been construed to allow Congress to delegate some of its power to make and implement laws to administrative agencies. The delegation is considered to be proper as long as Congress sets standards outlining the scope of the agency's authority.

Delegator One who delegates his or her duties under a contract to another, called the delegatee.

Delivery In contract law, one party's act of placing the subject matter of the contract within the other party's possession or control.

Delivery order A written order to deliver goods directed to a warehouser, carrier, or other person who, in the ordinary course of business, issues warehouse receipts or bills of lading [UCC 7–102(1)(d)].

Demand deposit Funds (accepted by a bank) subject to immediate withdrawal, in contrast to a time deposit, which requires that a depositor wait a specific time before withdrawing or pay a penalty for early withdrawal.

De novo Anew; afresh; a second time. In a hearing *de novo,* an appellate court hears the case as a court of original jurisdiction—that is, as if the case had not previously been tried and a decision rendered.

Depositary bank The first bank to receive a check for payment.

Deposition The testimony of a party to a lawsuit or a witness taken under oath before a trial.

Destination contract A contract in which the seller is required to ship the goods by carrier and deliver them at a particular destination. The seller assumes liability for any losses or damage to the goods until they are tendered at the destination specified in the contract.

Devise To make a gift of real property by will.

Digital cash Funds contained on computer software, in the form of secure programs stored on microchips and other computer devices.

Dilution With respect to trademarks, a doctrine under which distinctive or famous trademarks are protected from certain unauthorized uses of the marks regardless of a showing of competition or a likelihood of confusion. Congress created a federal cause of action for dilution in 1995 with the passage of the Federal Trademark Dilution Act.

Direct examination The examination of a witness by the attorney who calls the witness to the stand to testify on behalf of the attorney's client.

Directed verdict *See* Motion for a directed verdict

Disaffirmance The legal avoidance, or setting aside, of a contractual obligation.

Discharge The termination of an obligation. (1) In contract law, discharge occurs when the parties have fully performed their contractual obligations or when events, conduct of the parties, or operation of the law releases the parties from performance. (2) In bankruptcy proceedings, the extinction of the debtor's dischargeable debts.

Discharge in bankruptcy The release of a debtor from all debts that are provable, except those specifically excepted from discharge by statute.

Disclosed principal A principal whose identity is known to a third party at the time the agent makes a contract with the third party.

Discovery A phase in the litigation process during which the opposing parties may obtain information from each other and from third parties prior to trial.

Dishonor To refuse to accept or pay a draft or a promissory note when it is properly presented. An instrument is dishonored when presentment is properly made and acceptance or payment is refused or cannot be obtained within the prescribed time.

Disparagement of property An economically injurious false statement made about another's product or property. A general term for torts that are more specifically referred to as slander of quality or slander of title.

Disparate-impact discrimination A form of employment discrimination that results from certain employer practices or procedures that, although not discriminatory on their face, have a discriminatory effect.

Disparate-treatment discrimination A form of employment discrimination that results when an employer intentionally discriminates against employees who are members of protected classes.

Dissenting opinion A written opinion by a judge or justice who disagrees with the majority opinion.

Dissociation The severance of the relationship between a partner and a partnership when the partner ceases to be associated with the carrying on of the partnership business.

Dissolution The formal disbanding of a partnership or a corporation. It can take place by (1) acts of the partners or, in a corporation, of the shareholders and board of directors; (2) the death of a partner; (3) the expiration of a time period stated in a partnership agreement or a certificate of incorporation; or (4) judicial decree.

Distributed network A network that can be used by persons located (distributed) around the country or the globe to share computer files.

Distribution agreement A contract between a seller and a distributor of the seller's products setting out the terms and conditions of the distributorship.

Distributorship A business arrangement that is established when a manufacturer licenses a dealer to sell its product. An example of a distributorship is an automobile dealership.

Diversity of citizenship Under Article III, Section 2, of the Constitution, a basis for federal court jurisdiction over a lawsuit between (1) citizens of different states, (2) a foreign country and citizens of a state or of different states, or (3) citizens of a state and citizens or subjects of a foreign country. The amount in controversy must be more than $75,000 before a federal court can take jurisdiction in such cases.

Divestiture The act of selling one or more of a company's parts, such as a subsidiary or plant; often mandated by the courts in merger or monopolization cases.

Dividend A distribution to corporate shareholders of corporate profits or income, disbursed in proportion to the number of shares held.

Docket The list of cases entered on a court's calendar and thus scheduled to be heard by the court.

Document of title Paper exchanged in the regular course of business that evidences the right to possession of goods (for example, a bill of lading or a warehouse receipt).

Domain name The series of letters and symbols used to identify site operators on the Internet; Internet "addresses."

Domestic corporation In a given state, a corporation that does business in, and is organized under the laws of, that state.

Domestic relations court A court that deals with domestic (household) relationships, such as adoption, divorce, support payments, child custody, and the like.

Donee beneficiary A third party beneficiary who has rights under a contract as a direct result of the intention of the contract parties to make a gift to the third party.

Double jeopardy A situation occurring when a person is tried twice for the same criminal offense; prohibited by the Fifth Amendment to the U.S. Constitution.

Double taxation A feature (and disadvantage) of the corporate form of business. Because a corporation is a separate legal entity, corporate profits are taxed by state and federal governments. Dividends are again taxable as ordinary income to the shareholders receiving them.

Draft Any instrument (such as a check) drawn on a drawee (such as a bank) that orders the drawee to pay a certain sum of money, usually to a third party (the payee), on demand or at a definite future time.

Dram shop act A state statute that imposes liability on the owners of bars and taverns, as well as those who serve alcoholic drinks to the public, for injuries resulting from accidents caused by intoxicated persons when the sellers or servers of alcoholic drinks contributed to the intoxication.

Drawee The party that is ordered to pay a draft or check. With a check, a financial institution is always the drawee.

Drawer The party that initiates a draft (writes a check, for example), thereby ordering the drawee to pay.

Due diligence A required standard of care that certain professionals, such as accountants, must meet to avoid liability for securities violations. Under securities law, an accountant will be deemed to have exercised due diligence if he or she followed generally accepted accounting principles and generally accepted auditing standards and had, "after reasonable investigation, reasonable grounds to believe and did believe, at the time such part of the registration statement became effective, that the statements therein were true and that there was no omission of a material fact required to be stated therein or necessary to make the statements therein not misleading."

Due process clause The provisions of the Fifth and Fourteenth Amendments to the Constitution that guarantee that no person shall be deprived of life, liberty, or property without due process of law. Similar clauses are found in most state constitutions.

Dumping The selling of goods in a foreign country at a price below the price charged for the same goods in the domestic market.

Durable power of attorney A document that authorizes a person to act on behalf of a person—write checks, collect insurance proceeds, and otherwise manage the person's affairs, including health care—when he or she becomes incapacitated. Spouses often give each other durable power of attorney and, if they are advanced in age, may give a second such power of attorney to an older child.

Duress Unlawful pressure brought to bear on a person, causing the person to perform an act that he or she would not otherwise perform.

Duty of care The duty of all persons, as established by tort law, to exercise a reasonable amount of care in their dealings with others. Failure to exercise due care, which is normally determined by the "reasonable person standard," constitutes the tort of negligence.

E

E-agent A computer program, electronic, or other automated means used to perform specific tasks without review by an individual.

E-commerce Business transacted in cyberspace.

E-contract A contract that is entered into in cyberspace and is evidenced only by electronic impulses (such as those that make up a computer's memory), rather than, for example, a typewritten form.

E-evidence A type of evidence that consists of computer-generated or electronically recorded information, including e-mail, voice mail, spreadsheets, word-processing documents, and other data.

E-money Prepaid funds recorded on a computer or a card (such as a *smart card*).

E-signature As defined by the Uniform Electronic Transactions Act, "an electronic sound, symbol, or process attached to or logically associated with a record and executed or adopted by a person with the intent to sign the record."

Early neutral case evaluation A form of alternative dispute resolution in which a neutral third party evaluates the strengths and weakness of the disputing parties' positions; the evaluator's opinion forms the basis for negotiating a settlement.

Easement A nonpossessory right to use another's property in a manner established by either express or implied agreement.

Electronic fund transfer (EFT) A transfer of funds with the use of an electronic terminal, a telephone, a computer, or magnetic tape.

Emancipation In regard to minors, the act of being freed from parental control; occurs when a child's parent or legal guardian relinquishes the legal right to exercise control over the child. Normally, a minor who leaves home to support himself or herself is considered emancipated.

Embezzlement The fraudulent appropriation of money or other property by a person to whom the money or property has been entrusted.

Eminent domain The power of a government to take land for public use from private citizens for just compensation.

Employee A person who works for an employer for a salary or for wages.

Employer An individual or business entity that hires employees, pays them salaries or wages, and exercises control over their work.

Employment at will A common law doctrine under which either party may terminate an employment relationship at any time for any reason, unless a contract specifies otherwise.

Employment discrimination Treating employees or job applicants unequally on the basis of race, color, national origin, religion, gender, age, or disability; prohibited by federal statutes.

Enabling legislation A statute enacted by Congress that authorizes the creation of an administrative agency and specifies the name, composition, purpose, and powers of the agency being created.

Encryption The process by which a message (plaintext) is transformed into something (ciphertext) that the sender and receiver intend third parties not to understand.

Endowment insurance A type of insurance that combines life insurance with an investment so that if the insured outlives the policy, the face value is paid to him or her; if the insured does not outlive the policy, the face value is paid to his or her beneficiary.

Entrapment In criminal law, a defense in which the defendant claims that he or she was induced by a public official—usually an undercover agent or police officer—to commit a crime that he or she would otherwise not have committed.

Entrepreneur One who initiates and assumes the financial risks of a new enterprise and who undertakes to provide or control its management.

Entrustment rule The transfer of goods to a merchant who deals in goods of that kind and who may transfer those goods and all rights to them to a buyer in the ordinary course of business [UCC 2–403(2)].

Environmental impact statement (EIS) A statement required by the National Environmental Policy Act for any major federal action that will significantly affect the quality of the environment. The statement must analyze the action's impact on the environment and explore alternative actions that might be taken.

Environmental law The body of statutory, regulatory, and common law relating to the protection of the environment.

Equal dignity rule In most states, a rule stating that express authority given to an agent must be in writing if the contract to be made on behalf of the principal is required to be in writing.

Equal protection clause The provision in the Fourteenth Amendment to the Constitution that guarantees that no state will "deny to any person within its jurisdiction the equal protection of the laws." This clause mandates that state governments treat similarly situated individuals in a similar manner.

Equitable maxims General propositions or principles of law that have to do with fairness (equity).

Equity of redemption The right of a mortgagor who has breached the mortgage agreement to redeem or purchase the property prior to foreclosure proceedings.

Escheat The transfer of property to the state when the owner of the property dies without heirs.

Escrow account An account that is generally held in the name of the depositor and escrow agent; the funds in the account are paid to a third person only on fulfillment of the escrow condition.

Establishment clause The provision in the First Amendment to the U.S. Constitution that prohibits Congress from creating any law "respecting an establishment of religion."

Estate The interest that a person has in real and personal property.

Estate planning Planning in advance how one's property and obligations should be transferred on one's death. Wills and trusts are two basic devices used in the process of estate planning.

Estop To bar, impede, or preclude.

Estoppel The principle that a party's own acts prevent him or her from claiming a right to the detriment of another who was entitled to and did rely on those acts. *See also* Agency by estoppel; Promissory estoppel

Estray statute A statute defining finders' rights in property when the true owners are unknown.

Ethical reasoning A reasoning process in which an individual links his or her moral convictions or ethical standards to the particular situation at hand.

Ethics Moral principles and values applied to social behavior.

Evidence Proof offered at trial—in the form of testimony, documents, records, exhibits, objects, and the like—for the purpose of convincing the court or jury of the truth of a contention.

Eviction A landlord's act of depriving a tenant of possession of the leased premises.

Exclusionary rule In criminal procedure, a rule under which any evidence that is obtained in violation of the accused's constitutional rights guaranteed by the Fourth, Fifth, and Sixth Amendments, as well as any evidence derived from illegally obtained evidence, will not be admissible in court.

Exclusive distributorship A distributorship in which the seller and the distributor of the seller's products agree that the distributor has the exclusive right to distribute the seller's products in a certain geographic area.

Exclusive jurisdiction Jurisdiction that exists when a case can be heard only in a particular court or type of court, such as a federal court or a state court.

Exclusive-dealing contract An agreement under which a seller forbids a buyer to purchase products from the seller's competitors.

Exculpatory clause A clause that releases a contractual party from liability in the event of monetary or physical injury, no matter who is at fault.

Executed contract A contract that has been completely performed by both parties.

Execution An action to carry into effect the directions in a court decree or judgment.

Executive agency An administrative agency within the executive branch of government. At the federal level, executive agencies are those within the cabinet departments.

Executor A person appointed by a testator to see that his or her will is administered appropriately.

Executory contract A contract that has not as yet been fully performed.

Export To sell products to buyers located in other countries.

Express authority Authority expressly given by one party to another. In agency law, an agent has express authority to act for a principal if both parties agree, orally or in writing, that an agency relationship exists in which the agent had the power (authority) to act in the place of, and on behalf of, the principal.

Express contract A contract in which the terms of the agreement are fully and explicitly stated in words, oral or written.

Express warranty A seller's or lessor's oral or written promise, ancillary to an underlying sales or lease agreement, as to the quality, description, or performance of the goods being sold or leased.

Expropriation The seizure by a government of privately owned business or personal property for a proper public purpose and with just compensation.

Extension clause A clause in a time instrument that allows the instrument's date of maturity to be extended into the future.

F

F.A.S. Free alongside. A contract term that requires the seller, at his or her own expense and risk, to deliver the goods alongside the ship before risk passes to the buyer.

F.O.B. Free on board. A contract term that indicates that the selling price of the goods includes transportation costs (and that the seller carries the risk of loss) to the specific F.O.B. place named in the contract. The place can be either the place of initial shipment (for example, the seller's city or place of business) or the place of destination (for example, the buyer's city or place of business).

Family limited liability partnership (FLLP) A limited liability partnership (LLP) in which the majority of the partners are persons related to each other, essentially as spouses, parents, grandparents, siblings, cousins, nephews, or nieces. A person acting in a fiduciary capacity for persons so related could also be a partner. All of the partners must be natural persons or persons acting in a fiduciary capacity for the benefit of natural persons.

Federal form of government A system of government in which the states form a union and the sovereign power is divided between a central government and the member states.

Federal question A question that pertains to the U.S. Constitution, acts of Congress, or treaties. A federal question provides a basis for federal jurisdiction.

Federal Reserve System A network of twelve district banks, located around the country and headed by the Federal Reserve Board of Governors. Most banks in the United States have Federal Reserve accounts.

Federal Rules of Civil Procedure (FRCP) The rules controlling procedural matters in civil trials brought before the federal district courts.

Fee simple An absolute form of property ownership entitling the property owner to use, possess, or dispose of the property as he or she chooses during his or her lifetime. On death, the interest in the property passes to the owner's heirs; a fee simple absolute.

Fee simple absolute An ownership interest in land in which the owner has the greatest possible aggregation of rights, privileges, and power. Ownership in fee simple absolute is limited absolutely to a person and his or her heirs.

Felony A crime—such as arson, murder, rape, or robbery—that carries the most severe sanctions, usually ranging from one year in a state or federal prison to the forfeiture of one's life.

Fictitious payee A payee on a negotiable instrument whom the maker or drawer does not intend to have an interest in the instrument. Indorsements by fictitious payees are not treated as unauthorized under Article 3 of the Uniform Commercial Code.

Fiduciary As a noun, a person having a duty created by his or her undertaking to act primarily for another's benefit in matters connected with the undertaking. As an adjective, a relationship founded on trust and confidence.

Fiduciary duty The duty, imposed on a fiduciary by virtue of his or her position, to act primarily for another's benefit.

Filtering software A computer program that includes a pattern through which data are passed. When designed to block access to certain Web sites, the pattern blocks the retrieval of a site whose URL or key words are on a list within the program.

Final order The final decision of an administrative agency on an issue. If no appeal is taken, or if the case is not reviewed or considered anew by the agency commission, the administrative law judge's initial order becomes the final order of the agency.

Financial institution An organization authorized to do business under state or federal laws relating to financial institutions. Financial institutions may include banks, savings and loan associations, credit unions, and other business entities that directly or indirectly hold accounts belonging to consumers.

Financing statement A document prepared by a secured creditor and filed with the appropriate government official to give notice to the public that the creditor claims an interest in collateral belonging to the debtor named in the statement. The financing statement must contain the names and addresses of both the debtor and the creditor, and describe the collateral by type or item.

Firm offer An offer (by a merchant) that is irrevocable without consideration for a period of time (not longer than three months). A firm offer by a merchant must be in writing and must be signed by the offeror.

Fitness for a particular purpose *See* Implied warranty of fitness for a particular purpose

Fixed-term tenancy A type of tenancy under which property is leased for a specified period of time, such as a month, a year, or a period of years; also called a *tenancy for years.*

Fixture A thing that was once personal property but that has become attached to real property in such a way that it takes on the characteristics of real property and becomes part of that real property.

Floating lien A security interest in proceeds, after-acquired property, or property purchased under a line of credit (or all three); a security interest in collateral that is retained even when the collateral changes in character, classification, or location.

Forbearance The act of refraining from an action that one has a legal right to undertake.

Force majeure (pronounced mah-*zhure*) **clause** A provision in a contract stipulating that certain unforeseen events—such as war, political upheavals, acts of God, or other events—will excuse a party from liability for nonperformance of contractual obligations.

Foreclosure A proceeding in which a mortgagee either takes title to or forces the sale of the mortgagor's property in satisfaction of a debt.

Foreign corporation In a given state, a corporation that does business in the state without being incorporated therein.

Foreseeable risk In negligence law, the risk of harm or injury to another that a person of ordinary intelligence and prudence should have reasonably anticipated or foreseen when undertaking an action or refraining from undertaking an action.

Forfeiture The termination of a lease, according to its terms or the terms of a statute, when one of the parties fails to fulfill a condition under the lease and thereby breaches it.

Forgery The fraudulent making or altering of any writing in a way that changes the legal rights and liabilities of another.

Formal contract A contract that by law requires a specific form, such as being executed under seal, to be valid.

Forum A jurisdiction, court, or place in which disputes are litigated and legal remedies are sought.

Forum-selection clause A provision in a contract designating the court, jurisdiction, or tribunal that will decide any disputes arising under the contract.

Franchise Any arrangement in which the owner of a trademark, trade name, or copyright licenses another to use that trademark, trade name, or copyright, under specified conditions or limitations, in the selling of goods and services.

Franchise tax A state or local government tax on the right and privilege of carrying on a business in the form of a corporation.

Franchisee One receiving a license to use another's (the franchisor's) trademark, trade name, or copyright in the sale of goods and services.

Franchisor One licensing another (the franchisee) to use his or her trademark, trade name, or copyright in the sale of goods or services.

Fraud Any misrepresentation, either by misstatement or omission of a material fact, knowingly made with the intention of deceiving another and on which a reasonable person would and does rely to his or her detriment.

Fraud in the execution In the law of negotiable instruments, a type of fraud that occurs when a person is deceived into signing a negotiable instrument, believing that he or she is signing something else (such as a receipt); also called fraud in the inception. Fraud in the execution is a universal defense to payment on a negotiable instrument.

Fraud in the inducement Ordinary fraud. In the law of negotiable instruments, fraud in the inducement occurs when a person issues a negotiable instrument based on false statements by the other party. The issuing party will be able to avoid payment on that instrument unless the holder is a holder in due course; in other words, fraud in the inducement is a personal defense to payment on a negotiable instrument.

Fraudulent misrepresentation (fraud) Any misrepresentation, either by misstatement or omission of a material fact, knowingly made with the intention of deceiving another and on which a reasonable person would and does rely to his or her detriment.

Free exercise clause The provision in the First Amendment to the U.S. Constitution that prohibits Congress from making any law "prohibiting the free exercise" of religion.

Free writing prospectus A free writing prospectus is any type of written, electronic, or graphic offer that describes the issuing corporation or its securities and includes a legend indicating that the investor may obtain the prospectus at the SEC's Web site.

Frustration of purpose A court-created doctrine under which a party to a contract will be relieved of his or her duty to perform when the objective purpose for performance no longer exists (due to reasons beyond that party's control).

Full faith and credit clause A clause in Article IV, Section 1, of the Constitution that provides that "Full Faith and Credit shall be given in each State to the public Acts, Records, and Judicial Proceedings of every other State." The clause ensures that rights established under deeds, wills, contracts, and the like in one state will be honored by the other states and that any judicial decision with respect to such property rights will be honored and enforced in all states.

Full warranty A warranty as to full performance covering generally both labor and materials.

Fungible goods Goods that are alike by physical nature, by agreement, or by trade usage. Examples of fungible goods are wheat, oil, and wine that are identical in type and quality.

G

Garnishment A legal process used by a creditor to collect a debt by seizing property of the debtor (such as wages) that is being held by a third party (such as the debtor's employer).

General jurisdiction Exists when a court's subject-matter jurisdiction is not restricted. A court of general jurisdiction normally can hear any type of case.

General partner In a limited partnership, a partner who assumes responsibility for the management of the partnership and liability for all partnership debts.

General partnership *See* Partnership

Generally accepted accounting principles (GAAP) The conventions, rules, and procedures that define accepted accounting practices at a particular time. The source of the principles is the Financial Accounting Standards Board.

Generally accepted auditing standards (GAAS) Standards concerning an auditor's professional qualities and the judgment exercised by him or her in the performance of an examination and report. The source of the standards is the American Institute of Certified Public Accountants.

Genuineness of assent Knowing and voluntary assent to the terms of a contract. If a contract is formed as a result of a mistake, misrepresentation, undue influence, or duress, genuineness of assent is lacking, and the contract will be voidable.

Gift Any voluntary transfer of property made without consideration, past or present.

Gift *causa mortis* A gift made in contemplation of death. If the donor does not die of that ailment, the gift is revoked.

Gift *inter vivos* A gift made during one's lifetime and not in contemplation of imminent death, in contrast to a gift *causa mortis*.

Good faith Under the Uniform Commercial Code, good faith means honesty in fact; with regard to merchants, good faith means honesty in fact *and* the observance of reasonable commercial standards of fair dealing in the trade.

Good faith purchaser A purchaser who buys without notice of any circumstance that would put a person of ordinary prudence on inquiry as to whether the seller has valid title to the goods being sold.

Good Samaritan statute A state statute that provides that persons who rescue or provide emergency services to others in peril—unless they do so recklessly, thus causing further harm—cannot be sued for negligence.

Grand jury A group of citizens called to decide, after hearing the state's evidence, whether a reasonable basis (probable cause) exists for believing that a crime has been committed and whether a trial ought to be held.

Grant deed A deed that simply recites words of consideration and conveyance. Under statute, a grant deed may impliedly warrant that at least the grantor has not conveyed the property's title to someone else.

Grantee One to whom a grant (of land or property, for example) is made.

Grantor A person who makes a grant, such as a transferor of property or the creator of a trust.

Group boycott The refusal to deal with a particular person or firm by a group of competitors; prohibited by the Sherman Act.

Guarantor A person who agrees to satisfy the debt of another (the debtor) only after the principal debtor defaults; a guarantor's liability is thus secondary.

H

Habitability *See* Implied warranty of habitability

Hacker A person who uses one computer to break into another. Professional computer programmers refer to such persons as "crackers."

Health-care power of attorney A document that designates a person who will have the power to choose what type of and how much medical treatment a person who is unable to make such a choice will receive.

Hearsay An oral or written statement made out of court that is later offered in court by a witness (not the person who made the statement) to prove the truth of the matter asserted in the statement. Hearsay is generally inadmissible as evidence.

Hirfindahl-Hirschman Index (HHI) An index of market power used to calculate whether a merger of two businesses will result in sufficient monopoly power to violate antitrust laws.

Historical school A school of legal thought that emphasizes the evolutionary process of law and that looks to the past to discover what the principles of contemporary law should be.

Holder Any person in the possession of an instrument drawn, issued, or indorsed to him or her, to his or her order, to bearer, or in blank.

Holder in due course (HDC) A holder who acquires a negotiable instrument for value; in good faith; and without notice that the instrument is overdue, that it has been dishonored, that any person has a defense against it or a claim to it, or that the instrument contains unauthorized signatures, alterations, or is so irregular or incomplete as to call into question its authenticity.

Holding company A company whose business activity is holding shares in another company.

Holographic will A will written entirely in the signer's handwriting and usually not witnessed.

Homestead exemption A law permitting a debtor to retain the family home, either in its entirety or up to a specified dollar amount, free from the claims of unsecured creditors or trustees in bankruptcy.

Horizontal merger A merger between two firms that are competing in the same market.

Horizontal restraint Any agreement that in some way restrains competition between rival firms competing in the same market.

Hot-cargo agreement An agreement in which employers voluntarily agree with unions not to handle, use, or deal in nonunion-produced goods of other employers; a type of secondary boycott explicitly prohibited by the Labor-Management Reporting and Disclosure Act of 1959.

I

I-9 verification All employers must verify the employment eligibility and identity of any worker hired in the United States. To comply with the law, employers must complete an I-9 Employment Eligibility Verification Form for all new hires within three business days.

I-551 Alien Registration Receipt Commonly referred to as a "green card," the I-551 Alien Registration Receipt is proof that a foreign-born individual is Lawfully Admitted for Permanent Residence in the United States. Persons seeking employment can prove to prospective employers that they are legally within the U.S. by showing this receipt.

Identification In a sale of goods, the express designation of the specific goods provided for in the contract.

Identity theft The act of stealing another's identifying information—such as a name, date of birth, or Social Security number—and using that information to access the victim's financial resources.

Illusory promise A promise made without consideration, which renders the promise unenforceable.

Immunity A status of being exempt, or free, from certain duties or requirements. In criminal law, the state may grant an accused person immunity from prosecution—or agree to prosecute for a lesser offense—if the accused person agrees to give the state information that would assist the state in prosecuting other individuals for crimes. In tort law, freedom from liability for defamatory speech. *See also* Privilege

Implied authority Authority that is created not by an explicit oral or written agreement but by implication. In agency law, implied authority (of the agent) can be conferred by custom, inferred from the position the agent occupies, or implied by virtue of being reasonably necessary to carry out express authority.

Implied warranty A warranty that the law derives by implication or inference from the nature of the transaction or the relative situation or circumstances of the parties.

Implied warranty of fitness for a particular purpose A warranty that goods sold or leased are fit for a particular purpose. The warranty arises when any seller or lessor knows the particular purpose for which a buyer or lessee will use the goods and knows that the buyer or lessee is relying on the skill and judgment of the seller or lessor to select suitable goods.

Implied warranty of habitability An implied promise by a landlord that rented residential premises are fit for human habitation—that is, in a condition that is safe and suitable for people to live in.

Implied warranty of merchantability A warranty that goods being sold or leased are reasonably fit for the ordinary purpose for which they are sold or leased, are properly packaged and labeled, and are of fair quality. The warranty automatically arises in every sale or lease of goods made by a merchant who deals in goods of the kind sold or leased.

Implied-in-fact contract A contract formed in whole or in part from the conduct of the parties (as opposed to an express contract).

Impossibility of performance A doctrine under which a party to a contract is relieved of his or her duty to perform when performance becomes impossible or totally impracticable (through no fault of either party).

Imposter One who, by use of the mail, telephone, or personal appearance, induces a maker or drawer to issue an instrument in the name of an impersonated payee. Indorsements by imposters are not treated as unauthorized under Article 3 of the Uniform Commercial Code.

In pari delicto At equal fault.

***In personam* jurisdiction** Court jurisdiction over the "person" involved in a legal action; personal jurisdiction.

***In rem* jurisdiction** Court jurisdiction over a defendant's property.

Incidental beneficiary A third party who incidentally benefits from a contract but whose benefit was not the reason the contract was formed; an incidental beneficiary has no rights in a contract and cannot sue to have the contract enforced.

Incidental damages Losses reasonably associated with, or related to, actual damages resulting from a breach of contract.

Incontestability clause A clause within a life or health insurance policy that states after the policy has been in force for a specified length of time—most often two or three years—the insurer cannot contest statements made in the policyholder's application.

Indemnify To compensate or reimburse another for losses or expenses incurred.

Independent contractor One who works for, and receives payment from, an employer but whose working conditions and methods are not controlled by the employer. An independent contractor is not an employee but may be an agent.

Independent regulatory agency An administrative agency that is not considered part of the government's executive branch and is not subject to the authority of the president. Independent agency officials cannot be removed without cause.

Indictment (pronounced in-*dyte*-ment) A charge by a grand jury that a reasonable basis (probable cause)

exists for believing that a crime has been committed and that a trial should be held.

Indorsee The person to whom a negotiable instrument is transferred by indorsement.

Indorsement A signature placed on an instrument for the purpose of transferring one's ownership rights in the instrument.

Indorser A person who transfers an instrument by signing (indorsing) it and delivering it to another person.

Informal contract A contract that does not require a specified form or formality in order to be valid.

Information A formal accusation or complaint (without an indictment) issued in certain types of actions (usually criminal actions involving lesser crimes) by a law officer, such as a magistrate.

Information return A tax return submitted by a partnership that only reports the income earned by the business. The partnership as an entity does not pay taxes on the income received by the partnership. A partner's profit from the partnership (whether distributed or not) is taxed as individual income to the individual partner.

Infringement A violation of another's legally recognized right. The term is commonly used with reference to the invasion by one party of another party's rights in a patent, trademark, or copyright.

Initial order In the context of administrative law, an agency's disposition in a matter other than a rulemaking. An administrative law judge's initial order becomes final unless it is appealed.

Injunction A court decree ordering a person to do or refrain from doing a certain act or activity.

Innkeeper An owner of an inn, hotel, motel, or other lodgings.

Innkeeper's lien A possessory or statutory lien allowing the innkeeper to take the personal property of a guest, brought into the hotel, as security for nonpayment of the guest's bill (debt).

Innocent misrepresentation A false statement of fact or an act made in good faith that deceives and causes harm or injury to another.

Inside director A person on the board of directors who is also an officer of the corporation.

Insider A corporate director or officer, or other employee or agent, with access to confidential information and a duty not to disclose that information in violation of insider-trading laws.

Insider trading The purchase or sale of securities on the basis of "inside information" (information that has not been made available to the public) in violation of a duty owed to the company whose stock is being traded.

Insolvent Under the Uniform Commercial Code, a term describing a person who ceases to pay "his [or her] debts in the ordinary course of business or cannot pay his debts as they become due or is insolvent within the meaning of federal bankruptcy law" [UCC 1–201(23)].

Installment contract Under the Uniform Commercial Code, a contract that requires or authorizes delivery in two or more separate lots to be accepted and paid for separately.

Instrument *See* Negotiable instrument

Insurable interest An interest either in a person's life or well-being or in property that is sufficiently substantial that insuring against injury to (or the death of) the person or against damage to the property does not amount to a mere wagering (betting) contract.

Insurance A contract in which, for a stipulated consideration, one party agrees to compensate the other for loss on a specific subject by a specified peril.

Intangible property Property that is incapable of being apprehended by the senses (such as by sight or touch). Intellectual property is an example of intangible property.

Integrated contract A written contract that constitutes the final expression of the parties' agreement. If a contract is integrated, evidence extraneous to the contract that contradicts or alters the meaning of the contract in any way is inadmissible.

Intellectual property Property resulting from intellectual, creative processes. Patents, trademarks, and copyrights are examples of intellectual property.

Intended beneficiary A third party for whose benefit a contract is formed; an intended beneficiary can sue the promisor if such a contract is breached.

Intentional tort A wrongful act knowingly committed.

***Inter vivos* gift** *See* Gift *inter vivos*

***Inter vivos* trust** A trust created by the grantor (settlor) and effective during the grantor's lifetime (that is, a trust not established by a will).

Intermediary bank Any bank to which an item is transferred in the course of collection, except the depositary or payor bank.

International law The law that governs relations among nations. International customs and treaties are generally considered to be two of the most important sources of international law.

International organization In international law, a term that generally refers to an organization composed mainly of nations and usually established by treaty. The United States is a member of more than one hundred multilateral and bilateral organizations, including at least twenty through the United Nations.

Interpretive rule An administrative agency rule that is simply a statement or opinion issued by the agency explaining how it interprets and intends to apply the statutes it enforces. Such rules are not automatically binding on private individuals or organizations.

Interrogatories A series of written questions for which written answers are prepared and then signed under oath by a party to a lawsuit, usually with the assistance of the party's attorney.

Intestacy laws State statutes that specify how property will be distributed when a person dies intestate (without a valid will); statutes of descent and distribution.

Intestate   As a noun, one who has died without having created a valid will; as an adjective, the state of having died without a will.

Investment company   A company that acts on behalf of many smaller shareholder-owners by buying a large portfolio of securities and professionally managing that portfolio.

Investment contract   In securities law, a transaction in which a person invests in a common enterprise reasonably expecting profits that are derived primarily from the efforts of others.

Invitee   A person who, either expressly or impliedly, is privileged to enter onto another's land. The inviter owes the invitee (for example, a customer in a store) the duty to exercise reasonable care to protect the invitee from harm.

Irrevocable offer   An offer that cannot be revoked or recalled by the offeror without liability. A merchant's firm offer is an example of an irrevocable offer.

Issue   The first transfer, or delivery, of an instrument to a holder.

J

Joint and several liability   In partnership law, a doctrine under which a plaintiff may sue, and collect a judgment from, one or more of the partners separately (severally, or individually) or all of the partners together (jointly). This is true even if one of the partners sued did not participate in, ratify, or know about whatever it was that gave rise to the cause of action.

Joint liability   Shared liability. In partnership law, partners incur joint liability for partnership obligations and debts. For example, if a third party sues a partner on a partnership debt, the partner has the right to insist that the other partners be sued with him or her.

Joint stock company   A hybrid form of business organization that combines characteristics of a corporation (shareholder-owners, management by directors and officers of the company, and perpetual existence) and a partnership (it is formed by agreement, not statute; property is usually held in the names of the members; and the shareholders have personal liability for business debts). Usually, the joint stock company is regarded as a partnership for tax and other legally related purposes.

Joint tenancy   The joint ownership of property by two or more co-owners in which each co-owner owns an undivided portion of the property. On the death of one of the joint tenants, his or her interest automatically passes to the surviving joint tenants.

Joint venture   A joint undertaking of a specific commercial enterprise by an association of persons. A joint venture is normally not a legal entity and is treated like a partnership for federal income tax purposes.

Judgment   The final order or decision resulting from a legal action.

Judgment *n.o.v.*   *See* Motion for judgment *n.o.v.*

Judgment rate of interest   A rate of interest fixed by statute that is applied to a monetary judgment from the moment the judgment is awarded by a court until the judgment is paid or terminated.

Judicial lien   A lien on property created by a court order.

Judicial process   The procedures relating to, or connected with, the administration of justice through the judicial system.

Judicial review   The process by which courts decide on the constitutionality of legislative enactments and actions of the executive branch.

Junior lienholder   A person or business who holds a lien that is subordinate to one or more other liens on the same property.

Jurisdiction   The authority of a court to hear and decide a specific action.

Jurisprudence   The science or philosophy of law.

Justiciable (pronounced jus-*tish*-a-bul) **controversy**   A controversy that is not hypothetical or academic but real and substantial; a requirement that must be satisfied before a court will hear a case.

K

King's court   A medieval English court. The king's courts, or *curiae regis*, were established by the Norman conquerors of England. The body of law that developed in these courts was common to the entire English realm and thus became known as the common law.

L

Laches   The equitable doctrine that bars a party's right to legal action if the party has neglected for an unreasonable length of time to act on his or her rights.

Landlord   An owner of land or rental property who leases it to another person, called the tenant.

Larceny   The wrongful taking and carrying away of another person's personal property with the intent to permanently deprive the owner of the property. Some states classify larceny as either grand or petit, depending on the property's value.

Last clear chance   A doctrine under which a plaintiff may recover from a defendant for injuries or damages suffered, notwithstanding the plaintiff's own negligence, when the defendant had the opportunity—a last clear chance—to avoid harming the plaintiff through the exercise of reasonable care but failed to do so.

Law   A body of enforceable rules governing relationships among individuals and between individuals and their society.

Lawsuit   The litigation process. *See* Litigation

Lease   In real property law, a contract by which the owner of real property (the landlord, or lessor) grants to a person (the tenant, or lessee) an exclusive right to use and possess the property, usually for a specified period of time, in return for rent or some other form of payment.

Lease agreement In regard to the lease of goods, an agreement in which one person (the lessor) agrees to transfer the right to the possession and use of property to another person (the lessee) in exchange for rental payments.

Leasehold estate An estate in realty held by a tenant under a lease. In every leasehold estate, the tenant has a qualified right to possess and/or use the land.

Legacy A gift of personal property under a will.

Legal positivists Adherents to the positivist school of legal thought. This school holds that there can be no higher law than a nation's positive law—law created by a particular society at a particular point in time. In contrast to the natural law school, the positivist school maintains that there are no "natural" rights; rights come into existence only when there is a sovereign power (government) to confer and enforce those rights.

Legal rate of interest A rate of interest fixed by statute as either the maximum rate of interest allowed by law or a rate of interest applied when the parties to a contract intend, but do not fix, an interest rate in the contract. In the latter case, the rate is frequently the same as the statutory maximum rate permitted.

Legal realism A school of legal thought that was popular in the 1920s and 1930s and that challenged many existing jurisprudential assumptions, particularly the assumption that subjective elements play no part in judicial reasoning. Legal realists generally advocated a less abstract and more pragmatic approach to the law, an approach that would take into account customary practices and the circumstances in which transactions take place. The school left a lasting imprint on American jurisprudence.

Legal reasoning The process of reasoning by which a judge harmonizes his or her decision with the judicial decisions of previous cases.

Legatee One designated in a will to receive a gift of personal property.

Legislative rule An administrative agency rule that carries the same weight as a congressionally enacted statute.

Lessee A person who acquires the right to the possession and use of another's property in exchange for rental payments.

Lessor A person who sells the right to the possession and use of property to another in exchange for rental payments.

Letter of credit A written instrument, usually issued by a bank on behalf of a customer or other person, in which the issuer promises to honor drafts or other demands for payment by third persons in accordance with the terms of the instrument.

Leveraged buyout (LBO) A corporate takeover financed by loans secured by the acquired corpora-

tion's assets or by the issuance of corporate bonds, resulting in a high debt load for the corporation.

Levy The obtaining of money by legal process through the seizure and sale of property, usually done after a writ of execution has been issued.

Liability Any actual or potential legal obligation, duty, debt, or responsibility.

Libel Defamation in writing or other form (such as in a videotape) having the quality of permanence.

License A revocable right or privilege of a person to come on another person's land.

Licensee One who receives a license to use, or enter onto, another's property.

Lien (pronounced *leen*) A claim against specific property to satisfy a debt.

Lien creditor One whose claim is secured by a lien on particular property, as distinguished from a general creditor, who has no such security.

Life estate An interest in land that exists only for the duration of the life of some person, usually the holder of the estate.

Limited jurisdiction Exists when a court's subject-matter jurisdiction is limited. Bankruptcy courts and probate courts are examples of courts with limited jurisdiction.

Limited liability Exists when the liability of the owners of a business is limited to the amount of their investments in the firm.

Limited liability company (LLC) A hybrid form of business enterprise that offers the limited liability of the corporation but the tax advantages of a partnership.

Limited liability limited partnership (LLLP) A type of limited partnership. The difference between a limited partnership and an LLLP is that the liability of the general partner in an LLLP is the same as the liability of the limited partner. That is, the liability of all partners is limited to the amount of their investments in the firm.

Limited liability partnership (LLP) A form of partnership that allows professionals to enjoy the tax benefits of a partnership while limiting their personal liability for the malpractice of other partners.

Limited partner In a limited partnership, a partner who contributes capital to the partnership but has no right to participate in the management and operation of the business. The limited partner assumes no liability for partnership debts beyond the capital contributed.

Limited partnership A partnership consisting of one or more general partners (who manage the business and are liable to the full extent of their personal assets for debts of the partnership) and one or more limited partners (who contribute only assets and are liable only to the extent of their contributions).

Limited-payment life A type of life insurance for which premiums are payable for a definite period, after which the policy is fully paid.

Limited warranty A written warranty that fails to meet one or more of the minimum standards for a full warranty.

Liquidated damages An amount, stipulated in the contract, that the parties to a contract believe to be a reasonable estimation of the damages that will occur in the event of a breach.

Liquidated debt A debt that is due and certain in amount.

Liquidation (1) In regard to bankruptcy, the sale of all of the nonexempt assets of a debtor and the distribution of the proceeds to the debtor's creditors. Chapter 7 of the Bankruptcy Code provides for liquidation bankruptcy proceedings. (2) In regard to corporations, the process by which corporate assets are converted into cash and distributed among creditors and shareholders according to specific rules of preference.

Litigant A party to a lawsuit.

Litigation The process of resolving a dispute through the court system.

Living will A document that allows a person to control the methods of medical treatment that may be used after a serious accident or illness.

Long arm statute A state statute that permits a state to obtain personal jurisdiction over nonresident defendants. A defendant must have "minimum contacts" with that state for the statute to apply.

Lost property Property with which the owner has involuntarily parted and then cannot find or recover.

M

Magistrate's court A court of limited jurisdiction that is presided over by a public official (magistrate) with certain judicial authority, such as the power to set bail.

Mailbox rule A rule providing that an acceptance of an offer becomes effective on dispatch (on being placed in a mailbox), if mail is, expressly or impliedly, an authorized means of communication of acceptance to the offeror.

Main purpose rule A rule of contract law under which an exception to the Statute of Frauds is made if the main purpose in accepting secondary liability under a contract is to secure a personal benefit. If this situation exists, the contract need not be in writing to be enforceable.

Majority *See* Age of majority

Majority opinion A court's written opinion, outlining the views of the majority of the judges or justices deciding the case.

Maker One who promises to pay a certain sum to the holder of a promissory note or certificate of deposit (CD).

Malpractice Professional misconduct or the failure to exercise the requisite degree of skill as a professional. Negligence—the failure to exercise due care—on the part of a professional, such as a physician or an attorney, is commonly referred to as malpractice.

Manufacturing or processing-plant franchise A franchise that is created when the franchisor transmits to the franchisee the essential ingredients or formula to make a particular product. The franchisee then markets the product either at wholesale or at retail in accordance with the franchisor's standards. Examples of this type of franchise are Coca-Cola and other soft-drink bottling companies.

Marine insurance Insurance protecting shippers and vessel owners from losses or damages sustained by a vessel or its cargo during the transport of goods by water.

Mark *See* Trademark

Market concentration A situation that exists when a small number of firms share the market for a particular good or service. For example, if the four largest grocery stores in Chicago accounted for 80 percent of all retail food sales, the market clearly would be concentrated in those four firms.

Market power The power of a firm to control the market price of its product. A monopoly has the greatest degree of market power.

Marketable title Title to real estate that is reasonably free from encumbrances, defects in the chain of title, and other events that affect title, such as adverse possession.

Market-share liability A method of sharing liability among several firms that manufactured or marketed a particular product that may have caused a plaintiff's injury. This form of liability sharing is used when the true source of the product is unidentifiable. Each firm's liability is proportionate to its respective share of the relevant market for the product. Market-share liability applies only if the injuring product is fungible, the true manufacturer is unidentifiable, and the unknown character of the manufacturer is not the plaintiff's fault.

Market-share test The primary measure of monopoly power. A firm's market share is the percentage of a market that the firm controls.

Marshalling assets The arrangement or ranking of assets in a certain order toward the payment of debts. In equity, when two creditors have recourse to the same property of the debtor, but one has recourse to other property of the debtor, that creditor must resort first to those assets of the debtor that are not available to the other creditor.

Material fact A fact to which a reasonable person would attach importance in determining his or her course of action. In regard to tender offers, for example, a fact is material if there is a substantial likelihood that a reasonable shareholder would consider it important in deciding how to vote.

Mechanic's lien A statutory lien on the real property of another, created to ensure payment for work performed and materials furnished in the repair or improvement of real property, such as a building.

Mediation A method of settling disputes outside of court by using the services of a neutral third party, called a mediator. The mediator acts as a communicating agent between the parties and suggests ways in which the parties can resolve their dispute.

Member The term used to designate a person who has an ownership interest in a limited liability company.

Mens rea (pronounced *mehns ray-uh*) Mental state, or intent. A wrongful mental state is as necessary as a wrongful act to establish criminal liability. What constitutes a mental state varies according to the wrongful action. Thus, for murder, the *mens rea* is the intent to take a life; for theft, the *mens rea* must involve both the knowledge that the property belongs to another and the intent to deprive the owner of it.

Merchant A person who is engaged in the purchase and sale of goods. Under the Uniform Commercial Code, a person who deals in goods of the kind involved in the sales contract; for further definitions, see UCC 2–104.

Merger A contractual and statutory process in which one corporation (the surviving corporation) acquires all of the assets and liabilities of another corporation (the merged corporation). The shareholders of the merged corporation receive either payment for their shares or shares in the surviving corporation.

Meta tags Words inserted into a Web site's key-words field to increase the site's appearance in search engine results.

Metes and bounds A system of measuring boundary lines by the distance between two points, often using physical features of the local geography, such as roads, intersections, rivers, or bridges. The legal descriptions of real property contained in deeds often are phrased in terms of metes and bounds.

Minimum-contacts requirement The requirement that before a state court can exercise jurisdiction over a foreign corporation, the foreign corporation must have sufficient contacts with the state. A foreign corporation that has its home office in the state or that has manufacturing plants in the state meets this requirement.

Minimum wage The lowest wage, either by government regulation or union contract, that an employer may pay an hourly worker.

Mini-trial A private proceeding in which each party to a dispute argues its position before the other side and vice versa. A neutral third party may be present and act as an adviser if the parties fail to reach an agreement.

Mirror image rule A common law rule that requires, for a valid contractual agreement, that the terms of the offeree's acceptance adhere exactly to the terms of the offeror's offer.

Misdemeanor A lesser crime than a felony, punishable by a fine or imprisonment for up to one year in other than a state or federal penitentiary.

Mislaid property Property with which the owner has voluntarily parted and then cannot find or recover.

Misrepresentation A false statement of fact or an action that deceives and causes harm or injury to another. *See also* Fraudulent misrepresentation (fraud); Innocent misrepresentation

Mitigation of damages A rule requiring a plaintiff to have done whatever was reasonable to minimize the damages caused by the defendant.

Money laundering Falsely reporting income that has been obtained through criminal activity as income obtained through a legitimate business enterprise—in effect, "laundering" the "dirty money."

Monopolization The possession of monopoly power in the relevant market and the willful acquisition or maintenance of that power, as distinguished from growth or development as a consequence of a superior product, business acumen, or historic accident.

Monopoly A term generally used to describe a market in which there is a single seller or a limited number of sellers.

Monopoly power The ability of a monopoly to dictate what takes place in a given market.

Moral minimum The minimum degree of ethical behavior expected of a business firm, which is usually defined as compliance with the law.

Mortgage A written instrument giving a creditor (the mortgagee) an interest in (a lien on) the debtor's (mortgagor's) property as security for a debt.

Mortgage bond A bond that pledges specific property. If the corporation defaults on the bond, the bondholder can take the property.

Mortgagee Under a mortgage agreement, the creditor who takes a security interest in the debtor's property.

Mortgagor Under a mortgage agreement, the debtor who gives the creditor a security interest in the debtor's property in return for a mortgage loan.

Motion A procedural request or application presented by an attorney to the court on behalf of a client.

Motion for a directed verdict In a state court, a party's request that the judge enter a judgment in her or his favor before the case is submitted to a jury because the other party has not presented sufficient evidence to support the claim. The federal courts refer to this request as a *motion for judgment as a matter of law.*

Motion for a new trial A motion asserting that the trial was so fundamentally flawed (because of error, newly discovered evidence, prejudice, or other reason) that a new trial is necessary to prevent a miscarriage of justice.

Motion for judgment as a matter of law In a federal court, a party's request that the judge enter a judgment in her or his favor before the case is submitted to a jury because the other party has not presented sufficient evidence to support the claim. The state courts refer to this request as a *motion for a directed verdict.*

Motion for judgment *n.o.v.* A motion requesting the court to grant judgment in favor of the party making the motion on the ground that the jury verdict against him or her was unreasonable and erroneous.

Motion for judgment on the pleadings A motion by either party to a lawsuit at the close of the pleadings requesting the court to decide the issue solely on the pleadings without proceeding to trial. The motion will be granted only if no facts are in dispute.

Motion for summary judgment A motion requesting the court to enter a judgment without proceeding to trial. The motion can be based on evidence outside the pleadings and will be granted only if no facts are in dispute.

Motion to dismiss A pleading in which a defendant asserts that the plaintiff's claim fails to state a cause of action (that is, has no basis in law) or that there are other grounds on which a suit should be dismissed.

Multiple product order An order issued by the Federal Trade Commission to a firm that has engaged in deceptive advertising by which the firm is required to cease and desist from false advertising not only in regard to the product that was the subject of the action but also in regard to all the firm's other products.

Municipal court A city or community court with criminal jurisdiction over traffic violations and, less frequently, with civil jurisdiction over other minor matters.

Mutual assent The element of agreement in the formation of a contract. The manifestation of contract parties' mutual assent to the same bargain is required to establish a contract.

Mutual fund A specific type of investment company that continually buys or sells to investors shares of ownership in a portfolio.

Mutual rescission An agreement between the parties to cancel their contract, releasing the parties from further obligations under the contract. The object of the agreement is to restore the parties to the positions they would have occupied had no contract ever been formed. *See also* Rescission

N

National law Law that pertains to a particular nation (as opposed to international law).

Natural law The belief that government and the legal system should reflect universal moral and ethical principles that are inherent in human nature. The natural law school is the oldest and one of the most significant schools of legal thought.

Necessaries Necessities required for life, such as food, shelter, clothing, and medical attention; may include whatever is believed to be necessary to maintain a person's standard of living or financial and social status.

Necessity In criminal law, a defense against liability; under Section 3.02 of the Model Penal Code, this defense is justifiable if "the harm or evil sought to be avoided" by a given action "is greater than that sought to be prevented by the law defining the offense charged."

Negligence The failure to exercise the standard of care that a reasonable person would exercise in similar circumstances.

Negligence *per se* An act (or failure to act) in violation of a statutory requirement.

Negligent misrepresentation Any manifestation through words or conduct that amounts to an untrue statement of fact made in circumstances in which a reasonable and prudent person would not have done (or failed to do) that which led to the misrepresentation. A representation made with an honest belief in its truth may still be negligent due to (1) a lack of reasonable care in ascertaining the facts, (2) the manner of expression, or (3) the absence of the skill or competence required by a particular business or profession.

Negotiable instrument A signed writing that contains an unconditional promise or order to pay an exact sum of money, on demand or at an exact future time, to a specific person or order, or to bearer.

Negotiation (1) In regard to dispute settlement, a process in which parties attempt to settle their dispute without going to court, with or without attorneys to represent them. (2) In regard to instruments, the transfer of an instrument in such a way that the transferee (the person to whom the instrument is transferred) becomes a holder.

Nominal damages A small monetary award (often one dollar) granted to a plaintiff when no actual damage was suffered or when the plaintiff is unable to show such loss with sufficient certainty.

Nonconforming goods Goods that do not conform to contract specifications.

Nonpossessory interest An interest in land, such as a right-of-way, that does not include any right to possess the land, but only confers the right to use the real property of another for a specified purpose. Nonpossessory interests include easements, profits, and licenses.

No-par shares Corporate shares that have no face value—that is, no specific dollar amount is printed on their face.

Normal trade relations (NTR) status A status granted through an international treaty by which each member nation must treat other members at least as well as it treats the country that receives its most favorable treatment. This status was formerly known as most-favored-nation status.

Notary public A public official authorized to attest to the authenticity of signatures.

Note A written instrument signed by a maker unconditionally promising to pay a fixed amount of money to a payee or a holder on demand or on a specific date.

Notice-and-comment rulemaking An administrative rulemaking procedure that involves the publication of a notice of a proposed rulemaking in the *Federal Register*, a comment period for interested parties to express their views on the proposed rule, and the publication of the agency's final rule in the *Federal Register*.

Notice of Proposed Rulemaking A notice published (in the *Federal Register*) by an administrative agency describing a proposed rule. The notice must give the time and place for which agency proceedings on the proposed rule will be held, a description of the nature of the proceedings, the legal authority for the proceedings (which is usually the agency's enabling legislation), and the terms of the proposed rule or the subject matter of the proposed rule.

Novation The substitution, by agreement, of a new contract for an old one, with the rights under the old one being terminated. Typically, there is a substitution of a new person who is responsible for the contract and the removal of an original party's rights and duties under the contract.

Nuisance A common law doctrine under which persons may be held liable for using their property in a manner that unreasonably interferes with others' rights to use or enjoy their own property.

Nuncupative will An oral will (often called a deathbed will) made before witnesses; usually limited to transfers of personal property.

O

Objective theory of contracts A theory under which the intent to form a contract will be judged by outward, objective facts (what the party said when entering into the contract, how the party acted or appeared, and the circumstances surrounding the transaction) as interpreted by a reasonable person, rather than by the party's own secret, subjective intentions.

Obligee One to whom an obligation is owed.

Obligor One that owes an obligation to another.

Offer A promise or commitment to perform or refrain from performing some specified act in the future.

Offeree A person to whom an offer is made.

Offeror A person who makes an offer.

Omnibus clause A provision in an automobile insurance policy that protects the vehicle owner who has taken out the insurance policy and anyone who drives the vehicle with the owner's permission.

Online Dispute Resolution (ODR) The resolution of disputes with the assistance of organizations that offer dispute-resolution services via the Internet.

Opening statement A statement made to the jury at the beginning of a trial by a party's attorney, prior to the presentation of evidence. The attorney briefly outlines the evidence that will be offered and the legal theory that will be pursued.

Operating agreement In a limited liability company, an agreement in which the members set forth the details of how the business will be managed and operated.

Opinion A statement by the court expressing the reasons for its decision in a case.

Option contract A contract under which the offeror cannot revoke his or her offer for a stipulated time period and the offeree can accept or reject the offer dur-

ing this period without fear that the offer will be made to another person. The offeree must give consideration for the option (the irrevocable offer) to be enforceable.

Order for relief A court's grant of assistance to a complainant. In bankruptcy proceedings, the order relieves the debtor of the immediate obligation to pay the debts listed in the bankruptcy petition.

Order instrument A negotiable instrument that is payable "to the order of an identified person" or "to an identified person or order."

Ordinance A law passed by a local governing unit, such as a municipality or a county.

Original jurisdiction Jurisdiction that is exercised by courts of the first instance, or trial courts—that is, courts in which lawsuits begin, trials take place, and evidence is presented.

Output contract An agreement in which a seller agrees to sell and a buyer agrees to buy all or up to a stated amount of what the seller produces.

Outside director A person on the board of directors who does not hold a management position at the corporation.

Overdraft A check written on a checking account in which there are insufficient funds to cover the amount of the check.

P

Parent-subsidiary merger A merger of companies in which one company (the parent corporation) owns most of the stock of the other (the subsidiary corporation). A parent-subsidiary merger (short-form merger) can use a simplified procedure when the parent corporation owns at least 90 percent of the outstanding shares of each class of stock of the subsidiary corporation.

Parol evidence A term that originally meant "oral evidence," but which has come to refer to any negotiations or agreements made prior to a contract or any contemporaneous oral agreements made by the parties.

Parol evidence rule A substantive rule of contracts under which a court will not receive into evidence the parties' prior negotiations, prior agreements, or contemporaneous oral agreements if that evidence contradicts or varies the terms of the parties' written contract.

Partially disclosed principal A principal whose identity is unknown by a third person, but the third person knows that the agent is or may be acting for a principal at the time the agent and the third person form a contract.

Partner A co-owner of a partnership.

Partnering agreement An agreement between a seller and a buyer who frequently do business with each other on the terms and conditions that will apply to all subsequently formed electronic contracts.

Partnership An agreement by two or more persons to carry on, as co-owners, a business for profit.

Partnership by estoppel A judicially created partnership that may, at the court's discretion, be imposed for purposes of fairness. The court can prevent those who present themselves as partners (but who are not) from escaping liability if a third person relies on an alleged partnership in good faith and is harmed as a result.

Par-value shares Corporate shares that have a specific face value, or formal cash-in value, written on them, such as one dollar.

Past consideration An act done before the contract is made, which ordinarily, by itself, cannot be consideration for a later promise to pay for the act.

Patent A government grant that gives an inventor the exclusive right or privilege to make, use, or sell his or her invention for a limited time period. The word *patent* usually refers to some invention and designates either the instrument by which patent rights are evidenced or the patent itself.

Payee A person to whom an instrument is made payable.

Payor bank The bank on which a check is drawn (the drawee bank).

Peer-to-peer (P2P) networking The sharing of resources (such as files, hard drives, and processing styles) among multiple computers without necessarily requiring a central network server.

Penalty A sum inserted into a contract, not as a measure of compensation for its breach but rather as punishment for a default. The agreement as to the amount will not be enforced, and recovery will be limited to actual damages.

Per capita A Latin term meaning "per person." In the law governing estate distribution, a method of distributing the property of an intestate's estate in which each heir in a certain class (such as grandchildren) receives an equal share.

Per curiam By the whole court; a court opinion written by the court as a whole instead of being authored by a judge or justice.

Per se A Latin term meaning "in itself" or "by itself."

Per se violation A type of anticompetitive agreement—such as a horizontal price-fixing agreement—that is considered to be so injurious to the public that there is no need to determine whether it actually injures market competition; rather, it is in itself (*per se*) a violation of the Sherman Act.

Per stirpes A Latin term meaning "by the roots." In the law governing estate distribution, a method of distributing an intestate's estate in which each heir in a certain class (such as grandchildren) takes the share to which his or her deceased ancestor (such as a mother or father) would have been entitled.

Perfect tender rule A common law rule under which a seller was required to deliver to the buyer goods that conformed perfectly to the requirements stipulated in the sales contract. A tender of nonconforming goods would automatically constitute a breach of contract. Under the Uniform Commercial Code, the rule has been greatly modified.

Perfection The legal process by which secured parties protect themselves against the claims of third parties who may wish to have their debts satisfied out of the same collateral; usually accomplished by the filing of a financing statement with the appropriate government official.

Performance In contract law, the fulfillment of one's duties arising under a contract with another; the normal way of discharging one's contractual obligations.

Periodic tenancy A lease interest in land for an indefinite period involving payment of rent at fixed intervals, such as week to week, month to month, or year to year.

Personal defense A defense that can be used to avoid payment to an ordinary holder of a negotiable instrument but not a holder in due course (HDC) or a holder with the rights of an HDC.

Personal identification number (PIN) A number given to the holder of an access card (debit card, credit card, ATM card, or the like) that is used to conduct financial transactions electronically. Typically, the card will not provide access to a system without the number, which is meant to be kept secret to inhibit unauthorized use of the card.

Personal jurisdiction *See In personam* jurisdiction

Personal property Property that is movable; any property that is not real property.

Personalty Personal property.

Petition in bankruptcy The document that is filed with a bankruptcy court to initiate bankruptcy proceedings. The official forms required for a petition in bankruptcy must be completed accurately, sworn to under oath, and signed by the debtor.

Petitioner In equity practice, a party that initiates a lawsuit.

Petty offense In criminal law, the least serious kind of criminal offense, such as a traffic or building-code violation.

Pierce the corporate veil To disregard the corporate entity, which limits the liability of shareholders, and hold the shareholders personally liable for a corporate obligation.

Plaintiff One who initiates a lawsuit.

Plea In criminal law, a defendant's allegation, in response to the charges brought against him or her, of guilt or innocence.

Plea bargaining The process by which a criminal defendant and the prosecutor in a criminal case work out a mutually satisfactory disposition of the case, subject to court approval; usually involves the defendant's pleading guilty to a lesser offense in return for a lighter sentence.

Pleadings Statements made by the plaintiff and the defendant in a lawsuit that detail the facts, charges, and defenses involved in the litigation; the complaint and answer are part of the pleadings.

Pledge A common law security device (retained in Article 9 of the Uniform Commercial Code) in which personal property is turned over to the creditor as security for the payment of a debt and retained by the creditor until the debt is paid.

Police powers Powers possessed by states as part of their inherent sovereignty. These powers may be exercised to protect or promote the public order, health, safety, morals, and general welfare.

Policy In insurance law, a contract between the insurer and the insured in which, for a stipulated consideration, the insurer agrees to compensate the insured for loss on a specific subject by a specified peril.

Positive law The body of conventional, or written, law of a particular society at a particular point in time.

Positivist school A school of legal thought whose adherents believe that there can be no higher law than a nation's positive law—the body of conventional, or written, law of a particular society at a particular time.

Possessory lien A lien that allows one person to retain possession of another's property as security for a debt or obligation owed by the owner of the property to the lienholder. An example of a possessory lien is an artisan's lien.

Potentially responsible party (PRP) A potentially liable party under the Comprehensive Environmental Response, Compensation and Liability Act (CERCLA). Any person who generated the hazardous waste, transported the hazardous waste, owned or operated a waste site at the time of disposal, or currently owns or operates a site may be responsible for some or all of the clean-up costs involved in removing the hazardous chemicals.

Power of attorney A written document, which is usually notarized, authorizing another to act as one's agent; can be special (permitting the agent to do specified acts only) or general (permitting the agent to transact all business for the principal).

Preauthorized transfer A transaction authorized in advance to recur at substantially regular intervals. The terms and procedures for preauthorized electronic fund transfers through certain financial institutions are subject to the Electronic Fund Transfer Act.

Precedent A court decision that furnishes an example or authority for deciding subsequent cases involving identical or similar facts.

Predatory pricing The pricing of a product below cost with the intent to drive competitors out of the market.

Predominant-factor test A test courts use to determine whether a contract is primarily for the sale of goods or for the sale of services.

Preemption A doctrine under which certain federal laws preempt, or take precedence over, conflicting state or local laws.

Preemptive rights Rights held by shareholders that entitle them to purchase newly issued shares of a corporation's stock, equal in percentage to shares already held, before the stock is offered to any outside buyers. Preemptive rights enable shareholders to maintain their proportionate ownership and voice in the corporation.

Preference In bankruptcy proceedings, property transfers or payments made by the debtor that favor (give preference to) one creditor over others. The bankruptcy trustee is allowed to recover payments made both voluntarily and involuntarily to one creditor in preference over another.

Preferred creditor One who has received a preferential transfer from a debtor.

Preferred stock Classes of stock that have priority over common stock both as to payment of dividends and distribution of assets on the corporation's dissolution.

Prejudgment interest Interest that accrues on the amount of a court judgment from the time of the filing of a lawsuit to the court's issuance of a judgment.

Preliminary hearing An initial hearing used in many felony cases to establish whether it is proper to detain the defendant. A magistrate reviews the evidence and decides if there is probable cause to believe that the defendant committed the crime with which he or she has been charged.

Premium In insurance law, the price paid by the insured for insurance protection for a specified period of time.

Prenuptial agreement An agreement made before marriage that defines each partner's ownership rights in the other partner's property. Prenuptial agreements must be in writing to be enforceable.

Preponderance of the evidence A standard in civil law cases under which the plaintiff must convince the court that, based on the evidence presented by both parties, it is more likely than not that the plaintiff's allegation is true.

Presentment The act of presenting an instrument to the party liable on the instrument to collect payment; presentment also occurs when a person presents an instrument to a drawee for acceptance.

Presentment warranties Any person who presents an instrument for payment or acceptance impliedly warrants that (1) he or she is entitled to enforce the instrument or authorized to obtain payment or acceptance on behalf of a person who is entitled, (2) the instrument has not been altered, and (3) he or she has no knowledge that the signature of the drawer is unauthorized.

Pretrial conference A conference, scheduled before the trial begins, between the judge and the attorneys litigating the suit. The parties may settle the dispute, clarify the issues, schedule discovery, and the like during the conference.

Pretrial motion A written or oral application to a court for a ruling or order, made before trial.

Price discrimination Setting prices in such a way that two competing buyers pay two different prices for an identical product or service.

Price-fixing agreement An agreement between

competitors in which the competitors agree to fix the prices of products or services at a certain level; prohibited by the Sherman Act.

Prima facie case A case in which the plaintiff has produced sufficient evidence of his or her conclusion that the case can go to to a jury; a case in which the evidence compels the plaintiff's conclusion if the defendant produces no evidence to disprove it.

Primary liability In negotiable instruments law, absolute responsibility for paying a negotiable instrument. Makers and acceptors are primarily liable.

Principal In agency law, a person who agrees to have another, called the agent, act on his or her behalf.

Principle of rights The principle that human beings have certain fundamental rights (to life, freedom, and the pursuit of happiness, for example). Those who adhere to this "rights theory" believe that a key factor in determining whether a business decision is ethical is how that decision affects the rights of others. These others include the firm's owners, its employees, the consumers of its products or services, its suppliers, the community in which it does business, and society as a whole.

Private equity capital A financing method by which a company sells equity in an existing business to a private or institutional investor.

Privatization The replacement of government-provided products and services by private firms.

Privilege In tort law, the ability to act contrary to another person's right without that person's having legal redress for such acts. Privilege may be raised as a defense to defamation.

Privileges and immunities clause Special rights and exceptions provided by law. Article IV, Section 2, of the Constitution requires states not to discriminate against one another's citizens. A resident of one state cannot be treated as an alien when in another state; he or she may not be denied such privileges and immunities as legal protection, access to courts, travel rights, or property rights.

Privity of contract The relationship that exists between the promisor and the promisee of a contract.

Pro rata Proportionately; in proportion.

Probable cause Reasonable grounds to believe the existence of facts warranting certain actions, such as the search or arrest of a person.

Probate The process of proving and validating a will and the settling of all matters pertaining to administration, guardianship, and the like.

Probate court A state court of limited jurisdiction that conducts proceedings relating to the settlement of a deceased person's estate.

Procedural due process The requirement that any government decision to take life, liberty, or property be made fairly. For example, fair procedures must be used in determining whether a person will be subjected to punishment or have some burden imposed on him or her.

Procedural law Rules that define the manner in which the rights and duties of individuals may be enforced.

Procedural unconscionability Occurs when, due to one contractual party's vastly superior bargaining power, the other party lacks knowledge or understanding of the contract terms due to inconspicuous print or the lack of an opportunity to read the contract or to ask questions about its meaning. Procedural unconscionability often involves an *adhesion contract,* which is a contract drafted by the dominant party and then presented to the other—the adhering party—on a take-it-or-leave-it basis.

Proceeds Under Article 9 of the Uniform Commercial Code, whatever is received when the collateral is sold or otherwise disposed of, such as by exchange.

Product liability The legal liability of manufacturers, sellers, and lessors of goods to consumers, users, and bystanders for injuries or damages that are caused by the goods.

Product misuse A defense against product liability that may be raised when the plaintiff used a product in a manner not intended by the manufacturer. If the misuse is reasonably foreseeable, the seller will not escape liability unless measures were taken to guard against the harm that could result from the misuse.

Professional corporation A corporation formed by professional persons, such as physicians, lawyers, dentists, and accountants, to gain tax benefits. Subject to certain exceptions (when a court may treat a professional corporation as a partnership for liability purposes), the shareholders of a professional corporation have the limited liability characteristic of the corporate form of business.

Profit In real property law, the right to enter onto and remove things from the property of another (for example, the right to enter onto a person's land and remove sand and gravel therefrom).

Promise A person's assurance that he or she will or will not do something.

Promisee A person to whom a promise is made.

Promisor A person who makes a promise.

Promissory estoppel A doctrine that applies when a promisor makes a clear and definite promise on which the promisee justifiably relies; such a promise is binding if justice will be better served by the enforcement of the promise. *See also* Estoppel

Promissory note A written promise made by one person (the maker) to pay a fixed sum of money to another person (the payee or a subsequent holder) on demand or on a specified date.

Promoter A person who takes the preliminary steps in organizing a corporation, including (usually) issuing a prospectus, procuring stock subscriptions, making contract purchases, securing a corporate charter, and the like.

Property Legally protected rights and interests in

anything with an ascertainable value that is subject to ownership.

Prospectus   A document required by federal or state securities laws that describes the financial operations of the corporation, thus allowing investors to make informed decisions.

Protected class   A class of persons with identifiable characteristics who historically have been victimized by discriminatory treatment for certain purposes. Depending on the context, these characteristics include age, color, gender, national origin, race, and religion.

Proximate cause   Legal cause; exists when the connection between an act and an injury is strong enough to justify imposing liability.

Proxy   In corporation law, a written agreement between a stockholder and another under which the stockholder authorizes the other to vote the stockholder's shares in a certain manner.

Proxy fight   A conflict between an individual, group, or firm attempting to take control of a corporation and the corporation's management for the votes of the shareholders.

Public figures   Individuals who are thrust into the public limelight. Public figures include government officials and politicians, movie stars, well-known businesspersons, and generally anybody who becomes known to the public because of his or her position or activities.

Public policy   A government policy based on widely held societal values and (usually) expressed or implied in laws or regulations.

Public prosecutor   An individual, acting as a trial lawyer, who initiates and conducts criminal cases in the government's name and on behalf of the people.

Puffery   A salesperson's exaggerated claims concerning the quality of property offered for sale. Such claims involve opinions rather than facts and are not considered to be legally binding promises or warranties.

Punitive damages   Money damages that may be awarded to a plaintiff to punish the defendant and deter future similar conduct.

Purchase-money security interest (PMSI)   A security interest that arises when a seller or lender extends credit for part or all of the purchase price of goods purchased by a buyer.

Q

Qualified indorsement   An indorsement on a negotiable instrument in which the indorser disclaims any contract liability on the instrument; the notation "without recourse" is commonly used to create a qualified indorsement.

Quantum meruit (pronounced *kwahn*-tuhm *mehr*-oo-wuht)   Literally, "as much as he deserves"—an expression describing the extent of liability on a contract implied in law (quasi contract). An equitable doc-

trine based on the concept that one who benefits from another's labor and materials should not be unjustly enriched thereby but should be required to pay a reasonable amount for the benefits received, even absent a contract.

Quasi contract   A fictional contract imposed on parties by a court in the interests of fairness and justice; usually, quasi contracts are imposed to avoid the unjust enrichment of one party at the expense of another.

Question of fact   In a lawsuit, an issue involving a factual dispute that can be decided only by a judge (or, in a jury trial, a jury).

Question of law   In a lawsuit, an issue involving the application or interpretation of a law; therefore, the judge, and not the jury, decides the issue.

Quiet enjoyment   *See* Covenant of quiet enjoyment

Quitclaim deed   A deed intended to pass any title, interest, or claim that the grantor may have in the property but not warranting that such title is valid. A quitclaim deed offers the least amount of protection against defects in the title.

Quorum   The number of members of a decision-making body that must be present before business may be transacted.

Quota   An assigned import limit on goods.

R

Ratification   The act of accepting and giving legal force to an obligation that previously was not enforceable.

Reaffirmation agreement   An agreement between a debtor and a creditor in which the debtor reaffirms, or promises to pay, a debt dischargeable in bankruptcy. To be enforceable, the agreement must be made prior to the discharge of the debt by the bankruptcy court.

Real property   Land and everything attached to it, such as foliage and buildings.

Reasonable care   The degree of care that a person of ordinary prudence would exercise in the same or similar circumstances.

Reasonable doubt   *See* Beyond a reasonable doubt

Reasonable person standard   The standard of behavior expected of a hypothetical "reasonable person." The standard against which negligence is measured and that must be observed to avoid liability for negligence.

Rebuttal   The refutation of evidence introduced by an adverse party's attorney.

Receiver   In a corporate dissolution, a court-appointed person who winds up corporate affairs and liquidates corporate assets.

Record   According to the Uniform Electronic Transactions Act, information that is either inscribed on a tangible medium or stored in an electronic or other medium and that is retrievable. The Uniform Computer Information Transactions Act uses the term *record* instead of *writing*.

Recording statutes Statutes that allow deeds, mortgages, and other real property transactions to be recorded so as to provide notice to future purchasers or creditors of an existing claim on the property.

Red herring prospectus A preliminary prospectus that can be distributed to potential investors after the registration statement (for a securities offering) has been filed with the Securities and Exchange Commission. The name derives from the red legend printed across the prospectus stating that the registration has been filed but has not become effective.

Redemption A repurchase, or buying back. In secured transactions law, a debtor's repurchase of collateral securing a debt after a creditor has taken title to the collateral due to the debtor's default but before the secured party disposes of the collateral.

Reformation A court-ordered correction of a written contract so that it reflects the true intentions of the parties.

Regulation E A set of rules issued by the Federal Reserve System's Board of Governors under the authority of the Electronic Fund Transfer Act to protect users of electronic fund transfer systems.

Regulation Z A set of rules promulgated by the Federal Reserve Board to implement the provisions of the Truth-in-Lending Act.

Rejection In contract law, an offeree's express or implied manifestation not to accept an offer. In the law governing contracts for the sale of goods, a buyer's manifest refusal to accept goods on the ground that they do not conform to contract specifications.

Rejoinder The defendant's answer to the plaintiff's rebuttal.

Release A contract in which one party forfeits the right to pursue a legal claim against the other party.

Relevant evidence Evidence tending to make a fact at issue in the case more or less probable than it would be without the evidence. Only relevant evidence is admissible in court.

Remainder A future interest in property held by a person other than the original owner.

Remanded Sent back. If an appellate court disagrees with a lower court's judgment, the case may be remanded to the lower court for further proceedings in which the lower court's decision should be consistent with the appellate court's opinion on the matter.

Remedy The relief given to an innocent party to enforce a right or compensate for the violation of a right.

Remedy at law A remedy available in a court of law. Money damages are awarded as a remedy at law.

Remedy in equity A remedy allowed by courts in situations where remedies at law are not appropriate. Remedies in equity are based on settled rules of fairness, justice, and honesty, and include injunction, specific performance, rescission and restitution, and reformation.

Remitter A person who sends money, or remits payment.

Rent The consideration paid for the use or enjoyment of another's property. In landlord-tenant relationships, the payment made by the tenant to the landlord for the right to possess the premises.

Rent escalation clause A clause providing for an increase in rent during a lease term.

Repair-and-deduct statutes Statutes providing that a tenant may pay for repairs and deduct the cost of the repairs from the rent, as a remedy for a landlord's failure to maintain leased premises.

Replevin (pronounced ruh-*pleh*-vin) An action to recover specific goods in the hands of a party who is wrongfully withholding them from the other party.

Reply Procedurally, a plaintiff's response to a defendant's answer.

Reporter A publication in which court cases are published, or reported.

Repudiation The renunciation of a right or duty; the act of a buyer or seller in rejecting a contract either partially or totally. *See also* Anticipatory repudiation

Requirements contract An agreement in which a buyer agrees to purchase and the seller agrees to sell all or up to a stated amount of what the buyer needs or requires.

Res ipsa loquitur (pronounced *rehs ehp*-suh *low*-quuh-duhr) A doctrine under which negligence may be inferred simply because an event occurred, if it is the type of event that would not occur in the absence of negligence. Literally, the term means "the facts speak for themselves."

Resale price maintenance agreement An agreement between a manufacturer and a retailer in which the manufacturer specifies the minimum retail price of its products.

Rescind (pronounced reh-*sihnd*) To cancel. *See also* Rescission

Rescission (pronounced reh-*sih*-zhen) A remedy whereby a contract is canceled and the parties are returned to the positions they occupied before the contract was made; may be effected through the mutual consent of the parties, by their conduct, or by court decree.

Residuary The surplus of a testator's estate remaining after all of the debts and particular legacies have been discharged.

Respondeat superior (pronounced ree-*spahn*-dee-uht soo-*peer*-ee-your) In Latin, "Let the master respond." A doctrine under which a principal or an employer is held liable for the wrongful acts committed by agents or employees while acting within the course and scope of their agency or employment.

Respondent In equity practice, the party who answers a bill or other proceeding.

Restitution An equitable remedy under which a person is restored to his or her original position prior to loss or injury, or placed in the position he or she would have been in had the breach not occurred.

Restraint of trade Any contract or combination that tends to eliminate or reduce competition, effect a monopoly, artificially maintain prices, or otherwise hamper the course of trade and commerce as it would be carried on if left to the control of natural economic forces.

Restrictive covenant A private restriction on the use of land that is binding on the party that purchases the property originally as well as on subsequent purchasers. If its benefit or obligation passes with the land's ownership, it is said to "run with the land."

Restrictive indorsement Any indorsement on a negotiable instrument that requires the indorsee to comply with certain instructions regarding the funds involved. A restrictive indorsement does not prohibit the further negotiation of the instrument.

Resulting trust An implied trust arising from the conduct of the parties. A trust in which a party holds the actual legal title to another's property but only for that person's benefit.

Retained earnings The portion of a corporation's profits that has not been paid out as dividends to shareholders.

Retainer An advance payment made by a client to a law firm to cover part of the legal fees and/or costs that will need to be incurred on that client's behalf.

Retaliatory eviction The eviction of a tenant because of the tenant's complaints, participation in a tenant's union, or similar activity with which the landlord does not agree.

Reverse To reject or overrule a court's judgment. An appellate court, for example, might reverse a lower court's judgment on an issue if it feels that the lower court committed an error during the trial or that the jury was improperly instructed.

Reverse discrimination Discrimination against majority groups, such as white males, that results from affirmative action programs, in which preferences are given to minority members and women.

Reversible error An error by a lower court that is sufficiently substantial to justify an appellate court's reversal of the lower court's decision.

Revocation In contract law, the withdrawal of an offer by an offeror. Unless an offer is irrevocable, it can be revoked at any time prior to acceptance without liability.

Right of contribution The right of a co-surety who pays more than his or her proportionate share on a debtor's default to recover the excess paid from other co-sureties.

Right of entry The right to peaceably take or resume possession of real property.

Right of first refusal The right to purchase personal or real property—such as corporate shares or real estate—before the property is offered for sale to others.

Right of redemption See Equity of redemption; Redemption

Right of reimbursement The legal right of a person to be restored, repaid, or indemnified for costs, expenses, or losses incurred or expended on behalf of another.

Right of subrogation The right of a person to stand in the place of (be substituted for) another, giving the substituted party the same legal rights that the original party had.

Right-to-work law A state law providing that employees are not to be required to join a union as a condition of obtaining or retaining employment.

Risk A prediction concerning potential loss based on known and unknown factors.

Risk management Planning that is undertaken to protect one's interest should some event threaten to undermine its security. In the context of insurance, risk management involves transferring certain risks from the insured to the insurance company.

Robbery The act of forcefully and unlawfully taking personal property of any value from another; force or intimidation is usually necessary for an act of theft to be considered a robbery.

Rule of four A rule of the United States Supreme Court under which the Court will not issue a writ of *certiorari* unless at least four justices approve of the decision to issue the writ.

Rule of reason A test by which a court balances the positive effects (such as economic efficiency) of an agreement against its potentially anticompetitive effects. In antitrust litigation, many practices are analyzed under the rule of reason.

Rule 10b-5 *See* SEC Rule 10b-5

Rulemaking The process undertaken by an administrative agency when formally adopting a new regulation or amending an old one. Rulemaking involves notifying the public of a proposed rule or change and receiving and considering the public's comments.

Rules of evidence Rules governing the admissibility of evidence in trial courts.

S

S corporation A close business corporation that has met certain requirements as set out by the Internal Revenue Code and thus qualifies for special income tax treatment. Essentially, an S corporation is taxed the same as a partnership, but its owners enjoy the privilege of limited liability.

Sale The passing of title (evidence of ownership rights) from the seller to the buyer for a price.

Sale on approval A type of conditional sale in which the buyer may take the goods on a trial basis. The sale becomes absolute only when the buyer approves of (or is satisfied with) the goods being sold.

Sale or return A type of conditional sale in which title and possession pass from the seller to the buyer; however, the buyer retains the option to return the goods during a specified period even though the goods conform to the contract.

Sales contract A contract for the sale of goods under which the ownership of goods is transferred from a seller to a buyer for a price.

Satisfaction *See* Accord and satisfaction

Scienter (pronounced *sy-en*-ter) Knowledge by the misrepresenting party that material facts have been falsely represented or omitted with an intent to deceive.

Search warrant An order granted by a public authority, such as a judge, that authorizes law enforcement personnel to search particular premises or property.

Seasonably Within a specified time period, or, if no period is specified, within a reasonable time.

SEC Rule 10b-5 A rule of the Securities and Exchange Commission that makes it unlawful, in connection with the purchase or sale of any security, to make any untrue statement of a material fact or to omit a material fact if such omission causes the statement to be misleading.

Secondary boycott A union's refusal to work for, purchase from, or handle the products of a secondary employer, with whom the union has no dispute, for the purpose of forcing that employer to stop doing business with the primary employer, with whom the union has a labor dispute.

Secondary liability In negotiable instruments law, the contingent liability of drawers and indorsers. A secondarily liable party becomes liable on an instrument only if the party that is primarily liable on the instrument dishonors it or, in regard to drafts and checks, the drawee fails to pay or to accept the instrument, whichever is required.

Secured party A lender, seller, or any other person in whose favor there is a security interest, including a person to whom accounts or chattel paper has been sold.

Secured transaction Any transaction in which the payment of a debt is guaranteed, or secured, by personal property owned by the debtor or in which the debtor has a legal interest.

Securities Generally, corporate stocks and bonds. A security may also be a note, debenture, stock warrant, or any document given as evidence of an ownership interest in a corporation or as a promise of repayment by a corporation.

Security agreement An agreement that creates or provides for a security interest between the debtor and a secured party.

Security interest Any interest "in personal property or fixtures which secures payment or performance of an obligation" [UCC 1–201(37)].

Self-defense The legally recognized privilege to protect one's self or property against injury by another. The privilege of self-defense protects only acts that are reasonably necessary to protect one's self or property.

Seniority system In regard to employment relationships, a system in which those who have worked longest for the company are first in line for promotions, salary increases, and other benefits; they are also the last to be laid off if the workforce must be reduced.

Service mark A mark used in the sale or the advertising of services, such as to distinguish the services of one person from the services of others. Titles, character names, and other distinctive features of radio and television programs may be registered as service marks.

Service of process The delivery of the complaint and summons to a defendant.

Settlor One creating a trust; also called a *grantor*.

Severance pay A payment by an employer to an employee that exceeds the employee's wages due on termination.

Sexual harassment In the employment context, the granting of job promotions or other benefits in return for sexual favors or language or conduct that is so sexually offensive that it creates a hostile working environment.

Share A unit of stock. *See also* Stock

Share exchange In a share exchange, some or all of the shares of one corporation are exchanged for some or all of the shares of another corporation, but both corporations continue to exist. Share exchanges are often used to create *holding companies* (companies that own part or all of other companies' stock).

Shareholder One who purchases shares of a corporation's stock, thus acquiring an equity interest in the corporation.

Shareholder's derivative suit A suit brought by a shareholder to enforce a corporate cause of action against a third person.

Sharia Civil law principles of some Middle Eastern countries that are based on the Islamic directives that follow the teachings of the prophet Muhammad.

Shelter principle The principle that the holder of a negotiable instrument who cannot qualify as a holder in due course (HDC), but who derives his or her title through an HDC, acquires the rights of an HDC.

Sheriff's deed The deed given to the purchaser of property at a sheriff's sale as part of the foreclosure process against the owner of the property.

Shipment contract A contract in which the seller is required to ship the goods by carrier. The buyer assumes liability for any losses or damage to the goods after they are delivered to the carrier. Generally, all contracts are assumed to be shipment contracts if nothing to the contrary is stated in the contract.

Short-form merger A merger between a subsidiary corporation and a parent corporation that owns at least 90 percent of the outstanding shares of each class of stock issued by the subsidiary corporation. Short-form mergers can be accomplished without the approval of the shareholders of either corporation.

Short-swing profits Profits made by officers, directors, and certain large stockholders resulting from the use of nonpublic (inside) information about their companies; prohibited by Section 12 of the 1934 Securities Exchange Act.

Shrink-wrap agreement An agreement whose terms are expressed in a document located inside a box in which goods (usually software) are packaged; sometimes called a *shrink-wrap license.*

Sight draft In negotiable instruments law, a draft payable on sight—that is, when it is presented for payment.

Signature Under the Uniform Commercial Code, "any symbol executed or adopted by a party with a present intention to authenticate a writing."

Slander Defamation in oral form.

Slander of quality (trade libel) The publication of false information about another's product, alleging that it is not what its seller claims.

Slander of title The publication of a statement that denies or casts doubt on another's legal ownership of any property, causing financial loss to that property's owner.

Small claims courts Special courts in which parties may litigate small claims (usually, claims involving $2,500 or less). Attorneys are not required in small claims courts, and in many states attorneys are not allowed to represent the parties.

Smart card Prepaid funds recorded on a microprocessor chip embedded on a card. One type of *e-money.*

Sociological school A school of legal thought that views the law as a tool for promoting justice in society.

Sole proprietorship The simplest form of business, in which the owner is the business; the owner reports business income on his or her personal income tax return and is legally responsible for all debts and obligations incurred by the business.

Sovereign immunity A doctrine that immunizes foreign nations from the jurisdiction of U.S. courts when certain conditions are satisfied.

Spam Bulk, unsolicited ("junk") e-mail.

Special indorsement An indorsement on an instrument that indicates the specific person to whom the indorser intends to make the instrument payable; that is, it names the indorsee.

Special warranty deed A deed in which the grantor only covenants to warrant and defend the title against claims and demands of the grantor and all persons claiming by, through, and under the grantor.

Specific performance An equitable remedy requiring the breaching party to perform as promised under the contract; usually granted only when money damages would be an inadequate remedy and the subject matter of the contract is unique (for example, real property).

Spendthrift trust A trust created to prevent the beneficiary from spending all the money to which he or she is entitled. Only a certain portion of the total amount is given to the beneficiary at any one time, and

most states prohibit creditors from attaching assets of the trust.

Spot zoning Granting a zoning classification to a parcel of land that is different from the classification given to other land in the immediate area.

Stale check A check, other than a certified check, that is presented for payment more than six months after its date.

Standing to sue The requirement that an individual must have a sufficient stake in a controversy before he or she can bring a lawsuit. The plaintiff must demonstrate that he or she either has been injured or threatened with injury.

Stare decisis (pronounced *ster*-ay dih-*si*-ses) A common law doctrine under which judges are obligated to follow the precedents established in prior decisions.

Statute of Frauds A state statute under which certain types of contracts must be in writing to be enforceable.

Statute of limitations A federal or state statute setting the maximum time period during which a certain action can be brought or certain rights enforced.

Statute of repose Basically, a statute of limitations that is not dependent on the happening of a cause of action. Statutes of repose generally begin to run at an earlier date and run for a longer period of time than statutes of limitations.

Statutory law The body of law enacted by legislative bodies (as opposed to constitutional law, administrative law, or case law).

Statutory lien A lien created by statute.

Statutory period of redemption A time period (usually set by state statute) during which the property subject to a defaulted mortgage, land contract, or other contract can be redeemed by the debtor after foreclosure or judicial sale.

Stock An equity (ownership) interest in a corporation, measured in units of shares.

Stock certificate A certificate issued by a corporation evidencing the ownership of a specified number of shares in the corporation.

Stock option *See* Stock warrant

Stock warrant A certificate that grants the owner the option to buy a given number of shares of stock, usually within a set time period.

Stockholder *See* Shareholder

Stop-payment order An order by a bank customer to his or her bank not to pay or certify a certain check.

Strict liability Liability regardless of fault. In tort law, strict liability may be imposed on defendants in cases involving abnormally dangerous activities, dangerous animals, or defective products.

Strike An extreme action undertaken by unionized workers when collective bargaining fails; the workers leave their jobs, refuse to work, and (typically) picket the employer's workplace.

Subject-matter jurisdiction Jurisdiction over the subject matter of a lawsuit.

Sublease A lease executed by the lessee of real estate to a third person, conveying the same interest that the lessee enjoys but for a shorter term than that held by the lessee.

Subpoena A document commanding a person to appear at a certain time and place or give testimony concerning a certain matter.

Subrogation *See* Right of subrogation

Subscriber An investor who agrees, in a subscription agreement, to purchase capital stock in a corporation.

Substantial performance Performance that does not vary greatly from the performance promised in a contract; the performance must create substantially the same benefits as those promised in the contract.

Substantive due process A requirement that focuses on the content, or substance, of legislation. If a law or other governmental action limits a fundamental right, such as the right to travel or to vote, it will be held to violate substantive due process unless it promotes a compelling or overriding state interest.

Substantive law Law that defines the rights and duties of individuals with respect to each other, as opposed to procedural law, which defines the manner in which these rights and duties may be enforced.

Substantive unconscionability Results from contracts, or portions of contracts, that are oppressive or overly harsh. Courts generally focus on provisions that deprive one party of the benefits of the agreement or leave that party without remedy for nonperformance by the other. An example of substantive unconscionability is the agreement by a welfare recipient with a fourth-grade education to purchase a refrigerator for $2,000 under an installment contract.

Suit *See* Lawsuit; Litigation

Summary judgment *See* Motion for summary judgment

Summary jury trial (SJT) A method of settling disputes in which a trial is held, but the jury's verdict is not binding. The verdict acts only as a guide to both sides in reaching an agreement during the mandatory negotiations that immediately follow the summary jury trial.

Summons A document informing a defendant that a legal action has been commenced against him or her and that the defendant must appear in court on a certain date to answer the plaintiff's complaint. The document is delivered by a sheriff or any other person so authorized.

Superseding cause An intervening force or event that breaks the connection between a wrongful act and an injury to another; in negligence law, a defense to liability.

Supremacy clause The provision in Article VI of the Constitution that provides that the Constitution, laws, and treaties of the United States are "the supreme Law of the Land." Under this clause, state and local laws that directly conflict with federal law will be rendered invalid.

Surety A person, such as a cosigner on a note, who agrees to be primarily responsible for the debt of another.

Suretyship An express contract in which a third party to a debtor-creditor relationship (the surety) promises to be primarily responsible for the debtor's obligation.

Surviving corporation The remaining, or continuing, corporation following a merger. The surviving corporation is vested with the merged corporation's legal rights and obligations.

Syllogism A form of deductive reasoning consisting of a major premise, a minor premise, and a conclusion.

Symbolic speech Nonverbal conduct that expresses opinions or thoughts about a subject. Symbolic speech is protected under the First Amendment's guarantee of freedom of speech.

Syndicate An investment group of persons or firms brought together for the purpose of financing a project that they would not or could not undertake independently.

T

Tag In the context of the World Wide Web, a code in an HTML document. *See* Meta tags.

Takeover The acquisition of control over a corporation through the purchase of a substantial number of the voting shares of the corporation.

Taking The taking of private property by the government for public use. Under the Fifth Amendment to the Constitution, the government may not take private property for public use without "just compensation."

Tangible employment action A significant change in employment status, such as firing or failing to promote an employee, reassigning the employee to a position with significantly different responsibilities, or effecting a significant change in employment benefits.

Tangible property Property that has physical existence and can be distinguished by the senses of touch, sight, and so on. A car is tangible property; a patent right is intangible property.

Target corporation The corporation to be acquired in a corporate takeover; a corporation to whose shareholders a tender offer is submitted.

Tariff A tax on imported goods.

Technology licensing Allowing another to use and profit from intellectual property (patents, copyrights, trademarks, innovative products or processes, and so on) for consideration. In the context of international business transactions, technology licensing is sometimes an attractive alternative to the establishment of foreign production facilities.

Teller's check A negotiable instrument drawn by a bank on another bank or drawn by a bank and payable at or payable through a bank.

Tenancy at sufferance A type of tenancy under

which one who, after rightfully being in possession of leased premises, continues (wrongfully) to occupy the property after the lease has been terminated. The tenant has no rights to possess the property and occupies it only because the person entitled to evict the tenant has not done so.

Tenancy at will A type of tenancy under which either party can terminate the tenancy without notice; usually arises when a tenant who has been under a tenancy for years retains possession, with the landlord's consent, after the tenancy for years has terminated.

Tenancy by the entirety The joint ownership of property by a husband and wife. Neither party can transfer his or her interest in the property without the consent of the other.

Tenancy for years *See* Fixed-term tenancy.

Tenancy in common Co-ownership of property in which each party owns an undivided interest that passes to his or her heirs at death.

Tenant One who has the temporary use and occupation of real property owned by another person, called the landlord; the duration and terms of the tenancy are usually established by a lease.

Tender An unconditional offer to perform an obligation by a person who is ready, willing, and able to do so.

Tender of delivery Under the Uniform Commercial Code, a seller's or lessor's act of placing conforming goods at the disposal of the buyer or lessee and giving the buyer or lessee whatever notification is reasonably necessary to enable the buyer or lessee to take delivery.

Tender offer An offer to purchase made by one company directly to the shareholders of another (target) company; often referred to as a "takeover bid."

Term insurance A type of life insurance policy for which premiums are paid for a specified term. Payment on the policy is due only if death occurs within the term period. Premiums are less expensive than for whole life or limited-payment life, and there is usually no cash surrender value.

Testamentary trust A trust that is created by will and therefore does not take effect until the death of the testator.

Testate The condition of having died with a valid will.

Testator One who makes and executes a will.

Third party beneficiary One for whose benefit a promise is made in a contract but who is not a party to the contract.

Time draft A draft that is payable at a definite future time.

Tippee A person who receives inside information.

Title insurance Insurance commonly purchased by a purchaser of real property to protect against loss in the event that the title to the property is not free from liens or superior ownership claims.

Tombstone ad An advertisement, historically in a format resembling a tombstone, of a securities offering.

The ad informs potential investors of where and how they may obtain a prospectus.

Tort A civil wrong not arising from a breach of contract. A breach of a legal duty that proximately causes harm or injury to another.

Tortfeasor One who commits a tort.

Totten trust A trust created by the deposit of a person's own money in his or her own name as a trustee for another. It is a tentative trust, revocable at will until the depositor dies or completes the gift in his or her lifetime by some unequivocal act or declaration.

Toxic tort Failure to use or to clean up properly toxic chemicals that cause harm to a person or society.

Trade acceptance A draft that is drawn by a seller of goods ordering the buyer to pay a specified sum of money to the seller, usually at a stated time in the future. The buyer accepts the draft by signing the face of the draft, thus creating an enforceable obligation to pay the draft when it comes due. On a trade acceptance, the seller is both the drawer and the payee.

Trade dress The image and overall appearance of a product—for example, the distinctive decor, menu, layout, and style of service of a particular restaurant. Basically, trade dress is subject to the same protection as trademarks.

Trade fixture The personal property of a commercial tenant that has been installed or affixed to real property for a business purpose. When the lease ends, the tenant can remove the fixture but must repair any damage to the real property caused by the fixture's removal.

Trade libel The publication of false information about another's product, alleging it is not what its seller claims; also referred to as slander of quality.

Trade name A term that is used to indicate part or all of a business's name and that is directly related to the business's reputation and goodwill. Trade names are protected under the common law (and under trademark law, if the name is the same as the firm's trademarked property).

Trade secret Information or a process that gives a business an advantage over competitors who do not know the information or process.

Trademark A distinctive mark, motto, device, or implement that a manufacturer stamps, prints, or otherwise affixes to the goods it produces so that they may be identified on the market and their origins made known. Once a trademark is established (under the common law or through registration), the owner is entitled to its exclusive use.

Transfer warranties Implied warranties, made by any person who transfers an instrument for consideration to subsequent transferees and holders who take the instrument in good faith, that (1) the transferor is entitled to enforce the instrument; (2) all signatures are authentic and authorized; (3) the instrument has not been altered; (4) the instrument is not subject to a defense or claim of any party that can be asserted against the transferor; and (5) the transferor has no knowledge of any insolvency proceedings against the maker, the acceptor, or the drawer of the instrument.

Transferee In negotiable instruments law, one to whom a negotiable instrument is transferred (delivered).

Transferor In negotiable instruments law, one who transfers (delivers) a negotiable instrument to another.

Traveler's check A check that is payable on demand, drawn on or payable through a bank, and designated as a traveler's check.

Treasure trove Cash or coin, gold, silver, or bullion found hidden in the earth or other private place, the owner of which is unknown; literally, treasure found.

Treasury shares Corporate shares that are authorized by the corporation but that have not been issued.

Treaty An agreement formed between two or more independent nations.

Treble damages Damages consisting of three times the amount of damages determined by a jury in certain cases as required by statute.

Trespass to land The entry onto, above, or below the surface of land owned by another without the owner's permission or legal authorization.

Trespass to personal property The unlawful taking or harming of another's personal property; interference with another's right to the exclusive possession of his or her personal property.

Trespasser One who commits the tort of trespass in one of its forms.

Trial court A court in which trials are held and testimony taken.

Trust An arrangement in which title to property is held by one person (a trustee) for the benefit of another (a beneficiary).

Trust indorsement An indorsement for the benefit of the indorser or a third person; also known as an agency indorsement. The indorsement results in legal title vesting in the original indorsee.

Trustee One who holds title to property for the use or benefit of another (the beneficiary).

Tying arrangement An agreement between a buyer and a seller in which the buyer of a specific product or service becomes obligated to purchase additional products or services from the seller.

U

U.S. trustee A government official who performs certain administrative tasks that a bankruptcy judge would otherwise have to perform.

Ultra vires (pronounced *uhl*-trah *vye*-reez) A Latin term meaning "beyond the powers"; in corporate law, acts of a corporation that are beyond its express and implied powers to undertake.

Unanimous opinion A court opinion in which all of the judges or justices of the court agree to the court's decision.

Unconscionable (pronounced un-*kon*-shun-uh-bul) **contract or clause** A contract or clause that is void on the basis of public policy because one party, as a result of his or her disproportionate bargaining power, is forced to accept terms that are unfairly burdensome and that unfairly benefit the dominating party. *See also* Procedural unconscionability; Substantive unconscionability

Underwriter In insurance law, the insurer, or the one assuming a risk in return for the payment of a premium.

Undisclosed principal A principal whose identity is unknown by a third person, and the third person has no knowledge that the agent is acting for a principal at the time the agent and the third person form a contract.

Unenforceable contract A valid contract rendered unenforceable by some statute or law.

Uniform law A model law created by the National Conference of Commissioners on Uniform State Laws and/or the American Law Institute for the states to consider adopting. If the state adopts the law, it becomes statutory law in that state. Each state has the option of adopting or rejecting all or part of a uniform law.

Unilateral contract A contract that results when an offer can only be accepted by the offeree's performance.

Union shop A place of employment in which all workers, once employed, must become union members within a specified period of time as a condition of their continued employment.

Universal defense A defense that is valid against all holders of a negotiable instrument, including holders in due course (HDCs) and holders with the rights of HDCs. Universal defenses are also called real defenses.

Universal life A type of insurance that combines some aspects of term insurance with some aspects of whole life insurance.

Unlawful detainer The unjustifiable retention of the possession of real property by one whose right to possession has terminated—as when a tenant holds over after the end of the lease term in spite of the landlord's demand for possession.

Unliquidated debt A debt that is uncertain in amount.

Unreasonably dangerous product In product liability, a product that is defective to the point of threatening a consumer's health and safety. A product will be considered unreasonably dangerous if it is dangerous beyond the expectation of the ordinary consumer or if a less dangerous alternative was economically feasible for the manufacturer, but the manufacturer failed to produce it.

Usage of trade Any practice or method of dealing having such regularity of observance in a place,

Answers to Questions

Case No. 1

Paste v. Weber, et al.

1) You might disagree with the court and think punitive damages should have been awarded. The officer's excessive use of force appeared to be spiteful and wilful. The amount of force was considerably in excess of permissable limits. Under these circumstances punitive damages would be appropriate remedy.

Case No. 3

Cardiff v. Brooklyn Eagle, Inc.

1) This fact contributes to the conclusion that a false report of one's death does not demean or belittle the person. Since he or she has no control over the happening of the event, the false report does not suggest the person did any wrongful or shameful act.

2) Yes. A published statement that a person has engaged in the sale of drugs—which is an illegal act—does demean the person. Such a statement may well expose the person to hatred, contempt, disgrace or ridicule.

3) Yes. When a newspaper publishes false information about a public figure, the newspaper will not be liable unless the report was published maliciously (with knowledge that the information was untrue) or with reckless disregard of the standards for obtaining the truth. The constitutional rights of free press and free speech are the bases for this rule. Without such a rule the media would be inhibited from printing news unless every reported fact was verified to a certainty. Such inhibition would seriously threaten the availability of current news, a vital element of a free society.

In this case the newspaper failed to verify a report from an unidentified caller prior to publishing the information provided by that caller. Such conduct would likely be considered reckless disregard of the standards for obtaining the truth.

Case No. 4

Mahoney v. Adirondack Publishing Company

1) These facts show that it was possible that the reporter's opportunity to hear was less than perfect, thus demonstrating that the reporter's actions were the result of a misperception rather than a fabrication.

Case No. 5

Costanza v. Seinfeld

1) Statements of opinion are offered by the speaker not as fact but as one person's view. When information is presented as an opinion, the listener knows it is but one person's belief and it may or may not be consistent with the facts. The circumstance that causes damage to a person's reputation is false information presented as factual. A listener is much more apt to presume such information to be truthful.

Case No. 11

Shields v. Gross

1) She could have insisted on a more restricted consent form. Instead of authorizing the photographer to use the pictures at any time for any purpose whatsoever, she should have restricted in the consent form the authorized use to the magazine *Sugar and Spice*.

2) A person's interests in avoiding unwanted publicity and in controlling public exposure are protected by the tort of invasion of privacy. A person who poses for a photograph may wish to avoid unwanted public exposure or to control the manner in which public exposure is achieved. By requiring a model's permission before a photograph of that model can be used for commercial purposes, these interests are protected.

Case No. 13

Joseph and Ida Finger v. Omni Publications International, Ltd.

1) The following arguments support a decision for the Fingers in this case: the family pictured in the photograph was not involved with the caffeinated-sperm study, nor did

they use in vitro fertilization to conceive any of their children. Therefore, they had no actual connection to the article. To argue that a picture of a large family complements an article with a fertility theme is too great a stretch to justify disrupting the Fingers' privacy rights.

2) The judge or jury resolves disputed issues. If the issue is one of law—that is, one that is resolved by the application of law, such as the issue in this case—the issue is determined by the judge. If the issue is one of fact, such as whether a defendant went through a red light, it is resolved by the jury or, if the trial is a bench trial (no jury), by the judge.

3) No, a news story about a robbery arrest is newsworthy. The fact that the story is untruthful is not a defense to invasion of privacy. Query: Would these facts give rise to a defamation action? The answer would be no, unless the television station acted maliciously, since the person arrested would qualify as a public figure.

Case No. 16

Leary v. Punzi

1) The statute of limitations is a law that identifies a maximum time period within which a plaintiff can sue. If the would-be plaintiff fails to commence the lawsuit within the period specified by the statute of limitations, plaintiff is thereafter barred from pursuing the case.

2) The policy supporting the statute of limitations is that a defendant ought not to have to worry for in inordinate amount of time that s/he may be sued. If plaintiff has good grounds on which to sue, plaintiff should not be permitted to wait indefinitely to start the case.

Case No. 17

Click Model Management, Inc. v. Rachel Williams and Christy Turlington

1) Assuming that Williams had a contract with Click obligating her to model for Click for a period of time, and assuming that she left Click to join Ford prior to the end of that time period, and assuming Click had kept its promises to Williams, Click could sue Williams for breach of contract. It is possible that Click could win the breach of contract action even though it did not win the lawsuit for interference with contractual relations.

Case No. 19

<u>Gold Medal Farms v. Rutland County Cooperative Creamery, Inc.</u>

1) No. An element of the tort of wrongful inducement of a breach of contract is the inducement of the *breach*. In this example Vermont did not attempt to persuade Rutland to breach its contract with Gold Medal but rather proposed waiting until that contract expired before Rutland did business with Vermont. Therefore, Vermont would not be liable for wrongful inducement of a breach of contract.

2) No. For a party to commit the tort of wrongful inducement of a breach of contract that party must know that a contract exists.

3) The competing interests are, on the one hand, society's interest in maintaining the integrity of contractual relationships, and on the other hand, society's concern for open and free competition. When a person induces breach of an existing, valid contract, the interest in unrestricted competition is outweighed by the interest in maintaining respect for contract rights.

Case No. 23

<u>Palsgraf v. The Long Island Railroad Company</u>

1) The reasons for this rule, which is often called respondeat superior, include agency law and public policy. Concerning agency law: an employee is normally considered an agent of the employer while the employee is acting in furtherance of his or her job responsibilities. The party on whose behalf an agent acts, in addition to the agent, is legally liable for the negligent acts of the agent.

Concerning public policy: the purpose of holding an employer liable for the negligent acts of employees is to protect the injured person by expanding the parties who are liable to include a person who is often in a better position to bear the financial responsibility for the negligent act.

2) Yes. If the guards had known the package contained explosives, the injury to Palsgraf would likely have been foreseeable by the guards. By helping the passenger onto a moving train the guards should have foreseen the possibility that the passenger and/or the package would fall. Knowing that the package contained explosives, they should have foreseen the explosives might explode if dropped. Such an explosion would foreseeably cause injury to anyone in the train station.

3) Yes. Presumably the man knew that his package contained explosives. The risk of his falling or dropping the package was foreseeable when he attempted to board a moving train. He therefore could have foreseen the explosion and the resulting injury to anyone in the train station.

Case No. 25

Merrill v. the State of New York

1) The following precautions might have prevented a finding of negligence: installation of special lighting on the median where parking was to occur; maintenance of a trooper at the site until all parked cars had gone; installation of a foot bridge over the highway; utilization of an identification system to help fairgoers locate their cars; installation of signs on the interstate highway warning that pedestrians may be nearby.

2) No. The outcome would not have been different. The actions of the state trooper constituted negligence regardless of the physical characteristics of the injured party. Injury to fairgoers who parked in the median was foreseeable from the trooper's actions whether or not the fairgoers had full use of their senses.

Case No. 27

Gross v. Waldbaum

1) Waldbaum's knew shoppers often overload grocery carts. Without a protective flap on the cart, Waldbaum's could foresee that food could drop from the cart and hit the shopper pushing the cart or, as in this case, another shopper.

2) It is true that the shopper whose cart was broken may have been negligent by overloading her cart. Even without a broken or missing protective flap an overloaded cart may foreseeably result in food falling from the cart and injuring a shopper. In this case, however, Waldbaum's knew from experience that customers often overload their carts and therefore could foresee injury to customers if the flap was absent. Since Waldbaum's provided the carts and was responsible for their maintenance, and since Waldbaum's could foresee the injury occurring in this case, the shopper's negligence does not break the connection between Waldbaum's negligence and Gross's injury.

3) Gross would not have been able to recover for her injuries. Under the rule of contributory negligence, an injured plaintiff is barred from recovering from a negligent defendant if the plaintiff was also negligent and that negligence contributed to the accident that caused the plaintiff's injuries. The court in this case concluded that Gross's own negligence contributed to the cause of the accident. Therefore, under the rule of contributory negligence, Gross would be barred from recovery against Waldbaum's.

4) Your authors believe this is a reasonable allocation of the liability for the accident. If your authors were to change the result at all, it would be to increase Waldbaum's percentage of liability and decrease Gross's.

Case No. 28

Kosok v. Young Men's Christian Association

1) Yes. The court or jury should find the camp negligent. The camp was alerted from the first pail incident that the campers were engaging in potentially dangerous activity. The camp should have foreseen the possibility of continued dangerous activity unless more supervision was provided to the campers involved. The first incident constituted the warning that should have alerted the camp to the necessity of supervising the activities of the campers during the rest period.

2) With these conditions, the camp would be liable for the injuries. The camp should foresee that an inmate who had escaped from a maximum-security prison might be dangerous and that, given the proximity of the prison to the camp, such an inmate might be near the camp. Therefore tighter supervision than normal would be required for the camp to avoid liability.

Case No. 29

Herman v. State of New York

1) No, the fact that millions of swimmers swim injury-free at the beach suggests the absence of foreseeability of injury from sand bars. Although three prior swimmers over a period of 24 years may have suffered similar injuries, that number is minuscule in comparison to the total number of swimmers at the beach in the same time period. Since the beach operators had no warning of dangerous conditions, they could not foresee the risk of injury to Herman from the sand bars. Since the risk was not foreseeable, the beach did not owe a duty to warn against the danger.

2) Yes. The state was negligent. The operators of the beach could foresee that on a hot Saturday in July many people would be swimming in the public swimming areas. The operators could also foresee that failure to provide lifeguards could result in a troubled swimmer being unable to get necessary help. Therefore the beach owed a duty to the beachgoers and swimmers to provide lifeguards during normal swimming hours.

3) It is foreseeable that swimmers may injure themselves on debris on the ocean bottom by hitting their heads when surface diving, stubbing their feet, or otherwise. The beach operators should remove the debris as soon as possible. In the interim, the operators of the beach should display warning signs, prohibit swimming in the affected area, and assign guards to police the area to ensure no one swims in it.

Case No. 31

<u>Maddox v. The City of New York et al.</u>

1) If this case was decided today the rule of comparative negligence would apply. If Maddox could prove that part of the cause of the accident was negligent maintenance of the baseball field, the culpability for the accident would be allocated between Maddox and the defendant. Maddox would then be able to recover that percentage of his damages equal to the percentage of culpability allocated to New York City. Thus, if 85% of the culpability for the accident was allocated to New York City, and 15% to Maddox, he would be entitled to collect 85% of his damages from New York City.

2) Your authors believe comparative negligence is fairer. Often, although the negligence of a plaintiff who is injured in an accident contributed to the accident, it would not have occurred without the negligence of the defendant. Your authors believe that reducing plaintiff's recovery by a percentage equal to plaintiff's percentage of culpability is sufficient consequence for plaintiff's negligence. Eliminating plaintiff's right to collect any damages whenever plaintiff's negligence contributes to the occurrence of an accident is too great a penalty.

Case No. 32

<u>King v. Jordan</u>

1) Malpractice is negligence in the performance of one's professional duties. Malpractice applies to such professions as lawyers, accountants, doctors, dentists, architects, and others.

2) The legal concept of informed consent assures that a patient understands not only the possible benefits from a medical procedure but also the potential negative effects. Only when a patient knows all the pros and cons can s/he make an informed decision of whether to authorize the doctor to perform the procedure.

Case No. 33

<u>Nelson v. The State of New York</u>

1) This type of damages includes compensation for pain and suffering the injured party has had to endure for the period of time between the accident and the trial, and for pain and suffering reasonably certain to continue beyond the trial date. Because of the difficulty in measuring pain by any objective standard, New York State has no precise formula for determining an appropriate amount of money to award to the plaintiff. Instead the determination of the appropriate amount is left to the good sense and judgment of the jury. Among the factors the jury should consider include the

nature and extent of the injuries, the susceptibility of the particular injured party to pain, and his or her capacity to withstand it. Also to be considered is evidence that the injury has restricted the injured party from carrying on his or her normal activities.

2) In New York State, loss of consortium refers to a general loss of services between spouses. The term broadly encompasses love, affection, companionship, sexual relations, and contributions to the maintenance of the household.

In determining a proper sum of money to award for this loss the following factors are considered: the extent of the injured spouse's involvement with the noninjured spouse and the family prior to the injury; the injured party's temperament; the social life of the family; acts of affection and sexual intercourse between the spouses prior to the injury; the happiness and general welfare of the family members; and the extent to which the injured spouse is unable to continue normal family-related activities as a result of the injury.

3) Arguments for the bill include the following: a) the cost for insurance should decrease with a cap on recovery for pain and suffering; b) parties to a lawsuit would be encouraged to settle, thereby accelerating the time within which the injured party would receive compensation; c) the number of plaintiffs affected by a cap would be small; d) the pattern of unpredictable and seemingly arbitrary amounts awarded by juries for pain and suffering would become less arbitrary and more predictable and uniform.

Arguments against the bill include the following: a) an injured party should be entitled to recover that amount of money necessary to restore the person to his pre-injury situation; b) a cap would reduce the incentive on the public to act safely; c) a cap would discriminate against the seriously injured whose recovery might otherwise exceed the cap; d) although pain and suffering is intangible, it is a very real harm and the amount of compensation should reflect that fact.

Case No. 34

<u>Chandler v. Hodge & Hammer, Inc.</u>

1) Public policy seeks to protect an injured person from the catastrophic financial burden of a serious injury caused by a defective product. The injured person can seek recovery from the seller who can treat the expense as a cost of doing business. The seller can spread the expense among its customers by increasing the price of its goods. The costs of serious injury resulting from a defective product are thus spread throughout the consuming public.

Case No. 35

Trimmer v. Van Bomel

1) An express contract is a contract whose terms have been expressed by the parties, either orally or in writing. An implied contract is one whose terms have not been expressed but are inferred from the parties' actions.

2) A party claiming the existence of an express contract can prove the contract in court by: a) testifying himself as to the existence of the contract; b) presenting as evidence the testimony of witnesses, if any, who were present when the contract was made; or c) presenting the written document, if any, evidencing the contract. If the other party denies the existence of the contract, a classic "proof problem" exists and the judge or jury will determine, based on all the evidence, whether a contract existed. If one of the parties lies under oath while testifying, that party would be guilty of perjury, the crime of lying under oath. Penalties for perjury include jail and/or a fine. Parties to a contract can often avoid proof problems by reducing their agreement to writing.

Case No. 38

Joseph Martin Jr. Delicatessen, Inc. v. Schumacker

1) They could have specified the amount of rent the tenant would pay in the event of renewal, or included a formula for determining the rent. If the contract provided that the rent would be $700.00 or some other specified figure per month, or that the rent would be the fair market rental value at the time the original lease term expired, as determined by an appraiser, the renewal clause would have been upheld.

2) The courts do not want to guess what the parties intended. If a court's guess did not reflect the parties' intention, the parties would be stuck with a contract they did not intend to enter.

3) According to common law, a contract which does not specify material terms will be unenforceable due to indefiniteness. The Uniform Commercial Code relaxes the requirements of definiteness. For example, under the UCC, a contract for the sale of goods which omits the price is enforceable even though the price was not agreed upon by the parties. In such a case the Code provides that the price may be a reasonable price, such as the market price, at the time of delivery. Similarly, the Code provides rules to determine other contract terms that parties fail to specify.

Case No. 40

S.S.I. Investors, Ltd. v. Korea Tungsten Mining Co. Ltd.

1) S.S.I., the bidder, was the offeror. The Mining Company was the offeree. The Mining Company's statement that it would sell to the highest bidder was a solicitation of offers and not an offer.

2) At an auction the bidder is the offeror. The auctioneer accepts by bringing down the hammer. The bidder can withdraw the offer anytime before the acceptance occurs.

Case No. 42

John William Costello Associates, Inc. v. Standard Metals Corp.

1) To avoid a dispute on fees or price, the parties to a contract should clearly identify and agree to the price before any goods are delivered or services rendered. Had Costello insisted upon a signed agreement from Standard specifying the fee, Standard would have no basis to dispute the fee after the client was hired.

Case No. 45

1020 Park Avenue, Inc. v. Raynor

1) Normally an acceptance cannot be revoked. Once an offer is accepted a contract is created and the parties are bound to its terms. In unusual situations an offeree can revoke an acceptance.

2) An offeror can withdraw an offer anytime before the offeree accepts provided the offer was neither a firm offer (a written promise to keep an offer open signed by a merchant in a contract for the sale of goods) nor an option contract (an agreement in which the offeree gives the offeror consideration in return for the offeror's promise not to withdraw the offer for a specified period of time).

3) Once a contract is created the parties are legally bound to perform their obligations. Until that time no legal obligation exists. To create a contract both an offer and an acceptance are necessary. An unaccepted offer is not a contract nor is it legally binding. Therefore, it can be withdrawn at the will of the offeror absent a firm offer or an option contract.

Case No. 46

Camrex Contractors, Marine, Ltd. v. Reliance Marine Applicators, Inc.

1) No, the counteroffer of $1.47/$1.46 terminated the offer of $1.46. Plaintiff cannot accept a terminated, and therefore nonexistent, offer.

2) No, announcements of merchandise for sale sent to many potential buyers are considered invitations to negotiate or solicitations of offers. Such announcements are not treated as offers because they do not contain promises to sell nor do they specify any of the essential terms of an offer such as the quantity or the buyer's identity.

Case No. 47

Trevor v. Wood

1) An offer is effective when communicated to (received by) the offeree. When parties deal in person, knowledge of the offer by the offeror is immediate. When dealing from a distance the offer is effective when received.

2) The revocation of an offer is effective when received by the offeree.

3) Yes, a contract was created on December 3. An acceptance sent by mail is effective when it is mailed. A letter revoking an offer is not effective until the letter is received. In these facts the acceptance was sent before the revocation was received and therefore the acceptance created a contract.

Case No. 48

Kirshner v. Spinella

1) The concept of legally sufficient consideration requires that, to bind a contract, something must be given that the law recognizes as having legal value. The following are recognized by the law as having legal value and constitute sufficient consideration to bind a contract: payment of money, provision of goods, performance of services, forbearance from enforcing a legal right, and a promise to do any of the foregoing.

The concept of adequacy of consideration addresses whether the value of the consideration exchanged by the parties to a contract is relatively equal. Normally adequacy of consideration is not required for an enforceable contract to exist; only legally sufficient consideration is necessary. However, in the event a party claims to have been the victim of fraud, duress or undue influence and for that reason entered a contract in which she received inadequate consideration, the issue of adequacy of consideration may be examined as a means to prove the fraud, duress or undue influence.

2) a) The consideration given by Jane is the Pontiac. The consideration given by John is the five dollars.

    b) Yes, both have promised to give something of legal value.

    c) Yes. Unless evidence exists that Jane's friend used fraud, duress or undue influence to convince her to enter this contract, the question of adequacy of consideration is not relevant to the validity of the contract.

Case No. 49

Hammer v. Sidway

1) No, forbearance constitutes consideration only when a person refrains from doing something he has a legal right to do. In New York a person cannot legally purchase alcoholic beverages until age 21. Therefore when the nephew refrained from purchasing alcohol between ages 16-18 he did not forfeit any legal right.

2) No, a promise to make a gift is unenforceable because it is not supported by consideration.

Case No. 51

Century 21 Kaaterskill Realty v. Grasso

1) An accord is an agreement in which one party agrees to give, and the other to accept, in satisfaction of a claim, something different from, and usually less than, what was originally agreed upon.

2) A satisfaction is the performance of an accord.

3) The debtor had a pre-existing legal duty to pay the entire debt and did not dispute the amount owed. Therefore, Grasso gave no consideration for Century 21's alleged acceptance of the lesser amount in full satisfaction of the debt.

4) Yes, the outcome might have been different because an enforceable accord and satisfaction might have resulted. See Schnell v. Perlmon.

Case No. 52

Schnell v. Perlmon

1) The amount owed was disputed in good faith. Perlmon offered by checks less than the contract price as payment in full, and Schnell cashed the checks without objecting to the amount tendered.

Case No. 53

Horn Waterproofing Corp. v. Bushwick

1) In both cases the parties disputed in good faith the amount owed by the debtor, the debtor tendered as payment in full less than the full amount claimed due by the creditor, and the creditor cashed the checks by which payment was made.

2) In <u>Schnell v. Perlmon</u>, the creditor did not signify his objection to the accord proposed by the debtor. In the <u>Horn Waterproofing</u> case the creditor evidenced its objection to the accord by noting on the debtor's check the term "under protest", thereby preserving the right to collect the balance.

Case No. 54

Sullivan v. Conant Valley Associates, Ltd., et al.

1) To preserve her right to pursue Jerry for the $1200.00, Eileen could write, above her endorsement of the check, "all rights reserved". In the alternative, she can refrain from cashing the check. The latter option is not very appealing because it requires Eileen to delay benefiting from Jerry's partial payment. The change in the law provided by the UCC was to enable the creditor to both cash a partial payment check and retain the right to sue for the balance.

Case No. 55

Rodriguez v. Northern Auto Auction, Inc.

1) The reasons include protection of minors from their own immaturity and inexperience, and protection of minors from unscrupulous adults who might otherwise take advantage of their inexperience and youth.

2) While exceptions exist, a minor can generally disaffirm a contract any time during minority and for a reasonable period of time after reaching the age of majority. In New York the age of majority is 18.

Case No. 56

Fisher d/b/a Syosset Employment Services v. Cattani

1) The employment service could have protected itself by doing any of the following: a) refused to do business with Cattani until she reached the age of majority; b) refused to do business with Cattani unless an adult signed the contract in addition to Cattani; or c) refused to enter a contract with Cattani and instead contracted with her parent or other adult. In any of these situations the contract would have been enforceable.

Case No. 58

Braunstein v. Jason Tarentella, Inc.

1) In New York obscenity is defined as follows:

   Any material or performance is "obscene" if (a) the average person, applying contemporary community standards, would find that considered as a whole, its predominant appeal is to the prurient interest in sex, and (b) it depicts or describes in a patently offensive manner, actual or simulated sexual intercourse, sodomy, sexual bestiality, masturbation, sadism, masochism, excretion or lewd exhibition of the genitals, and (c) considered as a whole, it lacks serious literary, artistic, political, and scientific value.

2) Pornography is defined as follows: "a depiction (as in writing or painting) of licentiousness or lewdness: a portrayal of erotic behavior designed to cause sexual excitement." By permission from Webster's Third New International Dictionary 1986 by Merriam-Webster Inc., publisher of the Merriam-Webster dictionaries.

Case No. 59

East Coast Moving and Storage, Inc. v. Flappin

1) Yes, the contract between Flappin and East Coast would be enforceable. Where a person engages in a business for which a license is required for revenue raising purposes only, and the person is not licensed, that person's contracts are valid notwithstanding the person's failure to obtain the required license.

2) Flappin could present several types of evidence to establish East Coast's liability including: testimony from Flappin and any witnesses that, prior to the move, Flappin's furniture did not contain the scratches and dents it had after the move; videotape or photographic pictures of the furniture prior to the move to show the dents, etc. did not exist prior to the move; testimony that Flappin had in his apartment prior to the move the items of furniture claimed to have been lost; sales receipts evidencing Flappin's purchase of the furniture claimed to have been lost; testimony from Flappin that he has not seen the furniture since the move and that he did not authorize East Coast Moving to do anything with the furniture except move it to the new apartment; admit into evidence the damaged furniture or, if not feasible due to its size, weight or otherwise, photographs of the damaged furniture showing the dents, scratches and/or other damage.

   To prove the amount of money Flappin should be awarded in the case he could present the following types of evidence: testimony from a furniture repairer as to the cost of repairs; testimony from a furniture appraiser as to the value of the furniture that was lost.

Case No. 60

Sung v. Ramirez

1) A basic principle underlying our legal and economic systems is freedom of competition. The law promotes this objective by refusing to enforce contracts which significantly and/or unnecessarily limit competition.

2) Under New York law, an agreement not to compete made by a seller of a business is enforceable provided the restriction is reasonable in the time and territory within which competition is prohibited. Whether in a given case the restrictions are reasonable depends upon the type of business involved and the geographical area in which it does business. In this case the agreement not to compete restricted Ramirez from competing in all of Staten Island. The business involved was a corner deli-grocery, a type of business which customarily attracts most of its customers from the immediate neighborhood. Staten Island covers a greater area than necessary to protect the buyer from competition from the seller.

Case No. 62

Hartogs v. Employers Mutual Liability Insurance Company of Wisconsin

1) Malpractice is misconduct or negligence occurring in the course of performance of professional duties.

2) No, a contract to indemnify a professional for losses incurred as a result of malpractice is not illegal or otherwise contrary to public policy. Such contracts are enforceable risk-shifting agreements.

3) Hartogs' treatment of the patient was contrary to acceptable standards and immoral. To allow Hartogs recovery against the insurance company in the circumstances of this case ". . . would be to indemnify immorality and to pay the expenses of prurience."

Case No. 63

Harwood v. Lincoln Square Apartments Section Five, Inc.

1) The defense could have been eliminated had the contract contained a statement that identified a reasonable period of time within which the landlord could attempt to repair and restart interrupted services without liability. The following statement, if added at the end of the contract term quoted in the case facts, is an example of terminology that should eliminate the landlord's defense: "provided the services are interrupted no longer than a reasonable time necessary for the landlord to arrange for reinstatement of the curtailed services. In no event shall a reasonable time be more than ten days."

2) No, freedom of contract is a constitutional right which establishes a person's right to determine the terms of his contracts without interference by government. The government can, through the courts, refuse to enforce contracts that are contrary to public policy and such refusal is not in violation of the right to freedom of contract. Unconscionable contracts are contrary to public policy and thus considered unenforceable. Therefore the court's refusal in this case to enforce an unconscionable provision of the contract is not a violation of the landlord's freedom of contract.

3) An adhesion contract is one in which one party has no opportunity to negotiate and no meaningful choice concerning the contract terms. Instead, the other party, who is normally one with significantly greater bargaining power, provides and requires the use of a standard printed form contract. The first party is in a "take it or leave it" situation. If the resulting terms are grossly unfair such a contract will be treated as unconscionable and therefore void.

Case No. 64

St. John's Episcopal Hospital v. McAdoo

1) The contract provision requiring McAdoo to assume liability for his wife's medical treatment should have been in larger print with its own paragraph heading clearly alerting the reader to the provision's contents.

2) Contracts are private agreements which are enforceable in court. Parties to a contract rely on each other's performance of the contractual obligations. If a party could avoid the contract because he failed to read it at the appropriate time, the usefulness of contracts as a means to create enforceable obligations would be significantly impaired.

Case No. 65

BGW Associates, Inc. v. Valley Broadcasting

1) Generally these concepts suggest the absence of a meaningful choice by one party to a contract coupled with unreasonably favorable contract terms to the other. In considering the absence of a meaningful choice, the courts examine, among other things, the education and experience of the parties. Experienced business people are considered knowledgeable in their field and experienced in contractual negotiations. As such the opportunity for one party to take unfair advantage of the other is limited. Further, the terms of contracts between business people customarily result from negotiations between the parties rather than the imposition by one party of unfair terms on the other. Finally, the concept of unconscionability normally applies to contracts relating to necessities of life because, in contracts for such goods the opportunity for overreaching is the greatest. Business contracts do not normally involve necessities of life.

2) Generally, a court can do any of the following: a) refuse to enforce an unconscionable contract; b) enforce the contract without the unconscionable clause; or 3) limit the application of the unconscionable clause in order to avoid an unconscionable result. These choices give the court the option of either completely denying enforcement of an unconscionable contract or tailoring the effect of the unconscionable clause to eliminate or minimize the unfairness while leaving the remainder of the contract intact.

Case No. 66

Gross v. Sweet

1) An exculpatory clause is a term in a contract which seeks to limit a person's liability under specified circumstances. A phrase often used in exculpatory clauses is "hold harmless". This phrase means that one party agrees not to hold the other party liable in circumstances that might otherwise give rise to liability. An example of such a clause is as follows: "Customer agrees to hold seller harmless for property damage and personal injuries caused by the equipment and/or by the seller's negligence."

2) He could strengthen his position by mentioning negligence in the release, and by reviewing his training procedures to ensure adequate coverage of important information in parachute training.

Case No. 67

Public Service Mutual Insurance Company v. Royal Burglar and Fire Alarm Inc.

1) Some examples of contracts that are prohibited from containing exculpatory clauses are the following:

    a) contracts with a landlord for real property where the clause seeks to exempt the landlord from liability for negligence;

    b) contracts with a caterer where a clause seeks to exempt the caterer from liability for negligence;

    c) contracts with a construction company where a clause seeks to require the party who hires the construction company to hold it harmless;

    d) contracts with an architect, engineer or surveyor where a clause requires indemnification of the architect, engineer or surveyor for damage resulting from defects in maps, plans, designs or specifications prepared by the architect, engineer or surveyor;

    e) contracts with an operator of a service station or parking lot where a clause seeks to exempt the operator from liability for negligence;

f) contracts with the operator of a pool, gymnasium, place of amusement or recreation as part of which the operator receives compensation for the use of the facilities, where a clause seeks to exempt the operator from liability for negligence.

2) Such clauses are void as being against public policy and therefore unenforceable.

Case No. 69

Rodas v. Manitaras, et al.

1) Rodas could have required that Oyster House allow him to inspect the books before the sale.

Case No. 70

Austin Instruments, Inc. v. Loral Corp.

1) In both types of duress a party enters a contract to avoid threatened danger. In the case of physical duress the threatened danger is injury to person or property. In the case of economic duress the threatened danger is financial loss. Economic duress occurs where a seller threatens to breach a contract by failing to deliver the required goods, no alternative source for the goods exist, and the nonbreaching party would not be adequately compensated by recovery of damages for breach of contract. In this case Loral risked losing not only the profits on the contracts in issue, which it might have recovered in a breach of contract action, but also profits on future contracts with the Navy, the amount of damages for which would be too speculative to recover in a breach of contract action.

2) No, if other suppliers were available to deliver on time, Loral would have had a choice of suppliers and would not have risked financial loss by refusing to concede to Austin's demands. Thus if other suppliers were available but Loral nonetheless agreed to pay Austin the higher price, it could not avoid its promise on the basis of economic duress.

Case No. 71

Leasco Corp. v. Taussig

1) In deciding to enter a contract parties often reasonably assume the truth of certain material facts. If the parties' assumption is incorrect a mutual mistake exists and the contract will be unenforceable.

Where the parties project a fact which they know may or may not be true, they deliberately take a business risk if they enter a contract hoping the fact will prove true. If the fact does not materialize the law will not relieve the parties from the consequences of the risk they assumed.

2)   The problem could have been avoided if the contract included a provision that stated buyer's obligation to purchase the business would be void if the actual earnings for a specified period of time deviated from the projected earnings by more than a stated percentage. Leasco, however, may not have agreed to such a term in which case Taussig's problem might not have been avoidable.

Case No. 72

Ryan v. Boucher, et al

1)   Recission is an equitable remedy that undoes the contract and returns the parties to the positions they were in prior to entering the contract. The parties must return any property or money exchanged prior to the recission.

Case No. 73

Mangini v. McClurg

1)   The parties were mistaken about the cause of Mangini's pain. Whereas they believed the source was a back injury, in fact it was an unknown hip injury.

2)   The consideration was as follows: McClurg gave money and Mangini gave a promise not to sue for her injuries (forebearance).

3)   Had Mangini's pain been caused by the back injury she would not have been able successfully to sue McClurg for additional damages; the release would have been a bar to such an action. The release prevented her from suing for consequences of injuries known at the time the release was signed, even though the specific consequence might not have been known at that time.

Case No. 74

Marchello v. Lennox Hill Hospital

1)   In this case, unlike Mangini, the particular damages for which the plaintiff was suing involved an unknown consequence of an injury known at the time the release was signed. A release can be set aside when a mutual mistake exists as to injuries existing at the time the release was signed. If the injury is known but a particular consequence of the injury is not known, such does not constitute mutual mistake sufficient to set the release aside.

2)   A general release relieves the releasee from liability for both known and unknown consequences of known injuries. If a release is not a general release but rather has a

narrower application and applies by its terms only to known consequences of known injuries, it would not relieve the releasee from liability for unknown consequences of known injuries. If the application of the release in <u>Mangini v. McClurg</u> had been limited to known consequences of known injuries, the result of the case would have been the same; the release would not have relieved McClurg of liability. Mangini's problem that surfaced after the release was signed involved an unknown injury.

The result of Marchello v. Lennox Hill Hospital would have been different and the Hospital would have been liable had the release covered only known consequences of known injuries. Marchello's problem that surfaced after the release was signed involved an unknown consequence of a known injury.

Case No. 75

<u>Balabon-Gordon Company v. Brighton Sewer District No. 2</u>

1) A mathematical or clerical error is one in which a party incorrectly adds the component figures to determine the total bill, or incorrectly transposes aA figure from a worksheet to the final bid submission form. Such an error is evidenced by the fact that if the bid was recomputed by the bidder or another person, the error would be identified and corrected. Thus the error's existence can be objectively established. If a bidder makes a mathematical or clerical error the bidder would be entitled to withdraw the bid. The mistake made in this case was not strictly mathematical or clerical. Instead Balabon misconstrued the work specifications and added a figure into the cost for one job that should have been added to the cost for another job.

2) Where a construction company incorporates into a bid figures based on estimates of the time and effort a job will take, and those estimates are based on the exercise of business judgment, the bidder will not be able to withdraw the bid if the estimates turn out to be low. In such a case the bidder intentionally assumes a business risk.

The error made by Balabon was not one involving a business risk intentionally undertaken by Balabon. Instead it involved inadvertent misinterpretation of job specifications. Under these circumstances a bidder is entitled to withdraw its bid.

Case No. 76

<u>Farash v. Sykes Datatronics Inc.</u>

1) No, the Statute of Frauds requires a writing for leases only where the lease is for a period of more than one year. Had a writing not been required in this case, Farash would still have to prove that the oral lease existed. If Sykes denied the existence of the lease, Farash would have a proof problem. Such problems can be avoided by reducing all contracts to writing, not just those required to be in writing by the Statute

of Frauds.

2) Yes, the Statute of Frauds requires a writing for a contract for the sale of an interest in real property.

Case No. 79

P.J. Carlin Construction Company v. Whiffen Electric Company, Inc.

1) Such a guarantee is not viewed as a promise to perform for two years into the future. Instead, it is regarded as a guarantee of the present condition of the labor, materials and equipment. The guarantee is interpreted to mean the materials and services that will be provided will be of such quality that they should endure for two years. Because such guarantees are not viewed as promises to perform an act for more than a year into the future, the Statute of Frauds does not require a writing.

2) If the Statute of Frauds applies in a case, and the parties fail to satisfy its requirements, the oral contract is unenforceable. If the contract is unenforceable, issues concerning the terms of the contract are irrelevant. Therefore, in a case involving a contract which requires a writing, a court should ensure that enforcement of the contract is not barred by the statute of frauds before the court invests the time to address other issues of the case.

Case No. 83

Mitchill v. Lath

1) Exceptions to the parol evidence rule are situations in which evidence of an oral agreement can be introduced to modify a written contract. The exceptions include the following:

   a) Oral modifications made after the contract is signed;

   b) Evidence showing the contract was void or voidable, for example evidence showing the contract resulted from fraud, duress, undue influence, illegality, etc.;

   c) Evidence clarifying ambiguous contract terms;

   d) Evidence showing the contract is incomplete or not intended as the entire agreement between the parties;

   e) Evidence showing the parties agreed to a condition precedent to which the entire agreement is subject.

2) No. The parol evidence rule applies only to oral agreements made prior to signing a written agreement. The rule does not apply to modifications made after the written contract was signed.

Case No. 85

Potler, as Trustee in bankruptcy for Underwater Advisors Corp. v. MCP Facilities Corp.

1) The purpose of the parol evidence rule is to protect the integrity of a written contract complete on its face by preventing false claims by one party of the alleged existence of terms and conditions to which the parties never agreed.

Case No. 86

Ralston Purina Company v. Arthur G. McKee & Company, et al.

1) Another exception to the requirement of privity is an assignment of rights or a delegation of duties.

2) In a third party beneficiary contract, the rights of the third party arise at the time the contract is made, whereas in an assignment of rights or a delegation of duties, the rights of the third party arise at some time after the original contract is made.

Case No. 89

City of New York v. Local 333, United Marine Division International Longshoreman's Association and Moran Towing and Transportation Company

1) In this situation the court could conclude that Moran should have foreseen the possibility of a strike. When a circumstance that makes performance impossible is foreseeable, a contracting party will not be excused from performance when the circumstance occurs. Instead, the parties should negotiate a term in the contract addressing the issue in such a way that liability is avoided.

2) No, normally when a party to a contract fails to perform a contractual duty, the breaching party will be liable for damages.. However, the law recognizes an exception to liability where performance is objectively impossible due to the occurrence of an unforeseen event. In this situation the dancer's injury makes his performance objectively impossible. As a result he should be excused from liability for the loss suffered by the theater from cancellation of the performance. In negotiating the contract the theater might attempt to include a provision that would allocate the liability in some other way.

3) No, the defense of impossibility applies only when the performance is objectively impossible. Inability to pay a personal obligation constitutes subjective impossibility, that is, particular to the individual. Subjective impossibility will not excuse performance.

Case No. 90

Kenyon and Eckhardt, Inc. v. 808 Third Avenue Co.

1) Government approval for construction of a building in excess of a specified height was required by law. Approval was not guaranteed and thus denial was a foreseeable event. Therefore, 808 Third Avenue would not have been excused, based on impossibility of performance, from performance of its contractual obligation to provide eleven floors of space. 808 Third Avenue in the court case wisely attempted to protect itself against the foreseeable risk of denial of approval by stating that Kenyon would accept seven floors instead of eleven. By doing so it protected, itself against a breach of contract action by Kenyon based on inability to provide eleven floors of space. However, due to some unexplained reason, 808 Third Avenue, following denial of the required approval, attempted to disregard the contract term and avoid its obligation to Kenyon altogether. It therefore was in breach of its contract.

Case No. 91

Sure Fire Transport Corporation v. Garsite Products Inc.

1) To invoke the doctrine of impossibility, performance must in fact be impossible. The doctrine of frustration of purpose, on the other hand, does not require that performance be impossible. Instead, it excuses the party from performance where unforseen circumstances arise which frustrate the purpose of the contract and therefore deprive the parties of the value anticipated from performance of the contract. For example, assume that Jerry rented an apartment in New York City for one day, the day of Macy's Thanksgiving Day Parade. The apartment was located on a street down which the parade regularly passes. Known to the landlord, Jerry's intention in renting the apartment was to host a party for his friends and their children to enable their having a good view of the parade. The day before the parade a water main broke on the street on which the apartment is located. As a result the parade route was changed and it no longer was scheduled to pass the apartment. Due to these circumstances, the benefit anticipated from renting the apartment would no longer result. Jerry should be excused from performance without liability due to the doctrine of frustration of purpose.

Case No. 92

Tenavision v. Neuman

1) A breach of contract occurs when a party fails to perform contractual duties at the time they are due. An anticipatory breach occurs when a party clearly manifests an intention not to perform the contract prior to the date performance is due. Normally

in a breach of contract case, the nonbreaching party cannot sue for damages until the contract date for performance has passed and the breaching party has failed to perform. In a case involving an anticipatory breach, the nonbreaching party can sue for damages immediately upon the occurrence of the anticipatory breach and need not wait until the date performance is required by the contract.

2) No, to constitute an anticipatory breach, the breaching party must clearly evidence an intent to breach the contract. The letter sent by Raynor suggested that he was reconsidering his acceptance. It did not, however, clearly indicate an intention to breach the lease.

Case No. 93

Harbor Hill Lithographing Corp. v. Dittler Brothers, Inc.

1) The law seeks to give the nonbreaching party the benefit of the bargain by placing the nonbreaching party in as good a position as he would have been in had there been no breach.

2) No, consequential damages are recoverable by a nonbreaching party only when the loss is foreseeable by the breaching party.

3) No, a nonbreaching party has a duty to mitigate its damages. Failure to attempt to do so will preclude the nonbreaching party from recovering those damages it could have avoided.

Case No. 94

Neri v. Retail Marine Corporation

1) Where the buyer breaches a contract for the sale of goods and seller's supply of the goods is limited, the measure of damages is the difference between the contract price and the resale price plus incidental damages. In this case Marine resold the boat to a second buyer for the same price as Neri contracted to pay. Therefore the difference between the contract price and resale price was zero. The incidental damages of $674.00 Marine spent for insurance, upkeep and interest would be recoverable.

2) Marine would be entitled to recover nominal damages, which acknowledges a breach of contract occurred although the nonbreaching party suffered little, if any, loss. The amount awarded is usually $1.00.

Case No. 95

North American Foreign Trading Corp. v. Direct Mail Specialist a/k/a DMS, Inc.

1) a) The seller is entitled to collect storage fees. Without the breach, the seller would not have had to incur this expense.

    b) The seller is not entitled to collect the full contract price where it has been able to resell the goods. The seller must credit buyer's account with the proceeds of the resale. It can collect as damages the difference between the contract price and the resale price plus incidental damages.

    c) The advertising and auctioneer's fees are recoverable because, without the breach, the seller would not have had to incur them.

Case No. 98

American Standard. Inc, v. Schectman

1) A party substantially performs when, although it fails to render a perfect performance, it does perform sufficiently to give the other party essentially that for which she contracted.

2) The usual measure of damages in a construction contract where the construction company fails to fully perform is the same whether or not the construction company substantially performed. The measure of damages in such cases is the cost to the nonbreaching party of completing the work performed improperly or left undone by the breaching party.

Case No. 99

Reale v. Linder

1) The objective of this equitable doctrine is to provide contractors partial payment for construction work in cases where, although the work varies from contract specifications, it deviates in a relatively minor way only.

Case No. 101

Jacob & Youngs, Inc. v. Kent

1) Although the cost of completion is the usual measure of damages in a case involving breach of a construction contract, such a measure will not be used where economic waste will result. Rather, where the breaching parties substantially performed the

contract, the deviation from full performance was inadvertent and the cost to correct the deviation is excessive in relation to the benefit that would be achieved, the cost of completion would result in economic waste. To avoid that result an alternative measure of damages is used—the difference in value of the building as constructed and the value it would have had had it been built as required by the contract.

Case No. 102

Spring Valley Gardens Associates v. Earle

1) For a liquidated damage clause to be enforceable, the amount of damages identified in the clause must be reasonable in relation to the actual or anticipated loss, and the contract must be one in which damages are difficult to calculate.

2) By identifying the amount of damages in the contract the parties avoid the need to prove the amount of damages in the event of breach. Thus time is saved at trial and the expense of litigation reduced.

Case No. 103

The Stock Shop Inc. v. Bozell and Jacobs, Inc.

1) Yes, this clause would likely be enforceable because the amount of the damages would be difficult to measure and the $500.00 damage figure appears to be reasonably related to the actual loss the town would incur.